HEALTH AND DISEASE
IN
DEVELOPING COUNTRIES

Kari S. Lankinen

Staffan Bergström

P. Helena Mäkelä

Miikka Peltomaa

MACMILLAN

Macmillan Education
Between Towns Road, Oxford OX4 3PP
A division of Macmillan Publishers Limited
Companies and representatives throughout the world

www.macmillan-africa.com

ISBN 0 333 58900 9

Printed and bound in Malaysia

2006 2005 2004 2003 2002
13 12 11 10 9 8 7 6

The authors and publishers acknowledge with thanks the use of
figures and photographs from several sources. Sources are credited
below each photograph or given as a reference for each table and
figure. Where no credit is given, the illustration is an original from the
chapter authors.

The authors and publishers have made every effort to trace the
copyright holders, but if they have inadvertently overlooked any,
they will be pleased to make necessary arrangements at the first
opportunity.

Cover photographs by Heikki Peltola

CONTENTS

II BURDEN OF INFECTIOUS DISEASES

III CHALLENGES FOR HEALTH CARE

IV HEALTH SERVICES TO MEET THE CHALLENGES

Foreword

There are few subjects that are more prone to the stifling impact of conventional wisdom than health and disease, in both industrialised and developing countries. So many health professionals tend to react to the formidable challenges inherent in these subjects by just shrugging their shoulders and saying, 'do not think, there is always an easier way out by doing more of the same'. This well written, relevant and sensitive book is, in our opinion, an appetising and timely contribution to fresh thinking and action on a wide spectrum of health issues in developing countries.

Medical textbooks often deal with health problems in developing countries within the conventional panorama of tropical medicine. This book does not blame disease on geography or the weather. It traces the problems to their roots, to the pathology of poverty. A major section of the book deals with society, economy and health, with chapters covering topics ranging from politics to prostitution.

Conventional medical textbooks tend to deal with the diseases that people have, rather than with the people who have the diseases. The organisation of health services to meet the health needs of the people often recedes into the background, while glamorous technologies jump to the forefront. This book attempts to redress this imbalance.

The Alma-Ata declaration in 1978 stated that, 'The existing gross inequality in the health status of the people particularly between developed and developing countries, as well as within countries, is politically, socially and economically unacceptable, and is, therefore, of common concern to all countries'. We live in a new age of global consciousness. We are increasingly realising how all of us on board spaceship earth have become interdependent in all matters including health. The concern about the health of people in other countries is no longer a question of morals. It is a question of reason. It is in this spirit that we welcome this novel international textbook on health and disease in developing countries by a joint Finnish–Swedish group of editors and with authors from both industrialised and developing countries.

Mahmoud Fathalla

Halfdan Mahler

Preface

We have produced this book for medical and other professionals working or aiming to work in developing countries, or those working for international cooperation agencies. District medical officers should benefit especially from the parts on planning and management of health services. The volume is also essential reading for students taking courses in public health or tropical medicine.

Many historical, sociocultural, economic and political factors thwart general development in the Third World. To facilitate better understanding of the complexity of health sector development we have chosen to introduce the book with an interdisciplinary section discussing these essential background factors (Section I).

Clearly, communicable diseases are still major problems in developing countries, which is why they are reviewed extensively in this book (Section II). The multitude of environmental and socioeconomic factors influencing the transmission patterns, the clinical pictures and the outcomes of the diseases have been given special attention throughout the volume.

What is usually not appreciated, is the ongoing epidemiological transition in the Third World that already has moulded the disease profile in several countries to resemble that in industrialised countries (Section III). Noncommunicable diseases are entering the developing world and should receive immediate attention, as the true consequences of changes in lifestyle will not become fully evident until several decades have passed.

Ever since primary health care was recognised as the mainstay of health services in developing countries, the concept has been widely publicised. At this stage, it is important that primary health care concentrates on interventions that will reduce mortality and morbidity as effectively as possible. But effectiveness is not only a question of type of intervention, it very much depends on the effectiveness of the delivery system. Therefore, planning, organisation, management and financing of health care are essential issues in planning future strategies (Section IV).

Primary health care has also been emphasised in chapters relating to the different clinical specialities. The pivotal message in all chapters is clear: strengthening of the primary health care and the first referral level services will provide health benefits to the largest possible number of people. With only a few exceptions we have not given much attention to second and tertiary referral levels. It is nevertheless essential to understand that the credibility of primary health care in any country owes much to the existence of reliable and readily available referral services. Thus, hospitals are also essential, although currently the best pay-off comes from investments in primary health care.

The concluding part of the book reflects on the principles, practice and possibilities of international cooperation in the efforts to achieve better health for all (Section V). While both non-governmental and intergovernmental organisations do play significant roles in these efforts, it must be emphasised that, on a national level, only governments can effect the fundamental changes of reallocating resources for health care. At the same time the organisations should make the international community understand that priorities need to be set to address the pathology of poverty. This is not just a case for the health sector, but for all sectors of the community.

This book is a product of the joint efforts of 85 experts, all of whom made their contributions without any financial compensation. The editors would like to thank all authors for their most flexible cooperation. Special thanks are due to Dr Heikki Peltola, for letting us use his photographs on the front cover. Miikka Peltomaa produced the lay-out of the book.

The editorial process has been carried out under administrative and financial support from Physicians for Social Responsibility – Finland (PSR–Finland), for which the editors wish to express their gratitude. The editors would also like to acknowledge the significant financial contribution of the Finnish International Development Agency (FINNIDA), without which the publication of this volume would simply not have been possible. Together with the input from PSR–Finland the funding facilitates an international circulation of this book to a number of non-governmental organisations working in the health sector. The Finnish Medical Association also provided financial and technical assistance in the editorial process.

While we would have liked to produce a perfectly comprehensive book, both time and space have limited our aspirations. It is only too obvious that many important issues are not covered. However, we wish to continue the development of this book into new editions, and welcome all comments, corrections and suggestions for improvement. Please address all correspondence to Kari S. Lankinen, National Public Health Institute, Mannerheimintie 166, FIN-00300 Helsinki, Finland (Fax: +358 0 4744 238, E-mail/Internet: kari.lankinen@ ktl.fi).

A fresh, realistic view on the current problems in the Third World is truly needed. We need to confront the global dilemmas of inequity, injustice and poverty, and realise their impact on morbidity and mortality. In releasing this book we hope that it will act as an agent for a change in addressing health and disease in developing countries, and could induce a shift in our approaches from relieving symptoms to attending to the causes.

Kari S. Lankinen   Staffan Bergström   P. Helena Mäkelä   Miikka Peltomaa

Abbreviations

ADH	antidiuretic hormone
AFB	acid-fast bacilli
AfDB	African Development Bank
AFP	alpha fetoprotein
AIDS	Acquired Immunodeficiency Syndrome
AMREF	African Medical and Research Foundation
AOM	acute otitis media
ARI	acute respiratory infection
ARI	WHO Programme for the Control of Acute Respiratory infections
AsDB	Asian Development Bank
ATF	CEC AIDS Task Force
AZT	zidovudine
BB	bordeline borderline leprosy
BCG	Bacillus Calmette–Guérin
BHS	basic health services
BI	bacterial index
BL	borderline lepromatous leprosy
BMI	body mass index
BPD	IFRCS Blood Programme Department
BT	borderline tuberculoid leprosy
BTS	blood transfusion services
CATT	card agglutination test for trypanosomiasis
CBR	crude birth rate
CBR	community-based rehabilitation
$CCID_{50}$	cell culture infectious dose
CDD	WHO Diarrhoeal Disease Control Programme
CDR	WHO Division for the Control of Diarrhoeal and Acute Respiratory Infections
CEA	carcinoembryonic antigen
CEC	Commission of European Communities
CFR	case fatality ratio
CHD	coronary heart disease
CHW	community health worker
CL	cutaneous leishmaniasis
CNS	central nervous system
COM	chronic otitis media
CRP	C-reactive protein
CSF	cerebrospinal fluid
CSOM	chronic suppurative otitis media
CT	computerised tomography
CVD	cardiovascular disease (diseases)
CVI	Children's Vaccine Initiative
DAC	OECD Development Assistance Committee
DALY	disability-adjusted life years
DANIDA	Danish International Development Agency

DAP	WHO Drug Action Programme
DC	developing country
DCL	diffuse cutaneous leishmaniasis
DDC	zalcitabin
DDI	didanocin
DDS	dapsone
DFMO	eflornithine
DHF/DSS	dengue hemorrhagic fever/dengue shock syndrome
DMF-index	decayed–missed–filled (oral health index)
DRA	Drug Regulatory Authority
DTH	delayed type hypersensitivity
EBV	Epstein–Barr virus
ECG	electrocardiography
ECT	electroconvulsive therapy
EDL	Essential Drugs List
EIA	enzymeimmunoassay
EIPV	enhanced-potency inactivated polio vaccine
ELISA	enzyme-linked immunosorbent assay
ENL	erythema nodosum leprosum
EPI	WHO Expanded Programme on Immunization
ERB	Ethical Review Board
ESR	erythrocyte sedimentation rate
FAO	Food and Agricultural Organization
FAS	fetal alcohol syndrome
FINNIDA	Finnish International Development Agency
GAPC	Global AIDS Policy Coalition
GBS	Guillain–Barré syndrome
GBSI	Global Blood Safety Initiative
GCP	Good Clinical Practice
GI	gastrointestinal
GNP	gross national product
GPA	WHO Global Programme on AIDS
HAV	hepatitis A virus
HBIG	hepatitis B immunoglobulin
HBsAg	hepatitis B surface antigen
HBV	hepatitis B virus
HGIG	human rabies immunoglobulin
HIV	Human Immunodeficiency Virus
IBRD	International Bank for Reconstruction and Development
ICCE	intracapsular cataract extraction
ICRC	International Committee of the Red Cross
IDA	International Development Association
IFAD	International Fund for Agricultural Development
IFC	International Finance Corporation

IFRCS	International Federation of the Red Cross and Red Crescent Societies
IGO	intergovernmental organisation
ILO	International Labour Organization
IMF	International Monetary Fund
IMR	infant mortality rate
INN	International Non-proprietary Names (of drugs)
INRUD	International Network for the Rational Use of Drugs
IPPNW	International Physicians for the Prevention of Nuclear War
IPV	inactivated polio vaccine
IQ	intelligence quotient
IRB	Internal Review Board
ISBT	International Society of Blood Transfusion
IUGR	intrauterine growth retardation
LAM	lactational amenorrhea method
LBS	WHO Unit of Health Laboratory Technology and Blood Safety
LBW	low birth weight
LDC	least developed countries
LL	lepromatous leprosy
MAECT	miniature anion exhange centrifugation technique
MAL	WHO Malaria Unit
MCH	WHO Maternal and Child Health Programme
MCL	mucocutaneous leishmaniasis
MDT	multiple drug therapy
mf	microfilariae
MHW	multipurpose health worker
MI	morphological index
MIGA	Multilateral Investment Guarantee Agency
MRI	magnetic resonance imaging
NBTS	National Blood Transfusion Service
NCA	National Control Authority
NCE	new chemical entity
NCL	National Control Laboratory
NDD	National Drugs Policy
NEQAS	National Quality Assessment Schemes
NGO	non-governmental organisation
NIDDM	non-insulin dependent diabetes mellitus
NORAD	Norwegian Agency for Development Co-operation
nu/nu	homozygous nude gene in mice (nude/nude)
NUG	necrotising ulcerative gingivitis
NUT	WHO Nutrition Programme
OAU	Organization for African Unity
ODA	UK Overseas Development Administration
ODA	official development assistance
OECD	Organization for Economic Co-operation and Development
OHS	occupational health services
OPV	oral polio vaccine
ORH	WHO Oral Health Programme
OTC	over-the-counter (drugs)
PBL	WHO Programme for the Prevention of Blindness
PCR	polymerase chain reaction
PEM	protein energy malnutrition
PHC	primary health care
PHN	public health nurse
PKDL	post kala-azar dermal leishmaniasis
PO	people's organisation
PPD	purified protein derivative
PYLL	potential years of life lost
QCL	quality control laboratory
RBBB	right bundle branch block
SF	symphysis–fundus distance
SGA	smallness for gestational age
SNOPAD	Standardized Nomenclature of Parasitic Animal Diseases
SOM	secretory otitis media
SOP	Standard Operating Procedure
SSPE	subacute sclerosing panencephalitis
TB	tuberculosis
TBA	traditional birth attendant
TDR	UNDP/World Bank/WHO Special Programme for Research and Training in Tropical Diseases
TFR	total fertility rate
TSP	total suspended particles
TT	tuberculoid leprosy
TU	Tuberculin Unit
TU	tropical ulcer
ULV	ultra low volume
UNDP	United Nations Development Programme
UNHCR	United Nations High Commissioner for Refugees
UNICEF	United Nations Children's Fund
URI	upper respiratory infection
USD	U.S. dollar (dollars)
VA	visual acquity
VES	ventricular extrasystolies
VHW	village health worker
VL	visceral leishmaniasis
w/a	weight for age
WBC	white blood cell (count)
WFH	World Federation of Hemophilia
WHO	World Health Organization

I SOCIETY, ECONOMY AND HEALTH

Lankinen KS, Bergström S, Mäkelä PH and Peltomaa M, eds.
Health and disease in developing countries. London:The Macmillan Press Limited, 1994:3-12.

1 THE PATHOLOGY OF POVERTY

Staffan Bergström, M.D., Ph.D.
University of Oslo, Department of Obstetrics and Gynaecology,
Ullevål University Hospital, N-0407 Oslo,
Norway

INTRODUCTION

Traditional textbooks of tropical medicine focus upon infectious diseases and deal much less with other clinical specialties. During the past decade, however, the concept of tropical medicine has been widened and includes today issues of maternal and child health, nutrition, surgery and other disciplines. However, the attribute tropical still remains the hallmark of this specialty. In most countries, departments and chairs in tropical medicine are almost exclusively within departments of infectious diseases and the colonial heritage influences the discipline maintaining its traditional limitations.

The importance of communicable diseases in tropical areas is indisputable and infections will continue to be the major cause of death among both children and adults. However, this perspective seems incomplete if we look upon tropical areas from a different point of view. If we, for example, choose a maternal health perspective the following questions may be justified:

Is eclampsia a tropical disease? There is no exact data on the epidemiology of eclampsia in the world. Point prevalence studies indicate that eclampsia is much more common in tropical than in temperate areas and more common at low than at high altitudes. If we draw a map with the geography of eclampsia incidence in the world, it would correspond fairly well with a map drawn of malaria incidence: much higher figures would be found in the tropics, especially in low-land areas. Furthermore, we would see a striking seasonality in the eclampsia incidence, a phenomenon also encountered in malaria incidence.[1] What factors could provide an explanation of these features of eclampsia incidence? It is well known that, to a large extent, eclampsia is due to insufficient antenatal care. The absence of such care among the majority of Third World women implies that eclampsia is seen frequently there, but very seldom in areas with functioning antenatal care.

Is maternal death a significant issue in tropical medicine? It is now a recognised fact that maternal deaths in the world occur almost exclusively (99 per cent) in developing countries, mostly in the tropics. The geography of maternal mortality seems to correspond fairly closely to the geography of several communicable diseases almost exclusively occurring in the tropics.

Is low birth weight delivery a tropical entity? It has been calculated that 95 per cent of all low birth weight deliveries occur in developing countries, by and large corresponding to the tropics. The fact that approximately 20 out of a total of 21 million low birth weight deliveries occur in the tropics would seem to justify it as an issue of tropical medicine.

Are urovaginal fistulae of relevance as an issue in tropical medicine? This life-long complication of obstructed labour is common in the tropics due to unattended deliveries, particularly among young women. It is almost never seen outside the tropics. In most tropical areas the insufficient quality of birth attendance contributes to a high incidence of this disaster in many young parturients.

Table 1.1. The relationship between the infant mortality rate (IMR) and the gross national product *per capita* (GNP) is not linear. Several countries with very high GNP *per capita* have remarkably high IMR and *vice versa*. IMR figures are from 1991 and GNP *per capita* figures from 1990.[3]

Country	IMR (per 1000)	GNP *per capita* (USD)
Gabon	97	3 330
Libya	72	5 310
The Philippines	39	730
Saudi Arabia	33	7 050
China	22	370
Sri Lanka	16	470
Kuwait	14	16 150
Costa Rica	14	1 910
Cuba	11	1 170
USA	9	21 790
Sweden	4	23 660

If we consider the above four issues of relevance for tropical medicine and look for each of them in textbooks in tropical medicine, we will presumably be disappointed; these issues hardly ever appear in such books.

TROPICAL DISEASES IN ARCTIC AREAS

It is instructive and thought-provoking to have a retrospective look into the history of medicine in countries far away from the tropics and particularly into the morbidity patterns of such countries when they were poor. Sweden, Norway and Finland are among countries where malaria was still prevalent 100–200 years ago. A similar case can be made for leprosy, a well known, widespread disease in both Norway and Sweden 100 years ago. The prevalence of leprosy was presumably higher in Central Norway 100 years ago than it is in Central African countries at present.[2] Special leprosy hospitals are still maintained as medical museums in Norway and a Norwegian researcher, Armauer Hansen, is well known for his discovery of the *Mycobacterium leprae* (Chapter 26). Other diseases, which are presently prevalent in tropical countries and much more rare in arctic areas, such as tuberculosis, had epidemic proportions in Northern Europe during the 18th and 19th centuries.

The historical perspective is complementary to the geographical one since it brings into focus the past of presently affluent countries, when they were still poor like today's developing countries in the tropics. For many health workers in the tropics it complicates reality to hear that malaria, leprosy and other tropical diseases have been prevalent in arctic areas. It was also unexpected to many to witness how a large number of leprosy patients – without any known contacts with the tropics – were discovered in an asylum in Moscow a few years ago and shown to an astonished world.

The historical perspective teaches us that many so-called tropical diseases have occurred outside the tropics, but it also shows that several tropical diseases do not exist in typically tropical areas. Malaria has been eradicated in Cuba and was temporarily eradicated in Sri Lanka. We can thus conclude that malaria was a more significant public health problem in Sweden 200 years ago than it is today in Cuba.

THEIR LATITUDES OR OUR ATTITUDES?

It is instructive to reflect critically on the background of our tendency to stick to latitude-centred medicine instead of paying attention to other more important background variables at the community level that contribute to the high morbidity and mortality figures in the tropics. It is not difficult to see how the latitude orientation in conventional tropical medicine has side-tracked our attention away from basic etiological factors in impoverished societies. It is a well known fact that the infant mortality rates can be very different in one and the same tropical area depending on the degree of poverty.

In India the infant mortality rate is *ten times as high in lower income strata as in the uppermost stratum*.[3] In South Africa estimates by missionary doctors indicate that the Bantustan infant mortality rate may reach levels as high as ten times the infant mortality rate of the white, privileged population. This occurs in one and the same country, indicating that tropical morbidity like malaria, parasitic infections, other communicable diseases and malnutrition that cause the vast majority of infant deaths are much more prevalent – at the same latitude – among less privileged groups than among more privileged ones.

In international medicine these examples are well known and widely discussed in

Table 1.2. Populations estimated to be living in absolute poverty (1989).[6]

Region	Number of people (millions)	Share of total population (percent)
Asia	675	25
Sub-Saharan Africa	325	62
Latin America	150	35
Northern Africa and Middle East	75	28
Total	1 225	23

professional circles. Among the public, however, much of the information on the disease panorama of the tropics transmitted via mass media tends to blame climate, latitude and harmful environmental factors not possible to influence. Informed public opinion about important determinants of diseases and deaths in the tropics depends on an understanding of the relative roles of climate (impossible to influence) and impoverishment (possible to influence). From an operational point of view, and particularly regarding public willingness to assist impoverished countries to alleviate poverty, the latitude-centred interpretation seems to be simplistic and incomplete and contribute to fatalistic, non-interventional attitudes. Our attitudes may thus be at least as important as their latitudes in finding solutions to the problems evident in the challenges of the pathology of the tropics, which, rather, should be called the *pathology of poverty*.

POVERTY AND MORTALITY

The World Bank has provided important statistics to illustrate the relationship between various economic indicators and death rates. One well known comparison (Table 1.1) examines the relationship between GNP *per capita* and infant mortality rate (IMR).[3] The relationship is not straightforward. The IMR is quite low in some countries, like Cuba and Costa Rica, with a conspicuously low GNP *per capita*. Sri Lanka also has a remarkably low IMR in spite of its low GNP *per capita*. This lack of congruence between GNP *per capita* and IMR is evident at the international level and can also be found at the national level. In India, for instance, Punjab, which is among

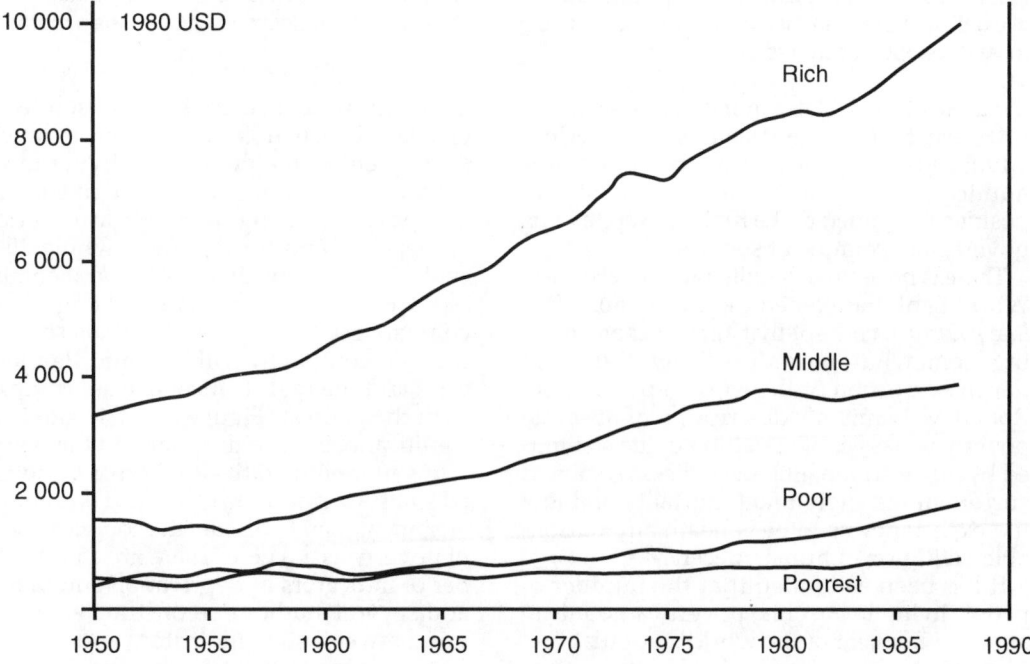

Figure 1.1. Adjusted income per person in four economic classes of nations, 1950–88.[6]

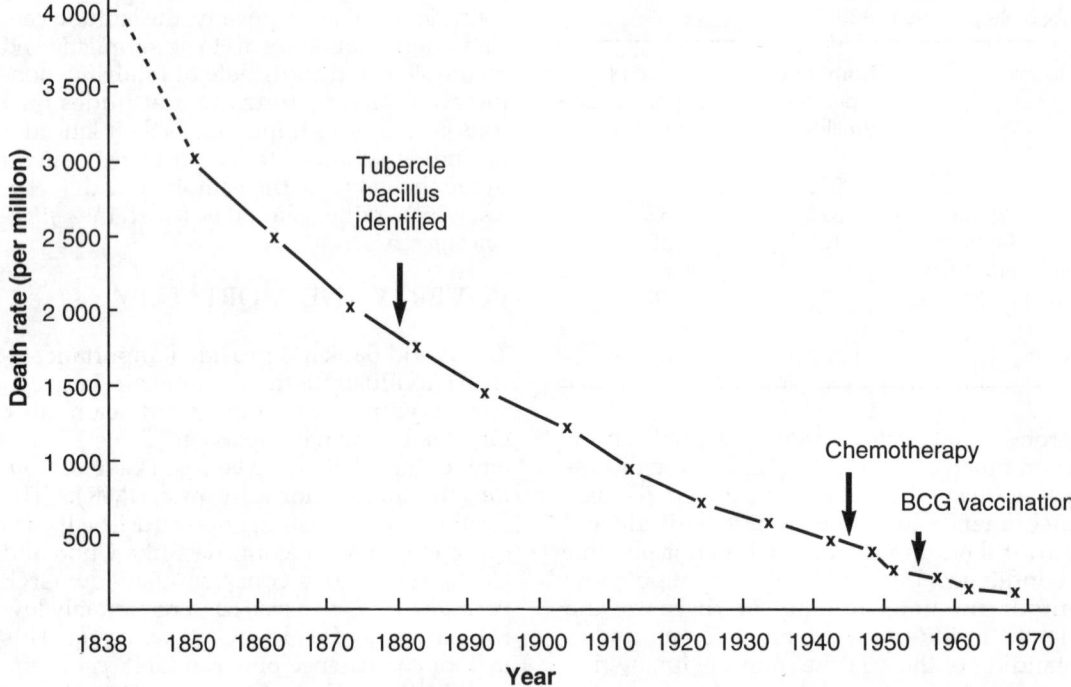

Figure 1.2. Number of deaths in lung tuberculosis in England and Wales over the last century. While the mortality has levelled off almost continuously, it was not until 1880 that Robert Koch discovered the tuberculosis bacteria. Chemotherapy and BCG vaccination were not available until the 1940s. Poverty alleviation, more than medical interventions, has guaranteed the steep decline of tuberculosis mortality in most developed countries.

the more affluent states in India, has far worse IMR level than the poor state of Kerala. More advanced social organisation, more pronounced equity and historically strong position of women make Kerala, in spite of its poverty, an example of success.

There is no simple definition of poverty. The World Bank has coined the expression *absolute poverty*, a concept that aims at characterising somewhat more precisely the most deprived portion of the world's population. Robert McNamara's description of absolute poverty is classic: 'A condition of life so limited by malnutrition, illiteracy, disease, squalid surroundings, high infant mortality and low life expectancy as to be beneath any reasonable definition of human decency'.[4]

It has been estimated that the number of people living in absolute poverty amounts to about 23 per cent of the world's population.[5] The figure is *increasing*, reflecting the widening gap between affluent and poor countries. This gap is illustrated in Figure 1.1 and the continent-wise distribution of absolute poverty can be seen in Table 1.2. While as much as 62 per cent of the population living in Sub-Saharan Africa are estimated to live in absolute poverty, the figure for Latin America is 35 per cent and for Asia as a whole 25 per cent.[6] It is obvious that the gap in income *per capita* is widening, not only among the rich compared with the poorest, but also between the rich compared with the middle income class and the middle income class compared with the poorest (Figure 1.1). The gap is also significant between the poor and the poorest.

It is more illustrative to discuss various vital statistics indicators associated with impoverishment than to discuss the complex concept of poverty as a whole. There are a great number of indicators of deprivation and scarcity, and several studies demonstrate an association between such indicators and mortality figures. One such example has shown a relationship between unemployment and early neonatal mortality in the USA.[7] There is

The pathology of poverty has a human face in Sinkat, Sudan. Photo: UNICEF/Roger Lemoyne

a striking *association* between a high unemployment rate and early neonatal mortality, although there is no possibility to state anything about a *causality*, because of the many confounding factors and intermediate circumstances that could explain the association.

POVERTY ALLEVIATION AND DECLINING MORBIDITY

The historical perspective is important for an understanding of the role of poverty alleviation in patterns of morbidity and mortality decline. One example, being perhaps the most clear-cut of all, is the declining mortality in lung tuberculosis over the last hundred years in Western Europe.[8] In England and Wales, figures from 1850 and onwards indicate that there has been a steady decrease in the mortality of lung tuberculosis long before the discovery of *Mycobacterium tuberculosis* by Robert Koch around 1880. Anti-tuberculosis drugs became widely used only in the 1940s and the

BCG vaccination came into public use somewhat later (Figure 1.2). At that time the bulk of the reduction had already occurred.

It is, of course, difficult to know exactly which factors were most important for this decline. Better housing, improved sanitation, declining illiteracy, better food, and generally improved standards of living certainly contributed. In other words, it may be stated that the contribution of medicine, in its strict sense, has been fairly limited in the decline of tuberculosis mortality over the last hundred years in England and Wales and probably in other European countries as well. Of course, the *maintenance* of low levels of tuberculosis mortality has been successful with the maintenance of protective immunisation.

In England, both measles prevalence and mortality have decreased dramatically. The fall in mortality has been quite similar to that of tuberculosis, with only a limited contribution from measles immunisation (Figure 1.3). In the same way as in tuberculosis, however, measles immunisation has maintained the low death rate among children. In developing countries, measles immunisation has brought a dramatic decline in mortality figures in a way different from the historical pattern of England. In some settings poverty alleviation has thus been the main determinant of falling mortality tuberculosis, while in other settings

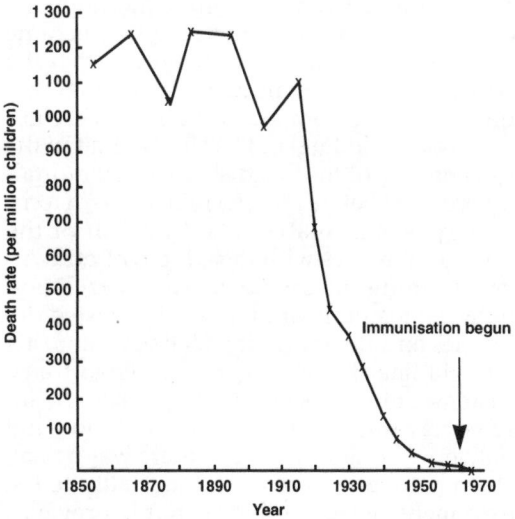

Figure 1.3. The decline in measles-related mortality shows a pattern similar to that of tuberculosis (Figure 1.2). The measles mortality reached almost zero before measles vaccination became a practice.

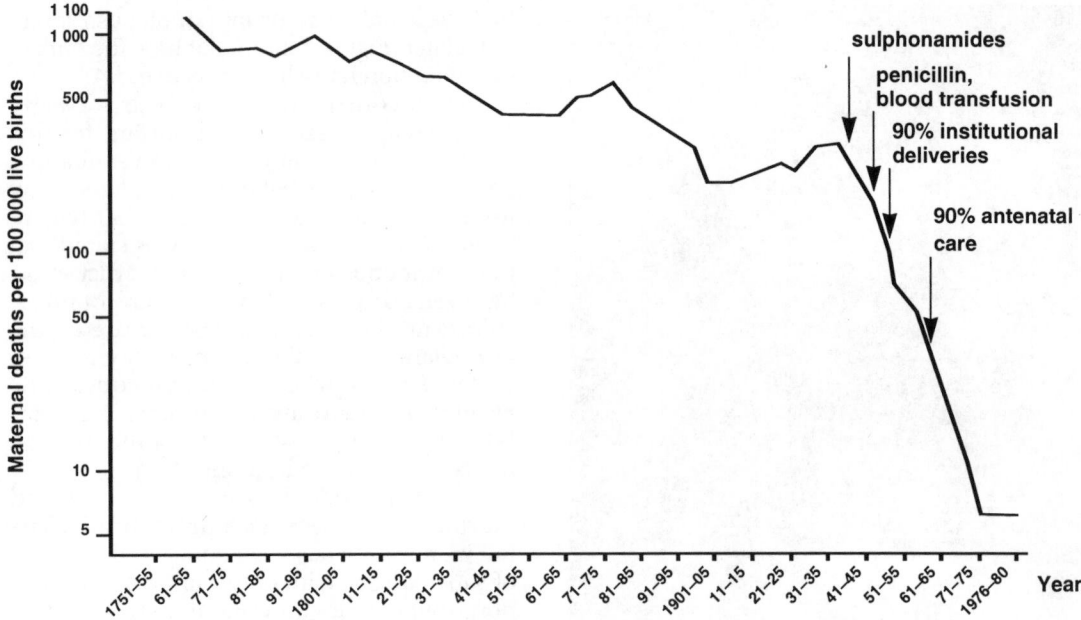

Figure 1.4. The decline in maternal mortality (logarithmic scale) in Sweden from 1750 to 1980 indicates that well over 50 per cent of the decline is attributable to interventions before the advent of modern maternal health technology.[9]

technical innovations like vaccines have contributed in the same direction.

A somewhat different example can be quoted from the field of maternal mortality (Figure 1.4). In Sweden the civil register existing since 1749 confirms that the maternal mortality declined long before modern technology became available. It is quite clear, however, that the pattern of maternal mortality in Sweden was quite different from the decline of tuberculosis mortality in England. Well over half of the total decline of the Swedish maternal mortality occurred before any essential modern technology was available. The first half of the decline coincides with the advent of midwifery training in Sweden. The correlation between the number of midwife-assisted deliveries and the mortality decline is almost a straight line (Figure 1.5). When blood transfusions, antibiotics and modern obstetric intensive care, antenatal care and hospital deliveries became available, there was a final, steep reduction in maternal mortality to the extremely low levels that currently prevail.[9]

That poverty alleviation cannot reduce maternal mortality without use of modern technology is clear from a study of fundamentalist religious groups in the US. In one such religious group, maternal mortality reaches ex-

tremely high levels (about 800 per 100 000 live births), which is significantly worse than in Bangladesh at present.[10] The explanation of these high maternal mortality levels is that some of these groups constantly avoid any modern health care even in emergencies that may be life-threatening. Such an attitude brings obstetric standards back to the era before the advent of blood transfusions, antibiotics, intensive care and other life-saving skills.

STRUCTURAL ADJUSTMENT PROGRAMMES AND HEALTH

The prevailing impoverishment, the health consequences of which are clearly visible in today's world, has been addressed in a number of ways over the last decades. The latest system of measures and undertakings can be summarised in the structural adjustment policies (Chapter 2) implemented in a number of countries by the World Bank and the International Monetary Fund (IMF).[11] The incentive to privatise and commercialise public sectors like health care and education is expected to lead to economic recovery in debt-burdened countries where the prevalence of absolute poverty is alarming.

In many of these countries the poverty has, however, already reached such levels that any belt-tightening of already minimal health budgets is a disastrous threat to public health. According to the IMF there is a falling trend in the *per capita* expenditures on health and education in most developing countries (Table 1.3).[12] These data show that in Latin America, from 1980 to 1984, expenditures on health *per capita* fell in 14 countries (16 per cent of the countries for which there are data). There were cuts in education expenditures *per capita* in about 30 per cent of the countries for which there are data in Africa, in ten countries (nearly 60 per cent) in Latin America and in several countries in Asia. The countries with most severe cuts in the *per capita* GNP and health/education expenditures are listed in Table 1.3.

Nigeria, a country where structural adjustment programmes have been introduced, is an illustrating example of how adjustment programmes can deteriorate health services. In Zaria, all aspects of maternity care at a hospital level were free in 1983. Two years later, following the reduction in government subsidy, health service fees were introduced and were high enough to lead to a fall in the number of pregnant women attending the hospital. Most patients stayed at home and came to the hospital only as a last resort if a serious complica-

tion developed. *Maternal mortality increased 1983–1988 by 56 per cent and the number of hospital deliveries declined by about 50 per cent. The percentage of complicated labour rose from 20 per cent to more than 60 per cent during the same years.*[13]

In Zimbabwe, attendances have declined substantially. The number of babies born before their mothers reached the Harare central hospital increased by 30 per cent during the first half year following the introduction of the adjustment programme.[14] In Zambia, malnutrition now affects half of the children below five years of age and nearly one-third of the adult population.[14] In Senegal, where one of the first structural adjustment programmes in Africa was undertaken in the early 1980s, malaria, tuberculosis and diarrhea cases are increasing.[14]

The scientific documentation supporting an association between structural adjustment programmes and deteriorating health services still remains to be consolidated. Most indicators, however, point to the fact that the debt burden must be examined as a determinant of rising figures of morbidity and mortality. In a recent review it was noted that less than three per cent of total African debt had been cancelled.[14] There has been an obvious failure to address the considerable amount of debt owed to the World Bank and IMF, which now absorb 36 per cent of total debt service payments.[15] A major problem remaining with all debt reduction schemes is that they are associated with adjustment programmes. It is remarkable that the latest offer of the USA to cancel 50 per cent of the loans to the very poorest African countries is conditional on their acceptance of such programmes.[16]

THE FEMINISATION OF POVERTY

A Telugu proverb says: 'Bringing up a girl is like watering a plant in your neighbour's garden'. This proverb illustrates one essential point in the gender discrimination prevailing in many less affluent countries. The International Labour Organization (ILO) indicated in a recent report that 'women are half the world's population, receive one-tenth of the world's income, account for two-thirds of the world's working hours and own only one-hundredth of the world's property'.[17]

In most countries female life expectancy is longer than that of males. In impoverished societies, above all in South-East Asia, the reverse is true and female mortality is higher than male

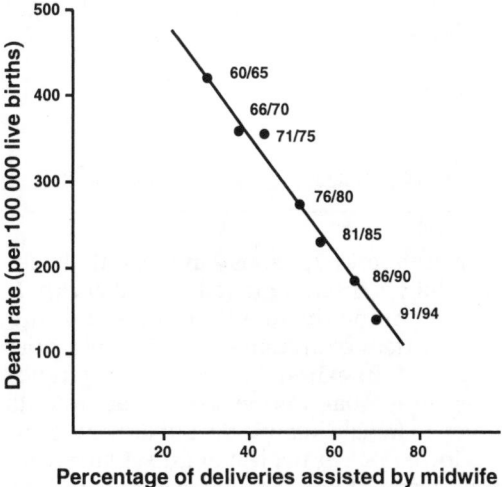

Figure 1.5. The decline in maternal mortality ratio 1850–1890 indicated that the training of rural midwives was a key factor in the decline. Although this is no proof of a cause-effect relationship, it is an indicator of the role of midwives in maternal mortality reduction in Sweden.[9]

Table 1.3. Countries with the most severe cuts in the *per capita* gross national product (GNP) and health/education expenditures (annual percentage change).[17]

Country	Health	Education	GNP
Africa	**1979–83**	**1979–83**	**1980–85**
Ghana	− 15.8	− 9.5	− 4.4
Malawi	− 9.8	+ 7.0	− 1.0
Sudan	− 9.5	− 16.8	− 2.6
Togo	− 7.5	+ 3.3	− 3.7
Liberia	− 6.9	− 0.6	− 7.1
Mauritius	− 6.6	− 7.7	N.A.
Tunisia	− 6.4	− 16.6	+ 1.4
Latin America	**1980–84**	**1979–83**	**1980–85**
Bolivia	− 77.7	− 14.1	− 27.5
Guatemala	− 58.3	N.A.	−14.8
Dominican Republic	− 46.5	− 4.1	+ 1.8
Surinam	− 44.2	N.A.	N.A.
El Salvador	− 32.4	− 8.1	− 25.6
Chile	− 23.8	+ 0.7	− 6.7
Barbados	− 21.3	N.A.	− 5.0
Jamaica	− 18.5	− 24.1	− 5.6
Costa Rica	− 16.5	− 16.5	− 12.3
Honduras	− 15.2	N.A.	− 11.5
Argentina	− 13.9	− 8.9	− 13.9
Uruguay	− 13.4	− 6.1	− 12.0
South and East Asia	**1979–83**	**1979–83**	**1980–83**
Sri Lanka	− 12.9	+ 1.6	+ 2.5
Philippines	− 1.3	+ 0.8	− 2.7
Middle East			
Israel	− 3.8	− 0.4	− 0.1
Jordan	− 3.1	+ 2.3	+1.3

mortality. This has been regarded as a consequence of culturally and economically motivated preference for sons. Such a preference has long since been both a consequence and a cause of a low status of women. It is a consequence because it arises as a result of women being considered as playing only unimportant roles and thus being less valued. It is also considered a cause because this under-valuation in turn leads to lower investment in females; as a result they are able to play only a peripheral role in society – causing a further lowering in their status. In either case, it indicates the pervasive prevalence of sexism, where allocation of prestige, power and resources depend on the physical characteristics of sex.

The preference for sons can mean that a female child is disadvantaged from its birth. It may determine the quality of parental care and the extent of investment in the child's development. In extreme cases, son preference may lead to abandonment of female infants or even to female infanticide, but its most common form is sheer neglect of girls. One recent announcement in Indian newspapers indicated that more than 50 per cent of families interrogated had carried out a female infanticide in their own family.

In countries where the social status of women is very low, the lack in care of girls is so great that this *environmental disadvantage* far outweighs the *genetic advantages*. This may

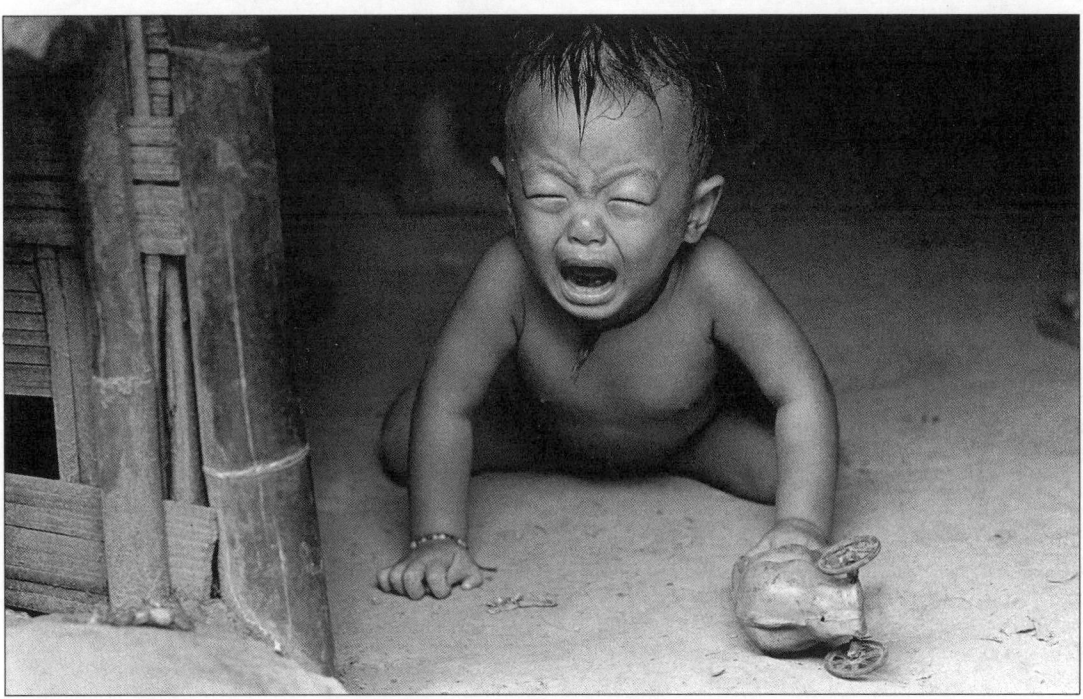

More than one billion people live in absolute poverty, a condition of life so limited by malnutrition, illiteracy, disease, squalid surroundings, high infant mortality and low life expectancy as to be beneath any reasonable definition of human decency. Photo: UNICEF/John K. Isaac

result in a complete reversal of the usual trend of higher male infant and child mortality in these countries, and a greater proportion of female infants and children dying than males. Excess female infant and child mortality may therefore be seen as a warning signal indicating serious neglect of girls in the society concerned.

There are regions in India where four times more girls than boys suffer from acute malnutrition and they may be up to 40 times less likely to be taken to hospital. It has been estimated that one in six female infant deaths in India, Bangladesh and Pakistan is due to neglect and discrimination. In India alone, this would amount to over 300 000 deaths annually.[17]

Female feticide in India and in other Asian countries deserves particular mention in this context. Fetal sex determination is a lucrative business. In spite of the relatively high cost of the procedure, most of the clients are women or couples from the middle or the lower classes, who say it is better to pay 20 USD for an abortion now than to have to finance money for a dowry when the girl is marrying. The desire for boys is not confined to Southern Asia. In a chain of clinics offering sex pre-selection services in 46 countries in

Europe, America, Asia, Latin-America, 248 out of 263 couples selected boys and 15 selected girls.[17]

CONCLUSION

It has long been obvious that there is a direct relationship between women's reproductive behaviour and various poverty indicators. In one study, comparing the 43 least developed countries with the 29 most developed countries in terms of GNP *per capita*, it was noted that almost 95 per cent of the poor countries had birth rates above 40 per 1000 while more than 95 per cent of the rich countries had birth rates below 25 per 1000.[18]

In the current interest in bringing down high birth rates in developing countries, it is easy to overlook their roots in impoverishment (the helicopter perspective). The dire consequences of absolute poverty in many countries are not sufficiently recognised in the affluent world. Structural adjustment programmes tend to focus upon symptoms of poverty rather than on mechanisms of impoverishment and powerlessness in the developing world (the grass-root perspective). These two perspectives are addressed in Chapter 4, but this concept has a wider applicability than in the field of population control. Our understanding of the pathology of poverty is dependent upon our willingness and preparedness to assume the grass-root perspective.

The conventional, latitude-oriented tropical medicine is a privileged outlook, consisting of a global overview that is more descriptive (geographical and meteorological) than analytical (economical and political). While the pathology of the tropics may leave most people without action-oriented challenges to counteract the widening poverty-gap in the world, the pathology of poverty is more thought-provoking as it puts us in a position of participation in the international economic order. Whereas drought, temperature, rain-fall and humidity at exotic latitudes seem less meaningful to try to influence, the moral challenge to the world of the pathology of poverty is obvious.

References

1. Bergström S, Povey G, Songane FF, Chong C. Seasonal incidence of eclampsia and its relationship to meteorological data. J Perinatal Med 1992;20:153–8.
2. Bjune G.Tuberkulose og lepra som folkehelseproblem. In: Ingstad B, Møgedal S, eds. Samfunnsmedisin. Oslo: Gyldendal norsk forlag, 1992, 167–77.
3. UNICEF. The state of the world's children 1993. Oxford: Oxford University Press, 1993.
4. MacNamara RS. The MacNamara years at the World Bank: major policy addresses of Robert MacNamara 1968–1981. Baltimore: Johns Hopkins University Press, 1981.
5. World Bank. World development report 1993. New York: Oxford University Press, 1993.
6. Durning AB. Poverty and the environment: reversing the downward spiral. New York: Worldwatch Institute, 1989. (Worldwatch paper)
7. Brenner MH. Fetal, infant and maternal mortality during periods of economic instability. Int J Health Serv 1973;3:145–59.
8. Fendall NRE. Medical care in the developing nations. In: Fry J, Verndale WAJ, eds. International medical care. A comparison and evaluation of medical care services throughout the world. Oxford: Medical and Technical Publishing, 1972, p. 204–48.
9. Högberg U. Maternal mortality in Sweden. Thesis. Umeå: Umeå University, 1985
10. Kaunitz AM, Spence C, Danielson TS, Rochat RW, Grimes, DA. Perinatal and maternal mortality in a religious groups avoiding obstetric care. Am J Obstet Gynecol 1984;158:826–31.
11. Gibbon P. Social dimensions of adjustment and the problem of poverty in Africa. Nytt från Nordiska Afrikainstitutet 1991;28:5–26.
12. Cornia GA, Jolly R, Stewart F, eds. Adjustment with a human face. Protecting the vulnerable and promoting growth. A study by UNICEF. Oxford: Clarendon Press, 1987.
13. Ekwempu CC, Maine D, Olorukooba MB, Essien ES, Kisseka MN. Structural adjustment and health in Africa. Lancet 1990;336:56–7.
14. Logie DE, Woodroffe J. Structural adjustment: the wrong prescription for Africa? Br Med J 1993;307:41–4.
15. Oxfam. Africa make or break. Oxford: Oxfam U.K., 1993.
16. Brummer A. US offers to write-off half debt of poorest countries in Africa as policy shifts to relieve 'crushing burdens'. Guardian 1993, May 14:15, Col. 4–6.
17. Smyke P eds. Women and health. London: Zed Books, 1991, p. 20.
18. Murdoch, W.W. The poverty of nations: the political economy of hunger and population. New York: Johns Hopkins University Press, 1980.

About the author

Staffan Bergström is Professor of International Health at the University of Oslo and Senior Physician at the Department of Obstetrics and Gynaecology, Ullevål University Hospital, Oslo, Norway. He is a specialist in obstetrics and gynaecology and responsible for several research projects in the area of reproductive health in developing countries. During 1982–86 he was the Director of the Department of Obstetrics, Central Hospital, Maputo, Mozambique. He is also involved in the human reproduction research programme (HRP) within the WHO.

Lankinen KS, Bergström S, Mäkelä PH and Peltomaa M, eds.
Health and disease in developing countries. London:The Macmillan Press Limited, 1994:13-18.

2 WORLD ECONOMY AND DEVELOPING COUNTRIES

Kimmo Kiljunen, Dr. Phil.
University of Helsinki, Institute of Development Studies
P.O. Box 47 (Hämeentie 153 B),
FIN-00014 University of Helsinki, Finland

INTRODUCTION

For many developing countries the 1980s was a lost decade. In most African countries and many Latin American ones, average incomes dropped by 10–25 per cent. Their share in world trade decreased considerably. The external debt service consumed a quarter of their export revenues – in many countries, over half. And on top of this, since the middle of the last decade, the net capital transfers in the developing world became negative *vis-à-vis* the industrial world. Wealth is now flowing from the poor South to the rich North.

THE WORLD INCOME GAP

Underdevelopment manifests itself most disturbingly in famine. According to current estimates almost 800 million people live in a permanent state of undernutrition. Every year, millions die of hunger or diseases caused by it. World *per capita* food production has risen, but so has the number of people living in absolute poverty. Moreover, in the poorest countries, as in the whole Africa, food production has decreased during the past ten years.

Also other socioeconomic indicators reveal the wide scope of the problems in developing countries. On average, one in five newborn infants will die before their fifth birthday. Over 1500 million people live without PHC. There are more than 900 million illiterate adults in the developing countries, about 40 per cent of the total adult population, and 150 million school-age children receive no schooling. There are 2000 million people without any organised water supply, and 1500 million have to use only wood for fuel.[1,2,3]

The average income level in industrial countries in 1990 was nearly 22 000 USD per capita, compared with 840 USD in developing countries – that is, the gulf in living standards is nearly 30-fold.[4] Surprisingly, 20 years earlier, the corresponding gap was 'only' 11-fold. Today, there are significantly more human and material resources which, shared more equally, would guarantee a satisfactory living standard for everybody in the world.

In 1990, the world average GNP was 4200 USD per capita, which is equivalent to the living standard of South Korea or Algeria. This is the average income level that would be reached if the global GNP were to be literally divided equally (Tables 2.1 and 2.2).

The present-day problems in the developing countries seem all the more startling compared with the optimism of a couple of decades ago. The Southern hemisphere had just been liberated from colonialism and it was believed that independence would lead to rapid progress. The industrial countries, too, were willing to support development efforts in the poorer countries. However, bitter experience has proven that to become politically independent was, after all, a relatively painless process compared with the difficulties to reform the prevailing economic and social structures both internationally and nationally.

Table 2.1. Population, GNP *per capita* and growth of GNP *per capita* in country groups.

Country group	1990 population (millions)	1990 GNP *per capita* (USD)	Average annual growth of GNP *per capita* (per cent)		
			1965-73	1973-80	1980-90
Low- and middle-income	4 100	840	4.3	2.6	1.5
Low-income	3 100	350	2.4	2.7	4.0
Middle-income	1 100	2 220	5.3	2.4	0.4
Sub-Saharan Africa	500	340	1.6	0.6	-1.1
East Asia and the Pacific	1 600	600	5.1	4.8	6.3
South Asia	1 200	330	1.2	1.8	2.9
Middle East	256	1 790	6.8	1.0	-1.5
Latin America	430	2 180	4.6	2.3	0.5
High-income	820	19 590	3.7	2.1	2.4
OECD members	780	21 170	3.7	2.1	2.5
World	5 300	4 200	2.8	1.3	1.4

DEVELOPING COUNTRIES IN THE WORLD TRADE

The colonial economic legacy was left for the newly independent countries: export-oriented, resource-based production structure and a one-sided basic infrastructure facilitating primarily the operation of export sector. Still today, two-thirds of the foreign trade in developing countries are with Western industrial countries, while mutual trade relations are modest. *Consequently, the structure of foreign trade is almost as one-sided as during the colonial period.* Basic raw materials still make up nearly 70 per cent of their exports.[5,6] Furthermore, the commodity export has concentrated on one, or at best a few, products: coffee comes from Colombia, cotton from Sudan, cocoa from Ghana, tea from Sri Lanka, peanuts from Senegal, sugar from Cuba, jute from Bangladesh, sisal from Tanzania, oil from Saudi Arabia, copper from Chile or Zambia, phosphate from Morocco, bananas from Central America, and so on. Half of the developing countries earn more than 50 per cent of their export income from one single commodity, and in several countries the share of that one product out of total export revenues is more than 90 per cent.

The development after the Second World War has meant marked structural change in the international economy. Multinational companies have emerged, controlling an increasing share of international trade and investment. *It is estimated that one-third of world trade is in fact intra-firm transactions within multinational corporations.* As to trade in basic commodities, 40–90 per cent, depending on the product, is in the hands of a few leading international companies. These have a decisive influence on the prices, the location of production and the revenues generated. The multinational companies are not particularly interested in increasing the processing capacity of developing countries.

For Third World countries the international division of labour is disadvantageous in the long run. They will lose the added value that would accrue from the processing industry. Moreover, they are suffering from the downward trend in the relative prices of commodities. During the period 1980–88, the developing countries had a cumulative loss of 93 billion dollars as a result of declining terms of trade in their foreign trade. That nearly corresponds to the revenues they receive in one year in their commodity exports, oil excluded.

Producers of raw materials also suffer sharp cyclical price fluctuations. Commodity prices in the world market vary greatly. During the last thirty years, the commodity prices have fluctuated by an average of 15–20 per cent annually. The greatest fluctuations have been for sugar, 62 per cent; and the smallest for jute, 13 per cent. Such sudden price changes make even a short-term economic planning well-nigh impossible (Figure 2.1).[6,7]

Price variations are frequently influenced by supply factors. However, primarily com-

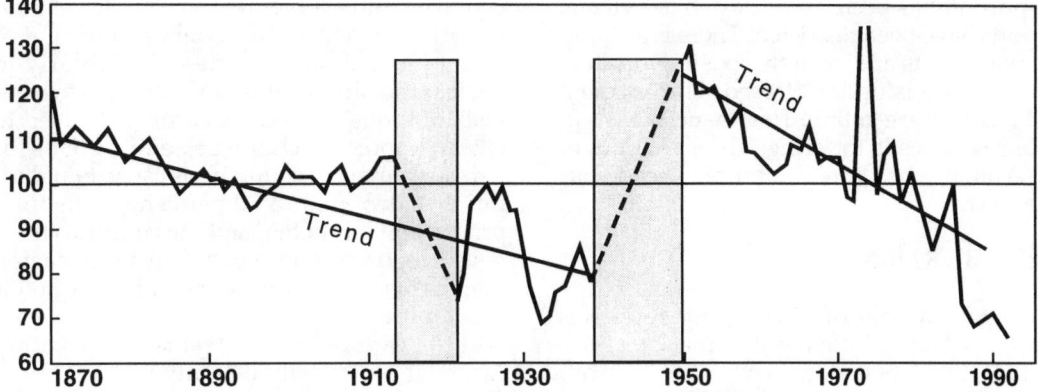

Figure 2.1. Price index of raw materials 1870–1992 (1980 = 100). Prices of raw materials (excluding oil) are deflated by prices of industrial products.

modity price fluctuations follow demand changes in the industrial countries. Even minor variations in their economic growth are directly reflected in the prices of raw materials.

At present, the relative commodity prices are at their lowest since the Great Depression in the 1930s. There are many reasons for this. Firstly, growth in the traditional raw material-intensive processing industries has been meagre. Secondly, substitutes for traditional raw

Table 2.2. Population and GNP *per capita* in selected countries.

Country	1990 population (millions)	1990 GNP *per capita* (USD)
Switzerland	7	32 680
Japan	123	25 430
Sweden	9	23 600
Germany	80	22 320
United States	250	21 790
Finland	5	18 000
Saudi Arabia	15	7 050
Hungary	11	5 900
South Korea	43	5 400
Russia	147	3 200
Thailand	56	1 420
Zimbabwe	10	640
China	1 134	370
Kenya	24	370
India	850	350
Ethiopia	51	120
Mozambique	16	80

materials have been developed. And thirdly, technical progress has enabled more efficient utilisation of raw materials and recycling.

Besides these demand factors, commodity price depression is caused by an excess supply, arising from the economic difficulties, particularly balance-of-payments and debt problems in developing countries. Countries are forced into export-oriented growth model in order to increase foreign exchange earnings to pay for debt service. This has led to oversupply and to a fall in commodity prices. The vicious circle is complete. The price decrease is compensated by export volume increase in order to maintain export revenues. The supply growth in saturated markets only accelerates the drop in prices.

In the period 1980–88, the commodity exports of developing countries (excluding fuels) grew in volume by 11 per cent, but their real export income was 20 per cent less in 1988 than in 1980. The real prices of commodities had dropped by 30 per cent.[8]

The industrialised countries gain a double benefit from the economic and financial difficulties of the developing countries. On the one hand they credit from the debt service payments of the developing countries; and on the other hand, the prices of the imported commodities have dropped drastically.

In the 1980s, the trade account in the developing countries became positive: their export surpassed the import. Nevertheless, their economic growth – with the exception of South-East Asian and Far Eastern countries – has in the main either halted or taken a downward turn. The export income has not been used for domestic investments – rather, too great a proportion has been used for debt servicing. Imports have been restricted. There is a slump in investments and even the existing production capacity is under-utilised. Employment and incomes are falling. The financial basis of public services is tottering. The dynamics of the economy has gone – a whole decade has been lost.

DEBT BURDEN

The external debt of developing countries overtook the 500 billion dollar mark in 1979. By 1987, the debt had grown to over 1000 billion USD, and at present (1993) it is around 1500 billion USD. The developing countries have been driven into a situation where in practice they receive new credit only for re-scheduling of the previous ones.

The scale of the problem is illustrated by the fact that in 1990, the developing countries paid to the industrial ones a total of 162 billion dollars in debt service payments, out of which mere interest payments amounted to 80 billion dollars. In the same year, they received 50 billion dollars in development assistance from Western industrial countries.

Development aid financing, has stagnated too. Since 1984, the net transfers of financial resources to developing countries have been reversed from the poor countries to the rich ones (Figure 2.2). Furthermore, aid budgets are growing more slowly than is the number of old and new claimants on these limited funds. The new claimants are primarily countries of Eastern Europe and the former Soviet Union.

The external debt burden is equivalent to some 50 per cent of the GNP in developing countries and an average one-quarter of their export income is used to debt servicing. For many individual countries, particularly in Africa, the situation is considerably worse. Lack of foreign exchange earnings has led to cuts in imports, including essential goods for industry. In many countries its capacity utilisation has dropped to 30 per cent. Thus total production has fallen, and the countries have fewer resources than ever before for managing their debts and restoring the balance of their economies.[3]

In the case of the poorest countries, debt cancellation is really the only viable option. This has in fact been partly implemented by official creditors. Within the banking community, the debt crisis of the past decade is all but over. Today, banks have made effective provisions against the Third World debt. For developing countries, the debt problem is far from resolved. Some claims have been reduced as a result of buy-backs in the secondary markets or debt swaps for equity investments associated with privatisation. Some new debt relief schemes have also been introduced in which outstanding external debt obligations have been converted into local currency contributions for natural resources or for social investment e.g. within approved UNICEF programmes.[7]

STRUCTURAL ADJUSTMENT PROGRAMMES

Many developing countries have ended up in an unbearable situation with the chronic deficits – aggravated by debt problems – in their balance of payments and their budgets. Inefficient, often unsocial and undemocratic administration, with bureaucracy that cripples economic activity, has been incapable of creating balance. The International Monetary Fund (IMF) and the World Bank have taken responsibility for carrying through of structural adjustment programmes. Debt rescheduling as well as development assistance transfers are more and more dependent on debtors' willingness to follow IMF direction.

Current adjustment programmes embody three typical elements. First, reliance upon contraction of aggregate demand, usually via credit squeezes, contraction of money supply, wage freezes and cuts in public expenditures. This, in turn, has caused consequent reduction in overall imports and, frequently, in the level of output and employment.

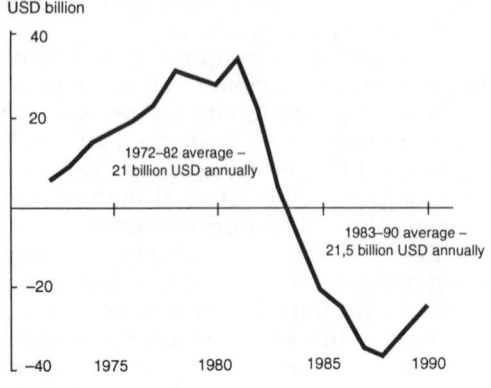

Figure 2.2. Net transfers to developing countries.

Women harvesting rice in Pate Bana, Sierra Leone.
Photo: UNICEF/Carolyn Watson

Second, there are efforts to restructure the economy by producing more tradeable goods and services or by increasing exports, principally via rationalising relative product and factor prices, including the exchange rate adjustment and efficiency-raising measures.

A third set of policies, generally part of conventional adjustment packages, consists of series of institutional economic reforms related to the overall development strategy of the country. These may include attempts towards greater market- and outward-orientation, reduced control of trade and foreign exchange, a reduced role of the public sector, new approaches to income distribution, etc.

While it is self-evident that countries have to adjust – taking into consideration present economic constraints, both external and internal – it is equally obvious that this should preferably be done in a way that protects the current level of output and employment, the potential for medium-term economic growth and the most vulnerable members of the society. The critics of the current conventional adjustment programmes have stressed four principal shortcomings in them.[9,10] First, adjustment programmes should respond to the particular needs of the developing countries, embodying selective, targeted and country-specific approaches instead of relying upon generalised and blunt policy instruments.

Second, the appropriateness of the conventional stabilisation programmes has been dubious in many cases, particularly when the developing countries are facing structural deficits in their balance of payments, being primary product exporters. Their exports are basically constrained by external demand due to slow growth in world demand for primary products. As countries try to expand their exports, they may only succeed in undermining the adjustment efforts of others, by further depressing global commodity prices. Hence, the adjustment of balance of payments has been made primarily by cutting back imports rather than by increasing exports. It has been a recessive adjustment.

Third, to be effective, domestic adjustment measures in developing countries should be supported by sufficient international measures including supportive, long-standing external resource flow and improvements in the international trading environment.

Fourth, doubts about adjustment programmes have been expressed on the grounds that they do not take sufficient account of their likely effects upon poverty and income distribution. In many developing countries, it cannot be a legitimate policy alternative to pursue expenditure cuts and to decrease the average consumption level in a situation where it is barely sufficient to ensure survival levels. Adjustment policies have caused a deterioration in the welfare of the poor in three broad ways: incomes fall, consumer prices rise and government social services are cut.

The effects of macroeconomic stabilisation and structural adjustment programmes upon poverty have already been subject of great concern to some international organisations such as UNICEF and ILO. Their basic conclusions have been that worsening economic conditions are indeed provoking a severe deterioration of child health, quality of education and nutrition in several developing countries. It appeared that the extent of the deterioration in human conditions had largely been dependent on the type of adjustment policies adopted. The UNICEF reports did not accuse anybody of having pursued regressive distributive policies *per se*. Adjustment programmes have not necessarily been biased against poor people, but neither, in general, have they been designed to protect the basic needs of the poorest.

Alarmed by the situation, the IMF and the World Bank have begun to draw attention to income distribution effects of the adjustment programmes. The aim has been particularly to support African governments to take into account the needs of the poorest sections of the population when implementing adjustment programmes.[11-14]

Why not to go further. The next phase would emphasise structural reforms that would permanently improve the social position of the poor. Such reforms would include a fairer distribution of income, a more efficient system for taxing income and wealth, land reform, more vigorous investments in human capital – that is, in basic education and health – and improvement in people's participation in decision making. Structural adjustment is a process that enables new policy orientation. Hence, it is a challenge for poverty alleviation too.

References

1. IFAD. The state of world rural poverty. An inquiry into its causes and consequences. New York: New York University Press, 1992:514 pp.
2. UNICEF. The state of the world's children 1990. Oxford: Oxford University Press, 1990:102 pp.
3. UNDP. Human development report 1992. New York: Oxford University Press, 1992:216 pp.
4. World Bank. World development report 1992. Oxford: Oxford University Press, 1992:308 pp.
5. UNCTAD. Revitalizing development, growth and international trade: Assessment and policy options. Geneva: UNCTAD, 1987. (TD/328)
6. South Commission. The challenge to the South. The report of the South Commission. Geneva: South Commission, 1990:325 pp.
7. Furtado C, Jayawardena L, Yoshitomi M. The world economic and financial crisis. Helsinki: WIDER, 1989:59 pp. (Research for Action)
8. Blanchard O, Dornbusch R, King MA, et al. World imbalances. Helsinki: WIDER, 1989:137 pp. (World Economy Group 1989 Report)
9. Cornia G, Jolly R, Stewart F, eds. Adjustment with a human face. Protecting the vulnerable and promoting growth. A study by UNICEF. Oxford: Clarendon Press, 1987:319 pp.
10. Kiljunen K. The World Bank and the world poverty. Helsinki: Institute of Development Studies, University of Helsinki, 1988:15 pp. (Occasional Papers No. 2)
11. World Bank. Protecting the poor during periods of adjustment. Washington: World Bank, 1987:53 pp. (SecM 87–128)
12. Demery L, Addison T. The alleviation of poverty under structural adjustment. London: Overseas Development Institute, 1987:47 pp.
13. Taylor L. Varieties of stabilization experience, towards sensible macroeconomics in the Third World. WIDER Studies: Development Economics. Oxford: Clarendon Press, 1988:180 pp.
14. Serageldin I, Nool M. Tackling the social dimensions of adjustment in Africa. Finance & Development 1990;27:18-20.

Additional reading

1. Drèze J, Sen A. Hunger and public action. Oxford: Clarendon Press, 1989:373 pp.
2. Kiljunen K. Toward a theory of the international division of industrial labour. World Development, 1989;1:109–38.
3. Kiljunen K, ed. Region to region cooperation between developed and developing countries. London: Avebury, 1990:179 pp.
4. Kiljunen K. Finland and the new international division of labour. London: Macmillan Press, 1991:240 pp.
5. United Nations. International development strategy for the Fourth United Nations Development Decade (1991–2000). New York: United Nations, 1990:7 pp.

About the author

Kimmo Kiljunen is development economist and since 1986 the Director of The Institute of Development Studies, University of Helsinki, Finland. During 1989–91 he worked as a UNICEF consultant in Kenya. He is an executive committee member of European Association of Development Research and Training Institutes. He has published extensively on global development problems including some dozen of books on e.g. Namibia, Cambodia, regional cooperation and Finland's role in the international system.

Lankinen KS, Bergström S, Mäkelä PH and Peltomaa M, eds.
Health and disease in developing countries. London:The Macmillan Press Limited, 1994:19-23.

3 THE ROOTS OF DEVELOPMENT COOPERATION

Mikko Juva, Ph.D., Th.D., LL.D., D.D., Litt.D.
Nuuksiontie 38, FIN-02820 Espoo,
Finland

INTRODUCTION

Development cooperation is a relatively recent chapter in the history of mankind. Of course, nations have always learned from each other ever since they became neighbours. The development has been driven by those who were able to find novel ideas and new ways of action in the continuous battles with nature and other nations. Their success then prompted the others to ponder the secrets of their neighbours, and then to follow their examples. This is the way that passed along axe and spear, wheel and lever, agriculture and animal husbandry, boat and sail, cloth and net, bronze and iron, writing and instrumental music.

The main responsibility for the dissemination of knowledge and promotion of development, however, has always been with the followers, the apprentices. The history of the world is full of stories about how those who made the innovations and discoveries jealously guarded their advantage and tried to prevent the spreading of the essential information to outsiders. But the history is equally full of stories about aggressive invaders and clever spies who managed to bring new know-how back to home.

But there are no records in history about periods when the affluent nations would have made any special efforts to develop the efficiency and wealth of the underprivileged. Admittedly, international collaboration has included both mutually profitable trade and the comparison and exchange of ideas and working methods within the sphere of shared religion or culture, but the political state always insisted that its own resources should benefit only the national needs and objectives.

Children and women deserve special attention, since they are the most vulnerable groups. Photo: UNICEF/Mariantonietta Peru

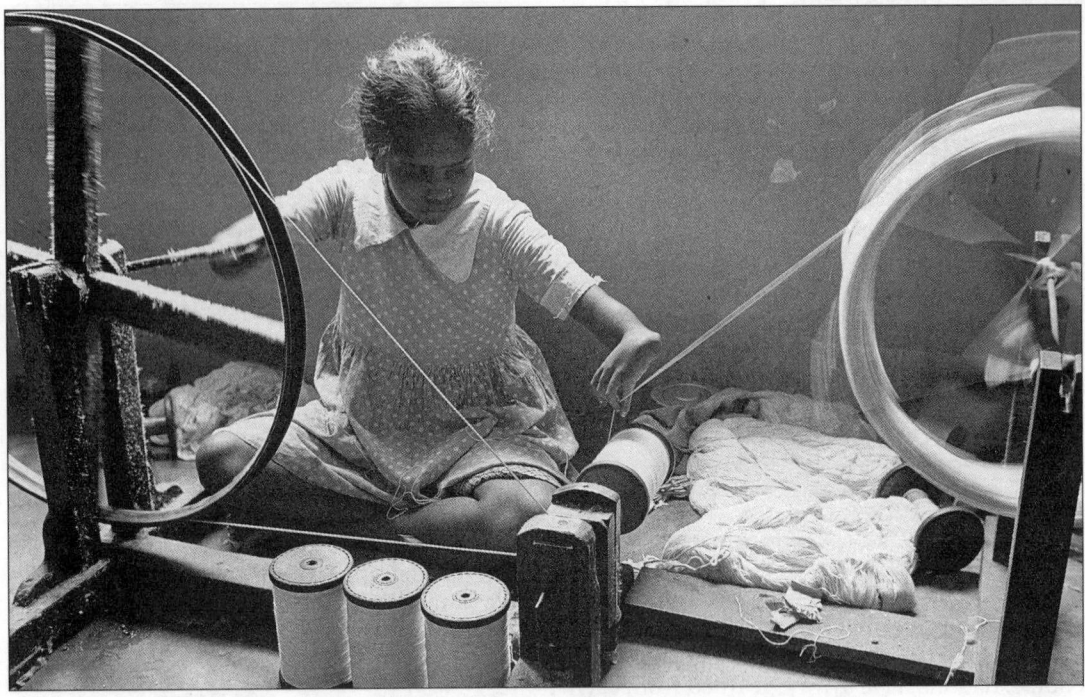

Disabled child in Bombay, India participating in a UNICEF program that will provide her with practical skills. Photo: UNICEF/Bernard P. Wolff

Each country took responsibility of the upbringing and welfare of its citizens, but they did not assume any liability of the well-being of other states.

Such was the world a thousand years ago and even a hundred years ago. During this century both the attitudes and practices have changed significantly. Of course, in all countries there are still those who feel that only the less developed themselves are responsible for their own situation, but it seems that these people have now been surpassed by those in favour of development assistance. The two World Wars of this century awakened the mankind to see that it will not survive without collaboration, joint planning and central world organisation. That common organisation, United Nations, has acknowledged this fact and stated that the responsibility of the current state and future of the mankind is common and not dividable.

THE ROAD TO COLONIALISM

To analyse the character and problems of development cooperation it is necessary to review the process that led to the current state of affairs. The great revolution was initiated in and distributed from Europe with the advent of modern times. Throughout the Middle Ages, European Christianity and Eastern and South Mediterranean Islam had fought fiercely for supremacy. The fight was mainly of political and military nature, but covered also areas of religion, culture and society. Islam had close contacts with the great civilisations of Asia, India and China, which meant a significant advantage for a considerable period of time. At the same time, this effectively closed the road from Europe to other parts of the world, a close-down that lasted for a millennium.

By the advent of modern times Europe raised this blockade. With the help of the superior technical skills and military powers accrued during the Renaissance, Europe sailed through oceans to Africa, to the Americas and, circumventing Islam, to India and China, and finally, round the world. At first, Europe conquered the seas and subsequently also the shores. Simultaneously it deprived the Islamic nations of the trade hegemony they had held for centuries; Europe was now dictating the terms of world trade. In many places, like in North America, Australia and South Africa, the European immigrants also settled down in the areas they had invaded, and either displaced or destroyed the original inhabitants. The invasion of other people's land by conquerors was by no means a new feature in the human history. What was new, was the extension of the conquests to faraway continents and the devastating results to the indigenous populations.

Where inconvenient climate, ancient culture or dense population prevented the displacement or destruction of the indigens, the conquered areas were taken into possession and put into the service of the trade and economy of the mother country. During three centuries Europe used its economic, technical and military supremacy to put the both Americas, almost the whole of Africa and a major part of Asia under its colonial rule. Even countries that retained their independence, China, Japan, Siam, Persia and Ethiopia, had to adjust to the European political and economic hegemony. By the end of the period Europe was no longer master of the seas but, in fact, master of the whole world.

Rudyard Kipling expressed the essential idea of the colonial rule with his well-known words about 'the burden of the white man'. To him, the white man represented the height of evolution of mankind whose responsibility was to make other nations share the higher civilisation, order and technologies. It was not attempted to make the indigenous populations European but to make them recognise the most important of European values, especially industriousness, law and order. Class division in the colonies remained clear, however high the original culture of the colonised country might have been.

COLONIAL RULE

Generally speaking, the colonial administrators did not force the original populations to the ruler's religion. Even if they sometimes did encourage conversion their attitude towards missionary activities was mostly negative. The reasoning was clear: the colonies were economically important to the mother country, and all activities causing trouble or unrest in the society were therefore undesirable.

More than two centuries of European colonial rule branded the world permanently. In Europe, the period from the beginning of 18th century to the middle of 20th century was an era of immense scientific, technical, economic and social advances. The benefits of this technical–economic growth were shared only minimally with other parts of the world.

When the British rule was established in the beginning of 19th century in India, the country had about 100 million people living mostly in the rural villages. The industries were traditional agriculture, animal husbandry and handicraft. The industrialisation in Great Britain suppressed the Indian weavers as the markets were taken over by cheap fabrics produced in the mother country. Millions of craftsmen were left without livelihood. As the rural population grew simultaneously, the jobless started flowing into rapidly swelling cities. An army of jobless, homeless and beggars soon evolved, an army that ever since is the hallmark of the impoverishment of the Indian people.

In Africa and East Asia the colonial rulers transformed the agriculture to serve the American and European consumers. Large areas were converted to coffee, tea, cocoa, sisal, rubber or peanut plantations, which effectively reduced the land areas available for local food production. Sadly, also the economic profits were totally channelled to European and American industries and consumers, leaving little for the development of the colonies themselves.

In a quite similar fashion, also minerals, copper, gold, diamonds and oil have been exported almost for free from the colonies. Local people were employed in the mines, often originating from several tribes, uprooted from their own societies. In the mining communities and industrial centres they had little means of maintaining their own traditions, not to mention the obvious impossibility of retaining the structures of the tribal societies.

The European colonial system collapsed finally after the Second World War. Without a deeper analysis of the circumstances that led to this change, it can be said that the system broke down just as it was starting to demand more money in expenditure than it could produce for the mother country. One by one, the colonies in Asia and Africa struggled for liberation and got their independence. What remained was their poverty and economic dependence. The new national governments were unable to raise the long-oppressed peoples to the level of the industrialised nations. Both the know-how and the financial means were simply insufficient. Such was the setting for the idea of development cooperation.

FROM ASSISTANCE TO COOPERATION

Initially the collaboration was described as development assistance, but as this was considered offensive in the newly independent nations, it was soon substituted by the more appropriate term development cooperation. To start with, the activities dealt mainly with the practical matters of the transition phase of independence. It would have looked too bad just to abandon the bankrupt territories and some financial arrangements by the previous mother country became necessary. Of course there was also a price to be paid for maintaining the advantageous trade connections. It was good foresight to keep in good terms with the old colonies as they now had the possibility to trade with other countries as well, many of them rivals to the previous mother country. This promoted close relations with the new rulers and, effectively, also support to at least some of their favourite projects.

Development cooperation was necessary in all walks of life. The administration and the judicial system had to be manned with able people who wanted to serve the new management. The economy was badly in need of upgrading. Transport and trade connections had to be established. A pivotal issue was of course the school system that had not been one of the priorities of the colonial administrations. The old rulers had taken good care of the health of the Europeans, but the local people had been largely left to local traditional healers. After the situation changed, all this needed both manpower and financial resources.

MISSIONS, SCHOOLS AND HOSPITALS

Actually there already existed a considerable network of schools and hospitals with professional staff, but they were not in the service of the local governments. These networks had been created by the missionary movement that from the beginning of the 19th century inspired the whole Western Christianity. This movement had not been initiated by official bodies of the churches, but rather by religious individuals at a time when the European society already had, to a considerable extent, turned against the church.

Following the conquerors and traders these missionaries now sailed to foreign continents.

Obviously, they could not have done this without the European rule of the seas and colonies. Nevertheless, they had objectives different from those of their countrymen. They were not seeking financial profit, but rather the souls of the people. It did not take long, however, before the missionaries extended their activities to two sectors which today count as development cooperation: they started schools and founded hospitals or health stations.

Historically, development cooperation thus has two origins: the European governments' responsibility for the colonial societies and, secondly, the school and health care systems created by the Christian missionaries on the other.

DEVELOPMENT AND BASIC RIGHTS

From an ethical point of view development cooperation is based on common basic rights of human beings. Such rights have their roots deep in the history of mankind. The obligation of helping also others and not only one's own family, admittedly, has been extended rather slowly to foreign nations. 'Love your neighbour and hate your enemy' was a long-lasting general rule determining the mutual relationships between peoples who were fighting over living space.

When United Nations in 1945 published its famous Universal Declaration of Human Rights it could refer to both old and general traditions. The Preamble of the Declaration spells out its justification in saying that 'recognition of the inherent dignity and of the equal and inalienable rights of all members of the human family is the foundation of freedom, justice and peace in the world'. The Declaration is in actual fact only a recommendation, but it has very much influenced public opinion and consequently also governments' policies.

In democracies public opinion is a significant factor both economically and politically. The missionary movement has demonstrated what endurance and devotion to a purpose can accomplish, e.g. by establishing wide networks of hospitals and schools in Asia and Africa. This work is now being continued by innumerable NGOs, both religious and secular. Voluntary fund raising amounts to substantial sums each year. Mass media has played a significant role in augmenting the people's will to help by bringing to the living

Bolivian children beg their daily bread by the main road. Photo: UNICEF/A. Graciano

rooms of industrialised countries the messages and images of malnourished children in Africa, the refugees on flight from guns of war and the miseries in slums of Asian megacities.

TO START BRIDGING THE GAP

But the ever worsening gap between the poor South and the affluent North cannot possibly be resolved by pretty speeches and voluntary movements or fund raising. To give the countries of the South a real start in development needs such large amounts of money that only governments can supply them. United Nations recommend that industrialised countries should allocate at least 0.7 per cent of their GNP to development cooperation. At the beginning of the 1990s only few European countries had met this recommendation. But in 1993, at the time when this is being written, economic recession at home has made even them to give up this level.

In the long term, the world has no other option than to start bridging the gap between the rich and poor. Development cooperation is one of the tools for this policy. We know only too well that wrong judgments have been made also within development cooperation,

especially when western technologies and management systems have been imported to developing countries without any adjustments. However, abuse and mistakes should not lead to rejection of the operation.

In the future the focus should be more on the structures of the world economy and trade so that the developing countries themselves will be able to benefit from their own products and so that the lion's share of profits will not fall to the tradesmen of the affluent countries. The world situation is intolerable in all respects. If the mankind opts for survival a change is inevitable. The current illness of the world is not only an ethical but also a political challenge.

About the author

Mikko Juva is an internationally known scholar and churchman. He has been Professor of History at the University of Turku and Professor of Church History at the University of Helsinki, Finland. Lastly, until his retirement in 1982 he served as the Lutheran Archbishop of Turku and Finland. For 25 years he chaired the Board of the Finnish Missionary Society which during that time worked mainly in Namibia. During 1970–77 he was the President of the Lutheran World Federation.

Lankinen KS, Bergström S, Mäkelä PH and Peltomaa M, eds.
Health and disease in developing countries. London:The Macmillan Press Limited, 1994:25-36.

4 POPULATION CONTROL: controlling the poor or the poverty?

Staffan Bergström, M.D., Ph.D.
University of Oslo, Department of
Obstetrics and Gynaecology
Ulleväl University Hospital,
N-0407 Oslo, Norway

Sher Shah Syed, M.D., M.R.C.O.G.
Dow Medical College, Department of
Obstetrics and Gynaecology
Civil Hospital, Karachi,
Pakistan

INTRODUCTION

Population control has been on the agenda of international discussion from the 1960s. The upsurge in the global interest in population issues culminated in 1974 at the first World Population Conference in Bucharest. The controversy between affluent and impoverished countries came to the surface. The population control-oriented approach of some experts and politicians was counterbalanced by the majority of impoverished countries calling for a recognition of the problems of world poverty and global distributive injustice. The health minister of India, Dr Karan Singh, pronounced the almost magic conclusion: 'The best pill is development'. In the years to come, influential circles gradually modified their positions and powerful western debaters admitted profound changes of opinion.[1]

In retrospect, it is instructive to note that while Karan Singh expressed the above slogan, the architects of the Indian emergency with compulsory sterilisation by law were already well organised in several states in northern India.[2] In the wake of the Bucharest conference there was thus a growing alertness among leaders of impoverished countries regarding the nature of the population problem. India and China followed their own paths, opting for control in the alleged national interests, while other countries opted for recognition of family planning as a human right to be integrated in maternal and child health care. Still others continued their pro-nationalist stand and did not adhere to the idea of birth control as a road to socioeconomic improvement.

THE MAGNITUDE OF THE POPULATION PROBLEM

Simple calculus tells us that a population growing at a constant rate will double, triple, quadruple etc. in so and so many years. The mathematical representation of this process is an exponential graph, theoretically ending in an almost infinite population in a comparatively short period of time.

In a historical perspective the world population has increased at a rather slow rate, presumably amounting to 0.1 per cent per year. This rate is assumed to have prevailed until the late 17th century. The improvement in general living conditions since then has resulted in a slowly declining mortality and rising global population growth rate. This trend was accentuated during the present century. The world population increased by about one billion from the early 1970s to 1987 and will grow by another billion by the year 2000. Most projections call for the addition of another billion by 2010.

There were 76 million more births than deaths in 1987, an excess that will grow to 100 million per year by the end of the century. The current population growth rate in the world is calculated to amount to 1.5–1.6 per cent. For most people such percentages are difficult to perceive. One attempt to clarify the implications of population growth rates has been to state the doubling period, that is the period during which a population will double assuming a specific growth rate. The formula to be utilised for calculating such a doubling period in years is approximately 72 years/p, where p

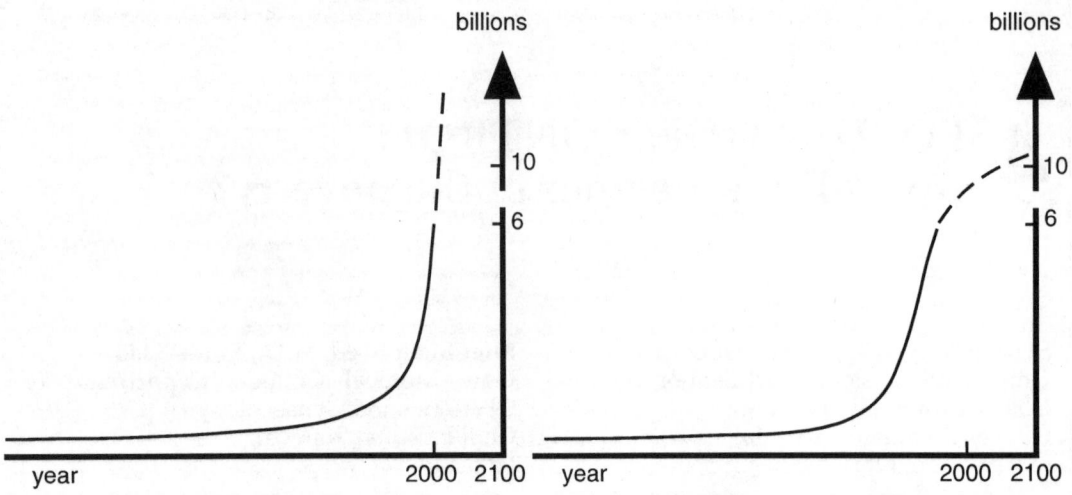

Figure 4.1. The conventional exponential graph of the 1960s and 1970s depicted the global population growth rate as an 'explosion' (graph on the left). The currently valid graph takes into consideration the falling global population growth rate, reflecting the declining total fertility rate (graph on the right), which by all probability implies the achievement of a steady state of the world's population size soon after the year 2100.

is the population growth rate in per cent. A growth rate of 1 per cent will result in a doubling in 72 years and a 3 per cent rate in about 24 years. A growth rate of 4 per cent, which a recent estimate has presented for Kenya, will mean a doubling in 18 years.

The doubling time mathematics led to a frightening scenario and constituted the basis of a doomsday perspective. This scenario characterised most of the 1960s until the breathtaking theoretical perspective was brought down by recognising the declining global population growth *rate* as a fact. It was soon discovered that the exponential graph had to be corrected to correspond to a forthcoming steady state. A comparison of these two graphic models can be seen in Figure 4.1.

The exponential graph is presumably almost correct in predicting the prevailing estimate of around 5.3 billion inhabitants in the world by the year 1990. Most evidence indicates that the world would reach approximately eight billion inhabitants by the year 2020. These figures may appear threatening, but they conceal the fact that fertility, particularly in the developing world, has turned substantially downward over the last decades. The total fertility rate (TFR), which amounted to around six children per woman in 1960 reached approximately four per woman in 1985.[3] In the United Nations medium variant projection

the TFR will reach 2.3 children per woman by the year 2025. This implies that the doubling time mathematics does not make sense, since it assumes the growth rate to be *constant*, which – as we have seen – is not the case.

UNCONTROVERSIAL ISSUES IN THE CONTROVERSY

The last two decades of debate on the population problem have demonstrated that much controversy has been linked to areas being fundamentally uncontroversial. In retrospect, and addressing the population problem ahead of us, it is appropriate and adequate to reaffirm that the population problem *is* a problem. Unprecedented growth of the world's population, particularly in poor countries, together with an appalling overconsumption and neglect of distributive global justice in the rich world, has conveyed a severe stress on the environment. This has resulted in pollution and overconsumption of non-renewable resources, resulting in exhaustion of fire-wood, water and basic means of survival in large parts of the world. Enormous resources have been wasted on armament and destructive weapons, while a growing number of starving children face an extremely troublesome future with increasing child mortality in several countries (Chapter 5).

Family planning, understood as an individual asset to regulate fertility according to individual preferences and needs, is usually considered inherently beneficial and uncontroversial, except in certain religious groups. Given our limited environment and its non-renewable resources, it is also uncontroversial to state that in the foreseeable future, the world must aim at a small-family norm, that is one to two children per family.

Even if much controversy exists concerning global distribution of consumable resources, one particular resource makes the small-family norm particularly essential in a growing number of impoverished areas: *water*. The growing number of populations already now living under water stress make the small family norm imperative. The global distribution of water is different from the global distribution of other consumable resources and the water question will presumably be the most important environmental issue in the coming decades.[4,5]

THE OVERCONSUMPTION PROBLEM

The recognition of the extremely skewed global distribution of wealth is of utmost relevance in any discussion of the population

Table 4.1. Daily supply of calories, protein and fat *per capita*, major regions.[7]

	1961–1963	1983–1985
Calories		
World	2 316	2 666
All developed countries	3 090	3 374
All developing countries	1 957	2 424
Africa	2 099	2 278
North and Central America	3 016	3 378
South America	2 401	2 617
Asia	1 916	2 437
Europe	3 122	3 390
Oceania	2 960	3 133
USSR	3 173	3 403
Protein (grams)		
World	62.4	68.2
All developed countries	89.8	97.3
All developing countries	49.7	58.2
Africa	54.5	56.4
North and Central America	87.8	93.2
South America	64.2	65.6
Asia	48.7	58.7
Europe	88.3	97.6
Oceania	86.9	87.3
USSR	94.0	98.3
Fat (grams)		
World	51.0	64.2
All developed countries	99.9	127.1
All developing countries	28.5	42.8
Africa	38.7	45.6
North and Central America	119.9	135.8
South America	52.5	62.2
Asia	24.6	40.9
Europe	107.8	136.7
Oceania	110.4	120.3
USSR	73.1	99.2

Table 4.2. *Per capita* consumption of energy in selected countries (1989).[28]

Country	Energy (kilograms of coal equivalent)
United States	10 127
Soviet Union	6 546
West Germany	5 377
Japan	4 032
Mexico	1 689
Turkey	958
China	810
Brazil	798
India	307
Indonesia	274
Nigeria	192
Bangladesh	69

problem. The enormous strain on the world's resources, exerted by the affluent minority of the world, should be emphasised when analysing the alleged problem of too many mouths to feed. According to an analysis carried out by the Food and Agricultural Organization (FAO) in the mid-1980s there had been an *increase* in the global food production *per capita* of 40 per cent during the period 1950–1980. While the number of starving people seems to have increased during the same period, the unprecedented growth of food production *per capita* has created severe storage problems both in Europe and in the US. The burden of over-production of food in affluent regions – unavailable for the starving masses of the planet due to their lack of purchasing capacity – is the most visible and clear illustration of the imbalance between impoverished and enriched countries (Table 4.1). Offering food to starving people without money would have meant dumping of food prices with ensuing loss of income for food producers in rich countries. The market mechanisms depriving the starving people from sharing the overproduction must be considered when analysing the population problem.

While the FAO figures testify to the fact that the food supply *per capita* has been growing worldwide, such documented surpluses of food are counterbalanced by large short-falls in the food supply in several countries of Sub-Saharan Africa. In Mozambique, the *per capita* daily caloric intake was reduced from an estimated 2075 to 1664 over the years 1970–1985.[7] Starvation has spread, particularly over Sub-Saharan Africa and in South-East Asia. According to the Worldwatch Institute:

'The world has 157 billionaires and perhaps two million millionaires, but 100 million people around the globe are homeless, living on sidewalks, in garbage dumps and under bridges. Americans spend five billion USD each year on special diets to lower calorie consumption, while the world's poorest 400 million people are so undernourished that they are likely to suffer stunted growth, mental retardation or death'.[6]

The overconsumption problem is not only related to food consumption in affluent countries, but also to other environmental resources. This pattern has been overwhelmingly demonstrated in the United States with 6 per cent of the world's population, but with a consumption of 40 per cent of its resources. It has been calcula-ted that the energy consumption of one American is equivalent to that of two Frenchmen, six Mexicans, 39 Indians, 57 Nigerians, 133 Haitians, or 456 residents of Nepal.[7]

Rapidly increasing, impoverished populations are commonly blamed for their deteriorating impact on the environment while, in reality they consume extremely small resources *per capita*. The attention geared towards the ecological collapse in impoverished countries conceals the real overconsumption pattern. As has been pointed out in an American report:

'Measured in constant dollars the world's people have consumed as many goods and services since 1950 as all previous generations put together. Since 1940, Americans alone have used up as large a share of earth's mineral resources as did everyone before them combined. ... The furnishings of our consumers´ lifestyle – things like automobiles, throwaway goods and packaging, a high fat diet and air-conditioning – can only be provided at great environmental cost. Our way of life depends on enormous and continuous inputs of the very commodities that are most damaging to the earth to produce: energy, chemicals, metals and paper.'[8]

The overconsumption pattern is particularly striking as regards energy. While the poor Bangladeshi peasant may worsen soil erosion by cutting down trees to get firewood, the reality is depicted in a more proper way in Table 4.2. It is important to note that the energy consumption figures are *per capita*. The *per capita* consumption pattern of other key issues in development are indicated in Table 4.3.

THE POVERTY TRAP AND THE DEMOGRAPHIC TRAP

In the population control debate the concept *demographic trap* has received increasing attention. The trap analogy implies a priority-setting among prevailing global threats with a tendency to isolate the demographic development *per se*, and to argue strongly in favour of population control.[9]

However, since fertility decisions depend on a number of fertility determinants, it would be more adequate, to address any alleged trap as constituted by the constellation of the most important fertility determinants. Considering such determinants there is general agreement that high infant mortality, inflated female illiteracy, low status of women etc. are directly related to impoverishment. It would therefore be adequate to pay more attention to the *poverty trap* in the demographic trap debate. The poverty trap has recently been analysed in four parts in the following way:[6]

1) *The lack of productive assets*: It is underscored that the poor are poor, not only because they do not earn sufficiently, but mainly because they do not own much. The ownership of farmland is well known to be highly concentrated in the hands of a fortunate few. In Latin America there are several countries with 1 per cent of landlords owning more than 40 per cent of the arable land.

2) *Physical weakness and illness*: Lacking means of subsistence implies consistent malnourish-

ment and lack of clean water, basic medical care and sufficient housing: 'Most pronounced among those one-third of the absolute poor who lack even enough calories to meet the metabolic requirements and the physical requirements, physical weakness can combine with low income to form a vicious circle. For lack of food, they have no energy to work, and for lack of work, they have no money to buy food.'[6]

3) *Population pressure*: While resources are poor, rapid population growth forces salaries down to survival level, since the poor have to compete with each other for scarce work. Poverty may stretch investment resources and may overtax natural resources whereby their productivity will diminish. In such a setting, poor couples may be driven by a complex set of circumstances into having large families as part of a strategy for economical security. In the constant struggle for survival, impoverished populations tend to see children as an economic asset: in the absence of such 'economic and institutional conditions, in which each individual has good chances of success, families see each child as an opportunity to broaden, diversify, and thereby strengthen their means of support. When times are bad for some, they may be better for others. This strength in numbers strategy, may lower the chances of pulling the whole family out of poverty, but that is a small price to pay if it reduces the risk of falling into starvation.'[6]

4) *Powerlessness*: Deprived of material goods, most absolute poor are often misled or

Table 4.3. *Per capita* consumption of steel (1987), paper (1989) and *per capita* production of cement (1990) in selected countries.[29]

Country	Steel	Paper (kilograms)	Cement
Japan	582	222	665
Soviet Union	582	36	470
West Germany	457	207	476
United States	417	308	284
Turkey	149	8	436
Brazil	99	27	167
Mexico	93	40	257
China	64	15	185
Indonesia	21	5	73
India	20	3	53
Nigeria	8	1	31
Bangladesh	5	1	3

Children and women line up for a meal near El Obeid, Sudan. Photo: UNICEF/Roger Lemoyne

intimidated into signing away their rights to land or accepting debt repayment terms that verge on extortion. Even in so-called democratic systems, legal systems and laws are often a dead end for impoverished couples, riddled, as they often are in the procedure of delays, mystifications and corruption: 'When the wealthy go to court against the illiterate poor, there is little competition. When they go to war, there is none.'[6]

The poverty trap at the global level can be illustrated by the existing terms of trade reflecting the deteriorating position of the poor. According to World Bank figures, commodity prices have undergone very marked decline over the last two decades, while the debt has gone steeply up (Figure 4.2).

The World Bank and the IMF have been instrumental in prescribing the remedy to avoid a further deterioration in the poverty trap. With a market-oriented *structural adjustment policy* major donors in affluent countries believe that the poverty trap can be opened. In the field of health there is fear, however, that increased privatisation and market orientation will have huge adverse repercussions for the absolute poor, which according to current World Bank figures means 200–300 million people in the world. The already visible

repercussions of the structural adjustment policy have forced the World Bank to initiate studies on its social dimensions.

Health care expenditures in low-income countries tend to decrease when structural adjustment policies are implemented. Shrinking health budgets tend to affect the most vulnerable part of impoverished populations, particularly women and children.[10] In this perspective the belt-tightening adjustments prescribed by the World Bank and the IMF constitute a threat to the underprivileged groups. Increasing prices of maintenance, living, food, antenatal care, hospital care, abortion services etc. tend to make people refrain from utilising live-saving skills in health units due to unbearable costs. In several countries in Africa the minimum wages have fallen by 30–50 per cent over the last years and the health expenditure on mothers and children have diminished sharply. This has reversed the trend of improving maternal and child health services in several countries.[10] In the early 1990s there will be a measurable decline in the utilisation of maternal health services also in big African capitals. The deterioration of such services implies the risk of increasing maternal mortality.

The adverse repercussions of structural adjustment policies on maternal health occur

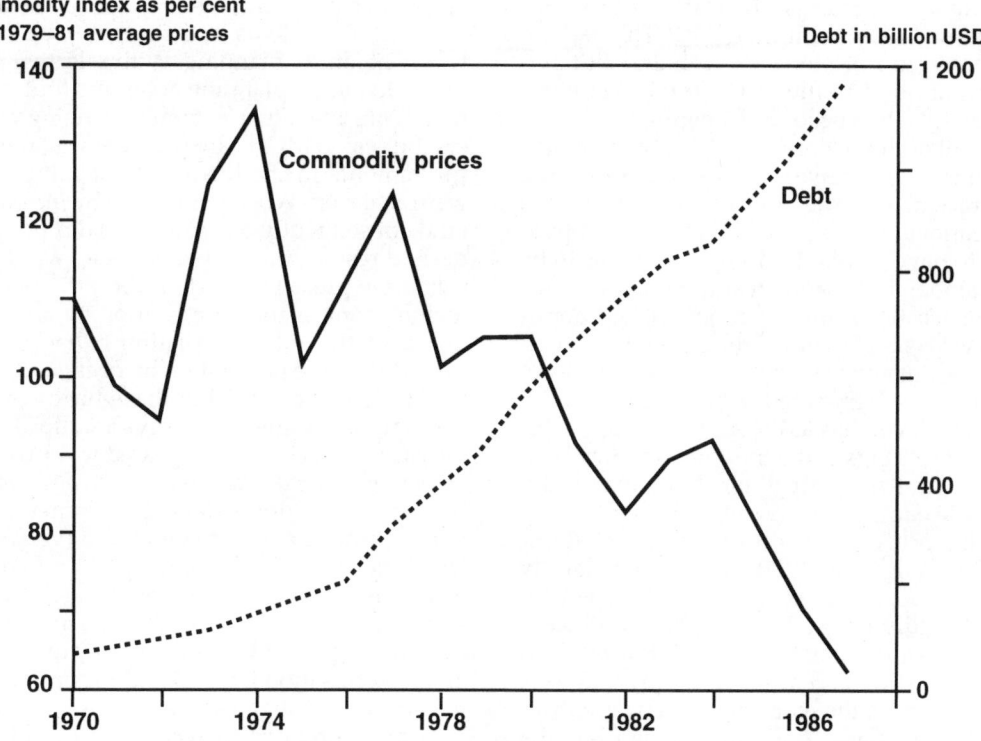

Commodity index as per cent of 1979–81 average prices

Debt in billion USD

Commodity prices

Debt

Figure 4.2. The rising Third World debt should be seen together with the declining commodity prices over the last two decades. Both phenomena contribute substantially to the aggravation of the impoverishment problem.[6]

simultaneously with an unforeseen rise in the incidence of HIV infection in pregnant women. Recent reports from Zimbabwe indicate that in some areas already 40 to 50 per cent of pregnant women are HIV positive.[11] This disastrous tendency in the HIV pandemic occurs simultaneously with the intensified financial stranglehold exerted by the affluent world on the economy of African countries. The net drain of resources from the African continent is an important reminder of the fact that the poverty trap threatens any fragile improvement in the safety of motherhood in Africa.

FREEDOM AND COERCION ISSUES IN POPULATION CONTROL

The concept control has an implication of setting limits to or checking and intervening at a defined stage of development. In one sense the word is positive: to keep an eye on the undesirable. There are few who would question the inherent good in pollution control, pesticide control, nuclear arms control etc. When it comes to birth control or population control

the control issue becomes more controversial. *In whose interest is the control to be executed? To whom is it desirable to control numbers of impoverished individuals rather than to control impoverishment?* It may be argued that potential threats should be controlled and limits should be set to avoid undesirable events. Such a threatening event would be over-population or too many births. In this sense control implies intervention in one of the most private of spheres. Much of the controversy surrounding population control stems undoubtedly from control measures taken without due attention to the integrity of privacy in fertility decisions, particularly among the poorest in the world.[12]

Few, except those being opposed for religious reasons, would deny the great value of fertility regulation technology, if used appropriately. There is, however, a risk of a confidence crisis in its application in practice, due to the renewed interest in more drastic control measures as a consequence of the insufficient outcome of population policies in various poor countries. The demographic trap debate is an obvious illustration of the up-surge of a new mentality.[9,13–15] This debate has emerged concomitantly with the belt-tightening implicit in the structural adjustment policies.[16] The risk of a deepening impoverishment of the poorest countries of the world is evident. In many of these populations the contraceptive prevalence remains low and the educational level – and thereby the motivation to have fewer children – continues to be low among both women and men.

The resistance among impoverished populations to comply with vertical population policies formulated from above at a national level and executed unrelated to health priorities at the local level, has led to a series of opportunistic renamings of the most controversial elements in the control mechanisms. India provides an illustrative example of this renaming process. After the compulsory sterilisation in the mid-1970s the concept family planning became so coercion-associated that it could hardly be used at all.[17] The contraceptive prevalence sank to extremely low levels in the population and a renaming process took place in which the word planning was substituted by welfare. Consequently, books in the area of family welfare methods comprised condoms, pills, IUDs, sterilisation etc., saying nothing about other aspects of family welfare in the more common sense of welfare. Likewise, family welfare centres provided welfare only in the limited sense of female contraceptive surgery, which, in actual fact, consisted of two – and only two – activities: abortion and sterilisation.[17]

FAMILY PLANNING AS A HUMAN RIGHT

Family planning is undoubtedly a valuable asset, particularly in the process of women's liberation. It is laudable that it is considered a human right. However, there are indications that the provision of this human right may imply the deprivation of freedom. A look into the process of freedom in fertility decisions may raise some doubts.

In the early era of birth control campaigns in South-East Asia, much attention was given to information, education and communication campaigns in order to spread the message of the advantages of family planning. Due to the non-responsiveness among the poor and the insufficient outcome of these campaigns, they escalated to include also persuasion and more aggressive interventions in order to convince resistant individuals in the target population to accept family planning. With selective payments to family planning acceptors (but *not* to MCH care attenders), to family planning workers (but *not* to MCH care providers), some improvements in the birth control campaigns were achieved. When persuasion by incentives (and subsequently disincentives) did not give desired results, the next logical step was to escalate the pressure exerted upon the poor to include compulsory sterilisation by law. The human right of family planning, hence, was provided to the population by coercion.

The resistance meeting these birth control campaigns entailed extensive manipulative measures, which were all geared towards *generation of demand where there is no demand*. In this approach donors and governments did not pay due attention to perceived (versus alleged) needs among poor people: 1) intensive mass communication aiming at target audiences; 2) persuasion efforts with incentives (like food given to a starving population to attain sterilisation targets) and 3) compulsion in the form of legalised violence. The three levels were related to each other even if the degree of violation of the needy poor populations became gradually more and more brutal. The isolation of perceived needs (recipients' opinion) from alleged needs (donors' opinion) runs parallel to a clearly visible tendency of *status quo*, giving most family planning programmes the character of no change programmes.[18]

The concept incentive would presumably seem to most people a positive word, implying encouragement of efforts made e.g. in the assumed societal interest of the common good. In impoverished societies with extremely small margins for survival, incentives may have much more controversial implications. In such societies there are areas of widespread poverty and starvation, where incentives undoubtedly can be coercive.[19] If incentives really were an attempt to improve the interest in maternal and child health (including family planning) among the population, incentives should naturally be paid to support the broad concept of MCH/FP. Instead, selective fertility regulation incentives (and disincentives) have been introduced in several poor countries, questioning the only tangible capital the poor people may be able to generate: their children. In the escalated form that incentives/disincentives issues took in India in the

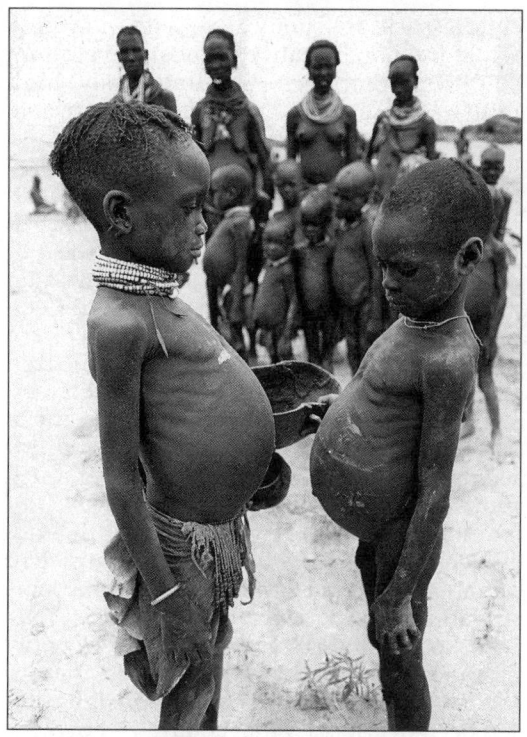

Children waiting for emergency supplies in Bume, Ethiopia. Photo: UNICEF/Peter Magubane

mid-1970s, the *de facto* coercion did not result in a fall of the birth rate but rather a fall of the government. The political implications of deprivation of freedom in fertility decisions can hardly be illustrated more clearly.

BIRTH CONTROL VERSUS MOTHERHOOD CONTROL

While it is obvious to all that zero fertility will automatically mean zero maternal mortality it is less clear what impact family planning will have on the maternal mortality ratio. This ratio is defined as the number of maternal deaths per 100 000 live births. In a carefully performed study from Bangladesh in the early 1980s it was shown that the impact of family planning was unexpectedly limited.[20] Two villages were set up for comparison, in which one was subject to an intense family planning drive over several years, while in the other no family planning propaganda was made. In the village where family planning was decisively promoted, village fertility was reduced by 26 per cent in relation to the reference village. Unexpectedly, the maternal mortality ratio was identical in the two villages.

The explanation was that the intensive family planning drive had not conveyed any increase in the *safety at birth*. The findings imply that wanted pregnancies did not enjoy any better protection in the family planning village than in the reference village. Family planning could even have been counterproductive to safer motherhood, because the few resources (doctors, nurse-midwives) available may have been drained to family planning activities. In fact, in the area studied 75 per cent women dying in childbirth did not see a doctor before their death and almost 90 per cent had no access to modern health facilities.[21]

It is a well-known fact that most maternal deaths occur at medium parity (one to four births) and at medium age (20–35 years).[22] This is derived from various findings, of which one, from a study in Bangladesh 1968–1970, is particularly revealing. It was calculated that if all births had been averted in women 1) below age 20, 2) above age 39 and 3) beyond parity 6, the maternal mortality ratio would have declined only from 570 to 430 per 100 000 live births.[23] Even with this extremely non-realistic achievement of virtually cutting off all births in recognised risk groups, a very limited gain in maternal mortality would have resulted.

Even if we assume an impoverished country with a high maternal mortality in the high parity range, we can still conclude, as shown in various data-simulation studies, that elimination of *all* grand multiparity (parity ≥ 5) may mean a *less than 5 per cent reduction of maternal deaths*.[23] This and similar findings indicate the limited value of targeting grand multiparous women for sterilisation in order to reduce the overall maternal mortality. However, it must be underscored that, beyond all doubt, a significant number of such grand multiparous women actually have an unmet need, perceived by themselves, of fertility control. This important maternal health aspect of grand multiparity is distinctly different from the one blaming grand multiparity as a major cause of maternal mortality.

In spite of the widespread belief that age and parity are exceptionally important in any strategy for the reduction of maternal deaths, it can be concluded that *it is not the age/parity distribution of births that explains the low maternal mortality in the developed world*. It is a well documented fact that grand multiparity is associated with high maternal mortality figures in impoverished countries, but not in more affluent countries. An illustration is the very low maternal mortality in the high parity range in Sweden and in other developed countries. It has been shown in Nigeria that high parity is associated with high maternal mortality, only if the child mortality is high.[24] This is a parallel to most industrialised countries: *what kills the mother is not parity but poverty*.[25]

In Sweden the maternal mortality ratio has dropped from levels of around 1000 to about five maternal deaths per 100 000 live births over a period of 250 years.[26] The bulk of this decline occurred before any kind of modern contraception was available. It is true, however, that the combined effect of increased availability of contraceptives and access to safe, legal abortion services meant a very important contribution to the final reduction in maternal mortality over the last five to six decades in Sweden. A similar pattern has been found in several other industrialised countries.

The need of health-oriented empowerment of women *and* men to plan for optimal reproductive health and voluntary spacing of births is uncontroversial. The controversial point lies in the priority given to birth control ahead of more comprehensive maternal health care. Winikoff and Sullivan concluded in a balanced review in 1987 that *'efficient health care is more effective than family planning in preventing maternal deaths'*.

FOUR DECADES OF ATTEMPTS TO SOLVE THE POPULATION PROBLEM

A critical review of the achievements in the area of population indicates that the initial optimism has turned into a relative pessimism mostly due to the understanding of the complexity of human reproductive behaviour.[18] The focusing on contraceptive technology has been criticised as obsession with a technique that implies that fertility has been regarded a disease, requiring particular remedies. This has conveyed a research orientation towards technical approaches with a focus on doctors and medical pharmaceutical solutions to essentially motivational problems. Many foreign initiatives have dominated and there has seldom been due recognition of perceived needs in the target populations.

It has been further argued that the one-sidedness in this approach did not recognise one particularly perceived need in the impoverished populations targeted: *reproductive failure and childlessness*.[12] In more affluent countries childlessness is synonymous with infertility, while the harsh reality in most developing countries comprises, simultaneously, high figures of pregnancy wastage/miscarriage, intrauterine fetal death and postpartum child loss. Childlessness in the Third World is a three-pronged problem comprising infertility, pregnancy wastage and child loss. All three entities clearly reveal and show the vulnerability of reproductive health of women and men in impoverished countries, reflecting particularly the disastrous effects of genital infections. Infections killing children under five years also contribute to child loss, thereby making such diseases important in the area of reproductive failure and childlessness. The latter concepts thus cover much more than gynecological problems.

Another experience gained is that the motivational aspect has been given insufficient attention.[18] It remains a fact that, for the poorest families in the Third World children may be the only tangible capital available, not only as child labour and as an economic guarantee, but also as a security at old age. It has often been overlooked that children – however malnourished and deprived of decent living conditions – may still imply a net advantage in poor families. However deplorably they are cared for, they may still produce a net surplus of income and social status. The problem of child labour has gradually come into focus and it has been demonstrated that having many children in labour, if looked upon from a mere capital-generating point of view, may be a rational decision.

The Caldwell hypothesis has gained widespread recognition. It postulates that human reproduction (number of children born) is associated with capital flow from children to parents and *vice versa*. If the net capital flow from children to parents is positive, children may constitute an economic advantage resulting in resistance to birth control. On the other hand, when children cost (school fees, clothes, child labour being illegal etc.) parents may tend to limit their number.

It has been learnt that a key concept in the freedom of fertility decisions is perceived need. In campaigns to force couples to accept contraceptives, it has been noted that insufficient motivation results in poor acceptance of fertility regulation. In order to overcome this hurdle, campaigns have been launched to generate demand. This shows clearly the conflict between perceived and alleged needs.

The conflict allows us to raise a number of critical questions:[19]

1) Is family planning/birth control in a setting enhancing self-determination and well-being of women, or does it remove control of fertility from women, placing it in the hands of birth control providers?

2) Is there a difference in the birth control need perceived by the potential clients and the need perceived by the birth control providers?

3) Can alleged needs (not perceived by potential clients) be discerned in programme documents?

4) Does family planning/birth control exist as a means of reducing social pressures resulting from economic and political inequities that family planning programmes are unwilling to confront?

5) Is family planning/birth control a substitute for economic and political reforms responsive to the needs perceived by the poor?

CONTINUING IMPOVERISHMENT OR CREDIBLE EMPOWERMENT?

The controversy that dominated so clearly the World Population Conference in Bucharest in 1974, focusing on birth control versus poverty control, was less obvious in Mexico 1984, but has been visible over the last years in the debate on priorities in international population assistance. Heated debates on the demographic trap or the ecological collapse are important reminders of this new tendency. While the impoverished village family obviously has no idea of the global population growth problem (the grass root perspective) the more privileged spectators with a global overview (the helicopter perspective) are painfully aware of the disastrous perspective emanating both from the backwardness of the majority of the world's population and from the escapistic justification of overconsumption in the rich world. In the forthcoming Cairo World Population Conference in 1994 the two perspectives would merit more profound attention.

According to World Bank figures, the net flow of economic resources is currently directed *from* poor countries *to* affluent countries.[10,27] In the absence of a new economical order it must be considered highly controversial to debate the truly threatening demographic perspective in the world over the next century without debating the economic stranglehold of

the majority of the world's poorest nations. Recently the total international assistance amounted to about 50 billion US dollars while the flow of financial resources from poor to affluent countries approached about 150 billion USD, or three times the flow of international assistance.[14] It has also been documented that given the existing debt *the annual total sum of payments for rates of interest from Africa to affluent countries recently amounted to more than all investments for all Africans in the areas of health and education.*[10] This has taken place when the devastating effects of AIDS are only beginning to become visible and when drought and aggression wars threaten the survival of the poorest of the poor.

There is a real challenge in what option to choose: continuing impoverishment or credible empowerment, above all among women. Empowering women, however, would seem improbable unless men are empowered to share the power. The common denominator is undoubtedly education.

References

1. Rockefeller IIIrd JD. Population growth: the role of the developed world. Pop Dev Rev 1978;4:509.

2. Shah Commission of Inquiry. Implementation of the family planning program during the emergency. Third and final report (August 6, 1978). New Delhi: Ministry of Health, 1978.

3. Mc Nicholl G. An argument yet to have its day. International Family Planning Perspectives 1990;16:146.

4. Postel S. Last oasis: facing water scarcity. Norton, New York: The Worldwatch Insitute, 1992. (The Worldwatch Environmental Alert Series)

5. Falkenmark M. The massive water scarcity now threatening Africa – why isn't it addressed? Ambio 1989;18:2.

6. Durning AB. Poverty and the environment: Reversing the downward spiral. Washington D.C.: The Worldwatch Institute, 1989. (Worldwatch Papers 92)

7. Basch PF. Textbook of international health. New York: Oxford University Press, 1990: 188 p.

8. Durning A. How much is enough? Norton, New York: The Worldwatch Institute, 1992. (The Worldwatch Environmental Alert Series, No. 2).

9. King M. Health is a sustainable state. Lancet 1990;336:664–7.

10. Grant J. The state of the world's children 1992. Oxford: Oxford University Press, 1992.

11. Health Minister Timothy Stamps: Interview, The Chronicle. Bulawayo, 30 July 1992

12. Bergström S. Fertility and subfertility as health problems – population control versus family planning by the family. In: Bergström S, Bondestam L. Poverty and population control. London: Academic Press, 1980.

13. King M. Overpopulation and death in childhood. Lancet 1990;336:1312–3.

14. Potts M, Rosenfield A. The fifth freedom revisited: II, the way forward. Lancet 1990;336: 1293–5.

15. Lithell UB, Rosling H, Hofvander Y. Children's deaths and population growth. Lancet 1992;339:377.

16. Gibbon P. Social dimensions of adjustment and the problem of poverty in Africa. Nytt från Nordiska Afrikainstitutet 1991;28:5–26.

17. Bergström S. Family welfare as health need in Indian population policy. Trop Doct 1982;12:182–4.

18. Demerath NJ. Birth control and foreign policy. The alternatives to family planning. New York: Harper & Row, 1976.

19. Lappé FM, Schurman R. Taking population seriously. London: Earthscan Publishers, 1989.

20. Lindpainter LS, Jahan N, Satterthwaite AP, Zimicki S. Maternal mortality in Matlab Thana, Bangladesh, 1982. Final report for Research Protocol 83–021 (P) of the Community Services Research Working Group, International Centre for Diarrhoeal Diseases Research. Mimeograph. 1982

21. Fauveau V, Wojtymak, B, Koenig MA, Chakraborty J, Chowdbury IA. Epidemiology and cause of deaths among women in rural Bangladesh. Int J Epidemiol 1989;18:139–45.

22. Winikoff B, Sullivan M. Assessing the role of family planning in reducing maternal mortality. Stud Fam Plann 1987;18:128–43.

23. Trussel J, Pebley AR. The potential impact of changes of fertility on infant child and maternal mortality. Stud Fam Plann 1984;15:253–66.

24. Harrison KA, Rossiter CE, Tan H. Family planning and maternal mortality in the Third World. Lancet 1986;i:1441.

25. Bergström S. Motherhood control. On the sustainability of maternal health in the debt trap. In: Stanseth NC, ed. The demographic trap. London: Academic Press, 1994 (in press).

26. Högberg U. Maternal mortality in Sweden. Thesis. Umeå: University of Umeå, 1985.

27. Cornia GA, Jolly R, Stewart F, eds. Adjustment with a human face. Protecting the vulnerable and promoting growth. A study by UNICEF. Oxford: Clarendon Press, 1987.

28. United Nations. Energy statistics yearbook. New York: United Nations, 1991.

29. Statistical Abstracts of the United States. USS Department of Commerce, Bureau of the Census, Washington, D.C., Government Printing Office, 1990.

About the authors

Staffan Bergström is Professor of International Health at the University of Oslo and Senior Physician at the Department of Obstetrics and Gynaecology, Ullevål University Hospital, Oslo, Norway. He is a specialist in obstetrics and gynaecology and responsible for several research projects in the area of reproductive health in developing countries. During 1982–86 he was the Director of the Department of Obstetrics, Central Hospital, Maputo, Mozambique. He is also involved in the human reproduction research programme (HRP) within the WHO.

Sher Shah Syed is Assistant Professor of Obstetrics and Gynaecology at Dow Medical College in Karachi, Pakistan. He is involved in teaching programmes of the University of Karachi for both postgraduate and undergraduate medical students and has also worked as a lecturer and registrar a Trinity College, Dublin (St. James' Hospital). His publications cover maternal health and problems related to maternal mortality.

Lankinen KS, Bergström S, Mäkelä PH and Peltomaa M, eds.
Health and disease in developing countries. London:The Macmillan Press Limited, 1994:37-48.

5 INFANT MORTALITY AND BIRTH RATES

Lars Åke Hanson, M.D., Ph.D.
University of Gothenburg, Departments of
Clinical Immunology and Paediatrics
Sahlgren's Hospital, Guldhedsgatan 10,
S-41346 Gothenburg, Sweden

Staffan Bergström, M.D., Ph.D.
University of Oslo, Department of Obstetrics
and Gynaecology, Ullevål University
Hospital, N-0407 Oslo,
Norway

Luis Rosero-Bixby, MPH, Ph.D.
University of Costa Rica, Institute for
Health Research (INISA)
Apartado 833–2050, Montes de Oca,
Costa Rica

INTRODUCTION

It has been suggested that decreasing infant mortality is a prerequisite for decreasing birth rates and the experience in several countries shows that decreasing infant mortality rates are indeed followed by declining birth rates. Actually, industrialised countries with their low infant mortality have low birth rates. In contrast, the highest birth rates are found in countries with the highest infant mortality (Tables 5.1a and b).[1] A few developing countries, such as Sri Lanka, China and Costa Rica, have managed to decrease the child death rates substantially.[2] This has been followed (or preceded) by a decline in birth rates to some of the lowest levels among developing countries. – But is this a true connection?

HISTORICAL AND RECENT EVIDENCE

Data from Sweden show that the striking decrease in infant mortality during the 19th century was soon followed by decreasing birth rates (Figure 5.1). A study of similar figures from 15 European countries showed a somewhat complex pattern. However, the conclusion after a detailed demographic analysis was that the data agree with the hypothesis that declining birth rates were preceded by decreasing infant mortality.[3] In only two instances the reverse was found. By the same

token, a recent extensive investigation on the fertility in Europe mostly in the 19th century showed that decreases in fertility followed upon declines in infant mortality in the great majority of areas.[4] However, in several provinces, especially in France, a tendency of fertility decline could be noted already before a decline in infant mortality.

Analysis of regional variations in fertility and child mortality during the late 19th and

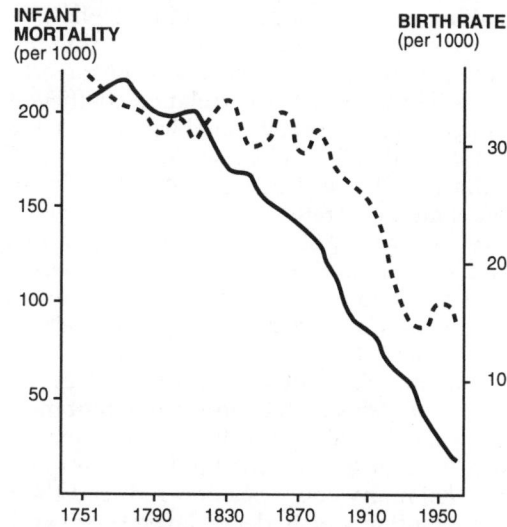

Figure 5.1. Infant mortality (———) and birth rates (- - -) in promille in Sweden during the 19th and 20th centuries.[34]

Table 5.1a. Infant and child mortality in the world population in relation to frequency of low birth weight, birth rate and literacy rate.[2]

1985 Mortality < 5 years of age	1985 Infant mortality	1982–83 Low birth weight	1985 Birth rate	1985 Adult literacy rate male/female
(promille)	(promille)	(per cent)	(promille)	(per cent)
>175	136	14	47	42/21
95–174	83	13	42	68/50
30–94	44	9	30	89/84
< 30	11	6	15	97/93

early 20th century in England and Wales disclosed a positive correlation between the two variables.[5] On the basis of this study the authors suggested that the factors determining mortality also influence fertility and both variables are affected within a relatively short interval.

A positive correlation has been found between infant mortality and fertility in Finland and Sweden in the 19th century.[6] Similarly, the remarkable decrease in infant mortality during the 1970s in Costa Rica showed a significant relation to decreasing fertility rates.[7]

We have analysed the contemporary relationship between infant mortality and birth rates across nearly 100 developing countries making use of data published by UNICEF.[2] These data show a positive association between the two rates, especially in most recent times (Figure 5.2). The correlation coefficient between infant mortality and birth rates is 0.58 in 1960 and 0.79 in 1985. No country (except India in 1985) exhibits simultaneously an infant mortality rate above 100 per 1000 and a birth rate below 35 per 1000. Thus, it seems that a moderate infant mortality is a necessary condition for fertility transition or, in other words, *a combination of high infant mortality and low fertility seems incompatible.*

The contrary is not true, however. There are many countries with a moderate infant mortality and a very high birth rate, with Jordan and Syria in 1985 as outstanding examples. By 1960 many countries had reduced their infant mortality to moderate levels but in very few of them fertility had started to decline. Singapore, with an infant mortality of 36 and a crude birth rate of 38, exemplifies this

situation in Figure 5.2. The six countries with a moderate birth rate of less than 35 in 1960 (Yugoslavia, Argentina, etc.) essentially lay in

Table 5.1b. Infant mortality and birth rates in selected countries 1985.[2]

Country	Infant mortality (promille)	Crude birth rate (promille)
Africa		
Somalia	152	48
Sudan	112	45
Egypt	93	35
South Africa	78	38
Asia		
Bangladesh	124	43
India	105	30
Thailand	44	26
Japan	6	13
Latin America		
Bolivia	117	43
Brazil	67	30
Chile	22	22
Cuba	15	17
North America		
USA	11	16
Canada	9	15
Europe		
USSR	24	19
Greece	14	15
UK	10	13
Sweden	6	11

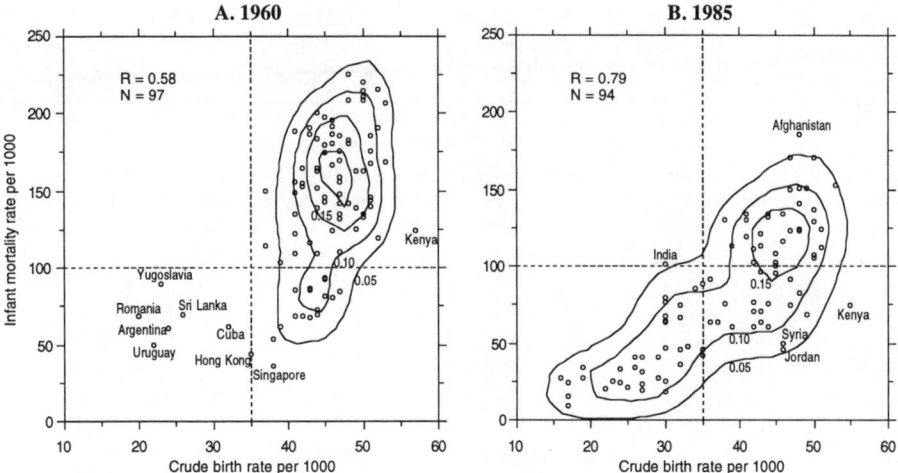

Figure 5.2. Scatterplot and smoothed density contours for the relationship between infant mortality and birth rate. Less developed countries, 1960 and 1985.[2]

a different category and their inclusion in the universe of less developed countries is questionable. It seems that a falling infant mortality rate has not been sufficient condition for fertility transition, at least by 1960. However, by 1985 the link between the two rates becomes much clearer (Figure 5.2, part B). Almost all countries with a birth rate below 30 per 1000 have also low infant mortality (below 50 per 1000). The emergence of this stronger association is compatible with claims that fertility declines boost infant mortality falls.

Statistical correlation alone, however, is not sufficient proof of a causal link. There is a distinct possibility that the correlation between infant mortality and birth rates is a spurious byproduct of underlying common determinants, such as women's education, social organisation, health infrastructure, or cultural practices. A first approach to get rid of some of these potential confounding variables (those that are constant over time) is by looking at the association between *changes* – rather than *levels* – in the two rates. In this regard, Figure 5.3 shows that the correlation between the decline in infant mortality and in birth rates stays high (0.74) during 1960–1985.

In countries like Hong Kong, Singapore, Costa Rica, and Cuba, spectacular fertility declines of about 50 per cent accompanied also spectacular infant mortality falls of about 80 per cent. In the other extreme, in backward countries, such as Kampuchea, Afghanistan, Ethiopia and Somalia, neither fertility nor

infant mortality have changed in a meaningful way. In turn, no country but Peru and India presents a meaningful fertility decline of at least 20 per cent without presenting simultaneously a significant infant mortality reduction of at least 40 per cent. The absence of this conjunction suggests that either an infant mortality decline is a necessary precondition for a birth rate decline or that a fertility decline always causes infant mortality falls. In contrast, Figure 5.3 shows many countries

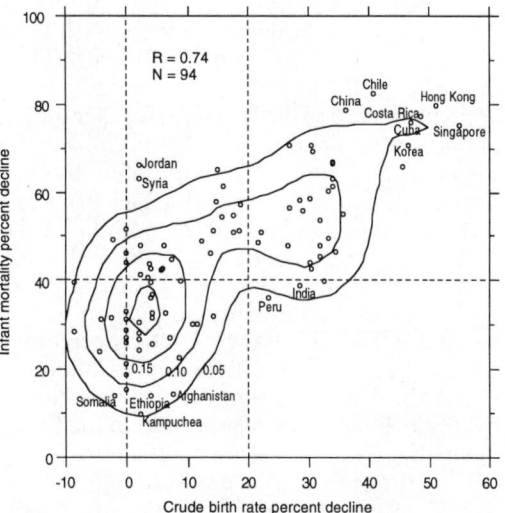

Figure 5.3. Scattergram and smoothed density contours for the relationship between the percentual decline in infant mortality and birth rates from 1960 to 1985. Less developed countries.[2]

Table 5.2. Multiple regression analysis of female illiteracy (FI), crude birth rate (CBR) and the ratio of population by physician (P/P) as explanatory variables for infant mortality rate (IMR). N = number of countries, R^2 = coefficient of determination, standard errors in parentheses. Discussion in text.

1960

| IMR = 5.78 | • | $FI^{0.40}$ | • | $CBR^{0.35}$ | • | $P/P^{0.07}$ | $N = 88$ |
| | | (0.08) | | (0.23) | | (0.02) | $R^2 = 0.69$ |

1985

| IMR = 1.39 | • | $FI^{0.36}$ | • | $CBR^{0.70}$ | • | $P/P^{0.09}$ | $N = 81$ |
| | | (0.06) | | (0.18) | | (0.03) | $R^2 = 0.80$ |

% Decline 1960-85

| IMR = 24.7 | + | 0.23•FI + | | 0.61•CBR + | | 0.05•P/P | $N = 77$ |
| | | (0.06) | | (0.08) | | (0.03) | $R^2 = 0.63$ |

in the quadrant where there is a conjunction of big infant mortality reductions and modest or nil birth rate declines, which means that either an infant mortality reduction is not a sufficient condition for a birth rate decline or that a fertility decline is not a precondition for an infant mortality reduction. Jordan and Syria are clear examples of this combination.

Multiple regression analysis gives a more precise indication of the magnitude of the relationship between infant mortality and fertility, and tests whether this relation is merely a residual byproduct of third variables. With data from about 80 developing countries, we have created multiple regression models on the country-level infant mortality with three explanatory variables: female illiteracy (FI) as indicator of (the lack of) socioeconomic development, the crude birth rate (CBR) as indicator of both fertility and the burden of children for a society, and the ratio of population by physician (P/P) as indicator of (the lack of) health care resources available to the population.[2]

Three regression equations were estimated: two multiplicative equations for both 1960 and 1985, and an additive equation for the percent 1960–1985 change. Partial derivatives demonstrate that a multiplicative relationship in the absolute values of the variables levels results in an additive relationship in their rates of change. The regression coefficients for the CBR estimate the per cent change in IMR resulting from one per cent change in the CBR, net of changes in the other two variables (Table 5.2).

Although the data do not support an independent association between IMR and CBR

in 1960*, a clear and significant association between these two variables emerges in 1985. A reduction of 1 per cent in the CBR would generate 0.70 per cent reduction in the IMR according to the 1985 equation. A similar figure (0.61 per cent) occurs in the more demanding equation for longitudinal changes. These effects of CBR on IMR, which are net of the influence of the other two variables in the regression, are higher than those of illiteracy and substantially higher than those of the population/physician ratio.

Thus, cross-country covariation in infant mortality and birth rates by 1985 and in their decline from 1960 to 1985 give strong support to the hypothesis of a connection – and probably one of a causal nature – between these two rates. Studies of many countries during the last few decades have repeatedly found similar results.[8,9] Analysis of 53 African, Latin American and Asian countries showed that when infant mortality decreased after World War II, birth rates declined at the same pace. A remarkably high correlation coefficient of –0.82 between the percentage of wives practising family planning and the infant mortality rate has been reported in 99 developing countries *circa* 1982, an association that is even higher than that corresponding to the variable education measured in several ways.[10] A study with data from 88 developing countries proposes that the combined effect of education

*The regression coefficient of 0.35 is lower than 1.96 x 0.23 = 0.45, where 1.96 is the 97.5 percentage point of the standard normal distribution and 0.23 the standard deviation.

and infant mortality explains about 70 per cent of the variation in birth rates.[11] This study also found that the effect of education on fertility increased considerably when infant mortality declined.

POSSIBLE MECHANISMS LINKING CHILD MORTALITY AND BIRTH RATE

Clearly the relation between the two variables is multifactorial and there is no single explanation. Moreover, causation probably is bidirectional – infant mortality effects fertility and the latter influences the former – or there can be even other variables, biological or socioeconomic.

Breast-feeding decreases both infant mortality and fertility

Since breast-feeding decreases both infant mortality and fertility, this clearly is an intervening variable linking infant deaths and subsequent fertility. Studies conducted since the late nineteenth century have shown that infant mortality is inversely linked to breast-feeding practices.[12] It is well known that breast-feeding decreases morbidity and mortality in diarrhea.[13] The risk of non-breast-fed babies in a developing country to die from diarrhea during the first months of life may be 25-fold compared with exclusively breast-fed babies.[13] A recent study showed that even partial breast-feeding could protect against 70–80 per cent of diarrhea attacks in young infants of poor population groups in Pakistan.[14] In the same population, partial breast-feeding decreased the risk of attracting neonatal septicemia 18 times compared with non-breast-fed controls.[15]

Such protection against the two most common causes of the high early infant mortality in poor areas, can strikingly decrease infant morbidity and mortality in developing countries where it is usually high.[16] Although previous evidence that breast-feeding also protects against respiratory infection has been less convincing, a well performed epidemiological study in Brazil has shown that breast-feeding significantly decreases mortality in respiratory infections as well.[17] This finding is of great importance since respiratory tract infections are a major cause of death in childhood in developing areas.

A major reason for the strong protective effect of breast-feeding is the high content in the milk of the secretory IgA antibodies which are specially adapted to protection of mucous membranes, e.g. the mucosa in the gastrointestinal and respiratory tracts, against infectious agents.[18] The mother's milk contains secretory IgA antibodies against all the microbes the mother has been exposed to and which her infant is likely to meet as well after delivery. It has been shown that the protection provided by breast-feeding against *Vibrio cholerae, Campylobacter* and enterotoxigenic *Escherichia coli* relate to the content of the maternal milk of secretory IgA antibodies against these pathogens.[19–21] In addition to secretory IgA, human milk contains several other components that might support the defence against infections in the breast-fed infant.[18]

The fact that breast-feeding has a contraceptive effect was noted by Aristotle: 'while women are suckling children, menstruation does not occur according to nature, nor do they conceive'. It is the stimulation of the nipple that induces the hormonal changes, resulting in prevention of ovulation and conception.

The term 'lactational amenorrhoea method' or LAM has been used for this form of contraception. In a study from Australia it was recently demonstrated that in well nourished,

Refugee mother breast-feeding in Wollo Province, Ethiopia. Photo: UNICEF/Bill Campbell

partially breast-feeding mothers the contraceptive effect was 98.3 per cent at 6 months of lactation, 93 per cent at 12 months and 87 per cent at 24 months.[22] A contraceptive effect of 90 per cent was obtained by breast-feeding six times daily for 2 years. In Chile LAM was also applied successfully during the first 6 months of lactation.[23] In a traditional society like Pakistan, where partial breast-feeding is the rule[24], a significant contraceptive effect was verified for the first 6 months of lactation. After that breast-feeding obviously becomes too irregular or infrequent to provide a continuous hormonal stimulus sufficient for full contraception (Ashraf *et al.*, unpublished observations).

Still, it is being claimed that LAM may prevent more conceptions in the developing world than all family planning programmes together.[25] LAM may be the only family planning method available for those 300 million couples or so in the world, who do not want a new pregnancy but are unaware of contraceptive possibilities. For them it is crucial to know that to be effective LAM requires frequent and persistent breast-feeding, although it can be partial.[22,26] It may be that in many, if not most traditional societies, breast-feeding is partial with other foods and fluids given from birth onwards and the interval between breast meals may vary.[24,27]

Studies have shown that a decrease in infant mortality tends to increase the duration of lactational amenorrhoea and result in better birth spacing.[28–31] A surviving infant means that the mother will continue to breast feed, which results in both a prolonged contraceptive effect and an improved defence against potentially lethal infections in the infant, decreasing infant mortality.

Worldwide evidence. Although the nutritional status of the mother can influence fertility demographic studies have demonstrated that its effect is less than a 10 per cent.[32] According to studies in Papua New Guinea variability in natural fertility may be explained to 75 per cent by breast-feeding practices.[33]

The striking decrease in infant mortality during the 19th century, followed some 20 years later by a decrease in fertility in Sweden (Figure 5.1), may certainly have several explanations including education and socioeconomic development. There is, however, data to suggest that an important factor could have been an increase in breast-feeding, which perhaps resulted from a campaign for better

nutrition and health care started in the 1830s.[5,34] Those studies also give the first good historical evidence of the fact that breast-feeding leads to a striking decrease in infant mortality caused by diarrhea.[5,35]

From Senegal it was reported that with no infant deaths in the family, the time interval between two deliveries increased by 9 months if weaning was postponed by 1 year beyond the first year of life.[36] The average interval between births was shortened from 3 to 2 years if an infant died during the first month of life so that breast-feeding was interrupted, according to a study from Kerala.[37]

In Nepal it was found that for a child born less than 18 months before or after a sibling the risk of dying was three times higher than for a child born with an interval of 24 months or more. This association was unrelated to the mother's age or the birth order.[38] In Senegal it was shown that one third of all children were weaned too early because of a new pregnancy. Too early weaning is followed by a much increased risk of infections that cause malnutrition and endanger growth, development and life. It was noted that for such a child the likelihood of dying within a year increased by 50 to 150 per cent.[39] Actually the African word 'kwashiorkor' means the deprivation of a child who is no longer breast-fed because the mother has become pregnant again.[40]

On the basis of a study of 25 developing countries it was determined that if the interval between births were at least 2 years, infant mortality would be reduced by 10 per cent and child mortality (one to four years) by 16 per cent.[37] Shorter spacing increases the risk not only by interrupting breast-feeding and impairing nutrition, but also by increasing the risk of low birth weight (LBW) deliveries.

Family size and infections

It has been stressed that demographic data are inadequate for really untangling the many factors involved in the relation between fertility and infant mortality, such as mother's age, parity, birth-spacing, nutrition, education, socioeconomic level and the likes.[41,42] However, birth spacing stands out as a dominant variable compared with maternal age and parity. Blacker suggested that, in addition to maternal depletion and sibling competition resulting from frequent deliveries, there may be another causal relationship between short birth interval and high infant mortality.[42] This would be the effect of infections in relation to birth-crowding which might be more important than the factors listed above.

Infectious diseases are the major cause of high infant mortality in developing countries. Poverty is followed by poor housing, lack of sanitation and potable water, unhygienic conditions and a continuous heavy exposure to microbes.[27] Besides being a major cause of morbidity and mortality, frequent infections also lead to undernutrition. Certain infections have a higher fatality rate in this setting, especially measles at young age. The presence of several young children in a family therefore increases the risk of a poor outcome.

It has recently been claimed that the declining fertility seen in England and Wales 1849–1950 accounted for at least a 24 per cent decrease in postneonatal mortality caused by pneumonia and bronchitis.[43] Suggestive evidence has been provided that the high measles mortality among children in developing countries is not related to undernutrition as often believed, but to crowding in families with many children. Crowding results in transmission of high infectious doses that may provoke severe disease (Chapter 17).[44]

The effect of child deaths on reproductive behaviour

The classic demographic transition theory sees high fertility as a response to high levels of infant and child mortality.[45,46] Parents have many children to replace those who have died

or parents set excess fertility goals in anticipation of children deaths.[47] The demographic literature calls these phenomena 'replacement' and 'insurance' effects, respectively.[48] In addition, in some societies parents want to compensate for the loss of a child, especially if they have lost a son.[49-51] One reason is that they strongly wish to have at least one son alive to support them when they grow old.[52] This is the case in India, where no social security system exists for the aged. To be sure with 95 per cent probability to have at least one surviving son when they are old, the parents may aim at having about six live born babies.[53] An expression of this as well as of other factors has been found in studies from Pakistan and Bangladesh showing a relationship between the experience of child deaths in the family and the family size (Table 5.3).[54]

Mothers with three or more child deaths have three times as many children as mothers who have not lost a child, all ages combined. This connection becomes even more striking when comparing the birth intervals for the Bangladeshi mothers. It was 37.2 months in families without child deaths, but 24.1 months in the families with deaths. However, this was not found for the Pakistani mothers. In some studies it has not been possible to establish a significant relationship between child deaths and family size.[54]

Other factors

After observing that numerous or ill-spaced children are likely to be also unwanted, some

Table 5.3. Mean number of children born to women of different ages in relation to the number of experienced child deaths.[54]

Number of child deaths	Mother's age (years)					
	15–24	25–29	30–34	35–39	40–49	Total
Pakistan						
0	1.1	2.8	4.0	4.5	4.7	2.4
1	2.4	3.9	5.2	5.5	6.1	4.5
2	3.6	4.8	6.0	7.2	7.0	6.2
>2	4.4	6.0	6.8	8.4	8.9	7.9
Bangladesh						
0	1.8	3.6	4.9	5.7	5.6	2.6
1	3.3	5.0	5.9	6.6	7.2	4.7
2	4.6	5.9	7.1	7.6	8.6	6.2
>2	6.3	7.4	8.6	9.4	10.4	8.3

authors have postulated that unwanted births have higher risk of death as consequence of parental neglect, underinvestment in resources to save their lives, and even other more obvious forms of infanticide.[55,56] Direct or indirect infanticide can occur especially under severe resource constraints. The relatively high mortality of female infants in many poor places in South Asia strongly suggests the existence of some kind of infanticide.

Some authors have also pointed out *indirect* links between family planning and improved child survival.[57,58] One of these indirect effects is the improvement in maternal and child health programmes originating in savings from prevented pregnancies, i.e. from fewer prenatal consultations and deliveries. Another extrafamilial effect is that some family planning programmes (especially in Latin America) target the prevention of high risk pregnancies, for example in diabetic women. Changes in the affective relation between mother and her planned children have been mentioned among these indirect links.

It has also been argued that improved health education and other developments bring about both a decreasing infant mortality and a fall in birth rates.[37] The undernourished, illiterate, unhealthy and oppressed may have little sense of freedom or capacity to influence their situation, including planning the size of the family. With education, better health and economy, it is probable that the family would welcome measures to increase birth spacing that would result in physically and mentally healthier children. However, it has not been possible to fully evaluate the weight of different factors as to their effect on mortality and fertility. Education is clearly of importance.[11] It seems as if 'modernisation' of societies will lead to a decrease in infant mortality as well as birth rates, probably in a number of ways.

A certain level of economic security is obviously accompanied by the choice of fewer children.[59] Only in very poor communities do children contribute to the income of the family. As soon as the family is better off, children are not used for work but are sent to school, and therefore start to cost instead. Evidence of a wish for fewer and healthier children after improvement of child survival has been given in a recent review sponsored by the Population Division of the UN, which confirms the connection between child mortality and fertility.[47] However, local variations are also stressed, e.g. related to the actual level of

mortality and attitudes. Emphasis is put on the importance of contraception, which when available reinforces the linkage between improvement in child survival and fertility decline. Furthermore, this connection between the two parameters is in agreement with the fact that the decrease in infant mortality during recent years, through a more frequent use of vaccines and ORS, has already been followed by a decrease in fertility rate in large parts of the developing world.[60]

Claims and controversies

Revisionists claim that the increasing world population is not an economic problem.[61] It is true that there is enough food available for a growing world population, although it is inadequately distributed.[62] It seems cynical to believe, however, that a yearly addition of 150 million children giving a 90 million world population increase, mainly in developing countries, can be managed, when already today there are severe deficiencies especially in the availability of health care. With the growth of family size the expenditure of food *per capita* decreases. There was a 500 kcal negative difference in food consumption between families with four compared with two children according to a study from Colombia.[39]

The effect on population growth of a 50 per cent reduction in infant and child mortality is illustrated in Figure 5.4. This is not an unrealistic task since about three million child deaths can be prevented yearly with the vaccines already available. Measles and poliomyelitis could actually be eradicated. Many of the about four million deaths of children in acute diarrhea every year could be prevented by availability of clean water, latrines, and health education and ORS. India would have about 4.4 million fewer child deaths and 7.5 million fewer births each year if the whole nation could have the same low mortality and birth rate as the State of Kerala.[26] That world population total will be reduced as a consequence if infant mortality rate is reduced by 50 per cent is important information, since it totally contradicts the opinion that measures aiming at reducing infant mortality might worsen the problem of rapid population growth.

In this connection it is of interest that it has been claimed in a recent publication that decreased public health efforts for children, such as ORS and vaccination programmes, might have to be accepted to reduce the

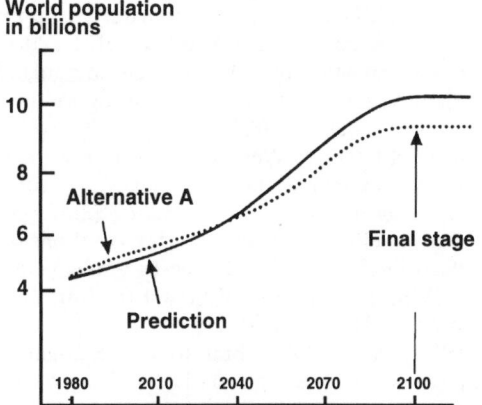

World population
in billions

Figure 5.4. The impact on population growth of a 50 per cent reduction in child deaths (Alternative A).[37] Discussion in text.

population increase. This was actually done because of deep concern about the ecological destruction following the dramatic population increase in some parts of the developing world, endangering the possibilities for future populations in these areas to support themselves. The statement is erroneous because an *increased infant mortality has very little demographic effect.* The population increase will continue due to the large fertile populations already born. This fact can be illustrated by the indications that all the cases of AIDS dying in Africa during the 1990s may still only correspond to one month of population increase on this continent – according to currently known incidence figures. There is, however, evidence of prevalence figures of HIV sero-positivity among antenatal care attenders approaching 50 per cent in Zimbabwe (MOH, Zimbabwe, unpublished).

The link between infant mortality and birth rates gives us the basis for public health policies that continue to try to decrease infant mortality, thereby also gaining decreasing fertility as reviewed above. This is strengthened further by a recent authoritative analysis of the involved factors by the Department of International Economy and Social Affairs at the United Nations.

CONCLUSIONS

When child mortality rates decrease, birth rates also decline. The relation between these two rates is quite complex but the weight of the evidence is in favour of the interpretation that decreasing infant mortality may lead to decreasing birth rates and vice versa. However, it is very difficult to evaluate the significance of the various components due to the multifactorial, bidirectional relationship.

Education, especially of women, is clearly important, but more diffuse factors, such as modernisation and improved socioeconomic conditions, are also involved. Breast-feeding leads to decreased infant mortality, increased birth spacing and decreased fertility. The important interrelation between education, breast-feeding, infant mortality and fertility is illustrated in Figure 5.5. Historical as well as recent data suggest that breast-feeding is an important factor in this connection. It is also the cheapest and most easily available nutrition and support of host defence for children. Up to 75 per cent of the variability in natural fertility has been related to breast-feeding practices, whereas maternal nutrition has been reported to have less than a 10 per cent effect. Large families run a higher risk of more frequent and more dangerous infections since the children are presumably subjected to them at a younger age with higher doses of the infectious agent. This risk is smaller when fertility is low. Some studies, but not all, show that the experience of child deaths in the family is followed by an increased number of births. These factors alone cannot explain the relation between decreasing infant mortality and birth rate. However, it can be stated generally that the measures that lead to a decreased infant mortality also lead to a decreasing birth rate, usually within a short time span. Availability of contraceptives enhances this linkage.

It is possible to further decrease the present infant mortality by preventing several million deaths per year, especially those caused by

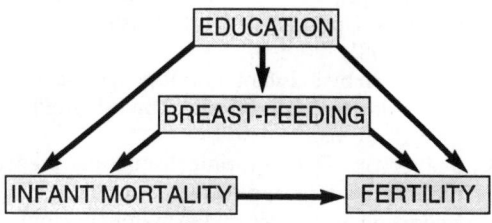

Figure 5.5. Education of mothers results in decreased infant mortality, decreased fertility and an increase in breast-feeding, which in itself decreases infant mortality and fertility. The interrelationship is illustrated.

diarrhea and infectious diseases preventable by vaccination. Such a decreased infant mortality would most likely be followed by decreased birth rates, resulting in many million fewer births per year in developing countries.

Acknowledgements

Our work in developing countries has been supported by the Swedish Agency for Research Cooperation with Developing Countries (SAREC), the Swedish Medical Research Council, and the World Health Organization, as well as by the Lennart, Ellen and Walter Hesselman Foundation for Research. This paper was initially written while L. Å. H. was the first Sir Clavering Fison Visiting Professor at the Institute of Child Health, London, U.K.

References

1. Visaria P, Visaria M. Indian population scene after 1981 census: a perspective. Economical Political Weekly, Nov. 1981:1727–80.
2. UNICEF. The state of the world's children. Oxford: Oxford University Press, 1987.
3. Matthiessen PC, McCann JC. The role of mortality in the European fertility transition: aggregate level relations. In: Preston SH, ed. The effects of infant and child mortality on fertility. New York: Academic Press, 1978: 47–68.
4. Coale AJ, Watkins SC. The revised proceedings of a conference on the Princeton European Fertility Project. Princeton: Princeton University Press, 1986.
5. Brass W, Kabir M. Regional variations in fertility and child mortality during the demographic transition in England and Wales. In: Hobcraft J, Rees P, eds. Regional demographic development. London: Croom Helm, 1977: 71–88.
6. Lithell UB. Breast-feeding and reproduction. Studies in marital fertility and infant mortality in 19th century Finland and Sweden. Acta Universitatis Upsaliensis. Studia Historica Upsaliensis 1981; 120: 1–87.
7. Rosero-Bixby L. Infant mortality in Costa Rica: explaining the recent decline. Stud Fam Plann 1986;17: 57–65.
8. Beaver SE. Demographic transition theory reinterpreted: an application to recent natality trends in Latin America. Lexington: Lexington Books, 1975.
9. WHO report. Health trends and prospects in relation to population and development. In: United Nations, Department of Economic and Social Affairs. The population debate: discussions and perspectives. Vol. I. Geneva: WHO, 1978.
10. Caldwell J. Routes to low mortality in poor countries. Pop Dev Rev 1986; 12(2):171–220.
11. Glassman MB, Ross JA. Two determinants of fertility decline: a test of competing models. Stud Fam Plann 1978; 9: 193–7.
12. Knodel J, van de Walle E. Breast feeding, fertility and infant mortality: and analysis of some early German data. Pop Stud 1967;21(2):109–31.
13. Feachem RG, Koblinsky MA. Interventions for the control of diarrhoeal diseases among young children: promotion of breast feeding. Bull WHO 1984; 62: 271–91.
14. Jalil F, Mahmud A, Ashraf RN, et al. Epidemiology of breast feeding and diarrhoea in a developing country. Acta Paediatrica (submitted).
15. Ashraf RN, Jalil F, Zaman S, et al. Breast feeding protects against neonatal sepsis in a high risk population. Arch Dis Child 1990;66: 488–490.
16. Zaman S, Jalil F, Karlberg J, Hanson LÅ. Early child health in Lahore II Morbidity. Acta Paediatr 1993;(Suppl 390):63-78.
17. Victora CG, Smith PG, Vaughan JP, et al. Evidence for protection by breast feeding against infant deaths from infectious diseases in Brazil. Lancet 1987; ii: 319–322.
18. Hanson LÅ, Brandtzaeg P. The mucosal defence system. In: Stiehm RT, ed. Immunologic disorders in infants and children. Philadelphia: Saunders, 3rd ed, 1989: 116–155.
19. Glass RE, Svennerholm A-M, Stoll BJ, et al. Protection against cholera in breast-fed children by antibodies in breast-milk. N Engl J Med 1983;308: 1389–1392.
20. Cruz JR, Gil L, Cano P, et al. Breastmilk anti-Escherichia coli heat-labile toxin IgA antibodies protect against toxin-induced infantile diarrhoea. Acta Paediatr Scand 1988;77: 658–662.
21. Ruiz-Palacios GM, Calva JJ, Pickering LK. Protection of breastfed infants against Campylobacter diarrhoea by antibodies in human milk. J Pediatr 1990;116:707–713.
22. Short RV, Lewis PR, Renfree MB, Shaw G. Contraceptive effects of extended lactational amenorrhoea: beyond the Bellagio Concensus. Lancet 1991;337: 715–717.
23. Perez A, Labbok MH, Queenan JT. Clinical study of the lactational amenorrhoea method for family planning. Lancet 1992;339: 968–970.
24. Ashraf RN, Jalil F, Khan SR, et al. Early child health in Lahore, Pakistan. IX. Feeding patterns. Acta Paediatr 1993 (Suppl 390):47-61.
25. Rosa FW. Breast feeding in family planning. PAG Bull 1975;5: 5–10.
26. Thapa S, Short RV, Potts M. Breast feeding, birth spacing and their effects on child survival. Nature 1988;335: 679–82.

27. Hanson LÅ, Adlerberth I, Carlsson B *et al.* Breast feeding in reality. In: Hamosh M, Goldman A, eds. Human lactation 2. Maternal-environmental factors. New York: Plenum Press, 1986: 1–12.

28. Ryder NB, Influence of declining mortality on Swedish reproductivity. In: Current research in human fertility. New York: Milbank Memorial Fund, 1955.

29. Coale AJ, Hoover EM. Population growth and economic development in low income countries. New Jersey: Princeton University Press, 1958.

30. Hyrenius H. Fertility and reproduction in a Swedish population group without family limitation. Popul Stud 1958;12: 121–30.

31. Potter RG, New ML, Wyon JB, Gordon JE. Application of field studies to research on the physiology of human reproduction. In: Sheps MC, Ridley JC, eds. Public health and population change. Current research issues. Pittsburgh: University of Pittsburgh Press, 1965; 143–73.

32. Habicht JP. Newsletter. Mammary gland biology and lactation 1987;6:2.

33. Wood JW. Newsletter. Mammary gland biology and lactation 1987;6:2.

34. Brändström A, Stenflo G. Dependence between birth intervals and infant mortality. The case of Nedertorneå 1818–1896. European Population Conference, Finland, 1987.

35. Brändström A. The loveless mothers. Acta Universitaris Umensis. Umeå studies in the Humanities 62, 1984. (In Swedish with English summary).

36. Cantrelle P, Leridon H. Breast feeding mortality in childhood and fertility in a rural zone in Senegal. Popul Stud 1971;25: 505–553.

37. UNICEF. The state of the world's children. Oxford: Oxford University Press, 1984;49–63, 92–99.

38. Charlaw RW, Waidya K. Birth interval and the survival of children to age five: some data from Nepal. J Trop Pediatr 1983;29: 31–34.

39. Huffman SL. Child spacing for maternal and child health. Mothers and children 1984;4: 1–12.

40. Williams CD. Child health in the Gold Coast. Lancet 1938, i: 97–102.

41. Preston SH. Mortality in childhood: lessons from World Fertility Survey. In: Cleland J, Hobcraft J, eds. Reproductive change in developing countries. Oxford: Oxford University Press, 1985: 252–272.

42. Blacker JGC. Health impacts of family planning. Health Policy and Planning 1987;2: 193–203.

43. Reves R. Declining fertility in England and Wales as a major cause of the twentieth century decline in mortality. The role of changing family size and age structure in infectious disease mortality in infancy. Am J Epidemiol 1985;122: 112–126.

44. Aaby P, Bukh J, Lisse IM, *et al.* Overcrowding and intensive exposure as determinants of measles mortality. Am J Epidemiol 1984;120: 49–63.

45. Notestein F. Economic problems of population change. In: Proceedings of the eight international conference of agricultural economists. London: Oxford University Press; 1953:13–31.

46. Davis K. Institutional patterns favoring high fertility in underdeveloped areas. Eugenics Q 1955;2(1):33–39.

47. Lloyd CB, Ivanov S. The effects of improved child survival on family planning practice and fertility. Studies in Family Planning 1988; 19(3):141–161.

48. Preston S. Introduction. In: Preston S., ed. The effects of infant and child mortality on fertility. New York: Academic Press, 1978:1–18.

49. Rutstein S. The relation of child mortality to fertility in Taiwan. In: Social statistics section. Proceedings of the American Statistical Association. 1970: 348–353.

50. Wyon JB, Gordon J. The Khanna study: population problems in rural Punjab. Cambridge: Harvard University Press, 1971.

51. Harrington J. The effect of high infant and childhood mortality on fertility: a simulation model study. In:Preston SH, ed. The effects of infant and child mortality on fertility. New York: Academic Press, 1978: 235–257.

52. Venkatacharya K. Influence of variation in child mortality on fertility: a simulation model study. In: Preston SH, ed. The effects of infant and child mortality on fertility. New York: Academic Press, 1978: 235–257.

53. Pottenberg T. Fertility and family life in an Indian village. Michigan papers on South and Southeast Asia. Ann Arbor: University of Michigan, 1975.

54. Chowdhury AKMA, Khan AR, Chan LC. Experience in Pakistan and Bangladesh. In: Preston SH, ed. The effects of infant and child mortality on fertility. New York: Academic Press, 1978: 113–33.

55. Scrimshaw S. Infant mortality and behaviour in the regulation of family size. Pop Dev Rev 1978; 4(3):383–403.

56. Scrimshaw S. Infanticide as deliberate fertility regulation. In: Bulatao RA, Lee RD, eds. Determinants of fertility in developing countries 2. New York: Academic Press; 1983:245–266.

57. Bongaarts J. Will family planning reduce infant mortality rates? Pop Dev Rev 1987;13(2):323–34.

58. Potter J. Does family planning reduce infant mortality? Comment. Pop Dev Rev 1988; 14(1):179–87.

59. Werner D. Health care in Cuba: a model service or a means of social control – or both? In: Morley D, Rohde J, Williams G, eds. Practicing health for all. Oxford: Oxford University Press, 1987:17–37.

60. UNICEF. The state of the world's children. Oxford: Oxford University Press, 1989.

61. Bauer PT. Are world population trends a problem? In: Wattenberg B, Zinsmeister K, eds. Washington DC: American Enterprise Institute for Public Policy Research, 1985: 19–24.

62. Editorial. Poverty, malnutrition and world food supplies. Lancet 1987; ii:487–490.

About the authors

Lars Åke Hanson is a specialist in pediatrics and clinical immunology and presently the Professor in Clinical Immunology at the University of Gothenburg, Sweden and Physician-in-Chief in clinical Immunology at the hospitals in Gothenburg. His research has concentrated on pediatric immunology including breast-feeding and its effect on the child. The research includes programmes in Costa Rica, Nicaragua and Pakistan.

Staffan Bergström is Professor of International Health at the University of Oslo and Senior Physician at the Department of Obstetrics and Gynaecology, Ullevål University Hospital, Oslo, Norway. He is a specialist in obstetrics and gynaecology and responsible for several research projects in the area of reproductive health in developing countries. During 1982–86 he was the Director of the Department of Obstetrics, Central Hospital, Maputo, Mozambique. He is also involved in the human reproduction research programme (HRP) within the WHO.

Luis Rosero-Bixby is a demographer, specialist in population planning and international health. Currently he is staff researcher at the Office of Population Research of the Princeton University and Coordinator of the Central American Population Program in the University of Costa Rica. His research interest is on the determinants of fertility transition in developing countries.

Lankinen KS, Bergström S, Mäkelä PH and Peltomaa M, eds.
Health and disease in developing countries. London:The Macmillan Press Limited, 1994:49-58.

6 PRIMARY HEALTH CARE IN PLURALISTIC SETTINGS

Ari Serkkola, Lic.Soc.Sci.
University of Helsinki, Institute of Development Studies
P.O. Box 47 (Hämeentie 153 B)
FIN-00014 University of Helsinki
Finland

PLURALISTIC MEDICAL SYSTEMS

In the developing countries, the majority of the population live within the influence of various coexisting medical systems. This situation where a patient and his family can use different treatment methods for the same illness is known as medical pluralism or a pluralistic medical system.[1] Medical pluralism includes both the cognitive and social-system aspects of healing and treatment traditions. The cognitive dimension relates to a wide range of medical concepts, values, attitudes, and beliefs that serve as guidelines for health action and practices. The social-system dimension refers to the different economic, institutional and organisational aspects of treatment and health care delivery systems.

In the health cultures of the developing countries, we can identify the local medical systems, with their traditional methods of treating illness and beliefs about its causes. These traditions are maintained by various traditional specialists, such as spiritual or religious healers, herbalists, technical specialists such as bonesetters and traditional birth attendants.[2] The norms and customs of the social environment, and its modes of interaction, are built into the local treatment methods. In the course of time, these traditions have been subjected to various influences and have changed as a result of contacts with other health cultures. With some forms of treatment, the external influences stem from the movement of people, such as immigration; and with other practices, from the spread of a religion, like Christianity or Islam.

Local conceptions have merged into regional medical systems. Oral and written sources tell us about the history and development of traditional Chinese medicine, of the Indian Ayurveda, of the Moslem Unani, of ancient Greek medicine and its modern descendant, the humoral pathology of Latin America. These traditions derive from different philosophies and theories of health care (e.g. the Hippocratic and Galenic theories of medicine); from religion (e.g. Ayurvedic medicine from Hindu philosophy, and Unani from Islam); or from practical experimentation (e.g. acupuncture in Chinese medicine, and homeopathy).

In the course of time, the traditions have been influenced by one another and have developed in directions of their own. The humoral theory (the categorisation of living and inanimate matter as hot or cold), though originating in Latin America, has spread to India and many other Asian countries. As to the Arabic or Islamic Unani medicine, it has its roots in the ancient Greek medicine developed in the period of the Arab civilisation.[3,4] Even Western medicine is based to a considerable extent on the utilisation and development of various herbalistic methods.

The most important health traditions have attained the status of cosmopolitan medicine. The Ayurveda, Unani, Chinese, Tibetan and Burmese medicines are well known over wide areas of South-East Asia and India. Humoral medicine, as mentioned, is known in both

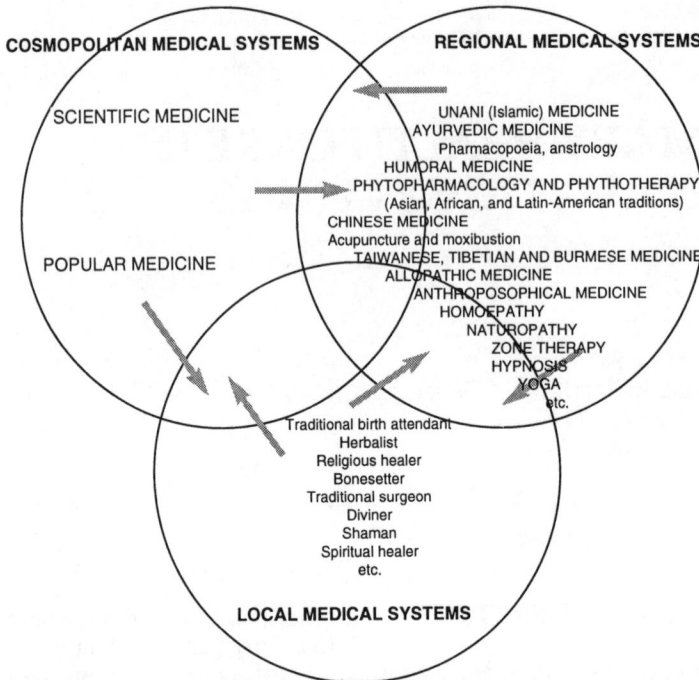

Figure 6.1. Local, regional, and cosmopolitan medical systems.

Latin America and Asia. Western medicine, to which the term cosmopolitan medicine most often refers, has achieved a leading position throughout the world. A growing number of developing countries have endeavoured to apply PHC to the specific needs of their own people (Figure 6.1).

Medical pluralism presents two challenges to PHC. Firstly, the coexistence of different medical systems offers multiple choices to the individual. PHC has to justify its activities within the field of alternatives: how can it gain general acceptance? Secondly, the coexistent traditions mean pluralism within a particular system, allowing access to various levels and types of care. In this situation PHC, its different branches and their mutual cooperation must fit in with the customs and demands of the surrounding health culture. *The question is, how can PHC adapt itself to become a part of the local culture?* These aspects are a test of the applicability and sustainability of PHC in developing countries.

STEREOTYPES IN PLURALISTIC SETTINGS

Examination of health and illness behaviour in a pluralistic health culture has revealed sever-

al stereotyped conceptions contrasting traditional and scientific medicine.[5] These stereotypes are both cognitive (linked to health knowledge and beliefs) and social (connected with illness behaviour and the organisation of treatment). If accepted uncritically as a basis for health planning, they may hinder the incorporation of useful aspects of traditional medicine into modern health care systems.

1) Illnesses are classified as attributable to either supernatural and magical causes, termed personalistic in ethnomedical literature, or natural causes, called naturalistic. This dichotomic thinking derives from the Cartesian mind and body dualism, on which earlier anthropological research was also based. However, in pluralistic health thinking, both naturalistic and personalistic reasons may be given simultaneously to explain illness; both are equally natural and normal. Explanations of more serious illnesses are structured into a rather semantic chain or cluster of causes, in which social and religious background factors are referred to along physiological sensations.

2) It is assumed that local people dichotomise illnesses as curable either by folk medicine or by a physician; and that a spiritual or religious therapist treats, and is believed to

cure, only supernatural illnesses, while a physician treats and cures only natural illnesses. In many developing countries, however, traditional healers also utilise modern medical procedures, pharmaceuticals, surgical instruments and so on. Just as stereotyped is the idea that people use exclusively either traditional or new methods. In fact, the use of parallel methods, such as medication together with religious treatment, is also common. In a pluralistic health culture, choices cannot be referred back to an adversarial model.

3) Traditional medicine is presumed to be holistic, while modern medicine considers only the disease. The basic argument is that traditional healers know their patients' family background and can therefore assess psychosocial as well as clinical factors in diagnosis and therapy. This assertion still holds for relatively isolated rural villages. However, traditional healers in large villages and towns in Africa and Asia are probably impersonal in their methods almost as often as are modern medical physicians. The holistic grounds for integrating traditional practitioners into PHC programmes may be weaker than frequently is presumed.

4) Traditional healers are perceived as elderly, highly respected people, who are also able, by virtue of their social status, to promote PHC in an area. The older healers do command a charismatic veneration among patients and their families. Nevertheless, the idea that the respect for a healer in traditional settings could serve the new health care has proved problematic. It is difficult for the carrier of tradition to adopt the role of an agent of change in health culture. Literate apprentices or journeymen who have a thirst for knowledge and whose status is not yet established may be better able to reorganise traditional medicine to be a part of PHC. Also with the new health care, however, the authority and blessing of elders and older healers are needed for moral support.

5) It is assumed that physicians working in traditional settings are unacquainted with indigenous beliefs and medicine, and do not understand the language and rationale of these; and that this causes difficulties in communicating with patients. In fact, now that more health professionals are trained locally, many may have a personal knowledge of traditional beliefs. Correct diagnosis of illness does presuppose that the doctor is familiar with the traditional symptom descriptions and

causal conceptions. However, the problem of communication between doctor, patient and therapeutic group exists both in modern and traditional environments.

Equally stereotyped is the idea that the local population is ignorant of the new health care and of pharmaceuticals. Western medicines are known in almost every village in the developing countries. The problem is more in the population using new treatment methods to an ever-increasing extent, but often in a different way than medical regimes recommend.

6) Healers and other authorities are seen as having a consistent, clearly defined status and task in health care. In fact, their status varies from one community to another, just as community structures vary. Furthermore, it is assumed that health services can be arranged in accordance with a consistent PHC model. PHC can at any rate be promoted with the eight PHC sectors as universal elements, but these can only be organised while taking into account the special characteristics of each community.

CAUSALITY AND ILLNESS BEHAVIOUR

In medically pluralistic settings, illness is explained from multifactorial – and not from solely naturalistic or solely personalistic – starting-points.[6] In almost every developing country, there are various different sources that contribute to the popular stock of etiological knowledge: environmental elements, bodily conditions, food, psychosocial emotions and feelings, spiritual beings and magical acts, poverty, etc. Already, in many strata of society, also microbes, bacteria and viruses are recognised as causing illnesses.

Regional health cultures have moulded the cultural content of causal explanations and the relationships between them. To give a brief outline, personalistic explanations have been particularly prevalent among indigenous inhabitants of Africa, North America, Oceania and Siberia. They also form a basis for the more complex medicine of contemporary China, South Asia and Latin America. Naturalistic explanations, on the other hand, are dominant in humoral pathology, Ayurveda, Unani, and traditional Chinese medicine (though not necessarily ruling out personalistic causes). Naturalistic concepts of causality also characterise homeopathy and naturopathy.[5]

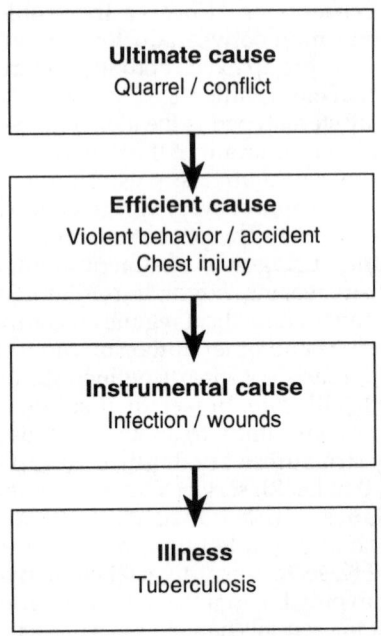

Figure 6.2. Causal chain of tuberculosis.

In addition, so-called culture-bound syndromes can be recognised – the term refers to mental disorders or changes in perception of reality. For instance, *susto* in Latin America, *latah* in Malayo-Indonesia, *amok* in Malaya, and *saar* (spirit possession) in the Sahel zone of Africa are illnesses or symptom combinations which cannot be explained by clinical diagnosis.[7] These illnesses consist of culturally specific behavioural repertoires which are legitimated in culturally sanctioned norms and concepts.

In lay thinking, illness is linked to the larger context of the socioenvironment, including also the biological context of the organism. Therefore, the same illness can be the result of a variety of causal factors, both naturalistic and personalistic. In Somalia, for example, tuberculosis can just as well be explained by malnutrition or stigma as by heredity or harmful spirits. Moreover, the same causal factor can provoke a variety of different illnesses. Malnutrition or harmful spirits, for instance, may contribute to the outbreak of many other infectious diseases.

Varietal causal explanations in the cultures under examination can often be represented as multiple aspects of causality (Figure 6.2). Local people sometimes refer to mechanisms, commonly termed instrumental causes: hot sun and cold wind, or contagion and infections are good examples of these. At other times, they refer to agents, termed efficient causes – e.g. bacteria or spirits – whose intervention accounts for the onset of an illness. And finally, they believe in an ultimate cause of their affliction, such as Allah's will in Unani, hot-cold balance in humoral theory, or Panchamahabhutus and Tridosha (balance of body, mind and soul) in Ayurveda. The ultimate cause tells something about the deepest origin of illness: it consists of events and circumstances whose occurrence explains why a particular illness strikes a particular person at a particular moment.

Taken as a whole, explanations for illnesses can be understood as a semantic chain of causes. Illnesses are labelled in the therapeutic process as due to some cause(s), which is in turn explained by various indirect factors connected with life experiences of the sufferer and those close to him/her. One cause follows another, and they carry a different weight.[6,8]

Each health culture – also biomedicine – has its own principles for conceptualising illnesses. Lay knowledge derived from or popularly attributed to biomedicine may not always be accurate. This is because, on the one hand, the information may be inadequately presented to the lay public; and on the other, people may reinterpret it from their own local, regional or cosmopolitan medical perspective.

THE PRACTITIONER AS AN INTERPRETER OF SICKNESS

Therapists – physicians as well as healers – seek solutions to the same basic questions: how sickness occurs (symptoms), why it occurs (causes), and how it can be cured (treatment). In addition, they draw their conclusions in a psychosocial environment, where other influencing factors will be linked to the therapeutic process.

However, the therapeutic rationality of practitioners often leads to varying solutions for the same illness. In brief, religious and spiritual healers draw special attention to the causes of illness. The primary role of the shaman, religious healer, or witch-finder is to identify the deity, ghost, or other agent that has caused the illness; and then to determine how to placate or overcome him. Until the causal agent has been discovered, therapy is believed to have little effect. Physicians are seen as diagnosing the symptoms, both clinically and by means of tests. In consequence, the local people accept the doctor's procedures – but at the same time, they hold on to the old beliefs and rituals by which they attempt to eliminate the causes of the illness.[5]

Healers and their clients share the same health care thinking – even if on a different level of consciousness. Herbalists like the *curanderos* of Latin America mirror their patients' symptoms in humoral theory, in which knowledge of the effect of herbs on illnesses is central; for them, the balance of health is concretised in relationships between cold and hot. African herbalists, likewise, know hundreds of healing herbs and their combinations, but they often connect their curative knowledge with various social incidents, harmful spirits, and ancestor cults. In both cases, the treatment is rational in the sense that it endeavours to cater for cultural beliefs (which themselves may appear irrational) besides the organic affliction.

The jointly held health conceptions mean that a patient can know already beforehand about the treatment he will receive. The healer's role varies from being a leading authority to being a member of a therapeutic group. A healer functioning as a member of a group, e.g. a traditional midwife, will assist the patient and those close to him/her in self-diagnosis or labelling of the illness; then, after confirming the medical picture, she will administer the appropriate remedies. As an authority, a healer will lead the diagnosis and prescribe the treatment.

Preventive health care is an integral part of traditional medicine also. For each cause of illness, there are cultural instructions or norms as to how it can be avoided. For the maintenance of health, a religious healer preaching the Unani doctrine will stress Islamic dietary habits, hygiene and a moral life. A spiritual healer will advise the avoidance of disputes with neighbours, so as to avoid witchcraft. Village elders will advise folk to stand upwind of a sick person to avoid infection. The principles in question have been internalised in numerous cultural beliefs, taboos and instructions for living.

Traditional medicine is of importance in the adapted nursing approach. This approach can, on the one hand, maintain and utilise scientifically grounded conceptions and forms of treatment found in traditional medicine. However meaningless isolated treatment procedures of healers might be, traditional medicine as a whole may have elements that are consistent with scientific medicine. On the other hand, the adapted approach can direct health education towards the eradication of harmful living habits and treatment forms. An adaptive strategy requires a serious study of the preventive and curative practices of traditional medicine, and this should not be limited merely to an evaluation of healers' work.

THE RANGE OF THERAPEUTIC OPTIONS

When people resort to local, regional or cosmopolitan medicine, their choices are anchored in the cognitive and value orientations of the popular culture. According to research, as many as 70 to 90 per cent of all illness episodes are managed within the popular sector.[9] Only in one-third of them do specialists and practitioners recommend and make therapeutical decisions.

Therefore, the interaction between the popular sector and local/regional/cosmopolitan medicine is crucial: lay people actually activate their health care by deciding whom to consult and when. The switching from one source of care to another depends on many factors, including medical knowledge, costs and time, accessibility, preferences, confidence, satisfaction, the experience of others, convenience, the affective behaviour of the provider, etc. In Kenya, for example, individuals and families can choose from 12 therapeutic options.[10]

In a pluralistic health culture, individuals and those close to them are constantly pacing the bounds between alternative services. The use of parallel treatment methods is usual, especially for chronic and serious illnesses. A person may, after self-medication, go to a traditional healer, and finally end up at a doctor's surgery or a hospital. Often, the sufferer endeavours to supplement the new chemotherapy with religious treatment. The treatment choices reflect the various conceptions and health care value systems upheld by the therapeutic group.

In most health cultures in Africa and Asia, choices of therapy are made by constellations of kinsmen, friends, and other associates. Patients and therapeutic specialists play a relatively minor role in determining the pattern of medical utilisation. This therapeutic group conceptualises and manages the various tasks of health care: it diagnoses, analyses causes, recommends treatment methods, and takes care of the social and economic consequences of the illness.[11] Characteristic of the group's operation is reliance on earlier experiences, on the collective memory. In addition, the group, acting as a support network for the sufferer, contributes toward paying the costs of treatment.

Therapeutic choices and decision-making are of integral importance also in PHC. One ethical principle of scientific medicine is privacy and confidentiality between the patient and the treating staff. In the patient–doctor relationship, the sufferer has to convince the doctor of his/her symptoms, and the doctor has to convince the patient concerning the therapy. In the developing countries, the interaction also includes a third party: it is a patient–doctor–therapeutic group relationship. Treatment solutions should, therefore, be communicated to the whole therapeutic group, not just to the patient. In this way, the cognitive consensus (awareness of the illness and of its treatment) as well as the social consensus (mutual understanding that the treatment rules will be followed) can be shared among all those involved.

DRUGS AND MEDICATION

A transitional medical system arises when new medicines are used in the developing countries. Sections of the population practice self-medication with the drugs in varying ways, without consulting experts. Pharmaceuticals have undergone a cultural reinterpretation on encountering local modes of understanding. Side by side with the generic content and trade-name of a medicine other meanings have appeared. The use of medicines is regulated by both cognitive reinterpretation and social accommodation.[12]

In some cultures, as in Somalia, the observable characteristics of medicines (colour, shape, taste) are linked with the traditional anatomical classification (head, stomach, back). Combinations of these concepts give rise to about a dozen different symbols for the same medicine. The symbols also contain within them semantic instructions on how the medicine is used (e.g. head medicine, syrupy stomach medicine, red back medicine). In cultures where people live within the sphere of influence of a dominant regional medical system, medicines are conceptualised according to that prevailing health philosophy. For example, Guatemalan villagers categorise Western drugs as hot or cold in accordance with their own illness classification. Medicines are used for hot or cold illnesses.

In certain cultures, e.g. in the Philippines, medicines are classified using local criteria of applicability. In Manila, the term *hiyang* (suit) defines a medicine as suitable for one, but wrong for another. The inefficacy of a therapy is explained by the concept of *hiyang*: if a drug does not work, then it apparently does not suit the individual.

The distribution and commercialisation of drugs is of vital significance in the formulation of medical regimes. As commodities, drugs are transformed into articles of exchange, and they change hands in the free market. In this situation, they easily pass out of the control of biomedical professionals. The public and private, the formal and informal sources of drugs are closely related.

In the developing countries, numerous unofficial delivery systems can be identified. In many African countries, for instance, pedlars move from village to village selling medicines along with other products. Doctors, nurses and other personnel in hospitals and health centres redistribute supplies obtained at work to relatives, friends, and relevant others. Sometimes they sell drugs clandestinely to drug vendors in the market. Town-dwellers send drugs to country areas on receiving an oral message about a case of illness in a related family. Furthermore, medicines are popular gift articles, particularly in mail sent from abroad. Whether official or unofficial, each delivery channel involves its own characteristic medical regime, custom or instruction for using the medicine.[13]

COMMUNITY, HEALTH ACTORS AND PHC

Community is one of the commonest words in the primary health care literature. The shortcomings of PHC frequently arise from misunderstanding or ignorance of the structure, dynamics, and capabilities of local communities.[14]

Communities are often simplified as being homogeneous, integrated, harmonious, relatively autonomous, and well-bounded entities. *In reality, communities are dynamic, often heterogeneous groupings of people, whose interests and identities converge and diverge in complex ways.*

Community versus village

In planning PHC, the community is often conceived of as a village. A village may well, as in many states and provinces of India, be coherent to the extent that it can be spoken of as an areal, ethnic and/or administrative community (*panchayat samity*). An African village, however, forms a highly inaccurate and dysfunctional basis for anticipating participation in PHC. In the first place, an African village may vary in size from two houses to a densely populated centre with many thousands of inhabitants.

Secondly, community participation may be inhibited because traditional society is not accustomed to collective action at the village level. Among the Hausa of Nigeria, the Bulu of Cameroon, and the pastoralists of Somalia, the operative social units are the patrilineages rather than the villages. Members of these societies think in terms of lineage interests, scarcely conceiving of common village interests.

And thirdly, over one quarter of African societies are fully or partly mobile. Among pastoralists in the Sahel region (e.g. Mali, Niger, Chad, Sudan) the size, composition and location of social groups varies according to the season. The pattern of dispersed settlements that is widely prevalent in eastern and southern Africa is also of significance with regard to community participation. Many of the people live in scattered, individual homesteads restricted to the extended family, rather than in densely inhabited villages.

Therefore, variations in the spatial pattern, degrees of isolation, ecological setting, size, mobility and cohesion of communities have profound significance for the organisation of community participation in PHC. In fact, it must be admitted that there are *communities within communities*. The criteria delineating a community depend in each case on how the people involved choose to define themselves.

Health priorities of the community

One cornerstone in planning health services is the priority order of health risks, based on epidemiological data. However, the health needs of the local population do not always correspond with epidemilogical evaluations. There prevails a gap between the plans and the needs of the population.

In many dry areas, for instance the Sahel zone of Africa, absolute food shortages at many times of the year make proper nutrition one of the most difficult aspects of community health to promote. Scarcities of food and of clean household water are the biggest problems to a nation's health.

A population's dependence on domestic animals may elevate the health of the animals to a position of greater importance than that of the people. Being quite aware of their health problems Nepali villagers give priority to health care for their agricultural animals. Similarly, Somali pastoralists consider the first task of PHC to be provision of medication for their camels.

Relief from personal suffering is clearly the top health priority of all individuals. It follows that curative care, backed by a dependable supply of essential drugs, is felt as one of the most pressing needs in a majority of communities. However, a substantial proportion of PHC outreach programmes have been specifically designed to focus on preventive and promotive activities. Nevertheless, the success of preventive health work is dependent on curative care. The use of health facilities diminishes proportionately as there are hitches in medicine supplies. A policy of no drugs also puts all other health work in jeopardy.

The challenge is to first find creative strategies that equip PHC services to meet curative needs and to offer preventive services that are in highest demand.

Organising the community for health work

The community health worker (CHW) has the role of a mediator, as a connecting link between community participation and the health administration. In theory, he/she should break down social and cultural barriers between the new health care and the collective health work of the community. In practice, the community health worker may find himself or herself at the interface of a technically complex delivery system and a socially complex community. Lack of a legitimate role, medicines and administrative support endanger the CHW's credibility and job motivation. From a broader perspective, the problem lies in the fact that the whole interaction of PHC with the community is narrowly based, depending on the CHW alone.[14]

The interests of the community can be more strongly represented in PHC by integrating into it also other specialists respected by the community, like village elders, healers, traditional birth attendants, agricultural workers, artisans, merchants, etc. The more effective community-based health programmes may be correlated with strong local movements, like the Harambee movement in Kenya, or Sarvodaya in Sri Lanka. Social structures for voluntarism and self-help can be strengthened, and new ones developed, in order to ensure popular participation in development activities – including health.

ADAPTATION OF HEALTH CULTURES

Through adaptation of health cultures, the scarce health service resources in developing countries can be reinforced, and the quality of the services improved. Such adaptation is a continual process, in which medical knowledge is brought into relation with the economic, social and cultural circumstances of local health care. It means meeting people's health needs at the lowest cost, using proper traditional and scientific methods. The adaptation can be aided by analysing the characteristics of health cultures side by side and deriving applicable health services from them. Cosmopolitan and traditional medicine may be more or less discrete entities, with greater or lesser contact, overlap, interdependence, or even congruence (as in the case of China).

Local beliefs – scientific conceptions

The idea of multiple aspects of causality helps us to understand the contents of and relationships between traditional conceptions, treatment and social sanctions. Put simply, in traditional treatment, elements that support the new health care can be found (e.g. preventive methods and clinical diagnosis), as well as meaningless and even harmful means of treatment. By examining the whole therapeutic process – besides the separate treatment practices – we can pinpoint similarities in which the adaptation of knowledge is possible.

Multiple aspects of causality link together different levels of consciousness and action. In indigenous knowledge, beneficial aspects can be singled out such as those concerning agricultural methods, medicinal plants, availability of underground water, etc. Indigenous communication systems – involving informal networks, interest groups, oral messages, religious meetings, balladeers, poets – can be recruited to give health information when transmitting new knowledge. A modern development of such a communication system

is constituted by the radio forums and discussion groups so well utilised in many African countries for distance learning. And the leaders of indigenous opinion – religious leaders, elders, healers, leaders of men's and women's groups, youth idols, merchants, artisans, farmers, etc. – are important promoters and appliers of new knowledge. In this way, local culture can be a help rather than a hindrance to change.[15]

People's needs – possibilities for health care

Patients and their therapeutic groups make the basic choice between the forms of treatment in a pluralistic health culture. This has led to informal linkage between traditional medicine and biomedicine through the therapy-seeking behaviour of patients. In the adaptive approach, we can examine side by side the questions 'What services do people want?' and 'What services is it possible to offer?'

The first question leads to a *segmentation of health services*, in which the needs are divided according to client groups.[16] Needs analysis helps us to recognise variations in the composition of a community and to pinpoint the health care interests of each group (e.g. children – nutritional care and vaccinations; women – gynecological services; male pastoralists – treatment of domestic animals). In addition, by mapping out the needs, one can identify groups and treatment methods that remain outside the domain of scientific services (e.g. the elderly – religious treatment).

The second question implies a *differentiation of services*, in which their importance and order of priority is evaluated by clients and community members.[16] Taking into account the needs of the different groups increases the credibility of PHC. By getting the groups involved in the production of the desired services, conventional PHC strategy can be reinforced and supplemented. The production of services is dependent, in the final analysis, on the people's participation and their ability to contribute towards the costs.

Healers' methods – scientific treatment

Traditional healers retain their popularity because they are accessible, available, acceptable and adaptable. They survive because they represent a culturally understood approach to managing many physical and psychosocial ills. Furthermore, traditional medicine remains a more or less integrated system of social control and curative procedures, with important individual and corporate health effects.[14] Therefore, the status of traditional specialists is recognised also in the adaptive approach.

In PHC, selective cooperation can be arranged with traditional healers. At national level, legislative control can be classified according to the following four types: 1) exclusive (monopolistic) systems; 2) tolerant systems; 3) inclusive systems; and 4) integrated systems, in which various traditional medical practices are legally permitted to a certain extent.[17] It is also the policy of the WHO (1985) to encourage some degree of integration of local, regional and cosmopolitan medicine. Integration of traditional health care into PHC has been taken furthest in China, Nepal and Sri Lanka. In most countries of Southern Africa nowadays, selected herbalists, bonesetters and midwives have a legal, licensed status. Adaptation of health cultures also presupposes that representatives of biomedicine acquire a deeper familiarity with the possibilities of traditional medicine and the needs of the community.

References

1. Frankel S, Gilbert L, eds. A continuing trial of treatment: medical pluralism in Papua New Guinea. Dordrecht: Kluwer Academic Publishers, 1989.
2. Slikkerveer LJ. Plural medical systems in the Horn of Africa. London, New York: Kegan Paul International, 1990.
3. Bannerman R, Burton J, Wen-Chieh C, eds. Traditional medicine and health care coverage. A reader for health administrators and practitioners. Geneva: World Health Organization, 1983.
4. Sheikh A, Sheikh K, eds. Eastern and Western approaches to healing: ancient wisdom and modern knowledge. New York: John Wiley & Sons, 1989.
5. Foster GM. Introduction to ethnomedicine. In: Bannerman R, Burton J, Wen-Chieh C, eds. Traditional medicine and health care coverage. A reader for health administrators and practitioners. Geneva: World Health Organization, 1983: 17–24. (References to 2–5)
6. Serkkola A. A sick man is advised by a hundred. Pluralistic control of tuberculosis in Southern Somalia (Thesis). University of Kuopio, Finland, 1994.
7. Good B, ed. Culture-bound syndromes (theme issue). Cult Med Psychiatry 1987;11(1).
8. Bibeau G. the circular semantic network in Ngbandi disease nosology. Soc Sci Med 1981; 15:295–307.
9. Kleinman A. Patients and healers in the context of culture. An exploration of the boderland between anthropology, medicine, and psychiatry. Berkeley, Los Angeles, London: University of California Press, 1980.
10. Good CM. Ethnomedical systems in Africa. Patterns of traditional medicine in rural and urban Kenya. New York, London: The Guilford Press, 1987.
11. Janzen JM. The quest for therapy. Medical pluralism in Lower Zaire. Berkeley, Los Angeles, London: University of California Press, 1978.
12. van der Geest S, Whyte S, eds. The context of medicines in developing countries. Dordrecht, Boston, London: Kluwer Academic Publishers, 1988.
13. van der Geest S, Hardon A, Whyte S. Planning for essential drugs: are we missing the cultural dimension? Health Policy and Planning 1990;5:182–185.
14. Good CM. The community in African primary health care. Strengthening participation and a proposed strategy. (Studies in African Health and Medicine; v. 2.) Lewiston, Queenstone, Lampeter: The Edwin Mellen Press, 1988.
15. Ebrahim GJ, Ranken IP, eds. Primary health care, reorienting organizational support. London: Macmillan Publishers, 1988.
16. Øvretveit J. Quality health services. Uxbridge: Brunel Institute of Organization and Social Studies, 1992
17. Stepan J. Patterns of legislation concerning traditional medicine. In: Bannerman R, Burton J, Wen-Chieh C, eds. Traditional medicine and health care coverage. A reader for health administrators and practitioners. Geneva: World Health Organization, 1983: 290–313.

Additional reading

1. Coreil J, Mull D, eds. Anthropology and primary health care. Boulder, San Francisco, Oxford: Westview Press, 1990.
2. Gray C, Baudouy J, Martin K, Bang M, Cash R, eds. Primary health care in Africa. A study of the Mali rural health project. Boulder, San Francisco, London: Westview Press, 1990.
3. Heggenhougen H. Medical anthropology and primary health care. London: EPC Publication No 22, 1990.

4. Justice J. Politics, plans and people. Culture and health development in Nepal. Berkeley, Los Angeles, London: University of California Press, 1986.

5. Last M, Chavunduka G, eds. The professionalisation of African medicine. Manchester: Mancester University Press, 1986.

6. Leslie C, ed. Asian medical systems: a comparative study. Berkeley, Los Angeles, London: University of California Press, 1976.

7. McElroy A, Townsend P, Medical anthropology in ecological perspective. Boulder, San Francisco, London: Westview Press, 1985.

8. Nichter M. Anthropology and international health. Dordrecht, Boston, London: Kluwer Academic Publishers, 1989.

9. Phillips D. Health and health care in the Third World. Harlow (Essex): Longman Scientific and Technical, 1990.

10. Spector R. Cultural diversity in health and illness. 2nd Norwalk, Conn.: Appleton-Century-Crofts, 1985.

11. Zeichner C, ed. Modern and traditional health care in developing societies: conflict and cooperation. Lanham: University Press of America, 1988.

12. Young J. Medical choice in a Mexican village. New Brunswick, New Jersey: Rutgers University Press, 1981.

About the author

Ari Serkkola is specialist in medical anthropology and health service administration working as a research fellow at the Institute of Development Studies, University of Helsinki. He has studied social sciences at the University of Tampere; and at the time of writing, was finalising his Ph.D. in public health for the University of Kuopio, Finland. He has done field research on Somali culture and health care under the auspices of the Finnish International Development Agency (FINNIDA) and the Tuberculosis Control Programme. He has published books and articles on these subjects.

Lankinen KS, Bergström S, Mäkelä PH and Peltomaa M, eds.
Health and disease in developing countries. London:The Macmillan Press Limited, 1994:59-66.

7 THE NEGLECTED EDUCATION

Arvi Hurskainen, Ph.D.
University of Helsinki, Department of Asian and African Studies
P.O. Box 13 (Meritullinkatu 1 B), FIN-00014 University of Helsinki,
Finland

INTRODUCTION

Health programmes need effective health education in order to succeed. This requirement concerns curative as well as preventive measures. The level and extent of health education may be a decisive determinant of their final results. Health education campaigns in industrialised countries have shown their effectiveness in reducing the risk of, for example, cardiovascular diseases and lung cancer.

Special campaigns are, however, only suited for tackling specific problems, while the general health of a population depends to a large extent on the general level of education and the multifaceted health education given in a number of contexts. Industrialised countries have the advantages of general primary education, and many kinds of information channels, through which health education can be distributed.

In developing countries it is far more problematic to convey the message to all those who need it. Not only are the infrastructures for communication insufficiently developed, but also conceptions of health education may be contradictory depending on who is giving it. Traditional conceptions of health and diseases may be different from the modern understanding of health.

UNIVERSAL PRIMARY EDUCATION STILL A DISTANT GOAL

The initiative of establishing primary schools in developing countries often came from the colonial government, but missionary agencies were also frequently involved in putting the plans into practice. The government needed literate local people for administrative tasks, and there were no plans to extend the education beyond these immediate needs. Consequently, during the colonial rule the number of schools increased only slowly.

The missionary agencies had their own motivations in joining the task of building and running schools, although the rationale for it was usually stated only vaguely. No doubt the missionary agencies saw school education as a means to further their general aim, i.e. to get converts into Christianity. It would be unjust, however, to conclude that mission agencies were involved in primary education *only* because of proselytism. General education was seen also as a means of elevating people's standard of life, including health. It should be remembered that in many places the same agencies had a responsibility in local modern health care. The primary education was to provide basic knowledge of the principles of health.

Although the number of schools during the colonial era increased in many areas, only a minority of the population was admitted. Significantly larger numbers received, however, modern medical services, often as one alternative along with the traditional health care systems. The medical staff communicated clearly that efficient medical care is not possible without general and well-planned health education, the natural place for which is the primary school.

After independence, one of the aims of the young nations was to put more emphasis on primary education, and ultimately, secondary education. As the statistics from Africa clearly

Spanish lesson in a rural school near San Christobal in Mexico. Photo: UNICEF/David Mangurian

show, this aim is still far from being achieved (Tables 7.1 to 7.3). Another serious problem is the lowering of the standard of education reported from many countries. In countries with a strong emphasis on good coverage of primary education, there has been a drop in standards of teaching and learning. Factors such as large teaching groups, inadequate teaching materials or a total lack of them, low and irregular salary, poor prospects of promotion etc. have disillusioned the atmosphere within the primary education system in many places.

Resources allocated for education have been directed in substantial amounts to adult education campaigns, which has in many cases disturbed normal school education. Senior pupils have been recruited as teachers for adult education classes, with only nominal pocket money, and schools have been temporarily closed during such campaigns. People have taken such programmes with ambiguous feelings. Although they might see the advantage of literacy in principle, it is not much use if there is no other reading available than the material used in the literacy campaigns.

PRIMARY EDUCATION AND NEEDS

In addition to the poor coverage of primary education and insufficient resources, there are also other serious problems with roots in the colonial school system. The models for schools were adopted from the systems of the colonial masters with little adaptation to local traditions and needs. What needed to be taught in schools was decided by the school authorities, which meant in practice copying the curricula of the colonising countries.

After independence, school curricula changed surprisingly little. The new governments may have had confidence in the already established school system. Obviously there was a common faith that education is one of the necessary conditions for development and that it should be structured according to the models which already had proved their efficiency elsewhere, i.e. in the colonising countries. Therefore, French, English and Portuguese school curricula continued, with a few exceptions, to dominate in developing countries.

This reinforced the deep-seated belief that real knowledge is available only from outside, while local knowledge is something inferior, bound to old disappearing traditions. Therefore, the quickest way to development would be through applying directly the most modern school system. An attempt to integrate it with traditional elements of knowledge would just delay development or, in the worst case, hamper it altogether. Consequently the local knowledge systems were virtually excluded from the modern school system, leading to alienation from traditional cultures.

One serious consequence of the neglect of local knowledge was the wholesale abandonment of the traditional healing systems. Those methods were viewed as something to be ignored because they were thought to be based on wrong reasoning. Only more recently has attention been paid to the knowledge and use of herbal medicines in traditional societies, although such medicines have always been an essential part of people's healing systems (Chapter 6).

Education in developing countries suffers from both quantitative and qualitative shortcomings. Primary education covers only part of the population and those attending modern schools face many kinds of problems. The lack of teaching materials or over large teaching groups are perhaps not the main problems in education. A more serious problem is the absence of a holistic view and philosophy of education, which would provide the basic guidelines for planning and action. In modern education knowledge is fragmented into separate subjects, the contents of which are often alien to the life situation of the students. Compared with traditional education, where teaching was anchored to the traditional culture and local needs, modern education alienates rather than integrates, and this has adverse consequences on traditional education.

LANGUAGE PROBLEMS

Many developing countries adhere to a language policy, that acknowledges a foreign language as the official language, although only a very small minority consider it their mother tongue. This is the case particularly in Africa, where the linguistic map is quite fragmented. It is often thought that the use of a foreign (colonial) language would ensure the integrity of the nation and that it would be a bridge to other countries worldwide. Although this may be partly true, it has the

effect of alienating educated people from the majority of the population. The foreign language has not become a real *lingua franca* in any of those countries where local languages are strong. It has maintained the illusion that things taught in schools in a foreign language are in some way superior to the matters at home, which are communicated through a local language. It is also true that the real capability of the students to communicate in French or English is often very limited.

Unfortunately, there is no easy way out of this situation. This concerns particularly countries with several local languages, where it is difficult to apply a monolingual policy based on one local language. Nevertheless, the use of several areal languages in school education, for example, would enable a large number of the students to use their own mother tongue in learning, which would certainly make the learning process more effective. The disadvantages are the high cost of producing teaching materials and the feared disintegrating effect, because such policy is thought to promote tribalism.

In any case it is important to note in this context that there is a lot of dissatisfaction among education authorities concerning the past language policies, where people were educated through a foreign medium. The disadvantages have also been increasingly recognised by the governments, and there is intensive discussion concerning the revision of language policies. Such rethinking raises hopes of a more viable and integrated educational system, where the needs of health education are taken into account more efficiently than before.

MODERN HEALTH EDUCATION

Health education has been traditionally given in a number of phases during man's life cycle; the following concentrates on health education in primary schools and within adult education programmes. The statistics clearly demonstrate that the percentage of children in developing countries who receive primary education is increasing steadily (Table 7.1). Obviously, 6–8 years of primary education offers the best forum for implementing plans for large scale health education. Health and hygiene is already a subject in several curricula in these countries, but it is difficult to estimate how these possibilities have been utilised in practice.

National and international organisations, including the WHO, have prepared a number of health education manuals for primary schools and primary health care workers. The presentation is simple and concrete enough to be useful in teaching. One gets the impression that poor results derive more from inadequate planning and implementation than from the lack of knowledge of what should be done to improve health education. Currently, the books and other teaching aids are available only to a small minority of teachers and educators.

Significant improvements in health could be achieved by quite simple methods of teaching community members basic facts of health (Figure 7.1). The students should be taught to look after themselves so that health risks would be minimised (teaching safe practices). Teaching the principles of healthy nutrition and personal hygiene are important in building a strong basis for healthy life. The students should also be taught about the health hazards of tobacco and alcohol, and possibly other drugs if relevant.

Healthy life is based on good relationships with the closest reference groups, such as the family and schoolmates. Teaching should also be related to the local traditions, thus integrating health education with the culture of the children. This is very important, because the pre-school socialisation of the children has taken place through indigenous education, which is also important later.

The community of the children and their environment are important subjects to teach, since the children are also members of the larger community. They should know what functions the community has and what kind of services are available. Caring for the environment is also an increasingly important subject to study.

HEALTH EDUCATION IN THE SCHOOL CURRICULUM

As can be seen from Figure 7.1, health education concerns a large number of elements which overlap with other teaching subjects. Therefore, it is not self-evident how health education in schools should be arranged. There are at least three ways of doing this.

First, health education can be taken as a separate subject in primary schools with one longer or two shorter teaching periods per week.

Second, health education can be integrated with other subjects and taught within them at relevant points. Such subjects are, for instance, biology (structure and function of human body, properties and nutritional values of various plants, the function of micro-organisms etc.).

Table 7.1. Level of primary education and life expectancy in Africa. Countries are grouped according to generality of primary education into three groups and compared with life expectancy. Note: Percentage exceeding 100 per cent could be explained by the fact that there are actually more students (e.g. those already past the age of apprenticeship) attending the school classes than the number of children in the eligible age group.

	Primary education % of			Life expectancy (years)	
	age group	males	females	males	females
Year 1965					
Low (I)	23.4	32.0	14.7	38.2	40.6
Mid (II)	53.5	64.9	33.4	40.5	44.6
High (III)	86.3	95.9	73.2	46.9	49.9
Total (average)	55.2	62.3	41.6	42.0	45.2
Year 1984					
Low (I)	45.0	58.4	36.2	44.1	46.9
Mid (II)	83.3	95.5	70.5	48.3	51.5
High (III)	98.8	103.3	93.8	54.4	58.5
Total (average)	74.7	84.6	67.5	49.2	52.6

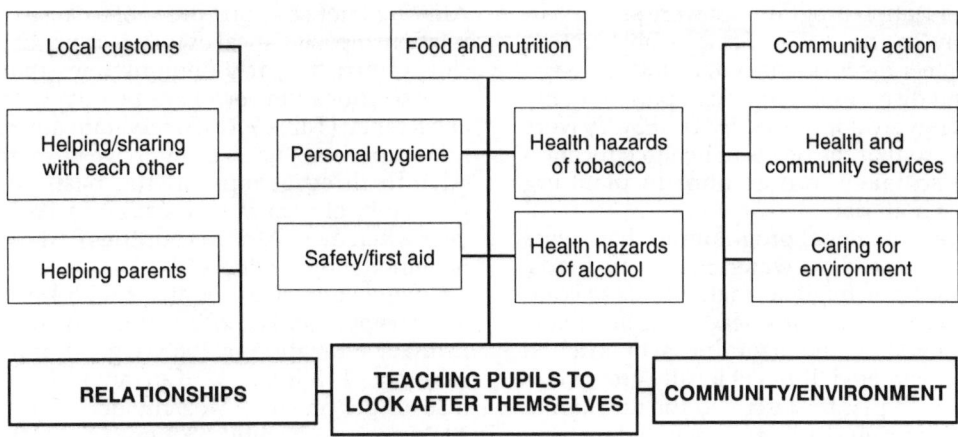

Figure 7.1. The structure of health education in primary schools.[2]

Geography offers possibilities for health education through studying the soil types, climate, water sources, production and distribution of food.

Third, where project work can be used as a form of modular education, health aspects can be taken as one element when studying the selected subject. Examples of topics with health components include water, plants with nutritional value, vitamins, malnutrition, germs, domestic hygiene etc.

INEFFECTIVE HEALTH EDUCATION IN PRIMARY SCHOOLS

It is one thing to plan a health education programme for primary schools and another to implement it effectively. There are a number of factors accounting for poor results:

1) First of all, the modern education system e.g. in Africa reaches about two -thirds of the population of school age, but more than half of the population of school age and above are still illiterate. The rate of primary education is improving in most countries, although some countries with political unrest have taken steps backwards (e.g. Somalia and Sudan).

2)Formal education has generally favoured the male population. This is regrettable, because females are in key positions in providing healthy conditions for their children and in teaching them the basics of a healthy life. The male:female ratio in primary education is improving to the advantage of females, but the situation is still far from satisfactory.

The low rate of females in primary schools is only one indication of the poor status of women. They also bear a double burden of duties. This has consequences on the level of knowledge among women and on the degree of interest they take in health problems. The equality between sexes is also still a distant ideal, and it is not known whether any of the developing countries seriously tries to achieve it.

3) The objectives of formal education in developing countries were formulated according to the models of the colonial masters, and hardly ever were the local needs taken into account. This has had several disadvantageous consequences on health education. It created the view that only school teaching had real value, and that traditional knowledge about health and curing was sheer ignorance. Nevertheless, people continued to use traditional healing systems extensively along with the modern health system. Because authorities showed no positive interest in traditional healing systems, they remained largely unknown, and the polarisation of the modern and traditional systems continued.

HEALTH IN ADULT EDUCATION PROGRAMMES

In countries that became free from the dominion of colonial powers it was felt that education was one cornerstone of development. Since the literacy rate of adults was low in almost all developing countries, special measures were taken to improve it. Massive adult education programmes were set up particularly in the 1970s. Factors obstructing development were identified, including ignorance and diseases. Literacy campaigns, many of which were supported by UNESCO, were planned so that the needs of health education were also taken into account in planning teaching material.

In these functional programmes there were topics such as: clean water, nutritious foods, vitamins, basic hygiene, many kinds of common diseases and their spread. Teaching material dealt with the usefulness of kitchen garden, evaluated different locally grown cultivated food plants, described the nutritional values of various fruits and included instructions on how to plant and nurse them.

In many countries the number of people participating in these campaigns was so high that nothing comparable had been experienced before. The rate of illiteracy dropped dramatically, and the useful teaching materials helped to raise the interest of the population to continue with practising reading skills. Such programmes involving illiterate adults have the additional value that the adults learn in the literacy classes to know the same basic health facts which their children learn in schools. Thus there is a possibility of developing mutual understanding between the children and their parents.

PRIMARY EDUCATION AND HEALTH INDICATORS

It is generally acknowledged that *formal education also improves health conditions*, even with-

out special emphasis on health education. Although not scientific proof of a cause-effect relationship, statistical evidence from 42 African countries clearly demonstrates that the level of education correlates positively to life expectancy (Table 7.1). To facilitate meaningful comparison, the countries have been divided into three groups on the basis of the generality of primary education in 1965, the year when most African countries had recently gained independence.

Group I comprises countries with less than 36 per cent of the school age children receiving primary education in 1965 (e.g. Somalia 10, Ethiopia 11, Nigeria 32, Tanzania 32), *Group II* 36–60 per cent (e.g. Mozambique 37, Angola 39, Malawi 44, Zambia 53, Kenya 54, Morocco 57), and *Group III* more than 60 per cent (e.g. Botswana 65, Madagascar 65, Uganda 67, Algeria 68, Cameroon 94, Zimbabwe 110*).

In Group I countries only 23.4 per cent of the children of school age participated in primary education, and the average life expectancy at birth was 38.2 years (males). Corresponding figures for Group II were 53.5 per cent and 40.5 years and for Group III 86.3 per cent and 46.9 years. The life expectancy of women was 2–4 years longer.

In 1984 the generality of primary education had increased in all three groups, with highest increase in the first two groups. In Group III with a high level of education already in 1965 the increase was less marked. Concurrently, the life expectancy had increased in all three groups. Still, Group I was in 1984 not yet on the same level in life expectancy where Group III had been in 1965. Nevertheless, the increase was impressive in all groups, demonstrating the positive correlation of the level of primary education and life expectancy at birth.

Also other development indicators correspond with the level of primary education. In a country with low education there are many inhabitants per physician and a high infant mortality rate (Table 7.2).

The general trend is obvious and shows the correlation between health and level of education. The statistics also show that the level of education and health are improving in all countries in question. There are, however, a few interesting exceptions in the generally improving statistics. The ratio of inhabitants per physician became worse between 1965 and 1984 in Ethiopia, Sudan, Angola, Tanzania,

Table 7.2. Level of primary education and the number of population per physician in Africa. Education levels for the three groups are shown in Table 7.1 (P/P = persons per physician, IMR = infant mortality rate).[1]

| Group | 1965 | | 1984 | |
	P/P	IMR	P/P	IMR
Low (I)	45 698	175.5	30 384	141.6
Mid (II)	24 890	159.8	17 187	120.3
High (III)	12 405	126.6	8 741	100.8

*See note in Table 7.1.

Mozambique, Ghana and Uganda. This adverse development is at least partly due to political restlessness and wars. It did not, however, prevent these countries from improving the level of primary education, the life expectancy at birth, and the infant mortality rate during those years.

Although the number of children receiving primary education has increased steadily in all African countries and had reached the level of 74.7 per cent of the whole age group in 1984 (Table 7.1), the overall literacy rate is still quite low. Table 7.3 shows the illiteracy rates in 36

African countries according to an estimate in 1990. These statistics are not available from all 42 countries in Tables 7.1 and 7.2, and therefore exact comparison of the data is not possible. However, overall more than half of those aged 15 years were still illiterate in 1990. What is significant is that the countries north of the Sahara were not above average in literacy.

Another significant observation is that female illiteracy was as high as 65.7 per cent. The low level of literacy among females has a strong connection to the level and quality

Table 7.3. Illiteracy of the population 15 years of age as a percentage in 36 African countries in 1990.[1]

Country	Total	Male	Female
Algeria	50.4	36.6	64.2
Angola	58.3	44.5	71.5
Benin	76.6	68.3	84.4
Botswana	26.4	16.3	34.9
Burkina Faso	81.8	72.1	91.1
Burundi	50.0	39.1	60.2
Cameroon	45.9	33.4	57.4
C.A. Republic	62.3	48.2	75.1
Congo	43.4	30.0	56.1
Egypt	51.6	37.1	66.2
Equatorial Guinea (1983)	38.0	22.6	51.5
Ethiopia (1984)	75.7	67.3	83.6
Gabon	39.3	26.3	51.5
Gambia	72.8	61.0	84.0
Ghana	39.7	30.0	49.0
Guinea-Bissau	63.5	49.8	76.0
Liberia	60.5	50.2	71.2
Libya	36.2	24.6	49.6
Mali	68.0	59.2	76.1
Mauritania	66.0	52.9	78.6
Morocco	50.5	38.7	62.0
Mozambique	67.1	54.9	78.7
Niger	71.6	79.6	83.2
Nigeria	49.3	37.7	60.5
Rwanda	49.8	36.1	62.9
Senegal	61.7	48.1	74.9
Sierra Leone	79.3	69.3	88.7
Somalia	75.9	63.9	86.0
South Africa (1980)	23.8	22.5	25.2
Sudan	72.9	57.3	88.3
Swaziland (1986)	32.7	30.3	34.8
Tanzania (1978)	53.7	37.8	68.6
Togo	56.7	43.6	69.3
Tunisia	34.7	25.8	43.7
Uganda	51.7	37.8	65.1
Zimbabwe	33.1	26.3	39.7
Africa (average)	**54.7**	**43.9**	**65.7**

of health education, since the mothers are in a key position to improve the standard of health in a society. Although literacy is not a necessary condition for improved health, and literacy itself does not guarantee ideal health conditions, it seems to be strongly linked to the openness of a person to acquire new knowledge about various spheres of life, and therefore also about factors related to health.

CONCLUSION

Formal education improves health conditions. However, primary education in developing countries is still far from satisfactory. Despite of recent advances in education, the comparatively high population growth and lack of resources have made general primary education a distant goal in many countries. Qualitative defects, such as the inadequacy of the European school system, neglect of indigenous knowledge, and language problems, weaken educational results.Because alternative healing methods will continue to operate side by side in the foreseeable future, primary education offers an effective information channel for knowledge of health problems and their cure. This should include information from all relevant health sectors, and not only from the modern health centre.

References

1. UNESCO. Statistical yearbook 1992. Paris: UNESCO, 1992.
2. Williams T, Moon A, Williams M. Food, environment and health. A guide for primary school teachers. Geneva: WHO, 1990.

Additional reading

1. Abbatt FR. Teaching for better learning. A guide for teachers of primary health care staff. 2nd ed. Geneva: WHO, 1992.
2. Cameron J, Hurst P, eds. International handbook of education systems, Vol. II (Sub-Saharan Africa and North Africa and the Middle East). Chichester: John Wiley & Sons, 1983.
3. Daun H. Childhood learning and adult life. The functions of indigenous, Islamic and western education in an African context. Stockholm: Stockholm University: Institute of International Education, 1992.
4. Erny P. L'enfant et son milieu en Afrique Noire: Essais sur l'éducation traditionelle. Paris: Payot, 1972.
5. King M, King F, Morley D, Burgess HJL, Burgess AP. Nutrition for developing countries. With special reference to the maize, cassava and millet areas of Africa. Nairobi: Oxford University Press, 1972.
6. Martin J, ed. Training health workers for primary health care. Gothenburg: The Nordic School of Public Health, 1985.
7. Staugård F. Traditional healers. Gaborone: Ipelegeng Publishers, 1985.
8. Staugård F. Traditional midwives. Gaborone: Ipelegeng Publishers, 1986.
9. Staugård F, ed. The role of women in health development. Gothenburg: The Nordic School of Public Health, 1990.
10. Uwechue R, ed. Africa today. 2nd ed. London: Africa Books Ltd, 1991.
11. World Health Organization. Education for health. A manual on health education in primary health care. Geneva: WHO, 1988.
12. World Health Organization. The primary health worker. Revised edition. WHO: Geneva, 1980.

About the author

Arvi Hurskainen is Professor of African Languages and Cultures at the University of Helsinki, Finland. He lived for 9 years in Tanzania and has carried out field research on languages and traditional knowledge systems in several phases since 1974. His current research interests include the problem of how cognitive systems are related to culture and environment, as well as computerised language-specific information management systems.

Lankinen KS, Bergström S, Mäkelä PH and Peltomaa M, eds.
Health and disease in developing countries. London:The Macmillan Press Limited, 1994:67–78.

8 ENVIRONMENTAL HEALTH HAZARDS

Paul Silfverberg, M.Sc.(Eng.)
Helsinki University Knowledge Services Ltd.
Teollisuuskatu 23, FIN-00510 Helsinki,
Finland

INTRODUCTION

Water supply, sanitation and waste disposal all contribute strongly to overall health and productive development in society. Therefore, they are discussed here as a part of infrastructural development of society.

A popular health promotion slogan has been 'Water is life!' It was used within the UN promoted International Water Supply and Sanitation Decade (1981–1991). In developing countries this slogan unfortunately often has two opposite meanings. It is very true that development of water supply may bring substantial improvements in health, especially in places where the scarcity of water is an acute problem. However, the slogan has also a very concrete opposite meaning indicating that there is life in water, i.e. that water may include numerous pathogens and other organisms or substances which cause health hazards. On the other hand, adequate supply of water is a prerequisite for hygienic environment. Thus, a more appropriate slogan could be 'Water is life – but clean water is better life!'

Because of the very concrete linkage between health and water supply, sanitation and waste disposal, they should be all components of primary health care (PHC). To be successful, any effort in PHC will require actions in environmental health. On the other hand, any improvement in water supply, sanitation and waste disposal requires support from other health factors (hygiene education, health monitoring, etc.).

Water and land use

Because of its continuous circulation water poured, e.g. on agricultural land becomes qualitatively affected by the condition of soil. This in turn is affected by the agricultural practices, use of chemicals or the possible use of excreta for fertilisation, etc. When this water is formed into ground water or slowly flows as surface runoff towards streams, the quality of ground water and downstream rivers and lakes also becomes affected by the land use practices. Deforestation affects the formation of ground water as well as the quality of surface waters through increased runoff. Type and location of industries and urban centres affect the quality and quantity of sewage, which in turn affects the quality of downstream water sources (Figure 8.1).

Contrary to popular belief, the amount of fresh water in lakes, rivers and streams is small, totalling about 200 000 km^3 of water. Still, at a global level even these limited usable fresh water resources are plentiful compared with the human needs. As they are, however, very unevenly scattered, there are already acute shortages of water in many regions.

The global hydrological system defines the regional variations in availability of water, ranging from the rain forests of Amazon to the deserts of Sahara. These set the limits in availability of water, and thus also the limits for human life. In stable cultures this has not been a problem as the population and level of agricultural production has been within the limits of water resources. The accelerated growth of the past decades, both in terms of population growth and increasing production has, however, in many places caused severe shortages of water. This in turn has serious effects on overall health situation.

Already now this global trend has serious impacts especially in the arid and semi-arid regions of the globe. As these regions include

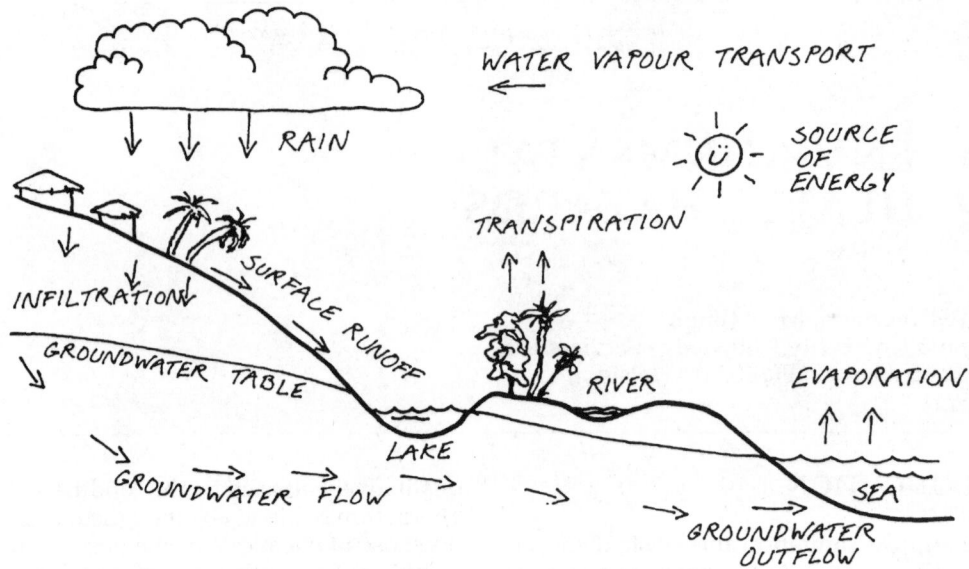

Figure 8.1. Hydrological cycle.

several of the poorest underdeveloped countries, the basic possibilities for improving the situation becomes more and more difficult, as it becomes more and more expensive to utilise potentially available water resources.

Water supply, environmental hygiene and health

It has been estimated that as many as 80 per cent of all diseases in the world are associated with unsafe water or poor environmental hygiene. The recent statistics based on the estimates of the International Water Supply and Sanitation Decade indicate that over 1.2 billion people still suffer from poor water supply. The percentage of unsafe sanitation (over 1.7 billion people) and waste disposal is even higher, as they usually have a lower priority among people's needs. In the long run, the improvement of the general situation requires extensive investments as well as remarkable efficiency reforms in water supply and sanitation (Figure 8.2).

TRANSMISSION OF WATER-RELATED DISEASES

Historical development

The history of safe hygiene behaviour and understanding of the relationships between diseases and environmental hygiene is rather short.

For example, it is often forgotten that as late as during the 19th century cholera pandemics, thousands died of waterborne cholera in such American cities as New York, New Orleans and St. Louis as well as in several European cities.

The industrial revolution and the rise of large urban populations requiring public water supplies during the 19th century were often accompanied by massive epidemics. It was only after some pioneering studies on cholera outbreaks that the sanitary revolution started in the late 19th century. The efforts in organising water supply, sewerage and waste disposal services and their safety were accompanied by improved hygiene behaviour, strongly promoted through public health education. Diseases associated with poor sanitation and crowded environments decreased in numbers even without planned medical interventions, curative medicine, or immunisation – and life-span increased.

It may be argued that many developing countries are repeating the Western history of decreasing water-related morbidity as a result of their infrastructural development. However, this process is facing serious constraints in the least developed countries where the high population growth, declining economic situation and environmental deterioration are increasing the health risks at an accelerating speed which hardly can be followed by development actions. Therefore, the historical approach where improvements were achieved through sole

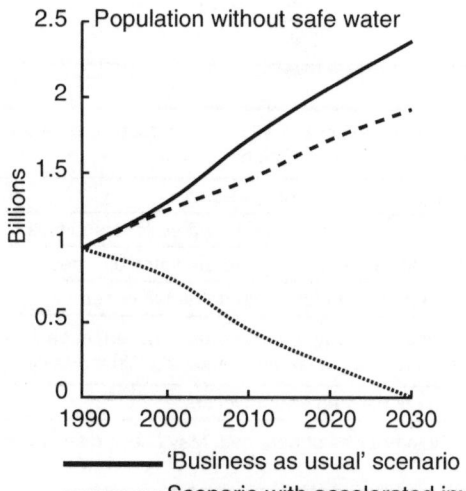 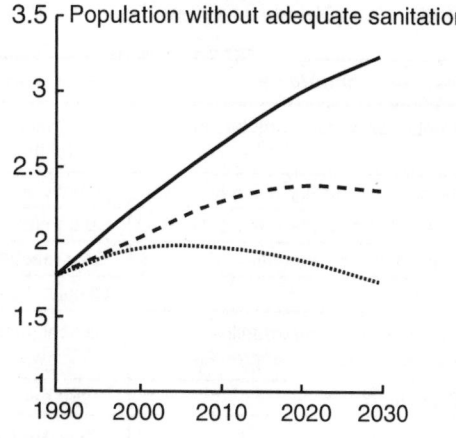

———— 'Business as usual' scenario

▪▪▪▪▪▪▪ Scenario with accelerated investment in water supply and in sanitation

••••••••••••• Scenario with accelerated investment and efficiency reforms

Figure 8.2. Scenarios for safe water supply and sanitation.

construction of safe water supplies, sewerage systems and waste disposal services, may not be adapted in poorest developing countries. Instead, the actions should be based on beneficiaries' own initiative and resources, and utilise simple and innovative approaches in problem-solving.

Transmission of water- and hygiene-related diseases

Water- and hygiene-related diseases are generally categorised in six main groups: 1)waterborne-microbiological diseases; 2) waterborne-chemical diseases; 3) water-washed diseases; 4) water contact diseases; 5) water vector habitat diseases; and 6) excreta disposal diseases.

Waterborne diseases. The pathogen enters the body through contaminated drinking water, or through food which has been contaminated via water used for irrigation or washing. The contamination is from human or animal origin. Most of the fecal–oral diseases are enteric, i.e. manifested in the intestinal tract. Therefore, these diseases are always dependent also on the level of sanitation and waste disposal. Their most common syndrome is diarrhea, caused by one or several pathogens (Table 8.1).

Another group are diseases due to inanimate toxic substances suspended or dissolved in water (Table 8.2). Some of these toxic substances may be of natural origin, like fluoride dissolved into ground water from soil. Several other toxic substances originate from various forms of pollution such as agricultural chemicals (fertilisers, pesticides), industrial wastes, etc. If the toxic chemicals are in high concentrations, diseases may be manifested in acute form. However, it is much more common, that the toxic substance is in such low concentration that it only has a cumulative effect leading to chronic disease.

In industrialised countries these diseases are nowadays the main problem, and the discussion focuses on the level of cancer risk, etc. In poor developing countries the core problem is, however, still the fecal–oral transmitted group of diseases.

Water-washed diseases. Diseases due to lack of water tend to be a serious health hazard. When people use very little water, either because there is little available or because it is too far away to be carried home in sufficient quantities, it is extremely difficult to maintain a reasonable personal as well as household and environmental hygiene.

Water-washed diseases include most of the fecal–oral transmission diseases, also listed as waterborne because many of them may also be transmitted by food, hand-to-mouth contact, and other means which may be affected by washing. Other water-washed diseases include various skin and eye infections which are heavily influenced by availability of water for washing.

When comparing the importance of quality of water (affects the incidence of waterborne diseases), and quantity of water (the key factor behind the water-washed diseases), one may

Table 8.1. Waterborne infections.[4]

Disease or syndrome	Fecal–oral pathways
Amebic dysentery (amebiasis)	Epidemics mainly by water, endemic spread by water, food, and hand-to-mouth contact. Resistance to chlorination.
Bacillary dysentery (shigellosis)	Usually soil-borne but also waterborne on occasion
Balantidial dysentery (balantidiasis)	Epidemics mainly by water. Endemic spread by water, food and flies.
Campylobacter enteritis	Only recently recognised as important cause of pediatric diarrhea.
Cholera	Classical waterborne disease. High fatality in untreated cases.
Diarrheas (inluding weanling diarrheas and gastroenteritis)	Clinical syndromes of varied etiology, generally unidentified, especially in LDCs, where frequently listed as the leading cause of child mortality.
Escherichia coli	Major cause for diarrheas of children and travellers.
Enteric viruses	Many are pathogenic. Role not well understood. May cause diseases of central nervous system.
Giardiasis	Common in LDCs. Resistant to chlorination.
Hepatitis A virus	Several transmission routes including fecal–oral.
Non-cholera vibrios	Increasingly recognised as a cause of diarrheal disease.
Norwalk virus infection	Apparantly a significant cause of diarrhea.
Paratyphoid fever	Direct or indirect contact with feces or urine of patient or carrier. Indirect spread mainly through food, and occasionally, through water supplies.
Rotavirus infection	Common agent of infantile diarrhea. Probably fecal–oral.
Typhoid fever	Spread through contamined water and food.
	Other pathways
Guinea worm disease (dracunculosis)	Complex transmission route with intermediate vector (cyclops). Not fecal–oral. Found only in LDCs and transmitted only by water.
Leptospirosis	A zoonosis. Transmission often by skin contact with contamined water.
Tularemia	Ingestion of untreated water from watersheds when infection prevails among wild animals, esp. rabbits, is one of the transmission mechanisms.

argue that quantity may be even more important than quality. The importance of water quality may remain marginal if the general household hygiene is very poor. For example, in such cases it is extremely difficult to arrange safe storage for water, which may easily contaminate the water that was originally safe at the water source. In very unhygienic conditions also the share of diseases obtained directly from drinking contaminated water may be smaller than the share of those diseases the pathways of which are affected by washing and the level of general hygiene (Table 8.3).

Generally, quantities less than 30 litres *per capita* per day (l/c/d) have been considered as the lowest quantity of water enabling reasonable personal hygiene. Compared to the physiological needs of a human being, this is about ten times more than the minimum daily water intake required for life (2.0–5.0 l/c/d).

However, in hot climate in hard work the water intake of men may be as high as 15 l/c/d. **Water contact diseases.** Water contact (or water-based) diseases do not spread directly from person to person. They are caused by infecting agents that for an essential part of their life-cycle develop in specific water animals, mainly snails and crustaceans. The diseases are transmitted via skin contact with pathogen or toxic-infested water. The most important of these diseases is schistosomosis (bilharzia).

The incidence of schistosomosis is heavily connected with the level of sanitation and sewage treatment. Without possibilities of extensive waste water treatment, the prospects for controlling schistosomosis are limited. Safe on-site sanitation connected with extensive health education are among the most effective means in bilharzia control, as well as provision of safe water for washing and bathing.

Table 8.2. Waterborne diseases, chemical and other sources.[4]

Source	Disease or syndrome	Remarks
Metals	Toxicoses	Intake of metals in drinking water and food from both natural sources and human activities. These include arsenic, cadmium, lead, copper, mercury, selenium, zinc, etc. Arsenic and cadmium may be especially important on a local basis. Industrial wastes include always chemical health hazards.
Organic chemicals	Toxicoses, cancers, mutations, birth defects	Intake of certain chemicals, esp. certain synthetic organic chemicals, is a health hazard. These include a.o. several pesticides. Organic byproducts of chlorination and industrial wastes may also include carcinogenic substances.
Hardness in water	Cardiovascular disease	Some epidemiologic evidence indicates an inverse correlation of cardiovascular diseases with hardness of drinking water. Not a high priority in LDCs.
Fluoride	Fluorosis	Damage to teeth and bones resulting from long-term ingestion of high concentrations of naturally occurring fluorides in ground water.
Nitrates	Methemoglobinemia	Serious, sometimes fatal poisoning of infants caused by ingestion of well water containing nitrates at concentrations higher than 30(45) mg/l. May be acute in areas under intensive agriculture (fertilisers) and near places where sewage has infiltrated into ground water.

Drug treatment for those infected has proven to have only a marginal overall effect. The risk of bilharzia is especially high for those working in contact with water (fishermen, farmers in irrigated fields) and for women and children during bathing, laundering, drawing water, and other domestic activities where water contact hardly can be avoided.

The occurrence of schistosomosis may be greatly affected by water development projects also in negative ways. Irrigation systems, storage dams for water supplies and hydropower plants, fisheries, etc. may actually increase the risk through creating environments favourable to the parasites and their intermediate snail hosts (Table 8.4).

Other water contact diseases of importance are leptospirosis and tularemia (Table 8.1). Many skin, eye, ear, nose, and throat diseases may also be acquired through water contact. **Water vector habitat diseases.** In tropical countries biting insects are common. Most of these, notably the mosquitoes, breed in pools or other open water bodies, and sometimes even in households in water containers. Tsetse flies are also active near water bodies.

The transmission of these diseases depends on the occurrence of their animal vectors which live all or part of their lives in a water habitat or near them. The most important vectors are snails, mosquitoes and flies.

Water supply and sanitation may have a two-fold impact on these diseases. For example, snail-vector diseases may to some extent be controlled by the provision of safe sanitation and water supply. On the other hand, mosquito-vector diseases may be increased through water supply actions if they increase the number of potential breeding places. Breeding may be promoted for example by spillage and wasted water by water points (wells and taps), uncovered water containers, or by flooding privies.

PREVENTION OF ENVIRONMENTAL HEALTH HAZARDS

Means of intervention in controlling water- and hygiene-related diseases

Improvement of water supply, sanitation, sewerage and waste disposal are among the most efficient means of controlling environmental health hazards together with measures in controlling use of chemicals and improvement of hygienic practices. The interventions for

Table 8.3. Water-washed diseases.[4]

Disease or syndrome	Remarks
Enteric diseases Diarrheas, bacillary and amebic dysenteries, gastroentritis, salmonellosis, etc.	Prevalence of most fecal–oral diseases is less with adequate quantity of water and safe sanitation and waste disposal.
Skin diseases Otitis externa, scabies, skin sepsis and ulcers, tineas (ringworm)	Prevented by personal hygiene, including frequent bathing and laundering with use of soap.
Louse-borne diseases Louse-borne fever, pediculosis, relapsing fever, typhoid fever, etc.	Prevented by personal hygiene, including bathing and laundering and change of clothing.
Treponematoses Endemic syphilis, pinta, yaws	Prevented by general public and personal hygiene.
Eye diseases Conjunctivitis, trachoma	Trachoma rare where water is available.

controlling waterborne and hygienic diseases include the following:

Water supply. 1) Selection of uncontaminated sources, for example deep wells or protected wells and springs; 2) treatment of raw water, especially chlorination and cooking; 3) replacement of contaminated water supplies by more convenient, reliable and safe supplies; 4) protection of watersheds; 5) water quality surveillance; 6) increasing the quantity of water to facilitate adequate hygiene.

Sanitation and waste disposal. 1) Protection of water supplies; 2) protection of environment; 3) support of excreta and waste control activities; 4) treatment, removal, isolation, or dilution of wastes and excreta.

Health education. 1) Personal and community hygiene; 2) protection of environment; 3) support of water supply and waste control activities.

In general, tackling just one of the above factors does not lead into any improvement. Instead, any substantial change usually requires a holistic approach where water supply improvements are supported with interventions in environmental hygiene and with extensive health education. As an example, the importance of the different measures in controlling excreta-related diseases is shown in Table 8.5.

Water supply

Level of water supply. In rural areas water supply has traditionally often been based on use of *surface water*, i.e. open streams, rivers, lakes and ponds, or unprotected water holes. In the past when population densities were smaller the risk might have been reasonable, but nowadays with intensive agriculture, high population density and increasing amount of pollution sources, *use of surface water without treatment is always a serious health hazard.* The reasons for the use of polluted surface water include: 1) there are no alternative water sources available; 2) poor knowledge on the risk of using untreated surface water; 3) use of surface water is a tradition; 4) poor know-how on alternative solutions (use of ground water, simple treatment methods); and 5) lack of organisational support and financing for improving water supplies.

Another common problem in rural areas is the long distance to the water sources. For example in Africa, there are places where water has to be fetched from a distance of more than 20 kilometres. In such circumstances it is obvious that the quantity of water fetched will remain very small and it is not possible to maintain a safe level of hygiene . Actually, always when the distance exceeds hundreds of metres, the quantity of water used will remain below the minimum level required for adequate hygiene.

In big cities as well as in some rural areas water supply is based on piped schemes. These encounter several problems causing serious health hazards. For example, inadequate quantity of water supplied, unsafe

Table 8.4. Examples of increased prevalence of schistosomosis resulting from water resource development projects.[4]

Country	Project (completion year)	Pre-project prevalence	Post-project prevalence
Egypt	Aswan dam (first, 1900)	6%	60% (3 years later)
Sudan	Gezira scheme (1925)	0%	30–60% (15 years later)
Tanzania	Arusha Chini (1937)	low	53–86% (30 years later)
Zambia and Zimbabwe	Lake Kariba	0%	16% adults, 69% children (10 years later)
Ghana	Volta Lake (1966)	low	90% (2 years later)
Nigeria	Lake Kainji (1969)	low	31% (1 year later), 45% (2 years later)
Iran	Dez pilot irrigation project	15%	27% (2 years later)

quality of tap water and/or unreliable functioning of the systems are common problems in most developing countries. In general, the reasons for inadequate functioning of piped water supplies are: 1) original installations are old and the growth of the cities has exceeded their capacity; 2) lack of chemicals for treatment; 3) high leakage which affects both the quantity of water through leakage from the network as well as the water quality through intrusion of pollution to the network; 4) high wastage caused by poor water use habits; 5) poor functioning of equipment due to neglected maintenance and poor operation; and 6) unreliable energy supply.

Unsafe water use habits are a general problem both in rural areas and in poor urban settlements. The reasons for these are poor knowledge on hygiene, inadequate hygienic traditions and inadequate and unsafe water containers at households.

Options for improving water supply

Water supply may be improved by various means which all depend on environmental conditions. In humid environments there are usually several options available (surface water, ground water, rainwater harvesting), whereas in arid areas there might be only one option, and even this may be far away.

Ground water may generally be considered as a safe water source. Ground water may be utilised through shallow (less than 20 metres) or deep (usually 20–100 metres) wells. Also protected springs may provide safe water. In general, deep borehole wells are hygienically safe, whereas shallow wells may become polluted if the surroundings are not kept clean. For example, the common small cracks on the well cover may become sources of pollution if the cover of a shallow ring-well is used for washing. Also nearby latrines are always a risk for the safety of the wells.

There are several limitations on the potential of ground water as a water source. Firstly, the availability of ground water is dependent on local circumstances. In many places it is just not possible to utilise ground water due to lack of adequate aquifers. In many occasions the chemical quality of ground water also limits its usability. For example, high concentrations of iron, manganese and fluoride are rather common, preventing the use of ground water for drinking and food preparation. In areas where intensive agriculture is practised the use of agricultural chemicals threatens the quality of shallow ground water.

Even the most simple protected wells require some equipment, mainly pumps. Especially in remote rural areas it is extremely difficult to establish reliable systems for their maintenance and spare part supply. In order to function reliably, even the most simple hand-pump equipped wells require reasonable technical know-how among the users and maintenance personnel, arrangement of spare part supply and securing of the maintenance and its financing. With adequate training, institutional support and community involvement it may, however, be possible to develop community-managed water supply systems which utilise shallow ground water (Figures 8.3 and 8.4).

Deep wells are rather expensive to construct and always require somewhat more complicated technology than shallow wells. Therefore, it is extremely difficult to establish

Table 8.5. The importance of different interventions for excreta-related diseases. 0 = no, 1 = little, 2 = moderate, 3 = great importance.[6]

	Water quality	Water availability	Excreta disposal	Excreta treatment	Personal and domestic cleanliness	Waste water disposal	Food hygiene
Diarrheal diseases							
Viruses	2	3	2	2	3	0	2
Bacteria	3	3	2	2	3	0	3
Protozoa	1	3	2	2	3	0	2
Worms with no intermediate host							
– Ascaris and trichuris	1	1	3	3	1	1	2
– Hookworm	1	1	3	3	1	0	0
– Enterobius	1	3	2	2	3	0	1
Worms with an aquatic intermediate host							
– Schistosomosis	1	1	3	2	1	0	0
Worms with an animal intermediate host							
– Beef and pork tapeworms	0	1	3	3	1	0	3
Insect-transmitted diseases							
– Bancroftian filariasis	0	0	3	0	1	3	0

reliably functioning, and still reasonably cheap deep-well systems.

As springs can be found only in some areas, spring protection may not provide a general solution for rural water supply in developing countries. Even in areas where springs are abundant, they are often located in difficult places and the walking distances become long, thus limiting the quantity of water below the level which enables safe hygienic conditions. However, in places where spring protection

Figure 8.3. Involvement of women in water development ensures adequate operation and maintenance of the wells. Photo: Paul Silfverberg

may easily be constructed, springs may provide a cheap and reasonably reliable water source for rural communities. In such occasions the nearby catchment area of the spring must, however, be adequately protected (Figure 8.5).

Spring protections may be constructed practically without equipment and imported materials. Therefore, they are the cheapest solution for improved water supply, material costs (some cement and reinforcement) easily remaining at the level of 50–200 USD. Protected, hand-pump equipped shallow wells are already about five times more expensive (500–800 USD). Deep borehole wells are about ten times more expensive than shallow wells, due to the high costs of ground water surveys and drilling. The cost of a hand-pump-operated deep well easily exceeds 10 000 USD.

Rainwater harvesting. In areas where rains are abundant, rainwater harvesting may provide a partial solution for household water supply. In principle, with adequate storing and hygienic harvesting systems, it might be possible to base all water supply on rainwater harvesting. However, as rains normally are somewhat irregular and because it is extremely difficult to ensure the hygiene of a rainwater system,

Figure 8.4. Shallow well at a rural school used for personal hygiene, drinking and irrigation of educational tree-nursery and vegetable garden. Photo: Paul Silfverberg

rainwater harvesting should generally be regarded as an additional water supply system in cases where the basic system may be based on wells or piped water supplies.

Rainwater harvesting has several advantages. Firstly, rainwater may be collected on the spot. Use of rainwater for washing and cleaning increases the amount of water used, which may enable the up-keeping of a reasonable hygienic level in the household. Rainwater is also free. In addition, the catchment systems are rather cheap to construct, especially if roofs or other existing structures are utilised (Figure 8.6).

Piped water supplies. Densely populated urban areas can hardly function without piped water. The problem of piped water supply is, however, its technical complexity and high cost, which easily are over ten-fold *per capita* compared with well systems.

In order to create any real health benefits, the whole process of piped water supply must function reliably on all occasions. In a typical case, the process of piped water supply covers the following components with the respective protective measures: 1) Raw water pumping, protection of the catchment area, pumping station and raw water channel or pipeline; 2) water purification; removal of suspended solids, chlorination, control of corrosiveness and hardness, control of treated water; 3) water distribution; control of leakage and wastage in the network, hygienic quality

control of network water; 4) use of communal taps and house connections; metering, hygiene control; and 5) storing at households; protection and cleaning of containers.

The technical complexity of piped water supply requires extensive systems for their management, operation and maintenance. Adequate technical know-how, motivated operational staff, reliable supply of chemicals, energy and spare parts, efficient management, adequate financing as well as reliable process control are all criteria which are difficult to fulfil in poor developing countries (Figure 8.7). Therefore, piped schemes should be utilised as the main option for water supply only in densely populated surroundings where alternative, simple solutions are not possible any more. Even in such cases a necessary prerequisite is good coverage of metering combined with adequate water tariffs.

Sanitation

The role of sanitation. The level of sanitation is crucial for the spreading of several waterborne and water-washed diseases. It also affects the prevalence of various vector-borne diseases. Environmental health conditions may not significantly be improved without provision of safe sanitation and/or sewerage facilities.

Financing is a major problem in sanitation development. Water supply is a necessity of life, and it may also be used for various productive purposes. Sanitation, instead, is in most cases seen only as a cost for the households, and in a larger scale, for municipalities. The benefits of sanitation are seen as mainly potential and hypothetical – it may be that improvement of sanitation reduces health risks, it may

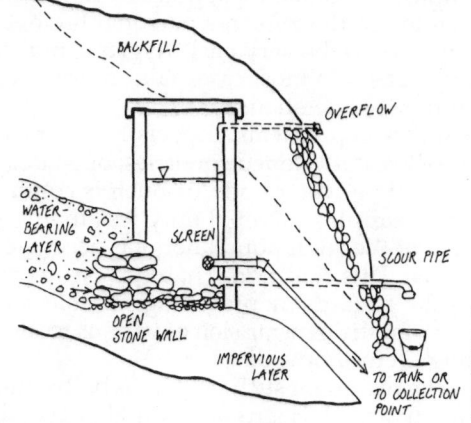

Figure 8.5. Typical spring protection.

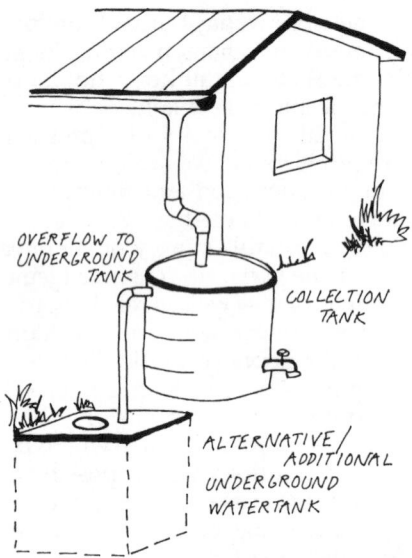

Figure 8.6. A rainwater harvesting system

be that in the long run the environmental costs of neglected sanitation and waste water treatment become higher than those accrued through active development of sanitation and sewerage. Therefore, the households and municipalities tend to neglect the development of sanitation especially in cases where there are several other, productive development needs. And this is usually the case in poor developing countries.

Sanitation is also a very culture-specific issue. Defecation is, in most cultures, an extremely personal practice, and controlled by strict taboos. Because of its strong culture-dependence, sanitation improvements are very difficult to introduce to the general public, as improving sanitation in practice means intervention to the person's personal life habits. Changes in the very basic hygienic practices of a person in most cases take at least years, or rather generations.

Sanitation problems. Especially in rural areas of least developed countries, open defecation into a water body or bush is common. For example, in Nepal only less than 1 per cent of the rural population has access to latrines. This traditional habit causes serious health hazards by providing suitable conditions for the transmission of various fecal–oral and vector-borne diseases.

The reason for such practice is both cultural and financial. Habits are strongly dependent on the level of knowledge and education.

Therefore, integrated health education at all levels is a necessity for any sanitation improvement. Another reason for the failure of various sanitation projects has been the high costs of proposed sanitation facilities. For example, the much promoted VIP-latrine (Ventilated Improved Pit latrine) seems to be much too expensive for poor rural households in several parts of Africa and Asia, but does provide safe sanitation for wealthier families (Figure 8.8).

In areas where latrines already are common, a major problem is their lacking hygiene. Flies are able to breed in poorly protected latrines, and there often is a high risk of infection through direct contact. This problem is especially acute in densely populated squatter areas. Therefore, improvement of sanitation is one of the top priority needs in slum upgrading. The key reasons for the poor quality of sanitation in slums are partially the same as in rural areas, namely poor knowledge of hygiene and expensiveness of the solutions. Another problem is the lack of space for simple latrines.

For big cities, in reality, traditional sewer systems are the only possibility to arrange adequate and environmentally safe sanitation. They are, however, extremely costly to construct and to maintain, even compared with the costs of water supply networks. In addition, a centralised sewer system normally requires full waste water treatment in order to avoid large-scale pollution in the receiving water body. Therefore, because of the lack of financing, commonly poor operation and maintenance, and aged equipment, the functioning of sewer systems is in many cases at least inadequate, if not disastrous. Common problems of sewerage include flooding and leaking of sewers as

Figure 8.7. Intermittent service due to electrical cuts threatens the safety and reliability of water supply. Photo: Paul Silfverberg

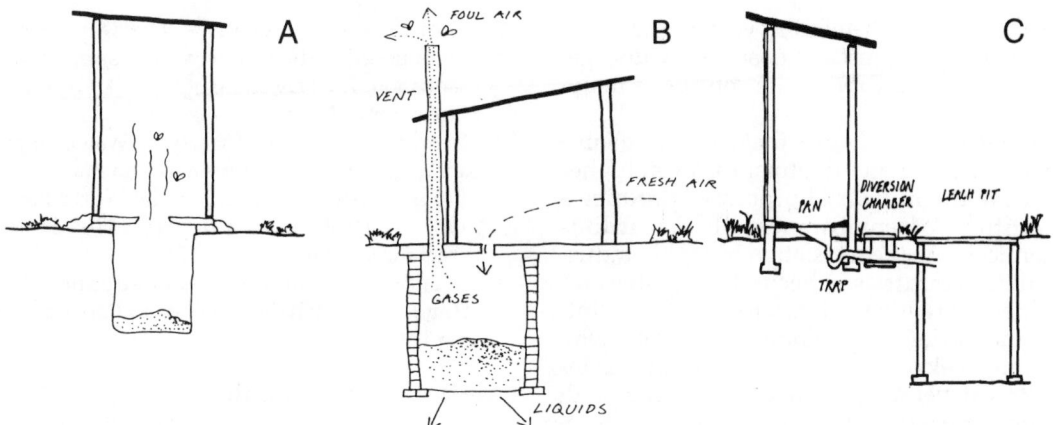

Figure 8.8. A. Traditional latrine, **B.** Ventilated Improved Pit (VIP) latrine and **C.** The pour-flush toilet

well as their filling with sediments and sand, all causing various health hazards.

Options in improving sanitation. Sanitation may be improved mainly through affecting behaviour through health education, introducing safe latrines, and by developing sewerage systems and waste water treatment facilities. The success of sanitation programmes depends mainly on how aware people are of the link between sanitation and health. If such awareness does not exist, people don't have enough motivation to improve their behaviour, especially if the improvements require relatively big investments from the household. Therefore, health education concentrating on problems in the society concerned, is of utmost importance. This health education must be done in close collaboration with the target groups themselves. The basis for health education should be in the local culture and traditional habits. The positive features of the traditions should be strengthened, whereas the risks should be discussed in practical terms.

Improved convenience is an effective motivating factor for households to improve their latrines. On the other hand, if the proposed improvements are more inconvenient than the traditional practices, major success may not be expected from a sanitation programme. Reducing the distance to the defecation place, for example through constructing latrines near the house, may be a motivating factor.

In most cultures the need for privacy may be used as a motivator, but in poorly planned projects it may also lead to the rejection or non-use of latrines. For example, in some cultures just the possibility of someone seeing a person enter a latrine may lead to the rejection of

its use. In other cultures, the potential to utilise feces more effectively as a fertiliser or for other productive purposes may be the most important motivating factor. Therefore, both socioeconomic and cultural problems and opportunities need to be recognised in connection with sanitation programmes.

Experience from various sanitation projects has revealed that lasting results may only be achieved through the active role of the beneficiaries themselves. Their needs and preferences should be the basis for planning, and they should also be the key actors in the concrete improvements and possible construction activities. Besides being a motivating factor, substantial contribution in cash and labour is necessary because it just is not possible for a society to construct latrines for larger populations. The selection of the type of latrine depends, besides on traditions and affordability, on environmental conditions and land-use (Figure 8.8).

Waste disposal

Problems in waste disposal. The third major group of environmental health hazards are those connected with waste disposal. In health terms, waste disposal in rural areas is usually of lower priority than water supply and sanitation, but even in rural settlements unorganised waste disposal may create severe health risks through providing breeding places for various disease-vector insects as well as food for rats.

Waste disposal suffers from the same financial problems as sanitation – there are several other, higher priority needs competing for the scarce resources, and it is recognised almost solely as a cost. Therefore, it is in most cities in developing countries almost totally unorganised, except maybe in the centres of major cities.

In industrialised areas the need for reliable waste disposal and treatment is even higher because the industrial processes produce a multitude of environmentally hazardous chemicals. As the legislation in highly industrialised countries is becoming tighter and tighter, there is a tendency to transfer polluting industries to developing countries, who warmly welcome new chances to enhance industrial development. Therefore, even though being at the moment mainly a local risk, disposal of industrial problem wastes may become a major health risk. The risk is usually multiplied by the almost non-existing awareness of the health hazards.

Options for waste disposal and treatment. In principle, organised waste disposal and treatment requires collection and transport of waste, waste disposal and treatment, as well as environmental monitoring – all requiring extensive financing, resources and sound management. In less densely populated areas, on-site waste treatment, as well as on-site sanitation, may be a potential and cheaper alternative. On-site systems must, however, be constructed and maintained adequately, as otherwise they may create even higher environmental health risks than unorganised waste disposal. The methods for on-site waste disposal include reuse, composting and burning. Reuse of waste is actually widely practised in developing countries. The poorer the country, the more effectively waste seems to be utilised. Therefore, the motivation for reuse of waste usually poses no major problems.

References

1. McJunkin E. Water and human health. Washington D.C.: U.S. Agency for International Development, 1983:134.
2. Wegelin-Schuringa M. On-site sanitation – Building on local practice. The Hague: IRC, 1991:74. (Occasional Paper Series No 16).

Additional reading

1. Arlosoroff S, Tschannerl G, Grey D, et al. Community water supply – The handpump option. Washington: The World Bank, 1987:202.
2. Boot M. Just stir gently – The way to mix hygiene education with water supply and sanitation. The Hague: IRC, 1987:171. (Technical Paper Series No 29).
3. Grover B, Burnett N, McGarry M. Water supply and sanitation project preparation handbook. Volumes I–III. Washington: The World Bank, 1983:172 (Vol. I), 332 (Vol. II), 288 (Vol. III) (Technical Paper Number 12).
4. IRC. Small community water supplies. The Hague: IRC, 1981:413 (Technical Paper Series No 18).

Additional information

International Water and Sanitation Centre IRC
P.O. Box 93190, 2509 AD The Hague, The Netherlands
– Manuals, guidelines, bibliographies and reports on water supply and sanitation. Also some publications dealing with waste disposal

World Health Organization WHO
Division of Public Information and Education for Health and Division of Environmental Health Avenue Appia, 1211 Geneva 27, Switzerland
– Several guidelines on training and health education related to water supply and sanitation projects
– Publishes bibliographies on reference literature

Water and Sanitation for Health Project WASH
1611 N. Kent Street, Room 1001, Arlington VA 22209–2111, U.S.A.
– Various practical manuals, guidelines and reports on water supply, sanitation, and health education

World Bank Publications
Publications Distribution Unit, 1818 H Street, N.W., Washington D.C. 20433, U.S.A.
– Technical manuals on water supply, sanitation and waste disposal, irrigation, etc.

About the author

Paul Silfverberg is a specialist in environmental protection and project planning as well as related training. He is currently the vice president of Helsinki University Knowledge Services Ltd. being responsible for environmental consulting and social development sectors. During 1988–90 he worked as the water supply adviser for FINNIDA and has thereafter acted as a specialist within several development projects in Asia, Africa and Eastern Europe. Mr Silfverberg has developed actively problem-based, objective-oriented and participatory planning methods and has been prepared several planning and training manuals on the subjects for FINNIDA and UN organisations, among others.

Lankinen KS, Bergström S, Mäkelä PH and Peltomaa M, eds.
Health and disease in developing countries. London:The Macmillan Press Limited, 1994:79–83.

9 CHEMICALS AND THE ENVIRONMENT

Olavi Pelkonen, M.D., Ph.D.
University of Oulu, Department of
Pharmacology and Toxicology
Kajaanintie 52 D, FIN-90220 Oulu,
Finland

Jorma T. Ahokas, Ph.D.
RMIT University, Key Toxicology Centre
GPO Box 2476V, Melbourne, Victoria 3001,
Australia

INTRODUCTION

Chemicalisation of the environment is a broad and multi-dimensional issue making it a very difficult problem to deal with. One possible approach could be to list compounds coming in contact with an individual during daily activities (Table 9.1). However, the adverse effects associated with chemicals are not particularly dependent on the numbers of chemicals, but rather on the concentrations of individual chemicals. For example, *poisoning epidemics* resulting from an exposure to a specific chemical are relatively common in developing countries.

Another approach could be to examine the importation, production and marketing of chemicals. Together with information on the use of pharmaceutical agents and pesticides, and on occupational exposures this should give an all-encompassing reflection of the use of chemicals.

Yet another approach is to monitor the overall flow of chemicals, including production, use, disposal, waste releases, dumping grounds, contamination of ground water and chemical catastrophes (Figure 9.1). Such an outline will help the community to control and direct the flow of chemicals and protect individuals. In attempting to do this it is necessary to concentrate on a few most important groups of chemicals for which adequate information is available. However, the field changes very rapidly when new compounds are introduced and new specific problems arise.

Many of the problems associated with chemical use in developing countries are illustrated also in the use of therapeutic drugs, these items are discussed in detail elsewhere (Chapter 49 and 50).

PESTICIDES

A broad range of pesticides is in extensive use in industrialised countries. Their use is monitored and controlled relatively tightly with several mechanisms both nationally and internationally. Many manufacturers actually claim that the control has been tuned too tight. In developing countries environmental and climatic conditions dictate wide-spread pesticide usage. The selection of pesticides is wider and to a significant extent different from that of affluent countries. The pesticides are marketed intensively and include products that may have been either prohibited or removed from the market elsewhere.

Since the 1960s several pesticides have been classified as too dangerous for use in industrialised countries. However, this has not prevented their marketing in the developing part of the world, largely due to the lack of mechanisms for monitoring and control both sale and use of pesticides. On the other hand the risk–benefit relationships are different in developing and affluent countries. For example,

Table 9.1. Examples of daily exposures to chemicals and of typical poisonings in developing countries. The individual exposure depends significantly on the locality, the living conditions and the nature of working conditions.

Chemical exposure	Typical poisons (examples)
Contaminants of air outdoors	SO_2, NO_x, Pb (specific environmental problems in Brazil, Mexico and other countries)
Contaminants of air indoors	Formaldehyde, polyaromatic hydrocarbon products (use of open fire, associated respiratory problems)
Cosmetic products	Many examples (use of lead colours)
Occupational chemicals	Heavy metals, mineral dusts, solvents (Bhopal accident and lead smelter in Yugoslavia)
Agricultural chemicals	Pesticides (pesticide poisonings in the Philippines, Sri Lanka, Egypt and so on)
Domestic chemicals	Solvents and cleaning agents
'Recreational' substances	Cigarettes, alcohol (diseases associated with cigarette smoking are increasing sharply in developing countries)
Food products	Adulterated foods (contaminated food oil in Spain and Morocco, pesticide treated seed grain in Iraq)
Additives and contaminants of food	Aflatoxins (liver cancer in Central Africa), pesticides
Therapeutic agents	

the incidence of malaria would almost certainly go up if use of DDT was stopped totally.

There is a lack of reliable information in this area, but it is apparent that the number of health problems and fatalities associated with pesticides is higher in developing countries. An estimated 10 000 people in developing countries die due to pesticides each year. This is not much in relation to the population, but in industrialised countries it would be intolerable (even though traffic fatalities are still accepted).

Use of pesticides in agriculture highlights the problems of developing countries. Highly toxic organophosphate compounds are still used despite the fact that they are known to cause severe poisoning manifested acutely as a cholinergic crisis and chronically as a paralysis.

In Sri Lanka there were 13 000 hospitalised poisoning cases between 1975–1980, and about 1000 of these patients died. Three-quarters of these poisonings were attempted suicides and one-quarter were accidental or due to occupational exposures. There are many reasons for the high prevalence of poisonings. For example, the poisons are readily available and secondary packaging of the poisons into unlabelled containers is common. The containers are often either sold or used subsequently for other purposes.

The circumstances under which the poisonings occur may appear unclear: even though there is no shortage of food in Indonesia, poverty nevertheless has forced people to eat seed grain that has been treated with rat poison for pest control. The victims of such poisonings may have been aware of the fact the grain was not intended for human consumption, as they usually have tried to remove the poison by washing. Pesticides have also been used for unintended purposes such as easy harvesting of fish from ponds or augmenting traditional food preparation such as fermentation and drying of fish (organophosphate sprays to prevent infestation by flies). Further problems of pesticide use are illustrated in Example 1.

EXAMPLE 1. PROBLEMS ASSOCIATED WITH THE PESTICIDE USAGE IN INDONESIA

Indonesia is an example of a country rapidly developing its industrial activities and depending heavily on domestic agricultural production. Examples presented here are from Malang, a very productive agricultural region situated in the eastern highlands of Java, with a population of one million. In the years 1980–84 the University Hospital of Malang listed 259 poisonings of which 25 (9.2 per cent) resulted in death. Pesticides accounted for 86 poisonings of which ten resulted in death and food poisonings included 67 with six fatalities. Therapeutic agents accounted for 53 poisonings, three of which were fatal, and miscellaneous chemicals caused 21 poisonings with one fatality.

Of the pesticide poisonings unquestionably the most common were those associated with organophosphates (35 cases) and propoxur (33 cases). According to the experts in the area the problem is much greater than would appear from the perspective of the University Hospital as poisoning cases in the countryside would not be taken to the major towns for hospital care and they would not be included in the data.

The difficulty of getting statistics can also be understood when one takes into consideration that nearly 60 per cent of the population of 90 million people are working in agriculture and the number of medical practitioners in 1980 was one per 11 500 people. No statistics are readily available with respect to the use of agricultural chemicals from the Department of Agriculture and it would appear that the statistics of the pesticide vendors are considered as commercially sensitive information.

Farmers themselves do not give a very clear picture of what they use. Regarding individual pesticides they have relatively limited information and the most important factor in the decision for selecting a pesticide is advertising.

The orchards in the vicinity of Malang utilise very high amounts of chemicals, e.g. in 1985 a farm of 2 hectares producing apples and asparagus spent 1000 USD on pesticides. This amount of money spent by the farmer would buy 100 litres of concentrate which when diluted would produce 100 000 litres of sprayable pesticide sprayed over a 1-year period on 2 hectares. The difficulty with this situation is that the villages are surrounded by the fields and the continuously flowing open irrigation channels flow into the villages where the water is used for bathing and washing laundry. No surveys of the long-term health effects have been carried out and for example the University of Malang has very limited means of undertaking such studies.

Manufacturers and importers of pesticides should be required to take a greater responsibility in phasing out the more toxic pesticides and training both the sales personnel and the end users. Industrialised countries could play a significant role assisting in the formulation of legislation, in training and in distribution of information. The industrialised countries could also prevent export of products considered too toxic or dangerous for their own use.

INDUSTRIAL CHEMICALS

Problems of industrial toxicology fall into two major categories: on one hand developing countries desire to develop their own industrial production in order to accelerate their economic development and fulfil the needs and aspirations of the population. On the other hand, western industry is shifting production facilities to developing countries in search of cheaper labour force, or because of tightening legislation in the home countries. As the industries focus primarily on efficient production with little consideration for occupational safety, many problems of occupational toxicology have emerged. Exposure to chemicals such as heavy metals, organic solvents, mineral dusts and organic dusts has become a major occupational problem in developing countries.

There is no reliable worldwide data on the incidence of occupational poisonings. In fact, this lack of information appears to be the main reason why no significant measures have been taken in developing countries for protecting workers. Even though illnesses related to occupational exposure result in reduced productivity, the immediate economic pressures work against attempts to improve the level of occupational hygiene.

In addition to chronic exposure to industrial chemicals there have been devastating accidents associated with the industrial use or production of chemicals. The most frightening example is the Bhopal accident in India on

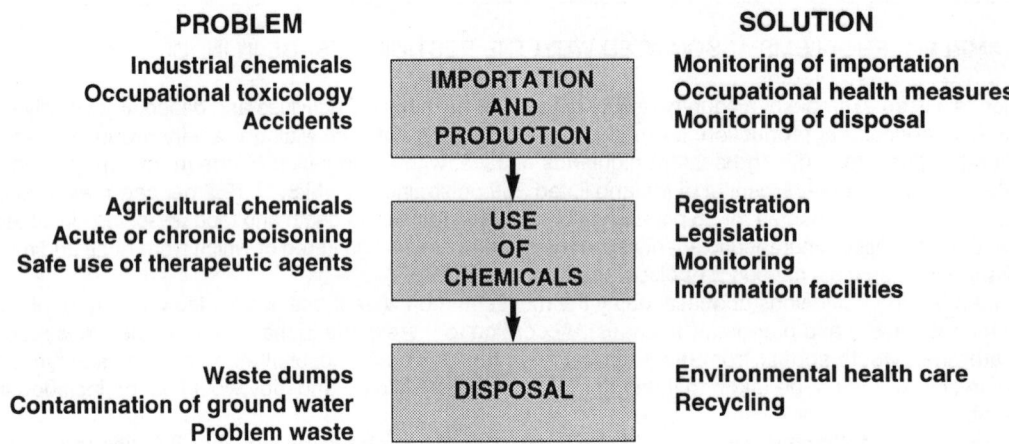

PROBLEM

Industrial chemicals
Occupational toxicology
Accidents

IMPORTATION
AND
PRODUCTION

SOLUTION

Monitoring of importation
Occupational health measures
Monitoring of disposal

Agricultural chemicals
Acute or chronic poisoning
Safe use of therapeutic agents

USE
OF
CHEMICALS

Registration
Legislation
Monitoring
Information facilities

Waste dumps
Contamination of ground water
Problem waste

DISPOSAL

Environmental health care
Recycling

Figure 9.1. Flow of chemicals in the society, related problems and possible solutions.

3 December 1984. In the middle of the night 40 tonnes of extremely poisonous methyl isocyanide leaked into the densely populated city of Bhopal with catastrophic results. Approximately 2800 people died immediately and about 200 000 people were injured to varying degrees. Methyl isocyanide affects mainly the eyes and the respiratory system. For thousands of people the injuries were permanent.

Methyl isocyanide was the raw material for the production of pesticides by Union Carbide at the Bhopal plant. The real cause of the gas leak is still unclear and legal battles related to the accident have continued for years. Nevertheless, several contributing factors have been identified, all of them typical problems of industry in developing countries:

1) Establishment of hazardous facilities in the more relaxed environment of developing countries without appropriate legislation and control for such a facility.

2) Complicated technology using hazardous materials in the middle of a densely populated city where the population is totally unprepared for a catastrophe.

3) Sub-optimally trained personnel in charge of production.

4) The local authorities determined to have international industry in the country at whatever cost, including neglecting the responsibility for monitoring and controlling the activity.

SUSCEPTIBILITY TO CHEMICAL HAZARDS

It is very likely that people of developing countries are more susceptible to chemicals

than people of industrialised countries. Chronic infectious diseases are common and there are indications that this may increase the susceptibility to certain carcinogens. The state of nutrition also affects the toxicity of chemicals by sensitising target organs and reducing the ability of the body to biotransform chemicals into less toxic products and to eliminate chemicals.

Poverty, ignorance and lack of education result in significant exposures in groups most likely to suffer from the exposure. Especially the high proportion of children represents an important risk factor. Although children may not be *physiologically* more sensitive than adults, they are usually first to suffer from poor living conditions and nutritional deficiencies. The inquisitiveness of children adds to the likelihood of accidental poisoning. They are more likely to smell and taste anything to which they have access.

INTERNATIONAL ACTIVITY

Many international organisations and agencies have taken up the problems discussed above. Addressing the issue of chemical safety is most advanced in the area of pharmaceutical products where both independent consumer organisations and United Nations organisations are active (Chapter 50).

The United Nations runs a programme called International Registry of Potentially Toxic Substances that plays a most important role in the collection and distribution of information on toxic substances. Also the activities of the International Labour Organization (ILO) are important in occupational safety with respect to chemicals. United Nations Food and Agricultural Organization (FAO) formulates recommendations on pesticide marketing and control in developing countries.

Unfortunately, the international programmes tend only to alleviate the symptoms without tackling the root of the problems. An essential issue is how to dismantle the double standards of the industry: what may be prohibited in the home country is permitted in developing countries. Often this occurs with the knowledge of the officials and with tacit consent or even public appeal to international competitiveness. All sovereign countries may and should make their own decisions concerning chemicals. It is important to guarantee that the decision making is based on information that is available already in the industrialised countries.

Additional reading

1. British Medical Association. The BMA guide to pesticides, chemicals and health. London: Edward Arnold, 1992.
2. Bull D. A growing problem: pesticides and the Third World Poor. Oxford: Oxfam, 1982.
3. Davies JE. Changing profile of pesticide poisoning. New Engl J Med 1987;316:807–8.
4. Loevinsohn ME. Insecticide use and increased mortality in rural central Luzon, Philippines. Lancet 1987;i:1359–62.
5. WHO Environmental Health Criteria Series.

Futher information can be obtained from

WHO publications, periodicals and report series contain a large number of useful entries on all aspects of chemicals and developing countries. A publications catalogue is published annually, and can be obtained from: WHO, Distribution and Sales, CH–1211 Geneva 27, Switzerland.

The Finnish Institute of Occupational Health publishes two series: African and East African Newsletter on Occupational Health and Safety. These contain important information on chemicals in developing countries in general, not merely on occuptional chemicals. For a subscription, write to: Institute of Occupational Health, Topeliuksenkatu 41 a A, FIN-00250 Helsinki, Finland

About the authors

Olavi Pelkonen is Professor of Pharmacology at the University of Oulu, Finland. He has been involved in IUPHAR- and EC-sponsored activities concerning differences of drug therapy between developed and developing countries. He has published extensively on drug metabolism and chemical carcinogenesis.
Jorma T. Ahokas is Professor of Toxicology at the Royal Melbourne Institute of Technology, Melbourne, Australia. In the late 1980s he worked as a toxicology consultant in Indonesia. His current research interests include the development of biological markers for monitoring environmental pollution. He has published extensively on pharmacology and toxicology.

Lankinen KS, Bergström S, Mäkelä PH and Peltomaa M, eds.
Health and disease in developing countries. London:The Macmillan Press Limited, 1994:85–94.

10 URBANISATION AND HEALTH

Trudy Harpham, Ph.D.
London School of Hygiene and Tropical
Medicine, Department of Public Health
and Policy, Health Policy Unit
Keppel Street, London WC1E 7HT,
Great Britain

Michael Reichenheim, M.Sc., Ph.D.
State University of Rio de Janeiro,
Institute of Social Medicine
Rua São Francisco Xavier 524/7 andar
20550 Rio de Janeiro,
Brazil

INTRODUCTION

Urbanisation and health in developing countries receive an increasing amount of attention from programme planners, funders and researchers for several reasons. One of the main reasons is the vast and rapidly growing number of people living in towns and cities of the developing world. Another reason is the inequity which is becoming increasingly visible and politically threatening as the number, and sometimes the proportion, of urban poor, living in slums, squatter settlements and shanty towns, grows.

The urban setting provides a particular challenge for national, international and nongovernmental organisations. The delivery of health services in urban areas is, theoretically, easier than in rural areas. The city has more health service infrastructure, the advantage of physical concentration, a larger tax base from which to raise revenue and, on first glance, apparently better health. However, the last decade has witnessed programme experience and research which demonstrates the complexities of health status and of improving health in urban areas of developing countries.

This chapter highlights selected issues that need to be considered in planning urban health. The chapter is not comprehensive as only certain health problems are selected to illustrate issues. The reader who wishes to have a more complete understanding of the processes and problems involved is referred to other texts.[1-3]

The chapter begins by describing briefly urbanisation trends in developing countries and the growth of low-income populations. Health problems are considered by examining differences within cities and within communities. The significance of the epidemiological transition is demonstrated by selected health problems in urban Brazil – infectious diseases, heart and lung diseases, cancers and psychoemotional problems.

URBANISATION AND THE URBAN POOR

Urbanisation is defined here as a relative increase in the urban population as a proportion of the total population. In 1990 most people lived in rural areas. If present trends continue, by 2030 the opposite will be true: urban populations will be twice the size of rural populations. Developing country cities as a group will grow by 160 per cent over this period, whereas rural populations will grow by only 10 per cent. Figure 10.1 shows the percentage change in the populations of urban and rural areas in developing countries up to the year 2025.

By 2000 there will be 21 cities in the world with more than 10 million inhabitants, and 17 of them will be in developing countries.[4] The pattern will vary substantially among regions.

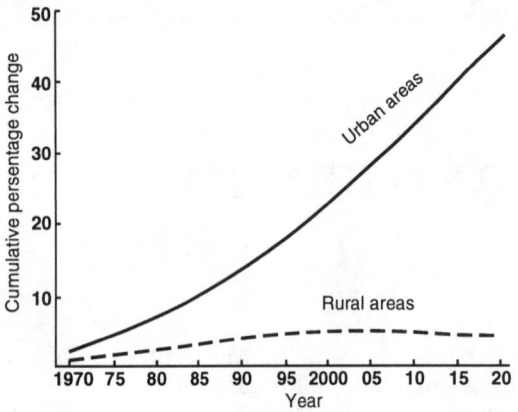

Figure 10.1. Percentage change in the populations of urban and rural areas in developing countries up to the year 2025 (base: 1970).

Over the next 30 years urban population growth will average 1.6 per cent a year in Latin America, 4.6 per cent in Sub-Saharan Africa and 3 per cent in Asia. Table 10.1 presents a categorisation of different patterns of urbanisation.

In addition to the pace of urbanisation, it is the growth of the urban poor and the inequity within the city that justifies research on urban health. Assessing the proportion of the urban population that lives below the poverty line is notoriously difficult. Case studies of specific cities in Africa, Asia and Latin America show that 'it is common for between 30 per cent and 60 per cent of the population to live either in illegal settlements with little or no infrastructure or services or in overcrowded and often deteriorating tenements and cheap boarding houses'.[5] The 1990 World Development Report concluded that urban poverty will become the most significant and politically explosive problem in the next century.

Two myths that appeared in the literature of the 1980s have now become generally appreciated. These concern the contribution of rural-urban migration to urbanisation and the number of people living in large cities. Natural increase is responsible for an average of 61 per cent of urban population growth in developing countries, compared with only 39 per cent from rural migration.[6] With regard to large cities, estimates for 1990 suggest that less than 2.5 per cent of the Third World's urban population lived in cities of more than 10 million inhabitants and less than 25 per cent in cities of more than 100 000 inhabitants.[2] The implications of

these facts are that stemming migration is not going to halt urbanisation and its associated problems (and opportunities) and that, although mega-cities will continue to present challenges, most urban health problems of the future will be found in small and intermediate sized cities and towns which will contain the most of the world's urban population.

Although the characteristics of the poor urban population differ between and within cities, some conditions are typically associated with life in poor urban areas. These have been listed in Table 10.2.

INTRA-URBAN HEALTH DIFFERENTIALS AND THE EPIDEMIOLOGICAL TRANSITION

One of the strong arguments for directing more attention and funds to improve the health status of low-income urban populations has been the exposure of intra-urban health differentials, that is, differences in health status within cities. When aggregate rural and urban health indicators are compared, urban areas often appear to have a better health profile. However, when urban data are disaggregated, intra-urban differences emerge to highlight inequity within the city. Basta was the first to point out such striking differences.[8] He showed that while the infant mortality for Manila, Philippines was 76/1000 live births, it was 210/1000 in Tondo, a squatter area within Manila.

Similar differentials in infant and child mortality, cause-specific mortality and morbidity now exist for many cities (see 3 for review) although a comprehensive set of data on health differentials for a particular city does not exist yet. In advocating action to improve the health of the urban poor the measurement of intra-urban health differentials is often useful.

On examining intra-urban differentials it is often possible to detect different stages of the epidemiological transition in different parts of the city – that is, different patterns of morbidity and mortality due to infectious diseases and chronic diseases respectively.[9] A crude comparison of urban and rural areas can also demonstrate this pattern as shown in Table 10.3. This shows that in Mexico the rural population is more likely to die of diseases of underdevelopment such as respiratory diseases, malnutrition and diarrhea while the urban population is more likely to die of heart disease, cancers, diabetes and accidents.

Table 10.1. Differences in urbanisation patterns of the developing countries (adapted from World Bank 1991 Urban Policy and Economic Development: An Agenda for the 1990s)

Group 1:	Heavily urbanised countries with more than 75 per cent of the population in the cities. Usually including mega-cities but declining rates of urban growth. Most growth attributable to natural increase rather than migration. Typical of Latin America, e.g. Argentina, Mexico, Colombia, Brazil.
Group 2:	Recently urbanising with about half living in urban areas. Growth rates have peaked and are beginning to decline. Typical of North Africa and some Asian countries e.g. Algeria, Morocco, Malaysia.
Group 3:	Primarily rural but rapidly urbanising. Migration a major source of urban growth although male migration replaced by household migration, leading to a shift towards natural increase as major growth. Typical of African countries, e.g. Senegal, Ivory Coast, Nigeria, Sudan, Kenya, Zaire.
Group 4:	Large, mostly rural countries. Major urban concentrations. Urban growth rates stabilised at high levels and projected to continue for next decade. Typical of large Asian countires, e.g. India, Indonesia, China

In turning the focus to what is happening within the city, some authors suggest that low income urban populations exhibit signs of multiple stages of the epidemiological transition and that they suffer the worst of both worlds – underdevelopment and modernisation.[1] Several studies support this. For example, in the peripheral settlements of Bombay, residents bear the disease burdens of both poverty and industrial pollution.[10]

The general view is that as urbanisation progresses, patterns of disease change dramatically, entailing discrete epidemiological periods. This model stems from an historical account taken from developed countries where a clear-cut epidemiological transition can be identified. In developing countries, though, this transition may not express itself so markedly, especially if the picture is disaggregated socioeconomically or geographically. There is evidence that in Brazil, for instance, the transition from one epidemiological period to another – e.g. infectious diseases to chronic-degenerative – took place in one segment of the population (better off) whereas in another group (poor) one finds a mixture of the various epidemiological periods. This model of intra-urban heterogeneity has important practical implications for both research and intervention activities.

Brazil will be examined below in order to illuminate these issues in more detail. Although there are still regional differences within Brazil – some regions being like many African countries while other parts tending to full urbanisation – as a whole the country may be regarded as typical in terms of recent and rapid urbanisation, and for having both traditional and modern epidemiological profiles.

The following account is not an exhaustive description of Brazilian urban epidemiology. The selection of the main health problems is based upon their present and projected magnitudes: the old and new infectious diseases; chronic diseases of the heart and lung; cancers; traumas, injuries and violence; and psychoemotional problems. Some attention is also given to environmental diseases and occupational diseases as they are peculiar to the urban context.

INFECTIOUS DISEASES: THE OLD AND THE NEW

Especially in the large conurbations, the progressive substitution of parasitic and infectious diseases by chronic-degenerative illness and injuries has been seen as a consequence of the social gains achieved by urbanisation. In

Table 10.2. Characteristics of poor urban populations.[2,7]

- dependence on a cash economy
- forced settlement on environmentally hazardous land
- household level and community level overcrowding
- insecurity of tenure with the threat of eviction
- replacement of the extended family by the nuclear family
- large number of female-headed households
- need for children to work away from family settlement and their subsequent exposure to hazards.

Brazil, the proportion of mortality due to infectious diseases has dropped from 45.7 per cent to 11.4 per cent since the 1930s. This reduction is still under way. The national mortality rate due to infectious diseases decreased from 62.7 to 45.0 per 100 000 population between 1979 and 1983.[11]

However, this downward trend is far from ubiquitous either from region to region or from community to community. In the medium sized city of Pelotas (State of Rio Grande do Sul), for instance, infant mortality – which is mainly attributed to perinatal and postnatal infectious diseases – among the lower socioeconomic stratum is at a level in line with most developing countries (80.1 per 1000), whereas among the better off this figure drops dramatically to 13.1 per 1000.[12] Viewed from another perspective, in the mega-city of São Paulo, in the upper socioeconomic stratum, the hospital admission rate for acute respiratory infections was 6 per 1000 children-years, while it was 131 per 1000 children-years among the poorer segments of society.[13]

Emulating the city structure as a whole, similar differentials can also be found within squatter communities, especially in large and well established ones. We have shown earlier that the chances of acquiring severe diarrhea, lower acute respiratory infection or malnutrition

are three times greater among the bottom income group of the slum as compared with the local elite within the slum.[14,15]

In addition to these poverty-related diseases a new pattern is emerging with the arrival of AIDS and dengue on one side and the resurgence of once eradicated or controlled ailments such as cholera and tuberculosis on the other. Environmental changes introduced by the construction of precarious dwellings in flood-stricken areas without adequate sanitation have resulted in an upsurge of hepatitis, leptospirosis and even schistosomosis. The recent cholera epidemics in Latin America put a vast urban population under threat.

Although the AIDS rate is not particularly high in Brazil – 5.3 per 100 000 – when compared with other developed countries or specific African countries, the number of cases in absolute terms is of great concern.[16] Even if AIDS cannot be characterised at a global level as an urban disease, in Brazil, it is heavily concentrated in the most developed regions and in the cities. Its transmission mechanisms are associated with characteristics of city life, such as drug addiction or liberal sexual habits. As in the developed countries, AIDS is becoming a heterosexual disease. In 1987 heterosexual transmission accounted for only 7.5 per cent of cases whereas in 1991 this figure

Table 10.3. Selected causes of mortality by rural and urban residence Mexico 1990. Rates by 100 000 inhabitants. Rural includes places with less than 2500 inhabitants, urban with 2500 or more.

Causes of mortality	Total rate	Rural rate	Urban rate	Relative risk (urban/rural)
Total	520.37	530.68	516.23	0.97
Heart disease	34.92	25.44	38.71	1.52
Diabetes	31.73	17.02	37.64	2.21
Cancers	27.48	20.77	30.17	1.45
Pneumonia	26.86	34.39	23.84	0.69
Accidents	25.67	22.16	27.07	1.22
Diarrhea and gastroenteritis	23.67	20.41	16.95	0.42
Liver diseases	23.03	19.94	22.87	1.15
Cerebrovascular diseases	16.95	16.07	17.30	1.08
Perinatal associated	16.40	12.62	17.92	1.42
Malnutrition	14.00	19.78	11.68	0.59
Asthma	11.85	13.91	11.02	0.79

reached 22.4 per cent. Drug addiction accounts for at least one-quarter of the cases.[16] Street children and adolescents – a bewildering problem in all the main cities of Brazil – are increasingly paying a heavy toll.

Estimates of numbers of street children are problematic as this population cannot be covered adequately by national census data and they are not normally reflected in educational or health statistics. Although not all street children use drugs, in general, drug use by them is greater than by other youths of similar age. The main drugs of street children in Latin America are coca paste, cocaine, cannabis, volatile substances, alcohol and tobacco. Drug use adds to the health problems of children but also leads them into a lifestyle which has additional health risks: violence, sexual exploitation, crime, lack of shelter and security. For some, street children culture is very much a drug culture.

Urban development and industrialisation have also lead to a rapid upsurge of environmental pollution. Sulphur dioxide and particulate complexes from power plants, and photochemical oxidants and nitrogen oxides produced by motor vehicle emissions have put São Paulo, Rio de Janeiro and Belo Horizonte (among other Latin American cities) on the World Health Organization's high concern list.[17] A study carried out in the metropolitan region of Rio de Janeiro showed, after controlling for socioeconomic status, a clear association between districts with high pollution and an excess infant mortality due to pneumonia.[18]

CHRONIC DISEASES: THE MAIN KILLERS

Turning to chronic diseases, chronic heart disease is the main cause of death and morbidity in Brazilian urban areas. Note that this is also true for urban Mexico as shown in Table 10.3. In 1980 heart disease accounted for 33 per cent of all deaths and 13 per cent of potential years of life lost. In São Paulo, the male mortality rate due to heart disease is 40 per cent above the median rates of 27 developed countries.[19]

Contrary to common belief, intra-urban differentials are not confined to infectious diseases. Regarding heart disease, there seems to be a concentration of hypertension and stroke among a specific stratum of the population. Even though there is some evidence of

a general decline in heart disease – possibly due to better treatment facilities and the growth of preventive habits – disaggregated data still show very high rates of stroke among economically disadvantaged groups as opposed to the better-off.[19] On the other hand, no major difference could be detected regarding myocardial infarction.

There is some evidence that both cardiovascular and chronic pulmonary diseases are partly due to air pollution. Long-term effects of sulphur oxides and particulate matters have been associated with chronic obstructive pulmonary disease, especially among the elderly.[17]

Table 10.4 shows figures on air quality in the metropolitan areas of São Paulo and Rio de Janeiro. Although the situation is clearly worse in São Paulo, especially where maximum 24 hour levels are concerned, the contrast between districts in Rio de Janeiro is particularly striking. They illustrate a marked socioeconomic differential with the rich areas of the metropolis, which are close to the sea side and forests, with much better environmental conditions.

CANCERS: REFLECTING THE DEVELOPED WORLD

All types of cancers increased about four-fold in the last 40 years in Brazil. In 1985, national mortality rates for both sexes combined was 51.5 per 100 000 population. Although this figure is still below levels found in developed countries, in the most industrialised regions of Brazil where the main cities are concentrated, levels tend to catch up with those in developed countries. For example, the mortality rate per 100 000 males in Rio de Janeiro (120.1) is close to that found in Japan (147.2) or Norway (146.0).[20]

Table 10.5 shows the crude mortality rates for selected cancers in four cities of Southern Brazil. As in developed countries, lung and breast cancers are the leading causes of death in males and females, respectively. These figures also reveal that in large cities some cancers usually linked to under-development such as those of the stomach and uterus are important causes of death. Thus, for the moment at least, among cancers there seems to be an epidemiological mix of patterns associated with both under-development and development. This is in contrast to the epidemiological transition that characterised the

Table 10.4. Summary of air quality measurements (Total Suspended Particles, TSP) in the metropolitan areas of São Paulo and Rio de Janeiro.[17]

Metropolitan area -City/District	TSP ($\mu g/m^3$)	
	Annual geometric mean	Maximum during 24 hours
São Paulo		
- Cambuci	66	326
- Santo Andre (Centre)	186	536
- Santo Amaro	140	1068
- São Bernardo do Campo	158	1160
Rio de Janeiro (1987)		
- São João de Meriti	123	448
- Bonsucesso	151	268
- Santa Tereza	45	106
- Copacabana	66	108
WHO guidelines	60–90	100–150
Brazilian standard	80	240

evolution of cancers in the developed countries where one group of cancers was gradually replaced by another group. Projections indicate that in the future, though, cancers associated with industrial development will predominate. Interestingly, although the average percentage of smokers in cities is 35–40 per cent, the figure is higher in rural areas in all age groups.

TRAUMA, INJURIES AND VIOLENCE: THE URBAN EPIDEMIC

In Brazil, injury and trauma due to external causes have become a real epidemic. Proportionate mortality increased three-fold since the 1930s.[21] Data from large cities show a mortality rate due to external causes as high as 81.1 per 100 000.[22] This figure rises to 99.6 in Rio de Janeiro. Age-aggregated data show that, to-

day, both intentional and unintentional injuries rank second among the major killers.[22] They are the leading causes of death in the population aged between 5 and 39 years.[23] In contrast to chronic-degenerative diseases which largely affect older people, injuries and violence are by far the main cause of potential years of life lost (PYLL) as they involve mainly children, adolescents and young adults.

In the city of Rio de Janeiro, for instance, 34 per cent of all PYLL are accountable to injuries and violence. It is worth noting that this PYLL level of 3315 per 100 000 population is far greater than in most Latin American countries and only comparable to El Salvador and Guatemala where there was recently civil war.[24,25] The full picture concerning the gender-disaggregated PYLL due to external causes and other leading causes of death is presented in Figure 10.2.

Table 10.5. Crude mortality rates (per 100 000) in 1979 for different types of cancers in four cities of Southern Brazil, by sex.[20]

Organ		São Paulo	Rio de Janeiro	Belo Horizonte	Porto Alegre
Lung	(M)	14.0	27.8	8.1	31.7
	(F)	4.1	7.6	3.5	7.5
Stomach	(M)	11.0	13.6	11.5	11.8
	(F)	5.9	8.4	7.0	6.1
Prostate		6.0	11.0	6.6	11.6
Uterus		3.6	6.1	3.1	4.0
Breast		12.5	21.4	9.4	19.8

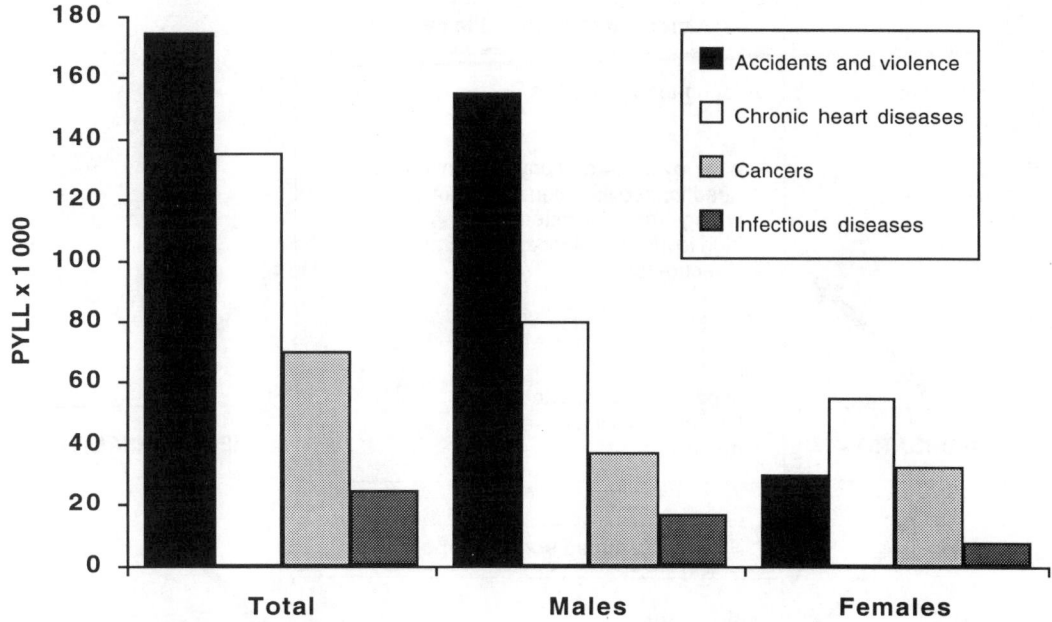

Figure 10.2. Potential years of life lost (PYLL) between age one and 70 according to leading causes by sex. Rio de Janeiro municipality, 1985.[24]

Within the group classified as external causes, motor vehicle injuries and homicides are the leading causes of death. This profile is qualitatively different from developed countries. Besides a very high mortality due to homicides, pedestrian deaths account for a large proportion within the motor vehicle group. In São Paulo, nearly half of the total deaths in males are caused by homicides. Injuries caused by people being run over by cars are five times greater in São Paulo than, for instance, Baltimore, USA.[19]

Occupational diseases, especially work related trauma, must also be brought into the picture. In Brazil, there are estimates that from 1970 to 1985, about 60 million work-related injuries occurred, 0.3 per cent being fatal.[26] In addition to motor vehicle related injuries and homicides, occupational trauma is partly responsible for the high prevalence of physically handicapped people estimated at about 7 per cent of the population.[11]

It is possible to identify patterns of trauma related to different phases of the evolution of cities. Thus, a first phase may be characterised by high rates of pedestrian injuries, disfiguring occupational injuries and homicides. In a second phase of the urbanisation process within-vehicular injuries or deaths and suicides predominate. Although good data is lacking at present, one may suggest that a specific population stratum is carrying the burden quite similarly to what has been outlined above for the other main causes of ill health and death. They are the people living in neighbourhoods with precarious intra-, peri- and extra-household conditions, and those involved in the informal, uncontrolled and low paid work force. In contrast, the better off, to whom labour or traffic regulations and interventions increasingly apply, are at present going through the second urban epidemiological phase outlined above. Possibly due to increasing uptake of safety measures, car crash injuries are slowly declining.

PSYCHOEMOTIONAL PROBLEMS: THE HIDDEN PROBLEM

Although not confined to urban areas, psychoemotional disturbances are frequently considered a by-product of urbanisation.[27] The urban environment and life style increases the long-term difficulties and life events and reduces the social support which are known to be associated with mental health (Figure 10.3). It is estimated that about 17 million Brazilians are affected by at least one type of mental problem. Of these 500 000 are confined to psychiatric hospitals.[11]

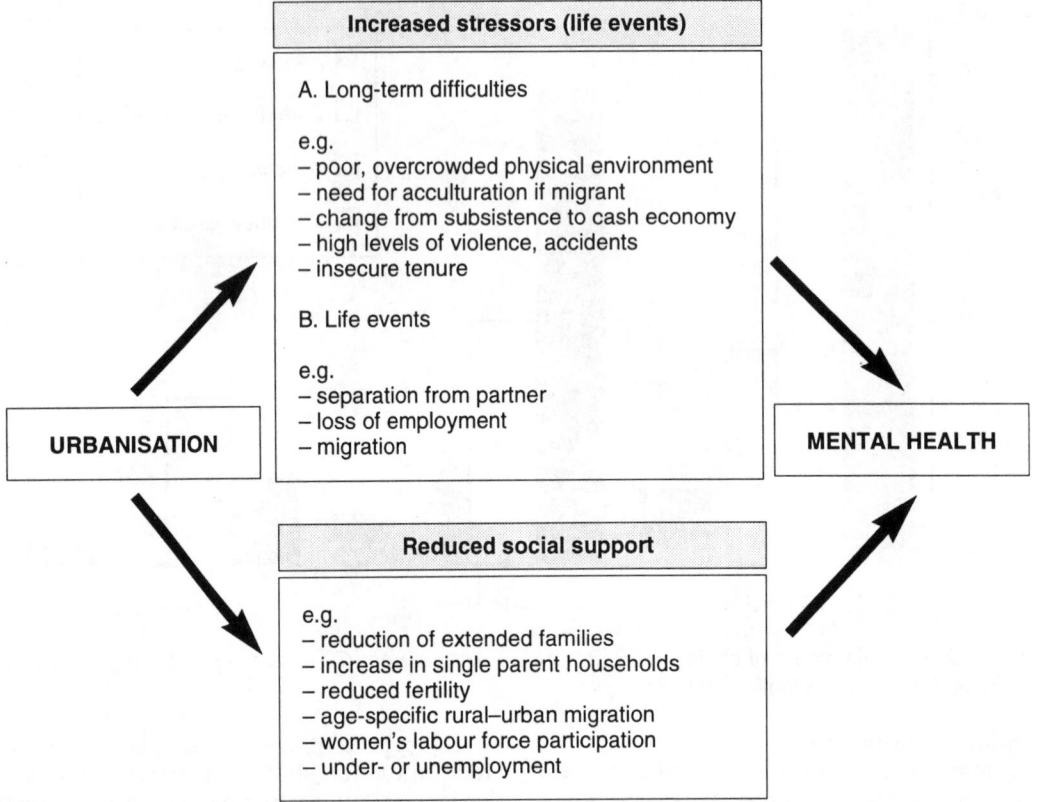

Figure 10.3. A model of social factors of urbanisation in developing countries associated with mental health.

Several studies have measured the prevalence of psychoemotional disturbances in the urban setting according to social differentials. For example, a study of the largest of Rio de Janeiro's *favelas* (squatter settlement) detected a high proportion of mothers with mental health problems. Even within this seemingly homogeneous setting, factors such as low socioeconomic status were associated with high levels of disturbances of this type. While the level of minor psychiatric problems (mainly depression and anxiety) stood at 30 per cent among mothers belonging to the highest income quartile, the prevalence reached 50 per cent among those mothers in the lowest income quartile.[27]

In the same line of investigation, data from the city of Pelotas show a prevalence of 36 per cent of psychoemotional disturbances among the most needy maternal population of the city, this being a six-fold risk as opposed to the better off.[28] In São Paulo, nearly half of the population attending health services showed affective disorders, this prevalence being even higher among users of health services close to unstable and poor squatter settlements.[29]

Again, it is possible to identify a mixed epidemiological model applying to mental health problems. The evidence points to a concentration of psychoemotional disturbances (stress, depression, etc.) among the worse off segments of the population, precisely those who also suffer from many other health problems. In addition, contrary to common belief, the higher income groups seem to be at lower risk of conspicuous mental health problems.

CONCLUSIONS

Interest in urban health in developing countries continues to grow. In the health sector this is reflected by, for example, the fact that the World Health Organization selected urban health as the theme of the 1991 Technical Discussions, has held an Expert Study Group on the topic and continues to promote the

Healthy Cities movement. In the wider development arena the productivity of urban populations is now acknowledged as crucial to the macroeconomic development of countries and we see a renewed emphasis on health in order to enhance productivity (for example, in the World Bank's urban policy agenda for the 1990s).

While this chapter has not been able to offer a comprehensive view of urban health in developing countries as a whole, the examples from Brazil highlight a number of issues which may be pertinent to other settings. The co-existence of two epidemiological profiles – infectious diseases and chronic diseases – means that primary health services in the city have to tackle a wide range of health problems. Even in discrete geographical areas (such as favelas) we see that socioeconomic differentials produce different health profiles. Urban primary health services face an increasing number of problems whose solution lies not in the health sector but in environmental improvement or strengthening social support within communities.

We still know little about how to respond to increased levels of violence and mental ill-health for example. To a large extent the problems have been measured and we now need comparative evaluations of either comprehensive or selective urban primary health care programmes in order to decide which approaches are most effective in particular settings.

Urbanisation will become one of the most critical development issues in the years ahead. Given the irreversible trend of urbanisation we need action and research which will ensure that, in terms of urban health, populations do not suffer the worst of both worlds but the best of both worlds. In health terms this means reducing infectious diseases and malnutrition – traditionally associated with rural areas – and, in the economists' language, turning agglomeration diseconomies into economies of scale.

The challenge to create effective and efficient urban health services, including primary preventive activities to reduce the risk of chronic diseases will involve re-allocation of health budgets, realistic intersectoral linkages and re-assessment of the role of urban local government versus central ministries. This creates a new agenda for national governments, non-governmental organisations, international agencies and researchers.

Acknowledgements

The Urban Health Programme at the London School of Hygiene and Tropical Medicine is funded by the Overseas Development Administration, UK. The authors are grateful to Vanessa Lavender for her efficient collation and word-processing of this chapter.

References

1. Harpham T, Lusty T, Vaughan P. In the shadow of the city: community health and the urban poor. Oxford: Oxford University Press, 1988.
2. Rossi-Espagnet A, Goldstein GB, Tabibzadeh I. Urbanisation and health in developing countries: a challenge for health for all. World Health Stat Q 1991;44(4):187–244.
3. Bradley D, Stephens C, Harpham T, Cairncross S. A review of environmental health impacts in developing country cities. Urban Management Program Discussion Paper no. 6. Washington D.C.: World Bank, 1992
4. World Bank. World Development Report 1992; Development and the environment. Oxford: Oxford University Press, 1992.
5. WHO. Our planet, our health, Report of the WHO Commission on Health and Environment. Geneva: WHO, 1992.
6. UN. Patterns of urban and rural population growth. United Nations Population Studies No. 68. New York: United Nations, 1980.
7. Stephens C, Harpham T. Policy directions in urban health in developing countries – the slum improvement approach. Soc Sc Med 1992;35 (2):111–20.
8. Basta SS. Nutrition and health in low income urban areas of the Third World. Ecol Food Nutr 1977; 6:113–24.
9. Omran AR. The epidemiological transition: A theory of the epidemiology of population change. Milbank Memorial Fund Q 1971;49(4): 509–38.
10. Cook N, Ramasubban R, Singh B. A multi-dimenional approach to the social analysis of the health transition in Bombay. In: Hill A, Cleland J, eds. The measurement of health transition concepts. Canberra: Australian National University Press, 1991.
11. Possas C. Epidemiologia e sociedade: heterogeneidade estrutural e saúde no Brasil. São Paulo: HUCITEC, 1989.
12. Victora CG, Smith PG, Barros FC, Vaughan JP, Fuchs SC. Risk factors for deaths due to respiratory infections among Brazilian infants. Int J Epidemiol 1989;18:918–25.

13. Monteiro CA. Saúde e nutrição das crianças de São Paulo. São Paulo: HUCITEC-EDUSP, 1988.
14. Reichenheim ME, Harpham T. Child health in a Brazilian squatter settlement: acute infections and associated risk factors. J Trop Pediatr 1989; 35:16–21.
15. Reichenheim ME, Harpham T. Perfil intra-comunitário da deficiência nutricional: um estudo de criancas abaixo de 5 anos numa comunidade de baixa renda do Rio de Janeiro. S. Paulo: Revista de Saúde Pública, 1990; 24:69–79.
16. AIDS-Boletim Epidemiológico. Semana epidemiológica – 27–31/92. Programa Nacional de Doenças Sexualmente Transmissíveis. Brasil: Ministério da Saúde, 1992.
17. Romieu I, Weitzenfeld H, Finkelman J. Urban air pollution in Latin America and the Caribbean: health perspectives. World Health Stat Q 1990; 43:153–67.
18. Penna MLF, Duchiade MP. Cantaminación del aire y mortalidad infantil por neumonía. Boletín de la Oficina Sanitária Panamericana 1991; 110:199–207.
19. World Bank. Adult health in Brazil: adjusting for new challenges. Brazil: Department Latin America and the Caribean Region, 1989.
20. FIOCRUZ-Dados. Escola Nacional de Saúde Pública. Câncer: mortalidade no Brasil. Dados, RADIS 1991;15:1–20.
21. Mello-Jorge MH, Marques MB. Violent childhood deaths in Brazil. Bull Pan Amer Health Organ 1985; 19:288–99.
22. FIOCRUZ-Dados. Regiões metropolitanas: violência na vida e na morte. Dados, RADIS 1990; 14:1–15.
23. FIOCRUZ-Dados. Escola Nacional de Saúde Pública. Mortalidade por causas externas no Brasil. Dados, RADIS 1985; 8:1–16.
24. Werneck GL, Reichenheim ME. Anos potenciais de vida perdidos no Rio de Janeiro, 1985. As mortes violentas em questão. Rio de Janeiro:

IMS/UERJ, Série Estudos em Saúde Coletiva n°4, 1992, p. 1–21.
25. Smith G, Barss P. Unintentional injuries in developing countries: the epidemiology of a neglected problem. Epidemiol Rev 1991;13: 228–66.
26. FIOCRUZ-Tema. Saúde do trabalhador: Um quadro dramático. Tema, RADIS 1987; 9:1–24.
27. Reichenheim M, Harpham T. Maternal mental health in a squatter settlement in Rio de Janeiro. Br J Psychiatry 1991;159:683–90.
28. Victora CG, Barros FC, Vaughan JP. Epidemiologia da desigualdade. São Paulo: HUCITEC, 1988.
29. Mari JJ. Minor psychiatric morbidity in three primary medical care clinics in the city of São Paulo. Thesis. London: Institute of Psychiatry, University of London, 1986.

About the authors

Trudy Harpham has a Ph.D. in Urban Geography and currently heads the Urban Health Research Programme in the Public Health and Policy Department of the London School of Hygiene and Tropical Medicine. She was co-editor of the first book on urban health in developing countries (In the shadow of the city, Oxford University Press, 1988). *Her current research interests are in the effects of urbanisation on the mental health of women. Dr Harpham teaches a course on the design and management of research to postgraduates at the London School.*

Michael Reichenheim is currently heading the Under- and Postgraduate Training Programmes of the Department of Epidemiology in the Institute of Social Medicine at the State University of Rio de Janeiro in Brazil. Since 1990, he has also been a research advisor for the Central Adolescent Clinic and the Institute of Paediatrics at the Federal University of Rio de Janeiro. His current research interests are epidemiological methods, maternal and child epidemiology and epidemiology of trauma and injuries.

Lankinen KS, Bergström S, Mäkelä PH and Peltomaa M, eds.
Health and disease in developing countries. London:The Macmillan Press Limited, 1994:95–104.

11 PROSTITUTION AND SEXUALLY TRANSMITTED DISEASES

Sophie Day, B.A., M.A., Ph.D.
University of London, Goldsmiths' College,
Department of Anthropology
New Cross, London SE14 6NW,
United Kingdom

Helen Ward, M.B., Ch.B., M.F.P.H.M.
University of London, Imperial College of
Science, Technology and Medicine,
St. Mary's Hospital Medical School,
Norfolk Place, London W2 1PG,
United Kingdom

'Historically, society has blamed prostitutes for spreading all kinds of disease. Syphilis was blamed on prostitutes. The plague was blamed on prostitutes. During World War One the government locked up prostitutes to protect enlisted men from VD... We prostitutes knew that, sooner or later, AIDS would spread into the heterosexual community and that when it did not only would we be blamed but, if history was any guide, we would also be arrested, quarantined, and worse.'[1]

INTRODUCTION

Prostitution has long been seen as both a medical and a social problem but the contemporary recognition of increasing poverty worldwide and increasing morbidity and mortality from sexually transmitted diseases (STD) has caused a new epidemic of publications about prostitutes from a wide range of competing perspectives.

Prostitution may be defined simply as commercial sex, that is, the exchange of sexual services for money. A prostitute is said to sell sexual services habitually, to more than one man, and to make most or all of her income in this manner. This chapter addresses the sale of such services by prostitute women. Prostitution also involves those who pay for sex, customers or clients; and those who manage the business. Prostitute–client contact is usually managed both directly and indirectly. Direct management refers to the plethora of businesses that put clients and prostitutes in touch with each other in order to make a profit. Indirect management refers to state control and especially to institutions responsible for the regulation of businesses, law and order.

The apparent ease of definition belies a complex history in which boundaries have been drawn and redrawn between prostitution, sexuality and work. In the context of pervasive gender inequalities, prostitution cannot necessarily be distinguished easily from marriage or other female careers. Moreover, the term itself provides a potent metaphor for popular unease with the financial dimensions to all sorts of relationships. The above definition is used in this chapter, but with two qualifications. First, prostitution is characterised by relations of inequality. Those who sell sexual services are disadvantaged by many factors including gender, social class, age and race. State control of prostitution commonly compounds these inequalities through policies that penalise the sale of sexual services.

Second, prostitution can be characterised by different points of view as to what counts as, and who is seen to participate in, commercial sex. Women who have been called prostitutes often contest the label. For example, white Australians thought that they were buying the services of prostitutes with goods while their Aborigine partners thought that they had been stolen forcibly or that they had entered into love affairs.[2]

FEMALE PROSTITUTION AND STD

Female prostitutes

Common sense suggests that individuals with above average numbers of sexual partners are more likely to acquire an STD than those with fewer partners. Similarly, if infected, they are more likely to transmit that infection.

Table 11.1. Prevalence of HIV-1 in prostitute samples.

Place	Year	N	Prevalence per cent	Reference
Nairobi	1981	116	4.0	10
Nairobi	1985	286	61.0	10
Nairobi	1988	500	80.0	7
Kinshasa	1986	377	27.0	3
Kinshasa	1988	1233	35.0	3
Chiangmai	1989	100	44.0	11
Chiangmai	1989	238	36.5	11
London	1986-88	188	1.6	5
London	1989-91	228	0.9	5

While some studies have reported low rates of STD, many others have reported high rates in groups of prostitute women (Table 11.1). High levels of STD continue to be reported among groups of prostitutes in all parts of the world. In Kinshasa, Zaire, 75 per cent of prostitutes presented with at least one STD; 24 per cent had a positive *Neisseria gonorrhoeae* culture.[3] In Honduras, 24 per cent of prostitutes had gonorrhoea, and 30 per cent had *Chlamydia trachomatis* infection.[4] In London, 14 per cent of prostitutes had an acute STD, including 4.7 per cent with gonorrhoea.[5]

Reported or documented past history of sexually transmitted pathogens indicates that the morbidity from STD for many prostitutes remains high over the course of a working life. Of particular concern to women is the potential of HIV infection, infertility following pelvic infection with *Neisseria gonorrhoeae* or *Chlamydia trachomatis*, and the possibility of transmitting infection to children *in utero*, during or after birth.

In STD epidemiology and public health, research has focused on STD transmission from prostitutes to their partners. Models with respect to the population as a whole have been formulated for gonococcal transmission in particular.[6] It has been suggested that a small number of people having high numbers of sexual partners could be seen as a core group, who would play a disproportionate role in transmission.

In recent years, research into STD has been driven by concerns to understand and control HIV infection. Rapid increases in HIV

prevalence have caused a re-evaluation of classical core group models. Prostitutes have been considered central to HIV transmission in the population at large. They have been described as 'high frequency STD transmitter core groups', sometimes together with their clients or other groups of mobile men, such as the military and truck drivers.[7] However, in contemporary research on STD/HIV transmission, prostitution is increasingly studied within the context of the population as a whole. Thus, it is suggested that the dynamics of transmission will depend less upon high rates of partner change per se than upon the variance in numbers of partners between different categories, which are generally formed on the basis of age and gender, and the sexual mixing between them.

Empirical support for core group models has been provided by some studies of classical STD as well as HIV. For example, in 1976, in Sheffield one-sixth of all locally acquired gonococcal infections in men were attributed to contact with 60 local prostitutes.[8] A review of penicillinase-producing *Neisseria gonorrhoeae* in the Netherlands reported that the proportion of cases related to prostitution ranged from 21 per cent to 79 per cent in different regions.[9]

High levels of HIV infection have been found among prostitutes in countries where the virus is transmitted primarily through heterosexual contact. In Nairobi, Kenya there was a rapid increase in the prevalence of HIV in one group of prostitutes studied in the early 1980s. Sera that had been stored in the course of other studies were tested. In 1981, the prevalence of HIV-1 was 4 per cent; by 1985, it had risen to 61 per cent and, by 1988, to over 80 per cent.[7,10] Similar dramatic rises in HIV prevalence have been reported for other groups of urban prostitutes in Africa, for example, in Abidjan, Ivory Coast, and in Ethiopia. More recently, a marked and rapid increase in the prevalence of HIV among prostitutes in India and in Thailand has been noted.[11]

In these groups, a complex relationship between HIV and STD has been reported. In addition to common behavioral risk factors, several interactions between STD have been suggested. A number of reports indicate that STD enhance HIV transmission. Prospective studies of female prostitutes and their clients in Nairobi showed that the acquisition of a genital ulcer was a highly significant risk factor for subsequent HIV seroconversion.[12,13]

Further evidence relating to non-ulcerative STD has been provided by prospective studies of prostitutes in both Nairobi and Kinshasa. For example, 76 of 431 HIV negative women enrolled in a cohort seroconverted during a period of 2 years in Kinshasa. The 4-month period before seroconversion in these women was compared with a concurrent period in controls. Chlamydial infection, gonorrhoea and trichomoniasis were significantly associated with HIV seroconversion, after controlling for sexual behaviour.[14]

Prostitutes' sexual partners

Little is known about the large numbers of men who pay for sex. Particular social situations have been associated with widespread prostitute contact, such as military bases, migrant workers, and travellers, including tourists. Even less is known about the men who have personal sexual relationships with prostitutes, who do not exchange money for sex.

The number of clients is likely to be far greater than the number of prostitutes and their characteristics are likely to be heterogeneous. A random study of the adult Danish population found 13 per cent of men reporting prostitute contact.[15]

Few studies have reported on STD prevalence among clients. In developed countries, HIV infection in clients has been explained primarily by other identified risk factors. In less developed countries, HIV infection has been associated with prostitute contact in some studies.[12,13]

Interpretation of data on STD and prostitutes

The studies cited above seem to confirm the common sense view that prostitutes are at increased risk of acquiring and transmitting STD. However, the difficulties of interpreting these data are so acute that this generalisation cannot be sustained.

In most parts of the world, the sale of sexual services is criminalised. In consequence, the population is 'hidden' and studies rely upon captive groups. Thus, samples are frequently drawn from women arrested, incarcerated or undergoing treatment. Furthermore, poorer and younger women are more accessible to research and public health interventions since they work more visibly, for example, on streets or in easily defined urban areas. Studies of STD have focused upon particular prostitution sectors and since the population from which these are drawn is unknown, reported rates of STD are difficult to interpret.

Interpretation is also hindered by problems of comparison, as there is no obvious control group for prostitutes. Commonly, samples of prostitutes are compared with a 'general population' or with STD clinic attenders. Such studies indicate that rates of STD in prostitutes reflect the prevalence in the local population. Some have also shown how levels of infection relate to the local organisation of prostitution. Thus, in Europe and north America the single most important risk factor for HIV in female prostitutes is a history of injecting drug use. A low prevalence or even absence of HIV has been reported in study groups, such as west European prostitutes, who do not inject drugs.[16]

A few studies have considered levels of disease in relation to sectors of prostitution. It has been found that women who worked on the streets in an economically depressed inner-city area in South Florida had an HIV-1 seroprevalence of 41 per cent, whereas women in the same state who worked for escort agencies showed no evidence of HIV infection.[17] A similar pattern was found in Nairobi, where 66 per cent of women of low socioeconomic status were HIV-1 positive, compared with 8 per cent of those of a higher socioeconomic status, working in a different prostitution sector.[18]

In numerous studies, but particularly in the industrialised world, prostitutes have been shown to construct differences between partners who pay for sex and those who do not. During the last 10 years, such studies have reported that condoms are used with the vast majority of clients but not with boyfriends or husbands. In a London study, the rate of STD was not associated with overall numbers of sexual partners but with the number of non-paying partners reported.[5]

The few studies published on prostitute partners suggest that distinct client behaviours may also be relevant to STD infection and transmission. In a London study of clients, for example, over a third of men reported past sex with men as well as women.[19]

The role of prostitution in a particular society will probably be as important to STD transmission as the internal organisation of prostitution. It has been suggested of Africa that, 'it is striking that countries with a typical "core group sexual pattern" (a large group of men having sex with a small number of women) have had the highest incidence rates of HIV, for example, Rwanda and Malawi'.[20]

Models of epidemics have contrasted this picture, where HIV infection will rise steeply soon after the virus is introduced, with a picture in which rates of partner change are more similar among different categories. In the latter situation, it has been suggested that infection will increase more gradually but may eventually reach similar levels.

Research has documented a great diversity in rates of STD in prostitute women, which have been associated with a range of epidemiological and sociological parameters. This research shows that STD in prostitutes cannot be understood purely in terms of rates of partner change, as suggested initially by calling upon common sense.

THE PROFESSIONAL PROSTITUTE

Contemporary images of prostitution in the literature on STD owe much to a relatively recent western history. In brief, poor women were, in the words of many historians, disciplined. Official accounts of sexuality, including medical studies, were deployed to encourage the unrespectable poor to adopt middle class norms relating to the sanctity of marriage and particular cultures of work.

Historians have shown that an image of the prostitute was created long before the fact.[21] During the 19th century in particular, respectable behaviour was constructed as all that was the opposite of informal sexual unions such

as common law marriage and concubinage, street life, lodging houses, and the sale of sex. Norms of respectability, backed by legal measures, were gradually adopted by the working classes as well as the middle classes. Poor women found it more difficult to combine sex work with other economic activities in their attempts to avoid impoverishment. Those who continued to sell sex eventually became professional prostitutes and professional outsiders. Medicine, especially public health attempts to control syphilis and gonorrhoea, constituted an important element in this process.[22]

By the end of the century, legislation that permitted prostitution within strictly defined limits had been exported to much of the world under colonial administrations, where it persists to the present day. In some countries, prostitution was regulated through official policy; elsewhere, prostitution was officially suppressed though unofficially tolerated. In recent years, a third type of system, decriminalisation, has been partially enacted in a very few places, such as New South Wales in Australia. Decriminalisation removes all specific laws relating to prostitution, which is controlled instead through general legislation on the conduct of businesses, public order and so forth. However, it seems that prostitute women continue to be effectively set apart from others by social sanctions attached to their work.[23]

Regulation and suppression forced many prostitutes underground, in association with previously unconnected sectors of the residuum, who were simultaneously redefined as deviants. For example, Judith Allen documents an association between prostitution and organised crime, particularly the marketing of illicit drugs, in New South Wales at the beginning of the century which continues in Sydney massage parlours today.[24]

Contemporary medical accounts seem to use a straightforward definition of prostitution. It appears to be simple common sense that prostitutes are at increased risk of STD, because they have a lot of sexual partners. It seems obvious that they will be important to the further spread of STD, because they are linked directly or indirectly with a wide sector of the rest of society. Moreover, this category of women appears to be the same the world over and through history. These brief comments about the creation of the professional prostitute are intended to challenge the simple

The growing number of street children is a major problem in all developing countries. They are especially prone to fall victim for prostitution. Photo: UNICEF/Eva Arnvig

definition used in most accounts of STD. Two features of this history are particularly relevant.

First, disease control measures were important in establishing differences between respectable and unrespectable women and were therefore instrumental in creating the modern professional prostitute.

Second, explicit references to respectability and morality were less common in medical than in non-medical accounts. Medical reports dealt with facts. The empiricist and positivist style make it difficult to see how these reports made possible and indeed depended upon the idea that prostitutes could be seen and easily distinguished from non-prostitutes.

From this perspective, it is apparent that medical understandings of prostitution are actually a complex historical construct, closely informed by ideas about the morality of sexual activity over the past 150 years. Therefore, it is important to ask why a prostitute is defined simply in terms of high levels of sexual activity, why references to poverty and the effects of stigma are so scarce, and why the mutual influences of poverty, stigma and sexual activity with multiple partners are not discussed.

PROSTITUTION IN CONTEXT

The sex industry: Thailand

Prostitution in Thailand has changed dramatically in the recent past. European travellers in the 17th and 18th centuries reported a growth in forms of prostitution, accompanying growing inequalities in landholdings and massive rural poverty. In the early 19th century, a category of prostitute was formalised in law. In 1909 registration was introduced by means of the Venereal Disease Control Act and many newly freed slaves were absorbed as prostitutes into a brothel system.

By the middle of the century, Thailand had ratified international agreements on trafficking in women and prostitution and therefore revoked, in 1960, the earlier registration system.

At the same time, legislation relating to the entertainment industry allowed female employees to provide special services, to sell sexual services informally and independently of their formal employment. In this way, prostitutes have been driven into the entertainment industry and street soliciting has been criminalised.

The recent development of the entertainment industry in Thailand has been linked to national and international policies.[25-27] The rise of the entertainment industry and of tourism more generally is related to the open economy pursued in Thailand since 1960. The interest of the US in an open economy was apparent after the Korean War and pre-dated Thai policies. Legislation relating to entertainments was designed initially to attract the US military as seen, for example, in a treaty of 1967 allowing US soldiers in Vietnam to visit Thailand on Rest and Recreation (R&R) leave. By 1970, US military personnel were spending 20 million USD in R&R activities, one-quarter of the value of rice exports for that year. By 1982, the tourist industry earned more foreign exchange than rice.

As the US withdrew from Indochina in the mid-1970s, US aid, loans and military support declined. Foreign exchange earnings from rice, rubber and tin declined at the same time. Tourism was then geared to a more mixed international market so as to diversify the export structure and attract foreign investment and exchange.

The mobilisation of female labour in the entertainment industry has been integral to government policies as well as business practices. Similar national policies have been reported for Japan, Korea and the Philippines. Impoverished rural communities, especially in Northeast and North Thailand, have exported their daughters into prostitution over the past 20–30 years.

Prostitutes remit earnings which form an important source of income for maintaining agricultural smallholdings and improving the standard of living. *The value of daughters' labour is now greater than that of sons* and the birth of a daughter is celebrated accordingly. Prostitute women see themselves as breadwinners for their families.

The tourist industry has created a demand for a very specific labour force. One of the most striking features of this industry is the development of sex tourism through package tours which are purchased by individuals,

groups and businesses. Moreover, this labour force is not confined to Thailand. An estimated 16 000 Thai prostitutes work overseas (as compared with a total number of perhaps 500 000 – 700 000). Indirect trafficking of women has also attracted interest in the form of mail order or catalogue brides and domestic servants.

In many of these commercial sexual exchanges, Thai women are interested in more than their immediate earnings. They may be drawn toward sex with foreigners as part of a wider relationship in which they can educate and westernise themselves or their children. This desire to marry a foreigner may have contributed to the out-migration of prostitutes and brides in Thailand and other Asian countries, such as the Philippines. Most women, however, maintain ties with their homes in rural areas where they return to marry in the hope of starting small businesses

Prostitution cannot be understood purely in terms of the employment alternatives open to women. Wider economic interests and policies are equally important to an understanding of contemporary prostitution in Thailand. It is unclear whether these policies will be reversed following the recent, rapid increase in AIDS cases associated with the entertainment industry.

Prostitution, marriage and work: Kenya

In much of Sub-Saharan Africa, poor urban women engage in a variety of jobs, including petty trade, beer brewing, the sale of food, sex and lodgings. Such work is located in the informal sector. Given the above example, it should be clear that prostitution cannot be explained simply in terms of the work options open to urban women. Nevertheless, studies of urban life illustrate the difficulties of categorising prostitutes, in contrast to non-prostitutes. Urban women may be involved in a series of temporary unions, some of which may involve commercial sex. While some women work as professional full-time prostitutes, most do not. Furthermore, all types of sexual union may involve the exchange of money for sex.

In Nairobi, Kenya, the term *malaya* (literally 'European') can be used to describe certain forms of commercial sex, adultery, promiscuity, particularly among divorced women, and vagrancy. In colonial Nairobi, the exchange of sex for money was only part of a relationship that involved, for example, the provision of food and lodgings as well. In the 1920s, as an African community was established in Nairobi, *malaya* prostitutes kept down the costs of labour and played an important part in its reproduction. Histories of *malaya* landlords in Pumwani, the oldest African settlement still existing in Nairobi and the area from which participants have been recruited to the studies of STD and HIV reported above, show that most women were migrants from rural Kenya and Tanzania.

Links with rural areas were maintained, often through the fostering of children. Commercial sex enabled these women to invest in property, which provided much greater security than marriage, as shown by this comment, '...an ex-prostitute when asked if she had ever been married, replied crossly, "Why do you insult me? My house is my husband"'.[28] In later life, from a base of economic independence, a variety of more or less permanent and formal relationships might be established with men.

Acts of prostitution range from a quick service of 20 minutes to a town 'marriage' lasting for years among the largely Kikuyu women in Mathare Valley, another poor area in Nairobi.[29]

Sexual relationships cannot be easily categorised as prostitution or marriage, they are better seen as points along a continuum. Thus, *malaya* prostitution is both like other forms of prostitution such as those associated with public soliciting or with the sale of sex alone and like other relatively informal unions, such as town marriages. Frequently, a variety of informal and formal unions are combined. A man may be married monogamously in a rural area and visit girlfriends or prostitutes in town. Equally, he may have one wife in the country and a second wife in town. A woman may be a steady or occasional partner of a man who is formally married elsewhere.

Two important points about these unions are evident from the literature. First, none of them can be distinguished readily through the idiom of commerce. Available accounts suggest a relatively instrumental view of sex in all types of union, in marriage as well as prostitution. Various forms of prostitution are simply short-term conjugal relationships in which sex is exchanged for money rather than food and rent. Husbands, boyfriends and customers pay for sex in different ways. Second, different unions may be distinguished through the filiation of children. Children of couples joined by some type of formal marriage are incorporated in a wider kin group while children of informal unions (including prostitution) stay with the mother.

These studies from Kenya are relevant to other African cities, where a similar continuum of unions has been described, which may all involve the exchange of sex for money or things of monetary value. In general, the distinction between formal and informal unions in terms of the ultimate destination of children seems important. However, data from Kenya cannot be generalised simply. For example, in West Africa, unlike East Africa, independent women known as prostitutes had a high status and were often associated with long distance trading. The free women described in several studies of West and Central Africa form associations to protect business and finance funerals, like other guilds.

Although these two examples do little justice to the rich data from which they are drawn, they serve to emphasise the inadequacy of representations of prostitutes in the literature on STD. While contemporary STD research focuses less on high rates of partner change among prostitutes than on behaviours in different groups and the sexual mixing between them, it still tends to rely upon a simple binary distinction between a core of STD transmitters and a non-core. Prostitutes continue to be identified with that core group. Contemporary STD research remains relatively blind to the social and economic context which structures behaviour and, thus, remains trapped in the old dilemma, reproducing the traditional imagery, where prostitutes are of interest because they are central to the wider sexual economy but continue to be represented as a discrete social group, which is marginal to society.

INTERVENTIONS

Negative attitudes towards prostitutes are clearly reflected in interventions associated with STD control. Many focus upon potential transmission from prostitutes to a notional general population; to clients and thence to innocent bystanders, such as monogamous wives or children. Few are concerned with the occupational risk posed to prostitutes. Most accounts are clearly unrealistic in their attempt to separate multi-partner sexual activity from other features of prostitution such as the machinery which effectively separates prostitutes from other people and the economic marginalisation of women.

As noted above, measures to control infectious disease have included the control of categories of people. During the current HIV epidemic, control measures have included compulsory screening and detention of those described or registered as prostitutes in many states, including parts of India, the US and Sweden.

However, there is no evidence that such strategies have prevented STD infection. Indeed, it has been argued that repression exacerbates the problem since women may be further marginalised from health care and health education in the attempt to evade state restrictions on their work. In this context, convincing arguments have been put forward for the decriminalisation of prostitution and the removal of all repressive measures that might discourage prostitutes from using health care services and practising safer sex.

Such arguments include a focus upon risk reduction in prostitutes and their partners and the development of accessible health care. These measures are comparable to harm minimisation strategies developed for other risk behaviours, such as injecting drug use. Evaluations of these strategies are complex but several studies have reported an increase in condom use and a decrease in STD incidence.

It has been argued that interventions towards prostitutes will be cost-effective in STD prevention. Some interventions may be more effective than others. Thus, while it is commonly recommended that men avoid sex with prostitutes, a reduction in prostitute contact may have unintended consequences. According to models of sexual mixing noted above, the effect of such interventions will depend upon the interrelationships between different rates of partner change in a community and may in fact increase transmission in some situations.

In areas where groups of prostitutes have very high levels of infection, accessible health care and STD control will be crucial. Detecting and treating STD will reduce morbidity among prostitutes and help decrease sexual transmission to partners and vertical transmission to children. Where indicated, vaccination may be recommended, for example, to prevent hepatitis B infection. In the context of HIV prevention, a reduction in the prevalence of other infections may help to decrease the transmission of HIV.

The distribution of condoms and information on STD prevention alone are unlikely to provide effective interventions since women may be unable to insist upon condom use and may be unwilling to prevent pregnancy. Alternative protective devices such as spermicides and the female condom have been introduced in some studies, but measures of their success are still unclear. In particular situations, mass prophylaxis with antibiotics may be indicated.

Innovative interventions have been developed in the last decade towards those involved in sex work. For example, interventions have been designed for managers of prostitutes. In Sydney, the Australian Prostitutes' Collective has developed a Safe House Scheme where symbols are awarded to parlours in which all clients are required to use condoms and in which working conditions are adequate. The Collective also encourages the distribution of introductory letters to clients of escort services which explain that condoms are required for all sexual contact. This prior notification by the management means that responsibility for negotiating safer sex does not lie solely with each individual prostitute.

In a number of cities, field workers, including women with experience in the sex industry, provide free condoms, equipment for injecting drugs and support in the negotiation of safer sex to women in various prostitution sectors. In Amsterdam, a group of clients has been set up to discuss safer sex and to hand out condoms to other clients in the Red Light district. Some interventions distinguish between different forms of prostitution. Several programmes have been developed for the most marginalised groups of prostitutes who, in different situations, may be defined as under-age (either with respect to employment or to sexual consent), illegal immigrants, unregistered workers, or who may be criminalised through other behaviours, such as the illicit use of drugs.

Finally, it should be noted that sex worker activists, in particular, have developed a wider platform related to STD prevention. Safer sex is seen as a *sine qua non* of professional prostitution. Condom use or non-penetrative sex are aspects of occupational health and safety in general and many prostitutes are skilled in encouraging safer sex among reluctant partners. Accordingly, sex workers have been seen and hired as professional educators in STD prevention for a range of at risk categories.

Since prostitution is best seen as a form of work rather than a deviant expression of sexuality, effective interventions are likely to extend beyond narrowly defined strategies of risk reduction. In many parts of the world, poor urban women have difficulties in making a living and sex work may provide one of the few realistic options. This situation has been addressed in a number of interventions, which have sought to provide alternative livelihoods to women on a small scale. Prostitute activists and others have made strong distinctions between forced and voluntary sex work. Alternatives to prostitution are essential for the first category but should be available for the second. Attempts to prevent STD through change in the larger political economy have attracted little practical support in the health field.

The definition of prostitution used in this chapter suggests that prostitution refers not only to multi-partner sexual activity but also to social stigma and inequality. Effective health care therefore requires a social as well as a medical understanding of prostitution so as to ensure, minimally, that services do not compound this situation of inequality. In order to provide services that do not reinforce existing stigma, staff training should be available both on general medical images of prostitution and on the local situation. Services should be accessible; this implies an approach that enhances the ability of prostitutes to negotiate sexual relationships so as to prevent STD acquisition and to have infections treated rapidly, rather than one which enforces a range of repressive measures. Additional strategies will vary locally but general parameters of STD transmission are likely to direct services and control measures in several directions, for example, to those who manage prostitution as well as those who take part in commercial sex, and to non-commercial relationships as well.

CONCLUSION

It may seem that medical and social perspectives on prostitution and STD are largely incompatible given their radically different understandings of the term prostitute and associated concepts of behaviour, populations, societies and social inequality. But, there are also points of contact. In medical studies, it has long been recognised that STD transmission is not random because social parameters, such as who has sex with whom, are important determinants of the epidemiology. In oth-

er words, populations are also societies. Equally, it has been recognised that peoples' own ideas about their behaviour will influence their risk of acquiring and transmitting STD. Thus, it is now a truism in many accounts of HIV and prostitution in the west that women are at little risk of acquiring infection at work because they are concerned about their safety and insist on condom use with clients. People's ideas inform their behaviour.

In STD medicine, it is beginning to be recognised that research paradigms, including the definition of the object of study, such as the prostitute, will shape research results. AIDS research provides an apt illustration once more, since many publications have exhibited a remarkable degree of historical self-consciousness about the unintended effects of using a particular vocabulary or model to describe infection. In this way, the object of study is less definitively constructed as a fact 'out there' that exists entirely independently of the men and women carrying out STD research, control and care.

In these three areas, there are indications of a growing congruence between medical and social approaches to the issue which may enhance our understanding of STD transmission and our attempts to prevent infection.

References

1. French, D. Working: my life as a prostitute. Gollanz: London, 1989:240.
2. McGrath A. Black velvet. In: Daniels K, ed. So much hard work: women and prostitution in Australian history. Sydney: Fontana/Collins, 1984:233–297.
3. Nzila N, Laga M, Thiam M A, *et al*. HIV and other sexually transmitted diseases among female prostitutes in Kinshasa. AIDS 1991;5:715–21.
4. Venegas VS, Villafrance P, Madrid JP, Cosenza H, Bygdeman S. Gonorrhoea and urogenital chlamydial infection in female prostitutes in Tegucigalpa, Honduras. Int J STD and AIDS 1992;2:195–9.
5. Ward H, Day S, Mezzone J, *et al*. Prostitution and risk of HIV: female prostitutes in London. Br Med J 1993;307:356–358.
6. Yorke JA, Hethcote HW, Nold A. Dynamics and control of the transmission of gonorrhea. Sex Transm Dis 1978;5:51–56.
7. Moses S, Plummer FA, Ngugi EN, Nagelkerke NJD, Anzala AO, Ndinya-Achola JO.

Controlling HIV in Africa: effectiveness and cost of an intervention in a high-frequency STD transmitter core group. AIDS 1991;5:407–11.

8. Turner EB, Morton RS. Prostitution in Sheffield. Br J Ven Dis 1976;52:197–203.

9. Ansink-Shipper MC, van Klineren B, Huikeshoven MH, et al. Epidemiology of PPNG infection in the Netherlands. Br J Ven Dis 1984;60:141–6.

10. Piot P, Plummer FA, Rey MA, et al. Retrospective seroepidemiology of AIDS virus infection in Nairobi populations. J Inf Dis 1987;155:1108–12.

11. Siraprapasiri T, Thanprasertsuk S, Rodklay A, Srivanichakorn S, Sawanpanyalert P, Temtanarak J. Risk factors for HIV among prostitutes in Chiangmai, Thailand. AIDS 1991;5:579–82.

12. Cameron DW, Simonsen JN, D'Costa LJ, et al. Female-to-male transmission of human immunodeficiency virus type 1: risk factors for seroconversion in men. Lancet 1989;ii:403–7.

13. Plummer FA, Simonsen JN, Cameron DW, et al. Co-factors in female-to-male sexual transmission of HIV. J Inf Dis 1991;163:233–9.

14. Laga M, Manoka A, Kivuvu M, et al. Nonulcerative sexually transmitted diseases as risk factors for HIV-1 transmission in women: results from a cohort study. AIDS 1993;7:95–102.

15. Melbye M, Biggar RJ. Interactions between persons at risk for AIDS and the general population in Denmark. Am J Epidemiol 1992;135:593–602.

16. European Working Group on HIV infection in Female Prostitutes. HIV infection in European female sex workers: epidemiological link with use of petroleum-based lubricants. AIDS 1993;7:393–400.

17. Fischl MA, Dickinson GM, Flanagan S, Fletcher MA. Human immunodeficiency virus among female prostitutes in South Florida. III International Conference on AIDS, Washington 1987. (Abstract W2.2)

18. Kreiss JK, Keoch D, Plummer FA, et al. AIDS virus infection in Nairobi prostitutes: spread of the epidemic to east Africa. N Engl J Med. 1986;314:414–8.

19. Day S, Ward H, Perrotta L. Prostitution and risk of HIV: male partners of female prostitutes. Br Med J 1993; 307:359–361.

20. Laga M, Nzila N, Goeman J. The interrelationship of sexually transmitted diseases and HIV infection: implications for the control of both epidemics in Africa. AIDS 1991;5: S55–63.

21. Corbin A. Women for hire. Prostitution and sexuality in France after 1850. Harvard: Harvard University Press, 1990.

22. Walkowitz J. Prostitution and victorian society: women, class and the state. Cambridge: Cambridge University Press, 1980.

23. Neave M. The failure of prostitution law reform. ANZJ Crim 1988;21:202–13.

24. Allen J. The making of a prostitute proletariat in early twentieth century New South Wales. In: Daniels K, ed. So much hard work: women and prostitution in Australian history. Sydney: Fontana/Collins, 1984:192–232.

25. Phongphaichit P. From peasant girls to Bangkok masseuses. Geneva: ILO, 1982.

26. Phongpaichit P. Economic and social transformation in Thailand: 1957–1976. Bangkok: Chulalongkorn University, Social Research Institute, 1980.

27. Truong TD. Sex, money and morality: Prostitution and tourism in Southeast Asia. London: Zed Books, 1990.

28. Bujra J. Women 'entrepreneurs' of early Nairobi. Can J Afr Stud 1975;9:213–34.

29. Nelson N. Selling her kisok: Kikuyu notions of sexuality and sex for sale in Mathere Valley, Kenya. In: Caplan P, ed. The cultural construction of sexuality. London: Tavistock Publicatons, 1987:217–39.

About the authors

Sophie Day is a social anthropologist who holds appointments both in the Department of Anthropology and in the Academic Department of Public Health at the University of London. She specialises in the anthropology of medicine, religion, gender and sexuality and has focused her work regionally on London and the Himalayas.

Helen Ward is a clinical epidemiologist and senior lecturer in academic public health. Since 1986 she has done, together with Sophie Day, research on commercial sex and sexually transmitted infections in London, collaborating on a number of similar studies in Europe. This research has led to the design and evaluation of interventions in various settings to reduce transmission of and morbidity from sexually transmitted infections.

Lankinen KS, Bergström S, Mäkelä PH and Peltomaa M, eds.
Health and disease in developing countries. London:The Macmillan Press Limited, 1994:105–114.

12 ALCOHOL AND TOBACCO

Heikki Jokinen, M. Pol. Sc.
Hauhontie 8 I 56, FIN-00550 Helsinki,
Finland

Y. Tapio Pitkänen, M.D. Ph.D.   **Leo Hirvonen, M.D., Ph.D.**
City of Helsinki, Herttoniemi Health Station
Kettutie 8 M, FIN-00800 Helsinki,
Finland

ALCOHOL AND COLONIAL POLICIES

Much like opium, alcohol was one of the cornerstones of colonialism. The British introduced the use of opium in China to boost trade, and fierce colonial wars were fought because of opium. The first slave traders brought distilled spirits to Africa. It was a good trade item, a bottle was much easier to transport from Europe than a sack of salt. Liberal use of spirits in trade negotiations often had a favourable effect on the prices of the slaves. Alcohol also counted as currency.

Once the colonies were formed, they favoured unrestricted import of alcohol because the import taxes constituted a major part of their income. Alcohol was one of the very few items that were exchanged according to the rules of money economy, while other forms of trade were much more difficult to tax. During one single quarter of a year in 1890 Dahomey imported more than one million litres of rum, a volume that equalled the total imports of French West Africa in 1957.[1]

Once the adverse effects of alcohol became obvious, the colonial rulers realised the threat of loosing their able workforce. The Brussels Conference in 1889–90 dealt with the cessation of slave trade and control trade of arms and alcohol; it decided to enact a prohibition law to cover practically the whole of Africa. The treaty was ratified when the colonial powers met again in 1919: the import, manufacture and possession of tradeable alcohol was prohibited, with the exception of the Arabic states and South Africa.

In India, the struggle against Western alcohol culture formed an important part of the national freedom movement. Alcohol did not belong to Indian culture and when the colonial masters introduced it, there was spontaneous resistance. The freedom movement, led by the Congress Party, demanded a prohibition law. Mahatma Gandhi supported the efforts towards temperance as a question of personal morals and of social and material advancement of the nation. He personally led several public protests against alcohol retail stores. Also in Sri Lanka anti-alcohol campaign was part of the struggle for independence.

NEW AND OLD COLONIALISM

Realising that alcohol trade was directly related to the objectives of colonialism made it easy for the newly formed national states to resist. Imported alcohol depleted financial resources and caused difficulties in cultures unfamiliar with industrially manufactured alcoholic beverages. Today, the situation is more problematic.

The international alcohol industry's interest in developing countries has steadily increased. The reasons are obvious: alcohol

Table 12.1. Alcohol consumption in selected countries, litres of absolute alcohol *per capita*.

	1980	**1985**	**1990**
France	14.9	13.3	12.7
Italy	13.0	11.6	8.7
Great Britain	7.1	7.1	7.6
Germany	11.4	10.8	10.6
Belgium	10.8	10.5	9.9
The Netherlands	8.8	8.5	8.2
Canada	8.7	8.0	7.5
Ireland	7.3	6.8	7.2
USA	8.2	8.0	7.5

consumption in industrialised countries has levelled off or taken a downward turn. The decline has been especially clear in countries with traditionally high consumption levels such as Italy and France (Table 12.1).

At the same time, the capacity of alcohol production has increased. During 1960–80 the production of both beer and distilled spirits doubled (Table 12.2). During many years the strong alcohol industry in industrialised countries had been accustomed to ever increasing sales as the use of alcohol became more and more common, and new user groups such as adolescents and women were introduced.

The ten leading alcohol exporters of the world are from countries where alcohol consumption has levelled off or is decreasing (Table 12.1). With a lack of new consumer groups in the domestic market it has been natural to look for trade in other areas, especially in developing countries where the use of industrially manufactured alcohol has been low.

In many developing countries the ruling elite and the affluent middle class tend to adopt Western values, transmitted so efficiently e.g. through television. This group prefers Western imported brands of industrially produced alcohol.

STRATEGIES OF ADVERTISING

Advertising is a new feature in comparison with the previous century. The market leaders of alcohol industry have vast turnovers and can afford large-scale advertising; in 1984 there were 27 multinational alcohol companies with annual sales exceeding one billion USD.

While advertising in Africa is usually rather limited (in comparison with Europe or USA), alcohol advertising certainly catches the eye. The strategies of selling alcohol are manifold, but usually they involve myths of modernisation and westernisation. Alcohol advertising in Africa emphasises also youth, strength and nutritional values.

In 1981, the most popular advertisement in the Ivory Coast featured an exhausted biker who was revived so efficiently after drinking a bottle of Bock beer that he even overtook cars. There are also clear messages to women and young people.

At a time when alcohol advertising is being more and more regulated in most industrialised countries there is no such trend in developing countries.

NATIONAL PRODUCTION LEAPS

Also the domestic alcohol production in developing countries has increased steeply. During 1960–80 the industrial beer production in developing countries increased by 400 per cent. Out of the ten countries that had increased their beer production most, eight were developing countries. The pace was most impressive in Brazil with an annual increase of 8.4 per cent.

The increased availability has its consequences. According to the annual report of the International Breweries' Association Gabon ranked fourth in the annual beer consumption per capita in 1981 preceded only by the traditional beer countries Federal Republic of Germany, and the late German Democratic Republic and Czechoslovakia.

Homemade alcohol is a traditional drink in many parts of Africa. Making of beer and palm wine is very common, even overflowing in some places. These drinks have sometimes a central role in the village rituals and symbolic functions. The homemade alcohol is often sold by women, as one of their few ways of making

Table 12.2. World production of absolute alcohol by type of product, annual averages in million kg (source: FAO, unpublished statistics).

	1961-65	1971-75	1981-83	Growth
Beer or barley	1 414	2 208	2 751	95%
Grape wine	2 616	3 128	3 451	32%
Fermented beverages (excluding grape wine)	550	550	658	20%
Vermouth and similar beverages	13	16	38	192%
Distilled alcoholic beverages	3 673	5 457	7 374	101%
Other alcoholic beverages*	406	577	526	30%
Non-food ethanol	1 409	1 870	7 364	423%
Total	10 081	13 806	22 162	120%

* Wheat or rice fermented beverage, beer of maize, millet and sorghum.

money. The alcohol content of the homemade brands is very variable (Table 12.3).

The homemade alcohols were estimated to account for 89 per cent of the absolute alcohol consumed in Tanzania in 1980s. Domestic industrial production accounted for 10 per cent and imports for only 1 per cent.

In many African countries, the production of traditional ales has now been converted to industrial scale. The ale is widely available in disposable 1 litre containers.

WHO DRINKS, WHO DOES NOT?

Considering the alcohol consumption in developing countries it is important to remember its concentration in urban areas. The alcohol industries are in the cities while the rural areas consume mostly homemade beers and wine. In addition, a significant part of the population both in Africa and Asia are non-drinkers.

Islam is traditionally against drinking. The Fourth Sura of the Quran proclaims that alcohol is from the devil and must be avoided. In practice the attitudes in Islamic countries are very variable. Some countries have strictly controlled prohibition laws, others are more tolerant.

The differences are not so much dependent on religious views, but largely due to differences in economic and cultural traditions. A tradition of abstinence creates social control that, at least, keeps the use of alcohol out of publicity. In most Islamic cultures it is absolutely impossible for women to drink alcohol.

An interview study conducted in Sri Lanka in 1987 concluded that alcohol was used by 58 per cent of the Buddhists, 78 per cent of the Christian, 15 per cent of the Hindus and 8 per cent of the Muslims.[2] Women in Sri Lanka appear to abstain completely.

ALCOHOL AND HEALTH

Excessive alcohol consumption has both social and health impacts. The children may miss their meals or schooling opportunities because of drinking parents as the meagre cash goes to satisfying their alcohol addiction. The vicious circle is made worse by the practice of giving maturing beer to infants and toddlers. In Cameroon 20 per cent of the parents gave alcohol to children under 15 years.[3]

Deaths due to malnutrition caused indirectly by the social consequences of alcohol use go largely unnoticed. Disrupted families, unemployment, violence, crimes and loss of work force may all be related to excessive use of alcohol.

A survey conducted in four rural hospitals in Kenya revealed features of alcoholism in 3.1 per cent of out-patients.[4] At the Department of Psychiatry at the University Hospital in Tanzania 6.4 per cent of the patients were alcoholics.[5]

Accidents and violence

Traffic accidents are increasing everywhere in developing countries, but especially in Africa. According to the statistics of Tanzanian police, the share of drunken drivers in car accidents increased from 2.2 per cent in 1981 to 8.0 per cent in 1986. In Dar es Salaam 9.5 per

Table 12.3. Alcohol content in traditional homemade drinks.

Traditional alcohol	Alcohol content %
Non-distilled	
Palm wine, Cameroon	3.0
Palm wine, Tanzania	5.5
Raphia wine, Cameroon	3.0
Honey wine, Tanzania	7.2
Millet beer, Cameroon	3.0
Busaa maize beer, Kenya	2.0–4.0
Maize beer, Tanzania	2.2–6.9
Banana beer, Tanzania	3.3
Sugarcane beer, Tanzania	4.9
Distilled*	
Haa and arki, Cameroon	40.0
Changaa, Kenya	24.2–46.4
Gongo, Tanzania	24.2–29.3

* Sales are usually illegal

cent of traffic accident were related to alcohol. A total of 254 people died during one year and in 34 per cent of these alcohol played a part.[5] Many developing countries still have no legislation on drunken driving, or the prevention and control measures are not implemented properly.

Again, in Dar es Salaam every fourth of the adult trauma patients had been drinking. The incidence of alcohol-related accidents in the capital is somewhere between 100 and 300 per 100 000 inhabitants, but in the rural areas significantly lower, maybe 60 per 100 000. Traffic accidents were rare in the countryside and only one in ten adult trauma patients were drunk.[6]

According to a study in Zambia 8 per cent of the in-patients, 3.6 per cent of the fatal cases and 9 per cent of the out-patients had trauma; 24 per cent of traumas were caused by violence and 15 per cent by traffic accidents. However, it is usual that the police take notice of the role of alcohol while the health care personnel only register specific trauma diagnoses. Similar problems exist also in several other countries.[7]

More than 1000 murders or manslaughters were reported annually in Kenya during the 1970s which amounts to eight per 100 000. Approximately 23 per cent of the cases were related to alcohol. Estimates of alcohol-related

killings range between 37–50 per cent in other African countries. Thus, the influence of alcohol on violence seems to be lower in developing countries than in Europe or Northern America.[8]

Neurological damage

Alcohol causes a variety of neurological diseases and syndromes, both directly and indirectly. Damage is frequent in both central and peripheral neural tissues. The exact mechanisms behind cortical atrophy, dementia or epilepsy in alcoholics are not clear, although the depletion of thiamin (Vitamin B_1) certainly contributes to the development of Wernicke encephalopathy.[9]

Alcoholics are subject to head traumas at least three times more frequently than normal population. Recurrent cerebral contusions favour the development of dementia and cerebral atrophy.[9]

Alcoholics also smoke often. Arterial diseases related to smoking may increase the possibility of ischemic attacks and arterial dissections. Alcohol drinking can also lower the convulsion threshold in epilepsy.[9]

Fetal alcohol syndrome

The fetal alcohol syndrome (FAS) affects children of mothers who have used alcohol during pregnancy. The condition was not recognised in the scientific literature until 1973.[10] FAS features of the neonate include microcephaly, dysmorphic face, mental handicap and epilepsy. In older children the syndrome is characterised by delayed growth, disturbances in the development of the CNS and typical face.

The safe limits of alcohol use during pregnancy are not known, but the adverse effects on the fetus are the more severe the longer the predisposition to alcohol. Malformations develop during the first trimester and intelligence is affected from the second trimester. The intelligence deficits often manifest themselves at school age. *Abstaining from alcohol during pregnancy benefits the child.*[11]

Other diseases

Alcohol is one of the direct causes of hepatitis and cirrhosis of the liver. Alcohol-induced hepatitis is one of the warning signals on the road to liver cirrhosis. The liver is usually able to regenerate after a bout of hepatitis, provided that the use of alcohol is discontinued. Women develop cirrhosis after a much smaller daily alcohol intake than men. Hepatitis B, so common in developing countries (Chapter 24), can make the illness worse.

Maize liqueurs have been connected with oesophageal cancer in African regions where its use is plentiful. This distilled drink contains several carcinogenic substances, but the high alcohol content may also play a role.[12]

HARMFUL SUBSTANCES IN ALCOHOL

More than 1300 chemical substances have been identified in bottled alcoholic drinks. These include taste giving substances, but also toxic heavy metals, methanol and fusal alcohols. Usually their concentrations are so small that they are not considered to pose major health risks. The situation may be quite different with regard to homemade drinks, but these have not been studied in detail.

Methanol is potent solvent for industrial use, but is sometimes, out of ignorance or pure irresponsibility, sold as an alcohol beverage. Consumption of methanol causes death, blindness or severe intoxication.

Aflatoxin

Aflatoxin is one particularly harmful substance in homemade alcohols. It is a mycotoxin produced by several moulds that can contaminate grain used for making food or drink. Aflatoxin B_1 is a most potent carcinogen. It has been estimated that aflatoxin could explain about half of all liver cancers.[13,14] Again, hepatitis B may be a contributing factor.

There are reports of aflatoxin in homemade millet or maize-based alcohols in Nigeria, Zambia and Tanzania. In the Quidong area in China the population receives annually more than 1 gram of aflatoxin B_1 in rice, maize and alcoholic beverages. There is an exceptional prevalence of liver cancer in this particular area.

In many places in Africa it is customary, in the initial stages of beer brewing, to give the gruel to children. The drink does not contain much alcohol, but may be contaminated by aflatoxin. In children with kwashiorkor the detoxification capacity of the liver may be impaired, which results in accumulation of aflatoxin.

POLICY AND ACTION PROBLEMS

The chances of developing countries to control the alcohol industry are severely limited by the size of the multinational companies and their expansion to multisectoral companies. Practically all leading alcohol companies have today other production and marketing branches, especially in the food industry.

The pricing policies in developing countries take only seldom into account the adverse effects of alcohol. There may be incoming funds from industrial production and imports of alcohol, but the funds are certainly not channelled to health care. In addition, homemade alcohols are usually completely uncontrollable. Furthermore, a counter-force to the promotion of alcohol is lacking as public health education campaigns on alcohol are few. Legislation and pressure groups limiting the sales and marketing are similarly scarce.

In international cooperation the adverse effects of alcohol have been largely neglected. The WHO employs only few people to work on alcohol issues. At the same time there are hundreds of employees within the UN system dealing with drug abuse. The situation reflects the general morals: the adverse impacts of alcohol are tremendous but because of the economic interests, concerted international efforts are not possible. Opium cultivation has been reduced in the Golden Triangle, but who would eradicate Guinness from Ireland?

TOWARDS HEALTH EDUCATION

In the beginning of 1980s the Blue Cross, an international temperance organisation, conducted an extensive survey on the knowledge and attitudes of 18–26 year olds in the Congo. It was a surprisingly common misbelief that the human body needs alcohol to function properly. Beer was believed to be nutritious and red wine considered a good remedy for anemia. The alcohol industry tends to reinforce similar images worldwide. Pointing out that beer-drinking makes your belly round is a nice marketing trick in countries where obesity is traditionally regarded as a sign of prosperity.

Temperance organisations, somewhat dormant in industrialised countries, have found new grounds in developing countries during the 1980s. Especially the politically and religiously non-aligned International Organization of Good Templars (IOGT) has started and helped many NGOs in developing countries. Abstinence is a mobilising ideology, much in the same way as it used to be in the beginning of this century in industrialised countries. In 1985 IOGT opened the Alcohol and Drugs Information Centre in Sri Lanka. As a centre working for health education and alcohol policies this is the first collaborative effort of an NGO and government officials.

It is evident that the increasing consumption of alcohol is an additional burden to the health care in developing countries. National alcohol legislation is in need of updating in several countries. Health education will need many more active NGOs that support healthy living by fighting alcoholic drinks.

The starting point to health education could be for example the family finances. Shall we buy 1 litre of milk to the children or 1 litre of homemade beer; 10 litres of milk or 1 litre of bottled beer? Health education on alcohol should be included in MCH activities. Fetal alcohol syndrome, aflatoxin and the safe development and growth of the children remain the challenges for the PHC personnel. Abstinence is a sound alternative.

TOBACCO IN DEVELOPING COUNTRIES

One of the most harmful consequences of the discovery of America a half millennium ago was the spread of tobacco to all parts of the world. In the past, smoking tobacco was regarded as a habit or cultural phenomenon only. There was a phase when tobacco was appreciated as a medicinal herb curing all diseases, but the discussion about the positive health effects of tobacco ceased a long time ago. Harmful health effects of tobacco have become the focus of attention, especially after the Second World War. This has led to an intensive war between health professionals and the tobacco industry, the health care policy and the economic policy. Tobacco legislation to reduce smoking has developed in many countries while nothing has happened in others.

TOBACCO OR HEALTH

Tobacco is used mainly by smoking but also as a smokeless tobacco (snuff, chewing tobacco). Rapid absorption of the various substances of tobacco smoke guarantees a rapid subjective experience. There are thousands of substances in the smoke. The main groups of the substances are tobacco tar, nicotine and carbon monoxide. From the medical point of view the main constituents of tobacco smoke are cancer-producing substances, irritant substances, nicotine, and carbon monoxide and other gases.

Morbidity and mortality

Apart from nicotine dependency, tobacco smoking does not cause a specific tobacco disease but it increases the incidence and prevalence of several diseases. This results in increased mortality, especially from diseases of the respiratory and circulatory systems and cancer.

Mortality from pulmonary cancer is 10.8 times more common among smokers than among non-smokers. The odds ratios (OR) are significantly increased also for mortality from bronchitis and bronchiectasia, laryngeal cancer, oral cancer, esophageal cancer, gastric and duodenal ulcer, liver cirrhosis, and cancer of the urinary bladder.

Extra mortality from the above diseases has less influence on total mortality than increased mortality from coronary heart disease (CHD) although the OR is only 1.7. This means that extra mortality from CHD among cigarette smokers is on average 70 per cent higher than among non-smokers.

In 1965 about one million people in the world died as the result of tobacco use. The vast majority of these were from developed countries.

If the present consumption trends continue, in 2025 there will be ten million deaths attributable to tobacco and seven million of these in developing countries. This means that about 15 per cent of the mortality in developing countries will be caused by the use of tobacco.

Respiratory diseases

Chronic bronchitis is common among smokers. It is frequently complicated by febrile episodes of exacerbation. Another serious complication of chronic bronchitis is emphysema.

Most emphysema patients are chronic tobacco smokers. Rare among non-smokers, pulmonary cancer is a well-known dangerous disease of smokers. Its incubation period is two decades or more.

Table 12.4. Adult *per capita* cigarette consumption in selected countries in 1990.

Cigarette consumption	Europe	Asia	Africa	Americas	Australia and Oceania
< 500		Papua New Guinea Nepal Afghanistan Myanmar India Bangladesh Sri Lanka	Chad Guinea Ethiopia Sudan Mozambique Niger Liberia Uganda Zaire Tanzania Nigeria Ghana Zambia Madagascar Kenya	Haiti Peru Bolivia Guatemala	
501–1000	Norway	Laos Vietnam Pakistan Cambodia Iran	Angola Senegal Congo Togo Cameroon Morocco	El Salvador Ecuador Jamaica Panama Honduras Mexico	
1001–1500	The Netherlands Albania	Thailand Syria North Korea Indonesia Yemen Saudi Arabia	Egypt Algeria South Africa	Paraguay Dominican Rep. Costa Rica Barbados Guyana Venezuela Chile Nicaragua Uruguay Argentina	Fiji West Samoa
1501–2000	Russia Belgium Luxemburg Sweden Romania Denmark Bulgaria Finland Great Britain	Hong Kong Singapore Jordan Philippines Malaysia	Tunisia Mauritius	Colombia Brazil Netherland's Antilles	
2001–2500	Italy France Austria Germany Ireland	China Turkey Taiwan Israel	Libya	Canada	New Zealand
2501–3000	Spain Iceland Switzerland	Kuwait Iraq South Korea		USA	Australia
>3000	Poland Yugoslavia Hungary Greece Malta Cyprus	Japan Brunei United Arab Emirates Lebanon Macau		Cuba	

Table 12.5. Preventive interventions in the tobacco problem.

Health information	Health education at school
	Health information for adults
Smoking withdrawal	Ambulatory guidance
	Stationary withdrawal
Legislation	Prohibiting smoking
	Protection of non-smokers
	Limitation of harmful substances
	Follow-up of harmful substances
	Prohibition of advertising
Price policy	Regulation of tobacco prices according to general price level
	Connection of prices and taxes with the quantity of harmful substances
Technological changes	Reduction of harmful substances of tobacco products
	Surrogates for tobacco
Research	

Involuntary smoking

The effects of tobacco smoking are not limited only to the smoker. So called involuntary or passive smoking is a great problem for people living with a smoker or working indoors together with them. It results in irritation of the eyes and nose, headache and cough. Incidence of infections among children is higher in families with smoking members.

The most unprotected passive smoker is the fetus of a smoking woman. Numerous studies have shown that the babies of smoking mothers are on average 200 grams lighter than those born to non-smoking mothers. The risk of spontaneous abortion, fetal death and neonatal death increases with maternal smoking during pregnancy. The smoking mother also transmits nicotine to her child through her milk.

Non-smoking husbands and wives who live for several decades with a smoking companion are at risk of developing cancer of the lungs and several other organs or cardiovascular diseases.

HUNTING GROUND FOR INDUSTRY

The rate of smoking has been highest in industrialised countries but has decreased there about 1 per cent per year. The transnational tobacco industry promotes tobacco marketing, especially in developing countries, because it is able to get new consumers there. Tobacco smoking has increased there more than the population. Women and children are special target groups as potential future smokers.

It is difficult to present exact numbers of tobacco consumption in various countries. Demographic differences between countries in the age structure distribution makes total consumption per head a misleading index of consumption. Table 12.4 shows adult consumption of cigarettes, the most commonly used form of tobacco, *per capita* by country in 1990. The location of various countries in the table tells something of their economic and cultural development.

There is special legislation to reduce smoking in many industrialised countries. Smoking is limited in public places, selling of tobacco to minors is prohibited, warning texts are included in tobacco packages, advertising of tobacco is limited or prohibited and the composition of tobacco products regulated. Although legislation alone is unable to reduce smoking, it is an important link in the chain of measures to reduce it. In countries with no tobacco legislation it is easy to promote the sale of tobacco. As long as there are no restrictions, the transnational tobacco industry will spread products in developing countries even if they were prohibited in industrial countries. In tobacco cultivating countries this problem is especially severe.

Cultivation of tobacco seems to have immediate favourable influences on the economy of the country but in the long term it is harmful. A considerable area of land which would be needed for the cultivation of food-stuffs is used to produce a harmful herb. Many tobacco cultivating countries are compelled to import food. Tobacco cultivation effectively promotes deforestation by eliminating trees from tobacco fields and burning wood for the processing of tobacco leaves. Deforestation in turn promotes soil erosion.

MEASURES TO REDUCE SMOKING

The is no single measure to solve the problem of tobacco smoking. The main points are health information and education, smoking withdrawal, legislation, price policy, technological changes in tobacco products and research (Table 12.5). To be effective all these means should be used. The work should be continuous.

Many promotion channels could be closed if legislation is up to date. The image of smoking as a status symbol or indication of prosperity and success should be changed. It depends on a false fantasy created by tobacco advertising.

Lack of money is one of the most important limiting factors for tobacco smoking. For example in Tanzania a package of tobacco costs as much as a worker's daily wage. When dependency is created increased prosperity is drained by increased tobacco consumption.

It is easiest to influence the male population in middle or older age. Stopping smoking spontaneously increases with age. Many consider stopping when they personally experience the harmful effect of smoking. Young people are not interested in consequences that may appear after years or decades. Therefore, it is important to stress the immediate effects e.g. impaired physical performance, acute diseases, negative effect on appearance and inhibiting effect on sex life.

References

1. Pan Lyn. Alcohol in colonial Africa. Forssa, Finland: Alkoholitutkimussäätiö, 1975. (The Finnish Foundation of Alcohol Studies, Volume 22)
2. Samarasinghe DS. The Buddhist, Hindu and Islamic influence on alcohol. In: Maula J, Lindblad M., Tigerstedt C, eds. Alcohol in developing countries. Proceedings from a meeting in Oslo, Norway, August 7–9, 1988. Helsinki: Nordic Council for Alcohol and Drug Research (NAD), 1990. (NAD-publication No. 18)
3. Yguel J. Consumption of alcoholic drinks in three different parts of Cameroon. In: Maula J, Lindblad M., Tigerstedt C, eds. Alcohol in developing countries. Proceedings from a meeting in Oslo, Norway, August 7–9, 1988. Helsinki: Nordic Council for Alcohol and Drug Research (NAD), 1990. (NAD-publication No. 18)
4. Acuda SW. International Review Series: Alcohol and alcohol problems research. 1. East Africa. Br J Addiction 1985;80:121–6.
5. Kilonzo GP. Tanzania. In: Kortteinen T, ed. State monopolies and alcohol prevention. Report and working papers of a collaborative international study. Helsinki: The Social Research Institute of Alcohol Studies, 1989: 591-624 (Report No. 181)
6. Kilonzo GP, Pitkänen YT, eds. Pombe. Report of alcohol research project in Tanzania, 1988–90. Helsinki: Helsinki University Printing House, 1992. (University of Helsinki, Institute of Development Studies, Report B 24/1992)
7. Haworth A. Alcohol-related casualties in Africa. In: Giesbrecht N, Gonzalez R, Grant M, *et al.* Drinking and casualties: accidents, poisonings and violence in an international perspective. London: Croom Helm Associated Publishers, 1990.
8. Partanen J. Sociability and intoxication. Alcohol and drinking in Kenya, Africa, and the modern world. Jyväskylä, Finland: Gummerus, 1991. (The Finnish Foundation for Alcohol Studies, Volume 39)
9. Thomas PK. Alcohol and disease: central nervous system. Acta Med Scand 1985;703 (Suppl):251–64.
10. Jones KL, Smith DW. Recognition of fetal alcohol syndrome in early infancy. Lancet 1973;ii:999–1001.
11. Autti-Rämö I. The outcome of children exposed to alcohol *in utero*. Academic dissertation. Jyväskylä: Gummerus, 1993.
12. Acuda SW. Alcohol research in developing countries: possibilities and limitations. In: Maula J, Lindblad M, Tigerstedt C, eds. Alcohol in developing countries. Proceedings from a meeting, Oslo, 1988. Helsinki: Nordic Council for Alcohol and Drug Research (NAD), 1990 (NAD-publication No 18)
13. Hsu IC, Metcalf RA, Sun T, Welsh JA, Wang NJ, Harris CC. Mutational hotspot in the p53 gene in human hepatocellular carcinomas. Nature 1991;350:427–8.
14. Bressac B, Kew M, Wands J, Ozturk M. Selective Grams to T mutations of p53 gene in hepatocellular carcinoma from southern Africa. Nature 1991;350:429–30.

Additional reading

1. Cavanagh J, Clairmonte FF. Alcoholic beverages: Dimensions of corporate power. The Globe 4/1983 (International Organisation of Good Templars, Oslo)
2. Clairmonte F, Cavanagh J. Merchants of drink. Transnational control of world beverages. Penang: Third World Network, 1988.
3. National Center for Chronic Disease Prevention and Health Promotion, Office on Smoking and Health. Smoking and health in the Americas. Atlanta, Georgia: U.S. Department of Health and Human Services, Public Health Service, Centers for Disease Control, 1992. (DHHS Publication No. CDC 92–8419)
4. Chapman S. Changes in adult cigarette consumption per head on 128 countries, 1986–90. Tobacco Control, 1992;1:282–4.
5. Hirvonen L. Avoiding the risk factors of noncommunicable diseases. Oulu: University of Oulu, Department of Physiology and ETRA Association, Turku, Finland, 1989.
6. Peto R, Lopez AD, Boreham J, Thun M, Healt C. Mortality from tobacco in developed countries: Indirect estimation from national statistics. Lancet, 1992;339:1268–1278.
7. Resisting tobacco in developing countries. Working papers in support of the 8th World Conference on Tobacco or Health: Building a tobacco-free world. Buenos Aires, Argentina 1992.

About the authors

Heikki Jokinen is a freelance journalist. He served in 1987–91 as a member of the State Delegation of Temperance and Alcohol Affairs, Finland. He has also been a board member in the Alcohol Researchers' Association for several years. Heikki Jokinen has done research on the alcohol policy of the European Community and published several papers on alcohol problems in developing countries.

Y. Tapio Pitkänen is medical officer and general practitioner in charge of Primary Health Care in Municipal Southeast Health Centre in Helsinki, Finland. Specialist in internal medicine and infectious diseases, he also holds the Diploma in Tropical Medicine and Hygiene from the University of Liverpool. In the 1970s he worked for 4 years in Tanzania and during 1988–90 was in charge of an alcohol research project conducted there.

Leo Hirvonen specialised in physiology and clinical physiology, and served as Professor of Physiology at the University of Oulu. He was one of the pioneers of cardiac physiology in Finland and was also deeply involved with health education activities, both as a writer and lecturer. Leo Hirvonen died in a traffic accident in July 1993.

Lankinen KS, Bergström S, Mäkelä PH and Peltomaa M, eds.
Health and disease in developing countries. London:The Macmillan Press Limited, 1994:115–121.

13 GLOBAL REFUGEE PROBLEMS

Eeva Kemppi-Repo, Reverend, M.Th.
The Finnchurchaid
Luotsikatu 1 A, FIN-00160 Helsinki,
Finland

INTRODUCTION

People on the move is an image used often to describe refugees, asylum seekers, displaced people and migrants. Today this group of people constitutes a growing population in all parts of the world. It is a widespread and dispersed people on the move.

During the past decade and a half the refugee issue has become a burning and complex global problem without any easy solutions. Hardly a day goes by without refugee or migration issues appearing in the global news agenda: in 1992 news items included, for instance, stories about Somalis leaving their country, ex-Yugoslavians escaping to neighbouring countries, Cambodians repatriating after a long history of war and violence, uprooted people from the ex-Soviet Union seeking better living conditions both in the newly independent states of Europe and in Western Europe. The list could continue.

Some scholars conclude that present situations are indications of the breakdown of the international system of refugee protection.[1] Some others emphasise that the refugee phenomenon is an indication of the interconnectedness of causes that threaten human survival. Such causes comprise the crisis in global economy, lack of democracy, environmental disasters, growing xenophobia, population growth, desertification etc.[1]

Irrespective of the different interpretations of the situation, scholars seem to share a common view about the global refugee issues turning into permanent and worldwide problems that require serious attention of the international community. Even though, every now and then, refugee-producing conflicts get settled, new wars and conflicts emerge, once again forcing people to flee. Characteristic of the situation is a tendency for prolonged periods of exile. The international community, which even after the Second World War could maintain hopes for solving refugee problems with international efforts, has been challenged with wider responsibilities than it was prepared to respond to.

ANNUAL AVERAGE ON THE INCREASE

There are estimates giving figures of some 75–85 million uprooted people, who had to leave their country after the Second World War.[2] The global annual average of refugees remained, however, rather small, from two to three millions, in the period between the late 1950s and the mid-1970s, with the exception of 1971–1972, when the fight for independence in Bangladesh drove some 10 million people out of East Pakistan into India.

Only in the late 1970s a major increase in the annual number occurred with a leap to 10–15 million. This was due to several coinciding factors in South-East Asia, the Horn of Africa and Afghanistan which all produced a regional exodus of people.[2]

The annual average of refugees has been growing steadily ever since without significant halts. The United Nations High Commissioner for Refugees (UNHCR) estimated

Table 13.1. Refugees in the world continents, UNHCR statistics as of 31 December 1992.

Continent	Approximate total population	1991 (millions)	1992
Africa	650	5	5
Asia and the Pacific	3 200	0.8	1
Europe	500	1.2	4.5
American continent	724	2	2
South-West Asia, North Africa and the Middle East	280	8	6.5
Total	5 000	17	19

that there were 18.8 million refugees at the end of the year 1992, the highest number ever (Table 13.1).

ROOT CAUSES MANIFOLD

The root causes of refugee problems are manifold, national and international, individual and social, political and economic. Generally speaking they relate to internal and external armed, ethnic or other conflicts, economic hardship of individuals and nations, governmental policies of control, foreign interventions and interference, and to natural and environmental disasters. Often several of these components are interconnected and intertwined and there is only seldom one single cause for the decision to seek protection from outside the country of origin.[1]

The massive movements of African people in the 1960s illustrate the catalytic factors generating from both national and international policies as well as from political, ethnic and economic causes. Formation of liberation movements, independence of African states, changes in economic and social infrastructures, and tensions in ethnic relations all resulted in refugees.

For instance, the independence movements produced refugees within the supporters of the colonial powers as well as within their own constituency when political and ideological orientation and differences in strategies

resulted in division. The conflict that led to the independence of Angola in 1975 generated in 1961–75 half a million refugees, most of whom crossed the border to Zaire. A similar development took place in Mozambique after the independence also in 1975, causing at that point some 80 000 people to move to Tanzania and other neighbouring countries.[2] Later on the war in Mozambique has produced one of Africa's largest refugee populations in Malawi.

The Cold War period intensified some refugee problems, like the flight of Afghan refugees in 1978–1979 after the invasion of the Soviet Union and the complex issues of the Indochinese refugees.[1] Even after the start of the repatriation the Afghan refugees still constitute the world's largest refugee population (beside the Palestinians) with 2.9 million still in Iran and 1.6 million in Pakistan, most of them living in camps at the end of 1992.

CONFLICTS, WARS, NATURAL DISASTERS

Emerging ethnic and religious conflicts often produce an influx of refugees when people feel that their ethnic or religious identity is threatened. In Sudan a new conflict started in 1983 over the national rule of the Islamic Sharia law in addition to a disagreement on the governance of the Southern Sudan. The UNHCR statistics of 1992 indicate that 260 000 Sudanese refugees have been admitted in the neighbouring countries. According to relief organisations, almost 2 million people were displaced at the same time within Sudan. In the same year in ex-Yugoslavia nearly 3 million persons were either internally displaced or living as refugees in neighbouring countries, because of ethnic conflicts.

War and violence constitute in many parts of the world a prolonged risk to life and provide reasons to seek security from outside the country of origin. In South-East Asia problems started in the mid-1970s with the end of the Vietnam war. The refugee situation culminated in 1979–81 with a massive exodus of about a million refugees from Vietnam in 1981, an estimated 850 000 from Kampuchea and some 250 000 from Laos.[2]

Often refugee issues are also seen as security issues. When large populations, for one reason or another, start to move in an uncontrolled way they pose problems of stability to societies.

Throughout the human history natural disasters, droughts, floods, volcano eruptions and hurricanes, have forced groups of people to seek shelter and care from outside the disaster area and in another country. According to some estimates, the devastating drought in Africa in the beginning of the 1990s affected over 20 million people, making large populations displaced and forcing rural populations to migrate to big cities.

Environmental disasters have become new threats to human survival, also producing refugees. The nuclear accident in Chernobyl in the former Soviet Union in 1986 contaminated large areas forcing people to leave the region for decades. Environmental degradation, such as erosion, deforestation and desertification, force more and more people to move from countryside to cities in search for opportunities for survival. Estimates of the number of 'environmental' refugees range from 10 to 15 million.

HUMAN RIGHTS VIOLATIONS AND ECONOMY

A dramatic development of the 1973 coup d'état in Chile resulted in the oppression of the opponents to the military junta. Some estimates end up with a figure of over 200 000 Chileans forced to seek for asylum after the coup.

Throughout the 1980s, death squads, military dictatorship, summary executions, forced relocation of indigenous people and massive human rights violations marked the policy of governments in many Latin and Central American countries from which people had to flee for their personal security. Coinciding with the international debt crisis, which affected severely many economies of the region, the living conditions worsened, adding an economic element to the political motivation for flight. The reasons why people seek protection outside their country of origin are quite often a mixture of political and economic factors. Flight becomes an option if there is no work or food available and the government is exercising restrictions in political freedoms.[1]

EMERGENCIES AND DEVELOPMENT ISSUES

There are differing approaches to refugee issues. To the public in the North, refugees are often seen as emergency and relief issues, or as issues relating to foreign and immigration policy. Refugees represent victims of violence and individual repression of authoritarian governments. This approach emphasises quick response with material and relief aid including preparedness for settlement. This approach has been increasingly challenged with addressing the root causes that make people leave.

A connection is made between general development and refugee problems more often in the Southern countries. Over 90 per cent of all refugees of the world live in developing countries, often crossing the border to the neighbouring countries as a reaction to repressive government policies of their country of origin. 'The poorest people in the world are knocking at the doors of the poorest countries', concluded Poul Hartling, a former United Nations High Commissioner for Refugees.

Refugees generate additional responsibilities and challenges to many developing countries in which resources are often overstretched in providing the minimum human standards of living to their own populations. When the international assistance is not sufficient, the burden for the care of refugees of Third World economies can become critical. Self-evidently refugee issues are seen as human rights issues. Refugee influx is often generated because of human rights violations in the country of origin.

INTERNATIONAL PROTECTION

International instruments have been developed for the protection of refugees. Soon after the Second World War in 1951 the UN adopted a Convention relating to the Status of Refugees. The Convention provides the basic definition of who is a refugee, provisions for the legal status of refugees and their rights and the duties in their country of refuge and other provisions with the implementation of the instruments from the administrative and diplomatic standpoint.[3]

At the time of adopting the Convention it was limited to refugee situations that were known to exist at that time, and to meet particularly the needs in Europe. With the passage of time and the emergence of new refugee situations the need was felt to make the provisions of the 1951 Convention global. As a result, the Protocol relating to the Status of Refugees was opened to governments for

Young refugee at Ban Nam Yao camp, Thailand.
Photo: UNHCR/N. van Praag

accession in 1967. Over one hundred governments have ratified either the Convention or the Protocol.

According to the 1951 Convention refugees are persons who, 'owing to a well-founded fear of being persecuted for reasons of race, religion, nationality, membership of a particular social group or political opinion, is outside the country of his nationality and is unable or, owing to such fear, unwilling to avail himself of the protection of that country, or who, not having a nationality and being outside the country of his former habitual residence, is unable or, owing to such fear, is unwilling to return to it.'[3]

REGIONAL APPROACHES

Because of the narrow UN definition of a refugee status, which fails for instance to provide a refugee status on grounds of general conditions of war or armed conflicts, regional approaches have been developed to broaden the definition, thus reflecting more realistically the refugee situation in the region.

The first regional convention was developed by the Organization of African Unity (OAU) in 1969 when it resolved that a refugee is a person to whom the UN refugee criteria can be applied and 'every person, owing to external aggression, occupation, foreign domination, or events seriously disturbing public order in either part or the whole of his country of origin or nationality, is compelled to leave his place of habitual residence in order to seek refuge in another place outside his country of origin or nationality.'[4] This OAU Convention has been adopted by over 40 African governments.

Another regional instrument was developed by ten Latin American governments in 1984 when they adopted the Declaration of Cartagena. This declaration includes as refugees those 'who have fled their country because their lives, safety or freedom have been threatened by generalised violence, foreign aggression, internal conflicts, massive violation of human rights or other circumstances which have seriously disturbed public order.'[1] The Cartagena Declaration is non-binding but Central American governments apply it in addition to the UN definition.

Discussion on the shortcomings of the UN definition is on the agenda of the international community. NGOs including many churches are advocating the broadening of the refugee definition to meet better with the *de facto* refugee situations. So far the international community has not been able to develop a commonly shared international protection system to the displaced persons.

HUMANITARIAN LAW

Humanitarian law has been developed for the protection of civilian non-combatants. The Geneva Conventions of 1949 are binding to all parties in conflict. They stipulate that persons taking no active part in the hostilities shall be cared for without discrimination.[5]

The Geneva Conventions prohibit certain acts, like torture and inhuman treatment, summary executions, deportation and destruction of civilian objects. They oblige all parties to provide for instance all sick and wounded with adequate medical care, to allow free passage to relief for civilian groups, and respect for the physical integrity.

Under the provisions of these four conventions the International Committee of the Red Cross (ICRC) is mandated to protect and assist both displaced persons and refugees who are victims of armed conflicts. They authorise the ICRC delegates to visit camps for prisoners of war and civilian internees, to deliver medical, food and material assistance, to set up reception facilities, to construct camps and to trace family members as well as to facilitate family reunification.

NON-REFOULEMENT AS A RULE

The UN Convention provides a set of rights for refugees, including the right to non-refoulement, i.e. not to be forcibly repatriated to the country of origin. This rule is one of the main cornerstones of international refugee protection. It means that under no circumstances shall a refugee be expelled or returned 'to the frontiers of territories where his life or freedom would be threatened on account of his race, religion, nationality, membership of a particular social group or political opinion'.[6]

Repatriation can take place only on the condition that there are proved guarantees of the personal safety of the returnee.

INDIVIDUAL TRAGEDIES

It is often said that no one wishes to be a refugee, but sometimes flight to another country is the only available option left for those who become refugees. When people decide to leave their home country they often see no future in their country and their only experience is that the present has become unbearable for them.

The decision to leave is always a difficult one, a jump to the unknown. Sometimes a persecuted family member has to leave secretly without even informing the family for fear of repression or detention of members of family. For security reasons many Vietnamese parents prepared their children for a visit to relatives before entering a refuge boat in hopes for a safe haven. Before taking the decision for flight, the individual or family history is often marked by fear, harassment and humiliation in the home country.

The journey of escape includes risks and dangers, particularly to the vulnerable groups, the children, the women, the aged and the disabled. Disintegration from family and cultural environment, experienced physical and psychological pressure traumatise to a certain extent the life of most refugees. Most refugees have been exposed to violence in one way or another. They or their family members have been victims of violence, terror, rape, physical abuse and other forms of humiliation. These incidents and memories, often purposely hidden because of their painfulness, provide the psychological background for the integration of refugees in a new environment.

Violence produces immediate consequences of pain, fear and death. Later on psychological effects appear, characterised by re-experiencing the traumatic events. This may be manifested in various kinds of symptoms like insomnia, moodiness, emotional numbness, dizziness and different kinds of pains.[7] Many have difficulties in expressing feelings, and they often hide guilt feelings about their survival because others did not survive.

Feelings of betrayal can be manifested in hostility towards authorities, including doctors. In a refugee's experience doctors may be connected to monitoring or even participating in torture sessions. Feelings of hostility can be provoked also by unknown countrymen who might be suspected of spying and therefore seen as a security risk to a refugee or to the family.[7]

Counselling services as well as mental and health care try to facilitate the rehabilitation and integration when settlement or resettlement is arranged. Among other measures used to fit refugees in the new environment are education, instruction in local language, vocational training and income-generating opportunities.

SPECIAL PROTECTION FOR WOMEN

Refugee women and girls represent the majority of the refugee populations in many countries hosting refugees. Characteristic of the situation of refugee women is a doubly disadvantaged position. In addition to the trauma of uprooting they often become responsible for the whole household after the loss of the husband. This situation entails both economic and cultural challenges to women whose social position gets changed.

Specific protection issues concerning refugee women include physical security, involving violations of the physical integrity of refugee women during flight, in camps, settlements and border areas. In 1987, the UNHCR issued a set of international guidelines, explaining the objectives of international protection of refugee women and girls.[8]

Incidence of rape, abduction, sexual harassment and the obligation to grant 'sexual favours' in return for documentation or relief goods remain distressing phenomena in the life of women refugees. In our time the horror stories about the fate of Indochinese women and girls at the South China Sea, and the Muslim women in ex-Yugoslavia have highlighted the need for special measures for the safety of refugee women.

EXODUS AFFECTS PARTICULARLY CHILDREN

Organised violence constitutes a threat particularly to the growth of a child, disturbing his or her physical and psychosocial development. Often children have experienced malnutrition before arriving in the host country. In many cases they are confronted with the breakdown of the family structure and the loss of family members. Children have often eye-witnessed the detention, disappearance or torture of their family members and they themselves may have been targets of violence. Their everyday life is marked by feelings of being aliens in a new cultural environment. Much like the adults also children often suffer from guilt for their survival.[9]

With exile new family structures need to be developed. Often this destabilises children who have learnt to relate to a certain social network of people typical of their culture. Depression, withdrawal and lack of interest can be symptoms of disturbance in a child's development. Children mourn the losses they have experienced, but in favourable conditions they start in due time to develop new networks of trust. In unfavourable conditions a child's development can get stagnated and result in behavioural aggression, anguish or hyperactivity.[9]

Refugee children suffer from uprootedness. They suffer from losing the identity of their culture which they as children never knew as well as their parents, and they have often difficulties in identifying their new cultural roles.

FAMILY REUNION HIGHLIGHTED

The UNHCR has a coordinating role with a view to promoting the reunion of separated refugee families through appropriate interventions with governments and inter- as well as non-governmental organisations. Even though the family reunification is not confirmed in the UN 1951 Convention, the unity of family is acknowledged as an essential right of the refugee and governments are requested by the UNHCR to apply liberal criteria in identifying those family members who can be admitted.

In many cases family reunion provides the healing component to the painful experiences. It invites the potential for personal resources, initiatives and creativity to bridge the present and the past. Family as the smallest unit of society also encourages cultural change and enrichment with the new environment.

DURABLE SOLUTIONS

The durable solutions promoted by the UNHCR are, in order of preference: voluntary repatriation, integration in the country of first asylum, or resettlement in a third country.

Voluntary repatriation can be considered only when conditions in the country of origin have changed so much that the refugees no longer believe their lives or liberty to be threatened. The UNHCR's role is to ensure that asylum can continue until the refugees have received sufficiently convincing evidence of the conditions in which their return can take place.

In Africa, where refugees have been moving since the 1960s into neighbouring countries, they have generally been admitted unconditionally. Ever since African states have become known as very generous to refugees in the international community. As most of the refugees came from a rural background, integration could often start without delay. People settled down in or near villages among local people. The intention of settlement is to bring refugees to the same level of self-sufficiency as the local population.[9]

When large populations move and stay in another country for long periods of time, like in Africa, it is important to facilitate the self-sufficiency of the refugees as much as possible. Rather quick integration in local life is necessary also because of maintaining local political and social stability.

When neither voluntary repatriation nor settlement is available, resettlement in a third country becomes an option. An illustrative example of a large international resettlement operation is the fate of of the Indochinese refugees. The UNHCR called for international action in 1978 and 1979 and, as a response to the UNHCR appeals, about 20 countries established immigration quotas and accepted 840 000 Indochinese refugees. Many of those have now been repatriated.

FUNDING RESPONSIBILITIES

The industrialised countries have admitted only a small percentage of refugees. Before the ex-Yugoslavian crisis only some 5 per cent of the world's refugee population was living in Western Europe. The trend of the 1990s is to make restrictions to refugee and asylum policies throughout the Western European continent. All this takes place in the climate of the harshening of public opinion towards refugees in general.

However, up to 90–95 per cent of the UNHCR's annual spending is covered by the industrialised world. The annual spending is around 500 million USD. Funding has not been equivalent to the needs, and with the decline in the world economy the industrialised world is also tightening the contributions to the UNHCR. The indicators for solving the global refugee problems in the 1990s are not too positive, quite the opposite.

International NGOs including churches and church-related agencies operate actively with the UNHCR in emergencies and relief operations, as well as in programmes for settlement and resettlement. The NGOs' involvement includes an advocacy role for refugee issues in the public and operational tasks both in developing and industrialised countries.

NGOs have expressed their concern on various international fora about the future of refugees. They draw the attention of governments to an urgent need to tackle the refugee issues on humanitarian, political and economic levels as an issue for a peaceful future.

References

1. Ferris EG. Beyond borders. Refugees, migrants and human rights in the post-cold war era. Geneva: World Council of Churches, 1993:310.
2. Hakovirta H. The world refugee problem. Tampere: Hillside Publications, 1991:109.
3. 1951 Convention relating to the status of refugees, article I. A. 2, Handbook on procedure and criteria for determining refugee status under the 1951 Convention and the 1967 Protocol relating to the status of refugees. Geneva: Office of the United Nations High Commissioner for Refugees, 1979:93.
4. OAU Convention governing the specific aspects of refugee problems in Africa. In: Collection of international instruments concerning refugees. Geneva: Office of the United Nations High Commissioner for Refugees, 1988: 193–200.
5. The International Committee of the Red Cross. What it is, what it does. Geneva: ICRC, 1992:22.
6. Goodwin-Gill GS. The refugee in international law. Oxford: Clarendon Press, 1985:318.
7. Mizerez D, ed. Refugees – the trauma of exile. The humanitarian role of Red Cross and Red Crescent. Belgium: Martinus Nijhoff Publishers, 1988:340.
8. Executive Committee of the High Commissioner's Programme. A role of refugee women, 1988. In: Working with refugee women. A practical guide. Geneva: UNHCR, 1989:85–93.
9. Zarjevski Y. A future preserved. International assistance to refugees. Oxford: Pergamon Press, 1988:280.

Additional reading

1. All Africa Conference of Churches. Handbook for refugee workers. Nairobi: All Africa Conference of Churches, 1983:176.
2. Sandler R, Jones T, eds. Medical care of refugees. New York: Oxford University Press, 1987.

About the author

Eeva Kemppi-Repo is a Finnish pastor and journalist. As a journalist she has travelled extensively for reporting in developing countries during 1983–1987. She has covered refugee issues on several continents, exploring them from the points of view of refugees, government administration and non-governmental organisations including churches. When serving with the World Council of Churches as a senior press officer during 1988–1991 she was familiarised with the efforts of the ecumenical community for advocating refugee issues and facilitating refugee projects. From 1993 she serves as an executive secretary for refugees with the Finnchurchaid, the development cooperation arm of the Evangelical Lutheran Church of Finland.

II BURDEN OF INFECTIOUS DISEASES

Lankinen KS, Bergström S, Mäkelä PH and Peltomaa M, eds.
Health and disease in developing countries. London:The Macmillan Press Limited, 1994:125–134.

14 RESPIRATORY INFECTIONS

Petri Ruutu, M.D., Ph.D.
Helsinki University Central Hospital
Second Department of Medicine
Division of Infectious Diseases
FIN-00290 Helsinki, Finland

Marilla G. Lucero, M.D., D.T.M.&H.
Research Institute for Tropical Medicine
Alabang, Muntinlupa, Metro Manila
The Philippines

INTRODUCTION

The multiplicity of presenting syndromes together with problems in both clinical and etiological diagnosis, as well as the unreliability of official statistics in many developing countries delayed the recognition of childhood pneumonia as a major problem until recently. As late as in 1979 a major report on infectious disease problems in developing countries *did not include* childhood pneumonia, referred to as Acute Respiratory Infection (ARI), as a high priority problem, because 'a specific causative agent could not be established in most patients'.

In 1982, however, WHO established a special programme for the control of ARI, linked with the diarrhea control programme. With the success of the latter in decreasing the mortality of children, the relative importance of the respiratory infections has increased. Following the pattern created for the diarrhea control efforts a programme was developed by the WHO that could be applied in PHC settings without diagnostic technology.

The broad spectrum of causative microbes and associated variable clinical syndromes in children delayed the development of simply defined clinical criteria and led to changes in terminology over a relatively short period of time. Traditionally the acute respiratory infections have been classified in three groups. Upper respiratory tract infections include pharyngitis, tonsillitis, sinusitis, and otitis media. Midrespiratory tract syndromes consist of laryngotracheobronchitis and epiglottitis. Acute lower respiratory tract infections include bronchiolitis and pneumonia. Commonly, however, infections manifest themselves simultaneously on several levels of the respiratory tract.

Acute infections of the lower respiratory tract in children have a major public health impact and are the focus of this chapter. It is of note that the definitions of lower respiratory tract infections used in various studies and other contexts differ from each other. The abbreviation ARI has sometimes been used to denote all acute respiratory tract infections, in other contexts only to denote clinically defined acute lower respiratory tract infections (ALRI) as separate from upper respiratory tract infections. Additional confusion has been caused by the fact that ALRI is not strictly identical to pneumonia verified as an infiltrate in a chest X-ray. However, with the present refined clinical criteria of the WHO case management guidelines, the correlation is sufficiently good to base treatment decisions on. In the early phases of its ARI control programme the WHO used the term ARI for clinically defined pneumonia requiring antimicrobial treatment, but has recently returned to using the term pneumonia instead of ARI for lower respiratory tract infections. Subsequently in this chapter, if not otherwise stated, the term pneumonia is used to denote both the clinically defined ALRI according to the WHO case management guidelines, and X-ray verified pneumonia.

Measles and whooping cough are commonly treated separately from childhood pneumonia. However, it is important to realise that pneumonia and other bacterial infections commonly complicate these two infections.

EPIDEMIOLOGY OF CHILDHOOD PNEUMONIA

Morbidity

ARI presents an immense disease burden both to the community and to the health services. At least one-third of symptomatic illnesses in children under five are due to such infections.

Widely ranging figures for the incidence of pneumonia in children have been reported in community-based studies. The gross morbidity in all ARI of children less than 5 years old in developing countries varies from equal to double to that of industrialised countries, partly reflecting varying definitions used.[1,2] However, in developing countries a larger proportion of ARI presents as bronchiolitis or pneumonia. In community-based studies it is frequently difficult to define separate episodes of respiratory infections, as the majority of children have respiratory symptoms at least 75 per cent of the days observed, and most could be considered ill at any one time.[3,4] Similar studies from six different developing countries reported incidences ranging from 0.2 to 4.0 new episodes of ALRI per child per year for age groups below 5 years of age, thus demonstrating a 20-fold difference in incidence rates.[3] Correspondingly the children spent 1–14 per cent of their time with ALRI.

Younger children consistently have a higher incidence of pneumonia. Children below 1 year of age have a 1.5–2.5-fold, sometimes as much as five-fold higher incidence than children between the ages of 2 to 5 years in the same populations.

Treatment of ARI consumes a major proportion of the health care resources: 20 to 40 per cent of outpatient visits are due to respiratory infections. The incidence of ARI leading to hospital admission is 3.2–4.8 per thousand children per year. These admissions constitute 13–40 per cent of all admissions.

Mortality

In spite of the fact that the gross morbidity from all ARI in developing countries does not greatly differ from that in industrialised countries, the impact of pneumonia on mortality equals or surpasses that of diarrheal disease in children under 5 years of age (Figure 14.1). Both cause approximately one-third of all deaths in children less than 5 years old. Children in industrialised countries have also

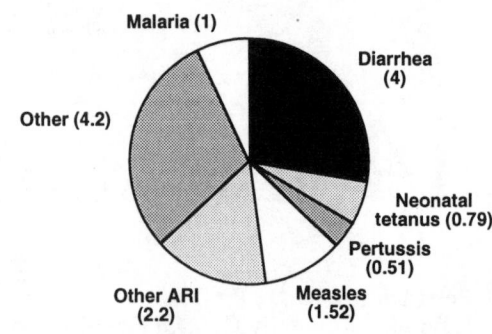

Figure 14.1. The causes of mortality in children less than 5 years of age in developing countries. The figures denote deaths in millions.[30]

until recently had a high mortality from pneumonia. Mortality from pneumonia during the first year of life in the USA in the 1910s was similar to that in Paraguay in the late 1970s (approximately 1500 deaths per 100 000 births), and the mortality in the USA in 1950 equalled that in Costa Rica about 30 years later.[2]

Globally ARI causes annually an estimated four million deaths in children.[5] In under-fives pneumonia causes approximately one-quarter of deaths, of which more than 90 per cent occur in developing countries. Children in this age group constitute approximately 15 per cent of the population in developing countries, but at least half of all deaths fall in this age group, and ARI causes one-third of the deaths. Pneumonia mortality is highest during the first year of life being three- to ten-fold higher than between the ages 1 to 4 years, and as much as 50- to 100-fold higher than in school age. Case fatality rates of children admitted to hospital for pneumonia range from 3 to 12 per cent, sometimes as high as 22 per cent.[6]

Risk factors

A number of risk factors related to the host and the environment increase the morbidity and/or mortality from pneumonia. These risk factors include low birth weight, malnutrition, lack of EPI coverage, low socioeconomic status and poor hygiene (Table 14.1). Many if not most of these risk factors are interacting with complex mechanisms, only some of which are known. An example of the interactions: the family income, the mother's education and her knowledge of appropriate foods for infants may interact to cause malnutrition

Table 14.1. Risk factors for morbidity and mortality from pneumonia in children in developing countries

Low birth weight
Absence of breast feeding
Missing EPI vaccinations
Malnutrition
Vitamin A deficiency
Indoor air pollution
Low socioeconomic status
Poor hygiene

in children and render them more susceptible to infection. Conditions related with poverty have also been strongly associated with mortality from pneumonia. For the subsequent discussion, only the relation of pneumonia to a few of the risk factors will be discussed.

Nutritional status. Malnutrition may increase the risk of acquiring pneumonia 10- to 12-fold.[7,8] Children in urban areas, frequently in slum-like conditions, commonly show higher pneumonia incidences than those in rural areas. The risk of dying has been reported to be seven-fold in children who are moderately malnourished.[9] Of severely malnourished children admitted to hospital for pneumonia almost 90 per cent die.[8,10,11] Studies in the Philippines have shown that the risk of death of malnourished children with severe pneumonia is two to three times higher than that of healthy children.[12]

Vitamin A deficiency. Interest in the relationship between vitamin A and ARI started in 1983 with the finding of Sommer *et al.* that vitamin A deficiency was associated with increased morbidity from respiratory infection and increased overall mortality. Subsequent controlled community-based and hospital-based trials have suggested that vitamin A supplementation reduces mortality from respiratory disease associated with measles, in addition to reducing mortality from all causes. A direct association of vitamin A deficiency with risk of ARI, however, has not been shown.[13] Theoretically, vitamin A is important in the maintenance of epithelisation of the respiratory tract and the pulmonary recovery process and plays a role in the host immune defence system.

Low birth weight. Low birth weight occurs in 15–30 per cent of newborns in developing countries and is associated with an increased risk of morbidity and mortality from pneumonia. Pneumonia is the leading cause of death from infection in this group.[1] A community-based case control study in the Philippines showed that low birth weight infants had twice the risk of dying from ARI compared with infants of 3–4 kilograms in weight.[14]

Breast-feeding. Results of studies in developing countries tend to support a protective effect of breast-feeding. Mortality from ALRI was lower in children less than 2 years old who had been hospitalised in Rwanda and who had been breast-fed.[15] In a community-based study in Brazil breast-feeding also reduced mortality from ARI among children.[16] The same findings were noted in a community-based case–control study in the Philippines.[14]

EPI immunisations. Diphtheria, pertussis and measles contribute significantly to the burden of ARI (Figure 14.2). It has been estimated that one-quarter of the deaths due to ARI in developing countries is related to whooping cough and measles. Studies conducted in the Philippines have shown that missing DPT immunisation among children less than 5 years of age is a risk factor for death due to ARI.[14,17]

Indoor air pollution. In a large proportion of the world's households biofuels (wood, crop residues and animal dung) are used for cooking daily, frequently without a chimney and with poor ventilation. Studies in developing countries have shown a wide range of levels of *indoor air particulate pollution*, suggesting that exposures to indoor particulate levels would be approximately 20 times higher in developing than in industrialised countries.[18] It is possible that smoke from biofuel is a risk factor for ARI but its relative significance in relation to other risk factors is difficult to establish.

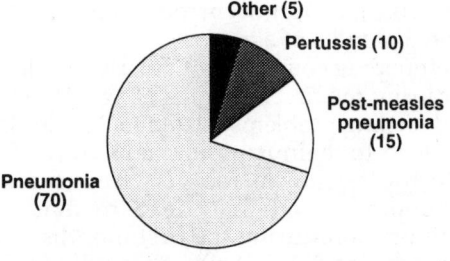

Figure 14.2. The significance of different ARI syndromes in causing death in children in developing countries. The figures denote per cent proportions.[30]

Table 14.2. Etiological agents in acute respiratory infections

Bacteria	Viruses	Others
Streptococcus pneumoniae	Measles	*Pneumocystis*
Haemophilus influenzae	RSV	*Ascaris*
Bordetella pertussis	Parainfluenzae 1–3	*Paragonimus*
Mycoplasma pneumoniae	Rhinoviruses	*Echinococcus*
Staphylococcus aureus	Adenoviruses	*Strongyloides*
Gram-negative rods	Influenza viruses	Fungi
Chlamydiae	Enteroviruses	
Rickettsiae	*Herpes simplex*	
	Cytomegalovirus	

Etiological agents and specific diagnostic methods

Overall, knowledge of the significance of the microbial causes of childhood pneumonia is deficient even in industrialised countries, and very limited in developing countries, due to problems of specific diagnosis (Table 14.2). Reliable laboratory methods have been available in only a few laboratories in developing countries, and the criteria for the selection of patients in different studies have varied. In pneumonia, blood cultures are very insensitive in children, and upper respiratory specimens are not valid for studying the bacterial etiology of pneumonia.

In studies employing lung aspiration with a needle, giving definitive information on the etiology, only patients with dense local infiltrates have been eligible, and frequently those already receiving antimicrobials have been excluded. The patient population thus selected represents the most severely ill group of pneumonia patients.

Bacterial infections. Most if not all young children in developing countries carry in their upper respiratory tract pneumococci (*Streptococcus pneumoniae*) and *Haemophilus influenzae* which are the most common causes of severe pneumonia. Studies employing lung puncture indicated bacterial etiology in 62 per cent of a total of 1080 patients.[2,19,20] *H. influenzae* and *S. pneumoniae* each constituted approximately 30 per cent of the bacteria isolated, and *Staphylococcus aureus* 20 per cent. Mortality was considerably higher among patients with a bacterial isolate than among those without.

The contribution of *Mycoplasma pneumoniae* and *Chlamydiae* has been investigated in only a few studies, but it seems evident that they are far less significant than the bacteria mentioned above.

Viral infections. Viruses cause the majority of ARI in industrialised countries, but mixed infections with viruses and bacteria are common. In developing countries the results of studies on viruses in ARI have varied greatly, but show the presence of a viral infection in up to 50 per cent of childhood pneumonia patients with a considerable proportion of virus–virus mixed infections.[2,6] In measles, mixed infection with bacteria is very common.[21] In areas with good measles vaccination coverage respiratory syncytial virus (RSV) is the most common virus involved in up to 20 per cent of cases. Parainfluenza virus, and less commonly adenovirus, influenza A or B virus are other viruses associated with ARI.

Whooping cough. Scant reliable information exists on the epidemiology of whooping cough in developing countries. The infectivity parallels that of measles and varicella viruses. It has been estimated that whooping cough causes 750 000 deaths per year in developing countries, mostly in very young children.[1,22]

In Nigeria, 55 per cent of children contracted symptomatic whooping cough by the age of 5 years, and 6 per cent of these died from the infection.[23] Half of the deaths due to whooping cough occurred in children less than 6 months of age.

Whooping cough is particularly problematic during the first 3 months of age. Vomiting and feeding problems related to the illness often lead to malnutrition, the recovery from which is as slow as recovery from measles. Whooping cough may lead to marasmic malnutrition during the first months of life when the incidence of measles is still very low. The clinical presentation in the young infant is frequently atypical; spells of breathing difficulty varying with symptomless periods during which the baby looks normal.

Table 14.3. Management of children aged 2 months to 4 years with cough or difficult breathing .[26]

SIGNS:	• Not able to drink • Convulsions • Abnormally sleepy or difficult to wake • Stridor in calm child, or • Severe malnutrition		
CLASSIFY AS:	**VERY SEVERE DISEASE**		
TREATMENT:	–> Refer URGENTLY to hospital –> Give first dose of antibiotic –> Treat wheezing, if present –> If cerebral malaria is possible, give an antimalarial		
SIGNS:	• Chest indrawning • If also recurrent wheezing go directly to –> Treat wheezing	• No chest indrawing and • Fast breathing (50 per minute or more if child 2 months up to 12 months; 40 per minute or more if child 12 months up to 5 years)	• No chest indrawing and • No fast breathing Less than 50 per minute if child 2 months up to 12 months; Less than 40 per minute if child 12 months up to 5 years
CLASSIFY AS:	**SEVERE PNEUMONIA**	**PNEUMONIA**	**NO PNEUMONIA: COUGH OR COLD**
TREATMENT:	–> Refer URGENTLY to hospital –> Give first dose of an antibiotic –> Treat fever, if present –> Treat wheezing, if present (If referral is not feasible, treat with an antibiotic and follow closely)	–> Advise mother to give home care –> Give an antibiotic –> Treat fever, if present –> Treat wheezing, if present –> Advise mother to return with child in 2 days for reassesment, or earlier if the child is getting worse	–> If coughing more than 30 days refer to reassessment –> Assess and treat ear problem or sore throat, if present –> Assess and treat other problems –> Advise mother to give home care –> Treat fever, if present –> Treat wheezing, if present

	Reassess in 2 days a child who is taking an antibiotic for pneumonia:		
SIGNS:	**WORSE** • Not able to drink • Has chest indrawning • Has other danger signs	**THE SAME**	**IMPROVING** • Breathing slower • Less fever • Eating better
TREATMENT:	–> Refer URGENTLY to hospital	–> Change antibiotic or refer	–> Finish 5 days of antibiotic

There is little information on the association of whooping cough and pneumonia. In Nigeria, complicating pneumonia often developed both at the whooping stage and after whooping had practically disappeared.[23] In another study in Uganda, 40 per cent of

Table 14.4. Antimicrobials used in ARI.[25]

Give an antibiotic
Give first dose of antibiotic in clinic
Instruct mother on how to give the antibiotic for five days at home (or return to clinic for daily procaine penicillin injection)

AGE or WEIGHT	CO-TRIMOXAZOLE trimethoprim + sulphamethoxazole Two times daily for five days			AMOXYCILLIN Three times daily for five days		AMPICILLIN Four times daily for five days		PROCAINE PENICILLIN Once daily for five days
	Adult tablet single strength (80 mg trimethoprim +400 mg sulphamethoxazole)	Pediatric tablet (20 mg trimethoprim +100 mg sulphamethoxazole)	Syrup (40 mg trimethoprim +200 mg sulphamethoxazole per five ml)	Tablet 250 mg	Syrup 125 mg in 5 ml	Tablet 250 mg	Syrup 250 mg in 5 ml	Intramuscular injection
Less than 2 months (< 5kg)**	quarter *	1†	2.5 ml†	quarter†	2.5 ml	half	2.5 ml	200 000 units
2 months up to 12 months (6-9 kg)	half	2	5 ml	half	5 ml	1	5 ml	400 000 units
12 months up to 5 years (10-19 kg)	1	3	7.5 ml	1	10 ml	1	5 ml	800 000 units

* Give oral antibiotic for 5 days at home only if referral is not feasible

† If the child is less than 1 month old, give 1/2 pediatric tablet or 1.25 ml syrup twice daily

Avoid co-trimoxazole in infants less than 1 month of age who are premature or jaundiced

patients admitted to hospital with whooping cough had a complicating bronchopneumonia.[24]

Other causative agents. Although many parasites and fungi occasionally can cause lower respiratory symptoms, the available evidence suggests they are not major contributors to the problem of ARI in developing countries. After the Second World War, *Pneumocystis carinii* caused major epidemics of pneumonia in malnourished children in Europe, but the limited information from developing countries does not indicate that the parasite would be a major causative agent in ARI.

STRATEGIES FOR INTERVENTION

The control of ARI is usually discussed in the context of intervention programmes geared towards the reduction of mortality due to pneumonia, which causes about 70 per cent of deaths in children with ARI. The WHO established in 1982 a global programme for the control of ARI using three major strategies: improving childhood immunisation rates against diphtheria, pertussis, measles and tuberculosis; case management; and health education.

Strategies in the long-term control of ARI include gradual reduction of other risk factors

for ARI dealt with above. At present ARI case management, combined with health education, is the core strategy of the ARI Control Programme.

Control programmes based on case management

Clinical aspects. The WHO Guideline for the management of ARI involves the differentiation of the clinical condition by degree of severity, appropriate referral, antimicrobial therapy, and supportive measures.[25] They emphasise critical signs that a minimally trained health worker can learn to recognise (Table 14.3), clearly defined signs that are relevant to two management decisions: should an antibiotic be given to a child with ARI, and should the child be treated at home or at a hospital. Thus, in the case management three main groups of children with ARI are to be identified: those with severe pneumonia or other very severe disease who require antibiotics and immediate referral for inpatient care; those who have pneumonia and need antibiotic treatment at home; and those who do not have pneumonia.[26]

The two entry criteria of the WHO case management are cough or difficulty of breathing (fast breathing). Fast breathing for infants 2–11 months old is defined as a respiratory rate (RR) of 50 per minute or above. For children 1–4 years old, the cut-off is 40 per minute. It is essential that the RR is recorded when the child is calm and not crying. *An important sign to look for is chest indrawing*, defined as an indrawing of the lower chest wall when the child breathes in. This is a sign of severe pneumonia. Chest indrawing does not include intercostal or supraclavicular retractions. Chest indrawing may also be caused by wheezing usually due to asthma or bronchiolitis.

The simple clinical criteria used in the case management decision algorithm correlate so well with diagnostics employing chest X-ray that radiological investigations are not necessary at the primary levels of health care. Laboratory investigations are not helpful in decisions concerning antibiotic use or referral of pneumonia cases

The decision algorithms provide instructions on how to manage these cases. Table 14.3 shows the case management chart for children 2 months to 5 years. Table 14.4 shows the antibiotics recommended for treating children with pneumonia.

The antimicrobials for pneumonia cases treated at home include a choice of injectable procaine penicillin and two oral antimicrobials: co-trimoxazole and amoxycillin. Oral phenoxymethyl-penicillin and benzathine penicillin should not be used to treat pneumonia in children because they do not reach high enough levels in the serum to be effective against *H. influenzae* or strains of *S. pneumoniae* with reduced sensitivity to penicillin. The standard antimicrobial for the treatment of severe pneumonia is intramuscular benzylpenicillin. Very severe cases are given chloramphenicol. Chloramphenicol is indicated for these cases because of its action against *S. aureus* and Gram-negative bacteria. Oxygen is indicated in very severe cases because the lungs are unable to transfer enough oxygen from the air into the bloodstream.

Further development of case management

Treatment of pneumonia in areas endemic for malaria. In areas endemic for malaria, problems arise in the use of the ARI case management. Control programmes for both diseases rely on detection of cases by clinical signs and empirical treatment with an antimicrobial or antimalarial.[27] Because of overlap in the clinical picture, children may be misclassified and given wrong or inadequate treatment. A study in Malawi showed that among children meeting the clinical case definition for pneumonia, 96 per cent also met that for malaria. With increasing prevalence of chloroquine resistance further schemes for combined therapy for pneumonia and malaria are needed. Use of co-trimoxazole is one promising possibility, as it has now been shown efficacious also in the treatment of malaria in young children.

The clinical signs as an indicator of pneumonia in children. Many studies have shown that fast breathing is a better predictor of pneumonia in children than other clinical signs such as chest indrawing, wheeze etc.[26] Recent studies on the use of respiratory rate have led the WHO to recommend different cut-off points for infants and older children. One has to make a balance between greater sensitivity on the one hand and simplicity (therefore easy implementation) on the other, so that health workers with little formal training including village health workers can adopt the recommendations. Should different or only one cut-off point be used for under-fives? Definitely children younger than 2 months old behave differently from older ones. Studies are currently under way to define the clinical signs and symptoms that would best predict the pneumonia in this population.

Impact of case management. On the assumption that early treatment with antimicrobials that are effective against *S. pneumonia* and *H. influenzae* can prevent deaths from pneumonia in children, the WHO sponsored seven studies during the 1980s to determine the impact of the standard case management strategy implemented through the PHC system, including community health workers. The studies were conducted in Haryana, India; Kediri, Indonesia; Jumla and Kathmandu Valley, Nepal; Abbottabad, Pakistan; Bohol Island, Philippines; and Bagamoyo, Tanzania. All these studies (except the Philippine study) have been reviewed recently.[28]

The results showed that overall, the *ARI control programme reduced mortality in infants by 20 per cent and in under-fives by 25 per cent*. The consistency of findings of all the studies, despite the differences in design and methods, shows that the case-management strategy has the potential for a substantial effect on infant and under-five mortality, at least in settings with infant mortality rates of 90 per 1000 live births or more.

Little information is so far available on the feasibility and sustainability of the ARI control programme as a part of PHC services outside the research context. The constraints on the availability of antibiotics, particularly in the poorest countries with high infant mortality, could severely limit the impact of this approach.

Health education

Health education is a basic component of ARI control programmes. Effective treatment is dependent on mothers and other child carers recognising the critical signs of pneumonia and acting immediately to seek help.[29] Health education should accomplish several tasks: increase the capability of families to recognise a child with pneumonia as separate from those without pneumonia (only cough and colds) and to decide when to seek help; educate the community in simple supportive therapy of ARI and to refrain from using such expensive, ineffective remedies as cough syrups; promote the timely immunisation against measles, pertussis, diphtheria and tuberculosis; promote breast-feeding; and reduce parental smoking and other causes of domestic air pollution.

Global implementation of the ARI control programme

One of the major targets of the WHO is the establishment of operational control programmes by 1995 in all countries with an infant mortality rate greater than 40 per 1000 live births per year. By the end of 1992, plans of operation for ARI control programmes had been prepared in 83 countries.[31] In 47 countries, activities consisting of training, supervision, and supplies in the first-level health facilities and first-referral hospitals had been implemented in at least one province or region. Operational programmes had been implemented in 53 per cent of the Programme's target countries.

FUTURE DEVELOPMENT IN ARI CONTROL

Priorities of research

Research activities for improved control of ARI are taking place in four main areas: 1) improvement of the case management control strategy; 2) behavioural research; 3) health systems research; and 4) prevention research. Several types of research in case management aim at improving the existing case management strategy promoted by the WHO, including improved guidelines for young infants and severely malnourished children and for areas highly endemic for malaria, better antibiotic regimens, and supporting technology. Behavioural studies are investigating practices related to ARI, and aim at improving, by health education, the ARI-related behaviour of guardians at home and in seeking health care services. Health systems research focuses on analysing the epidemiology of ARI, related health services utilisation, the impact and cost of the ARI control programme activities, and the surveillance of resistance of respiratory pathogens to the drugs used in the case management strategy.

The limitations of the case management strategy, above all the difficulty of arranging sufficient access to health services for a large proportion of particularly rural populations and regular supply of the necessary antibiotics, have made the development of disease prevention strategies urgent. This is also underscored by signs of increasing resistance in the main respiratory pathogens to the drugs used, mainly due to the widespread use of inappropriate, broad-spectrum antibiotics.

New vaccines against *Haemophilus influenzae* type b (Hib) are in wide use in industrialised countries and are highly efficacious in preventing meningitis as well as other invasive disease caused by this bacterium from a very early age. The vaccines hold great potential also in preventing childhood pneumonia caused by Hib, but their efficacy in preventing this disease has not yet been proven, as severe Hib pneumonia is much less common in industrialised countries. New pneumococcal vaccines, prepared in a similar manner to the Hib vaccine to be highly immunogenic already in early infancy, are being tested in industrialised countries, and will soon be available for studies in developing countries.

It has been estimated that the Hib vaccines and new pneumococcal vaccines have the potential to prevent half of severe pneumonias in developing countries, but this needs to be proven in real-life settings. Another potential way of improving the protection of infants even before they are immunised within the EPI schedule would be to vaccinate mothers during pregnancy concomitantly with tetanus vaccination.

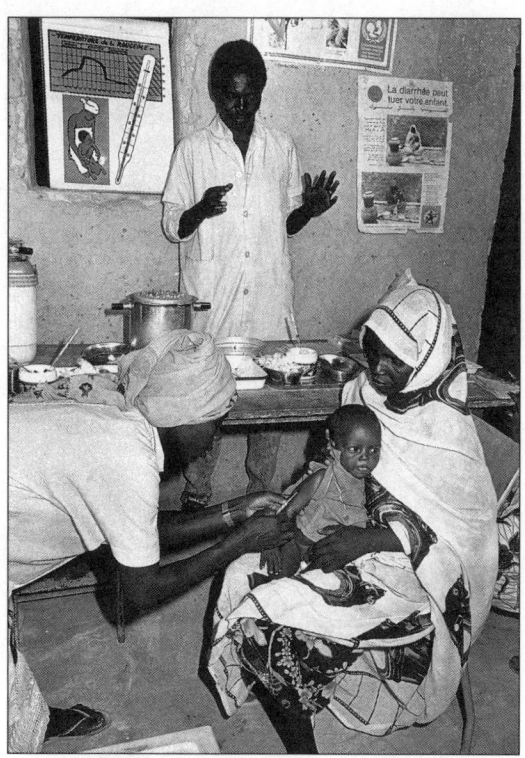

Measles vaccination is part of the Expanded Programme on Immunization. Vaccination clinic in Mao, Chad. Photo: UNICEF/Maggie Murray-Lee

The antibodies would be transferred to the infant and afford protection for the most vulnerable period for ARI, the first few months of life.

Information services

A global newsletter ARI News is produced by the Appropriate Health Resources and Technologies Action Group (AHRTAG). The newsletter contains articles related to ARI with a broad spectrum of topics and is meant for all levels of health services in developing countries. The ARI control programme of the WHO produces and updates guidelines and training materials for the case management control strategy.

References

1. Pio A, Leowski J, ten Dam HG. The magnitude of the problem of acute respiratory infections. In: Douglas RM, Kerby-Eaton E, eds. Acute respiratory infections in childhood. Proceedings of an international workshop. Adelaide, Australia: University of Adelaide Press. 1985:3–16.

2. Berman S, McIntosh K. Selective primary health care: Strategies for control of disease in the developing world. XXI. Acute respiratory infections. Rev Infect Dis 1985;7:674–91

3. Selwyn B, for the Bostid Group. The epidemiology of acute respiratory infection in young children: comparison of findings from several developing countries. Rev Infect Dis 1990;S8:S870–88.

4. Arruda E, Hayden F, McAuliffe J, et al. Acute respiratory viral infections in ambulatory children of urban Northeast Brazil. J Infect Dis 1991;164:252–8

5. Leowski J. Mortality from acute respiratory infections in children under 5 years of age: global estimates. World Health Stat Q 1986;39:138–44

6. Ruutu P, Halonen P, Meurman O, et al. Viral lower respiratory tract infections in Filipino children. J Infect Dis 1990;161:175–9

7. Herrero L. Respiratory infections in Central America. Pediatr Res 1983;17:1035–8

8. Berman S, Duenas A, Bedoya A, Constain V, Borero I, Murphy J. Acute lower respiratory illness in Cali, Colombia: a two-year ambulatory study. Pediatrics 1983;71: 10-2.

9. Escobar JA, Dover AS, Duenas A et al. Etiology of respiratory tract infection in children in Cali, Colombia. Pediatrics 1976;57:123–30

10. Tunbridge WMG, Wicks ACB. A review of bronchopneumonia in African children. Cent Afr J Med 1967;13:22–34.

11. Kielmann AA, McCord C. Weight for age as an index of risk of death in children. Lancet 1978;i:1247.

12. Tupasi TE, et al. Malnutrition and acute respiratory tract infection in Filipino children. Rev Infect Dis 1990;12:1047–54.

13. Glasziou P, Mackerras D. Vitamin A supplementation in infectious diseases: a meta-analysis. Br Med J 1993;306:366–70

14. ARI-Bohol Project Final Report. Mortality determinants in the general population. Research Institute for Tropical Medicine (Philippines) and the Tropical Health Program, University of Queensland (Australia), 1992:130–59.

15. Lepage P, Munyakazi C, Hennart P. Breast feeding and hospital mortality in children in Rwanda. Lancet 1981;ii: 409–11.

16. Victora CG, Smith PG, Vaughn JP, et al. Evidence for protection by breast-feeding against infant deaths from infectious diseases in Brazil. Lancet 1987;ii:319–21

17. Tupasi T, Velmonte A, Sanvictores M, et al. Determinants of mortality due to acute respiratory infections: implications for intervention. J Infect Dis 1988;157:615–23

18. Pandey MR, Boleij JSM, Smith KR, Wafula EM. Indoor air pollution in developing countries and acute respiratory infection in children. Lancet 1989;i:427–429

19. Shann F. Etiology of severe pneumonia in children in developing countries. Ped Infect Dis 1986;5:247–252

20. Wall R, Torrah P, Mabey D, Greenwood B. The etiology of lobar pneumonia in the Gambia. Bull WHO 1986;64:553–558

21. Morton R, Mee J. Measles pneumonia: lung puncture findings in 56 cases related to chest X-ray changes and clinical features. Ann Trop Paed 1986;6:41–45

22. Wright PF. Pertussis in developing countries: Definition of the problem and prospects for control. Rev Infect Dis 1991;13(suppl 6):S528–S534

23. Morley D, Woodland M, Martin W. Whooping cough in Nigerian children. Trop Geogr Med 1966;18:169–182

24. Bwibo N. Whooping cough in Uganda. Scand J Infect Dis 1971;3:41–43

25. World Health Organization. Acute respiratory infections in children: case management in small hospitals in developing countries. Geneva, Switzerland: WHO, 1990. (WHO/ARI/90.5)

26. World Health Organization. Technical bases for the WHO recommendations on the management of pneumonia in children at first-level health facilities. Geneva, Switzerland: WHO, 1991. (WHO/ARI/91.20)

27. World Health Organization. Programme for control of acute respiratory infections. Fifth Programme Report. Geneva, Switzerland: WHO, 1992. (WHO/ARI/92.22)

28. Sazawal S, Black R. Meta-analysis of intervention trials on case-management of pneumonia in community settings. Lancet 1992; 340:528–33

29. World Health Organization. Basic principles for control of acute respiratory infections in children in developing countries. Geneva, Switzerland: WHO, 1986. (WHO/UNICEF 1986:11)

30. World Health Organization. Implementation of the Global Strategy for Health for All by the Year 2000, Second Evaluation; and Eighth Report on the World Health Situation. Geneva Switzerland: WHO, 1991. (EB89/10/1991).

31. World Health Organization. Interim programme report. Programme for control of acute respiratory infections. Geneva: WHO, 1993. (WHO/ARI/93.25)

Additional reading

1. Feigin RD, Cherry JD eds. Textbook of pediatric infectious diseases. 3rd ed. Philadelphia: WB Saunders, 1992.

About the authors

Petri Ruutu is a specialist in internal medicine and infectious diseases and a consultant in Helsinki University Central Hospital in Helsinki, Finland. During 1983–84 he worked at the Research Institute for Tropical Medicine (RITM), Manila, the Philippines, and has since coordinated research collaboration on acute respiratory infections between RITM and the National Public Health Institute, Helsinki, Finland. His other interests and publications deal mainly with infections in immunosuppressed patients.

Marilla G. Lucero is a specialist in internal medicine and infectious diseases, and currently the head of the Acute Respiratory Infections Study Group at RITM. She has been deeply involved in the large ARI Case Management Intervention Study carried out between 1984 and 1992 on Bohol Island, the Philippines.

Lankinen KS, Bergström S, Mäkelä PH and Peltomaa M, eds.
Health and disease in developing countries. London:The Macmillan Press Limited, 1994:135-146.

15 DIARRHEAL DISEASES

Timo Vesikari, M.D., Ph.D.
Tampere University Hospital,
Department of Pediatrics
and University of Tampere, Department
of Biomedical Sciences
P.O. Box 607, FIN-33101 Tampere,
Finland

Benjamin Torun, M.D., Ph.D.
Instituto de Nutricion de Centro America y
Panama, Metabolism and Clinical Nutrition
Program
P.O. Box 1188, Guatemala,
Guatemala

INTRODUCTION

A cautious estimate in the beginning of the 1980s concluded that approximately 4.6 million children under 5 years of age in developing countries die from diarrheal diseases each year and the annual number of diarrheal episodes in this age group is above one billion.[1] Although the majority of diarrheal episodes are not severe and may not require specific intervention, a large number are potentially fatal. Identification and proper management of the severe episodes is the most urgent target of control efforts, while prevention of all mild episodes is of lower priority.

Approximately two-thirds of diarrheal deaths are attributable to dehydration and, therefore, preventable by adequate fluid therapy. Introduction and worldwide implementation of oral rehydration therapy (ORT) has had a significant impact in reducing diarrheal mortality, although exact figures are difficult to obtain. Moreover, after initial success, progress seems to have slowed down in recent years.

The remaining one-third of diarrheal deaths are due to a number of causes, and no single intervention is available to prevent them. These deaths include those from *shigellosis* with septicemia and various gastro-intestinal complications and deaths from *measles-associated diarrhea. Persistent and prolonged diarrhea* may follow an episode initiated by any of a variety of enteropathogens. Loss of nutrients associated with persistent or repeated diarrhea results in malnutrition, failure to thrive, increased susceptibility to secondary infections, and ultimately death.

CAUSAL ORGANISMS AND DISEASE ENTITIES

The enteric pathogens causing acute diarrhea in developing countries are largely the same that are encountered in developed countries, but their proportions are different. In general, bacterial pathogens are more important in countries with poor hygienic conditions. Rotavirus is an important pathogen in developing as well as developed countries, but in developing countries it is outnumbered by the excess of bacterial pathogens.

Regional differences in the etiology of acute diarrhea of children are relatively minor. Rather, several longitudinal etiology studies of acute diarrhea have revealed a surprisingly similar distribution of causative organisms in different parts of the world.[2] Many enteropathogens are frequently found in the stools of healthy children, and detection of a potential pathogen from a patient does not necessarily imply a causal relationship with diarrhea.

Even though an etiological agent can be determined in 70–80 per cent of cases of acute diarrhea in developing countries, microbiological diagnosis is seldom required for case management. The same general principles of management are applicable in most cases of acute diarrhea, regardless of etiology.

Table 15.1. Main causative organisms of acute diarrhea in developing countries.

Pathogen	Significance
Rotavirus	Over 800 000 deaths/year 30% of diarrheal mortality in age group 6-24 months
Shigellae	Over 500 000 deaths/year Dysentery, watery diarrhea
Enterotoxigenic *E. coli* (ETEC)	Over 500 000 deaths/year Most cases in children under 2 years of age
Vibrio cholerae	Over 100 000 deaths/year Pandemic spread from Asia to Africa to Latin America
Campylobacter jejuni	Significant pathogen in infants under 6 months of age
Enteropathogenic *E. coli* (EPEC)	Significant pathogen in infants under 6 months of age
Salmonella sp.	In 'transitional' urban areas

Knowledge of etiology is needed, however, to plan preventive measures and, especially, for development of vaccines.[2] The most common etiological agents are listed in Table 15.1 and discussed briefly below.

Rotavirus

Rotavirus is the single most important causal agent of acute watery diarrhea leading to severe dehydration. Rotavirus disease is characterised by vomiting, fever, and profuse watery diarrhea; this combination rapidly results in dehydration and necessitates a visit to treatment centre, if accessible. Because of the severity of the clinical picture, rotavirus is over-represented in hospital-based etiological studies, in which it may account for up to 40 per cent of all cases. In contrast, in community-based studies the etiological role of rotavirus is less than 10 per cent of all episodes of diarrhea.

The typical age for rotavirus diarrhea is between 6 and 11 months of age, but in developing countries cases begin from 2 months and extend beyond 2 years of age. In the age group 6–23 months rotavirus has been estimated to be responsible for 30 per cent of all diarrheal deaths.[3]

Rotavirus disease typically occurs only once, but in developing countries symptomatic reinfections are more common than in developed countries. In temperate climates rotavirus occurs seasonally with a peak in the cold season; in tropical countries seasonal variation is less clear or absent. Lack of seasonality may also be a sign of poor hygienic conditions and faecal–oral spread, in contrast to aerosol transmission thought to occur in developed countries. In some countries there are two patterns of rotavirus disease: for example, in South Africa rotavirus occurs seasonally in the white population and year round in the black population.

Group B rotavirus is a distinct agent that has caused large outbreaks of acute diarrhea in China, but not elsewhere. Most of the cases have been in adults, hence the name adult rotavirus. Other viral agents appear to play only a minor role in acute diarrhea in developing countries.

Escherichia coli

Enterotoxigenic *E. coli* (ETEC) are found in 10 to 50 per cent (average about 20 per cent) of cases in hospital- or clinic-based etiological studies of acute diarrhea in developing countries.[2] ETEC may be after rotavirus the second most common cause of dehydrating diarrhea in young children, particularly in children under 2 years of age; by age 5, children in developing countries have generally acquired immunity to these bacteria. In contrast, ETEC cause traveller's diarrhea among visitors to developing countries even in adult age, due to lack of immunity.

Two types of ETEC toxins, LT (heat-labile) and ST (heat-stable) can cause diarrhea. Phenotypically, the bacteria may be ST only, LT only or both ST/LT. To cause diarrhea, ETEC must first adhere to the gut mucosa with colonisation factor antigens. These antigens appear to be targets of acquired immunity to ETEC and hence potentially useful in experimental vaccines.

Enteropathogenic *E. coli* (EPEC) also cause diarrhea in developing countries, but only in the first months of life. Later, EPEC are found as commonly in healthy controls as is in patients with diarrhea.

Shigellae

Shigellosis commonly refers to dysentery, the clinical picture of which includes fever, abdominal cramps and bloody diarrhea with frequent, small and mucoid stools. Dysentery may be complicated by convulsions, paralytic ileus, septicemia and hemolytic-uremic syndrome, and may lead to persistent diarrhea and protein losing enteropathy. More than 500 000 children, mostly under the age of five, die annually from the various complications of shigellosis. In addition, *Shigellae* cause watery diarrhea, accounting for 10–20 per cent of cases of acute childhood diarrhea in treatment centres.

Both *S. flexneri* and *S. dysenteriae* 1 are important causes of dysentery in developing countries. In 1969, *S. dysenteriae* 1 reappeared after several decades in Central America, starting a new pandemic. Shigellosis is one of the few diarrheal infections in which antibiotics are indicated. The bacteria are often resistant to several common antibiotics, and the choice of antimicrobial therapy may pose a difficult problem. In developing countries bloody diarrhea (dysentery) should be regarded as suggestive of shigellosis and treated with antimicrobials without waiting for laboratory confirmation. Local knowledge of antimicrobial sensitivity is helpful for the choice of drug (Table 15.5). If available and affordable, new fluorokinolones are the most effective agents against multiply resistant shigellae.

Salmonellae

In contrast to the great public health significance of *Salmonella* sp. in developed countries, *Salmonellae* are generally not regarded as significant causative agents of diarrhea in developing countries. However, this may be true only for rural conditions, whereas in urban areas where processed foods are used the etiological role of *Salmonellae* in childhood diarrhea may be significant.

Apart from diarrhea, *Salmonellae* cause a disease entity called *enteric fever*. When caused by *S. typhi* the disease is *typhoid fever*, but a similar clinical picture may be associated with infection by *S. paratyphi* and occasionally other *Salmonellae*. Clinical symptoms include fever, abdominal pains, headache, and cough, and clinical signs include coated tongue, splenomegaly, rales in lungs and relative bradycardia. Usually there is no diarrhea.

Typhoid fever, although not a diarrheal disease, is transmitted by contaminated food and water like other enteric infections. In developing countries the source of infection is more often food than water, and open kitchens on street sides, which are common in many developing countries, often transmit the disease. Typically, school-age children are infected, but typhoid fever occurs from age one onwards. Typhoid fever is endemic in large parts of the world and carries an estimated death toll of 500–600 000 per year.

Campylobacter

Campylobacter infections are very common in developing countries. The source is often chickens that run freely around human dwellings. Immunity apparently develops at an early age and *Campylobacter jejuni* is usually established as a causal agent of acute diarrhea only in infants less than 6 months of age.

Vibrio cholerae

Cholera is endemic in the Indian subcontinent, where the classical biotype of *Vibrio cholerae* is encountered. The epidemic type of cholera that occurs in large parts of the world Asia, Africa and South America is caused by biotype El Tor. The El Tor pandemic (the seventh) began in Indonesia in 1961 and continues to spread. An estimated 120 000 deaths are caused annually by cholera, one-third of them in children under five, a quarter in children aged 5–14, and the remainder in adults.[3]

The number of cholera cases and associated deaths are difficult to estimate since many countries intentionally underreport cholera. When cholera broke out in the coastal region of Peru in 1991, exact figures were obtained. In 1991 there were 366 228 cases and 3893 deaths (case–fatality rate about 1 per cent) reported to the WHO by ten Latin American countries.[4]

Today most cases of cholera are manageable with ORT, although intravenous fluid therapy is commonly applied in specialised treatment centres. In addition, antimicrobials are routinely given.

Table 15.2. General principles of case management of acute diarrhea.

---

1. ORT = oral rehydration therapy
   - Correction of fluid deficit: ORS 70–100 ml/kg body weight in 4–6 hours.
   - Replacement of continuous fluid losses: ORS to substitute for stool volume and vomiting.
2. Dietary management
   - Breast-feeding must not be interrupted.
   - Start feeding according to age as soon as clinical signs of dehydration disappear, and continue feeding even if severe diarrhea persists.
3. Antimicrobials
   - Should be used only in special circumstances: dysentery, enteric fever, cholera.
4. Anti-diarrheal drugs
   - Should be generally avoided.

CASE MANAGEMENT OF ACUTE DIARRHEA

The general principles of case management (Table 15.2) are applicable to most cases of acute diarrhea regardless of etiology and pathogenetic mechanisms.[5]

Dehydration

Recognition of dehydration and its correction is the first priority in the treatment of acute diarrhea. Not all diarrheal episodes in developing countries are associated with dehydration and, consequently, do not require rehydration therapy. However, promotion of the basic concept that diarrhea and vomiting are likely to result in life-threatening dehydration continues to be of great importance. This educational promotion should be aimed at all levels from families to doctors.

Clinical signs of dehydration (Figure 15.1) include: sunken eyes, thirst and dry mouth, a sunken fontanelle in infants, reduced skin turgor, low urinary output, lethargy and apathy. In severe cases the patient can go into hypovolemic shock with cold sweat, a fast and weak pulse and reduced consciousness. This happens when the dehydration is equivalent to a loss of 15 per cent of body weight. Young infants may lose more fluid before critical signs appear. However, an exact estimation of the degree of dehydration is difficult without information about the child's weight before the diarrheal episode; this is usually unavailable. On the other hand, oral rehydration can be carried out safely and effectively without knowledge of the exact degree of dehydration. The WHO now recognises two intensities of dehydration, based on clinical signs: 1) some degree of dehydration; and 2) severe dehydration. Clinical signs to assess the severity of dehydration are listed in Table 15.3.[5]

Most episodes of dehydration are *isotonic*, that is the child has lost water and electrolytes in the same proportion. However, hypertonic and hypotonic dehydration can also occur and are more common in developing than developed countries.

Hypertonic dehydration occurs in young infants who are not breast-fed but receive commercial milk substitutes and carbohydrate-rich foods. It is characterised by central nervous system symptoms, such as irritability and restlessness. Such a child is severely ill even though he has not lost much weight. These cases are manageable by ORT but the rehydration should be done at a slower rate.[6]

Hypotonic dehydration is common especially in severely malnourished children, or when rehydration has been attempted with plain water, teas, or herb infusions. Treatment is not much different from isotonic dehydration.[6]

ORS

The physiological principles of oral rehydration, established in the 1960s, include: 1) water is absorbed from the intestine together with

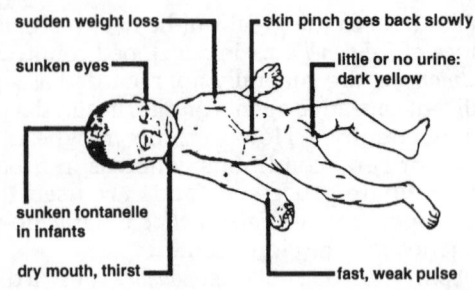

DANGER SIGNS OF DEHYDRATION IN THE CHILD

Figure 15.1. Signs of dehydration in a child (courtesy of Dr M. Merson, WHO Diarrhoeal Diseases Control Programme).

Table 15.3. Clinical signs to assess the severity of dehydration.

Sign	No dehydration	Mild/moderate	Severe
Patient's appearance	well, alert	* restless, irritable	* unconscious or limp, or too weak to move or drink (shock)
Radial pulse	normal	rapid	* very weak or absent
Thirst	not thirsty	some thirst or * thirsty, drinks eagerly	* very thirsty drinks poorly, or not able to drink
Eyes, fontanelle	normal, tears present	slightly sunken, tears present or absent	sunken, dry eyes, tears absent
Urine flow	normal	decreased	none for several hours
Skin elasticity	normal	less than normal, * skin pinch goes back somewhat slowly	poor, skin pinch goes back very slowly
Mouth and tongue	moist	dry	very dry
Hands and feet	warm or slightly cold	slightly cold	cold, usually moist and pale

* Especially important signs. Two or more signs in the column, including at least one especially important sign (*), indicates mild/moderate or severe dehydration.

sodium (Na+), hence salt is required in the solution; 2) absorption of sodium is coupled with absorption of organic substances like glucose, amino acids or dipeptides. For this reason the solution should contain an organic molecule, usually glucose; 3) for maximal absorption of water, sodium and glucose should be present in approximately equimolar proportions.[7]

Based on these principles, a consensus was reached in the 1970s about a formula, which since then has been the ORS (oral rehydration salts) recommended by the WHO and UNICEF (Table 15.4). The composition of this ORS is a compromise between high sodium solutions required for the treatment of cholera and those of lower sodium concentration which would be sufficient for treatment of non-cholera diarrhea.

Thus the ORS-WHO may be regarded as a universal, all-purpose, solution; but does not mean that it is the optimal solution. However, it is important to have a single acceptable formula that can be recommended and promoted worldwide. ORS-WHO is an extremely safe therapeutic tool: over two billion units of ORS have been administered without serious complications.

ORS-WHO with its relatively high concentration of sodium (90 mmol/l) is particularly suitable for treatment of cholera, in which the loss of sodium (and chloride) is greater than in other types of diarrhea. The relatively high sodium content also makes ORS-WHO suitable for the correction of the sodium deficit that usually develops in the initial days of acute non-cholera diarrhea.

ORS contains a small amount of potassium which will correct only partially the potassium deficit of diarrhea that has developed if diarrhea lasted for several days or the potassium deficit that is characteristic of severe malnutrition. However, since oral rehydration should be accomplished within 4–12 hours, the remaining potassium deficit can be replenished with the introduction of foods, particularly fruits and vegetables.

Citrate acts as a base precursor and helps to correct acidosis sooner than rehydration alone would do. The ORS formula originally recommended by WHO contained bicarbonate instead of citrate; however, even when packed in sachets, bicarbonate absorbs moisture when kept in a warm and humid environment, common in developing countries. Citrate keeps much better and has substituted bicarbonate in ORS for logistic reasons. Even so, also the bicarbonate-containing formula continues to be endorsed. This is the only change that has been made in the composition of ORS over the past 20 years.

Several modifications of ORS have been attempted in the last decade. A so-called super-ORS, which contained various amino acids in

Table 15.4. Composition of oral rehydration salts solution (ORS).

Standard ORS recommended by the WHO and UNICEF

Composition in mmol/l		Recipe for preparation	
Na+	90	NaCl	3.5 g
K+	20	KCl	1.5 g
Cl-	80	Na-citrate*	2.9 g
citrate	10		
glucose	111	Glucose[†]	20.0 g
Total osmolality	311	Water	1000.0 ml

Hypotonic ORS (not officially endorsed by the WHO)

Composition in mmol/l		Recipe for preparation	
Na+	60	NaCl	1.8 g
K+	20	KCl	1.5 g
Cl-	50	Na-citrate*	2.9 g
citrate	10		
glucose	84	Glucose[†]	15.1 g
Total osmolality	224	Water	1000.0 ml

*Trisodium citrate dihydrate
[†]Anhydrous glucose

addition to glucose, has been abandoned. Rice-based or cereal-based ORS are actually somewhat more effective than the standard ORS.[8] These can be made locally, and rice-ORS is also available as dry powder. Disadvantages of rice-ORS include large size of the package, jelly-like consistency when reconstituted, and relatively short shelf-life.

A recent improvement has been the discovery that a hypotonic ORS has better absorption properties than an isotonic solution.[9] Although it has not been officially endorsed by the WHO, the use of hypotonic ORS has given good results in the treatment of dehydration due to non-cholera diarrhea. One formula for hypotonic ORS is presented in Table 15.4.

Home-made salt–sugar solutions are widely used as substitutes for ORS. These are acceptable alternatives for home use to prevent dehydration when ORS is not available, but are inadequate for treatment of dehydration at treatment centres, except in emergency. The use of home-made solutions has been often associated with hypernatremic complications.

ORS is usually packaged in aluminium sachets (Figure 15.2). On reconstitution the contents of a sachet is mixed with 1 litre of water.

Oral rehydration therapy (ORT)

In developing country conditions it usually is not possible to calculate the degree of dehydration at the onset of therapy. Fortunately this is not essential with the use of ORT, as ORS is extremely safe within a large dose range.

In all cases of moderate and moderately severe dehydration it is customary to give within the first four hours between 70 and 100 ml of the reconstituted ORS per kilogram of body weight, depending on the degree of dehydration. In milder cases, 50 ml per kilogram may be sufficient. These amounts of ORS should be given in small quantities at few minute intervals. If too much ORS is given, some periorbital puffiness may appear, but this is by no means dangerous and will soon disappear. Plain water may be given to substitute up to one third the volume of ORS. Breast feeding must not be interrupted during ORT.[5]

The success rate of ORT can be as high as 99 per cent, but to reach this figure it is necessary to be patient and continue giving ORS to the child. ORS may be given from a cup or with a spoon, in small volumes each time. In case of vomiting a pause of 15–30 minutes is

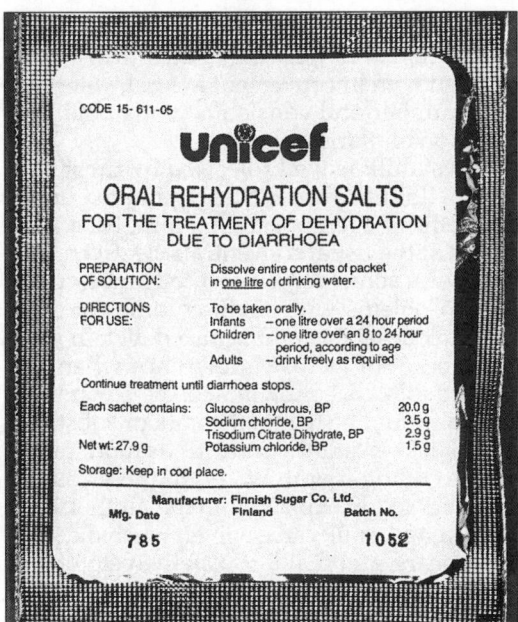

Figure 15.2. A sachet of ORS prepared for distribution by UNICEF.

acceptable, but after that another try must follow. In practice, the person who gives ORS is usually the mother, often supervised by health care personnel. Children who vomit constantly or cannot drink may require rehydration through a nasogastric tube, using an intermittent drip.

After initial rehydration, ORS should be given to compensate for the volume of fluid lost in diarrheal stools and vomit. The amount of ORS required may be about 100 ml per kilogram of body weight per day for most children, but it can be two to four times higher in cases of severe diarrhea.

ORT, using the WHO formula, is suitable for the management of all types of dehydration. In cases of hypertonic dehydration (especially if serum sodium is known to be 160 mmol/l or above), rehydration must be slower, and the required volume of fluid should be given in 12 hours rather than four hours.[6] The same is true in the case of severely malnourished children.[5]

Drug treatment

Symptomatic antidiarrheal drugs are usually not recommended for the treatment of acute diarrhea in children. Some antimotility drugs such as opiates and loperamide may cause paralytic

ileus and death in children. Drugs that improve the consistency of stools, such as smectite, are advocated by some as it is believed that normalisation of stools may encourage mothers for better feeding during a diarrheal episode. However, there is no consensus on this issue.

In addition to established pharmaceuticals, many traditional antidiarrheal substances usually derived from herbs are widely used. Most are of questionable purity, and the pharmacologically active component is often not known. Some of these agents have been ineffective when investigated in controlled trials. In some areas, belief in local antidiarrheals may be so strong that they should be tolerated as long as the treatment guidelines shown in Table 15.2 are otherwise followed.

Perhaps the greatest problem associated with the widespread use of antidiarrheals is the cost, as drugs divert resources and attention from ORT and nutritional therapy. One approach to this problem is education of drug dispensers and, possibly, an increase of the price of ORS in the free market, to allow sales at a profit. It is believed that such measures might encourage drug retailers to promote ORS, rather than antidiarrheals.

Antimicrobials are not effective in uncomplicated acute diarrhea and their use should be discouraged. In contrast, antimicrobials are indicated in dysentery, cholera and typhoid fever. The drugs of choice and their alternatives are given in Table 15.5.

NUTRITIONAL THERAPY

Adequate dietary management during and after diarrheal disease is very important in order to:[10,11]

1) Reduce or prevent the damage of intestinal functions induced by withholding food.

2) Prevent or decrease the nutritional damage caused by the disease. Even though appetite is reduced, most children will eat amounts of food that are nutritionally important, and significant proportions of nutrients are absorbed during acute and persistent diarrhea.[10]

3) Shorten the duration of the disease. Many foods that are commonly eaten in developing countries produce this effect, especially in acute diarrhea.[10,11] This reduces the risk of dehydration, makes the children more comfortable, and reduces the caretaking chores of their mothers.

Table 15.5. Antimicrobial therapy for acute bacterial gastroenteritis.

Disease	Alternative antimicrobials	Comment
Dysentery	co-trimoxazole ampicillin ciprofloxacin*	bloody diarrhea is usually due to shigellosis
Typhoid fever	chloramphenicol co-trimoxazole ciprofloxacin*	antibiotics are not required for salmonellosis without enteric fever
Cholera	tetracycline furazolidone	furazolidone is recommended instead of tetracycline for children under two years of age
Traveller's diarrhea	co-trimoxazole doxycycline ciprofloxacin*	

*Other fluorokinolones may also be used

4) Allow catch-up growth and a return to good nutritional condition during convalescence.[10,12] This is especially important for children who live in unsanitary environments, and go through recurrent cycles of disease – poor dietary practices – disease.

Worsening or persistence of the disease due to food intolerance is not a frequent occurrence. Misconceptions among the general public and many health workers may lead to the reduction or rejection of the milk intake, including interruption of breast feeding, and of the intake of many common foods, based on the belief that their lactose, fibre or fat contents make the diarrhea worse. This is very unfortunate, as it is often necessary to offer familiar and palatable foods to overcome a sick child's low appetite.

Economic constraints are an important cause of poor dietary practices during diarrhea. Some of the foods often recommended by doctors are too expensive for many families. Emphasis should be placed on foods commonly available in low-income households.[10,12]

Breast milk is the food of choice for infants. In addition to its nutritional qualities, it is associated with improvement in fecal water output, number and consistency of stools, and duration of diarrhea.

Cows' milk is well tolerated by most children with diarrhea, including infants under 6 months of age who are fed milk-based formulas at the usual concentrations. Even children with some degree of intolerance do not have problems with small volumes of milk, either alone or as part of a mixed diet. In identified cases of lactose intolerance when it is desired to reduce milk intake, the recommendation should be to mix the milk or substitute part of it with another nutritious food, rather than to dilute it with water. In these cases it must be clearly explained to the mothers that full-strength milk can be given when diarrhea disappears, and that it is usually well tolerated during convalescence. When they are culturally acceptable, fermented milks and yoghurt are good options for lactose intolerance patients, or for children whose mothers are reluctant to use regular milk. It should be noted, however, that many yoghurts have as much lactose as unprocessed milk.

Many cereal-based gruels and paps are readily accepted by mothers of children with diarrhea. Rice is probably the cereal used by a wider variety of cultures. Other good cereal products that have been fed as gruels, paps or solid foods, are from maize (flour, dough, tortillas), wheat (flour, toasted grain, bread, noodles) and sorghum (flour, dough).

Good results have been obtained with mixed diets, largely of vegetable origin, previously thought to be inadequate for children with diarrhea because of their high fibre and fat content, or because they included products such as lentils and black beans.[10–12] Table 15.6 lists some examples. Good protein quality has been achieved by combining cereals with pulses, using mixtures of vegetable flours, or adding food of animal origin. Energy density has been increased with vegetable oil and sugar.

Practical recommendations

1) Food should be offered frequently, six to seven times daily to infants under 1 year and five to six times to older children, or more often if the child's appetite is markedly depressed. The mother and other care-givers must be patient and understanding to overcome the lack of appetite.

Table 15.6. Examples of diets prepared with local foods, well tolerated by most children with diarrhea. Vegetable oil and sugar are added to increase energy density.

Milk and vegetable combinations
    Milk, and wheat noodles
    Milk, potatoes and carrots
    Milk and chickpeas
    Milk and corn
    Milk, rice and lentils

Other animal foods, with or without vegetables
    Minced chicken
    Chicken, rice and pulses
    Fish, rice and banana
    Egg and rice

All vegetable diets
    Rice, pulses and banana
    Corn-cottonseed flour, rice, corn, beans
    Wheat, peas, carrots
    Corn and cowpea

Mixed diets
    Chicken, lentils, rice, egg, milk, bread, bananas
    Corn, beans, egg, bread, vegetables, with or without corn-cottonseed flour
    Corn, beans, rice, egg, bread, chicken, fruit, vegetables and corn-soy flour or corn-cottonseed flour

---

2) Most children with diarrhea tolerate well cows' and other animals' milk. Practical advises for their use include: a) feed the type of milk used by the child before the disease; b) when skim milk is used, increase its energy density with 2 ml vegetable oil or 4–5 grams sucrose per 100 ml; c) feed full-strength (undiluted) milk and milk-based formulas – if signs such as increased volume of stools, weight loss, vomiting or dehydration appear, mix full-strength milk with equal amounts of other foods for one or two days, followed by full-strength milk; d) soy- and chicken-based formulas, other non-dairy foods, yoghurt or low-lactose milk can be used for children with intolerance to milk or lactose – availability, cost and cultural acceptance must be considered before recommending them; and e) tolerance to milk must be assessed again during convalescence in those children who were intolerant during diarrhea. Milk should be reintroduced in their diet according to the results.

3) Many local animal- and vegetable-based diets, which include cereals, some pulses, hard-boiled eggs, ground chicken meat, fish, sugar and vegetable oil, are well tolerated and assimilated during diarrhea. Some of these diets reduce the duration of the disease. Diets that will make stools appear more normal may influence mothers to accept the recommended feeding practices.

4) Good feeding practices are particularly important during convalescence to allow catch-up growth and nutritional recovery.

PERSISTENT OR PROLONGED DIARRHEA

This term refers to diarrheal episodes of presumed infectious etiology that have an unusually long duration. It does not include chronic or recurrent diarrheal disorders of hereditary, dietary or other acquired origins, such as gluten-sensitive enteropathy, monosaccharide intolerance, tropical sprue, blind loop syndrome or the chronic diarrhea of AIDS.

The definition of unusually long is arbitrary. Most episodes of childhood diarrhea resolve within one week or less, and the duration of the disease follows a continuous distribution that is skewed to the right. As Figure 15.3 shows, there is no clear breakpoint between episodes of shorter and longer duration. Based on the association of duration with impairment in nutritional status and an increased risk of death, most people define persistent diarrhea as that which lasts at least 14 days.[5]

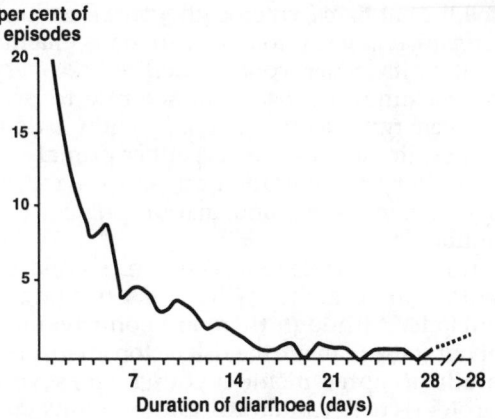

Figure 15.3. Frequency distribution of duration of diarrhea (composite data from Guatemala, Peru and Bangladesh).

Incidence and consequences

Using this definition, about 10 per cent (range 3–23 per cent) of diarrheas in children from developing countries become persistent, especially among those less than 3 years old, and more so among infants under 1 year.[4,5] Due to their long duration, as many as half of all recorded diarrhea days in a population may be from persistent episodes.

Persistent diarrhea causes substantial weight loss in most patients through a combination of reduced appetite, prolongation of malabsorption and fecal loss of nutrients, and poor – or suboptimal – dietary practices. It may be responsible for about one-third to half of all diarrhea-related deaths. Case fatality ranges widely, from less than 1 per cent in community studies to 14 per cent in hospital-based reports. From these epidemiological and clinical observations it can be concluded that while most episodes are not too severe, do not require hospitalisation and have a low mortality rate, severe cases have a high mortality. Furthermore, since persistent diarrhea is a major cause of malnutrition in developing countries, even the milder, non-fatal episodes contribute to the overall high mortality rates that are frequently associated with malnutrition in these countries.

Causes and risk factors

The pathogenesis of persistent diarrhea is not known. Several causes, probably in combination, have been proposed, including: infection with specific enteropathogens, such as enteroadherent E. coli, enteropathogenic E. coli and Cryptosporidium; intolerance to foods, mainly milk or its lactose content; delayed recovery of intestinal mucosal damage due to protein–energy malnutrition or vitamin A deficiency; immunodeficiency, either primary or secondary to malnutrition or to a recent systemic infections; and, inappropriate use of antibiotics.

It is not possible to foresee which children with acute diarrhea will have a prolonged episode. Although there are controversies about some of them, the risk factors more generally accepted include: young age, severe protein–energy malnutrition, previous episodes of persistent diarrhea, acute diarrhea within the preceding two months, and presence of blood and mucus in feces during acute diarrhea. Of the infectious agents, enteroad-

herent E. coli (EAEC) with autoaggregative adherence have the strongest correlation with persistent diarrhea. Moreover, infection with two or more enteric pathogens, especially with EAEC or Cryptosporidium is suggestive of high risk.

The role of diet and feeding practices before the illness or during an acute episode has not been clearly established. There are some suggestions that diarrhea is prolonged when it occurs shortly after the introduction of non-human milk into the diet, or when soy-based, low-fibre diets are used in the dietary management of acute diarrhea. However, there is not enough evidence to consider those foods as risk factors of persistent diarrhea.

Management

The inability to provide a rational explanation for most cases of persistent diarrhea has led to empirical treatment of the disease. The most important factors to consider are maintenance of hydration and avoiding malnutrition. Successful dietary management is usually a compromise between the nutritional demands of the patients, their altered intestinal functions and the foods that are accessible and culturally acceptable. In general, management of persistent diarrhea includes:

1) Prevention or correction of dehydration, as in the management of acute diarrhea.

2) Continued feeding to correct or prevent nutritional damage. Breast-feeding should be encouraged. Diets rich in fibre and vegetable fats do not seem to have deleterious effects. Cows' milk and milk of other animals may be fed as part of mixed diets. Non-dairy diets that have been successfully used in developing countries include minced chicken, and mixtures of rice with egg (whole or egg white), or of either rice or corn with pulses (soy, beans, lentils). Energy density should be raised in all those diets to about 250 kJ (60 kcal)/100 grams with vegetable oil and sugar.

Zinc and vitamin A supplements seem to reduce the duration of diarrhea, but their effectiveness has not been fully established. Blind use of antibiotics is not effective, and they should be given only in dysenteric persistent diarrhea. Other pharmacological agents, such as cholestyramine and antisecretory/antimotility drugs, have given inconsistent results and their routine use is not recommended.

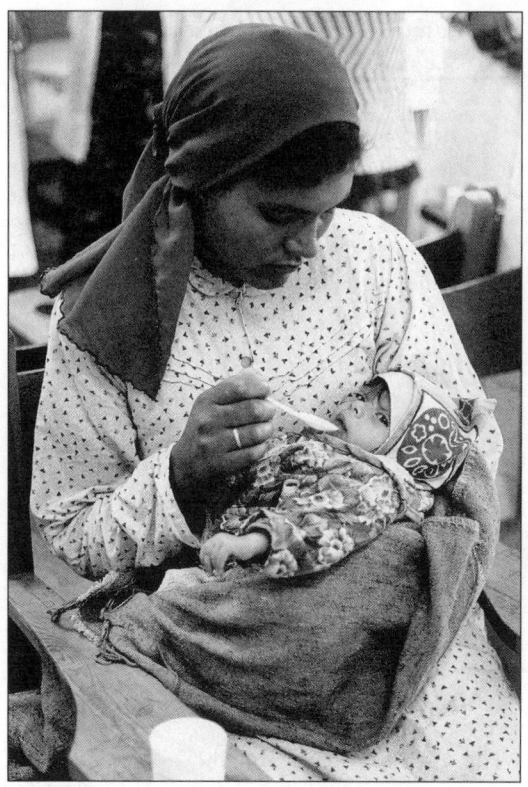

Mother feeding her baby with ORS-solution in Egypt. Photo: UNICEF/Sean Sprague

PREVENTION OF DIARRHEAL DISEASES AND THEIR CONSEQUENCES

The incidence of and mortality from diarrheal diseases in developing countries today is comparable to the situation in industrialised countries about one hundred years ago. Clean, running, chlorinated water, sewage disposal, sanitation, high standards of hygiene in food processing, refrigeration and generally improved nutrition of children have all contributed to the reduced incidence of diarrheal diseases in developed countries, and access to good medical management has controlled mortality.

The WHO Diarrhoeal Diseases Control Programme and other organisations have given first priority to the prevention of diarrheal deaths, rather than prevention of cases, and focused on promotion of ORT. The current production of ORS-sachets is equivalent to about 350 million litres per year. Most of that quantity is produced in developing countries.

It is estimated that ORS is accessible to more than 60 per cent of children, and used in about 20 per cent of all diarrheal episodes. Other forms of ORT are given in a further 10 per cent of the cases.[4]

Further training on the use of ORT is required since currently less than 20 per cent of health personnel in developing countries have received formal training on the subject. In addition to ORT, the training includes nutritional management of diarrhea. Other target groups for training are medical and nursing students, pharmacists and drug sellers, and, naturally, mothers. Promotion of adequate feeding practices, including breast-feeding and weaning foods, should be emphasised.[13] Other interventions that are likely to have an effect on both the incidence and mortality include hygienic preparation and storage of foods, vitamin A supplementation, and improvement of sanitary practices such as use of latrines and hand washing.

Vaccines against diarrheal diseases may also play a role in the prevention of diarrheal diseases mortality, and morbidity, in the future. Of the existing vaccines, measles vaccine certainly has a potential in reducing mortality attributed to diarrheal diseases, since measles is associated with diarrhea in some 20 per cent of the cases. This potential has been estimated between 6 and 26 per cent.[14]

Live oral rotavirus vaccine, based on rhesus rotavirus, is being tested in field trials in both developed and developing counties.[15] Preliminary results suggest that this vaccine is efficacious in the prevention of rotavirus diarrhea in the USA, but not in Peru.

A *killed oral cholera vaccine* has recently been licensed in Sweden and is available to travellers. The vaccine has been tested in Bangladesh where it showed over 60 per cent efficacy in the native population.[16]

Typhoid vaccines could potentially have a much greater use in developing countries than currently is the case. Live attenuated oral typhoid vaccine Ty 21a is licensed in a number of countries and used primarily for the immunisation of travellers. A full immunisation schedule consists of three or four oral doses.[17]

Even if effective vaccines against diarrheal diseases become available, a final decision on their use will be with the countries. The vaccines may be cost-effective in calculations, but still not affordable to many developing countries without substantial support from outside.

References

1. Snyder JD, Merson MH. The magnitude of the global problem of acute diarrhoeal disease: a review of active surveillance data. Bull WHO 1982;60:605–13.
2. Black RE. Epidemiology of diarrhoeal disease: implications for control by vaccines. Vaccine 1993;11(2):100–6.
3. de Zoysa I, Feachem RG. Intervention for the control of diarrhoeal diseases among young children: rotavirus and cholera immunization. Bull WHO 1985;63:569–83.
4. Programme for Control of Diarrhoeal Diseases. Eight programme report 1990–1991. Geneva: WHO,1992. (WHO/CDD/92/38).
5. Programme for Control of Diarrhoeal Diseases. A manual for the treatment of diarrhoea – for use by physicians and other senior health workers. Geneva: WHO. 1990. (WHO/CDD/SER/80.2 Rev. 2)
6. Pizarro D, Posada Grams, Villavicencio N, *et al.* Hypernatremic and hyponatremic dehydration treated with oral glucose/electrolyte solution (90 mmol/l sodium). Am J Dis Child 1983;137:730–4
7. Hirschorn N. The treatment of acute diarrhea in children. An historical and physiological perspective. Am J Clin Nutr 1980;33:637–63.
8. Molla AM, Ahmed SM, Greenough WB III. Rice-based oral rehydration solution decreases the stool volume in acute diarrhoea. Bull WHO 1985;63:751–6.
9. Cunha Ferreira RMC, Elliott EJ, Watson AJM *et al.* Dominant role for osmolality in the efficacy of glucose and glycine-containing oral rehydration solutions. Acta Paediatr 1992;81:46–50.
10. Torun B, Chew F. Practical approaches towards dietary management of acute diarrhoea in developing communities. Trans R Soc Trop Med Hygiene 1991;85:12–7.
11. Molla AM, Molla A, Rohde J, Greenough WB. Turning off the diarrhea: the role of food and ORS. J Ped Gastroenterol Nutr 1989;8:81–4.
12. Shaikh S, Molla AM, Islam A, Billoo AG, Hendricks K, Snyder J. A traditional diet as part of oral rehydration therapy in severe acute diarrhoea in young children. J Diarrhoeal Dis Res 1991;3:258–63.
13. Feachem RG, Koblinsky MA. Interventions for the control of diarrhoeal diseases among young children: promotion of breast-feeding. Bull WHO 1984;62:271–9.
14. Feachem RG, Koblinsky MA. Interventions for the control of diarrhoeal diseases among young children: measles immunization. Bull WHO 1983;61:641–52.
15. Vesikari T. Clinical trials of live oral rotavirus vaccines: the Finnish experience. Vaccine 1993;11:255–61.
16. Clemens JD, Sack DA, Harris JR, *et al.*Field trial of oral cholera vaccines in Bangladesh. Lancet 1986;ii:124–7.
17. Levine MM, Taylor DN, Ferreccio C. Typhoid vaccines come of age. Pediatr Infect Dis J 1989;8:374–81.

Additional reading

1. Persistent diarrhea in children in developing countries. Acta Paediatr Scand 1992;81(Suppl 381):1–154.
2. Readings on diarrhoea: Student manual. Geneva: WHO, 1990. (Document WHO/CDD/SER/90.13.)
3. Strengthening the teaching of diarrhoeal diseases to medical students. Geneva: WHO, 1991. (Document CDD/SER/91.1.)

Further information can be obtained from

WHO, Division of Diarrhoeal and Acute Respiratory Disease Control, CH-1211 Geneva 27, Switzerland. – Training materials, manuals, and technical papers on diarrheal diseases.

About the authors

Timo Vesikari is a specialist in pediatrics and virology. He is currently Professor of Virology and consulting pediatric infectious disease specialist at Tampere University Central Hospital. During 1981–87 he was acting Professor of Pediatrics in the same setting. From 1987 to 1990 he served as a scientist in the Diarrhoeal Diseases Control Programme at the WHO. He was then based in Geneva but was involved in research on diarrheal disease and enteric vaccines in several developing countries. His current research interests are rotavirus vaccine and case management of diarrheal diseases.
Benjamin Torun *is a specialist in physiology and human nutrition. For more than 20 years he has worked at the Institute of Nutrition of Central America and Panama in Guatemala City. His research has included clinical, metabolic and field studies on malnutrition and on diarrheal diseases. In 1986–89 he was a member of the WHO Diarrhoeal Diseases Control Programme's Scientific Working Group on Case Management, and has served as a consultant for several other international organisations. He has published extensively on nutrition and physical activity of children and adults, energy and nutrition requirements and functional consequences of malnutrition.*

Lankinen KS, Bergström S, Mäkelä PH and Peltomaa M, eds.
Health and disease in developing countries. London:The Macmillan Press Limited, 1994:147–162.

16 MALARIA

Hilton Whittle, M.D.
Medical Research Council Laboratories
Fajara, P.O. Box, 273 Banjul,
The Gambia

Michael Boele van Hemsbroek, M.D.
Medical Research Council Laboratories
Fajara, P.O. Box, 273 Banjul,
The Gambia

INTRODUCTION

Malaria is one of mankind's most feared and serious afflictions that causes more morbidity and mortality than any other human disease. About 55 per cent of the world's population is exposed to the infection which exerts its toll mainly on the young and the pregnant. Attempts in the 1960s to eradicate the disease by spraying the anopheline mosquito vector soon failed as insecticide resistance developed. Now the mosquitoes have shifted to new ecological niches as man becomes increasingly urbanised or as large scale irrigation has been extended. A further complication has been the rapid and widespread development of drug resistance in many areas of the world resulting in an added threat not only to local inhabitants but also to invading armies, tourists and travelling salesmen. The situation is deteriorating rapidly in many parts of the world. *P. falciparum*, the deadliest of the malaria parasites, kills alone in Africa 1–2 per cent of its children and is responsible for at least one million deaths each year.

PARASITES AND ANTIGENS

Malaria in man is due to infection with either *Plasmodium falciparum*, *P. malariae*, *P. vivax* or *P. ovale*. *P. falciparum* is the most common and most virulent species as it multiplies most rapidly and is able to sequester in small blood vessels causing damage to the brain and other organs. The others seldom cause death but can be difficult to cure because of relapses due to cryptic forms in liver or red cells. The infection is caused by the bite of an infected female *Anopheles* mosquito. Each parasite has a distinctive morphology and characteristic antigens at each stage of its life cycle which takes place in both the mosquito and in the liver and blood of man (Figure 16.1).

The developmental characteristics of the four species differ (Table 16.1). *P. falciparum* does not have a secondary liver cycle, and relapses are thus unknown after treatment has eradicated the parasite from the blood.

The parasite releases a toxin which is responsible for the fever. This is a phospholipid which

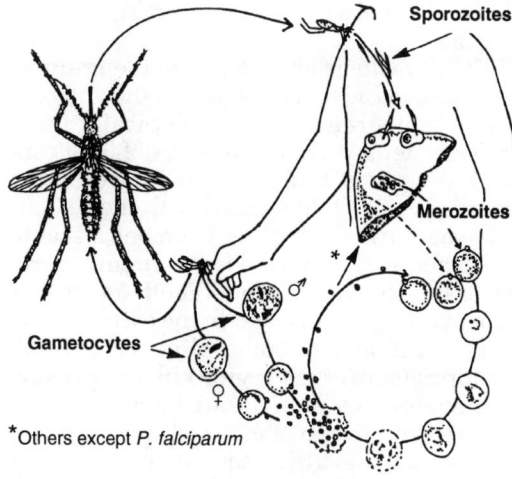

Figure 16.1. Life cycle of human malarial parasites.

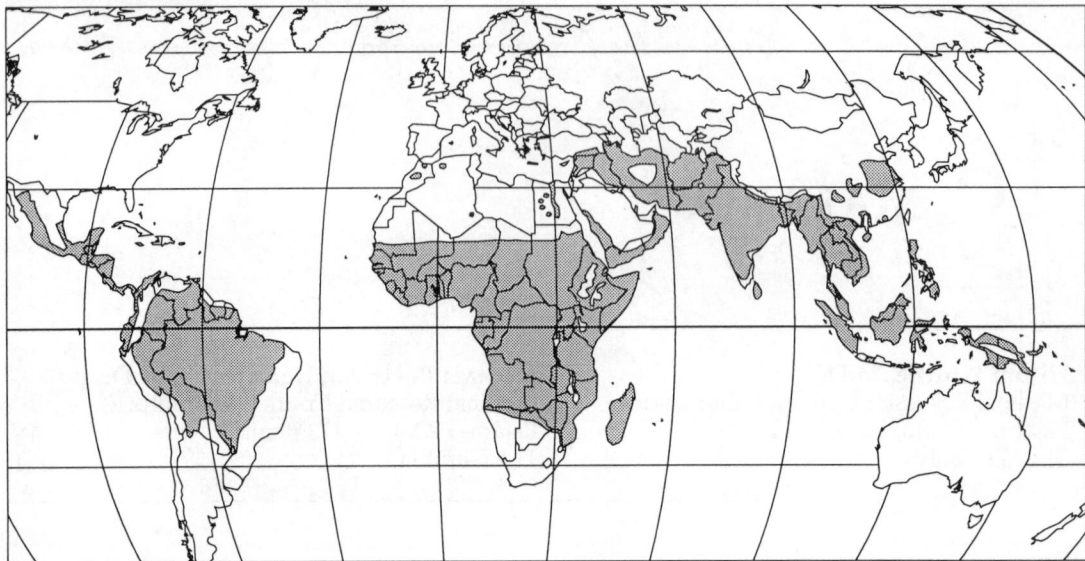

Figure 16.2. Distribution of human malaria in the world.[18]

stimulates the host's mononuclear cells to produce pyrogenic cytokines.[1] The parasite breaks down hemoglobin with consequent formation of the pigment hemozoin. Iron deficiency limits parasite growth due to a relative deficiency of hemoglobin in the red cell. The parasite causes changes in erythrocyte size, shape, and deformability. Insertion of parasite antigens in the internal surface of the erythrocyte membrane is associated with the formation of protuberances known as 'knobs'. This makes the cells sticky so that red cells infected with schizonts bind to capillary endothelia in the spleen, brain and other organs.

The parasite is able to evade the immune response because the stage-specific antigens vary from strain to strain. Typically these large proteins consist of a series of long conserved regions, built up of repeated amino acid sequences, interspersed with shorter variable regions which differ from one strain to the other. A typical case is the circumsporozoite antigen which is found both on the surface of the sporozoite and in the early stage of liver infection. Antibodies directed to B cell epitopes (conserved region) block invasion of hepatocytes *in vivo* but have not been found protective in man. T cell epitopes (variable region) have been shown in mice to trigger cytotoxic T cells which kill the parasite when it is in the hepatic cells. However, such cells have been extremely difficult to show in man.

The unusual repeating structures of malaria antigens form shared epitopes either within the same antigen or in different antigens within the same stage of the life cycle or at different stages.[2] These multiple cross-reacting epitopes may impair the development of a protective immune response either by absorption of antibodies or by induction of antibodies of low affinity which are inefficient in parasite elimination.

EPIDEMIOLOGY

Malaria is widely distributed throughout the tropics (Figure 16.2). *P. falciparum* predominates in Africa, Haiti, Dominican Republic, French Guinea, Surinam, parts of Asia and Papua New Guinea. *P. vivax* predominates in Latin America, Turkey, the Indian subcontinent and China. *P. malariae* is widely distributed but much less common than either of the former species. *P. ovale* occurs mainly in Africa.

The epidemiological features of malaria, mainly determined by the climate and the ecology of the mosquito vectors, influence immunity in the population. Thus, at one extreme in the forest zones of West Africa children are infected in the second 6 months of life, parasitemia reaches 80–100 per cent in childhood, disease occurs throughout the year, and death occurs mainly in the first 5 years of life. In contrast, the disease is seasonal in the dry savannah of Africa and mortality is spread

Table 16.1. Characteristics of human malaria parasites.

Species	P. falciparum	P. vivax	P. ovale	P. malariae
Pre-patent period	8–25 days	8–27 days	9–17 days	15–30 days
Length of asexual cycle	48 hours	48 hours	48 hours	72 hours
Number of merozoites in liver schizont	40 000	10 000	15 000	2 000
Number of merozoites in blood schizont	8–32	12–24	4–16	6–12
Type of red cell parasitised	any	reticulocytes	reticulocytes	mature
Chloroquine resistance	Yes	Rare	No	No
Fatal attack	Yes	No	No	No

over a wider age range (Figure 16.3). At the other extreme the disease may be epidemic, as in parts of North India or Thailand, and affect all ages.

The mosquito. Human malarial parasites are transmitted by the females of the genus *Anophelinae*. The females of this genus can be differentiated from other mosquitoes by their posture when feeding: she inclines her whole body at an angle to the skin of her prey. There are over 400 species of *Anopheles* which differ in their preference of habitat and whether they prefer to bite man or animals. *All feed at night,* some more frequently than others. However mosquitoes are remarkably adaptive changing their behaviour according to local circumstances. Thus, if houses are heavily sprayed they will rest outside.

The vectorial capacity of a mosquito population is determined by: 1) density of vectors in relation to man; 2) number of blood meals taken on man per day (*An. gambiae*, a highly efficient vector, feeds on man on alternate days whereas *An. culcifacies*, a less efficient vector, may feed only every third day and only 10 per cent of its meals are enjoyed from man); 3) longevity which determines the proportion of vectors surviving per day; and 4) incubation period of the parasite in the vector. The last two temperature dependent factors are very important. An efficient vector will be long-lived, occur at high density and frequently bite man: such are the characteristics of *An. gambiae*.

Climate. Temperature is the major determinant. Parasites do not develop in the vector below 15°C; the optimal temperature is between 20 and 30°C but *P. vivax* can adapt also to colder climates. Thus malaria is largely a lowland disease. Rainfall is also important for the mosquito needs high humidity and standing water in which to breed. In

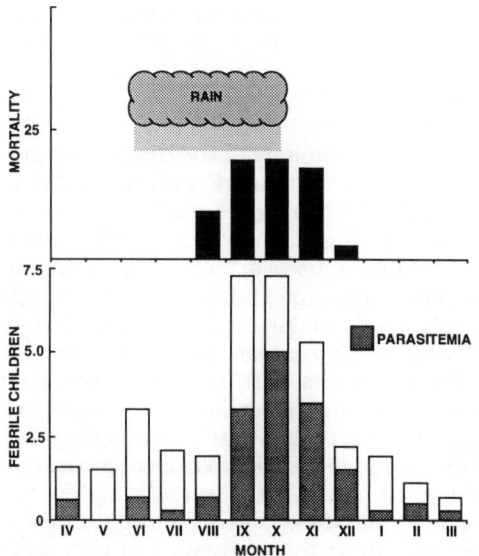

Figure 16.3. Prevalence of fever, parasitemia and proportion of deaths by *P. falciparum* malaria in Gambian children.[19]

Table 16.2. Patterns of malaria infections.[15]

	HIGHLY ENDEMIC (HOLO-ENDEMIC)	INTERMEDIATE	EPIDEMIC
Malaria transmission			
	Heavy throughout the year	Transmission for a few months each year	Intense during epidemics None in nonepidemic periods
Severe clinical malaria			
	Children only	Mainly children, but sometimes adults	Children and adults equally during epidemics
Splenomegaly in the community			
	Very high in children (more than 50%) Low in adults	Moderate in children (20-50%) Variable in adults	Low in adults and children between epidemics (less than 10%)
Parasitemia in the community			
	Very high in children Low in adults	Moderate in children Low in adults Seasonal variation	Low in adults and children between epidemics
Immunity			
	High in adults Low in small children	Moderate in adults Low in children	Low in adults and children

endemic areas such as the Sahel of Africa the seasonal pattern of transmission is determined by rainfall being high during the rains and shortly afterward and very low during the dry season.

Man. Man and his habits, including his attempts to control malaria, obviously influence the epidemiology of the disease. Migration of non-immune workers from highland areas to lowland irrigation or mining areas, such as the Thai–Cambodian border, often leads to severe disease. Non-immune travellers from Europe may become ill with malaria after staying in malaria endemic areas. Irrigation schemes have opened huge areas suitable for the *Anopheles* and the transmission of malaria. Rapid urbanisation without adequate drainage has created new ecological niches for the mosquito with a consequent increase of malaria. The widespread but intermittent use of inadequate doses of chloroquine in these cities may defer the acquisition of immunity until later ages and may increase the likelihood of resistant strains of *P. falciparum*.

Patterns of malaria infections. These are the result of the interplay of the duration of

malaria transmission, the infectivity rate of mosquitoes, the extent of man–mosquito contact and the degree of immunity of the population. Thus malaria endemicity varies from highly endemic to epidemic according to these factors (Table 16.2).

IMMUNITY TO MALARIA

Types of immunity

Genetic factors. By killing many children over the centuries malaria has selected for a number of genetic traits that reduce susceptibility to clinical infection.[3,4] Thus in populations from malarial areas such as West Africa there is a high frequency of the *sickle cell gene*. This gene alters the polymerisation of hemoglobin so that under low oxygen tension abnormal gelling and distortion of the red cells occurs. These changes inhibit both the invasion and growth of the parasite within the red cells, and children who carry this gene are protected from severe malaria. However, individuals homozygous for the gene seldom survive as their cells distort and sickle under the

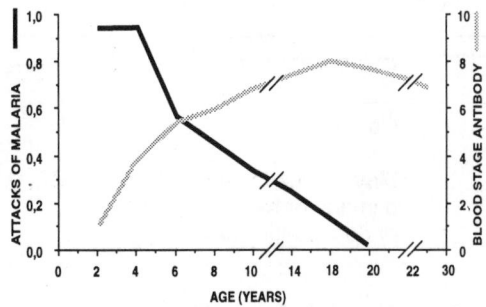

Figure 16.4. Clinical attacks of *P. falciparum* malaria (fever with parasitemia) related to age and the level of immunofluorescent antibody to blood stages of parasite (courtesy of K. Marsh).

slightest stress leading to severe anemia and infarction of various organs.[3]

A number of other genetic traits that affect the red cell, possibly making them less susceptible to malaria infection, are found in high frequency in malarious areas. These include the hemoglobin C and E genes, the glucose-6-phosphate dehydrogenase deficiency gene (G6PD) and gamma and beta thalassemia genes. Certain Duffy blood group antigens are necessary for invasion of red cells by *P. vivax*: as the genes for these antigens are rare in Negroes, this type of malaria is seldom seen in Africa. Certain HLA antigens which are frequent in West Africans, but not in Caucasians, may confer resistance to severe malaria.[3]

Passive immunity. IgG acquired transplacentally from the mother protects the infant against clinical disease during the first 6 months of life thus demonstrating that antibodies alone are sufficient to confer immunity to malaria. The amount of antibody transferred from mother to child depends on the immune status of the mother so that children of partially immune or non-immune mothers are susceptible to malaria before 6 months of age. Additional evidence for the protective effect of antibody was obtained in an early experiment which demonstrated that globulin derived from *P. falciparum* immune adults could cure children with parasitemia.

Acquired immunity. Immunity in endemic areas is acquired slowly after repeated infections and is never complete in that adults often harbour asymptomatic parasitemias. At first children become tolerant to infection so that clinical signs and symptoms diminish for a given level of parasitemia; later parasitemia drops to low levels. In endemic areas the brunt

of *P. falciparum* morbidity and mortality falls between 1 and 4 years of age but may fall even earlier in areas of very high transmission.

Acquired immunity wanes if inhabitants leave endemic areas. Students who study for long periods abroad may suffer severe attacks on returning home. Pregnancy diminishes immunity to *P. falciparum* through unknown mechanisms resulting in anemia, a parasitised placenta and a lower birth weight of the baby (200 grams less than average in The Gambia). These effects are particularly marked in primigravids.

Mechanisms of immunity

Antibody. High titres of antibody to the blood stage antigens such as the red cell surface antigen, the merozoite surface antigen or the soluble S antigens develop relatively early in children in endemic areas, but clinical attacks still occur in the face of these antibodies (Figure 16.4). The probable explanation is that effective antibody must be both species- and strain-specific. Only after repeated attacks does the full repertoire of antibody develop to all strains of the parasite present in the community.[5]

Specific and non-specific cellular immunity. Less is known of this phenomenon than about humoral immunity. Cytokines produced by helper T cells, notably gamma interferon and TNF, probably play a central role in the inhibition of parasite growth either in the red cell or in the hepatocyte. They are also involved in the pathogenesis of cerebral malaria.[6]

Immunosuppression and other immunological effects of malaria. An attack of *P. falciparum* malaria has profound effects on the immune system.[7] Cellular proliferation to malaria antigens is inhibited, large amounts of non-specific immunoglobulin are produced by activated B cells and cytotoxic immunity to latent viruses like the Epstein–Barr virus is abrogated. These disturbances may also be central to the development of a number of immunopathological syndromes such as *P. malariae* nephrosis, tropical splenomegaly syndrome and Burkitt's lymphoma.

CLINICAL FEATURES AND THEIR PATHOGENESIS

This section relates largely to the more severe forms of *P. falciparum* malaria seen in non-immune adults who are foreign to endemic

Table 16.3. Differences between severe malaria in adults and children.[8]

Sign or symptom	Adults	Children
Cough	Uncommon	Common
Convulsions	Indicates cerebral involvement or hypoglycemia	May be due to cerebral damage or hypoglycemia or due to high fever
Duration of symptoms	Several days	Shorter 2–3 days
Jaundice	Common	Uncommon
Duration of coma after start of treatment	2–4 days	1–2 days
Hypoglycemia	Uncommon but occurs after quinine	Common before treatment
Pulmonary edema	Common	Rare
Renal failure	Common	Rare
Neurological sequelae	Uncommon	10% of cases
Severe anemia	Uncommon	Common not necessarily associated with cerebral signs

areas and semi-immune children and pregnant women who are natives of these areas. It is not clear why only 1–2 per cent of children in an endemic area suffer severe disease. Parasite factors such as the dose, virulence, and drug resistance are important; host factors such as state of immunity to the invading strain and, perhaps, HLA type also play a role.[8] There is no convincing evidence that nutritional or sociological factors are implicated. However there are differences between severe malaria in adults and children, these are summarised in Table 16.3.

History of illness. This is of less importance for indigens in the endemic areas. In them fever during the malaria transmission season is likely to be due to malaria though this should be substantiated by microscopy of a blood film. However, at any one time a large proportion of individuals with low grade parasitemia remain asymptomatic, and other causes of fever should also be looked for.

In non-immune patients, especially travellers who have returned from endemic areas, the history is of vital importance because it provides the clue to diagnosis and dictates also the treatment. The incubation period between infection and symptoms varies with the parasite (Table 16.1) and may be further delayed by inadequate prophylaxis or chemotherapy due to drug resistance. The majority of travellers infected with P. falciparum fall ill within 6 weeks of return to their native country.

The history gives a guide to the speed of the illness and the rapidity of neurological onset of signs or coma which are major determinants of outcome. Children frequently die within 2–3 days from the onset of severe symptoms.

Fever. The clinical hallmark of malaria is said to be periodic fever. Typically it recurs every second day in tertian malaria (due to P. falciparum, P. vivax and P. ovale) and every third day in quartan malaria (due to P. malariae). The fever occurs when schizonts rupture releasing their phospholipid toxin and is recurrent because parasites undergo repeated cycles of growth in the erythrocytes of the host. However, in practice the pattern of fever is not necessarily periodic as the cycles of growth frequently become asynchronous. As immunity develops in older children and adults who live in endemic areas fever becomes less marked and less periodic until eventually non-symptomatic parasitemia occurs.

In non-immune patients fever is often high (above 40°C) and paroxysmal being preceded by rigours. In young children the fever may provoke short-lived convulsions that are not necessarily the herald of cerebral malaria unless associated with coma. Headache is a common accompaniment, but photophobia or a stiff neck are not. In adults joint pains and myalgia are common and in young children, as in so many other febrile illness, vomiting and diarrhea are frequent.

Hepatomegaly and/or splenomegaly. Enlargement of these organs accompanied by tenderness should not be confused with the chronic, non-tender non-symptomatic hypertrophy of liver and spleen which is found in endemic areas and is used as an epidemiological marker of endemicity (Table 16.2).

Anemia. Anemia, sometimes associated with mild jaundice, may progress rapidly in patients with high parasitemia. The primary mechanism is disruption of the red blood cells by the parasite. Beware the anemic child (Hb less than 7.0 g/dl) who has a high parasitemia (more than 250 parasites per high power field) for the hemoglobin may fall precipitously

Table 16.4. Modified Glasgow coma score for use in children with cerebral malaria.[16]

a) Best motor response	Score
Localises painful stimulus*	2
Withdraws limb from pain†	1
Non-specific or absent response	0
b) Verbal response to above stimuli	
Appropriate cry	2
Moaning or inappropriate cry	1
None	0
c) Eye movements	
directed (e.g. follows face)	1
not directed	0

Notes: *Rub knuckles on patients sternum.
  †Firm pressure on thumbnail bed with pencil.

during treatment before blood can be obtained for transfusion. Hemorrhage due to clotting abnormalities and petechiae are *not* a usual feature of severe malaria, but are more likely to be due to bacteremia or viremia. Deep jaundice is a bad sign which is found in patients with hemoglobinopathies such as sickle cell disease or G6PD deficiency or those with blackwater fever (see below).

A more chronic form of anemia is often found in young indigens towards the end of the malaria season. Repeated or prolonged attacks of malaria are responsible for red cell destruction and perhaps for bone marrow suppression also. Folic acid deficiency is not involved and these patients usually respond to antimalarials and oral iron therapy. Transfusion is indicated in cardiac failure or if the patient is not responding to treatment. Severe anemia due to drug-resistant parasites is becoming an increasing problem especially in children. Anemic children need careful follow-up, including parasitological assessment coupled with correct treatment.

Cerebral malaria. This is defined as an unconscious person with a febrile illness and malaria parasites in their blood. Those with postconvulsive coma should only be included in this category if unconsciousness persists for more than 30 minutes after a convulsion. The patient is desperately ill, may have repeated and prolonged seizures and often shows signs of widespread neurological abnormalities such as decorticate rigidity with oculogyric crises, dysconjugate gaze or hemiplegia. The depth of coma which in children should be assessed according to the modified Glasgow scale (Table 16.4), and the blood glucose level are the major prognostic indicators (Table 16.5). Other factors also influence the outcome, for example the level of parasitemia, extremes of age (less than three or over 60 years) and late pregnancy (third trimester). Even in the best hands the mortality ranges between 10–30 per cent.

The pathophysiology of cerebral malaria is complex and incompletely understood (Figure 16.5). Parasitised erythrocytes may become sticky due to knob formation or they may bind to non-infected red blood cells forming rosettes. The parasitised erythrocytes may bind to the endothelia of small vessels in the brain causing patchy local damage with possible reduction in blood flow in these areas and resultant stagnant anoxia. Toxins released from the ruptured schizonts are also known

Table 16.5. Prognostic features on admission in children with cerebral malaria.[17]

Feature	Relative risk of death or sequelae
Blood glucose	
≤2.2 nmol/L	6.3
Deep coma (Coma score 0)	6.0
Parasitemia	
≥1 x 10^6 trophs per µl	3.6
White blood count	
≥15 000 per µl	3.2
Age	
< 3 years	1.72
Bedside score	8.4
(any 4 or more above)	

to play a role by triggering the release of TNF from mononuclear cells.[9]

Cardiopulmonary damage. The heart is relatively unaffected although heart failure in severely anemic patients is always a threat. Pulmonary edema which is probably due to increase capillary permeability rather than heart failure is a terminal event in adults. Hyperventilation caused by systemic acidosis is a common and useful sign of severe malaria. The patient is often confused and smells ketotic. The respiratory rate is raised even in children with moderate or mild malaria thus confusing the diagnosis of pneumonia (Chapter 14).

Renal damage. Renal impairment resulting in low urine output, and increased blood urea is found in some 30 per cent of severe malaria cases. Around 5 per cent of patients, usually adults, develop oliguric renal failure which may require dialysis. The renal damage is due to diminished blood flow coupled with hemoglobin deposition in the tubules. Massive intravascular hemolysis with jaundice occurs in G6PD-deficient patients given oxidant antimalarial drugs like primaquine. *Blackwater fever* is a syndrome, classically found in non-immune Caucasians whose erythrocyte G6PD is normal, characterised by hemoglobinemia, hemoglobinuria and renal failure. It may be coupled to hypotension and coma and has a poor prognosis.

Gastrointestinal damage. Parasitised erythrocytes also lodge in the vessels of the gut causing pain and diarrhea. The resulting breakdown in the mucosal barrier can be associated with endotoxemia and Gram-negative bacteremia.

Severe malaria and pregnancy. *P. falciparum* malaria is particularly severe in the later stages of pregnancy and is a major cause of maternal death, abortion, stillbirth and low birth weight babies. The effects are worst in areas of unstable transmission. Particular care should be taken if quinine is use in treatment, because it readily precipitates hypoglycemia.

Transfusion malaria. Malaria can be transmitted by blood transfusion from apparently healthy donors. After leaving an endemic area donors may remain infective for up to five years with *P. falciparum* and *P. vivax*, seven years for *P. ovale* and 46 years for *P. malariae*. Incubation periods are around 12 days for *P. falciparum* and *P. vivax* and up to 100 days for *P. malariae*. Patients receiving transfusion are often undiagnosed until high parasitemia are reached. In endemic areas recipients of blood transfusion should be given antimalarial chemotherapy as a precaution.

Clinical features of benign malarias (*P. vivax*, *P. ovale* and *P. malariae*). Incubation periods are longer (Table 16.1). Malaria due to *P. vivax* and *P. ovale* may relapse months or years after the original infection because the exoerythrocytic cycle has persisted. The so called benign malarias cause bouts of fever no less distressing than *P. falciparum* malaria, but the acute mortality is very low. *P. vivax* infection leads to chronic anemia and to acute splenomegaly which on rare occasions leads to rupture.

CHRONIC IMMUNOLOGICAL COMPLICATIONS OF MALARIA

***P. malariae* nephrotic syndrome.** In East and West Africa, South America, South-East Asia and in Papua New Guinea *P. malariae* is a common cause of the nephrotic syndrome. Circulating immune complexes are deposited in the basement membrane of the glomerulus leading to irreversible membranous damage. At the time of presentation damage is advanced and therapy with steroids or other immunosuppressants is seldom successful. Diuretics and salt restriction are advised. Only eradication of malaria or large scale prophylaxis will prevent this syndrome.[7]

Tropical splenomegaly syndrome (TSS). In endemic areas some people develop massive splenomegaly in the course of acquiring immunity to *P. falciparum*, *P. malariae* or *P. vivax* malaria. The characteristics of the syndrome which is also known as *hyperreactive*

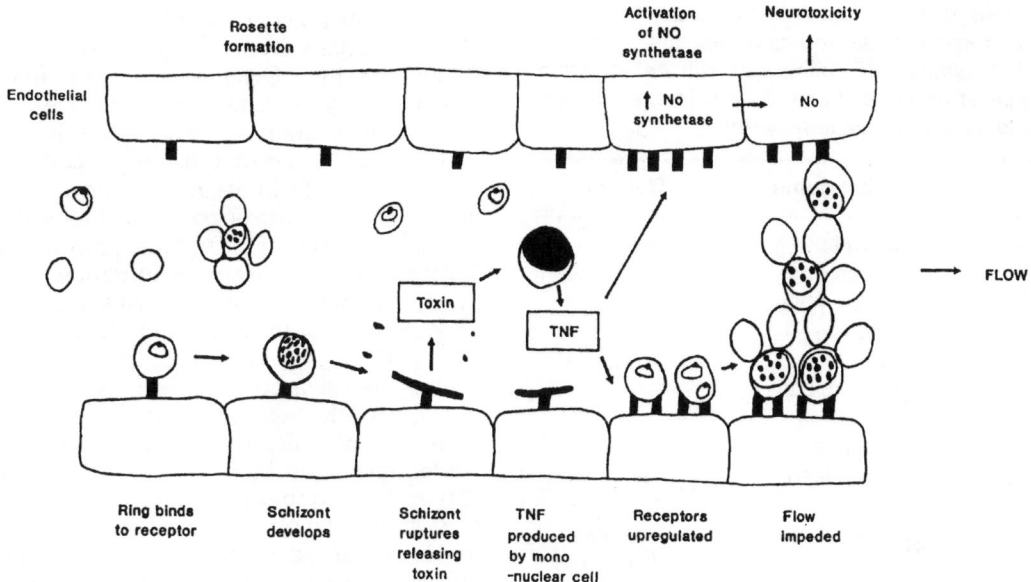

Figure 16.5. A view of the pathogenesis of cerebral malaria.[20]

malarious splenomegaly (HMS) are: 1) massively enlarged spleen (> 10 cm) with moderate hepatomegaly in a teenager or adult living in a malaria endemic area; 2) high malarial antibodies in the blood; 3) high serum levels of IgM (> 2.5 mg/ml); 4) lymphocytes in the sinusoids of the liver; 5) hemolysis and hypersplenism often with a raised lymphocyte count in the blood; and 6) regression of the syndrome with prolonged antimalarial prophylaxis.

The syndrome, which occurs in families, is in essence due to an abnormal IgM antibody response to malaria. Large molecular weight complexes of malaria antigen and IgM are engulfed by the cells of the reticulo-endothelial system in spleen and liver causing hypertrophy of these organs. Patients with this condition have a poor prognosis, if untreated, for reasons not clearly understood.

Endemic Burkitt's lymphoma is a B lymphocyte tumour due to infection with Epstein–Barr Virus (EBV). The tumour cells contain a characteristic chromosome translocation from chromosome 8 to the heavy chain immunoglobulin locus on chromosome 14. It is the commonest tumour of children (1 in 10 000 per year) who live in the hyperendemic malarious areas of Africa and Papua New Guinea. Typically it presents either as a large lump in the jaw or an abdominal mass in a child between the ages of 3 and 15 years.

Malaria probably causes a disturbance of T lymphocyte control over B cells which are infected with EBV. This defect allows the virus to activate such B cells which then proliferate in uncontrolled fashion so increasing the chances of the chromosomal translocation. Once this happens, autonomous growth becomes entirely established leading to the appearance of a large and rapidly growing tumour.

LABORATORY INVESTIGATIONS

Diagnosis. In practice this still rests on a high index of suspicion and a well prepared thick blood film. The simplest procedure is to spread a small drop of blood (5 µl) on a microscope slide, allow it to dry and then stain with Field's or Giemsa stain. The result is recorded as the number of parasites seen per high power field; 100 per high power field is equivalent to 1 per cent of the red blood cells being infected. This is a moderate parasitemia for *P. falciparum*, which can infect over 30 per cent of red blood cells. The other malarias usually cause much lower parasitemia (less than 1 per cent) so a long and careful search is necessary. Immunological tests or the use of DNA probes have little clinical application but may be useful in epidemiological studies. Follow-up blood films at 7 and 28 days after treatment are becoming increasingly necessary in areas where drug resistance is common.

Table 16.6. Geography of clinically important chloroquine and/or quinine resistant strains of *P. falciparum*. Quinine can still be effective against resistant strains if used in high dosage and combined with tetracycline.

	Chloroquine	Quinine
Africa	Burundi	None
	Cameroon	
	The Gambia	
	Kenya	
	Malawi	
	Mozambique	
	Nigeria	
	Tanzania	
Asia	Bangladesh	Cambodia
	China	Irian Jaya
	Kampuchea	Thailand
	India	Vietnam
	Indonesia	
	Laos	
	Malaysia	
	Myanmar	
	Papua New Guinea	
	Philippines	
	Solomon Islands	
	Thailand	
	Vietnam	
America	Brazil	Brazil
	Colombia	
	Ecuador	
	Surinam	
	Venezuela	

Other laboratory tests. Hemoglobin levels should be determined on admission and repeated during treatment in anemic patients. Blood glucose should be measured with a dipstick in all cases of severe malaria with cerebral signs. Total WBC and serum urea are also useful laboratory guides to severity. Unless contraindicated, due to signs of raised intracranial pressure, patients in coma or those with repeated convulsions should have a lumbar puncture in order to exclude other infections. Some authorities advocate a routine blood culture as Gram-negative septicemia is a common complication especially in anemic children with malaria.

TREATMENT

Anti-malarial chemotherapy is such a complex issue that the following notes must only be regarded as a general guide. Regional variations in sensitivity to drugs are very important (Table 16.6). Drug resistance is defined as the ability of a parasite strain to survive despite the administration of a drug given in a dose equal to or higher than usually recommended but within the limits of tolerance of the subject. Drug response is graded as follows:

1) Sensitive (S): if the asexual parasites have cleared by day six from the initiation of treatment, without subsequent recrudescence until day 28 (day 0 = first day of treatment).

2) Resistant grade I (RI): if the asexual parasites have cleared for at least two consecutive days, latest on day six after the initiation of treatment, followed by recrudescence. Recrudescences can be either early (before day 14) or delayed (between days 15 and 28).

3) Resistant grade II (RII): showing a marked reduction of asexual parasitemia to less than 25 per cent of the pretreatment count within 48 hours of the initiation of treatment, but no subsequent disappearance of asexual parasites (positive on day six after the initiation of treatment).

4) Resistant grade III (RIII): showing only a modest reduction, no change or an increase of asexual parasitemia, during the first 48 hours following the implementation of treatment, and no subsequent clearance of asexual parasites.

Whenever possible, the advice of local experts should also be obtained. A clear distinction must be made between the treatment of the three benign malarias which are rarely chloroquine resistant, mild *P. falciparum* malaria in a semi-immune or immune individual and life-threatening severe *P. falciparum* malaria in non-immune children and adults. The former two rarely require more than oral chemotherapy whereas the latter usually requires parental therapy given in correct dose as soon as possible. *Dosage should be prescribed clearly in terms of the base or the salt of the base and whenever possible dosage should be calculated according to body weight.* Tables 16.7. and 16.8. summarise some relatively simple drug regimes for the treatment of malaria, for full descriptions consult references.[8]

Antimalarial drugs

Artemisinin (Qinghasou). This compound was first extracted from the herb *Artemisia annua* (sweet wormwood) and has been used for the treatment of fever in China for hundreds of years.[10] Its efficacy has been evaluated in China and is now under trial for severe malaria in Vietnam, East Africa and The Gambia. It is very active against *P. falciparum* rings as well as the later stages of the parasite. Thus parasite and fever clearance times are shorter than with other antimalarials, but recrudescence rates are high. The parent compound artemisinin is given orally or by rectal suppository. Artemether and artesunate are even more potent than artemisinin. Artemether can only be given by intramuscular injection whereas artesunate can be given intravenously, intramuscularly or orally. In humans little evidence of toxicity has been found but there is evidence of neurotoxicity in dogs and rodents. The drugs should only be used for treatment, and not for prophylaxis. The official licensure of the compounds is still pending, and they are not generally available in the West.

Chloroquine. This is the treatment of choice for all *P. vivax, P. ovale* and *P. malariae* infections and for *P. falciparum* malaria when the parasite is sensitive. The drug is cheap (8 US cents per dose) and widely available both in oral and parenteral form. It is bitter and unpleasant to taste; therefore care should be taken to ensure that patients, especially children, do indeed ingest it. Given parenterally, in high dose, the drug can cause hypotension and deaths have been reported in young children if too large a dose is given intramuscularly: hence the recommendation to use the oral route wherever possible. The drug may cause itching which is relatively common in Africans.

Halofantrine. This antimalarial, developed by the US Army, has been found to be effective in multidrug-resistant *P. falciparum* infections.[10] However in South-East Asia failure rates of conventional doses reach 30 per cent. A higher dose of 72 mg/kg given over 3 days is still effective but is associated with cardiotoxicity as evidenced by prolonged QT intervals on the ECG. The drug is expensive (5 USD per dose).

Mefloquine. This drug is effective against multidrug-resistant strains, but resistance is developing fast in South-East Asia.[11] It is given orally in a single dose and apart from mild gastrointestinal symptoms is well tolerated. It is relatively expensive at 2 USD per dose. It is not recommended for children below 8 years of age and should not be given in therapeutic dose to people who have neurological or psychiatric illnesses or who are undergoing therapy with cardioactive drugs.

Quinine. This is another unpleasantly bitter drug which is rapidly and almost completely absorbed when given by mouth, producing, like chloroquine, peak plasma concentrations in 1–3 hours. Bolus intravenous injection, as opposed to slow infusion, is dangerous and can cause fatal hypotension and arrhythmias. Hypoglycemia is the most common complication of high dose parental therapy especially in pregnant women. Compliance is a major problem for the drug is most unpalatable.

Primaquine. This the only drug that is effective against the hepatic forms of *P. vivax* and *P. ovale*. It can cause severe hemolysis in G6PD-deficient patients and should not be used in pregnancy or lactation in areas where the enzyme deficiency is prevalent. The drug should be given daily from days 4 to 17 in a dose of 15 mg/day for adults and 0.25 mg/kg per day for children.

Pyrimethamine + sulfadoxine (Fansidar®). Fansidar was widely used in the treatment of uncomplicated mild to moderate chloroquine-resistant *P. falciparum* malaria. Resistance is now developing in many areas of the world, notably South-East Asia, Latin America and East Africa. It should be reserved for treatment only. In people hypersensitive to sulphonamides the drug may cause systemic vasculitis, Stevens–Johnson syndrome or toxic epidermal necrolysis. Agranulocytosis and aplastic anemia can also occur. In the USA the risk of fatal reactions is about one in 20 000 people given the drug. It is not recommended for treatment during pregnancy or lactation as sulphonamides which are excreted in breast milk can displace bilirubin from plasma binding sites and cause kernicterus in the child.

Mild malaria

Chloroquine is still recommended for treatment of *P. vivax, P. malariae* or *P. ovale* infections although chloroquine resistant strains of *P. vivax* have been found in Papua New Guinea and Indonesia (Table 16.7).

In South-East Asia *P. falciparum* is resistant to chloroquine and in the majority of the areas to Fansidar as well. Quinine or mefloquine are now the treatments of choice for mild malaria in these areas. Mefloquine has been combined with Fansidar (Fansimef®) but this combination should not be used any more because of high Fansidar resistance. New combinations with artemisinin derivatives are under investigation.

In Africa chloroquine may still be the drug of choice in the majority of countries, but resistance is spreading fast. Malawi is the first country in Africa to abandon chloroquine and to use Fansidar as the first line drug for mild malaria.

The safest treatment for a non-immune visitor to an endemic area with uncomplicated *P. falciparum* malaria is oral quinine. If in an area of quinine resistance (Table 16.6) oral tetracycline (250 mg four times a day for 7 days) should be added but only for non-pregnant patients and those over the age of 10 years. Alternatively, if the infection is derived from Africa, mefloquine or halofantrine, which are more palatable, can be used.

Severe malaria

In general parenteral therapy with quinine is the treatment of choice (Table 16.8). In South-East Asia resistance to quinine is increasing so here in older children or non-pregnant adults this drug is combined with tetracycline in an oral dose of 250 mg four times a day for 7 days. Alternatively an artemisinin derivative (artemether or artesunate) should be considered.
Other measures. Hypoglycemic patients who may have repeated episodes should be treated first with intravenous 50 per cent glucose followed by 5 per cent glucose infusion or glucose by nasogastric tube. An antipyretic is useful for high fever. Convulsions, which may be difficult to control, are best treated with intrarectal diazepam (0.5–1.0 mg/kg). A broadspectrum antibiotic should be used if bacterial infection is suspected, which is common occurrence in comatose severely ill patients and in severely anemic children. Careful attention needs to be paid to electrolyte and fluid balance as renal function may be impaired. Blood transfusion is necessary in anemic patients with high parasitemia. Corticosteroids are not recommended, neither is the use of heparin.

PREVENTION AND CONTROL

A variety of strategies have been formulated either around the human or the mosquito (Figure 16.6).

Chemoprophylaxis

Individual chemoprophylaxis. This is easiest to apply in the case of the occasional non-immune visitor or traveller to an endemic area.[12] Under these circumstances compliance is good and, as visits are often short, problems of long-term toxicity do not arise. The major determinant is the prevalence of drug resistant strains of the parasite. Whatever prophylaxis is used it should be started 1 week before travel and continued for 4–6 weeks following return from endemic areas. The greatest risk of acquiring *P. falciparum* malaria is in travellers to Africa.

Table 16.7. Oral treatment of mild to moderate malaria.

	Adults	Children
Chloroquine	600 mg base stat 300 mg/12 hourly x 3	10 mg base/kg stat 5 mg/kg 12 hourly x 3
Fansidar	3 tablets (1500 mg sulfadoxine/75 mg pyrimethamine) stat.	25 mg sulfadoxine and 1.25 mg pyrimethamine/kg stat.
Quinine	600 mg salt/8 hourly for 7 days	10 mg/kg/8 hourly for 7 days
Mefloquine	15 mg/kg single dose, or 25 mg/kg (given as 15 mg followed by 10 mg after 12 hours).	15 mg/kg single dose, or 25 mg/kg (given as 15 mg followed by 10 mg after 12 hours).
Halofantrine	8 mg/kg/8 hourly x 3	8 mg/kg 8 hourly x 3

Note: In areas of quinine resistance non-pregnant adults and children over 10 years may, in addition, be given oral tetracycline 250 mg four times a day for 7 days.

Table 16.8. Treatment of severe malaria.

	Adult	Children
Quinine	IV: 20 mg salt/kg loading dose over 4 hours followed by 10 mg/kg/ 8 hourly for 7 days[1]	IV: 20 mg salt/kg loading dose over 4 hours followed by 10 mg/kg 8 hourly for 7 days.
	IM: 20 mg salt/kg loading dose in two divided doses followed by 10 mg/kg/8 hourly for 7 days[1]	IM: 20 mg salt/kg loading dose in two divided doses followed by 10 mg/kg/8 hourly for 7 days.
Artemether	IM: 3.2 mg/kg loading dose followed 1.6 mg/kg/24 hourly for 4 days.	IM: 3.2 mg/kg loading dose followed by 1.6 mg/kg/24 hourly for 4 days.

Note: In areas of quinine resistance non-pregnant adults and children over ten years may, in addition, be given oral tetracycline 250 mg 4 times per day for 7 days.

The problems are different for non-immune people who live in endemic areas. Here toxicity from long-term prophylactics may become a problem so that a safe regime which prevents most attacks plus clinical and laboratory vigilance for malaria infection is best.

Table 16.9. provides a guide to common chemoprophylactic drug regimes for falciparum malaria. Apart from chloroquine, which is useful if *P. vivax* is sensitive to the drug, they give poor protection against *P. vivax*, *P. ovale* or *P. malariae*. The combination of chloroquine and proguanil is still widely used in those areas of Africa where chloroquine resistance is still at a low level. In areas of high resistance mefloquine should be used. A study of Peace Corps Volunteers working in Sub-Saharan Africa showed that this drug taken weekly was 86 per cent more effective than chloroquine plus proguanil in preventing infection. If mefloquine cannot be tolerated use doxycycline but only for a short while.

Advice for travellers can be obtained from reference centres such as the Center for Communicable Diseases, Atlanta, Georgia, USA or London School of Tropical Medicine and Hygiene, London, UK. In addition, local advice on suitable regimes is invaluable for transmission of each species of parasite varies with locality and season. The chances of the salesman contracting malaria in an air-conditioned hotel in the Sahel of Africa during the dry season are low compared with those of an agricultural expert living in the bush in the wet coastal areas. Non-immune pregnant women and their fetuses are at high risk so they must always receive prophylaxis. The same applies to young babies.

Chemoprophylaxis at the community level. This is a much more contentious issue and, at the moment, it is not advised by the WHO because of the potential dangers of drug resistance, toxicity and delay in the development of natural immunity. However, a recent well conducted study in a rural area in The Gambia has unequivocally shown that prophylaxis with Maloprim (a combination of pyrimethamine and dapsone) is more effective than treatment of fevers with chloroquine which is the strategy recommended by the WHO. Subsequent studies have shown that immunity to *P. falciparum* was in no way diminished or delayed after 3 years of Maloprim chemoprophylaxis. There may well be a place for chemoprophylaxis at a community level provided it is properly targeted (e.g. young children, primigravid women) and given at times of maximal transmission.

Treatment at the community level. The WHO and UNICEF currently recommend treatment of fevers in malarious areas with antimalarials by village health workers or others as the optimal strategy for the control of malaria in children. This approach needs further validation since studies both in Kenya and in The Gambia have failed to show that it had any significant effect in reducing either mortality or morbidity from malaria.

Side-effects of chemoprophylactic drugs. Both chloroquine and proguanil, which is

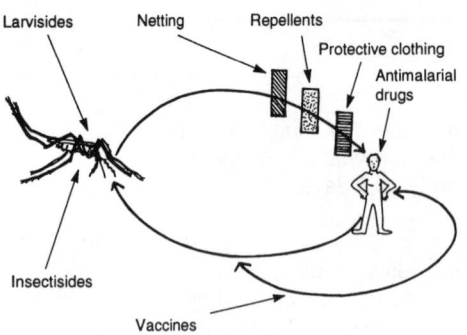

Figure 16.6. Strategies to prevent or control malaria.

excreted in breast milk, are of low toxicity and are safe to use in pregnancy. The risk of retinopathy following the long-term use of chloroquine is only apparent once the total cumulative dose reaches 100 grams of base. This amount is reached after 6 years' use of a standard prophylactic regime. Africans are prone to itching when taking chloroquine and some people discontinue the use of proguanil due to recurrent mouth ulcers. Mefloquine is remarkably safe, though a few individuals complain of nausea and bad dreams and the manufacturers do not recommend it for young children or pregnant women. Doxycycline, a tetracycline derivative, is more toxic. It should not be used in pregnancy or in children under the age of ten. It is associated with nausea, vomiting and photosensitivity reactions. Thus it is recommended for short courses only.

The widespread use of antimalarial drugs either for chemoprophylaxis or for treatment pose a number of potential problems relating to the development of drug-resistance. There is some evidence from Tanzania that pyrimethamine and chloroquine resistance may have increased in areas where mass chemoprophylaxis was attempted. The effects of the widespread use of chloroquine for treatment in the field are unknown, but it is likely that this will also increase resistance as has happened in the cities where many people treat their own fevers with inadequate doses.

VECTOR CONTROL

Individual efforts. There are also non-pharmaceutical ways of reducing the risk of malaria for the individual. Mosquito netting over doors and windows and bed nets have been used for centuries. In the colonial days expatriates used to wear mosquito boots and other protective clothing. Knockdown aerosol sprays are now popular for good reason.
The use of insecticide-impregnated bednets in the community. The incidence of clinical attacks of malaria in The Gambia was significantly less in children who slept in villages where all bed nets were treated with permethrin (a synthetic pyrethroid) than in villages which were issued with untreated nets. In a later trial mortality from malaria in children aged 1–4 years was reduced by 70 per cent by use of insecticide-treated bed nets.[13] The efficacy of this strategy, which is currently being evaluated in a number of countries, is likely

Table 16.9. Chemoprophylaxis of *P. falciparum* malaria.[1]

Drug	Adults	Children
Chloroquine plus	300 mg base weekly	5 mg base/kg weekly
Proguanil	200 mg daily	3 mg/kg daily
Mefloquine	250 mg weekly	5 mg/kg weekly
Doxycycline	100 mg daily	not advised

Prophylaxis should be taken 1 week before and 4–6 weeks after leaving an endemic area.

Mefloquine or doxycycline should only be used for short courses and is not recommended for children (less than 10 years of age) or pregnant women.

to vary according to the nature and habits of the dominant malaria vector.

Genetic manipulation of mosquitoes. Molecular biology offers an exciting new approach to vector control. Some strains of mosquitoes are naturally resistant to malaria infection. When the genes conferring resistance have been identified they could be inserted by genetic transfer techniques into normal mosquitoes. Ultimately the parasite-resistant mosquitoes should displace the wild type strain so that man will then be subject to malaria-free mosquito bites.

In general, the major difficulty of vector control is to maintain its continuity at a meaningful level. What often happens is that transmission of malaria is intercepted for a few years with a consequent waning of immunity in the population. When the mosquito comes back, an epidemic of severe malaria breaks out among the increased number of non-immune people.

Public health measures such as spraying and drainage. Various governments have been grappling with this problem since early times. Spraying of insecticide has been most successful in easily isolated areas such as the islands of the Mediterranean. Widespread eradication over large areas as in tropical Africa has been impossible to achieve due to the high costs of the operation and more importantly the lack of infrastructure and money to maintain the effort. On top of this, insecticide resistance has developed rapidly in many of the vectors. Drainage and other sanitary methods while simple in the concept of destroying mosquito breeding sites have largely remained unimplemented. The coffers of government are usually used for more important political purposes with the result that most cities and towns of the developing world remain good breeding areas for the mosquito. The rural areas are even more uncontrolled.

VACCINES

A massive international effort by the scientific community is now underway to try and develop a malaria vaccine for use in humans.[1] The tools of molecular biology have been usefully applied to define important antigens produced by the parasite at different stages of its cycle. A successful vaccine against malaria is likely to consist of a variety of antigens, derived from different stages of the cycle which ideally will raise both humoral and cellular immunity. One of the major stumbling blocks is the lack of a safe suitable adjuvant, which is necessary to raise strong cell-mediated immunity against the parasite. A number of vaccine candidate antigens are now being produced by genetic engineering. Many have been tested in animals and a few have been tried in man. Vaccine requirements and strategies will probably have to be tailored to different needs. Thus invading troops or expatriate aid workers will expect full protection whereas for the indigens of an endemic country a vaccine that reduces infection by 50 per cent and severe attacks by 90 per cent might well prove very useful.

Circumsporozoite (CS) antigen. Experiments in man have proven that the repeat sequences of the CS protein are highly antigenic but unfortunately the antibody has little *in vivo* effect on the invasion and growth of the parasite. Three trials in malaria-endemic areas have been unsuccessful.

Blood stage antigens. A whole variety have been defined. One, the 155 kilodalton antigen, found in the membrane of infected red cells is highly conserved. Antibody to this molecule inhibits the *in vitro* invasion of the parasite into red blood cells but was not found protective in monkeys. Another antigen (195 kDa) is the precursor of three proteins found on the surface of merozoites. A mixture of three synthetic peptides representing parts of these proteins induced protection against *P. falciparum* in *Aotus* monkeys. Vaccination of men with two hybrid protein polymers which included these protective epitopes induced partial protection. A recent randomised double blind trial of this vaccine, called Spf166, in Colombia has shown about 50 per cent protection against *P. falciparum* malaria.[14]

Gametocyte antigens. Vaccines against the sexual stage of the parasite are intended to block transmission of the parasite but will not directly benefit the vaccinee. A vaccine based on a 25 kDa antigen found in the ookinete has been found to be very effective at inducing transmission blocking antibodies in experimental animals. Trials in man are due to start soon.

It must be obvious from the above that while vaccination against malaria in man holds promise there is still a long way to progress before a practical vaccine for the use of people living in endemic areas becomes available. The best that might be achieved in the near future is a vaccine that offers some clinical protection against severe malaria but does not give complete sterilising immunity. This will have to be coupled to other control measures such as the use of insecticide impregnated bed nets.

References

1. Bates CAW, Taverne J, Roman E, Moreno C, Playfair JHL. TNF induction by malaria exoantigens depends on a phospholipid. Immunology 1991;75:129–35.
2. Moelans II MD, Schoenmakers JGG. Cross-reactive antigens between life cycle stages of *Plasmodium falciparum*. Parasitology Today 1992;8:118–23.
3. Playfair JHL. Immunity to malaria. Br Med Bull 1986;38:153–9.
4. Hill AVS. Haemglobinopathies and malaria: new approaches to an old hypothesis. Parasitology Today 1987;3:83–5.
5. Miller LH, Howard RJ, Carter R, Good MF, Nussenzweig V, Nussenzweig RS. Research towards malaria vaccines. Science 1986;234:1349–56.
6. Clark IA, Rockett KA, Cowden WB. Proposed link between cytokines, nitric oxide and human cerebral malaria. Immunology Today 1991;7:205–7
7. Marsh KM, Greenwood BM. Immunopathology of malaria. In: Clinics in Tropical Medicine and Communicable Diseases, 1986; 1:91–125.
8. World Health Organization. Severe and complicated malaria. Trans R Soc Trop Med Hyg 1990;84(Suppl 2):1–65.
9. Kwiatowski D, Hill AVS, Sambou I, *et al*. TNF concentration in fatal cerebral, non-fatal cerebral, and uncomplicated *Plasmodium falciparum* malaria. Lancet 1990; 336: 1301–4.
10. Hien TT, White N J. Qinghasou. Lancet 1993;341:603–8.
11. Ter Kuile FO, Dolan Grams, Nosten F, *et al*. Halofantrine versus mefloquine in treatment of multidrug resistant falciparum malaria. Lancet 1993;341:1044–9.
12. Steffen R, Behrens RH. Traveller's malaria. Parasitology Today 1992;8:61–6.
13. Alonso PL, Lindsay SW, Armstrong JRM, *et al*. The effect of insecticide-treated bednets on mortality of Gambian children. Lancet 1991;337:1499–502.
14. Valero MV, Amador LR, Galindo C, *et al*. Vaccination with SPf66, a chemically synthesized vaccine, against *Plasmodium falciparum* malaria in Colombia. Lancet 1993;341:705–10.
15. Greenwood BM. Malaria. In: Parry EHOP, ed. Principles of medicine in Africa. Oxford: Oxford Medical Publications, 1984:445.
16. Teasdale Grams, Jennett B. Assessment of coma and impaired consciousness. A practical scale. Lancet 1974;ii:81–4.
17. Molyneux ME, Taylor TE, Uirima JJ, Borgstein J. Clinical features and prognostic indicators in paediatric cerebral malaria: a study of 131 comatose malarian children with falciparum malaria. Q J Med 1989;265,441–59.
18. World Health Organization. Vaccination certificate requirements and health advice for International Travel. Geneva: WHO, 1985.
19. Greenwood BM, *et al*. Mortality and morbidity from malaria among children in a rural area of The Gambia, West Africa. Trans R Soc Trop Med Hyg 1987;81,478–86.
20. Greenwood BM. Malaria. Recent advances in paediatrics. London: Churchill Livingstone, 1993.

Additional reading

1. Bruce-Chwatt LJ. Essential malariology. London: Heinemann Medical Books, 1985.
2. Garnham PCC. Malaria parasites and other Haemosporidia. Oxford: Blackwell, 1966.
3. Harrison G. Mosquitoes, malaria and man: a history of the hostilities since 1880. London: John Murray, 1978.
4. Knell AJ. Malaria. Oxford: Oxford University Press, 1991.
5. Service MV. Lecture notes on medical entomology. London: Blackwell Scientific Publications, 1986.
6. Wernsdorfer WH, MacGregor I. Malaria. London: Churchill Livingstone, 1988.
7. Berendt AR, Ferguson DJP, Newbold C. Sequestration in *Plasmodium falciparum* malaria: sticky cells and sticky problems. Parasitology Today 1990;6:247–54.
8. Hill AVS, Allsopp CEM, Kwiatowski D, *et al*. Common West African HLA antigens are associated with protection from severe malaria. Nature 1991;352:595–600.

About the authors

Hilton Whittle has worked for the Medical Research Council (MRC, UK) in West Africa for the last 20 years. His main research interests are measles, hepatitis B virus, HIV and malaria. He resides in The Gambia where he is Deputy Director of the MRC unit and a consultant paediatrician to the Gambian Government.

Michael Boele van Hembsbroek *studied medicine at the University of Amsterdam. He worked in Kenya on a study of chloroquine resistance before moving to The Gambia where he is conducting trials of treatment of mild and severe malaria in Gambian children.*

Lankinen KS, Bergström S, Mäkelä PH and Peltomaa M, eds.
Health and disease in developing countries. London:The Macmillan Press Limited, 1994:163–176.

17 MEASLES AND ITS CONTROL: dogmas and new perspectives

Peter Aaby, M.Sc. (Anthropology)
Statens Seruminstitut, Epidemiology
Research Unit
Artillerivej 5, DK–2300 Copenhagen S,
Denmark

Badara Samb, M.D.
ORSTOM
BP 1386, Dakar,
Senegal

INTRODUCTION

The WHO estimated in 1987 that measles kills two million children annually, making it the major killer among vaccine preventable diseases. The estimate has declined in recent years to 0.9 million (1991) due to the improved immunisation coverage in developing countries (DCs). Though the accuracy of these estimates can be discussed (see below), it is clear that measles poses a major public health problem in DCs. Since the long-term effects of measles have not been included in the above estimates, measles is likely to present a larger problem than usually understood.

Measles has often been considered 'the simplest of all infectious diseases' (Maxcy). It is probably the most 'visible' infection due to a consistent clinical picture and the fact that virtually everyone contracted it before vaccination was introduced in the early 1960s. However, 'simple' does not imply that measles is well-understood. Several recent studies have succeeded in disproving common beliefs about measles.

Measles in DCs had hardly been studied before the 1960s.[1] There are few community studies of this important infection. This chapter presents some divergent interpretations of existing data on measles. In order to improve control of measles, much further research is needed.

SEVERE MEASLES

Clinical and immunological features

The following account focuses on measles mortality, which in epidemiological studies means any death occurring within one month of the rash. The common complication leading to death is pneumonia. In one South African study of 21 children who died of pneumonia, one-quarter had active measles virus pneumonia, half had adenovirus or *Herpes simplex* pneumonia and one quarter had bacterial bronchopneumonia due to *Klebsiella*, *Staphylococcus*, or *Pseudomonas*.[2] In some areas, diarrhea has been found to be a major complication of measles. *Salmonella* has been associated with particularly severe diarrhea following measles.

Giant cell pneumonia without a rash has been reported in children with kwashiorkor dying of measles, similar to what happens in leukemic children. Malnourished children with severe measles excrete giant cells for up to 4 weeks. This would suggest that they excrete more virus and are infectious for a longer period than children with measles in industrialised countries.[1]

Immunological studies indicate that severe measles measured in terms of death or pneumonia is associated with a low lymphocyte count (≤ 2.000 cells/ml), raised complement

Table 17.1. Measles case fatality rates (CFR) in prospective community studies.[9]

Country	Immunization*	CFR (number of measles cases)	
		0–4 years	All ages
Africa – Rural			
Guinea-Bissau	NI	34% (101)	24% (162)
Gambia	NI	22% (259)	
Senegal	NI	20% (44)	13% (68)
Senegal	NI	18% (537)	
Kenya	I (20%)	8% (331)	6% (424)
Nigeria	NI	7% (222)	
Africa – Urban			
Guinea-Bissau	NI	21% (356)	17% (459)
Guinea-Bissau	I	15% (124)	14% (161)
Zaire	I	6% (1069)	
Other areas – Rural			
Guatemala	NI	5% (292)	4% (449)
Guatemala	NI	4% (231)	3% (276)
India	NI	3% (72)	1% (181)
Bangladesh	NI	4% (510)	4% (896)
Bangladesh	NI	2% (3458)	
Other areas – Urban			
India	NI	0% (318)	

* NI=no immunization; I=immunization programme (% coverage)

component C3, low antibody response and depletion of T-helper and T-suppressor cells.[3]

Though emphasis is on mortality as the expression of severe measles, measles virus may have many other severe consequences. In one study from Nigeria, 25 per cent of the children lost 10 per cent or more of their weight during measles.[1] Measles often precipitates kwashiorkor. It may lead to *cancrum oris* (Chapters 28 and 54) and is one of the major causes of deafness (Chapter 37). Most important is the fact that measles often precipitates blindness (Chapter 36).[4] Several studies from Africa have shown that more than 50 per cent of childhood blindness is related to measles infection. The mechanisms are still under discussion, but one study from Tanzania found that measles-precipitated blindness was associated with vitamin A deficiency (50 per cent), herpes simplex infection (21 per cent) or use of traditional eye medicine (17 per cent).[4] It is not clear whether vitamin A deficiency was a preexisting condition or a result of the acute infection.

Popular beliefs

In most cultures measles has a specific name and is often a feared disease. In studies from West Africa, a good correspondence has been found between parental diagnosis and clinical or immunological findings. There may be some underdiagnosis of measles cases. However, a positive parental diagnosis is nearly always correct.

The popular understanding of measles is usually centred around the rash. In some societies, the rash is believed to be the menstrual blood retained during pregnancy which comes out.[1] It is a common belief in all continents that if the rash stays inside the body and does not come out the disease will be more severe. In a sense this is a correct observation since the prodromal period is prolonged in severe cases and in very severe epidemics, a large proportion of the deaths have occurred before the appearance of the rash.[5,6] Given this emphasis on the rash, therapeutic practices are often geared to get the rash out, e.g. by rubbing the skin with palm oil or kerosene. In West Africa, attempts are made to maintain the temperature since it is believed that cooling will keep the rash inside the body. Thus, the child may be bedded in hot sand, covered with blankets and not washed or given cold water to drink since this could cool the body, all practices that are likely to aggravate dehydration.

Though some believe that measles can be caught several times, there is often a close correspondence with Western medical understanding; everybody has to get measles but only once in a lifetime and it is more severe if caught as an adult. However, in contrast to the scientific understanding that measles infection in vaccinated children is due to vaccine failure, African mothers often believe that vaccinated children get milder measles infection.[7]

ESTIMATING MEASLES MORTALITY

The WHO estimate (1987) of two million measles deaths annually was based on the assumption that of the 83.3 million children in DCs surviving annually to the age of one year, only 24 per cent were protected by vaccination. The remaining children all get measles and the case fatality rate (CFR) of these children is 3.2 per cent on the average. The CFR has been assessed to be 3–4 per cent throughout Africa and Asia, and 2 per cent in the major countries of South America.[8] It is very difficult to assess the CFR in many of these areas due to lack of reliable registration. The available data of CFRs in longitudinal community studies are summarised in Table 17.1.[9] With few exceptions, the CFRs in these studies exceed the WHO estimate. For West and Central Africa, mortality in the community may well be two to three times higher than the estimated 3 per cent. During recent years, immunisation coverage has increased, and by 1991 the estimated number of deaths from measles had decreased to 0.9 million children.

INTERPRETATIONS OF SEVERE MEASLES

An adequate understanding of the epidemiology of measles should be able to account for the major variations in measles mortality as outlined in Table 17.2.[9–20] Measles virus is considered to be stable, and differences in its virulence are therefore unlikely to play a major role in the pathogenesis of severe measles.[1]

Table 17.2. Relative contrasts in measles case fatality rates (CFR).

High CFR	Low CFR
Africa	Asia, Latin America
West Africa	East Africa
Rural areas	Urban areas
Virgin soil epidemics	Endemic situation
Europe 1900	Europe 1940
Extended/polygynous families	Monogamous families
High birth rate/many siblings	Low birth rate/few siblings
Short spacing	Long spacing
Twins	Singletons
Multi-family dwellings	Single family housing
Small apartments (few rooms)	Many rooms
Institutions (refugee camps, military camps, orphanages)	
Genetic (HLA-Aw32)	
Chronic conditions: TB, leukemia, kwashiorkor	
Infants, adults	Children
Males	Females
Female closed societies	
Females	Males
Unimmunised	Immunised
	Immunoglobulin prophylaxis
	Treated with Vitamin A

Table 17.3. State of nutrition and severity of measles in community studies (w/h = weight-for-height; w/a = weight-for-age; muac = mid upper-arm circumference).

Country	Age (years)	Index	Nutritional status (% standard)		Type of control
			Fatal cases *(N)*	Controls *(N)*	
Bangladesh	0–9	w/h	86% (33)	88 % (33)	No measles
	0–2	w/h	93% (4)	86 % (148)	Measles survivors
	3–9	w/h	85% (5)	88 % (170)	Measles survivors
Guinea-Bissau	0–4	w/a	87% (17)	90 % (27)	Measles survivors
	0–5	w/a	92% (60)	92 % (1188)	All children
		h/a	97% (60)	97 % (1172)	All children
		w/h	97% (60)	98 % (1167)	All children
	0–1	w/a	88% (10)	89 % (36)	Measles survivors
Kenya		muac	84% (31)	86 % (36)	Measles survivors
Zaire	0–4	w/a	12% (6/51)	<3rd; 53%	<50th centile
		w/h	6% (3/50)	<3rd; 56%	<50th centile
		muac/a	12% (6/51)	<3rd; 55%	<50th centile
Gambia		w/a	29% (2/7) of fatal cases were malnourished. More than 29% malnourished among controls		
Gambia	0–2	w/a	State of nutrition did not affect severity		
Nigeria		w/a	No relation between malnutrition and severe measles		
India	0–2	w/a	Among malnourished children, 29% had severe measles and 29% lost weight; among children of normal nutrition 33% had severe disease and 56% lost weight		
India	0–4	w/a	Severely malnourished children (<60% of w/a) had the same rate of complications and the same immunological responses		
Philippines			Well-nourished and undernourished had similar course and outcome of their illnes		

Instead, most explanations have emphasised host and care factors, particularly malnutrition, age at infection, type of complications and availability of medical care.[1,17]

Host and care factors

Malnutrition. Only one community study, from Bangladesh, has documented higher mortality among malnourished children. In this study, 2019 children aged 12–23 months were followed for 2 years. During this period, children with a weight-for-age (w/a) of less than 65 per cent of standard had a mortality risk of 1.5 per cent compared with 0.6 per cent for the children with a w/a of more than 65 per cent.[18] However, this comparison may be partly confounded because it is based on deaths in relation to the total population rather than in relation to the number of children catching infection. Since children from large families have lower w/a and a higher risk of contracting measles, part of the reason for the higher risk of dying of measles among children under the w/a percentage of 65 may be a higher incidence of measles. Furthermore, in this community, females had lower w/a and a higher CFR in measles. overrepresentation of females in the < 65 per cent group could also partly explain the higher mortality.

Table 17.4. Case fatality rate (CFR) in measles infection by age and type of exposure. Bandim, Guinea-Bissau, 1979.

Age (months)	CFR (%) (deaths/no. ill)		
		Houses with multiple cases	
	Isolated cases	Index cases	Secondary cases
0–5	0% (0/1)		24% (4/17)
6–11	14% (1/7)	0% (0/15)	42% (11/26)
12–23	11% (2/19)	21% (3/14)	33% (14/43)
24–35	0% (0/10)	14% (2/14)	38% (14/37)
36–59	0% (0/10)	5% (2/38)	13% (5/39)
60+	33% (1/3)	6% (2/36)	0% (0/50)
Total	8% (4/50)	8% (9/117)	23% (48/212)

Hence, there seems to be no evidence (Table 17.3) that malnutrition is a major determinant of measles mortality. Even though future studies may find some association between nutritional state and measles mortality, it could explain only a small part of the variation in mortality. For example, children in West Africa have a better nutritional status than children in Bangladesh or India but the mortality is much higher in West Africa (Table 17.1). In Guinea-Bissau, weight-for-height (w/h) of children under 3 years of age was 98 per cent of standard and the CFR was 25 per cent. In Bangladesh, w/h was only 87 per cent, but the CFR was no more than 3 per cent.[9]

Vitamin A deficiency has been suggested as a major determinant, but no community study has examined whether the pre-morbid vitamin A status had an effect on the outcome. This is possible, but West Africa, where CFR is highest, is not known to be the most deficient area in vitamin A. The observation that survival was increased among patients who received vitamin A treatment may reflect the fact that severe measles had depleted vitamin A stores rather than indicating that vitamin A deficiency was the cause of the severe disease.[16]

Age at infection. Since the CFR is usually highest among the youngest children, it has been suggested that measles mortality should be particularly high where many children contract measles at an early age.[10,17] From this perspective, it has been predicted that measles mortality would be lower in rural areas, where age at infection is higher, than in urban areas. However, there is good evidence that the CFR is higher in rural than in urban areas.[9]

It has also been suggested that the decline in measles mortality in the industrialised world at the beginning of this century is related to an increase in the age at infection. There is, however, no data to show that the age at infection did in fact go up when fertility rates decreased, although children in small families supposedly get infected at a later age.[10] On the contrary, it is known that the age at infection fell from 5.5 to 4.4 years between 1944 and 1968.

In Guinea-Bissau, CFR fell as the nutritional state deteriorated and the mean age at infection decreased.[19] Differences in age of infection explain only a small part of the variation in mortality across different societies. The major differences are due to different age-specific CFRs.[1]

Type and severity of complications. Differences in the incidence of potential complicating infections and pre-existing diseases (tuberculosis, kwashiorkor etc.) may account for some of the variation in severity of measles. For example, intercurrent malaria has been suggested to be the major cause of the high mortality in Africa. Furthermore, also the severity of the underlying measles infection could influence the risk of complications. For example, in Guinea-Bissau, secondary cases had more pneumonia and diarrhea.

Availability of medical care. It is usually assumed that mortality is lower where medical assistance is available.[17] Reconvalescence serum and later immunoglobulin (Ig) undoubtedly helped reduce measles mortality in the industrialised countries, because it provided protection for the most important risk group: young children exposed at home to a sibling with measles. In virgin-soil outbreaks, mortality has also been lower among individuals who received Ig. However, Ig has only rarely, if ever, been used in measles control in DCs. For the usual symptomatic treatment there are no

Table 17.5. Case fatality rate (CFR) in houses with two cases of measles. According to sex constellation.

Age group	CFR in houses with two cases(deaths/cases)			
	MF pairs		MM or FF pairs	
Guinea-Bissau				
6–35 months	13%	(5/39)	38%	(14/37)
36–59 months	6%	(1/17)	8%	(2/24)
Total	11%	(6/56)	26%	(16/61)
Senegal				
4-41 months	8%	(7/84)	12%	(17/137)
42-65 months	0%	(0/54)	4%	(2/45)
Total	5%	(7/138)	10%	(19/182)

good community studies which have analysed whether the type of medical care available has an impact on mortality or not.

Transmission factors

In contrast to the emphasis on host factors in the pathogenesis of severe measles, recent studies from Africa have emphasised that variation in transmission may influence the severity of infection.[9] Children contracting infection from someone outside the home, the so-called index cases, have a much lower CFR, comparable with the mortality of children in houses with only a single case (Table 17.4). These tendencies have been found in several studies from Senegal, The Gambia, Guinea-Bissau, Kenya, Bangladesh, England, Germany and Denmark.[9]
Intensive exposure and dose of infection. Confounding factors cannot explain why secondary cases have higher mortality than index cases.[9] Since secondary cases are more intensively exposed within the house than index cases, it may be the intensity of exposure which determines severity of infection. Secondary cases presumably absorb a higher dose of measles virus and may also be more likely to contract complicating infection than the index case. The possibility that dose of measles virus is important for outcome of infection has rarely been considered, although, in experimental animal studies, it is well known that a high dose leads to a short period of incubation and a high CFR. Human studies seem to indicate an association between short period of incubation, long prodromes and more severe course of infection.[5,6]
Cross-sex transmission. Surprisingly, studies from Guinea-Bissau and Senegal have found that secondary cases have a higher mortality when infected by someone of the opposite sex instead of their own sex.[20] As a consequence, mortality was higher in houses where a boy and a girl had measles together compared with houses with two boys or two girls (Table 17.5). There is no apparent sociological reason why cross-sex transmission should lead to more severe infection.

Variation in exposure and mortality

If exposure is a major determinant of mortality, it is expected that the proportion of secondary cases is high where CFR is high. That is indeed what has been found so far (Table 17.6). For example, there is an enormous difference in the risk of intensive exposure between the two countries which we compared before; in Guinea-Bissau 61 per cent of the children under 3 years of age were secondary cases and the CFR was 25 per cent, in Bangladesh 14 per cent of the children of the same age group were secondary cases and the CFR was only 3 per cent.

The emphasis on exposure as a risk factor in severe measles suggests that socioeconomic and cultural conditions leading to the concentration of many susceptible children are major determinants of the risk of high mortality. Hence, institutions like polygyny, extended families, high birth rate and multifamily dwellings would increase the risk of intensive exposure and mortality.[9]
Geographical variation. There is no doubt that West Africa has the world's highest CFR in measles. This is related to the fact that West Africa has the highest proportion of polygynous families and the largest compounds and households.[9]

Table 17.6. Frequency of secondary cases and case fatality rate (CFR) in measles community studies.

Country	Age (years)	Rate of secondary cases (N)		CFR (N)	
Guinea-Bissau	0–2	61%	(203)	25 %	(203)
Senegal	0–2	56%	(171)	20 %	(171)
England (1885)	0–2	46%	(90)	14 %	(100)
Guinea-Bissau	0–2	45%	(77)	14 %	(77)
Guatemala	0–4	38%	(260)	5 %	(292)
Kenya	0–2	22%	(999)	6 %	(592)
Bangladesh	0–4	20%	(3181)	2 %	(3458)
USA	0–4	14%	(71)	10 %	(30)
Bangladesh	0–2	14%	(156)	3 %	(156)
Gambia	0–2	8%	(13)	0 %	(13)

The rural–urban difference in mortality is also influenced by the pattern of measles transmission. In urban areas, where measles is endemic, siblings in a household will tend to be infected at a young age and not in the same year. Therefore, the risk of becoming a secondary case is relatively small. Conversely, in rural areas, where there is a long interval between epidemics, siblings are likely to become infected at the same time. The mean age at infection will be higher than in urban areas. Thus, children in rural areas have a higher risk of becoming exposed at home as a secondary case. This should increase the mortality of rural children relative to urban ones. This pattern has been documented in Guinea-Bissau, where the same ethnic group has been studied both in an urban and a rural environment.[19]

Age. Other aspects of the epidemiology of severe measles may also be related to the risk of intensive exposure. Virtually all studies have shown that measles is most severe for the youngest children under one year of age.

Usually, severity increases again for teenagers and young adults, supporting the popular belief that childhood infections are more severe for adults. This U-shaped curve (Table 17.7) corresponds not to a biological model but to a social reality. Infections are transmitted between families in the age group with a high concentration of susceptible individuals. This age may vary according to social patterns of contact, e.g. age at schooling or the frequency of kindergartens. Most children infected at the age of inter-family transmission will be index cases infected outside the house. Children infected before or after that age have a much higher risk of being infected by a sibling who has brought the disease home. Since the secondary cases are more severe, part of the explanation for the higher CFR among the youngest children and young adults lies in their higher risk of having been intensively exposed.

Sex. Sex-related difference in severity could likewise be the result of variation in the risk of intensive exposure. Several studies from

Table 17.7. Case fatality rate (CFR) by age group.

England (1963)* Age (years)	CFR (N)		Guinea-Bissau (1979–83)† Age (years)	CFR (N)	
0	1.11%	(21 570)	0	46.7%	(15)
1	0.54%	(62 942)	1	52.4%	(21)
2–4	0.13%	(266 984)	2	26.9%	(26)
			3	40.0%	(20)
			4	5.3%	(19)
5–9	0.07%	(294 555)	5–9	4.5%	(44)
10–14	0.44%	(18 059)	10–	11.8%	(17)
15–	1.75%	(6 272)			

* Notifications
† Community study in rural area.

Table 17.8. Mortality during nine months of follow-up for measles patients and community controls in the Gambia.[21]

Age at infection	Mortality of measles cases		Mortality of controls
	Acute	1–9 months later	0–9 months later
3–11 months	18% (2/11)	56% (5/9)	3% (3/94)
1–2 years	9% (3/35)	13% (4/32)	2% (3/190)
3–4 years	6% (2/31)	7% (2/29)	1% (1/182)
5–6 years	0% (0/36)	6% (2/36)	1% (2/188)

developed countries have indicated that girls contract infection at a younger age than boys. Apparently, they contract infection more easily outside the home. Therefore, boys should have a greater risk of being exposed at home, and this may explain some of their excess mortality in industrialised countries. However, in cultures where girls are more confined to the home and boys attend school more frequently, girls may have a higher risk of being infected as a secondary case at home. In the one study from Senegal where this hypothesis has been examined, excess mortality among girls could indeed be explained on this basis.[20]

Decline in mortality. At the turn of the century, when measles mortality was high, the proportion of secondary cases in industrialised countries was very high (Table 17.6). The risk of intensive exposure within the family has been greatly reduced due to diminished family size, urbanisation and public child care. In Guinea-Bissau, measles mortality fell simultaneously with a fall in the frequency of secondary cases.[19] However, this cannot explain the whole change in mortality, because there are still secondary cases in the industrialised world and there is virtually no mortality any longer. Though *improved medical treatment* may have played some role, it is likely that positive feed-back in disease transmission has been important. Studies from Denmark and Kenya have shown that the severity of secondary cases depends on the severity of the index case. When the proportion of secondary cases is reduced in a community, more and more of the index cases will be mild due to infection from mild index cases rather than severe secondary cases. The implication is that secondary cases also

become milder and that the general severity of measles in the community is gradually reduced.

Delayed impact of measles

Acute measles mortality is counted as death within one month of a measles rash. Though it is well recognised that measles may give rise to prolonged complications, such as diarrhea and respiratory problems, until recently there have been no studies of the long-term impact of measles infection. Within the last years, however, it has become clear that measles may have a profound effect on morbidity and mortality, also after the acute infection.[8,21]

Delayed mortality after measles infection. The five studies available from West Africa all suggest that delayed mortality is at least two to three times higher among previous measles cases than among controls.[8] One of these studies from Gambia is summarised in Table 17.8.[21] After acute infection and during the 9 months of follow-up, mortality among the previous measles cases was nine times higher than among community controls. These results could be confounded by background factors distinguishing cases from controls. However, the difference in mortality seems so large that confounding is unlikely to be the whole explanation.

Studies to date suggest that the risk is particularly high for children who have had measles before one year of age. Most studies have emphasised the period of 1–6 months after infection as the critical one. Intensity of exposure has also been found to be important for the long-term consequences. Hence, index cases have lower post-measles mortality than do secondary cases.

There is some indication in studies from Guinea-Bissau and Senegal that excess mortality may not be very high if comparison is made with non-immunised controls rather than immunised controls. Hence, part of the excess mortality after measles infection may in fact be due to a non-specific beneficial effect of measles immunisation among the controls selected for comparison.

Early exposure to measles. Several studies from Guinea-Bissau have shown that children who live in houses where measles occurred during the first 6 months of their life had a mortality three to four times higher than community controls between 3 months and 5 years of age.[22] The difference in mortality could not be explained as a result of confounding factors. Diarrhea deaths were particularly common among the exposed children. Excess mortality was found among both the 20 per cent who had a history of measles and among those who did not. It is, however, possible that some of the children without a history of measles had, in fact, subclinical measles and that this infection could explain some excess mortality.

The delayed, fatal form of measles known as subacute sclerosing panencephalitis (SSPE) occurs mostly among children who have had measles early in life.

Exposure during pregnancy. Measles during pregnancy has been a rare event in the industrialised countries in the last decades. However, at the turn of the century it was a dreaded condition for both the mother and the fetus. Studies from virgin-soil epidemics have shown that pregnant women with measles have a higher mortality than non-pregnant women. In Greenland, mortality was 4.8 per cent (4/83) among pregnant but only 0.6 per cent (4/641) among other women aged 15–34 years.[6] Studies from Guinea-Bissau suggest that exposure during pregnancy may be dangerous even when the mother does not develop clinical measles. Children of a mother who lived in a house with a case of measles had four times the risk of being stillborn or dying within the first week of life (Table 17.9).

Conclusion. So far there are very few studies of the delayed impact of measles. There may therefore be doubts about the magnitude of the problem, and there are no explanations for the mechanisms leading to delayed mortality. However, this area of study is potentially very important because it may ultimately demonstrate that measles virus has a much higher impact than commonly assumed.

Immunity

Measles immunity is usually considered an either–or phenomenon. However, observations from DCs suggest that in some situations, immunity is only relative.

Maternal immunity. Children of immune mothers are usually assumed to be protected by maternal antibodies, at least to the age of 6 months. However, in DCs cases of measles are seen in children down to the age of 2–3 months without the mother necessarily having measles concurrently. When children younger than 6 months have measles, it almost always follows intensive exposure at home (or at a hospital). Antibody studies also indicate that many children under 6 months develop subclinical infection when exposed to a sibling with measles.

Vaccine-induced immunity. It has been commonly assumed that measles vaccine would produce a protective and lifelong immunity similar to natural infection. The large number of cases of measles in vaccinated children

Table 17.9. Perinatal mortality among children of mothers exposed to measles during pregnancy, Bandim, Guinea-Bissau, 1979. OR = Odds ratio (95 % confidence interval).

Type of mortality	Perinatal mortality risk (deaths/at risk)		
	Exposed	Controls	OR (95% CI)
Stillbirths	6.5% (7/107)	1.4% (5/346)	4.8 (1.7–13.8)
Died 1st week	9.0% (9/100)	2.6% (9/341)	3.6 (2.3–5.6)
Perinatal	15.0% (16/107)	4.0% (14/346)	4.2 (2.1–8.5)

observed in DCs have therefore been explained as vaccine failures, i.e. children who did not seroconvert due to improper storage or handling of the vaccine or because of interference from maternal antibodies. This explanation contrasts with popular perceptions in many parts of Africa that vaccinated children have a milder form of infection. Epidemiological studies have shown that mothers are correct. Vaccinated children who develop measles have lower mortality.[7] Vaccinated children are more likely to be secondary cases, which suggests that they contracted measles only because of the intensity of exposure. This would indicate that some of the children have indeed had partial immunity from vaccination. There are also a few reports of children who seroconverted after vaccination and subsequently developed clinical measles.

The relative importance of different causes of vaccine failure are likely to vary in different regions. It is important to detect these causes in measles control programmes. In most regions, vaccine failure may be due to breakdown of the cold chain and interference from maternal antibodies. However, it is important to recognise that partial immunity exists, since this has implications for the current vaccination strategy (see below).

Immunisation strategies

Measles vaccination and mortality. Since measles is believed to kill mostly malnourished children, it has sometimes been suggested that measles immunisation may have a limited impact on survival. It is thought that children saved from dying of measles will die of other infections instead. By this reasoning, nutrition and nutritional education is considered more important than immunisation. Since intensity of exposure is the major determinant of severe measles, it may not be the particularly weak children who die. Neither would they be more likely to die of other infections if surviving measles. Immunisation against measles should therefore have strong impact on mortality.

A study from Zaire is often quoted as having shown that immunisation had little impact on mortality.[23] In fact, the study found that in the critical period for child mortality, between 7 and 35 months of age, vaccinated children had a mortality of 3.8 per cent, i.e. 45–60 per cent lower than the three unvaccinated control groups (7.0–9.5 per cent). In spite of large variations in social settings and organisations,

other studies of the impact of measles immunisation have found very similar trends. The available studies from West Africa, Zaire, Bangladesh and Haiti suggest a reduction in child mortality after the age of vaccination of at least 30 per cent, and eight of the 12 studies found a reduction of 45–50 per cent or more. The beneficial impact of measles vaccination has been found both in urban and rural areas and in countries with both high and low overall child mortality.

All studies suggest that the reduction in mortality is larger than would be expected from a reduction in the number of acute measles deaths. One possible explanation is in the delayed excess mortality of children with measles. This effect is likely to be preventable by vaccination as well. Thus, there is no support for the view that measles infection functions as a mechanism of natural selection, merely taking the weakest children likely to die anyway. However, the impact of measles immunisation on mortality seems larger than can explained by the prevention of the acute and long-term consequences of measles.[8]

Herd immunity effect of vaccination. Apart from the direct effect of vaccination in protecting some children from catching measles, vaccination also has an indirect effect. When some individuals are vaccinated in a community, there are fewer families where several children get measles simultaneously. As a consequence, the risk of intensive exposure is reduced. The implication is that vaccination also reduces mortality among unvaccinated children who catch measles.[19]

Measles immunisation policy in developing countries

The EPI (Expanded Programme on Immunization) of WHO recommends immunization with a *single dose of Schwarz attenuated live measles vaccine at the age of 9 months in DCs*. Due to maternal antibodies, not more than 80–90 per cent may seroconvert at this age. In the industrialised countries, measles vaccination is delayed to the age of 15 months or later in order to prevent interference from maternal antibodies. However, if immunisation was delayed that long in DCs, an unacceptably large proportion of the children would already have contracted measles before the age of vaccination. The 9-month age limit is a compromise between the need to protect children early and the lower seroconversion rate at lower ages.

Studies from Kenya on measles incidence and seroconversion rate in different age groups predicted that vaccination at 8 or 9 months would yield the same number of prevented cases, whereas postponement of vaccination to 10 months would imply that too many children had already had measles. The age of 9 months was then selected because vaccination at 8 months would mean more vaccine failures, presumably leading to popular lack of confidence in the vaccine. However, this line of reasoning is debatable. Very often mothers view mild measles as an advantage of the vaccine and not as a reason to lack confidence. If vaccinated children indeed have milder measles and early cases have strong delayed mortality, it might save more lives to vaccinate at 7 or 8 months instead of waiting to 9 months of age.[7]

Alternative immunisation strategies. With vaccination at 9 months, as many as 10–20 per cent may not seroconvert, and as many as 5–10 per cent of the children may get measles before this age. To find a strategy which could overcome these problems, experiments have been made with high-dose measles vaccine. The Edmonston–Zagreb (EZ) high-titre vaccine induces a good serological response and provides clinical protection even when given as early as 4–5 months. In 1989, WHO therefore recommended the use of EZ high-titre vaccine from the age of 6 months in areas with a high incidence before 9 months. However, subsequent follow-up to the age of 3 years in studies in Guinea-Bissau, Senegal and Haiti has documented that girls who have received high-titre vaccines had significantly higher mortality than girls who had received the standard low dose Schwarz measles vaccine. There was no difference for the boys.[24] Hence, WHO has been obliged to change the recommendation back to one dose at 9 months of age.[25]

It is worth emphasising that there is no simple explanation of the higher mortality among female recipients of high-titre vaccines. The difference in mortality had nothing to do with differences in protection against measles.[24] Since the high-titre vaccine was not associated with higher mortality in areas with low mortality or compared with control children who had not received the standard measles vaccine, it seems unlikely that the vaccine is dangerous in itself. Hence, the main problem may be that it does not entail the non-specific beneficial effect associated with standard Schwarz measles vaccine.

Given the failure of high-titre vaccination, researchers are looking for a new vaccine. At the present time (1993), it seems likely that this may be a genetically engineered vaccine based on the canarypox virus as carrier. However, if the failure of the high-titre strategy is really due to the standard vaccine having non-specific beneficial effect, a new vaccine may also end up showing increased mortality compared with the standard vaccine. It may therefore be advisable to consider the benefit of a *two-dose schedule* with Schwarz measles vaccine; the first probably at six months and the second at 9 or 12 months of age. Non-randomised studies from both Guinea-Bissau and Senegal have shown much better survival for children who received standard Schwarz measles vaccine at 4–8 months of age than for children immunised at 9–11 months. *Without a vaccine which can be used at 5–6 months of age, it will be impossible to stop the transmission of measles.*

Transmission patterns and control of measles

Measles transmission depends on contact between infectious cases and susceptible individuals. *There are no infectious carriers or non-human reservoirs.* Measles is extremely infectious; when susceptible individuals are exposed at home, they nearly all catch the infection. In studies in DCs, the secondary attack rate, i.e. the proportion who develop infection after exposure at home, has been very high.

Endemic–epidemic tendencies. Theoretical studies have suggested that a population of 300 000 is needed for continuous transmission of measles. Hence, the infection is endemic only in larger cities. However, even in cities there are seasonal fluctuations and cycles in the incidence pattern, with more cases every second or third year. One important consequence of the endemic pattern is that children in urban areas are much more likely to contract infection early in life. However, since their older siblings have usually already had measles there is less risk that measles cases will occur in groups of two or more.

In smaller towns and rural areas, the pattern will be epidemic with introductions from the outside. Most of the susceptibles will be infected at the same time, after which the disease disappears again. The interval between epidemics depends on both the size of the community and its degree of isolation. In small isolated communities there may be long intervals, up to 10–15 years. Housing traditions may also be important for the way epidemics proceed in rural areas. Where compounds are close together, the epidemic will sweep through the village, attacking most susceptibles. In dispersed villages, an introduction of measles may attack only a few compounds.

Age and institutions of transmission. Inter-family transmission of measles occurs mainly in the age group where there is a high concentration of susceptible children. Individuals outside this age range will have a higher risk of being secondary cases infected at home.

The role of health care institutions needs to be particularly emphasised. Several community studies have shown that health centres and hospitals without isolation wards play a major role in the transmission of measles. In one urban community in Guinea-Bissau having a high vaccination coverage (> 80 per cent), half of the new introductions from outside the district were due to transmission at the hospital. It is also worth noting that children who catch measles at the hospital have much higher mortality compared with those hospitalised with measles.

Control measures

Improved vaccination coverage. Improving participation in vaccination programmes must have priority in measles control programmes. Lowering the age at vaccination is likely to increase the coverage. Most studies have shown that coverage for vaccines received before 4–5 months of age (DPT and polio) is much higher than for those given at 9 months. Acceptance of the rule of vaccinating all children attending health centres, even when sick would help improve coverage significantly.

Prevention of intensive exposure. Since secondary cases are a particular high risk group, intensive exposure at home should be prevented. Control of intensive exposure has not been attempted in DCs and the cost of immunoglobulin will be prohibitive in most places. However, if the index case is detected in the early phase of the rash, the effect of vaccinating susceptible contacts should be studied. Since the vaccine has a shorter period of incubation than the natural infection, it might be possible to prevent or attenuate some of the secondary cases.

Priorities in measles control. It seems likely that the source of outbreaks in rural areas is often introduced from the cities. Transmission in the rural areas would not be continued unless constant reintroduction from the cities took place. Therefore, a priority to high coverage in urban areas may be indicated. There also seem to be good reasons to attempt containment of outbreaks in rural areas. In outbreak campaigns, the age limit for vaccination has often been set at 2 or 5 years of age. However, experience from many rural areas suggests that a large proportion of the cases occur among children who are more than 5 years old.

Countrywide control or eradication of measles. Measles is reported to have been absent from The Gambia in a 2-year period in the 1960s, shortly after major campaigns were carried out simultaneously with the smallpox eradication programme. No other DC has attempted countrywide eradication of measles. A high degree of control requires at least the following:
1) A new vaccination strategy which provides effective immunisation at the age of 5–6 months. A two-dose schedule is probably necessary to prevent accumulation of susceptible non-seroconverters.
2) Systematic vaccination at all health institutions, including pediatric departments.
3) Some initiating vaccination campaigns to prevent outbreaks among susceptible older children who have accumulated due to isolation or previous vaccination activities.
4) Annual campaigns just before the local measles season.
5) Improved surveillance and containment vaccination when measles is introduced in a community.

CONCLUSION

Severe measles has usually been understood as a mechanism of natural selection which takes the weakest children. However, available data now suggest a quite different interpretation. Not only does measles kill many normal children in the acute phase of the infection, it may also weaken many children so that they become susceptible to delayed morbidity. It seems likely that future studies of the effects of measles will show that it kills considerably more than two million children annually.

The importance of transmission factors suggests that disease specific interventions may be very important, in addition to improvements in nutrition and hygiene.[23] It is likely that measles control is one of the most important public health interventions in terms of reducing child mortality.[1,8]

Future research

Much more research is needed to improve understanding and control of measles. Some of the major research questions include:
1) What are the pathogenic mechanisms of severe measles?
2) Why is measles infection connected with delayed morbidity and mortality?
3) How can intensive exposure be prevented?
4) Why does standard measles vaccine have non-specific beneficial effects?
5) Why was high-titre vaccine associated with higher mortality?
6) What is the basis of the sex specific effects of the disease and of the vaccines?
7) What is the best vaccine and vaccination strategy?
8) What happens to immunity when there is little re-exposure to measles? Will immunity wane and make revaccination necessary?

References

1. Morley D. Pediatric priorities in the developing world. London: Butterworth, 1973.
2. Kaschula ROC, Druker J, Kipps A. Late morphologic consequences of measles: a lethal and debilitating lung disease among the poor. Rev Infect Dis 1983;5:395–404.
3. Kiepiela P, Coovadia HM, Coward P. T Helper cell defect related to severity in measles. Scand J Dis 1987;19:185–92.
4. Foster A, Sommer A. Corneal ulceration, measles, and childhood blindness in Tanzania. Br J Ophthalmol 1987;71:331–43.
5. Aaby P, Bukh J, Lisse IM, Smits AJ. Severe measles in Sunderland, 1885: a European-African comparison of causes of severe infection. Int J Epidemiol 1986;15:101–7.
6. Christensen PE, Schmidt H, Bang HO, Andersen V, Jordal B, Jensen O. An epidemic of measles in southern Greenland, 1951. Acta Med Scand 1953;144:313–22,430–54.
7. Aaby P, Bukh J, Leerhøy J, Lisse IM, Mordhorst CH, Pedersen IR. Vaccinated children get milder measles infection: a community study from Guinea-Bissau. J Infect Dis 1986;154:858–63.
8. Aaby P, Clements J, Cohen N. Key issues in measles immunization research: a review of the literature. Geneva: WHO, 1987. (EPI/GAG/1987).
9. Aaby P. Malnutrition and overcrowding-exposure in severe measles infection. A review of community studies. Rev Infect Dis 1988;10:478–491
10. Reves R. Declining fertility in England and Wales as a major cause of the twentieth century decline in mortality. The role of changing family size and age structure in infectious disease mortality in infancy. Am J Epidemiol 1985;122:112–26.
11. Picken RMF. The epidemiology of measles in rural and residential area. Lancet 1921;i:1349–53.
12. Babbott FL, Gordon JE. Modern measles. Am J Med Sci 1954;228:334–61.
13. Bhuiya A, Wojtyniak B, D'Souza S, Nahar L, Shaikh K. Measles case fatality among under-fives: a multivariate analysis of risk factors in a rural area of Bangladesh. Soc Sci Med 1987;24:439–43.
14. Koster FT, Curlin GC, Aziz KMA, Haque A. Synergistic impact of measles and diarrhoea on nutrition and mortality in Bangladesh. Bull WHO 1981;59:901–08.
15. Bhaskaram P, Madhusudhan J, Radhakrishna RV, Reddy V. Immune responses in malnourished children with measles. J Trop Pediatr 1986;32:123–6.
16. Barclay AJG, Foster A, Sommer A. Vitamin A supplements and mortality related to measles: a randomised clinical trial. Br Med J 1987;294:294–6.
17. Foster SO. Immunizable and respiratory diseases and child mortality. Popul Dev Rev 1984;10(Suppl):119–40.
18. Chen LC, Chowdhury AKMA, Huffman SL. Anthropometric assessment of energy-protein malnutrition and subsequent risk of mortality among pre-school aged children. Am J Clin Nutr 1980:33:1836–45.
19. Aaby P, Bukh J, Lisse IM, da Silva CM. Measles mortality decline: Nutrition, age at infection or exposure? Br Med J 1988;296:1225–1228
20. Aaby P. Influence of cross-sex transmission on measles mortality in rural Senegal. Lancet 1992;340:388–391.
21. Hull HF, Williams PJ, Oldfield F. Measles mortality and vaccine efficacy in rural West Africa. Lancet 1983;i:972–975.
22. Aaby P, Bukh J, Kronborg D, Lisse IM, da Silva MC. Delayed excess mortality after exposure to measles during the first six months of life. Am J Epidemiol 1990;132:211–19.
23. The Kasongo Project Team. Influence of measles vaccination on survival pattern of 7–35-month-old children in Kasongo, Zaire. Lancet 1981;i:764–767.

24. Aaby P, Knudsen K, Whittle H, *et al.* Long-term survival after Edmonston–Zagreb measles vaccination: Increased female mortality. J Pediatr 1993;122:904-8.
25. EPI. Safety of high titre measles vaccines. Weekly Epidemiological Record 1992;67:357–361.

About the authors

Peter Aaby is a social anthropologist by training and currently the research coordinator of a long-term community study of the impact of infectious diseases in Guinea-Bissau. He has studied measles mortality and measles control for 15 years. His other research interests include the epidemiology of diarrhea and HIV-2, and – medical thinking.

Badara Samb *has worked as a physician for 5 years on the impact of measles and high-titre measles vaccination in a rural community in Niakhar, Senegal. He is currently writing a thesis on the short- and long-term consequences of measles infection and measles immunizations.*

Lankinen KS, Bergström S, Mäkelä PH and Peltomaa M, eds.
Health and disease in developing countries. London:The Macmillan Press Limited, 1994:177–184.

18 TUBERCULOSIS

Markku Kuusi, M.D.
Helsinki University Central Hospital, Second Department of Medicine
Haartmaninkatu 4, FIN-00290 Helsinki,
Finland

INTRODUCTION

There is evidence that tuberculosis was already an important disease thousands of years ago. There are signs of spinal tuberculosis in neolithic skeletons and early Egyptian remains.[1] It became a major problem in the Western World when the industrial revolution created crowded urban living conditions favouring the spread of the bacillus. Today tuberculosis has been largely controlled in industrialised countries, but in other parts of the world it is an important cause of death.

The incidence of tuberculosis in many developing countries has been rather stable for years, but in the late 1980s many Sub-Saharan countries have experienced a dramatic increase in its rates. The reason for this sudden change is almost certainly infection by Human Immunodeficiency Virus (HIV), which enables the dormant tuberculous infection to erupt into disease in the immunocompromised host.

EPIDEMIOLOGY

It has been estimated that worldwide about 1.7 billion people are infected with tuberculosis, and each year eight to ten million new cases are thought to occur leading to 2.9 million deaths annually (Table 18.1). This constitutes about 7 per cent of all deaths from any cause worldwide and 26 per cent of all potentially preventable deaths. About 95 per cent of new cases and 99 per cent of tuberculosis fatalities occur in developing countries where the greatest incidence and mortality concentrate in the

Table 18.1. The global toll of tuberculosis.

Region	People infected (millions)	New cases annually	Deaths annually
Africa	171	1 400 000	660 000
Americas*	117	560 000	220 000
Eastern Mediterranean	52	594 000	160 000
South-East Asia	426	2 480 000	940 000
Western Pacific†	574	2 560 000	890 000
Europe‡	382	410 000	40 000
Total	1722	8 004 000	2 910 000

*Excluding USA and Canada
†Excluding Japan, Australia and New Zealand
‡And other industrialised countries

most productive age group from 15 to 59 years making the disease economically extremely important.

Countries can be divided into four groups in terms of the current level and past trends of the annual rate of infection and health resource availability:

1) In industrialised countries tuberculosis has been declining very rapidly as transmission has diminished. This downward trend started in the 19th century with socioeconomic development, but after the Second World War the decline increased drastically, coinciding with the introduction of antituberculous chemotherapy. At the moment the favourable trend has changed in some of these countries (USA and Japan).

2) In some middle-income developing countries in Latin America, West Asia and North Africa tuberculosis is losing its status as a major health problem.

3) In other middle-income countries in East and South-East Asia the decline of tuberculosis is slow and the disease remains very important.

4) In the majority of low-income countries in Sub-Saharan Africa and the Indian subcontinent the absolute number of cases is increasing.[2]

The impact of HIV infection on tuberculosis is most important in Sub-Saharan Africa. At the moment less than 5 per cent of tuberculosis cases in the world are associated with HIV infection, but these cases are concentrated in ten African countries, where the AIDS epidemic is ruining the tuberculosis control programmes. The highest incidence of tuberculosis in 1990 was in Sub-Saharan Africa (229/100 000), followed by Asia, North Africa and Latin America. In industrialised countries the incidences vary between 10/100 000 and 40/100 000.

TRANSMISSION OF TUBERCULOSIS AND PROGRESSION TO DISEASE

The parasite

Tuberculosis is caused by *Mycobacterium tuberculosis*, an acid-fast bacillus (AFB) first identified by Robert Koch in 1882. It is an obligate parasite infecting humans, other primates and other mammalian species in contact with humans. However, man is the only reservoir of the organism. It can be recognised by direct staining of sputum or other specimens, which is still the most important diagnostic method in developing countries.

Transmission

Tuberculous infection is transmitted almost entirely by the aerial route. Persons having pulmonary tuberculosis aerosolise bacilli as droplet nuclei while talking, coughing or sneezing. These nuclei are sufficiently small to dry while airborne and remain suspended in the environmental air for long periods. When they are inhaled by a new host the infection begins. Extrapulmonary tuberculosis is not infective. *M. tuberculosis* is resistant to desiccation, but is rapidly killed by ultraviolet light including open daylight, so that transmission is almost always an indoor event.[3]

The infectivity of the tuberculosis patient is directly related to the presence and number of micro-organisms in sputum. The number of bacilli can be estimated by microscopic examination of stained sputum. Individuals on antituberculous chemotherapy become rapidly non-infectious, mostly within 2 weeks even if they may secrete organisms for months.[4] Isolation of patients does not alter the amount of tuberculosis in family contacts, probably because most susceptible contacts have already been infected at the time of diagnosis of the index case. On the average 25–50 per cent of a patient's close contacts are infected and in crowded conditions the percentage may be higher.[4] This can result in ten or more persons becoming infected from each untreated case of pulmonary tuberculosis.

The infection

Probably only a few bacilli reach the pulmonary air spaces to establish a primary tuberculous infection. In most cases the infection will be contained by the immune response and is recognised only if a tuberculin test is made and found to be positive. The microbes may spread by blood and lymphatics to other parts of lungs and other organs, even if the patient is asymptomatic. Up to 10 per cent of newly infected individuals will progress to disease.

Clinical tuberculosis can result from direct progression of an initial infection or can be a reactivation of a latent focus seeded years earlier. Malnutrition or other infections, especially HIV, can activate the tuberculous infection. Measles vaccination and other live virus vaccines may suppress the tuberculin test, but they do not reactivate tuberculosis.

PULMONARY TUBERCULOSIS

Symptoms

Primary tuberculous infection usually does not produce clinical illness. Reactivated pulmonary tuberculosis is a chronic or subacute disease characterised by respiratory symptoms. The most common symptom is persistent cough, which may be dry, productive or bloody. Chest pain and shortness of breath may be present. More severe disease is mostly accompanied by systemic symptoms like fever, night sweats, weight loss and fatigue. In developing countries persistent cough is often ignored and medical attention is sought too late. Thus, persistent cough should be used as the initial screening point in case-finding efforts. It is essential to educate health workers to understand the importance of identifying and evaluating persons with a chronic cough.

How to collect sputum samples

Because the cough is often most productive when one wakes up, it is best to collect one sputum specimen at the clinic , and then give the patient two containers with instructions to collect first-morning sputums for the next 2 days. Microscopy for AFB is only as good as the sample obtained, the equipment used and the microscopist doing the examination. The patient should be thoroughly instructed to get good sputum samples.

Diagnosis by bacteriology

The diagnosis of pulmonary tuberculosis is based on the identification of *M. tuberculosis* in sputum specimens. In countries where resources are limited, sputum smears are the principal means of diagnosis. By examining three separate sputum smears of each patient about 50–70 per cent of culture-positive patients can be found.[5] Repeated examinations increase the yield, but the maximum is reached at about five samples.

Under good conditions sputum cultures are more sensitive than sputum smear results. However, facilities for culturing mycobacteria are difficult to set up and to maintain. Thus, culture facilities in developing countries should be maintained only at the reference laboratory level.

The quality control of the laboratory should be organised to avoid both under- and over-diagnosis. The methods of this quality assurance include rereading of slides, the use of test slides and sending samples to a reference laboratory.

Diagnosis by X-ray

Chest X-rays are helpful in evaluating the extent of pulmonary tuberculosis and following its progression and response to therapy. The most common finding is chronic infiltrative disease with cavitation located in the apices, but there is no radiographic finding that would be pathognomonic for tuberculosis. Thus, diagnosis made on the basis of X-ray should be regarded as presumptive until confirmed by bacteriological investigations. When financial resources are limited, X-ray surveys for case detection are not rational because of their high cost and low specificity.

The resources are better used for screening by sputum smear. While it certainly misses early and mild cases, it brings the most sick and contagious patients under treatment.[3] Consequently, effective treatment of smear-positive patients has a definite impact on the epidemiological situation.

EXTRAPULMONARY TUBERCULOSIS

Mycobacterium tuberculosis can cause a symptomatic disease in any organ of the body, usually as a result of reactivation of a latent site of infection. The most common sites of reactivation are lymph nodes, bones and joints and the genitourinary tract. Less frequently the disease involves the gastrointestinal tract, peritoneum, pericardium or skin. Tuberculous meningitis and miliary tuberculosis, which result in high mortality, are more common in children.

Treatment based on clinical evidence only is often justified for lymphatic or spinal tuberculosis, because clinical features are sufficiently characteristic. It is usually difficult to obtain material for bacteriologic examination in extrapulmonary tuberculosis and smears often give false-negative results. Also radiologic findings are less helpful than in pulmonary tuberculosis.

When hematogeneously disseminated disease follows directly after primary infection,

Table 18.2. Principal drugs used in the treatment of tuberculosis.

Drug	Dosage	Adverse reactions	Antimicrobial activity
Isoniazid	5 – 10mg/kg up to 300 mg	peripheral neuritis, hepatitis	bactericidal
Rifampicin	10mg/kg up to 600 mg	hepatitis, fever, GI-intolerance	bactericidal
Streptomycin	15mg/kg up to 1 g	deafness, renal failure	bactericidal
Pyrazinamide	30 – 35mg/kg up to 2 g	hepatitis, hyperuricemia	bactericidal
Thiacetazone	2 – 3 mg/kg up to 150 mg	exfoliative dermatitis, hepatitis	bacteriostatic
Ethambutol	15 mg/kg	optic neuritis	bacteriostatic

all the lesions develop at the same rate and produce classical miliary (millet seed) tuberculosis in the lungs, spleen, liver and elsewhere. These patients present with persistent fever and splenomegaly, but appear rather healthy with an apparently normal X-ray until several weeks of the illness have passed. When dissemination occurs as reactivation disease, the course is much more fulminant.

Disseminated tuberculosis is particularly common in young children. Thus, children with chronic febrile disease or wasting should be suspected of having pulmonary, miliary or meningeal tuberculosis. If diagnostic facilities are limited, and antibiotic therapy has been unsuccessful, an antituberculous therapy based on clinical findings should be considered.[4]

TUBERCULIN SKIN TESTING

The tuberculin test has made its greatest contribution to the epidemiological surveillance of tuberculosis. The purified protein derivative (PPD) was prepared by Seibert in 1934 and it is used as standard material for all tuberculin testing. Trials of different concentrations have demonstrated that a dose of five Tuberculin Units (TU) of PPD produced the highest proportion of positives in people who were virtually all infected.[1]

Mantoux test

The testing is performed by injecting 0.1 cc of 5 TU PPD intracutaneously on the volar aspect of the forearm using a short, bevelled No 26 or 27 needle. Precise intracutaneous injection producing a raised, blanched wheal is necessary. Deeper injections are washed out by vascular flow leading to uncertain dosage. The reaction is read in 48–72 hours, a positive test being defined as greater than 10 mm of induration, not only erythema. A positive reaction to the test means prior primary tuberculous infection and it does not discriminate between those who have had asymptomatic primary infection without sequelae and those who have active tuberculosis.

Prior BCG vaccination also leads to a positive reaction, which is not reliably differentiated from tuberculous infection. About 15 per cent of acutely ill tuberculous patients may have negative tuberculin tests. – Thus, *the importance of tuberculin testing is essentially epidemiologic in developing countries and it is not very useful as a diagnostic test*, moreover because environmental mycobacteria also cause cross-reactions.[4]

TREATMENT OF TUBERCULOSIS

Successful chemotherapy of tuberculosis has two basic requirements: a combination of antituberculous drugs must be used and the treatment must be prolonged.[6] Hospitalisation, dietary supplements and rest are not necessary. The most important reason to treatment failure is patient's non-compliance resulting in uncompleted drug therapy. This leads to relapses of the disease and accelerates the development of drug resistance. Therefore, it is important for the motivation of the patient, that he can rely on the diagnosis of the disease. The health workers must also be active in keeping the patients on therapy. Individual chemotherapy under optimal circumstances has usually produced greater than 90 per cent favourable outcomes. The principal drugs available for the treatment of tuberculosis are listed in Table 18.2.

The treatment regimens are divided into an initial intensive phase and the continuation phase. During the intensive phase, which consists of four drugs used daily, the bactericidal effect leads to rapid bacteriological sputum conversion and relief of clinical symptoms. During the continuation phase, with fewer drugs, the sterilising effect of the therapy eliminates remaining bacilli and prevents subsequent relapse. Table 18.3 presents the priority categories for treatment with the recommended drug regimens.[7]

Retreatment and management of drug resistance are difficult problems. If sensitivity tests are not available, retreatment should be started with a combination which includes at least two new agents. Drug resistance is most common in Asia. The factors behind this are many: extremely high levels of tuberculosis; crowding, which favours person-to-person transmission; and uncontrolled dispensing of medications. For example, in Pakistan 31 per cent of patients with a prior history of treatment were shedding resistant organisms.[8]

To be able to monitor treatment outcome, it is recommended that all patients who are initially smear-positive should have repeat sputum smears examined at the end of the second month of treatment. Additional smears should be taken after 4 months and at the end of therapy for the 6-month regimens, and after 5 months and at the end of therapy for the 8-month regimens.

If resources are available, a chest radiograph should be taken at the end of therapy to serve as a reference film if the symptoms occur again.[7]

Table 18.3. Different categories of tuberculosis patients and the choice of treatment regimens.

Category I
– New cases of AFB smear-positive pulmonary tuberculosis and other newly diagnosed seriously ill patients with severe forms of tuberculosis
– priority: highest for smear-positive pulmonary tuberculosis
– recommended regimens:
    – initial intensive phase: isoniazid, rifampicin, pyrazinamide and either streptomycin or ethambutol daily for 2 months
    – continuation phase: isoniazid and rifampicin for 4 months daily or three times a week or isoniazid and ethambutol/thiacetazone daily for 6 months

Category II
– relapse and failure smear-positive tuberculosis patients
– priority: highest
– recommmended regimens:
    – initial intensive phase: rifampicin combined with isoniazid, pyrazinamide and ethambutol plus streptomycin for 2 months, followed by same drugs without streptomycin for 1 month
    – continuation phase: isoniazid, rifampicin and ethambutol daily or three times a week for 5 months

Category III
– pulmonary smear-negative tuberculosis with limited parenchymal involvement and extrapulmonary tuberculosis
– priority: higher for pulmonary tuberculosis, because it can become contagious
– recommended regimen:
    – initial phase: isoniazid, rifampicin and pyrazinamide daily or three times a week for 2 months
    – continuation phase: isoniazid and rifampicin for 2 months or isoniazid and ethambutol/thiacetazone for 6 months

Category IV
– chronic tuberculosis
– priority: low
– treatment may be attempted only in resource-rich nations

HIV INFECTION AND TUBERCULOSIS

In Africa, five million people have been HIV infected. Many of them live in areas where tuberculosis is prevalent and this is reflected in the 3–31 per cent increase in tuberculosis incidence experienced in many African countries in the late 1980s.

In Dar-es-Salaam, Tanzania, 51 per cent of HIV infected patients evaluated because of lung disease were found to have pulmonary tuberculosis. In a follow-up study in Rwanda, in a group of urban women of childbearing age, the incidence of tuberculosis was about 2.5 per cent annually. In comparison with HIV negative women, the risk ratio for HIV positive women was 23.[9]

The importance of tuberculosis in the context of HIV infection relates to at least four factors. The first is the high prevalence of tuberculosis in certain HIV infected groups. Second, tuberculosis is probably the only HIV-related infection that is transmitted from person to person regardless of whether the exposed person is infected with HIV. Third, if tuberculosis is diagnosed promptly and treated appropriately, it is very likely that it will be cured. Finally, there is evidence that tuberculosis can be prevented in HIV-infected populations.[9]

Patients with tuberculosis and HIV infection can be treated with standard therapeutic regimens including isoniazid and rifampicin. However, the treatment should be prolonged to 9 months or 6 months beyond the time of sputum conversion. Patients who cannot take isoniazid and rifampicin simultaneously should be treated for a minimum of 18 months, usually with isoniazid or rifampicin and ethambutol plus pyrazinamide in the initial phase. Recently there have been several outbreaks of multidrug-resistant tuberculosis with high mortality among HIV-infected persons in the USA, and this combination can also cause serious problems in developing countries.

GOALS AND METHODS OF TUBERCULOSIS CONTROL

Control activities

Tuberculosis control activities in developing countries were examined in 1989 by WHO and it was found that fewer than 15 countries had a monitoring system that would produce, on a regular basis, information on patients who were cured, had died or absconded.

In many developing countries fewer than half of the tuberculosis patients who started treatment were cured or completed their course of chemotherapy. In a few countries with a built-in system to monitor treatment outcome, cure rates of over 80 per cent were achieved. Roughly less than 50 per cent of existing tuberculosis patients have access to treatment services, and the proportion varies greatly among different WHO regions. Over the past 15 years there has not been significant change in the coverage rate.[2]

The WHO Tuberculosis Programme: policy and objectives

The objectives of the programme are to reduce: 1) tuberculosis mortality; 2) the prevalence of the disease; and 3) the incidence of tuberculosis. The control policy is based on effective treatment and case finding and BCG vaccination at birth.[10] It was formulated more than 25 years ago and is based on a comprehensive understanding of the natural history and epidemiology of the disease, and on the availability of relatively effective and simple intervention techniques. Since then no major policy changes have occurred.

The control policy was first implemented in industrialised countries and some middle-income developing countries, leading to a rapid decrease in the mortality of tuberculosis. While the incidence of tuberculosis has reached very low levels in industrialised countries, the rate of annual decline has slowed down, since the majority of cases originate from the pool of persons infected in the past.

The situation is quite different in developing countries. Most of them can only apply the basic programme appropriate for their own socioeconomic situation. On the other hand the coverage of these methods is inadequate and probably about 40 per cent of the population in developing countries has no easy access to basic tuberculosis control methods.[10]

BCG vaccination

BCG vaccination is part of the WHO's Expanded Programme on Immunization. The vaccine was developed at the beginning of 20th century from *Mycobacterium bovis*. There are several studies concerning the efficacy of this vaccine and the results are controversial.[11] It seems clear that the preventive effect of the vaccination on the infectious types of adult tuberculosis is limited and that the vaccination does not have an important effect on the transmission of the disease.[10]

However, all available information is consistent with a high protection against childhood tuberculosis and particularly the most severe forms: meningitis and miliary tuberculosis. Because still half a million children die every year from tuberculosis in developing countries, it seems reasonable to vaccinate all infants with BCG.[12] *HIV infected patients should not be vaccinated because the vaccine can cause an active disease in them.*

The new tuberculosis control strategy of the WHO

The prime objective of the WHO's control programme is to improve the cure rate of tuberculosis patients under treatment. The target rate is 85 per cent in developing countries and 95 per cent in industrialised countries.[10] Experience from tuberculosis control programmes in different countries demonstrates that the introduction of short-course chemotherapy and improved systems for the management of treatment are necessary for the achievement of the improved cure rate in developing countries. In fact short-course chemotherapy is more cost-effective than standard chemotherapy. It makes it easier to achieve a high cure rate by securing patient compliance, reducing the number of patients under treatment at a given time and preventing the emergence of drug-resistant bacilli.

To be able to achieve high cure rates it is important to *maximise efforts for case holding.* This means: 1) education of health workers, patients and their families; 2) medication free of charge; 3) effective treatment regimen; 4) administration of drugs directly observed by health workers, whenever possible; 5) minimal patient waiting time at the clinic; 6) rapid reaction of health workers (within 24 to 48 hours) if patients miss appointments. *A regular supply of antituberculous drugs and careful evaluation of treatment outcomes are the essentials for high cure rates.*[4]

Expansion of tuberculosis services should not be actively pursued until the targeted high cure rate has been achieved.[2] The long-term objective is to expand tuberculosis services by utilising existing health services, at least to district hospital level, to detect more cases. It is not necessarily effective to establish microscopy services below this level, because the microscopist should receive enough samples to maintain a high quality of sputum examination. A high cure rate increases service coverage by attracting patients also from other areas. In Tanzania, a 65 per cent case-finding coverage has been achieved by effectively diagnosing tuberculosis in all district hospitals by microscopy and X-ray screening.[2]

Global targets of the WHO

The proposed global target of the WHO's control strategy by the year 2000 is to achieve an 85 per cent cure rate of all sputum-positive patients under treatment and a 70 per cent case detection.[2] Different targets are set according to the health resources of various countries. By reaching these targets it is expected that the annual tuberculosis death rate will be reduced by 40 per cent and the prevalence of tuberculosis will be reduced by 50 per cent from the current level of more than 20 million by curing vast numbers of cases by short-course chemotherapy.

However, given the pace of socioeconomic development of the poor countries and the effectiveness of current methods of disease cure, detection and prevention, it is not realistic to expect a rapid reduction in the global tuberculosis situation in the near future. It would be important to develop new diagnostic methods for case-finding and new potent drugs that would make it possible to cure tuberculosis patients in a short period, to be able to achieve the objectives of the WHO's new control strategy.

Acknowledgement

The author received valuable comments on the manuscript from professor Eero Tala, M.D., Ph.D., Professor of Pulmonary Diseases, Turku University Hospital, Paimio Hospital.

References

1. Des Prez RM, Heim CR. Mycobacterium tuberculosis. In: Mandell GL, Douglas RG, Bennett JE, eds. Principles and practice of infectious diseases. 3rd ed. Edinburgh: Churchill Livingstone, 1990, pp. 1877–906.

2. Kochi A. The global tuberculosis situation and the new control strategy of the World Health Organization. Tubercle 1991; 72: 1–6.

3. Daniel TM, Tripathy SP. Tuberculosis. In: Warren KS, Mahmoud AAF, eds. Tropical and geographical medicine. 2nd ed. New York: McGraw-Hill, 1990, 839–51.

4. Slutkin G. Tuberculosis: the patient and the program. In: Sandler RH, Jones TC, eds. Medical care of refugees. Oxford: Oxford University Press,1987, 345–63.

5. Daniel TM. Rapid diagnosis of tuberculosis: laboratory techniques applicable in developing countries. Rev Inf Dis 1989; 11; 471–7.

6. Magnussen H, Nowak D. Die Standardtherapie der Tuberkulose und ihre Varianten. Pneumologie 1991; 45:549–552.

7. WHO. Guidelines for tuberculosis treatment in adults and children in national tuberculosis programmes. WHO/TUB/91.161.

8. Iseman MD, Sbarbaro JA. The increasing prevalence of resistance to antituberculosis chemotherapeutic agents: implications for global tuberculosis control. In: Remington JS, Swartz MN, eds. Current clinical topics in infectious diseases 12. Oxford: Blackwell Scientific, 1992, 188–207.

9. Hopewell PC. Impact of Human Immunodeficiency Virus infection on the epidemiology, clinical features, management, and control of tuberculosis. Clin Inf Dis 1992; 15:540–7.

10. Pio A. Impact of present control methods on the problem of tuberculosis. Rev Inf Dis 1989; 11: 360–365.

11. Fine PEM. The BCG story: Lessons from the past and implications for the future. Rev Inf Dis 1989; 11: 353–9.

12. Styblo K. Overview and epidemiologic assessment of the current global tuberculosis situation with an emphasis on control in developing countries. Rev Inf Dis 1989; 11: 339–46.

Additional reading

1. Murray GDL, Styblo K, Rouillon A. Tuberculosis in developing countries: burden, intervention and cost. Bull IUATLD 1990; 65(1): 6–24.

2. Crofton J, Horne N, Miller F. Clinical tuberculosis. Basingstoke: Macmillan Press, 1992.

3. World Health Organization. Treatment of tuberculosis. Guidelines for national programmes. Geneva: WHO, 1993.

About the author

Markku Kuusi works currently as a Senior House Officer at the Helsinki University Central Hospital specialising in internal medicine. During 1984–86 he worked in Senegal in a primary health care project, where tuberculosis was one of the principal health problems.

Lankinen KS, Bergström S, Mäkelä PH and Peltomaa M, eds.
Health and disease in developing countries. London:The Macmillan Press Limited, 1994:185–194.

19 THE AIDS PANDEMIC

Daniel Tarantola, M.D.
Harvard School of Public Health,
François-Xavier Bagnoud Center for Health
and Human Rights, International AIDS
Program, 665 Huntington Avenue,
Boston, MA 02115, USA

Jonathan Mann, M.D., M.P.H.
Harvard School of Public Health,
François-Xavier Bagnoud Center for Health
and Human Rights
665 Huntington Avenue,
Boston, MA 02115, USA

INTRODUCTION

In its second decade, the HIV/AIDS pandemic continues to expand, relentlessly. Its magnitude has increased over hundredfold since AIDS was discovered in 1981. As of 1 January 1993, 19.5 million people worldwide had been infected with HIV since the beginning of the pandemic. Of these, 18.3 million were adults (10.2 million men and 8.1 million women) and 1.2 million were children. The largest numbers of HIV infected people were in Sub-Saharan Africa (12 million; 61 per cent of global total) and South-East Asia (3.7 million; 19 per cent). For the first time, the number of HIV infected people in South-East Asia exceeds the total of infected people in the entire industrialised world. The large majority of HIV infected people (17.3 million; 89 per cent) live in the developing world. Worldwide, an estimated 16 million people were living with HIV on 1 January 1993 (Table 19.1).

Of the 3.7 million people who have developed AIDS from the start of the pandemic until the beginning of 1993, 2.5 million (67 per cent) were in Sub-Saharan Africa, about 0.5 million in North America, Western Europe and Oceania combined (13 per cent) and over 400 000 in South-East Asia (11 per cent). Of the nearly 770 000 children with AIDS, the large majority (660 000; 86 per cent) were in Sub-Saharan Africa (Table 19.2). During 1992, an estimated one million people newly developed AIDS, including 775 000 adults and 200 000 children.

While in some communities some success has been observed in slowing down the transmission of HIV, its spread has not been stopped in any community or country. In the United States, 40 000 to 80 000 new HIV infections are anticipated during 1993, and a similar number is expected to occur in Europe. HIV continues to spread unabated in the Caribbean, and Central and South America. In just 6 years, the cumulative number of HIV infected Africans has increased almost five-fold, from 2.5 million to over 12 million by early 1993 and worldwide, over 1.2 million children have been born with HIV infection.

The HIV pandemic is reaching new communities and countries around the world – in some areas with great rapidity. An explosion of HIV has recently occurred in South-East Asia – in particular in Thailand, Myanmar and India – where within only a few years nearly 3.7 million people may have been infected. AIDS is now reported from areas which had been left relatively untouched, such as Paraguay, Greenland, and the Pacific island nations of Fiji, Papua New Guinea and Samoa. The global implications are clear: during the next decade, HIV will reach most communities around the world.

Becoming more complex as it matures, the pandemic is now composed of thousands of separate and linked community epidemics. The impact of the pandemic on women is increasing dramatically as heterosexual mode of transmission accounts for the largest proportion (71 per cent) of HIV infections.

Table 19.1. Estimated cumulative numbers of HIV infections in adults and children in January 1993. (Source: Global AIDS Policy Coalition)

GEOGRAPHICAL AREA	HIV ADULTS	HIV WOMEN	HIV MEN	HIV CHILDREN	ADULTS AND CHILDREN
North America	1 261 000	139 000	1 122 000	15 000	1 276 000
Western Europe	834 000	142 000	692 000	8 000	842 000
Oceania	32 000	5 000	27 000	<1 000	33 000
Latin America	1 050 000	210 000	840 000	36 000	1 086 000
Sub-Saharan Africa	10 985 000	5 822 000	5 163 000	1 021 000	12 006 000
Caribbean	461 000	184 000	277 000	19 000	480 000
Eastern Europe	24 000	2 000	22 000	<1 000	24 000
South-East Mediterranean	48 000	8 000	40 000	<1 000	48 000
North-East Asia	49 000	8 000	41 000	<1 000	49 000
South-East Asia	3 567 000	1 605 000	1 962 000	102 000	3 669 000
World	18 311 000	8 125 000	10 186 000	1 203 000	19 513 000

Figures in table may not add up exectly to column totals due to rounding off to nearest thousand.

Worldwide, the proportion of HIV infected adults who are women rose rapidly, from 25 per cent in 1990 to 45 per cent by early 1993. The people most affected by the epidemic also change over time: in Brazil, the proportion of HIV infections linked with injection drug use has increased over ten-fold since the early 1980s; in the Caribbean, heterosexual transmission has now replaced homosexual transmission as the major mode of HIV spread.

Given current trends, the cumulative global total of HIV infections is projected to exceed 28 million by the beginning of 1996, including 26 million adults (15 million men, 11 million women) and over 2 million children. At that time, the cumulative global total of people with AIDS will be 7.7 million. Approximately 4 million people will develop AIDS from 1993 to 1996. Thus, more new AIDS cases will occur during the present 3-year period than during the entire history of the pandemic until now. If no major breakthrough in AIDS treatment and mean survival occurs, as many as 7 million people may have died of AIDS worldwide by 1996. The epidemic has not peaked in any country – no community or country can claim victory against AIDS.

By the year 2000, the largest proportion of HIV infections will be in Asia (42 per cent), surpassing Africa (31 per cent), Latin America (8 per cent) and the Caribbean (6 per cent). By the end of this decade, up to 24 million adults

and several million children may have developed AIDS – or ten times as many as today (Figure 19.1).

THE GLOBAL MOBILISATION

Following a phase of intense scientific research and remarkable discoveries in the early 1980s, enough understanding of the means to prevent the further spread of the pandemic had been acquired, and enough political commitment had been expressed internationally to launch a global mobilisation against AIDS. A declaration by the 167 member states of the WHO at the World Health Assembly in 1987 described AIDS as a global emergency. The Global Strategy for the Prevention and Control of AIDS was evolved and served as the reference framework for a newly created Global Programme on AIDS (GPA) launched by the WHO in 1987. The strategy had three objectives: preventing HIV transmission, reducing the personal and social impact of the pandemic and unifying national and international efforts against AIDS.

By 1990, virtually every country had a national AIDS programme albeit in different phases of maturity and quality, the importance of non-governmental efforts had been recognised and an unprecedented level of resources had been mobilised nationally and internationally. The concerted global response also revealed important weaknesses and deficiencies. Among

Table 19.2. Estimated cumulative numbers of AIDS cases in adults and children in January 1993. (Source: Global AIDS Policy Coalition.)

GEOGRAPHICAL AREA	AIDS ADULTS	AIDS WOMEN	AIDS MEN	AIDS CHILDREN	ADULTS AND CHILDREN
North America	320 000	36 000	285 000	11 000	332 000
Western Europe	134 000	22 000	112 000	5 000	140 000
Oceania	6 000	<1 000	5 000	<1 000	6 000
Latin America	198 000	40 000	159 000	23 000	222 000
Sub-Saharan Africa	1 800 000	947 000	853 000	658 000	2 458 000
Caribbean	67 000	27 000	40 000	12 000	79 000
Eastern Europe	3 000	<1 000	3 000	<1 000	3 000
Southeast Mediterranean	4 000	<1 000	3 000	<1 000	4 000
North-East Asia	4 000	<1 000	4 000	1 000	5 000
South-East Asia	353 000	160 000	192 000	57 000	409 000
World	2 890 000	1 235 000	1 655 000	768 000	3 658 000

Figures in table may not add up exectly to column totals due to rounding off to nearest thousand.

them, the implementation capacity of many national programmes was constrained by the shortage of resources, the inadequacy of structures and the lack of trained staff. There were difficulties in articulating effective relationships between AIDS and other health or social programmes.

Community and national response

The creation of national AIDS programmes in industrialised countries, starting in the early 1980s, resulted largely from the pressure exercised by community-based organisations. These programmes consisted of focused interventions intended to respond to groups and communities affected by AIDS early in the epidemic: gay or bisexual men, recipients of blood and blood products, and, to a lesser extent, injecting drug users. However, these initiatives often lacked resources, coordination and official legitimacy. By the mid-1980s, governments in industrialised countries created programmes which emphasised mass media campaigns, introduced HIV screening in blood transfusion centres and collected epidemiological information to track the epidemic.

In developing countries, most programmes were created during or after 1987. In the following years, several meetings brought together government representatives, creating a sense of globalism with an intensity not seen

before in any disease control programme. Indeed, unlike smallpox, tropical diseases or even tuberculosis before the recognition of its resurgence in affluent countries in the 1990s, AIDS had become a reality for both industrialised and developing nations.

After some initial hesitation, countries in the Sub-Saharan Africa began to mobilise earlier and somewhat in a more concerted manner than the rest of the developing world. By 1988, 144 of the 167 member states of the WHO had received support from GPA and by the end of 1989, this number rose to 159; a global response was clearly underway. By

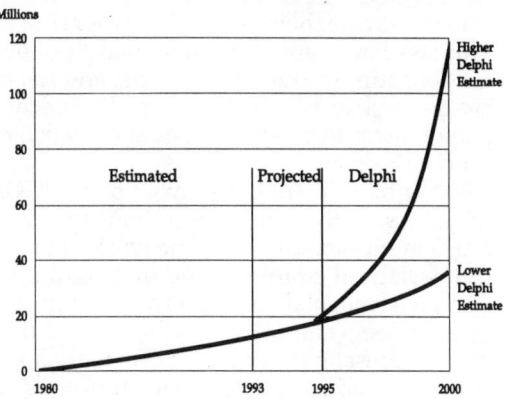

Figure 19.1. Cumulative HIV infections in the world, 1980–2000.[1]

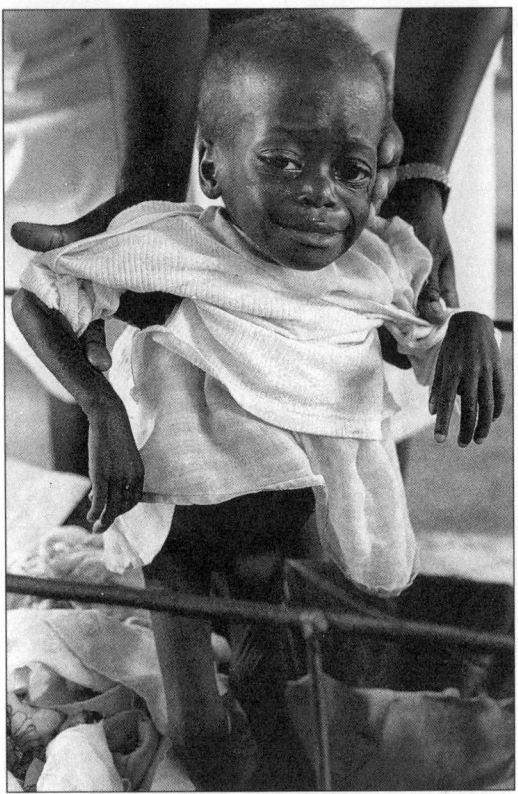

Two years old AIDS-patient from Masaka, Uganda.
Photo: UNICEF/Douglas Clement

1990, virtually all countries in the world had established their programme.

The programme development process, while well established, continues to evolve as political realities change. The ongoing redefinition of the map of Eastern Europe, for example, has created a need for newly reconstituted states to create their own AIDS programmes. This task began and continues amidst political tension, administrative confusion, and the increased risk of HIV transmission that accompanies disruptive social change and deepening economic crisis.

Non-governmental organisations (NGOs) have been at the forefront of the response to AIDS in most countries of the world. In most industrialised countries, the first significant non-governmental response was from groups of volunteers and activists who formed their own organisations to provide care to their sick friends, to educate their peers and to advocate for more attention and funds. Already by 1991 there were over 200 NGOs working on AIDS issues in Africa; at least 500 NGOs in

Latin America and 16 000 in the United States alone.

Today, there is a widening gap between efforts against AIDS in communities and at the national and international levels. Many communities have developed effective programmes for HIV prevention and care which demonstrate quite clearly how best to face the pandemic. White gay men in San Francisco, Paris and Sydney, sex workers in Athens, Kinshasa and Bangkok; injection drug users in Amsterdam, New York City and Stockholm have all demonstrated that individual and community action has a positive effect in reducing the spread of HIV. Yet, at the national and international level there is a widespread and growing sense of inadequacy, confusion about how best to proceed, failure to link AIDS with other health issues, increasing bureaucratisation and a lack of commitment to caring for people with HIV and AIDS.

Programme evaluation

The success of AIDS programmes is defined by the extent to which they help curb the course of the HIV epidemic and provide quality care to those already affected. On this basis, no programme in the world can yet claim success.

The monitoring systems created by these programmes usually have not been sensitive enough to measure their own impact. To date, their achievements have therefore been measured by the degree to which they have raised awareness about AIDS and distributed commodities such as condoms, and more generally on the managerial efficiency with which activities have been planned, implemented and financed. In addition, the commitment to programme evaluation is in no way universal: to-date, almost half of the programmes in industrialised countries and one-third of those in the developing world have not undergone any broad-scale evaluation.

In general, the evaluation findings can be summarised as follows: once created, programmes became operational rapidly; they were successful in enhancing public awareness on AIDS issues although they did not always prevent (and at times even generated) misperceptions among certain communities; they raised appropriate human rights issues and in some instances managed to prevent violations of these rights; and they exchanged information – and in some cases made funds and skills available – at the international level. Industrialised countries were generally able to secure financial, human and technological resources required to increase drastically the safety of blood and blood products, and to establish diagnostic and treatment schemes reaching most – but not all – people in need. Regrettably, the same could not be said about developing countries.

A common criticism, however, was a lack of focus and priority setting, weak management, and inability to involve other health programmes, sectors and NGOs more actively. There were also major concerns about the sustainability of prevention and care efforts, confronted with declining resources and rising care demands and costs.

Actually, programme evaluations were often called programme reviews, a term which carries a less threatening connotation – to pave the way for collective learning. These reviews provide crucial opportunities to learn from experience in an expanding field which demands creativity, innovation and, in some situations, risk taking. Switzerland, with the creation of areas in Zürich and Bern where injection drug users could access drugs and sterile injection equipment without the interference of law-enforcers, offers an example of such a situation. A trial period of several months, followed by an evaluation concluded that the negative consequences of the approach on the vulnerable population living near the trial sites were not offset by the risk reduction among those who were the intended primary beneficiaries of the projects. In contrast, projects in Greece, Kenya, Tanzania and the United States showed that the promotion of condoms among sex workers lead to a lower infection rate in this population and impacted positively on the acceptance of safer sexual practices among their clients. All programmes should build an evaluation element in their initial design, specifying criteria of success and failure and how these will be assessed.

THE COST OF AIDS

Since the early years of the response to AIDS, policies and programmes were guided by two motives misperceived by many as antagonistic: a human rights or humanitarian approach and a public health perspective. The economic argument was seldom raised. Until recently, it did not seem necessary or politically advantageous to make the cost of AIDS a major public issue. It did not conform to the humanitarian agenda (cost is secondary to human rights), nor to the public health perspective (the population must be protected). With the rising number of people and communities affected by the pandemic, the spending on prevention, care and the general economic impact of AIDS have now become critical issues.

An estimation was made by the Global AIDS Policy Coalition (GAPC) of the amount of spending on AIDS prevention, care and research in the world in a 1-year period during 1990–91. It concluded that this amount was in the range of 1.4–1.5 billion USD for prevention, approximately 3.5 billion USD for adult AIDS care alone, and 1.6 billion USD for research, for a total world cost which, after adjustment for under-reporting and inflation, ranged from 7.1 billion USD to 7.6 billion USD. Interestingly, about 95 per cent of this spending occurred in industrialised countries which have less than 25 per cent of the world population, 18 per cent of the people with AIDS and 15 per cent of HIV infections worldwide (Figure 19.2).

In industrialised countries, the majority of national AIDS programme spending is on care and research. In developing countries, the larger share of resources goes to the strengthening of programme management, blood safety and prevention. In countries in Sub-Saharan Africa, where the needs for care are enormous, only small amounts of funds are allocated to this area of activity. Individual studies have indicated that the annual cost of care for an adult with AIDS varied in 1990–1991 from 32 000 USD in the USA to 22 000 USD in Western Europe, 2000 USD in Latin America and 393 USD in Sub-Saharan Africa. This wide variation reflects the uneven quality of care in the world – for example whether the treatment regimen includes anti-virals such as AZT and the biomedical monitoring which it requires. Both life expectancy and quality of life of people with AIDS depend ultimately on their access to comprehensive, quality, and therefore more costly care.

Both industrialised and developing countries have great difficulties keeping up with the increasing demand for AIDS care. The cost of treatment of an adult with AIDS in one year approximates (in developing countries) or significantly exceeds (in industrialised countries) the GNP *per capita*. Everywhere in the world,

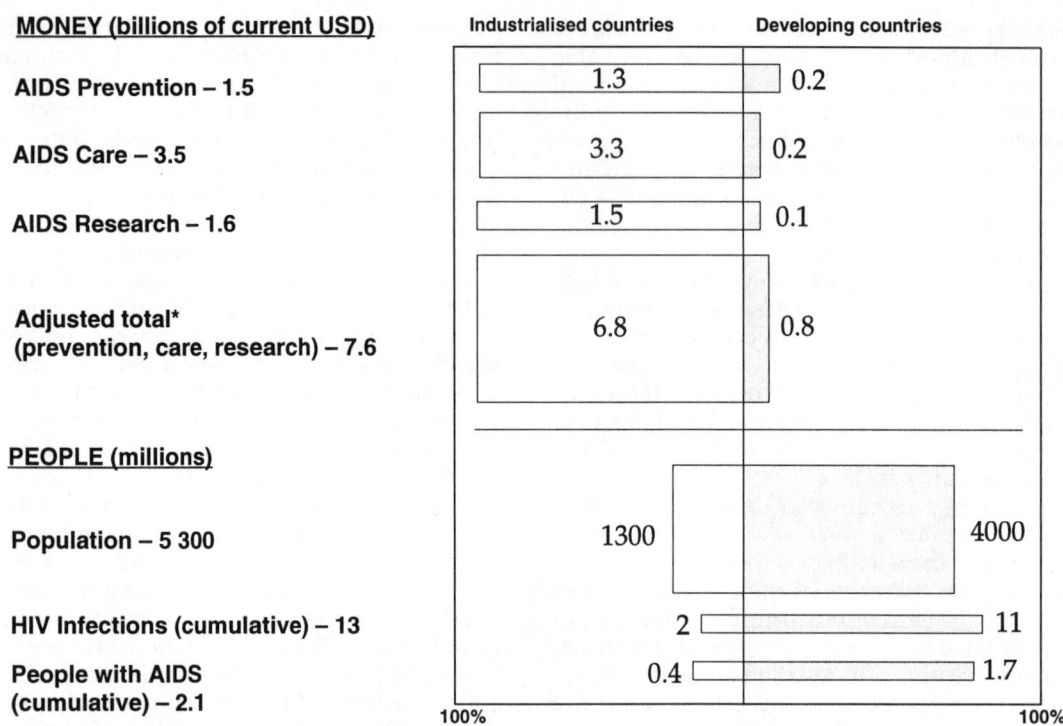

Figure 19.2. Global inequity: estimated costs of AIDS prevention, care and research in industrialised and developing countries, 1991–1992 (one year).[1]

the cost of AIDS care largely surpasses the annual overall spending per person and can represent as much as 15 to 50 times the annual per capita spending on health care. In countries that do not have national medical insurance schemes (countries in the developing world, but also the USA), the financial burden of AIDS care rests first and foremost on people with AIDS, their family and friends, on care facilities which must draw the needed resources from other health care activities and on public financing schemes such as Medicaid in the USA.

Between 1984 and 1987 in the United States, public financing rose from 25 to 41 per cent of total spending on AIDS care. This trend is indicative of several concurrent factors: the cost of AIDS care continues to increase, some people with AIDS have gradually consumed their personal resources, more people from socially and economically deprived communities require AIDS care, private insurance companies are finding ways to exclude people with AIDS from their subscribers.

On the prevention side, the situation is hardly better. In the United States, federal funding for AIDS prevention declined from 497 million USD in 1990 to 480 million USD in 1992. In Sub-Saharan Africa, where large scale programmes with significant international cofinancing were undertaken in the late 1980s, governments are not willing or able to commit extra financial resources when the needs are growing and international support is lagging behind.

Typically, governments have not spent more than 3 per cent of their health budget and less than 0.1 per cent of their total national budget on AIDS prevention and care in the early 1990s, while the reported ratio of military expenditure to combined health and education expenditure ranged from an average of 38 in industrial countries to 109 in developing ones.

Thailand and Nigeria are examples of countries that have significantly increased the national resources allocated to AIDS but the general picture is one of reluctance on the part of strained economies to invest in health and social programmes considered as big spenders with no obvious immediate return.

When considered in the context of national economies, the health and social costs of AIDS are affordable if efforts are made simultaneously in three directions. First, the cost of AIDS care can be reduced and the well-being of people with AIDS enhanced by improving services. Studies in France, Zambia, the USA and several other countries have shown that alternative approaches to inpatient care, with a focus on home, community based or ambulatory care improve quality of life of people with AIDS and reduce cost.

Second, information, education and legislation must create a societal environment that protects the individual rights' of people with AIDS as they relate specifically to free movement, housing, employment, access to education and to health insurance schemes where they exist.

Third, pressure must be exercised by constituencies onto their representatives and their governments to re-examine the priority accorded to the health and social sectors, at a time when enormous savings can be made on military expenditures. In order to do this, people concerned about health and social issues must learn how to place these issues on political agendas, from a political perspective, with politically meaningful messages.

AIDS AND INTERNATIONAL SOLIDARITY

Global policy leadership is becoming scattered and international solidarity is threatened. Industrialised nations are turning away from coordinated efforts, showing a growing preference to work independently, on a bilateral basis, with few developing countries chosen on historical or political grounds. Fragmentation of efforts by industrialised countries has led to competition among donors in some countries. For example, seven donor countries are supporting AIDS programmes in Kenya, Tanzania and Uganda, while in 35 other countries, only one donor country is present.

International financial assistance is not keeping up with the growth of the pandemic. In 1991, less than 72 million USD was provided for AIDS work to the WHO, 30 per cent less than its initial budget of 100 million for that year, and the first decline in resources since its AIDS programme began. In the period 1986–91, the industrialised nations provided a global total of about 864 million USD (an average of about 144 million USD per year) for the prevention and care of AIDS in the developing world. These resources grew steadily from 1986 to 1990, when it peaked at 255 million USD globally, before declining to 237 million USD in 1991. The declining trend in the international financing of AIDS programmes in the developing world is confirmed by data which are becoming available for 1992. It is clear that as the pandemic continues to worsen, AIDS programmes will be forced to struggle with insufficient funds. In developing countries, programme sustainability is vital and the entire world should be deeply concerned about the capacity of these countries to finance adequately their national programmes over time.

Estimating how much should be spent to create a significant impact on the AIDS pandemic is purely speculative. For example, addressing societal issues which condition vulnerability to AIDS may require major investments in the health and social sectors. In return, however, investing resources in AIDS is anticipated to impact positively on other health and social problems which may no longer warrant isolated, impact-limited funding. International funding should continue to accord priority to an equitable matching of resources and needs worldwide.

Thus, funding through international organisations – both intergovernmental and nongovernmental – should reach countries or programmes that do not receive sufficient bilateral aid. As these agencies increasingly draw funds for AIDS programmes from general resources allocated broadly to development with no disease-specific monitoring system, they must develop ways of tracking the type and the amount of resources that, directly or indirectly, may have a bearing on the pandemic.

To reverse the observed trend towards the fragmentation of the international response to AIDS calls for a number of synergistic actions: the development of a new global strategy which places AIDS in the broader context of society and development; the analysis of the multi-faceted implications of the pandemic and the creation of programmes in every sector concerned; and the demand imposed on international agencies to share in the global effort and increase their accountability for what they have done and what they have not, within their respective mandate, to address AIDS issues and coordinate their action.

BRIDGING THE VULNERABILITY GAP

Worldwide experience during the past decade has demonstrated that successful HIV prevention requires three elements which contribute to individual empowerment: information and health education; health and social services; and a supportive social environment. Personal vulnerability to HIV infection increases with lack of accurate, relevant and comprehensible information about HIV. It also increases when the individual lacks skills, the access to needed services, supplies or equipment, and the power or confidence to sustain behavioural changes. HIV prevention requires individuals to learn and respond.

In designing and evaluating AIDS programmes, a focus on the individual is necessary as behavioural and consequent health changes will reflect the ultimate outcome of National AIDS Programmes prevention strategies.

On this basis, an index can be developed which provides a measure of individual vulnerability to HIV, both present and future, granted that individual behaviour is both mutable and societally connected. The key questions then become: How can preconditions for reducing individual vulnerability be met? How can countries best promote individual's empowerment for HIV prevention?

In practice, this process will be mediated through two sets of factors: first, access to information and education, health and social services that depend on the quality and nature of the community, and national AIDS programmes; second, the broad societal influences that increase, sustain or reduce personal empowerment. Henceforth emerges a triangular relationship of interdependency between individuals, programmes and societal environment. The power of people to reduce their vulnerability to AIDS will be contingent upon the capacity of communities, nations and international agencies to create both a favourable societal context and effective programmes.

An agenda for action

It is abundantly clear that the AIDS pandemic will not be controlled simply by sustaining already existing prevention and care activities.

A three-pronged strategy is proposed to confront the pandemic more successfully.

The first approach is to stimulate the more widespread application of lessons from existing programmes that have demonstrated a reasonable measure of effectiveness. Apparently, successful pilot programmes in HIV prevention have been created in many diverse communities, including among gay men, adolescent heterosexuals, injecting drug users, commercial sex workers and street children. As just one example, the incidence of HIV infection among women commercial sex workers in Kinshasa, Zaire, was dramatically reduced – from 18 per cent per year to 2 per cent – through a programme which combined information and education, specific health and social services (counselling, diagnosis and treatment of other sexually transmitted diseases, and condom provision), and social support (group identity and cohesiveness).

Yet broadly, two failings can be identified. First, a systematic and critical analysis of these apparently successful programmes has not yet been conducted; learning the specific lessons from the enormous community-based experience of the past decade must be a high priority. This kind of meta-evaluation could be coordinated by an independent group, like the GAPC, or could operate under academic or foundation auspices.

The second failing has been the lack of further generalisation of apparently successful pilot efforts. It is vital to learn why these pilot programmes have not been replicated in many other communities, nor extended to larger population groups.

The second approach is to strengthen the capacity of existing HIV prevention and care programmes. Given the increases in numbers of HIV infected people becoming ill, virtually all care and support programmes will require concomitant increases in funding and staff capability during the next several years.

However, it is the third element that is most complex and also most necessary. The societal factors fuelling the spread of HIV must be clearly identified and addressed. The analysis of societal vulnerability presented in 'AIDS in the World' suggests that societal discrimination is the factor most closely linked to an increased risk of exposure to HIV. For example, studies have now demonstrated that married, monogamous women in East Africa are becoming HIV infected. They are informed

HIV INFECTION AND AIDS AT A GLANCE

The Acquired Immune Deficiency Syndrome (AIDS) is a disease caused by the Human Immunodeficiency virus (HIV), of which at least two types exist – HIV-1 and HIV-2, identified in 1983 and 1985, respectively. HIV is transmitted sexually, through blood and blood products and from mother to fetus/infant.

HIV affects the immune system over a period of several years by disabling or destroying cells which bear the CD4 surface antigen. A particular subset of lymphocytes, called CD4-T lymphocytes are the primary target for HIV. Having penetrated the cell, the virus transcribes its genes from RNA to DNA, which can then be inserted into the host cell's own genes. Immediately after, or later in the course of infection, it will replicate its genes, direct the host cell to make the proteins it needs, and start to reproduce itself before infecting new cells.

The mechanisms which lead to the disablement and destruction of host cells have yet to be fully elucidated. As HIV infection evolves and immunodeficiency sets in, the number of CD4-T lymphocytes declines from its normal level of greater than 500 CD4-T lymphocytes/mm^3 to less than 200/mm^3, a level considered by the US Centers for Disease Control as one of the markers of severe HIV related immunosuppression.

Following a silent latency period which, for more than half of the persons infected, may exceed ten years in industrialised countries, but be much shorter in developing ones, a wide variety of illnesses appear. Accompanied by or following a decline in the number of CD4-T lymphocytes, these illnesses mark the evolution of HIV infection to AIDS. The HIV related illnesses may include opportunistic viral, bacterial or fungal infections, and certain types of cancers, in particular high grade B cell lymphomas and Kaposi sarcoma. Tuberculosis is often the first opportunistic infection to appear in the course of HIV infection. The relationship between HIV and TB is synergistic, so the combined affect of both – or individuals and public health – is worse than their separate effects added together. HIV associated illnesses and cancers are preceded or accompanied by a deterioration of the general physical state reflected, among other signs, by a gradual and severe weight loss.

The prevention and early treatment of opportunistic infections and appropriate medical and social support can extend the survival of people with AIDS from one to several years and improve the quality of their life. The drugs for prophylaxis and treatment of *Pneumocystis carinii* pneumonia and antiviral therapies such as AZT are available to most people with AIDS in industrialised countries but to few among marginalised groups in these countries and to even fewer in the developing world where most of the people with AIDS reside. Because of their toxicity and the emergence of resistant HIV strains in the course of treatment, antiviral therapies with AZT, DDI and DDC require close biomedical monitoring.

While several diagnostic tests are available widely to detect HIV antibodies, others, more complex and expensive, can detect HIV antigen, a type of test mostly used in research. AIDS is diagnosed according to case definitions which differ from one world region to another depending on the ease with which marker diseases can be diagnosed and on the availability of serologic tests or tests measuring the loss of immunity via depression of CD4-T lymphocyte counts. Following the onset of AIDS, the length of survival will vary with the degree of care and support provided to people with AIDS. People with AIDS who have access to medical and social services, including the option of anti-viral treatment may survive for several years after the onset of the disease. Survival is shorter among children, older adults and people who have limited access to health care and social support.

The growing resistance of certain HIV strains to antivirals and of *Mycobacterium tuberculosis* to chemotherapy hamper the development of effective therapies, thus the need to continue to pursue research efforts and reinforce prevention programmes.

about AIDS and accessibility of condoms; their risk factor is their powerlessness to control their husband's sexual behaviour. They cannot refuse either unprotected or unwanted sexual intercourse. Therefore, in this setting, efforts to reform laws governing property distribution after divorce, will likely be of benefit.

Similarly, a common factor among public health efforts to work constructively with marginalised groups (commercial sex workers, sexual minorities, injecting drug users) is the assurance of a modicum of respect for rights and dignity. This suggests that priority must be given to identifying and redressing societal discrimination, marginalisation and stigmatisation, whether based on sex, race or ethnicity, national origin, sexual preference, social class, or any other status.

Clearly, efforts to improve respect for human rights and dignity go far beyond the normal definition of public health work, and will mandate collaboration with many organisations, both official and non-governmental, which have no specific health mandate.

Only such a global and strategic approach will be capable of controlling the AIDS pandemic. Even when considering an AIDS vaccine, a strategy limited to one country or one part of the world will likely fail. If the AIDS vaccine is only effective against the currently dominant strain of HIV in one part of the (industrialised) world, it will only be a matter of time before resistant strains spread to the areas of high vaccine use. In addition, if the hoped-for vaccine is only available to the wealthy nations, and only to the rich elsewhere, it cannot achieve its potential to help control the global epidemic.

A realistic and clear understanding of the pandemic and the response is the essential first step towards bringing AIDS under control. Yet the design and implementation of a new global strategy, taking full account of lessons learned during the first decade of this struggle, is a major challenge to communities around the world, to countries, and to global society.

Reference

1. Mann J, Tarantola D, Netter T, eds. AIDS in the world. Cambridge: Harvard University Press, 1992.

Additional reading

1. Kirp D, Bayer R, eds. AIDS in the industrialized democracies: passions, politics and policies. New Brunswick: Rutgers University Press, 1992.
2. Barnett T, Baikie P. AIDS in Africa: its present and future impact. London: Belhaven Press, 1992.
3. Mane P, Maitra SA. AIDS prevention – the socio-cultural context in India. Bombay: Tata Institute of Social Sciences, 1992.
4. AIDS prevention and control. World Summit of Ministers of Health on Programmes for AIDS Prevention; London 26–28 January 1988. World Health Organization, Geneva. Oxford: Pergamon Press, 1989.
5. Fee E, Fox D, eds. AIDS. The making of a chronic disease. Berkley: University of California Press, 1992.
6.
7. Gostin L, Porter L, eds. International law and AIDS: international response, current issues, and future directions. Chicago: American Bar Association, 1993.
8. Sepulveda J, Fineberg H, Mann J. AIDS: prevention through education: a world view. New York: Oxford University Press, 1992.
9. The Panos Institute. Triple jeopardy – women and AIDS. PANOS Dossier. London: The Panos Institute, 1992.
10. The Panos Institute. The hidden cost of AIDS. The challenge of HIV to development. PANOS Dossier. London: The Panos Institute, 1993.
11. Cross S, Whiteside A, eds. Facing up to AIDS: The socio-economic impact in southern Africa. New York: St. Martin's Press, 1993.

About the authors

Daniel Tarantola is a Lecturer in Population and International Health at the François-Xavier Bagnoud Center for Health and Human Rights at the Harvard School of Public Health. He participated in the early stages of the global initiatives of the WHO including smallpox eradication, childhood immunisation, and the control of diarrheal diseases and acute respiratory infections in Asia and the Pacific. In 1987 Dr Tarantola helped to create the WHO Global Programme on AIDS, heading its National AIDS Programs unit.

Jonathan Mann is François-Xavier Bagnoud Professor of Health and Human Rights and Professor of Epidemiology and International Health at the Harvard School of Public Health. He is the Director of the International AIDS Center of the Harvard AIDS Institute and the Chairman of the Global AIDS Policy Coalition. From 1986 to 1990 Dr Mann was the founding Director of the Global Programme on AIDS at the WHO, Geneva. Dr Mann co-edited with Daniel Tarantola and Thomas Netter 'AIDS in the World', a global report published in 1992 on behalf of the Global AIDS Policy Coalition.

Lankinen KS, Bergström S, Mäkelä PH and Peltomaa M, eds.
Health and disease in developing countries. London:The Macmillan Press Limited, 1994:195–209.

20 HELMINTHOSES

Ralph Muller, D.Sc., Ph.D., FIBiol
International Institute of Parasitology
395A Hatfield Road, St. Albans,
Herts AL4 0XU,
Great Britain

Pedro Morera, Ph.D.
University of Costa Rica, School of
Medicine
P.O. Box 2117-1000, San José,
Costa Rica

INTRODUCTION

Helminths are common and ubiquitous parasites of man in almost all developing countries. It has been estimated that in Asia and Central and South America each individual will harbour on average at least one species of helminth, while in Africa the average figure is two species per person. There are about 20 species of helminths which are natural parasites of man but many others cause zoonoses (i.e. infections of animals which can also infect man).

Unlike viruses, bacteria or protozoa, helminths (with very few exceptions) do not multiply within the human body. As a result, helminth diseases do not have a sudden acute crisis but tend to be chronic afflictions; the severity of disease is proportional to the worm load which is often affected by the intensity of transmission in the area.

Severe manifestations of disease can depend on an accumulation of parasites from repeated exposure so that the onset of symptoms is very insidious. For most of the common human helminth infections there is marked overdispersion of parasite numbers, so that, although in many endemic areas almost everyone is infected, only a small percentage of 'wormy' persons have heavy helminth burdens and suffer severe disease; they are also responsible for a large part of the transmission.

FLUKE INFECTIONS

Trematodes, often known as flukes, inhabit the intestinal tract, bile ducts, lungs or blood of man. They are characteristically flat, hermaphroditic organisms (except for the schistosomes). All have complicated life cycles with an alternating sexual cycle in the human host without multiplication and an asexual multiplicative cycle in a gastropod snail intermediate host. In addition many trematodes have a second intermediate host.

The most widely distributed and important human trematode disease is schistosomosis* but clonorchosis and paragonimosis are of local importance in areas of the Far East. Most trematode infections are zoonoses. Only those of widespread importance are considered here but others with more local distribution and minor pathology are listed in Table 20.1.

Schistosomosis

The blood flukes or schistosomes cause one of the most important helminth diseases in many tropical countries. They were first recovered from the vesical veins by Bilharz in Cairo in 1851. It has been estimated that there are over 200 million cases of schistosomosis in the world, principally in agricultural workers or, in Africa, fishermen. There are four major species involved, three of which (*Schistosoma japonicum*, *S. mansoni* and *S. intercalatum*) cause intestinal schistosomosis while the fourth (*S. haematobium*) causes urinary schistosomosis.

---

*The terminology of the chapter follows the Standardized Nomenclature of Parasitic Animal Diseases (SNOPAD) recommendations for parasitic diseases names which are now widely accepted.

Table 20.1. Trematodes and features of fluke infections.

Name of trematode	Site in body	Habitat of snail intermediate host (and genus)
Schistosoma mansoni	Blood	Slow flowing rivers, canals and lakes (*Biomphalaria*)
S. japonicum	Blood	Banks of rivers and rice paddies (*Oncomelania*)
S. haematobium and S. intercalatum	Blood	Ponds and margins of lakes (*Bulinus*)
Paragonimus westermani	Lungs	Fast flowing mountain streams (*Semisulcospira, Thiara, Oncomelania*)
Clonorchis sinensis	Bile ducts	Slow flowing streams (*Bulinus, Parafossarulus*)
Opisthorchis viverrini	Bile ducts	Slow flowing streams (*Bithynia*)
Fasciola hepatica and F. gigantica	Bile ducts	Damp pastures or ponds (*Lymnaea*)
Fasciolopsis buski	Small intestine	Ponds and slow flowing streams (*Polypylis*)
Heterophyes heterophyes	Small intestine	Lakes, ponds and streams (*Pirenella, Cerithidea*)
Metagonimus yokogawai	Small intestine	Lakes, ponds and streams (*Semisulcospira*)
Gastrodiscoides hominis	Large intestine	Ponds (*Helicorbis*)

The parasites. The adults differ from all other human trematodes in having separate sexes, the male having a gynecophoric canal in which the long slender female is held during copulation and oviposition. They inhabit the posterior mesenteric veins (or the veins of the vesical plexus in the case of *S. haematobium*). With the help of enzymes produced by the larval stage, eggs pass through the walls of the venules and into the lumen of the large gut to be passed out in feces (or into the bladder and out in urine in the case of *S. haematobium*).

When an egg containing a *miracidium larva* reaches fresh water, it hatches in minutes and swims actively, searching for a suitable *gastropod snail host*. After penetrating into the snail a process of asexual multiplication takes place, the miracidium transforming into a *primary sporocyst* containing numerous germinal cells each of which develops into a daughter sporocyst. These are then released and enter the digestive gland of the snail. Within each secondary sporocyst many thousands of the next free-living stage, the *cercaria*, develop and are released into the water. The whole process takes 4–8 weeks depending on the species.

Many fork-tailed cercariae can be released each day and can swim around in the water for a few hours before penetrating through the skin of another human. The immature schistosomes are carried in the lymph to the lungs and reach the portal vessels, where they mature, mate and migrate to their final sites, producing eggs 4–8 weeks after infection.

Pathology. Penetration of cercariae after primary exposure produces a transient dermatitis (swimmer's itch). Infection with *S. japonicum* can cause acute allergic manifestations at the time when eggs are first produced, with lymphadenopathy, splenomegaly, diarrhea, lung eosinophilia and liver tenderness (*Katayama fever*).

Beginning about 10–12 weeks after infection there is an intense production of eggs which penetrate through the mucosa of the colon (or bladder with *S. haematobium*). Many eggs, however, get trapped in the tissues where they become surrounded by inflammatory cells, leading to the formation of granulomas or pseudotubercles. These are the cause of all the important pathological effects of schistosomosis.

Intestinal schistosomosis is found in infections due to all species except *S. haematobium*. The colon becomes thickened and the mucosa may have many small ulcers surrounding granulomas. In Egypt in particular, papillomas

Table 20.1. Trematodes and features of fluke infections, continued.

Mode of infection of man	Definitive hosts
Active penetration of skin by cercariae	Man, Rodents (Baboon)
Active penetration of skin by cercariae	Man, Dog, Cattle, Rat
Active penetration of skin by cercariae	Man
Cercariae encyst as metacercariae in crabs and crayfish	Man, Carnivores
Cercariae encyst as metacercariae in freshwater fish	Man, Carnivores
Cercariae encyst as metacercariae in freshwater fish	Civet cat, Man
Cercariae encyst as metacercariae on herbage	Ruminants (Man)
Cercariae encyst as metacercariae on herbage	Man, Pigs
Cercariae encyst as metacercariae in freshwater fish	Man, Carnivores
Cercariae encyst as metacercariae in freshwater fish	Man, Carnivores
Cercariae encyst as metacercariae on herbage	Man, Pigs

and inflammatory polyps develop and can even lead to obstruction of the lumen of the colon.

The eggs of *S. haematobium* cause granulomatous lesions of the bladder and ureters. There may also be papilloma formation and bladder cancer is more common in areas where prevalence is high, although other factors also appear to be involved.

In heavy infections with *S. japonicum* and *S. mansoni* many eggs are carried to the liver and the granulomas formed around them can lead to a coarse periportal fibrosis. The resulting portal hypertension causes liver and spleen enlargement and possibly ascites, and leads to a varicose enlargement of the esophageal and gastric veins which sometimes burst. Eggs can reach other sites also and those deposited in the small pulmonary arterioles may cause pulmonary hypertension and cor pulmonale. Cerebral granulomatous lesions are usually caused by the eggs of *S. japonicum*.

Clinical features. In the majority of patients with intestinal schistosomosis the phase of intestinal damage is accompanied by few symptoms, apart from a vague feeling of ill health. Liver fibrosis occurs 5–15 years after infection. Schistosomosis haematobium is usually a mild infection and the only sign in children

is a recurrent painless hematuria. In many endemic areas almost all children are infected at a young age.

Diagnosis. The most important method is parasitological by finding the characteristic eggs in a sample of feces (except for *S. haematobium*) examined microscopically. For light infections, the sedimentation concentration method is dependable and simple and can be easily carried out in the field. It involves mixing 10 grams of feces with at least 100 ml of tap water containing 0.5 per cent glycerol and allowing the sediment to settle in urinalysis glasses. This is repeated at hourly intervals until the supernatant fluid is clear and the sediment is then examined under the microscope.

For *S. haematobium* infections most eggs are passed out in the urine and the deposit of centrifuged or sedimented urine, preferably obtained near midday, is examined microscopically. A rough guide to the presence of *S. haematobium* infection can also be obtained by measuring hematuria by the dipstick method.

Treatment. Praziquantel is effective against all species of schistosome and can be given in a single oral dose of 40 mg/kg for *S. haematobium* and *S. intercalatum*, in two doses of 25 mg/kg each 4 hours apart for *S. mansoni*, and in three doses of 20 mg/kg each at intervals of 4 hours for *S. japonicum*. It is well tolerated with few side effects.

Oxamniquine has been widely used to treat *S. mansoni* infection in a single oral dose of 15 mg/kg. It is generally well tolerated, with dizziness and drowsiness the most frequent side effects but very occasionally there are effects on the central nervous system. Metrifonate can be used orally against *S. haematobium* (three doses of 7.5 to 10 mg/kg each at 2-week intervals). Side effects are usually mild and transient. Niridazole can no longer be recommended because of possible severe side effects.

Epidemiology. *Schistosoma japonicum* is confined to the Far East, occurring principally in China, The Philippines, Central Sulawesi and southern Japan. *S. mansoni* is found over much of Africa, Saudi Arabia, the Yemen, South America and the Caribbean. *S. haematobium* also exists over a large part of Africa and occurs in the Middle East. *S. intercalatum* is found only in Central and West Africa.

The distribution and ecological factors associated with transmission of the human schistosomes depend on contamination of fresh water with human or animal feces or urine containing eggs, the presence in the water of suitable snail hosts and on human contact with the water containing cercariae.

The amphibious snail hosts of *S. japonicum* (*Oncomelania* spp.) live principally in rice paddies and on the muddy banks of rivers in the Far East. The aquatic snail hosts of *S. mansoni* (*Biomphalaria* spp.) live in slowly flowing water such as irrigation channels, streams and lakes. Snails transmitting *S. haematobium* and *S. intercalatum* (*Bulinus* spp.) live almost entirely in still water such as ponds, pools and lakes and the spread of water hyacinth in Africa is increasing their numbers. Irrigation is a major factor in the transmission of *S. mansoni* and its prevalence is increasing in many countries as more large-scale water schemes are built.

Control. There are four main methods for controlling schistosomosis: environmental sanitation, prevention and destruction of snails, mass chemotherapy and prevention of water contact. Snail control by mollusciciding has been effectively used in China and in Egypt but often has to be carried out repeatedly over a long period of time. Integrated control measures in conjunction with mass chemotherapy have also been used successfully in many countries. Targeted mass chemotherapy can be very effective in reducing intensity of infection and thus clinical effects even if less effective in reducing prevalence.

Paragonimosis

Many species of the lung flukes, *Paragonimus*, occur in carnivores throughout the world but most of the estimated five million human infections are caused by *P. westermani* in the Far East. Although several species have been described in Latin America, *P. mexicanus* causes most human infections.

The adult trematodes measure about 12 x 6 mm and live in pulmonary cysts, usually in pairs. Eggs travel up the trachea and are passed out in the feces after being swallowed. For further development they have to reach fresh water and the miracidium larva, which develops inside the egg in a few weeks, bursts out and enters a suitable snail host. After multiplication stages inside the snail, the next free-living stage, the cercaria, emerges and penetrates into a freshwater crustacean (crab or crayfish). When these are eaten uncooked, the metacercarial larvae excyst and reach the lungs after migrating through the intestinal wall and diaphragm.

The developing worms in the lungs provoke inflammatory and granulomatous reactions, forming a cyst with an opening into a bronchiole. Cysts contain a brown, purulent fluid and there may be up to 25 of them, each measuring about 2 cm in diameter. The majority of infections are asymptomatic but in a heavy infection there is dry cough, chest pain, dyspnea and hemoptysis, which may last for years.

Characteristic eggs can be found in the feces or sputum, but concentration methods are likely to be necessary in light infections.

Praziquantel given orally in three divided doses of 25 mg/kg daily for 2 days is extremely effective. Niclofolan in a single dose of 2 mg/kg is also effective but has more severe side effects. The older drug bithionol is still in use but at least 13 doses, given on alternate days, are necessary.

Epidemiology and control. Dishes containing raw crabs or crayfishes are often eaten in endemic mountainous areas. In Latin America only crabs are involved in the transmission. Control is by changes in the preparation of crustaceans for food and to a less extent by sanitary disposal of feces.

Fasciolosis

The sheep and cattle liver fluke *Fasciola hepatica* is endemic in many areas of the world and causes some human infections in South America, Cuba, North Africa and Western Europe.

The adult worms live within the bile ducts where they produce eggs; the intermediate host is a *lymnaeid snail*. The migrating young worms penetrate the gut wall and then eat their way to the bile ducts, causing necrosis and inflammatory reactions along their path.

Early symptoms consist of abdominal pain in the right upper quadrant, nausea, fever and hepatomegaly. Definitive diagnosis is made by finding eggs in the feces or by duodenal aspiration. Bithionol given at a dose of 1 gram three times a day to a total of 45 grams is the preferred drug and has little toxicity. Praziquantel is less effective.

Epidemiology and control. Fasciolosis is a cosmopolitan animal disease, more prevalent in sheep-raising areas. Most human infections are by ingesting watercress or radishes in salads contaminated with metacercariae.

Clonorchiosis

The human liver flukes *Clonorchis sinensis* and the closely related *Opisthorchis viverrini* are endemic in areas of South-East Asia where freshwater fish are eaten uncooked. There are an estimated 28 million cases in the world.

The adults inhabit the bile ducts; the intermediate hosts are gastropod snails. The emergent cercariae penetrate many different types of freshwater fish and encyst as metacercariae. When infected fish are ingested uncooked by man, the excysted immature worms pass up the main bile duct.

About 70 per cent of infections are very light (below 100 worms) and completely symptomless. Moderate infections result in diarrhea, abdominal discomfort and some degree of splenomegaly. With heavy infections (over 1000 worms) there is likely to be fever, acute liver pain, recurrent cholangitis, pancreatitis, slight jaundice and perhaps death in a few years with ascites and cachexia.

Eggs are passed in the feces and concentration techniques can be employed if necessary. Praziquantel given in a single oral dose of 40 mg/kg or at 3 x 25 mg/kg over 24 hours is very effective.

Epidemiology and control. Infection is widespread in many endemic areas of Korea, Vietnam, China, Taiwan and Japan where it also occurs in cats and dogs. In China human feces are commonly used to enrich ponds containing food fish but are now usually stored or treated first.

TAPEWORM INFECTIONS

All adult cestodes or tapeworms of man inhabit the intestinal tract. They are flat ribbon-shaped worms without a gut, consisting of a chain (strobila) of separate segments (proglottids) and attach to the intestinal wall by an anterior scolex. Infection with larval cestodes is potentially very serious and in some countries cysticercosis (infection with larvae of *Taenia solium*) and echinococcosis (infection with larvae of *Echinococcus* spp.) are important public health problems.

Taeniosis

Taenia saginata is the beef tapeworm and is common with an estimated 45 million cases worldwide in countries where beef is eaten raw or undercooked, while the pork tapeworm, *T. solium*, is rather less widely distributed with an estimated three million cases occurring where pork and pork products are eaten raw or undercooked. Man is the only definitive host for both species.

Adult taenias are located in the ileum with their anterior end (scolex) embedded in the mucosa and the rest of the organism, measuring about 5 metres in length, hanging free in the lumen. Posterior (gravid) segments filled with eggs pass out of the anus. Eggs are released on soil and are ingested by the intermediate hosts; these are cattle for *T. saginata* and pigs for *T. solium*.

Inside the intermediate host, the larvae penetrate the intestinal mucosa, and are carried to the muscles. When the meat is eaten by man cysts transform into adult tapeworms. Most infections are symptomless but nausea and a feeling of epigastric distension with pain may develop.

Praziquantel in a single oral dose of 10 mg/kg is very effective with virtually no side effects. Niclosamide can be taken orally in two 1-gram doses 1 hour apart for an adult. Albendazole is effective against *T. saginata* at a dose of 400 mg for adults and children over 2 years.

Prevention and control. Prevention is by thorough cooking or freezing of meat. Control is by thorough meat inspection for cysts and by mass diagnosis and treatment campaigns.

Hymenolepiosis

Hymenolepis nana, the dwarf tapeworm, is cosmopolitan with an estimated 43 million cases worldwide usually in children, particularly in warm countries and in southern and eastern Europe.

This tapeworm has no intermediate host and eggs passed in the feces can infect another individual by mouth. Headache, enteritis with abdominal pain, diarrhea, nausea and vomiting, and dizziness may occur.

Praziquantel is effective against at a single oral dose of 40 mg/kg. Niclosamide only kills adult worms (oral dose of 60–80 mg/kg for 6 days, repeated 10 days later if necessary).
Prevention and control. Hygienic measures should be directed at personal hygiene and washing of clothes and bedclothes but chemotherapeutic campaigns are also likely to be most successful.

Larval tapeworm infection

Cysticercosis. This is caused by infection with the larval stage (cysticercus) of *Taenia solium* and is endemic wherever adult tapeworm infection occurs, particularly in Mexico, South America, Indonesia and South Africa. Cysts of *T. saginata* do not infect man.

Pathology depends on the localisation of the cysts in the body; they are usually spread throughout the body roughly in proportion to the weight of each organ. The most serious pathology is caused by cysts in the central nervous system. Cysts in most other parts of the body are benign and often the calcified cysts are only recognised on X-ray. In the brain the most common manifestation is epileptiform attacks of the Jacksonian type occurring a few years after infection. Cysticerci scattered throughout the brain may produce a variety of symptoms, motor, sensory or mental, with the resulting classical features of any focal lesion, and various focal symptoms and signs may occur in the same patient. The most frequent are transient paraesthesia, visual and aural symptoms, aphasia and amnesia. Headaches can be severe. The course and prognosis of cerebral cysticercosis is unpredictable.

Praziquantel has revolutionised treatment and cerebral cysticercosis is now amenable to chemotherapy. A dose of 30 mg/kg daily for 6 days appears to be effective.

Control depends on treatment of *T. solium* infection in the community and at the personal level through thorough washing of salad vegetables contaminated with eggs.

Echinococcosis. Echinococcosis is caused by infection with the larval stage of a minute tapeworm of the dog, *Echinococcus granulosus*. Eggs are passed out in the feces of dogs and normally infect sheep, cattle, goats or camels by ingestion on pasture. Dogs are usually infected by eating discarded offal and human infection occurs from ingestion of eggs on foodstuffs or by contact with dogs.

The pathology caused by the presence of a single unilocular cyst depends very much on its site in the body and is due principally to pressure effects. Cysts are most commonly found in the liver (50 per cent) and cause compression of the liver cells which can lead to biliary stasis and cholangitis due to secondary infection. Lung cysts (40 per cent of total) are more spherical than those in the liver and their rupture can result in hemoptysis from bursting of pulmonary capillaries.

Infection usually occurs in childhood but the cysts are very slow-growing and symptoms, if they occur at all, are usually found only in middle age except for cysts in the brain or eyes which may be present in childhood. If a cyst ruptures there may be acute anaphylactic shock with fever, urticaria, gastrointestinal disturbances, dyspnea and cyanosis and the protoscolices released can develop into new cysts.

Surgical removal of large cysts is usually possible but to obviate the possibility of rupture and spillage of the contents of a cyst, with consequent anaphylactic shock and dissemination of new cysts, it can be injected first with 0.1 per cent centrimide solution.

Chemotherapy is not very effective although albendazole at high doses (15 mg/kg daily for 30 days repeated four times) is showing promise. High doses of mebendazole (10–40 mg/kg daily for many months or even years) probably cause cysts to regress but are likely to be much more toxic.

Echinococcosis (unilocular) is found extensively in sheep rearing countries but is particularly common in southern Kenya, the Middle East, South America, Vietnam, Australasia and southern Europe. Mass treatment of dogs with praziquantel is possible and should be coupled with sanitary disposal of offal.

ROUNDWORM INFECTIONS

The nematodes or roundworms are a ubiquitous group of organisms occupying a wide range of habitats but with a marked uniformity of structure. About 12 species are natural parasites of humans although many more can cause zoonoses. The soil-transmitted nematodes (known as geohelminths) are the most common human parasites and are second in importance only to the schistosomes among helminths as causes of disease. Their life cycles are shown in Figure 20.1. Tissue nematodes all have an indirect life-cycle which involves another host, usually an arthropod (but *Trichinella* larvae are ingested in meat of other mammals).

Hookworm

Hookworm is very common in almost all developing countries with about 800 million infections worldwide. Two species, *Ancylostoma duodenale* and *Necator americanus*, infect man, both attaching to the wall of the small intestine from which they suck blood and can cause anemia.

The females of both species deposit eggs into the lumen of the ileum, and the eggs then pass out in the feces. On reaching soil, a larva hatches out from the egg, feeds on bacteria, and transforms into an infective larva which can penetrate through the skin of a new individual, usually between the toes. Larvae enter venules and reach the heart and then the lungs where they penetrate into the alveoli, ascend the bronchi and trachea, and are swallowed to reach maturity in the ileum. Larvae of *Ancylostoma* are also commonly ingested on salad vegetables.

The adult worms attach to the intestinal mucosa by their anterior ends and cause small hemorrhages. The worms suck blood, change their position frequently, and secrete an anticoagulant so that in heavy infections there is a daily blood loss of about 100 ml and also a protein-losing enteropathy.

There may be an intense pruritis with papular eruptions at the site of entry, in the lungs the larvae may cause a cough, sore throat and nausea (*Wakana disease*). Early symptoms of adult infections are epigastric pain simulating a duodenal ulcer, diarrhea with blood and mucus, and eosinophilia of 30–60 per cent.

A hypochromic microcytic anemia develops in chronic heavy infections (with about 800 worms) or even in light ones where dietary intake of iron is insufficient (e.g. with about 100 worms). In children, stunting of growth is a characteristic feature of the persistent anemia accompanying heavy infections (Figure 20.2).

Eggs can be recovered from the stool, those of the two species being identical. Concentration techniques can be employed if necessary.

Albendazole in a single oral dose of 400 mg is effective against hookworms and other soil-transmitted nematodes. Other antihelmintics such as mebendazole, pyrantel pamoate and levamisole are also effective. Any drug treatment should be accompanied by iron replacement therapy.

Epidemiology and control. Hookworm disease is almost entirely a disease of rural communities in all the tropics and sub-tropics. It is most common in areas with over 100 cm of rain per year where the infection rates may be very high. Provision of footwear for children can help to prevent infection. Control is by sanitary disposal of feces and repeated mass chemotherapy campaigns.

Strongyloidosis

The causative parasite is cosmopolitan with a similar distribution to the hookworms but the infection is less common.

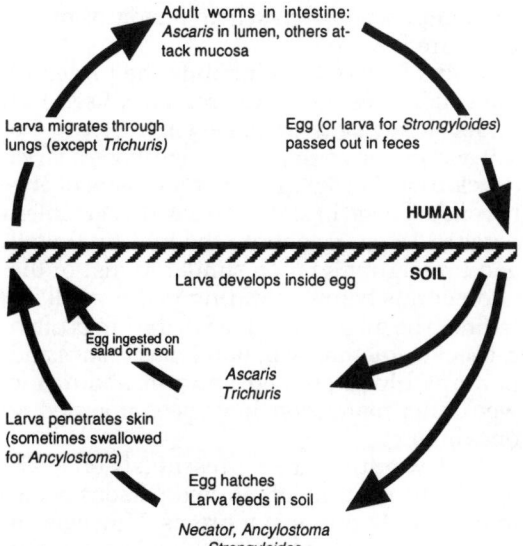

Figure 20.1. The life-cycles of the soil-transmitted nematodes.

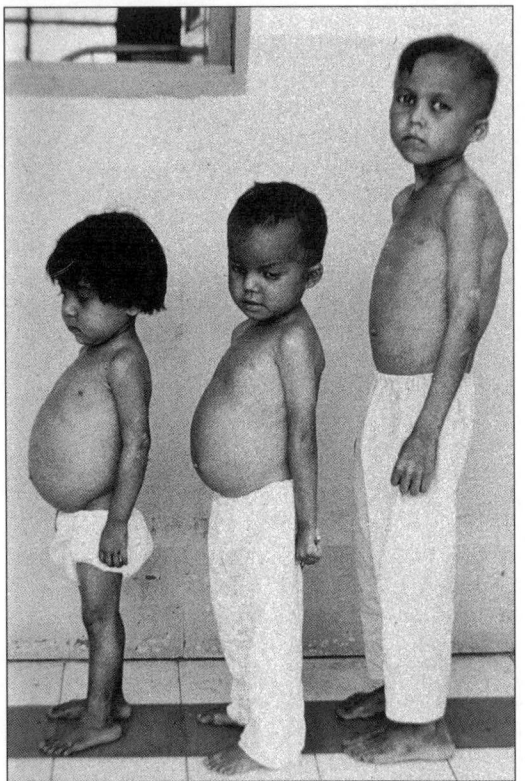

Figure 20.2. Severe stunting of growth in children in Colombia with heavy hookworm loads. Eldest child is 15 with a hemoglobin level of 1.8 g/dl (height of windowsill = 85 cm). Photo: D.B. Holliman

Strongyloides stercoralis females produce eggs which develop into larvae within the mucosal tissues, reach the intestinal lumen and are passed out in the feces. These feed, grow, and moult in soil and infect new individuals in the same way as hookworms. Autoinfection can also occur as infective larvae develop in the anal region and penetrate the skin.

A 'ground itch' can develop at the site of penetration and a pneumonitis can result from the migrating larvae in the lungs. The presence of larvae in the mesenteric lymph glands also causes a granulomatous lymphangitis so that there is a great loss in elasticity of the gut. Death can occur from septicemia. In immunocompromised hosts larvae penetrate through the gut into the lymphatics and can invade most organs of the body (e.g. patients undergoing immunosuppressive therapy for lymphoma, but apparently not AIDS patients).

Most cases are asymptomatic but there may be abdominal discomfort with intermittent gastric pain and diarrhea. In cases of autoin-fection there may be an itchy rash, usually in the perianal region marking the progress of the larvae, which lasts for a few hours (*larva currens*). In cases of massive hyperinfection, death almost always results and the symptoms may be protean, depending on the organs infected by the larvae.

The presence of characteristic first-stage larvae in a fecal sample is diagnostic. Larvae are often difficult to find and formol–ether concentration can be tried or larvae trapped on a swallowed brushed nylon string which is then withdrawn. A fecal sample can also be incubated with charcoal until the larger infective larvae develop; these are then fixed and examined microscopically.

Albendazole orally at 400 mg daily for 3 days is probably the best drug available. Mebendazole orally at 300 mg daily in divided doses for seven days has some effect.

Epidemiology and control. The larvae in the soil require warmth, shade and moisture and a light loamy soil as do hookworm larvae. Control is by sanitary disposal of feces, use of footwear and mass chemotherapy.

Ascariosis

The large roundworm of man has been known since ancient times. It is one of the commonest and most widespread of human infections with an estimated 1300 million cases worldwide. It is found in all tropical, subtropical and temperate regions where standards of hygiene are low.

Ascaris lumbricoides inhabits the lumen of the small intestine. Numerous fertilised but undeveloped eggs are passed in the feces. On soil and under warm, moist conditions a larva develops inside the egg. After ingestion of embryonated eggs in soil or on salad vegetables, hatched larvae penetrate the intestinal wall and undergo migration similar to that of the hookworms before maturing in the small intestine. The migrating larvae in the lungs often cause pneumonitis with numerous lesions and perhaps blood-stained sputum about one week after many eggs have been ingested at one time.

The few adult worms present (six on average) in the majority of infected persons result in no or only minor symptoms. However, it has been estimated that worldwide ascariosis causes over one million cases of disease annually with 20 000 deaths. Many worms (over 100) can result in digestive disorders and, in

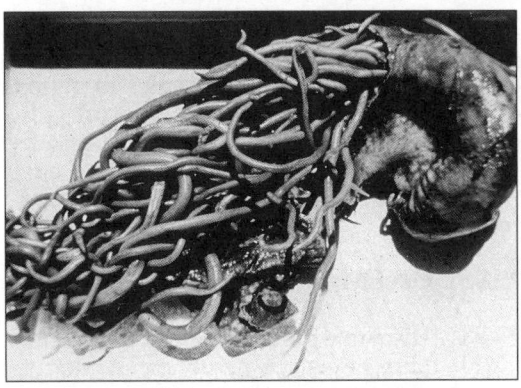

Figure 20.3. Intestinal blockage caused by large numbers of *Ascaris*. Photo: D.B. Holliman

children particularly, a protein–energy malnutrition. The importance of intestinal nematodes on nutritional status is being increasingly recognised. Intestinal obstruction results in severe abdominal pain, nausea and vomiting, worms in the bile duct in severe colicky pains, nausea, fever and slight jaundice (Figure 20.3). Eggs are usually plentiful in the feces and can be diagnosed under the microscope.

Many antihelmintics are effective but for convenience the newer broad-spectrum compounds are recommended. It is advisable to treat any patient from a developing country passing eggs who is about to undergo intestinal surgery, since adult worms sometimes wriggle through sutures, leading to peritonitis. Intestinal obstruction and bile duct infection should be treated medically if possible and surgery only considered as a last resort.

Single doses of albendazole at 400 mg, pyrantel pamoate at 10 mg/kg body weight, or levamisole at 4 mg/kg can all be used as can mebendazole at 100 mg twice daily for 3 days. Piperazine citrate at a single dose of 4 g has been used effectively for many years but has little effect on most other nematodes.

Epidemiology and control. Ascariosis is prevalent in most moist tropical countries often with very high infection rates, particularly in children. It tends to have a peridomestic transmission cycle with soil around houses being heavily polluted with eggs in both rural and urban areas.

Prevention is by thorough washing of salad vegetables while control is best achieved by a rise in standards of sanitation and in periodic mass chemotherapy campaigns.

Toxocara. Eggs of the cosmopolitan dog and cat roundworms, *Toxocara canis* and *T. cati* are passed in the feces of young animals and contaminate the soil. When ingested by young children they can hatch in the intestine and the larvae reach the bloodstream. They do not develop further and usually end up in the liver where they elicit a strong inflammatory response giving rise to granulomas. Rarely, there is long lasting hepatomegaly or, if larvae reach the brain, epileptiform attacks or, if the eye, retinal lesions.

Trichuriosis

Trichuriosis or whipworm infection is a worldwide infection of warm countries with about 750 million cases in the world and often occurs in the same areas as ascariosis.

Trichuris trichiura measures about 30 mm in length. Unembryonated eggs are passed out in the feces and, when they reach soil under warm moist conditions, a larva develops inside the egg. Eggs contain infective larvae in 2 weeks or more depending on temperature. When ingested the hatched larvae develop in the gut without undergoing a somatic migration.

In the great majority of cases no clinical symptoms can be attributed to the presence of the worms. In heavy infections there may be dysentery, abdominal pain, anorexia and weight loss with rectal prolapse in children. In children with chronic whipworm dysentery, severe hypochromic anemia and stunting of growth results.

Albendazole at a single oral dose of 400 mg is effective as is mebendazole at a dose of 100 mg twice daily for 3 days. For heavy infections, treatment may have to be repeated in a few weeks.

Epidemiology and control. Factors contributing to a high prevalence of trichuriosis, such as warmth, high humidity and shade, are similar to those for ascariosis and the highest infection rates are in children. Control measures are also similar.

Capillaria. *Capillaria philippinensis* was first reported from the Philippines in 1963 and cases have been reported since from Thailand and Iran. Clinical manifestations can be severe with malabsorption and emaciation and until mebendazole was found to be effective a mortality rate of 20 per cent was found. Intermediate hosts are probably small brackish-water fish with birds as the normal definitive hosts.

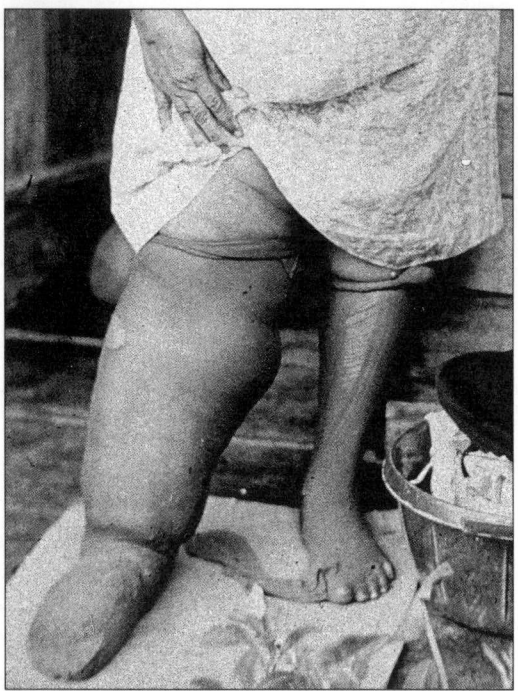

Figure 20.4. Patient with elephantiasis of right leg caused by *W. bancrofti*.

Enterobiosis

Enterobiosis or pinworm infection has a worldwide distribution with most transmission occurring inside houses. It is extremely common with about 750 million infections worldwide.

Adult *Enterobius vermicularis* inhabit the lumen of the cecum and appendix. Gravid female worms migrate out of the anus at night and deposit masses of sticky eggs on the skin around the anus. A larva develops inside the egg in a few hours and infection is usually transmitted to a new host from hand to mouth or possibly in house dust.

Mild catarrhal inflammation with diarrhea has been reported and very occasionally worms may block the lumen of the appendix. The eggs cause irritation of the anal, and in girls the vulval, region with pruritis. Eggs are rarely found in the feces and are best looked for in the anal region first thing in the morning by swabbing with transparent sticky tape and then examining this stuck on to a microscope slide.

Albendazole in a single dose of 400 mg or 10 mg/kg for young children can be used. Mebendazole, pyrantel pamoate and piperazine are also effective.

Epidemiology and control. Enteròbiosis is principally a group infection, particularly of children, and is a minor nuisance in almost every country of the world. Control is by chemotherapy of the whole family and by measures to prevent dissemination of eggs from anus to hand or into the domestic environment.

TISSUE NEMATODES

This is a disparate group of nematodes all having an indirect life-cycle involving an intermediate host. Some are natural parasites of man, such as the filariae which have insect vectors and the guinea worm which utilises water fleas; others are accidental guests of man, such as the trichina worm, in which larvae are transmitted in the flesh of food animals.

Lymphatic filariosis

This is an important and spreading helminth disease with about 90 million cases worldwide. *Wuchereria bancrofti* infections are widely distributed in the tropics in Africa, Asia, the Pacific, South america and the Caribbean; *Brugia malayi* infections are confined to areas of Asia. The adult worms inhabit the lymphatics.

Female worms produce sheathed pre-larval stages known as microfilariae which reach the blood and in most parts of the world are found in the peripheral bloodstream only at night (*nocturnal periodicity*). If microfilariae are ingested in a bloodmeal by a suitable species of mosquito, they develop into infective third-stage larvae that can leave the feeding fly and penetrate the puncture wound to infect a new human host.

Early effects of clinically evident cases consist of a recurrent adenolymphangitis. Lymphatic obstruction results in grotesque elephantiasis (Figure 20.4), usually of the lower limbs in malayan filariosis, but possibly affecting the arms, breasts in females and scrotum in males. Typically, the first clinical effects develop in about 8 months and consist of recurrent episodes of fever, nausea, headaches and possibly a rash lasting for about 2 weeks. This filarial fever may continue for many years and can also be accompanied by episodes of lymphangitis and lymphadenitis with painful inflammation and edema of the lymph trunks. A proportion of individuals infected in childhood remain symptomless.

The characteristic sheathed microfilariae can be found in a stained thick, dehemoglobinised blood smear taken at night. In symptomatic cases concentration methods have to be used (e.g. 10 ml of blood in a hypodermic syringe can be passed through a nuclepore filter, which is then stained).

Diethylcarbamazine citrate has been used as a microfilaricide for the last 40 years. It is given orally, 6 ml/kg body weight daily in three divided doses for 2–3 weeks. There is a slight action against adult worms and in some areas low doses for many months are being advocated to kill adults. Treatment is most effective in asymptomatic cases but side effects can be severe. Surgical treatment of hydrocele and elephantiasis can be attempted and symptomatic treatment of the various clinical effects is also possible.

Epidemiology and control. Infection is particularly common in the warm, humid tropics where mosquitoes can breed in large numbers. Many man-biting genera of mosquitoes are involved in transmission but rural bancroftian filariosis is adapted to *Anopheles* species while urban disease utilises ubiquitous and spreading *Culex* vectors, particularly *C. quinquefasciatus*. Control measures include mass chemotherapy programmes and insect larviciding campaigns.

Onchocercosis

Onchocercosis is an important filarial disease found principally in East, Central and West Africa with smaller foci in Central and South America. It is estimated that there are about 17 million cases worldwide. (Figure 20.5)

Adult female *Onchocerca volvulus* produce unsheathed microfilariae which wander through the dermal layers of the skin. If microfilariae are ingested by flies of the genus *Simulium* (in Africa known as blackflies), they develop into infective larvae. When the fly bites another host, these larvae enter through the puncture wound and set up a new infection.

In contrast to lymphatic filariosis nearly all the severe effects are produced by the microfilariae rather than by the adults. In the early patent stages the microfilariae usually cause pruritis with a persistent itchy rash and foci of inflammation surrounding dead microfilariae.

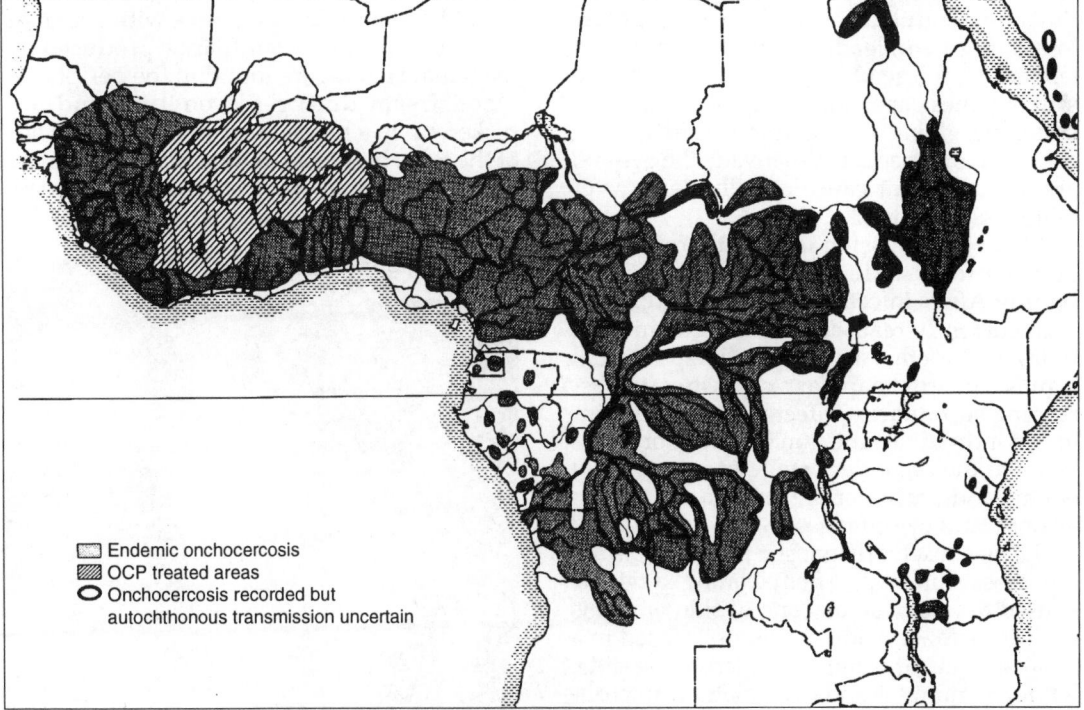

Figure 20.5. Geographical distribution of onchocercosis in Africa and Arabian Peninsula. Small foci exist also in Brazil, Colombia, Guatemala, Ecuador and Mexico; OCP = Onchocerciasis Control Programme. (Source: WHO)

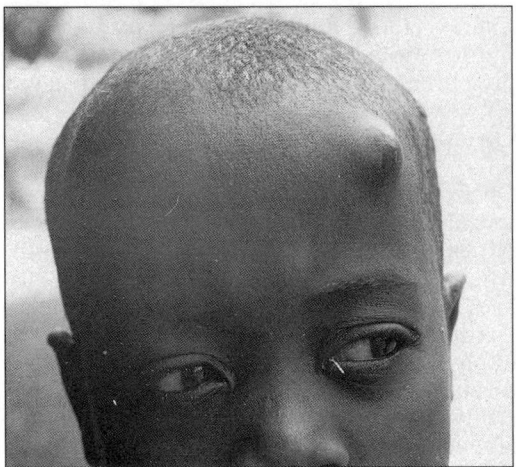

Figure 20.6. Child with *Onchocerca* on head. This location is especially dangerous because of the likelihood of eye damage. Photo: J. Anderson, H. Fuglsang

In heavier infections there may be an edematous reaction and later pachydermia and increasing destruction of elastic fibres. The last effect can result in hanging groin, in which the enlarged inguinal or femoral glands hang down in pendulous sacs. There is also often loss of pigment, leading to the condition of leopard skin resembling leprosy. Finally the skin becomes paper-thin, atrophied, and presbydermic, giving a prematurely aged appearance. Microfilariae can also invade the eye and are an important cause of blindness (river blindness, Chapter 36).

Where transmission is light there may be no symptoms and it is likely that in many parts of Africa infection is far more prevalent than currently realised. In infected children living in endemic areas the principal initial sign is a pruritic papular skin rash, often becoming secondarily infected. In heavily infected individuals this can lead in months or years to the secondary stage of intradermal edema and pachydermia and finally to skin atrophy and eye changes.

The most useful diagnostic procedure is the bloodless skin snip. After cleaning, a needle is used to raise a small cone of skin which is cut with a razor blade or scissors, teased in a drop of saline or water on a microscope slide, left for 30 minutes and examined for microfilariae under a low power microscope.

The drug of choice is ivermectin which kills microfilariae and sterilises female worms at very low dosages (0.15 mg/kg body weight in a single dose) with almost no side effects. Diethylcarbamazine (200 mg three times a day for 5–21 days) also kills microfilariae but often provokes severe side reactions. Suramin was formerly used to kill adults but is too dangerous for general use. Removal of nodules containing adults worms is practised in Central America, where they are principally localised on the head (Figure 20.6).

Epidemiology and control. Although onchocercosis does not kill, it can severely affect agricultural communities and has rendered areas of West Africa uninhabitable. The vector flies breed on vegetation and rocks in a great variety of river systems provided that these are well oxygenated. Heavily infected communities with 5–10 per cent blindness rates are always located within a few kilometres of rivers. An ambitious international control scheme has been underway in savanna areas of several countries of West Africa for the past two decades and shown remarkable success (Chapter 36).

Loaosis

Loaosis is found in man only in rain forest areas of West and Central Africa with a total of 2–13 million cases. Microfilariae produced by the female *Loa loa* are found in the peripheral bloodstream during the daytime and are picked up in a blood meal by various species of the large biting tabanid fly *Chrysops*. Larvae developing inside the fly are infective to a new host when the fly bites again.

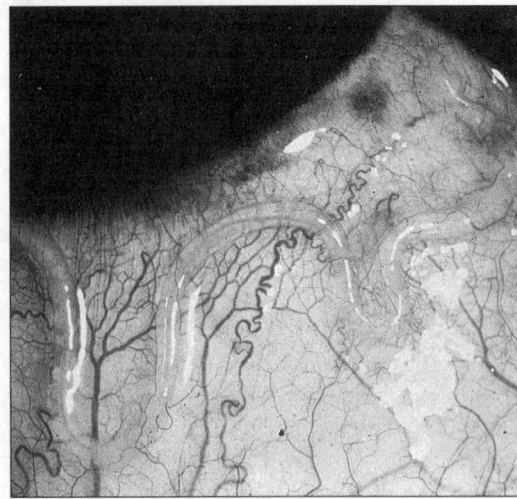

Figure 20.7. Adult *Loa loa* migrating across the eye beneath the conjunctiva. Photo: J. Anderson

Worms migrate through the connective tissues in any part of the body, the resulting hypersensitivity reaction eliciting painless fugitive (*Calabar*) swellings which disappear in a few days to reappear elsewhere. The swellings are usually painless but may also be accompanied by intense itching, pruritis and fever, with a high eosinophilia. Worms sometimes cross the eye under the conjunctiva and can then be extracted (Figure 20.7). Infection often causes vague symptoms of a general malaise. High levels of microfilaremia can result in encephalitis and have been associated with endomyocardial fibrosis and low fertility.

The presence of fugitive swellings with high eosinophilia in a patient from an endemic region is indicative of an early infection. Characteristic sheathed microfilariae can be found in a stained, thick, dehemoglobinised blood smear taken during the day.

Diethylcarbamazine given orally at 2–6 mg/kg body weight daily for 2–4 weeks kills both microfilariae and adults. However, there may be numerous side effects and with high microfilaremias there is a great risk of encephalitis.

Epidemiology and control. The vector breeds in densely shaded streams in the forest and adult flies are particularly common in the rainy season. The flies live in the high canopy and are attracted to movement below so infections are particularly common in cleared areas of forest such as rubber plantations or forest fringes. Control is not feasible.

Three species of the filarial genus *Mansonella* occur in man, all transmitted by tiny biting midges, *Culicoides*. *M. ozzardi* occurs in Central and South America and the Caribbean, *M. perstans* in Central and West Africa and areas of South America and *M. streptocerca* in Central and West Africa.

Dracunculosis

An adult female *Dracunculus medinensis* emerges from the subcutaneous tissues, usually of the foot, at patency. When an affected portion of the body is placed in fresh water, the anterior end of the emerging female bursts and releases thousands of first stage larvae into the water. For further development these need to be ingested by the small crustacean, *cyclops* (water flea), which inhabit ponds and open step wells. After about 2 weeks the larvae inside the cyclops are infective and, when the latter are

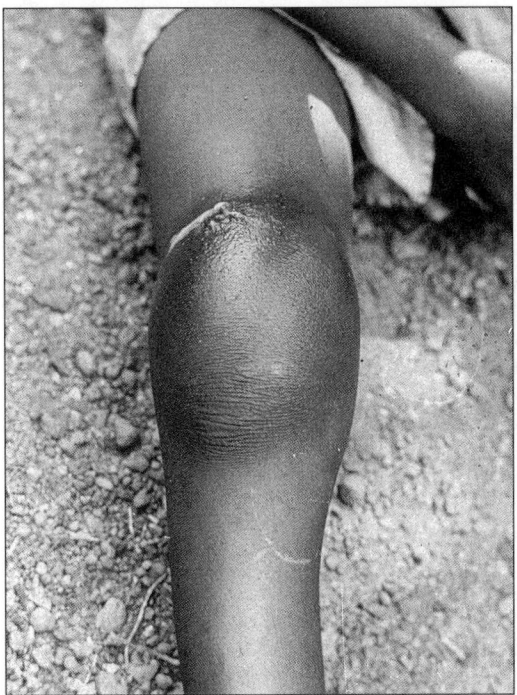

Figure 20.8. Child with adult *D. medinensis* emerging from right knee. Traditional treatment with palm oil has contributed to secondary infection and painful swelling.

ingested in drinking water, the larvae penetrate the intestinal and body walls, mature and mate in the subcutaneous connective tissue and the females emerge one year later (Figure 20.8).

Once a worm has begun to emerge there is a cellular reaction along the track of the worm: in about 50 per cent of cases secondary bacterial infection along the track follows and disability may last for months. The lesion may also provide an entry point for tetanus spores. If a worm bursts in the tissues before emergence, many thousands of larvae are released and a large abscess results. Possible sequelae include fibrous ankylosis of joints, contractures of tendons and chronic ulceration.

When a female worm is about to emerge there may be allergic symptoms of urticaria and fever. The small blister grows in a few days to one centimetre in diameter and becomes very painful. The pain is relieved by immersion of the affected region in water and a portion of the worm can then be extracted; but breakage of the worm can cause serious myositis.

Various benzimidazole compounds appear to act as anti-inflammatory agents, thus allowing worms to be withdrawn more easily.

Worms can be wound out on a stick a few centimetres a day and bandaging of the sore will prevent bacterial contamination.

Epidemiology and control. The disease is confined to rural communities in East, Central and West Africa, India and Pakistan. Most cases are in Nigeria. Safe drinking water supplies would eradicate the disease from the world, an aim resolved by the World Health Assembly in 1986 with a deadline of 1996. Many countries, such as India, Pakistan and various African countries now have eradication campaigns and the disease has almost, if not completely, vanished from Asia. Where the provision of safe drinking water is unfeasible, control is by health education, by provision of monofilament nylon filters and by treatment of ponds with insecticides (temephos).

Angiostrongylosis

Angiostrongylosis can be caused by larvae of two species of *Angiostrongylus*, which are natural parasites of rodents: *A. cantonensis* is widespread in the oriental basin of the Pacific and causes an eosinophilic meningoencephalitis; *A. costaricensis* has been reported from humans over much of the New World and recently also in Zaire, and causes an eosinophilic granulomatous inflammatory reaction in the intestinal wall.

Larvae passed by rodents in the feces develop in terrestrial molluscs such as slugs and snails. Infective larvae are ingested from the slime in salad vegetables. They are both diagnosed by serological tests. *A. costaricensis* is resistant to all known drugs.

Trichinellosis

Trichinellosis has a worldwide distribution in animals but is not of human importance in most developing countries except in Mexico, Brazil, Chile, Kenya and Senegal. Human infection is contracted by eating raw or undercooked pork or pork products containing encysted larvae.

The adult *Trichinella spiralis* is a small worm living partially embedded in the mucosa of the ileum. The adults live for only about one month but each female produces up to 2000 larvae which penetrate the mucosa and reach the skeletal muscles via the lymphatics and blood vessels. In the muscles the larvae grow and each becomes surrounded by a cyst. Important pathology is caused by the muscle larvae. These cause myositis with edema and inflammatory cells between the muscle cells.

Trichinellosis is a self-limiting infection lasting only a matter of weeks or months and light infections are usually asymptomatic. High dosages of mebendazole (20 mg/kg body weight every 6 hours for 2 weeks) kill the larvae. Massive doses of corticosteroids are necessary for neurological cases. Many antihelmintics will kill the adult worms.

Epidemiology and control. Domestic pigs (hogs) provide the main source of human infections in all areas except Africa, where wild pigs and hogs transmit the disease, and in the Far North among Eskimo peoples, where polar bears are most important. The larvae in pork are killed by thorough cooking or deep freezing.

CONCLUSION

In comparison with respiratory infections, diarrheal diseases or measles, helminth diseases are not a major cause of mortality in developing countries. The most important killer is schistosomosis with approximately 0.5 million deaths annually. Heavy infections with schistosomes, hookworms, *Ascaris*, or rare zoonotic infections such as larval tapeworms, cause obvious and often florid morbidity. However, the majority of individuals in developing countries harbour only moderate or low chronic helminth loads and it is difficult to evaluate the public health importance these. Recent studies have demonstrated that schistosomes and soil-transmitted nematodes (including *Trichuris*) cause widespread ill-health and loss of working capacity in adults and stunted physical and mental development in children, particularly where nutrition is inadequate. Heavier worm loads are almost always found in children and this is the age group in which the importance of these infections is greatest also from the public health perspective.

Control measures against helminth infections consist of:

1) *Personal prevention of infection.* Measures include wearing shoes (hookworms and strongyloidosis), avoidance of entering ponds, lakes, rivers and canals (schistosomosis), washing of salad vegetables (larval tapeworms, ascariosis, trichuriosis), thorough cooking of food (clonorchiosis, paragonimosis, trichinellosis) and use of bed nets at night (filariosis).

2) *Prevention of contamination.* Measures include the hygienic disposal of feces and urine, provision of safe water supplies and awareness of health hazards in the design of irrigation channels, ponds and lakes.

3) *Chemical control measures* include mass or targeted chemotherapy (for a specific age group such as children or for heavily infected individuals) and attack on vectors (e.g. insects or snails).

The transmission of helminth diseases is potentiated by conditions in warm, humid countries. In countries with a marked rise in living standards such as in Japan or the southern USA these diseases are no longer of clinical importance.

Recent emphasis on socioeconomic factors in developing countries by international agencies has decreased interest in specific control measures, as have also the failures in the past (particularly against hookworms and malaria). Effective drugs for mass chemotherapy of schistosomes and soil-transmitted nematodes are available but they are too expensive in poor, often rural, communities for the repeated treatments necessary.

Targeted chemotherapy appears to have little effect on transmission but can be economically used as part of a PHC programme to prevent morbidity due to these chronic diseases. This will require adequate and cheap diagnostic techniques which are now becoming available.

Additional reading

1. Bergquist NR, ed. Immmunodiagnostic approaches in schistosomiasis. Chichester: Wiley, 1992.
2. Cook GC. Parasitic diseases in clinical practice. London: Springer-Verlag, 1990.
3. Englund PJ, Sher A, eds. The biology of parasitism. New York: Alan R. Liss, 1988.
4. Esrey SA, Potash JB, Roberts L, Shiff C. Effects of improved water supply and sanitation on ascariasis, diarrhoea, dracunculiasis, hookworm infection, schistosomiasis and trachoma. Bull WHO 1991;69:609–21.
5. Haswell-Elkins MR, Elkins DB, Anderson RM. Evidence for predisposition in humans to infections with *Ascaris*, hookworm. *Enterobius* and *Trichuris* in a south Indian fishing community. Parasitology 1987;9S:323–37.
6. Jordan P, Webbe G, Sturrock RF. Human schistosomiasis. Wallingford: CABI, 1993.
7. McAdam KPWJ, ed. New strategies in parasitology. Edinburgh: Churchill Livingstone, 1989.
8. Mott KE, Desjeux P, Moncayo A, Ranque P, de Raadt P. Parasitic diseases and urban development. Bull WHO 1990;68:691–8.
9. Pawlowski ZS. Intestinal helminthiases and human health: recent advances and future needs. Int J Parasitol 1987;17:159–67.
10. Rollinson D, Simpson AGJG, eds. The biology of schistosomes: from genes to latrines. London: Academic Press, 1987.
11. Stephenson LS, Holland C. The impact of helminth infections on human nutrition. London: Taylor and Francis, 1987.
12. Walls K, Schantz P, eds. Immunodiagnosis of parasitic diseases. I. Helminthic diseases. New York: Academic Press, 1986.
13. Walzer PD, Genta RM, eds. Parasitic infections in the immunocompromised host. New York: Marcel Decker, 1989.
14. WHO Expert Committee. The control of schistosomiasis. Geneva: WHO, 1993. (Technical Report Series 830)

About the authors

Ralph Muller has been Director of the International Institute of Parasitology in St. Albans, Great Britain, since 1981. Before that he lectured at the London School of Hygiene and Tropical Medicine (1966–81) and the University of Ibadan, Nigeria (1961–66). He is a past President of the European Federation of Parasitologists, Editor of Advances in Parasitology and Journal of Helminthology. Dr Muller has written three textbooks and worked in several developing countries as a consultant to WHO, UNICEF, USAID etc.

Pedro Morera is specialist in parasitology (helminthology) and currently Professor of Medical Parasitology at the School of Medicine, University of Costa Rica. For more than two and half decades he has focused his research on Angiostrongylus costaricensis *and the syndrome of abdominal angiostrogylosis caused by it. From 1982 to 1986 he was the President of the World Federation of Parasitologists.*

Lankinen KS, Bergström S, Mäkelä PH and Peltomaa M, eds.
Health and disease in developing countries. London:The Macmillan Press Limited, 1994:211–220.

21 TRYPANOSOMIASES AND LEISHMANIASES

Alvaro Moncayo, M.D.
Trypanosomiases and Leishmaniases Control
World Health Organization, 1211 Geneva 27,
Switzerland

Felix Kuzoe, B.Sc., M.Sc.
UNDP/WORLD BANK/WHO Special Programme for Research and Training in Tropical Diseases, World Health Organization,
CH-1211 Geneva 27,
Switzerland

Farrokh Modabber, B.A., Ph.D.
UNDP/WORLD BANK/WHO Special Programme on Research and Training in Tropical Diseases, World Health Organization,
CH-1211 Geneva 27,
Switzerland

CHAGAS DISEASE

American trypanosomiasis or Chagas disease, originally a zoonosis, is endemic in Central and South America. In most endemic countries, the disease is recognised as an important public health problem and receives increasing priority for control.

Chagas disease is caused by infection with a protozoan parasite, *Trypanosoma cruzi* transmitted to man by an blood-sucking insect vector of the triatomine family and by blood transfusion. Some 2–3 weeks after infection, acute manifestations may be diagnosed in some patients. These manifestations are usually mild except in very young children who may develop myocarditis and meningo-encephalitis, the latter being fatal in 50 per cent of cases. However, the most important complications of Chagas disease develop some 10–20 years later in a third of those infected, and include chronic cardiopathy (in 27 per cent of those infected) as well as chronic digestive lesions (in 6 per cent) and neurological disorders (in 3 per cent). Patients with severe chronic disease become progressively sick and may ultimately die, usually as a result of heart failure.

It has been estimated that 16–18 million people are currently infected with *T. cruzi*. Of these, some 2–3 million may already have developed chronic complications, while over 3 million are still in the incubation period and likely to develop chronic Chagas disease in the future. The incidence of infection is probably close to 1 million cases per year.

Mortality due to Chagas disease is difficult to estimate but extrapolation from the results of some longitudinal studies would suggest that the disease causes more than 45 000 deaths per year. The number of disability-adjusted life years (DALYs) lost amounts currently to 2 740 000 which places the burden of disease due to Chagas disease in a global perspective on the third place after malaria and schistosomosis.[1]

The risk of infection with Chagas disease is directly related to socioeconomic factors: the triatomine bugs find a favourable habitat in crevices in the walls of poor-quality houses in many rural areas and in unplanned urban developments. Furthermore, rural to urban human migration is a factor which contributes to the spread of the infection by blood transfusion.

DISEASE CONTROL AND TRENDS

During the last decade there has been a steady decline in the incidence of infection, at least in those countries which have active control programmes, such as Argentina, Brazil, Uruguay and Venezuela. The incidence of

Table 21.1. Cardiac lesions and *T. cruzi* infection: incidence of right bundle branch block (RBBB) per 1000 person-years.

Age group	Seropositive	Seronegative
10 – 14 years	19.2	0.0
20 – 39	3.5	0.0
40 – 59	2.8	0.0

chronic morbidity is much slower to respond to control initiatives because of the long incubation period of the disease.

There is no effective chemotherapy for treating infected patients, and there is no vaccine for Chagas disease nor any prospect for such one in the near future. Fortunately, traditional vector control methods based on insecticide spraying, and especially newer approaches using fumigant canisters and insecticidal paints, have been shown to be highly effective, not only in reducing vector densities, but in reducing domestic transmission and the incidence of infection. Housing improvement schemes have also shown good results, and have the great advantage of not just being a method of control but of directly improving the living standards of the population.

The second most important mode of *T. cruzi* transmission is through transfusion with infected blood. It is not uncommon to find a 10–20 per cent seropositivity rate in blood banks in cities of the endemic areas, and serological screening of blood donors and in blood banks should be another pillar of Chagas disease control.

T. cruzi has an important sylvatic transmission cycle, and it is therefore not feasible to eradicate the infection in all endemic areas. However, in the Southern Cone countries (Argentina, Brazil, Bolivia, Chile, Paraguay and Uruguay) the parasite is mainly transmitted by *Triatoma infestans*, an intra-domiciliary vector species. These countries have therefore felt able to launch a joint initiative for the elimination of Chagas disease from their area. The backbone of the Southern Cone initiative, and of other attempts to control the disease as a public health problem in the remaining endemic countries, are control strategies based on a combination of vector control and blood screening. In the coming decade, the main research questions relating to control will concern the development of cost-effective and sustainable ways of implementing these strategies.

COURSE OF INFECTION AND CLINICAL PATHOLOGY

Some well controlled follow-up studies which describe the clinical evolution of the cardiac form have been carried out and provide accurate data on the evolution of infection and clinical pathology of Chagas disease. In a prospective electrocardiographic (ECG) survey of a Brazilian community it was observed that the incidence of cardiac lesions developed soon after infection and was highest in younger age groups, most of which had become infected before 20 years of age.

The incidence rate per 1000 person-years of the right bundle branch block (RBBB) – a characteristic conduction defect of chronic Chagasic myocardiopathy – was 19.2 in the age group 10–14 years, but less than four in older age groups (Table 21.1). In contrast, in the seronegative control groups there was no development of this characteristic conduction lesion.

Moreover, the mortality rate per 1000 person-years for seropositive patients with RBBB was 33.5 and with ventricular extrasystoles (VES) 39.2, whereas with the two conditions combined (RBBB and VES) the mortality rate rose to 116.3 per 1000 person-years (Table 21.2). In the seronegative group with normal ECG the mortality was 3.9 per 1000 person-years.[2] These and other similar data clearly indicate the much higher relative risk of developing myocardial lesions and death as a consequence of these lesions in seropositive than in seronegative individuals.[2,3]

Table 21.2. Mortality rates with cardiac lesions in *T. cruzi* infection per 1000 person-years. ECG=electrocardiogram, RBBB=right bundle branch block, VES=ventricular extrasystolies.

Lesion	Seropositive	Seronegative
RBBB	33.5	0.0
VES	39.2	0.0
RBBB and VES	116.3	0.0
Normal ECG	0.0	3.9

DRUG TREATMENT

Nifurtimox and benznidazole are the currently available drugs against Chagas disease. They are active as parasiticides only in the acute phase of the disease and have several

Table 21.3. Efficacy of triatomine control tools: percentage of reinfested houses after 12 months of different interventions in Argentina, Chile, Honduras and Paraguay (April 1993). Source: Progress Reports of field research projects, Geneva, June 1993.

Experimental groups (Number of houses)	Chile	Honduras	Argentina	Paraguay
Group I (150) Peri-domicile: Traditional insecticide Intra-domicile: Paints	3.1%*	8.0%*	2.5%*	5.6%
Group II (150) Peri-domicile: Traditional insecticide Intra-domicile: Canisters	N.D.	18.6%	0.66%*	8.0%
Group III (150) Peri-domicile: Paints Intra-domicile: Paints	0.0%*	4.0%*	2.3%*	2.6%*
Control group (300) Peri-domicile: Traditional insecticide Intra-domicile: Traditional insecticide	4.9%	11.0%	3.6%	4.3%

* Differences with Control group statistically significant.

serious side effects. The irreversible cardiac or digestive lesions of the chronic phase are not affected by the use of either of the available drugs. There is therefore a clear need for safe and effective new drugs.

IMMUNE MECHANISMS OF CHRONIC LESIONS

Basic research aimed at the elucidation of pathogenic mechanisms of chronic lesions involving damage of the heart and digestive autonomic nervous system, has advanced in recent years. Some experimental data involving molecular mimicry have been found to support the hypothesis of autoimmunity phenomena present in the pathogenesis of chronic cardiac and digestive irreversible lesions.[4]

Research has also progressed regarding the study of T-cell-dependent mechanisms of parasite resistance during the chronic phase in mice. It has been found that T-cell activation is not the only way for controlling parasitemia, tissular parasitism in myocardium or skeletal muscle in the chronic phase of *T. cruzi* infection.[5]

VACCINE DEVELOPMENT

In considering a possible vaccine for Chagas disease, there are at least two alternatives. One is an anti-parasite vaccine, mainly to control the acute parasitemia peak, and the other a control of the development of chronic pathology, that is, an anti-disease vaccine.

At present, there is no indication whether these two alternatives are related to each other or not. The expectation is that controlling the parasitemia might help to decrease the incidence or the severity of the chronic pathology. Due to the fairly high presence of parasitemia early after infection, there is a significant immune suppression and polyclonal activation, which if prevented, might result in the absence of pathology.

A large number of different *T. cruzi* antigens have been shown to contain different repeated epitopes which are highly antigenic. These molecules may provoke an imbalance in the immune response. If this is prevented through control of parasite growth during the acute period, the course of the infection may differ.

ADVANCES IN DISEASE CONTROL

Vector control

Two new tools for triatomine control have been developed: fumigant canisters and insecticidal paints. Initial results from Argentina, Chile, Honduras and Paraguay are very encouraging 12 months post-intervention. The rates of house re-infestation when using the insecticide paints are two to three times lower than those observed in the group of houses sprayed using the traditional insecticides (Table 21.3).

Blood banks control

In order to prevent transmission of Chagas disease through transfusion, blood is screened by serology and the positive units discarded. Some countries have already established systems to screen transfusion blood in blood banks that are compulsory by law (Argentina, Brazil, and Uruguay). There is, however, a need for well-defined antigens at the molecular level in view of the high sensitivity and specificity needed in blood banks control, as false negative results are not acceptable.

Two kits using recombinant defined antigens have been developed and are being commercially produced by the Institute Fatala Chaben (FATALAKIT) and Laboratorios Gador (BIO-CHAGAS) in Buenos Aires. Also the polymerase chain reaction (PCR) technique used for *T. cruzi* kDNA detection will be tested in sera panels provided by the reference laboratories of the continental network.

Initiative for the Southern Cone

Since *Triatoma infestans* is intradomiciliary in the countries of the Southern Cone (Argentina, Brazil, Bolivia, Chile, Paraguay and Uruguay), sustained implementation of multisectoral control measures could interrupt transmission within the coming decade. The Ministers of Health of the above-mentioned countries launched in June 1991 in Brazil the *Initiative for the elimination of Chagas disease* in these countries in the coming decade.

AFRICAN TRYPANOSOMIASIS

African trypanosomiasis, or sleeping sickness, is endemic in 36 Sub-Saharan African countries. It occurs in some 200 discrete foci, where the resurgence of the disease occurs, and where some 50 million people are at risk of contracting the disease. At the local level it is an important public health and socioeconomic problem that carries a continuous threat of severe epidemics, which are difficult and costly to control. The risk of epidemics makes African trypanosomiasis a major public health problem in Sub-Saharan Africa.

The disease is caused by infection with trypanosomes pathogenic to humans, *Trypanosoma brucei gambiense* and *T. b. rhodesiense*, which are transmitted by tsetse flies (*Glossina*). Clinical signs and symptoms of sleeping sickness may be suggestive but non-specific. Hence, a demonstration of the trypanosome in the blood or cerebrospinal fluid (CSF) is necessary to confirm diagnosis. The principal clinical manifestations in the early stage of the disease are intermittent fever, headache, joint pains and signs of reticulo-endothelial hyperplasia (e.g. enlarged lymph glands and spleen) and, in the advanced stage, neurological symptoms and endocrine disorders. The development and progression of disease may take several years in infections due to *T. b. gambiense*. In *T. b. rhodesiense* infections, it could be a matter of weeks and the early symptoms are more severe and acute. Once the disease has developed, it is fatal in all untreated cases. Other forms of African trypanosomiasis also affect domestic livestock and are a major obstacle to agricultural development and livestock production.

Around 15 000 to 20 000 new cases of trypanosomiasis are reported annually but the actual number has been estimated to be in the range of 200 000 to 300 000 per year. During epidemics, these numbers can increase significantly. The disease may be responsible for 25 000 to 50 000 deaths annually. During the first decade of the century, severe epidemics occurred in Central and East Africa, resulting in 750 000 deaths and in diminishing populations in several endemic areas.

Though such massive epidemics no longer occur, the disease causes much suffering among the inhabitants of endemic foci and serious social and economic hardship due to factors such as loss in manpower for cultivation and harvesting of crops, cost of treatment, care of patients, and death of the main income earners in the family. Neurological complications of sleeping sickness could lead to mental retardation in children and break up of families, as a result of changes in behaviour of a spouse.

EPIDEMIOLOGY AND DYNAMICS OF TRANSMISSION

The epidemiology of African trypanosomiasis is complex and transmission cycles are subject to interactions between humans, tsetse flies and trypanosomes and significantly, in rhodesiense sleeping sickness, domestic and wild animals. Improved understanding of the epidemiology of African trypanosomiasis is needed as a basis for its control.

Does the maintenance of sleeping sickness foci during endemic periods and their eruption into epidemics depend on variation generated by mutation or genetic exchange in trypanosomes? Information available from the study of strain variation in *T. b. rhodesiense* suggest that there is a set of stocks of circulating trypanosomes in tsetse and non-human hosts and that each sleeping sickness focus constitutes a separate set of human infective stocks.[1]

Tsetse distribution and mortality rate are key factors in the transmission of African trypanosomiasis. It has recently been demonstrated that weather satellites can be used to predict these factors over large areas of Africa.[2] Such predictions would assist in defining strategies for African trypanosomiases and for many other vector-borne diseases.

DIAGNOSIS

Many immunodiagnostic tests have been developed to detect antibodies to *T. b. gambiense*. The card agglutination test for trypanosomiasis (CATT) is best adapted for field use and is being used in 12 endemic countries for mass screening of people. The need to detect current infection led to the development of a monoclonal-based antigen-ELISA for the detection of trypanosome antigens in serum and cerebrospinal fluid of patients.[3] The test has a high sensitivity and specificity and has potential for diagnosis of both gambiense and rhodesiense sleeping sickness.[4,5] Parasitological confirmation is necessary before commencing treatment of the serologically positive cases and the Miniature Anion Exchange Centrifugation Technique (MAECT) is the most sensitive parasitological test currently in use.

PATHOGENESIS

The presence of trypanosomes in the CSF is one of the criteria in diagnosing late stage sleeping sickness. The sequence of events by which the parasite enters the CNS is not clearly understood, although previous studies have indicated that preferred route of entry may be via the choroid plexus to the CSF or regions lacking a blood–brain barrier or nerve–brain barrier. Certain signs and symptoms of the disease may be related to the early invasion of the trypanosome into these areas of the CNS.

Large numbers of parasites have been found in sub-arachnoid spaces and their extensions along the blood vessels, although only few parasites seem to penetrate the parenchyma. This finding has implications for chemotherapy since drugs used in the treatment of early stage sleeping sickness do not cross the blood brain barrier and may account for treatment failures of wrongly diagnosed early stage patients.

CHEMOTHERAPY AND DRUG DEVELOPMENT

Available chemotherapy

Few drugs are available for the treatment of sleeping sickness and have limitations. Pentamidine and suramin used for early stage sleeping sickness have undesirable side effects and do not enter the central nervous system.[6] Melarsoprol, which until recently has been the only drug available for late stage sleeping sickness, is associated with reactive encephalopathy, a serious adverse effect involving up to 10 per cent of patients, with a fatal outcome in 1–5 per cent.

The recent development of eflornithine (Ornidyl®, also known as DFMO) was a major breakthrough, in view of its safety. It was registered for the treatment of gambiense African trypanosomiasis in the USA in 1990, and approved for marketing in the European Community countries in 1991. Applications for registration in African countries have been submitted. In spite of the development of eflornithine, the chemotherapy of African trypanosomiasis is still beset with many problems and is far from satisfactory.

Eflornithine is effective for gambiense but not rhodesiense sleeping sickness and hence there is no alternative drug for melarsoprol-resistant infections of *T. b. rhodesiense*. In spite of its efficacy and safety it has a complicated mode of application which restricts its use to hospitals. The current cost of the drug alone for a 14-day treatment course is 250 USD and together with other paraphernalia and hospitalisation costs amounts to almost 500 USD per patient. In view of these constraints, it would be unrealistic to envisage the replacement of melarsoprol or any of the old drugs with eflornithine.

Novel approaches to chemotherapy

It has been suggested that a combination of eflornithine and melarsoprol in humans would enable reduced doses of the arsenicals and reduce substantially the number of relapses, which in certain areas is as high as 25 per cent. However, the problem of encephalopathies, which is probably an immune-mediated response, is likely to remain. It has also been suggested that the treatment of late stage sleeping sickness with currently available drugs might eventually include pretreatment with immunosuppressants, such as azathioprine and prednisolone to minimise the incidence of reactive encephalopathies. However, these suggestions are yet to be tried in humans for safety and efficacy.

DISEASE CONTROL AND TRENDS

The current control strategy is based on *medical surveillance of the population at risk and vector control*, where feasible. Regular medical surveillance provides an indication of the local epidemiological situation as an early warning of increases in prevalence. It allows the reduction of the reservoir of infection in humans and early detection and treatment of individuals and thereby avoids the complications of late-stage disease.

Vector control is also effective as an additional control measure. Simple tsetse control methods, such as insecticide impregnated traps, targets and screens, have been developed which are acceptable to communities and have been shown to be effective in reducing tsetse fly densities in several trials and in the control of sleeping sickness in Uganda. However, in the absence of disease or nuisance from tsetse fly bites, it is unlikely that this method will be sustained by the communities.

The development of new tools through research during the past decade has raised hopes for improved control of sleeping sickness but their integration into health care systems has been slow. The prospects of a vaccine in the near future are bleak due to the phenomenon of antigenic variation in trypanosomes which allows them to change their surface coat and evade the hosts' immune response.

The severe economic problems and political instability of many endemic countries have seriously affected African trypanosomiasis control during the last decade, especially in Central and East Africa. Prospects of any significant improvement in the African trypanosomiasis situation would largely depend on the successful mobilisation of external resources.

UNDP/World Bank/WHO Special Programme for Research and Training in Tropical Diseases supports several projects in prevention, diagnosis and treatment of trypanosomiases. Details of these can be found in WHO publications.[7,8]

LEISHMANIASES

The organisms of genus *Leishmania* are transmitted by female sandflies from infected animal reservoirs or infected humans. The *Leishmania* species vary with respect to their vector specificity or preference, biological activity (therefore clinical manifestations) and geographical distribution. The clinical manifestations may appear as asymptomatic infection, self-healing skin lesions, non-healing and generalised skin lesions, progressive mucocutaneous lesions or systemic visceral disease which is lethal if untreated. At present the role of asymptomatic infection in perpetuating transmission of leishmaniasis is not known. Asymptomatic infection may become full-blown disease when the immune response is suppressed due to HIV infection or immunosuppressive drug therapy.

In spite of the considerable progress made in molecular biology and immunology of leishmaniasis, definitive diagnosis of leishmaniasis depends, as it did 70 years ago, on the demonstration of the parasite in biopsy material. Because of the epidemic or endemic nature of the disease, diagnosis is usually clinical and relatively accurately made by local health workers. It is only in sporadic cases or with concomitant other diseases that diagnosis becomes a problem. In some parts of the world it is important to distinguish the causal parasite as it may determine the course of treatment.

THE DISEASES

Leishmaniasis is a group of diseases with very different clinical manifestations and public

Table 21.4. The major *Leishmania* species and the most common form of disease they produce. CL = cutaneous leishmaniasis, DCL = diffuse cutaneous leishmaniasis, MCL = mucocutaneous leishmaniasis, VL = visceral leishmaniasis.

Parasite	Disease	Comments
Old world		
L. major	CL	Zoonotic, gerbils are reservoir
L. aethiopica	CL, DCL, MCL	
L. tropica	CL, recidivans	Anthroponotic
L. infantum	VL, some variants CL	Zoonotic, dog is reservoir
L. donovani	VL	Anthroponotic
New world		
L. mexicana	CL	Chiclero's ulcer
L. amazonensis	CL	same group as *L. mexicana*
L. venezuelensis	CL	same group as *L. mexicana*
L. braziliensis	CL and MCL	
L. peruviana	CL	known as uta; same group as *L. braziliensis*
L. guyanensis	CL	
L. panamensis	CL, MCL	same group as *L. guyanensis*
L. chagasi	VL	Most likely identical to *L. infantum*

health consequences, ranging from self-healing but disfiguring cutaneous lesions in South-West Asia, Latin America and the Mediterranean region to severe epidemics with high mortality in the Indian subcontinent and Sudan. There are three general forms of leishmaniases: cutaneous (CL), visceral (VL) and mucocutaneous (MCL). Cutaneous leishmaniasis is the most prevalent, producing skin ulcers which may take more than a year to heal. Visceral leishmaniasis is a systemic disease which is nearly always fatal if left untreated.

A certain number (5–18 per cent reported in India and Sudan, respectively) of treated patients develop a skin condition called post kala azar dermal leishmaniasis (PKDL). This form is believed to develop as a result of incomplete treatment and is highly important as a reservoir of infection in the transmission of VL.

Mucocutaneous leishmaniasis initially appears as a CL which may heal but later develops a hideous tissue destruction that, if allowed to progress, will completely destroy the nose and the oral cavity. Mucocutaneous leishmaniasis is not very prevalent and only 5 per cent of CL cases may develop MCL in some regions (Brazil, Bolivia, Peru). The social consequences are obvious. Treatment is long, recurrence is frequent and patients often require corrective surgery to be accepted in the society.

More than twenty species of the protozoan parasite *Leishmania* are known of which over a dozen are associated with various forms of leishmaniasis (Table 21.4).[1] All forms of leishmaniases are transmitted by sandflies (*Lutzomiya* species in Latin America and *Phlebotomus* species in the Old World). The reservoir of the infection may be human during an epidemic, like in the VL of the Indian sub-continent known as *kala azar*, and the CL of some large cities in the Old World (Baghdad, Kabul, Damascus) known as *oriental sore*. The reservoir may be animals like dogs for VL in Southern Europe, Northern Africa and Latin America and gerbils for CL in Asian countries.

DISEASE TRENDS

There has been a general increase in the number of leishmaniasis cases of all groups during the last decade. Most cases occur as epidemics. Major causes are war and mass migration, new settlement or development projects in rural areas of zoonotic leishmaniasis, environmental changes and unplanned urbanisation. The reduction in malaria vector control programmes has also played a role as sandflies are highly sensitive to the insecticides used.

Some 12 million people are thought to be infected and a further 350 million are within the risk of getting infected.[1] These are only rough estimates as leishmaniases tend to occur in remote areas and in epidemics. Leishmaniases exist in over 80 countries in the world with different public health consequences.[2,3]

The epidemic in Sudan probably peaked in 1991–92 and killed an estimated 40 000 to 60 000 people and is still ravaging in the Western Upper Nile province and spreading in the Eastern province of Gadarif. The epidemic in Bihar state of India continues with over 75 000 cases reported in 1992. Since case-fatality is generally between 5 and 10 per cent in those diagnosed and treated (up to 14 per cent in Sudan), and 100 per cent in those who do not get treatment, it is estimated that visceral leishmaniasis may have killed over 100 000 people in 1992.[4]

The impact of cutaneous leishmaniasis is less dramatic, but it causes severe suffering in endemic areas not least because of the social and psychological trauma associated with disfigurement. During the Iran–Iraq war the severity of the CL problem was such that the Iranians resorted to the ancient practice of *leishmanization* and inoculated over two million people with live virulent organism in the arm in order to prevent multiple lesions elsewhere on the body. Reportedly in 2–3 per cent the lesion did not heal within the usual 9–12 months and in 1 per cent the lesion continued for 5 years and required treatment.

CONTROL

In the Indian subcontinent where the number of reported cases of VL has been rising in the recent years, vector control (spraying insecticide) is feasible and believed to be an effective method of control particularly if it is combined with case finding and treatment. This is because the vector lives in close proximity of human dwellings and the disease is believed to be anthroponotic during an epidemic (the reservoir of the parasite, *L. donovani*, is the infected human). However, this approach would not be feasible in controlling the zoonotic CL in Yucatan, Mexico (*Chiclero's ulcer*) where, *L. mexicana* infection is zoonotic in the wild animals in forests where humans are infected.

In the zoonotic VL, control of infected dogs is important e.g. in Brazil and in the Mediterranean region, where dogs rather than humans are the reservoir of infection. In the case of zoonotic CL in many dry zones where the gerbils (*Psammomys opimus*) are the reservoir, control may be feasible as was demonstrated in the Central Asian Republics and Eastern Saudi Arabia.

Control requires elimination of gerbil colonies from the periphery of human dwellings (by ploughing and sometimes introducing anticoagulants or other poisons), and elimination of vegetation on which the gerbils depend for survival. Once this is done, recolonisation must be prevented, for example by physical barriers (irrigation canals) or elimination of the plants. This operation for a small area near Al-Ahsa, Saudi Arabia costs about 1 000 000 USD a year. Hence even when feasible, the application of presently available tools require vast infrastructure and funds which are often beyond the means of most governments.

Usually only integrated programmes involving both vector and reservoir control can succeed. In any foci, this should start from identification of vectors and reservoirs, fluctuations of vector and reservoir density, infectivity rates of vectors and reservoirs, etc. As far as possible health education and community participation must be included in the control programmes, otherwise cessation of the programmes would give rise to large epidemics when the eradication of zoonotic infection is not possible. This is because the number of non-immune individuals in a population increases during an effective control programme.

Patients with MCL require long treatment of over 2–3 months and relapse is frequent. Often not knowing the possibilities of cure and reconstruction surgery, patients in remote areas accept the consequences of MCL as inevitable. In Peru, a patient organisation has been formed with the help of a non-governmental organisation, Ministry of Health and The University of Peruana to provide health education and assistance for chemotherapy and corrective surgery. The cost of treatment of all cases would certainly be beyond the resources of the Ministry of Health of many inflicted countries, but the demands of patients through such organisations would not go unnoticed.

All in all, the progress in controlling leishmaniases has been very slow. In contrast research in many aspects of long-term goals for developing new drugs, diagnostics and a vaccine against different forms have progressed considerably.[4]

VACCINE DEVELOPMENT

Vaccination is probably the only single tool that could be applied for controlling all forms of leishmaniases, but the target populations must be identified for cost effectiveness of the intervention. There are several reasons to believe that it would be possible to produce a single vaccine that could protect against all forms of leishmaniases.[5,6] All *Leishmania* species share many antigens and it has been experimentally possible to produce cross protection. The most direct evidence is epidemiological. It has recently been shown that previous infection with *L. major* producing CL would induce protection against VL in Sudan. Killed *Leishmania* mixed with a small dose of BCG is being tested in clinical trials as an experimental vaccine against cutaneous leishmaniasis. Avirulent parasites or single molecules produced by genetic engineering are at various stages of development in animal models.

DIAGNOSIS

Cutaneous and visceral leishmaniases were recognised as disease entities in the 9th and 18th centuries respectively, although their causal agents were not identified until early this century. Diagnosis of cutaneous lesions and for many geographical areas, visceral disease was done clinically with considerable accuracy and reliability. This is primarily because these diseases tend to appear as epidemic or endemic and therefore are easily recognised by local health workers.

Diagnosis becomes a major challenge when a case is displaced to a new non-endemic area or when different signs and symptoms appear because of superinfection with other agents. Clinical diagnosis is not sufficient for starting treatment even in endemic areas, although this unfortunately is a widespread practice due to lack of access to a diagnostic laboratory. Definitive diagnosis is based on demonstration of parasite in direct smear, or in animal or culture inoculation. Unfortunately, this old criterion is still held as the Golden Rule for all forms but hopefully will be changed to less invasive serological tests (at least for VL) that are now being evaluated. Parasites may be demonstrated in smears made from samples taken from the lesion (for CL and MCL) or lymph node, bone marrow and spleen for VL.

Lymph node aspiration is by far the most convenient method for VL patients. Lymphadenopathy is an important clinical feature of VL in many parts but parasites may also be found in lymph nodes that are not enlarged. Bone marrow aspiration is painful and unlike lymph node or splenic aspiration, is often resented by patients. Splenic aspiration is generally accepted as the most sensitive method but must be done with care and according to the recommended method.[1] There are certain precaution guidelines by the WHO before attempting splenic aspiration (prothrombin time and platelet count) but these are not always observed in the field. However, the technique and the experience of the person performing the aspiration may be more important.

TREATMENT

The first line drug against leishmaniasis is pentavalent antimony. Daily injections are required for a period of 4 weeks for VL or longer if signs and symptom persist (20 mg of antimony per kilogram of body weight). The cost of treatment ranges from 80 to 120 USD per VL patient. As this is not affordable for most of the patients in many hyperendemic foci, the patients are left without adequate treatment. The result is reflected in the increase in non-responders and in cases of PKDL (up to 18 per cent) who remain as the reservoir of the infection.

In most developing/endemic countries the drug is purchased and provided by the government as far as possible. Yet in many countries there is an illicit market for the drug. Extensive research activities are being supported by TDR on development of new drugs also for leishmaniases.[7]

References

Chagas disease

1. World Bank. World Development Report 1993. New York: Oxford University Press, 1993:216–8.
2. Maguire JH, Hoff R, Sherlock I, *et al.* Cardiac morbidity and mortality due to Chagas disease: prospective electrocardiographic study of a Brazilian community, Circulation 1987;75(6): 1140–5.
3. Mota EA, Guimaraes AC, Santana OO, *et al.* A nine year prospective study of Chagas disease in a defined rural population in Northeast Brazil. Am J Trop Med and Hygiene 1990;42(5): 429–40.
4. Van Voorhis WC, Schekewy L, Trong HL, *et al.* Molecular mimicry by *Trypanosoma cruzi*: the F1–160 epitope that mimics mammalian nerve can be mapped to a 12-aminoacid peptide. Proc Natl Acad Sci USA 1991;88:5993–7.

5. Rottenberg M, Cardoni R, Sinagra A, *et al.* *Trypanosoma cruzi*: T cell-dependent mechanisms of resistance during chronic infection. Exp Parasitol 1991;73:127–36.

African trypanosomiasis

1. Tait A. The epidemiological relevance of trypanosome strain variation. Ann Soc Belge Med Trop, 1989;69(Suppl. 1):197–203.
2. Rogers DJ, Randolph SE. Mortality rates and population density of tsetse flies correlated with satellite imagery. Nature 1991;351:739–41.
3. Nantulya VM. An antigen detection enzyme immunoassay for the diagnosis of rhodesiense sleeping sickness. Parasite Immunol 1989;11: 69–75.
4. Nantulya VM, Doua F, Molisho S. Diagnosis of *Trypanosoma brucei gambiense* sleeping sickness using an antigen detection enzyme-linked immunosorbent assay. Trans R Soc Trop Med Hyg 1992;86:42–5.
5. Komba EK, Odiit M, Mbulamberi DB, Chimfwembe EC, Nantulya VM. Multicenter evaluation of an antigen-detection ELISA for the diagnosis of *Trypanosoma brucei rhodesiense* sleeping sickness. Bull WHO 1992;70:57–61.
6. Bronner U, Doua F, Ericsson O, *et al.* Pentamidine concentrations in plasma, whole blood and cerebrospinal fluid during treatment of *Trypanosoma gambiense* infection in Cote d'Ivoire. Trans R Soc Trop Med Hyg 1991;85: 563–706.
7. World Health Organization. Epidemiology and control of African trypanosomiasis. Report of WHO Expert Committee, Geneva: WHO, 1986. (Technical Report Series No. 739)
8. Tropical Disease Research. Progress 1911–92. Eleventh Programme Report. UNDP/World Bank/WHO Special Programme for Research and Training in Tropical Diseases. Geneva: WHO, 1993.

Leishmaniases

1. World Health Organization. Control of the leishmaniases. Report of a WHO Expert Committee. Geneva: WHO, 1990. (Technical Report Series 793)
2. Desjeux P. Information on the epidemiology and control of the leishmaniasis by country or territory. Geneva: WHO, 1991. (WHO/LEISH/91.30)
3. World Bank. World development report. New York: Oxford University Press, 1993.

4. Modabber F. Leishmaniasis. In: Walgate R, Simpson K, eds. Tropical disease research. Eleventh programme report. UNDP/World Bank/WHO Special Programme for Research and Training in Tropical Diseases. Geneva: WHO, 1993.
5. Antunes CMF, Mayrink W, Magalhaes PA, *et al.* Controlled field trials of a vaccine against New World cutaneous leishmaniasis. Int J Epidemiol 1986;15:572–80.
6. Modabber F. Experiences with vaccine against cutaneous leishmaniasis: Of men and mice. Parasitol 1989;89:(Suppl)S49–S60.
7. Behbehani K. Integrated chemotherapy for African trypanosomiasis, Chagas disease and leishmaniasis. In: Tropical disease research. Eleventh programme report. UNDP/World Bank/WHO Special Programme for Research and Training in Tropical Diseases. Geneva: WHO, 1993.

About the authors

Alvaro Moncayo is a Doctor of Medicine and a specialist in epidemiology. He is currently the Chief of Trypanosomiases and Leishmaniases Control Unit in the Division of Control of Tropical Diseases (CTD) and Secretary of the Steering Committee on Chagas disease of the UNDP/World Bank/WHO special Programme for Research and Training in Tropical Diseases (TDR) at the WHO in Geneva. Dr Moncayo wrote the part on Chagas disease in this chapter.

Felix Kuzoe joined the WHO in 1974 as an entomologist with experience in the control of onchocerciasis and African trypanosomiasis. During 1978–1981 he worked as Project Leader for the WHO Inter-Regional Project for applied Research on African trypanosomiasis in Burkina Faso and Côte d'Ivoire. He joined the TDR in 1981 as Secretary of the Steering Committee on African Trypanosomiases. He has published a number of articles on the subject and wrote the part on African trypanosomiasis in this chapter.

Farrokh Modabber is an immunologist and currently works as a scientist and Secretary of the Steering Committee on Leishmaniases and Coordinator for Leismaniases in TDR. His previous posts include Assistant Professor and Lecturer, Harvard School of Public Health, Boston, USA (1973–82), Director of Pasteur Insitute, Teheran, Iran (1978–79), and Head of Immunology Department at Syntex Research Institute, Palo Alto, USA (1982–84). Dr Modabber wrote the part on leishmaniases in this chapter.

Lankinen KS, Bergström S, Mäkelä PH and Peltomaa M, eds.
Health and disease in developing countries. London:The Macmillan Press Limited, 1994:221–228.

22 AMEBIASIS AND OTHER ENTERIC PROTOZOAN INFECTIONS

Vinodh Gathiram, M.D.
University of Natal, Faculty of Medicine
Natal,
South Africa

Jonathan I. Ravdin, M.D.
Case Western Reserve University
Medical Service 111 (W), Cleveland V.A.
Medical Center, 10701 East Boulevard,
Cleveland, Ohio 44106,
USA

INTRODUCTION

The focus of this chapter is the enteric ameba, *Entamoeba histolytica*, which is the third leading parasitic cause of morbidity and mortality in the developing world. Giardiasis and cryptosporidiosis are also highly prevalent protozoan infections and important causes of chronic diarrhea. These and some others are discussed briefly at the end of this chapter. Paradoxically, the Programme for Control of Diarrhoeal Diseases of the WHO gives amebiasis a low priority rating in comparison to other causes of diarrhea. Consequently, research on *Entamoeba histolytica* has been confined to only a few centres

Losch first demonstrated the presence of amebae in colonic ulcers of a dysenteric patient in 1875. Schaudinn clearly distinguished the dysentery producing ameba from the non-pathogenic *Entamoeba coli*, naming the parasite *E. histolytica* due to its lytic effect on host tissues. Subsequently, a subgroup of *E. histolytica* was reclassified as *E. hartmanni*, a separate non-pathogenic species.

E. histolytica is truly a cosmopolitan parasite: it infects some 10 per cent of the world's population. However, disease is manifest in only a small minority of infected individuals most of whom live in or have visited the tropics or subtropical areas. It appears that there are distinct pathogenic and non-pathogenic strains of *E. histolytica* and that pathogenicity is influenced by bacterial flora and environmental conditions in the gut.

THE ORGANISM AND ITS LIFE CYCLE

E. histolytica trophozoites are uninucleate and range in size from 10 to 50 μm (average 25 μm). In fixed specimens the trophozoites have a spherical nucleus usually with a central karyosome. Chromatoid bodies which vary in size and shape are frequently seen in both cysts and trophozoites. The cysts range in size from 12 to 17 μm and depending on their maturity have one to four nuclei which are morphologically similar to those of the trophozoites.

Ingestion of cysts results in *excystment* in the small intestine with the production of trophozoites which infect the colon and multiply by binary fission. *Encystment* occurs in the large intestine. Trophozoites do not play any role in parasite transmission due to their sensitivity to temperature, desiccation and gastric acidity. Mature cysts survive for long periods of time in water, damp soil and feces.

EPIDEMIOLOGY

Man is the most important reservoir of *E. histolytica*. An asymptomatic carrier excretes up to 15 million cysts per day. Transmission of cysts via fecal contamination of water or vegetables or direct fecal–oral contact is

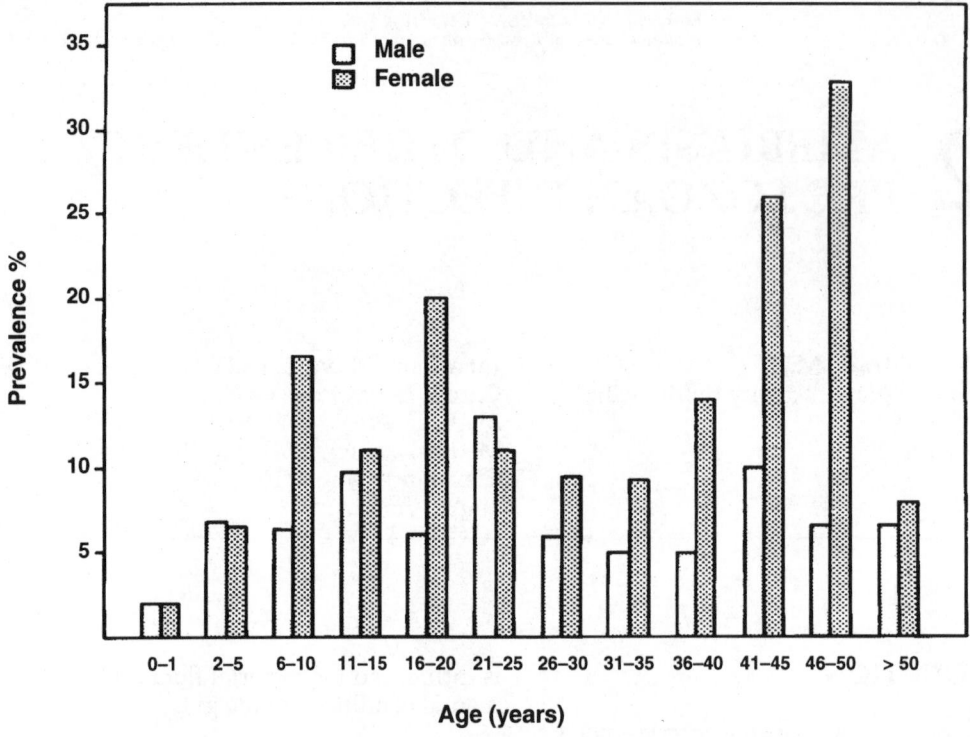

Figure 22.1. Prevalence of *E. histolytica* by age and sex in South Africa.

responsible for the world-wide prevalence of *E. histolytica*.

Risk factors for infection

Risk factors for infection and its severity are summarised in Table 22.1. Within developed countries the prevalence of infection is highest in the lower socioeconomic groups, immigrants from developing countries and sexually promiscuous male homosexuals. In tropical and subtropical developing countries, the damp conditions and high humidity favour survival of cysts. These factors coupled with poverty, poor sanitation and hygiene and overcrowded living conditions result in a much higher prevalence of infection reaching 50 per cent in certain areas of India and Mexico. Cultural rejection of latrine use may also contribute in certain circumstances, resulting in soil pollution and contamination of water supplies after heavy rains.

Cysts survive up to 10 minutes on hands and remain viable for up to 45 minutes in moist fecal material under fingernails. Where personal hygiene is not scrupulously observed infectious material may easily be carried from one individual to another. Thus, intrafamilial transmission results in clustering of infection.

Water plays an important role in transmission, both in the quality available and the per capita consumption. Personal hygiene is directly dependent on the amount, rather than the quality, of water available for personal cleanliness, the preparation of food, and cleaning of utensils and cloths.

The use of human waste as an agricultural fertiliser is an important method of parasite transmission and should be discouraged, especially if the agricultural products are eaten raw. Alternatively, application of such fertilisers should be halted a week or two before harvesting so that any viable cysts are killed by desiccation.

Parasite virulence and risk factors for disease

The majority of infected individuals (90–99 per cent) remain asymptomatic even in areas of high endemicity. There is now abundant evidence to support the existence of pathogenic

Table 22.1. Risk factors for infection and increased severity of infection.

For infection:
- lower socioeconomic status
- inadequate sanitation and water supplies
- poor hygiene
- crowding and communal living
- oral/anal sexual practices

For severe disease:
- malnutrition
- corticosteroid use in pregnancy
- young age (less than 12 years)

and non-pathogenic strains of *E. histolytica*. Amebae can be classified into different zymodemes by the use of isoenzyme electrophoresis. Some of the zymodemes are pathogenic while the remainder are non-pathogenic and exist as commensals even in patients with the severe immunosuppression of AIDS.

In endemic areas isolation of pathogenic zymodemes have, without exception, been made from patients with symptomatic amebiasis while asymptomatic cyst passers predominantly harbour non-pathogenic zymodemes. In large population-based surveys in Durban, South Africa (Figure 22.1.), where invasive amebiasis is common, 9 per cent of the periurban population were infected with non-pathogenic zymodemes and 1 per cent had pathogenic infections. In an area of South Africa free of invasive disease all *E. histolytica* isolates were non-pathogenic. The non-pathogenic zymodemes are distributed widely, while pathogenic zymodemes II, XI, and XX occur predominantly in South Africa and Mexico and pathogenic zymodeme XIV almost exclusively on the Indian subcontinent. However, disease patterns attributed to these pathogenic strains are identical.

In a longitudinal study of carriers of pathogenic zymodemes it was found that the majority (90 per cent) remained asymptomatic, eventually spontaneously clearing their infection in 6–12 months. However, all these carriers did develop a strong anti-amebic antibody response.

The events which predispose to deeper tissue invasion by pathogenic strains of *E. histolytica* with concomitant clinical disease have not been fully elucidated, but some associations are listed in Table 22.1. Overcrowding and consequently rapid transmission of the parasite from one human host to another may be a factor resulting in increased virulence of a pathogenic zymodeme. Malnutrition enhances the severity of invasive amebiasis, resulting in increased mortality. Similarly, the role of a high iron intake on disease severity has yet to be studied further. However, invasive amebiasis does tend to be more severe in very young children (especially neonates), in adult women during pregnancy, in immunosuppressed patients and in those with alcoholic liver disease.

PATHOGENESIS AND PATHOLOGY

Adherence of *E. histolytica* to colonic mucins is an important step in the pathogenesis of tissue invasion. Attachment of trophozoites to host cells results in lysis of the target cell, and proteolytic enzymes are released. The trophozoite also has enterotoxigenic activity which may be involved in the diarrheal symptoms associated with intestinal amebiasis.

There is now evidence that once deeper tissue invasion has occurred the amebae invade blood vessels causing a *vasculitis* with subsequent thrombosis and infarction leading to the characteristic sharply demarcated lesions seen in transmural colitis. Neovascularisation and re-epithelialisation leads to subsequent healing which is invariably associated with *stenosis* of the affected colonic segment.

Amebae reach the liver via the portal circulation. It is generally accepted that the liver 'abscess' is an area of liquefactive necrosis caused by a combination of hepatocellular lysis, tissue damage secondary to amebic and neutrophil enzymatic activity, and infarction caused by vasculitis and thrombosis.

HOST IMMUNITY

It is not known to what extent past invasive disease protects against recurrence of symptomatic infection. Studies in Mexico suggest that recurrence of amebic liver abscess is rare implying that there is protective immunity. Recently, it was found that subjects in India with serum anti-amebic antibodies have a lower incidence of intestinal colonisation with *E. histolytica*. In an endemic area in South Africa the prevalence of serum antibodies in subjects infected with non-pathogenic zymodemes is approximately 20 per cent. This is identical to that in subjects free of *E. histolytica* infection and probably indicates past asymptomatic infection with pathogenic zymodemes.

Table 22.2. Clinical syndromes of amebiasis.

Intestinal infection:
    Asymptomatic cyst passer (carrier)

Mucosal disease:
    Acute rectocolitis
    Chronic non-dysenteric colitis

Transmural disease:
    Perforation and peritonitis
    Mass (ameboma)
    Profuse hemorrhage
    Toxic megacolon
    Perianal ulceration

Extraintestinal disease:
    Liver abscess
    Liver abscess complicated by
        peritonitis
        empyema
        pericarditis
    Lung abscess
    Brain abscess
    Genitourinary disease

Serum anti-amebic antibody levels are elevated in both asymptomatic individuals colonised with pathogenic zymodemes and patients with invasive amebiasis. In more than 95% of the patients the antibody response is directed to the adherence protein. The use of this glycoprotein as a candidate vaccine has proved successful in preventing experimental amebic liver abscesses in gerbils.

Cell-mediated immune responses may play a role in protective immunity to recurrent infection. The observation that corticosteroid therapy results in exacerbation of intestinal disease further indicates that host cellular immune mechanisms play a role in limiting disease progression.

CLINICAL MANIFESTATIONS

The clinical syndromes of amebiasis are summarised in Table 22.2.

Intestinal disease

Carriage of non-pathogenic zymodemes is not associated with clinical disease. The occurrence of mild diarrhea in these patients can usually be attributed to other colonic pathogens. *Mucosal disease* usually presents as dysentery (diarrhea with blood and mucous) with a gradual onset over 1–3 weeks. In addition, there may also be abdominal pain and tenesmus; only a third of patients are febrile. A less common presentation is a *chronic non-dysenteric colitis* which manifests as intermittent mucoid diarrhea with abdominal pain, flatulence and weight loss. Amebae can be identified in their stools, they have specific serum antibodies, and respond to antiamebic therapy.

Transmural disease may be due to vasculitis caused by amebic invasion and subsequent colonic infarction. An acute presentation with fulminant bacterial peritonitis secondary to bowel perforation may occur. These patients are usually toxic, febrile and hypotensive with profuse bloody mucoid diarrhea. Other patients develop a slow leak from the site of perforation and the resultant inflamed bowel with omental wraps will lead to the development of an abdominal mass. Toxic megacolon and profuse intestinal hemorrhage can also occur from transmural disease.

Perianal disease may result from direct extension of mucosal disease to the skin or from a fistulous tract. The lesions can be ulcerative or condylomatous resulting in pain and bleeding.

Extraintestinal disease

Liver abscess is the commonest extraintestinal manifestation of amebiasis. Symptoms develop gradually over days to weeks. Pain is the cardinal symptom; it is usually of a pleuritic nature and in the right hypochondrium. Pain referred to the right shoulder tip may occur when the abscess encroaches on the diaphragm. Cough is common as is anorexia, weight loss and pyrexia. Concomitant dysentery may be present in 10 per cent of cases. The patient is usually febrile, jaundice is infrequent, and the liver is almost always palpably enlarged. Where the abscess is situated high up against the diaphragm, there may be no apparent hepatomegaly; chest signs including an impaired percussion note, decreased breath sounds, crackles and a pleural rub may be present. Intercostal tenderness or point tenderness in a palpable liver are useful clinical signs.

Abscesses close to a serosal surface may rupture into the peritoneum resulting in peritonitis or, if the leak is slow, a walled off abscess. Extension into the pleura is usually preceded by a sympathetic effusion. Occasionally extension could occur directly into the lungs resulting in a lung abscess or a bronchohepatic fistula. Pericardial extension usually complicates left lobe abscesses. Secondary bacterial infection of an amebic liver abscess occurs only following percutaneous aspiration of the abscess; this complication requires vigorous treatment with appropriate antibiotics together with drainage.

DIAGNOSIS

The diagnosis of intestinal amebiasis is made by identifying cysts or trophozoites in the stools. The dysentery associated with rectocolitis may be difficult to differentiate from bacillary dysentery. Sigmoidoscopy will show ulcers in 80 per cent of cases. Microscopic examination of a freshly voided stool or rectal scrape will usually reveal hematophagous trophozoites, erythrocytes; scanty leukocytes and Charcot–Leyden crystals are important differentiating features. Wet mount saline preparations on fresh specimens are helpful; however, the smear must be fixed and stained for definitive examination.

Detection of cysts in stools may be problematic. Firstly, many laboratories cannot correctly identify *E. histolytica* cysts: differentiation from macrophages, and other amebic cysts may cause problems. Secondly, cyst passage is usually episodic and up to three consecutive stools have to be examined to correctly identify infected subjects. To increase the yield cysts may first have to be concentrated. A number of techniques are available, formalin–ether sedimentation and zinc sulphate flotation are commonly employed. The preparation can be stained e.g. with iodine. It is important to appreciate that a number of substances can interfere with the stool examination including antibiotics, antiparasitic agents, laxatives, various enemas and antidiarrheal preparations.

At the PHC level of the rural clinic, microscopes may not be available and the technical expertise to correctly identify *E. histolytica* may be non-existent. In such situations a diagnosis of amebic colitis can be made following a successful trial of treatment with antiamebic drugs.

Liver abscess usually needs to be differentiated from other causes of tender hepatomegaly including pyogenic liver abscess, primary or secondary liver neoplasms, subphrenic abscess as well as gallbladder disease, pseudocyst and hydatid cyst. Ultrasound scanning is non-invasive, rules out biliary tract disease and demonstrates a hyperechoic lesion (which is difficult to differentiate from a neoplasm). Following successful treatment, the hepatic defect may persist for a variable period (up to one year) depending on its initial size. Hematological and biochemical tests are nonspecific and usually not helpful. Aspiration of the abscess may be therapeutic as well as aid diagnosis: amebic pus is bacteriologically sterile with scanty neutrophils. *E. histolytica* may occasionally be identified in the necrotic material.

Many serological tests are available to detect anti-amebic antibodies. The antibody response tends to persist for years after symptomatic disease or asymptomatic pathogenic infection. Therefore, in an endemic area, serology is not as useful for diagnosing active disease, as up to 25 per cent of the population may be seropositive. However, a negative test is of value in excluding invasive amebiasis. Serum anti-amebic antibodies are usually not present until the seventh day of symptoms.

TREATMENT

General supportive measures include relief of pain with analgesics, correction of anemia and rehydration. Mucosal intestinal disease responds well to metronidazole or tinidazole. Tinidazole is much better tolerated with less nausea and vomiting. Ingestion of alcohol should be avoided. In addition to metronidazole, use of a luminal amebicide such as diloxanide furoate is essential to eradicate intestinal colonisation. Patients with suspected transmural intestinal amebiasis will require referral to hospital and possible surgery. The use of antibiotics is indicated if there is evidence of septic peritonitis or septicemia.

Liver abscess responds also well to metronidazole or tinidazole. It is prudent to add a luminal amebicide (diloxanide furoate or paromomycin) since intestinal infection has been found to persist in up to a third of patients following cure of invasive disease.

Percutaneous aspiration of liver abscesses is usually not necessary, but it does reduce pain, shortens the duration of symptoms and may have diagnostic value. Although the procedure can be safely performed at the bedside, aseptic aspiration under direct visualisation by ultrasound scan is preferred. Open surgical drainage is rarely indicated, a poor response to therapy for 3–5 days can usually be managed simply by needle aspiration.

Amebic empyema or pericarditis requires immediate percutaneous drainage in addition to amebicidal drug therapy. The response is generally good and healing occurs without scarring.

The treatment of asymptomatic cyst passers remains controversial. In developed countries the majority of cyst passers are infected with non-pathogenic zymodemes and therefore do not require treatment. Infection with a pathogenic zymodeme can be detected by a positive serological test and treatment should be directed against this group of patients. In developing countries where stool microscopy may not be feasible and serological tests too costly, it may be prudent not to treat asymptomatic subjects. A number of luminal agents are available including diloxanide furoate, paromomycin, and di-iodohydroxyquin.

PREVENTION

Amebiasis is a disease of poverty associated with poor socioeconomic conditions, poor personal hygiene and sanitation. Improvement of the living standards of the individuals in developing countries may be the only way of decreasing the prevalence of the disease.

Mass chemotherapy is not feasible because luminal amebicides have to be administered for at least 10–20 days and are not entirely effective. Females are predominant carriers and, being food handlers, are likely to spread the infection. Targeting this group of the population has only been partially successful.

The role of immunity in preventing reinfection remains controversial. The increasing prevalence of asymptomatic intestinal infection with age indicates a lack of protective immunity. On the other hand, the low incidence of recurrence of liver abscess implies the development of protective immunity to invasive disease. A controlled prospective trial to establish the role of protective immunity in persons asymptomatically colonised, or convalescent patients with previous invasive amebiasis is required.

OTHER PROTOZOA

The two other most important causes of protozoal enteropathies are *Cryptosporidium* and *Giardia lamblia*. Much less commonly, other intestinal amebae cause disease in non-immunosuppressed hosts.

Cryptosporidiosis is the most common protozoan etiology of diarrheal disease worldwide, causing especially prolonged disease. Infection is associated with fecal–oral contamination and exposure to farm animals; it is a zoonosis. Severe, prolonged cryptosporidiosis has been associated with AIDS, hypogammaglobulinemia, and corticosteroid use.

The organisms are small (2–6 μm) coccidias with a life cycle that includes sporozoite, trophozoite and merozoite stages. Both trophozoites or merozoites infect mucosal epithelial cells. Oocysts develop in epithelial cells and are released in feces. The pathogenesis of cryptosporidiosis is not well understood, but infection can induce voluminous watery diarrhea. Clinical infection is self-limited in immunocompetent individuals.

Illness due to *Cryptosporidium* is characterised by malaise, abdominal pain, fever, and watery diarrhea without blood or mucus in stools. Diarrhea resolves within 6–14 days. However, in immunosuppressed individuals severe watery diarrhea and weight loss can persist indefinitely. Diagnosis is established by modified acid-fast stain of feces, usually three samples are required. Concentration techniques may be helpful, especially in subacute disease in which fecal shedding can be irregular. Therapy is mainly rehydration, nonspecific antimotility agents such as loperamide are clinically beneficial. There are no drugs documented to be effective *in vivo* against cryptosporidia although studies with spiramycin, a macrolide antibiotic, show limited promise. Prevention rests upon avoidance of fecal contamination.

Giardia lamblia infects 2 per cent of the world's population, both water-borne outbreaks and person to person transmission are important. Animal reservoirs, such as the beaver, may be important in contamination of surface water. Like *E. histolytica*, the cyst (8 to 12 μm) is the infective form, the trophozoites (12 to 15 μm) reside in the small bowel lumen. The malabsorption and diarrhea caused by giardia infection may result in host inflammatory responses, mechanical interference with gut absorption, bacterial overgrowth, parasitic toxins, or deconjugation of bile salts. In the majority of individuals, infection is self-limited.

Over half of giardia infections are asymptomatic; when present, symptoms consist of characteristic bloating, upper abdominal discomfort, flatulence, and watery diarrhea. A small subset go on to manifest chronic disease with malabsorption and weight loss. Diagnosis requires three separate stool microscopy examinations for cysts or trophozoites. If there is prolonged diarrhea and a high suspicion despite negative diagnostic studies, a therapeutic trial is indicated. In adults, metronidazole is the drug of choice, mepracrine or paromomycin are alternatives. Paromomycin is very useful in pregnant women as it is not absorbed. Furazolidone is often preferred for treating children. Prevention rests upon proper sanitation, boiling of water, and avoidance of raw fruits or vegetables.

Dientamoeba fragilis is a flagellate that infects the large bowel, causing non-invasive diarrhea. Symptoms such as intermittent diarrhea, abdominal pain, and anorexia are more likely to be present in children, eosinophilia may be observed. Therapy with di-iodohydroxyquin or metronidazole has been effective. *Balantidium coli* is a ciliate that can result in ulcerative colonic disease. This is a zoonosis, most associated with infection of swine. Diagnosis results from examination of stool or endoscopy with biopsy. Tetracycline, metronidazole or di-iodohydroxyquin are all effective in eradicating the infection.

Isospora belli is a coccidia similar to cryptosporidia and infects the small intestine of man. This infection is more frequent in the tropics and is manifest as watery diarrhea, cramps, and weight loss. No blood or pus is found in stool, the elliptical organisms are identified by acid-fast stain. Infection may persist for months but responds promptly to therapy with oral co-trimoxazole for 7 days.

CONCLUSION

Protozoans are important causes of gastrointestinal disease. Familiarity with the characteristic epidemiology and clinical syndromes provides effective use of the laboratory, when available, to make a diagnosis. These diseases will be with us for some time, as their spread is primarily due to difficult socioeconomic problems and the worldwide movement of people. AIDS has enhanced the awareness of some of these infective agents. However, in their own right, enteric protozoa lead to substantial suffering and, in some cases, mortality. Further understanding of disease pathogenesis and host immunity will hopefully lead to development of efficacious vaccines. However, a public health approach is crucial to the control of protozoan enteropathies by prevention of fecal-oral spread.

Additional reading

1. Ravdin JI, Weikel CS, Guerrant RL. Protozoal enteropathies. Baillieres Clin Trop Med Comm Dis: International Practice and Research 1988;3:503–36.
2. Ravdin JI, Schain DC, Kelsall B. Antigenicity, immunogenicity and vaccine efficacy of the galactose-specific adherence protein of *Entamoeba histolytica*. Vaccine 1993;11:241–6.
3. Aucott J, Ravdin JI. Clinical problems in management of amebiasis. Infect Dis Clin North Am 1993;1:467-86
4. Ravdin JI. Diagnosis and treatment of amebiasis and giardiasis. In: Kass EH, Platt R, eds. Current therapy in infectious diseases. Ontario: Decker Inc., 1989: 366–71.
5. Ravdin JI. Intestinal disease caused by *Entamoeba histolytica*. In: Rawdin JI, ed. Amebiasis: human infection by *Entamoeba histolytica*. New York: John Wiley and Sons, 1988: 495–509.
6. Adams EB, MacLeod IN. Invasive amebiasis. 1. Amebic dysentery and its complications. Medicine (Baltimore) 1977;56:315–23.
7. Katzenstein D, Rickerson V, Braude A. New concepts of amebic liver abscess derived from hepatic imaging, serodiagnosis, and hepatic enzymes in 67 consecutive cases in San Diego. Medicine (Baltimore) 1982;61:237–46.
8. Gathiram V, Jackson TFHG. Frequency distribution of *Entamoeba histolytica* zymodemes in a rural South African population. Lancet 1985;i:719–21.
9. Gathiram V, Jackson TFHG. Pathogenic zymodemes of *Entamoeba histolytica* remain unchanged throughout their life-cycle. Trans R Soc Trop Med Hyg 1990;84:806–7.
10. Irusen EM, Jackson TFHG, Simjee AE. Asymptomatic intestinal colonization by pathogenic *Entamoeba histolytica* in amebic liver abscess: prevalence, response to therapy and pathogenic potential. Clin Infect Dis 1992;14: 889–93.
11. Ravdin JI, Jackson TF, Petri WA, *et al*. Association of serum antibodies to adherence lectin with invasive amebiasis and asymptomatic infection with *Entamoeba histolytica*. J Infect Dis 1991;162:768–72.
12. Yang J, Scholten TH. *Dientamoeba fragilis*: a review with notes on its epidemiology, pathogenicity, mode of transmission, and diagnosis. Am J Trop Med Hyg 1977;26:16–22.

13. Current WL, Reese NC, Ernst JV, *et al.* Human cryptosporidiosis in immunocompetent and immunodeficient persons. N Engl J Med 1983;308:1252–7.

14. Jokipii L, Jokipii AMM. Timing of symptoms and oocyst excretion in human cryptosporidiosis. N Engl J Med 1986;315:1643–7.

15. Nash TE, Harrington DA, Losonsky GA, Levine MM. Experimental human infections with *Giardia lamblia.* J Infect Dis 1987;156:974–84.

16. Soave R, Armstrong D. *Cryptosporidium* and cryptosporidiosis. Review of Infect Dis 1986;8:1012–23.

About the authors

Vinodh Gathiram is a Senior lecturer in Medicine at the University of Natal and Attending Physician at the King Edward VIII Hospital in Durban. He has worked extensively on the epidemiology of Entamoeba histolytica *and has helped define the natural history of asymptomatic pathogenic and non-pathogenic intestinal infection. His interests include gastroenterology, infectious diseases, and recently, clinical studies of AIDS patients in South Africa.*

Jonathan I. Ravdin is Professor and Vice Chairman of Medicine and Professor of International Health at the Case Western Reserve University School of Medicine and is Chief of Medicine at the Cleveland Veteran's Affairs Medical Center. He is one of the leading researchers and authorities on E. histolytica, having contributed over 100 articles, reviews and chapters to the field and edited the definitive text 'Amebiasis, Human Infection by Entamoeba histolytica'. *His research is focused on development of an amebiasis subunit vaccine based upon use of parasite antigens. Dr Ravdin served as the Secretary-Treasurer for the American Society of Tropical Medicine and Hygiene from 1989–1991 and has given numerous invited lectureships on amebiasis in the United States, Europe and Africa.*

Lankinen KS, Bergström S, Mäkelä PH and Peltomaa M, eds.
Health and disease in developing countries. London:The Macmillan Press Limited, 1994:229–237.

23 DENGUE, YELLOW FEVER AND RABIES

Scott B. Halstead, M.D.
Rockefeller Foundation, Health Sciences Division
1133 Avenue of the Americas, New York, N.Y. 10036,
USA

INTRODUCTION

The three diseases in this chapter are linked by their high incidence in developing countries, their relatively high profile as diseases exciting fear and the fact that adequate tools for their control have been developed and have been applied successfully in industrialised countries. Given organisation, commitment and political will their impact on human health could be reduced greatly or eliminated altogether.

DENGUE

Global perspective

Dengue is an acute febrile illness syndrome caused by dengue viruses and also by several other mosquito-borne viruses, such as chikungunya (Africa and South-East Asia), o'nyong nyong (Africa) and West Nile (Africa and India). Although dengue fever caused by dengue viruses produces a memorable illness in adults, the reason to fear dengue is the severe disease it causes in children. Dengue hemorrhagic fever or dengue shock syndrome (DHF/DSS) is an acute capillary permeability syndrome complicated by abnormalities in the blood clotting system, a combination which produces a rapid decrease in blood volume and, in some cases, hemorrhaging. Case fatality rates for DHF/DSS may be as high as 5–10 per cent.

There are four dengue viruses (types 1–4) all in the viral family *Flaviviridae*, of which the type species is the yellow fever virus.[1]

Dengue viruses are transmitted from man to man principally by the domestic day-biting mosquito *Aedes aegypti*. These viruses are also maintained in jungle cycles in African, Indian and South-East Asian monkeys.[2,3] Dengue transmission occurs in virtually every tropical country. It is estimated that between 50 million and 100 million individuals are infected yearly; of these between 200 000 and 500 000 are children in tropical Asia and America hospitalised with DHF/DSS.[4]

Clinical features

Dengue fever gives a biphasic febrile exanthem with classic features observed only in adults.[5] In children clinical manifestations are milder, often resembling an upper respiratory infection with coryza, pharyngeal and conjunctival injection and mild gastrointestinal symptoms. A rash may be evident. In adults, dengue usually begins with a retro-orbital headache, proceeds to fever, myalgia and altered taste sensation. During the height of the 4–7 day illness, there may be severe prostration, multiple gastrointestinal disturbances, inappetence, continuing myalgia and sensations of anxiety and depression.

The appearance of a generalised maculopapular rash which accompanies or follows defervescence heralds the end of the disease. Dengue fever is normally accompanied by the destruction of circulating mature polymorphonuclear leucocytes which, together with a modest reduction in lymphocytes, results in a profound leucopenia. A moderate thrombocytopenia occurs in many instances. There is evidence that dengue induces a hemostatic defect which, in the presence of underlying disease such as peptic ulcer, leads to severe gastrointestinal bleeding.[6] Women who acquire dengue infection during menstrual periods may have severe menorrhagia.[7]

DHF/DSS is seen predominantly in children.[8] Initially, there is a mild febrile illness for 4–7 days. Towards the end of this illness, the child may develop mid-epigastric pain, cool extremities, a flushed face with circumoral pallor and severe weakness. During or following the return of fever to normal, hypotension, bleeding phenomena and, in severe cases, shock may occur. Physiological changes include severe thrombocytopenia, increased vascular permeability, complement consumption, elevation of liver enzymes and metabolic acidosis. Vascular permeability with loss of fluid into tissue spaces is the hallmark of DHF/DSS. This produces an illness remarkably similar to severe diarrhea. Without being able to observe fluid loss from the body, the physician may fail to recognise the signs and symptoms of severe hypovolemia.[8]

Dengue infections may be diagnosed by isolation of virus from blood during the acute phase illness or demonstrating specific IgM antibodies in the blood for up to 2–3 months after infection.[9,10]

Epidemiology

Dengue viruses are transmitted to man and monkeys by mosquitoes of the *Aedes* genus.[11] Taking a blood meal twice at an interval of 8–12 days is an obligatory requirement for the biological transmission of dengue viruses. During this extrinsic incubation period, the virus replicates in the mosquito.

Aedes aegypti is a markedly anthropophilic species and is such an efficient vector that in endemic areas virtually every person is infected. Further, a dengue infection nearly always results in clinical disease in adults.[12] This means that when dengue outbreaks occur in virgin populations, dengue fever may occur in almost 100 per cent of the adult population.

Aedes aegypti feeds preferentially on people, breeds in clean water, and hence is most abundant in and around human habitation. The species breeds in containers used to store water or in artificial containers, for example flower vases, tin cans, rubber tires, bottles, or coconut husks. Dengue transmission is increased at high temperatures and at a high relative humidity, but reduced in cool or dry weather.[13] Thus, in the tropics, epidemics generally coincide with the hot, rainy season, and in temperate countries, dengue dies out during the cold season.

An astonishing fact about dengue viruses, only recognised 30 years ago, is that the first dengue infection has an adverse effect on the outcome of a succeeding infection.[14] Thus DHF/DSS occurs only in children experiencing a second dengue infection or in infants who are borne to dengue-immune mothers.[14–17] Presently recognised epidemiological features of DHF/DSS include the following:

Age restriction. Typical cases of hypovolemic dengue hemorrhagic fever occur at high frequency in children up to age 10 years, decreasing progressively thereafter.[18]

Higher susceptibility of girls. Girls over the age of 4 years have a significantly higher attack rate of DHF/DSS than boys.[19]

Sparing effect of malnutrition. DHF/DSS is not seen in severely malnourished children. The severity of disease is inversely related to a child's nutritional status.[18,20]

Lower susceptibility of blacks. A very large dengue epidemic in Cuba demonstrated that black people were hospitalised for DHF/DSS five times less frequently than whites.[21] The explanation of this phenomenon may be that there exists a human gene regulating the severity of DHF/DSS.

Infection sequence. As suggested by epidemiological studies in tropical Asia, secondary dengue 2 and 3 infections are more severe than secondary dengue 1 or 4 infections.[15,17]

Virus virulence. Secondary infections with South-East Asian dengue viruses cause DHF/DSS while secondary infection with Caribbean dengue viruses do not.[20,22]

Role of antibodies. Severe secondary infections occur in individuals lacking heterotypic neutralising antibodies. The strongest risk factor for DHF/DSS yet discovered is the presence of enhancing antibodies in the absence of crossreactive dengue 2 neutralising antibody in individuals with a secondary infection by dengue 2 after a primary dengue 1, 3 or 4 infection.[23,24]

Socioeconomic factors contributing to transmission

Aedes aegypti owes its present distribution and abundance to human beings. The transport and global distribution of yellow fever,

Table 23.1. Criteria for diagnosing dengue hemorrhagic fever (DHF) or dengue shock syndrome (DSS).

Clinical case definition for dengue hemorrhagic fever

A)   A child presents with history of fever (of 4–5 days duration).

B)   With thrombocytopenia (< 50 000/mm^3).

C)   Hemorrhagic manifestations, as evidenced by at least one of the following:
1) Positive tourniquet test.
2) Bleeding from mucosa, gastrointestinal tract, injection sites, or others.
3) Ecchymoses, petechiae, purpura, and/or
4) Other abnormalities documented by coagulation tests.

D)   Decreased plasma volume due to increased capillary permeability as manifested by at least one of the following:
1) Hematocrit on presentation that is > 20% above average for that age and population.
2) > 20% drop in hematocrit following treatment.
3) Commonly associated signs of increased capillary permeability.
       – pleural effusion
       – ascites
       – enlargement of liver

Clinical case definition for dengue shock syndrome

Elements of each of the above, plus circulatory failure manifested by rapid and weak pulse, narrowing of pulse pressure (20 mmHg or less) or hypotension, with the presence of cold clammy skin and restlessness.

Confirmed cases of DHF or DSS will have the above, plus

1) Virological or serological evidence of acute dengue infection, or
2) recognising that during epidemics it is unlikely that many cases will have laboratory confirmation, or
3) a history of exposure in dengue endemic or epidemic areas.

chikungunga and dengue viruses were enhanced by colonialism and by the slave trade.[25]

Sailing ships carried large amounts of fresh water in casks. All of these provided excellent breeding places for *Aedes aegypti*. Shipboard epidemics were the reason why ships sailing from endemic countries were held in quarantine. In the case of yellow fever, for example, a ship's company was forced to remain at sea until the passage of the extrinsic (mosquito) and intrinsic (human) incubation period without the occurrence of a case.[26]

Late in the British raj, dengue became a disease of socioeconomic and national status – that is, it was almost completely restricted to indigens. The British who lived in cantonment residential areas observed *Aedes aegypti Friday*, a sound hygienic practice in which all water containers were emptied, scrubbed and refilled weekly.[27] This simple, labour-intensive practice essentially eradicated *Aedes aegypti* breeding in British households and prevented dengue transmission.

General sanitary hygiene practices of the 20th century and the specific *anti-Aedes campaigns* of the 1930s, 40s and 50s gradually reduced the prevalence of this species in the Western hemisphere, South Africa and Australia.[28] But, forces were building in Asia for a dengue explosion. In the months after the bombing of Pearl Harbor, large numbers of dengue-susceptible combatants in Japanese, American and Australian troops entered the dengue-endemic Asian tropics. By 1942, epidemics of dengue began to reach out across the Pacific. The cities which emerged from the Second World War were crowded with refugees, filled with ramshackled housing and abundant water storage containers which substituted for piped water. During the post-war era the population began to grow, and a rural to urban migration began. Bangkok grew from 1.5 million in 1960 to 7.5 million in 1990. The large urban slums of Bangkok, Rangoon, Jakarta, Manila and Ho Chi Minh City fuelled a multi-type South-East Asian dengue epidemic and the subsequent global dengue pandemic. Dengue viruses have now spread to every South-East Asian village while viremic individuals transport dengue viruses to India, Africa, the Pacific Islands, the Caribbean and South America.[4,29]

Treatment, prevention and control

Treatment. DHF/DSS is one of the few potentially fatal viral infections for which treatment can be life saving.[8,10] It is crucial to make an early diagnosis which depends upon applying criteria listed in Table 23.1.

Fluid loss and corresponding replacement can be managed by frequent measurement of the hematocrit. This can be done using fingerprick blood collected in capillary tubes. A small hematocrit centrifuge can be placed on the paediatric ward and nurses trained to take blood samples and measure hematocrits. This should be done every 2 hours with pulse, blood pressure and respiratory rate measured every 15–30 minutes.

Very serious problems can result from the overuse of invasive procedures. Unless scrupulous asepsis is maintained and a laboratory is at hand to detect bacteremia, children may contract and die of septic shock – often with gastrointestinal hemorrhage, which simulates dengue shock syndrome. The clue is fever. Dengue shock syndrome occurs as the fever of dengue remits; during the most severe stage of vascular permeability and hemorrhage, the child is afebrile or hypothermic. Return of fever is a danger sign suggesting secondary infection.

Prevention. A tetravalent live-attenuated dengue vaccine is in the late stages of development. Dengue viral transmission can be prevented by measures described below.

Control of *Aedes aegypti*. This species was once eradicated from virtually the whole of South America. Unfortunately, an eradication campaign in the United States was abandoned and replaced by a programme of disease surveillance and containment of introduced virus. With time, after this decision, the species successfully re-established itself throughout Central and South America.[28]

Mosquito control or eradication programmes require the simultaneous use of two approaches: reduction in breeding sites and application of larvicides. Alternatively, a significant reduction in mosquito populations may be effected by the closely spaced application of ultra-low volume adulticide spray.[10]

Source reduction requires the support of the population either by legal sanctions or with voluntary actions (see below: Health education). This includes proper disposal of discarded cans, bottles, tyres, and other potential breeding sites not used for storage of drinking or bathing water.[27,28] Sides of water storage containers should be scrubbed to remove eggs at regular intervals and specifically when the water level is low. Water storage containers for drinking and bathing and flower vases should be emptied completely once weekly. Water containers that cannot be emptied should be treated with temephos 1 per cent sand granules at a dosage of 1 p.p.m. (e.g. 10 grams of sand to 100 litres of water). Treatments should be repeated at intervals of two to three months.[10]

Vehicle-mounted or portable ULV aerosol generators or mist-blowers can be used to apply technical grade malathion of fenitrothion at 438 ml/ha. Three applications made at 1-week intervals can suppress *Aedes aegypti* populations for about 2 months.

Health education. *Aedes aegypti* control has been maintained effectively in some tropical areas through the simple expedient of regular emptying of water containers. During the yellow fever campaigns, strong sanitary laws made the breeding of mosquitoes on premises a crime punishable by fine or jail.[26] In the modern era, Singapore has successfully applied the same measures.[27]

The goals of health education are to make the population aware of the identity of the vector of DHF, to describe its biting habits (daytime feeding) and its breeding habits (containers holding clean water), and to motivate people to reduce breeding sources as discussed above.[28] The use of piped water rather than stored water should be encouraged.

YELLOW FEVER

Global perspective

Yellow fever is an acute infectious disease in which liver damage is accompanied by moderate to severe hemorrhages. Yellow fever is caused by a Flavivirus which is transmitted to man principally by the mosquito *Aedes aegypti*, and maintained in nature by monkey–mosquito cycles in the jungles of South America and Africa. Yellow fever is classified as a viral hemorrhagic fever, along with Lassa fever, the African hemorrhagic fevers, due to

Ebola and Marburg viruses, Argentine and Bolivian hemorrhagic fever (caused by Junin and Machupo viruses), hemorrhagic fever with renal syndrome and dengue hemorrhagic fever.

Along with cholera, plague and typhus, yellow fever is listed among history's most feared pestilences. The global system of quarantine and notification was developed to limit the spread of these diseases.[30] Yellow fever was particularly devastating in colonial America where large epidemics with high attack and case fatality rates devastated major cities such as Havana, Rio de Janeiro and New Orleans. Yellow fever destroyed new settlements in French Guiana, a British army attacking the Dominican Republic (Hispaniola) and the French attempt to build the Panama Canal.[26]

The story of yellow fever is one of success and frustration. In 1919, fearful that the Panama Canal would result in the transport of yellow fever to Asia where *Aedes aegypti* was abundant, the Rockefeller Foundation organised a successful effort which culminated in the eradication of *Aedes aegypti* from 13 Latin American countries and the elimination of urban yellow fever in the Americas.[26] Further, the Foundation developed an excellent vaccine against yellow fever. The eradication or control of *Aedes aegypti* plus use of the yellow fever vaccine has reduced yellow fever in the American tropics to a few hundred cases a year, all acquired from exposure to mosquitoes infected from the jungle cycle.

Unfortunately, the same success story has not been repeated in Africa where yellow fever is transmitted by the periurban *Aedes africanus* and the more urban *Aedes aegypti*. There appear to be extensive connections between humans and a highly complex monkey cycle of transmission. Extensive African outbreaks have occurred from Senegal to Nigeria and Cameroon in West Africa, in the recent past in Ethiopia and Somalia and very recently in the West Nile district of Kenya.

Clinical features

Yellow fever and DHF/DSS are clinically rather similar.[31] The principal differences are a greater degree of liver and kidney involvement in yellow fever. In typical cases of yellow fever, perhaps 10–20 per cent of individuals with clinical disease have jaundice, hemorrhages and protein in the urine (albuminuria). After an incubation period of 3–6 days, onset is abrupt with fever rising to 40°C, severe headache, myalgia, anxiety, anorexia, nausea, vomiting, constipation and minor hemorrhages. After 2 days or more, and following a reduction in fever, severe symptoms return – epigastric pain, prostration, jaundice, decreased urinary volume, albuminuria and gastrointestinal bleeding. Patients usually die on the seventh to tenth day of illness.

Epidemiology

Urban outbreaks have been reported in West Africa since the 18th century. From about the time of the Second World War yellow fever vaccines were manufactured in Lagos, Nigeria and Dakar, Senegal.[26] These were used in immunisation campaigns which largely prevented yellow fever epidemics. But with the coming of independence in the 1960s, African vaccine manufacture, vaccine quality and vaccine coverage declined steeply. Large outbreaks occurred in rural West Africa, such as the one in Senegal in 1965 where high *Aedes aegypti* indices were due to the practice of storing water in containers buried in the ground.[32] In 1987, over 120 000 cases of yellow fever occurred in the cities of western Nigeria.[33] The outbreak was preceded by an epizootic of monkey yellow fever from which the virus might have been introduced into the human population.[34]

Socioeconomic factors contributing to transmission

Much of what is said about the socioeconomic factors contributing to the maintenance and spread of dengue should logically apply to yellow fever because both have exactly the same mosquito vector. Strangely, this is not so. Dengue viruses are now present in countries inhabited by more than 3.5 billion people, are endemic in virtually all tropical cities located between 20°N and 20°S at or near sea level, and particularly in the Asian and American tropics. By contrast, yellow fever in South America is a disease of the forest fringe; of wood cutters, persons who harvest forestry products, miners, campers and hikers.

In Africa, where yellow fever is a major health problem, the disease occurs in the villages, towns and cities of the savannah and tropical rain forests. It seems probable that the virus does not survive indefinitely in the urban *Aedes aegypti*-man cycle, but is fed at intervals into this cycle from monkey epizootics.[34] The reason why yellow fever has never occurred in Asia is not known.[35]

Treatment, prevention and control

Treatment for yellow fever is supportive. The principles described for dengue probably apply to yellow fever.

Prevention. Yellow fever differs from dengue in that a safe and effective vaccine been available since 1937.[26] This vaccine is produced by serial passage in chicken embryos. Supply of vaccine is not restricted by limited production, but the ability to purchase and distribute vaccines.

Accumulating experience suggests that yellow fever vaccine induces circulating antibodies which persist and protect against disease for a life-time. The WHO recommends that yellow fever vaccine be given to children in Africa along with measles vaccine at 9–12 months of age.[36] International regulations require that travellers from or to yellow fever endemic countries be immunised against yellow fever at an interval of not longer than 10 years.

In Latin America, yellow fever vaccine is given on a mass scale to persons living in rural areas who might be in contact with jungle yellow fever. Large supplies of vaccine are held in reserve against the possible introduction of virus into urban areas, an increasingly likely scenario.

Mosquito control. See section on dengue.

RABIES

Global perspective

Rabies, an inevitably fatal viral encephalitis, occurs as the result of the bites from infected animals, often carnivores, but, occasionally bites of cattle and fruit-eating bats. The virus belong to a subgroup of rhabdoviruses called lyssaviruses. Despite minor antigenic differences between strains, the current generation of vaccines are fully effective in treating rabies after animal bites or preventing rabies if given before exposure.[37]

Rabies is a problem in 87 developing countries and territories with a total population of 2.4 billion; each year 35 000 die of this disease.[38] Human beings are at risk to rabies principally in countries on the Indian subcontinent, Africa, South-East Asia and China. The problem, principally, is one of stray dogs. The most significant clinical problem with rabies is the

fear caused by dog bites. It is estimated that 3.5 million persons receive vaccine treatment for dog bites each year. In developing countries this often means the use of potentially dangerous vaccines which have been produced in neurological tissues.

Table 23.2. Steps for treating animal bites.

1) Wash wound well with water and detergent. Debride dead tissue.
2) Inoculate human rabies immune serum (20 IU/kg body weight) into and around the bite and another portion intramuscularly in the deltoid or gluteal areas.
3) Inoculate rabies vaccine intradermally (0.1 ml dose) at the following schedule: days 0, 3, 7, 14, 30 and 90.

Clinical features

For the public health worker *it is more important to recognise rabies in domestic animals than to be able to diagnose human rabies*. While a tragedy to the individual, human rabies is not contagious. Recognition of a rabid animal in association with a bite incident should lead to the prompt institution of treatment and possibly saving a life.[39]

The earliest signs of infection in the animal are restlessness or change in personality.[39] The clinical course progresses rapidly to dumb or furious rabies. In addition to lethargy, paralysis of throat muscles may occur, resulting in drooling due to difficulty in swallowing. Furious rabies is characterised by an unusual state of alertness in which any stimulus may excite an attack. Animals may roam indiscriminately, frequently feeding on stones, twigs or other non-foods. Pets may exhibit affectionate, playful behaviour alternating with vicious biting. Both dumb and furious rabies have a rapid clinical course with death occurring 7–10 days after onset of first signs. Wild animals with rabies may lose their fear of human beings and move about at abnormal times.

After an infectious bite, human rabies occurs at an interval that is directly related to the number of nerve endings at the site of the bite.[40,41] The disease progresses in 2–10 days from a prodrome that may include anxiety and itching, tingling or pain at the site of the bite to either furious or dumb (paralytic) rabies.[40,41] Classically there are severe pharyngeal spasms which are extremely painful and

Table 23.3. Guide to treatment of possible rabies virus exposures.

Bite by	Status of the animal	Actions
dog or cat	healthy, available for 10-day observation	no vaccines given unless signs of rabies appear in the animal
	rabid or suspected	HRIG plus rabies vaccine
	escaped	HRIG plus vaccine in rabies enzootic area
skunk, raccoon, bat, fox, mongoose	rabid unless proved otherwise	HRIG plus vaccine
livestock, rabbits, rodents	observe for rabies; consider circumstances	HRIG plus vaccine after consultation with public health officials

prevent swallowing (hydrophobia). Tragically, mental status remains normal. Death occurs rapidly after onset of coma.

Epidemiology

Dogs and cats are the largest source of exposure in developing countries. The incubation period in dogs is relatively long, 2 weeks to 6 months. In many tropical countries dogs roam freely and assemble into packs in which virus is maintained through biting. Virus appears in saliva at least 2 days before onset of the behavioural signs of rabies. In some areas of Africa, jackals and mongooses are common sources of rabies exposure. In Central and South America, vampire bats are of considerable importance. These bats live in caves, trees, mines and abandoned buildings in colonies of 50 to 1000 or more.

Socioeconomic factors contributing to transmission

Today, developing countries devote more resources to post-exposure treatment than to prevention. In spite of an average of 800 to 900 persons per million inhabitants treated annually for animal bites, vaccination coverage for dogs hardly exceeds 15 per cent, a figure far too low to eliminate disease in dogs.[38] Studies commissioned by the WHO have shown that rabies prevention is essentially a problem of responsible dog ownership.[38]

Why then, are there so few successful dog vaccination programmes? At least in part, this is due to the lack of knowledge of the role of household pets in exposing human beings to rabies. Imported veterinary rabies vaccines are also moderately expensive. Finally, many anti-rabies programmes focus on the elimination of stray dogs. Householders in many Hindu and Buddhist countries are taught to value life and become the protectors of all dogs, whether pets or strays.

Treatment, prevention and control

Treatment. Rabies infection can be aborted by the prompt treatment of animal bites.[42] The attachment of virus to nerve cells is a relatively slow process and can be interrupted by antibody. Once the virus is in nerve cells, it may be destroyed by a specific immune response, presumably cell-mediated immunity. These two mechanisms are the aim of treating the bite of a potentially rabid animal (Tables 23.2 and 23.3).[43]

Potent and safe rabies vaccines based on tissue culture are produced by reputable pharmaceutical manufacturers.[43] These vaccines given with gamma globulin obtained from rabies-vaccinated human blood donors (human rabies immune globulin, HRIG) constitute the optimal treatment for rabies. Anti-rabies serum is also prepared in horses. Horse serum can be purified by removing proteins other than gamma globulin and modifying IgG to the Fab 2 portion. Unmodified horse serum may produce serum sickness.

In many of the larger developing countries in Africa and Asia, rabies vaccines are still made in neural tissues. This product may cause demyelinating encephalitis in one of 1000 vaccinated individuals.[44]

When to vaccinate? The most important decision to make in regard to rabies is when to vaccinate. Table 23.3 tells what to do.

Prevention and control. The control of rabies requires a health education effort aimed at defining human rabies deaths as unacceptable to a modern society. To prevent rabies deaths, dogs and cats must be vaccinated. Usually, this requires a national dog licensing programme. Dogs and cats are given one dose (2 IU) intramuscularly at age 6 months and thereafter at 2-year intervals.

Pre-exposure vaccination. Veterinarians, Peace Corps workers, hikers, field-workers and others who may be exposed to rabid animals should be vaccinated against rabies. For pre-exposure, standard rabies vaccine is given 0.1 ml intradermally or 1.0 ml intramuscularly on days 0, 7 and 28.[43,45]

References

1. Westaway EG, Brinton MA, Gaidamovich SYA, *et al. Flaviviridae*. Intervirology 1985;24:183–92.
2. Roche JC, Cordellier R, Hervey JP, *et al.* Isolement de 96 souches de virus dengue 2. A partier de moustique captures en Cote-D'lvoire et Haute-Volta. Ann. Virology (Inst. Pasteur) 1983;134E:233–44.
3. Rudnick A. Ecology of Dengue virus. Conference on DHF. Oct. 24–28, 1977, Singapore. Asian J Inf Dis 1978;2:156–60.
4. Halstead SB. The 20th century dengue pandemic: need for surveillance and research. World Health Stat Q 1992;45(2–3):292–8.
5. Halstead SB. Arboviruses of the Pacific and Southeast Asia: Dengue and dengue hemorrhagic fever. In: Feigin RD, Cherry JD, eds. Textbook of pediatric infectious diseases. Philadelphia: WB Saunders, 1992;138:1475–83.
6. Tsai CJ, Kuo CH, Chen PC, Chang Chen CS. Upper gastrointestinal bleeding in dengue fever. Am J Gastroenterol 1991;86:33–5.
7. Rice L. Dengue fever. A clinical report of the Galveston epidemic of 1922. Am J Trop Med 1923;40:571–8.
8. Cohen SN, Halstead SB. Shock associated with dengue infection I. The clinical and physiologic manifestations of dengue hemorrhagic fever in Thailand 1964. J Pediatr 1966;68:448–56.
9. Innis BL, Nisalak A, Nimmannitya S, *et al.* An enzyme-linked immunosorbent assay to characterize dengue infections where dengue and Japanese encephalitis co-circulate. Am J Trop Med Hyg 1989;40:418–27.
10. Technical Advisory Committee on Dengue Haemorrhagic Fever for the South-East Asian and Western Pacific Regions. Technical guides for diagnosis, treatment, surveillance, prevention and control of dengue haemorrhagic fever. WHO/SEARO: Manila, 1980.
11. Lumley GF, Taylor FH. Dengue School of Public Health and Tropical Medicine Service Publication Number 3. Glebe: N.S.W. Australasian Medical Publishing Company 1943:74.
12. Halstead SB, Marchette NJ, Diwan AR, Palumbo NE, Putvatana R. Selection of attenuated dengue 4 viruses by serial passage in primary kidney cells. II. Attributes of virus cloned at different dog kidney passage levels. Am J Trop Med Hyg 1984;33:666–71.
13. Derrick DH, Bicks VA. The limiting temperature for the transmission of dengue. Australas Ann Med 1958;7:102.
14. Halstead SB, Nimmannitya S, Yamarat C, *et al.* Hemorrhagic fever in Thailand. Newer knowledge regarding etiology. Jpn J Med Sci Biol 1967;20(Suppl.):96–102.
15. Burke DS, Nisalak A, Johnson DE, *et al.* A prospective study of dengue infectious in Bangkok. Am J Trop Med Hyg 1988;38:172–80.
16. Russell PK, Yuill TM, Nisalak A, *et al.* An insular outbreak of dengue hemorrhagic fever. II. Virologic and serologic studies. Am J Trop Med Hyg 1968;17:600–8.
17. Sangkawibha N, Rojansuphot S, Ahandrik S, *et al.* Risk factors in dengue shock syndrome: a prospective epidemiologic study in Rayong, Thailand. Am J Epidemiol 1984;120:653–69.
18. Kouri GP, Guzman MG, Bravo JR, *et al.* Dengue haemorrhagic fever/dengue shock syndrome: lessons from the Cuban epidemic. Bull WHO 1989;67:375–80.
19. Halstead SB, Eckels KH, Putvatana R, Larsen LK, Marchette NJ. Selection of attenuated dengue 4 viruses by serial passage in primary kidney cells. IV. Preparation and characteristics of a vaccine candidate prepared in fetal rhesus lung cells. Am J Trop Med Hyg 1984;33:679–83.
20. Halstead SB. Immunological parameters of Togavirus disease syndromes. In: Schlesinger RW, ed. The togaviruses, biology, structure, replication. New York: Academic Press, 1980:107–73.
21. Guzman MG, Kouri GP, Bravo J, *et al.* Dengue hemorrhagic fever in Cuba, 1981: a retrospective seroepidemiologic study. Am J Trop Med Hyg 1990;42:179–84.
22. Rico-Hesse R. Molecular evolution and distribution of dengue viruses type 1 and 2 in nature. Virology 1990;174:479–93.

23. Kliks S, Nisalak A, Brandt WE, *et al*. Evidence that maternal dengue antibodies are important in the development of dengue hemorrhagic fever in infants. Am J Trop Med Hyg 1988;38:411–9.

24. Kliks S, Nisalak A, Brandt WE, *et al*. Antibody dependent enhancement of dengue virus growth in human monocytes as a risk factor for dengue hemorrhagic fever. Am J Trop Med Hyg 1989;40:444–51.

25. Mattingly PF. Symposium on the evolution of arbovirus diseases. II. Ecological aspects of the evolution of mosquito-borne virus diseases. Trans Soc Trop Med Hyg 1960;54:97–112.

26. Strode GK. ed. Yellow fever. New York: McGraw-Hill, 1951.

27. Halstead SB. Selective primary health care: strategies for control of disease in the developing world. XI. Dengue. Rev Infect Dis 1984;6:251–264.

28. Gubler DJ. *Aedes aegypti* and *Aedes aegypti*-borne disease control in the 1990s: top down or bottom up. Am J Trop Med Hyg 1989;40:571–8.

29. Halstead SB. Pathogenesis of dengue: challenges to molecular biology. Science 1988;239:476–81.

30. Bres PLJ. A century of progress in combating yellow fever. Bull WHO, 1986;64:775.

31. Francis TI, Moore DL, Edington GM, Smith JA. A clinicopathological study of human yellow fever. Bull WHO, 1972;46:659.

32. Chambon L, Wone I, Bres P, *et al*. Une epidemie de fievre jaune au Senegal en 1965: l'epidemie humaine. Bull WHO, 1967;36:113–50.

33. Nasidi A, Monath TP, DeCock K, *et al*. Urban yellow fever epidemic in western Nigeria, 1987. Trans R Soc Trop Med Hyg 1989;83:401.

34. Germain M, Cornet M, Mouchet J, *et al*. La fievre jaune selvatique en Afrique: donnees recentes et conceptions actuelles. Med Trop 1981;41:31–3.

35. Smith HH, Downs WG. Historical perspectives on yellow fever vector research. Curr Top Vector Res 1983;1:1.

36. Recommendations of the Immunization Practices Advisory Committee (ACIP). 1990-Yellow fever vaccine. Morbid Mortal Wkly Rep 1990;39:RR-6;1–6.

37. Wiktor TJ, Koprowski H. Antigenic variants of rabies virus. J Exp Med 1980;152:99–112.

38. Bogel K, Meslin F-X. Economics of human and canine rabies elimination: guidelines for programme orientation. Bull WHO 1990;68:281–91.

39. Eng TR, Fishbein DB. Epidemiologic factors, clinical findings and vaccination status of rabies in cats and dogs in the United States in 1988. J Am Vet Med Assoc 1990;197:201–9.

40. Hattwick MAW, Gregg MB. The disease in man. In: Baer GM, ed. The natural history of rabies. New York: Academic Press, 1975:281–304.

41. Warrell DA. The clinical picture of rabies in man. Trans R Soc Trop Med Hyg 1976;70:175–8.

42. Kaplan MM, Cohen D, Koprowski H, *et al*. Studies on the local treatment of wounds for the prevention of rabies. Bull WHO 1962;26:765–75.

43. Centers for Disease Control: Recommendation of the Immunization Practices Advisory Committee, Rabies Prevention-United States, Atlanta, GA: CDC, 1990.

44. Applebaum E, Greenberg M, Nelson J. Neurological complications following antirabies vaccine. JAMA 1953;151:188–91.

45. Warrell DA, Warrell MJ. Human rabies and its prevention: an overview. Rev Infect Dis 1988;10:S726–S731.

About the author

Scott Halstead is a specialist in virology and epidemiology and currently Deputy Director, Health Sciences Division at the Rockefeller Foundation in New York. Dr Halstead has directed dengue virus research programmes in Tokyo, Washington, Bangkok and at Yale University. His special interest is the pathogenesis of dengue hemorrhagic fever. During 1968–83 he was Professor and Chairman, Department of Tropical Medicine and Medical Microbiology, University of Hawaii School of Medicine. Since 1967 he has served as a consultant to the WHO in most Asian countries on the treatment and control of dengue hemorrhagic fever. At the Rockefeller Foundation he directs numerous programmes designed to strengthen global vaccine delivery, medical education, public health practice and data-based decision making.

Lankinen KS, Bergström S, Mäkelä PH and Peltomaa M, eds.
Health and disease in developing countries. London:The Macmillan Press Limited, 1994:239–246.

24 VIRAL HEPATITIS

Andrew J. Hall, M.B.B.S., M.Sc., Ph.D., M.R.C.P., M.F.P.H.M.
London School of Hygiene and Tropical Medicine,
Communicable Disease Epidemiology Unit
Keppel Street, London, WC1E 7HT,
United Kingdom

INTRODUCTION

Hepatitis means, literally, inflammation of the liver. This can have a multiplicity of causes but the most frequent, and the basis of this chapter, is the hepatitis due to viruses. Many viruses can cause hepatitis but there are six which have it as their predominant manifestation. They are known as the hepatitis viruses A, B, C, D, E and the yellow fever virus (Chapter 23). The acute manifestations of these viruses are remarkably similar but they differ in terms of viral structure, modes of transmission, epidemiology and most important their propensity to lead to chronic hepatitis and liver cancer.

CLINICAL MANIFESTATIONS

The common feature of all of these viruses is that they produce a syndrome of acute clinical hepatitis (Table 24.1). All infected individuals will not develop acute hepatitis, and their proportion varies from virus to virus and with the age of the person infected. However, the virus causing acute clinical hepatitis can not be determined on the basis of symptoms or physical examination, but requires specific serological tests.

Three of these viruses, B, C and D, will persist in a proportion of infected individuals and lead to chronic infection and damage to the liver. The severity of this varies from individual to individual and is partly determined by the virus and other co-factors such as alcohol consumption. Finally two of the viruses (B and C) may lead to primary liver cancer. There is no specific treatment for acute viral hepatitis.

THE VIRUSES

The common feature of the six viruses is that they infect the liver cell (hepatocyte). In other

Table 24.1. Clinical manifestations of viral hepatitis.

Clinical syndrome	Viruses	Clinical features
Acute hepatitis	A, B, C, D, E, yellow fever	Fever, jaundice lethargy
Chronic hepatitis, cirrhosis	B, C, D	Lethargy, enlarged liver, intermittent jaundice, ascites
Primary liver cancer	B, C	Weight loss, enlarged liver, hepatic pain

Table 24.2. Characteristics of the hepatitis viruses.

Hepatitis	Agent	Incubation period	Special features
A	Picornavirus	14–45 days	No carrier state
B	Hepadnavirus	6 weeks to 6 months	Carrier state, cancer and cirrhosis
C	RNA virus	2–26 weeks and cirrhosis	Carrier state, cancer
D	Similar to satellite plant viruses	2–10 weeks	Carrier state, needs HBV
E	RNA virus	Mode 38 days	Kills pregnant women
Yellow fewer	Flavivirus	3–6 days	Mosquito vector

respects they are completely different, classified into different families of viruses (Table 24.2). Hepatitis B is a DNA virus whereas all of the others are RNA viruses. After serological tests for hepatitis B were developed, the precise epidemiology of this virus could be described in the early 1970s. Subsequently, tests for hepatitis A virus made the epidemiological studies of this agent possible and the presence of viruses that were neither A nor B was confirmed. Since 1989, specific tests for hepatitis C (transfusion hepatitis) and for hepatitis E have become available illuminating the global epidemiology of these infections. The current serological markers for hepatitis viruses are summarised in Table 24.3.

Yellow fever has been recognised as a distinct entity for some decades because of its epidemic propensity, limited geographical distribution and association with a mosquito vector. It is likely that there are at least one, and possibly more, other hepatitis viruses yet to be discovered but they are likely to be uncommon and not of major public health concern.

The significance of each virus is determined by two factors, the mode of transmission and the persistence of the infection. In public health terms the viruses can be regarded as falling into three groups: 1) the agents transmitted by the fecal–oral route, which cause acute hepatitis and no persistent infection (hepatitis A and E); 2) the sexually and parenterally transmitted viruses, which lead to persistence and chronic liver disease (hepatitis B, C and D); and 3) yellow fever, which is

mosquito borne, does not cause persistent infection but has a high case fatality rate in epidemics.

FECAL–ORAL TRANSMISSION

Epidemiology

Hepatitis A is spread in much the same way as the common diarrheal diseases through food and water contaminated by human feces or from hand to mouth in societies with poor sanitation and hygiene. This makes it a frequent infection of children in most developing countries. In Africa and most of Asia all children are infected by the age of 10 years as determined by serological surveys. The importance of this age distribution of infection lies in its relationship to clinical disease (Figure 24.1). Infection in those less than 10 years of age rarely leads to clinical hepatitis. Most children have no illness or only a minor illness which is not recognisable as hepatitis. Mortality is extremely rare, perhaps one in every 1000 with clinical hepatitis.

In contrast, infection at an older age, in adolescence or adult life, leads to jaundice, fever and marked lethargy – all the manifestations of acute hepatitis. The severity, and associated mortality, increases with age so that in the middle-aged or old person this is often a serious disease. Since in most developing countries the whole population has been infected, and is therefore life-long immune by the age of 10 years this infection presents no public health problem.

Table 24.3. Serological tests for viral hepatitis.

Virus	Serological Marker	Meaning
Hepatitis A (Hepatovirus)	IgM antibody IgG antibody	Recent infection Immunity
Hepatitis B	Surface antigen Surface antibody IgM core antibody IgG core antibody e antigen e antibody	Current infection Immunity Recent infection Past infection Infected and infectious Infected and non-infectious
Hepatitis C	Various antibody assays Tests for virus	Immunity or infection Infection
Hepatitis D	Antigen IgM antibody IgG antibody	Active infection Recent infection Past infection but does not persist
Hepatitis E	Antibody	Past infection? how long?
Yellow fever	Antibody	Past infection - difficult to interpret because of other similar viruses

However, one of the ironies of improving sanitation and hygiene is that the age at which infection with hepatitis A occurs moves into older age groups in which clinical disease becomes a problem. This phenomenon is now being seen in some wealthier urban populations and in countries such as Singapore, Hong Kong and Korea which are in the transition from developing to developed. The effects of this transition were highlighted by a massive epidemic of hepatitis A in Shanghai in 1988 that affected more than 200 000 people. This epidemic was traced to clams.

Thus, hepatitis A is a public health problem in these countries and it is likely to be an increasing problem in other countries also as development progresses. It also makes it a significant risk for those from developed countries who choose to travel or live in developing countries. These individuals are not likely to have met the virus before and are thus non-immune adults, susceptible to acute hepatitis when infected.

Hepatitis E appears to be transmitted by similar routes to hepatitis A. Until very recently it has only been recognised by its epidemic behaviour since serology was not available. These epidemics have occurred after fecal contamination of the water supply. Thus a major epidemic affecting more than 50 000 people occurred in Delhi in 1955 when the city's water supply was contaminated by sewage. Outbreaks are frequent in refugee camps where the water supply is precarious.

The particular feature of this virus is that it particularly affects pregnant women. They suffer acute severe clinical hepatitis which frequently leads to the loss of the fetus and may also kill the mother. In some epidemics the case fatality rate in pregnant women has been as high as 25 per cent. This feature of the virus, and the fact that adult epidemics occur in developing countries with poor sanitation is surprising. If the virus was similar to hepatitis A in its transmission then one would predict that the majority of infections would occur in childhood with ensuing immunity.

It is possible that the efficiency of transmission of the virus is much poorer than that of hepatitis A, requiring heavy fecal contamination to lead to infection, or that the immunity induced is not long lasting. The high attack rate in pregnancy when immunity is suppressed, suggests the latter mechanism. This virus is an important cause of epidemics in South Asia, South-East Asia and the Middle East. It is a particular threat to refugees living in camps without a secure supply of potable water.

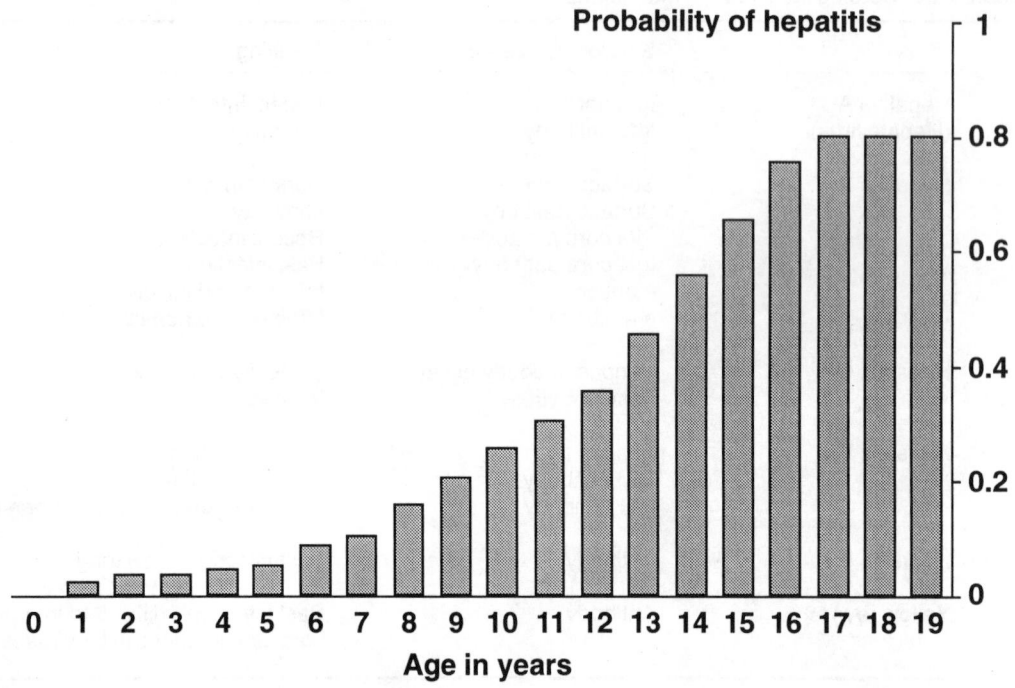

Figure 24.1. Hepatitis A: probability of disease if infected.

Control

A clean water supply, uncontaminated food and personal hygiene are the primary methods of preventing these infections. Ironically the period when these are being established makes the population less susceptible to infection but increasingly likely to suffer disease.

Specific preventive measures are available for hepatitis A. Injection of hyperimmune globulin which contains antibody to the virus can protect the individual for up to 4 months. While this is helpful to the traveller and temporary resident in an area of high risk, it is not useful for indigenous populations. This globulin does not appear to be effective against hepatitis E nor does it interrupt epidemics of hepatitis A, although it may be used to protect household contacts of index cases.

Quite recently, in 1993, an inactivated hepatitis A vaccine has been launched in a number of countries. This vaccine has minimal side effects, is highly immunogenic and has a protective efficacy of over 90 per cent against clinical disease both in the endemic and epidemic setting. It is likely that protection will persist for at least 10 years. These features have led to its widespread use among travellers to endemic areas. The WHO has suggested its use in those areas of the developing world that are in transition from a developing to a developed situation in terms of sanitation. Furthermore, the WHO proposes that the vaccine is introduced as part of the routine childhood immunisation programme.

The vaccine is, however, quite expensive. So far only China has accepted the WHO proposal but bases its programme on locally produced live attenuated hepatitis A vaccine. No doubt as the price and availability of the inactivated vaccine become more favourable other countries will add hepatitis A vaccine to the Expanded Programme on Immunization. However in the next decade this is unlikely to include the majority of developing countries for which hepatitis A is not a significant problem and who have much higher priorities of vaccine-preventable diseases.

SEXUAL AND PARENTERAL TRANSMISSION

Epidemiology

Hepatitis B is not only the first of these viruses to be isolated but also the most important in public health terms. This is because of the serious consequences associated with long-term persistent infection with the virus. Infection with the virus occurs at three ages.

Women who are themselves persistently infected, so-called carriers, and who are infectious (serologically positive for the hepatitis B surface antigen s and hepatitis B e antigen) transmit the infection to around 90 per cent of their children at the time of birth. Carrier women make up some 10–20 per cent of the population in the highly endemic areas of the world such as China and Sub-Saharan Africa. However, the proportion of infectious women is much higher in China at 50 per cent than in Africa or other parts of the world where it is 10 per cent or less.

The second age of infection is in childhood. This is particularly between the ages of 2 and 5 years with a second wave of infection in some societies at school entry. The risk factors at this age are predominantly contacts with other children who are infectious, whether from acute infection or because they are persistently infected. These other children are frequently siblings of the child and the infection shows marked household clustering. The precise mode of transmission at this age is unknown but saliva or open skin sores seem the most likely routes.

Finally, in adult life sexual transmission becomes predominant, with both heterosexual and homosexual intercourse transmitting the infection. Again, this is usually from an infectious carrier of the virus. Formerly blood transfusion was a significant contributor to transmission, but the introduction of blood donor screening has greatly reduced this risk in virtually all countries of the world.

The major importance of the age at infection lies in two factors. First, as with hepatitis A, infection in the first decade of life rarely leads to clinical disease and morbidity increases in severity with increasing age. But secondly, and crucially, the age at infection determines the probability that a person will be persistently infected (Figure 24.2) . This is highest for those infected around the time of birth (approximately 80 per cent of those infected become carriers), falls to a level of 20–40 per cent for those infected between 2 and 5 years of age while those infected older than this have only a 7 per cent chance of becoming carriers. Since this persistent infection with its role in chronic liver disease is the major impact of hepatitis B virus on public health the

pattern of age at infection in a country determines the priority for control.

In general, countries are classified by the proportion of the adult population who are carriers of the virus. In most West European countries, Australasia, North America and the majority of Latin America hepatitis B infection is quite rare, with a carrier rate of less than 1 per cent, and the predominant mode of transmission is sexual and parenteral in adult life. The Amazon basin is an exception to this with intermediate to high rates of carriage (greater than 5 per cent). Here child to child transmission plays an important role. Countries of Southern Europe and those African countries with Mediterranean coasts have intermediate levels of endemicity with carriage rates of 2–7 per cent. Eastern Europe and South Asia share this intermediate level of infection with a mixture of child and adult infection.

Perinatal and child infections predominate in the highly endemic areas of the world with carriage rates in excess of 7 per cent. In South-East China and Sub-Saharan Africa these rates are frequently as high as 15 per cent. In some of the islands of the South Pacific carriage rates as high as 50 per cent are found. Sexual spread is less important in these communities as a large proportion of the population is infected before the age of sexual activity commences. In these communities chronic hepatitis, cirrhosis and primary liver cancer become major causes of morbidity and mortality in adult life.

The interval between the establishment of persistent infection and the development of the complications is in the range of 10–30 years. Thus, childhood infection often first becomes manifest as liver cancer at the age of 30 or 40 years. In parts of China and Sahelian Africa hepatitis B related liver cancer alone causes more than 10 per cent of adult deaths. The middle-aged deaths in particular have a profound effect on economic productivity of the communities and on the dependents of these adults.

Hepatitis D or delta hepatitis was first recognised in 1977. The D virus is peculiar in that it requires the presence of the hepatitis B virus for its transmission. This is because the surface antigen of hepatitis B virus, a protein produced in great excess by liver cells infected with hepatitis B, forms the coat of hepatitis D. This gives rise to two forms of natural infection with hepatitis D: 1) co-infection in which there is simultaneous primary infection with

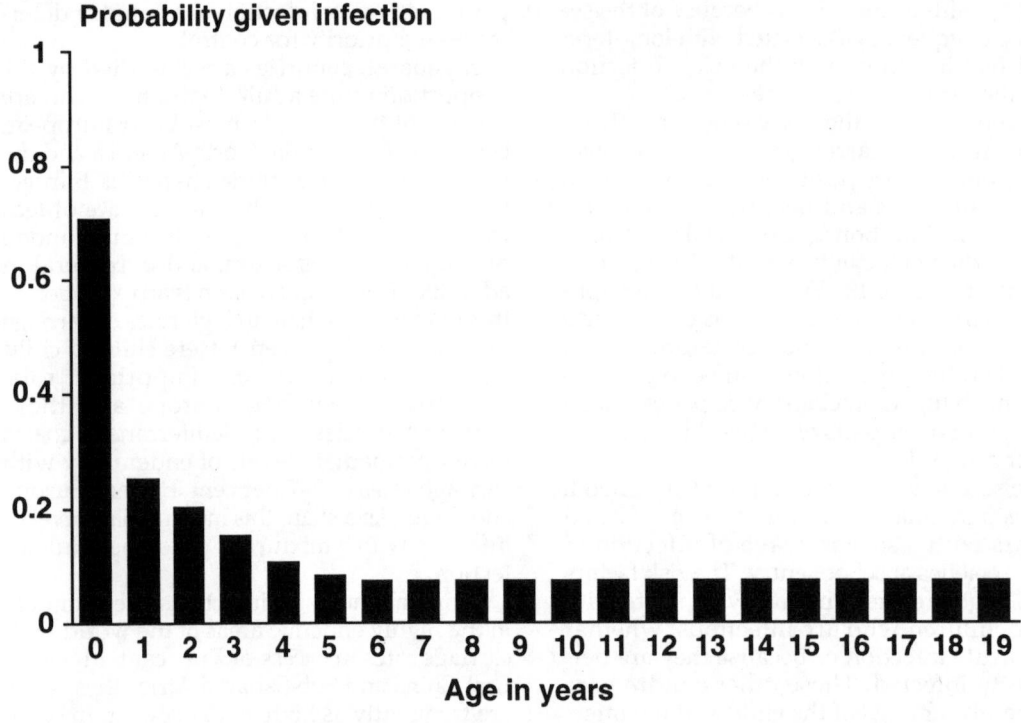

Figure 24.2. Hepatitis B: probability of persistence if infected.

both hepatitis B and D viruses; and 2) super-infection where a person who is already persistently infected with hepatitis B, a carrier, is additionally infected with hepatitis D. This close relationship between these two viruses means that they are likely to share the same routes of transmission.

In developed countries this infection is particularly a problem for intravenous drug users but relatively uncommon in other groups, even highly promiscuous gay men, despite their high rate of hepatitis B infection. In developing countries the picture is also surprising. Hepatitis D infection seems to be highly focal affecting some countries but not their neighbours, affecting one tribe but not adjacent ones and showing marked variation from one village to another.

The Amazon basin is the area in which it represents the largest public health problem. Here it is a frequent infection affecting children and adults, both as a co-infection and as superinfection. Some tribal groups have suffered epidemics of the infection leading to outbreaks of jaundice and high mortality from both acute severe hepatitis and chronic liver disease. *Labrea hepatitis*, an alternative name for acute hepatitis D, comes from a town in Colombia which suffered such an epidemic.

Acute co-infection has a high rate of severe acute hepatitis with an appreciable mortality. In superinfection the severity of the acute infection is less but it leads on to a rapid development of chronic hepatitis and cirrhosis, with the accompanying mortality. It does not appear that hepatitis D infection is related to liver cancer.

Hepatitis C virus was first recognised as the cause of acute hepatitis following blood transfusion that was not due to the A or B viruses. The development of tests for A and B made it clear that there was at least one other virus transmitted by blood transfusion although it has been only in the last 5 years that molecular biology has provided the tools which have allowed tests for this virus to be developed.

Hepatitis C is considerably less transmissible than B. This is thought to be because the amount of virus in the blood of those who are persistently infected is very small. There is, however, a large amount of circulating virus around the time of the acute hepatitis. Transmission is relatively unusual by the sexual route or from mother to child. The infection occurs in both developed and developing countries primarily in adult life.

Surveys around the world suggest that between 0.3 and 2 per cent of most populations are persistently infected with the virus, but there are a few reports of higher prevalence (5–10 per cent in Egypt, Cameroon and Gabon).

There is mounting evidence that persistent infection with this virus is also a cause of liver cancer. Since the infection occurs later in life than hepatitis B it appears that the cancer also occurs predominantly in an older age group. The mechanism for this is unclear but cirrhosis is probably an important intermediate step to liver cancer.

Control

The multiple routes of infection for these agents in developing countries, particularly hepatitis B, has made any uniform control strategy difficult. That is until the price of *hepatitis B vaccine* began to approach the level at which poor countries could afford it. *Screening of blood donors* has been a major means of control in developed countries and has significantly reduced the risk of hepatitis B and more recently hepatitis C. Screening for B has the added advantage of virtually eliminating hepatitis D infection. More recently the *behavioural changes* associated with public knowledge of the human immunodeficiency virus have affected sexual transmission of the hepatitis viruses.

In developing countries the introduction of screening for hepatitis B has been more recent. It has been greatly facilitated by the provision of equipment and training for HIV screening at blood transfusion centres and hospitals. In some areas where hepatitis B is a universal infection at a young age the need for screening has been questioned (Chapter 52). Screening of blood for transfusion for hepatitis C is currently expensive and until the public health implications of the infection in developing countries become clearer it is likely to remain of low priority.

The major means of control for hepatitis B infection and the sequelae of chronic infection are the use of hepatitis B immune globulin (HBIG) and hepatitis B vaccine. HBIG is derived from the blood of persons immune to the virus. It is purified and treated to ensure that there is no risk of transmission of other viruses. The original vaccine was also derived from blood or plasma of those persistently infected with the virus. The vaccine consisted of the excess surface antigen produced by the liver of these individuals. It was also purified and treated to make it safe. There is clear evidence that neither of these preparations transmit HIV.

Subsequently, genetic engineering has been used to produce the hepatitis B surface antigen in yeast cells. These engineered hepatitis B vaccines are somewhat less immunogenic than the plasma-derived vaccines but effective in preventing infection.

The globulin provides protection against infection when it is administered soon after exposure. For developing countries this primarily means after birth for children born to infectious mothers. The vaccine is also highly effective in these situations, providing 70–90 per cent protection against infection and carriage of the virus. A combination of both HBIG and vaccine is highly protective in the range of 90–95 per cent. Protection from the globulin only lasts some 4 months, which is as long as the injected antibodies last in the recipient. In contrast, the vaccine-induced immunity lasts at least 10 years.

While screening of mothers for infectivity is widely practised in developed countries this is not usually considered a cost-effective option in developing countries. The use of HBIG is also not necessary outside Chinese societies since the infectivity of mothers in other populations is considerably less. Thus for most of the world three doses of hepatitis B vaccine in the first 6 months of life provide the best defence against hepatitis B. Protection, as measured by antibodies, declines after vaccination. This has led to suggestions that booster doses of vaccine may be necessary. All of the evidence published to date shows that although antibodies decline, and infection may occur as shown by serological status, protection against acute hepatitis, and most important of all persistent infection, remains solid. Thus the current recommendation for developing countries is that booster doses are not necessary. This is under constant review as the duration of follow-up of vaccinated children increases.

Some 33 developing countries had implemented hepatitis B immunisation of infants by 1993. The major hindrance to wider use is the relatively high market price of the vaccine, between 50 and 100 US cents. It is hoped that this situation will change in the next decade. Interestingly in the last 2 years the USA, Italy and Bulgaria have also introduced universal infant vaccination because they judge it the most cost-effective approach to hepatitis B control.

The only cause for concern in this otherwise clear-cut story is that in a few vaccinated children some viruses have been found that appear able to avoid the vaccine-induced protection. These viruses have a different amino acid sequence in their surface antigen to that used in the vaccine. While this is a cause of interest and investigation, if it proves to be of public health significance, a simple change in the formulation of the vaccine should be sufficient to control it.

This strategy of control of hepatitis B infection serves the additional purpose of controlling hepatitis D. Since this cannot exist without the hepatitis B virus protection against the latter effectively protects against the former. Brazil has introduced universal hepatitis B vaccination of infants in the Amazon region and this is expected to virtually eliminate the public health impact of hepatitis D for this generation.

HBIG and vaccine do not help the approximately 250 million people in the world already persistently infected with hepatitis B. There is no treatment currently available at a population level to eliminate the virus from them. They are at high risk of hepatitis D infection as well as chronic hepatitis, cirrhosis and liver cancer. Screening programmes for liver cancer in this group have been suggested to allow early detection and treatment. However, this is expensive and the detection and treatment facilities are scarce in developing countries.

Control of hepatitis C, apart from blood transfusion screening, is problematic. The epidemiology of the infection is ill-understood and it is unlikely that there will be any specific control programmes. Vaccines are under development but are likely to prove difficult to make given the variation in strains of virus around the world.

CONCLUSION

Hepatitis viruses represent a fascinating range of infectious agents. The importance of each varies around the world, but persistent hepatitis B virus infection represents a major public health problem for the majority of developing countries. It can be readily controlled through infant immunisation. This makes liver cancer the first cancer to be controlled by vaccination and hepatitis B the next major cause of adult mortality after smallpox which can be removed by vaccination. The means is there, what is required is the funding and the political will.

Additional reading

1. Hadler SC, Margolis HS. Viral hepatitis. In: Evans AS, ed. Viral infections of humans. Epidemiology and control. New York: Plenum Medical, 1989.
2. Hall AJ. Hepatitis in travellers: epidemiology and prevention. Br Med Bull 1993;49:382–93.
3. Szmuness W. Hepatocellular carcinoma and hepatitis B virus. Evidence for a causal association. Prog Med Virol 1978;24:40–69
4. Beasley RP, Hwang LY, Lin CC, Chien CS. Hepatocellular carcinoma and hepatitis B virus. Lancet 1981;ii:1129–1132

About the author

Andrew Hall is an epidemiologist at the London School of Hygiene and Tropical Medicine. He originally trained in infectious disease and internal medicine. After spending two years as a Provincial Medical Officer in Papua New Guinea he trained in epidemiology. Between 1986–1990 he was Principal Investigator of a large scale intervention study against liver cancer in The Gambia, West Africa, employed by the International Agency for Research on Cancer (WHO). His current interests are in the epidemiology and control of hepatitis and poliomyelitis, epidemiological methods and vaccine trials.

Lankinen KS, Bergström S, Mäkelä PH and Peltomaa M, eds.
Health and disease in developing countries. London:The Macmillan Press Limited, 1994:247–253.

25 POLIOMYELITIS

U. Tapani Hovi, M.D., Ph.D.
National Public Health Institute,
Department of Viral Diseases
Mannerheimintie 166, FIN-00300 Helsinki,
Finland

T. Jacob John, Ph.D., FRCP(E)
Christian Medical College and Hospital,
Department of Microbiology
Vellore, Tamil Nadu 632 004,
India

INTRODUCTION

Poliomyelitis is an illness characterised by an acute onset of flaccid paralysis of muscles, due to neuronal destruction or damage, caused by any of the three serotypes of poliovirus. Groups of muscles of the lower limbs are most commonly affected; however, upper limbs, trunk muscles, the diaphragm, and muscles innervated by cranial nerves may also be affected. In the acute phase of the disease the case fatality rate is 5–10 per cent, mostly due to paralysis of respiratory muscles. Partial or near complete recovery from paralysis occurs over several weeks or months in about a quarter of the patients. The majority will have residual paralysis of some of the affected muscles for the rest of their life. By common usage the term poliomyelitis is also used to denote this chronic *post-poliomyelitis paralysis*.

EPIDEMIOLOGY

Poliovirus types 1, 2 and 3 belong to the *Enterovirus* genus of the family *Picornaviridae*. Other enteroviruses are coxsackieviruses and echoviruses. Other picornaviruses include rhinoviruses, hepatitis A virus (presently called *Hepatovirus*) and the foot-and-mouth disease virus of cattle. Man is the only natural host of polioviruses.

Polioviruses, like other enteroviruses, infect primarily the gastrointestinal tract. The oro-pharynx and the lower small intestine are the predominant regions infected. Poliomyelitis occurs in only about 0.1–1 per cent of infected persons. Thus, the infected individual usually remains symptom-free, but sheds large quantities of virus in the feces for several days and lesser quantities for several weeks. Intermittent or low level virus shedding may continue for months, especially in children infected for the first time. Poliovirus can withstand a range of pH and temperatures and survive for long periods outside the human body. These features contribute to its spread via the fecal–oral route.

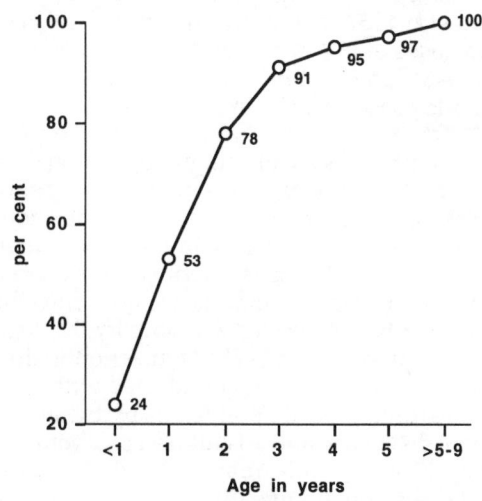

Figure 25.1. Acute poliomyelitis cases in rural South India in 1988–90. The age distribution of children with poliomyelitis as cumulative percentage. Note that 50 per cent of cases were below 2 years and 75 per cent of cases below 3 years.

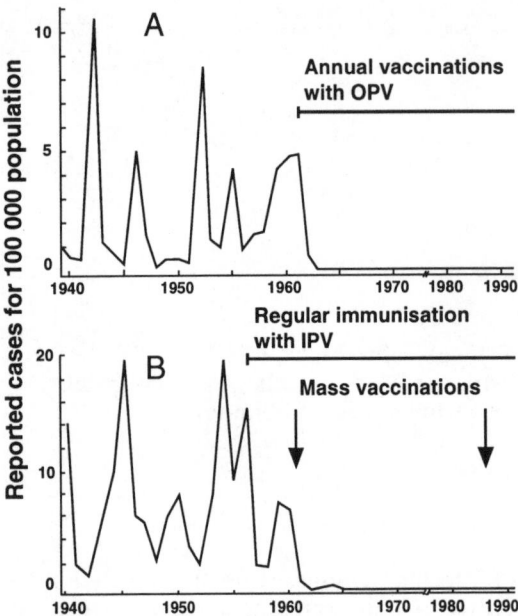

Figure 25.2. Effect of immunisations on incidence of poliomyelitis in (A) Cuba and (B) Finland. A programme of two annual vaccination days with a 6-week interval was started in Cuba in 1962. On a vaccination day, a dose of trivalent OPV is offered to every child younger than 3 years. Children up to 14 years were included in the target group in the first years of the programme. In Finland, a more classical strategy was used. Regular immunisation of infants and children with 5–6 doses of IPV was started in 1957. In addition, an early campaign of two doses of IPV was given to all age groups in 1960–61, and another with one dose of OPV in 1985 to cease an outbreak (arrows).[2]

In communities with a high population density, high birth-rate and poor hygiene, poliovirus transmission may be intensive, infections occurring very frequently in the very young. Circulation of the virus is more or less continuous as susceptible infants are born into the community, get infected and amplify the virus in the environment.[1] Where infection is thus *endemic*, most children get infected with each of the three types of poliovirus by the age of about 2–3 years, and all children by about 5–6 years. Consequently, practically all of the clinical cases of poliomyelitis also occur in infancy and early preschool period (Figure 25.1). Hence the name infantile paralysis.

Improvement of hygiene results in decreasing contamination of the environment with feces and fecal viruses; hence poliovirus circu-

lation becomes slow, or intermittent. As susceptible children, adolescents and adults accumulate, re-introduction of poliovirus may result in an *epidemic* of infection, and the consequent epidemic of poliomyelitis across a wide range of age. Under these circumstances the exact mode of virus transmission is not clearly understood; it appears to be due to person-to-person contact, probably via contaminated fingers and hands or on account of oropharyngeal shedding of virus. Many industrialised nations had experienced the transition from the endemic phase to a period of several years or a few decades during which periodic epidemics occurred, until immunisation became available in the mid 1950s and early 1960s (Figure 25.2).

Poliomyelitis is no longer a public health problem in most if not all industrialised countries on account of improvements in hygiene and effective immunisation. Many developing countries also have been able to control or even eliminate poliomyelitis using effective strategies of immunisation.[2] However, it continues to be an important public health problem in many countries in Asia and Africa (Figure 25.3), either due to insufficient immunisation coverage of infants and young preschool children or in some instances even in spite of high levels of coverage.

This paradox may be explained by the combination of two factors: the less than satisfactory vaccine efficacy and the intensity of virus transmission among the very young. In such regions more intensive immunisation will have to be applied, as will be described later.

NATURAL COURSE OF INFECTION AND PATHOGENESIS

Poliovirus enters the body through the mouth. Initial infection and replication take place in the lymphoid tissues under pharyngeal and ileal mucosa. Virus then reaches the blood circulation and can spread to secondary replication sites, including the central nervous system (CNS). While it is generally assumed that viremia is a common phase in the natural course of poliovirus infection, symptomatic CNS infection is a rare occurrence with less than 1 per cent of all infected persons showing paralytic symptoms. The typical course of events is shown in Figure 25.4. The incubation period from the time of infection to paralysis ranges from 1 to 4 weeks.

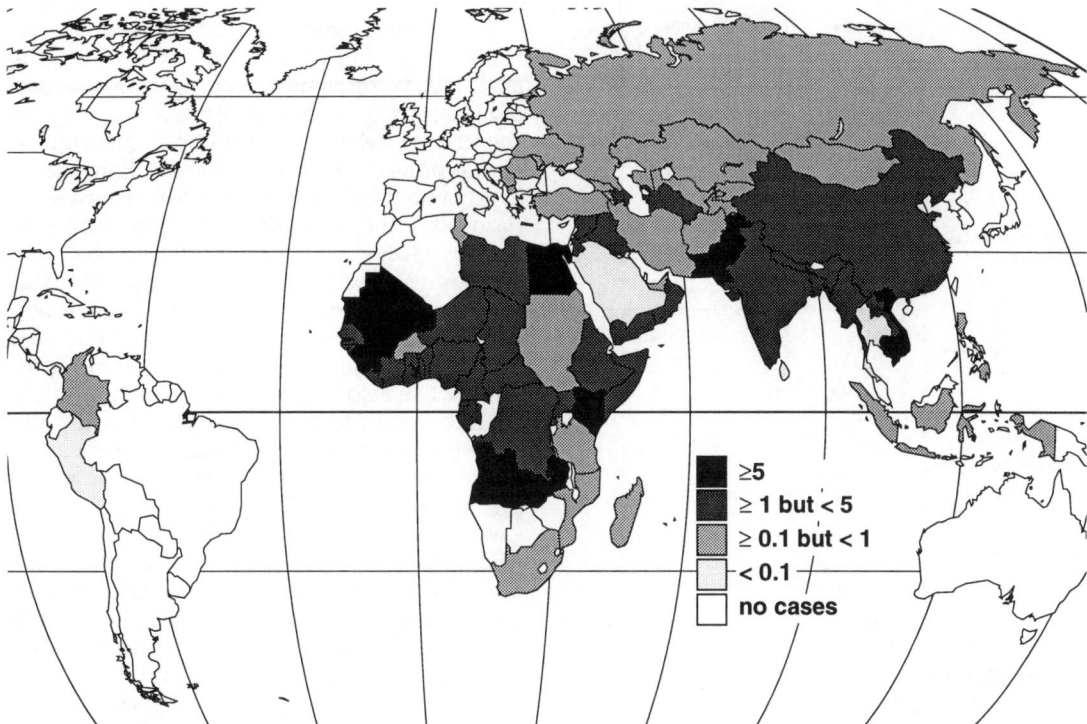

Figure 25.3. Persisting endemic poliomyelitis. Based on cases of acute poliomyelitis reported to WHO for 1991 and 1992 as by 1 January 1993, with vaccine-associated cases excluded. The approximate incidences (cases per million) are calculated without any correction in spite of the general assumption that true values are about tenfold the reported ones in many developing countries. Likewise, putative differences between districts within a given country are ignored.

An unresolved question in the pathogenesis is whether the virus enters CNS through viremia or centripetal movement via nerve fibres, or a combination of both. The neural route is supported by some epidemiological observations and also by data from work with experimental animals. Intramuscular injection or other tissue trauma during the incubation period significantly increases the risk of paralytic disease especially in the extremity that was the target of trauma. – A possible explanation of the latter observation would be that the trauma has enabled transfer of the virus from circulation to local motor nerve endings, and subsequent retrograde movement of the virus to the neurons in the anterior horn of the spinal cord.

Other risk factors for paralytic disease in poliovirus-infected persons include older age, male gender and pregnancy. There also seems to be a familial trend for increased susceptibility to paralytic disease but it has not been established if it is truly based on genetics of the host rather than on variation of

virus virulence or on the dose of virus inoculum.

The virus replicates in the motor neuronal cells. Since neurones cannot regenerate, paralysis once developed often remains persistent. Partial recovery, however, occurs in some cases. This is due to two factors. First, paralysis may have been partly due to transient nearby inflammatory reaction rather than complete destruction of the neuronal cells themselves. Secondly, it appears that axons of healthy neurones adjacent to the virus-destroyed ones can branch and the new sprouting nerve fibres can renervate the orphaned muscle fibres.

CLINICAL FEATURES

In most individuals, poliovirus infection is clinically unapparent. In a small proportion, the oropharyngeal and intestinal infection with viremia may cause a short-lasting fever with or without malaise and pharyngitis (minor illness). The CNS involvement (major illness)

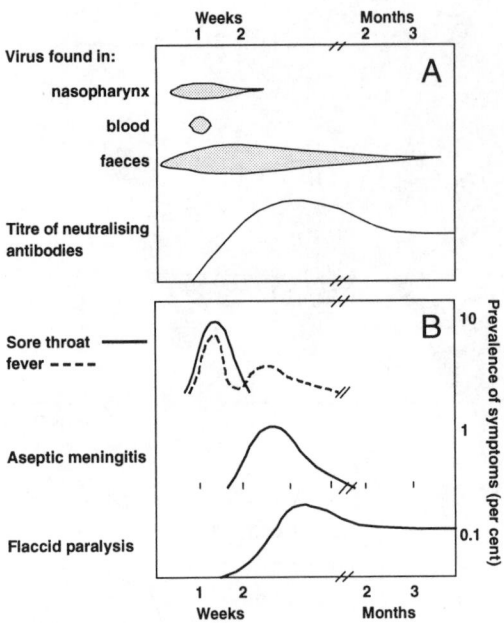

Figure 25.4. Natural course of poliovirus infection. Panel A: Upper part, infectious virus in the body. The vertical widths of the shaded areas represent both relative proportions of tests positive and relative amounts of virus positive specimens. Lower part, relative antibody concentration in serum. Note life-long persistence of neutralising antibodies. Panel B: Prevalence and timing of symptoms in wild-poliovirus-infected unvaccinated persons. The prevalence of acute-phase paralytic symptoms varies between 0.5 and 0.1 per cent.

usually occurs after an afebrile interval of 1 to 2 days, or sometimes without a preceding minor illness. The major illness itself may start with moderate or high fever. The CNS pathology may include aseptic meningitis, spinal poliomyelitis, bulbar poliomyelitis, facial paralysis, encephalitis or any combination of these. Muscle pain, often severe, may precede or coincide with the onset of paralysis.

Spinal poliomyelitis, the commonest major illness, may itself have a wide range of severity, from paresis of a few muscles, to paralysis of one limb, paralysis of more than one limb, quadriplegia, and to paralysis of muscles of respiration (diaphragm and intercostal muscles). In infants and young children, severe neck muscle weakness (head lag) and localised abdominal muscle paralysis causing a bulge when the child cries (pseudo-tumour or pseudo-hernia) are characteristic features in a proportion of cases, irrespective of severity.

The most common mode of presentation is the paralysis of one lower limb. Here, the asymmetry, the rapidity of progression of paralysis to its maximum within 2–4 days and the unaffected sensory functions distinguish spinal poliomyelitis from the Guillain–Barré syndrome (GBS). When both lower limbs are paralysed, the similarity to GBS may be confusing. However, when most persons with GBS show early clinical recovery, poliomyelitis paralysis persists beyond 60 days, a feature often used for defining poliomyelitis for public health reporting. Many other enteroviruses can also rarely cause mild poliomyelitis-like symptoms, but early and complete recovery is the rule in such cases. Other alternatives to consider for differential diagnosis are shown in Table 25.1.

Where poliomyelitis is endemic its clinical diagnosis is reasonably accurate based on the above features, including persistence of paralysis, and laboratory tests do not contribute much. Similarly, during an epidemic, the clinical diagnosis is highly specific. Where its incidence has become very low, and disease occurs in adults, a clinical diagnosis is not sufficient, especially from the public health point of view. Here, the etiology has to be established and if found to be due to poliovirus, then rigorous remedial measures must be taken to prevent further spread and more disease.

Routine laboratory tests of blood are not helpful. If hypokalemic paralysis needs to be excluded, serum potassium level should be measured. The cerebrospinal fluid (CSF) usually shows pleocytosis, granulocytes predominating transiently very early, and lymphocytes predominating subsequently and persisting over several days. CSF protein levels are only slightly, if at all, elevated in the early phase. In GBS, more marked increase in protein and the absence of pleocytosis are the characteristic findings. Nerve conduction studies may further assist in distinguishing between poliomyelitis (normal conduction time) and GBS (delayed conduction).

ESTABLISHING POLIOVIRUS ETIOLOGY IN POLIOMYELITIS

Where the disease is common, it is not very important to establish etiological diagnosis of poliomyelitis. Where disease is not endemic, correct etiological diagnosis is important to understand the transmission dynamics of poliovirus and to design control measures. The

Table 25.1. Differential diagnosis of poliomyelitis

Guillain–Barré syndrome
Poliomyelitis-like paralysis due to
        Sabin (OPV) strains of poliovirus
        coxsackieviruses
        echoviruses
        enterovirus type 70 and 71
        mumps virus
Hypokalemic paralysis
Post-diphtheria paralysis
Bell's palsy
Sciatic nerve injury due to gluteal
   intramuscular injection
Transverse myelitis
Spinal cord compression or tumour
Pseudoparalysis due to
        arthritis of hip (pyogenic, tuberculous)
        Perthe's disease
        congenital dislocation of hip
        osteomyelitis
        trauma with or without fracture
        arthritis of knee
        myositis/pyomyositis
Acute viral encephalitis/meningoencephalitis
Cerebral palsy
Muscular dystrophy

detection of poliovirus in feces is accepted as reasonable evidence for etiology of the concurrent paralytic illness. However, the virus isolate should be tested to distinguish between wild (virulent) strains and vaccine (attenuated) strains. A stool sample should be collected as soon as possible after the onset of paralysis and submitted either immediately to a virus laboratory, or kept frozen at –20ºC until analysed.

A serum sample may also be collected, for the detection of virus-specific IgM antibodies. If two samples of sera are collected with an interval of 7–14 days, a rising titre of virus-neutralising antibodies may be shown. CSF sample collected within 2 weeks of onset of paralytic disease may also be useful for the demonstration of virus-specific IgM antibodies.

TREATMENT AND REHABILITATION

There is no antiviral therapy against polioviruses. Therefore therapy is essentially palliative, supportive, preventive for deformities and rehabilitative. In the acute phase no intramuscular or subcutaneous injections should be given. The paralysed limb should be kept in the neutral position to prevent pain and deformity, with support using pillows or warm packs. The respiratory movements should be carefully observed. Weak movements, diaphragm moving down and anterior abdominal wall moving forward during inspiration (paradoxical respiration), cyanosis and drowsiness are indications of respiratory insufficiency. If the throat is dry, there is no risk of aspiration. If pooling of saliva is observed in the pharynx, the muscles of deglutition are also weak, indicating bulbar involvement; the throat should be frequently sucked to keep the airway clear. If necessary, the patient should be put on assisted ventilation.

Rehabilitative exercises should be started for the paralysed muscles after the pain and tenderness have disappeared and the general condition is stable. Passive movements to keep the affected joint supple are started first, about 4 weeks after the acute illness. Active exercises, splints, orthotic supporting devices, etc. are needed in the majority of cases and experienced staff are needed for their evaluation, application and follow-up. The purpose is to rehabilitate those who can walk to walk without support; those who cannot walk to walk with support; those who cannot be mobile to become mobile with wheelchairs. A further purpose is to prevent deformities and to perform corrective surgery when necessary and possible.

It is important to remember that poliomyelitis does not affect the brain. Children should attend schools like all other children. Emotional support and acceptance in play groups are important.

Some 25–35 years after the onset of paralysis and a subsequent stable state, some persons develop deterioration due to muscular atrophy (*post-polio muscular atrophy*). Additional physical rehabilitation will be necessary for them. Table 25.2 summarises guidelines for management of acute poliomyelitis.

IMMUNISATION

Both inactivated poliovirus (IPV) and oral, live poliovirus vaccines (OPV) have been available for more than three decades. Both vaccines are effective and safe but have important differences. The present version of IPV, containing relatively large amounts of immunising antigens, induces neutralising serum antibodies to all three serotypes after two doses in nearly all vaccinees (hence: enhanced-potency IPV or EIPV). The drawbacks

Table 25.2. What to do when acute poliomyelitis is suspected?

1. Review detailed history and physical findings to ensure that diagnosis is correct.
2. Check respiratory system. Shallow breathing, paradoxical breathing or cyanosis indicates respiratory involvement. The child requires hospitalisation.
3. Examine the throat. If dry, the respiratory involvement is muscular, affecting diaphragm or intercostal muscles. Prepare for assisted ventilation if condition deteriorates.
4. If throat shows pooling of saliva, respiratory involvement may be central, namely bulbar poliomyelitis. Assisted ventilation may be life-saving.
5. Limb paralysis without respiratory involvement may be managed at home. Rest, relief of pain, prevention of deformities and no injections are the main points to remember.
6. Passive movements may be started about 2 weeks after the onset of paralysis. Active movement may be started about 4 weeks after the onset of paralysis.
7. Physical medicine review, physiotheraphy and rehabilitation services are necessary in all cases in whom paralysis persists.

of IPV are the need of multiple injections and the fact that immunisation does not give as good protection against intestinal infection as does the OPV.

In contrast, OPV is easy to give. It is also relatively inexpensive, and hence, has been the vaccine of choice in most countries. In developing countries it is recommended by the EPI programme of the WHO (Chapter 48) in a four-dose schedule, at birth and at 6, 10 and 14 weeks. Although a three- or four-dose schedule will effectively immunise nearly all children in industrialised countries, experience in developing countries has often been less satisfactory.

To follow the WHO recommendations the quantities of vaccine virus in one dose of OPV should be at least 10^6, 10^5 and 3×10^5 cell culture infectious doses ($CCID_{50}$), for type 1, 2 and 3 polioviruses, respectively. Exposure of OPV to increased temperatures will inactivate the vaccine viruses, which compounds the sub-optimal vaccine efficacy. Such geographic problems are virtually absent with IPV since it is injected and since it is more heat-stable. IPV is free from serious adverse effects while OPV can cause poliomyelitis on rare occasions, especially in immunodeficient children and non-immune adults.

Immunisations are organised in different ways in different countries. In some places they are arranged within the primary health care system, in other places a separate organisation provides the regular immunisations. In Central and Southern America, good results have been obtained by a different strategy, originally developed in Cuba. Rather than trying to vaccinate all children at the age of 6, 10 and 14 weeks, specific national vaccination days are arranged twice a year. On the vaccination days every child under 5 years of age is offered a dose of OPV. This practice brings about a strong *herd effect* against the circulating wild poliovirus; its transmission appears to have ceased on the entire continent of the Americas. However, the total requirement of OPV doses for such campaigns are two to three times that needed for the entire routine schedule, and the campaigns do not help to enforce the utilisation of other childhood vaccines recommended by the EPI to be offered at the same time as polio vaccine.

GLOBAL ERADICATION BY THE YEAR 2000

WHO, UNICEF and some other organisations agreed in 1987 for a joint programme in order to eradicate poliomyelitis from the world by the year 2000.[3] Rotary International donated a considerable amount of money for purchasing the vaccine. The goal itself is feasible in the sense that man is the only natural host species of polioviruses, chronic infections do not occur normally and effective vaccines are already available.[4] Furthermore, rapid progress in the elimination of the disease and of wild poliovirus circulation in the Americas in the 1980s has been encouraging. In spite of a steady decrease in the number of globally reported cases of poliomyelitis, the progress of immunisations has been clearly less dramatic in Africa and Asia where endemic poliovirus infection persists.

The organisation of the immunisations simply is not sufficiently effective in many countries. Political turbulence and economic difficulties, together with health problems that are locally more demanding, such as AIDS, will further delay the execution of the programme in many countries. Eradication of poliomyelitis can and will succeed some day, but the year 2000 is too close for that to happen, unless more rigorous and concerted efforts are applied. The optimum methods to interrupt the transmission of polioviruses under different epidemiological situations have not been worked out. The surveillance system, both for disease and for virus isolation, is not yet in place in some regions of the world.[5]

References

1. Nathanson N, Martin JR. The epidemiology of poliomyelitis: enigmas surrounding its appearance, epidemicity, and disappearance. Am J Epidemiol 1979;110:672–692.
2. Horstman DM, Quinn TC, Robbins FC, eds. International symposium on poliomyelitis control. Rev Infect Dis 1984;6, Suppl. 2.
3. World Health Organization. Global eradication of poliomyelitis by the year 2000. Wkly Epidemiol Rec 1988;63:161–162.
4. Wright PF, Kim-Farley RJ, de Quadros CA, et al. Strategies for the global eradication of poliomyelitis by the year 2000. N Engl J Med 1991;325:1774–1779.
5. World Health Organization. Responding to a suspected polio outbreak: Case investigation, surveillance and control. A manager's checklist. Geneva: WHO, 1991. (WHO/EPI/POL/91.3)

About the authors

U. Tapani Hovi, is a Specialist in Clinical Microbiology and Virology, and presently Research Professor and Head, Department of Viral Diseases, National Public Health Institute (KTL), Helsinki, Finland. Within the department he is the Head of the Enterovirus Laboratory that serves as the WHO Collaborating Centre for Reference and Research on Poliomyelitis for the European region. He is also an Assistant Professor (Docent) in Virology at the University of Helsinki. His present research interest is in immunology, molecular pathogenesis and epidemiology of enterovirus infections.

T. Jacob John is the Professor and Head of the Department of Microbiology and Virology at the Christian Medical College, Vellore, India. He has been a pioneer in the study of the epidemiology and prevention of paediatric infections diseases in India. He serves on the WHO EPI Research and Development Group, EPI Technical Committee, and the Strategy Planning Task Force of the Children s Vaccine Initiative. Dr John was the recipient of the Medical Man of the year National Award, India, 1990.

Lankinen KS, Bergström S, Mäkelä PH and Peltomaa M, eds.
Health and disease in developing countries. London:The Macmillan Press Limited, 1994:255–264.

26 LEPROSY

Morten Harboe, M.D., Ph.D.
University of Oslo, Institute of Immunology and Rheumatology
Frederikke Qvamsgate 1, N-0172 Oslo,
Norway

INTRODUCTION

Leprosy is a chronic disease due to infection with *Mycobacterium leprae*, often characterised by a protracted course with exacerbations. To a large extent it may be considered an immunological disease. Most symptoms of the disease are due to immune reactions against antigenic constituents liberated from the bacilli. The disease chiefly affects the skin and peripheral nerves, and reactions that result in loss of nerve function are a major cause of the chronic disability often associated with the disease. The clinical course is highly variable.

For several decades 12–15 million patients were estimated to suffer from leprosy throughout the world. Following the introduction of multiple drug therapy (MDT) the number of registered patients has decreased dramatically both in individual programmes and worldwide.[1,2] These relatively short, intensive treatment regimens reduce the amount of live, infectious leprosy bacilli in individual patients more rapidly than monotherapy with dapsone that was previously used for extensive periods, often for the rest of life-time. The declining numbers of registered leprosy patients reflect to a great extent the early discharge policy associated with MDT.[3] The effect of MDT on the leprosy endemic itself still remains uncertain.

The leprosy bacillus was first seen and recognised as such in 1873 by Hansen in Norway.[4] At that time areas of Western Norway were severely affected with prevalence rates above 20 per 1000. Later, during an 80-year period the disease virtually disap-

peared from the country. This decline, typical of industrialised countries with improving socioeconomic conditions, has not been observed during the same period in developing countries.

Hansen's approach that led to the detection of the bacillus was logical, step-wise, and to a great extent based on epidemiological considerations. It is still informative today as a model for the study of a 'new' infectious disease.

The first step consisted of clinical and anatomical studies of the disease. Based on these, he concluded that leprosy was 'a specific disease', that is 'a distinct, well-defined disease, and therefore probably with a definite cause'.

The second step was epidemiological, studying the disease in the society. In particular he studied 69 families where some members were affected by leprosy and found that the major hypothesis of the time, heredity, could not account for the observations made. In contrast, his observations strongly indicated an infectious origin of the disease.

The third step was to search for the bacillus which he saw and recognised for the first time on 28 February 1873. These observations then formed the basis for his work to reduce the transmission of the infectious agent in the society, and thus for prevention of the disease.

THE LEPROSY BACILLUS AND EXPERIMENTAL MODELS

Mycobacterium leprae is an acid-fast Gram-positive rod that has not yet been cultured *in vitro*.

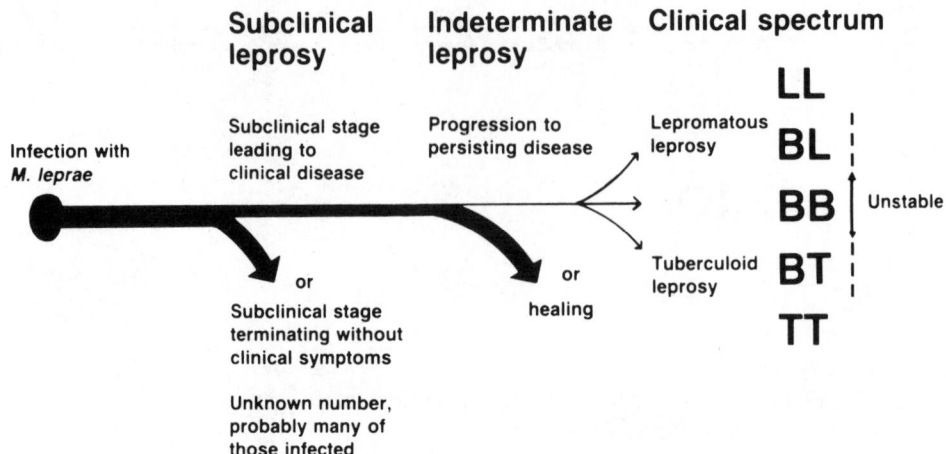

Figure 26.1. The course of infection with *Mycobacterium leprae*. (Reproduced with permission from the editor and the publisher from Figure 4.3 in: Hastings RC, ed. Leprosy. Edinburgh: Churchill Livingstone, 1985. Medicine in the Tropics Series).

In vivo it is an obligate intracellular parasite growing mainly in macrophages and Schwann cells of peripheral nerves. Some bacilli may remain dormant within cells for years, and represent a risk for relapse up to several years after cessation of chemotherapy. Experimental models have been essential for understanding the mechanisms of the disease and for development of preventive measures, and therefore deserve to be discussed here.

Shepard originally demonstrated local multiplication of *M. leprae* in the footpad of the normal mouse.[5] This growth is strictly local, with bacillary multiplication indicating a generation time of around 12 days, longer than for other mycobacteria. This slow growth fits well with the clinical evidence of a long incubation time, in most cases 2–7 years, and with the slow progression of the disease in its initial phases. This model has been of tremendous importance, particularly for testing the efficiency of drug treatment, for screening of new drugs, and for the demonstration of drug resistance.

The thymectomised mouse model has shown that resistance depends on reactions mediated by T lymphocytes. Furthermore, transfer of normal lymphoid cells to these mice that develop systemic *M. leprae* infection leads to an immunological attack on the bacilli and a violent reaction resulting in tissue damage and clinical symptoms similar to severe reversal reactions in humans.[6] In nude mice with no development of the thymus on a genetic basis (*nu/nu* mice), *M. leprae* multiplies even

more.[7] These models have also been used to demonstrate persisting viable *M. leprae* in various tissues after prolonged drug treatment explaining the pronounced risk of relapse in lepromatous leprosy.

In 1971 Kirchheimer and Storrs demonstrated that, upon intravenous inoculation, a systemic *M. leprae* infection can be established in the nine-banded armadillo.[8] The infection model in armadillos was shown to be quite similar to severe lepromatous leprosy in humans. The bacillary content is high in the tissues of armadillos sacrificed 1.5–2 years after inoculation. This model completely changed the availability of *M. leprae* for bacteriological and immunological studies and provided a basis for development of a new leprosy vaccine. In recent years recombinant DNA-technology has been of increasing importance for production and characterisation of different antigenic proteins of *M. leprae*.[9]

THE IMMUNOLOGY OF LEPROSY

Since *M. leprae* is an obligate intracellular parasite cell-mediated immune reactions are essential for protective immunity since antibodies do not have access to bacilli inside living cells.[10] While cell-mediated immune reactions are essential for development of protective immunity, reactions mediated by T lymphocytes are also responsible for delayed type hypersensitivity (DTH) reactions against antigens liberated from the bacilli, and in this way for development of neuritis and complications of the

Table 26.1. The clinical spectrum of leprosy.

Classification	Tuberculoid		Borderline		Lepromatous
Ridley and Jopling[12]	TT	BT	BB	BL	LL
Paucibacillary					
Multibacillary					
Skin smear Bacterial Index (untreated)	0	0–2+	2–3+	3–4+	3–6+
Antibodies to *M. leprae*	Low amounts				Usually high amounts
Resistance	Relatively high				Low
Cellular immunodeficiency	No				Yes
Delayed type hypersensitivity		Frequent			Absent
Reaction type		Reversal reaction			Erythema nodosum leprosum

disease.[10] The relationship between the two forms of cellular immune reactions has not been established. In experimental mycobacterial infections the onset of DTH reactions often occurs at the time when protective immunity becomes evident with arrest of bacterial multiplication. However efficient protective immunity can also occur without detectable DTH.

THE COURSE OF INFECTION

The clinical course after infection with *M. leprae* is highly variable as illustrated in Figure 26.1. The transfer of bacilli from an infectious individual is mainly by droplet infection, like in tuberculosis, and the port of entry is probably the nose. Poverty with crowded living is therefore an important risk factor for infection. The majority of those infected are sufficiently resistant to limit the multiplication of *M. leprae* without clinical signs of the infection. In many instances, immunological tests can still reveal the infection.[11]

The frequency of subsequent development of clinical disease varies in different populations. Improvement of the nutritional status and standard of living tends to decrease the proportion of individuals developing clinical disease. *M. leprae may thus be able to uphold a sufficient infectious reservoir only in societies with extensive poverty and poor socioeconomic conditions.*

Indeterminate leprosy mainly occurs in children and is difficult to recognise with certainty: there may be a few slightly hypo-pigmented lesions with vague borders. These lesions contain only few bacilli, and most of them heal spontaneously.

Patients with *determinate, persisting disease* constitute a spectrum between two polar groups, *tuberculoid leprosy* (TT) with few lesions containing few bacilli, and *lepromatous leprosy* (LL) with multiple lesions in which there is unihibited bacillary growth due to deficient cell-mediated immunity. Essential features of the clinical spectrum of leprosy are summarised in Table 26.1.

Ridley and Jopling have divided leprosy into five major groups.[12] The classification has been widely accepted and provides a good basis for accurate clinical diagnosis and evaluation of prognosis. Figure 26.2 shows a single lesion of tuberculoid leprosy, and Figure 26.3 the multiple nodular lesions characteristic of lepromatous leprosy. These lesions contain large

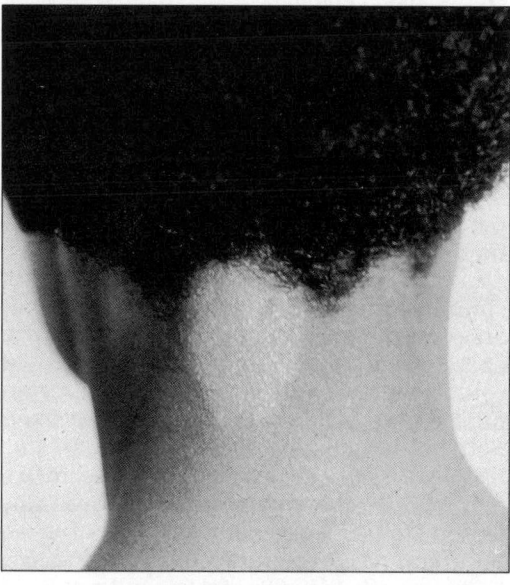

Figure 26.2. Tuberculoid (TT) leprosy. The patient had a single hypopigmented lesion in the neck. Courtesy of Armauer Hansen Research Institute, Addis Ababa, Ethiopia.

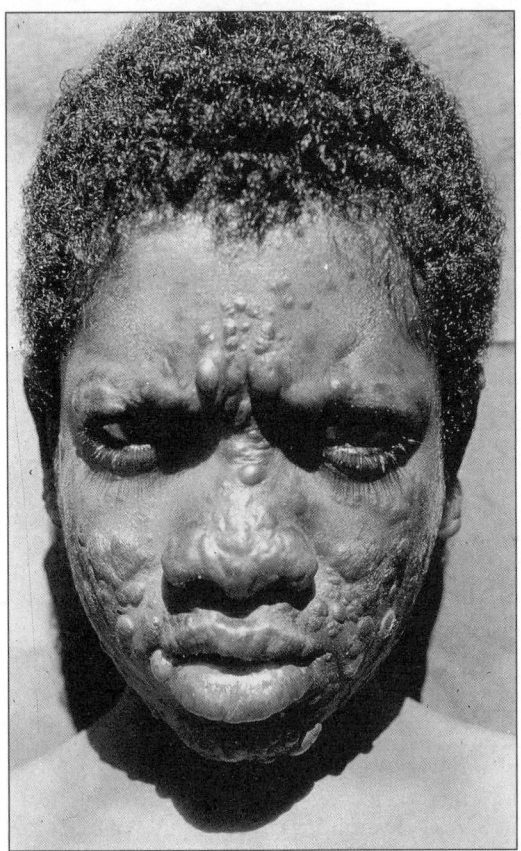

Figure 26.3. Lepromatous (LL) leprosy. Multiple nodular lesions. Note loss of eyebrows. Courtesy of Armauer Hansen Research Institute.

numbers of acid-fast bacilli as shown in Figure 26.4. In the classification the abbreviation B stands for 'Borderline'. It could as well stand for 'Be aware of reactions' since these are the patients most prone to develop serious reactions with nerve damage.

In field work there is an obvious need for simplification of classification. The patients are conveniently grouped into two major categories. *Paucibacillary leprosy* with skin lesions containing few bacilli corresponds to indeterminate leprosy, tuberculoid, and most patients with borderline tuberculoid leprosy. In *multibacillary leprosy* the lesions contain many bacilli. Most of these patients have borderline lepromatous or lepromatous leprosy. The latter group has greater infectivity, a tendency to relapse after drug treatment, and a marked deficiency in cellular immune reactions. These two main categories are also used as basis for the current treatment recommendations by WHO.[1,2]

Reactions

Mycobacterium leprae is virtually non-toxic and may occur in vast numbers in various tissues almost without any clinical symptoms. Therefore, immune reactions against antigens liberated from the bacilli are of major importance in the development of clinical symptoms and complications. The term *reactions* is used to denote acute or subacute states with increased inflammation in the lesions of leprosy patients. They are of two distinct categories, induced by different kinds of immune reactions.[10]

The term *reversal reaction* is used for episodes of increased cellular immune reactions associated with delayed type hypersensitivity against antigens of *M. leprae*. DTH reactions against antigens liberated from bacilli in Schwann cells damage the nerve as an innocent bystander, with typical clinical signs of neuritis. This neuritis leads to loss of function in sensory and motor nerves. If not prevented or reversed by treatment, neuritis may lead to permanent loss of nerve function with claw hands, drop foot, or insensitivity of hands and feet which in turn often results in chronic infection in wounds of various kind (Figure 26.5).

Erythema nodosum leprosum (ENL) is an immune complex disease. Antigens liberated from the bacilli react with circulating antibodies, resulting in formation of immune complexes with secondary activation of complement and induction of inflammatory reac-

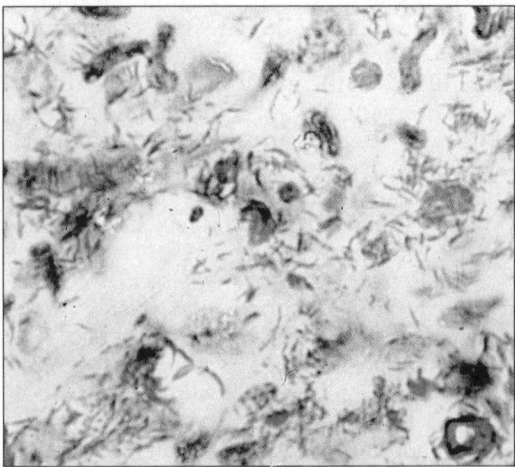

Figure 26.4. Biopsy of a nodule in lepromatous leprosy showing large amounts of acid-fast bacilli in the tissue.

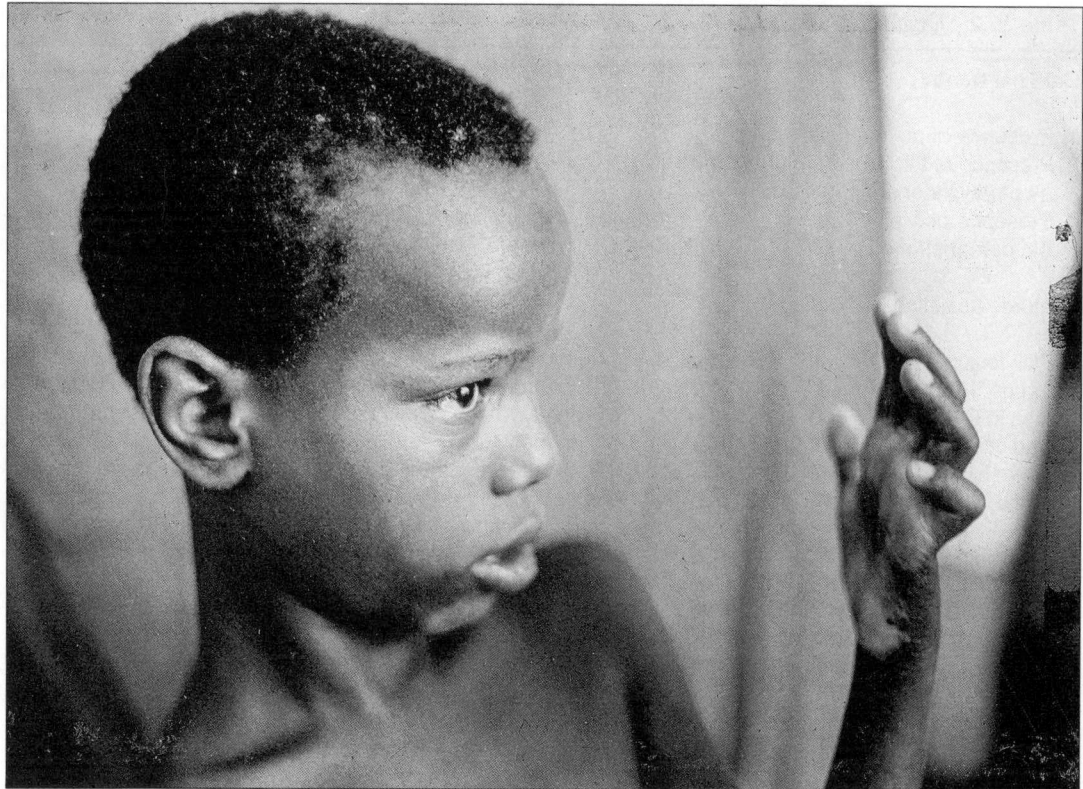

Figure 26.5. Reversal reaction. We see a hypopigmented lesion in the face. He is unable to extend the fingers due to neuritis with loss of function in extensor muscles. If untreated, continued loss of function lead to flexion contracture with long-lasting deformity. Courtesy of Armauer Hansen Research Institute.

tions. Tender subcutaneous nodules, mainly on the arms and legs, are the main symptom in ENL. They appear suddenly and usually disappear after a few days. The condition can also present with general malaise and fever.

Diagnosis

The diagnosis of leprosy should be made with caution. If there remains *any* doubt, the patient should be observed until further evidence confirms or excludes the disease. This will obviate psychological, social and other damage to the patient that could be caused by an incorrect diagnosis. Criteria for the diagnosis of leprosy are listed in Table 26.2.

The skin provides the most readily available tissue to look for *M. leprae*. Smears of skin-slits stained for acid-fast bacilli is the standard technique to estimate the number of *M. leprae* in the lesions, recorded on a logarithmic scale as a *bacterial index* (BI).[13] Reliable determination of the BI is an essential requirement for

introduction and proper evaluation of chemotherapy according to WHO recommendations. Upon effective chemotherapy the BI falls distinctly, and proper recording of the BI is thus also a necessary requirement for evaluation of the effect of the instituted chemotherapy. In untreated patients live *M. leprae* tend to be solidly stained. During treatment dying and dead bacilli become granular. These features are recorded in a *morphological index* (MI) giving the proportion of regularly stained, solid bacilli of the scored total. Properly executed this index is very informative, but technically too demanding for most programmes.

The organisation of leprosy care has undergone dramatic changes in many societies. For a long time it was based on vertical programmes developed for this disease. Today integration of leprosy into the general health services is the declared policy in most developing countries. This is a positive development, and necessary to provide sufficient care for the majority of leprosy patients living in

Table 26.2. Diagnosis of leprosy.

Cardinal signs

1. Presence of an insensitive patch.
2. Presence of thickened peripheral nerves, particularly when associated with signs of nerve damage such as paralysis or sensory loss.
3. Presence of *Mycobacterium leprae* in the skin, mucous membranes, or nerves. In practice this means the demonstration of acid-fast bacilli at one or more of these sites.

Features assisting in the diagnosis

1. Skin lesions are of various kinds and care should be taken to avoid misinterpretation due to racial differences. In dark-skinned people, the patch of tuberculoid leprosy is hypopigmented, whereas it is reddish in Caucasians. Lesions may be flat, with slightly raised borders, or nodular toward the lepromatous end of the spectrum. The progression is slow, in most cases tending to be prolonged over years.
2. There is often a history of numbness and hot and cold sensations in arms and feet, especially in the area of the ulnar, median and lateral popliteal nerves. These changes may be followed by loss of cutaneous sensitivity and later by muscular weakness, paralysis and atrophy.
3. Thickening of nerve trunks and superficial nerves occurs. During acute neuritis, nerve trunks are tender. Neuritis of other neurological diseases is very rarely accompanied by thickening of nerves. On a global scale, leprosy is the most frequent cause of peripheral neuropathy.
4. Demonstration of acid-fast bacilli in skin smears is essential for diagnosis of lepromatous cases, but these tests are often negative in tuberculoid leprosy.

remote areas.[14] Teaching activities are essential to ensure a sufficient level of knowledge at all levels of the health services. Establishment of a proper referral system to ensure that patients with special problems can be evaluated and cared for in more central institutions is also important.

EPIDEMIOLOGY AND SOCIOECONOMIC ASPECTS

The data on the prevalence of leprosy are unreliable in many countries because of insufficient case finding and reporting. Therefore, the number of registered patients and estimated cases have probably been too low. The figure of 12–15 million has often been given. About 40 per cent of the patients live in India. Africa occupies the second position, followed by South-East Asia, The Pacific region and Latin America. Following the introduction of MDT there has been a dramatic reduction in the reported number of patients. At the end of 1990, there were about 3.74 million registered patients in the world.

In many instances the number of leprosy patients is recorded as the number of patients under active treatment. When the treatment period is shortened, this leads to a statistical artifact, and the number of registered patients may be markedly reduced without a similar reduction in the number of individuals affected by the disease.

The consequences of the disease in terms of disability and deformity are often life-long, implying that the official figures often underestimate the public health problem of leprosy in the society. It is therefore essential that the term 'leprosy patient' includes not only those requiring or receiving chemotherapy but also those under continued surveillance and in need of care or assistance because of disabilities.[2]

There are marked regional variations in prevalence rates. In countries with prevalence rates above one per 1000 leprosy constitutes a significant public health problem. In many countries the occurrence of leprosy is patchy, affecting certain regions only, and this pattern is difficult to explain on epidemiological terms today. The patchy occurrence is at least partially due to variation in genetic, nutritional and migratory patterns. As discussed above, socioeconomic factors undoubtedly play a major role.

TREATMENT

Dapsone (DDS) has been the major drug for treatment of leprosy since its introduction in

Table 26.3. Standard regimens for treatment of leprosy recommended by WHO.[1,2]

Paucibacillary patients

    Rifampicin: 600 mg once monthly, for 6 months;
    Dapsone: 100 mg daily, for 6 months.
    The administration of rifampicin should invariably be fully supervised, but dapsone may be given unsupervised. The treatment should be completed within a period of 9 months.

Multibacillary patients

    Rifampicin: 600 mg once monthly, supervised;
    Dapsone: 100 mg daily, self-administered;
    Clofazimine: 300 mg once monthly, supervised, and 500 mg daily, self-administered.
    Treatment should be continued for at least 2 years and, whenever possible, until smear-negativity. In many programmes, dapsone-treated multibacillary patients continue to receive dapsone monotherapy indefinitely, even after becoming smear-negative. Where resources permit, it is recommended that such patients should be given multi-drug therapy for 2 years and that chemotherapy should then stop.

the late 1940s. DDS is bacteriostatic, acts slowly, and needs prolonged administration. Application as monotherapy led to increasing DDS resistance, and the required very long treatment led to poor compliance. The introduction of MDT, as intensely recommended by WHO since 1982[1], has resulted in a dramatic change in both attitudes and logistics of treatment. The recommended regimens are shown in Table 26.3.

These shorter, and more intensive treatment regimens have resulted in better compliance, a reduced risk for development of drug resistance, and the recorded relapse rates have generally been low.[15] WHO has recommended intensification of the application of MDT regimens, emphasising effective drug therapy as the prime mechanism to reduce the infectivity of individual patients and to break the chain of infection. In 1991, the 44th World Health Assembly approved a statement committing WHO 'to attain the global elimination of leprosy as a public health problem by the year 2000'. The goal is further specified: 'Elimination of leprosy as a public health problem is defined as the reduction of prevalence to a level below one case per 10 000 population'.

To monitor the elimination of a chronic disease, incidence rates are more informative than prevalence rates. The MDT regimens are without any doubt far superior to monotherapy with dapsone. Increased coverage with MDT should therefore have top priority.[16] At the same time, there is a need of caution: it remains to be seen whether relapse rates will continue to be low in the long term. It also remains to be proven that MDT will have the

required effect on the infectious reservoir to reduce the frequency of new cases to sufficiently low levels in the face of extensive poverty and weak infrastructure in developing countries today and in the years to come.

Treatment of reactions is summarised in Table 26.4. Clinically it is difficult to distinguish between relapse, with renewed bacterial multiplication, and late reversal reactions resulting in nerve damage after cessation of 6–9 months treatment in BT leprosy. It must be realised that a substantial proportion of the reversal reactions in BT patients occur *after* cessation of MDT, and these reactions usually respond well to treatment with prednisolone.[17] Continued care and clinical observation of these patients are essential to recognising signs of neuritis at a sufficiently early stage to prevent further nerve damage and risk of long-lasting disability and deformity. *Release from treatment must not imply release from care!*

PREVENTION

Prevention continues to be the most essential part of leprosy work at the level of the community as well as the individual.

Prevention at community level

At community level efforts to brake the chain of infection are essential to reduce the total infectious reservoir in the society which in turn would lead to reduction in the number of new cases.

Untreated patients with multibacillary leprosy are highly infectious. The local lower tem-

Table 26.4. Treatment of reactions.

1. The basic chemotherapy against *M.leprae* should not be discontinued.

2. Additional drug treatment is given to reduce the inflammatory reaction.

In **reversal reactions** high-dose corticosteroids are essential in patients with neuritis, and should be given as long as there is active neuritis.

This treatment can also be administered in the field, although careful control and follow-up are essential. It is important to start with a sufficiently high dose of steroids, prednisone or prednisolone given as a single daily dose of 40 mg, gradually being reduced.

In **erythema nodosum leprosum** mild symptoms are often sufficiently reduced by non-steroidal anti-inflammatory agents like aspirin and chloroquine. The combination is often better than either alone. In severe cases high-dose corticosteroids are essential.

Thalidomide is very efficient in ENL. However, this drug should only be used with great caution in view of its marked teratogenic effects with a high risk of serious fetal damage during early pregnancy. Clofazimine has a marked anti-inflammatory activity in higher doses than for regular anti-bacterial activity and should be used in patients with recurrent ENL.

---

perature favours growth of *M. leprae* in the nasal mucosa, and a single patient can shed millions of bacilli per day in nose-blows with rapid transfer of droplet infection in crowded housing conditions, during public transport etc. Effective chemotherapy usually results in the individuals rapidly becoming non-infectious. Early diagnosis combined with effective therapy are therefore essential features to break the chain of infection. Good care and relevant information at a community level remain essential in inducing patients to report early after recognition of clinical symptoms, rather than hiding themselves and thus transmitting the infection.

The effect of BCG vaccination in relation to leprosy remains an important issue. In tuberculosis, the main point is not whether BCG is effective but to realise and understand the marked variation in different trials. Estimated vaccination efficacy regarding protection against tuberculosis was 75–80 per cent in four trials (in Haiti, British school children, North-American Indians and Chicago infants), lower in other trials, while no protective effect was demonstrable in several instances including the major recent trial in South India. The same is the case in leprosy, BCG vaccine efficacy ranging from 80 per cent protection in the trial in Uganda to about 20 per cent in Karimui, New Guinea.[18] Thus there is a definite need for improved vaccines both for tuberculosis and leprosy.

In an attempt to develop a vaccine giving greater and more consistent protection against leprosy than BCG, Convit and collaborators[19] compared the effect of BCG with BCG plus killed *M. leprae* in close contacts of leprosy cases in Venezuela. There was no evidence in the first 5 years of follow-up of this extensive trial that BCG plus killed *M. leprae* offers better protection against leprosy than BCG alone. Analysis of data on the number of BCG scars found on each contact screened suggested that BCG alone confers substantial protection against leprosy in Venezuela as well. Additional vaccine trials are under way in Malawi and India providing additional, important points for analysis.[20]

The relative contribution of improved chemotherapy in the form of MDT programmes and extended BCG vaccination to leprosy control should be carefully evaluated in the years to come. Continued emphasis on BCG vaccination is important in view of its effect on tuberculosis as well as leprosy. Recombinant DNA technology is now intensively explored for development of second generation vaccines.[21]

Individual prevention

The patients themselves play an essential role in preventive work. They are important in detecting new patients, encouraging them to seek treatment, and helping to keep them under treatment. Equally important is the fact that most of the deformities associated with leprosy are preventable. Recognition of early symptoms of reactions with neuritis and prompt institution of adequate therapy are essential to reduce the risk of long lasting nerve damage with significant loss of sensitivity and function.

In case of permanent loss of function, the patients still can prevent a lot of deformity by knowing how to prevent contractions and to protect insensitive hands and feet.

Provision and use of adequate footwear are essential. It extends the mechanical stress of the daily gait on to a larger area of the sole of the foot since repetitive higher pressure at local sites is a main ulcer-inducing factor.

Soaking of the feet in water and use of an ointment also reduce the tendency of the skin to form thick keratin layers which increase the risk of inflammation and ulcer formation. For insensitive hands it is important to vary frequently used procedures to avoid repetitive pressure at certain sites and to avoid damage by heat during cooking procedures etc. Plastic gutter splints may protect wounded or infected fingers. These efforts reduce the risk of ulcer formation. Early detection of ulcers and adequate care reduce the risk of secondary chronic infection so important in induction of the chronic deformity and disfiguration still often associated with leprosy and which contributes greatly to the stigma of the disease. The greatest factor impeding progress in this area is not lack of knowledge, but the influence of poverty on many of these patients.

Social aspects

In many cultures the social consequences of leprosy are far greater than the medical consequences. The deformities and disfiguration in advanced cases are important causes of the stigmatisation of leprosy patients. It is essential not only to break the chain of infection, but to break the effects of stigmatisation. Prevention of deformity in individual patients and health education of the general community are important to reduce the stigma of the disease. Every effort should be made to consider leprosy as a curable disease. This would lessen the fear of the disease in the individual patient as well as in the community. Any factor contributing to bring the patients for early treatment, to keep them under treatment, and to reduce the frequency and severity of nerve damage would contribute to better control.

References

1. Chemotherapy of leprosy for control programmes. Report of a WHO Study Group. Geneva: WHO, 1982. (Techn Rep Ser No 675)
2. WHO Expert Committee on Leprosy. Sixth Report. Techn Rep Ser No 768. Geneva: WHO, 1988.
3. Fine PEM. Reflections on the elimination of leprosy. Int J Leprosy 1992;60:71–80.
4. Harboe M. Armauer Hansen – the man and his work. Int J Leprosy 1973;41:417–24.
5. Shepard CC. The experimental disease that follows the injection of human leprosy bacilli into foot pads of mice. J Exp Med 1960;112:445–54.
6. Rees RJW, Weddell AGM. Experimental models for studying leprosy. Ann NY Acad Sci 1968;154:214–36.
7. Chehl S, Ruby J, Job CK, Hastings RC. The growth of *Mycobacterium leprae* in nude mice. Lepr Rev 1983;54:283–304.
8. Kirchheimer WF, Storrs EE. Attempts to establish the armadillo (*Dasypus novemcinctus* Linn) as a model for the study of leprosy. I. Report of lepromatoid leprosy in an experimentally infected armadillo. Int J Leprosy 1971; 39:693–702.
9. Young RA, Mehra V, Sweetser D, *et al.* Genes for the major protein antigens of the leprosy parasite *Mycobacterium leprae*. Nature 1985;316: 450–2.
10. Harboe M. The immunology of leprosy. In: Hastings RC, ed. Leprosy. Edinburgh: Churchill Livingstone, 1985:53–87.
11. Godal T, Löfgren M, Negassi K. Immune response to *M. leprae* of healthy leprosy contacts. Int J Leprosy 1972;40:243–50.
12. Ridley DS, Jopling WH. Classification of leprosy according to immunity: a five-group system. Int J leprosy 1966;34:255–73.
13. Rees RJW. The microbiology of leprosy. In: Hastings RC, ed. Leprosy. Edinburgh: Churchill Livingstone, 1985:31–52.
14. Feenstra P. Leprosy control through general health services and/or combined programmes. Lepr Rev 1993;64:89–96.
15. Becx-Bleumink M. Relapses among leprosy patients treated with multidrug therapy: Experience in the leprosy control program of the All Africa Leprosy and Rehabilitation Training Center (ALERT) in Ethiopia; practical difficulties with diagnosing relapses; operational procedures and criteria for diagnosing relapses. Int J Leprosy 1992; 60:421–35.
16. Yuasa Y. MDT for all; target oriented leprosy control program in the 1990s. Int J Leprosy 1991;59:624–38.
17. Becx-Bleumink M, Berhe D. Occurrence of reactions, their diagnosis and management in leprosy patients treated with multi drug therapy; experience in the leprosy control program of the All Africa Leprosy and Rehabilitation Training Center (ALERT) in Ethiopia. Int J Leprosy 1992; 60:173–84.
18. Fine PEM. BCG vaccination against tuberculosis and leprosy. Br Med Bull 1988;44:691–703.
19. Convit J, Sampson C, Zuniga M, *et al.* Immunoprophylactic trial with combined *Mycobacterium leprae*/BCG vaccine against leprosy: preliminary results. Lancet 1992;339: 446–50.

20. Anonymous. Bettering BCG. Lancet 1992;339:462–3.
21. Stover CK, Cruz VF de la, Fuerst TR, *et al*. New use of BCG for recombinant vaccines. Nature 1991;351: 456–60.

About the author

Morten Harboe is a professor of medicine (immunology) at the University of Oslo and is currently the head of the Institute of Immunology and Rheumatology in Oslo, Norway. During 1969–70 he was the director of the Armauer Hansen Research Institute (AHRI) in Addis Ababa, Ethiopia, establishing the Institute and initiating its work in basic studies of leprosy. Since then he has been closely connected with the Institute serving as member and as Chairman of its Board, with the All Africa Leprosy and Rehabilitation Training Centre (ALERT) and various organisations working on leprosy. His current research interest is mainly immunological aspects of mycobacterial infections and complement. He has also published extensively on immunoglobulins, particularly on genetically determined factors (allotypes) of human immunoglobulins and diseases associated with monoclonal immunoglobulins.

APPENDIX

Training and teaching materials for leprosy

INTERNATIONAL JOURNAL OF LEPROSY published quarterly has a section NEWS and NOTES in each issue. 'This department furnishes information concerning institutions, organisations, and individuals engaged in work on leprosy and other mycobacterial diseases, and makes note of scientific meetings and other matters of interest.' The information is extensive and given country by country.

LEPNnews is published by World Health Organization, Leprosy Unit, Division of Control of Tropical Diseases, CH-1211 Geneva, Switzerland. The unit provides all types of information on WHO supported activities concerning leprosy and related diseases.

LEPROSY REVIEW is published quarterly and has a section *Teaching Materials and Services* in almost every issue of the journal providing up-to-date information with relevant addresses on training courses in different institutions and various types of teaching materials.

GERMAN LEPROSY RELIEF ASSOCIATION is in charge of the working group on training in the International Federation of Anti-Leprosy Associations (ILEP) and is in this capacity in possession of extensive information on international training activities and teaching materials concerning leprosy. Post Box 348, D-8700 Wurzburg 11, Germany.

THE LEPROSY MISSION INTERNATIONAL. Lists of the mission's extensive collection of teaching and learning materials in leprosy are available from 80 Windmill Road, Brentford, Middlesex TW8 0QH, United Kingdom.

THE NETHERLANDS LEPROSY RELIEF ASSOCIATION is in charge of INFOLEP. These Leprosy Information Services function as 'a library and documentation centre offering its services to all those who need information on leprosy, in all its various aspects.' Wibautstraat 135 II, NL-1097 DN Amsterdam, The Netherlands.

ALL AFRICA LEPROSY AND REHABILITATION TRAINING CENTRE in Ethiopia is an international training centre providing courses and in service training for various kinds of health personnel, medical doctors, rural area supervisors, physiotherapists etc. engaged in leprosy work. The institution has also produced a series of written manuals concerning leprosy, diagnosis, treatment, foot care, prevention etc. P.O. Box 165, Addis Ababa, Ethiopia.

SCHIEFFELIN LEPROSY RESEARCH AND TRAINING COURSES. Information on the courses at Karigiri for medical officers and other categories of health personnel can be obtained from the Training Officer, SLRTC, SLR Sanatorium PO, Karigiri 632 106, Tamil Nadu, India.

L'ASSOCIATION FRANCAISE RAOUL FOLLEREAU. Teaching and learning materials on leprosy for francophone countries. 31 rue de Dantzig, BP 79, 75722 Paris Cedex 15, France.

Lankinen KS, Bergström S, Mäkelä PH and Peltomaa M, eds.
Health and disease in developing countries. London:The Macmillan Press Limited, 1994:265–270.

27 BACTERIAL MENINGITIS

Heikki Peltola, M.D., Ph.D., D.T.M.&H.
University of Helsinki, Department of Paediatrics
Children's Hospital, Stenbäckinkatu 11,
FIN-00290 Helsinki,
Finland

INTRODUCTION

Meningitis due to bacteria is the most important infection of the central nervous system. It is an example of a disease that is well known in industrialised countries but takes its greatest toll in developing countries. Poor housing conditions, insufficient hygiene and malnutrition all contribute to spread of meningitis.

Almost any bacteria may cause meningitis but *Haemophilus influenzae*, meningococci (*Neisseria meningitidis*) and pneumococci (*Streptococcus pneumoniae*) are the most prevalent causative agents beyond the neonatal period (Figure 27.1). Meningococci cause mainly meningitis or sepsis, whereas *H. influenzae* and pneumococci may present as a variety of clinical entities, such as pneumonia, arthritis, cellulitis, or epiglottitis.

Only meningococcal disease occurs as extensive epidemics and these have been known for centuries.[1,2] In many countries meningococcal disease is the only meningitis that is officially reportable. This may give an erroneous overall picture since

H. influenzae and pneumococcal diseases are more common in circumstances without an ongoing epidemic.

EPIDEMIOLOGICAL FEATURES

The statistics are unreliable particularly in developing countries but show, at least, periods of highest and lowest incidence in a given area. A meningitis zone extends across Africa

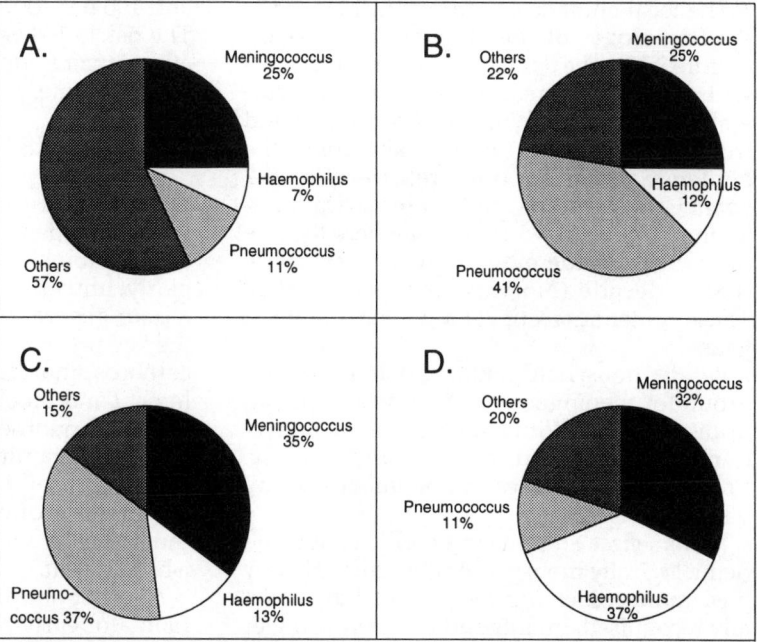

Figure 27.1. Main causative agents of bacterial meningitis in a) Brazil, b) Egypt, c) Senegal and d) Finland.

Figure 27.2. The Sub-Saharan meningitis belt.[3,4]

(Figure 27.2). It is an area where the annual rainfall varies between 300 mm (in north) and 1100 mm (in south). The eastern boundary goes through the eastern regions of Ethiopia and the western boundary through the savannas of Senegal.[3,4]

The local climatic conditions influence the epidemiology of meningococcal disease (Figure 27.3). The epidemic spreads in the area within weeks and reaches sometimes considerable proportions. When the *harmattan*, wind from north, subsides and the rains come, the epidemic wanes but often returns after 1–2 years.[4] The epidemic pattern in Africa mimics that of cholera, whereas elsewhere the meningococcal epidemics last years, even more than a decade (Norway in the 1970–80s). Those epidemics recur at long intervals, 10–30 years.[1]

Besides household contacts, one special risk group for meningococcal disease are the pilgrims to Mecca. With modern tourism an epidemic may spread rapidly and widely. Progress of epidemics can be intervened by vaccinations.

H. influenzae and pneumococci behave epidemiologically more peacefully, although they have more epidemiogenic potential than usually recognised. Infants and children younger than 5 years are at greatest risk. If one member of the family falls ill, the risk of the sister or brother is several hundred-fold as compared with the general population.

Incidence and age distribution

Although many developing countries are familiar with meningitis and consider it as one of their public health problems, hard data is scanty. Only seldom has it been possible to create a system that collects the information on all cases, not only on those verified in hospitals. Many patients are, however, lost before reaching hospital.

One of the few incidence rate reports in a non-epidemic time is from Senegal where two studies estimate the annual incidence of bacterial meningitis as approximately 50 per 100 000 inhabitants, i.e. every 20 000th inhabitant contracts meningitis annually.[5,6] The incidence is ten-fold in comparison with Finland or USA.

Children are at an increased risk of meningitis compared with adults. The main reason lies in the fact that protection from the disease is largely dependent on antibodies. As protective antibodies inherited from the mother wane within months, the infant is susceptible until his/her own antibodies gradually develop. Infants are the most susceptible, with an annual incidence rate of 400 per 100 000 among those under one year of age in Senegal and 100 per 100 000 in Finland (Figure 27.4).[6] The risk in 1–4 year olds is still high but thereafter remains approximately the same through one's lifetime.

DIAGNOSIS

A classical case of meningitis is easily identified: the patient presents with an acute onset of symptoms and signs, high fever, neck rigidity, impaired consciousness, petechiae and a poor general condition. *Lumbar puncture* is the key procedure with which a sample of the cerebrospinal fluid is obtained for bacteriological and biochemical examination. In developing countries, there are not many choices, but Gram staining of the specimen and simple microscopy suffice in most situations. Diagnosis is often made by the naked eye if the normally water-clear fluid looks yellowish, purulent.

Another simple method is *latex agglutination*: a of cerebrospinal fluid is mixed on a glass slide with a latex reagent specific for *H. influenzae*, meningococci or pneumococci and

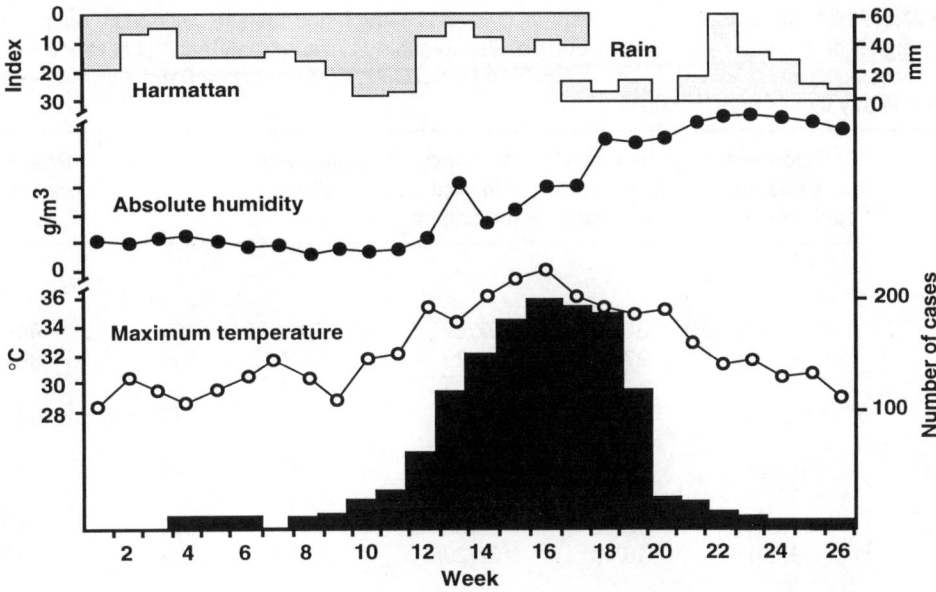

Figure 27.3. During meningococcal epidemic, one eagerly waits for the rains because then wanes the epidemic, northern Nigeria.[18]

in positive cases pinpoint-sized conglomerates distinguishable by the naked eye are generated. Because the test is specific for each pathogen, one always has to use many reagents and this is one of the restrictions of the method. On the other hand, precise information on etiology is obtained, and the test has been utilised in remote areas and extreme circumstances.

Blood and cerebrospinal fluid can be analysed with numerous laboratory methods but a few only are handy and reliable enough to be used in conditions in poor countries, where

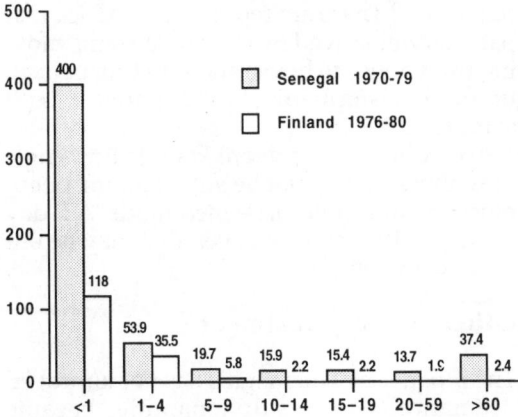

Figure 27.4. Age distribution of bacterial meningitis in Senegal and Finland.[6]

most cases occur. When five cerebrospinal fluid and five blood tests were evaluated for their ability to distinguish bacterial from viral meningitis, most routine tests proved surprisingly poor (Table 27.1). In summary, taking into account the realities, the three aforementioned very simple methods – visual examination, Gram staining, and latex agglutination of the cerebrospinal fluid – are challenged by only one blood test, determination of *serum C-reactive protein* (CRP). With modern techniques, even whole blood may be used instead of serum.

CRP can be determined quantitatively from a finger prick sample or semiquantitatively with a moderate accuracy by latex agglutination. CRP is not a specific indicator of bacterial meningitis but shows with 90 per cent probability that the patient has severe bacterial disease.[7] This information together with the characteristic symptoms and signs makes correct diagnosis very reliable.

TREATMENT

Antimicrobial treatment

Recent years have brought new alternatives for antimicrobial therapy (third generation cephalosporins) but high cost restricts their use in many parts of the world. On the other hand, although low-cost penicillin is the most

Table 27.1. Ability of the routine cerebrospinal fluid (CSF) and blood tests to distinguish bacterial from viral meningitis of children.[7] Accuracy = correct distinguishing/cases examined; * Difference from serum CRP almost significant ($P<0.05$); ** Difference from serum CRP significant ($P<0.01$); *** Difference from serum CRP highly significant ($P<0.001$).

Test	Reference value for bact. meningitis	Accuracy in bacterial meningitis	Accuracy in viral meningitis	Sensitivity (%)	Specificity (%)	Positive predictive value
CSF						
WBC	$>5 \times 10^6$/l	33/35	27/29	94	93	94
	$>10 \times 10^5$/l	27/35	29/29	77**	100	88*
Rods	>0.5 (>50%)	34/34	17/24	100	71*	88
Glucose	<2.2 mmol/l	22/34	27/29	65***	93	78***
Protein	>1.0 g/l	23/30	25/29	77**	86	81**
	>1.5 g/l	16/30	27/29	53***	93	73***
Gram st.	positive	26/31	26/26	84*	100	91
BLOOD						
CRP	≥ 20 mg/l	37/37	24/25	100	96	98
ESR	≥ 30 mm/h	17/21	11/13	81*	85	82*
WBC	$>15 \times 10^5$/l	9/37	21/26	24***	81	48***
Granulocytes	$>10 \times 10^9$/l	10/32	16/20	31***	80	50***
Rods	$>0.5 \times 10^9$/l	29/32	11/20	91	55**	77***

effective drug with regard to meningococcal and pneumococcal diseases (provided there is no resistance problem), the 3rd generation cephalosporins are also very effective.

Meningitis caused by *H. influenzae* would be a problem, without the availability of another low-cost medicine, chloramphenicol. There are recognised toxicity problems but these are very infrequent. In addition to being cheap, chloramphenicol has another advantage: it is also absorbed when given orally and penetrates well into the central nervous system.

Because hospital beds are in short supply, duration of the medication is critical; the shorter the course the better. In two studies (Table 27.2), patients with meningococcal meningitis were treated in three ways: 5 days with penicillin (2 days intravenously, 3 days intramuscularly) versus one single dose of penicillin or

chloramphenicol intramuscularly. There was no difference in mortality, treatment failures, or sequelae.[8,9] There are reports from Africa that patients were saved by treatment teams moving from house to house and injecting penicillin or chloramphenicol to all patients with symptoms.[10]

According to the present knowledge, single dose therapy may not be sufficient for pneumococcal or *H. influenzae* meningitis. A 7-day course is efficacious but even that may be unnecessarily long.[11]

Other medical treatment

The prognosis of meningitis has not improved dramatically since sulphonamides became available in the 1930s, and penicillin and chloramphenicol in the 1940s. Several attempts have been made to reduce the relatively high

Table 27.2. Short treatment of bacterial meningitis.[8,9] PEN = penicillin; i.m. = intramuscularly i.v. = intravenously; Failures = poor clinical response or CSF culture positive after 72 hours.

Comparison of therapies	Patients (N)	Recovered (%)	Failures (%)	Sequelae (%)	Died (%)
Penicillin for 5 days G-PEN 3 days i.m./i.v. + procain-PEN 2 days i.m.	64	83	11	16	5
Long acting penicillin One single dose i.m.	59	78	18	8	3
Penicillin for 5 days G-PEN 3 days i.m. + procain-PEN 2 days i.m.	66	89	6	11	5
Long acting chloramphenicol One single dose i.m.	65	94	5	11	2

mortality and frequency of permanent sequelae. Since dexamethasone is known to reduce the increased intracranial pressure – probably an essential cause of death in meningitis – *intravenous dexamethasone* looked promising in the late 1980s, but was soon challenged by less encouraging results.[12,13] Recent work suggests that it could be of use, but only when given early in the course of disease.[14]

Instead, *oral glycerol* seems to prevent severe hearing impairment at least as efficiently as dexamethasone.[13] Should the finding be confirmed, it would have great potential in the developing world since, in contrast to dexamethasone, glycerol is inexpensive, readily available and can be administered orally.

Fluid therapy

Attention has to be paid also to fluid therapy. Some patients may have succumbed because of excessive volumes of fluids which have worsened the intracranial pressure. On the other hand, one may be faced with a hypovolemic patient who needs immediate fluid resuscitation. The concomitant measurement of serum and urine sodium gives information on potential inappropriate secretion of antidiuretic hormone (ADH), but such determinations are not always feasible. Therefore, after correction of the estimated fluid deficit, the amount of fluids administered should be limited to 1000 ml/m^2 per day. Several studies show that the prognosis is better than one would think on account of Western experience.

PREVENTION

Most cases of bacterial meningitis should be, at least in principle, preventable since several meningococcal, pneumococcal and *H. influenzae* vaccines have been developed in recent years.

Against *meningococcal* disease, caused by group A, a *polysaccharide vaccine* has proved efficacious e.g. in Nigeria, Egypt, Brazil and the Sudan. Because most epidemics are due to group A, it is an important vaccine for developing countries and often coupled with a vaccine against the group C (A+C). The groups Y and W_{135} are of minor importance, and the group B (against which no vaccine is commercially available) has so far been the problem of industrialised countries. A or A+C vaccine is to be used in combatting epidemics at the earliest possible stage. In shortage of vaccine, as often is the case, children (up to 15 years of age) should be the primary target group. A single dose of vaccine is sufficient.

The polysaccharide vaccines have two problems: the relatively short (3–10 years) duration of efficacy without an immunological memory, and poor or non-existent efficacy of many of them in children under 2 years old.[15]

Chemical conjugation of the capsular polysaccharide to a carrier protein has led to a great success of elimination of *H. influenzae* meningitis in several countries.[16,17] At present, there are four slightly different conjugate vaccines on the market, all effective and with a great potential of decreasing the incidence of *H. influenzae* diseases, if widely used in the first months of life. Two or three doses are required, and they may be combined with other routine vaccines of infancy. This approach would decrease the otherwise high cost of the vaccine.

The basic problem with the *pneumococcal vaccines* is that over 80 types of pneumococci are capable of causing infection. Fortunately, not all types are equally common in meningitis but, on the other hand, the prevalence of each type varies from country to country. Hence, an effective vaccine should always comprise at least several capsular polysaccharides of pneumococci. Because many components of the present polysaccharide vaccines are not immunogenic and protective in infants, one anticipates an approach similar to that with *H. influenzae* vaccines; the conjugation technology hopefully solves the greatest theoretical problems – after which come those of logistics and economics.

References

1. Peltola H. Meningococcal disease: still with us. Rev Infect Dis 1983; 5: 71–91.
2. Schwartz B, Moore PS, Broome CV. The global epidemiology of meningococcal disease. Clin Microbiol Rev 1989; 2: S118–24.
3. Lapeyssonnie L. La méningite cérébrospinale en Afrique. Bull WHO 1963;28(Suppl): 1–114.
4. Moore PS. Meningococcal meningitis in Sub-Saharan Africa: a model for the epidemic process. Clin Infect Dis 1992; 14: 515–25.
5. Rey M, Lafaix Ch, Diop Mar I, Trevoux C. Aspects épidémiologiques des méningites purulents en Afrique tropicale (d'apres 1052 cas observés à Dakar). Lyon Medical 1972;228: 503–8.
6. Cadoz M, Denis F, Diop Mar I. Etude épidémiologique des cas de méningites purulents hospitalisés à Dakar pendant la décenne 1970–1979. Bull WHO 1981;59:575–84.
7. Valmari P, Peltola H. Serum C-reactive protein: A valuable differentiator between viral and bacterial meningitis. Infections in Medicine 1987;4:308–11.
8. MacFarlane JT, Anjorin FI, Cleland PG, et al. Single injection treatment of meningococcal meningitis. 1. Long-acting penicillin. Trans R Soc Med Hyg 1979;73:693–7.
9. Wali SS, MacFarlane JT, Weir WRC, et al. Single injection treatment of meningococcal meningi-
tis. 2. Long-acting chloramphenicol. Trans R Soc Trop Med Hyg 1979;73:698–702.
10. Liebowitz LD, Koornhof HJ, Barrett M, et al. Bacterial meningitis in Johannesburg 1980–1982. S Afr Med J 1984;66:677–9.
11. Peltola H, Anttila M, Renkonen O-V, The Finnish Study Group. Randomised comparison of chloramphenicol, ampicillin, cefotaxime, and ceftriaxone for childhood bacterial meningitis. Lancet 1989;i: 1281–7.
12. Lebel MH, Freij BJ, Syrogiannopoulos GA, et al. Dexamethasone therapy for bacterial meningitis. Results of two double-flind, placebo-controlled trials. N Engl J Med 1988;319:964–71.
13. Kilpi T, Peltola H, Kallio MK, et al. Oral glycerol and intravenous dexamethasone in preventing hearing impairment due to childhood bacterial meningitis. 33rd Interscience Conference on Antimicrobial Agents and Chemotherapy, 17-20 October 1993, New Orleans LA. Abstract 1148.
14. Schaad UB, Lips U, Gnehm HE, et al. Dexamaethasone therapy for bacterial meningitis in children. Lancet 1993;342:457–61.
15. Reingold AL, Broome CV, Hightower AW, et al. Age-specific differences in duration of clinical protection after vaccination with meningococcal polysaccharide A vaccine. Lancet 1985;ii:114–8.
16. Eskola J, Peltola H, Takala AK, et al. Efficacy of *Haemophilus influenzae* type b polysaccharide-diphtheria toxoid conjugate vaccine in infancy. N Engl J Med 1987;317:717–22.
17. Peltola H, Kilpi T, Anttila M. Rapid disappearance of *Haemophilus influenzae* type b meningitis after routine childhood immunisation with conjugate vaccines. Lancet 1992; 340: 592–4.
18. Greenwood B, Bradley AK, Cleland PG, et al. An epidemic of meningococcal infection at Zaria, northern Nigeria. I General epidemiological features. Trans R Soc Trop Med Hyg 1979;73:557-62.

About the author

Heikki Peltola is specialist in pediatrics, pediatric infectious diseases, and general surgery and traumatology. He also holds the Diploma in Tropical Medicine and Hygiene from London. For 20 years he has participated in the national programmes on meningococcal, H. influenzae, and measles–mumps–rubella vaccinations in Finland. As a clinician, Heikki Peltola is currently focusing in treatment of bacterial meningitis and orthopedic infections especially in Latin America. At the University of Helsinki he is the Head of the Division of Infectious Diseases in the Department of Pediatrics.

Lankinen KS, Bergström S, Mäkelä PH and Peltomaa M, eds.
Health and disease in developing countries. London:The Macmillan Press Limited, 1994:271–280.

28 COMMON SKIN DISEASES

Hannu Paajanen, M.D.
Oulaskangas Regional Hospital
FIN-86301 Oulainen
Finland

INTRODUCTION

Poverty, over-crowding and inadequate hygiene contribute to the spread of many skin diseases making them common in developing countries. They are seldom life-threatening but can cause notable disability. Leprosy can be physically debilitating and often leads to social segregation. Scabies, on the other hand, is primarily a relatively trivial problem, although a very itchy one. At the same time it is a major cause of acquired heart and kidney diseases, due to secondary infection of the skin lesions.

In principle the prevention of many skin infections is easy: water and soap are enough. Producing sufficient quantities of water, however, may require considerable changes and investments in the community. Perhaps a new water and sanitation system is needed, and housing has to be improved. The workload of women who fetch the water has to be alleviated, etc. Inadequate hygiene is not only due to material short-comings but also to ignorance. Therefore health education is of utmost importance in the prevention of skin infections.

DIAGNOSTICS AND TREATMENT

The diagnosis of skin diseases is mainly based on observations of the nature of skin lesions, their distribution in different parts of the body, behaviour (itching, spreading, tenderness, loss of sensation) and the duration of symptoms. Similar skin changes in family members may give a clue to diagnosis, and knowledge of

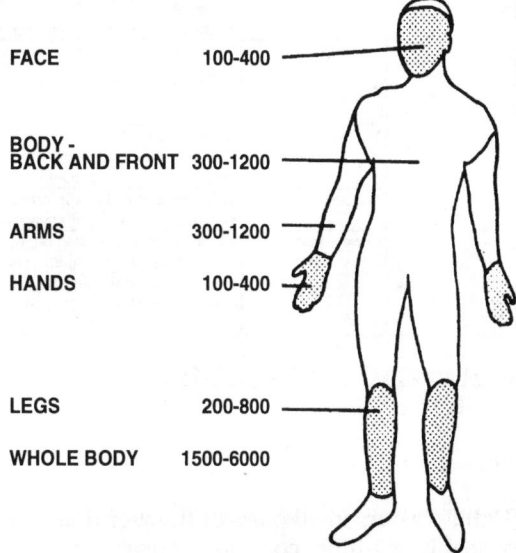

FACE	100-400
BODY - BACK AND FRONT	300-1200
ARMS	300-1200
HANDS	100-400
LEGS	200-800
WHOLE BODY	1500-6000

Figure 28.1. Guideline for estimating the monthly consumption of ointments (g/month) when the treatment is applied twice daily. Courtesy of Orion-Farmos, Finland.

local epidemiology is also valuable. Table 28.1 outlines the diseases according to their clinical characteristics and also briefly describes the treatment.

A particular problem in developing countries is the extent of skin changes. For example the lesions of a fungal infection, scabies or dermatitis may cover the whole body from top to toe. Hence the consumption of ointments can be extraordinarily high. Figure 28.1 gives an idea of how much ointment may be needed in a month for different parts of the body.

Table 28.1. Common skin conditions: nature of lesion, possible causes and treatment in short.[4]

Nature of lesion	Possible causes	Description of lesions	Treatment
Itchy rash	Scabies	very itchy symmetrically distributed papules, vesicles or pustules between fingers and toes, on wrists, elbows, ankles buttocks and genitals similar lesions in family members	wash properly apply 25% benzyl benzoate or 1% gamma benzene hexachloride for 24 hours treat the whole family at the same time wash clothes, blankets, etc.
	Fungal infection	typically a slowly growing ring with raised edges and a tendency to central healing and scaling ('ringworm') anywhere on the body, also in the scalp itchy fissures and sogginess of the skin between the toes	wash with water and soap Whitfield's ointment or benzoic acid ointment b.d. until the lesions disappear imidazole derivatives topically or orally if available gentian violet or Castellani's solution for moist lesions
	Lice	itchy, pinpoint, flat and reddish lesions behind the ears, in the nape, around the waist	the same as in scabies
	Eczema	symmetrical, itchy, raised, scaly, sometimes oozing lesions on legs and arms, in the buttocks	Whitfield's or sulphur ointment to dry lesions gentian violet or Castellani's solution to oozing lesions steroid ointments if available
	Urticaria, hives	itchy white wheals on reddish base; disappear quickly while new ones emerge at other sites	try to define the cause, if a drug reaction is suspected, discontinue the drug, calamine lotion topically, antihistamine to control the itching
	Strongyloidosis	transient, linear, itchy wheals, move rapidly, disappear in 1-2 hours on the trunk and buttocks, near the anus	thiabendazole 50 mg/kg in two doses for 3 days albendazole
	Onchocercosis	intensely itchy papular rash may be confined to one anatomical region only	ivermectin
	Chigger	very itchy small abscess typically under or at the root of a nail	dissect the roof of the abscess and remove the flea apply an antiseptic in the cavity
	Myiasis	itchy, quite painless boil any part of the body that has contact with the seams of infected clothing	obstruct the respiratory spiracles of the larva with an oily substance to force it out
	Sunburn	erythema of the skin with itching or burning sensation, blistering in severe cases	cool, wet dressings, emulsion ointments
	Prickly heat rash	papular or vesicular rash on an erythematous skin with severe itching and prickling which may come on in waves in the bends of the elbows and knees, in the axillae, round the waist and over the sternum	cool and dry the involved areas, avoid sweating, use loose and light clothing apply zinc oxide powder or calamine lotion to the lesions, peroral antihistamine for the itch

PARASITIC DISEASES WITH SKIN LESIONS

Scabies

Scabies occurs in all parts of the world and is probably the most common cause of itching skin lesions in developing countries. The itch mite, *Sarcoptes scabiei*, causes human scabies by spreading from person to person in direct contact and through bedding and clothing. Scabies affects persons of all ages but infants and young children tend to suffer more. A chronically infected person develops an immunological tolerance to the mite, which lessens itching and controls the expansion of infection.

Usually scabies is a disease of the whole family. The source of the infection is frequently the mother, whose own disease gives only mild symptoms. Secondary streptococcal infection of the lesions is the cause of major morbidity and may result in glomerulonephritis or acquired valvular disease of the heart.

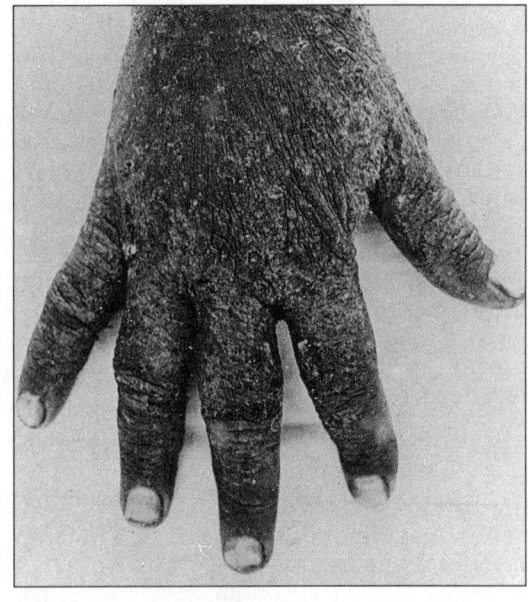

Norwegian or crusted scabies affecting fingers.
Photo: C. James Webb

Table 28.1. Continued

Nature of lesion	Possible causes	Description of lesions	Treatment
Ulcers	Tropical ulcer	round or ovoid single lesions with a deep crater base covered with slough >90% in the lower leg or foot	remove the pus daily with antiseptic soaks (e.g. hydrogen peroxide or sodium hypochlorite) cover the ulcer with gauze soaked in the antiseptic, use non-adherent dressings when the ulcer is dry and change them once a week give a course of penicillin or metronidazole at the initial stage
	Cancrum oris	painful, develops rapidly involves the mouth and may cause a large defect affects malnourished children	large doses of penicillin the earliest possible improve the nutritional status surgical repair may be needed
	Cutaneous leishmaniasis	single or multiple, quite painless ulcers, usually on the face or extremities the ulcers have a raised, firm and not undermined edge tendency to spontaneous cure	prevention of secondary infection may suffice
	Yaws	the primary lesion is papilloma-like, round or ovoid, 2-5 cm in diameter, in distal parts of extremities the early lesions are papillomas or papules and exude highly infective liquid the late lesions are destructive gummas	long-acting penicillin is the drug of choice at all stages of the disease
	Syphilis	the primary lesion is a painless ulcer with indurated base the secondary lesions are pinkish or pigmented spots on flexor surfaces of the body; they tend to become confluent and indurated the tertiary lesions are slow growing painless ulcerations or punched-out ulcers that appear on the upper trunk, face, scalp and below the knee	long-acting penicillin for 12 days tetracycline for 10 days treat all sexual contacts
	Lymphogranuloma venereum	enlarged lymph nodes (buboes) in groin that undergo suppuration painful, oozing sores in the anus in females	tetracycline for at least 2 weeks treat all sexual contacts
Skin infections	Impetigo	start as reddish spots which develop quickly into superficial blisters that rupture and form crusts typical locations are the face, neck, scalp, hands and feet	wash with water and soap apply gentian violet or antibiotic ointment give systemic antibiotics if the lesions are extensive or don't respond to local treatment
	Pyoderma	septic skin lesions anywhere on the body, which may be secondarily infected insect bites, wounds, etc.	as for impetigo
	Erysipelas	a swollen, red and very tender area with a sharply defined, slightly elevated edge fever, prostration usually on a leg, arm or on the face	give penicillin parenterally or perorally give an analgesic for pain
	Boils	a consequence of minor injuries or unsterile injections	drain the abscess in its softest spot give antibiotics if the patient has fever or there are signs of cellulitis

Clinical features and diagnosis. Itching is the chief symptom of scabies and is maximal at night. At the initial stage the skin lesions are itchy papules. There may also be vesicles and pustules, burrows and scrapings. They appear first in the finger-webs and the sides of fingers, wrists and between toes. Later the lesions spread to elbows, armpits, nipples and inframammary folds, buttocks, genitals and ankles. Infants may have lesions also in the face, scalp, neck, palms and soles. The diagnosis is based on the typically distributed, symmetrical and very itchy lesions. If the rash doesn't itch, its most probably not scabies! A history of similar skin lesions in family members strongly suggests scabies. Scabies mites can be directly demonstrated in the burrows but it is rarely necessary.

Treatment. Benzyl benzoate is an inexpensive and effective treatment for scabies. Adults and children over 3 years of age are treated with a 25 per cent emulsion of benzyl benzoate; for younger children dilute the emulsion 1:1. According to local availability, gamma benzene hexachloride (1 per cent solution), sulphur ointment (5–10 per cent), crotamiton (Eurax®) or monosulfiram can also be used. Some traditional medicinal plants may also be effective. For children under 4 years and especially infants sulphur ointment twice a day is advisable because other medications tend to cause skin irritation.

Wash the body thoroughly with water and soap and spread the lotion all over the body, avoiding face and mucous membranes. Leave the lotion on for 24 hours during which time itching is significantly reduced. Wash the lotion off on the following day and change into clean clothes. Wash the clothes and bedding at the time of treatment. Always treat the whole family simultaneously. Repeat treatment should be after 5–7 days to destroy the mites hatching from the eggs, not killed in the first round of treatment.

Lice

There are three types of lice, namely the head louse, the body louse and the pubic louse. The head louse and pubic louse lay the eggs (so called nits) at the base of hairs, the body louse in the seams of clothing. Lack of cleanliness and infrequent washing of the clothes favour the spread of lice. The pubic louse is transmitted in sexual contacts.

Being blood-suckers the lice can transmit diseases from man to man. In particular body louse can be the vector of relapsing fever and epidemic typhus. Relapsing fever is caused by *Borrelia* species and encountered in most parts of the world where the hygienic conditions are suitable. Epidemic typhus (louse-borne typhus) is a rickettsial disease that is endemic in Andean Highlands in South America and found also in Eastern Africa and in parts of the Himalayas.

Clinical features and diagnosis. Itching is the main symptom of louse infestations. The lice pierce the skin to suck blood causing pinpoint, flat, reddish lesions. The head lice especially involve areas behind the ears and the nape. Scratching the lesions may cause secondary infection. The diagnosis is based on demonstrating the nits or adult lice in the hair or seams of clothing.

Treatment. Benzyl benzoate and gamma benzene hexachloride are effective agents to destroy lice. They are applied to the affected areas and washed off after 24 hours. The whole family ought to be treated at the same time. Repeat the treatment after a week to kill the newly hatched lice. The nits can be removed with a fine comb. Body lice are killed by washing the clothes and the bedding.

Sand flea, jigger, chigger

Sand flea, *Tunga penetrans*, is endemic in Central and South America, Africa and the west coast of India. Its main host is the pig but it can also live in man. The fertilised female sand flea causes the symptoms by attaching itself to the sole, a toe or to the side of foot. In children the fleas can also establish themselves in the thighs, buttocks or genitals.

Clinical features and treatment. The infection is acquired by walking barefoot. The first sign is an intense itching at the site where the sand flea is penetrating the skin. Its favourite site is under or at the root of a nail. It matures in a few days and creates a small swelling, which contains the egg-filled body of the female flea. The expanding flea causes irritation and itching. If left undisturbed, the flea matures in 8–12 days and the eggs are discharged through a small ulceration which may develop into a septic ulcer or cause tetanus.

Treatment consists of dissecting the roof of the cavity with a needle and removing the flea intact. In endemic areas the procedure is done with great skill by local people. Some antiseptic should be applied in the cavity to prevent secondary infection.

Myiasis

Myiasis means a condition in which the maggots of some flies develop in living tissue. *Cordylobia anthropophaga* (tumbu fly) is the cause of subcutaneous myiasis in Sub-Saharan Africa. The female fly lays its eggs on sandy ground or in the seams of clothing hanging in shaded areas. It the warmth of the body the eggs develop into invasive larvae, which penetrate the skin quickly and painlessly. The initial lesion is a papule that may be itchy. The papule grows into a boil-like, quite painless lesion in about a week. The respiratory spiracles of the larva emerge as black marks as they penetrate the head of the boil, which distinguishes it from an ordinary boil. The lesions may be numerous and situated on the arms, genitals and other areas of the body that have had contact with the seams of infected clothing.

The larvae of *Dermatobia hominis* cause a similar condition in tropical America but the mode of transmission is different. The female fly lays its eggs directly on foliage or other insects that convey them to the host.

Treatment. When the respiratory spiracles of the larva are obstructed with an oily substance, it starts wriggling out and can be removed with forceps or by manual expression.

Prevention. All clothing and towels should be dried in direct sunlight and ironed carefully to prevent the African form of subcutaneous myiasis. Prevention of the American form requires measures to control the fly.

Other skin conditions caused by parasites

Cutaneous leishmaniasis (CL) is one of the commonest causes of chronic skin ulcerations in the world. The clinical picture of CL is manifold and depends on the species of *Leishmania* For details, see Chapter 21.

Strongyloidosis and onchocercosis also involve skin symptoms and problems, which are presented in Chapter 20.

FUNGAL SKIN INFECTIONS

Fungal infections of the skin and scalp are also associated with inadequate hygiene and the best prevention is water and soap. Warm and humid conditions increase susceptibility.

Clinical features and diagnosis. A fungal skin lesion starts as a papule, which grows slowly larger from its edges. Typically it is a well-demarcated ring (ringworm) with raised, reddish edges and perhaps small vesicles. As the ring grows, the centre starts healing and may appear quite normal or be covered with scales. The lesions may itch mildly and become secondarily infected due to scratching. In the scalp the fungus also infects the hair, which breaks off forming bald lesions covered with scales or crusts. In nails fungi cause deformation, thickening, yellow discolouration and fragility.

Fungal infections of the feet are especially a problem for shoe wearers. Fungi like the warm and moist space between the toes and cause itching, fissuring and sogginess of the interdigital space.

Pityriasis versicolor (*versi color* = different colour) is widespread in hot and humid environments. It presents with mild pruritis and superficial scaly patches, which become hypopigmented. The lesions are readily visible in pigmented races. They tend to unite and form large hypopigmented areas, sometimes hiding the normal skin colour. The diagnosis is based on the typical skin changes and can be confirmed by scraping scales from the edge of a lesion. Spores and other fungal structures can be demonstrated microscopically after incubating the scales for a few minutes in a drop of potassium hydroxide (KOH).

Treatment. Various ointments based on salicylic or benzoic acid e.g. Whitfield's ointment (6 per cent benzoic acid and 3 per cent salicylic acid) are the most economical way to treat fungal infections. The ointment is applied to the affected areas twice a day after washing. Treatment should continue for some

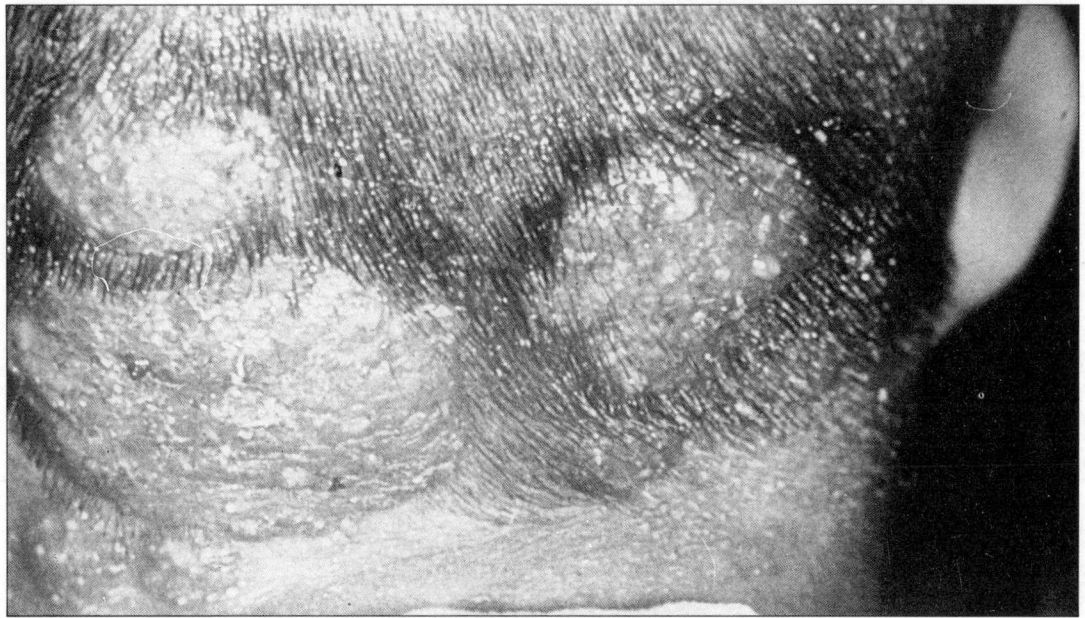

Ringworm at back of the neck. Photo: C.James Webb

time after the lesions have clinically healed. Castellani's solution and gentian violet are also effective, particularly for moist lesions. Imidazole derivatives are effective but costly fungicides that are available both in topical and oral form.

Fungal infections of the feet are treated in the same way as described above. Good hygiene should be maintained by washing the feet often and by changing the socks daily. The shoes should be as open as possible to allow free evaporation of sweat.

BACTERIAL SKIN INFECTIONS

Impetigo and secondary skin infections

Oozing lesions with crust formation are typical for bacterial skin infections. The infection is often secondary to a primary lesion, e.g. fungal infection, scabies or insect bite. Infected insect bites may lead to a condition called multiple skin sepsis. All infections of the skin can be dangerous because of the possibility of generalised infection.

Impetigo is a very contagious primary skin infection caused usually by streptococci and staphylococci. The lesions are normally on the face, neck, scalp, hands and feet but can appear in any part of the body. They start usually as reddish spots which develop quickly into superficial blisters. The blisters break easily leaving a moist surface that forms crusts. The

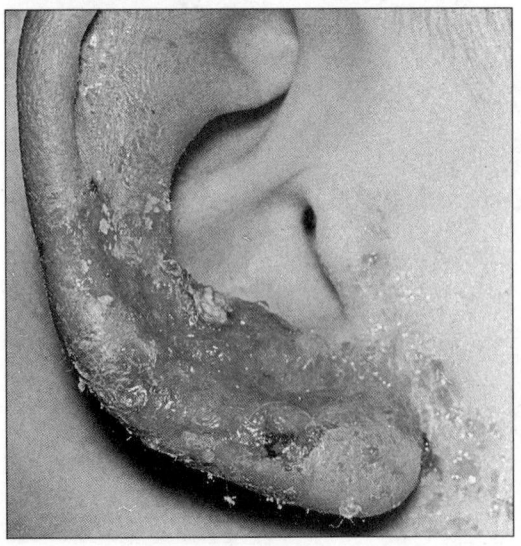

Impetigo on ear lobe. Photo: C. James Webb

lesions spread rapidly into other parts of the body.

Treatment. Wash the infected areas with water and soap to remove the crusts. Potassium permanganate or hypochlorite solution can be added to the water. Washing is followed by local application of gentian violet or antibiotic ointment. Systemic antibiotics like penicillin, sulphonamide or erythromycin should be used if the lesions are extensive or do not respond to local treatment.

Erysipelas

Erysipelas is an acute streptococcal infection of the skin and the underlying connective tissue (= cellulitis). Most often it affects the face, an arm or a leg. The skin over the affected area is swollen, red and very tender. There may be vesicles or bullae. A characteristic finding is a sharply defined, slightly elevated border. The patient has also fever and other signs of septic infection.

Other forms of cellulitis without a sharply demarcated border are caused by bacteria like staphylococci and *Haemophilus influenzae*.

Treatment. Erysipelas responds well to systemic penicillin, which may initially be given parenterally. Erythromycin is an alternative. In other forms of cellulitis the antibiotic must be chosen according to the local resistance situation of the likely causative agent.

Abscesses

Deficiencies in general hygiene, unsterile injections and various minor injuries are probably one explanation for the common occurrence of abscesses in developing countries. A developing abscess is hard and tender and the skin over the area is reddish. A ripe abscess feels warm and fluctuant. Its diameter may be more than 10 cm.

An injection abscess develops slowly, sometimes in the course of a couple of weeks. The inflammation reaction is moderate and the contents of the abscess may be sterile. In principle, injection abscesses shouldn't occur at all. They indicate inappropriate techniques in administering injections and necessitate a revision of the practices.

Treatment. Opening the abscess is sufficient if there is no fever, malaise or other general symptoms. The abscess is drained with an incision in its softest spot. Rinse the cavity with saline when pus has come out and insert a strip of rubber or wet gauze in the opening to prevent it from closing too early. A systemic antibiotic is necessary if the patient is febrile or if the local reaction around the abscess is extensive or in the case of multiple abscesses.

Wound infections

Wounds and wound infections are common in developing countries. The principles for treating wound infections are the same as for tropical ulcer. Tetanus infection is in most cases acquired through wounds, and its possibility should always be kept in mind when treating wounds. Therefore, tetanus vaccination or a booster dose must be given to every person, who has not been previously vaccinated or who has received the last booster more than 5 years ago.

Tropical ulcer

Tropical ulcer (TU) is a common, acute or chronic skin disease that affects mainly children and young adults in tropical and subtropical areas. Several researchers have observed anaerobic fusiform bacteria and spirochetes in samples taken from the ulcers. Therefore infection is a likely cause of TU. Malnutrition, trauma, poor personal hygiene, poor sanitation and exposure to mud or slow-moving water may contribute to the disease. **Clinical features.** Tropical ulcer usually involves the skin and the superficial subcutaneous tissue but in severe cases the underlying muscle, tendons and even bone can also be affected. More than 90 per cent of TUs are in the lower leg or foot. The first sign of TU is a local, tender swelling, followed by a vesicle that bursts and sloughs leading to the development of ulcer. Early ulcers are painful and may enlarge for many weeks. Fully formed ulcers are usually round or ovoid single lesions with deep crater and base covered by yellow slough. The edges are raised and sometimes slightly undermined. TU may become chronic persisting for months or even years but sometimes it heals spontaneously.

The commonest complications of TU are infections that can spread to the underlying bone and cause osteomyelitis or to a joint and result in bacterial arthritis. Contamination of the wound with *Clostridium tetani* causes tetanus if the person is not adequately vaccinated. A malignant transformation of the ulceration is also a possibility, although a rare one.

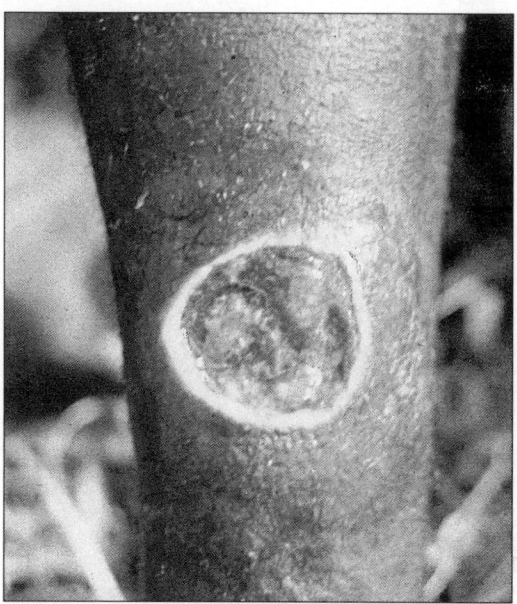

Tropical ulcer on lower leg. Photo: C. James Webb

Treatment. Procaine penicillin or metronidazole for 5–7 days at the acute stage relieves the pain and inflammation. The basis of the treatment of TU, however, is local treatment. Initially its aim is to create optimal conditions for the healing process by removing pus and slough. The local treatment aims at protecting the ulceration from trauma and re-infection when healing is under way.

Antiseptic soaks clean the ulcer. Suitable alternatives are potassium permanganate solution ($KMnO_4$, 1 gram or pinch in a litre of water), sodium hypochlorite, hydrogen peroxide (1–3 per cent) or saline, if nothing else is available. Remove pus and slough daily and cover the ulcer with gauze soaked in the solution or paint it with gentian violet. A plastic occlusion prevents the dressing from drying out and adhering to the ulceration. If an occlusion can not be used, the dressing must be removed very gently by soaking it thoroughly in saline in order not to destroy the newly formed epithelium. This phase continues until the floor of the ulcer is completely clean.

Non-adherent dressings protect the fragile, healthy granulation of the ulcer. This kind of dressing can be made by impregnating gauze with any locally available oil or petroleum jelly and sterilising it. Commercial brands are also available but they are costly. Change the dressing about once a week. If the ulcer is clean, reapply a new non-adherent dressing. If

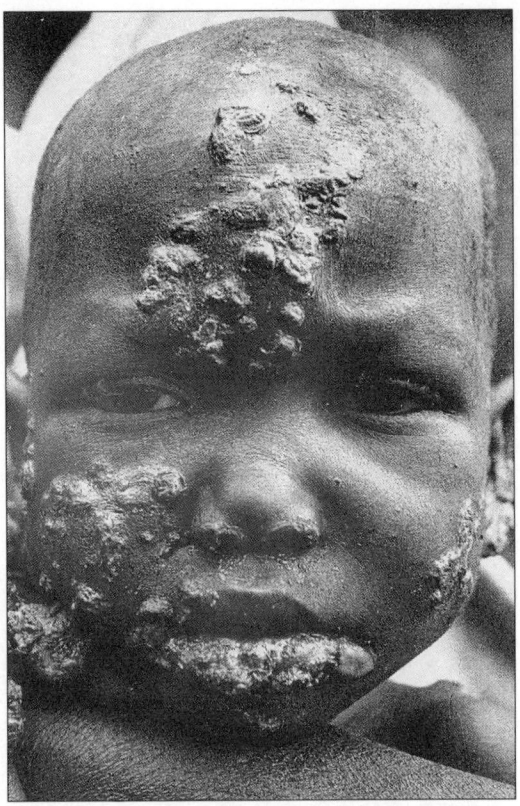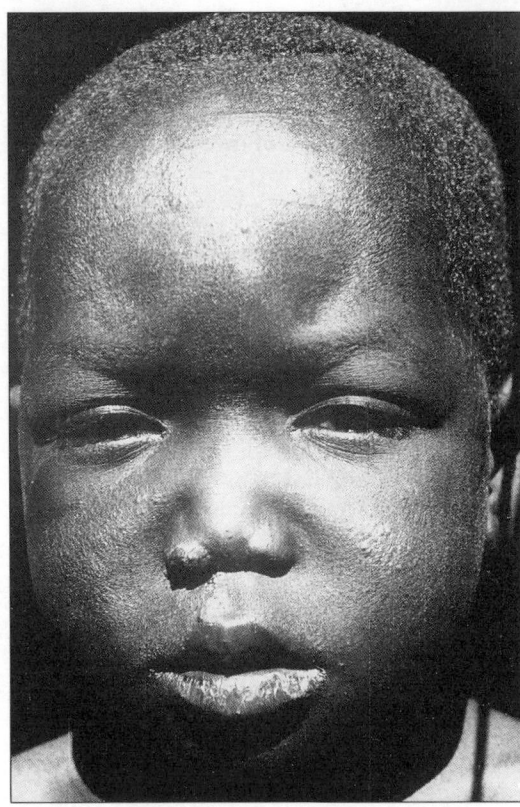

Yaws lesions on the face of a Liberian boy. Photo on the right is taken two weeks after treament with penicillin. Lesions have cleared almost completely. Photo: WHO/Dr Hackett

there are signs of infection, return to treatment with wet antiseptic dressings until the infection abates.

Cancrum oris

Cancrum oris is a necrotic ulceration of the face caused by the same bacteria that are present in early tropical ulcers (Chapter 54). It affects mainly malnourished children. Cancrum oris is very painful and develops rapidly. It involves the mouth and may cause a large defect revealing the mouth cavity.

Cancrum oris is treated with large doses of penicillin as soon as possible. Improving the nutritional status is also important. The defect may require surgical repair.

Skin manifestations of the treponematoses

Syphilis has various cutaneous manifestations. The primary lesion is a red papule that soon forms a painless ulcer with a hard base.

It occurs normally in the genital area and heals in 4–8 months in untreated patients. In secondary syphilis the lesions are usually symmetrical spots that are pinkish or pale red in whites and pigmented in dark skinned persons. The lesions are on flexor surfaces of the body and tend to become confluent and indurated. The lesions of tertiary syphilis develop years after primary infection. They may be slowly growing non-tender ulcerations or punched-out ulcers. They may occur anywhere in the body although the typical sites are the upper trunk, the face, the scalp and the leg just below the knee.

In congenital syphilis the characteristic lesions are bullous eruptions of the palms and soles and papular rashes around the mouth and nose and in the nappy area. A generalised lymphadenopathy is also present.

Yaws is a disease of hot and humid conditions. It is found in tropical South American countries as well as in West and Central Africa. It transmits on direct contact from infective lesions. The initial lesion develops usually in the distal parts of the extremities. It is 2–5 centimetres in diameter, round or oval resembling a papilloma, persists for many months and resolves spontaneously. The initial lesion is followed by early lesions which are divided into two types, major and minor. The major lesions are large papillomas and papules of the size of grain of rice. The lesions exude highly infective liquid. The minor lesions are small, dry papules which are scattered all over the body and may itch. There may also be numerous plantar papillomas which develop many years (up to 20) after the primary lesion and are very painful. The late lesions of the skin are destructive gummas which may persist for years.

Treatment. Long-acting penicillin is the drug of choice both in syphilis and yaws.

MISCELLANEOUS SKIN CONDITIONS

Eczemas

Various infections (bacterial, fungal or parasitic) constitute more than half of all skin ailments in developing countries. Of the rest, eczema along with allergic skin reactions form a notable part. Eczema is characterised by raised, itching, scaling and sometimes oozing lesions, which demarcate quite clearly from the surrounding skin. Due to scratching and secondary infection the affected skin becomes thickened.

Nummular eczema is common in adults. It has well-defined discoid or round lesions, which appear symmetrically on the legs and arms. Atopic eczema is a children's complaint, which starts often during the first year of life with very itchy lesions in the proximity of joints, in the face and in the buttocks. It is a common problem in industrialised countries but relatively unusual in developing countries with significant regional variations. It is in many cases associated with food allergies, and therefore presumably more prevalent in areas where the breast-feeding period is short and the consumption of formulas, dairy products, eggs, fish and tomatoes starts early.

Adverse effects of various drugs are a common cause of skin reactions in developing countries, because all kinds of medicaments are freely available. Hives (urticaria) is probably the most common one reaction form. It starts with a sudden appearance of white edematous wheals on reddish base, which are very itchy. The lesions tend to disappear quickly while new ones emerge at other sites.

Treatment. Oozing and crusted lesions have to be washed with water and soap to remove the crusts. Gentian violet can be applied to dry up the lesions. It should be available even at the most distant clinics. Castellani's solution (magenta paint) is another alternative. When the lesions are dry, the treatment can be continued with Whitfield's ointment or sulphur ointments. Steroid ointments are very useful when available. Treat secondary infections with penicillin or sulphonamides besides the local treatment. If a drug reaction is suspected, discontinue the drug. Antihistamines are useful for controlling the itching.

Cracking of the feet

Walking barefoot subjects the feet constantly to trauma and leads to thickening of the skin in the exposed areas. New trauma and the skin-drying effect of walking barefoot cause cracking of the feet. The cracks may be painful and predispose to deep infections of the foot.

Treatment. Vaseline or any local (cooking) oil are suitable for softening the skin. Ointments containing salicylic acid (e.g. Whitfield's) or carbamide can also be used due to their keratolytic and antibacterial effect. Infections are treated according to the principles described above.

Effects of the sun

Sunburn is a common complaint among fair skinned expatriates in developing countries, because they lack the protective pigment of the indigenous population. Usually sunburn is a result of overexposure of the skin to the ultraviolet radiation of sunshine, but in some cases the culprit is a drug (e.g. tetracyclines, sulpha derivatives, phenothiazines, thiazides and topical antihistamine ointments) that enhances the effect of the sun on the skin. Skin changes range from mild erythema with subsequent scaling to pain, swelling, skin tenderness and blisters from prolonged exposure. Constitutional symptoms may appear if a large portion of the body is affected. Secondary infection is the most common late complication of sunburn and a long-term, unprotected exposure to sunshine increases the risk of skin malignancies.

Prickly heat or *miliaria* is an acute pruritic eruption which is found in those parts of the skin where evaporation is poor. It is caused by obstruction of the sweat ducts which retains the sweat in the skin and causes severe itching and prickling which may come on in waves. The rash consists of papules or vesicles on an erythematous skin. The lesions are typically in the bends of the elbows and knees, in the axillae, round the waist and over the sternum.

Treatment and prevention. In sunburn watery ointments (emulsion) and wet dressings cool down the skin. Peroral antihistamines alleviate itching and in severe cases hydrocortisone emulsion relieves the symptoms effectively. It can be prevented by using appropriate clothing and sun-barrier ointments and by avoiding excessive exposure to sun. A very effective and cheap sun-barrier is 5–10 per cent para-amino benzoic acid in ethyl alcohol or in a gel.

Prickly heat can be prevented and relieved by cooling and drying the involved areas and by avoiding sweating and using loose, airy and light clothing. Zinc oxide powder or calamine lotion can be applied to the lesions and peroral antihistamines control the itching and prickling. Air-conditioning is useful if available.

Skin changes in nutritional deficiencies

Pellagra is caused by a deficiency of nicotinic acid. It is prevalent in areas where the diet consists mostly of maize without any supplements. The clinical features of pellagra are manifold but the triad: diarrhea, dermatitis and dementia is well known. The exposed surfaces of the skin become sensitive to sunshine (solar eczema). The eruption starts with a symmetrical, painful erythema of the hands, forearms, neck, face and feet that becomes gradually hyperpigmented, scaly and rough. A ring and collar round the neck is a characteristic eruption.

Kwashiorkor (protein–energy malnutrition, Chapter 31) presents sometimes with a flaky paint rash. It appears in the arms and legs, especially near the big joints. It starts with hyperpigmentation of the skin which is followed by peeling off the skin in large pieces (flakes). The remaining skin is hypopigmented and atrophic. Edema and other signs of malnutrition are usually also present.

Cutaneous manifestations of HIV infection

Cutaneous manifestations of HIV infection are common. They include a wide variety of infectious and inflammatory disorders and may precede the development actual immune deficiency. The most common skin changes are various bacterial, fungal and viral infections, severe scabies, eczemas and Kaposi's sarcoma.

Additional reading

1. Bell DR. Lecture notes on tropical medicine. 2nd ed. London: Blackwell Scientific, 1985.
2. King M, King F, Martodipoero S. Primary child care. Book 1. Oxford: Oxford Medical, 1984.
3. Manson-Bahr PEC, Bell DR. Manson's tropical diseases. 19th ed. London: Baillière Tindall, 1987.
4. Hoverd C, Brown R. Tropical diseases: including aspects of hygiene, malnutrition and injuries. London: Macmillan, 1986.

About the author

Hannu Paajanen is a specialist in paediatrics and works currently as a consultant in paediatrics in Oulaskangas Regional Hospital, Finland. During 1986-88 he worked as a medical officer at a Namibian refugee centre in Central Angola. After returning from Angola he completed his specialisation in paediatrics in Oulu University Children's Hospital. Since 1991 he has been in his current position.

III CHALLENGES FOR HEALTH CARE

Lankinen KS, Bergström S, Mäkelä PH and Peltomaa M, eds.
Health and disease in developing countries. London:The Macmillan Press Limited, 1994:281–286.

29 INTEGRATED MANAGEMENT OF THE SICK CHILD

Sandy Gove M.D., MPH
World Health Organization, Division of Diarrhoeal and Acute Respiratory Disease Control
CH-1211 Geneva 27,
Switzerland

INTRODUCTION

The WHO and UNICEF are currently collaborating in the development of an integrated approach to the management of the sick child. Globally, ARI (mostly pneumonia), diarrhea, malaria, measles, and malnutrition cause seven out of ten deaths in children under 5 years of age in developing countries (Figure 29.1). The integrated guidelines for the management of the sick child focus the health workers' training and attention not on one but on all of the leading killers of young children which can be effectively managed with simple and affordable treatments.

These main contributors to death are also responsible for tremendous morbidity and disability, accounting for a large proportion of outpatient clinic visits. The integrated guidelines instruct the health workers to prevent serious disabilities, such as blindness resulting from measles and vitamin A deficiency. They also cover the management of the common illnesses that cause mothers to seek care, such as otitis media, a common cause of fever in young children and the leading preventable cause of deafness.

The relevant programmes and units at the WHO and UNICEF are working together to integrate their advice on clinical management

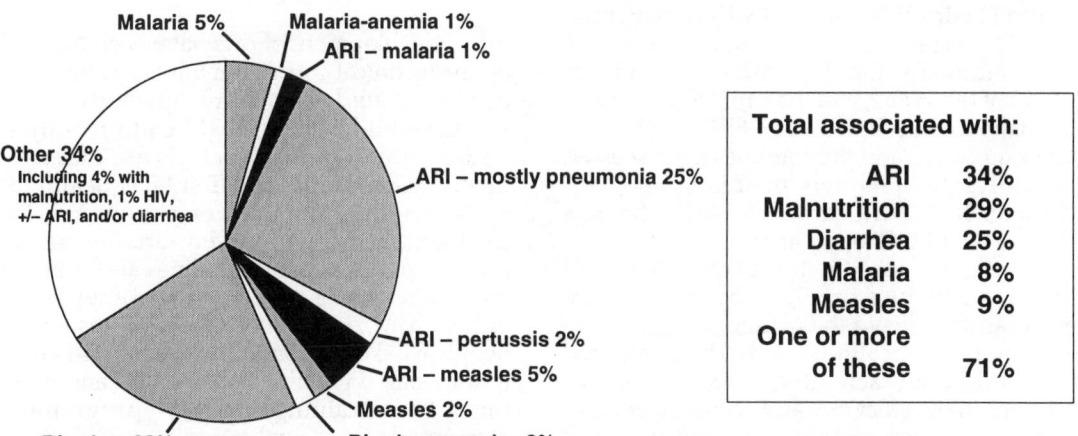

Figure 29.1. Distribution of 12.9 million deaths among children under 5 years old in all developing countries in 1990.

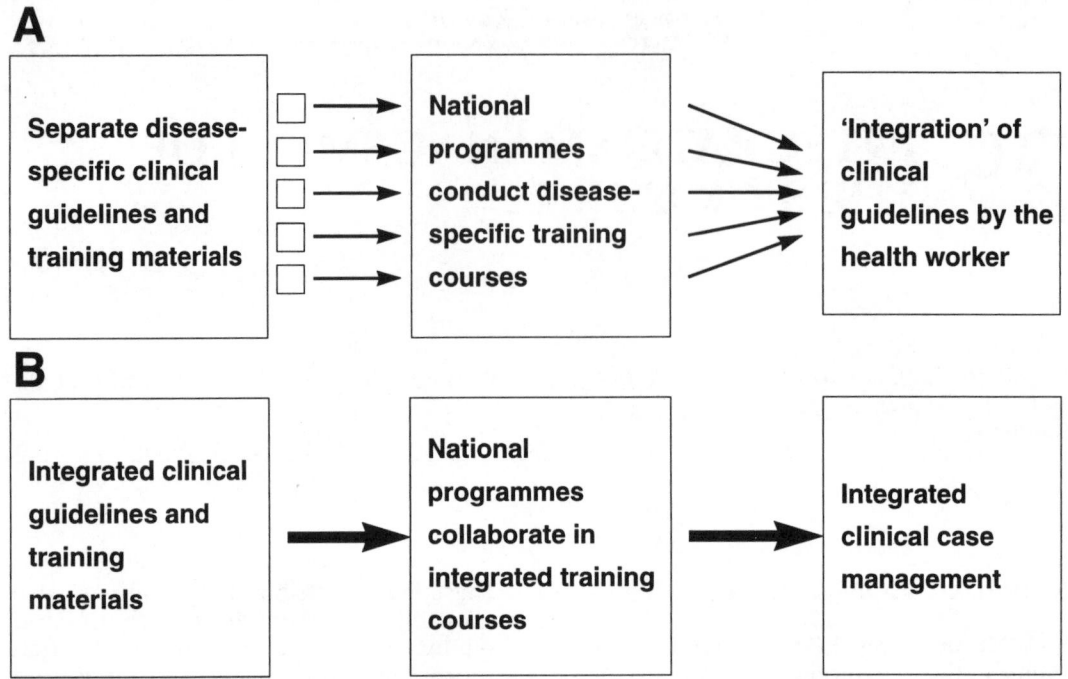

Figure 29.2. Old (A) and new (B) options for integrated management of the sick child.

and on the organisation of health services (Figure 29.2). This effort is coordinated by the WHO Division for the Control of Diarrhoeal and Acute Respiratory Disease (CDR) and involves the Programme for the Control of Acute Respiratory Infections (ARI), Diarrhoeal Disease Control Programme (CDD), Drug Action Programme (DAP), Expanded Programme on Immunization (EPI), Malaria Unit of CTD and TDR (MAL), Maternal and Child Health Programme (MCH), Nutrition (NUT), Oral Health (ORH), and the Programme for the Prevention of Blindness (PBL) of the WHO, and the Child Survival and Bamako Initiative Units of UNICEF. The separate questions and programmes are discussed in individual chapters of this book (ARI: Chapter 14, CDD: Chapter 15, DAP: Chapters 49 and 50, EPI: Chapter 48).

The disease-specific clinical guidelines and training activities provided by the separate programmes leave the difficult task of integration to the health worker. The integrated sick child approach offers a substantial advantage in the efficiency and economy of training, supervision and management of health facilities, including standard drugs and job aides. Efficient triage and case management of sick children in outpatient settings should ensure urgent referral or treatment of severely ill children and appropriate management of key major illnesses present. Another advantage of this approach is that a young infant with a life-threatening illness commonly presents with non-specific clinical signs making a disease-specific approach difficult.

INTEGRATED CLINICAL GUIDELINES

Initial development efforts have been focused on the technical core of the initiative, integrated clinical guidelines for the management of the sick child at first level health facilities. These bring together a set of case management interventions. The first level health facility is where the bulk of patients go for treatment and thus is an important starting point. From this core, guidelines and training materials will be developed for other levels of health workers (doctors and other senior health workers at small hospitals and community-based practitioners; medical and nursing school training) and for programme management and evaluation.

The integrated guidelines bring together the simplest possible expression of what needs to be done to treat children in order to reduce mortality or to avert significant disability. *The guidelines rely on detection of cases based on simple clinical signs and empirical treatment, without laboratory tests.* A careful balance has been struck between sensitivity and specificity using as few clinical signs as possible and ones that health workers of varying backgrounds can be trained to recognise accurately.

The guidelines define the minimal level of knowledge, skill and supplies required to ensure quality health care for children presenting to a first-level outpatient facility. They are based on a few essential drugs for outpatient use – oral rehydration salts, an antibiotic (usually co-trimoxazole), an oral antimalarial, vitamin A, iron tablets, an oral antipyretic (usually paracetamol), an antibiotic eye ointment and gentian violet. For severely ill children a parenteral antibiotic and antimalarial and intravenous fluids are needed before referral to hospital.

In terms of equipment, the health worker needs only a timing device (a watch or other timer) to allow an accurate count of the respiratory rate, a litre measure for the preparation of oral rehydration salts, a scale and a thermometer. If health workers are already trained and equipped to use an otoscope, a growth chart or a height board, their use in classifying the child's illness or nutritional status are explained. Cold chain and vaccination equipment are needed as all children's vaccination status will be updated.

The charts

The integrated clinical guidelines for sick children aged from 2 months up to 5 years by first-level facility health workers are summarised on three case management charts. The first, *Assess and Classify the Sick Child Age 2 Months Up to 5 Years*, summarises how to assess the sick child and classify the illness. First, the health worker checks for danger signs: a child abnormally sleepy or difficult to wake or not able to drink or with convulsions during this illness. Then, the caretaker is asked a series of key questions: Is the child coughing? Does the child have diarrhea? Has the child had fever? Does the child have an ear problem?

Depending on the answer to each question, further questions are asked and the child is examined for key clinical signs. Then all sick children are checked for signs of malnutrition. This information is used to classify the illness

using a colour-coded triage system already made familiar to health workers by the existing diarrhea and ARI case management charts.

The classification leads to treatment instructions which are summarised on a second chart, *Treat the Child*. A third chart, *Advise the Mother*, summarised the advice on treatment that must be given to the caretaker. All these charts are expected to be available in 1994 and will be distributed widely soon after that.

The integrated clinical guidelines for the assessment of the young infant aged less than 2 months and classification of the illness and treatment instructions specific to this age group will be summarised on a separate chart.

These fully-integrated case management charts (Figure 29.3) serve both as a learning and job aide, to guide the health worker in the assessment and classification of the illness, and the treatment of young children. This will include teaching the mother to administer drugs and care for infections as well as good communication of priority messages. The charts do not stand on their own. Health workers are instructed to use them with training modules and visual training aids to improve recognition of important clinical signs, including video, colour photographs, and line drawings. Guides have been prepared for the course director, facilitators and clinical instructors to ensure effective use of the modules and training on the necessary hands-on clinical practice.

In addition to the clinical modules, instructional material is being developed on how to organise the work at a health centre and at the district level. This will cover identification of the population to be served, planning and work scheduling, monitoring performance and output, and maintaining adequate supplies and materials, including inventory control. A guide is also being prepared to help national programmes to adapt the guidelines to their national conditions.

Synergies for preventive measures

Although the focus of the sick child approach is integrated case management of childhood illness, its implementation will allow efficient use of clinical encounters for several key preventive interventions: immunisation, promotion of breast-feeding and improved infant feeding, and vitamin A. Health workers are instructed to use all sick child encounters to check the immunisation status and vaccinate

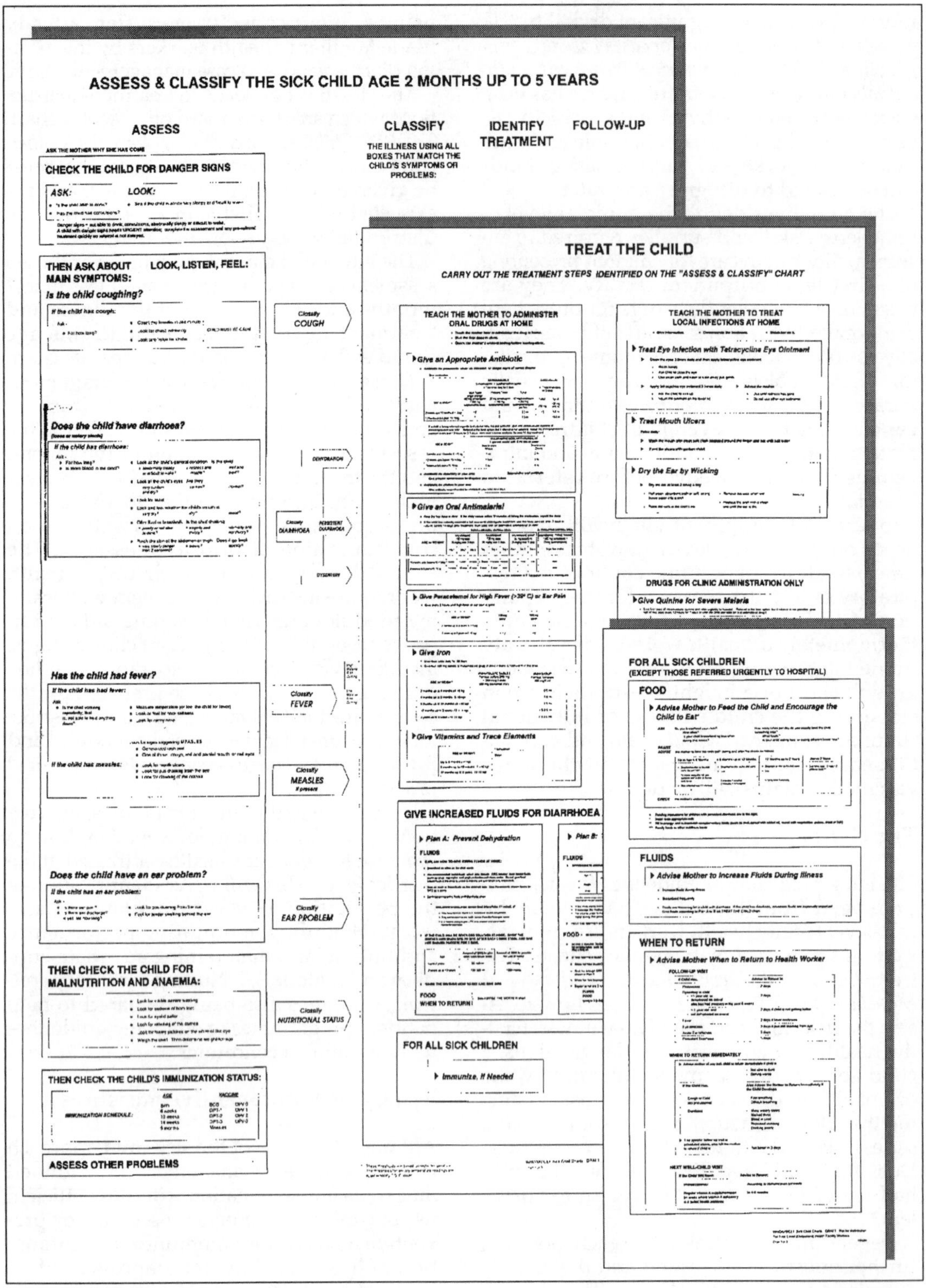

Figure 29.3. The fully-integrated case management charts serve both as a learning and job aide, to guide the health worker in the assessment and classification of the illness, and the treatment of young children.

the children, when indicated. The importance and safety of immunising sick children who are not being referred to hospital can be consistently taught and reinforced, resulting in fewer missed opportunities for immunisation (Chapter 48). Children with eye signs suggesting vitamin A deficiency and all children with measles are given vitamin A. In countries that have decided on regular vitamin A supplementation, sick child encounters can be used to update the child's vitamin A supplementation status.

Sick child encounters also provide an opportunity for the delivery of sound, consistent advice on the nutrition of the young child both during and after illness which may have a significant impact in reducing the adverse effect of infections on the nutrition of infants and young children. This includes the promotion of breast-feeding and improved weaning practices with locally appropriate energy- and nutrient-rich foods.

TECHNICAL BACKGROUND TO THE APPROACH

Why is this approach being developed now? Interest in supporting improved case management of measles has grown in recent years. Despite substantial success in improving immunisation coverage in many developing countries, many measles cases will continue to occur. It will therefore be necessary to reduce the case–fatality rate by good case management. Several recent studies suggest that this is possible by the use of vitamin A and by good management of the common complications.[1,2] In the integrated guidelines for the management of the sick child, all children with measles are given vitamin A. Urgent referral to hospital is recommended for those with severe pneumonia, stridor when calm (which may indicate life-threatening laryngotracheitis), corneal clouding, severe malnutrition, or general danger signs.

Mothers are taught to manage mouth ulcers and conjunctivitis at home and to administer antibiotics for otitis media and pneumonia. The management of diarrhea complicating measles is the same as that for diarrhea of any cause, with the exception of a follow-up visit in 2 days for children with dysentery who have had measles within the last 6 weeks.

Research has recently been completed to elucidate the overlap in both the clinical presentation and the treatment of pneumonia and malaria, leading to an important simplification in treatment.[3–5] In settings where *P. falciparum* malaria is sensitive to sulfadoxine-pyrimethamine and where *P. vivax* is not a major component of the malaria disease problem, children presenting with cough, fast breathing and fever can be treated with co-trimoxazole alone. Co-trimoxazole twice daily for 5 days has been shown to be an efficacious antimalarial in young children, which eliminates the need to use both an antibiotic and an antimalarial. Given the substantial overlap in the clinical signs of pneumonia and malaria in young children, this is an useful simplification which will hopefully both reduce the cost of drug treatment and improve compliance by simplifying the drug regimen.

The importance of promoting breast-feeding and improving the complementary foods both during and after illness to counter malnutrition, has gained increased scientific support (Chapter 31).

Substantial experience is available in case management training in diarrheal disease and acute respiratory infection control programmes which can now be expanded to include children with malaria, measles and malnutrition. Since most children who attend an outpatient clinic have more than one problem and these five constitute a logical cluster since they are similar, not from an anatomical, biomedical, microbiological or pathophysiological perspective, but from the perspective of delivery of health services. These have the same target audience, mothers and other caretakers of children under five. The same health workers are trying to deliver services for these problems in the same place – the first level health facility. The conditions are all amenable to similar interventions which require training of health workers and the availability of a limited number of drugs, although for each problem additional preventive interventions exist which are not included in the package.

COST-EFFECTIVENESS OF THE APPROACH

The 1993 World Development Report prepared by the World Bank in partnership with WHO provides a framework for rationalising investment in health based on comparing the relative cost of health interventions to achieve an additional year of healthy life (disability-life adjusted years).[6] The report endorses essential packages for both clinical services and for public health. Among these, the sick child approach was one of the most cost-effective. The report identifies nine packages of interventions with high potential effectiveness at an affordable cost in both low- and middle-income countries. Among these packages, management of the sick child in low-income countries averts the largest percentage of the disease burden (14 per cent) at only 1.60 USD *per capita* annually or 30 to 50 USD per disability-life adjusted year saved.

References

1. Garenne M, Leroy O, Beau JP, Sene I. Child mortality after high-titre measles vaccines: prospective study in Senegal. Lancet 1991;338:903-6.
2. Hussey GD, Klein M. A randomised controlled trial of vitamin A in children with severe measles. N Engl J Med 1990;323:160-4.
3. World Health Organization. The overlap in the clinical presentation and treatment of malaria and pneumonia in children. Report of a meeting. Geneva 8 April 1991. Geneva: WHO, 1992. (WHO/ARI/92.23 WHO/MAL/92.1065)
4. Daramola OO, Alonso PL, O'Dempsey TJD, *et al*. Sensitivity of *Plasmodium falciparum* in the gambia to cotrimoxazole. Trans R Soc Trop Med Hyg 1991;84:345-8.
5. Redd SC, Bloland PB, Kazembe PN, *et al*. Usefulness of clinical case-definitions in guiding therapy for African children with malaria or pneumonia. Lancet 1992;340:1140-3.
6. World Bank. World development report. New York: Oxford University Press, 1993.

About the author

Sandy Gove received her medical degree from the University of California, San Francisco and did her MPH at the University of California, Berkeley. She is also specialist in internal medicine. Currently, she coordinates research and development for the WHO's Programme for the Control of Acute Respiratory Infections within the Division of Diarrhoeal and Acute Respiratory Disease Control. She has been responsible for the technical coordination of the Sick Child case management charts, clinical modules and other training materials for the WHO/UNICEF course 'Management of Childhood Illness'. During 1985-87 she worked with the Refugee Health Unit of the Ministry of Health, Somalia, as Senior Medical Advisor.

Lankinen KS, Bergström S, Mäkelä PH and Peltomaa M, eds.
Health and disease in developing countries. London:The Macmillan Press Limited, 1994:287–296.

30 PERINATAL HEALTH

Staffan Bergström, M.D., Ph.D.
University of Oslo, Department of Obstetrics and Gynaecology
Ullevål University Hospital, N-0407 Oslo,
Norway

INTRODUCTION

In medical terminology the perinatal period refers to time surrounding birth. More exactly the WHO has recommended the following definition: 'The perinatal period is the one extending from the gestational age at which the average fetus attains the weight of 1000 g (equivalent to 28 completed weeks of gestation) to the end of the seventh completed day of life'.[1] Reference is not made to anything else than antenatal and postnatal age. More specifically it should be noted that the concept *perinatal* alludes neither to the fetus/neonate nor to the pregnant/puerperal woman. Current use of 'perinatal', however, excludes most maternal aspects by focusing on fetal/infant events. Maternal morbidity or mortality in the perinatal period is normally not included in the scope of perinatal medicine; this is particularly remarkable since there is evidence that more than 50 per cent of all maternal deaths occur in the perinatal period.[2]

It is obvious that the road to health in the perinatal period is dependent upon the health of the mother. Her pregnancy health depends on her living conditions before becoming pregnant. The young girl living under nutritionally adverse conditions during childhood will be at risk of skeletal stunting, deficiency diseases (anemia and rickets) and infections (e.g. polio with limp leg and pelvic asymmetry). Such a girl will often run a high risk of early pregnancy. The road to perinatal health for the young mother is threatened by a number of complications potentially affecting both the mother and the fetus. Either of the two may die from complications originating in the woman's early years.

LOW BIRTH WEIGHT – A GLOBAL PROBLEM

The problems arising in the perinatal period are almost always associated with maternal disease. One outstanding common denominator in this regard is low birth weight (LBW). The proportion of newborns with a birth weight below 2500 g varies considerably from country to country. It is often used an indicator of the general health situation and living standard in a given country. It has been calculated that about 95 per cent of all LBW births, or 20 out of 21 millions per year, occur in low-income countries. This problem is particularly important in southern Asia where 20–30 per cent of newborns have a birth weight below 2500 g. Any setting with a LBW incidence above 7–8 per cent is at risk of having high perinatal mortality, which would be possible to counteract by analysing the roots of the LBW problem. In Third World countries a significant portion of this problem is considered to be associated with the problem of smallness for gestational age (SGA), due to a combination of factors including maternal malnutrition, anemia, malaria, placental insufficiency, pre-eclampsia and other unknown factors.[3] Very limited data exist, however, regarding the etiological role of various maternal diseases for the development of SGA. Only a proportion of SGA newborns suffers from intrauterine growth retardation (IUGR); some normally-grown fetuses may still be in the SGA category for genetic and other reasons.

Among LBW newborns there is a variety of causes of perinatal infant deaths. Vulnerability to infections, particularly maternal genital infections, seems to play a predominant role in some deprived populations.[4] Such maternal infections may lead to uterine contractions and finally to expulsion of the baby, sometimes with IUGR. Asphyxia, hypothermia and infections, especially neonatal tetanus, are other causes of neonatal death.

There are few tools available to predict LBW. Anthropometry is one useful approach in this regard ('tape measure obstetrics'). The SF (symphysis–fundus) distance can be used for the recognition of early deviations in fetal growth.[5]

SMALLNESS FOR GESTATIONAL AGE (SGA)

Any newborn with birth weight below the 10th percentile is said to be small for that particular gestational age. These newborns comprise various groups of infants, among whom the long-term prognosis can vary between severe persistent growth retardation and psychomotor retardation, to completely normal growth and development. In many cases it is not possible to predict the outcome before the child has reached the age of 6 months or more.

Asymmetrical growth retardation. The weight is abnormally low compared with length. In countries where severe maternal malnutrition is prevalent, e.g. in India and parts of Africa, these infants are common in the LBW category. Their length and head circumference are in most cases normal for full term infants. These newborns have, for some reason, suffered from intrauterine malnutrition, frequently without overt maternal disease. This pattern is encountered also in multiple pregnancy, in pre-eclampsia and in other conditions with inadequate placental nutritional supply. These newborns may be born at term or preterm.

Infants with asymmetrical (late) growth retardation have drastically reduced fat stores at birth. This disadvantage is aggravated by a high metabolic rate. Starvation must therefore not continue after birth and appropriate early feeding with breast milk within 1–2 hours after birth is mandatory. These babies are easy to feed and take large amounts of breast milk. If there is hypoglycemia (blood glucose values below 1.5 mmol/l) clinical signs such as convulsions, apnoeic spells or other neurological symptoms can occur. Intravenous glucose infusion with 10 per cent glucose 150 ml/kg birth weight is recommended.

These newborns may also suffer from meconium aspiration and neonatal asphyxia. This may be the reason for some late neurological complications (e.g. intracranial hemorrhage and convulsions), contributing to long-term disability. The prognosis in cases with late growth retardation is, however, good. With adequate care the child will grow fast and catch up most of the initial weight loss. If, however, the prenatal malnutrition is followed by severe postnatal starvation the situation is precarious and the risk of permanent brain damage high.

Genetically small newborns. Short mothers and fathers often have small children. Social factors and early teenage pregnancy may be in the background. These infants usually have small heads and normal mid-upper arm skinfold thickness; they will remain small and their prognosis is generally good.

There is in this group, however, also a subgroup of infants with very early intrauterine growth retardation either due to embryopathy, maternal diseases, infections, drug or alcohol abuse. They have small heads, short stature and low birth weight. In some cases congenital malformations are present and in some so-called syndromes stigmata and malformations occur. These infants are frequently suffering from poor growth and development. In most cases the true reason for the early embryonal lesion cannot be determined.

PRETERM BIRTH

The word *preterm* refers to any gestational age earlier than 37 completed weeks of pregnancy. The word premature is *not* synonymous with preterm. In actual practice 'premature' is often (bad) jargon for 'less than 2500 g', which is, correctly, LBW. *The word premature should therefore never be used, since it is obsolete, unclear and misleading.* Refer *either* to weight (e.g. LBW) *or* to gestational age (e.g. preterm).

It may be of clinical interest to know whether an LBW baby is born preterm or at term. The estimation of gestational age is thus important and if the maternal menstrual data are reliable there is no problem in calculating it. If the data is absent or inaccurate it may be of some help to use a maturation-scoring system. At present there is, unfortunately, no maturity-scoring system tested in both developed and developing countries. An optimum scoring system should be based on external and easily defined signs rather than neurological signs, since these are influenced by the time elapsed after birth and by the general condition of the baby.

It is common that maturation scoring systems underestimate the gestational age of children with intrauterine growth retardation. There is also a considerable margin of error in the determination of gestational age when using a scoring system. No system gives a better estimate of gestational age than plus/minus 2 weeks.

In current practice in most developing countries efforts to save preterm babies start when the babies have reached approximately 28 weeks of gestation, corresponding to a birth weight of around 1000 g. In developing countries this is a necessity due to limited economic and manpower resources. The expenditures of modern neonatal intensive care for infants born before 28 weeks of gestation are exorbitant and are very difficult to cover even in the industrialised world.

THERMAL CONTROL OF THE NEWBORN

Over the last decades *hypothermia* has been recognised as a problem in tropical countries. The low temperature problem has previously been given insufficient attention, since room temperature in these countries is usually high, at least during the day. Body temperature has usually been measured with rectal thermometers, which do not record temperatures below 35°C. Thus the temperature of a baby admitted to a neonatal ward, may have been reported to be 35°C though the actual temperature might actually have been as low as 30°C.

Perinatal death is clearly associated with hypothermia.[6] By the beginning of this century it was shown that preterm babies with a rectal temperature of less than 36°C had a mortality rate above 75 per cent. If they were kept warm, the mortality rate dropped to less than 20 per cent. Avoiding hypothermia is probably the most important single factor in reducing neonatal mortality among LBW newborns. It has been estimated that during the last decades, prevention of hypothermia

has contributed to a 25 per cent increase in survival rate in industrialised countries.

Mild hypothermia is best managed by fast rewarming, provided that the method is safe. Burns may occur when focused radiant heat sources or uncontrolled methods such as hot water bottles or heated stones are used. Such methods should be replaced by the efficient kangaroo method, using skin to skin contact. This method uses the mother as the source of extra heat. There are many obvious advantages with this: the closeness to the mother's breast for feeding and the maternal attention provided. It is of utmost importance that the baby and the mother are kept together and that breast-feeding is started and maintained during the stay in hospital.

FEEDING THE NEWBORN

Breast-feeding is the basis for infant feeding. For most children in developing countries it is a prerequisite for survival during the first few months after birth. Particularly for preterm and underweight babies the key to future health and development is successful breast-feeding. The skin-to-skin contact guarantee the mother/infant-bonding from the moment of birth that is of utmost importance for uneventful perinatal outcome. *Warmth, love* and *breast milk* are rightly said to be the cornerstones of perinatal survival. Even if not immediately relevant during the perinatal period it is important to underscore that successful breast-feeding prepares the ground for a forthcoming lactational amenorrhea and anovulation in the woman breast-feeding her child frequently. There is evidence that on demand breast-feeding without resumption of menstruation will give more than 95 per cent protection against pregnancy during the first 6 months after delivery.[7] There is also evidence that in practice no other contraceptive is needed during the first 12 month after delivery as long as menstruation has not started.[8,9]

In most low-income countries, mothers and their newborn babies are discharged within the first day after delivery in a health unit. Prevailing home conditions with heavy work and malnutrition may impair breast-feeding with subsequent risk of early malnutrition of the newborn infant. In this situation breast-feeding is crucial. Gastrointestinal infections are much more prevalent in infants who have been given water or other supplements to breast milk. Such infections can also occur due to the artificial separation of mother and infant, which is by and large a consequence of misguided heritage from affluent countries. In home deliveries there is often a natural close contact between mother and child and early breast-feeding is initiated. Colostrum may erroneously, however, often be regarded as harmful and not given to the baby, but thrown away. Before introduction of Western medicine in the 1940s and 1950s breast-feeding 10–20 times a day appears to have been the norm in most cultures. In modern medicine a number of recommendations regarding the minimum interval between feeds etc. were introduced without any supporting scientific data. Such unfounded advice disturbed the natural contact between mother and child.

The encouragement of early contact between mother and child after birth is the first step on the road to successful breast-feeding. A set of simple rules are the following ones:

• Avoid unnecessary separation of mother and child
• Stimulate frequent suckling
• Assist the mother in the positioning of the infant so that the infant has a comfortable resting position at the mother's breast and starts suckling with both nipple and areola in its mouth
• Avoid unnecessary weight checks before and after feeding and restrict weight checks in hospital wards to one a day
• Do not give any extra fluids or nutrients during the first few months of life

INFECTIONS IN THE PERINATAL PERIOD

Infections are one of the main causes of maternal death and perinatal infant death, HIV/AIDS being the most prominently growing of the threats to perinatal health. Puerperal endometritis with sepsis is a largely preventable complication, which kills many mothers. Unhygienic handling at birth is also a threat of infection that may be fatal in combination with other negative circumstances such as LBW birth.

Both transplacental and transcervical infections are common during pregnancy in low-income countries. Many viruses that infect the mother may pass the placenta, while only few bacterial or parasitic infections, such as syphilis and malaria, pass via this route. Ascending infections make the birth canal an important route of entry for any bacteria or occasionally even virus that the mother may have in her vagina or cervix. At birth, a baby may thus carry an infection acquired during pregnancy or while passing through the birth canal.

The healthy, well-nourished, breast-fed, term newborn has a good protection against infections during the first few months of life. This is due in part to the antibodies transferred to the infant transplacentally or through the breast milk. The colonisation of the skin and the intestinal canal of the infant by the bacterial flora of the family is essential for the protective mechanisms of the infant. On the other hand, the defence mechanisms of LBW and/or malnourished newborns are poor. The threat of a serious infection is increased by the high risk of acquiring hypothermia and poor suckling ability, leading to starvation. All this contributes to impaired defence mechanisms in the newborn. In such cases overcrowded neonatal units are particularly dangerous places, since cross-contamination from one infant to another or from staff members to the child is common.

At birth there is an increased risk of infection for the mother and for the infant. Infections are commonly transmitted from hospital staff to patients. It is important that the newborn is colonised with maternal bacteria (more benign) rather than with hospital staff bacteria (less benign and more drug-resistant). Some of the measures, such as separation of the child from the mother, care in closed neonatal units and the use of protective clothing have turned out to be ineffective. Still more important is that these routines have seriously affected the possibilities of establishing close contact (bonding) between the mother and her newborn.

HOW TO ORGANISE FOR IMPROVED PERINATAL SURVIVAL?

The ambition to prevent perinatal deaths assumes that it is possible to foresee and predict certain complications of pregnancy and delivery. In addition, some maternal risk factors that are associated with an adverse pregnancy outcome for both the mother and the baby (e.g. short stature, previous Cesarean section, limp leg) are relevant in all subsequent pregnancies, and a longitudinal perspective is therefore useful.

Over half of all deliveries in the world are home deliveries, unattended by trained staff. These deliveries take place under poor conditions, but most of them occur without complications. Improving the quality of home deliveries is therefore extremely important in order to reduce maternal mortality and perinatal infant mortality. The first objective must be to create conditions for the hygienic home delivery, compatible with *the 'three cleans': clean hands, clean perineum, and clean cord care* (China). If the three cleans could be achieved for all childbirths that take place in the developing world a drastic decline in perinatal deaths would be achieved. Of domiciliary parturients few give birth totally alone. Local women with their varied own experience, traditional birth attendants, assist most home deliveries.

Traditional birth attendants (TBAs)

The TBA has usually learnt to assist at childbirth from other local women or female relatives. She may give traditional treatments during pregnancy, or recommend certain behaviour. The TBA is usually illiterate without any formal health education. She shares the experiences, fears, beliefs and traditions of the birthing women. She often has considerable social status and prestige in the area in which she is working. A TBA usually only works part-time: some payment may be received after completion of the delivery but the great bulk of her daily work is agricultural and domestic duties. Some countries have launched training programmes for TBAs. A fruitful dialogue between the local health care network and the TBAs has thereby been achieved.

Midwives and nurses

The most important perinatal health care workers are nurses and midwives. Some countries have recognised the need to train midwives quite late, but today practically all countries of the world have midwifery education (except parts of Latin America). It has been shown that *the enhancement of national midwifery coverage has been the single most important measure in reducing maternal mortality in developed countries.*[10] However, in most low-income countries it is difficult to achieve a national coverage of midwives. Inadequate numbers of trained midwives, or budget constraints in employing existing midwives are further challenges. They are often badly paid for long working hours. Midwives in health posts and health centres often work without sufficient drugs and equipment and without regular contact with the local hospital.

Overburdened antenatal clinics constitute a demanding challenge. Midwives may serve independently in ordinary antenatal care, usually without support from doctors. The need for encouragement, feedback, and re-training is great. Providers (midwives) and consumers (pregnant women) of antenatal care are increasingly in need of improved quality of antenatal care.

Globally, midwives also play an increasingly important role in delivery care, their traditional main task. Giving emphasis to safe motherhood and to safe birth, the setting will undoubtedly demand more obstetric skills from midwives, much like the pattern in many affluent countries, where midwives have taken over several tasks conventionally carried out by doctors. On the other hand, nurses and midwives in several developing countries (more than in developed countries) have to take over some of the doctors' tasks (minor surgery, tubal ligation, legal abortions, symphysiotomies and even Cesarean sections) due to the unavailability of doctors in rural areas. They should then be carefully trained for such interventions. The *delegation of responsibility* is an important area of debate in the organisation of perinatal health care.

Medical assistants

In non-urban settings there are few, if any, doctors in perinatal care. Some countries have trained staff at a level that combines superior nursing training with diagnostic and therapeutic skills. A medical assistant is often in charge of a health centre, and he or she may be the first extra support upon whom a midwife can call when in difficulty. When duly trained, medical assistants may give anaesthesia and perform some surgery independently. In some countries like Mozambique and Zaire they have specialised in surgery (surgical assistants, *técnicos de cirurgia* etc.) and have in actual fact the position of general surgeons.[11–14]

Doctors

For the organisation of perinatal care there is a need of qualified medical staff to inspire and maintain efforts for improved perinatal survival. Specialised doctors, however, such as obstetricians and pediatricians only rarely work outside the big cities. Increasing urban populations, with higher hospital attendance, tie these

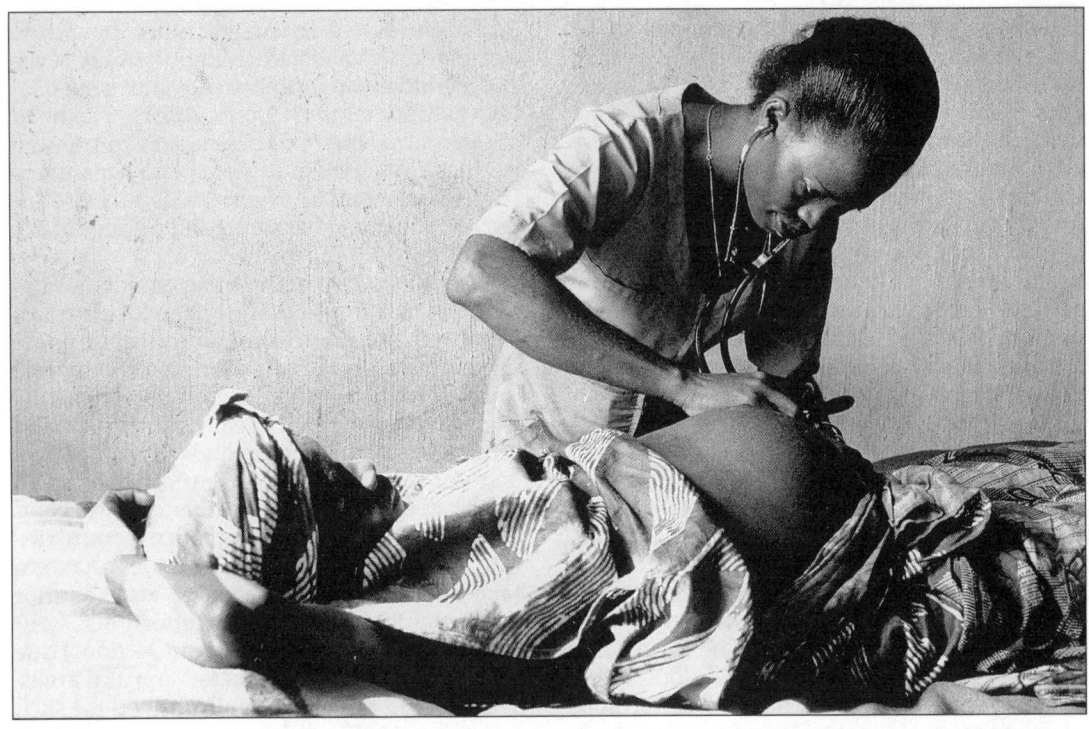

Systematic antenatal care is a prerequisite for better perinatal health. Photo: UNICEF/Carolyn Watson

specialists to the cities, as do professional (equipment, development) and personal (career, private practice) motives.

PERINATAL CARE AT DIFFERENT LEVELS

Antenatal care

Antenatal care is a prerequisite for better perinatal health. It should consist of motherhood education, prevention of pregnancy complications, treatment of common diseases, and risk screening/referral. In antenatal care pregnant women are introduced to the health care system. This introduction should foster confidence and satisfaction to encourage continuation. Referral of some pregnant women to clinics for high risk patients is an important function of antenatal care. High risk cases can be managed as outpatients or as inpatients if any complications (membrane rupture preterm, hypertension, preterm labour, vaginal hemorrhage etc.) should occur. *Inpatient antenatal* care is thereby a necessary corollary to outpatient antenatal care in case of referral need. Predelivery care is inpatient antenatal care before birth.

Predelivery care

A safe delivery for the woman affected by any significant complication should always be preceded by adequate predelivery care. It is particularly crucial for high risk pregnancies. Even when delivery (intrapartum) care is well organised, the outcome of pregnancy may be poor if predelivery care has not functioned properly.

Outpatient care of high risk pregnancies requires more frequent check-ups. Several pregnancy complications in the third trimester also require periods of observation and treatment in hospital. The importance of inpatient care is best illustrated by the detrimental effect on pregnancy outcome of a heavy daily workload for a poor pregnant woman – carrying water, food, and firewood. An insufficient number of available beds necessitates restrictions regarding inpatient care, but it is often advisable to aim at combining short periods of inpatient care with frequent outpatient check-ups. This is particularly important for women living far from the antenatal clinic.

At the organisational level there are three different levels of predelivery care. The *first level* corresponds to the concept of maternal waiting area (maternal village), not too far from a hospital with a surgical theatre (Chapter 32). The *second level* is designed for women, whose pregnancies are complicated by, for instance, pre-eclampsia, preterm labour, or prelabour rupture of membranes preterm. Such women require rest and some supervision, e.g. by a midwife or by a nurse, but not daily care by a doctor. Wards at this level may be similar to a maternal waiting area but should ideally be supervised by a midwife or by another trained person. The *third level* caters to more severe cases with bleeding complications, threatening preterm birth, cervical insufficiency, intrauterine growth retardation, and severe cases of pre-eclampsia. These high risk wards should be situated close to qualified delivery care with surgical facilities. It is important that the three levels collaborate closely and that a rotation of the patients can be achieved.

Delivery care

In the delivery ward each patient must have her own patient record. Its character and quality will be crucial for individual patient care and also for further data collection and feedback/follow-up. It should have two features: it should be operational (oriented towards patient care) and optimal for scrutiny (oriented towards collection of relevant data for each individual, mother and newborn baby). A patient's progress in active labour should be recorded on a partogram. A modification of the classical partogram has been called a cervicogram, since it simply follows the dilatation of the cervix and is oriented towards early observation of deviations in progress of labour.[15]

For proper delivery care the action-oriented perspective is mandatory when antenatal cards are elaborated. Such cards should be operational by giving concrete help whom to refer. It is important to use all available information from the antenatal card. A maternal health card should have one part for use during antenatal care (the antenatal card), but it should also contain information on delivery events (the delivery card). Ideally it should also contain information on the postpartum/puerperal period and furthermore summarise information of each previous pregnancy outcome, with any infant and maternal complications.[16]

The delivery ward book is the key document in delivery care. Even if patient care at delivery must be individualised it is difficult to judge the quality of obstetric care from individual patient records unless they are written so as to make a retrospective follow-up of each case possible. The condition of the delivery ward book is therefore an important quality criterion. It should be comprehensive and completely filled in every day with all relevant details of each delivering woman. Pregnancy outcome for both mother and newborn should be given in detail, and the objective should be to lay the basis for forthcoming audit and feed-back to improve obstetric outcome (for both mother and newborn). The delivery ward book is also the basis for calculating an important portion of the perinatal mortality rate. It should be possible to discern the number of low birth weight babies, preterm births, and other risk deliveries such as twins, breech presentations, eclampsias, etc.There are also simplified delivery records for TBAs.[6]

Perinatal audit (action-oriented review) is of importance for the improvement of perinatal care. There is nothing magical about audit: it simply allows for a careful follow-up of what has happened in a health unit over a certain period (week or month) in order to trace causes of bad outcome of management (perinatal deaths, severe neonatal asphyxia, serious maternal disease and death, etc.). It is most important for an audit to be straightforward, honest, and open-minded and imply constructive dialogue between doctors, chief midwives, and other persons in key positions. Regular audit sessions at which all the staff is present are one of the cornerstones of good perinatal care.[17]

In Maputo the mere introduction of a new registration routine in the delivery ward (without any other quality-improving measure in patient care) led to a 30 per cent reduction in the intrapartum death rate for newborns because the improved registration quality oriented the staff towards better patient care.[18] The staff found its own performance regularly recorded and made public, a circumstance that empirically leads to better patient care. In small health units, as well as in big hospitals, any improvement in maternal care at delivery starts with a carefully filled-in delivery book. Professional neglect, prestige and individual shame should never be allowed to conceal obstetrical mismanagement.

PERINATAL TERMINOLOGY

The perinatal period. The perinatal period comprises the period from 28 completed weeks of gestation to the end of the 7th completed day of life.

Birth weight. The birth weight is the weight of the newborn infant obtained preferably within 1 hour of birth (before significant postnatal weight loss has occurred). The concept low birth weight (LBW) refers to a birth weight of less than 2500 g (that is up to and including 2499 g).

It has been recommended that all fetuses and newborn infants weighing 500 g or more – alive or otherwise – should be reported in a country's statistics. Obviously, in the developing world, this is not a realistic limit. Hence, WHO has recommended that mortality statistics reported for purposes of international comparison should include only those newborns weighing 1000 g or more (corresponding approximately to 28 weeks of gestation).

Gestational age. The duration of gestation is measured from the first day of the last normal menstrual period. Gestational age should always be expressed in completed weeks.

The preterm period. Preterm refers to less than 37 completed weeks. The concept premature is unclear and obsolete in modern perinatal terminology and should not therefore be used. It was previously used as a synonym to LBW but reference should be made either to the gestational age or to the birth weight. The concept premature has a functional significance (before attaining maturity), which is confusing and obsolete, since it is used (incorrectly) as a synonym of LBW.

The term period. This period starts after 37 completed weeks and continues to the end of the 42nd week. It has a duration of 5 full weeks (38–42).

The post-term period. This period refers to a pregnancy length of more than 42 completed weeks. Sometimes other synonyms are used, e.g. post-date or post-mature. Post-term is recommended instead of these synonyms.

Live birth. A live birth has occurred when the newborn infant breathes or shows any other sign of life, such as heartbeat, pulsation in the umbilical cord or movements of the voluntary muscles.

Stillbirth. Stillbirth refers to the birth of a fetus showing no sign of life. For international comparisons of perinatal mortality rates only such stillborn infants with a birth weight of 1000 g or more are included.[*] Sometimes stillborn babies are not weighed. In this case a gestational age of 28 completed weeks or a body length of 35 cm should be taken as equivalent to 1000 g birth weight. The stillbirth rate is defined as the number of stillborn infants per 1000 total births (stillborn infants + liveborn infants).

Early neonatal death. This refers to the death of a liveborn infant during the first 7 days of life. The early neonatal mortality rate is defined as the number of early neonatally dead infants weighing 1000 g or more occurring 0–7 days after birth, expressed per 1000 livebirths.

Late neonatal death. This refers to the death of a liveborn infant after 7 completed days, but before 28 completed days, after birth.

Perinatal death. Perinatal deaths comprise the sum of all stillbirths and early neonatal deaths. The perinatal mortality rate is the sum of all such deaths in relation to the sum of all stillborn and liveborn infants. In other words, it expresses the total fetal/neonatal loss in relation to all infants born (stillborn and liveborn).

Maternal death. A maternal death is defined as the death of a woman while pregnant or within 42 completed days of termination of pregnancy, irrespective of the duration and site of the pregnancy, from any cause related to or aggravated by the pregnancy or by its management but not due to accidental or incidental causes. Maternal deaths can be either direct or indirect obstetric deaths. For details, see Chapter 32.

The maternal mortality ratio is the number of maternal deaths per 1000 total births. However, the currently most frequently used definition utilises a denominator of 100 000 live births. Ideally the denominator should comprise all pregnancies but this figure is virtually impossible to obtain. It is also difficult to calculate the total number of births. The number of liveborn babies is, in practice, therefore considered an acceptable approximation of the total number of births.

---

[*]For national perinatal statistics the Ninth Revision of the International Classification of Diseases (ICD 9) from 1980 recommends that the lower limit should be 500 g.

Neonatal care

Neonatal care is an integral part of delivery care. Perinatal care of the newborn comprises, however, the whole first week post partum. In the immediate care of the newborn some issues are particularly important. The most important procedures to give a newborn the best chance of a healthy life are to: 1) check the baby's vital signs; 2) dry the baby; 3) cut and clamp the cord; 4) keep the baby warm; 5) put the baby close to the mother's skin; and 6) let the baby suck the mother's breast.[6]

Except for a small minority of newborns the baby can be given to the mother within two minutes after birth after due recognition of the six items above. When there are no complications the baby can be kept at the mother's breast or in a separate cot. Suckling should be allowed as soon as the baby seems to want to suck. This will stimulate the milk production and most mothers will have milk in their breasts within 2–3 days after delivery. The mother and her baby should preferably stay at the health centre or in the hospital for at least 24 hours. Before they leave the centre the mother and the baby should be examined by a nurse or a midwife. The observations should be written down in the mother's record. With the deliveries at home the birth attendant should ideally visit the mother and perform a similar examination about 24 hours after delivery.

Some newborn babies will need additional treatment depending on their condition and available facilities. Newborn babies that need further treatment will usually be kept in a separate room or in a separate ward. It is important that this is close to the place where the mother is staying. The facilities have to be arranged to permit close supervision by well trained nurses and to carry out procedures, that may be necessary. The room should have a fairly stable day and night temperature of 22–25°C. The number of visitors has to be limited, but the mothers (and their husbands, if possible) should always be permitted to stay with the babies. Clean water, safe electricity, and oxygen supply should preferably be available. All observations made, tests performed, and treatments given should be written down in the records with the day, time, and name of the staff member who has written down the note clearly stated.

Puerperal care

A short inpatient period amounting to about 24 hours is normal after an uneventful birth in a small health unit or in a hospital. Complicated deliveries associated with various diseases require a prolonged stay and, hence, a classification of post-partum women according to risk may be desirable in the puerperal ward. Immediate post-delivery complications are rare in the majority of women while late, sudden bleedings, endometritis, meningitis, malaria, etc., may occur many days or even weeks after delivery, with ensuing risk of maternal death.

At discharge the continuity of maternal health care should be emphasised and mothers should be encouraged to return to maternal and child health care after delivery. Attention should be paid to maternal nutrition, family planning, and maternal health education.

TOWARDS ANOTHER CARE IN THE PERINATAL PERIOD

For the vast majority of delivering women of the world even the basic concept of hygienic delivery is far beyond reach. There is little doubt that knowledge can improve the perinatal health of mothers and children in low-income countries, without the introduction of more sophisticated equipment. The few obstetricians and pediatricians available (if any), being at the top of the health care pyramid, have a privileged perspective (though sometimes incomplete and skewed) of the pyramid and therefore a special responsibility in spreading knowledge of the significance of appropriate technology. Doctors in general also have the responsibility of supervising and maintaining the perinatal care chain by frequent visits to primary health care workers and health stations, an outreach activity often more important than giving curative care in hospital.

There are many obstacles to an improved perinatal health care. One such obstacle may be lack of cooperation between obstetricians and paediatricians. All experience shows that a continuous dialogue between the specialists at the top of the pyramid greatly improves perinatal care all the way down to the general population. Supporting the perinatal care chain means providing education, supervision, and information about the results of work at other levels of the chain, including for instance the very important feed-back to the midwife in the field about mothers referred by her to higher levels of care.

In several low-income countries the low status of midwives and nurses constitutes a serious problem. Underpayment or irregular wages often leads to absence from work in order to earn the means of living in other ways. Perinatal care needs staff, and in hospitals there must be staff around the clock. Inexperienced and inadequate staff have little chance of solving the problems of overcrowding, and lack of drugs and equipment.

Only when more importance is given to the status of women and the improvement of basic preventive care may a significant reduction in maternal mortality be achieved during the next decades to come. A 50 per cent reduction in neonatal mortality and the eradication of neonatal tetanus within 5 years are goals that WHO has formulated. They can be attained provided that the affluent countries offer substantial increases in support and commitment to deprived and impoverished countries.

References

1. WHO. Recommended definitions, terminology and format for statistical tables related to the perinatal period and use of a new certificate for cause of perinatal deaths. Acta Obstet Gynecol Scand 1977;56:247–53.
2. Bergström S. Is there an 'M' in perinatal medicine? J Trop Pediatr 1991;37:89–90.
3. Sterky G, Mellander L, eds. Low birth weight – a social indicator. Stockholm: SAREC, 1977. (SAREC Report)
4. Axemo P, Ching C, Machungo F, Osman NB, Bergström S. Intrauterine infections and their association to stillbirth and pre-term birth in Maputo. Gynecol Obstet Invest 1993;35:108–113.
5. Bergström S, Liljestrand J. Parturient fundal height and its relation to fetal weight. J Trop Pediatr 1989;35: 27–30.
6. Bergström S, Höjer B, Liljestrand J, Tunell R. Perinatal health care with limited resources. London: Macmillan, 1994.
7. Winikoff B and Mench B. Rethinking postpartum family planning. Stud Fam Plann 1991;22:294–307.
8. Short RV, Lewis PR, Renfree MB and Shaw G. Contraceptive effects of extended lactational amenorrhea: beyond the Bellagio Consensus. Lancet 1991;i:715–717.
9. Bhatia S, Becker S and Kim YJ. The effect of oral contraceptive on fertility in the postpartum period. Int J Gynaecol Obstet 1987;25(Suppl):1–11.
10. Högberg U. Maternal mortality in Sweden. Umeå: Umeå University, 1985. (Medical dissertation No 156)
11. da Luz Vaz M, Bergström S. Mozambique – delegation of responsibility in the area of maternal care. Int J Gynaecol Obstet 1992;38(Suppl): S37–S39.
12. Dusitsin N, Satayapan S. Sterilization of women by nurse-midwives in Thailand. World Health Forum 1984;5:259.
13. Potter AR. Letter. Br Med J 1984;289:495.
14. Satayapan S, Varakamin S, Suwannus P, Chalapati S, Onthuam Y, Susitsin N. Postpartum tubal ligation by nurse-midwives in Thailand: a field trial. Stud Fam Plann 1983;14:115.
15. Bird GC. Cervicographic management of labour in primigravidae and multigravidae with vertex presentation. Trop Doct 1978;8:78.
16. Essex BJ and Everett VJ. Use of an action-oriented record card for antenatal screening. Trop Doct 1977; 7:134–138.
17. Ali L, Kifle G, Mbaruku G, et al. Audit of maternal health care. In: Bergström S, Molin A Povey GW, eds. International maternal health care 1992 – The challenge beyond the year 2000. Uppsala: University of Uppsala, 1993.
18. Bugalho A, Bergström S. The value of perinatal audit in obstetric care in the developing world. Gynecol Obstet Invest (in press).

About the author

Staffan Bergström is Professor of International Health at the University of Oslo and Senior Physician at the Department of Obstetrics and Gynaecology, Ullevål University Hospital, Oslo, Norway. He is a specialist in obstetrics and gynaecology and responsible for several research projects in the area of reproductive health in developing countries. During 1982–86 he was the Director of the Department of Obstetrics, Central Hospital, Maputo, Mozambique. He is also involved in the human reproduction research programme (HRP) within the WHO.

Lankinen KS, Bergström S, Mäkelä PH and Peltomaa M, eds.
Health and disease in developing countries. London:The Macmillan Press Limited, 1994:297–304.

31 MALNUTRITION IN CHILDREN

David Morley, C.B.E., M.D., FRCP
51 Eastmoor Park, Harpenden, Herts. AL5 1BN,
United Kingdom

INTRODUCTION

There is mention of starvation and nutritional disorders in European history back to the 16th century. At various times it was called atrophy, infantile pellagra, Mehlnährschaden, wetmarasmus and, most recently, protein energy malnutrition. However, it was Cicely Williams who published in 1933 a letter in *The Lancet*, in which she called the condition kwashiorkor. This was the name given by the Ga tribe in Ghana and its meaning is related to the displacement of the older child from the place on the mother's back when another child is born, and the illness that then affects the older child.

Every health worker knows that protein energy malnutrition (PEM) is a name used to cover a range of nutritional disorders. These include growth failure, marasmus and kwashiorkor. However, the name is misleading because it implies that lack of protein and energy are the sole causes of these conditions. Unfortunately, when the condition was first studied lack of protein was considered to be most important. We now know that in almost every circumstance energy is the major lack. Lack of some minerals and vitamins such as zinc and vitamin A also contribute to growth failure.

EPIDEMIOLOGY

PEM presents most frequently in the preschool child, particularly between the ages of 6 months and 5 years. However, the origins of the condition go back to early fetal life, to low birth weight, and sometimes to inadequate growth in the first 6 months of life, particularly when bottle feeding is attempted by the mother. However, PEM can occur at any age and, in older children and adults, is often a complication of a wasting disease such as tuberculosis.

PEM is closely linked to socioeconomic development of a community and is most common in the poorest countries with a large population living in poverty in rural areas and urban slums. Malnutrition can reach epidemic proportions when there are catastrophes, civil disturbance and war.

In *urban areas*, malnutrition occurs mostly in the families of low socioeconomic status and where the home is broken. It is particularly likely to occur when families try and exist on just one staple. Among those who by tradition have a very mixed diet, such as the Chinese, severe malnutrition is less frequent. The worldwide drift from rural to urban areas and the rapid growth of shanty towns with poor sanitation, water supply and distribution of services is leading to a rapid increase of children with malnutrition in urban situations.

In *rural areas* in poor countries, malnutrition is endemic and often seasonal. This is related to a period of the year when food for the whole family is in short supply and the child's limited food intake is diminished by frequent infections such as measles.

The prevalence of malnutrition in communities varies but severe forms are frequently found in 2–3 per cent of the child population, with up to 60 per cent suffering from various degrees of stunting.

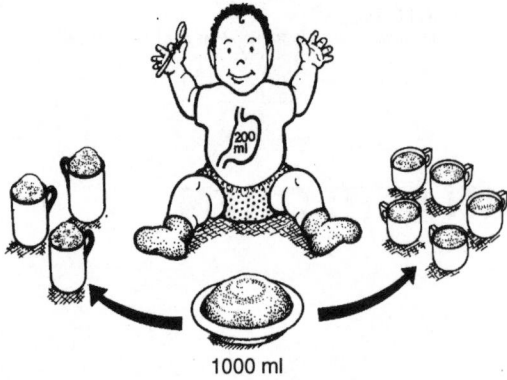

Figure 31.1. Why small children need to eat often. Artist: Sara Kionga-Kamau

Malnutrition is closely related also to the political situation of a country. It is frequent in countries with a marked disparity between the rich and poor. In countries such as China, Sri Lanka, Kerala and Cuba, where there has been a more appropriate distribution of resources, severe forms of malnutrition may become infrequent or disappear. However, stunting may still remain.

CAUSES OF MALNUTRITION

Children who are fed inadequate quantities of protein and energy for their growth and health are likely to suffer from malnutrition. However, infections also have a pivotal role in development of almost all severe cases of malnutrition. For many years, emphasis was placed on the poor protein intake of children in developing countries, and many health workers unfortunately associated the name kwashiorkor with protein deficiency. However, research has shown that the diet of children admitted to hospital with marasmus and kwashiorkor is similar in all respects and it is now realised that, in most diets, the limiting factor is energy rather than protein.

The stomach of small children is small, usually the size of their fist. However, because of growth requirements, the child's energy requirements are almost half those of an adult. Unfortunately most diets in the developing world fed to young children are largely made up of dilute paps or porridges with less than one calorie per gram. For this reason the first and most important rule is that two to three meals is not enough for a child, but five meals are required with possible snacks as well (Figure 31.1).

Fats and oils the priority, not protein

After increasing the frequency of meals the next most important step is to increase the energy content of the food. As shown in Figure 31.2, the addition of fat or vegetable oil to the food is one very efficient way of increasing its energy content. The food containing fat has a greater energy content per gram, partly because of the large calorie content of fats and oils. But it is probably even more important that because foods cooked with oils and fats contain less water they are more easily eaten by children. This difference can be demonstrated practically by comparing the result of cooking a cupful of rice, which is about the requirement of a child, into a fluffy, soft boiled rice or into a much smaller volume of fried rice.

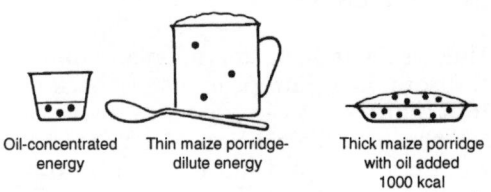

Oil-concentrated energy   Thin maize porridge-dilute energy   Thick maize porridge with oil added 1000 kcal

Figure 31.2. Energy concentration of oil and thin porridge (one dot = 100 kcal).

In Europe children show their innate understanding of nutrition by their choice of French fries rather than boiled potatoes much to the profit of international fast food chains! Table 31.1 shows the intake of fats in developed and developing countries. In these countries, the quantity taken by the poorest is likely to be only a small fraction of the average figure.

As mentioned already, infections play a major part in the causation of malnutrition. Infection increases the energy, protein and vitamin requirements of a child and may also affect their absorption. However, the major influence of infection is in reducing the appetite of the child and unfortunately too often also the amount of food that she is encouraged to take. Following an infection, a refeeding period of at least a week and frequently longer may be required, during which the child's intake needs to be higher than normal. As well as preventing and treating infections, health workers have a particular responsibility to supervise and encourage this increased feeding of children during convalescence following even a minor illness.

Table 31.1. Fats and oils in North and South. There is a much greater relative difference in consumption compared with protein.

	Grams per day	Proportion of total calories consumed
Industrialised countries	126	34 per cent
Developing countries	41	16 per cent

PATHOGENESIS

Growth failure (nutritional dwarfing)

The early effects of malnutrition on the child are shown by loss of activity; slowing or cessation of linear growth; slowing increase or loss of weight; decrease in mid-upper arm circumference; delayed bone maturation; normal or diminished weight/height ratio; normal or diminished skinfold thickness.

A *single weight* alone is a poor method of assessing nutrition of a child. However, at community level comparison of the *weight for age* of a group of children can be an excellent measure of local nutritional state. For the individual child the *weight for age growth curve* remains the most sensitive indicator of nutritional state. Where no recent weighing

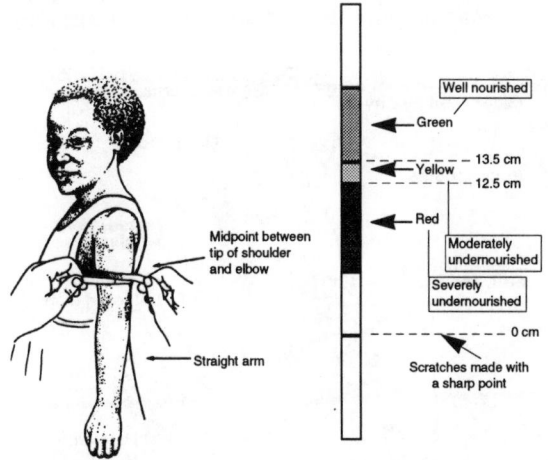

Figure 31.3. Measuring mid-upper arm circumference with a Shakir strip that is made from an old X-ray film.

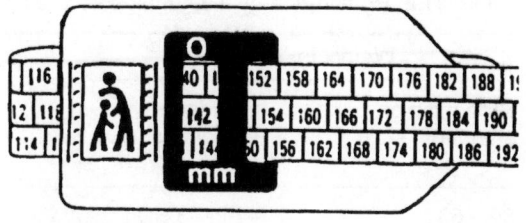

Figure 31.4. An insertion tape (available from TALC).

has occurred weight for height is usually used, although it involves two measurements and a calculation, and is therefore liable to error. The simplest assessment of nutritional state is mid-upper arm circumference measured with a coloured Shakir strip (Figure 31.3), or preferably with an insertion tape (Figure 31.4). Those doing the measurements must be trained so that they get reproducible results.

Appropriate standards to assess growth

Frequent debates arise as to whether domestic or international standards for children should be used. The consensus among anthropometrists is that, although there is considerable genetic variation *within* any population, the variation *between* populations is small. It has been suggested that between Europeans and South-East Asians, in children of the ages from 5 to 7 years, a racial variation in height of 3 centimetres occurs. However, in terms of nutrition, a variation of 12 centimetres between the well-off and the under-privileged in a community is a frequent finding.

Patterns of growth failure

There are many patterns of growth failure. The most common is a chronic low intake of energy, which leads to a failure of weight and height with little or no change in the weight-height ratio. This is stunting and is common in less privileged groups in developing countries. The more acute loss with sudden restriction of energy, usually in association with an acute infection or diarrhea, may result in the syndrome of kwashiorkor. Between these two extremes lies the child in whom growth has been limited from an early age and in whom there may be no weight gain over a period of 6 months or even 2 years. An attempt to

Table 31.2. Protein-energy malnutrition according to the Wellcome Classification.

Weight for age			
Proportion of standard	Standard Deviations (SD)	Edema present	Edema absent
80 – 60 %	–1 to –3 SD	Kwashiorkor	Underweight
Under 60 %	below 3 SD	Marasmic kwashiorkor	Marasmus

classify these more accurately has been made e.g. in the Wellcome Classification (Table 31.2).

However, none of the available classifications are fully satisfactory. Before developing kwashiorkor and after recovery most children show some degree of marasmus. Underweight children are very common and, in many countries, make up 10–60 per cent or more of the population. Contrary to what has been stated in the past, recent studies now show that these stunted children do not suffer from a higher mortality than children of normal stature. *Only when the weight for age of the child falls below 60 per cent from the mean, there is an increase in mortality.*

KWASHIORKOR

This is the most severe, fatal and characteristic form of PEM. It is most frequent after weaning and occurs usually between 9 months and 2 years, but can occur also later. Clinical examination shows growth failure with a low body weight and decreased length for age.

Typically, there is marked edema, which may give the child a 'chubby' appearance in the face. There is marked muscle wasting, which is part of the reason for the inactivity of these children, who are frequently unable to walk or at times to sit and hold their heads up (Figure 31.5).

The skin changes are pellagroid in type, with increased pigmentation and desquamation. Unlike pellagra, the lesions are not in exposed places, but are most frequent in the perineum and buttock. The mouth also shows reddening, with atrophy of the tongue papillae and a fissuring at the corners of the mouth. The hair is sparse, thin and easily pulled out and may change to a reddish colour. However, colour changes may also be related to sun and, in coastal regions, to salt. Following measles, the rash of kwashiorkor may cover the whole body and difficulty arises in deciding how much of the rash is due to measles and how much to kwashiorkor.

There are mental and neurological changes; apathy and irritability are always present. The child is always unhappy and the history of failure to smile is useful.

The liver is palpable and firm. There is frequently anemia associated with iron, folic acid and protein deficiency. Infections of all kinds, particularly pneumonia, septicemia, gastroenteritis and tuberculosis are frequent and often difficult to diagnose. Diarrhea is nearly always persistent and debilitating.

There is a depressed immunity which makes underlying infections worse and septicemia common (mostly Gram-negative, frequently with candidosis). Herpes infection may disseminate and may be related to a cancrum oris or sudden death. Due to severe infection, hypothermia, hypoglycemia, jaundice and collapse from dehydration are common. The prognosis may be poor immediately after admission.

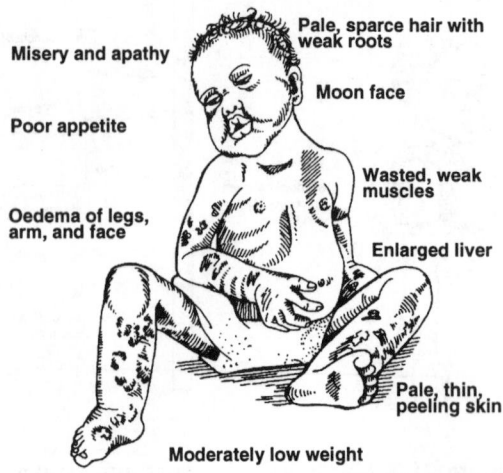

Figure 31.5. A child with kwashiorkor. Artist: Sara Kionga-Kamau

There is a great change in body composition; the distribution of body water, body fat, minerals, trace elements and total body protein, with particularly muscle wasting, are all involved.

Course of the disease

The majority of deaths occur in the first few days and are related to uncontrollable infection, diarrhea, electrolyte imbalance and hypothermia. With good treatment, the mortality even in severe cases, however, can be reduced to well below 10 per cent. The reappearance of the smile is a good indication of recovery and, if home conditions permit, may allow discharge of the child.

MARASMUS

Severe stunting and particularly a loss of subcutaneous fat characterise marasmus. If weights are available, it may be apparent that the child has made no gain in weight for over a year, as shown in Figure 31.6.

Marasmus may appear in the first few months of life particularly if bottle (formula) feeding is attempted. The marasmic child presents typically with a history of failure to thrive, an irritable cry or apathy but may also present with diarrhea, dehydration and vomiting. Usually these children are ravenously hungry, but some may be anorexic. On examination, the child has a shrunken wizened appearance of an old man with even some loss of the buccal pad of fat. In the differential diagnosis, it is important to distinguish severe weight loss from chronic pyogenic or urinary infections, tuberculosis, syphilis and tropical infestations. Child abuse may also present as marasmus.

Probably the most common pattern of malnutrition is a marasmic child who then develops kwashiorkor, frequently following an infection.

MALNUTRITION AND INFECTION

Malnutrition and infection are closely linked. The actual frequency of infection may be only slightly increased, but infections which would have passed as sub-clinical may become sever in the malnourished child. Before the advent of widespread vaccination measles was a most common precipitating cause of malnutrition (Chapter 17). Today, marasmus or marasmic

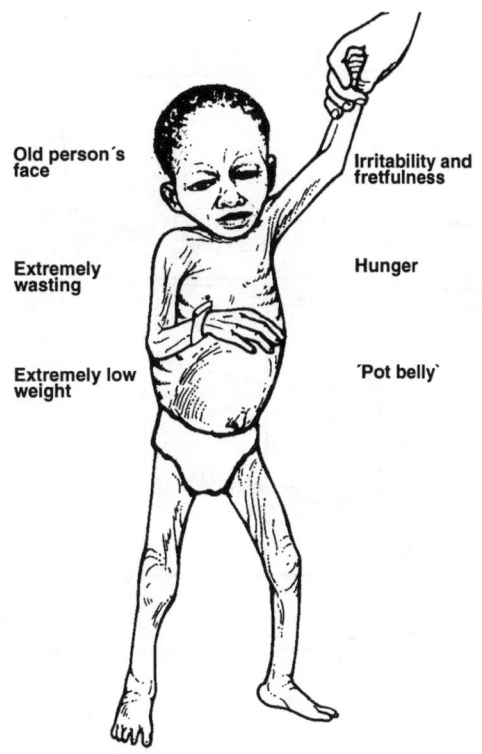

Figure 31.6. A child with marasmus. Marasmic children are easy to recognise. Artist: Sara Kionga-Kamau

kwashiorkor are likely to be frequent presentations of AIDS.

LONG-TERM EFFECTS OF MALNUTRITION

Kwashiorkor is an acute episode, and follow-up of cases does not show significant difference in later growth from other children in the same community. Stunting, on the other hand, can clearly have a long term effect. This is particularly serious in women (Figure 31.7). Short mothers have small babies and provide less breast milk.

LABORATORY FINDINGS

The classical biochemical finding in malnutrition is a reduced serum albumin concentration (Table 31.3). It is a relatively insensitive measure compared with anthropometric measures, but when reduced it is pathognomonic of malnutrition.

Many other proposed biochemical tests have not proved valuable. Abnormalities of serum

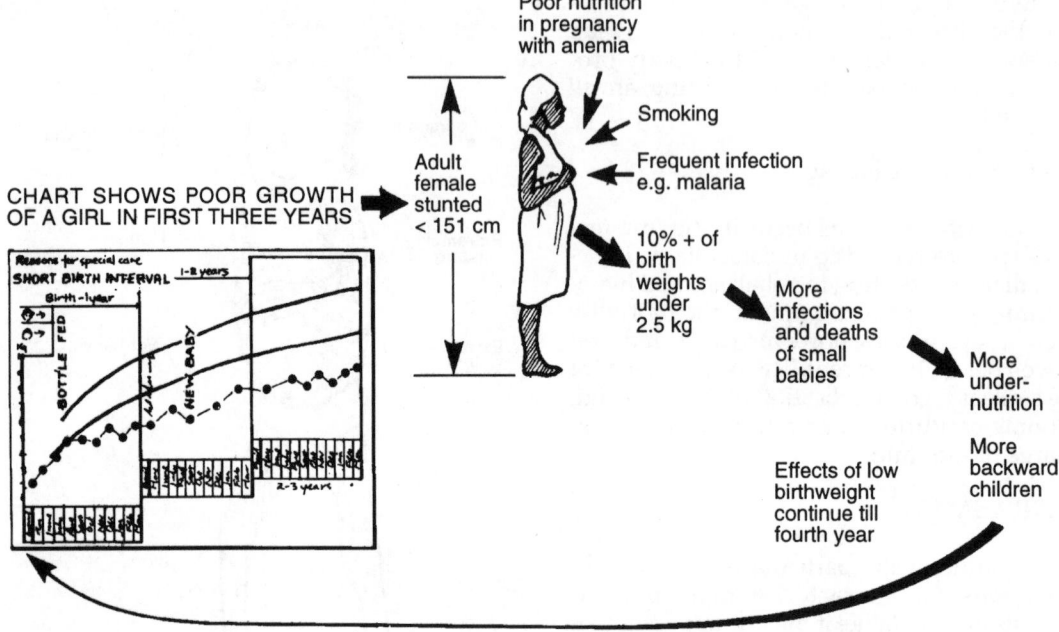

Figure 31.7. Malnutrition cycle.

electrolyte concentrations may help in management, but are not diagnostic of malnutrition. Hypoglycemia is a feature in severe cases and should be screened for, using Dextrostix®, if suspected.

TREATMENT

Mild cases are treated along the principles of prevention (see below). Severe cases should be hospitalised because of danger of sudden death from dehydration, electrolyte disturbances, hypoglycemia or infection. Treatment can be divided into the following phases.

Resuscitation. Dehydration, severe anemia, hypoglycemia and electrolyte imbalances must be managed as a matter of urgency. In many units, during the first 24 hours, a half-strength Darrow's solution or equivalent should be given by mouth or intravenously at a level of 100–150 ml/kg per day. If there is severe dehydration, additional fluids may be required. If the child is shocked or has severe anemia, plasma or blood may be required. Mineral supplements in the form of potassium, to a level of 6 mmol/kg per day, calcium 3 g/day and magnesium 1–1.6 mmol/kg per day have been found helpful in correcting growth deficiencies and cardiac arrhythmias that are frequently present. In severe

cases, in the first 24-hour period of resuscitation, no food or milk should be given. This precaution lessens the complications of vomiting and gastric distension.

Hypoglycemia. Mild asymptomatic hypoglycemia requires 25 per cent dextrose orally. For severe cases with less than 20 mg/100 ml, often complicated with hypothermia, dextrose needs to be given intravenously in the form of a 50 per cent solution, and maintained with 10 per cent dextrose electrolyte solution.

Infection. Children appearing septicemic or who are critically ill should be given antibiotics immediately. Penicillin and streptomycin or co-trimoxazole have proved effective. Malaria or amoebiasis require also urgent treatment. Underlying tuberculosis is a frequent concern, and must be treated.

Diets and supplements after resuscitation. After initial resuscitation, feeding can be recommenced. Small, frequent milk feeds orally

Table 31.3. Interpretation of serum albumin levels (g/litre).

≥35	Normal
30-34	Subnormal
25-29	Low
≤ 25	Pathological

or by nasogastric tube should be started. This can usually be given first at a level of 20 ml/kg per day, and increased to 100 ml/kg per day. This is usually required for 3 or 4 days, until the child can be on a full diet. Where milk is not available, or poorly tolerated because of lactose intolerance, milk substitutes, e.g. soya milk, egg added to porridge or other lactose-free formula, may be used. A useful hospital formula is shown in Table 31.4.

To make up the feed, 100 g of this formula is diluted with 800 ml of water. Vitamin A should be given as there is a real danger of xerophthalmia in many areas, and in all areas there is likely to be some deficit of this. Other vitamin supplements are usually unnecessary. However, iron and folic acid should be given to anemic patients from the second or third day. Usually there is an obvious improvement in the child within the first 2–3 days of treatment. Appetite returns and apathy and irritability lessen.

During the onset of the illness, interaction between the child and its mother will have become minimal, and it is important to encourage the mother to talk and handle the child. Close contact with her may also be a method of preventing hypothermia. Once the child begins to recover, play therapy and attention are of great importance in speeding recovery.

PREVENTION OF MALNUTRITION

Malnutrition is essentially a problem of poverty and its prevention is the responsibility of politicians and those concerned with improving socioeconomic conditions. Food hand-outs by medical centres are not appropriate. The responsibility of the health worker is to evaluate the state of nutrition in a population and to try and ensure that all children grow regularly and adequately. *Children who are growing adequately never suffer from malnutrition.*

To see that children grow regularly, some system of monitoring is essential and, in an attempt to make this possible, growth charts have been widely recommended by international organisations such as WHO, UNICEF and Save the Children Fund. Unfortunately, there have been difficulties in such programmes, partly due to lack of resources but even more to lack of training amongst village and front-line workers. In most school systems in developing countries, graph paper is not found in primary schools and the whole

Table 31.4. A hospital formula for feeding of the malnourished child after the initial resuscitation. Cream can be substituted by local cooking oil.

Casilan	38	parts
Glucose	32	parts
Cream	25	parts
Salt mixture	5	parts
Salt mixture	%	
Calcium carbonate	10	
Potassium	33	
Calcium phosphate	7	
Sodium chloride	40	
Magnesium sulphate	10	

concept of graphs and histograms is not easily understood by large sections of the population.

For this reason, a simple growth chart is not easily understood by the mother and, too frequently the significance of variations in the growth curve are not comprehended even by health workers. The movements of the growth curve are not easily interpreted into appropriate advice and action. For many years, the standard equipment for weighing children, particularly at village level, has been the hanging Salter scales. However, these are quite expensive and the reading of a dial and completing of a chart may be difficult. Fortunately, a new development of a direct recording scale, in which the chart is fitted and a mark is made at the top of a spring which stretches accurately 1 cm a kilogram and records the next point on the child's growth curve, has been introduced (Figure 31.8).

It is hoped that these TALC direct recording scales may take the weighing of children away from the clinic into the community, where the grandmother, father and other members of the household can be involved in discussing the child's growth and making decisions which are often difficult for the mother to make. Instructions to help the mother must be simple and must be in terms of a discussion with her – a discussion in which she is fully involved.

Promotion of growth must be part of PHC with growth monitoring as one of the central issues. If weighing of the small child can be undertaken in or near the home, this should be an occasion for discussing other health measures, such as immunisation, oral rehydration

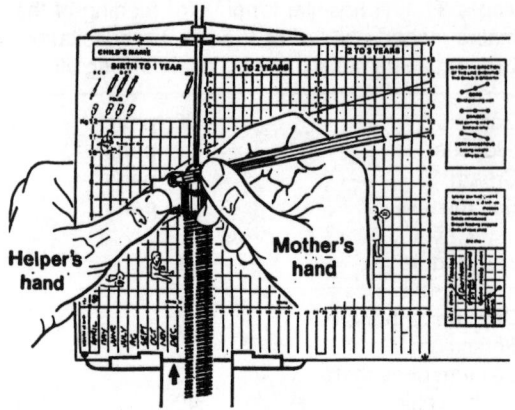

Figure 31.8. TALC direct recording scale.

and eye care. At the same time, any health problems affecting the whole family can be considered. Weighing the small child can be made an entry point for considering the total family health and welfare.

Additional reading

1. Dean P, Ebrahim GJ. Practical care of sick children. London: Macmillan Publishers Ltd, 1986.
2. Ebrahim GJ. Paediatric practice in developing countries. London: Macmillan Education Ltd, 1981.
3. Ghosh S. Nutrition of children under five. In: Wallace HM, Giri K, eds. Health care of women and children in developing countries. Oakland, California: Third Party Publishing Company, 1990:316–26.

4. Morley D, Lovel H. My name is Today. London: Macmillan Publishers Ltd, 1986.
5. Savage King F, Burgess A. Nutrition for developing countries. Oxford: Oxford University Press, 1992.
6. Waterlow JC. Protein energy malnutrition. London: TALC, 1992.

Additional information

Teaching-aids at Low Cost, TALC. P.O. Box 49, St. Albans, Herts. AL1 4AX, Great Britain. A non-profit organisation which supplies a large selection of teaching aids and books to raise standards of health care worldwide.

About the author

David Morley worked in West Africa where he undertook one of the first longitudinal studies of children growing up in a village. He identified and described severe measles, showed the importance of an adequate birth interval, and was responsible for introducing home based growth charts. During the last 20 years of his professional career he set up the Tropical Child Health Unit at the Institute of Child Health in London. He developed Teaching-aids at Low Cost (TALC), the biggest distributor of slides and books to developing countries, and was involved in the initiation of the Child-to-Child Programme. In retirement, he is interested in introducing consumer-friendly methods of measurement such as the TALC Direct Recording Scale and a new method of children measuring each other's height. Many of his numerous publications and books have already become classics.

Lankinen KS, Bergström S, Mäkelä PH and Peltomaa M, eds.
Health and disease in developing countries. London:The Macmillan Press Limited, 1994:305–315.

32 MATERNAL HEALTH:
a priority in reproductive health

Staffan Bergström. M.D., Ph.D.
University of Oslo, Department of Obstetrics and Gynaecology,
Ulleval University Hospital, N-0407 Oslo,
Norway

INTRODUCTION

The definition of reproductive health is variable. The concept has been coined during the latter half of the 1980s and various attempts have been made to clarify what it covers and does not cover. It is obvious that it focuses on prevention and treatment of diseases that impair reproduction. The concept has both male and female dimensions. Among males the fertile age comprises most years from puberty to senescence or death. Among females the fertile age is defined by the more limited period between menarche/pubescence and menopause.

FEMALE AND MALE REPRODUCTIVE HEALTH

Re-production denotes the process of producing a new generation. While the starting point of reproduction can be said to be the gametogenesis it is less clear what would be a relevant end of the process of reproduction. It can be argued that reproduction ends by delivery. It has been argued that the most vulnerable period of the newborn's life, infancy or even childhood up to 5 years, should be included in the scope of reproductive health. Under-five mortality in some rural areas may reach 50 per cent and infant mortality rates around 30 per cent have been reported from several areas. The dependence of the newborn on the mother for warming and feeding makes it relevant and reasonable to include health of the mother and her infant in the scope of reproductive health.

It is important to note that reproductive health is not only pregnancy-oriented. There are reasons to subdivide further the concept of reproductive health as an area focusing on at least three different categories of diseases affecting reproductive health: 1) diseases affecting fertility, i.e. the capacity of a couple to conceive; 2) diseases of both mothers and newborns affecting pregnancy, puerperium and infancy; and 3) diseases affecting reproductive organs in both females and males, but not related to fertility functions or occurring outside fertile age.

Female reproductive health may be threatened by diseases belonging to all three categories in the list given above. There are several prevalent diseases having far-reaching influences on female fertility, most of which affect tubal function. While anovulatory diseases are fairly common worldwide, unilateral or bilateral tubal occlusion is particularly prevalent in areas where gonorrhea and *Chlamydia* infection are common.

The infertility issue is only one part of a greater problem, which would more correctly be called childlessness. It is pertinent and relevant to stress that the problem of childlessness can be subdivided into at least three principal categories: 1) infertility; 2) pregnancy wastage; and 3) child loss.

The health of a pregnant woman and the outcome of her pregnancy are threatened by a number of diseases and adverse environmental conditions. Some infectious diseases, e.g. rubella, syphilis, *Herpes simplex*, cytomegalovirus, *Streptococcus* and *Chlamydia* infection, are related to adverse pregnancy outcomes.

Table 32.1. Maternal deaths as a proportion of deaths of women of reproductive age (1980 to 1985).[6]

Country	% of deaths from maternal causes	Maternal mortality ratio*	Year
Bangladesh (Rural Jamalpur)	46	623	1982–1983
India (Rural Andhra Pradesh)	45	874	1984–1985
Bangladesh (Rural Tangail)	33	566	1982–1983
India (Urban Andhra Pradesh)	28	545	1984–1985
Paraguay	27	275	1984
Bangladesh (Matlab)	26	510	1983
Indonesia (Bali)	23	718	1980–1982
Egypt (Menoufia)	23	190	1981–1983
Egypt (South)	21	300	1984–1985
Ecuador	15	190	1980
Romania	10	149	1984
Mexico	10	88	1984
El Salvador	8	70	1984
Mauritius	6	103	1985
Costa Rica	5	26	1983
Cuba	3	45	1983
Japan	1	16	1985
United States	1	8	1983
Hong Kong	1	5	1985
Sweden	0	2	1984

*Deaths per 100 000 live births.

Pregnancy wastage should be understood as any loss of the fetus from conception to delivery, including early and late miscarriage, late fetal death and stillbirth.

The socioeconomic determinants influencing reproductive health can be seen most clearly in the pattern of childlessness in poor and rich countries. In affluent countries childlessness is almost exclusively an infertility problem. In impoverished countries infertility takes a heavy toll due to tubal obstruction in women and also obstruction to sperm transport in men. In addition to that, however, diseases like syphilis and various viral infections are widespread, resulting in much higher figures of pregnancy wastage than in affluent countries. This is particularly true of fetal death and ensuing stillbirth in the second and third trimesters. Because of this, perinatal mortality ranks much higher in impoverished than in affluent countries.

There are significant threats to female reproductive health also outside the area of fertility and pregnancy. The magnitude of this problem is far greater among women than among men due to the (mostly neglected) problem of uterine malignancies in impoverished countries. About 500 000 female deaths due to cancer of the uterine cervix are estimated to occur annually in the world. Incidentally, this figure is the same as the often quoted figure of maternal deaths annually in the world. In practice there is no screening, nor efficient cure to this half a million women dying a painful death. Even if the bulk of these women may die outside fertile age, cervical cancer has particularly serious consequences to female reproductive health. This is particularly pertinent in the light of recent evidence of this disease being due to papilloma virus infection, presumably transmitted sexually. In this perspective it is noteworthy that long before AIDS the world has had a fatal, sexually transmitted disease selectively killing women (but not men) to an extent overshadowing the present disaster of another acquired, sexually transmitted disease, HIV infection.

Male reproductive health has been somewhat overshadowed by the relevant and adequate focus of interest on female reproductive health. It is, however, well known that disorders affecting male fertility are prevalent in most countries. In affluent countries the relative contribution of the male to the etiology of a couple's infertility problem is considered as almost as important as that of the female. Male reproductive function depends on normal gametogenesis, gamete transport and normal sexual function. Widespread diseases in developing countries affect both gamete production and transport. Inflammatory changes in testicular tissues and in the epididymis may create obstruction to gamete transport with ensuing male infertility. Diseases like mumps, gonorrhea and filariosis may affect male fertility in several ways. Mumps may lead to orchitis with ensuing azoospermia and infertility, and gonorrhea may cause epididymitis with blockage of sperm transport. Filariosis may create lymph obstruction in the groins with ensuing swelling, hydrocele and warming of testicular tissue, leading to impaired gamete production and infertility.

THE MATERNAL DIMENSION OF REPRODUCTIVE HEALTH

In medical jargon maternal health is almost exclusively understood as pregnancy-related health. The concept maternal derives from the Latin word *mater* (mother). In the normal sense of the word a mother is a woman having had children but in the medical jargon it is most often synonymous with a pregnant woman or an early puerperal woman. This meaning of the word mother is clear when we look upon concepts like maternal health care, maternal leave, maternal mortality, maternal morbidity etc. In everyday language maternal actually means a *child-bearing* woman or

a *child-rearing* woman. Still, maternal health care in health care terminology is most often understood as merely pregnancy-related health care.

The wider sense of maternal health care has not won wide international acceptance as yet. By including care of the child-rearing women in the concept of maternal health care, due attention would be paid to *a longitudinal perspective* of reproductive health care. Using this wider concept in maternal health care, the target group must be all women of reproductive age, whether pregnant or not. In most low-income countries these women constitute about 20 per cent of the population. They are subject to pregnancy-related risks in a substantial way (Table 32.1). Between 20 and 45 per cent of their deaths are pregnancy-related (maternal mortality in a strict sense).[1]

The prevention of maternal disease and death should include *the prevention of undesired motherhood* for those most likely to get pregnant and to suffer illicit abortion. Adolescents are most at risk, since young girls are prone to be victims of sexist exploitation. These young women should be particular targets for *preventive maternal health care* due to their need for prevention of undesired motherhood and should not be excluded from safe motherhood initiatives. Conventional family planning clinics may not, however, be suitable as service providers, since unmarried adolescents needing contraceptives do not have any family to plan. It is simply an individual question of fertility control by contraception in order to avoid an undesired motherhood.

Maternal and child health were key components given much attention in Alma-Ata in 1978, but the maternal health component - in its own right and not only as a vehicle for the child - was given remarkably little emphasis. There is plenty of evidence of this imbalance, which has been also clearly visible in bilateral and multilateral assistance. The bias also applies to research related to human reproduction. Fertility regulation research was long given highest priority, while little or no attention was paid to research in maternal health assistance or maternal health care. The alleged priority of birth control and fertility regulation thereby obscured development needs in maternal health care.

Only recently there have been significant efforts in donor countries to support safe motherhood-oriented research and the concept of the road to death has become appreciated. It is easy to say that a woman has died from fatal hemorrhage or from eclamptic convulsions. But the analysis of cause of death should comprise a more holistic approach. A longitudinal perspective, covering the period from the birth of a girl child onwards, reveals important determinants of maternal deaths on the woman's road to death.[2,3] Poverty, son preference, illiteracy, malnutrition and lack of primary maternal health care may have paved the road. An investigation of this road to death in terms of *avoidability* may show that the vast majority of all maternal deaths are avoidable by access to simple and basic maternity care.[4] It should be recognised that medical problems often have non-medical solutions: several investigations confirm that oppressed, impoverished, ill-informed and deprived women have by far the highest maternal morbidity and mortality.[5]

Women living far away from health facilities may suffer a maternal mortality four times as high as similar women living close by. Gender attitudes may be an important reason of lacking maternal health. Experiences from various health services show that approaches for the improvement of maternal survival and female reproductive health are dependent on prevailing gender roles and their determinants.

MATERNAL MORTALITY: THE TIP OF THE ICEBERG

Maternal death is internationally defined as the death of a woman while pregnant or within 42 days from the termination of pregnancy, irrespective of the duration and the site of the pregnancy, from any cause related to or aggravated by the pregnancy or by its management but not due to accidental or incidental causes. Usually maternal deaths are grouped in two categories: direct and indirect obstetric deaths. *Direct* obstetric deaths result from obstetric complications of pregnancy, labour or puerperium, from interventions, omissions, incorrect treatment or from a chain of events resulting from any of the above. Such direct obstetric deaths may be consequences of e.g. eclampsia, uterine rupture, post partum endometritis with septicemia or complications following abortions. *Indirect* obstetric deaths comprise deaths resulting from previously existing disease or a disease developed during pregnancy and aggravated by the physiological effects of pregnancy. Examples of such diseases include diabetes, tuberculosis and heart disease.

The *maternal mortality ratio* is the number of maternal deaths per 100 000 live births. A much less utilised expression is *maternal mortality rate*, which is the number of maternal deaths per 1000 women of reproductive age. While the *rate* expresses the risk of maternal death per women exposed to pregnancy, the *ratio* expresses the risk of maternal death per pregnancy. The ideal denominator in the maternal mortality *ratio* would be total number of pregnancies. This number is virtually impossible to obtain and it is also most difficult to obtain total births. Therefore the currently used approximation, live births, is considered appropriate for practical use.

The wider concept of mortality among women of reproductive age has been given more attention over the last decade. Currently available data reveal the wide gap between poor and rich countries regarding the proportion of maternal deaths in this category of women's deaths (Tables 32.1 and 32.2).

It has been estimated that each year at least half a million women die from causes related to pregnancy and childbirth. More than 99 per cent of these maternal deaths occur in developing countries, which account for about 85 per cent of the world's births.[6] Of the world's maternal deaths more than 50 per cent occur in Asia. India is a particularly typical case in that there are more maternal deaths in one day than there are in the whole affluent world in one month.[7]

Hospital data on maternal deaths point to high rates but the majority of figures (also in affluent countries) are misleading when it comes to exact levels. Most civil registration data are incomplete and even in the USA registration data may underestimate the number of maternal deaths by as much as 25 per cent.[8] Similarly, a recent independent study in Jamaica indicated that there were more than twice as many maternal deaths as the official figure.[9] In India there is evidence that the degree of under-registration is even more pronounced.[6] For many countries the national estimates, crude as they are, are official government or UN estimates. Fortunately, in recent years there have been a growing number of community surveys, which have given some information on the problem of maternal mortality in localities, where very little was known before. In other deprived areas of low-income countries a large number of orphan children or many more female deaths than male deaths in reproductive age groups may point to high levels of maternal mortality.

It has been estimated that 25–40 per cent of maternal deaths imply the loss, for remaining children, of the only parent.[10] Often, then, a maternal death means the end of a socially functioning family. The consequences are brutal: as many as 95 per cent of the remaining infants may not survive their fifth birthday.[11] Those children who do survive, add to the growing number of abandoned orphans, an increasing problem in low-income countries. Some of these abandoned children may also be the consequence of the less visible maternal morbidity.

MATERNAL MORBIDITY: THE BASE OF THE ICEBERG

It has been estimated that for each maternal death there are at least 15–20 cases of severe maternal morbidity.[12] Severe alludes to long-lasting disease and handicap and not only to anemia, infectious diseases and short-lasting periods of common ailments. Maternal morbidity as an indicator of deficient maternal health can be measured in several ways. Firstly, maternal disease might be diagnosed clinically. This is *the carrier expression* of maternal morbidity. Secondly, carrier health is necessarily reflected in its dependent passenger, the fetus. *The passenger expression* of maternal morbidity is found in the health status of the offspring. Many examples of this can be given.

The prevalence of low birth weight (LBW) births is one relevant expression of this carrier morbidity. The stillbirth rate is another. Improving maternal health in various ways can be expected to result in the reduction of the number of both LBW newborns and stillborns. Studies in the Gambia have shown that a specific food supplementation of pregnant women during seasons of nutritional hardship reduced the prevalence of LBW newborns to levels prevailing in affluent countries like Sweden.[13] Adoption of suitable nutritional screening and antenatal follow-up of fetal growth among pregnant women has resulted in a new interest in anthropometry, including mid-upper-arm circumference and fundal height.[14-16] These simple measures can improve monitoring of maternal health.

The pattern of maternal puerperal morbidity is variable. In some areas, but not in others, devastating consequences of complicated pregnancies and deliveries include chronic conditions like fistulae and tubal sterility after postpartum endometritis–myometritis.[17] The wide variation in morbidity patterns can be illustrated by the prevalence of prolapse conditions, being reportedly different in some African and Asian populations studied.[17] Diseases occurring during pregnancy show an even wider variation than the puerperal morbidity. Such diseases comprise cerebral malaria, severe anemia, tuberculosis, nutritional deficiency-related conditions, HIV-related infections and complications arising from illicit abortion.[17]

MATERNAL HEALTH CARE: EXPERIENCE OF INTERVENTIONS

Recent studies have confirmed that suitable technology and appropriate approaches can contribute substantially to improved maternal health. Growing interest in maternal health care has produced a large amount of valuable experience. Published results have hitherto applied mostly to child-bearing women and perinatal outcome. Since maternal mortality is a comparatively distinct entity to study and to assess, *organisational* consequences of analyses of avoidability of maternal deaths have been given more attention.[18] The organisation of the referral chain is an example.

The recognition of the value of the first referral level is an important improvement in maternal health care. The establishment of a simple referral system from a peripheral area to a hospital will significantly reduce maternal mortality.[19] Health service research is another recent approach to improve maternal care. Studies from Guatemala show that personal, human support from lay women through labour and delivery means improved perinatal outcome.[20] Such extremely simple but rewarding interventions, in cost–benefit terms, are often overshadowed by more sophisticated measures. The sustainability of efforts, such as those mentioned here, obviously depends on their appropriateness, viability and acceptability in the traditional setting.

An action-oriented approach to maternal health care can be defined in various ways. The problem may not be to find relevant alternatives to existing routines, but rather to motivate decision-making key staff – mostly male – to utilise available information. Women are mostly underprivileged and have seldom

Table 32.2. Distribution of maternal deaths by cause in selected countries of the Americas.[6]

Country	Year	Direct obstetric causes					Indirect obstetric causes
		Abortion	Hemorrhage	Toxemia	Puerperal	Other	
Argentina	81	35.8	14.4	13.1	14.4	20.6	1.7
Brazil	83	13.5	19.6	31.6	14.7	17.7	3.0
Chile	84	40.4	6.4	20.2	13.8	11.7	7.4
Colombia	81	17.2	18.6	23.5	6.5	31.3	2.9
Cuba	84	15.6	3.9	–	13.0	35.1	32.5
Dominican Republic	84	21.7	18.3	31.7	–	17.5	10.8
Ecuador	84	8.9	21.4	27.9	8.6	32.0	1.3
El Salvador	84	7.1	7.1	5.1	8.1	71.7	1.0
Guatemala	81	8.6	4.6	3.4	9.2	74.2	–
Honduras	82	6.0	3.4	0.7	1.3	88.6	–
Mexico	82	8.2	21.2	5.9	8.6	53.0	3.0
Paraguay	84	12.3	27.7	18.7	16.1	21.3	3.9
Peru	82	12.5	29.3	7.5	12.3	38.0	0.3
U.S.A.	83	17.2	10.3	13.8	29.0	26.9	2.8
Venezuela	83	19.8	15.8	20.5	18.8	18.2	6.9

anyone to speak for them. Education is therefore a crucial starting point for change. At the community level female (and male) education is therefore a prerequisite for female empowerment.

Community education

The objective of this education is to make the community aware (through newspapers, radio and so on) of the importance of maternal health and pregnancy care. Families may be unaware or ignorant and, for cultural and religious reasons, pregnant women may be reluctant to enroll early enough for antenatal care. A community education approach may even include programmes for an improved enrolment of traditional birth attendants (TBA), though several such programmes have met with severe difficulties due to deficient sustainability in governmental supervision and support.[21]

The community health education should also focus upon the recognition of dangerous signs during pregnancy. Encouraging the enrolment in antenatal care of pregnant women is a process over several years that must run concomitantly with an improvement in existing, peripheral health posts. Resources to strengthen the referral chain are often scarce, however, and innovative approaches are necessary.

In community education a particularly important component is sex education. This is most clearly demonstrated regarding safe motherhood during adolescence. The provision of school-based sex education is culturally controversial in many countries but should nevertheless be a long-term goal in community education for safe motherhood.

Traditional community birthing care

In a number of programmes in maternal health care there has been a focus on prevailing traditions in birthing care at the community level.[21] Most programmes have stimulated great interest at first but many of them have not maintained momentum and have not been sustainable. If vigorously supervised and integrated into peripheral maternal health services, with transport and communication available, TBAs may improve conditions for hygienic delivery and give some prenatal and postnatal care. TBAs have also been shown to successfully identify simple risk factors for referral.[22] In many rural areas a sound operational attitude, recognising both limitations and possibilities, should opt for the selective enrolment of some TBAs for appropriate training. Expanding their responsibility and participation in peripheral maternal health care has been tried with some success in several countries. On the other hand, studies from the Gambia suggest that maternal mortality and efficiency in perinatal screening have been unchanged over periods of intense TBA training.[23] Another problem is that TBAs traditionally attend very few deliveries, maybe 15–25, per year. Hence, in order to have a substantial impact on maternal health and quality of peripheral pregnancy care, a great number of them have to be upgraded by training. In conclusion, TBAs would seem to play a relatively minor role in reducing maternal mortality but play a potentially major role in the prevention of unhygienic deliveries, thereby reducing the risk of neonatal and other diseases.

Antenatal care

The care of the pregnant woman has three essential functions: 1) selection of women at risk for subsequent referral to a level with better competence and facilities; 2) prevention and treatment of severe maternal morbidity; and 3) maternal health education.

The *first* function, screening for risk, rests on the fact that certain women have an increased tendency for serious pregnancy or delivery complications. Such complications comprise eclampsia, severe anemia, obstructed labour, abnormal fetal presentation etc. Some risk factors are related to the patient's own history, while others are associated with clinical signs appearing only during the current pregnancy.

The foremost problem related to the risk classification of pregnant women is that *most alleged risk factors tend to have a low predictive value.*[24] Among the minority of women with an alleged risk factor the number of maternal deaths or severe maternal diseases may be very low, while maternal deaths also occur among the larger number of women without distinguishable risk factors. A concrete example is anemia, which may increase the risk of maternal death, e.g. when there is abundant bleeding *postpartum*. In absolute numbers such cases are, however, limited and the abundant hemorrhage, in itself, may be fatal to all women, whether anemic or not.

Since severely anemic women are a minority of all pregnant women a life-threatening bleeding more often affects women without severe anemia. The same can be said about infections, particularly *postpartum* endometritis–myometritis. The possibility to foresee that disease in antenatal care is in practice nil.

Bleedings, infections, some eclampsia cases and a number of less frequent complications affect, in absolute numbers, more low risk women (without risk factors) than high risk women (with risk factors). It is therefore important to stress that *the majority of women dying a maternal death are low risk women.*[25] This fact indicates clearly that antenatal care must be supplemented with access to emergency care in case of unforeseen complications. Up to one fifth of all pregnant women, on the average, will need some form of advanced, emergency obstetric care in order to guarantee safe motherhood and uneventful perinatal outcome for the newborn. Such emergency care comprises life-saving skills at the midwifery level, measures to stop life-threatening bleeding, Cesarean section in obstructed labour, extraction with vacuum extractor or forceps, blood transfusion, anti-convulsant treatment, antibiotic infusion, symphysiotomy, and others.

Prevention and treatment of maternal morbidity is the *second* principal function of antenatal care. Such care comprises diseases like anemia, syphilis, malaria, genital tract infections and in some cases also prophylaxis. While chemoprophylaxis in malaria is disputed especially because of the development of resistance, it seems to be less disputable among certain high risk groups, e.g. in young mothers during their first pregnancy and in some high risk groups of pregnant women.

Maternal health education is the *third* principal component in antenatal care. Information of the importance of compliance in antenatal care and delivery care is underscored here as well as the importance of adhering to established rules and treatment routines. Antenatal care is an important *meeting place* for pregnant women and the formal and informal exchange of information is an important means of spreading messages for an improved maternal health. The maternal health education should embrace not only pregnancy and delivery care but also neonatal care, family planning etc.

It is common to see antenatal cards in low-income countries copied from affluent countries with minor changes. Such a copying often

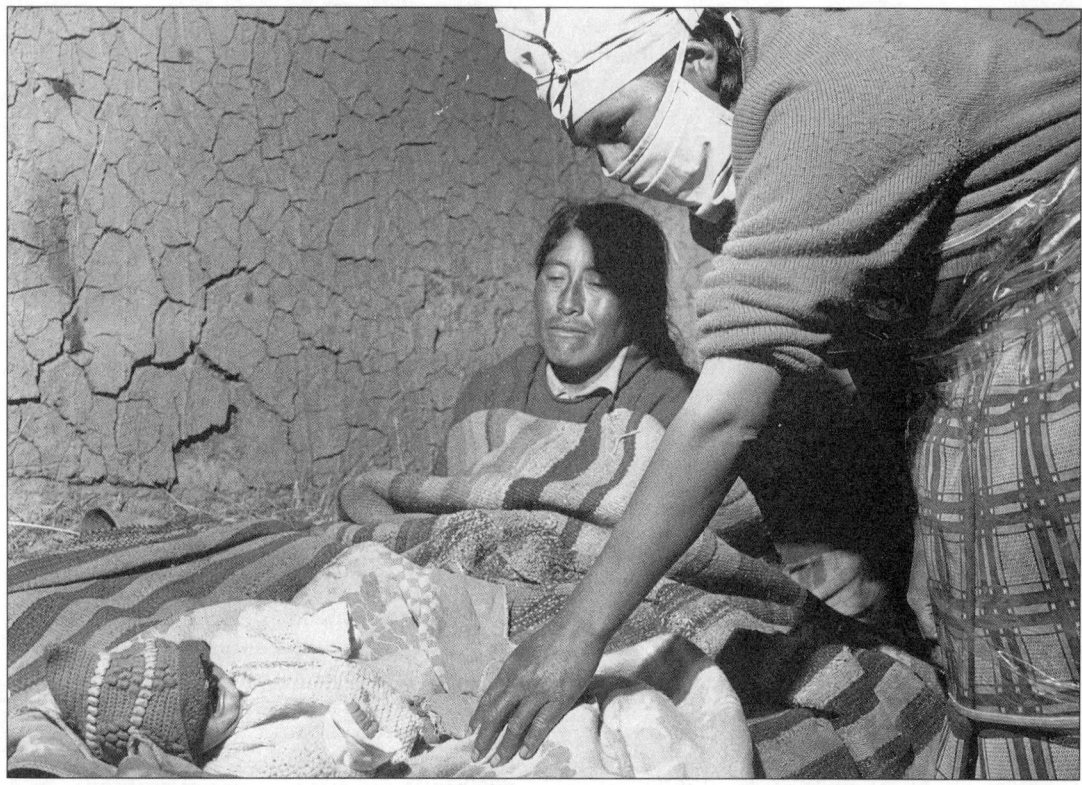

A new life just arrived under the trained hands of a traditional midwife from the Altiplano of Puno, Peru.
Photo: UNICEF/Alexander Røsler

implies the application of unsuitable criteria with ensuing overloading of antenatal clinics with low risk pregnancies (allegedly high risk), while unrecognised high risk groups (allegedly low risk) escape attention.

Antenatal care has often been thought to prevent a large portion of maternal deaths. This is a conclusion from the concentration of maternal deaths and severe maternal morbidity among women who never receive antenatal care. However, it is inappropriate to conclude from this that adding antenatal care to such a setting, leaving other variables as they are, will improve perinatal outcome both for the mother and her newborn. It is quite probable that it is the low socioeconomic status which generates *both* the high risk of maternal death *and* the low utilisation of antenatal care.

An operational attitude aims at excluding the merely ritual attendance to conventional antenatal care without critical questioning of its quality and relevance. Also in developed countries discussion of the value of antenatal care has started over the last few years.

Ingredients in the maternal health care of affluent countries have been questioned. Recent scientific findings suggest that conventionally used risk factors must be questioned and better ones sought.[26]

While recognising the importance of prophylactic measures during pregnancy, it is essential to emphasise that preventive health measures also include *pre-pregnancy health care*. Since the aim is to reduce maternal morbidity and mortality any comprehensive health care should include pre-pregnancy interventions, such as sexual education and contraception counselling. This *longitudinal* perspective should consider pregnancies and intervals between pregnancies to be links in the chain of reproductive life. Preventive delivery care should be broadly based on preventive antenatal care and organically linked to it. While antenatal care should make an effort to foresee and prevent complications both before and during motherhood, preventive delivery care should attempt to foresee and to prevent complications immediately before and during the delivery itself. Appropriate documentation of delivery care is most important. The basis of such documentation is the patient´s record, the quality of which should be given particular attention.

Maternity villages

In order to overcome problems of distance and to avoid dangerous and mutilating traditional birth practices, maternity waiting homes or maternity villages have been established in some developing countries. The intention is to offer resting areas during the last month of pregnancy to women being at particular risk or living very far from a hospital. Such villages should ideally be situated close to a delivery facility with resources of a first referral level (see below). Though theoretically efficient, these villages have often appeared alien and logistical problems have been difficult to solve. A woman may be unable to stay away from home for several weeks. However, in Cuba and in some African countries waiting homes and villages have worked well. If socially acceptable and feasible as to food and lodging, they may guarantee a hygienic delivery and early referral when this is called for.

Beyond primary mother care: the first referral level

While the Alma Ata conference in 1978 was a significant step forward in recognising the priority of primary health care, the concept safe motherhood was not coined until some 10 years later. The prevention of maternal deaths has been characterised as *'an area in which no amount of primary care or community effort can make a significant impact unless it is built around adequate medical services'*. It is estimated that approximately one fifth of pregnant women will develop serious complications, such as obstructed labour, placental abruption, pre-eclampsia, severe anemia, pre-labour rupture of the membranes preterm etc., regardless of the antenatal care they receive. A recent WHO meeting concluded that 'in the larger proportion of cases in which complications cannot be predicted more effective means of treating complications need to be available at the first referral level'. The improvement of maternal health care beyond primary health care embraces particularly the concept of the first referral level. Some factors currently given emphasis in this concept are the following:

Improving obstetric first aid. Three frequent killers of pregnant women are postpartum hemorrhage, eclampsia and puerperal sepsis. Counteracting postpartum hemorrhage by abdominal compression of the aorta is a technique that can be learnt by anyone. Eclampsia can be easily and safely treated by injection of magnesium sulphate, a cheap and safe drug that could be made available almost everywhere. If available early enough, antibiotics can cure potentially fatal postpartum endometritis–myometritis.

Upgrading of small rural hospitals. The crucial role of rural hospitals in preventing maternal deaths is beyond doubt. Appropriate technologies, including Cesarean section under local anesthesia and symphysiotomy, might mean a revolutionary improvement. The most serious problem is staffing. Technical upgrading should be thoroughly planned and might enable staff to undertake for example symphysiotomy and Cesarean section without undue risk to the mother or newborn.

Expanding role of mid-level health workers. In countries like Mozambique, Zaire and Thailand, medical assistants and nurses have been trained to perform laparotomies, Cesarean sections, tubal ligations and legal abortions, and the results are good.[27-29] These innovations are often met with opposition from the established medical profession. The results are, nevertheless, rewarding and thought-provoking. In Mozambique, medical assistants have been trained to substitute for surgeons with good results.[27]

The fact that many obstetric complications are unpredictable and rapidly life-threatening makes the availability of emergency obstetric care most important. Irrespective of the presence of risk factors any pregnant or parturient woman should have access to life-saving skills among trained health workers, available near the place where the unforeseen, severe complication occurs. This is, in essence, the consideration on which the concept of the first referral level rests. In a sense this is beyond primary mother care if the latter concept is interpreted to mean non-hospital-oriented care. It was, however, never inherent in the Alma-Ata spirit to deny the value of hospital services but rather to give more emphasis to primary care outside institutions. In obstetrics, the need of such back-up services is very clear and the simplistic approach of overlooking or paying less attention to the first referral level than to antenatal care is now less

Table 32.3. Eight essential obstetric functions at the first referral level.

Surgical functions
Cesarean section, symphysiotomy, surgical repair of high vaginal and cervical tears and lacerations, including uterine rupture, surgical treatment of sepsis, removal of ectopic pregnancy, evacuation of uterus in incomplete abortion etc.

Anesthetic functions
Local and general anesthesia, regional block etc.

Medical treatment
Parenteral treatment of shock, intravenous administration of antibiotics in the control of sepsis, administration of iron in severe anemia or blood loss, control of hypertensive disorders of pregnancy and eclamptic convulsions.

Blood replacement
The availability of a small blood bank is essential.

Manual and/or assessment functions
Vacuum extraction to hasten delivery in the second stage of labour, manual removal of placenta, partogram routines.

Family planning functions
Tubal ligation and vasectomy, insertion of intrauterine devices.

Management of women at particular risk
Access to a maternal waiting area where women living at a long distance or women with a particular risk factor may stay for a period at the end of pregnancy.

Neonatal special care
Resuscitation, thermal control and feeding.

---

common than in the wake of the Alma-Ata conference in the early 1980s.

The concept of first referral level in maternal health care consists of *eight essential obstetric functions* (Table 32.3). In reality these essential obstetric functions are unavailable outside most provincial hospitals or central hospitals in low-income countries. The virtual absence of surgically trained obstetric staff makes the problem of *responsibility delegation* more prominent. The implementation of the essential obstetric functions at first referral level requires training of a large number of qualified staff which cannot possibly be recruited among doctors. The growing experience of delega-

tion of responsibility, *also for surgical functions like Cesarean sections and laparotomies,* is an encouraging fact in considering ways for improved maternal survival.

Highly trained personnel are often reluctant to work in rural areas. Such a reluctance may be exacerbated by the fact that most training at medical faculties is predominantly urban-oriented and frequently western-influenced. Recognition of the value of middle-level workers is important, in particular midwives and medical assistants, who are usually trained in peripheral areas.

In the referral chain of pregnant and parturient women the concept of the health team is most important. All staff, from the doctors at first referral level to the health worker or TBA close to the patient, should work together in constructive cooperation with support and supervision being offered down the line. In order to make such a collaboration possible and fruitful, the artificial barriers that separate categories of staff need to be abolished. Team work should become part and parcel of the training curriculum of all health workers right from the very beginning of their training. Practical field work and on-the-job training could further enhance the process of creating the spirit of team work.

With the hierarchical system prevailing in many low-income countries the possibility of team work will depend on good supervision and guidance. Health personnel at the periphery are in constant need of *encouragement, instruction* and *technical guidance*. Besides, good morale throughout a team will help to guarantee that all members are fulfilling their professional potential, referring adequately and avoiding unnecessary referrals.

The current threat to maternal survival due to structural adjustment policies has become glaringly visible in several African countries.[30] The debt trap has become a potential disaster for most vulnerable among Third World adolescents and adults: women in reproductive age. While the dramatic improvement of maternal mortality figures would have been within reach at a highly bearable cost we may have to witness that maternal mortality figures continue to increase. There is reason for concern in the era of safe motherhood rhetorics.

References

1. Basch PF. Textbook of international health. Oxford: Oxford University Press, 1990:160.

2. Kwast BE. Roads to maternal death. Case histories, including comments on preventive strategies. Informal paper No. 1, Safe Motherhood Conference, Nairobi 1987.
3. The girl child – an investment in the future. New York: UNICEF, 1991.
4. Mahler H. The Safe Motherhood Initiative: a call to action. Lancet 1987;i(8534):668–70.
5. Bhatia JC. A study of maternal mortality in Anantapur district, Andhra Pradesh, India. Bangalore, 1986.
6. Royston E, Armstrong S, eds. Preventing maternal deaths. Geneva: WHO, 1989.
7. World health statistics annual, 1986. Geneva: WHO, 1986.
8. Ziskin LZ, Gregory M, Kreitzer M. Improved surveillance of maternal deaths. Int J Gynaecol Obstet 1979;16:282–6.
9. Walker GJ, Ashley DEC, McCaw AM, Bernard GW. Maternal mortality in Jamaica. Lancet 1986; i(8479):486–8.
10. The World Bank. Gender and poverty in India. Washington DC: World Bank, 1991.
11. Chen L, Gesche MC, Ahamed S, Chowdhury AI, Mosley EWH. Maternal mortality in rural Bangladesh. Stud Fam Plann 1974;17:243–51.
12. Koblinsky MA, Campbell OMR, Harlow S. Mother and more: a broader perspective on women's health. In: Koblinsky M, Timyan J, Gay J, eds. The health of women: global perspective. Boulder, Colorado, USA: West View Press, 1992.
13. Whitehead RG, Prentice AM, Lamb W, Paul AA. Maternal dietary supplementation during lactation and pregnancy in a rural African village in the Gambia. In: Campbell BD, Gillmer MDG, eds. Nutrition in pregnancy. London: Perinatology Press, 1983:133-41.
14. Liljestrand J, Bergström S. Antenatal nutritional assessment: the value of upper-arm circumference. Gynaecol Obstet Invest 1991; 32:81–3.
15. Bergström S, Liljestrand J. Parturient fundal height and its relation to fetal weight. J Trop Pediatr 1989;35:27–30.
16. Bergström S, Libombo A. Puerperal measurement of the symphysis-fundus distance. Gynecol Obstet Invest 1992;34:76–8.
17. Omran AR, Standley CC. Family formation and maternal health. In: Further studies on family formation patterns and health. Geneva: WHO, 1981:271–302.
18. Maine D. Safe motherhood programmes: options and issues. Columbia University Center for Population and Family Health, NY, 1990.
19. Essential elements of obstetric care at first referral level. Geneva: WHO, 1991.
20. Klaus MH, Kennell JH, Robertson SS, Sosa R. Effects of social support during parturition on maternal and infant morbidity. Br Med J 1986;293:586–7.
21. Leedam E. Traditional birth attendants. Int J Gynaecol Obstet 1985;23:249–74.
22. Poovan P, Kifle F, Kwast B. A maternity waiting home reduces obstetric catastrophes. World Health Forum 1990;11:440–5.
23. Greenwood A. The Farafenni project. Proceedings of a Workshop on guidelines for safe motherhood programming. Washington D.C.: The World Bank/Mother care, 1991.
24. Maine D. Too far to walk. New York: Colombia University Center for Population and Family Health, 1991.
25. Winikoff B, Sullivan M. Assessing the role of family planning in reducing maternal mortality. Stud Fam Plann 1987;18:128–43.
26. Lindmark G, Cnattingius S, eds.The scientific basis of antenatal care routines: the state of the art. Int J Technol Assess Health Care 1992;8 (Suppl 1).
27. da Luz Vaz M, Bergström S. Mozambique – delegation of responsibility in the area of maternal care. Int J Gynaecol Obstet 1992;38(Suppl): 41–3.
28. White SM, Thorpe RG, Maine D. Emergency obstetric surgery performed by nurses in Zaire. Lancet 1987;ii:612–3.
29. Kanchanasinith K, Piyapinyo P, Pitaktepsombati P, et al. Postpartum sterilization by nurse-midwives in Thailand. Internat Fam Plann Perspect 1990;16:55–8.
30. Ekwempu CC, Maine D, Olorukoba MB, Essien B, Kisseka MN. Structural adjustments and health in Africa. Lancet 1990;336:56–7.

About the author

Staffan Bergström is Professor of International Health at the University of Oslo and Senior Physician at the Department of Obstetrics and Gynaecology, Ullevål University Hospital, Oslo, Norway. He is a specialist in obstetrics and gynaecology and responsible for many research projects in the area of reproductive health in developing countries. During 1982–86 he was the Director of the Department of Obstetrics, Central Hospital, Maputo, Mozambique. He is also involved in the human reproduction research programme (HRP) within the WHO.

Lankinen KS, Bergström S, Mäkelä PH and Peltomaa M, eds.
Health and disease in developing countries. London:The Macmillan Press Limited, 1994:317–322.

33 THE INCREASING IMPORTANCE OF CHRONIC DISEASES

Aulikki Nissinen, M.D., Ph.D.
University of Kuopio, Department of Public
Health and Primary Care
P.O. Box 1627, FIN-70211 Kuopio,
Finland

Geoffrey Kiangi, M.D.
University of Kuopio, Department of
Public Health and Primary Care
P.O. Box 1627, FIN-70211 Kuopio,
Finland

INTRODUCTION

The aging of populations in developing countries results in both a demographic and an epidemiological transition that will affect the impact of chronic degenerative diseases on the health of the populations. The epidemiological transition phenomena have been well recognised only recently.[1-4] As economies develop and societies meet their needs for sanitation and for maternal and child health services, life expectancy increases and life styles associated with injury and chronic diseases tend to become more common. The change may include a shift in the health-related behaviour which may augment the dietary consumption of fats and alcohol, increase obesity, increase smoking and decrease physical activity.

Changes in risk factor levels increase the prevalence of chronic diseases which manifest themselves at advanced age. As a matter of fact, in populations with life expectancy in the age range of 60 years and above, chronic degenerative diseases may become the major determinants of health. In every country, depending upon the status of development, non-communicable diseases are either emerging, rapidly increasing or already established at high levels.[5]

CHANGE IN NON-COMMUNICABLE DISEASES

A comparison of the mortality data reported for Chile and Finland in 1954 and 1989 demonstrates clearly the epidemiological transition. In Finland the proportion of deaths from non-communicable diseases such as cancer, stroke, diabetes, liver diseases, accidents, suicide and homicide rose slowly from 71 per cent in 1954 to 80 per cent in 1989. The corresponding figures from Chile were 39 per cent in 1954 and 67 per cent in 1988.[6]

Cardiovascular diseases (CVD) account for a major proportion of all deaths during adulthood in both developed and developing countries (Table 33.1).[7] In the developing countries, CVD account for a smaller proportion of all deaths than in developed ones, but the greater contribution of CVD deaths in developing countries to mortality worldwide means that the total number of deaths from these diseases is even greater there than in the developed

Table 33.1. Mortality from cardiovascular disease in developing coutries, 1990.[7]

	Deaths (x 1000)	Sex-ratio (male/female)
Rheumatic heart disease	440	0.5
Ischemic heart disease	2 470	1.2
Stroke	3 180	0.9
Pericarditis, endocarditis, myocarditis and cardiomyopathies	1 230	1.1
Total	9 000	1.0

Table 33.2. Leading causes of death, 1990.[7]

Cause of deaths	Millions of deaths	%
Developing regions		
Cardiovascular diseases	9.0	23.0
Acute respiratory infections	3.9	10.0
Cancer	3.7	9.5
Accidents and injuries	3.4	8.7
Diarrheal diseases	2.8	7.2
Tuberculosis	2.0	5.1
Chronic obstructive pulmonary disease	1.7	4.4
Measles	1.0	2.6
Malaria	1.0	2.6
Cirrhosis	0.5	1.3
Diabetes	0.5	1.3
Developed regions, EME and FSE		
Ischemic heart diseases	2.7	24.8
Cancer	2.4	22.0
Stroke	1.4	12.8
Accidents and injuries	0.8	7.3
Infectious/acute respiratory infections	0.5	4.6
Chronic obstructive pulmonary disease	0.4	3.7
Diabetes	0.2	1.8
Cirrhosis	0.2	1.8

countries.[7,8] The broad categories of conditions of concern include atherosclerotic cardiovascular diseases (including some cerebrovascular diseases), hypertensive diseases, rheumatic fever and rheumatic heart diseases, congenital heart diseases, specific heart muscle diseases and cardiomyopathies and pulmonary heart diseases (Table 33.2). The arterial lesions which may lead to atherosclerotic cardiovascular diseases in the forth decade and later are already commonly present by the age of 20 at frequencies differing markedly from one population to another (Figure 33.1).[9]

Cancer is the third cause of death, stomach, lung and liver cancers being the most prevalent (Tables 33.2 and 33.3).[7]

It is often assumed that chronic diseases develop as countries become more affluent. However, there is evidence that striking increases in deaths from these causes occur both in poor and affluent countries. The age-adjusted mortality of men and women aged 35–69 years is dominated by cardiovascular

diseases and cancers irrespective of the GNP (Figure 33.2).[10] In countries with a GNP of 3000–4000 USD, the burden of cardiovascular diseases and cancers is nearly as great as in the very affluent countries with an average income three times greater. Thus already a modest increase in prosperity in populations with low GNP seems to be associated with the most marked increases in the prevalence of these diseases, which then pose a major long-term burden on the health services of the country.[11]

Among the majority of the world's population, *rheumatic heart disease* remains the most common cardiovascular cause of death in the first four decades of life. In many developing countries rheumatic fever and rheumatic heart disease account for about half of all CVD, whereas they have almost disappeared from the industrialised countries. The favourable trend in developed countries has parallelled the improvements in living standards that have taken place in these countries since the turn of the century. The low incidence of rheumatic heart disease is in keeping with the low incidence of rheumatic fever in developed

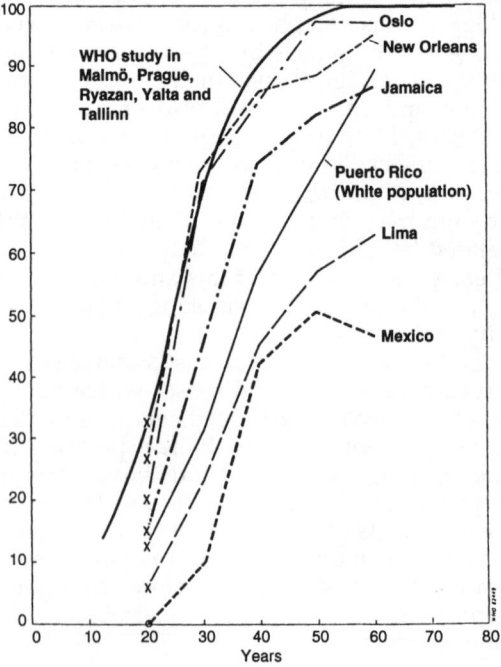

Figure 33.1. Age-related dynamics of incidence of atherosclerotic plaques in selected populations, data derived from autopsy studies, prevalence rates at age 20.[9]

Table 33.3. Cancer mortality in developing countries, 1990.[7]

Site	Deaths (x 1000)	Sex-ratio (male/female)
Stomach	522	1.8
Lung	440	3.0
Liver	420	2.5
Esophagus	332	2.0
Oral cavity/pharynx	315	2.0
Colon/rectum	215	1.2
Cervix	183	–
Breast	158	–
Leukemia	143	1.2
Lymphomas	121	1.7
All sites	3 700	1.4

countries. But the prevalence of the disease in school-age children in many developing countries is alarmingly high (Table 33.4).[12]

These observations suggest that new initiatives need to be taken in health promotion and in provision of improved adult health services for control of non-communicable diseases.

RISK FACTORS

Smoking is undoubtedly a major cause of illness and premature death. It is responsible for as many as 90 per cent of all cases of lung cancer, 75 per cent of chronic bronchitis and emphysema and 25 per cent of cases of ischemic heart diseases in men under 65 years, as well as for a number of other types of cancer, for pregnancy complications and for more frequent respiratory ailments in children in smoking families. In South-East Asia, tobacco chewing is estimated to cause about 90 per cent of the deaths due to oral cancer. Worldwide cigarette consumption per adult has increased only very slightly, by 7.1 per cent between 1970 and 1985. In many industrialised countries the percentage of smokers has started to fall in recent years. In developing countries, however, the prevalence of smoking is frequently higher than in affluent countries. For instance, 62 per cent of men in China, 84 per cent in Bolivia and 80 per cent in Swaziland smoke compared to 30 per cent in United States of the 35 per cent in Finland.[13]

Smoking is also prevalent among young people worldwide. The prevalence of smoking among young males in Argentina is 57 per

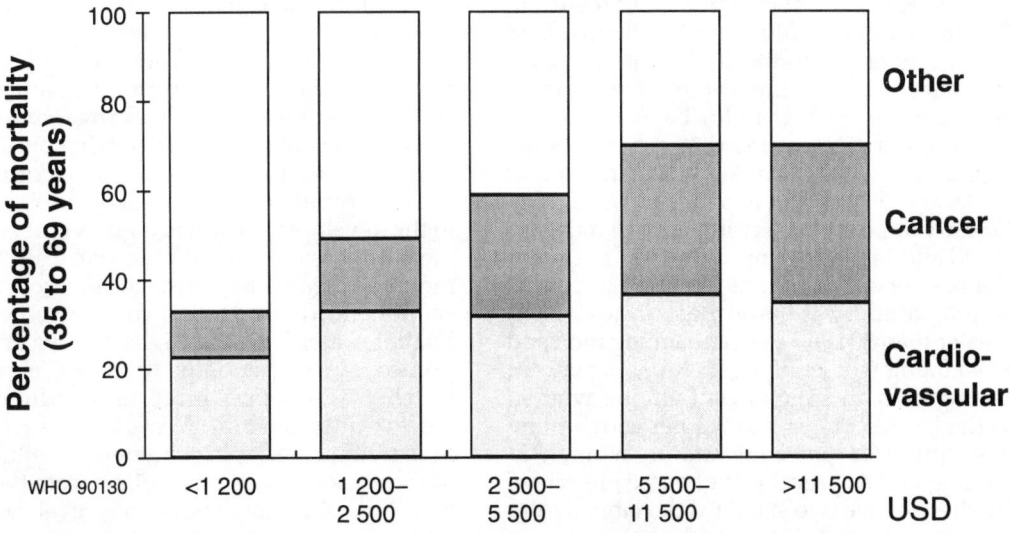

This diagram is based on an analysis of cause-specific mortality rates for the ages 35-69 years, from the WHO international mortality data base, adjusted to the world population, standard-age distribution. Fifty-two countries satisfied selection criteria for this analysis; information was available on national mortality by age group and GNP *per capita*, and the population numbered more than one million. Countries were divided into five groups according to GNP.

Figure 33.2. Proportion of deaths from cardiovascular diseases, cancer and other diseases, for both sexes aged 35–69, in relation to GNP *per capita*.[10]

Table 33.4. Prevalence of rheumatic heart disease in school-age children in different regions of the world.[12]

Country, territory or locality		Year	Prevalence per 1 000
Africa			
	Algeria	1970	15.0
	Côte d'Ivoire	1985	1.9
	Morocco	1973	9.9
	South Africa, Soweto	1975	6.9
Asia			
	China	1979	0.4–2.7
	India	1970s	6.0–11.0
	Pakistan	1970s	1.8–11.0
	Thailand	1974	1.2–21.0
Latin America			
	Bolivia, La Paz	1973	17.0
	Mexico, Mexico City	1977	8.5
	Puerto Rico, San Juan	1980	1.6
	Uruguay, Montevideo	1970	1.0
Pacific			
	Cook Islands, Rarotonga	1982	18.6
	French Polynesia	1985	8.0

cent, in Senegal (Dakar) 71 per cent, in Colombia and Italy 51 per cent, in Switzerland 36 per cent and in India 10 per cent. It is striking that in some countries prevalence rates are higher for girls than for boys: in Italy 55 per cent and in Switzerland 46 per cent. Some 30 per cent of girls smoke in Argentina and Chile, and 52 per cent in Senegal (Dakar).[14]

Obesity appears to be rising both in industrialised and in developing countries. The prevalence of obesity in adults in national surveys as indicated by a body mass index (BMI) greater than 30 is 5.7 per cent among men and 14.4 among women in Costa Rica, 12 per cent among men and 15 per cent among women in the United States and 3.3 per cent among men and 16.4 per cent among women in Nicaragua. The prevalence of obese pre-school children (above two standard deviations from the reference median weight for height) varies from zero in Papua New Guinea to over 10 per cent in Chile (Figure 33.3).[15]

Hypertension. Population surveys carried out since 1970 in developing countries including 23 population groups show that the prevalence of hypertension varies from as low as 1 per cent in some African countries to over 30

per cent in Brazil. The trend analyses of the mortality statistics for the group aged 35–74 years in 16 countries (from which data are available) show a falling trend in mortality from hypertension and cerebrovascular diseases in most of these countries. In spite of the currently low prevalence in some countries the total number of hypertensive individuals in the developing world is high. A cost assessment of possible antihypertensive drug treatments indicates that developing countries cannot afford an adequate drug treatment.[16]

Diabetes mellitus. The highest prevalence of non-insulin-dependent diabetes mellitus (NIDDM) is found in certain indigenous North-American and West-Pacific societies. In extreme cases approximately one-third of the adult population now suffers from the disease. NIDDM is also common (prevalence approximately 5 per cent) in Europe and in communities of European descent. Data from the United States suggest that approximately one-fifth of the white North-Americans can expect to develop NIDDM if they live to the seventh decade of life. Of populations of South-East Asian ethnicity, Indians appear to be the most susceptible. Indian migrants to

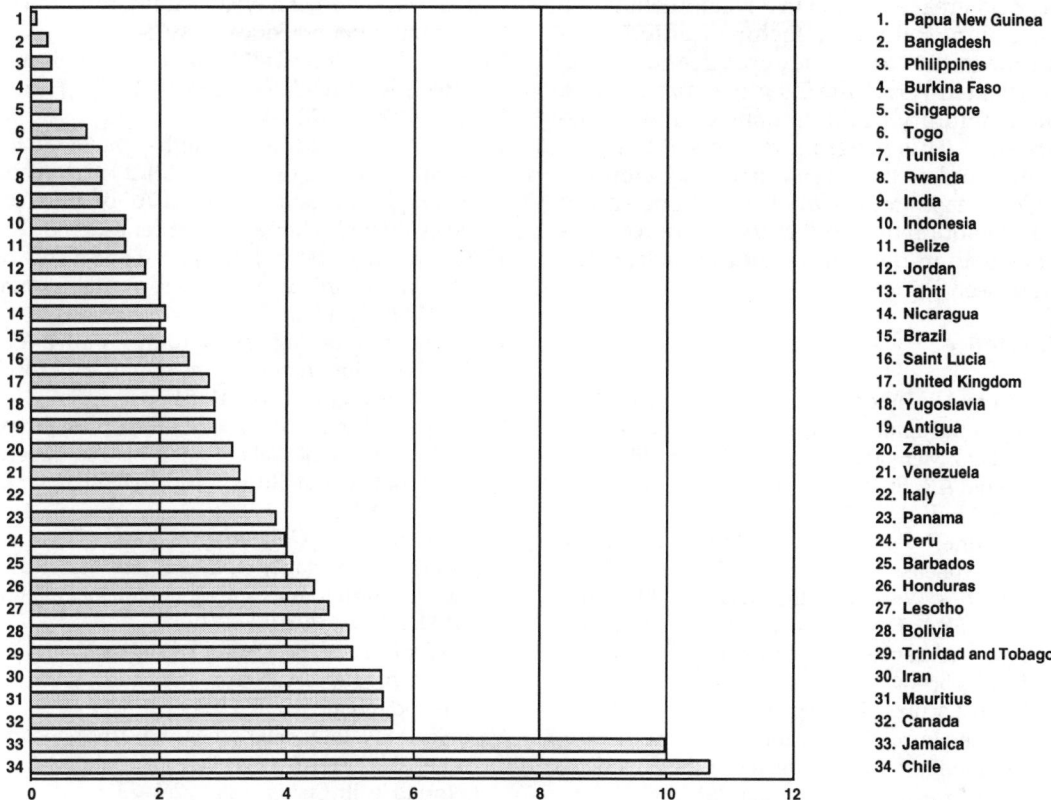

Figure 33.3. Prevalence of obese preschool children (above 2 SD from the reference median weight-for-height (0–59 months.)[15]

Fiji, South Africa, South America all demonstrate prevalence of NIDDM of 10 per cent or more.[17]

POTENTIAL FOR PREVENTION

All non-communicable diseases have a multifactorial etiology. In order to decrease mortality or morbidity rates the influence of predominant negative socioeconomic, behavioural, environmental and medical-biological etiology factors should be reduced or preferably eliminated, and health care systems should be improved.

Comparative analysis of changing epidemiological patterns is likely to become increasingly important for planning of public health services in developing countries. The most encouraging trend is the mortality decrease in cardiovascular diseases and some other non-communicable diseases seen in Finland and other economically stronger countries where

both disease rates and risk factors are declining.[18,19] It will be of interest to observe whether this will also occur in other developed economies and to see in other populations how serious the problem becomes before public health programmes and other positive trends appear. It has been noted that *acceleration of the rate of transition may be preferable to its retardation*.[2] If populations develop more rapidly they need not linger in phases of traumatic or chronic, lifestyle related mortality. Educational programmes for both non-communicable disease risk factor reduction and overall cultural development, may hasten the extension of life expectancy beyond the limits imposed by unhealthy products and inadequate health services.

Taking into account the importance of risk factors for many non-communicable diseases, there is much activity at present in programmes dealing with campaigns against smoking, alcohol and drug use, for improved diet and for increased physical activity. WHO has paid great attention to development of the most important risk factor-oriented programmes. In 1986 a new programme was launched in WHO, the integrated programme for community health in non-communicable diseases.[6] This programme aims at the prevention and control of selected non-communicable diseases and related conditions and to the promotion of health in the entire communities both in developing and industrialised countries.[6,20]

References

1. Omran AR. The epidemiological transition – a theory of the epidemiology of population change. Milbank Memorial Fund Q 1971;4:509–38.
2. Omran AR. Epidemiologic transition in the US. Popul Bull 1977:32
3. Uemura K, Pisa Z. Recent trends in cardiovascular disease mortality in 27 industrialized countries. World Health Stat Q 1985;38:142–62.
4. Dodu SRA: Emergence of cardiovascular diseases in developing countries. Cardiology 1988;75:56–64.
5. Litvak J, Ruiz L, Restrepo HE, McAlister A. The growing burden of noncommunicable disease: a challenge for the countries of the Americas. Bull Pan Amer Health Organ 1987;21:156–69.
6. InterHealth Steering Committee. Demonstration projects for the integrated prevention and control of noncommunicable diseases (InterHealth programme): Epidemiological background and rationale. World Health Stat Q 1991;44:48–54.
7. Murray CJL, Lopez AD. Global cause of death patterns in 1990: new methods and results. Bull WHO 1994;72 (in press).
8. WHO. Prevention in childhood and youth of adult cardiovascular diseases: time for action. Report of a WHO Expert Committee. WHO Technical Report Series. 1990;792.
9. WHO. Prevention of coronary heart disease. Report of a WHO Expert Committee. WHO Technical Report Series. 1982;678.
10. World Bank. World tables. 3rd ed. Vol I. Economic data. Washington, DC: John Hopkins University Press, 1983.
11. WHO. Diet, nutrition and the prevention of chronic diseases. Report of a WHO Study Group. WHO Technical Report Series. 1990;797.
12. WHO. Rheumatic fever and rheumatic heart disease. Report of a WHO Study Group. WHO Technical Report Series. 1988;764.
13. Masironi R, Rothwell K. Smoking trends and effects worldwide (summary). World Health Stat Q 1988;41:239–41.
14. WHO. Young people's health – challenge for society. Report of a WHO Study Group on Young People and Health for All by the Year 2000. WHO Technical Report Series. 1986;731.
15. Gurney M, Gorstein J. The global prevalence of obesity – an initial overview of available data. World Health Stat Q 1988;41:251–4.
16. Nissinen A, Böthig S, Granroth H, Lopez AD. Hypertension in developing countries. World Health Stat Q 1988;41:141–54.
17. King H, Zimmet P. Trends in the prevalence and incidence of diabetes: non-insulin-dependent diabetes mellitus. World Health Stat Q 1988;41:190–6.
18. Tuomilehto J, Geboers J, Salonen JT, et al. Decline in mortality from coronary heart disease in North Karelia and other parts of Finland. Br Med J 1986;293:1068–71.
19. Puska P. The North Karelia Project: Nearly 20 years of succesful prevention of CVD in Finland. Hygie XI, 1992;1:33–5.
20. Shigan EN. Integrated programme for noncommunicable diseases prevention and control (NCD). World Health Stat Q 1988;41:267–73.

About the authors

Aulikki Nissinen is Professor of Public Hhealth and currently the Head of the Department of Community Health and General Practice at the University of Kuopio, Finland. She started her scientific work in the framework of the North Karelia Project and has focused her research on epidemiology of chronic diseases. During 1986–88 she worked as a Medical Officer in the Division of Noncommunicable Diseases at the WHO, Geneva. Currently, she is the Coordinator of the WHO InterHealth programme, which involves both developing and industrialised countries to fight against the chronic diseases.

Geoffrey Kiangi got medical degree from the University of Dar es Salaam and is currently a Ph.D. student on public health at the Department of community Health and General Practice at the University of Kuopio, Finland. His research topic is the occurrence of tobacco smoking and alcohol drinking among school children in Tanzania and the preventive measures against these habits.

Lankinen KS, Bergström S, Mäkelä PH and Peltomaa M, eds.
Health and disease in developing countries. London:The Macmillan Press Limited, 1994:323–329.

34 MENTAL HEALTH

Sixten Bondestam, M.D., Ph.D.
East Helsinki Health Division, Department of Mental Health,
Tallinnanaukio 6, 3rd floor
FIN-00930 Helsinki
Finland

INTRODUCTION

Many of the early papers dealing with psychiatry in developing countries were clearly within a racist framework. That does not exclude the fact that there may be differences between races in the psychological behaviour. The subject is controversial since ethnocentrisism or racism, i.e. the feeling that *the way we do things is the only right way*, is to a certain degree part of all human beings. Cultural differences do exist and are in fact much greater than racial differences.

In developing countries psychiatric services are commonly neglected altogether or limited in extent and suffer from a constant lack of resources. Most donor organisations are not interested in development cooperation in mental health, the one exception being Danish International Development Agency (DANIDA). Most countries with an Essential Drugs Programme cannot afford appropriate amounts of drugs for psychiatric illness and epilepsy. In the meetings of the African Mental Health Action Group most of the participants report on shortages of qualified personnel like psychiatrists, psychologists, occupational therapists, of transport and communication, and on a lack of adequate infrastructure and essential psychotropic drugs. Mental health legislation is ancient, or is lacking altogether. Centralisation of services is excessive and forces patients

to travel long distances which makes continued treatment impossible and often results in relapse.

New problems like increasing alcohol and drug abuse or victims of torture arise. Neuropsychiatric features in mentally ill patients with HIV infection with or without AIDS, the problems of unemployed and disadvantaged youth including the mentally handicapped, mental illness in refugees, prisoners and so forth are other examples of more recent challenges.

Outpatient studies have shown that psychiatric morbidity is more prevalent than suggested by health statistics.[1] In East Africa the percentage of mental disorders is 20–25 in patients visiting outpatient clinics.[2,3,4] Although these data cannot be used to estimate the prevalence of psychiatric disorders in the community, considerable quantitative evidence indicates that psychiatric disorders are no less frequent in Africa than in developed countries.[5]

An epidemiological study from Finland reported a prevalence of 17 per cent for clinically diagnosed mental disorders, psychotic disorders occurring in 2.3 per cent of the subjects.[6] One half of the subjects diagnosed as having some type of mental disorder needed treatment at specialised health care level. Only 42 per cent of those in need of therapy actually did receive some kind of treatment and, furthermore, the treatment was considered adequate in only half of the cases. Thus, there is clearly a need for both qualitative and quantitative development of mental health services even in highly developed countries. Third World countries will have a long way to go before psychiatric services can be considered adequate.

The same applies to neurology which is commonly included in psychiatry in developing countries. The scope of the task of treating epileptic patients is evident from prevalence rates of 4–7.5 per 1000 reported from developed countries. Prevalence rates of epilepsy for adults in developing countries have been found to range from 4 to 49 per 1000 population.[7] A considerable problem is posed by tropical infections in the nervous system such as echinococcosis, cysticercosis, trypanosomiasis and a variety of viral diseases. Leprosy and AIDS involvement of the central nervous system must not be forgotten.

Also the mentally retarded are often included in services for psychiatric patients in Third World countries. Prevalence rates for serious mental retardation (IQ less than 55) in developing countries have been reported[8] to range from 5.0 to 40.3 per 1000. – All put together, the task facing those responsible for mental health services in Third World countries is immense.

The following concentrates on psychiatry in an East African setting and the differences in psychiatric disease panorama in different parts of the world are not discussed in detail. For those interested there are textbooks on this subject[9,10] as well as reviews of regional problems, e.g. in South-East Asia[11], Latin America[12] and Sub-Saharan Africa.[5,13]

SERIOUS MENTAL DISORDERS

The main burden of psychiatric morbidity, serious mental disorder, in the adult population in East African countries consists of the categories presented below. They are actually more or less consistent for all Sub-Saharan countries and, with certain reservations, also in a global perspective.

Acute or subacute mental disorders

The most common type is the acute confusional state characterised by restlessness, confusion, and vivid hallucinations. The etiology is often mixed, with psychological background and infection with malaria or other infectious disease with or without cerebral involvement. The prognosis is usually very good indeed. The exception is a debilitating disease of the central nervous system such as tuberculosis, epilepsy or infections with a chronic course if untreated.

In addition to psychological and infectious origins, acute confusion can also be provoked by many toxic agents, ranging from indigenous herbal drugs to new drugs such as mefloquine. Although the traditional healers are sometimes doing a very good job with these cases, the treatment of confusional states is most efficiently arranged by western type psychiatric services.

Chronic mental and neuropsychiatric disorders

This category includes the psychoses, of which schizophrenia is the most important, like elsewhere. The prevalence of schizophrenia is commonly held to be close to 1 per cent throughout the world. The clinical picture of patients with schizophrenia differs according to educational level. Those with an illiterate rural background have more of an amorphous form of psychosis with less paranoid features. The prognosis is usually better than in cases with a more sophisticated literate educational background. Social rehabilitation is easier when working skills are limited to the use of an hoe. Educated individuals develop a picture of schizophrenia more similar to that found in European individuals with a poorer prognosis.

In Nigeria and subsequently in Tanzania and some other African countries the concept of psychiatric rehabilitation villages has been developed. In Tanzania the first village was constructed as a response to the overcrowded wards of an old western type mental hospital. It was consequently decided to move the most chronic and long-standing patients to live in a village to relieve the hospital of part of its burden. The patients built their own village and were given some land to cultivate, livestock and a lake with fish.[14]

A mental health assistant moved to live in the village together with the patients. He was in charge of the management of the village and dispensation of drugs. After one year, more than half of the patients were rehabilitated and had moved back to live into the community.[15] The outcome of the scheme was completely unanticipated by the management of the hospital. Subsequently, more psychiatric rehabilitation villages have been started in different regions of Tanzania. The majority of patients in institutions and psychiatric villages are classified with schizophrenia.

Major affective disorders (disorders with typical changes in the mood), such as manic disorder, occurs throughout Africa. Affective or manic symptoms associated with other psychoses are more common. The prevalence of major depression is difficult to assess. Depressive patients according to European standards are not commonly seen. There might be local variations linked to urbanisation and Christian religion with more emphasis on individual responsibility and guilt.

A study from Colombia, India, Sudan and the Philippines emphasises that primary health workers recognise only a minority of mental disorders among their patients.[16] Missing psychiatric cases at primary care level is a worldwide phenomenon and the need for greater awareness of psychological disturbance and for improved diagnostic skills is a general one. Improved diagnosis will not, however, be sufficient to reach those patients with severe mental disorders, such as schizophrenia or depressive psychosis who do not normally present themselves at PHC facilities.

Many depressive patients attend with somatic complaints or are left in some corner of the hut until the depressive phase is once again over. This probably applies even more to depressive psychotic patients with a tendency to withdraw completely. These facts combined with the common belief that severe mental disease is caused by supernatural forces mean that these patients will never be seen by health authorities.

Psychoses associated with epilepsy, infections or chronic organic disease occur commonly. The problem associated with these is the lack of sophisticated examinations, laboratory and X-ray facilities. Shortage of appropriate drugs is an equally severe problem. In many conditions simple laboratory tests, e.g. microscopy for malaria, can help a lot and modern treatment can achieve stable remissions or reduce disability in a significant proportion of the cases.

Emotional illness

Anxiety states and neuroses are ubiquitous throughout the world and the developing countries make no exception. It may really not be necessary any more to state that the noble, happy, carefree individual of a tropical paradise is merely a wishful European projection. Anxiety and emotional symptoms exist in a variety of forms, usually not similar to those encountered in western patients. Africans present more often with physical complaints of psychological origin. The problem might quite simply be the stomach or the head or, even more diffusely, dizziness or fatigue.

The African medical assistant or rural medical aide will usually react to somatisation in much the same way as his colleagues with a more sophisticated training in the Western World; he will prescribe more investigations and several drugs. In one study the rate of mental disorder as the main diagnosis was in excess of 13 per cent in patients presenting with a complaint of cough and fever or in women coming for family planning advice.[16]

One aim in the training of manpower at the PHC level will in fact be to train them to avoid inappropriate investigations and treatment and to avoid building up a treatment system of frequent attendances and drug trials. Instead there should be an emphasis on training to deal with underlying psychological and social problems.

Alcohol and drug abuse

Alcohol abuse, alcoholism, drug abuse and dependence appear to be a growing problem in many countries. Prevention based on community sensitisation, public information and focus on distribution of drugs and alcohol deserves a greater emphasis than the treatment of cases of advanced dependence. For further discussion of alcohol problems see Chapter 12.

THE NATIONAL MENTAL HEALTH PROGRAMME IN TANZANIA

The Tanzanian experience can be used as an example of what can be done by bringing forward different problem areas.[14] Since 1981, strategies for mental health care have been developed within the National Mental Health Programme in Tanzania. It is a joint project including the Tanzanian government, the WHO and DANIDA. The main objective of the programme is to integrate mental health care into the existing PHC system.

The Tanzanian programme is an ambitious one with initial involvement of DANIDA and

Mental patient in a children's hospital in Lima, Peru. Photo: UNICEF/Alexander Røsler

the WHO. The initial technical cooperation was vital indeed for the establishment of a psychiatric resource centre in connection with the Psychiatric Unit in Dar es Salaam. In the first phase there was support to the conceptual formulation of the programme and provision of consultants.

In starting a new health scheme the least difficult part is the actual training of manpower. Much more important is *administrative and managerial support*. The most difficult and important part of the programme is the administration and the local management and implementation at all levels of psychiatric services.

The goal of the programme was to extend and improve the psychiatric services by decentralising care and establishing a community psychiatry service integrated in PHC and backed up by a psychiatric unit and a rehabilitation village in all regions of Tanzania. This involved the construction of some new buildings, and support of transport (cars, motorbikes or bicycles) for mental health coordinators.

Training seminars were also conducted, including seminars for the teaching staff. The required mental health skills for the different echelons of mental health workers involved diagnostic skills, therapeutic skills, skills in

the field of service provision, skills in public health and in organising health education. Typical items of the training programme were orientation to the unit routine, the psychiatric examination, how to conduct outpatient clinics, and psychiatric management. Appropriate skills required of mental health workers involved specific problems like diagnosing epileptic fits or acute excitement, the assessment technologies like observation and history taking and management technologies like drug treatment, guidance and instruction and safe methods of physical restraining.

Another goal of the programme was to raise community awareness of the importance of mental health as a component of general health. This is sought through seminars for community leaders and through programmes on radio and television.

The programme has gradually spread from one region to the next through seminars conducted by those connected to the Psychiatric Resource Centre and those recently trained in the neighbouring region. The implementation of the programme, which started in 1981, is still not complete. It represents an important milestone in the development of mental health care in the African region, and is likely to benefit public health planners throughout the developing world by providing an example of a strategy and technology for implementing psychiatric services in a variety of settings.

Lessons learned

The following summarises some of the most important things the programme in Tanzania has taught.

Closed wards. Psychiatric services do need closed wards. Not many beds and big hospitals are needed, but there will always be a need for some psychiatric beds for the acutely psychotic patients. The island of Pemba, off the East African coast, is only one example of an area without any psychiatric in-patient services. The acute patient is still tied to a tree or tied in the corner of the hut or his legs are secured through holes in a log. To get medical treatment, the patient is dependent on whether the mental health coordinator is called upon, whether there is petrol for his motorbike or whether his bike has spare parts! So what is needed is some funds for starting small psychiatric units with male and female wards.

Drugs. Comprehensive psychiatric services cannot be run without psychiatric drugs. Again, not many drugs are needed. The most important are the neuroleptics. Chlorpromazine can be recommended since no other neuroleptic drug offers significantly better overall therapeutic properties. A second, less sedative neuroleptic, e.g. fluphenazine is also needed. Fluphenazine decanoate injections are convenient.

Neuroleptics often induce side-effects and a small amount of biperidene tablets and injections are needed. An anti-convulsant is also necessary, either phenobarbitone, which is cheap, or phenytoin, which has fewer side-effects and is more effective. For epileptic states diazepam injections are the treatment of choice. Depending on the prevalence of depressive disorder in the community some antidepressants are needed, e.g. amitriptyline.

As the government health budget is usually very restricted and the budget for the mental health programme even more so it is usually best to avoid the use of tranquilisers. Drug companies are very prone to convince Ministers of Health and Principal Secretaries that tranquillisers are the drugs of choice. The role of experts and advisers to governments is to resist squandering government funds on less important drugs.

The most important thing related to drug treatment of psychiatric patients in developing countries is that *drug treatment should not be started unless there is an absolute certainty of continuous drug supply*. In the case of epileptic patients it is nearly malpractice to start drug treatment without certainty of a stable supply. Also those psychiatric patients who have been convinced about the profits of drug treatment and who walk considerable distances to get them, should not be discouraged with repeated frustrating reports that there are no drugs. Whether the drug supply is through the Essential Drugs Programme or through Government Pharmaceutical Store, all steps should be taken to secure a constant supply of drugs.

In many countries it is a fact that there simply are not enough funds to treat even a minority of patients with adequate doses of drugs. Hence there is no reason to make community surveys to find new patients who could not be treated anyway. The common practice to treat patients with inadequate doses of neuroleptics and antiepileptics is understandable but should be avoided. It is better to treat those who are motivated properly and to hope for better times for those we cannot afford to treat now.

Vehicles and equipment. Psychiatric services in rural areas cannot be run properly without transport. In Third World countries public transport is far from satisfactory. The vehicles are usually old and in a miserable condition. Roads are deteriorating and add to the wear of cars. Distances to be covered by foot from the village to nearest dispensary may be up to 10 kilometres. Each psychiatric unit should have a vehicle, preferably with a four-wheel drive, or at least a motorbike for the mental health coordinator. Transport is needed for all those things that are commonly executed by using public transport in developed countries. Patients must sometimes be taken to hospital, or sent back home to the village. Often transport has to be provided for food, firewood, drugs or diesel.

Other necessities include office equipment, the standard office furniture, typewriters, an adequate constant supply of stationary, a filing system and a telephone connection. Duplicating machines are also needed. Clinical equipment includes diagnostic sets, an ECT machine and occupational therapy equipment. Educational material and training equipment, textbooks and medical journals can be requested through the WHO.

Traditional healers. Traditional healers are often doing a good job especially with anxious or neurotic patients and in some countries their cooperation with government medical services has been arranged. The example should be considered in other countries also. As throughout Africa belief in supernatural forces as the cause of misfortune and disease will continue to persist for many years, the role of the traditional healer will continue to be central.

The aim of the representatives of western medicine should be to train the traditional healer to discriminate those cases which need treatment with western medicine (e.g. cerebral malaria). Also the fresh nurse student or medical assistant, who has recently been introduced into the world of western medicine and who is eager to teach patients to refrain from traditional procedures, should be guided to use his new knowledge without contempt for the work of the traditional healer.

RESEARCH

For expatriates, psychiatric research in Third World countries certainly gives a good introduction to the community. Through the mental hospital or the psychiatric unit a lot about tradition, culture and beliefs in the country can be learned. Before starting on any research project it is advisable to talk to the Division of Mental Health at the WHO in Geneva. They can provide valuable support in the form of research tools. The research project will be more successful if local people participate. At the Ministry of Health there may be a demographer or a population statistician, the local university may have anthropologists or sociologists. In planning, training of the field workers, in pilot studies and in the implementation of the field work a lot more will be gained than just the specific research goals. Simultaneously, a lot of indirect public health education can be done both in villages and in the ministries.

MENTAL HEALTH OF THE EXPATRIATE

Those who go to work in a foreign developing country are likely to react to the differences in culture. If the circumstances are extreme, and the conditions differ too much from those he/she is accustomed to, as in countries with severe famine, it may be difficult to adapt. If the initial experience proves to be too much to cope with one should not hesitate to consider premature termination of one's contract. Some experiences, e.g. the death of many small children, will normally force your apative mechanisms to an extreme and are surely not to be experienced without personal involvement. In such situations every effort to get supervision and guidance from those more experienced should be taken.

Those who go to work for a period in a Third World country can be roughly divided in two groups. Naturally there are all kinds of people in between, but these two are the most typical ones.

First, there are young people who are still looking for a personal identity and along with this want to do something for a suffering humanity. They may have an attitude that those who work for other than meagre salaries should feel ashamed. The host country and the local people are idealised and local customs and fashions adopted. To a lesser degree this is probably a sound way of finding one's identity; in more severe cases of identification with the local people the inevitably following disappointment may be bitter.

In the works of David Livingstone and H.M. Stanley on their research travels typical stories are told of how they wanted to trust in some specific individual and how they later were bitterly frustrated when they found out that they had been deceived and used for other purposes. To trust (and to be deceived!) are typical concepts of the guilt-prone western world and cannot as such directly be applied to other cultures. The young Europeans, for example, who are separated from their own way of living and their own conceptual world are equally seldom understood by the alien environment. Sometimes they are taken advantage of much in the same way as some kind of natural resource.

The other characteristic way of relating to a foreign culture is to despise it from the start and to measure people and life with western standards. Much of the time is used ridiculing and despising the host country.

To avoid these extremes, it would be wise to remember, that you some day will return back to your home country and there is no need to burn bridges. Although it is important to get thoroughly acquainted with the host country, it is a good practice to meet your fellow countrymen once in a while to let off some steam. When things get really tough, it is better to talk them over with your own fellows than to let relations become too strained on your job. It is also a good practice to take your annual leave in your own country. Often those who go home for their leave are more able to keep a distance from cultural differences and also see better the problems they have in their home countries. Those who go home for their annual leave will also tend to stay healthier during their stay abroad.

To return to your home country after a period in a developing country will invariably provide you with an even greater culture shock. You have adapted to life in the host country with all its peculiar ways of dealing with people. When you return back home you will again feel all the differences – and this time more painfully. The worst symptoms will be over if you can stand it for about half a year. Friends with similar experiences as yours will provide valuable help through sharing experiences and feelings. Do not plan to undertake any big projects immediately you have returned; a lot of energy will just be needed to adapt. After 6–8 months you gradually start forgetting, you stop thinking and talking about your experiences and the present reality will be more important. For most people the period abroad will remain a precious memory.

To work in an alien culture offers a unique chance to observe your own culture from an orbit and to take a more objective view of its good and bad qualities and all its deficiencies. This is a valuable experience for anybody and will enable you to get a more distinct picture of behaviour as part of community and culture.

References

1. Bondestam S, Garssen J, Abdulwakil AI. Prevalence and treatment of mental disorders and epilepsy in Zanzibar. Acta Psychiatr Scand 1990;81:327–31.
2. Ndetei DH, Muhangi J. The prevalence and clinical presentation of psychiatric illness in a rural setting in Kenya. Br J Psychiatry 1979;135:269–72.
3. Jacobsson L. Psychiatric morbidity and psychosocial background in an out–patient population of a general hospital in western Ethiopia. Acta Psychiatr Scand 1985;71:417–26.
4. Dhadphale M, Ellison RH, Griffin L. The frequency of psychiatric disorders among patients attending semi-urban and rural general out-patient clinics in Kenya. Br J Psychiatry 1983; 142:379–83.
5. German GA. Aspects of clinical psychiatry in Sub-Saharan Africa. Br J Psychiatry 1972;145: 187–92.
6. Lehtinen V, Joukamaa M, Jyrkinen T, et al. Mental health and mental disorders in the Finnish adult population. Helsinki: The Social Insurance Institution, 1991.
7. Osuntokun BO, Adeuja AOG, Nottidge VA, et al. Prevalence of the epilepsies in Nigerian Africans: a community-based study. Epilepsia 1987;28(3):272–9.
8. Stein Z, Durkin M, Belmont L. 'Serious' mental retardation in developing countries: an epidemiological approach. Ann N Y Acad Sci 1986;477: 8–21.
9. Kiev A. Transcultural psychiatry. London: Cox & Wyman, 1972.
10. Fernando S. Mental health, race & culture. London: Macmillan, 1991.
11. Neki JS. Psychiatry in South-East Asia. Br J Psychiatry 1973;123:257–69.
12. Leon CA. Psychiatry in Latin America. Br J Psychiatry 1972;121:121–36.
13. Carothers JC. The African mind in health and disease. A study in ethnopsychiatry. Geneva: WHO, 1953.
14. World Health Organization. A programme for mental health in a country struggling for development: The Tanzanian experience. A report on the cooperation between the United Republic of Tanzania, The World Health Organization and the Danish International Development Agency. Geneva: WHO, 1986.
15. Bondestam S. Report on a visit to a psychiatric village settlement in Tanzania. Psychiatria Fennica Year Book, 1976:21–3.
16. Harding TW, de Arango MV, Baltazar J, et al. Mental disorders in primary health care: a study of their frequency and diagnosis in four developing countries. Psychol Med 1980;10:231–41.

About the author

Sixten Bondestam is specialist in psychiatry. He is currently head of community mental health services in the eastern parts of Helsinki, Finland. In the early 1970s he started the psyciatric outpatient and hospital services at the Kilimanjaro Christian Medical Centre in northern Tanzania. During 1985-89 he served as an appointed consultant psychiatrist in the WHO-DANIDA-Zanzibar Government Joint Mental Health Project in Zanzibar.

Lankinen KS, Bergström S, Mäkelä PH and Peltomaa M, eds.
Health and disease in developing countries. London:The Macmillan Press Limited, 1994:331–340.

35 MALIGNANCIES: a growing problem

Olle Kjellgren, M.D., Ph.D., F.I.A.C.
University of Umeå, Department of Oncology
S-901 85 Umeå,
Sweden

OVERALL CANCER INCIDENCE AND MORTALITY

The prevalent view regards cancer as a problem of industrialised countries only, but the facts tell a different story. Even though cancer is frequent in the highly industrialised countries, especially in the elderly population, it is also very frequent in developing countries, not because of a high age specific rate but because of the high number of individuals living there.

WHO has estimated that there are about seven million new cancer cases every year in the world and half of these occur in developing countries.[1] It is also estimated that about five million die from cancer every year. The number of cancer deaths is twice as high in developing as in industrialised countries due to the scarcity of diagnostic and treatment facilities. Death from cancer accounts for about one tenth of all deaths worldwide. By the turn of the century the number of cancer deaths will be about eight million. Advanced cancer cases with severe pain, mainly in developing countries, is estimated to four million – a tremendous human, medical and social challenge.

CANCER INCIDENCE IN FIVE CONTINENTS

An increasing number of national and regional cancer registries report on cancer incidence and mortality.[2] A useful compilation has been made by International Union Against Cancer giving age-adjusted data for 137 populations in 36 countries in five continents.[3] The volume also includes different age adjusted hypothetical population estimates, e.g. World, European with a high proportion of elderly persons or African with a high proportion of children. In the discussion below, figures are standardised to world population and 'per 100 000 per annum' will be omitted. It should be noted that the efficacy and validity of registration varies in different countries.

The overall incidence of cancer in all sites, except cancer of the skin other than melanoma, varies among different countries (Tables 35.1 and 35.2). At the two extremes, the highest rate in males is reported in blacks in Detroit, USA (400.1), and the lowest in Kuwaitis in Kuwait (71.9). Specific incidence figures for different cancers are best found in the publication 'Cancer incidence in five continents'.[3–6]

Industrialisation changes the panorama of cancer. This has been clearly demonstrated in Japan during the last few decades.[7] Previously cancer of the esophagus and stomach were very frequent but during the last 30 years their incidence has decreased while cancers of the breast, colon, prostate and lungs have increased and now reached about the same level as in western countries. These changes depend on environmental factors e.g. smoking and eating habits, changes of lifestyle and increasing exposure to industrial carcinogens contaminating air, food and water. There is also a positive correlation between the incidence of cancer of the colon and the production of energy or the consumption of meat.[7]

Table 35.1. Age standardised cancer incidence for all cancers in selected countries.

Country			Male	Female
AFRICA[5]				
Mozambique	Maputo		186.7	123.3
South Africa	Natal Bantu		208.9	162.6
Uganda	Kyadondo[4]		58.9	70.5
ASIA				
India	Madras		91.2	119.8
Japan	Hiroshima		233.2	224.1
	Osaka		242.9	150.9
Kuwait		Kuwaitis	71.9	72.0
		Non-Kuwaitis	191.3	139.0
EUROPE				
Sweden			233.2	224.1
Switzerland			314.1	204.4
NORTH AMERICA				
USA	Bay Area	White	312.0	295.0
		Black	386.4	249.2
		Chinese	224.4	197.5
		Japanese	189.0	176.5
SOUTH AMERICA				
Brazil	Porto Alegre		325.5	247.6
Colombia	Cali		209.9	220.8
OCEANIA				
Australia	Victoria		308.2	233.2
Hawaii		White	346.1	289.1
		Hawaiian	311.9	297.6
		Filipino	175.1	154.8

When people move from one country to another with a different cancer panorama, they tend to adopt the same pattern as the population of the new country, especially in new generations born in that country. Japanese migrants to the USA and black Africans living in the USA for many generations illustrate this phenomenon.[8] Thus, environmental factors are more important than genetic for cancer development.

CAUSES OF CANCER

The development of a cancer proceeds in multiple steps, beginning with a mutation in the DNA in a cell nucleus. Many factors can act as mutagenic agents and initiate the cancer degeneration process. In most cases promotor factors are needed to allow the changed cell to develop into a cancer tumour. Some of the most important factors responsible for the development of cancer in man are discussed below. See also Table 35.3.

Heredity. Very few cancers in man are caused by hereditary factors – examples of such are retinoblastomas and some leukemias of children. There seems to be a contributing hereditary factor in breast, stomach and colon cancers.

Chemicals. Many chemicals can cause cancer in man. Polycyclic hydrocarbons like benz(a)pyren, nitrosamine, aflatoxin, asbestos, vinylchloride and phenacetin are a few examples. The most important chemical causing cancer in man is tobacco smoke, which contains several agents possessing a carcinogenic potential.

The enormous increase in lung cancer in industrialised countries is due to tobacco

Table 35.2. Cumulative risk (0–74 years) for cancer (all sites) in different countries.

Country			Cumulative risk (per cent)	
			Male	Female
USA	Bay Area	Black	46.7	27.4
	Detroit	Black	38.3	30.0
Switzerland	Basel		34.5	22.5
Japan	Hiroshima		27.8	18.8
Sweden			26.4	24.7
Colombia	Cali		22.8	23.6
Puerto Rico			21.7	16.6
Singapore		Malay	13.6	12.6
India	Madras		10.4	12.6
Kuwait		Kuwaitis	8.3	7.8

smoking only. As tobacco smoking increases in developing countries a dramatic increase in lung cancer incidence is to be expected (Chapter 12). – Not only cancer of the lung is dependent of tobacco smoking, but also to some extent cancer of the lip, mouth, pharynx, larynx, pancreas and urinary bladder. Chewing or sniffing tobacco can cause cancer of the mouth. The mixture of tobacco and betel used in certain countries is carcinogenic to the buccal mucosa.

Ethanol. Heavy use of alcohol increases the risk of developing cancer of the mouth, pharynx, esophagus and liver.

Dietary factors. Cancers of the stomach, colon and rectum are dependent on dietary factors. Western style food with a high fat and low fibre content favours the development of colorectal cancer. Even cancer of the breast and prostate depends on hormonal changes brought about by the high fat content of the food.

Hormonal factors. Exogenous supply of estrogens enhances the risk of developing cancer of the endometrium and the breast. Women with no or only few pregnancies have a higher risk of developing cancer of the breast and of the ovary.

Viruses. Only a few oncogenic viruses are known in man. Burkitt's lymphoma and cancer of the nasopharynx are associated with Epstein–Barr virus (EBV) infection. This virus is spread worldwide and causes a benign infection of certain lymph glands in the industrialised world. In tropical Africa and in New Guinea, where malaria is endemic, it can cause cancer (Chapter 16). Infection with human papilloma virus (HPV) types 16 and 18 seem to be involved in cancer of the cervix (see be-

low). Viral (HBV) hepatitis causing cirrhosis plays an important role in the development of cancer of the liver.

Chronic infection. Chronic infection in nasal sinuses and the middle ear can cause cancer. Cancer of the skin can develop in ulcers after fistulas and burns. In developing countries tropical parasites like *Schistosoma* can cause cancer of the urinary bladder and *Clonorchis sinensis* cancer of the liver.

Sexual habits. Sexual habits play an essential role in the development of cancer of the cervix and penis (see below).

Immunologic factors. Immunologic surveillance (by the lymphatic tissue) seems to be most important in taking care of mutating cells. Mutation of cells in the enormous amount of cells in the body is not infrequent, but is efficiently counteracted by the defence systems of the body. – When the immunological surveillance is impaired e.g. by inborn or acquired (AIDS) immunodeficiency or immunosuppressive therapy, the cancer incidence increases.

Irradiation. Ultraviolet light of short wavelength can cause cancer of the skin and lip (see below). Ionising radiation, even though of little importance for the total cancer incidence, has been thoroughly studied. Such radiation can cause different kinds of cancer e.g. in the thyroid, breast, skin, lung, bone marrow, mucous membranes and connective tissue. The experiences from the Hiroshima and Nagasaki bombing have contributed to this knowledge. Under normal circumstances radon exposure in mines and houses is the most important type of irradiation and contributes to development of lung cancer.

Table 35.3. Importance of different factors for the development of cancer.[9]

Factors	Per cent of all cancer	
	Male	Female
Tobacco and alcohol	32	9
Dietary	40	57
Environment	4	2
Irradiation	8	8
Extrinsic hormones	4	
Unknown and hereditary	16	20

Synergistic factors. Factors can work together in a synergistic way like asbestos and tobacco smoke. There are also factors in the food active against the development of cancer e.g. some vitamins, fibres and selenium. Attempts have been made to evaluate the importance of different factors causing cancer for the entire cancer panorama (Table 35.3).[9]

The age-specific pattern for different cancer sites observed in a population can give a hint as to what kind of agent is involved. The common pattern observed when an exogenous agent is acting continuously during life is a steadily increasing incidence during life. If the agent has to act for many years the incidence curve starts rising in mid-life. (e.g. cancer of the gastrointestinal tract and cancer of the lung.)

When the carcinogenic agent is strongest in early life the incidence curve decreases in the older age groups (e.g. cancer of the cervix, see below.) On the other hand, when the agent is most active in early life and the susceptibility decreases in later life, as in cancer of the liver in Africa, a plateau type of incidence curve is seen.

Different stimuli in early and late life, as in cancer of the breast or endometrium, give a bimodal type of incidence curve. A double peak incidence curve with one peak in childhood and one in later life may also indicate a factor of immunological deficiency (e.g. Hodgkin's disease).

Some cancers are culturally dependent like cancer of the oral cavity in India (chewing of betel) and cancer of the lung in the western world (cigarette smoking).

SPECIFIC CANCER SITES

Cancer of the lip is most frequent in whites living in sunny countries and working outdoors and is rare in black people. It is also connected with smoking and with the use of clay or metal pipes.

Cancer of the mouth is also associated with smoking of tobacco or different mixtures of tobacco and dried leaves e.g. temburni and banana. The very high incidence in women in India is noteworthy.

Cancer of the nasopharynx is most frequent in the Chinese population both in China, especially southern China, and also in countries where Chinese people are living abroad. In high incidence areas most nasopharynx tumours are of epithelial origin. In low incidence areas there are a higher proportion of lymphomas, possibly associated with EBV.

Cancer of the esophagus is rare in the western world but in some parts of Asia and Africa it is very frequent. The highest figures are seen in the Mazandaran province of Iran close to the Caspian Sea. The adjacent states of Kazakhstan and Turkmenistan and some African regions like Transkei and Natal in South Africa and Bulawayo also have a high incidence.[10] Cancer of the esophagus demonstrates the widest variation between high and low incidence of cancer. In Iran there are low incidence areas close to the above mentioned high incidence areas. This is an indication of a powerful exogenous carcinogen.

Cancer of the stomach. High incidences are seen in western countries and Japan, low in most developing countries. The incidence of cancer of the stomach has been decreasing in the western countries as preparation and conservation of food has changed from salted, smoked and fermented to frozen. Formation of nitrosamines and polycyclic hydrocarbons during food conservation and preparation is believed to be important.

Cancer of the colon. Industrialised countries have a much higher incidence of cancer of the colon than developing countries. It is of interest that a high frequency of colon and rectal cancer has not been reported in any country in which the population consumes bulky natural diets. The exact protective element of such diets is unknown, but the possibility that they may cause dilution and more rapid passage of intraluminal carcinogens, or reduce the chance of their formation, remains attractive.[7]

Cancer of the liver. Primary cancer of the liver is uncommon in the Western World and Australia but very common in the Sub-Saharan Africa. The highest rate is reported in males with low socioeconomic status in Maputo, Mozambique. In the age group 25–34 years the rate is 500 times higher than in the USA. Mycotoxins and chronic infection with HBV are widely suspected to be an important agent in primary cancer of the liver, especially aflatoxin.[7]

Cancer of the lung. During the last few decades the incidence of cancer of the bronchus and lung has increased rapidly in the western world. The highest figures are seen in the USA and Great Britain and the increase affects males more than females. The age-specific incidence increases with age. Numerous studies indicate that tobacco is the most important etiological factor, especially cigarette smoking. The ongoing introduction of cigarette smoking in developing countries will cause increase in the incidence of cancer of the lung in these countries during the next decades. The exposure to radon radiation in mines and houses also contributes to development of cancer of the lung, but to a much lesser extent.

Cancer of the breast. The highest incidence of cancer of the female breast is found in the western world. In developing countries it is uncommon. This may be dependent upon the fact that early first pregnancy, as is common in developing countries, is the best protective factor known.

Cancer of the uterine cervix. In the developing countries cancer of the uterine cervix is one of the most frequent cancers among the female population. The incidence in Recife, Brazil is 21 times higher than that in Israel. The peak incidence of this cancer comes rather early in life – in the forties. An estimated 0.5 million women worldwide die from cancer of the cervix each year, most of them in developing countries.

Most patients with cancer of the cervix in developing countries come for examination when the tumour is far advanced and inoperable. Radiation which would be the treatment of choice in these advanced cases, is rarely available in such countries.

Early sexual debut, many sexual partners, early first pregnancy and promiscuity are well known risk factors for cancer of the cervix, probably due to a causative role of infection with HPV type 16 or 18. – There is also a link between cancer of the cervix and cancer of the penis. Wives of males with penile cancer have higher incidence of cancer of the cervix than expected.[11]

Cancer of the cervix is preventable by population-based screening with cytological tests. Precancerous conditions and early invasive cancer can be diagnosed and successfully treated without loss of fertility.

Other cancers of the genital organs. Cancer of the endometrium is uncommon in the developing countries. Most cases are operable with good prognosis. Cancer of the ovary is also infrequent in developing countries. Many ovulations during lifetime is a predisposing factor, and many pregnancies and long lactation periods are protective factors. When diagnosed the cases are usually advanced and incurable. Palliative treatment with cytostatic drugs are expensive and mostly not available in developing countries.

Cancer of the testis and of the penis is rare in both developing and industrialised countries. Cancer of the prostate and of the bladder is rare in Asia and Africa. In Latin America the incidence is about the same as in the western world.

Leukemia and malignant lymphomas. Leukemia and malignant lymphomas are not more frequent in developing than in industrialised countries, even though there is a special type seen in tropical Africa – the Burkitt's lymphoma.

Cancer of the skin. Cancer of the skin and malignant melanoma, which seem to be increasing in the western world and in Australia, are much less frequent in developing countries. Apparently dark skin gives protection against the ultraviolet radiation. Squamous cell cancer is often seen to develop in depigmented skin scars after burns.

Choriocarcinoma is a rare tumour in the Western World, but seems to be much more frequent in South-East Asia and East Africa.

DIAGNOSIS

The ultimate goal of the diagnostic procedures in oncology is to establish: 1) the diagnosis of cancer; 2) the extension and spread of the tumour; and 3) to get information of the biological nature of the cancer through histological, cytological and biochemical analyses. In most cancer diseases early diagnosis means easier treatment and better prognosis.

The patient's delay. The patient's delay can be reduced by increased knowledge of early symptoms and signs of cancer diseases. This can be obtained by public information through mass media about early warning symptoms

Table 35.4. Early warning signals for cancer.

– Spontaneous ulceration or vulnuses that do not heal in proper time.
– Abnormal bleeding or discharge such as bloody nasal catarrh, hemoptysis, hematemesis, melena, hematuria and bleeding and bloody discharge from the vagina.
– Palpable masses, even painless, in the breast, lip, tongue or anywhere on the body surface.
– Naevi in the skin, that start to grow or bleed (very suspicious of being malignant).
– Unexplained changes in digestion and bowel function.
– Pain is seldom an early symptom of cancer, but a typical symptom, when the tumour is growing into nerves, periost or is obstructing the passage in tubal organs.

like the ones listed in Table 35.4. Symptoms like these should always be thoroughly investigated by a physician.

The doctor's delay. Unfortunately there is often also a doctor's delay in the diagnosis of cancer. This can be reduced by making the doctors more 'cancerminded' and to increase the doctors' knowledge of the diagnostic procedures in oncology. The first essential steps are a careful case history and a thorough physical examination. Many cancers can be diagnosed by inspection and palpation, e.g. cancer of the skin, lip, mouth, tongue, pharynx, mammae, thyroid, prostate, uterine cervix and rectum.

Diagnostic methods

The use of simple and cheap instruments can increase the diagnostic ability e.g. the use of specula to inspect the mouth, nasopharynx, hypopharynx, larynx, uterine cervix and rectum. Even though a little more expensive, different kinds of endoscopic examinations can significantly increase the diagnostic ability (e.g. cystoscopy, gastroscopy, colonoscopy, bronchoscopy, laparoscopy, pleuroscopy).

X-ray examination plays an important role in diagnosing and monitoring of cancer diseases. Routine X-ray machines, despite rather expensive, are usually available in developing countries. Mammography is an important diagnostic method for breast cancer, but it requires special equipment that is often not readily available.

Ultrasound examination (sonogram) is getting more and more important in the examination of cancer patients. It is not too expensive and can be complementary to X-ray examination. The more advanced examinations such as computed tomography (CT) or magnetic resonance imaging (MRI) are too expensive for developing and also for many industrialised countries.

Microscopic examination of tissue from tumours is a corner-stone in the diagnosis of cancer. Different kinds of biopsies can be used to obtain tissue for examination e.g. incision, extirpation, aspiration, and exfoliative surface biopsies. All types of microscopic examination require extensive training and knowledge which are often a problem in developing countries.

Biochemical markers (e.g. AFP or CEA) have a certain value for diagnosis and monitoring of some cancers. Such biochemical surveillance requires laboratory supplies and a trained staff, that often are not readily available in developing countries.

Radioisotope examinations with different types of isotopes and a gamma camera are useful for diagnosis of tumours in e.g. the thyroid, kidneys, liver, brain, lymph nodes and bones. The equipment is rather expensive and the examinations require specially trained staff.

PREVENTION OF CANCER

Primary prevention. By avoiding the different kinds of agents that can cause cancer the risk of getting cancer can be considerably decreased. The most important factors to avoid are smoking and excessive alcohol and fat consumption. This requires awareness and motivation, which can be brought about by public education. Primary prevention also includes avoiding the carcinogenic hazard from air pollutants, food additives and industrial pollution and extensive sun exposure.
Secondary prevention. Secondary prevention includes different measures to reduce the effect of cancer diseases, e.g. early diagnosis and treatment as early as possible to avoid complications and sequelae of the disease.

Screening procedures

It is a tempting challenge to introduce screening procedures for early diagnosis of cancer or precancerous conditions. For most cancers, however, screening procedures are not available or practical. The requisites for meaningful screening are that the cancer in question is 1) common, 2) easy to diagnose with simple methods, and 3) that there is an effective treatment to offer. The screening method employed must have a high sensitivity and specificity. Currently, there are actually only two types of cancer that fulfil these requirements, i.e. cancer of the breast and cancer of the uterine cervix.

Screening for cancer of the breast with mammography has been used in some industrialised countries but its true benefit is still under discussion. There seems to be a reduction of mortality in the climacteric and postclimacteric ages, but so far not in the youngest age groups.

Mass screening for cancer of the uterine cervix with exfoliative cytology is well established in many industrialised countries. In Sweden screening was introduced in 1965. Now it includes the age group 20–59 year with the test taken every third year. This means 1.1 million smears every year in the country of 8.5 million inhabitants. About 1–2 per cent of the smears are positive or suspicious. The cost of the programme is estimated at 36 million USD per year. The effect of the programme has been dramatic.[12,13] Before the screening programme cancer of the uterine cervix was scoring number three among female cancers – today it is number 15. The age adjusted incidence has dropped from 30 to 11.5 and the mortality from 5 to 1.5.

Cancer of the uterine cervix kills about 0.5 million women every year worldwide, most of them in developing countries. There would obviously be a need for a mass screening suitable for developing countries. There are, however, many obstacles: need of laboratories, specially trained nurses to take the smears and trained cytotechnicians and experienced pathologists/cytologists to examine them, i.e. a lot of money.

It has been stated that while the effectiveness of well organised cytological screening programmes in reducing cervical cancer mortality is now well confirmed, controversy still continues on its viability and value in less developed countries. Such efforts in developing countries have been few and mostly short-term, but there is accumulating evidence that the mounting of successful screening programmes may not be possible within existing socioeconomic frameworks. To date, despite several promising pilot projects, not a single developing country has been able to design a national screening programme, that could work in the face of the social, administrative and infrastructural impediments.[14]

THERAPEUTIC CONSIDERATIONS

The main methods for treatment of cancer are surgery, radiotherapy, chemotherapy and hormonal treatment. The first consideration must be to decide if any treatment is indicated at all. Some patients with low grade malignancy and slowly growing tumours might not benefit from treatment. Some cases of prostatic or mammary cancer and elderly patients with chronic, lymphatic leukemia are better off without treatment. Palliative treatment for pain, of course, should never be denied.

There are many factors to take into consideration when planning treatment of the patient. The type of cancer, tumour stage, other complicating diseases, the patient's age, general condition and social situation are some factors. The aim of the treatment should be to give as long life expectancy as possible with the best possible quality of life with the resources available. The side effects of treatment should always be less than the gain of treatment.

Surgery

Radical surgery has long been a predominant method of treatment, where the tumour has a limited local and regional spread. Local extirpation (tumours of the skin) or extirpation of an organ (mastectomy, cystectomy, hysterectomy, laryngectomy, extirpation of the rectum) can be resorted to depending upon circumstances. Regional extirpation of lymph nodes is often added. Partial or segmental resection of organs is often used for treatment of cancer of e.g. lung and colon. Palliative reduction of tumour mass, Witzel-fistula or bypass operation can be beneficial to the patient.

Massive regional spread to the lymph nodes or very advanced local tumour indicate that surgery alone cannot be the method of choice. In most cases of advanced cancer radiotherapy or chemotherapy is the first treatment of choice. On the other hand, in many developing countries surgery is the only available method of treatment. The fact that most patients come late to treatment makes the situation very difficult.

Table 35.5. High-energy radiotherapy resources by WHO regions, 1989.[15]

WHO region	Countries with high energy radiotherapy facilities	Number of high energy centres
Africa*	12/44	14
Americas†	23/34	250
Eastern Mediterranean	20/22	40
Europe‡	35/35	500
South-East Asia§	7/11	80
Western pacific	11/20	200

Excluding: *South Africa, †USA and Canada, ‡USSR, §China

Radiotherapy

Radiotherapy centres are frequent in industrialised countries but scarce in developing countries. In Africa (excluding South Africa) 12 out of 44 countries have high energy radiotherapy facilities in 14 centres (Table 35.5).[15] South of the Sahara only the Republic of South Africa has more than one cobalt unit. In Nigeria the single cobalt unit in Ibadan serves the whole of west Africa with a population of 180 million people.[16]

External radiation with different types of radiation plays an important role in the treatment of cancer, especially in advanced cases. Many tumours are best treated with a combination of radiation and surgery, e.g. cancer of the breast, head and neck tumours, cancer of the esophagus, urinary bladder and rectum.

Intracavitary radiation, usually gamma radiation from radium or caesium, inserted into the uterine canal and the vagina is successfully used in the treatment of cancer of the uterine cervix.

Chemotherapy

Today there are many different cytostatic drugs available for various tumour types and indications. Most cytotoxic drugs interact with the DNA or the synthesis of DNA. Some interact with enzymes in the cell metabolism, with the microtubuli or with the mechanism of mitosis.

Rapidly growing cells like tumour cells, hair follicle cells, bone marrow cells and the cells of the intestinal mucosa are most sensitive to cytotoxic drugs. This explains the side effects of chemotherapy with leukopenia, alopecia and diarrhea. Germinal cells are also very sensitive causing azoospermia and anovulation during treatment.

Chemotherapy is indicated in a variety of situations. Some tumours can be cured completely with cytotoxic drugs e.g. choriocarcinoma, which is rather frequent in developing countries. In most cases, however, the indication is relative. Chemotherapy may give remission of symptoms and signs for varying length of time in different kinds of cancer. Treatment with cytotoxic drugs is very expensive, which is an obstacle to most developing countries.

Hormonal treatment

Some tumours have receptors for steroid hormones, e.g. cancer of the breast, prostate, endometrium, some leukemia and lymphomas. Estrogens, progestogens, androgens and corticosteroids bind to specific proteins on the cell surface of tumour cells.

Withdrawal of as well as exposure to steroids can change the activity of the tumour. Surgical withdrawal can be achieved by e.g. oophorectomy, orchidectomy, adrenalectomy or hypophysectomy.

Hormones and antihormones can be used for cancer treatment. Estrogen medication as well as withdrawal of testosterone by orchidectomy can give good palliation for years to patients with disseminated cancer of the prostate. Advanced cancer of the breast can be palliated with antiestrogens as well as by surgical hormone withdrawal through oophorectomy, adrenalectomy, hypophysectomy or through cortisone treatment.

Cancer of the endometrium, which is estrogen dependent, can be palliated by treatment with progestogens or antiestrogens. About 30 per cent of patients with generalised disease get a good remission. Lung metastases, without further spread, are palliated in 60 per cent.

Hormonal treatment is not expensive like chemotherapy and is therefore more available for developing countries.

Palliative treatment

In industrialised countries about 50 per cent of cancer patients are not cured, but have to live with chronic and eventually fatal cancer. In developing countries most of the patients are not cured. There is therefore a great need of palliative treatment methods against a variety of symptoms e.g. pain, anxiety, depression, nausea, vomiting, intestinal obstruction, dryness of the mouth and pulmonary symptoms.
Pain. Pain from many different causes is a very common symptom in advanced cancer. There can e.g. be an inflammatory component in ulcerating and/or necrotic tumours, compression or infiltration of nerves or periost, obstruction of tubal organs or expansion of organs infiltrated by cancer. It is essential to analyse the mechanism of pain to be able to give adequate palliation. In some cases local radiotherapy can give good pain relief by decreasing the tumour mass and sometimes the same can be achieved by chemotherapy. Nerve-blocking at different levels can sometimes be the best solution e.g. by percutaneous cordotomy or continuous epidural analgesia at different levels.

Most cases need some kind of pain relief. There is a variety of drugs to choose from. Many patients are helped for a long time with aspirin combined with sedatives and/or neuroleptics. Codeine or dextropropoxifen is the next kind of analgesics to be used. In very severe pain the drug of choice is morphine which can be administrated in different ways. If possible morphine should be taken by mouth in liquid solution in sufficiently high doses at regular intervals to achieve continuous pain relief. If necessary morphine should be given intramuscularly or by continuous intravenous drip. Morphine administration to cancer patients with severe pain does not make them addicts, but the dose has to be increased somewhat as time goes by.

Adequate pain relief in patients with tumours may be difficult to get in developing countries because of shortages of trained staff and drugs. The fact that most cancer patients are seen in developing countries and most of them have to live with chronic and fatal disease should accelerate the efforts for solving these problems.
Anxiety. Most cancer patients experience some degree of anxiety and depression during their illness. It is therefore important that they are taken care of by their relatives and the district nurse and doctor in a proper way to minimise the psychological burden of the illness. Sedatives and neuroleptics may be indicated to help some patients.
Nausea and vomiting. Beside the illness in itself also chemotherapy, analgesics and uremia can cause nausea and vomiting. Antihistamines, neuroleptics, antiemetics and cortisone can be used, if available, to minimise these symptoms. A nasal tube to the stomach can sometimes be helpful. Intestinal obstruction can be treated by enterostomy or by-pass operations.
Dryness of the mouth. Local radiation that involves the mouth and throat and a variety of drugs can give dryness of the mouth, which can be very distressing. This can in developing countries be alleviated by mouth-wash containing methylcellulose or simply by cream in water.
Pulmonary symptoms. Cough and dyspnea can be caused by pleural effusion or pulmonary metastases. Palliation can be achieved by pleurocentesis. Severe cough can be relieved by codeine and morphine.

Patients with advanced cancer and distressing symptoms mostly cannot be treated in hospitals in developing countries like in developed countries. One has to rely on the existing health service infrastructure in the village or location, where health workers and nurses have to take care of the patients with the scarce resources that are available.

MORTALITY

In most industrialised countries there are registers for cause of death that are reliable at least to some extent. In some instances, however, cancer may be recorded as cause of death when a cancer patient dies from another disease. In most developing countries there are currently hardly any reliable registers for cause of death. It is therefore not possible to know how many patients really survive and for how long.

In an industrialised country like Sweden the overall 5-year survival for men and women during 1980–1984 was 52 per cent. The survival for men was 47 per cent and for women 57 per cent. – For cancer patients less than 20 years old the overall 5-year survival was 69.7 per cent; male survival was 65.7 per cent and for females it was 73.6 per cent.[17]

For developing countries it is not possible to give corresponding figures, but with reasonable certainty it can be assumed that they are considerably lower.

References

1. Stjernswärd J. WHO statement at the International Conference on Cancer of the Cervix in Developing Countries. Nairobi 17–23 September, 1989.
2. National Board of Health and Welfare. The Cancer Registry. Cancer Incidence in Sweden 1988. Stockholm: Socialstyrelsen, 1991.
3. UICC. Cancer Incidence in five continents. Vol. V. Muir C, Waterhouse J, Mack T, Powell J, Whelan S, eds. IARC: Lyon, 1987.
4. UICC. Cancer incidence in five continents. A Technical Report. Vol. I. Doll R, Payne P, Waterhouse J, eds. Berlin: Springer Verlag, 1966.
5. UICC. Cancer incidence in five continents. Vol. II. Doll R, Muir CS, Waterhouse J, eds. Berlin: Springer Verlag, 1970.
6. UICC. Cancer incidence in five continents. Vol. III. Waterhouse J, Muir C, Correa P, Powell J, eds. Lyon: IARC, 1976.
7. Higginson J, Muir CS. Epidemiology. In: Holland JF, Frei E. Cancer medicine. Philadelphia: Lea and Fibiger, 1973.
8. Haenszel W, Kurihara M. Studies of Japanese migrants 1. Mortality from cancer and other diseases among Japanese in the U.S.A. J Natl Cancer Inst 1968:40;43.
9. Wynder EL, Gori GB. Contribution of the environment to cancer incidence. An epidemiological exercise. J Natl Cancer Inst 1977:58;825.
10. Kmet J, Mahboubi E. Esophageal cancer in the Caspian littoral of Iran: initial studies. Science 1972;175:846.
11. Martinez J. Relationship of squamous cell carcinoma of the cervix uteri to squamous cell carcinoma of the penis among Puerto Rican women married to men with penile carcinoma. Cancer 1969;24:777.
12. Kjellgren O. Mass screening in Sweden for cancer of the uterine cervix. Effect on incidence and mortality. Gynecol Obstet Invest 1977;22:57.
13. Pettersson F, Näslund I, Malker B. Evaluation of the effect of Papanicolaou screening in Sweden: Record linkage between a central screening registry and the national cancer registry. In: WHO, IARC and UICC: Screening for cancer of the uterine cervix. Hakama M, Miller A, Day N, eds. Lyon: IARC, 1986. (Scientific Publications No.76:91)
14. Machoki J, Rogo K. Knowledge and attitudinal study of Kenyan women in relation to cervical carcinoma. Int J Gynaecol Obstet 1991;34:55.
15. Hanson GP. Statement at the International Conference on Cancer of the Cervix in Developing countries, Nairobi 17–23 September 1989.
16. Rogo KO. Human papillomavirus and human immunodeficiency virus infection in relation to cervical cancer. Umeå University medical dissertations. New Series No. 293, 1990.
17. Adami HO, Rutqvist LE. Cancerbekämpningen gör framsteg (Swedish) Läkartidningen 1989;45:3877.

About the author

Olle Kjellgren is a specialist in gynaecological oncology and has trained also in obstetrics and gynaecology, and surgery. During 1962–84 he was the Head of the Department of Gynaecological Oncology at the University of Umeå, Sweden, and is currently an Emeritus Professor at the same university. In 1974 he served as a visiting professor at the Department of Obstetrics and Gynaecology, Kenyatta Hospital, Nairobi, Kenya, where he designed and started the Department of Gynaecological Oncology and trained its staff. Professor Kjellgren has published numerous papers in his specialty and coauthored textbooks of general and gynaecological oncology, and pathology.

Lankinen KS, Bergström S, Mäkelä PH and Peltomaa M, eds.
Health and disease in developing countries. London:The Macmillan Press Limited, 1994:341–353.

36 EYE DISEASES AND BLINDNESS

Paula Summanen, M.D., Ph.D.
University of Helsinki, Department of
Ophthalmology
Haartmaninkatu 4 C, FIN-00290 Helsinki,
Finland

**Hadi El-Sheikh, M.B., B.CH., D.O., Ph.D.,
F.C.Opth.**
University of Khartoum, Department of
Ophthalmology, Khartoum,
Sudan

INTRODUCTION

According to the WHO there were 27–35 million blind persons in the world in 1984. This estimate is based on more than 150 references for a total of 90 countries.[1]

Definition of blindness

According to the WHO definition, a person is regarded blind when the visual acuity (VA) in the better eye is less than 3/60 (categories 3 to 5, Table 36.1) which corresponds to an impairment ranging from total blindness (no light perception) to inability to count fingers in daylight at a distance of 3 metres.[2] Blindness defined in this way precludes an individual from functioning effectively in his community without special assistance.[2]

In some eye diseases, e.g. onchocercosis, glaucoma and many hereditary retinal degenerations, the VA remains normal until late in the course of the disease, while the visual fields become progressively narrower. Therefore, the WHO defines also a person with a visual field radius no greater than 10 degrees around central fixation as blind (categories 3 and 4, Table 36.1).[2]

In terms of social services and rehabilitation in the industrialised countries, blindness is often defined as a VA less than 6/60 in the better eye (categories 2 to 5, Table 36.1).[2] Were this used worldwide, the blindness estimate would rise to 41–52 million persons, or 1 per cent of the world population.[1]

Assessment of vision

Visual acuity is the most easily tested indicator of visual function. It is important that each person examined is carefully instructed in his or her own language, and has sufficient time to understand and respond in the test. The person examined should wear any corrective eyeglasses that he habitually uses, so that the test reflects his everyday situation.[2] Lack of spectacles causes a considerable amount of visual impairment in developing countries.

In clinical practice, the best corrected VA is assessed using testing charts with appropriate optotypes (letters or numbers, the illiterate E or Landolt's rings, Sjögren's hand etc.), and corrective lenses. However, in epidemiological field studies and screening, only levels which define the different WHO categories of visual impairment (Table 36.1), or at least the level of 3/60, might be tested.[2]

OVER-BURDEN OF AVOIDABLE BLINDNESS

Up to 80 per cent of the blindness that afflicts the world occurs in less developed areas (Figure 36.1).[1] The prevalence of blindness is typically ten times higher in developing countries than in industrialised ones (Figure 36.2).[1]

In industrialised countries, the main causes of blindness are congenital and hereditary diseases in children, hereditary retinal degenerations and diabetic eye disease in adults, and senile macular degeneration and glaucoma in

Table 36.1. Categories of visual impairment according to the World Health Organization.[2]

Category of visual impairment[†]	Visual acuity in the better eye[*]	
	Maximum less than	Minimum equal or better
1	6/18 (0.3) 20/70	6/60 (0.1) 20/200
2	6/60 20/200	3/60 (CF at 3 m) 20/400
3[‡]	3/60 (CF at 3 m) 20/400	1/60 (CF at 1 m) 5/300 (20/1200)
4[‡]	1/60 (CF at 1 m) 5/300 (20/1200)	Light perception
5	No light perception	

[*]The same level of visual acuity is expressed according to the Snellen six-metre scale (and, where applicable, the corresponding ability to count extended fingers (CF) at a set distance (metres, m); the second line gives the equivalent notation used with the 20–foot scale.
[†]Categories 1 and 2 refer to low-vision, categories 3–5 to blindness.
[‡]Visual field radius, in the better eye, >5–10 degrees applies to category 3, and 1–5 degrees to category 4, even if the central acuity is not impaired.

elderly people (Figure 36.3).[1] Most of these diseases cannot be prevented, and their management requires special techniques and expensive equipment (e.g. laser therapy, vitreoretinal surgery).

On the other hand, in developing countries the leading causes of blindness are cataract, infectious and parasitic diseases (trachoma, leprosy, onchocercosis), malnutrition (xerophthalmia-keratomalacia) and, glaucoma (Figure 36.3).[1,3,4] Most of these diseases (except chorioretinitis and optic nerve damage caused by onchocercosis, and glaucoma) affect the anterior part of the eye, therefore the changes can easily be observed even by laymen (Figure 36.4). However, diabetic eye disease is an evolving problem in urban areas in developing countries.

Loss of vision is a tremendous personal tragedy everywhere, but especially in societies where there are no social services for blind. Incapacity to work puts a heavy burden on the rest of the family, and blind people and their families are often the poorest of the poor. High prevalence of blindness among the adult population of the best working age (e.g. as caused by onchocercosis) has severe socioeconomic repercussions on the whole community.[5]

THE MAJOR BLINDING DISEASES AND STRATEGIES TO COMBAT THEM

Cataract

Visual impairment due to opacity of the lens causes the pupil to appear grey or white (cataract refers to the waterfalls of the Nile, and e.g. in Arabic *moya beeda* means white water, or in Hindi *moti pani* means pearl water). It is the single, most common cause of blindness responsible for 50 per cent of all world blindness, and in some countries for up to 67 per cent (Figures 36.3 and 36.4).[1,6] Cataract occurs with increasing age everywhere; however, excessive amount of ultraviolet light, diet, nutritional status or severe dehydration crises may possibly cause it to occur, at an earlier age in the South-East Asia and Africa than elsewhere. It cannot be prevented, but is readily curable by operation.

The ancient way to treat cataract by pushing the lens downwards into the vitreous cavity, known as couching, originated in the 19th century BC Babylonia, and is still used in some parts of the world. The modern surgical technique, extracapsular cataract extraction with lens implantation is not always possible in de-

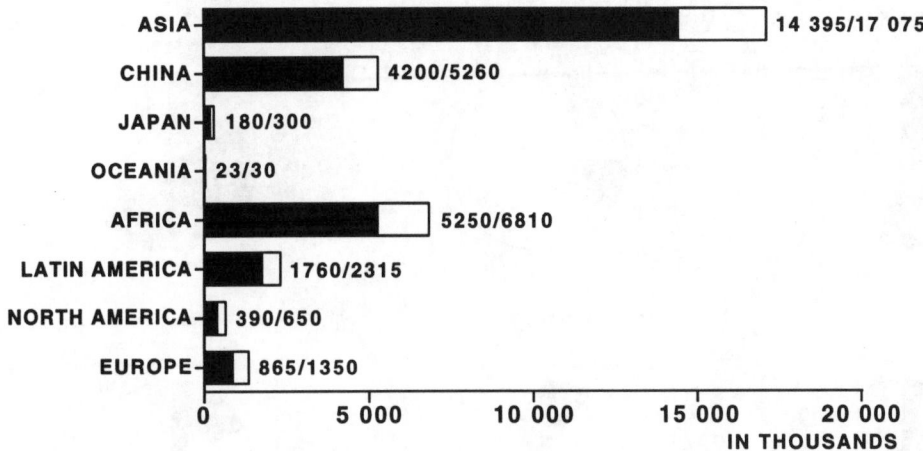

Figure 36.1. Distribution of blindness in the world in 1984 (minimum and maximum estimates with 95% confidence limit). The number of blind persons in absolute figures.[1] China and Japan are not included in Asia, but presented separately. Australia and New Zealand are not included in Oceania.

veloping countries, since it requires operation microscope, a costly lens and prolonged operation time and postoperative care.[6,7]

The safety, speed and simplicity of the intracapsular cataract extraction (ICCE) done under local anesthesia is the recommended method of choice by WHO in large-scale cataract surgery.[6,7] The ICCE technique is relatively easy to be taught for non-ophthalmologists (general surgeons, medical officers and even paramedical personnel such as ophthalmic assistants) where eye specialists are lacking.[8]

There is only one ophthalmologist per one million people in Africa, one per 100 000 in Asia, and up to five per 100 000 in capital cities of Latin America.[8,9] Mobile cataract teams with doctors from hospitals travelling out to the countryside (eye camps) provide good possibilities for teaching of local personnel, in addition to the service given. After cataract surgery spectacles for aphakic correction are needed: they should be provided as part of the service, and local low-cost spectacle manufacturing is therefore important. At

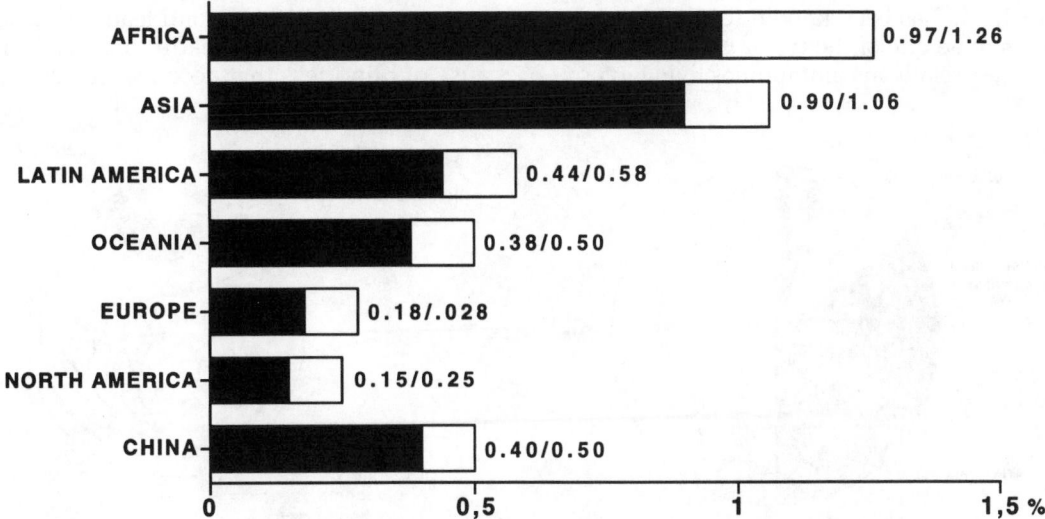

Figure 36.2. Prevalences of blindness in the main regions in the world.[1] China and Japan are not included in Asia, but China is presented separately. Australia and New Zealand are not included in Oceania.

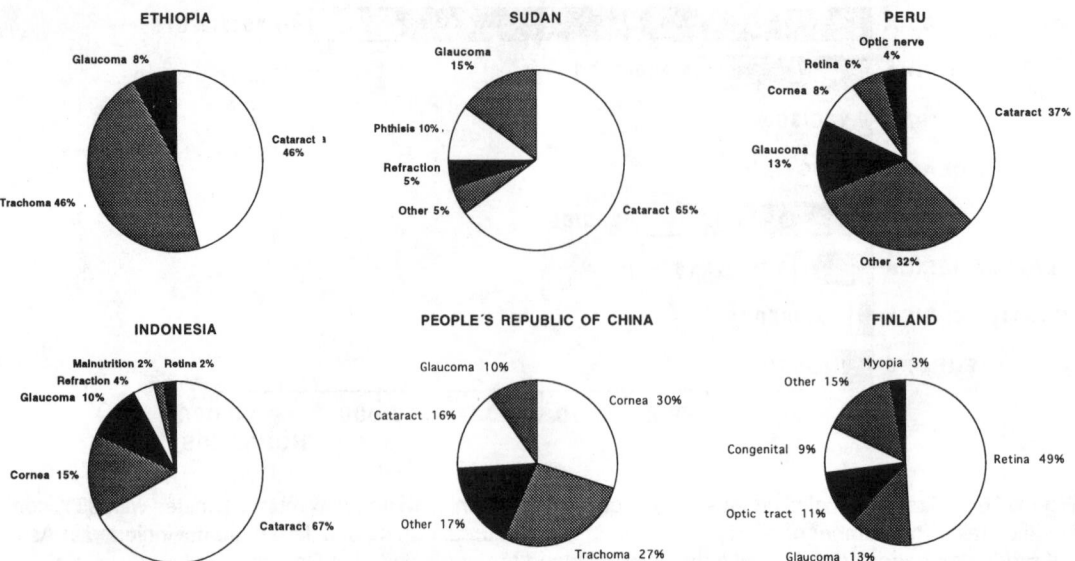

Figure 36.3. Examples of prevalences (in brackets) and causes of blindness in some countries around the world (representing the whole country, if not mentioned otherwise)[1]: a) Ethiopia (0.9%, rural area, 1981), b) Sudan (Eastern region, 1989), c) Peru (1.0%, jungle zone, 1983), d) Indonesia (1.2%, 1982), e) China (Beijing suburb, 0.5%, 1984), and f) Finland (The Finnish Register for Visual Impairment,1992).

present the annual number of cataract operations done per million population varies e.g. in Latin America from 150 in poor countries to 600 in Brazil, and to over 1000 in countries with better services.[9]

Trachoma, an ancient disease still active

Trachoma has been known for thousands of years to be one of the major causes of blindness, especially in communities living in poverty. It was in China where trachoma was known as early as the 27th century BC that the causative organism, *Chlamydia trachomatis*, was finally isolated in 1957. In the pathogenesis of trachoma, microtrauma caused by windborne dust, sand and smoke further contribute the to damage of the eye.[10]

Trachoma is still, a major public health problem in rural communities of many developing countries. It is the second leading cause, and the most common readily preventable cause of blindness that accounts for 25 per

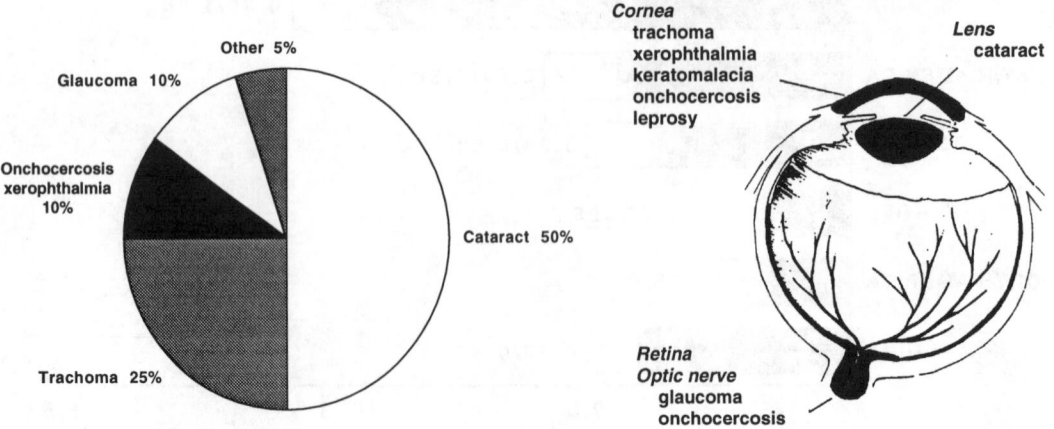

Figure 36.4. Causes of blindness worldwide and the principal part of the eye involved in the disease process.

Key findings

Five of more follicles
in the upper tarsal conjunctiva (TF)
    i) current infection
    ii) how widespread trachoma is

Inflammation obscures more than half of
the normal deep tarsal vessels (TI)
    i) severe current infection
    ii) how severe trachoma is

Scars - white lines, bands or sheets (TS)
    i) present or past trachoma
    ii) how common trachoma was in the past

Trichiasis, at least one eyelash rubs on
the eyeball, or eyelashes recently removed (TT)
    i) a potentially disabling lesion-lid
      surgery needed
    ii) magnitude of the immediate need for
      surgical services

Corneal opacity over the pupil (CO)
    i) a disabling lesion causing visual
      impairment or blindness
    ii) the impact of trachoma in terms of
      visual loss

Evert the upper eye lid

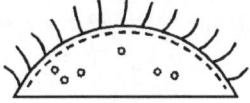
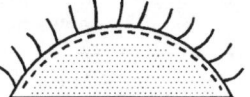
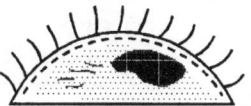
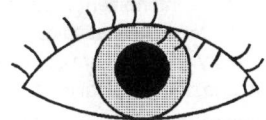
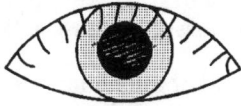

Figure 36.5. A simplified grading system for trachoma and its complications, and their significance i) for an individual person, and ii) for a community.[11]

cent of the world blindness (Figure 36.4).[1,3] Blinding trachoma is typically a family disease. Extended families, overcrowding, low standards of personal hygiene and short interpersonal distances between family members characterise it.[3,10] Transmission occurs both by touch and flies.

In hyperendemic areas, active trachoma can be found in babies as young as 2–3 months old. Reinfections, actually leading to persistent trachomatous conjunctivitis, are common in pre-school children. Blinding complications of trachoma, i.e. damage and opacification of the normally transparent cornea, result from the deformity of the lids caused by severe and excessive scarring. Each re-infection increases the scarring most probably due to over-stimulation of cell mediated immunity. In addition, contracture of the scar tissue occurs with time even without further active infection and distorts the eyelids. Blinding complications generally occur in persons over 35–40 years of age after 15–20 years of repeated exposure of the conjunctiva

to *Chlamydia* and severe inflammation. Women are about four times as likely as men to go blind from trachoma.

People in rural areas commonly accept trachoma without complaint. However, in urban populations, patients with active trachoma may complain of watering, slight mucopurulent discharge, redness, swelling of lids or irritation. If the cornea is affected, the eyes are sensitive to light. Most difficult symptoms occur as the lid scarring causes the lid deformities; the inward deviation of the lid margin (entropion) and the eyelashes (trichiasis). As the lashes touch the cornea, they cause constant foreign body sensation and discomfort. To seek temporary relief, patients themselves pluck out the irritating eyelashes or family members help each other.

The WHO has developed a simplified grading system for trachoma and its complications.[11] The presence of five or more follicles in the upper tarsal conjunctiva is used as the key sign of active inflammation (Figure 36.5).[11] Follicles are seen typically in pre-school

Table 36.2. Strategies for the treatment of trachoma.[11]

Proportion of children 1–10 years old with trachoma	Basic treatment	Additional treatment
TF: 20% or more, or TI: 5% or more	Mass topical antibiotic treatment	Selective systemic treatment of severe cases
TF: 5% to 20%	Mass or individual/family topical antibiotic treatment	As above
TF: Less than 5%	Individual topical antibiotic treatment	Not indicated

Mass treatment (all members of all families in the community): tetracycline one per cent eye ointment, either twice per day for six weeks, or as intermittent treatment with ointment twice a day for five consecutive days per month, or a once daily application for ten consecutive days, each month for at least six consecutive months per year.
Family treatment: identify and treat families where there are one or more members with TF or TI; treat the whole family in accordance with one of the topical antibiotic regimens for mass treatment, as above.[11]

children. They vary in size between 0.2–2 mm in diameter and consist of a dense collection of inflammatory cells.

The ultimate goal of trachoma intervention would be its elimination. Since that will not be possible in the foreseeable future, a more realistic objective is the prevention of blindness due to it. This can be achieved through mass intermittent topical antibiotic treatment or selective intervention, and surgery to correct entropion and trichiasis in high risk communities.[10–12]

Chlamydia trachomatis is sensitive to sulphonamides, tetracyclines, erythromycin and rifampicin. Individual patients with active trachoma, especially in urban areas, can be effectively treated with a 1 per cent tetracycline ointment one to two times a day for 6 weeks, or systemic therapy for 3 weeks.[11]

In mass interventions the classic regimen is application of a 1 per cent tetracycline eye ointment to both eyes twice a day for 5 consecutive days once a month, or once daily for 10 consecutive days, each month for at least 6 consecutive months a year. It should be continued as long as blinding trachoma is detected. Short campaigns have short term success. This therapy should be given to all members of all families in a community (blanket treatment), to all affected families, to all infected persons, or at least to all those with moderate to severe intensity of inflammation (Table 36.2).[11,12] Treating only school children is not advisable. However, every school child with active disease is an indicator of a family at risk.

Successful topical mass therapy will eventually reduce the ocular reservoir of *Chlamydia* and its transmission in the community. Also, it significantly reduces the intensity of active infection in the individuals thus preventing all those who do not yet have excessive lid scarring from going blind. Systemic mass therapy would be more effective than local since it would reduce also the non-ocular reservoirs of *Chlamydia* (nasopharyngeal infections), but it is more difficult to administer and more costly.

A successful intervention programme requires active participation of the communities involved, both in planning and implementing. Ideally, it mobilises auxiliary staff, community leaders, school teachers and specially trained village workers, but it should also be integrated with the general PHC delivery systems. Trachoma control should always include health education, and attempts to improve personal and environmental hygiene.

Recently several community-based health education programmes have been undertaken with the simple message: *Keep the children's faces clean!* It is essential that the long-term control of blinding trachoma is not based on only a hope of socioeconomic development, but rather encourages those behavioural changes at the grass root level that are possible now. Access to water is, however, crucial.[3]

Trachoma control must include services for lid surgery on the spot in the rural communities to correct potentially blinding lid distortions. A backlog of lid surgery is always an urgent task to clear. Simple surgical methods (e.g. tarsal rotation) are suitable and effective, also for paramedical workers to perform, and costs only one to 2 USD.[7] Recurrent cases must, however, be referred for more sophisticated surgery.

Xerophthalmia and keratomalacia

Xerophthalmia has been recognised for thousands of years, and been a common cause of blindness throughout the world. The ancient Egyptians correctly prescribed liver as a cure. It was in Denmark in 1920s that the lack of a fat-soluble element found in dairy products, vitamin A, was thought to be the reason of xerophthalmia. The disease was at that time relatively common in Denmark since most of the butter produced was exported.[13]

At present, it is estimated that 70 per cent of the 1.5 million blind children in the world are blind because of vitamin A deficiency, and the condition still blinds 350 000 children annually.[3,4] However, 60–80 per cent die within one year of becoming blind, either from the condition which led to the blindness (vitamin A deficiency, malnutrition, infections, especially measles) or from the consequences of being blind.[4,8,9] There is excess mortality even with sub-clinical deficiency, and the risk of death is highest in children between 6 and 12 months of age.[4] The main xerophthalmia areas are in the rice-eating South Asia, but it occurs also in Africa, Latin America, The Caribbean, and the Eastern Mediterranean.[13,14]

Vitamin A is essential for the wellbeing of skin and mucous membranes, and it is part of the visual purple, rhodopsin. The most obvious example of vitamin A deficiency is seen in the eye. The first symptom, difficulty in seeing in dim light, so called night blindness, is reversible, but more advanced cases will result in xerophthalmia (dry eye) and keratomalacia.

Dairy products, eggs, liver, fish, carrots, tomatoes are the most important sources of vitamin A. However, these are not available (or not consumed) in a majority of poor families in developing countries, especially not for children.

Blinding complications due to vitamin A deficiency are most common in children of 0.5–3 years of age.[13] Risk groups are especially children living in impoverished villages,

slums in urban areas, refugee camps, and orphanages. Vitamin A deficiency starts at the cessation of breast feeding. Relatively low vitamin A values have been measured (borderline 100–200 µg/l, pathological < 100 µg/l) without eye symptoms, but if the general nutritional status deteriorates e.g. during infectious disease, xerophthalmia is found. Severe xerophthalmia and danger of visual loss is thus linked with upper respiratory infections, gastroenteritis and measles.

Vitamin A deficiency causes keratinisation of skin and mucous membranes. The first finding is xerosis (dryness) of the conjunctiva. Bitot's spots are also typical, i.e. small areas covered with a fine foamy or cheesy material.[13] They can, however, be sequelae of past deficiency and occur when vitamin A status is already normalised.

Corneal xerosis, due to keratinisation itself and lack of mucin in tears, is more dangerous. It varies from a mild haziness of the lower part of the cornea to an entire dry, pebbly surface. Erosions are common as well as the typical punched-out ulcers. The most serious finding is keratomalacia, a rapidly destructive full thickness liquefactive necrosis of the cornea, often leading to perforation, extrusion of intraocular contents, and loss of the eye.[13]

With proper treatment, alterations in the retina (night blindness) and conjunctiva (xerosis and Bitot's spots) clear without harm. But corneal involvement (xerosis, ulcers and keratomalacia) usually result in some opacification and loss of vision. Even in those cases therapy is important, since it may limit the corneal damage and prevent it in the opposite eye if it is not yet affected.[13]

The most important xerophthalmia treatment is immediate administration of a large dose of vitamin A by mouth (200 000 IU if over 1 year of age, half dose if younger) in 2 consecutive days, and again after 1–4 weeks.[13-15] In addition, protein-rich diet should be given to correct general malnutrition. Local antibiotics will help to prevent secondary infections if the cornea is involved. Corneal ulcers need frequent topical and systemic antibiotics. The globe must be protected by a shield and all pressure on the eye must be prevented.[13]

The WHO, FAO and UNICEF all encourage vitamin A deficiency control to reduce blindness and save lives.[14] Vitamin A supplementation (usually 200 000 IU, half that amount if under 1 year or weight less than 8 kg) is an emergency measure to all children at high risk, i.e. those up to 6 years of age each time, but not more than once a month, when presenting with measles, acute or prolonged diarrhea, acute lower respiratory infections, or moderate to severe malnutrition, as well as to all children with corneal ulcer regardless of the origin of the ulcer.[14,15] It is recommended that in Africa, where measles is particularly severe, a full treatment regimen (see above) should be given.[14,15]

The WHO recommends also broader prevention programmes which attempt to improve the vitamin A status of all children in communities at risk of the disease.[4,13,14] Three basic approaches exist: 1) Periodic (every 4–6 months) administration of a 200 000 IU vitamin A capsule to children 1–5 years of age, as well as 200 000 IU to mothers shortly following delivery. (Pregnant and lactating women could be given smaller doses, not exceeding 10 000 IU daily); 2) Fortification of a commonly consumed item with vitamin A, such as sugar in Latin America, or monosodium glutamate (MSG) in Asia; 3) Increased dietary intake of foods rich in vitamin A is the preferred, long-term solution.

Health education to mothers of the dietary needs of the children is essential. Breastfeeding is encouraged. Advice to use the locally, often abundantly, available food rich in provitamin A, i.e. beta-carotene rich fruits such as mango and papaya, dark green leafy vegetables, or even leaves of some trees like drumstick or horseradish tree, or red palm oil, is essential. Home gardens and milk-producing animals are encouraged.[13]

The problem requires interdisciplinary awareness. Ophthalmologists and pediatricians could cooperate in the vitamin A distribution which in turn should be incorporated into programmes for vaccination (EPI) and control of diarrheal and respiratory diseases.[4] At the community level, PHC workers should be taught to recognise xerophthalmia. A quick method of assessing the vitamin A status of a community is to estimate the number of 1–5-year-old children with Bitot's spots.[4]

Onchocercosis, river blindness

Onchocercosis is caused by the worm, *Onchocerca volvulus*, the microfilariae (mf) of which are responsible for the lesions in the skin (Chapter 20) and the eye. The localisation of the blackfly vector on fast-flowing watercourses has given the name river blindness to onchocercosis. According to the estimates in 1985, out of the 86 million persons living in endemic onchocercosis areas, 18 million are infested, and at least one million people are blind or have severely impaired vision due to the disease.[3,5] More than 95 per cent of those live in Africa. In the worst afflicted villages in the savanna up to 15 per cent of the whole population, and more than 40 per cent of the males of working age may be blind from onchocercosis.[5] In these villages, blind adults, over 30 years of age, have a significantly reduced life expectancy compared with sighted persons in the same age groups.[5]

The risk of developing eye lesions is directly related to the intensity of the infection. Invasion of mf into the cornea causes temporary 'snowflake' opacities around dead mf, but permanent exposure leads to opacities which eventually transform the whole cornea to fibrotic, vascularised and pigmented tissue (sclerosing keratitis). Iridocyclitis may lead to secondary glaucoma and acute painful visual loss. More often the low-grade inflammation causes early cataract. The posterior pole invasion by mf causes chorioretinitis, optic neuritis and optic atrophy, which lead to severe visual loss by narrowing the visual field.

The diagnosis is based on the history, and typical skin and ocular lesions, and is confirmed by the skin snip test (Chapter 20). The test can easily be carried out in field conditions.

The most recent development for prevention of blindness from onchocercosis is ivermectin, a non-toxic microfilaricide, suitable also for large-scale treatment. Present contraindications to ivermectin include pregnant women; mothers in the first month of lactation, children under the age of 5 years and those severely ill.[5] Ivermectin is, since 1987, supplied free of charge by Merck, Sharp & Dohme to individuals and organisations who are competent to distribute it safely in the endemic areas.[5] Annual ivermectin treatment is recommended at a dose of 150 µg/kg.

In 1974 the Onchocerciasis Control Programme (OCP) was started by the WHO together with UNDP, FAO and the World Bank. Weekly aerial application of larvicides to the breeding sites of blackflies, has effectively interrupted the disease transmission, farming communities are regaining their lost land, and people are again planting crops and reaping harvest. Some four million children born in the OCP area since 1974 are no longer in risk of onchocercosis blindness.[5]

In heavily infected areas as much as 15 per cent of the village population may be blind as a result of onchocercosis and groups of the blind must be led by young people. Photo: UNICEF

Leprosy

The description 'to lose the eyesight when the sense of touch is already gone' underlines the impact of the ocular complications of leprosy. – It is estimated that out of the 10–12 million leprosy patients in the world, one third suffers from disabilities such as sensory impairment of the extremities, and roughly the same number have eye complications. About 250 000 – 500 000 (4–7 per cent) of them are blind.[15,16] Early detection of patients at risk, and appropriate management can prevent blindness.[15,16] Therefore, the training of PHC personnel dealing with leprosy patients and patient education is needed. Recently clear guidelines have been provided for paramedical workers (Table 36.3). Briefly, PHC workers dealing with leprosy patients should at certain intervals test visual acuity, and lid function, check eyelids for malposition and trichiasis, test corneal sensation and examine the pupil reactions.

There are two main pathways to blindness from leprosy, resulting from either corneal or uveal complications of the disease. Corneal involvement occurs in both paucibacillary and multibacillary leprosy, whereas iridocyclitis is characteristic of the latter.

Predisposing factors for corneal damage are involvement of the fifth and seventh cranial nerves leading to reduced corneal sensation and impaired lid closure (lagophthalmos). Such patients are at risk of corneal drying, trauma or infections.[15,16] Measures to protect the cornea include active exercises to close the lids frequently which can help the patient to restore full lid closure and keep it functional, and approximation of the eyelids by non-allergenic tape. In more severe cases, the palpebral fissure may be shortened by surgery (tarsorrhaphy). Frequent use of artificial tears during daytime and lubricating ointment (clean vaseline) or oily drops at night is advisable, if available. Evaporation of tears can be reduced and the cornea protected from foreign bodies by the use of goggles or shields, both at daytime and during sleep.[15,16] If a corneal ulcer occurs, it is an ophthalmic emergency and the patient must be referred further if appropriate antibiotics are not available where the diagnosis is made.

Blindness due to acute iridocyclitis not uncommon during a reaction phase can be prevented with prompt therapy with topical mydriatics and steroids. Leprosy patients

Table 36.3. Guidelines for paramedical workers to prevent blindness in lepers.[16]

Clinical sign	Diagnostic criteria	Therapeutic intervention
Visual acuity* (pinhole)		
Visual impairment	<0.3 (6/18)	Refer
	<0.1 (6/60)	Refer
	<0.05 (3/60)	Refer
Lagophthalmos		
Recent lagophthalmos	Less than 6 months	Refer for steroids
Involuntary blinking	Weak, incomplete lid closure	Exercise
Gentle closure as in sleep	Drift open	Exercise, eye ointment at night
Forced closure	Cornea exposed	Protect cornea and refer
Trichiasis	One or more lashes rubbing on globe	Epilate if few. Apply ointment. Refer if many lashes rubbing
Cornea		
Surface	Dull/rough	Ointment and refer.
Sensation	Diminished	Ointment, lid exercise. Patient instruction. Refer if trichiasis and/or corneal damage
Red eye		
Discharge and clear cornea	Visual acuity unaffected	Antibiotic eye ointment[†]
Pain and photophobia	Visual acuity diminished	Refer
Pupil/Lens		
Constricted pupil		Phenylephrine and refer
Cataract		Refer

In addtion, patients should be referred from the PHC centre to the secondary level of eye care if they have:
*rapidly progressing diminution of vision; or
[†]no response to topical antibiotic therapy.

undergoing cataract surgery need meticulous perioperative and postoperative care.

Other conditions

All eye disorders occur in developing countries, some, such as congenital cataract and glaucoma, retinoblastoma and retinal degenerations, even more frequently than in the industrialised world due the common practice of consanguine marriage. Furthermore, gonococcal ophthalmia neonatorum is re-emerging in some parts of the world, especially in Asia. For a prophylaxis in the newborn either a single application of tetracycline 1 per cent ointment or 1 per cent silver nitrate is crucial and highly recommended.[15]

Ocular traumas. Ocular traumas are also common both in children and in adults. It is typical that help is sought too late: even corneal foreign bodies and erosions, common in agricultural occupations, may lead to loss of the eye if infected. Appropriate first aid, bandage and antibiotics is essential and can prevent blindness.[15] Indiscriminate use of steroid and anesthetic containing eye medication, often as a self-medication, must be discouraged.[15]

Glaucoma. It is suspected that in parts of the tropics glaucoma occurs in age-groups younger than in the Western World. It requires lifelong treatment and follow-up. It is easy to understand that regular treatment e.g. eye drops two to four times a day is seldom realistic in the setting of developing countries.

In some areas (South-East Asia) narrow-angle glaucoma is frequent due to an anatomically narrow anterior chamber. It may cause blindness in a day or two with a high pressure attack. In those areas, prophylactic iridotomy should be performed, either surgically, or with laser equipment, for all those who have already lost one eye, and to those who are found to have very narrow, occludable chamber angles.

PREVENTION OF BLINDNESS

In 1976 the World Health Day was devoted to eye diseases and blindness with the theme 'Foresight prevents blindness'. Since 1978 the prevention of blindness has been one of the priorities of the WHO. The goal of the WHO Programme for the Prevention of Blindness is to eliminate the burden of avoidable blindness in developing countries by reducing national blindness rates to less than 0.5 per cent with no more than 1.0 per cent in individual communities.[2] In order to reach this goal WHO encourages and helps national authorities to assess the nature and extent of the problem. In terms of cost-effectiveness and improvement in the quality of life, prevention of blindness programs are highly recommended.

The WHO Programme for the Prevention of Blindness collects data and collaborates with Ministries of Health. There are presently national blindness prevention programmes in 93 countries. International Agency for Prevention of Blindness (IAPB) is a non-governmental umbrella organisation with national committees in several countries.

Prevention of blindness on a national level should always start with identifying communities with a high prevalence of blindness and determining its causes.[2] Worst affected communities should have highest priority and interventions by preventive and therapeutic means should first attack the major causes of blindness. Furthermore, it is of utmost importance that primary health care should deliver also *primary eye care*. When specific programmes, e.g. mass tetracycline ointment

or vitamin A capsule treatment, are needed these should be combined with PHC.[2]

PHC and eye care as part of it

PHC is preferably given by persons who belong to the community concerned. Primary eye care must include therapeutic and preventive activities and the promotion of eye health.[2]

Primary health workers should be provided with essential drugs such as topical tetracycline, and other topical antibiotic, with vitamin A capsules and with bandages and shields thus being able to treat conjunctivitis, trachoma, superficial foreign bodies, minor trauma, and xerophthalmia.[2] They should be able to recognise, give first aid treatment for, and refer further more serious eye conditions, such as corneal ulcers, severe eye injuries (perforations), painful eyes and visual impairment not alleviated by simple refractive correction.[2] They should screen for major blinding diseases prevalent in their communities e.g. cataract, trachoma, xerophthalmia, onchocercosis, and possibly glaucoma, and participate in interventions, and health education.[2]

Secondary and tertiary health care and eye care

Strengthening of intermediate and central (tertiary) ophthalmic services is often required in order to provide an adequate referral system, and for supervision and training. Secondary care facilities should be appropriate in location, capacity and technical capability for the management of the main diseases such as trauma, cataract, corneal ulceration, intraocular infections, severe recurrent trichiasis/entropion, pterygium and glaucoma.[2]

Tertiary centres often provide high-cost services for the immediate urban area, and fail to provide services appropriate to the ophthalmic needs of the whole country.[2] Ideally, they should be more involved in preventive ophthalmology and the promotion of eye health throughout the country. They should closely cooperate with peripheral units in terms of training manpower in their facilities as well as their staff to participate in the work of the primary and secondary units.[2]

Ophthalmology must be emphasised in the curricula of undergraduate medical students in developing countries due to the high prevalence of avoidable blindness. Furthermore, the

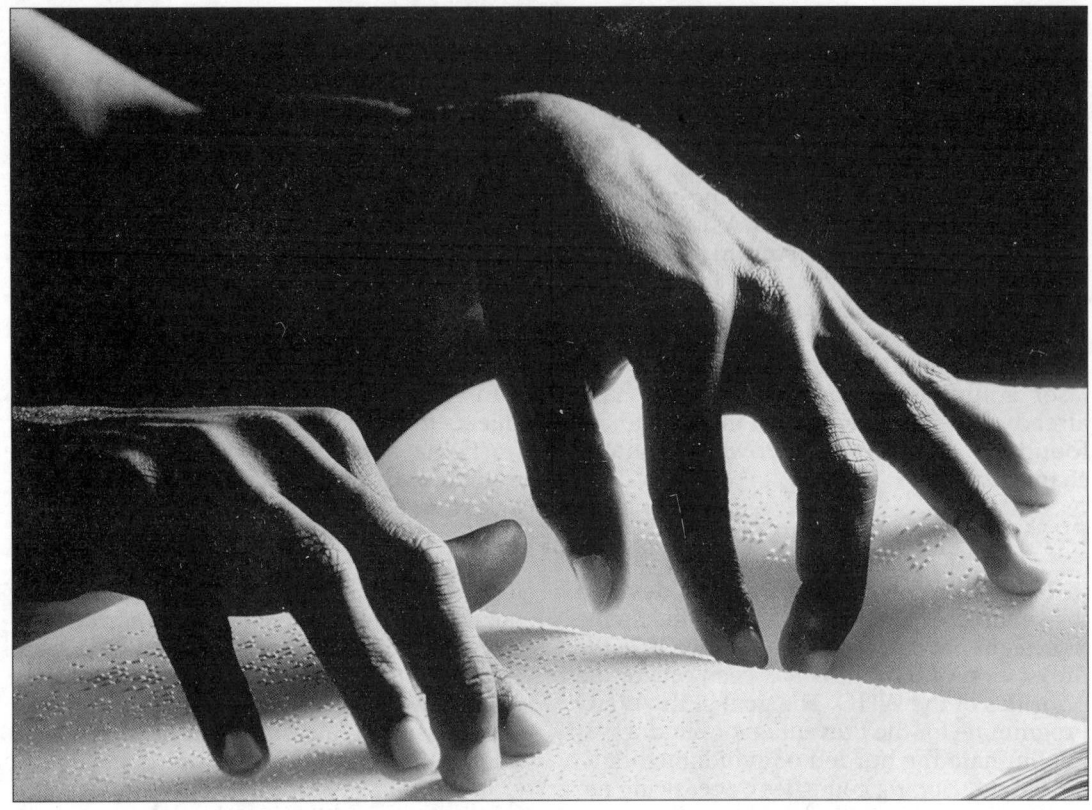

Braille, low vision aids and rehabilitation services are out of reach for most of the blind in developing countries. Photo: UNICEF

content of these curricula should be made relevant to the patterns of eye diseases in the country. This applies also to the training of specialists in ophthalmology and paramedical workers. Active participation in field activities should be an integral part of all these courses.[2] Research relevant to the regional problems should be conducted in tertiary centres.[2,8]

References

1. World Health Organization. Available data on blindness (Update 1987). Geneva: WHO, 1987. (WHO Publication 14)
2. World Health Organization. Guidelines for programmes for the prevention of blindness. Geneva: WHO, 1979.
3. Thylefors B, Négrel A-D, Pararajasegaram R. Epidemiologic aspects of global blindness prevention. Curr Opin Ophthalmol 1992;3:824–34.
4. World Health Organization. Report of the Ninth Meeting of the WHO Programme Advisory Group on the Prevention of Blindness. Geneva: WHO, 1991. (WHO Publication 22)
5. Luke BOL. Human onchocerciasis. An overview of the disease. In: van der Kaay HJ, Overbosch D, eds. O-NOW! Proceedings of the symposium on onchocerciasis. Acta Leiden 1990;59(1–2):9–24.
6. World Health Organization. Report of the interregional meeting on the management of cataract within primary care system. Geneva: WHO, 1987. (WHO Publication 13)
7. World Health Organization. Report on an informal working group on essential eye surgery. Geneva: WHO, 1985. (WHO Publication 11)
8. World Health Organization. Report on the third meeting of the consultative group of nongovernmental organizations to the WHO Programme for the Prevention of Blindness. Geneva: WHO, 1990. (WHO Publication 1)
9. World Health Organization. Report on the fourth meeting of the consultative group of nongovernmental organizations to the WHO Programme for the Prevention of Blindness. Geneva: WHO, 1992. (WHO Publication 26)
10. Darougar S, Jones BR. Trachoma. Br Med Bull 1983;39:117–22.

11. World Health Organization. Primary health care level management of trachoma. Geneva: WHO, Programme for the Prevention of Blindness, undated.

12. Dawson CR, Jones BR, Tarizzo ML. Guide to trachoma control. Geneva: WHO, 1981.

13. Sommer A. Field guide to the detection and control of xerophthalmia. 2nd ed. Geneva: WHO, 1982.

14. World Health Organization. Vitamin A supplements. A guide to their use in the treatment and prevention of vitamin A deficiency and xerophthalmia. Geneva: WHO, 1988.

15. World Health Organization. Report of the interregional meeting on control of corneal blindness within primary health care systems. Geneva: WHO, 1989. (WHO Publication 16)

16. Courtright P, Johnson GJ. Prevention of blindness in leprosy. Revised ed. London: International Centre for Eye Health, 1991.

Additional reading

1. Jones BR. The epidemiology of trachoma and other communicable ophthalmia. In: Perkins ES, Hill DW, eds. Scientific foundations of ophthalmology. London: Heineman Medical Books Ltd, 1977:149–59.

2. Venkataswamy G. The epidemiology of keratomalacia. In: Perkins ES, Hill DW, eds. Scientific foundations of ophthalmology. London: Heineman Medical Books Ltd, 1977: 164-8.

3. Reviews of Infectious Diseases 1985:7:711–843.

4. Javitt J, Sommer A, Venkataswamy G. The economic and social impact of restoring sight. In: Henkind P, ed. Acta: XXIV International Congress of Ophthalmology. Philadelphia, Pa:JB Lippincott; 1983:1308–12.

5. Schwab L. Eye care in developing nations. 2nd ed. Oxford: Oxford Medical Publications, 1990.

About the authors

Paula Summanen is a specialist in ophthalmology and currently Clinical Instructor at the Department of Ophthalmology, Helsinki University and consulting ophthalmologist at the Helsinki University Central Hospital. During 1979–81 she was in Sudan and, in collaboration with Professor Hadi, initiated the ophthalmic survey among leprosy patients. She also worked as a resident in Khartoum Eye Hospital. She was research fellow at King Khaled Eye Specialist Hospital in 1984 and participated in the National Eye Survey in Saudi Arabia and in several trachoma interventions among school children. Her current research interests are malignant melanoma of the uvea and diabetic eye disease.

Hadi El-Sheikh graduated from Cairo University and got his Diploma in Ophthalmology in London 1964, where he later did his Ph.D. thesis on 'Feline chlamydial keratoconjunctivitis as an analogue of trachoma'. He has wide experience on the main worldwide blinding diseases trachoma, onchocercosis, cataract and xerophthalmia as he has conducted and participated in several field studies and research projects. He was promoted to Senior Lecturer in Ophthalmology in the University of Khartoum in 1973, and Associate Professor and Head of the Department of Ophthalmology in 1980 and subsequently became the first Professor in Ophthalmology.

Lankinen KS, Bergström S, Mäkelä PH and Peltomaa M, eds.
Health and disease in developing countries. London:The Macmillan Press Limited, 1994:355–362.

37 EAR AND HEARING DISORDERS

Inga Pereira Bastos, M.D.
University of Lund, Malmö General Hospital,
WHO Collaborating Center for Prevention of Deafness and Hearing Impairment
S-214 01 Malmö,
Sweden

INTRODUCTION

Deafness and profound hearing impairment prevent an individual from hearing the spoken language. A child who is born deaf, or one who develops profound hearing impairment in early childhood, will not learn to speak. The lack of stimulation by sound may affect the child's development. There will be a communication barrier, leading to isolation and frustration. Integration into the human community will be affected.

Deafness is a hidden disability because damaged hearing cannot be seen or estimated as easily as for example a missing limb. The etiology is often unknown. Epidemiological data of its prevalence are, especially in developing countries, incomplete and fragmentary.

About 10 per cent of the world population is affected by hearing loss of significant degree. According to an estimation by the WHO, in 1985 there were about 42 million people over the age of 3 years with moderate to profound hearing impairment. This number is most probably an underestimate. The number of hearing-impaired persons in developing countries is increasing. As health care in developing countries improves, more children can be expected to recover from diseases that cause hearing impairment and, as the average length of life increases, more individuals are prone to hearing loss because of old age.

DEAFNESS

Hearing loss can be conductive, sensory or neural (Table 37.1). The term deafness should be reserved for those who cannot hear speech at all, even with the aid of a hearing instrument. Sometimes, the terms deaf-mute or deaf and dumb have been used. These expressions should be avoided, since they may be regarded as pejorative. Hearing loss simply means that hearing is less accurate than normal.

When working with hearing loss or deafness, one often finds the misunderstanding that deaf people are stupid. They are not – but they cannot hear. If they were deaf from

Table 37.1. Different types of hearing loss.

Type of hearing loss	Site of pathology	Restoration of hearing
Conductive	outer ear canal middle ear	often possible with medication or surgery
Sensory	cochlea	not possible
Neural	acoustic nerve brain stem	not possible

Table 37.2. Grades of hearing impairment.[3]

Grade of impairment	Corresponding audiometric ISO value (Average of 500, 1000 and 2000 Hz)*	Performance	Recommendations	Comments
0 No impairment	25 dB or better (better ear) 20 dB also recommended	No or very slight hearing problems Able to hear whispers		People with 15-20 dB levels may experience hearing problems People with unilateral hearing losses may experience hearing problems even if better ear normal
1 Slight impairment	26-40 dB (better ear)	Able to hear and repeat words spoken in normal voice at 1 metre	Counselling Hearing aids may be needed	Some difficulty in hearing but can usually hear normal level of conversation
2 Moderate impairment	41-60 dB (better ear)	Able to hear and repeat words using raised voice at 1 metre	Hearing aids usually recommended	
3 Severe impairment	61-80 dB (better ear)	Able to hear some words when shouted into better ear	Hearing aids needed If no hearing aids available, lipreading and signing should be taught	Discrepancies between pure tone thresholds and speech discrimination score should be noted
4 Profound impairment including deafness	81 dB or greater (better ear)	Unable to hear and understand even a shouted voice	Hearing aids may help in understanding words Additional rehabilitation needed Lipreading and sometimes signing essential	Spoken speech distorted the degree depending of the age at which hearing was lost

*Speech discrimination in a background of noice requires good high frequency hearing. It is therefore recommended that epidemiological studies include testing and reporting of hearing thresholds at 4000 Hz.
Note: Performance test for speech discrimination levels should be carried out using the hearing alone, i.e. without any visual clues.

early childhood, they are not able to learn to speak, since speech is a form of communication that is not suited to them. They and their parents should learn sign language as soon as possible. Lip-reading is for those who have lost their hearing after they had already learnt to speak.

CLASSIFICATION OF HEARING IMPAIRMENT

Table 37.2 gives an idea of the level of hearing impairment and the performance ability. However, it says little of the individual's hearing handicap. Handicap, being defined as a social phenomenon, depends on the attitudes of the society, and the barriers set up by this society. Slight or moderate hearing impair-

ment may not always be considered as a hearing handicap in e.g. rural societies in developing countries. On the other hand, in a community where the spoken word is more common than the written word as a means of communication, even a slight hearing impairment can have repercussions on the individual's development and his ability to fulfil his role in the community. Thus, when judging a hearing handicap it is necessary to see how the individual functions in his society, not looking at the hearing level alone.

PREVENTION

Two thirds of the world's hearing-impaired persons live in developing countries. Only 1 per cent of them are subject to some kind of rehabilitation. The ultimate goal for those who work with hearing impairment must be prevention. About 50 per cent of hearing impairment and deafness in developing countries is potentially preventable. Priority should be given to the most common preventable causes. The major causes of avoidable hearing impairment must be identified. In order to prevent a disease or disability, it is mandatory to have good knowledge about its epidemiology and etiology in the country or region concerned. Prevalence studies, based on internationally accepted criteria of pathology and epidemiological methods, give a good view of the magnitude and the geographical distribution of hearing impairment. These studies are necessary for a national strategy, but the prevention of hearing impairment must not be delayed while waiting for epidemiological results.

Areas of major concern

The etiology profile of hearing impairment looks different in different countries (Figure 37.1). Some infectious diseases, like measles, malaria, meningitis and enteric disease, are important because they are common causes of mortality among children in developing countries. But they are also important because they may cause hearing impairment. Malnutrition aggravates these diseases but is also alone a cause of severe hearing impairment. Respiratory infections often spread to the middle ear, causing otitis media and leading to hearing impairment.

Low socioeconomic status, poor hygiene, poverty, and illiteracy are important contributing factors in the occurrence of these diseases. Chronic otitis media among children in developing countries is associated with low education and deficient hygiene.

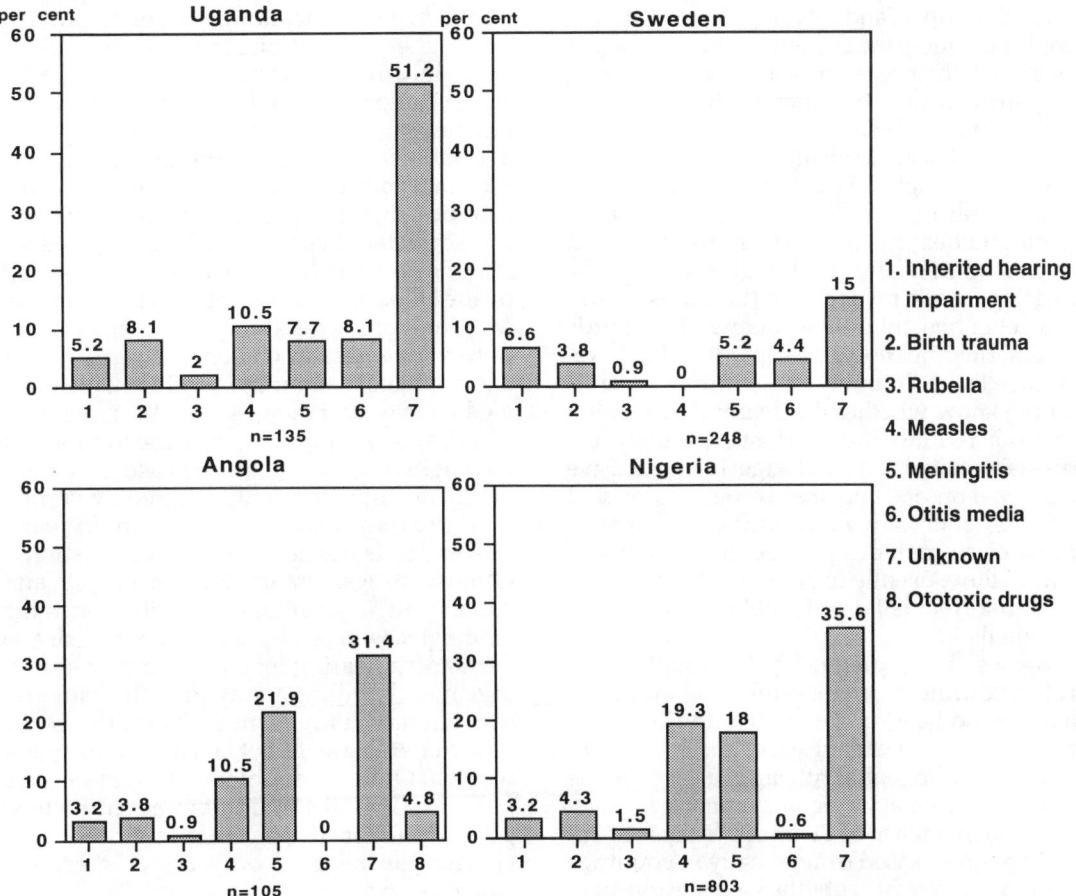

Figure 37.1. Etiology of hearing impairment in children in four different countries. Uganda and Sweden: all degrees of hearing loss; Angola and Nigeria: severe to profound hearing loss.

Table 37.3. Causes of hearing loss with approximate percentage in developing and developed countries.

			Developing countries	Developed countries
Hereditary (genetic)			5-10 per cent	55 per cent
Non-genetic			40-60 per cent	30 per cent
	Prenatal	rubella, syphilis, ototoxic drugs		
	Perinatal	birth damage, prematurity, anoxia, jaundice		
	Postnatal	meningitis, measles, mumps malaria, ototoxic drugs, noise, otitis media		
Unknown			30-50 per cent	15 per cent

Table 37.3 gives some of the more important causes of hearing impairment and shows the approximate percentages of occurrence in both developed and developing counties. In countries where the custom of intermarriage is practised, the prevalence of inherited hearing impairment may be much higher than suggested in the table.

Inherited hearing disorders can be of all degrees, from slight hearing impairment, to profound hearing loss or deafness. Hereditary, profound hearing loss or deafness may affect approximately one child in 2000 births. The hearing loss is progressive (becomes slowly worse) in one out of five patients. Two thirds of inherited hearing impairment is due to recessive traits. In many cases it may be difficult to know whether the deafness or hearing loss is hereditary or not. Most commonly, the disease is noted at an early age, but some have a delayed onset. There may be other associated defects, such as eye or kidney disorders. Prevention includes genetic evaluation and counselling, usually to parents who have had one abnormal child or to siblings of deaf individuals.

Diseases during pregnancy. If the mother has rubella during pregnancy, the child may have a profound hearing deficit. In addition, there may be eye or heart disease, and mental retardation. Congenital rubella is a preventable disease. Vaccination against rubella is effective; the incidence of deafness because of rubella has decreased dramatically in countries with a successful rubella vaccination programme.

If the mother has active syphilis, the child may be affected with a hearing loss that may be evident only at a much later time. Treatment of the pregnant mother can prevent hearing loss in the child, but the best prevention is health education in order to prevent the mother from getting the disease at all.

Birth injuries. Asphyxia or cerebral hemorrhage can occur at delivery. This can affect also hearing, and a combination of brain damage and hearing loss is sometimes seen.

Neonatal period. If there is severe neonatal jaundice, due to e.g. ABO or Rh incompatibility, kernicterus can result. This term means that the nuclei in the brain stem are damaged by the bilirubin. Hearing loss can be profound.

Meningitis. Bacterial meningitis may result in total deafness in one or both ears. As for haemophilus meningitis in children, the hearing loss may start months after the meningitis. Measles and mumps may give rise to a form of meningitis where the patient is usually not severely ill, but is suddenly affected by vertigo and hearing loss in one or both ears. Prevention is possible through vaccination.

Ototoxic drugs. Streptomycin, neomycin and kanamycin are examples of antibiotics in the aminoglycoside group that often give rise to permanent hearing loss. Gentamycin, tobramycin and amikacin may give the same result, but more infrequently. They all cross the placenta, and should not be given to pregnant women. Ototoxic antibiotics should only be used on very strict indications at central hospital level. Ear drops containing these substances can be used only under specialist supervision.

Chloroquine is ototoxic in large doses, and quinine produces toxic effects already at therapeutic doses. The hearing loss is sometimes permanent. If chloroquine is taken during the first trimester it may result in profound hearing loss in the child. However, malaria is even more dangerous to the unborn child.

Aspirin causes a reversible hearing loss and tinnitus (buzzing in the ears). Chlorhexidine, a disinfectant, is toxic, and should not be used in the ear. Some anticancer drugs are ototoxic, especially cisplatin.

Noise. Firearms, industry noise, loud music, or any other source of loud sound may cause permanent hearing impairment. The main problem with noise damage is that noise is not very painful. Simple noise meters are not very expensive and it is desirable that all industries have their noise levels measured. If the noise level is not known, hearing protection should always be recommended. A homemade ear plug of cotton is better than nothing at all. Noise damage is one of the major causes of hearing loss in industrialised countries.

Otitis media. The most common cause of conductive hearing impairment is otitis media. Otitis media is defined as an inflammatory condition with effusion in the middle ear. Depending on symptoms, the appearance of the tympanic membrane, the character of the middle ear fluid, and the duration of symptoms, otitis media is divided into acute otitis media (AOM), secretory otitis media (SOM), and chronic otitis media (COM) (Figure 37.2).

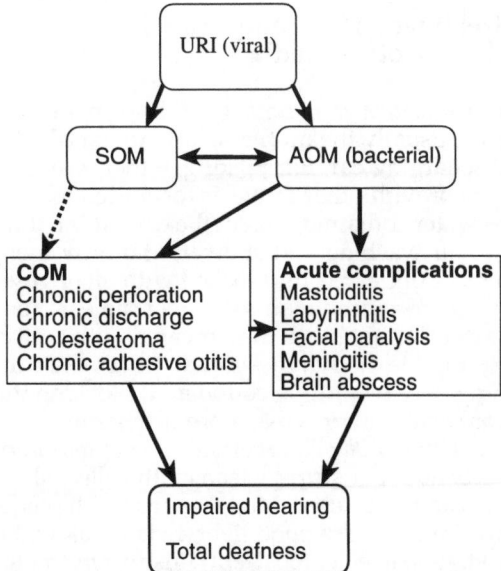

Figure 37.2. The relationship between upper respiratory infection (URI), AOM, SOM, and COM, and their complications.

Common cold or other viral respiratory infections often precede an acute middle ear infection. Acute otitis media (AOM) can be considered as a bacterial complication these viral diseases.

The symptoms of AOM include pain, fever, bulging and sometimes red ear drum, ear discharge and conductive hearing loss. The cornerstone of treatment is antibiotics, analgesics can be used if necessary. It is important also to control healing at the latest after 3 months.

If the eardrum cannot be seen, but the patient has purulent discharge from the ear, pain and fever, always consider AOM. If there is only discharge for some time but no pain, chronic suppurative otitis media (CSOM) is a possible diagnosis.

Acute otitis media is treated with antibiotics in order to relieve symptoms quickly and to prevent serious complications, like mastoiditis or chronic otitis media. Penicillin V is the drug of choice, given in a dose of 25 mg/kg bodyweight twice daily for 5 days. If penicillin V is not available, ampicillin or amoxicillin can be used. If the child is allergic to penicillin, give erythromycin or cotrimoxazole. Never use streptomycin or other ototoxic antibiotics!

Mastoiditis is a serious complication of AOM, where the primary infection of the middle ear has spread to the surrounding bone in the mastoid process. The infection can also spread to the inner ear, meninges, and the brain. These complications are life-threatening.

Signs and symptoms of mastoiditis are painful swelling behind the ear, increased ear pain, profuse discharge and fever.

If signs of mastoiditis or other otogenic complications are suspected (dizziness, stiffness of the neck, facial palsy) the patient should immediately be referred to the nearest hospital or ENT clinic for surgery. Start treatment with antibiotics.

Secretory otitis media is one of the most common causes of slight hearing impairment in childhood. The diagnosis can only be made by otoscopy and assessment of the movement of the ear drum.

Signs and symptoms of SOM are retracted, yellowish ear drum, mild conductive hearing loss, inattentive child, never discharge. SOM often heals spontaneously. Follow-up is necessary and in chronic cases ventilation tubes through the ear drum can be inserted.

Chronic suppurative otitis media is the result of untreated or inadequately treated AOM

Patient's complaints						Questions?	Test	Probable disease	First treatment without seeing ear drum	Treatment after otoscopy		Further treatment	
	Fever	Pain	Discharge	Itching	Hearing loss					Appearance of ear drum	Action to be taken	Medical officer	ENT-clinic
Pain (Discharge)	+	+/-	+/-	I	(±)	After a cold? < 3 weeks of discharge		Acute otitis media	Antibiotics (systemic)	 Drum swollen red (pus)	Continue treatment	Assesment if new ACM < 4 weeks	Some for surgery
	+	+	+	I	(±)	Increasing discharge over weeks	Redness and swelling behind the ear	Acute mastoiditis	Antibiotics (systemic) and referral			Drain if abscess	Surgery
Pain (Discharge)	I	I	+	I	(I)	With itching Now or earlier? Discharge	Pain on moving ear	Otitis externa	Clean ear - if wet: syringe gently Ear-drops, antibiotics if fever	Meatal walls swollen White depris 	Continue treatment		Very few
Discharge Hearing loss	I	I	+	I	+	Discharge > 3 weeks Foulsmelling?		Chronic otitis media	Dry mopping or syringing Ear-drops		Continue treatment	Those that discharge after 12 weeks	Some for assessment and ear surgery
						Dizziness Pain		Complications	Antibiotics, Dry-mopping or syringing Ear drops		Continue treatment	All soon	Possible ear surgery
Transient pain	I	(±)	I	I	(±)	After injury?		Traumatic perforation	Keep ear dry and clean		Keep dry and clean until healed	Failure to heal within 6 months	Very few

Figure 37.3. Treatment of ear disease: chart to assist primary health care workers and health workers without otological training. Modified by Bastos I and co-workers (Moshi Project), after Holborow C and Corcoran A. Commonwealth Society for the Deaf (Botswana Project), 1985.

or SOM. CSOM is the most common cause of moderate hearing impairment among children in developing countries. In some poor countries as many as 15 per cent of the children in schools for the deaf are there because of chronic otitis media.

The result of CSOM is bad hearing, and if the patient is a child, speech development will be poor. The disease is progressive: if the ear is allowed to discharge without adequate treatment, the perforation will slowly increase in size, and the fine structures in the middle ear (the ossicles) will be destroyed. If the ear is kept dry by adequate local treatment, the progression of the disease is stopped. Aural cleaning by primary health care workers and simple eardrops constitute the treatment of choice where doctors and otologists are not available and adequate equipment non-existing (Figure 37.3).

Signs and symptoms of COM are continuous or intermittent, often foul smelling discharge, perforation of the ear drum and conductive hearing loss. Ear pain is uncommon and, if present, indicates a risk of complications. Dizziness, facial nerve palsy, high fever (> 39°C), chills, severe headache also indicate serious complications. These patients should be referred immediately.

Treatment of uncomplicated chronic otitis media

1. *Information about ear hygiene.* Inform the parents, usually the mothers, how to handle the discharging ear. Ear picking, either with fingers or with other things is forbidden as well as water contamination of the ear. At the time of hair washing and shower, and only then, a piece of clean cotton soaked with oil or vaseline is recommended to protect the ear from water. Do not block the ear canal with cotton to stop the discharge – you do not stop a running nose by putting cotton in it! Blocking the ear canal will provoke more discharge.

2. *Dry-mopping.* Use cotton-tipped pins or absorbent paper strips. Clean cloth rolled like a pin can also be used. Mop away as much pus as you can see. Use good light. Do not allow the cotton-tip to enter too deeply. Instruct the mother or some family member to do the same thing with clean cloth. Let her train while you are watching. This dry-mopping should be repeated three times daily until the ear is dry.

3. *Gentle syringing.* This should only be done at the clinic. Use sterile (or boiled), lukewarm water in a 5 cc syringe. Syringe gently – you are not removing wax! Dry-mop afterwards.

4. *After dry-mopping, eardrops can be instilled into the ear.* Use 1.5 per cent boric acid or 1–2 per cent acetic acid solutions. These eardrops are cheap and can usually be produced at any hospital pharmacy. Instruct the mother how to give eardrops: let the child lie down with the ear upwards, fill the ear with the drops, and wait for 5 minutes. Do not put any cotton in the ear afterwards. Give eardrops three times daily.

5. *Regular controls.* See the patient once a week or every second week until the ear is dry. Tell the mother that the controls are very important.

If this treatment is not successful within 3–9 months (depending on the severity of the disease), refer the patient to a more specialised level. *Do not prescribe systemic antibiotics in cases of chronic otitis media.* They do not help to cure the infection.

EARLY IDENTIFICATION OF HEARING IMPAIRMENT

It is important that children with hearing impairment get proper training and treatment as early as possible in order to prevent serious handicap. One should suspect hearing loss if speech development is slow or absent, and try to test the hearing of the child.[1,2] The diagnosis should not be delayed. The ideal treatment is a hearing aid and special training, directed towards communication. If these are not possible, support the parents with advice how to start non-verbal communication. They will have to invent signs for food, members of the family, and important objects. A developed sign language helps the child to learn lip-reading and talking, provided that there is some residual hearing.

In older children and adults, hearing tests can be performed at different levels of technical sophistication. The simplest way of testing is by conversational voice test. Audiometry requires trained personnel and technical equipment not always available. When properly used it gives information about the level of hearing impairment.

Conversational voice test. Let the person cover one ear and ask him to repeat numbers or words. Make sure he cannot see your lips. Use ordinary conversational voice strength. If the person can hear your voice at a distance of 3–6 metres, the hearing is normal, or at least adequate.

Schools. Some developing countries have schools for special training of deaf children. The number of schools usually does not correspond to the amount of children in need. The schools are expensive to run. The training of special teachers is also expensive. The Community Based Rehabilitation concept is a different approach to the problem of training of handicapped persons, described in Chapter 55.

PRIMARY EAR AND HEARING CARE

Specialists of otology are few in most developing countries. Therefore, and in accord with the principle 'the greatest possible good to the largest number', ear and hearing care has to be an integral part of primary health care. As such it forms the basis of prevention of hearing impairment and deafness. At the same time, primary ear care has to be backed up by strengthening of the referral levels.

The basic elements of otology often exist in the curricula for education of medical staff, but lack of training opportunities and appropriate equipment is an obstacle to their adequate implementation. The ideal situation is that all medical staff, especially those working with children, at the different levels of the health care delivery system have some knowledge of otology, and that each level is properly equipped. The creation of new 'mini-specialists' should be avoided.

Not only medical staff are involved in the prevention of hearing impairment. In the first line, as always, are the families and especially the mothers. Information about causes of hearing impairment, and the possibilities of prevention is not separated from any other health education. It can be given while teaching a group of mothers about better nutrition, or while monitoring a child's weight at the MCH clinic. It can be given through posters at any clinic or at schools. By education on the prevention of hearing impairment, awareness of the problem is created.

Training opportunities for medical staff at primary and district level must be created locally. The aim would be practical skill of diagnosing ear disease and hearing problems at the primary health care level with scarce resources, and using appropriate and available technology.

Many cases of hearing impairment can be prevented:

- early diagnosis and adequate treatment of acute otitis media can prevent the development of chronic otitis media;
- conservative treatment of chronic otitis media can prevent the disease from getting more serious;
- good hygiene will prevent the spread of infectious diseases;
- vaccination will prevent children from getting infections like measles, meningitis, and tuberculosis;
- vaccination of the girl will prevent her from getting rubella during pregnancy;
- good and healthy food will make the child strong and more resistant to infections;
- ototoxic antibiotics are to be used only by specialists and only if the doctor is fully aware of the risk of hearing loss;
- protect the ears from noise: always ask industrial workers and military personnel if they use hearing protection;
- remember that one of your most important missions is to be a teacher to your patients and co-workers. Your knowledge can prevent disease, reduce symptoms, diminish suffering, and save money.

References

1. Helander E, Mendis P, Nelson G, Goerdt A. Training in the community for people with disabilities. Geneva: WHO, 1989.
2. Werner, D. Disabled village children. Palo Alto: The Hesperian Foundation, 1988. (Pages 257–76)
3. World Health Organization. Report of the Informal Working Group on Prevention of Deafness and Hearing Impairment, Programme Planning, Geneva, 18-21 June 1991. Geneva: WHO, 1991. (WHO/PDH/91.1).

Additional reading

1. Bastos I. Ear diseases and hearing loss. A manual for nurses. Malmö, Sweden: WHO Collaborating Centre, ENT-department, 1993.
2. Wirz S, Winyard S. Hearing and communication disorders. Basingstoke: Macmillan, 1993.

About the author

Inga Bastos is a specialist in otorhinolaryngology, and is currently the head of WHO Collaborating Centre for the Prevention of Deafness and Hearing Impairment at the ENT-department, Malmö, Sweden. During 1975–1983 she worked in Angola mainly with ear problems among children, and has since acted several times as adviser to projects on pediatric otology in African countries. She is a member of the WHO Expert Advisory Panel on Prevention of Deafness and Hearing Impairment since 1989, and since 1993 a member of the Advisory Board of Hearing International. Her main research interest is in the epidemiology of chronic otitis media and hearing impairment among children in developing countries.

Lankinen KS, Bergström S, Mäkelä PH and Peltomaa M, eds.
Health and disease in developing countries. London:The Macmillan Press Limited, 1994:363–379.

38 MANAGEMENT OF TRAUMA

Ari Leppäniemi, M.D., Ph.D.
Helsinki University Central Hospital,
Second Department of Surgery
Haartmaninkatu 4, FIN-00290 Helsinki,
Finland

Hannu Savolainen, M.D., Ph.D.
Helsinki University Central Hospital,
Third Department of Surgery
Haartmaninkatu 4, FIN-00290 Helsinki,
Finland

**James Lawrie, OBE, M.D., DCH, FRCS (Edin.
Eng. Glas.), FWACS**
College of Medicine, Department of Surgery
P/B 360, Blantyre 3,
Malawi

INTRODUCTION

A 36-year-old man was brought by relatives to the Princess Margaret Hospital in Tuvalu in the central Pacific after falling about 10 metres from a coconut tree. He was dyspnoeic and complained of pain on the right side of the chest aggravated by breathing. A chest X-ray showed multiple costal fractures and a hemothorax on the right side.

A chest drain set was constructed using available material: a Foley catheter, piece of plastic tubing, a glass jar with two holes drilled through the lid, and adhesive tape to seal the connections. The Foley catheter was inserted into the right pleural cavity under local anesthesia, and 800 millilitres of blood was aspirated. The catheter was connected to the jar with water-lock, and the level of the normal saline in the bottle was marked on the side. The patient was admitted, and placed on an elevated hospital bed (Figure 38.1).

Repeated intercostal blockade was used for analgesia, breathing exercises were started, and the clinical condition was monitored daily with regular measurements of the chest tube discharge. X-ray controls were taken as needed. The tube was removed after 10 days, and the patient discharged with supportive bandage and analgesics 2 days later.

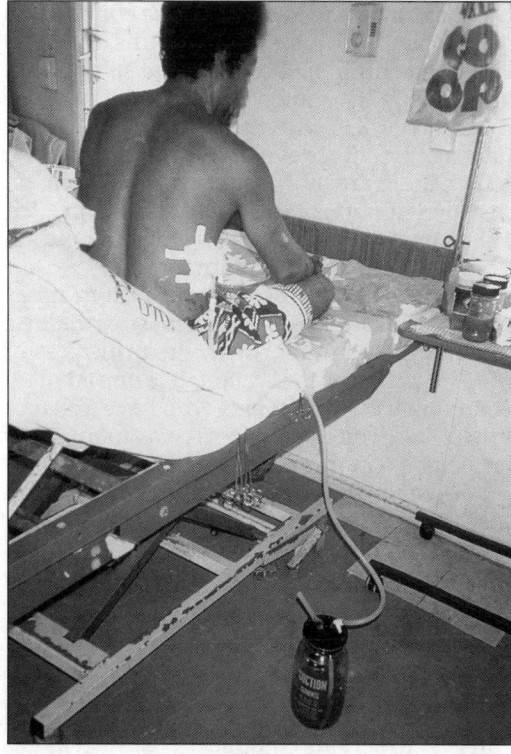

Figure 38.1. An improvised chest tube drainage system in a patient with traumatic hemothorax. Photo: Ari Leppäniemi

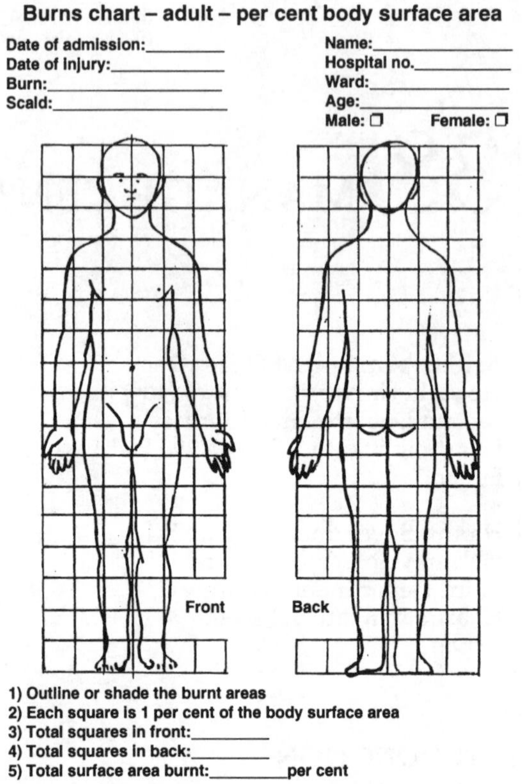

This example gives a true picture of the conditions and problems facing a physician working in developing countries where 25–50 per cent of patients suffer from injuries. Therefore, every doctor working in such countries should have the basic knowledge, skills and flexibility to manage all kinds of injuries from the beginning to the end using all available resources.

CAUSES OF INJURIES

Of all causes of external trauma, traffic accidents carry the highest mortality rate. Annually, six million people are injured and 200 000 die in traffic accidents worldwide. In developing countries, transport vehicles are always crowded. A typical way of mass transport is a truck with tens of passengers on board. In buses, the roofs are full of passengers, and open doors and windows are full of them as well. Roads are bad, and drunken driving is common. Roads are full of people, animals, rickshaws and other vehicles. Seat belts are hardly ever used, and head-lights are used sparingly. Sometimes one bulb is removed to save them.

Other man-made accidents are common as well. Open fire causes a lot of burns, especially among children. Occupational safety is often inadequate. Violence is common in cities.

Most conflicts after the Second World War have occurred in developing countries. Even today, there are more than ten wars going on in different parts of the world. Civil wars, tribal disputes, and cattle raids increase injuries. Gunshot wounds are common.

Most Third World countries are in areas prone to natural disasters. In mass casualties, one has to be familiar with the principles of *triage* or patient classification. It is important to concentrate on the patients who have a chance to survive. The idea is to save as many lives and limbs – in this order – as possible.

Poisonous, stinging, and biting animals and insects cause a large number of the injuries. During the rainy season, up to 10 per cent of hospital beds can be occupied by patients suffering from snake bites.

Open fractures are up to ten times more common in Africa than in industrialised countries. Not closing a wound can seem strange to a western-trained doctor, but closing a wound can lead to serious complications, such as gas gangrene or tetanus.

Long transportation distances are problematic, patients are brought from distances that

Burns chart – adult – per cent body surface area

Date of admission:_____
Date of Injury:_____
Burn:_____
Scald:_____

Name:_____
Hospital no._____
Ward:_____
Age:_____
Male: ☐   Female: ☐

Front   Back

1) Outline or shade the burnt areas
2) Each square is 1 per cent of the body surface area
3) Total squares in front:_____
4) Total squares in back:_____
5) Total surface area burnt:_____per cent

Figure 38.2a. Burns chart for estimating percentage of body surface area in adults (from College of Medicine, Blantyre, Professor James Lawrie).

take days, on miserable roads. Dust and dirt may enter the wound easily. The conditions at the hospital may be less than optimal. Lack of well-trained staff is common. Electricity and water are not always available. The equipment can be outdated, broken, lost or stolen. The X-ray machine can be out of order for weeks. Or there is no film or liquids for developing. Medicines and infusions are scarce. The patients are often malnourished. Parasites are ubiquitous. Most people are not vaccinated against tetanus.

Because of all this, diagnosis and treating the patients are the responsibility of an individual doctor relying on his or her knowledge, skills and ethics. Often it is impossible to refer patients to hospitals with better facilities. Possibilities for intensive care are limited. A patient requiring institutionalised care may have extremely poor prognosis. Most of the time, however, discharging a patient is no problem, since families are quite willing to take care of their relatives. Striving towards

Burns chart – child – per cent body surface area

Date of admission:_____
Date of injury:_____
Burn:_____
Scald:_____

Name:_____
Hospital no._____
Ward:_____
Age:_____
Male: ☐   Female: ☐

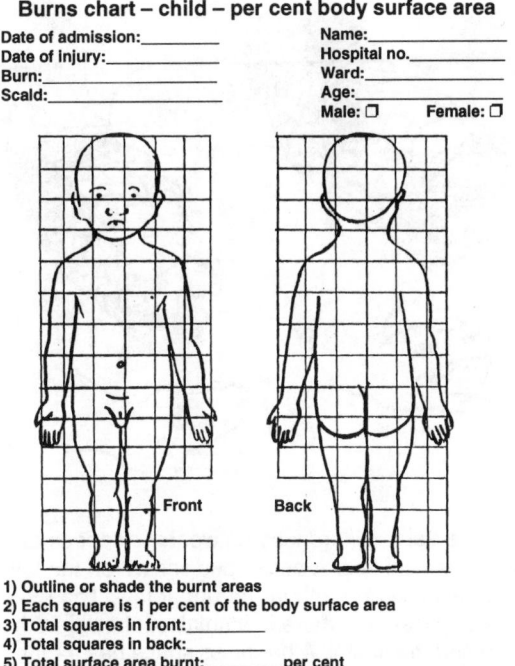

Front   Back

1) Outline or shade the burnt areas
2) Each square is 1 per cent of the body surface area
3) Total squares in front:_____
4) Total squares in back:_____
5) Total surface area burnt:_____per cent

Figure 38.2b. Burns chart for estimating percentage of body surface area in children (from College of Medicine, Blantyre, Professor James Lawrie).

optimal functional result is crucial in the treatment. Without comprehensive social security system, the future of the whole family may depend on the recovery of a single member.

It is important to recognise cultural differences also. For example, a Moslem patient may rather die than have his leg amputated. Many patients may initially have been treated by traditional healers, and seek conventional medical help only if the traditional treatment has failed. Nevertheless, one should not underestimate the importance of the support traditional healers give.

In spite of the difficulties, results of treatment are often good. An active attitude, and the ability to improvise are the basis of successful treatment.

WOUND MANAGEMENT

Unlike in industrialised countries, wounds in developing countries tend to be old. A delay of a few days or even more is the rule. The main aim is to prevent infection, particularly *gas gangrene*. Removal of all dead tissue is crucial in proper wound management. Only after reaching healthy tissue, a wound is closed

with sutures or adhesive, but never under tension. In gaping wounds, a split skin graft is often more practical.

Wounds older than 12 hours should always be left open after revision, and covered with lightly moistened fluffy dressings. Wounds should never be packed; the skin will only macerate. Dressings are changed daily or, if there is a lot of pus, even more often. Continuing secretion is a sign of inadequate revision, osteomyelitis, or a missed foreign body. The wound can be closed only when it is completely clean which normally takes 1–2 weeks. – The same principles of delayed closure apply to fresh wounds caused by animal or human bites, high-energy gunshot wounds and badly contaminated wounds.

Proper wound care prevents tetanus. In high risk patients, hyperimmunoglobulin should be used, if available. In frank infections, antibiotics do not replace adequate wound care. In patients with septicemia, however, antibiotics are indicated. One should not forget that in many countries, where malaria is endemic, postoperative fever may be caused by parasitemia.

BURNS AND SCALDS

In the management of thermal injuries a confusing variety of options exits, both for treating initial hypovolemic shock, and for the local care of the burned area. There is no treatment of choice, but the site, extent and depth of a burn wound determine the treatment.

The extent can be estimated using burns charts for adults (Figure 38.2a) and children (Figure 38.2b). Patients with burns less than

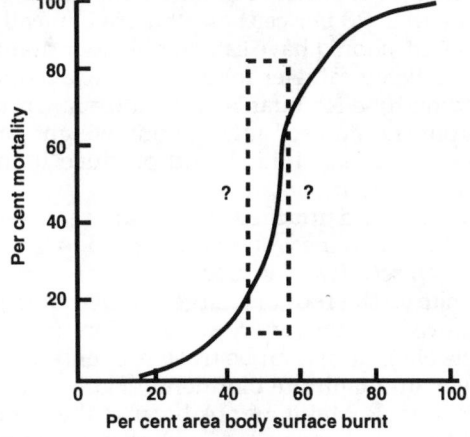

Figure 38.3. The relationship between body surface area burned and mortality, the 'critical area'.

20 per cent should survive, and those with 70 per cent or more will not. The group of patients whose management is critical, and who need most care and attention are those around 50 per cent (Figure 38.3). With care they will survive, neglected they will die.

All burns larger than 20 per cent, and even smaller ones on the face or hands require admission. Sufficient fluid replacement is important. As small children form a large group of burned patients in rural societies in the poorer countries, body weight and surface area burned are the key factors in estimating intravenous fluid requirements.

A useful formula is: fluid requirements (volume in millilitres) = percentage of surface area burned x body weight in kilograms x 3 ml. Thus, a boy weighing 10 kg with 30 per cent surface burned will require 900 ml in the first 24 hours.

If the patient is brought soon after the burn injury (in about 2 hours) he should be given half this volume in the first 8 hours, and a quarter in each of the following 8-hour periods. Usually, however, they arrive a day late, and the estimated volume can be given at a constant rate over 24 hours. Ringer-lactate or similar balanced electrolytic solution is used. *Do not forget the basic maintenance requirements.* This same 10 kg child has a daily fluid maintenance requirement of 1000 ml (100 ml per kg body weight) so that his total fluid requirement is doubled.

As important as any formula is the need to monitor each patient individually, as one would with any acutely ill patient – from trauma, peritonitis or anything else. Urine output is the best monitor. Patients with burns of more than 20 per cent or who are clinically shocked, should have catheter bladder drainage, a Foley catheter for adults, a size 5 or 8 feeding tube for infants and children. Urine output should be: 1 ml/kg body weight per hour, i.e. 10 kg child should produce 10 ml urine per hour.

Burned and attached clothes are removed carefully, and the wound is irrigated. A greyish, non-sensitive skin area is a sign of a deeper injury. The roof of a large infected bleb is removed. Under very clean conditions (no insects etc.), burns can be treated openly with silver sulphanitrate ointments (Flamazine®, Silvadene®, Mafylon®). A burn of the hand can be kept clean in a sterile plastic bag which allows the important early mobilisation of the fingers.

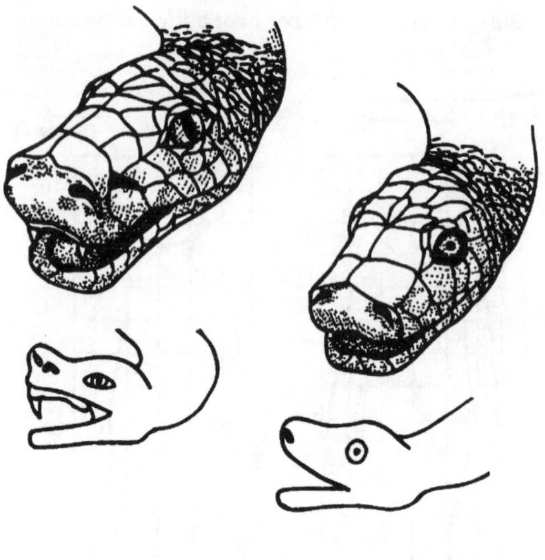

Figure 38.4. Differences between poisonous and harmless snakes. A poisonous snake (on the left) has two poison teeth in the upper jaw. The eyes are elliptical, and there is a small pit between the eye and the nostril. A harmless snake has a round eye and has no poison teeth.

If burns need to be dressed the dressing should not be changed too frequently, *practically never daily.* Even in infected cases there is deep granulation and epithelialisation takes place at the margins. Dressings should include gentle lavage with normal saline only – not any chemical or antiseptic, as these do as much damage to newly forming tissues as they do to infecting organisms.

In deep burns, early excision and skin grafting give the best results. In general, prophylactic antibiotics are not required.

STINGS AND BITES

Stings and bites are often less dangerous than generally thought and most victims need no medical attention. In the United States, it is estimated that 45 000 people are bitten by snakes every year, and even there only 8000 seek professional help. Each year only some 15 people die from snake bites. Worldwide, however, 30 000 to 40 000 people die annually. In Africa alone, there are more than 140 species of snakes. Of them, only about 30 are dangerous to man. A doctor should be able to recognise the poisonous snakes in his own area (Figure 38.4).

If more than 2 hours have passed after a bite from a snake of the adder-family (*Viperidae*),

FRACTURE	OP	IMMOBILISATION	WEIGHT-BEARING
VERTEBRAL COLUMN			
Atlas		3 months	
Axis (epistropheus) – dens		3 months	
Other cervical			
fracture dislocations		2–3 months	
compression fractures		a few weeks	
PELVIS			
stable and mild		0–2 weeks	
double–vertical (unstable)		6 weeks	
UPPER EXTREMITY			
clavicle		3 weeks (elderly 0 weeks)	
humeral neck (major tubercle)		3–4 weeks	immediate mobilisation
humeral shaft		6–8 weeks	mobilisation after 4 weeks
humeral condyles	x	6–8 weeks	
capitulum radii		1 week	
antebrachium	x	2–3 months (cons. tr.)	
Colles' fracture		4–6 weeks	
scaphoideum		6–12 weeks	
other carpal bones		3 weeks	
metacarpal shaft		5–8 weeks	
metacarpal base or head		3–4 weeks	
Bennett's fracture		6–8 weeks	
phalanx		3–4 weeks	

Table 1a. The immobilisation and non-weight-bearing times of common adult fractures of vertebral column, pelvis and upper extremity.[13] Immobilisation refers here to the time required to maintain the position of an operatively or conservatively treated fracture using a plaster of Paris (POP), different splints or bed rest. An operation does not shorten the time of immobilisation as such, but allows earlier mobilisation of joints. Walking with crutches should be started as soon as possible. Weight-bearing is allowed when the fracture is clinically stable and callus formation can be seen on X-rays (OP = usually treated operatively)

and the patient has no symptoms, the patient is usually safe. Nevertheless, the patient should be admitted for observation.

In fresh bites, species-specific anti-snake serum is administered if the patient has general symptoms. Up to 15 per cent of patients will get a severe allergic reaction from the antiserum itself. The treatment of other snake bites is more complex, since the symptoms are hidden and develop more slowly.

Incision, sucking the wound, or a tourniquet are not needed. The bite itself often gets infected from the Gram-negative rod bacteria

commonly found in the mouth of a snake. The bites of some snakes such as cobras, cause extensive tissue necrosis. After demarcation, they are treated with revisions and skin grafting. The affected limb should be immobilised.

Infections require antibiotics as well. The value of fasciotomies is questionable. Possible cardiovascular collapse is managed with volume substitution, and epinephrine or other inotropic agents. *Corticosteroids are not required.*

Only few scorpion species are lethal to man: the Central American *Centruroides*, the African

FRACTURE	OP	IMMOBILISATION	WEIGHT–BEARING
LOWER EXTREMITY			
femoral neck	x	3 months (cons. tr. with 2 months in traction, hip–spica 1 month)	3 months (earliest)
femoral shaft		5–6 weeks in traction, 5–6 weeks in hip–spica	2–3 months
femoral condyle	x	as above	as above
patella		4 weeks (long cylinder POP)	full weight immediately
tibial condyle			
undislocated and stable		no POP	1/3 of weight after 3 weeks, full 6 weeks
dislocated < 5mm, stable		4 weeks (long cylinder POP)	1/3 of weight after 6 weeks
dislocated > 5mm, unstable	x	4 weeks (long cylinder POP)	1/3 of weight after 1.5–2 months
tibial shaft		2–3 months (long POP)	weight of the leg immediately, full weight after 2–3 months
fibula		2–3 months (POP)	weight of the leg immediately, full 1.5 months
malleolar, stable		1.5–2 months (below knee POP)	1/3 of weight after 4, full at 5–6 weeks
calcaneus			
undislocated or very comminuted		compressive bandage	weight of the leg immediately full weight after 4 weeks
dislocated or extending to the subtalar joint		1.5–3 months (below knee POP)	1/3 of weight after 1 month, full 1–2 months (1.5–3 months in very comminuted)
talus		1.5–3 months (below knee POP)	1/3 of weight after 1–2, full 2–3 months
naviculare			
undislocated		none	full weight immediately
dislocated		1.5–2 months (below knee POP)	1/3 of weight after 2–4, full 4–6 weeks
cuboideum, cuneiforme		none	full weight immediately
metatarsal, mild		none	full weight immediately
dislocated, painful		3–4 weeks (below knee POP)	full weight immediately (in POP)
toes (painful)		bandage to next toe 2 weeks	full weight immediately

Table 1b. The immobilisation and non-weight-bearing times of common adult fractures in lower extremity.[13]

Table 38.2. Indications for operative and conservative management of acute (less than 2 weeks old) fractures.[13]

Tubular bone
Conservative management
– small dislocation
– limited soft tissue injury
– limited or very severe comminution
Operative management
– acceptable position not achieved with conservative treatment
– large dislocation
– large, complicated fractures

Cancellous bone
Conservative management
– compression fractures
– juxta-articular fractures
Operative management
– intra-articular fractures (in lower extremities especially)
– avulsion fractures causing instability in the joint

Androctonus, the *Leiurus* of Africa and the Middle East, the Asian *Buthus*, and the South American *Tityus*. In the United States, it has been estimated that one out of a thousand stings is deadly. In these cases, the patient is often a young child.

Antitoxins are rarely available. Often the most cumbersome problem is the excruciating pain. It can be managed with local or regional anesthesia. Infections are rare, and usually symptomatic treatment of a couple of days is enough.

Practically all spiders are poisonous but very few can penetrate the human skin. In the United States, a few people die from spider bites every year. Spiders move at night which makes the incidents less common. The black widow (*Latrodectus mactans*) and its relatives can cause a generalised toxic reaction. The bite of the brown recluse spider (*Loxosceles*) of the temperate zone causes a deep and progressing tissue necrosis.

A centipede bite is treated with topical cold which is analgesic.

There is an abundance of stinging and biting sea animals. The sting of a stingray can cause general malaise, and loss of consciousness. The patient may sweat profusely, have shortness of breath, and even convulse. Shock is treated symptomatically. The sting wound is irrigated with hot water.

LIMB INJURIES

Loosing the function of a limb in a developing country is disastrous. The aim of the treatment is full functional recovery. Open comminuted fractures are common and often old.

Soft tissue injuries

The wound itself is managed as described above. If the revision requires additional incisions, they are performed along the long axis of the limb, except over the joints where they are done transversally along skin creases. Adequate incision of the fascia allows good exposure, and removal of all dead muscle.

Primary repair of nerves and tendons is seldom successful. In general, it can be carried out after 3 weeks, provided there is no infection. A vessel injury threatening the vitality of the limb requires arterial reconstruction within a few hours, if the limb is to be saved. If the transportation to another facility is needed, the patient needs an intravenous line for fluid resuscitation. The reconstruction is performed with an autogenous vein graft. Prosthetic material cannot be used in contaminated wounds.

In severe bleeding, proximal ligation of a major artery is lifesaving. If the collateral circulation is sufficient, the limb is not always lost. During transport to hospital abundant bleeding from leg wounds can be efficiently stopped by compressing the aorta at the umbilical level. Same technique can be applied in cases of uterine bleeding.

Fractures and dislocations

Because X-rays are not always available the diagnosis of a fracture is based on clinical examination. Local tenderness, crepitation, hematoma, and malalignment suggest a fracture. The diagnosis is more difficult if the fracture is in the proximity of a joint. *When X-rays are not available, a suspected fracture is treated as one.*

A closed fracture is managed with plaster of Paris or traction, if the alignment can be retained after reposition. The first cast is always split. A doctor working in developing countries should be familiar with the basic casts and traction techniques. The management principles and immobilisation times are presented in Tables 38.1 to 38.5.

Table 38.3. Average healing times of fractures.[13]

Fracture	Consolidation (weeks)	Ossification (weeks)
Cancellous bone	3	6
Upper extremity, oblique	3	6
transverse	6	12
Lower extremity	Twice compared with similar fracture of upper extremity	
Children's fractures	Half of the time compared with adult fractures	

Table 38.4. Fractures apt for early mobilisation.[13]

- Mild compression fracture of the thoracic and lumbar vertebrae
- Pubic ramus fracture without tenderness in the sacro-iliac joint
- Iliac bone fracture of the pelvis
- Fractures of the anterior iliac spine and tuber ossis ischii
- Fracture of the neck of the humerus
- Fracture of the olecranon without dislocation
- Fracture of the capitulum radii
- Oblique fracture of a metacarpal bone
- Fracture of the distal phalang of a finger
- Fracture of the shaft of the fibula
- Calcaneal fracture
- Fracture of the base of the fifth metatarsal bone
- Oblique fractures of the II–IV metatarsal bones
- Fractures of the toes

The position of the healing fracture is controlled by X-ray if possible. If not, rotation and angulation are corrected visually. This is especially important in the fractures of the hand, because the hand is so important in developing countries.

In fractures of the lower limbs, mobilisation too early should be discouraged and, in the mean time, non-weight bearing exercise encouraged. It is very important to teach the patient how to *gradually* put more weight on the leg. The disappearance of pain, and lack of crepitation on passive movement are signs of consolidation. A non-union is tender and unstable.

Operative treatment is required, if the fracture is associated with an arterial or nerve injury, or if acceptable position can not be retained. Internal fixation is only appropriate in well equipped hospitals.

A dislocated joint has to be repositioned quickly, usually under anesthesia. The limb is immobilised for approximately 3 weeks.

A penetrating joint injury is debrided, irrigated, and immobilised after removal of possible foreign bodies which is particularly important in the knee. The joint capsule has to be closed, and meticulous attention paid to the sterility. Inadequate treatment can lead to a stiff joint. Prophylactic antibiotics are necessary.

A painful hemarthron should be aspirated. If fat droplets are seen in the aspirate, an intra-articular fracture is likely and a prolonged immobilisation required.

Complications of limb injuries

Complications of fracture management include malalignment, chronic osteomyelitis and non-union (pseudoarthrosis).

Prevention is the best treatment. Late corrections require expertise and well-equipped facilities. Removal of dead bone (sequestrectomy) is essential for infection control. Gentamycin beads are useful, but cannot replace thorough revision. They remain active in tissue for weeks.

Pseudoarthrosis is treated with debridement and bone grafting. A painless non-union can be managed with an orthosis made of locally available materials.

Table 38.5. Fractures of growing bones where operative treatment is often required.[13]

- Epiphyseal fractures with threathening growth disturbance, non-union or incongruence of the joint
- Avulsion fractures of the apophyses
- Juxta-articular fractures with unsatisfactory reposition or retention
- Fractures of the femoral neck and trochanter region
- Fractures associated wih vascular or nerve damage
- Fractures associated with severe soft tissue injury
- Fractures in patients with multiple injuries
- Fractures in patients with a brain injury
- Antebrachium fractures in older children

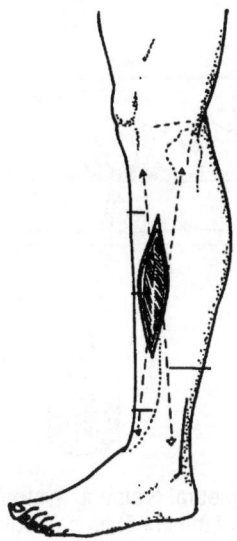

Figure 38.5. Fasciotomy of the leg requires two skin incisions. The lateral incision is placed half-way between the anterior margin of the tibia and the fibula. The medial incision should be 2 cm dorsally from the posteromedial margin of the tibia. The skin incisions can be shorter than the actual fasciotomies, since the fascial incision can be continued under the skin with the tip of the scissors.

Compartment syndrome. Swelling of an injured limb may cause a compartment syndrome leading to muscle necrosis. The vitality and function of the limb are endangered. To prevent this, the injured limb should be elevated. If compartment syndrome is suspected, early fasciotomy is indicated (Figure 38.5). It is always carried out after arterial reconstruction.

Amputations

A frank gangrene or uncontrollable infection warrant amputation. Complete loss of function may also be an indication for amputation.

One should be familiar with the basic amputation techniques (below and above knee). Of more distal amputations, the transmetatarsal is practical. The Syme amputation requires special footwear; barefoot one can walk on it for a year or two, but late infections may ruin the result.

Exarticulations are not practical in lower extremities in adults, because they make prosthesis fitting more difficult. In children exarticulation allows a bone to grow to its full length. Reconstructions can be carried out after cessation of growth. When performing an amputation, sufficient soft tissue coverage of the bone should be secured with flaps long enough. The wound is left open and closed after 4–7 days.

HEAD AND NECK INJURIES

The severity of the injury determines the prognosis of a patient with a brain injury. Even under the best conditions, the outlook after a major penetrating head injury or brain contusion is grim. The level of consciousness is the best indicator of the severity of the injury. A patient with an acute extradural hematoma may have a lucid interval before final loss of consciousness. It can be treated with a burr hole to evacuate the hematoma in order to decrease the intracranial pressure. Permanent hemostasis often requires a formal craniotomy to control the bleeding. A chronic subdural hematoma can often be managed with a burr hole and irrigation.

An open cranial fracture is treated with wound revision, hemostasis and closure. Liquorrhea or bleeding from the ears suggest a fracture of the base of the skull. Prophylactic antibiotics (penicillin or chloramphenicol) are needed until there is no more liquorrhea which usually takes a couple of weeks. If it does not stop, neurosurgery cannot be avoided.

Impression fractures deeper than the thickness of the bone should be elevated. It can be done under local anesthesia. A burr hole near but outside the impression and nibbling of the

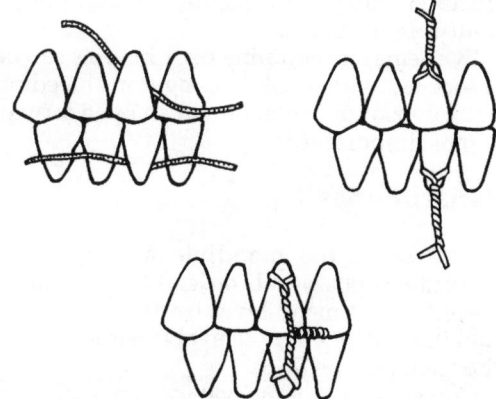

Figure 38.6. A simple way to immobilise jaws in mandibular fractures is to insert metal threads around opposing upper and lower teeth and tie the ends together. The connection should be easily dismantled in case the patient starts vomiting.

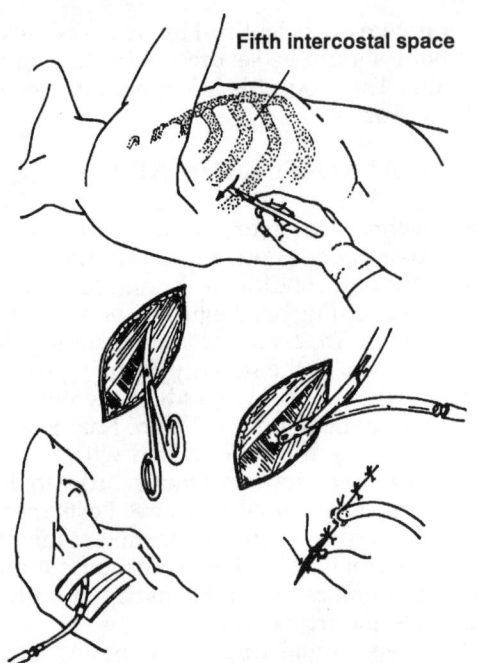

Fifth intercostal space

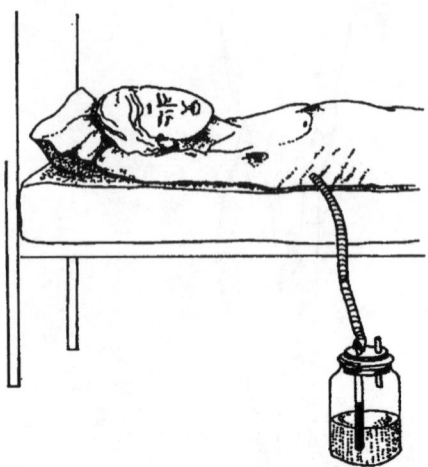

Figure 38.8. A simple pleural drainage system using gravitation. The tip of the chest tube should not be deeper than 4 cm for the system to work efficiently. The chest tube can be connected to a collection bottle for easy emptying (see also Figure 38.1).

Figure 38.7. Insertion of a chest tube. The fifth intercostal space in the anterior axillary line is a safe place. If more caudal spaces are used, the drain can go into the abdominal cavity due to the unexpectedly high position of the diaphragm during expirium. No trocar is needed. The free route can be checked with a finger before insertion. The drain should always be secured with two stitches to prevent it from sliding out.

hole is needed to place an elevator under the fracture. Other skull fractures without brain injury are harmless.

Even small penetrating neck injuries can be associated with a risk of dangerous bleeding or asphyxiation. To maintain an open airway is most important.

Facial injuries

Fractures of the mandible are common. Accurate reposition is crucial to maintain a correct bite. A mandibular fracture can be immobilised using simple eyelet wires around the teeth (Figure 38.6).

Corneal and conjunctival foreign bodies are removed under local anesthesia using for example the tip of a hypodermic needle. An antibiotic ointment is required for a couple of days.

Removal of an intraocular foreign body requires experience in ophthalmic surgery. First aid with systemic and local antibiotics, and

covering both eyes may save some eyesight. Other severe eye injuries are initially managed with the same principles.

The possibility of sympathetic ophthalmia should be kept in mind. It is rare and usually develops a few weeks after the incident. One can try to treat an angry red eye or a soft eyeball with systemic steroids, but if does not help the eye has to be removed. Otherwise the healthy eye may be at risk.

VERTEBRAL FRACTURES

The prognosis of a paraplegic or tetraplegic patient in a developing country is poor. Even if the families eagerly participate in the rehabilitation, complications such as urinary infections, pneumonia and bedsores leading to sepsis are difficult to avoid. The patient may live for some months or even years, but long-term survival is rare.

There is no cure for spinal dissection. At an early stage, however, it is difficult to determine the extent of the injury, and therefore active treatment should be started. One can expect improvement up to a year. Rehabilitation is particularly important at this stage to avoid recurrent infections. It is very important to advise the relatives how to prevent bedsores by turning the patient frequently.

Most vertebral fractures leave no permanent damage. If the fracture seems stable in an X-ray, bed rest until the pain is relieved is sufficient. An unstable cervical fracture requires skull traction for 6 weeks, and a collar for another 6 weeks. Operative treatment is needed for unstable fractures of the thoracic or lumbar vertebrae. If it is not available, extended bed rest and supportive corsets can be tried.

CHEST INJURIES

Up to 90 per cent of chest injuries can be managed with simple chest tube drainage. The most important thing is to prevent complications by removing air and blood from the chest cavity. One should not hesitate to insert a chest drain, but proper technique is important (Figures 38.7 and 38.8).

Rib fractures

In a simple uncomplicated rib fracture, pain relief is the treatment. Maintaining painless breathing is essential in the management of a multiple fracture, which can best be achieved by repeated intercostal blockades. If necessary, this can be carried out two or three times daily.

A flail chest can lead to respiratory insufficiency. An increased breathing frequency is an early sign. The pathological movement of the chest wall can be stabilised using towel clip traction (Figure 38.9). For first aid the patient can be turned on the injured side.

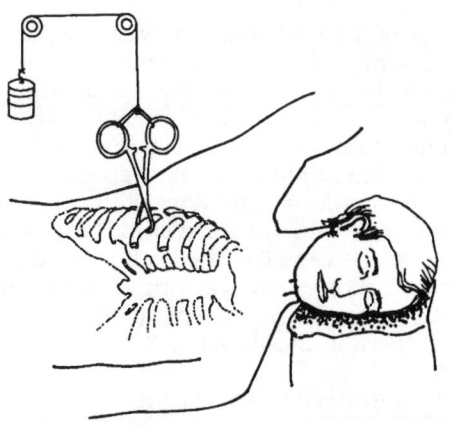

Figure 38.9. If a ventilator is not available for a patient with a flail chest, the unstable segment can be immobilised with towel clips connected to a one kilogram weight. Adequate analgesia is important; repeated intercostal blockades are useful.

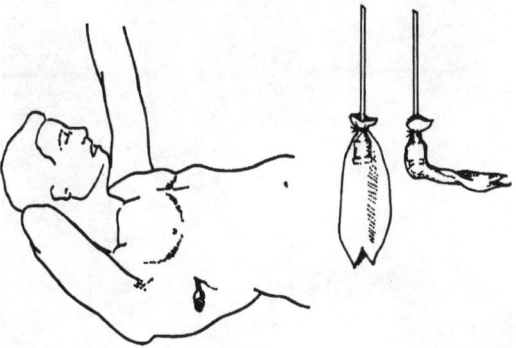

Figure 38.10. A tension pneumothorax is a life-threatening condition requiring immediate care. Inserting a large bore needle into the pleural cavity is good for first aid. The air can be prevented to enter the cavity using a simple valve constructed from a tip of a rubber glove or condom with a small hole at the tip.

Hemothorax or pneumothorax

If a pneumothorax or hemothorax is suspected on auscultation, a chest tube should be inserted. An X-ray is not necessary.

Air alone can be drained by any sterile tubing via the second or third intercostal space in the mid-clavicular line. A hemothorax requires a thick tube through the fifth or sixth space in the anterior or mid-axillary line. The patient is asked to inhale during the insertion of the drain. An untreated hemothorax may lead to an empyema.

Penetrating chest injuries also require drainage. The connection between the pleural space and the outside should be closed.

The drains are connected to a suction device. If not available, the drain is placed under a water-seal and the bed elevated. If nothing else is available, a Heimlich-type valve can be constructed with a finger of a glove or a condom to treat or prevent a tension pneumothorax (Figure 38.10).

Indications for thoracotomy are: hemothorax draining initially more than 1.5 litres, continuing bleeding of more than 100 millilitres per hour, air leakage continuing for more than 3 days, mediastinal injuries, diaphragmatic rupture, and injuries causing defects in the thoracic wall.

The prevention of post-traumatic respiratory insufficiency is important, because mechanical ventilators are seldom available. An improvised PEEP system (PEEP = positive

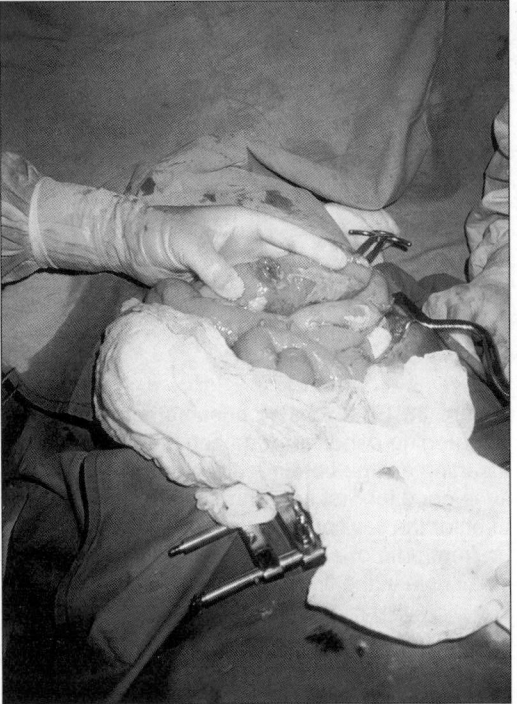

Figure 38.11. A small bowel perforation caused by an abdominal gunshot wound requiring operative repair.

end-expiratory pressure) is helpful, and can be achieved by asking the patient to exhale through a tube. The other end of the tube is placed into a bottle with water, and the bubbles show the PEEP effect.

ABDOMINAL INJURIES

Injuries to the abdominal organs usually require operative repair. Hemorrhage from ruptured parenchymatous organs or blood vessels can lead to hypovolemic shock and exsanguination. Perforations of the gastrointestinal tract (Figure 38.11) cause generalised peritonitis and septic shock.

Penetrating abdominal injuries caused by stab or gunshot wounds are best treated with early explorative laparotomy. Intra-abdominal hemorrhage following blunt abdominal trauma can be detected with a simple technique of diagnostic peritoneal lavage. A small infraumbilical midline incision is made under local anesthesia and the peritoneal cavity is reached under visual control. A sterile irrigation tube is inserted and 1 litre of warm normal saline is infused into the peritoneal cavity.

The fluid is let out with the same tube for analysis. If it contains visible blood, bile or food particles, laparotomy should be carried out.

Prophylactic antibiotics in patients with abdominal injuries should cover both aerobic and anaerobic bacteria. If cephalosporins or aminoglycosides, and metronidazole are not available, chloramphenicol is a good alternative.

UROGENITAL INJURIES

Hematuria is usually a sign of a renal injury following blunt abdominal trauma. A patient with pelvic fracture may be unable to pass urine suggesting a ruptured urinary bladder or urethra. A blood drop at the tip of urethra also points to a urethral injury. Injuries of the penis are often associated with lesions in the anterior urethra.

Excluding renal contusions, the management of urogenital injuries requires operative repair. The initial step is always to secure the flow of urine. If bladder catheterisation is unsuccessful, a suprapubic cystostomy should be inserted under local anesthesia. Before insertion the bladder should be full.

In partial urethral injuries or small extraperitoneal bladder ruptures, keeping the Foley catheter in place for 1–2 weeks is sufficient. In scrotal lacerations, the exposed testis should be covered under skin sometimes using the inner side of thighs.

ANESTHESIA

Lack of a qualified anesthetist is a common problem in developing countries, especially in rural areas. Because the administration of general inhalation anesthesia with controlled ventilation requires special knowledge and experience, a physician managing trauma patients should be confident with some of the alternative forms of anesthesia. The majority of operations can be carried out using one or a combination of the following anesthetic methods: local infiltration, spinal, axillary block, or ketamine anesthesia.

Preoperative preparation

Unless the patient requires immediate operation, a good preoperative preparation with the correction of disturbances in the fluid, electrolyte and acid–base balances is important. In trauma patients, hypovolemia is common. The severity of hypovolemia should be estimated and properly corrected with intravenous fluids. If no laboratory services are available, the estimate of fluid and electrolyte requirements is based on clinical judgement.

If, for example, the patient has not been able to eat and drink for several days or has been vomiting, fluid resuscitation with electrolyte solutions would seem appropriate. Urine output, blood pressure and heart rate are easily measured and give a rough estimate of the amount of fluid required. Respiration rate is a good measure for the adequacy of ventilation.

After the severity of the injuries have been estimated, and the decision to operate is made, there is no reason not to use adequate amounts of analgesics to relieve the pain caused by the injuries, which also reduces the preoperative stress reaction of the patient.

Except for limited local infiltration anesthesia, preoperative medication is useful. Easily available and commonly used premedication include promethazine and pethidine intramuscularly. When ketamine is used, atropine and diazepam should be given shortly before induction. Before spinal anesthesia, prehydration with 1000 ml lactated Ringer's solution (for adults) reduces the risk of severe hypotension. Patients undergoing Cesarean section should only be given promethazine for premedication, and when the umbilical cord has been cut, opiates should be administered, if required.

Local infiltration anesthesia

The majority of small surgical procedures involving the skin and subcutaneous tissue can be carried out using local infiltration anesthesia, or digital blocks in fingers or toes. The limiting factor is usually the maximum dose, which with lignocaine is 200 mg (7 mg/kg for children) without and 500 mg (9 mg/kg) with adrenaline. A mild solution of lignocaine should be preferred, and adrenaline must not be used in fingers, toes, nose, earlobes and penis. With accidental intravascular injection, a severe toxic reaction is possible, and should be treated with oxygen and intravenous fluids, and using atropine, anticonvulsive and inotropic drugs if required.

Spinal anesthesia

Almost any operation involving the lower extremities or the lower part of the trunk up to the umbilical or even subcostal level can be performed using spinal anesthesia. If laparotomy is carried out, the relaxation of the abdominal wall musculature is usually sufficient. The patient may feel discomfort when peritoneal surfaces are stretched, but with added analgesic (pethidine, ketamine) this is seldom a problem.

Short-acting, hyperbaric spinal anesthetics are most useful. With the patient lying on the operation table with one side up, a thin spinal needle in inserted usually through the L 2–3 interspace into the subarachnoid space. After the injection of the anesthetic (e.g. lignocaine 50 mg/ml or mepivacaine 1.2–2.0 ml), the patient is placed supine (unless only a one-sided anesthesia is required), and the head is tilted down to reach the required level of anesthesia which can be checked with the 'pinprick' method. A short-acting anesthetic will fixate within 5–20 minutes after which the change of the patient's position does not affect the level of anesthesia.

The blood pressure and heart rate should be closely monitored, and hypotension or bradycardia should be promptly corrected with intravenous fluid infusion and inotropic drugs, or atropine, respectively. The administration of oxygen is important.

Axillary block

The block of the axillary plexus is very useful in surgical procedures involving the upper extremity. It is time-consuming and can only be done on one side at the time. Lignocaine (1.5 per cent) with adrenaline can be used up to 20–40 ml. Using a small needle, the anesthetic is injected around the axillary artery in the armpit. Intravascular injection must be avoided, and sufficient time used to wait for the maximum effect to emerge.

Ketamine anesthesia

Ketamine is an efficient analgesic which causes dissociative anesthesia. Using proper doses, it does not suppress respiration or circulation. It can be used for surgical procedures anywhere in the body except the head, and it is especially suitable for trauma patients with hypovolemia requiring urgent operation. It should not be used for patients with brain or eye injuries (most of the simple surgical procedures such as cranial burr holes or elevation of impression fractures can be done under local infiltration anesthesia of the scalp).

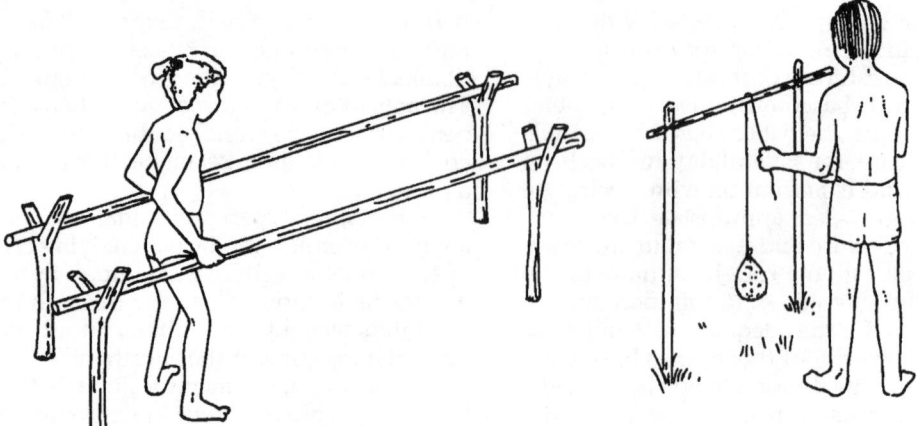

Figure 38.12. Physical rehabilitation requires inventiveness (adapted from Operation Handicap International, OHI).

After premedication with atropine (and diazepam for adults) the anesthesia is induced with 1–2 mg/kg of ketamine given intravenously as a bolus. The anesthesia can be maintained using doses half of the original, as required. With small children, intramuscular ketamine injections are more appropriate. At the end of the operation, an additional dose of diazepam (for adults) is useful in reducing the postoperative restlessness and hallucinations which are common after ketamine. Quiet environment and the presence of relatives usually limit the problems caused by postoperative hallucinations which may need additional sedative medication.

PRACTICAL ASPECTS OF REHABILITATION

In most industrialised countries, a patient unable to recover from injuries in reasonable time can retire with sufficient economic and social security. In addition to physical rehabilitation, occupational retraining and psychosocial rehabilitation are usually available. Special institutions for rehabilitation exist.

In developing countries, the social security system is often inadequate. Basic services and trained personnel cannot easily be found. Therefore, a very important part of the management of injuries is to train the patient to adapt to the new circumstances caused by his invalidity. But it is also necessary to *adapt the society* to accept and take care of persons with a variety of handicaps (Chapter 55). The support given by the patient's family is crucial although it does not replace adequate professional care and training of the patient in the early stage. This can be facilitated by longer hospitalisation times, which are not usually a problem.

Rehabilitation has to be a part of every medical specialty, and its requirements should be kept in mind while making the initial plan of treatment. Knowledge of the locally available physiotherapeutic services is useful. Where is the nearest prosthesis manufacturer? Could local facilities be used to construct prostheses or orthoses? What about crutches or wheel-chairs? Is there any place for the blind and deaf?

There are many groups who would benefit from rehabilitation: the blind, pulmonary chronics, patients with deforming joint diseases, children with polio, neurological patients etc. Limited resources should be used as efficiently as possible, even if this would mean that costly and demanding rehabilitation of a tetraplegic patient, for example, sometimes should not be started. The decisions are not easy, and require always consultation with the patient, the relatives, and local colleagues.

Basic requirements

In planning rehabilitation facilities, the space available should be large enough to accommodate several groups at the same time. With a larger population base, a works for manufacturing prostheses and orthoses is useful. Self-made and simple devices for physical rehabilitation can be constructed (Figure 38.12). A class-room for children is important, and enough room outside for playing and sports should not be forgotten.

When training local personnel, the language must be simple, clear and non-technical. The

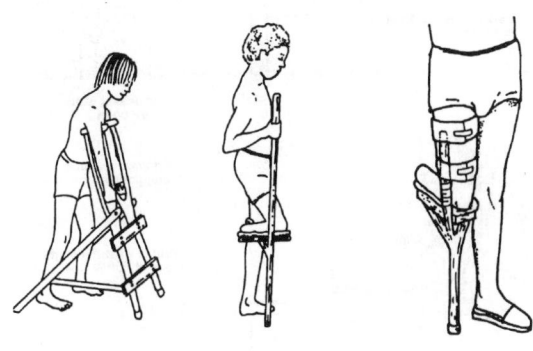

Figure 38.13. Different types of walking aids and prostheses. A stick with a knee support is a temporary help which, if used for a longer period, impairs the mobilisation of the knee joint (adapted from OHI).

emphasis should be on practical matters related to the actual needs of the patients. A mutually active attitude is essential. A more advanced student can teach the others.

Rehabilitation of special groups

Pulmonary diseases. Physical exercise improves the general condition of the patient. Breathing exercises increasing the general mobility of the chest are an essential part of physical treatment. The patient should learn the correct technique for breathing and mucus extraction. The tapping of mucus can be taught to the relatives whose motivation is important. Occupational therapy is helpful in restoring activity.

Hearing problems. In a child, the development of speech, verbal thought functions and personality is dependent on proper hearing. The first years are the most important. Teachers should be familiar with the special problems caused by impaired hearing. Early diagnosis and rehabilitation give the best results.

Problems of vision. The degree and type of visual impairment vary. Loss of central vision is the most common, but peripheral visual defects also occur. It may be caused by a treatable disease which should be looked for. In post-traumatic loss of eye, an eye-prosthesis is important in preventing recurrent infections of the empty orbit. It is not just a cosmetic problem.

In the case of a *blind child*, rehabilitation should be started early to achieve as great mobility as possible. There is no reason why visually impaired children should not go to school, even if the special equipment and skills are not available. Even limited ability to move and read may be essential for the development and survival of the child.

Prostheses

Manufacturing prostheses does not require heavy investment; local carpenter and blacksmith can help. Suitable materials can be found everywhere: wood, leather, metal bars and rubber which can be obtained from old car tyres, for example. This makes also maintenance and repair of the prostheses easy even in the most remote places.

Leather is better than plastic in constructing the prosthesis. It is more pleasant for the user, and allows inaccuracies in measurements and repairs. Even a less satisfactory stump can be prosthetised.

Below knee prosthesis. This is the most common prosthesis needed. There are several types available. The most simple is a walking support, but it should be used only temporarily. Mobilising the knee from the beginning is important in order to prevent later stiffness of the joint (contracture) which will impair the use of a prosthesis (Figure 38.13).

The main principle is to distribute the weight evenly on the stump. During the first weeks the stump will swell. It should be bandaged always when the prosthesis is not used. The patient must be taught to do the bandaging correctly so that the stump will form into a shape of a blunt cone.

Before starting adjustments of the prosthesis, the stump must be carefully inspected. The position of the muscles and the patella should be noted. Most of the weight should rest on the muscles, not the bones. The point of support should be below the patella. There ought to be enough space for the stump to sink downwards without damaging its tip.

The stump must be measured carefully. The circumference measurement starts at the level of the upper margin of the patella and continues downwards 2–3 centimetres apart (Figure 38.14). The width of the stump, the distance from the mid-patella to the heel, the longest circumference in the healthy extremity, and the circumference of the healthy ankle are also needed. In a difficult terrain, the prosthesis can be a little shorter than the healthy leg.

Above knee prosthesis. A child learns to walk even with a jointless above knee prosthesis.

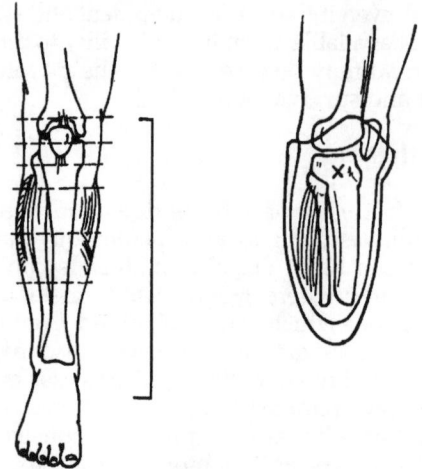

Figure 38.14. The measurements of the healthy leg are important when designing a prosthesis. The cross on the right side shows the place where the support for the prosthesis should be (adapted from OHI).

It can be made along the same principles as the below knee prosthesis described above. The posterior part rests on the buttock. In adults, a prosthesis with a knee joint is more feasible (Figure 38.15). Some kind of foot part is important when moving on uneven terrain, as well as for cosmetic reasons. A sharp stick would sink easily in a rice field (Figure 38.16).

Orthoses

Orthoses are useful in the management of acute injuries as well as chronic instability problems. They equalise the weight, and can improve the function. They can be used to support fractures and prevent malpositions. It allows the mobilisation of the limb during the healing of the fracture.

A hand may be useless after radial palsy, but become a functional gripping instrument with the aide of a simple orthosis. Slowly healing fractures can be supported with orthoses. Even a pseudoarthrosis may gain enough stability to allow the use of the limb.

Construction of orthoses requires imagination. Load to the thigh can be transferred upwards to the buttock and iliac tubercle. Below the knee, the support point could be in the patella or upper part of the tibia. An unstable knee can be stabilised with an orthosis, and a drop foot following peroneal palsy can be supported to prevent problems while walking on uneven terrain.

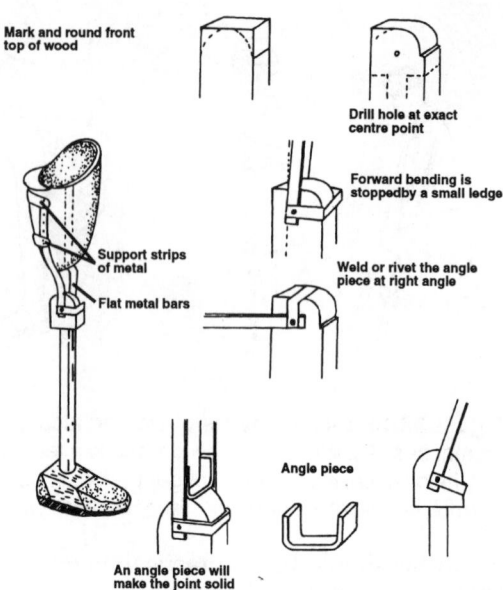

Figure 38.15. Reconstruction of an above knee prosthesis with a mobile knee joint is not difficult (adapted from OHI).

In developing countries, the use of hand is very important. The principles of active splints should be familiar. The construction of braces and vests for the paraplegic patients may be difficult.

Scarce resources do not prevent rehabilitation

All kinds of physical activities should be encouraged. The mobility will increase, balance and coordination improve, and even a lost function can be partially regained. Games and sports are useful. Everyone gains from mobility in every-day life.

Even if the resources for rehabilitation are limited in developing countries, a lot can be achieved with an active attitude. Creativity, ability to improvise, and willingness to learn can change the life of many patients otherwise doomed to misery. A state is not always needed to improve the quality of life for its citizens.

Additional reading

Accidents and injuries:

1. Adeloye A, ed. Davey's companion to surgery in Africa 1987. Edinburgh: Churchill Livingstone, 1987.

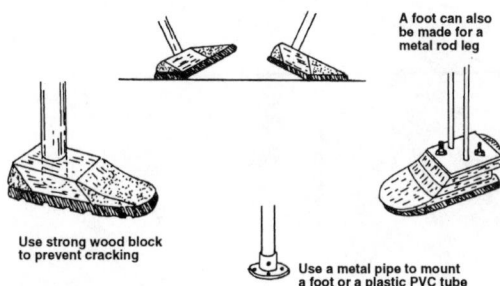

Use strong wood block to prevent cracking

A foot can also be made for a metal rod leg

Use a metal pipe to mount a foot or a plastic PVC tube

Figure 38.16. There are many ways to construct the foot part of the prosthesis (adapted from OHI).

2. Asensio JA, Weigelt JA, eds. Contemporary problems in trauma surgery. Surg Clin North Am 1991, 71: 209–437.
3. Burgess E. Amputation. Surg Clin North Am 1983; 63: 749–64.
4. Cannon S, Taylor A, Lynch A. Simple external fixation of open and complicated fractures. Injury 1985; 16: 363–70.
5. Coupland RM. Technical aspects of war wound excision. Br J Surg 1989; 76: 663–667.
6. Coupland RM, Pesonen PE. Craniocerebral war wounds: non-specialist management. Injury 1992; 23: 21–24.
7. Demetriades D, Rabinowitz B. Indications for operation in abdominal stab wounds. A prospective study of 651 patients. Ann Surg 1987; 205: 129–132.
8. Dudley H, ed. Hamilton Bailey's emergency surgery. 11th ed. Bristol: John Wright and Sons Ltd., 1986.
9. Efem SEE. Noninvasive technique of intraoperative autologous blood transfusion in abdominal vascular accidents. Vasc Surg 1987; 21: 1–4.
10. Leppäniemi AK. Where there is no anaesthetist... Br J Surg 1991; 78: 245–246.
11. Mubarak S, Hargens A. Acute compartment syndromes. Surg Clin North Am 1983; 63: 539–563.
12. Naraynsingh V, Ariyanayagam D, Pooran S. Primary repair of colon injuries in a developing country. Br J Surg 1991; 78: 319–320.
13. Rokkanen P, Slätis P, Alho A, Ryöppy S, Huittinen VM, eds. Traumatologia, 4th ed. Helsinki: Kandidaattikustannus Oy, 1987.

Rehabilitation:

14. Richardier J, Werner D. Rehabilitation medicine in refugee camps. In: Sandler R, Jones T, eds. Medical care of refugees. New York: Oxford University Press, 1987.
15. Dartnell C. Simple orthopedic aids. Appropriate designs for a developing country. London: Leonard Cheshire Foundation International, 1983.
16. Operation Handicap International. Simple above-knee prosthesis. Simple below-knee prosthesis. Lyon: OHI, 1983.
17. United Nations High Commissioner on Refugees. Hand book for social services. Geneva: UNHCR, 1984.
18. Werner D. Where there is no doctor. A village health care handbook. Palo Alto: Hesperian Foundation, 1977.
19. World Health Organization. The primary health worker. Geneva: WHO, 1980.
20. World Health Organization. Training disabled people in community. Geneva: WHO, 1983.

About the authors

Ari Leppäniemi is a specialist in general and gastroenterological surgery and is currently working as the Clinical Instructor in the Second Department of Surgery at the Helsinki University Central Hospital. He has worked in developing countries as a field surgeon for the International Committee of the Red Cross in Thailand, Kenya and Pakistan, and spent 1 year in Nigeria (1983–4) and 2 years in Tuvalu in the central Pacific (1988–9) as clinical surgeon working for a bilateral aid project and for United Nations Volunteers, respectively. The majority of his publications deal with abdominal injuries.

Hannu Savolainen is a specialist in general and thoracic surgery and works currently as a Staff Surgeon in the Third Department of Surgery at the Helsinki University Central Hospital. He has extensive experience from war surgery while working as a field surgeon and medical coordinator for the International Committee of the Red Cross in Lebanon, Thailand, Pakistan, Kenya, Somalia and the Persian Gulf. Most of his publications are about cardiovascular surgery and, especially, laser angioplasty.

James Lawrie is a general and paediatric surgeon currently working as Professor of Surgery at the College of Medicine in Blantyre, Malawi. He has been working in developing countries since 1969. He spent 15 years as professor of surgery in Zaria, Nigeria, and 5 years in Saudi Arabia. He has extensive experience in all fields of surgery in developing countries and has published many articles on the subject. A large number of surgical residents in Nigeria, Saudi Arabia and Malawi have enjoyed his fascinating lectures during the years.

Lankinen KS, Bergström S, Mäkelä PH and Peltomaa M, eds.
Health and disease in developing countries. London:The Macmillan Press Limited, 1994:381–389.

39 MANAGEMENT OF ACUTE MEDICAL AND SURGICAL PROBLEMS

Erkki Tukiainen, M.D., Ph.D.
Helsinki University Central Hospital
Topeliuksenkatu 5, FIN-00260 Helsinki,
Finland

INTRODUCTION

The gulf between western medicine and medicine practised in developing countries is widening. Doctors in developing countries are struggling with basic shortages and overwhelming numbers of patients. As living standards in the industrial countries have improved, many diseases, which once occurred everywhere, are now confined to the impoverished countries. Although they are often thought of being 'tropical', many of them are in fact a result of poverty.

In developing countries the basic health care is given in small clinics or health centres equipped with the most elementary facilities. The transportation of patients is often difficult and slow. The selection of drugs is restricted and the technical and diagnostic resources are limited. However, these restrictions should not prevent adequate clinical work. Basic clinical skills, good training, experience and sound judgement become of utmost importance.

For the expatriate physician, the consulting specialists are not available. New circumstances demand patience, adaptability, respect and new ideas. The details of the project and the local circumstances on the area must be studied in advance. One must be prepared to meet tasks and duties extending outside one's speciality.

The equipment and instruments must be simple, reliable and tested. Most wishes (favourite drugs or instruments etc.) of every newcomer cannot and should not be fulfilled. It is often better to adapt to proven methods and equipment. The repair and maintenance of the equipment must often be performed by the medical personnel. The assortment of drugs must be carefully planned, it must tolerate transportation and storage under changing temperatures.

In practical patient work the carefully obtained history is essential. *Despite difficulties caused by foreign culture and language, relevant history must be taken.* Underlying diseases, procedures performed previously and treatment received, also traditional therapy, must be recorded. As long as the interpreter and family members are present, the details of fever, vomiting, diarrhea, obstipation, last meals and fluid intake must be clarified. An epidemiological tip may be crucial: have there been similar symptoms in the family, in the village etc.

The patient must be examined discretely but thoroughly, taking into account the cultural restrictions. Inspection, palpation and auscultation are often the only available diagnostic methods – very often adequate enough. The diagnosis may become evident only after repeated examinations and a follow-up period.

The different alternatives of treatment, especially operative procedures, must be carefully considered. Certain conservatism may be advisable – the risks and benefits, own experience and skills, and local facilities must be weighed. The treatment must not be more strenuous or risky than the illness itself!

Malnutrition impairs both wound healing and the immune response. During severe malnutrition operative procedures should be performed on vital indications only. For example, an elective hernia operation may lead to severe complications. Supplementary feeding is important. Mostly in can be carried out perorally, using nasogastric tube if indicated.

Diarrhea, fever, sweating and vomiting may lead to dehydration. Anemia is often caused by both malnutrition and parasitic infections (malaria, intestinal parasites). Acquired coagulopathy may result from complicated labour or illegal abortion. Transfusion can be risky, and should be performed only after careful consideration.

SOFT TISSUE INFECTIONS

Subcutaneous infections

Subcutaneous infections may be acute, severe and have poor prognosis without adequate treatment. The infection may arise from injection, skin laceration, wound, bite, stoma, decubitus, drain etc. Poor general condition, malnutrition, diabetes, heart disease, vascular disease or alcoholism are important risk factors. The causative bacteria may be anaerobic or aerobic, Gram-positive cocci or Gram-negative rods.

Anaerobic cellulitis is a necrotising infection of the subcutaneous tissue, which does not affect the fascia or muscle. Gas production may be marked (crepitation). Especially the fecally contaminated wounds of the lower trunk or thighs are at risk of this infection. The exudate often has a bad smell. The treatment is radical excision, removal of infected and dead tissue, the wound is left open, closed secondarily and a broad-spectrum antibiotic is given.

Necrotising fascitis is a serious, spreading infection of the superficial fascia caused by hemolytic streptococci or staphylococci. It may be fulminant or lie dormant for a week or more before a rapid spread. Skin is affected only secondarily, after its vessels have become thrombosed resulting in necrosis. The treatment must be urgent with excision of the entire area of necrosis, a broad-spectrum antibiotic and appropriate systemic support.

Infections of the muscle

Pyomyositis is an acute bacterial infection of striated muscle. It is typical of impoverished areas, especially in children. The most common causative agent is *Staphylococcus aureus*, sometimes *Streptococcus* or *Escherichia coli*. The typical symptoms arise from one or several abscesses, which are formed in large muscles of the extremities or the retroperitoneal space. The symptoms start with fever, local muscle spasm, induration and at last abscess formation. In the beginning antibiotic therapy may be sufficient, but an obvious abscess must be canalised. If the diagnosis is uncertain, an aspiration by large needle may help.

Pyomyositis of the psoas muscle is a typical disease of children and teenagers in these countries. The hip is in flexion contracture and there is a swelling medial to the anterior superior iliac spine. Several important differential diagnoses should be considered. In septic arthritis of the hip or osteomyelitis of the trochanter region the muscles of the hip area are in spasm, all the movements are restricted and the compression of the trochanter is painful. A descending abscess from thoracolumbar osteomyelitis of the spine may cause similar symptoms: examination of the spine is important. Tuberculosis of the spine destroys one of the intervertebral discs and the adjacent vertebrae, leading to kyphosis and very often abscess formation. The pus tracks downwards behind the fascia of the psoas muscle to form a palpable abscess. The abscess must be drained extraperitoneally.

Gas gangrene or clostridial myonecrosis is a life-threatening anaerobic infection of the muscle caused by *Clostridium* species. Delayed or inadequate wound debridement, retained foreign bodies or dead tissue, and primary closure of a contaminated wound are typical risk factors. Gas gangrene often follows war wounds, high energy open fractures, and heavily contaminated farming injuries.

The local symptoms arise acutely: the wound area becomes swollen and very painful, the skin gets cool, dark and at last desquamates, and may become blue-red and crepitate due to gas in the tissue. The muscles are first red and friable, progressing to a purple and black mass. The exudate is dark, coloured by blood and necrotic muscle, bubbles and smells very offensive. Toxic general symptoms arise quickly with high fever, agitation, confusion and shock.

Delay in diagnosis and treatment is fatal. Very radical wound excision, often amputation and large doses of penicillin are indicated. Mortality is 25–40 per cent.

ACUTE ABDOMEN

Acute abdominal pain is a common problem in developing countries. The reasons behind acute abdominal conditions are partially different from those in industrialised countries. Gallstone disease, colon cancer, ulcerative colitis, Crohn´s disease, and diverticulosis of colon are rare, possibly due to dietary reasons. On the other hand parasitic and other infectious abdominal diseases are common. In certain areas peptic ulcer disease or special types of small bowel or colonic volvulus are common.

Every patient with acute abdominal pain lasting more than 6 hours should be sent to a doctor – especially so, if there is fever, vomiting or deterioration of the general condition.

Intestinal obstruction

Intestinal obstruction may be caused by hernial incarceration, adhesions and bands, acute appendicitis, volvulus, or by intestinal contents (ascariosis, undigested bolus etc.).

Incarceration of a hernia is common reason for intestinal obstruction. Although congenital umbilical hernia is common, it usually subsides spontaneously and is very seldom complicated by incarceration. Inguinal or femoral hernia may lead to incarceration. In the early phase, reposition should be tried. The patient is placed in Trendelenburg's position, analgesics and sedative are given and the hernia is gently compressed long enough. A lurp sound is promising. If the situation has lasted for hours, and the inguinal area is very painful, or patient presents with signs of severe obstruction or even peritonitis, reposition should not be tried. The abdomen should be decompressed by the use of nasogastric tube, fluid and electrolytic resuscitation started and operation performed.

An incarcerated hernia, which presents late, may perforate. Aside from the signs of obstruction, usually peritonitis and local soft tissue infection of the groin and scrotal area develop. If an intestinal fistula arises, it should be operated upon in an elective phase, after the general condition of the patient has been improved.

Obstruction due to *Ascaris*

Ascariosis is common in all developing countries, but dense infestations and obstructions are common in areas with a mild winter. A child, usually 2–14 years of age, may develop intestinal obstruction caused by the worms. The patient usually has had several attacks of moderate abdominal pain and vomiting before the obstruction of the small bowel. Abdominal distension is mild to moderate. There is often visible peristalsis and a mobile, irregular mass palpable in the centre of abdomen. There are no signs of peritonitis and the general condition is good. The diagnosis can be confirmed from a plain abdominal film, on which the intraluminal mass shows as 'soap bubble'. Acute intestinal obstruction may follow an attempt of deworming by drugs.

The obstruction usually resolves conservatively. Nothing should be given by mouth. A nasogastric tube is inserted, and intravenous fluids given. Deworming should be performed only 2–3 days after the obstruction is gone. Laparotomy is indicated if perforation, associated intussusception or volvulus is suspected, or if the obstruction fails to resolve. If possible the mass formed by the worms is broken up and the worms milked down to caecum or, from the proximal small bowel, up to stomach to relieve obstruction. If milking downwards or upwards is not possible a longitudinal antimesenteric 2 cm enterotomy is performed, worms are removed and the enterotomy closed transversely.

Volvulus

Volvulus of the small gut is relatively common in the developing world, especially in young men. A longer or smaller segment of small bowel rotates on its mesentery (primary volvulus), or on a band (secondary volvulus) from ileocecal area to the posterior abdominal wall.

The symptoms of acute obstruction (sudden colic, distension and vomiting) are soon followed by signs of strangulation (severe pain, marked distension, and shock). After fluid resuscitation, a laparotomy is performed. The gut is untwisted and decompressed. Often the ugly-looking, dark segment of gut partially or totally recovers during 10–15 minutes' observation. A devitalised segment is resected.

Volvulus of the midgut may occur in African females after childbirth. The symptoms may be acute or subacute. On plain film a distended loop of the caecum with haustration can be seen. If necrosis is evident, right hemicolectomy must be performed.

Volvulus of the sigmoid colon may present in two forms. The subacute sigmoid volvulus (thick-walled type) is more common. It occurs typically in adult males. It is connected with a

PROCEDURES, WHICH SHOULD BE MASTERED BY A PHYSICIAN WORKING IN DEVELOPING COUNTRIES.

Fluid and electrolyte resuscitation
- insertion of nasogastric tube
- insertion of intravenous cannula
- dissection and cannulation of vein
- intramedullary or intraperitoneal infusion
Cardiopulmonary resuscitation
- endotracheal intubation
- emegency tracheostomy
Catheterisation of the urinary bladder, suprapubic cystotomy
Intercostal drainage
Peritoneal drainage
Principles of closed fracture treatment (plaster casts)
Supracondylar femoral, upper tibial and os calcis tractions
Basic X-ray technique (most common films) positioning, exposure and development
Principles of wound care
- radical wound excision, suture, skin grafting
Drainage of abscesses
Curettage of uterus
Treatment of normal delivery, Cesarean section
Principles of local, intravenous, spinal and ketamine anesthesia

high-fibre diet. First symptom is difficulty in passing flatus. During the following days the abdomen distends hugely and gets tympanist. Abdomen is usually soft, and the dilatated sigmoid loop can be felt. The general condition remains good for days.

The acute sigmoid volvulus affects mainly women. Abdominal colics, urge to defecate, vomiting, anxiety, raised pulse and temperature, and abdominal distension are the characteristic signs. About 50 per cent of the patients develop gangrene, peritonitis and shock within 24 hours.

The subacute sigmoid volvulus can usually be treated by passing a soft rectal tube through a rigid sigmoidoscope in the knee-to-chest or right lateral position. If this fails or if the sigmoid is gangrenous, a laparotomy with Hartmann procedure is indicated.

Ileo-sigmoid knot (compound volvulus) is seen in certain countries. A loop of the small bowel is twisted together with the loop of pelvic colon. The onset is acute. Pain, vomiting, and distension, are due to early necrosis of small intestine segment and sigmoid colon. At operation the necrosis it evident, and necrotic loops are resected in block. Reduction and twisting of necrotic loops should not be done because it will release bacteria and toxins into the portal circulation and leads to further complications. Preoperative fluid resuscitation, gastric decompression, and antibiotic treatment are crucial like in any cases with intestinal obstruction, strangulation or peritonitis.

Peptic ulcer

Peptic ulcers are common in most parts of the world. Perforation of duodenal or gastric ulcer will cause a sudden agonising pain. The patient lies still, breathes shallowly, is pale, sweating, hypotensive with a fast pulse. In the beginning the temperature is normal, and the abdomen is not distended. After 3–6 hours the pain and rigidity lessen, patient feels better (silent interval). Thereafter the signs of diffuse peritonitis develop: abdominal distension, absent bowel sounds, fever, dehydration, sepsis and shock.

Treatment consists of nasogastric tube, fluid and electrolytic resuscitation, antibiotics and operation as soon as fluid depletion is corrected. The perforation is closed with one to three deep, resorbing stitches, and a fold of the omentum is sewed over the perforation site.

Vagotomy and pyloroplasty or gastroenterostomy at the primary operation is considered only if patient's general condition is good, he is operated early, he has severe ulcer disease *and* the surgeon is experienced.

The treatment of chronic peptic ulcer disease is problematic everywhere. Antacids, correct diet and abandoning alcohol and cigarettes often help. The H_2-receptor antagonists are expensive and not available. However, constant pain, pyloric stenosis, recurrent bleeding or perforations may indicate an elective operation (truncal vagotomy and gastroenterotomy or pyloroplasty)

Typhoid fever

Typhoid fever is an acute, systemic febrile infection caused by *Salmonella typhi*. The incubation period lasts 7–14 days. Common symptoms are fever, headache and constipation. A reactive bradycardia, 'rose spots' on the trunk and hepatosplenomegaly may be present. Patients with typhoid fever must be carefully followed, including the daily clinical examination of the abdomen, to detect early possible abdominal complications, such as intestinal perforation or bleeding. Typically the perforation occurs in the third or forth week, but sometimes also earlier and affects 2–6 per cent of patients.

Nasogastric tube, aggressive antibiotic and fluid resuscitation, and operation are usually indicated. At laparotomy usually one small hole (sometimes two to three holes) are detected in the terminal ileum. The ulcers are excised and closed in two layers. Occasionally, a small bowel resection is indicated. Meticulous peritoneal toilet and irrigation are at least as important as the suture of holes. After operation the recovery may be complicated by intra-abdominal abscess, wound dehiscence and prolonged illness.

Necrotising enteritis

Necrotising enteritis (pigbel) is caused by beta toxins of *Clostridium perfringens* which multiply in the gut, often after a large meal, classically a feast of pork. The disease has caused epidemics among children and young adults in South-East Asia, Papua New Guinea and Africa. Often the patients are malnourished. The extent of mucosal necrosis explains the different severity of the illness; colicky pain, vomiting, and foul flatus or rapidly progressing general symptoms and shock leading to death in few hours. Weeks or months after acute illness, strictures and adhesions may provoke obstruction or malabsorption.

Non-operative treatment with nasogastric tube, fluid resuscitation, and large doses of penicillin is started. Deterioration of the general condition and peritonitis indicate surgery. Necrotic segments of small intestine are resected with a wide margin.

Acute necrotising colitis is a similar entity affecting the colonic mucosa in young patients. In a few hours long segments of colon may become necrotic, causing severe symptoms. Often the colon has to be resected down to the pelvic colon: terminal ileostomy is performed, and later ileosigmoid anastomosis.

Abdominal tuberculosis

Abdominal tuberculosis can present in many ways. The three main types are: 1) ascites-type, common in Africa; 2) plastic type with obstruction in India and Nepal; and 3) glandular-type in African children. Abdominal tuberculosis may also present with symptoms caused by strictures, ulcers or fistulas of the intestine.

In the ascites-type the patient has 'a balloon abdomen and matchstick legs'. Straw-coloured fluid accumulates as a result of many miliary nodules, each about 1–2 mm in size, on the peritoneum. If the clinical diagnosis is uncertain; a 'minilaparotomy' with biopsies will confirm the diagnosis.

The plastic abdominal tuberculosis results from granuloma which cause adherences. The obstruction is commonly incomplete. The patient has weight loss, weakness, malaise, fatigue, anorexia, fever, and abdominal pain. If the diagnosis is uncertain, laparotomy and biopsy are indicated. The adhesions are difficult to separate at operation – too much should not be attempted at surgery, only the necessary. The granuloma usually resolves after antituberculous treatment. Ileocecal fibrosis or stenosis may follow.

In the glandular type, in addition to the general symptoms of tuberculosis, the mesenteric nodes are enlarged and palpable as irregular lumps in abdomen. Other lymph nodes may also be involved (axilla, neck, groin, mediastinum).

Acute proctocolitis

Ulcerative colitis and Crohn's disease are rare in developing countries. In some areas acute hemorrhagic proctocolitis may follow traditional enemas. Sigmoidoscopy reveals ulcerations and hemorrhage. If there are no signs of perforation, the treatment is conservative. – Amebic colitis causes recurrent diarrhea, abdominal cramping pain and mucus or even blood in the stool (Chapter 22).

Appendicitis

Appendicitis is the most frequent abdominal emergency in the industrialised world. It is unusual in the people of developing countries living in the traditional way, but is seen more frequently as the dietary habits are changing.

If the patient has signs of appendicitis, and is seen early, he should be operated upon. If the patient presents later, with signs of abscess and no signs of peritonitis, the treatment is non-operative with appendectomy, if performed, after 6 weeks. If the abscess is enlarging, it should be drained. If there are signs of local or generalised peritonitis, the patient should be resuscitated and operated.

OTHER ACUTE DISEASES

Abscess in the breast

Acute mastitis is common during the first weeks after child birth. *Staphylococcus aureus* enters through small abrasions in the nipple. Poor hygiene predisposes to breast infection. Fever, pain, heat, redness are the first symptoms, which may subside with antibiotic treatment. *Breast-feeding should be continued.*

Local hardening, induration and fluctuation indicate *abscess formation*. In unclear cases a puncture with large needle is diagnostic. It is a common mistake to incise abscesses too late. After incision, the wound is kept open with a rubber drain. Breast feeding must be stopped from the affected breast for a couple of days, but the breast must be emptied by milking to avoid congestion. Anti-inflammatory drugs and support of the breast relieve the pain.

Infection after abortion

Unsterile instrumentation of the uterus or septic abortion may cause a life-threatening infection. The causative organisms are often anaerobic bacteria. Gas may be visible in the uterine wall, it may crepitate, and it may be seen in native X-ray. The exudate flowing out from the cervix is dark and foul-smelling. The situation may progress until perforation, peritonitis or severe anaerobic infection of the abdominal wall develops. – Treatment consists of antibiotic therapy, emptying of the uterine cavity, and often laparotomy with hysterectomy.

Acute renal failure

The etiology of renal failure can be difficult to identify. Often it is associated with severe infection and dehydration. Low blood pressure, fluid and electrolytic depletion and infection must be treated. Oliguria may last from a few days to months. During this period acidosis and excessive amount of fluid and potassium should be avoided. During the diuresis period the need of fluid and electrolytes is great.

Pericarditis

Pericarditis may be caused by rheumatoid fever, viruses, bacteria or parasites. Pyogenic pericarditis usually affects children as a complication after severe systemic infection (pneumonia, osteomyelitis or measles with secondary staphylococcal infection). If the patient presents late, there may be tamponation demanding aspiration.

Rheumatoid fever

Rheumatoid fever is a complication of group A streptococcal infection, usually tonsillitis. The disease is common in developing countries among children and young adults. The preceding streptococcal infection can be asymptomatic. The classical signs are carditis, migratory polyarthritis, chorea, subcutaneous rheumatic nodules, erythema nodosum over the tibiae, and erythema marginatum on the trunk. Tachycardia and especially atrial fibrillation are indicators of cardiac involvement.

The mitral and aortic valves are the most frequent sites of endocarditis. Pericarditis may also develop. Bed rest, penicillin therapy and anti-inflammatory medication are indicated. Prophylactic penicillin (or erythromycin) is indicated, but seldom possible. Cardiac surgery is rarely available.

THERMOREGULATION AND HEAT-RELATED DISORDERS

The human body adjusts to high ambient temperatures by several mechanisms. Muscles adapt to work by generating less heat. Sweat volume capacity increases and the sweat sodium concentration decreases. Also potassium loss in the sweat becomes less. As a result of acclimatisation effective sweating starts already at a lower temperature. The whole adaptation process takes several weeks.

Heat-related disorders can be divided into four groups: heat syncope, heat cramps, heat exhaustion and heat stroke. The disorders are often overlapping. The three first are often prodromal to the most serious condition, heat stroke.

Heat syncope means fainting due to peripheral vasodilatation, when the central circulation is disturbed. The patient recovers rapidly in supine position in a cool place. The condition is not severe, but the individual may be susceptible to more serious heat-related problems.

Heat cramps are painful contractions of large muscles of the trunk or the extremities. They

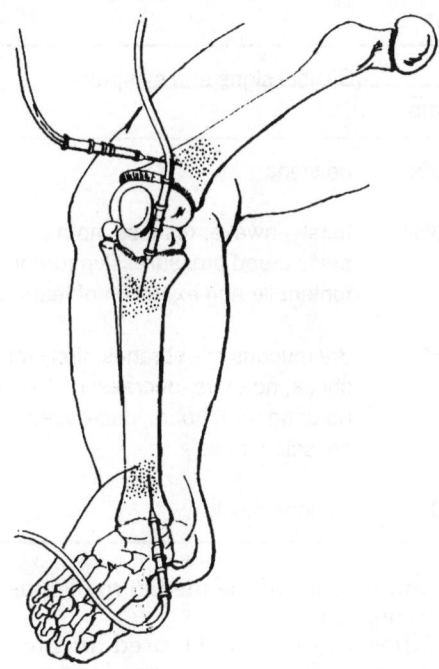

Figure 39.1. Appropriate needle sites for intra-osseus infusion.[2]

appear after hours of muscular activity and are due to sodium depletion. Often the patient has had adequate amount of fluid during the activity, but it did not contain enough salt. If the heat cramps affect abdominal muscles, the situation may mimic acute abdomen. The treatment consists of cool, salted juice (0.2–0.5 per cent of salt). Intravenous infusion is not necessary.

Heat exhaustion develops after sustained effort in a hot and humid environment. Large amounts of fluid and electrolytes are lost. Headache, painful thigh and calf muscle contractions are characteristic. Vomiting makes the dehydration worse, the patient becomes restless, agitated, and apathetic. The therapy is rest and fluid and electrolytic replacement, mostly by the oral route.

Heat stroke implies a severe disturbance of the central thermoregulatory system with core temperature up to 41–42ºC. The extreme hyperpyrexia will damage many organs and tissues. The patient has been in too hot an environment for hours or days. He may have had prodromal symptoms (heat syncope, cramps or exhaustion), but sometimes confusion and coma arise quickly. The main symptoms are high fever and confusion progressing

to coma. In the beginning the patient has tachycardia and tachypnea.

The treatment of hyperthermia and any possible underlying cause must start urgently. The patient is sponged with cool water – wet sheets and moving air (exposure during transportation, a fan in the ward) enhance the cooling effect. Open airways and breathing must be secured, and fluid depletion is corrected with intravenous replacement. The rectal temperature is monitored every fifth minute, and vigorous cooling is stopped when 38.5ºC is reached.

In prevention of heat-related diseases adequate fluid and salt intake is crucial. At temperatures above 30ºC an adult must drink 5 litres and take 15–20 grams salt daily. Also regular meals and rest are important. Excessive alcohol intake and sedative drugs are predisposing factors. Light, loose cotton clothes are most practical. Local working hours (breaks, siesta) should be followed and heavy effort avoided when the temperature is more than 30ºC and humidity more than 50 per cent. The vulnerable groups (the elderly people, or patients with poor general condition) must be specially protected. The prodromal symptoms must be taken seriously.

Hypothermia

In hypothermia the core temperature is below 35ºC. Even in tropical or subtropical areas the diurnal temperature variations may be considerable. Severe disease or injury, prolonged exposure, and hemorrhage may form lethal combination with hypothermia.

The symptoms are cold skin (also on the trunk), slow pulse, low blood pressure, shivering, slow muscular reflexes, a hoarse voice and confusion. Deeply hypothermic patient may look clinically dead: missing respiration, non-reacting pupils, missing heart sounds in auscultation, cold skin, and rigid muscles. In these occasions the diagnosis of death is reliable only after hypothermia has been treated and the treatment has proved ineffective.

The treatment starts by stopping further heat loss. The patient should be handled gently and protected from rain and wind to avoid cardiac arrythmia. Warm blankets, prewarmed infusion fluids, oxygen, and correction of acidosis and volume depletion are the means of treatment. Passive slow rewarming (less than 1ºC/h) is the safest method, especially if hypothermia has developed gradually.

Table 39.1. Clinical assessment of severity of dehydration.

Severity of dehydration		Weight loss		Clinical signs and symptoms
		< 3 years	> 3 years	
Mild	<50 ml/kg	5%	< 3%	no signs
Moderate	50 ml/kg	5%	3%	thirsty, awake, restless, normal pulse blood pressure, skin turgor, fontanelle and excretion of tears
Severe	60-90 ml/kg	10%	6%	dry mucous membranes, first signs of shock, no tears, decreased skin turgor, no urine for 8 hours, decreased consciousness
Critical	100 ml/kg	> 15%	< 9%	evident shock

FLUID AND ELECTROLYTIC THERAPY

Oral rehydration therapy (ORT) is often the safest and most efficient method to correct fluid and electrolytic losses. Often the result is better by giving the fluid repeatedly in small doses with a spoon. Drinking large amounts may provoke nausea and vomiting. If oral fluid intake is not possible, the second alternative is nasogastric tube. The correct position of the tube must be checked to avoid aspiration. Air is passed with a large syringe, and the epigastrium is auscultated with a stethoscope. A sound will indicate the right position.

Severe vomiting, unconscious patients, intestinal obstruction or paralysis, or shock make the use of the enteral route impossible, and parenteral routes are indicated. Insertion of an intravenous cannula is often most difficult in urgent situations. In a small child with severe dehydration and hypothermia it is often very difficult to find a suitable peripheral vein. Warming and gentle massage of the lower arm, cubitum or arm may bring the constricted veins visible. In a newborn a scalp vein may be visible. Also the veins of the lower extremities are available in a critical situation. Sometimes the jugular vein is visible on the neck. A good assistant and light are needed to cannulate small veins.

If a peripheral vein is not visible, a vein can be cannulated after skin incision and dissection. In small children the saphenous vein is cannulated below the inguinal ligament, and in adults and older children a vein is to be found in front of the medial malleolus or in the cubitum.

Intraosseus line can be used during emergency resuscitation if peripheral venous access is not immediately obtained. Fluid absorbtion from the intramedullar space into the blood circulation is quick even in shock.[1,2] The method is applicable in children under the age of 6 years in emergency situation. The best sites for intraosseus infusion are the anterior aspect of distal metaphysis of the femur and the anteromedial aspect of proximal or distal metaphysis of the tibia (Figure 39.1). The technique involves insertion of strong needle (13 to 20-gauge intravenous, bone-marrow or spinal needle) perpendicular to the bone directed away from the adjoining epiphysis.

To avoid extravasation of the fluid repeated penetrations of the cortex must be avoided, only the first cortex is penetrated (the position of the needle is confirmed with aspiration of the marrow contents). The displacement of the needle must be prevented with a splint. The limb must be carefully observed for any sings of compartment syndrome (presence of distal pulses, diameter of the limb, soft tissue turgor, skin colour). To avoid local infection (abscess, osteomyelitis) only healthy skin areas should be used as insertion sites. Intraosseus needle should be removed as early as possible and conventional intravenous cannula inserted.

A further possibility in emergency situations is the *intraperitoneal route*: an intravenous cannula is inserted besides the umbilicus into the peritoneal cavity.

Fluid resuscitation in dehydration

Severe dehydration is a common problem in tropical areas. Diarrhea, many difficult infectious diseases, heat-related disorders and burns easily cause critical dehydration. The severity of dehydration must be judged clinically (Table 39.1).

Dehydration shock in small children must be treated especially quickly. Plasma would be optimal, 10–20 ml/kg, but it may not be available. Ringer-lactate or 0.9 per cent saline is given at 20 ml/kg intravenously, or via another parenteral route. After this rapid initial expansion of plasma volume the extracellular volume is filled with Ringer or saline. The necessary amount depends on the weight of the patient, severity of dehydration and response to replacement in signs of shock, state of consciousness, peripheral temperature, state of jugular veins, auscultation of the lungs and urine output. When urine output starts, potassium is added to the fluid. Peroral resuscitation is started as soon as possible.

CONCLUSION

Acute medical and surgical problems in poverty-stricken countries demand appropriately organised peripheral health services. A few simple principles, based on common sense and clinical skills, may guide the devoted health staff in the provision of essential help and care so as to avoid death and disease in such emergency situations.

References

1. Hodge D. Intraosseus infusion: a review. Pediat Emerg Care 1985;1:215-8.
2. Burke T, Kehl K. Intraosseus infusion in infants. Case report of a complication. J Bone Joint Surg 1993;75:428-9.

Additional reading

1. King M, Bewes P, Cairns J, Thornton J. Primary surgery. Volume One. Non-trauma. Oxford: Oxford University Press, 1990
2. Dudley HAF, Hamilton Bailey's Emergency Surgery. Bristol: Wright, 1986.
3. Wiener SL, Barret J. Trauma Management for Civilian and Military Physicians. Philadelphia: W.B. Saunders Company, 1986.
4. Sandler R, Jones T. Medical Care of Refugees. Oxford: Oxford University Press, 1987.
5. Cook GC. Communicable and tropical diseases. London: Mainstream Medicine, 1988.

About the author

Erkki Tukiainen is a general surgeon with subspecialties in plastic surgery, orthopedics and traumatology. He is working as a reconstructive surgeon on the Department of Plastic Surgery at the Helsinki University Central Hospital, Finland. On three occasions he has been working in ICRC field hospitals delegated by the Finnish Red Cross, and once in Sri Lanka delegated by the Ministry of Foreign Affairs, Finland. His current interests is reconstructive surgery after tissue loss caused by open fractures, burns and tumours.

IV HEALTH SERVICES TO MEET THE CHALLENGES

Lankinen KS, Bergström S, Mäkelä PH and Peltomaa M, eds.
Health and disease in developing countries. London:The Macmillan Press Limited, 1994:393–401.

40 LEVELS OF HEALTH CARE

Marjukka Mäkelä, M.D., Ph.D.
STAKES, National Research and
Development Centre for Welfare and Health
P.O. Box 220, FIN-00531 Helsinki,
Finland

Debabar Banerji, M.D.
Jawaharlal Nehru University, Centre of
Social Medicine and Community Health
New Delhi 10067,
India

INTRODUCTION

In most countries, the health care organisation is divided into primary care and hospital care, and several functional levels may actually exist. Health care budgets are often drawn separately for hospitals and primary care, and training schemes commonly aim at either primary or secondary care.

The education of a health care professional provides both formal and implicit knowledge about health care organisations in the country of training. In working life, this knowledge becomes more concrete and detailed. The professional also develops contacts outside the health care system, with schools, social sector and others. Even within a country, the nature and amount of these contacts varies from place to place. A new job brings along acquaintance with new and often different practices, even if the basic structure is similar.

It is thus understandable that a health care professional carries along the structural principles of health care from his or her own country, and tries to apply observations of a new culture and environment to the familiar frame. Many basic assumptions do not hold, however, when transferred to a developing country. An outline of the principles and utilisation of health care levels is useful.

Relating one's own work to the structure of health care in the country may enhance the practical planning and coordination of the work, and provide a basis for the evaluation of the results. The model of health care funding can also influence the structures in a major way.

WHY LEVELS?

Resources for health care are always limited. Therefore one must aim at *efficiency*, i.e. producing as much health as possible with the available resources. *Accessibility* is another important principle: people should be able to reach health care services from wherever they live. It is not economical to bring specialised, high-technology care to every village, or to transport each case of common diseases to the central hospital. Stepped care is an efficient solution of distribution problems.

In this article, *stepped care* means the planned and conscious organisation of health care into different referral levels. This theoretical model aims at an efficient division of labour between the actual levels of care, based on the incidence and severity of diseases and the available technology.

The levels of health care are defined with the help of three factors: epidemiology, technology and personnel. The fundamental one is *local epidemiology*, or the type and frequency of health problems. Starting with this data, one can determine the necessary *material and technological level*. The third factor, the *level of skills and knowledge of the personnel*, is determined by epidemiology and technology.

PHC is responsible for prevention and health promotion; recognition, treatment, and rehabilitation of common diseases and injuries; and first aid in cases where delayed treatment would increase the risk for permanent handicap or death. The more uncommon a health problem is, the more likely the patient benefits from a hospital referral. On the other hand, if the treatment of a frequent problem requires high technology or the cooperation of several specialties, again, hospital is the right place for it.

For historical reasons, health services may have been organised along other lines. Separate, vertical programmes and institutions have been created for specific diseases, such as tuberculosis or psychiatric illness. Systems may cover population groups according to age, religion, occupation, or type of funding. It is common for an institution to limit the provision of services to a certain geographical area. – Hospitals may provide an abundance of high-technology, tertiary-level services, while there is a lack of secondary-care hospitals; or a hospital may produce both primary care and specialised services.

LEVELS OF CARE IN AN INDUSTRIAL COUNTRY: FINLAND

Health care in Finland is divided in three levels: primary health *and* medical care in health centres, secondary care in local or regional hospitals, and tertiary care in teaching hospitals, where top technology and rare subspecialties are located. The personnel structure in Finnish health care is suitable for this type of organisation. There are six trained nurses to one physician, and a well-trained supply of allied health personnel. The level of technology is rather high, and the primary care units are large and well funded.

The technology of health care in Finland depends on the type of problems treated on each level. Primary care treats most diabetics on dietary and/or oral treatment. When diabetes causes eye problems, the patient is remitted to secondary care. New or experimental treatments (insulin pumps or pancreatic transplants) are reserved for university hospitals.

The collaboration in health care is smooth. Information passes fairly reliably between the levels, and division of labour can be and has been changed when needed. Although health centres do not have a gatekeeping role, people can usually choose the right level of care for

their need, and public funding provides equal opportunities for care. The parallel organisation of private practitioners is partly publicly funded as well, and provides an alternative route of services for a large number of people especially in the cities.

Preconditions for a well-functioning health care in Finland are good: a high standard of living and literacy rate; reliable transport of people, goods, and information; and a comprehensive network of social services. Like most industrial countries, Finland discusses the priorities in health care, as techniques for cure advance faster than the funding available. Stepped care is seen as a major tool to keep the health care budget in check.

HEALTH CARE SYSTEMS IN DEVELOPING COUNTRIES

Most health care organisations have been built from several independent structures without a methodical scheme for stepped care. Many developing countries have inherited parts of their health care structure – most often hospitals – from the industrial mother country, where the structure served a completely different society. Often health services were originally provided for the needs of educated city-dwellers. The building blocks of epidemiology, technology, and health care personnel were not always used in the planning.

The common health problems in developing countries differ greatly from those of an industrial society. A hospital-based professional sees and treats only the tip of the iceberg: the patients who seek for help and for whom the resources suffice. Malnutrition, lack of clean water, and illiteracy create basic health problems that can be treated effectively only by prevention. Medical knowledge applied through team work to populations as a whole, not just patients, and aiming at prevention may help more people than the most devoted cure around the clock. Sound epidemiological approach with knowledge of the local culture brings about and supports structural and functional health-promoting changes.

Even if health care technology theoretically fits the level of care it is used in, defects in the basic structures of the society can make the application of technology impossible. Complex technology is most vulnerable, but lack of electricity or clean water can hinder even the use of simple tools. It is difficult to assist a delivery in the dark, or to give oral rehydration without safe water. Equipment wears and breaks down, needs spare parts and maintenance skills. Thus, a logical base for stepped care may be the availability of electricity or a technician.[1,2]

In developing countries, the least-trained health care workers are closest to the population. This solution provides accessibility in an economical manner. The supervision of the village health workers is often scant. In well-functioning stepped care, workers with wider training act as consultants for less trained personnel.

Networks of primary care are patchy in many countries, there is lack of well-trained personnel, and those with most training often remain in the cities, where they have trained.[3]

In Zimbabwe, for example, only a quarter of the population of eight million lives in the cities, whereas 80 per cent of the 1100 physicians in the country work in the cities. The 90-million population of Nigeria has only 10 000 physicians and 30 000 nurses; the yearly population increase rate is 2.5 per cent, and medical schools cannot provide a corresponding relative growth of the personnel. Most medical schools have a traditional hospital-based curriculum with only a short visit to rural health care. Although the professionals are required to work in the countryside for a year after graduation, most want to return to the cities.[4,5]

LEVELS OF CARE IN A DEVELOPING COUNTRY: INDIA

Health care in India is built on the British colonial tradition, with the conscious objective of stepped care from the village level all the way to tertiary and super-specialised care. The construction of the system started in the 1950s, and the principles are exemplary, although in practice the system is far from complete.[5,6]

India is a federal democracy that during the 1970s belonged to the group of the least developed countries. Three quarters of the 850 million inhabitants live in the rural areas. The GNP per capita is 350 dollars. One third of the babies born in early 1980s were under-weight, infant mortality rate was 120 per 1000, and life expectancy was 52 years. In 1990, the infant mortality rate was down at 92 per thousand, and life expectancy had risen to 59 years. Half of the men and a third of the women were literate. The country has

Picture 40.1. Multipurpose health worker, Poona area. Photo: Marjukka Mäkelä

a good network of roads and railroads, and a well-functioning information network. Overall 72 per cent of the population have access to safe water. India produces enough food for the population, but there are still malnutrition problems.[5]

The entire health care system is funded by the state. Prosperous areas can increase the number of workers or functions with tax money; this is rather exceptional.

The strategy: vertical programmes

The health policy is formulated in the federal 5-year plans. These are based on twelve national programmes, and for the implementation of these, the 22 states and nine Union territories receive a federal grant. The resources are bound to each programme, and the state may not reallocate the money from one programme to another. The share of health care has been 2–3 per cent of the gross national product. In addition, the country receives foreign aid, which covers about one-tenth of the federal budget for new programmes.

The most important of the vertical programmes is Family Welfare Programme (including maternal and child health care and family planning) which receives one third of all health budget. Another third is allocated to the Programme for Water and Sanitation. Other programmes include the extended programme of immunisation, programmes of health care training and services, and national programmes against tuberculosis, malaria, and goitre.

The states are divided into 10–30 districts, with an average population of 1.5 million. Districts are further divided to tashils or taluks and these again to Community development blocks with some 100 000 people in each. The smallest unit is the village, of which there are nearly 600 000 in India. Each village has 1000 to 10 000 inhabitants. Larger villages are often divided to hamlets, which lack administrative independence. The population density in the country is variable: the seven smallest states together account for only 2 per cent of the population. The economy of the states also differ greatly from one another.

Seven levels of health care

In India, health care is divided into primary and secondary care, which have four and three levels respectively (Figure 40.1.). The quality of care is assumed to be higher on each successive step, and on the 'primary care side' this assumption holds true. The stepped care of the hospitals is more haphazard in nature. Besides, the patient goes or is sent to the *closest* institution that can offer help to his or her health problem. If the university hospital is closer than a health centre, the pregnant mother or the remitting village health worker may choose the hospital for delivery, even if the primary health centre would have the skills and equipment for the case.

Patients are never turned down even when they present their problems at the 'wrong' level. The patient has to pay for treatment only in the hospitals, and the fees are ranked according to wealth. Some 80 per cent of the population are so poor they do not need to pay the hospital either. The Central Government Health Scheme provides health insurance to six million government employees, and some 29 million industrial workers with their families are covered by another health insurance policy. For others, no chance exists for even private insurance.

Primary health care

Village level. The smallest health care unit in India is the village. Health care areas are based on the population, not the number of hamlets or villages. According to the general plan, there should be a subcentre per 5000 inhabitants, but in practice these still cover 10 000 people. Each subcentre has a building where the medical equipment, drugs, and the health statistics of the village are kept. The subcentre features a delivery room where most births take place with trained assistance. Only 15 to 20 per cent of deliveries are done in the hospitals.

Each subcentre is staffed by two Multipurpose Health Workers (MHWs), one man and one woman. After 10 years of public school, they must complete a year of theoretical studies and 6 months of applied training in the villages to receive their degree.

The MHW is a federal employee and is responsible for 32 specific functions. They implement the vertical programmes in the villages (vaccinations, maternal health care, malaria etc.), treat minor injuries, and maintain the statistics. The MHWs can use some 20 essential drugs for the treatment of the common diseases. In smaller villages without a subcentre house, the MHWs can keep their equipment in the village office building.

MHWs have been trained since the 1960s. Before this, there were some self-educated midwives (*dais*) and traditional health workers in the villages. These two groups have received additional training, and are called Village Health Guides (VHGs). They continue to take care of normal deliveries, and they also can sell condoms with a small profit they can keep, motivating them to promote family planning. The VHGs can assist the MHWs in many ways.[7,8]

Primary Health Centre. The next level of care is the Primary Health Centre, which in the optimal model would provide services for five or six subcentres, or some 30 000 inhabitants. At present, the population bases are between 70 000 and 100 000 per center. The health centre provides integrated health services: in addition to prevention and cure, it is the office for environmental health and intersectoral collaboration. Patients from the subcentres are sent here for treatment, when the disease is too complicated to be handled in the village. The MHW might for example decide during pregnancy check-ups, that a more experienced

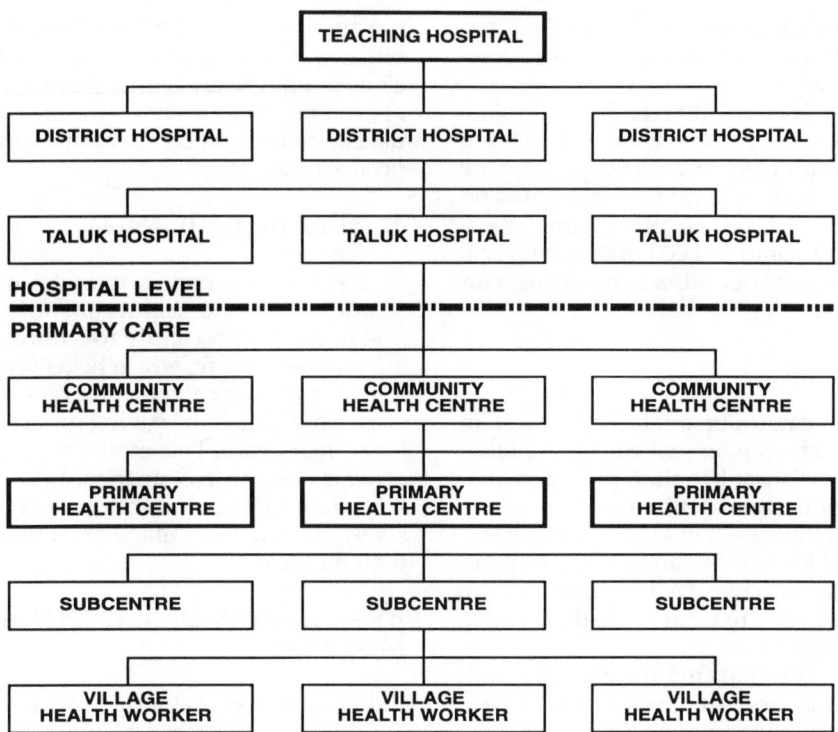

Figure 40.1. Organisation of health care levels in India

health worker should take care of the delivery, and recommend that the mother consults the primary health centre when the labour begins.

The health centre also functions as the headquarters for the Health Visitors. They have usually completed the MHW training, worked in the villages 3–4 years, and been accepted for a 1-year postgraduate training. They have personal experience of the MHW work they coordinate, and their additional training is on administration and management.

An optional route to the work of Health Visitors for a high school graduate (i.e. with 12 years of school) is to get a degree by 2.5 years of training in one of the few private institutions offering the study programme. One year of the degree studies takes place in the villages.

One of the Health Visitors is responsible for health care in the villages. He or she trains and supervises MHWs in four to six villages, visiting them regularly on a Fixed Tour Programme. The other Health Visitors run the vertical programmes with the help of the Village Health Guides, MHWs and the various technicians of the health sector.

The Public Health Nurse (PHN) supervises 10–20 Health Visitors in one area. It is possible to specialise as a PHN through the long route: an experienced Health Visitor studies epidemiology, administration and management for a year. The other option is to study 4 years in a teaching hospital after 12 years of public school and high school. In primary care, the Health Visitors and PHNs with long on-the-job training are considered far more useful than the graduates from academic programmes.

Each health centre will usually employ four physicians, one with the traditional (*Ayurveda*) training and the others with western-style medical training. The health centre building usually includes a laboratory and a six–bed ward. Every health centre has a refrigerator for vaccines, which then are transported to the subcentres in cold bags for the daily need.

The diagnostic possibilities include recognition of at least tuberculosis, urinary tract infection, leprosy, and malaria: the MHW can take the samples in the village, and they are transported to the health centre with the vaccine courier. Intravenous hydration can be given, if oral rehydration is not sufficient.

Health centres also take care of snake bites, smaller fractures, and some of the more complicated deliveries.

Community Health Centre. Since the late 1980s, a new level has been established between health centres and hospitals. One Community Health Centre will supervise and service three Primary Health Centres, i.e. a population of some 100 000. Each CHC will have 25 beds and specialists in medicine, surgery, midwifery, and pediatrics.

Hospital level

If the patient cannot be treated in the health centre, he or she can be sent to either a taluk hospital or a district hospital, provided that the traffic connections are suitable.

Although taluks are subordinate to districts, the degree of knowledge and technology can be equal in the two types of hospitals. A taluk hospital may feature even specialties that a district hospital lacks.

The district hospitals run the district health administration, and all national health programmes are coordinated there. District hospitals stock up vaccines for 2 months' use for their district, as required by the EPI programme.

The teaching hospitals educate physicians, hospital nurses, pharmacists, health care administrators, and specialists in environmental health. A teaching hospital can either be connected with a medical school or receive the teaching rights by application – a district hospital or even a taluk hospital may consequently be also a teaching hospital.

A teaching hospital must include departments of certain clinical specialties and a number of elective other medical experts work either in or near these hospitals as consultants.

Private health care

The public health services are complemented by private organisations. A sizable portion is funded by employers: e.g. extensive health services are offered to the railway staff and their families. Many industrial corporations have health services of their own, and the army also runs a hospital network. Non-governmental organisations have built health centres, hospitals, and schools to train health care personnel often with foreign support.

According to the criteria of the WHO, India has a surplus of physicians, and private practitioners abound especially in the cities. In Bombay, there are as many as a dozen physicians per block, and consultation rooms may open their doors right to the street – potential customers can compare the skills of these professionals in action.

Training for health care

Two special features in training are of great importance to the health care structure. The first one is the possibility for continued training after field work, which helps professionals to increase their competence. Secondly, there is a clear division in training for hospitals and for primary care. This model is used in many other developing countries. In India, those who train for primary care participate extensively in practical village level work during their studies.

EVALUATION OF THE INDIAN MODEL

India has strived toward strong PHC, but *the function of a principally healthy structure is undermined by lack of personnel and economic constraint.* Vertical programmes are implemented through primary care, but they have at times inflicted serious damage to the balance of health care. An attempt has been made to include a possibility for the collection of nationwide health statistics, but it has been difficult to get dependable data. The results are clearest in population growth. The fertility rates have gone down in all age groups, most notably among the youngest. The infant mortality rate is decreasing steadily.

For communicable diseases, the data is scant and partly conflicting. Vaccination coverage for children is followed by the amount of vaccines used, but there is no information on the prevalence of childhood diseases, and the efficiency of the cold chain cannot be evaluated. The effective treatment of leprosy suffers from the cultural position of this disease: even the nurses of leprosy patients are shunned.

The social structure of the villages and the caste system causes problems. Wealthy families utilise health services more than others, and the professionals may not always be willing to work for the poorest people. Not all health workers in the villages have received appropriate training, and lack of knowledge and motivation causes problems.

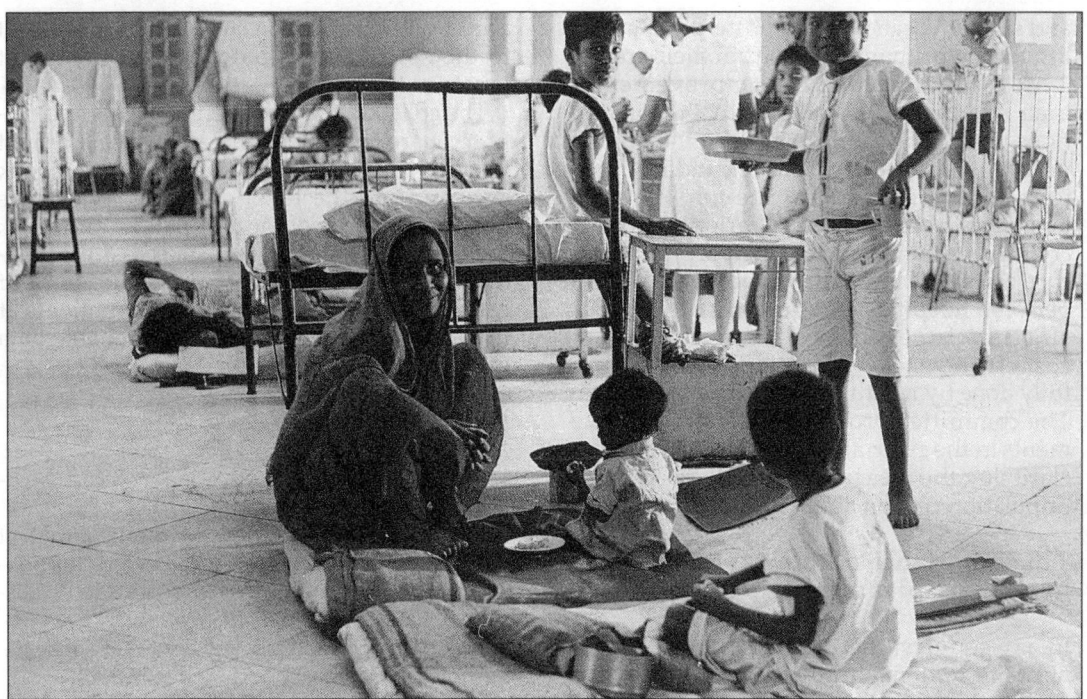

Picture 40.2. University Hospital of Bombay, India. Photo: Marjukka Mäkelä

FUNCTIONAL PROBLEMS IN HEALTH CARE SYSTEMS

In 1987, a WHO expert committee considered the difficulties in collaboration between hospitals and PHC.[9] The work is based on collaboration studies in several countries. The regional organisation of health care was presented as the basic model, and the health services in the region were divided into six levels: 1) Home and the family; 2) Community health action; 3) First level of health care; 4) First referral level (hospital/local health office); 5) Second referral level; 6) Third referral level.

Hospitals on the first referral level were considered as part of PHC instead of secondary care. Here the committee wanted to stress that it is absurd to think that hospitals function separately from the rest of health care.

Health care systems were divided in five types. In the ideal model (I), clear responsibility for the health care of a certain area is assumed, with successful coordination between primary care and the hospitals. Model countries for this type were Finland and China. In the next type (II), the borders are less clear and collaboration weaker, and both levels can be funded either publicly or privately. Here, the models were Indian rural

areas and Kenya. Examples of type III or a weak coordination were several countries in Western Europe, the USA and Mexico; the areal borders are undefined, private and public sectors provide similar services, and hospitals are numerous. The last two types are developing health care systems with either a fairly weak primary care sector (IV) or a deficient hospital level (V).

From type II system on, the remedial tasks were listed as: 1) strengthening connections between PHC and the hospitals; 2) clarifying the population bases; and 3) coordination of multisectoral work. Levels IV and V would need in addition strengthening the weaker level of health care and increased funding.

Different health care systems face other common problems than lack of coordination. Both the population and the personnel do well to check their attitudes toward health services – especially the staff attitudes can be strongly influenced by training. The importance of the selection criteria for medical schools and of field experience during training were stressed. By improving the quality and location of services, the demand for health care can be partly controlled. The committee recommended that hospitals should participate in preventive and promotive health care in their area and supply vocational and postgraduate training for the primary care staff in their area.

Most countries need an improvement in their information systems, so that the institutions would have information on the population basis, socioeconomic level, and resources in their respective areas. The funding problems stem from the political priorities in each country. Even if resource increases in health care are slow, internal resource reallocation between hospitals and primary care for best efficiency is possible. Cost containment and cost-effectiveness evaluations are most usefully done by health professionals themselves. The committee proposes detailed improvements in the referral systems, with the aim of clarifying the ideas of stepped care and local population responsibility.

The importance of referral levels in health care planning and evaluation

In any country, the health care professional needs to understand the type of health care system, referral system, and cooperation between the different levels. In practice, the position of one's own unit in the referral system and the physical units above and below it should be familiar to the entire staff. The services produced by the nearest levels must be well-known, as well as the responsibilities and practical ways of giving and receiving either material or educational support. People working in a vertical programme must know the interface between the programme and the country's system of health care.

Knowledge of the levels of health care also helps in planning and development. Statistics from one's own unit give very little information of the health in the population. The accessibility and cost-effectiveness of treatment and preventive care should be critically assessed considering areas and populations instead of treated individuals only. When double work or unmet needs are noticed, rearrangement of services is called for.[10]

When one unit tries to cope with both primary and secondary care, the effectiveness usually suffers. The level of knowledge and technology in the units defines their most productive level of care. Each unit should state clear and binding targets that are suitable for the referral level. For each target, ways of measuring the achieved level must be enumerated and the population or the area of services defined. When the results are com-

pared with the targets, large differences point to the need of reevaluating either the target levels or the ways of action.

The collaboration between hospitals and primary care units of the same area is most important. Both should plan their work according to the level of health as well as health care needs of the population, and work together with other sectors. Successful collaboration leads to an efficient division of resources and labour, treatment of patients at the appropriate level of care, and reliable data of the quality and coverage of care.

References

1. Appropriate technology. London: British Medical Association, 1985.
2. Bloom G, Temple-Bird C. Medical equipment in Sub-Saharan Africa. A framework for policy formulation. IDS research reports Rr19. Sussex: IDS Publications, 1988, pp. 167.
3. Anthropology and primary health care in developing countries. Soc Sci Med 1984;19(4).
4. Fry J, Hasler JC, eds. Primary health care 2000. Churchill Livingstone, London 1986.
5. Social indicators of development 1991–92. Published for the World Bank. Baltimore: The Johns Hopkins University Press, 1992.
6. Banerji D. Health and family planning services in India. An epidemiological, socio-cultural and political analysis and a perspective. New Delhi: Lok Paksh, 1985.
7. Haraldson SSR. Community health aides for sparse populations. World Health Forum 1988;9;234–8.
8. Ramprasad V. Community health workers – an evolving force. World Health Forum 1988;9:229–34.
9. Hospitals and Health for All. Report of a WHO expert committee on the role of hospitals at the first referral level. Geneva: WHO, 1987. (WHO Tech Rep Ser 744)
10. Health Programme Evaluation: Guiding Principles. Geneva: WHO, 1981. (Health for All Series, No. 6)

Additional reading

1. Development of indicators for monitoring progress towards Health For All by the year 2000. Geneva: WHO, 1981. (Health for All Series, No. 4)
2. Health that goes out to meet people. Technical discussions at the 34th World Health Assembly. WHO Chron 1981;35:168–71.

3. Kleczkowski BM, Pibouleau R. Approaches to planning and design of health care facilities in developing areas. Volumes 1–4. Geneva: WHO 1976, 1977, 1979 and 1983. (WHO Offset Publications no. 29, 37, 45 and 72)

4. Kleczkowski BM, Montoya-Aquilar C, Nilsson NO. Approaches to planning and design of health care facilities in developing areas. Volume 5. Geneva: WHO, 1985. (WHO Offset Publication no. 91)

5. Research for the reorientation of national health systems: Report of a WHO study group. Geneva: WHO, 1983, pp. 694 (WHO Tech Rep Ser 1983)

About the authors

Marjukka Mäkelä is a specialist in general practice in Helsinki, Finland. She works at the National Research and Development Centre for Welfare and Health (STAKES) as Head of Research and Development in Primary Care, and is responsible for the programmes of quality assurance and functional development in primary care. These are also the areas of her current research, with methodology from health economics. Since 1985 she has participated in a Physicians for Social Responsibility, Finland collaborative primary care development project in Tanzania. She is a member of the World Organization of National Colleges, Academies and Academic Associations of General Practitioners/Family Physicians (WONCA) European group for Quality in primary care, and has acted as a Temporary Advisor for the WHO in primary care.

Debabar Banerji has opened up the new field of relating medical technology to the people of India and has been active in the area for more than four decades. He has worked as a physician in the interior Himalayan regions and in the Western Tibet (1956–59) and later at the National Tuberculosis Institute (1959–64), the National Institute for Health Administration and Education (1964–71) and at the Centre of Social Medicine and Community Health, where he is currently a Professor Emeritus. He has contributed to the conceptualisation of New Public Health, as distinct from the conventional public health evolved in the industrialised countries. He has articulated his ideas in a number of books and research papers.

Lankinen KS, Bergström S, Mäkelä PH and Peltomaa M, eds.
Health and disease in developing countries. London:The Macmillan Press Limited, 1994:403–415.

41 HEALTH SYSTEMS AND THEIR MANAGEMENT

Mikko A. Vienonen, M.D., Ph.D.
World Health Organization,
Regional Office for Europe
Scherfigsvej 8, DK-2100 Copenhagen,
Denmark

INTRODUCTION

Systems and management – two words that hold a magic promise of a quick solution to the problems that developing countries are facing today, at a time of economic recession and structural adjustment. However, just as we know that in real life *'abracadabra'* does not make the tricks to work, we should be aware that much more is needed than the jargon of planners and consultants. We need to demystify these words, because nothing will change as long as we fail to call a spade a spade.

The term *health systems* refers to the fact that services are interdependent. Health professionals know that an imbalance in the functions of an organism is called disease, but imbalances between primary and secondary levels of health care, nursing and medical manpower, essential and less-essential drugs, geographical distribution of services, curative and preventive services etc., often are not recognised at all.

The reasons behind this are many and often connected with power politics. Those with influence usually benefit the most from specialised urban-based services. The same is true of the of the medical profession. No wonder then that this part of health systems has become like a cancer, which grows out of control and demands endlessly more and more resources at the expense of others. Just like in any other malignant disease, death will result unless radical surgery is performed.

A *balanced health system* is built on the actual needs and priorities of the population, not on the demands of professionals. Overall 80–90 per cent of services should and could be produced at the primary level, and that is where the main emphasis should be. Preventive services are also important, because that is where the biggest savings can be expected. However, even preventive programmes must be kept in balance with other services in order to avoid rigid vertical structures, which duplicate efforts and waste resources.

Of course hospitals and specialised care are needed also, but their task is to provide the necessary services which the primary level cannot. Furthermore, their role is to counsel, consult and give feed-back to the primary level.

If this is what the health services are, what then is *management*? It is a difficult and unfortunate word, because it translates badly into other languages – so badly that is often taken as a direct loan from English. Its etymology comes from Latin (*manus* = hand, *agere* = to act). So we could say that management is 'hand-making'. Truly, good management means nothing else than good housekeeping. Perhaps that also explains, why many women make good managers.

Planning was the magic slogan in the 1970s and even in the 1980s. Since then its reputation has been tarnished by bad experience. The usual gap between planning and implementation indicates that close attention must be paid to the implementation of plans and

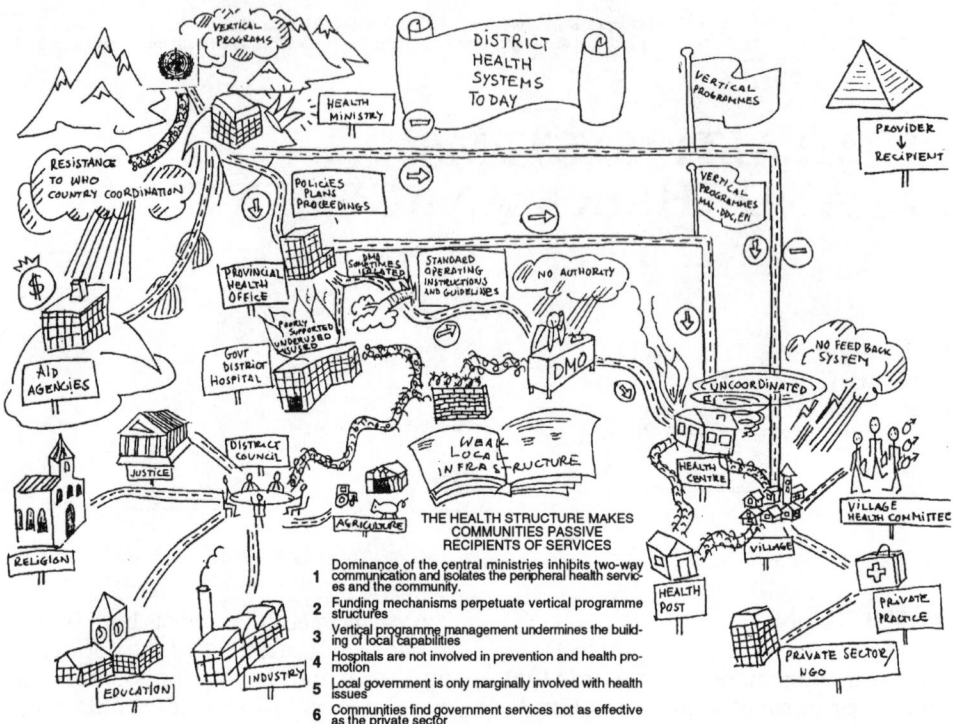

Figure 41.1. The patterns of district health systems today (source: Division of Strengthening of Health Services, WHO Headquarters, CH-1211 Geneva 27, Switzerland).

achieving development targets. It also argues in favour of setting development targets which can be achieved under existing conditions, and sustained in the foreseeable future.

Central planning is easily divorced from implementation and reality. Producing plan documents may become more important than the frustrating, messy and much less logical process of operational planning. Yet, the ultimate performance of the health sector will depend on the implementation and the operational plans of those doing it. It is imperative that the link between development planning, operational planning and implementation be strengthened.[1] This theme is further developed in Chapter 44 which discusses participation of the community in both planning and implementation.

EFFICIENCY, EFFECTIVENESS AND EQUITY

Three E's of health services management are important to keep in mind: *efficiency, effectiveness* and *equity*. The economists and managers, by definition, are mainly concerned with the efficiency of health systems – that the work

gets done with the minimum of financial inputs and as quickly as possible. The epidemiologists, and hopefully more and more also the clinicians, are interested in improving the effectiveness of the system – that is the ability to deliver interventions which improve the health status of individuals. Everyone should be concerned with equity – the ability to allocate the interventions according to the needs and expected health benefits. Unfortunately, equity tends to be the step-sister of the other two E's, remembered before political elections and in official speeches, then soon again forgotten.

For health professionals not used to managerial thinking it may be useful to clarify the terms by examples from outside the sector. For example, if the aim of a transport squadron was to fly material aid from Italy to Sarajevo and they did it by direct flight, were able to land on the airport, deliver the goods to the needy ones and fly back, one could say that they were both efficient and effective. However, if they could not land in Sarajevo, had to unload their cargo in Zagreb and to take it by land to the destination, they were effective, but less efficient than the former group. If they lost half of their freight, they were not only less efficient but also 50 per cent less effective. If again they were able to land in Sarajevo, but were not able to deliver the goods to the needy people, they were efficient but ineffective.

Equity is always connected with the population served and it brings the ethical aspect into the picture. Equity is connected with the relative importance of the service. If our squadron had decided to deliver the goods only to one ethnic group, we would all agree that the service was not equitable no matter how efficient or effective. But if priorities had to be decided, what would be just: to give to those who are the neediest (the most famished and dying anyway), to those who gain most in life expectation (the children), to those from whom most direct benefit is to be expected (defending soldiers and working population) – or to those who can pay the most?

This example illustrates the most crucial questions that health professionals too often refuse to think about: Where do we want to go and with whom? Why? How? The result of such indecision is *inefficiency, ineffectiveness* and *inequity*.

WHO MAKES A GOOD MANAGER?

In the industrialised world the trend in recent years has been that professional managers, are more and more coming to replace the doctors and head nurses, who 10–20 years ago took care of most managerial tasks within the health services. The reason behind this change is that professional staff was often reluctant to accept and see the importance of management in the running of a modern service system. Too many considered that their managerial duties were fulfilled by signing some papers after a busy surgery, or maintaining discipline and taking care of work shift lists. We all know what will happen to a hotel without a manager, and yet a hospital or a primary health service network must handle much more complicated matters. No wonder our clients or patients are widely dissatisfied.

In developing countries specialised managers can seldom come into question. The nurses and doctors simply have to resume the managerial responsibilities and train themselves into it. This can be done quite satisfactorily with courses, motivation and – common sense.

Training should be very concrete and practical. Too often the academic training courses are like learning to ride a bicycle through studying theoretical mechanics. To avoid such an approach the WHO has developed good manuals and even simulation models.[2–4]

DISTRICT HEALTH SYSTEMS APPROACH

In most developing countries the health systems are still based on centralised administration, and interference in even the smallest details in decision-making is not uncommon. Such systems are often detrimental from the management point of view, because the temptation to become blind obeyers of orders is often too great. Anything which is not explicitly allowed becomes forbidden.

The process of decentralisation is not easy. It involves power conflicts and it can be argued that decentralisation is not possible in lack of adequate intermediate or local level staff. This creates a vicious circle because expertise and know-how do not develop before the responsibilities for real decision-making are given.

For several years the WHO has advocated the district health approach.[5,6,7] This means that the smallest comprehensive administrative unit in a country is chosen as the focal point. The more decentralised the system is the more powerful this approach can be. It is generally believed that in order to make the most efficient use of the scarce resources, all PHC services should be fully integrated under management of a district health team, led by district health manager.

However, decentralisation can de dangerous, if management development is not given emphasis at the same time. Badly administered freedom can be worse than well-run central regulation. For example, Papua New Guinea decentralised a wide range of health functions to provincial governments between 1977 and 1983. The national health budget was split into the health components of provincial budgets. The impact on health workforce development was particularly severe and largely unforeseen. Many problems arose as a result of the administrative confusion and inflamed relationships that accompanied the forceful transfer of power from a very reluctant Department of Health to the provinces. Even though policy formulation and planning were retained as national functions, decentralisation hampered effective execution. Human capital deteriorated and responsibility of planning became confused. In reality, health

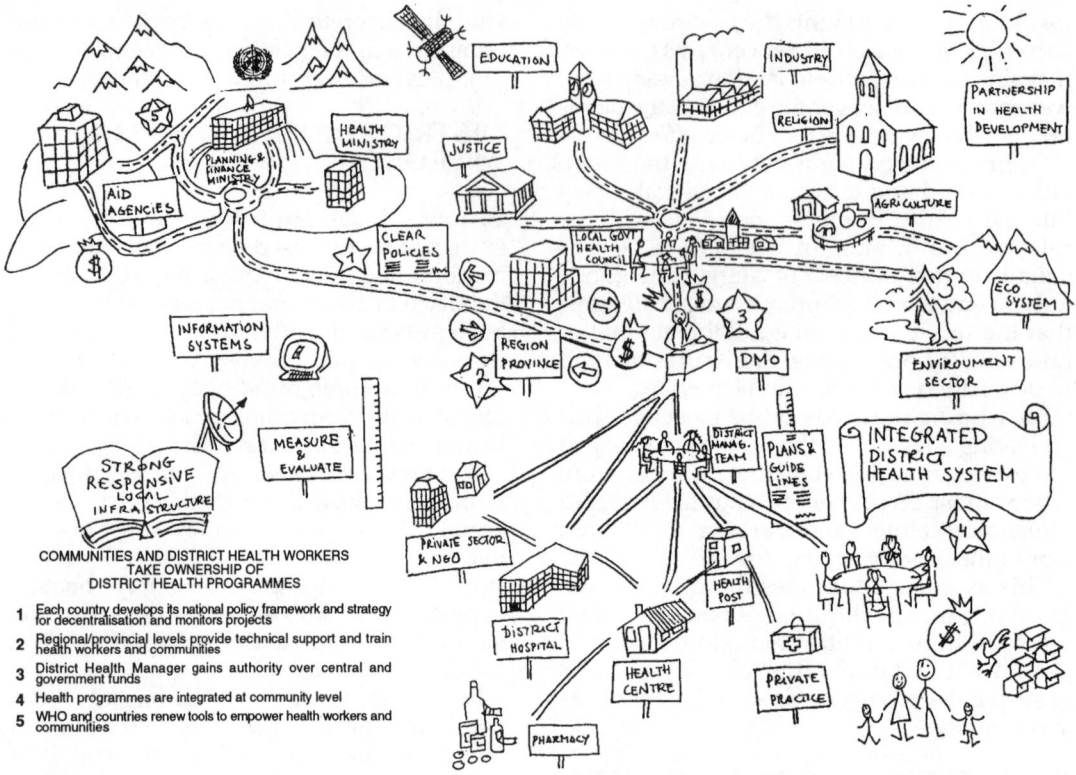

Figure 41.2. The patterns of integrated district health systems (source: Division of Strengthening of Health Services, WHO Headquarters, CH-1211 Geneva 27, Switzerland)

workforce planning was carried out by the Departments of Finance and Planning without any attempt to assess health service needs either in the country as a whole or between the provinces.[8]

Figure 41.1. illustrates how the present problems of district health systems can be conceptualised when the local infrastructure is weak. The lines of authority are not clear and many 'natural catastrophes' occur. An *integrated* district health system is presented in Figure 41.2., where the connecting links are two-way roads, responsibilities are clear, communication functions, and emphasis is on local services and decision-making is subordinate to them.

In the districts the four components of a health system become clearly apparent. *Diseases* call action in medical care and preventive services, *individual behaviour* is a target for health promotion, *environmental hazards* need to be tackled through health protection, and better housing, clean water, education and nutrition are enhanced through *economic development* (Figure 41.3.).

To devote increasingly scarce resources to areas, where they would achieve the greatest impact was largely the rationale behind the concept of *selective primary health care*. Though the case was simplistic in its initial formulation, it forced those arguing for 'comprehensive' primary health care to consider the implications to resource limitations.

Community health development refers to activities that help individuals, families and communities to deal with the many problems of living, in particular with health problems. It recognises the dynamic interaction between health, socioeconomic and environmental factors promoting personal and community responsibility and involvement. It also stresses the importance of health promotion, without overemphasising treatment of diseases.

Table 41.1. shows examples that illustrate the nature of most frequent and persistent management problems in PHC. These problems are due to variety of factors: lack of skills, lack of resources, lack of information, unclear procedures, poorly motivated staff. To move from basic health services and traditional disease control programmes to health systems based on PHC requires not only reorientation and training of staff, but fundamental changes in the whole organisation.[9]

INFORMATION SUPPORT FOR HEALTH MANAGEMENT

A reform of *health information systems* has been made a priority by health managers, public health specialists and technocrats alike. However, improved efficiency and rational allocation of resources do not automatically follow from improvements in information technology or increased amount of data.

Reforms in health information systems can certainly improve health management, but only if the process is action-led rather than, as usually, data-led. The latter approach sees data as an end in themselves. In contrast, the action-led approach regards information as a prerequisite of interventions. If improvements in information are to result in improved health, there must be strategies which ensure that information really influences decisions routinely.[10]

In much the same way that monitoring data looses operational significance when processed at the national level, centralised disease surveillance systems are normally of little use for the detection and control of outbreaks. Typically, disease episodes are reported to a national office where responses, if they occur at all, are far too slow to be effective. In situations where disease surveillance is carried out locally, a more rapid response to outbreaks is possible. The danger remains, however, that the action will be an *ad hoc* fire-fighting approach. A more rational action could often be planned ahead, knowing that outbreaks of many illnesses can be predicted on the basis of seasonal variation.

In places where there is no tradition of regular analyses of routinely collected data, it will be difficult to ensure that data is used for decision making. Therefore, data analysis and interpretation should be 'ritualised'. A surgical team is able to detect and treat post-operative complications such as infection not simply because the nurses regularly take the patients' temperature but because the data is plotted on a chart which is inspected on ward rounds (unfortunately it may sometimes happen that even then information is only collected, not interpreted). The ward round serves to ritualise analysis and interpretation of routinely collected patient data. This does not only help to identify the problems but also ensures that existing problems are not swept under the rug.

Table 41.1. Examples of frequent and persistent management problems in PHC.

- In District A there is no common work plan for the outreach activities of the district health team. The district public health nurse does not know when the public health inspector is next going to village X. There is no system for sharing transport.
- The job descriptions of the medical assistant running the health centre and the district health team are outdated and irrelevant. They do not describe the responsibilities detailed at a recent PHC workshop.
- The public health nurse reports directly to the MCH Director at headquarters about family planning results. A similar procedure exists for most other district officers. The district medical officer's role as a team leader is, therefore, undermined.
- Two different district officers are involved in EPI. Each uses a separate and different information system.
- The district medical officer does not know which of the health centres in the district operate more efficiently. Although he knows the number of outpatients seen at each facility, the accounting system does not provide him with information on their operating cost.
- Village health committees have been established at the request of the PHC coordinator at ministry headquarters. But the committees have never met, and utilisation of health services continues to be very low.
- The director of MCH and the director of the EPI programme work in isolation of each other. Each programme is funded by a different donor and has a separate information and reporting system, separate accounts and separate supply systems.
- The District Medical Officer has just attended a PHC management workshop in the regional capital. When she returns to the district, she finds it impossible to hold an intersectoral workshop because all available funds have been earmarked for specific programmes.

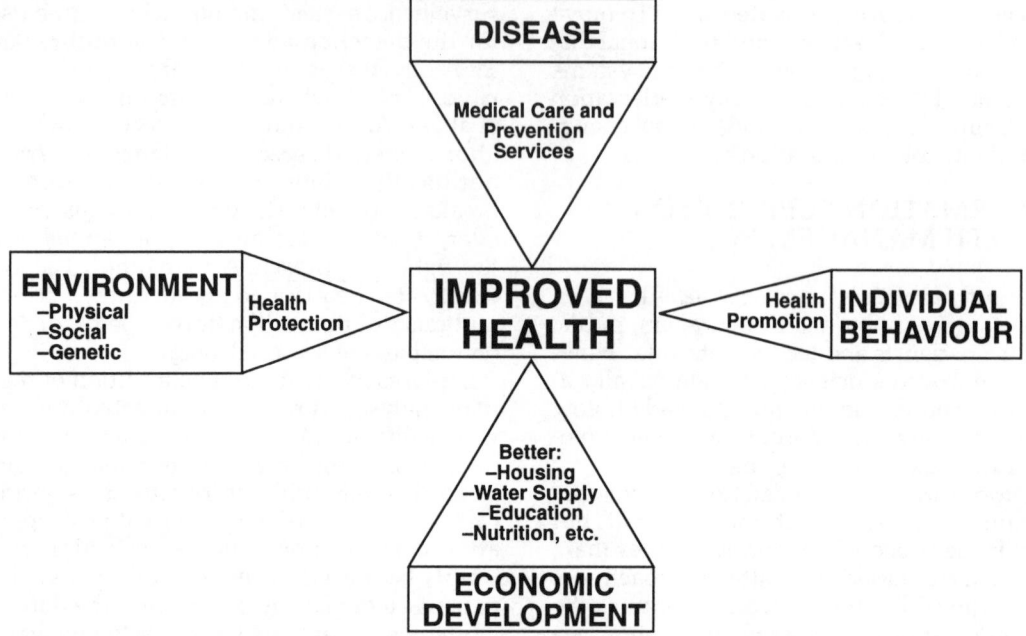

Figure 41.3. The four components of health systems in districts.

There is no reason why public health specialists and management teams could not organise regular rounds during which indicators of service efficiency, effectiveness and equity are regularly analysed to identify areas where action or further investigation is necessary. This is sometimes done – for example in Tanzania the District Medical Officers produce comprehensive annual reports. As such reports are time-consuming to prepare, a verbal presentation may be an alternative, perhaps made more frequently. One month the report might be on bed occupancy in health centres, the next month on immunisation coverage, etc.

The possibility of using microcomputers for information handling and analysis has revolutionised data management – for better and for worse. The relative ease in handling the data has created a temptation to put everything on computer – just in case. The crucial issue remains that the quality of data does not improve itself automatically when it comes out through a printer. Therefore, careful and stringent planning on the really essential data is important.

It is often thought that appropriate technology for the developing countries cannot include high-tech. Behind this thinking there is a concept that the developing countries should have to go through the same steps that the industrialised countries did. However, a well planned computerised information system based on e.g. on portable PCs can be very appropriate in developing country circumstances.

PERSONNEL MANAGEMENT

Managing a community of highly educated experts is a demanding task. They say it is like guarding a basket full of kittens. – Or like in another story: One day an academic manager died and unfortunately had to go to the door of hell. The devil at the door asked his profession and said that he had come at a good time: the management post of the University of Hell was vacant and he could get it. That could not be so bad, thought our mortal. 'Just you wait', said the devil, 'in our university we have two medical faculties'.

It is generally accepted that health services should be based on the work of a multi-disciplinary team. In reality there is much left for improvement and the manager's attention. Often the most urgent work is to clarify job-descriptions of the professionals, so that tasks and lines of authority are clear and appropriate.

Remuneration of staff is a difficult issue, especially in developing countries. On the other hand, if the salary scales are such that a worker simply cannot live on it, then it is useless to grumble if the staff are looking for extra jobs, the morale is low, and consumables disappear.

Already the old Roman military commanders knew that *principis est virtus maxima nosse suos* (the strength of a leader is to know those who work for you). To conduct regular development discussions with your team members is the beginning in this process. Especially physician managers must pay attention to and respect the wisdom of their subordinates, who do not always express it with medical vocabulary. Process thinking may be more natural for nursing personnel, and it is the manager's challenge to discover that wisdom.

QUALITY MANAGEMENT

The aim of introducing or strengthening quality assurance is to achieve the best possible quality consistent with the available resources and equity at all levels.

The first term used widely in this process was *quality control*. The word control was abandoned because it gave an impression of police actions. Then the term *quality assessment* was used which in turn was rejected as it gave the process an impression of a passive, theoretical exercise. The term *quality assurance* is the most recent term, introduced to mean quality assessment, action to correct deficiencies detected and monitoring results of that action.

The common approach in quality assurance is to set performance standards and then establish a system of surveillance with appropriate measurements to detect deficiencies. Remedial interventions are then implemented as indicated by the findings. Standards and periodic assessment by independent outside groups can also help to prevent the internal laxity to which organisations tend to fall victim.

There are, however, problems in the traditional quality assurance approach. Once standards have been reached, further improvement has little appeal. Secondly, as standards are usually imposed from outside, there is little drive for local initiatives that are not directly related to the standards. Thirdly, quality assurance has tended to focus on errors of individuals, and not so much on the organisation and management. Yet it is well known that many problems encountered in the implementation of PHC are due to defects of the systems in which people work and not so much to errors of individual persons.[11]

The quality assurance approach known as *total quality management* is based on a participatory philosophy. It emphasises continuous improvement and not just meeting the standards. Quality assurance is seen as the responsibility of all health workers and not of a person or unit charged with monitoring the standards.

In many health systems, managers' routine assessments tend to be rather rudimentary comparisons of a given indicator with a centrally set target value, or of one year's performance with that of the preceding year. It would often be more informative to make comparisons between similar health facilities or areas.

Total quality management is not only fulfilling a norm, but a constant strive towards the best. For instance, you should compare your unit´s postoperative infections with other similar units in your vicinity but also abroad. Finding out why someone is performing better than you, implementing the necessary changes in your behaviour, and monitoring whether you are improving will guide you on your way becoming the centre of excellence. Sometimes it is difficult to find appropriate indicators, but even the existing ones are not in widespread use: the DMF-index for oral health, vaccination coverage figures (not pooled), bed sores of chronic hospitalised patients, statistics on the use of antibiotics, just to name a few.

Interestingly, improved quality seldom results in significant cost increases, in fact, the facilities with lower quality often have higher pharmaceutical costs. Many of the perceived quality differences between private and public facilities relate to aspects such as friendliness of staff, cleanliness of facilities and newness of equipment.[12]

Managers have traditionally not been very keen on evaluating their own efficiency. In order to create a positive atmosphere towards quality management it may be a good idea to start evaluating your own management performance by for instance the instruments provided by the WHO shown in Annex 1.[13]

CONCLUSIONS

To change from administered into managed health services requires a revolution in

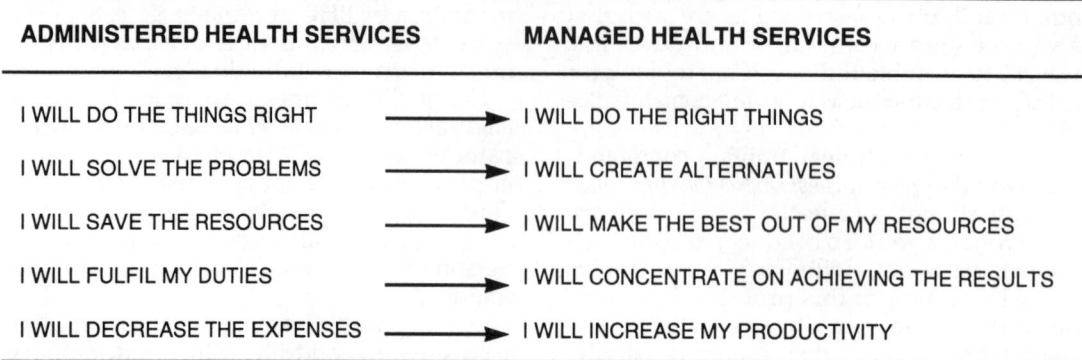

Figure 41.4. The survival strategy for managers of health care systems.

thinking. Doing things right, solving the problems, saving resources, fulfilling the duties and decreasing expenses is not enough. Additionally we need to do the right things, create alternatives, make the best of our resources, concentrate on achieving results and increase productivity (Figure 41.4).

References

1. Cassels A, Janovsky K. A time of change. Health policy, planning and organization in Ghana. Current Concerns, SHS Paper number 4. WHO/SHS/CC/91.2.1992.
2. McMahon R, Barton E, Piot M. On being in charge. A guide to management in primary health care. Geneva: WHO, 1992.
3. Dorros G. Planning and management of change in health systems. World Health Forum 1993;14:86–8.
4. Vaughan JP, Morrow RH, eds. Manual of epidemiology for district health management. Geneva: WHO, 1989.
5. Janovsky K. The challenge of implementation. District health systems for primary health care. Geneva: WHO, 1988. (WHO/SHS/DHS/88.1/Rev.1).
6. Amonoo-Lartson R, Ebrahim GJ, Lovel HJ, Ranken JP. District health care. Challenges for planning organisation and evaluation in developing countries. Basingstoke: The Macmillan Press Ltd., 1984.
7. Tarimo E. Towards a healthy district. Organizing and managing district health systems based on primary health care. Geneva: WHO, 1991.
8. Kolehmainen-Aitken R. The impact of decentralization on health workforce development in Papua New Guinea. Public Administration and Development 1992;12:175–91.
9. WHO/SHS/DHS. Management Development for Primary Health Care. Report of a consultation 28 May-1 June 1990. WHO: Geneva, 1990.
10. Sandiford P, Annett H, Cibulskis R. What can information systems do for primary health care? An international perspective. Soc Sci Med 1992;10:1077–87.
11. Kaluzny AD, McLaughlin CP, Simpson K. Applying total quality management concepts to public health organizations. Public Health Reports. Journal of the US Public Health Services. 1992;107:257.
12. Newbrander W, Parker D. The public and private sectors in health: economic issues. International Journal of Health Planning and Management 1992;7:37–49.
13. Rotem A, Fay J. Self assessment of managers of health care. How can I be a better manager? Geneva: WHO, 1987. (WHO Offset Publication No 97)

About the author

Mikko Vienonen is a specialist in general practice and administration. His Ph.D. thesis dealt with maternal health care, the aspects of improving collaboration between primary and secondary health care. During 1990–1992 he worked as Project Director for the Health and Social Development Cooperation Group HEDEC assisting FINNIDA, the Finnish International Development Agency, in the planning, monitoring and evaluation of projects in Asia, Africa and Latin-America. Since 1993 he has worked for the WHO/EURO as Health Services Management Adviser assisting the countries of Central and East-

ANNEX 1. Five instruments for self-assessment of health care managers.[13]

INSTRUMENT NO. 1 – PROVIDING SERVICES

Please circle a rating from 1 to 5 in response to the first series of statements – 1 if you strongly agree with the statement, 2 if you generally agree, and so on up to 5 if you strongly disagree.

In the comments section, please provide information you feel will be helpful, especially regarding those statements you either strongly agree or disagree with. Thoughtful and frank comments will be very welcome.

	Strongly agree				Strongly disagree
1. The services provided are focused on the major health problems as seen by the community	1	2	3	4	5
2. Services are in line with the national health plan	1	2	3	4	5
3. The manager understands the needs and priorities of the community	1	2	3	4	5
4. Community members are involved in the planning process	1	2	3	4	5
5. Services have been designed as an integral unit in the referral system	1	2	3	4	5
6. There is an appropriate emphasis on prevention as well as treatment of illness	1	2	3	4	5
7. Services are designed to reach all social and economic groups	1	2	3	4	5
8. The technology used is appropriate to the level of services	1	2	3	4	5
9. Equipment is well used and is out of order for a minimum of time	1	2	3	4	5
10. The number of staff is adequate	1	2	3	4	5
11. The qualifications of staff are appropriate	1	2	3	4	5
12. Evaluation is made a part of routine operations	1	2	3	4	5
13. When problems are identified, a clear plan for corrective action is followed	1	2	3	4	5

Comments: (Please begin by showing the number of the statement concerned)

Questions:
1. What are the health needs that you are aware of in the community that have not been adequately met by the health centre?

2. What new services or programmes can you identify that show that the health centre is keeping up with the needs of the community?

3. Can you cite an example to show that the management is creative in developing new services?

INSTRUMENT NO. 2 – PERSONNEL MANAGEMENT

Please circle a rating from 1 to 5 in response to the first series of statements – 1 if you strongly agree with the statement, 2 if you generally agree, and so on up to 5 if you strongly disagree.

In the comments section, please provide information you feel will be helpful, especially regarding those statements you either strongly agree or disagree with. Thoughtful and frank comments will be very welcome.

	Strongly agree			Strongly disagree	
1. I have a clear job description that describes my routine duties in detail	1	2	3	4	5
2. My education and experience are appropriate to my duties	1	2	3	4	5
3. I understand clearly the kind of decisions I can make on my own	1	2	3	4	5
4. When I need approval, I don't have to wait long before decisions are made	1	2	3	4	5
5. I feel comfortable about discussing problems with my supervisors	1	2	3	4	5
6. My supervisors are capable and qualified	1	2	3	4	5
7. Supervisors usually discuss new plans with me before changes are made	1	2	3	4	5
8. There are resources available to improve my effectiveness	1	2	3	4	5
9. I have opportunities available for promotion	1	2	3	4	5
10. There are sufficient materials available to perform each task	1	2	3	4	5
11. There is usually enough time available to perform each task	1	2	3	4	5
12. I have the right equipment available	1	2	3	4	5
13. When equipment breaks down, it is usually repaired without a long delay	1	2	3	4	5

Comments: (Please begin by showing the number of the statement concerned)

Questions:
1. What do you feel is the role or purpose of the health centre?
2. What is the purpose of your particular department?
3. What changes would you make to make better use of the staff and equipment already available?
4. Are there other tasks you feel qualified for but have not had a chance to pursue?
5. Do you feel that your last personnel evaluation was helpful to you?
6. Why would you, or would you not, encourage a friend to apply for a position in the health centre?

INSTRUMENT NO. 3 – LEADERSHIP SKILLS

Please circle a rating from 1 to 5 in response to the first series of statements – 1 if you strongly agree with the statement, 2 if you generally agree, and so on up to 5 if you strongly disagree.

In the comments section, please provide information you feel will be helpful, especially regarding those statements you either strongly agree or disagree with. Thoughtful and frank comments will be very welcome.

	Strongly agree				Strongly disagree
1. The manager enjoys the respect of his staff	1	2	3	4	5
2. He sets a good example for junior staff to follow	1	2	3	4	5
3. He understands the needs of staff and treats them as individuals	1	2	3	4	5
4. He handles personnel matters fairly and consistently	1	2	3	4	5
5. He acknowledges jobs well done and provides rewards without letting personal bias interfere	1	2	3	4	5
6. He disciplines staff when necessary without letting personal bias interfere	1	2	3	4	5
7. He shows his concern for the professional advancement of staff	1	2	3	4	5

Comments: (Please begin by showing the number of the statement concerned)

Questions:
1. What example can you point to that shows that the manager knows how to use both rewards and discipline in managing personnel?
2. How do you feel junior staff would rate the manager as a leader?
3. What specific leadership skills need improvement?

INSTRUMENT NO. 4 – COMMUNITY RELATIONS

Please circle a rating from 1 to 5 in response to the first series of statements – 1 if you strongly agree with the statement, 2 if you generally agree, and so on up to 5 if you strongly disagree.

In the comments section, please provide information you feel will be helpful, especially regarding those statements you either strongly agree or disagree with. Thoughtful and frank comments will be very welcome.

	Strongly agree				**Strongly disagree**
1. There is regular communication between the centre staff and the community	1	2	3	4	5
2. The services provided are in line with the needs of the community	1	2	3	4	5
3. Community members are aware of the services offered	1	2	3	4	5
4. The centre makes good use of volunteer staff available in the community	1	2	3	4	5
5. There are special services available for specific groups such as malnourished children, young mothers, tuberculosis patients, etc.	1	2	3	4	5
6. Appropriate educational services are provided and used	1	2	3	4	5
7. The staff are able to guide patients to other facilities when special care is needed	1	2	3	4	5
8. The staff works with other providers in the community (traditional healers, birth attendants, etc.)	1	2	3	4	5
9. Home visits are made for families at high risk or with special needs	1	2	3	4	5
10. Regular discussions show that the staff has a good understanding of the needs of the community	1	2	3	4	5

Comments: (Please begin by showing the number of the statement concerned)

Questions:
1. What access do different groups in the community have to discuss their needs with the health staff?
2. Which groups in the community find it difficult to make full use of the services available?
3. Are some of the services provided using resources that could be more effectively used on more serious problems?
4. What recent services have been started that show that the staff really understand the needs of the community?

INSTRUMENT NO. 5 – MANAGING FINANCIAL RESOURCES

Please circle a rating from 1 to 5 in response to the first series of statements – 1 if you strongly agree with the statement, 2 if you generally agree, and so on up to 5 if you strongly disagree.

In the comments section, please provide information you feel will be helpful, especially regarding those statements you either strongly agree or disagree with. Thoughtful and frank comments will be very welcome.

	Strongly agree				Strongly disagree
1. Personnel and materials are used wisely	1	2	3	4	5
2. Money needed to maintain equipment and purchase parts is generally available	1	2	3	4	5
3. The equipment purchased is not too sophisticated or expensive	1	2	3	4	5
4. A reasonable amount of the budget is devoted to administrative expenses	1	2	3	4	5
5. Vehicles and equipment are efficiently shared among different units	1	2	3	4	5
6. The actual expenditures are reasonably close to the levels predicted in the budget	1	2	3	4	5
7. Funds are available to respond to unforeseen situations and emergencies	1	2	3	4	5
8. Minor adjustments can be made when needed without lengthy delays	1	2	3	4	5
9. The reporting system is simple and not too time-consuming	1	2	3	4	5
10. The reports provide only usable and necessary information	1	2	3	4	5

Comments: (Please begin by showing the number of the statement concerned)

Questions:
1. Can you describe areas where financial resources are not being efficiently used?
2. What suggestions can you make to improve the efficiency?
3. What safeguards are there to avoid misuse of funds?
4. How might the reporting system be simplified and still provide information needed by management?

Lankinen KS, Bergström S, Mäkelä PH and Peltomaa M, eds.
Health and disease in developing countries. London:The Macmillan Press Limited, 1994:417–426.

42 HEALTH SYSTEMS FINANCING

Hannu Valtonen, D.Phil. (York)
University of Vaasa
P.O. Box 700, FIN-65101 Vaasa,
Finland

INTRODUCTION

The history of economic thinking about development and developing countries after the Second World War is a story of increasing pessimism. The expectations were high after the war, especially so in many newly independent developing countries. It was thought that economic policies would soon boost growth in developing countries and that the route to welfare was imminent. In health care, this optimism was reflected in hopes of eradicating diseases such as tuberculosis or malaria. It seemed that the knowledge and the technologies for this were available. The principal concern was to use them in a rational way.

Since those days, the optimism has vanished. In 1983 for instance, the Economic Commission for Africa envisioned the future in nightmarish terms: in developing countries *'the socioeconomic conditions would be characterized by a degradation of the very essence of human dignity'*. This could happen in spite of economic growth. In fact even in Sub-Saharan Africa, the growth of GNP per capita has been about 1 per cent annually from the 1960s to the 1980s. In developed countries, the future does not seem bright, either. There was a promise in the 1950s and 1960s that the economic problems of development could be solved by economic growth, but even the developed countries as the locomotives of growth have not succeeded in doing this.

There are, of course, countries where the situation does not look bad at all. In some developing countries the health status of the population and the functional capacity of the health care system actually have improved. This is the case of several countries in Asia.

The funding difficulties do not exist only in developing countries. In fact, both in developing and in industrialised countries the public sector faces constant difficulties in securing funding. The levels of the actual spending on health care are vastly different, but the problem of finding the necessary funds is the same. Our ability to solve these problems seems to be weak worldwide. It seems today that economic growth cannot secure increasing funds for health care, or at least this can happen only very slowly.

The thinking concerning health and health care in developing countries reflects the more general ideas about development. After the Second World War the most prominent idea was W.W. Rostow's theory of stages of growth. Even today it seems as if growth is a phenomenon, that can be generated by an initial push.

This is reflected, e.g. in the concepts of sustainable or self–supporting development. The history of developing countries, especially during the last two decades, shows that the inducement of sustainable growth has not been successful.

In the public sector, the changes in the way of functioning of economy have led to a constant crisis. The potential of the public sector in developing countries to finance various welfare services has declined. Thus, the financial problems are not only problems of the health care, and they can, in the long run, only be solved from outside the health care. There are, however, some things that can be done also within the health care.

The economic problems in developing countries have intensified since the first oil crisis in the 1970s and since the debt crisis in the 1980s. These problems have immediately affected the public sector, including health care. Once again it is time to view the problems from a new perspective. In the 1970s the focus of health care development was moved to PHC. Since then, a new evaluation of the financing options has been done in the Bamako initiative, reflecting the actualisation of the funding problems.

RECURRENT FUNDING CRISIS

Financing the public sector is a persistent problem in developing countries. The most important provider of health care is the public sector, and if there are no funds for education, there may be little funds for health care. For health care this usually means a shortage of *recurrent funds*. The situation is caused by factors from mainly outside the health care. The national economic problems have an effect on health care through the governmental budget, in the same way as they have their effects on education or social services.

Governments' revenues are heavily dependent on the world market prices of primary products, oil, and foreign debt servicing. The worsening economic situation has decreased the potential to finance the public sector, including health care. The problem of public sector financing is worst in Africa, but if the international debt crisis worsens, all countries with large foreign debt will face the same problem.

Previously, it was thought that a suitable cooperation in health care implies donors' help in creating the system and facilities (i.e. investments), recipient countries taking care of the rest and actually running the created systems. As in the general ideas of development the presumption was that after an initial push from the donors' side, the developing countries would find a path of cumulative development in all sectors. During the last decades this belief has lost its credibility and the basic concept has changed. The main lesson is that *a sustainable solution for health care financing can only be found from outside the actual health care.*

Originally, the idea of sustainability meant only economic sustainability. An ideal case would be an income-generating industrial investment, which after some time is able to cover not only the production costs, but also to give an economic surplus. Some developing countries have diverted their revenues from the social sector to projects that promise economic gains in terms of money surplus. This implicit or explicit idea of economic sustainability relies on the old concept of development, which has not proved to be successful.

In most instances, health services cannot be sustainable in the same sense. Even in developed countries health services are not producing an income surplus and, because of considerations of equity and distribution, hardly ever will. Health care is usually seen as a necessity (like education), a welfare service, and every individual should have free access to health care. Equity cannot be achieved, if health care (or education) is not financed from outside.

THE VULNERABLE POSITION OF PUBLIC SERVICES

Because the funding of health care depends mainly on public resources it is in a much more vulnerable position than e.g. industrial development. The availability of public funding is dependent e.g. on the volume and the terms of international trade, and on the expansion of the tax basis of government. The future of health care therefore depends on things that are far beyond the control of health care decision makers.

Developing countries not only lack capital funds, but they increasingly face difficulties with recurrent funding of the existing health care: 'many countries have found it increasingly impossible to meet recurrent costs from their own budgets, since as producers of primary products they have been subject to the vagaries of the physical environment, and fluctuations in world prices. Further, the two oil price crises left many of these countries heavily indebted, with repayments being a major claim on public funds'.[1]

Recurrent costs are expenditures, that are borne repeatedly over the whole life time of an activity. Typically these include salaries and wages; equipment maintenance and spare parts; supplies such as drugs, food, dressings, fuel; utilities, such as electricity, water, and maintenance of human capital, i.e. on–the–job training. These costs are connected with actual service provision, not with system building.

Children from Jakarta, Indonesia. Photo: UNICEF/Sean Sprague

The recurrent costs comprise the actual running costs of *the service provision*.

Recurrent funding difficulties most probably will ensue if the amount of capital expenditure (investments) exceeds one quarter (or one third, in individual cases) of the amount of recurrent funding available for the same period. Such level of investments may be possible only if the GNP and the revenue base are expanding at an exceptional rate. Otherwise the only escape is if donors are willing to provide budgetary support in increasing amounts indefinitely.[2]

This rule is based on the observation that unless the financial basis for government activities expands exceptionally quickly, the pace of investments is often too rapid. The new investments create an increasing demand for recurrent funding, and some part of this demand cannot be met. The attempt to hold investments at a third of recurrent expenditures causes a need for about 9 per cent annual recurrent cost funding increase. A growth of 9 per cent per annum again would imply, that the size of health care expenditure would double in every 8 years. In developing countries this growth pace cannot be achieved at present. In comparison, Finland as a rapidly growing developed country has experienced a very swift growth of health care system since the 1960s. The health expenditures increased

from 1960 to 1986 more than five-fold, but still only about 6 per cent per year.

LEVEL OF NATIONAL ECONOMY – EXAMPLE FROM MALI

At the level of the whole economy the financial situation of the health sector may look as in the example from Mali.[3] The economic characteristics of health care system in Mali are as follows: National public financing is the main source of funding. Altogether 86 per cent of health care expenditure comes from national sources, public and private, and the remaining 14 per cent comes from abroad. However, while 96 per cent of recurrent costs (in 1987) are financed by national resources, external aid covered 81 per cent of investment costs. What is also important is that the share of foreign funding for investments has increased in the 1980s. The external aid covers more and more of investments in health care.

The share of health in the national budget is decreasing. In the beginning of the 1970s, estimates put it at 9 per cent and in 1986 it was only 4 per cent of the national budget. Additionally, the share of government budget from GNP has decreased from about 4 per cent in 1981 to 1 per cent in 1985. All this means that the allocations in the whole public sector, including education, social services

Table 42.1. Estimates of recurrent costs in health care for 1986 in Mali.[3] FCFA = Malian Franc, in January 1986 1 USD = 374 Francs; i.e. 20256 Million Francs = 54 Million US Dollars.

Categories of recurrent cost financing	Millions of FCFA	per cent
Public financing		
State (government)	4 200	
Other public institutions	90	
Development operations	8	
Social security	380	
Total	4 678	23
Households' financing		
Fees	236	
Drugs	12 000	
Traditional medicine	2 000	
Transportation expenditures	300	
Illicit private fees	500	
Total	15 036	74
External aid	542	3
TOTAL	20 256	100

and health care have decreased. Especially the recurrent funds have decreased. The investment funds, especially external aid, have not undergone the same decreasing path. Because of this change, it is *relatively easier in developing countries to get funds for new investments than to recurrent funding of the existing facilities.*

The breakdown of health expenditures as a whole is presented in Table 42.1. The households cover a very large share of the total health expenditures. It must be noted that this purchasing power is not evenly distributed, either socially or geographically. As can also be seen in this table is, that drugs take about 60 per cent of the total health care costs (compared with about 10 percent in developed countries). In relation to the total health expenditures the external aid is small (3 per cent), about the same amount is used to transport and illicit private fees. – Two major problems have been noted:

1) The state lacks financial resources. This is quite apparent when considering the increasing gap between the funds required to reach the planned modest objectives and the resources effectively made available, either nationally or internationally. In fact, although the domestic deficit in the Malian consolidated budget has greatly diminished in percentage of the GNP, the value of the GNP has nevertheless declined in real terms during this period.[3]

2) Health services run by the public authorities lack resources. This results in a decreasing quality of care and in increasing cost for equipment; a shortage of maintenance allowances, for example, necessitates earlier replacement of equipment before it would have been necessary, had adequate repair been available.[3]

DAMAGE MINIMISATION STRATEGY

It has been stated that 'This downturn in the fortunes of the health sector came at a particularly unfortunate time. The need to increase trained health manpower had been one of the priorities of the sixties and seventies. There had been a rapid expansion of medical schools and the costly hospitals associated with them. The lack of trained manpower was at last being overcome. The new problem which was presenting itself was how to maintain the costly hospitals which had been built and how to pay the staff who had been trained'.[4] The recurrent cost crisis not only slows the further development of health services, and it is not a temporary recession, it threatens also the existing structures.

When health care decision makers in any country are facing increasing difficulties of financing the recurrent costs, they may try to minimise the damage by cutting some expenditures. Expecting that the public sector funding potential improves in future, they may try to protect the existing health care structures as far as possible. A hierarchy of such damage minimisation could be the following: The first item to be cut is building, the next are acquisition of new capital equipment, building maintenance and repair, materials, supplies and, as the last resort, personnel.[1] – This strategy, however logical it may be, finally leads to a situation, where the only funded item is personnel. In practice this implies a stepwise closing of activities. Attempts to solve the problem also may lead to chronically low wages in the public sector, with difficulties in employing personnel.

Because of strategies of this kind, the recurrent cost problem might become visible in two ways (which may overlap in time). Before the

Table 42.2. Main sources for financing health care.

---

1) Public funding:
- taxation
- other central and local government revenues
- social insurance

2) Private funding:
- user fees
- revolving drug funds (partly private)
- private insurance

3) Donor contributions:
- intergovernmental cooperation
- non-governmental cooperation

---

recurrent cost problem occurs, the proportion of investment budget and recurrent budget is weighted towards investment. The investment budget may be large in relation to future recurrent financing possibilities when the investment expenditure is between a quarter and a third of recurrent expenditures. The problems may occur afterwards: 1) the proportion of government expenditure on investments compared with that of foreign assistance tends to decrease; and 2) the proportion of personnel expenditures in the recurrent budget tends to rise, and the share of materials, maintenance, supplies, and transport tends to decrease.

In practice, the recurrent cost problem manifests itself when health centres have drugs and other supplies for only a part of the year, equipment is not maintained, transport does not function, buildings are slowly deteriorating, and confidence in public health services is decreasing. The shortage of recurrent funding causes severe deterioration of health services. The existence of the recurrent cost problem can be seen when examining the relative sizes of recurrent cost allocations to wages and salaries and to 'other goods and services' within health care, or even in individual health facilities. An example from El Salvador shows that the budget allocations for supplies may become almost non-existent: 'It is certainly true that when budgets are cut, salaries are defended as much as possible. ... during the years 1977–85 there was (in El Salvador) an increase from 56 to 92 per cent in the percentage of expenditure devoted to salaries in the non–hospital sector of

the Ministry of Health'.[2] This is a very clear indication of imbalance in the use of resources – unfortunately, personnel without drugs or transportation cannot do very much. If the public sector funding does not improve, the regress of health services cumulates until both the patients and the staff have left the facilities.

SOLUTIONS FOR THE RECURRENT COST PROBLEM

The first thing that could be done is to increase awareness of these problems and to improve planning and operation of health care. The proposed solutions can be divided into different categories. The finding of extra funding is the last one, indicating that the scarcity of funds is not the problem *per se*. The most crucial problems are usually the health problems.

When appraising the different solutions some basic truths must be kept in mind. The purpose of fundraising systems is not only to collect funds. There are other important things to be considered, and the ability to collect funds is only one criterion. In fact, *the funding systems should be evaluated in the context of national health and development policy.* Important tasks for a financing system could be the financing system's contribution to these policies, (these are examples, the actual contents of policies may vary from country to another), e.g.: 1) to extend equitable access to primary health care; 2) to involve communities in decision-making; 3) to implement appropriate, professionalised medical technology; and 4) to initiate a generally self-reliant health system.

Main sources for financing health care are listed in Table 42.2. The forms of financing are not similar in their effects on society and health care. All alternatives have their positive and negative features. An ideal funding system would not only support the national health policy, but it would also provide a secure flow of funds. In developed economies, taxation and insurance systems have been this kind of stable sources of funds. In developing countries, both the tax and insurance basis is often quite narrow.

From the economic point of view some important aspects should be considered. Before implementing any fundraising systems one should ask what is the administrative capacity at different tiers of health care and different organisations to raise, control, and use the collected funds? Before implementing

Table 42.3. Alternative forms of fee or local fundraising systems.[10]

- a fixed payment for each service provided,
- payment for each service, depending on the ability to pay
- payment that varies according to the type of service provided
- payment for a drug prescription, which may vary according to the type of drug and/or ability to pay
- payment through an insurance scheme, in which individuals or families make continued regular payments to provide for services when they are sick
- donations for services, the amount depending on the patient's willingness or ability to pay
- payment through an insurance scheme covering preventive and promotive activities as well as individual illnesses in the community
- periodic donations (for example, by the local cooperative)
- periodic fund–raising campaigns, which may include athletic or cultural activities organised by communities

systems of fund creation, it should be ascertained that the organisations can smoothly accomplish the task of fund collection. A simple rule is, that the collection costs should be only a small fraction of the collected funds. The organisational tiers should be prepared to do the work, otherwise it may cost more in labour and effort to collect the funds, than the amount collected.

EVALUATION OF VARIOUS FUNDING ALTERNATIVES

What are the implications of the various forms of financing on health policy objectives through their effects on access and functioning of health care? It needs to be asked what is the effect of a fundraising solution on:

1) *demand* for health care goods and services. Which groups of population are affected? How does the composition of clients change, regarding socioeconomic status or type of disease? What kind of services are affected (e.g. visits to health centres or use of drugs)? Do fees decrease demand for important services?

2) *distribution* of health care goods and services between different geographical areas, groups of population. How the poor, women, and children are protected? How various priority groups are supported?

3) *functional efficiency* of health care. What effect do the various forms of financing have on the functioning of referral system, or on the emphasis on preventive services? How is the management of the use of health services affected, e.g. is the appropriate use of drugs affected? Do the forms of financing increase local confidence in health services?

4) *quality of service delivery*. Financing mechanisms can imply both positive and negative incentives for health workers to supply good quality care, e.g. fees per drug purchased may encourage over-prescription whereas fees per episode of illness might encourage continuity of care.

5) *integration*. In the case of foreign aid, how the forms of financing (capital investments and maybe also recurrent funding) support the integration of aid into the society of recipient country. E.g. how do the form and quantity of finance support existing health care and social structures.[5]

The various fundraising solutions are administratively different. The smaller the items collected at one time, the more expensive and complicated is the fundraising. The potential uses of the collected funds should also be discussed more. We might, e.g. combine two forms of financing: a hypothetical example could be one, where a donor covers the salaries and wages for a health facility, and the government covers the other recurrent costs.

The most discussed option to raise funds for recurrent costs are user charges. User charges decrease demand for health care services, and unfortunately the demand of health care of the most vulnerable groups, the poor, women and children. When discussing user fees, it must be noted, that in most countries health care customers are already paying various charges, fees and prices. Private households are reported to contribute up to 50 per cent of the total health expenditure in many developing countries. A large share of these private expenditures is on drug purchases. This was also the case in Mali (Table 42.1).

According to some studies, it seems that initially a large scale introduction of user fees decreases the demand for health care services for a year or two, but after some time the demand rises again (especially if the quality of services can be improved), perhaps almost to the previous level. The crucial pre-condition for a political justification of the user charges is that the quality of services improves with the introduction of charges. If the other alternative is cessation of health care services provision altogether, the fees, carefully administered and monitored, may be a better choice.

There are some estimates of ways of raising income. It has been estimated (in 1987) that e.g. in Kenya the introduction of user fees would make a significant contribution to health care financing.[6] Between 10 and 20 per cent of the total MOH recurrent expenditures could be covered by user fees. In 34 developing countries the average revenue collected from user fees was 7 per cent of the current MOH budget. In 1986 it was estimated in Kenya that the total welfare effects of the user charges is ambiguous, and that the charges may prove to be socially and politically unacceptable.[7] The reasons for this are long tradition of free health services and the inequity-increasing effects of user fees.

It has been argued that the problem of the protection of the poor is a very severe one: '... these fees may impede access of the most needy to medical care and thereby may have a negative impact on the health of the individuals. ... This evidence should not be used to conclude that user fees should receive no further consideration for use in developing or transitional countries. Rather, it suggests that their imposition should be done in a cautious and experimental fashion'.[8]

Altogether 'the bulk of the available evidence appears to confirm that, while user charges for health care can generate additional income, they also deter the patients at greatest risk. ... Equity in health care is thus deteriorating – already measurably, in terms of access to care, and probably also in health status differentials between socioeconomic groups'.[9] If user fees are accepted, the protection of the poor and other vulnerable groups must be organised by alternative free services. The method of identifying the poor is dependent on local conditions, but it should be the simplest possible. It is very likely that the coverage of preventive services is severe-

ly lowered if fees are charged. The user fees can at their best bring in a substantial addition to the recurrent costs, but they cannot solve the whole problem. – Alternatives for fundraising systems have been listed in Table 42.3.

A SKETCH FOR EVALUATION MATRIX

As a whole, the potential funding systems should be analysed and compared more carefully than so far has been done. Not only the technical side, the administrative processing need analysing, but also more general features; the relationship of the funding systems to the national development strategies. Table 42.4. presents a comparison framework. The idea is, that the potential funding systems should be compared in this kind of framework.

There is no perfect funding system, and the policy makers have to choose between the alternatives giving appropriate weights to various characteristics. In each case the items to be considered depend on local conditions and relevant funding alternatives, thus the items mentioned in the table are only examples. The table considers only public, private and donor funding, and the potential alternatives in an actual comparison have to be classified in more detail.

We may, for instance, assume that the more there is local involvement in the funding, the more the communities feel the health facilities as their own, and the more the funding system encourages local initiatives and self–confidence. In this sense, user contributions (in cash or in kind) also emphasise the value of health services. The positive feature of outside funding, governmental or donor funds, is that they often provide a considerable amount of support for poor communities, which on their own never could support properly functioning PHC.

In all developed countries, the main option for financing health care is health insurance in one form or another. The patients receiving health care may pay directly a minor part of the costs of public health care, and the majority of costs is covered collectively. In the long run, a widespread availability of health insurance is necessary to relieve the government of subsidising the high costs of hospital-based curative care.[11] Consequently, this would free governmental resources to be

Table 42.4. A sketch for a characteristics matrix of various funding systems (yes = improvement, e.g. increased public funding improves access to care, no = impairment, e.g. increasing private funding impairs access to care for the poor).

Various characteristics to be compared	Funding systems		
	Public	Private	Donors
Related to the national health policy			
Access to care	yes	no	yes
Community involvement	no	yes	no
Appropriate medical care	yes	??	yes
Self-reliant health care	no	yes	no
Related to the administration of the funding system			
Funding potential (per cent of costs)	??	varying	large
Preferred use of funds	salaries, wages?	drugs consumables?	system maintenance wages?
Collection costs (administrative complexity)	??	??	??

directed to PHC, and possibly help to change the skewed distribution of health expenditures.

Insurance funds may help to raise standards of care for the whole health system. However, the insurance systems are difficult to organise. They can often only cover employed workers, and they are thus socially divisive and inequitable. They may also encourage cost escalation. Currently, insurance programmes cover only a small proportion of low-income households in most developing countries.

Donor contributions to recurrent costs is a political question: Are donors willing to finance recurrent costs? The arguments in favour of this are that health is a basic right, and thus it has a special status. The recurrent cost problems are not caused by developing countries alone, and especially not caused

inside health sector in developing countries. Furthermore, cost-effective health care programmes may be abandoned, because of worsening public finances. Health care is subsidised everywhere, and it is nowhere self-sustainable (so that it would create economic surplus through private markets) in the strictest sense of the word. However, much of health care in developing countries is sustainable, in the sense that resources used are used for cost-effective and productive projects.

NEED FOR INTERNATIONAL REDISTRIBUTION OF RESOURCES

It seems obvious that the financial position of the governments of most developing countries is not improving, at least not with a pace necessary for appropriate development of public services, including health care. The financial potential in developing countries cannot meet the requirements of adequate health care. Well-intended projects, in which new investments are made, do not presently solve the problem; on the contrary they may worsen the recurrent cost funding crisis. From the discussions concerning economic problems, one thing is clear: the public sector in developing countries needs a constant and hopefully also increasing source of funds. This kind of financial basis in the developed countries is a broad tax basis and the various insurance systems, that have provided the necessary flow of health care funds. Without this kind of source the growth of health care experienced is not possible.

In developing countries, there is unused potential for funding (such as insurance systems and fees for services). These systems, however, are not socially oriented, i.e. if they discourage some people from using the services, it is always the poor, women and children. Unfortunately in the present state of world economy public finances cannot provide this kind of flow of funds. In many instances, the question is not of developing the health services, but preserving the existing systems.

The developed countries are presently (1993) experiencing an economic recession, and we can more frequently hear comments such as 'the possibility for getting increased funding from rich countries is rather slim'. However, the differences between developed and developing economies are so large, that aid should not be dependent on the business cycles of the developed world. There is still demand for an increased role of the donors to finance recurrent costs in developing countries. For the donors, this is after all a relatively cheap alternative, because the price levels (and salaries and wages) are low in developing countries compared to the levels of developed countries.

For instance, the health care costs per capita in developing countries are extremely small compared with those any developed country (Table 42.5). The costs of public health care in Finland are, e.g. 85 times higher than in Kenya, or 770 times higher than in Pakistan. – The comparison does not take into account the differences in the price levels, which means that although the Finnish health care is 85 times more expensive than the Kenyan health care system, the Finns do not get 85 times 'more' health care. Nevertheless, the numbers perhaps do give an impression of the magnitude of the differences.

The total costs of public health care in Pakistan, Kenya and Tanzania summed together are only 12 per cent of the costs of the Finnish health care. The total population of these three countries summed together is 167 millions compared to the 5 million Finns.

Although the developed countries are presently facing a worldwide recession, it is still true that they are rich countries. The developing countries are facing the same recession, and the consequences are very much worse for them. The financing problems of health care presently cannot be solved by economic growth neither in developing nor in developed countries. The situation should lead to more equitable redistribution of the resources among the rich and poor.

Table 42.5. Health care costs *per capita* in US Dollars (Encyclopedia Britannica 1990, latest available figures).

Country	Public health costs per capita	Population millions	Total costs of public health care (1 x 2, million USD)
Brazil	26.80	147	3840
Kenya	5.40	24	130
Pakistan	0.60	119	71
Tanzania	3.50	24	84
Finland	462.90	5	2315

References

1. Lee K. Symptoms, causes and proposed solutions. In: Abel–Smith B, Creese A, eds. Recurrent costs in the health sector – problems and policy options in three countries. Geneva, Washington D.C.: World Health Organization, USAID, no year:11–44.
2. Waddington C, Thomas M. Recurrent costs in the health sector of developing countries. International Journal of Health Planning and Management 1988;3:151–166.
3. Diarra K, Coulibaly S. Financing of recurrent health costs in Mali. Health Policy and Planning 1990;5(2):126–138.
4. Abel–Smith B. Financing health for all. World Health Forum 1991;12:191–200.
5. Valtonen H. Guidelines, 1: Economic aspects of health sector development projects. Helsinki: Health and Social Development Cooperation Group, National Research and Development Centre for Welfare and Health, 1993.
6. Ellis RP. The revenue generating potential of user fees in Kenyan government health facilities. Soc Sci Med 1987;25(9):995–1002.
7. Mwabu G, Mwangi WM. Health care financing in Kenya: A simulation of welfare effects of user fees. Soc Sci Med 1986;22(7):763–767.
8. Stanton B, Clemens J. User fees for health care in developing countries: A case study of Bangladesh. Soc Sci Med 1989;29(10):119–205.
9. Creese A. User charges for health care: a review of recent experience. Health Policy and Planning 1991;6(4):309–319.
10. Tarimo E. Towards a healthy district. Organizing and managing district health systems based on primary health care. Geneva: World Health Organization, 1991.
11. Akin J, Birdsall N. Financing of health services in LDCs. An agenda for reform that would rationalize official expenditures in order to improve basic services for the poor. Finance and Development 1987:40–43.

About the author

Hannu Valtonen is an economist working at the Department of Economics, University of Vaasa, Finland. His main research interests have been the economics of public sector and public services (such as health care, cultural services, and education) and microeconomic theory. His most recent work in the field of health care is 'Application of cost benefit thinking in health care' (Acta Wasaensia, 1993).

Lankinen KS, Bergström S, Mäkelä PH and Peltomaa M, eds.
Health and disease in developing countries. London:The Macmillan Press Limited, 1994:427–432.

43 TRAINING OF HEALTH WORKERS

Kati Juva, M.D.
University of Helsinki, Department of
Neurology, Memory Research Unit
Haartmaninkatu 4, FIN-00290 Helsinki,
Finland

Matti Mäkelä, M.D., Ph.D.
Koskela Hospital
Käpyläntie 11, FIN-00600 Helsinki,
Finland

INTRODUCTION

The training of health workers varies from
one developing country to another even more
than between industrialised countries. The
experience presented in this chapter is mostly
related to Tanzania, where a hierarchically
organised health care system with focused
training programmes at different levels has
been systematically created.

In Tanzania, there is a development project
that aims at developing the participatory
aspects in health worker training. This is a collaboration between the organisation of Physicians for Social Responsibility in Finland and
the local Ministry of Health. In this project,
new educational material has been produced,
the teachers in different health training institutes have been trained and cooperation
between different levels of education and
between the institutions and health authorities has been enhanced. The main goal has
been to lay a basis for community participation, to support sustainable development at
the community level. Plans also exist to support the continuing education in Tanzania.

HEALTH WORKER TRAINING IN DEVELOPING COUNTRIES

The manpower structure

The structure of health care staff in developing
countries is heterogeneous. There are several
different professional groups, some of which
are unknown in industrialised countries. The
level of education varies, with many workers
getting only an on-the-job training.

In many developing countries the health
care system is based on various medical assistants and barefoot doctors. They have a significantly shorter education than medical doctors,
and their theoretical training is sparse. In spite
of this, they are expected to work independently and treat common diseases. In Tanzania the Rural Medical Aides are responsible
for rural dispensaries and Medical Assistants
take care of health centres. The former have
3 years of education after 7 years of primary
school and the latter have studied 3 years after
secondary school.

Besides medical assistants and aides, there is
a large number of nurses working in developing countries. They have an education similar to that of nurses in industrialised countries
and work mostly in hospitals. Community
nurses and workers specialised in mother and
child health care work closer to the community. In Tanzania these Mother and Child
Health Care Aides (MCH-Aide) receive 3
years of training after primary school. They
take care of deliveries, immunisations, health
checks and health education.

Problems related to environment and hygiene
are common in developing countries, and health
inspectors play an important role in health care.
In Tanzania, there are two differently trained
groups, Health Assistants and Health Officers,
who are responsible for meat inspection, for
housing and latrines, and for pest control.

Besides these professionally trained health
workers there are workers with only a short,
local training. They work in their community
by giving advice on health-related problems,
by treating the most simple diseases (diarrhea,
simple traumas) and by promoting hygiene.

In Tanzania the goal is to train Village Health Workers for every village (2000 to 10 000 inhabitants), one male and one female worker to each village. These Village Health Workers should be members of the community, and they are trained in a nearby hospital or health centre for a period of six to nine months.

Quantitative relations and placement of staff

An antithesis to the variety of staff categories is the sparseness of personnel at all levels. When there is one physician for an average of 20 000 inhabitants and one nurse for 2500 inhabitants (Tanzania 1984) one might think that any increase in the number of personnel is better than the existing situation. Still, the situation can be worsened by a distorted structure of staff. In some countries there are actually more doctors than nurses. In most cases the relation between the quantity of doctors and nurses resembles that in industrialised countries (Table 43.1). Attempts to compensate the scarcity with too highly educated staff can lead to difficulties by consuming the small development budget.

The health workers do not always work where the need is greatest. The doctors are mainly located in cities, where hospitals and other paraclinical services make their technology-oriented occupation easier to practise. Many less educated workers find their work more convenient in cities, where they can work in hospitals rather than in the restricted conditions of rural areas.

The problem of getting well-trained workers to distant regions is well known even in industrialised countries. The problem is magnified in developing countries, where the health problems accumulate in rural areas, and there

is no possibility of monetary compensation for working in faraway places. The more educated the person is, the more difficult it is for him or her to feel professional satisfaction in conditions where there is no equipment for laboratory tests or even drugs to treat diagnosed diseases. Selecting and training suitable staff are the best means of getting people to work also far away from hospitals.

In Tanzania, an attempt to counteract the tendency of health workers to migrate to towns has been made by selecting village health workers. It has been recommended, that only married people be selected. The family keeps the person at home more effectively than abstract duty.

In Bangladesh a non-governmental organisation, Gonoshasthaya Kendra (People's Health Centre), trains local people as paramedics. Candidates are selected from villages and advantage is given to applicants from poor families. About 70 per cent of trainees are female. The course lasts for one year and puts special emphasis on understanding social factors behind diseases. Communication skills and service delivery to villagers are also an essential part of the curriculum.

More recently, Gonoshastaya Kendra has started planning similar community based, but university level training for medical doctors as a measure of counteracting the physicians' tendency to stay in cities where they have trained, near university hospital referral services.

Every health worker should be able to satisfy his or her capabilities. This pleasure is endangered, if a worker with a sophisticated training is frustrated by not being able to do what his or her training would make possible. It is also important to be able to share the experiences of the day's work with other

Table 43.1. The skewed distribution of health care personnel in 1983.

| Country | Inhabitants | | Nurses |
	per doctor	per nurse	per doctor
Bangladesh	10 940	24 450	0.45
Nigeria	12 550	3 010	4.16
Guatemala	8 600	1 620	5.30
Ivory Coast	21 040	1 590	13.23
Iran	2 320	2 520	0.92
USA	520	150	3.56
Finland	480	75	6.40

professionals. The more lonely and isolated the worker, the more important it is that the language and concepts used in the training are familiar and comprehensible to the people with whom he or she lives and works.

The content of training does not always reflect the fact that the demands of work vary on different levels of the health care system. The Rural Medical Aides in Tanzania work in rural dispensaries, but their training is conducted in English and in a much more technical environment. The future worker may thus feel that 'real' work is done in a hospital-like environment and with concepts incomprehensible to rural people.

The role of a doctor

The western doctor-centred health care is not optimal for developing countries. A trained doctor is far too valuable a resource to be used only in curative work. Training and employing doctors is expensive and so also is the treatment given by them, as it is usually drug- and technology-oriented. A less trained worker can adjust more easily to local conditions and is more likely to use local resources and appropriate technology.

In developing countries there is usually a lack of doctors in rural areas. In hospitals doctors often focus on curative work, but they also educate other staff. Many doctors work in administrative assignments in planning and organising the health care system or training other staff.

Traditional medicine

Besides the modern health care system there are usually plenty of traditional healers in developing countries (Chapter 6). The People's Republic of China has successfully connected the means and principles of traditional medicine with modern medicine, and in India and in Indonesia the traditional and modern healers work officially together. In many countries these traditional healers work outside the official system without any legitimation or supervision, often in a clandestine way.

Traditional healing constitutes an important part of the praxis of health care in developing countries. The modern system cannot meet all needs, and some of the people will seek alternative help anyway. Traditional beliefs also influence people's attitudes towards health services.

The group of traditional healers is very heterogeneous. In many regions traditional birth attendants have a central role in deliveries and healers are often very influential in the society. Urbanisation has also created a large group of healers who have weak connections with both traditional healing and with modern medicine.

DEVELOPING THE TRAINING OF HEALTH WORKERS

Community participation

Health workers should work in close contact with the local community (village, tribe etc.), and be well aware of its life and attitudes. Good plans can be catastrophic, if the local conditions or values have not been taken into account. In Tanzania they once began to produce latrine covers with a rectangular hole. Nobody used these latrines, because the rectangular hole was associated with a grave, and who would relieve himself into a grave. The problem was solved easily by making the holes round.

The concept of community participation in health work and especially in health training has risen from a need to improve the knowledge of health workers about the community, to enhance their capability to work within the community and to strengthen the people's own participation in health-promoting activities. Community participation means, that one has to work *with* the people, not *for* the people (Chapter 44). People themselves have the best knowledge of values related to their own life and they should participate from the very beginning in planning and implementing health services and in working out the priorities. The health worker acts as a specialist giving advice and, by listening to the people, learns about the life of the community. The learning process should be interactive.

The principles of community participation should penetrate all health training. Besides the specific skills of the future health profession, the students should also learn to listen to people, to make community diagnoses and to find means to activate the community to promote health.

A *common language* is a prerequisite for successful work within a community. The health workers should speak the local language or languages, and use comprehensible concepts. This should be taken into account in their training. Teaching in local languages helps future work in the community. If this is not possible (there are many languages in the country or the teachers are expatriates), the importance of language and communication should be stressed in other ways.

The importance of women in health training

Taking care of ill people is often the work of women, and women are always responsible for most health-related tasks, such as preparing (often also producing) food, carrying drinking water and nursing the children. Looking at things from the women's point of view improves the effectiveness of all health education. Professional training of women, e.g. to health workers, also strengthens the status of women in the society. A woman with a profession can move around more easily and cannot is no longer completely dominated by a man. She will also have some money of her own, which improves the nutrition and health of both women and children.

The increase in women's literacy and basic education directly benefits the health of families. In both developing and industrialised countries the level of women's education is one of the main predicting factor for infant mortality (Chapters 5 and 7).

Appropriate technology

Poverty is the hallmark of developing countries. It is a major constraint against doing things in the way prescribed in textbooks. Therefore, it is necessary to find cheaper ways of action within the existing resources.

Technology is equipment and material as well as ways to use them. *Appropriate technology is a concept that emphasises the fact that the most sophisticated technology is not always the best.* Technology has to fit the society in which it is used, not only the task it is used for.

In training, the concept of appropriate technology requires that the constraints of the student's work are taken into account and that appropriate teaching methods and materials are used. In cultures where the tradition of story-telling is stronger than the use of written information, one could use narrative stories, allegories and proverbs instead of books full of cold facts.

Constraints

The constraints of training in developing countries are the same as in all work. Lack of materials such as books or slide projectors hampers training in a very concrete way. Local conditions must be taken into account at planning stage, and training should not depend on vulnerable technology.

It requires more expertise to recognise the constraints related to the social life of the students and teachers. Travelling and living far away from home can cause problems. These are often economic, because the economy of students (and often also of teachers) relies on work done in the fields at home. Intensive seminars or courses should not be conducted at the time of harvest, and travel problems can delay students in rainy seasons. There can also be religious or other local habits which make certain times or days of the year unsuitable for training.

Teaching methods and materials

Methods and means of teaching are excellent objects for appropriate technology development. Instead of blankly lecturing, a creative teacher transforms the content of learning into a story, which adjusts to the narrative tradition of the students. Role plays, puppet shows and learning by discussing and experimenting are examples of cheap and often effective means of teaching.

An important line of argument in selecting the teaching method is to keep the students keen and active. The best method for this can vary according to the level and cultural background of the students, of which the teacher must thus be well aware.

Teaching materials designed especially for developing countries exist in growing amounts. Still, much of the training has to be conducted with material prepared for industrialised countries. This implies a risk of admiring and overvaluing inappropriate technology. The local production of learning materials is highly recommended. In this way the local conditions and traditions can be taken into account and the many difficulties of foreign language and foreign authors are avoided.

In most cases the teacher has to provide most of the learning material him/herself. Good knowledge of the subject taught, simple language, clear pictures, clear thinking and elimination of the non-essential combined with good knowledge of the background of the students are basic elements of good teaching.

It is also very important to get practical experience during the study period. All

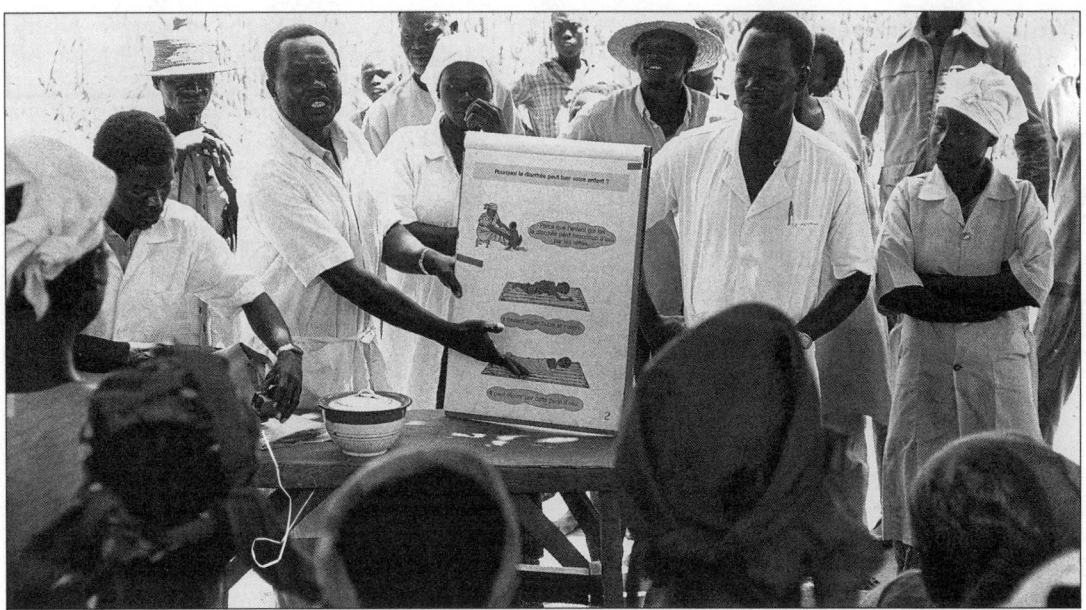

Training health workers in Chad. Photo: UNICEF/Maggie Murray-Lee

training should include field work, where knowledge achieved and skills learned could be practised in real life. This field work should be organised together with the community involved and it should preferably take place in rural areas.

CONTINUING EDUCATION

The effect of training is diluted, if knowledge is not updated and if one does not get feedback from one's work. In developing countries, networks of medical journals, newsletters, meetings, consultations and exchange of information between health workers are much more scarce and vulnerable than in industrialised countries. Trainers and planners have to take responsibility for the extension of education after the basic training. A dialogue between different levels of the health care system is as important for a village health worker as it is for a specialist in the hospital, and it must be seen as part of continuing education.

Private and non-governmental health care units often constitute independent organisations and separate nets of information flow. Those working in these hospitals should find out the situation of other PHC units and health workers in their catchment area. The same is of course true for government workers. Without this it is impossible to use and support all the health care capacity in the area.

Connections with traditional medicine

Western medicine has long been arrogant or even hostile towards traditional healing (Chapter 6). This has created a near total communication block between modern and traditional medicine. The training curricula of health workers seldom include information about the existing traditional healing methods, or any kind of dialogue.

Still, dialogue and cooperation between modern and traditional medicine are necessary elements in the development of effective and comprehensive health care systems in developing countries. It is not only a question of a unilateral process, where the representatives of traditional healing are told the truths of modern medicine. The health workers need the information of traditional healing methods in order to know what services are available and to learn new and different methods to approach people and their illnesses.

Often it is possible to agree about the division of labour, e.g. when the patient should be referred to a hospital. On the other hand many illnesses heal equally well with traditional as with modern methods. In many countries, for example, in India, Tanzania and Zaire, the training of traditional birth attendants to become village health workers has proved a successful solution for developing primary health care on the village level.

Connections between projects, sectors and authorities

A health worker does not work in isolation from other sectors of the society, e.g. water supply, agriculture and traffic. Most health problems in developing (and also in industrialised) countries are caused by matters beyond the reach of the health care system. Health workers and health trainers should learn to become people with influence who can inform the authorities about weaknesses and drawbacks and, when needed, organise common (also non-medical) actions.

Training health workers is essential to every country. Local resources and traditions determine the practical organisation of the training. Health worker training is a valuable form of development cooperation. It provides chances for the growth of resources in a poor country tactfully and with respect. The results will be good, if attention is paid to the universal principles of training, conditions in the developing country and the culture of the population served.

Additional reading

1. Government report. Analysis of the situation of children and women, and priorities for child survival and development. Dar es Salaam: Government of Tanzania and UNICEF, 1985.
2. Johnston MP, Rifkin SB, eds. Health care together. Training exercises for health workers in community based programmes. London: Macmillan, 1987.
3. Morley D, Rohde J, Williams G, eds. Practicing Health for All. London: Oxford Medical Publications, 1983.
4. Pizurki H, Mejia A, Butter I, Ewart L. Women as providers of health care. Geneva: WHO, 1987.
5. Sanders D, Craver R. The struggle for health. Medicine and the politics of underdevelopment. London: Macmillan, 1985.
6. Shaffer R. Beyond the dispensary. Nairobi: AMREF (undated).
7. Werner D. Where there is no doctor. London: Macmillan, 1980.
8. Werner D, Bower B. Helping health workers learn. Palo Alto, CA: The Hesperian Foundation, 1982.
9. WHO Study Group. Learning together to work together for health. Geneva: WHO, 1988.
10. WHO Study Group. Community based education of health personnel. Geneva: WHO, 1987.

About the authors

Kati Juva is a specialist in neurology. She works currently as a researcher at the Memory Research Unit, Department of Neurology, University of Helsinki, Finland. Her research subject is the social capacity of demented patients. Previously, she worked for several years as a consultant neurologist at the Helsinki City Hospital, Kivelä hospital. Dr Juva has also participated in a development cooperation project in Tanzania run by Physicians for Social Responsibility (PSR) in Finland about Community Participation in Health Worker Training, and has visited Tanzania repeatedly within this project. Kati Juva has also been the Secretary General of PSR since 1990. Her publications have dealt with dementia, ethics and development cooperation.

Matti Mäkelä started his career as a research fellow in community medicine. During 1985-1993 he has also been responsible for a project dealing with Community Participation in Health Worker Training in Tanzania, run by the organisation Physicians for Social Responsibility in Finland. Currently, he is specialising in clinical geriatrics, working as resident in Koskela Hospital, Helsinki. His main research interests are in the relationship between musculoskeletal disorders and disability in the community.

Lankinen KS, Bergström S, Mäkelä PH and Peltomaa M, eds.
Health and disease in developing countries. London:The Macmillan Press Limited, 1994:433–441.

44 COMMUNITY PARTICIPATION IN HEALTH CARE

Marja Liisa Swantz, M.A., Phil. Lic., Ph.D. (Uppsala), Professor (H.C.)
Tunturikatu 7 A 4, FIN-00100 Helsinki,
Finland

INTRODUCTION

The logic of community participation in health care derives from two basic principles, health as a total well-being, not only of individuals but of communities, and health care as the responsibility of people themselves, not only of professionals trained for the purpose. The main thrust of this chapter is to show that the concept of health and health care, as defined by the WHO, not only permits but demands participation of communities. It reflects on ways in which people can influence their own well-being, the conditions of their own lives and the communities of which they are part; in general, how people can be active in their own health care and in the health care of their communities.

At the WHO conference in Alma-Ata in 1978, the concept of health was interpreted as something more than absence of illness. Health was given the meaning of people's total well-being. As such it requires conditions in which such well-being can thrive. Since Alma-Ata, the concept of primary health care (PHC) has been common currency at least in the health rhetoric. An essential part of it is that a *community takes responsibility for its own health.* Consequently, issues outside the field of medicine, such as people's economic state, intra-household distribution of income and division of labour are decisive factors in determining the state of health. They have an impact on the standard of living quarters and latrines, on the level of maternity and child care, availability of

nutritious food and adequate diet, potable water and hygiene in general. This in turn makes it difficult for the medical personnel to see that this kind of general community welfare would be their concern.

We can legitimately ask whose responsibility communal health care is and how it best could be implemented? One simple answer is that it is people's own responsibility and they are the only ones who can coordinate the various aspects of their lives. Even if a single community cannot possibly implement everything that pertains to the upkeep of its health, the practical situation which people of the same locality share is the only level on which all the needs and resources of the community converge and have to be met in one way or another. People in all circumstances have to find time, space and resources to manage the problems they face daily. But they need the support of the state and the whole society in this endeavour.

For these reasons, a community should be involved in the planning phase as well as in implementation of the improved conditions in which its health care is carried out. The concern, the needs, the knowledge of available resources and the basic care are the basis on which community health care is built. What community participation is not, is taking part in an action which the health authorities plan from top. The community should be able to come into a consensus of how to balance its needs, and to call for external services from the authorities and from the institutionalised health system for those aspects which it cannot manage itself. The community needs to be equipped and empowered to do this. This requires flexibility from the institutional system, ability to link up with the local needs and local resources and to be ready to serve in the ways which the community requests.

Usually PHC is not defined in these broad terms. In practical situations, the medical personnel deal with health in terms of cure in an institutional setting and limit the preventive measures to medical aspects, such as vaccination or use of medicines rather than promoting general communal measures for prevention. This is reflected in the way allocations of finances and personnel are made, and thus also the emphasis in the training of health workers.

It is not surprising that the PHC personnel are primarily concerned of the lack of facilities for delivering health services. A recent meeting of a regional PHC committee serves as an illustration (PHC Committee Meeting of the Kilimanjaro Region, Mwanga town, March 1993). The main concerns were in themselves important issues: lack of medicines, syringes and gloves, lack of ambulances and poor transport in general, vaccines spoiled because of failing cold-chain, villages failing to pay for their health workers and AIDS programme halting because the donor funds did not reach the health workers. But there was nothing on the agenda on the causes of such failing facilities or of improving the economic conditions in which the service is delivered. The regional and district administrative staff was present to answer when their part in deliveries of goods or passing on information from the Ministry of Health was called into question, but not in order to plan together how to cooperate with the communities in improvement of hygiene or conditions of life in general.

It is naturally also in the interest of the common people to secure medical facilities for acutely ill patients in their communities. No enthusiasm for PHC can ignore people's preference for curative aspects of health care. But where the primary conditions of life are low and the causes of illnesses need to be urgently tackled *the preconditions for good health cannot be neglected*. The health institutions alone cannot be relied on to supply the basic health care system. Yet, they commonly become the ambition of both politicians and highly specialised medical personnel, for the former as a matter of prestige, for the latter for professional reasons.

The fragmented scientific system of the West with greater and greater specialisation often either prevents the formation of health care systems in which communities could be developed as the locii of health care, or makes its organisation unnecessarily complicated and costly. Similar difficulties prevent the system from taking care of an individual as a human being or a person. The person is rather divided into body parts and thrusted from one specialist to another, who seldom treat her as a whole being. This makes it difficult for the individual to find her own role in the process of gaining health. In these circumstances it is equally difficult to make room for the relatives or neighbours in the care of one another.

Thus the lessons from communal health care are for Westerners not only a matter of knowing something about health care in developing countries, they also force them to confront the same questions in their own society and to compare the growing ill health of Western communities with health care of other cultures.

The Nordic welfare societies have transferred the communal responsibility of people's health to the state through democratic government structures. But deteriorating economic conditions have brought social health care systems increasingly into crisis also in the countries in which people's health needs are extensively covered. Furthermore, it appears that the crisis is not only economic. The diminishing personal responsibility over the neighbour's needs within Western societies has brought about social ills which cannot be divorced from personal health. Experience shows that countries that build their health systems on voluntary health insurance, the USA as the prime example, also fail miserably in delivering adequate health care. In the USA 40 million citizens are outside any health insurance system. Some rethinking needs to be done, not only in developing countries, but also in the industrialised countries in which social health care is well established.

In what way can people influence their own well-being, the conditions of their lives and the lives of the communities of which they are part? What does the community participate in and how? How can people incorporate their own practices into the health care. These are questions that need to be asked when dealing with the topic of community participation in health care.

Table 44.1. Community participation requires people's cooperation at least in the following aspects of health care.

- in planning together with health planners and implementers the aspects of health care that concern them directly
- in improving economic and social conditions of the community, of its environment, of its households and of its individual members
- in improving the general hygiene of the community
- in engaging in a communal learning process about factors affecting health
- in developing a consensus in communal and individual health goals, and in preventive health measures, such as vaccinations, nutritional diets, and reduction of use of intoxicating and polluting substances
- taking part in communally organised work and services or in neighbourhood action
- in taking care of one's own and one's family's health to the best of one's ability

WHAT IS COMMUNITY PARTICIPATION?

Community participation in health care simply means that people in a community share in the responsibility of caring for their own health, in creating and preserving a healthy environment, in preventing any factors that could threaten people's health from getting a foothold in that community, and in doing their part for the maintenance of health in general. People's cooperation is required at least in the manifold aspects listed in Table 44.1.

A word of caution is, however, in order: the word participation has often been used in ways which makes mockery of the whole concept. Decision makers from the top or specialists and experts determine what is to be done in the communities and common people are then mobilised to take part in what has been planned and decided by others. *Making a community participate in predetermined measures is not worthy of being called participation.* Planning has too often been a top-down exercise in all areas of planning as long as planning for social or health services or for development in general has been an administrative practice.

The same is the case with the concept of health education. Educational theories have long since refuted the idea that children or hu-

man beings are like *tabula rasa*, empty boards which only wait to be written on. Yet in practice, people are continually treated as if they had no previous knowledge; they are made targets or objects of education. 'We have to educate them to follow the rules for good health' is the common way of putting it. People's ignorance in health matters is blamed to the point that other reasons for not adopting recommended health practices are often ignored.

People's poor participation is only partly due to lack of knowledge; head knowledge does not translate into action if there are reasons that prevent people from absorbing it. The reasons can be economic, social, cultural or simply attitudinal and motivational. The question of how valid these reasons are and how they can be overcome will be further discussed later on.

COMMUNITY PARTICIPATION IN PLANNING

What complicates direct participation?

In the Western democracies people participate in planning their health care mainly through elected representatives who on the national level influence matters through legislation and on the local level are members of health boards. However, most decisions bypass ordinary citizens who often become aware of what is happening only when they face the reality of reduced services, changed locations of health facilities, and changes in the fees or in the mode of delivery of the health care. Furthermore, in a welfare society in which services are organised by the state or by communal bodies, voluntary action for improvement of the environment or health care has become rare. With the deteriorating economic situation the idea of voluntary action has again come to the fore, as it has always been in the USA where the public Medicare has never been fully adopted.

A complicated society requires well educated and concerned people who are aware of their opportunies for decisions that concern them. Both in industrial and in developing countries ordinary citizens face the same difficulty that decisions concerning public services are removed away from them, but the obstacles in overcoming this difficulty are even bigger in the latter because the modern health service culture differs greatly from people's own ways of taking care of their health.

How can a whole community be involved in planning?

Direct community participation in planning is possible only on a local level. But there should also be channels for feedback from the local level up to the national level so that the public services would better correspond with people's own ways of thinking and acting.
Tanzanian experience. Participation of local people is greatly enhanced where there are institutional structures that facilitate communication. Tanzania serves as an illustrative case: the country created a ten-house cell-structure which linked up with administrative and party levels of village or branch, ward, division, district and region. This gave a political and institutional base for communication from top to bottom and, at least in theory, from bottom to top. The same message can be communicated throughout the nation and people can gather to debate the same issues countrywide. An innovation can be disseminated from one locality to other communities through such channels. In practice, however, it requires very special efforts from the bureaucrats and politicians to involve people in innovative action nationwide. In Tanzania it has been done through countrywide campaigns which have been organised for educational purposes. A participatory learning process turns in practice into planning, when people's awareness of their own situation is broadened.

In the Tanzanian case, the village government could choose whether they wanted to elect a special health committee or whether the committee for social and educational affairs could manage the health issues. Where externally induced and supported health programmes were carried out it was more likely that health committees came into being. The suggestion that each ten-house cell would have elected a person, preferably a woman, to be in charge of channelling health information and in being responsible if any special needs occurred in their unit, was never implemented in a larger scale, although good opportunities for it would have existed. The village council, or the village, branch or ward committees or corresponding other organs can take up health issues and act as the local planning agencies. The village assembly, consisting of all adult villagers, can also be called together to discuss and plan health matters.

Before meetings can make informed decisions, special participatory enquiries can be made whereby groups of health personnel, social and community workers and/or participatory researchers and representatives of the villages concerned involve themselves in face to face discussions with people in small groups and/or dividing themselves in teams of two contacting individuals randomly or selectively from different age and gender groups.

More often than not, instead of engaging people in debates and discussions, social and health surveys are made whereby people's only role is to answer questions that they have had no part in formulating. While such surveys do gather data about the communities, they do not allow people to participate in the issues that they themselves consider to be the most important ones. People should not be participating only in matters that outsiders think are necessary. People's participation in planning means giving them voice from the start and joining them in those plans which they initiate. Other ideas from outside can then be also introduced and put into practice.

Planning through practice

Planning in a bureaucratic system is done as a theoretical exercise, not integrated with practice. Educated and modernised groups at times formalise even their own social planning for weddings and funerals to the point of a minute detail in written agendas. But the African traditional way of planning for a ritual process or a celebration begins implementation after the first stage of planning. The planning evolves while the activities are carried out in gradual implementation of the mentally formed plan. The ritual preparations begin after the invited people have arrived in the place of celebration. Each has a task to perform.

What is needed is a mental image of what is going to take place, but not a carefully written document with many details. The details are worked out when the implementation begins and there is something concrete to relate to. The initial plan can be modified according to the situational need. Concrete steps are needed soon after the ideas have been discussed to sustain commitment; the common people have too often seen plans that remain empty words, and cannot afford to put forth an effort for something that never materialises.

Formal and informal ways of planning

An often seen form of externally imposed planning is to go to a village, to gather a few people together who happen to be available and then start asking questions. Another extreme is to contact only the officials and not the authentic representatives of the communities. Listening to officials, teachers, government workers, etc., who are not long-time members of the community, is an easy way of getting information because they speak the same language as the planners, but this will give often a distorted picture.

In their work, the outsiders have probably met resistance; the local people have been unwilling to cooperate in whatever measures they have tried to promote. The external workers have formed a basically negative attitude toward 'these people here', as they call them. This attitude in itself already cautions against the engagement of this category of people as the guides to the community. They need to be drawn into the community action and to be counted as members of the community, but not consulted as the primary category.

Any agency, internal or external, government or otherwise, engaged in an effort to gain the cooperation of a community has to make some initial contacts to gain knowledge of the institutional forms through which the local people operate. In this, a period of participation in the everyday life of the community is of great help. Participation in this sense means taking part in people's daily activities, talking with them on the road, in the places where they wait around, in bars and cafes, in the fields and other places of work. Through free, yet in suitable places slightly directed, discussions more understanding of how the community operates can be gained than through formal surveys and questionnaires. But these contacts cannot replace the formal contact and formal meetings.

Recently, I was asked to make a brief visit to a project area to find out how the social measures that a project was to implement had been carried out. I visited some of the villages and talked to a few people at random, but also got hold of the village secretary and an elderly member of the village council. To my question whether the project had communicated with the village the answer was: '*Amekuja lakini amesema na watoto tu*' (He came but he only talked with 'children'), meaning that the people the person had contacted were not those with any authority to speak for the village. Yet the village opinion was being quoted within the project on the basis of such contacts.

It is not easy to balance between the formal and informal structures, since the formal channels get often blocked if even one person in a position of authority has his own axe to grind and does not think of the good of the community. But the formal channels cannot be completely by-passed if the community is to act on its own initiative. Even when people do not agree with their leadership, they are seldom willing to start any action if the formal leaders have not been contacted. People have experienced that their efforts can be easily hampered if they do not follow the proper channels. Yet the danger is probably greater that people mind the authorities too much rather than too little and do not take action before the authorities have been consulted. There is much ambiguity about the matter at this time, when the previous one-party structures are being abolished in many African countries.

The role of indigenous institutions in planning

Indigenous organisational forms have seldom been taken seriously or become part of the modern system because they have been considered too traditional and thus negative in the light of the scientifically based medical profession. In Tanzania, people themselves introduced a traditional guarding system, *sungusungu*, which the political party was first suspicious of. Later the party realised its benefits and adopted the system of people's own patrolling teams for the whole country.

In the same vein, the health authorities have at times contacted traditional health practitioners and their practice has been used for channelling health information, but less often have they been involved in planning the cooperation between the traditional and modern health services. They have rather been incorporated in pre-planned measures, as is the case in fighting cholera or more recently AIDS. Yet the involvement of the traditional health personnel, whether they are healers, diviners who diagnose the illnesses or birth attendants, would give much initial information and basic knowledge about the communities at the planning stage. This requires, however, a participatory research effort.

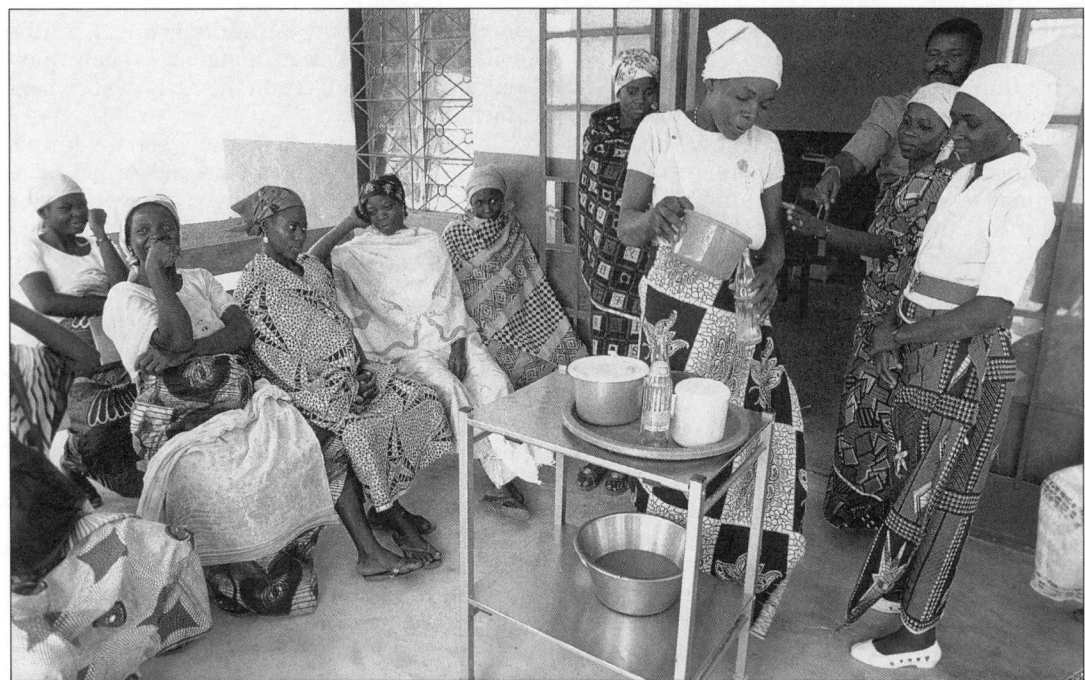

Community participation in health care simply means that people in a community share in the responsibility of caring for their own health like the Nigerian women here, teaching the use of ORS to each other.
Photo: UNICEF/Sean Sprague

WHAT MOTIVATES PEOPLE?

The implementation of health care should not be dependent on the funds allocated from outside the community. In fact, a lot of preventive health measures can be taken with no financial contributions. The question is how to balance between rules, regulations, orders, campaigns, mobilisation (which tend to dominate) and free voluntary action motivated by people's own initiatives and interest. People are motivated if matters which are central to them are taken seriously. If a group considers water the most important issue and there are water sources available but not open to them, ways have to be found to accommodate to their primary need, if the group's cooperation is sought further.

Involving people in the planning and implementation of health measures must start from some positive action. Recent campaigns in Dar es Salaam for cleaning up the city have been a one-man show, but people have cooperated at times very well, because what he is doing meets an acutely felt need. The Minister for Home Affairs of Tanzania has taken it upon himself to cleanse the country from corruption and filth and has been relentlessly pursuing

the cause with only little money incentives. The media coverage that he has got and the sympathetic attitude of people towards his efforts have given him a lot of cooperation.

In contrast, the city authorities, on their part, have carried a constant war of harassment against people who try to make their living by engaging in a great variety of income-earning activities.[1] The city meets its people with rules and regulations, but the whole population knows that their enforcement has become the main channel for the police and city personnel to gain extra income. The city has done little to assist its residents to clean up their corners nor has it provided the trucks or other services to do so. It comes with demands that the latrine pits have to be emptied, but people with small material means do not have the funds each individually to hire refuse trucks to suck the muck. In these conditions people have no motivation to cooperate with the city authorities.

SOCIOECONOMIC IMPROVEMENT OF LIVING CONDITIONS

A Kenyan researcher doing his doctoral work in nutritional sociology in Finland was asked to participate in a Kenyan–Finnish health project in Western Kenya. His interest was to do a study of the nutritional status in the communities in which the project was carried out. He was told that if that was his interest he did not fit into the planned project. This he could not accept and it led him to adopt an approach to his study of nutritional sociology that he named a SPEC (socio-political-economic-cultural) approach. He wanted to show that nutrition as part of health care could not be tackled as an isolated issue if all aspects of communal life were not considered at the same time. He worked out a participatory approach in which he included all aspects that affected people's ways of maintaining good nutritional status and thus health.[2]

It was not surprising that the researcher had a difficult time working out such a broad basis for his study and even harder time to have it accepted as a sociological thesis. The good scientific rule of limiting the field of one's study did not make sense to him in the practical situation which he faced. It made it clear to him that science alone is not the best guide for practical life, not even for communal health. Medical personnel are trained to deal with health problems primarily as part of the medical system. PHC requires openness for cooperation with many other field workers.

It is self-evident today that without eradication of the basic poverty, decisive steps in improving people's health cannot be taken. But health hazards have become even more obvious with the new technologies in industrial countries, requiring the same participation and alertness as is required from the people in developing countries. Both poverty and wealth require the same degree of people's participation in protecting their health.

Health personnel need to work in cooperation with nutrition, agricultural, livestock and fishing extension workers and to assist in holistic planning for improvement of the economic standard in specific communities. Milking goats for family use, planting vegetable gardens and fruit trees, growing beans, collecting leaves, roots, berries and mushrooms, etc. can become communal thrusts, if the personnel from different sectors decide to work together and lead the way with their own example.

Hospitals and clinics, where patients and above all the relatives often spend hours in waiting, could have special spaces for training purposes which combine ideas and practice for nutrition and income earning. There is no reason why an agriculturalist could not spend some hours a week in talking to clients in health institutions, especially because the standard complaint is that they cannot do their work because of lack of transportation. The patients have to pay for their own transport and make their way to the hospital or clinic. The extension officers could make use of this opportunity, if their interest really was in incorporating men and women in embetterment of life.

In many countries the relatives stay near the hospital compounds and cook their own meals. Organising proper stalls for acquiring their provisions or encouraging local entrepreneurs to keep hygienic eating places in close neighbourhood of the health institutions would offer a market for many. Institutions can also make catering arrangements with local producers and traders in order to create local links and networks which could provide a steady supply of food supplies and thereby strengthen the local market. The decreased transport costs would allow cheaper price range and more sales. Convenience and expediency often compel caterers for local institutions to by-pass the local markets. Yet with cooperation and initial hard effort new opportunities can be offered for local producers for example by organising product collection points for small producers from which bigger transporters could collect the supplies for the institutions, much like milk is collected for dairies.

The crucial point is that in organising the health services sufficient attention is simultaneously paid to strengthening the underlying economic base and structural factors, which maintain the conditions of poverty. Community committees, in which the educated members of community can meet local people in an intense effort to improve the conditions of the community, would go a long way in engaging also the health personnel in community effort. Associations established for economic and social improvement by city-dwelling members of rural communities in Africa would be natural partners in such efforts.

Class differences prevent the wealthier sections of population from seeing the acute problems of their neighbours. The participation of the civil servants or private entrepreneurs should be visible in examples shown and in putting forth financial resources. The plans for costing services are too often concerned about the payments of the poor and poorest rather than charging according to capacity or counting the physical work done by the poor as the payment. Communal voluntary work needs to be recorded and credited as payments made by the individuals and households that participate in a communal action.

HOW TO WORK WITH PEOPLE FOR IMPROVED CONDITIONS?

Earlier, when the health care system included public health nurses who visited homes, they had better opportunity for challenging people to improve hygiene and for guiding them to grow nutritious food and to adopt sound health habits which then could become part of their daily routine. The public health nurses worked in cooperation or parallel with citizens' movements. This kind of development is familiar from the history of many developed and even developing countries.

There are many fewer home-visits today than before. Because of lack of funds, the coverage for home consultations has been minimised and thus one of the most effective means of mutual cooperation has been abolished. This vacuum is in many places being filled with voluntary community action and with citizens' self-help movements. Especially women have set up new kinds of organisations, which serve both their own economic needs in a modest way, but also give support to special needs in the form of small scale support in kind or capital, training for income earning purposes, legal advice and defence, care of orphans where parents have died of AIDS and in other forms geared to specific situational needs.[3]

In Tanzania, such programmes as *Wakati wa Furaha* (Time of joy or happy time), *Mtu Ni Afya* (To be a human being means being healthy), or *Chakula Ni Uhai* (Food is life) were organised in the 1970s to motivate people to action in regard to their own health. Village level committees and study groups were formed which gathered to listen to health lessons on radio and to plan and to put into action in their immediate surroundings what they learned. A high degree of participation was accomplished through these programmes, but their success depended naturally on the degree of local work accomplished before the radio programmes started and during and after the programme.[4]

Another way of using the means of communication has been to involve writers and drama groups, creating and using local channels for communicating health information and engaging press and media people in the training for these efforts. An example of this was a programme organised in cooperation between the Tampere University and Tanzanian health and media institutions. It was a significant pioneering effort with good local results, even spreading to the national media.[5]

The AIDS programmes and other community action programmes have employed popular theatre. People in Africa have a tremendous gift for acting out their problems and then discussing them with the audience in a way which makes an impression and can lead to action.

PARALLEL HEALTH SYSTEMS

The traditional therapies are often more holistic than modern medicine and could give the modern practitioner new understanding of people's needs for health care. Listening to people would also show how the same people use parallel medical systems. The motivation cannot be raised simply by giving education. There is a need to understand more deeply the reasons for treating both the cause and the symptoms of illnesses and threats of illnesses within parallel systems. The modern system deals with the symptoms while the more traditional ways are used for feeling at home in one's body, for warding off ills and diseases and for determining the causes for them (Chapter 6).

The medical practitioners in a developing country come to see the negative effects of the traditional practices and thus seldom see anything worth adopting in them or even worth knowing about. Patients are brought into hospitals after they have been treated by traditional practitioners and cannot any longer be saved. Overdoses of drugs are given and modern medicines are at times mixed in with the traditional ones.

Misuse is not the whole picture. How the patient feels about the *mganga*, the healer, is more important to him or her than the effectiveness of the substance itself. The way the illness is diagnosed and the medicine or therapy prescribed, the way the medicine is acquired and therapy applied in personal terms may have a psychological effect and it gives social support which is perhaps more than half the cure.

Thus when community participation is the aim, it has to start from where the people are and what they have to contribute to their own health care. It does not mean that people would not want to accept modern health services, but they might be passive or even react against them if they do not correspond with their experience or are too difficult to adopt. However, the main difficulty is not lack of community participation in the curative services. They are usually overburdened, short of facilities and medicines or make business with people's health. – The difficulty is in creating a healthy environment and needed economic standard for overcoming the health hazards that accompany poverty.

CONCLUSION

Community participation in health care can be accomplished if people are sufficiently motivated to care for their own health and to improve their own situation. The reason why most efforts for involving people in their own health measures have only meagre results depends on a top-down approach, lack of communication on the local level, not taking seriously the people's own ideas and primary needs, not putting forth sufficient resources for general health measures, and above all, not making an integrated effort to improve the total well-being of the people concerned.

People's own ways of health care and cure and maternal and child care need to be incorporated by a positive approach to their good intention and by upgrading or improving the local practices. The educated and wealthier sections of the population must be involved financially and through example and the community action by the poor credited as their payments toward their health care.

Positive measures can be taken if the medical people do not take too narrow a professional view of health care and are able to cooperate and support measures from other sectors as well as citizens voluntary efforts to supplement the official public services. Yet the main responsibility for public health and conditions amenable to maintaining health remains in the hands of the state.

References

1. Tripp A. The urban informal economy and the State in Tanzania. Evanston: Northwestern University, 1991. (Dissertation.)
2. K'Okul R. Maternal and child health in Kenya. Monograph of the Finnish Society for Development Studies No 4, in cooperation with the Scandinavian Institute of African Studies, Jyväskylä, 1991
3. Hall, B. Wakati wa furaha. An evaluation of a Radio Study Group Campaign. Uppsala: Scandinavian Institute of African Studies, 1973. (Research Report 13.)
4. Kivikuru UM. Timed novelties or creative culture? A study on the role of mass communication in peripheral nations. Helsinki: University of Helsinki, Department of Communication, 1990. (Publications IF/10/90).
5. Swantz ML. Community and Healing among the Zaramo in Tanzania. Soc Sci Med 1979;138:169–73.

About the author

Marja Liisa Swantz has specialised in grassroots development research. As an anthropologist she has centered her research on the role of culture in the development process with special reference to women. She has pioneered participatory research approaches in development studies incorporating the communities under study into the research process. In cooperation with the Ministry of Health in Tanzania she has initiated a Village Participation Programme for the health workers training institutes. Before her recent retirement she was the Director and Research Director of the Institute of Development Studies at the University of Helsinki. Besides articles on participatory approach to development and anthropology of health she has published the books 'Transfer of technology as an intercultural process', and 'Women in development: a creative role denied?'.

Lankinen KS, Bergström S, Mäkelä PH and Peltomaa M, eds.
Health and disease in developing countries. London:The Macmillan Press Limited, 1994:443–451.

45 INFORMATION FOR A CHANGE

Sarah B J Macfarlane, B.A., M.Sc.
Liverpool School of Tropical Medicine,
Unit for Statistics and Epidemiology
Pembroke Place, Liverpool L3 5QA,
United Kingdom

Assefaw Tekeste, M.D.
Liverpool School of Tropical Medicine,
Unit for Statistics and Epidemiology
Pembroke Place, Liverpool L3 5QA,
United Kingdom

INTRODUCTION

'Better a handful of produce than a mountain of information.'
— *An Eritrean proverb*

Information is available to all who look for it. The skill is to know why to look, what to look for, where to look and how to look at it.

Most ministries of health expect staff at all levels to contribute to the routine reporting of financial, management and epidemiological information. This involves a process of observing, recording, transcribing, reporting, manipulating and interpreting *data* in order to provide the *information* required to set priorities, allocate resources and to evaluate interventions. The management of the data may be more or less sophisticated, particularly with the widespread availability of computers.

The whole process may be referred to as a health information system, a management information system, a health management information system, a management information and evaluation system or a public health surveillance system. Each term represents a difference of emphasis but all have the word *system* in common. Unfortunately, this terminology has led to certain misconceptions about the management of health information.

The use of the word system implies a degree of organisational efficiency, which may not exist and which may actually be counter-productive to achieve. Furthermore, to equate the collection of information with routine recording and reporting is to relieve individuals of their own initiative to look for and use information.

If change is the goal of the health care system, then the focus of attention should not be on the organisation of the information but on the milieux in which informed decisions can be made.

CHANGE

Desirable change can be defined as an improvement in health that is recognised and maintained by pressure from the people. Change that is imposed from above, without any attempt to gain the awareness of the people, is seldom sustainable. If information is to be used to facilitate sustainable change then consideration has to be given not only to the requirements of the government but also to the requirements of the people. The availability of information cannot facilitate the process of change without political commitment and participation of the people. What, then, is information and how can it be harnessed to achieve change?

Information is produced as part of a process of enquiry. Facts and figures, or data, are assembled and interpreted to answer questions. Data become information when conclusions are drawn. The transformation is sometimes intangible but usually involves comparison with other data. For example, the infant mortality rate for a country remains a piece of data unless it can be assessed in relation to other values such as those of other countries in a similar state of development. Comparisons may be made, for example, over time, between population groups, with an achievement target or with a financial constraint, depending on the nature of the question. The data for the

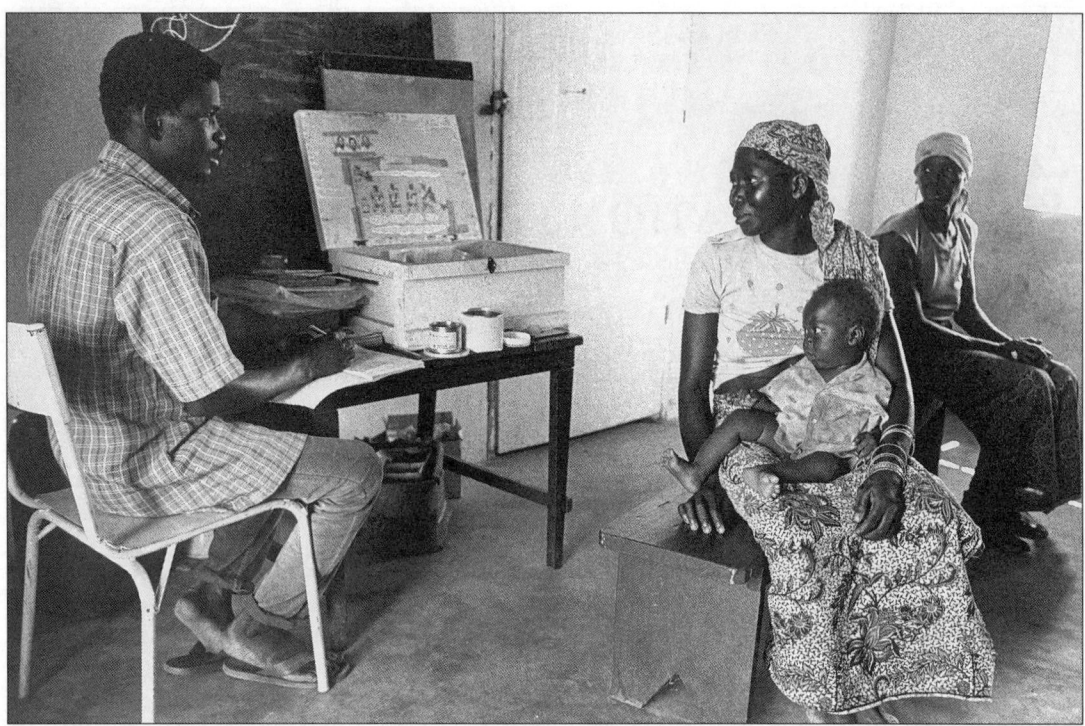

Descriptive information relating to health care delivery is best obtained from routine health service records. A health worker and his patients in Chad. Photo: UNICEF/Maggie Murray-Lee

comparison may be in the mind of the questioner or may be provided as part of the answer to the question. Only a small proportion of questions result, or are even intended to result, in any action. This depends on the motivation behind the question and the availability of resources.

Questions may be descriptive in their nature like 'what is the size of the problem?', for example 'What are the immunisation coverage rates in different districts?' The answer can be used for reporting purposes but in isolation this type of question leads to no action. If the motivation behind the question is to identify and encourage those districts that are falling behind their targets then it is necessary to find out why. The question becomes analytical, for example 'why does the problem occur?' or, in this case, 'why are these districts falling behind?' There may be shortages of resources or some inefficiency in their management. Another possibility is that the community has not recognised the need for this intervention and that time would be best spent discussing the situation with the community leaders and finding out their priorities. This provides the community with the opportunity to ask the questions and

obtain the information that it requires to assess the possibility that immunisation will bring about a desired change in the health of its children. The transfer of this type of information is difficult to incorporate into an information system and is often ignored.

INFORMATION REQUIREMENTS

Information requirements depend on the decisions being made at all levels of the health care system: politicians, professionals and people. They have differing resources at their disposal and differing abilities to make decisions and to achieve change. It is important to recognise the contribution of each to the other's decisions and to facilitate the flow of information within the decision-making structure.

Over the last two decades the need for decentralised health systems has become very obvious.[1] This is achieved by delegating the power of decision making and the control of resources from the centre to the periphery, that is from the state to region, district and finally to the people. As decentralisation cannot exist without centralisation, the challenge is to strike a balance between the two. The ethical base of any information system should be to provide the data required at both ends.

The people

Community participation has become a popular slogan repeated alike by democratic governments, by military dictators and by multilateral aid agencies. The issue is whether or not communities can acquire all the information needed to understand the factors that affect their health.

Most communities have opinion leaders selected or elected to assess and represent the needs of the community. When health workers listen to the opinions of community leaders they gain a more comprehensive picture than is possible through any routine reporting. The role of community leaders can be strengthened, however, by providing them with the additional information they need to evaluate the services provided. The information exchanged may relate to disease experience, environmental development, health promotion or perceived need.

The health workers

Staff in the department of health (or in regional offices) account for the allocation of resources by describing their distribution and measuring the efficiency and effectiveness of health policy. Their requirements for information range from the assessment of epidemiological risk to the calculation of economic costs and benefits. The department of health will also be expected to produce information to meet agendas other than its own, for example, for other ministries and for international agencies. This can result in an overambitious and poorly focused collection of information.

The problems at this level are a heavy dependence on others for the provision of information, the types of information collected and also the top down nature of the response. There is no reason why regional or district level managers should not specify their own additional information requirements, particularly in the context of decentralisation. Regrettably, the format is usually accepted from above.

The management information requirements of district level managers tend to focus more on accountability for resources received, supervision of staff and the redistribution of existing resources. But epidemiological information is also important because it provides an indication of the risk groups to which resources should be allocated. For practitioners, decisions relate not only to individual patients but also to the implementation of prevention and control programmes. Their concern is to deliver services to the community in line with their plans and targets.

THE CONCEPT OF SURVEILLANCE

The term surveillance was first used by epidemiologists to describe a systematic method of monitoring the occurrence of disease in individuals in order to control its spread in the community.[2] The concept has recently been broadened to include other events of public health interest, for example: low birth weight, malnutrition, disability, accidents, death etc. The aim of a surveillance system is to provide information for planning, implementation and evaluation of public health programmes.

Surveillance is primarily concerned with the incidence and magnitude of health events. This requires not only the selection of health events for surveillance but also the definition of both the numerator (the event) and the denominator (the population base). Selection of health events to be recorded depends on the priorities of the country and also on the requirements of international reporting. Definition of the health event (e.g. a person acquiring a specific condition) is likely to invoke more serious problems than definition of the population base. Gross errors in population estimates will undermine the comparison of rates between populations but are less important in time trend comparisons within the same population. The definition of the health event, on the other hand, depends on the availability of a recognised classification that can be modified to suit the qualifications of the health worker responsible for reporting the event and the facilities available.

Disease surveillance is practised worldwide for a number of internationally reportable diseases.[3] However, the choice of specific diseases for national surveillance should relate to their public health importance and to the potential for their prevention and control. Standard case definitions are available, for example in the International Classification of Diseases.[4] It is important to differentiate between medical and lay definitions depending on the educational background of the health worker and the laboratory facilities available to confirm the diagnosis. There may also be problems in recording and reporting multiple diagnoses and in differentiating new cases from old. Because of the poor coverage of health care in many countries, disease surveillance usually provides only a picture of diseases seen and their relative importance rather than any accurate estimates of prevalence or incidence.

Disease incidence is not the sole focus of disease surveillance. Other activities include the assessment of control measures. The targeting of specific diseases has resulted in a number of vertical control programmes, for example malaria, tuberculosis, AIDS etc. One programme which has been developed internationally and received considerable donor funding is the Expanded Programme on Immunization (Chapter 48). This brings with it a recommended information system which includes not only the reporting of targeted diseases but also evaluations of the cold chain and immunisation coverage surveys.

Nutritional surveillance is practised in many countries and provides important indicators of health and development. The event in this case is usually the occurrence of malnutrition in a young child. The magnitude of the problem varies according to the definition of malnutrition and the reference population with which the children are compared. The tendency to focus on anthropometry reflects the desire to measure rather than observe. Comprehensive nutritional surveillance needs to take into account food availability, food habits and the purchasing power of risk groups.

Surveillance is most comprehensive when information is based on populations rather than facilities. There are some projects which have successfully involved community members in the surveillance process. The emphasis of *national surveillance*, however, is on events identified by health professionals. The challenge is to add another dimension to surveillance systems by including events identified by the community.

OBTAINING INFORMATION

It is important to explore all possible sources of information, both formal and informal, and to consider ways of collecting, managing and interpreting it to be as useful as possible. The choice depends on information requirements and the resources available. The following section describes some of the formal methods that can be used by health workers to build up profiles of the communities that they serve. More informal methods may also be used, particularly by community leaders.

Collection

Routine health service records. Descriptive information relating to health care delivery is best obtained from routine health service records. Ongoing records are kept at each health facility and data are extracted regularly and transcribed onto the report forms required by the next administrative level. Records relate to patient characteristics (medical records), laboratory results, preventive and promotive activities, stock control and staff management.

At health centres it is common for patient diagnoses to be kept in outpatient or inpatient registers making it very difficult to cross-reference between patient visits. Individual cards may be used for maternal and child health activities, for example to follow a mother and child from first antenatal visit to completion of immunisation of the child. Files of family records have been successfully introduced into some health centres. In some cases patients keep their own records, for example 'Road to Health' charts track the child's progress from birth to 5 years in terms of growth and immunisation status.

The quality and quantity of hospital records vary enormously. In addition to information required for hospital management and individual patient management, the hospitals are usually required to report to the government on the use of pharmaceuticals, finance, bed occupancy and disease occurrence. Some hospitals have a very sophisticated computerised records system whereas in others the operational centre is a large room piled high with dusty forms.

Household registration. Health service records are demand-based and should ideally be complemented by population-based information. Community health workers are often expected to maintain records about the families or households in their catchment area. These may take the form of a series of registers of different population groups, for example children under five or couples eligible for family planning advice. Sometimes household records are more comprehensive containing demographic, epidemiological and environmental information about the household and its members. A family diary may even be kept by the family itself.

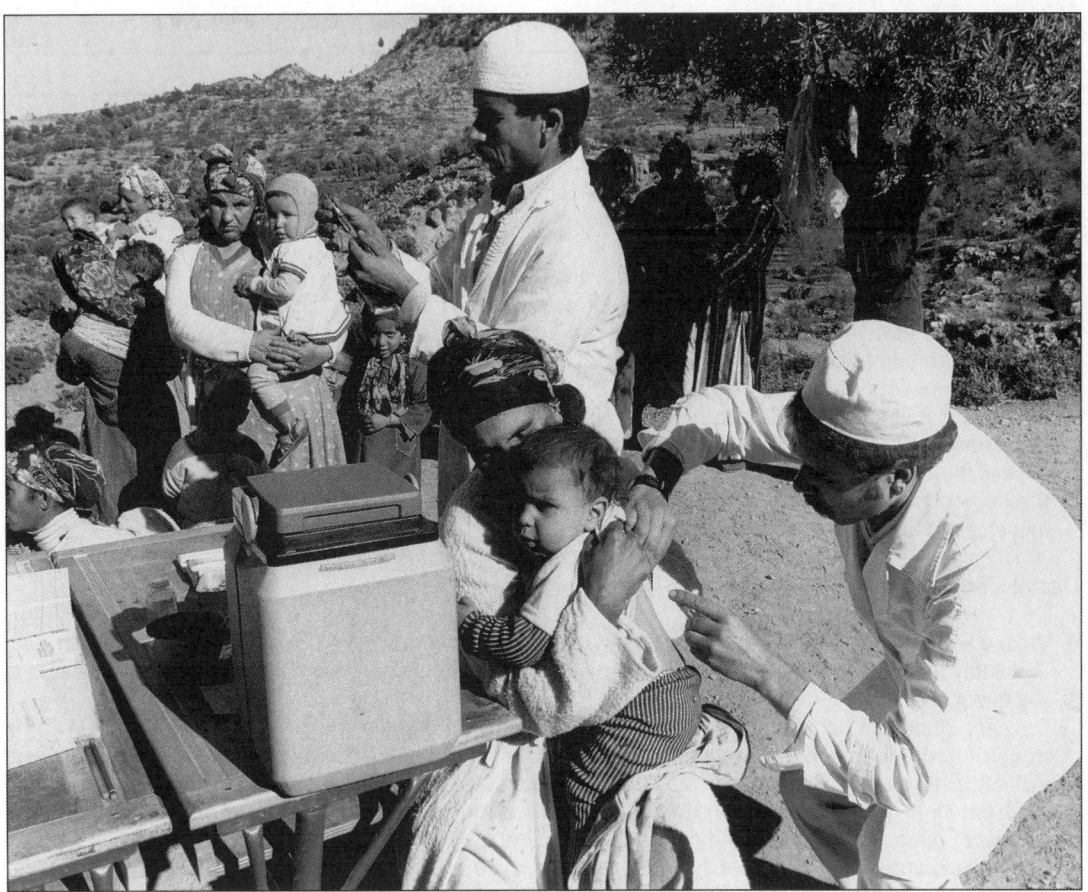

Extended Programme on Immunization includes a comprehensive information system which reports targeted diseases, but also facilitates evaluation of the cold chain and immunisation coverage. Vaccination day in Morocco. Photo: UNICEF/Amy Zuckerman

The primary motive for keeping such records may be unclear even to the community health worker. If the motivation appears solely to come from above then recording and reporting will become a burden with very little action on the ground. When the motivation is clearly to involve the community and the health worker in the identification of their own problems it is more likely that they will be solved not only for the individual but also for the village.

Special surveys. Cross-sectional surveys are conducted to describe population characteristics, for example mortality, fertility, prevalence of disease, coverage of services, knowledge, attitudes and practice in relation to health and health care.[5] Large scale surveys are conducted at national or regional level but smaller scale surveys can be undertaken within the district or even by health centre staff. Time and resources can be saved by keeping questionnaires short, giving careful consideration to selecting the sample size and by choosing a convenient means of sampling which is both rapid and efficient.

Baseline information, such as demographic trends in mortality and fertility, is best obtained by sampling the population and administering a household questionnaire. The effectiveness of intervention programmes is sometimes evaluated by comparing cross-sectional information on the population before and after the intervention, for example: immunisation coverage surveys to assess vaccination campaigns; surveys of nutritional status to assess supplementary feeding programmes; surveys of tuberculosis to assess its control programmes. While the surveys will provide

Table 45.1. Guidelines for manager practitioners in evaluating the availability of information.

Collection and management

1. Make a list of all the reports received and transmitted. Describe the reporting process including why the data are being collected and whose responsibility it is to collect and transcribe them.
2. Make a list of the items of data contained in each report and assess their reliability in terms of accuracy of recording and reporting, speed of reporting, representativeness with respect to the population being covered and their sensitivity and specificity.
3. How are the data handled? Are the staff involved carefully supervised? If computers are used, seek some outside expertise to assess the use of software and hardware. This can be done at a modest level but it is always worth updating knowledge and seeking advice.
4. Consider the primary use of the data which are transmitted to or within the health facility. Are they used for any purpose at the point of collection? Discuss the value of the data with the staff involved. How could the data be used in discussion with community leaders to solve their perceived health problems? What additional information do staff and community leaders need?
5. Assess the communication system. Is there an effective means of listening to the views of staff and to the opinion leaders of the community? How good is communication with the next administrative level? Is it efficient and effective? How could it be improved?

Usefulness

6. Make a list of the questions that are important to the running of the facility. Using the list compiled in Step 2, identify the subset of data items which provide information at this level. Can they provide answers to the questions?
7. For each question, think about how the data could provide the information required. Can the data be transformed into indicators by taking denominators into account (coverage rates, prevalence and incidence rates etc.)? Can the indicators be dis-aggregated: is it possible to make comparisons between different time periods and/or between different population groups (geographic, demographic, socioeconomic etc.)? Can the indicators be displayed graphically for ease of presentation?
8. Could the same questions be answered with alternative or additional information? Consider here the possibilities of focus group discussions, rapid assessment and epidemiological surveys before suggesting additional routine data collection. Assess the resources required and the feasibility in terms of skills available.
9. What action could be taken on the basis of the answers to these questions? These might include management of resources (reallocation or requests for more), or management of health programmes (follow up of an epidemic outbreak and initiation of preventive activities).
10. Consider the overall objectives of the health facility and list additional questions and the information required to answer them. Is additional information collection required?

---

a record of change in population characteristics it may not be easy to associate the change specifically with the intervention.

Rapid assessment. Traditional epidemiological survey methods may not be appropriate when there are shortages of skilled staff and financial resources. Furthermore, formal surveys are not necessarily the most efficient or the most appropriate method of obtaining qualitative information. Procedures for rapid assessment are becoming increasingly popular in the assessment of health and development needs.[6,7] They provide a balance of qualitative and quantitative approaches and can be applied in almost any context and utilised by different planning sectors. Small teams of investigators from a wide spectrum of backgrounds, both community and professional, can assess the sociological, agricultural, economic and health characteristics of a community within a short time by using a variety of methods such as: semi-structured interviewing, focus group discussions, direct observations of carefully chosen indicators and ranking exercises. The participatory approach necessitates the transfer of skills to the community and their involvement in the analysis of their own health and development needs.

The approach has been used predominantly by non-governmental organisations in situations requiring rapid assessment, for example amongst refugees. It has been beneficial in the preparation, implementation and evaluation of community projects, and complements the more traditional approaches to research and health information activities. It is tempting to think that rapid assessment is easier to conduct than more traditional survey methodology, but the skills are varied and require training to implement.

Management

Communication. This the point at which to introduce the technocrats, that is epidemiologists, statisticians and health information specialists, who are professionally responsible for the management of the information. Their network of staff may extend from the epidemiology section of the department of health as far as the district or even the health centre, depending on the country. Reporting systems are commonly criticised for focusing on the upward flow of information without any responding feedback. Another problem lies in poor horizontal communication between the professionals and decision makers. In extreme situations information is seen as the domain of the technocrats to transmit vertically between themselves without its use by decision makers at the point of collection.

Information exchange is the key to good management and epidemiology. Management issues and epidemics can be controlled by observation, communication and action. Transmission may be by messenger, telephone, radio or satellite so long as the information communicated is relevant, accurate and timely. Communication only exists when there is a two-way horizontal and vertical response.

The role of computers. The role of computers has to be continually reassessed in pace with technological developments.[8] Feasibility can be measured in terms of the physical size of the computer, its processing speed and memory capacity, the maintenance requirements of the computer and its peripherals, the availability of suitable software and of relevant computer expertise and the financial outlay involved in establishing a computer system. Another dimension has been added with the introduction of networking facilities and the possibilities of satellite communication.

Justification for the introduction of computers can be made on the grounds of ease of manipulation and speed of data processing, improved supervision of quality of data recorded, greater coordination of different types of information, more sophistication and flexibility in the analysis of data and improvement in presentation of reports and speed of feedback. Experience has shown, however, that the introduction of computers can result in overambitious collection of data, backlogs of records to be entered into the computer, inadequate supervision of the quality of data, misuse of sophisticated software packages, delays in the production of reports and little improvement in feedback.

Psychological dependence on the computer for processing the data into information may replace intelligent and common sense interpretation. Another problem is that it is easier to enter quantitative data into a computer than to enter qualitative data resulting in a tendency to ignore the information which can be provided directly by the community.

Interpretation

Straight counts of the numbers of events are useful to community leaders but are only informative to managers if the event is very rare. It is easier to interpret information once the data have been transformed into indices or indicators, for example bed occupancy rate, immunisation coverage rate, low birth weight rate, infant mortality rate, malnutrition rate, morbidity rates etc. These are formed by relating the number of events to the population at risk. The indicators provide a means of comparison in time and place. Trends in time of morbidity rates, for example, can be examined in order to identify unusual occurrence of disease. The geographical distribution of indicators is important for targeting inequalities in health status and also in the assessment of efficiency of health care delivery.

Reporting systems demand that an aggregate figure is passed to the next level up. The department of health will require the antenatal coverage rate for each region (aggregated from aggregate reports from all the districts in the region) from which it will calculate an overall antenatal coverage rate for the country. The resulting figure may be compared with some target but if improvements are required it is the distribution of the rates between regions that should be examined in order to identify those regions which need to improve. Similarly at regional level, while it is the aggregate figure that has been reported to the department, the figure dis-aggregated by district provides more information. This argument can be extended as far as the community health worker who should be able to identify those women in a village who have not received antenatal care and why. It is the responsibility of the reporter to retain the disaggregated figure for local use while reporting the aggregated figure to the next level up.

Sophisticated skills of data analysis are not usually required out of the context of research. Care needs to be taken in the interpretation of the information but *careful trend analysis can usually substitute for statistical tests of significance.* The focus of attention should be a careful evaluation of the information in order to be confident of its reliability as the basis for decision making.

The role of epidemiology needs emphasis, too often seen as an activity which can only be practised by professionals trained in its theory.[9] This is unfortunate since the primary skills of epidemiology are empirical and are practised naturally in the course of everyday life. Villagers may observe and interpret events in an epidemiological way but their conclusions are seldom communicated. Health workers, on the other hand, busy themselves with the collection and reporting of data without having the time to observe and interpret. It is difficult to train people to observe but they can be encouraged to ask the questions: what, who, where, when, why and how?

EVALUATING THE INFORMATION

Controversy abounds in any discussion of health information systems. Debate focuses on the value of the information, the resources required to obtain it and its eventual use. Many national health information systems are cumbersome in the amount of data collected and in the method of managing the data but they have become so institutionalised that they are difficult to change. Guidelines have been proposed for the evaluation of surveillance systems and these have some relevance in the evaluation of health information systems.[10] It must be emphasised that the evaluation should be a team effort involving staff at all levels and discussions with community leaders.

Guidelines for manager practitioners in evaluating the information which is or should be available to them are shown in Table 45.1. The most logical starting point for an evaluation is the identification of the objectives of the health facility. But it is probably easier to start the evaluation with an assessment of the information

available and to compile the objectives gradually during the iterative evaluation process.

The steps outlined in Table 45.1 can be repeated any number of times within the evaluation and the evaluation itself should be repeated at regular intervals. The very act of evaluation will serve as a training exercise and naturally lead to improvements in the collection and use of information.

The evaluation should be conducted with the intention of taking action or making improvements. There may be little scope for change within the overall reporting system but the challenge is to make maximum use of the information and thereby insure its relevance and reliability. This will require regular discussions about the information, relevant training, careful supervision and above all good communication.

THE STATE OF BABEL

Health is not the sole responsibility of the department of health and its staff. There are other key players whose opinions and influence should be considered especially when discussing the information network. These include other government departments, international donors, politicians and of course the people.

A typical state organogram is composed of clearly delineated vertical departments functioning unilaterally within defined policy agendas. Interdepartmental coordination is sometimes indicated by a faint horizontal line. *Other government departments*, for example of agriculture, education, social services, sanitation, construction, communication and industry are all involved in providing the basic material needs of health. Intersectoral collaboration, however, although desirable, may be hindered by competition and conflicting interests between departments.

Nevertheless, the exchange of information between each department must be considered if only to prevent unnecessary duplication. The example is set at the level of the community where all factors that affect health are naturally integrated and their separation is only imposed for administrative and professional convenience. An information network which is built on the premise of community participation is by definition intersectoral.

International donors play a significant role in the implementation of health interventions. Their decisions about project support are based on priorities identified only in part on information from the country itself. Their approach is to review all available information and to assess it in the light of their own priorities. It is essential, therefore, that reliable in-country information is available and that it correctly reflects national priorities.

Having established an aid programme the donor is answerable to its own administration for its implementation. Donors demand information and are prepared to allocate funds to make it available, if necessary by implementing programme-specific information systems. This adds a further dimension to the problems of vertical and horizontal communication of information, that is the compartmentalisation of information for specific purposes.

One major purpose for which donors collect information is to assess the impact of the interventions in as short a time period as possible. The process of change, is slow; it takes time for any impact to appear, longer to be recognised and ultimately it may be difficult to measure and to attribute to any one intervention. It is popular to attempt to quantify health impact in terms of morbidity and mortality rather than through the community's awareness.

Health is not always high on the agenda of the ultimate decision makers, the *politicians*. Furthermore, their information requirements do not necessarily match those of the health planners. Their objectives may be disguised and their means of evaluating success are unlikely to coincide with those of the health professionals. Theirs is a political rather than a scientific environment and their interpretation of information may appear irrational to the health practitioners. Health planners should attempt to understand the political rationale and to convey information to politicians in such a way that the scientific rationale is at least considered.

The common goal of creating a sustainable healthy society is frustrated by the failure to communicate, creating instead a state of Babel. Change is most likely to be achieved through a common language, that is *through a system of communicating information rather than through a system of health information*.

References

1. Mills A, Vaughan JP, Smith DL, Tabizadeh I, eds. Health system decentralization: concepts, issues and country experience. Geneva: World Health Organization, 1990.

2. Eylenbosch WJ, Noah ND, eds. Surveillance in health and disease. Oxford: Oxford University Press, 1988.

4. International statistical classification of diseases and related health problems. 10th Revision, Volume 1. Geneva: WHO, 1992.

5. Vaughan JP, Morrow RH, eds. Manual for epidemiology for district health management. Geneva: WHO, 1989.

6. Scrimshaw NS, Gleason GR, eds. RAP Rapid Assessment Procedures: qualitative methodologies for planning and evaluation of health related programmes. Boston: International Nutrition Foundation for Developing Countries (INFDC), 1992.

7. World Health Statistics Quarterly 1991; Vol.44, No.3.

8. Wilson RG, Echols BE, Bryant JH, Abrantes A, eds. Management information systems and microcomputers in primary health care. Geneva: Aga Khan Foundation, 1988.

9. The place of epidemiology in local health work: The experience of a group of developing countries. Geneva: WHO, 1982. (WHO Offset Publication No. 70)

10. Klaucke DN, Buehler JW, Thacker SB, *et al.* Guidelines for evaluation surveillance systems. MMWR (Suppl). May 6, 1988.

About the authors

Sarah Macfarlane is a Senior Lecturer in the Unit for Statistics and Epidemiology at the Liverpool School of Tropical Medicine and Programme Manager of the Liverpool Epidemiology Programme. She assisted in the development of a health information system during the war in Eritrea and has advised on information and surveillance systems in several countries. Her major interest is in the promotion of the epidemiological approach with an emphasis on innovative training programmes. Assefaw Tekeste, a Visiting Fellow with the Liverpool Epidemiology Programme at the Liverpool School of Tropical Medicine, was previously head of the civilian health services provided by the Eritrean People's Liberation Front. Dr Assefaw was responsible for setting up the health information system in the liberated areas of Eritrea during its armed struggle. He is currently exploring ways of encouraging the involvement of communities in making decisions about their health.

Lankinen KS, Bergström S, Mäkelä PH and Peltomaa M, eds.
Health and disease in developing countries. London:The Macmillan Press Limited, 1994:453–459.

46 HEALTH RESEARCH

Manuel M. Dayrit, M.D., M.Sc.
Department of Health, Office of Public
Health Services,
San Lazaro, Sta. Cruz, Manila 1014,
Philippines

Hanna M. Nohynek, M.D.
National Public Health Institute, Department
of Infectious Disease Epidemiology
Mannerheimintie 166, FIN-00300 Helsinki
Finland

INTRODUCTION

Health research can be defined in multiple
ways. In its broadest sense health research can
be viewed as research on health problems
done jointly or separately by biomedical scientists, other natural scientists, social scientists,
and scientists in the quantitative sciences.

Unfortunately, health research remains mystifying to non-scientists. Although research
often involves high technology, sophisticated
computers and software, a vast area of health
research is close to everyday problems of the
real world. Health research can generate new
understanding and fresh interventions and
may provide immediate solutions to facilitate
health action.

In health research the questions are strongly influenced by politics and power: who sets
the priorities, that is what information is to be
collected and analysed and how that information is to be utilised in order to bring about
change. When resources are scarce, the more
important it is to make best use of them. An
anecdote puts this: 'Gentlemen, we have run
out of money, now we have to start thinking'.

Research provides a tool for planning, maintaining and evaluating existing health systems.
*Optimally, research should be a natural element
of health systems rather than a separate function
performed by those from outside the actual health
services delivery system.* A prerequisite for
research is a reasonable infrastructure for data
collection and analysis, laboratory studies,
intervention trials and so on. But conversely,
by promoting research, one creates the opportunity to upgrade the existing infrastructures.

THE VICIOUS CIRCLES
SUPPRESSING RESEARCH

In developing countries, research activity is
often fragmented and poorly funded. The
three vicious circles of health research, that is
decision-making, health services, and training are illustrated in Figure 46.1.

Low levels of health research beget poor
data which in turn result in poor decision-making. This leads to substandard health services, unsatisfied customers and weak public
support for investments in health services.
These translate to small budget allocations for
health services and, as is often the case, almost
negligible allocations for health research.
These in turn discourage young professionals from pursuing careers in research and further contribute to low levels of research
activity.

To promote the role of health research, the
Commission on Health Research for Development, an independent international initiative formed in 1987 with 12 members, has
suggested that a minimum of 5 per cent of the
international development aid funds put into
upgrading health services should be allocated
to health research. Similarly, developing countries are encouraged to allocate at least 2 per
cent of their budgeted health spendings into
research.

While circumstances in different developing countries may vary, few decision-makers
substantially support research. Those who
want it, often lack the needed resources to
encourage it. Some pay lip-service to it, but
do not actively develop it. Others may tolerate

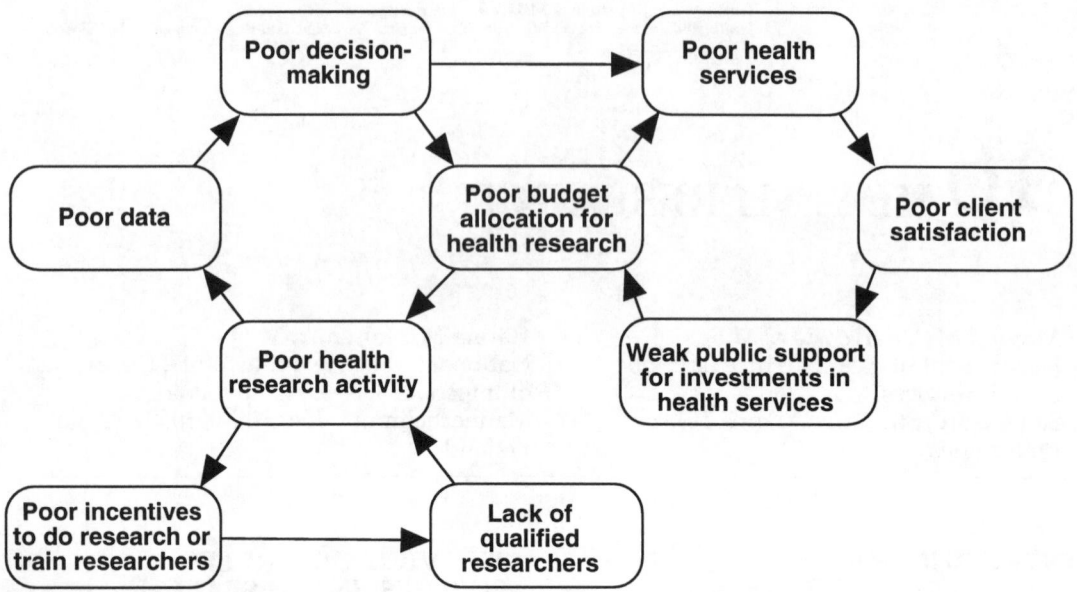

Figure 46.1. The vicious circles of health research in developing countries which involve decision-making, health services, and training.

it, allowing token levels of activity to continue. Research is often viewed as a peripheral activity that has little impact on the provision of better services. This view was expressed by a budget minister who said that research mainly concerned a few scientists who produced papers that were largely irrelevant to the business of procuring medicines which health centres constantly needed. He thus opposed wasting government funds to support research.

As a result, the constraints of health research in developing countries are manifold (Figure 46.2). Since research seldom pays well, few researchers can devote their entire working time to it, but are often loaded with clinical, administrative and training work. A chronic lack of trained supportive staff and of experienced seniors renders the developing country researcher a lonely explorer. Difficulties in subscribing to journals, in getting copies of important references, and in joining computer networks as well as difficulties in financing participation in international meetings add to the burden. Research is also constantly threatened by political instability and deterioration of the national economy, which takes the form of frequent power shortages, lack of sufficient equipment, reagents and other items and which at worst may fatally harm already well-laid work.

BREAKING THE VICIOUS CIRCLE

How could the vicious circles engulfing health research be broken? First, *it must be proven that research pays off*. This means showing that the new knowledge and understanding resulting from research does make a difference in the way problems are identified and solved. Decision-makers must be convinced that research is an investment that will lead to better decisions and outcomes: more astute planning and budgeting, more efficient use of resources, higher quality of services, better control of diseases, more satisfied constituents and clients.

The following examples illustrate this point. Measles epidemics in the Philippines indicate gaps in the national immunisation programme and call attention to the public health officials concerned. Despite the average 87 per cent national measles immunisation coverage, field studies have shown pockets of non-immunised children in urban slums and remote rural areas. Poor coverage in these areas results in a build-up of susceptibles whose health is already compromised by malnutrition and parasites. When outbreaks occur, there are many deaths. Vaccine coverage surveys and outbreak investigations help to identify the groups at risk and lead to adjustments in the age of measles immunisation especially in remote and underserved areas.

Furthermore, these coverage surveys are used as instruments for acknowledging health personnel who achieve high levels of performance. This simple field research activity facilitates better services, prevention of measles, and rewards those who do their jobs well.

The eruption of Mount Pinatubo in June 1991 displaced thousands of residents living in the provinces near the volcano. Hardest hit among these refugees were the Aetas – upland tribesmen who lived on the slopes of Mount Pinatubo, at the margins of mainstream Filipino society. Disease surveillance in the evacuation camps showed that death rates among the Aetas were ten times higher than those in lowlanders. Surveys showed that the Aetas refused to eat food rations and to have their children immunised. Because of this finding, the Department of Health developed a 700 000 USD project in partnership with a foreign donor and a local non-governmental agency. The special attention given to the Aetas who were placed in resettlement areas paid off. Follow-up showed that Aeta survival rates rose and approximated those of lowlanders as their malnutrition rates and immunisation coverage improved. This outcome was publicised by the media which credited government health services for addressing the refugee problem intelligently.

In the early 1980s, a number of researchers based in medical schools and a research institute banded together to study the epidemiology of hepatitis B infection among Filipinos. Since it had been shown that the carrier state of hepatitis B surface antigen was associated with hepatic carcinoma and chronic hepatitis, the group was looking for appropriate strategies for preventing hepatitis B infection given its local patterns of transmission. The group's efforts finally paid off when their recommendation for hepatitis B immunisation of infants was accepted by the Secretary of Health and incorporated into the Expanded Programme on Immunization. Presently, the Philippines Department of Health is undertaking a phased implementation of these recommendations.

From a broader perspective, the aforementioned successes are relatively isolated and limited in scope compared with the enormity of problems. Developing countries have a long way to go in institutionalising research-based decision making within their political and bureaucratic systems. This is partly because the infrastructure to undertake and utilise meaningful research needs to be developed further. For example, health and management

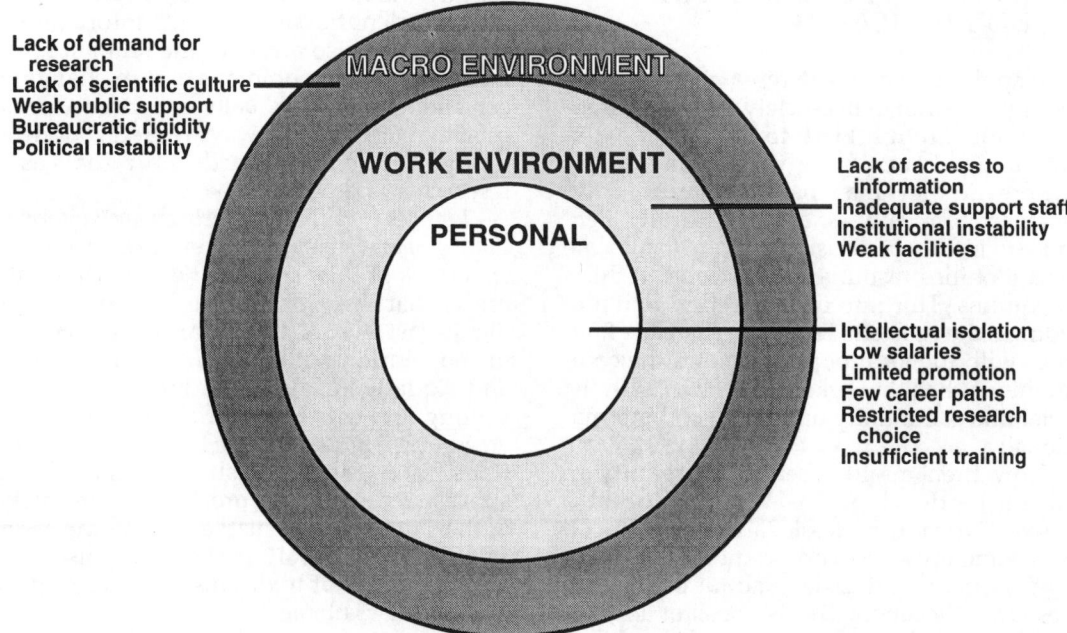

Figure 46.2. Constraints on researchers in developing countries.[3]

information systems often do not provide managers with the pertinent information with which to manage effectively. It is not uncommon for health authorities to use data that are 3–4 years old to plan the programmes and budgets for the next year. As a result, managers become inured to the inertia of decision-making without good information. Their decisions therefore tend to be arbitrary and prey to political pressures.

In many developing countries political representatives present constant requests to build hospitals in their districts. Operations research has shown this an unwise policy. When other cost-effective alternatives to building hospitals are presented, discussions become more rational and productive. It is thus the paramount contribution of health research for equity to set out as lucidly as possible the common menu of options for policy making and resource allocation which can be the basis for public debate. Political and market forces will exert their constant pressure on the decision-making environment. The potency of good research can, however, act as a shield against the biases and seeming irrationality of these forces to create pockets, islands, even continents of deprivation and inequity in society.

PROMOTING RESEARCH FOR EQUITY IN HEALTH

The application of health research to promote equity in health in the society involves essentially four things. First, to identify the disadvantaged and marginalised in society wherever they may be – geographically, socioeconomically, or cross-culturally. Second, to influence decision-makers to allocate and mobilise resources to respond to these inequities. Third, to take effective action to address the problem. Fourth, to share the findings with the local population and the community of health workers as well as with the scientific community nationally and internationally.

How then might research for equity in health be developed? – We must build a research-friendly professional *and* popular culture which respects and promotes the use of data in making decisions about policy and resource allocation. This is a task of advocacy. We must also build our research capability; a task of institutional and human resources development. Both tasks need adequate,

mutual support. We must safeguard the ethical standards and technical quality of research for these are the true foundations for political decision-making on equity issues. The following lessons have been learned in the Philippines.

1. *Begin with the constant promotion of the value that good decision-making must be based on valid data.* This is particularly important for health service programmes in which targets are too often set without a thorough study of the people to be served and how best to go about the task.

2. *Make information meaningful to the public so that they can act on it in their everyday lives.* For example, in a social marketing campaign, the focus was on the occurrence of pneumonia as a complication of measles. This became the basis for exhorting mothers to bring their children to the health centres for immunisation. This media campaign contributed greatly to increasing national immunisation coverage rates.

– *Establish a partnership with media (usually with health reporters) to disseminate accurate news and features reports.* Inform and educate journalists about the technical intricacies of health problems so they provide people with accurate information and not with wrong ideas. Given time, well-trained health reporters will acquire the habit of inquiring more deeply into the scientific basis of health information. However, be also aware of the limitations of media in forming opinions and in changing behaviour patterns. Equally important, do not trust that media will always respect confidentiality or function towards your goals as a researcher and policy maker.

– *In times of controversy, rely on good information to manage conflict.* There are countless examples of this. During the Red Tide outbreaks that have afflicted the Philippines during the last 5 years, the Department of Health in cooperation with the Bureau of Fisheries and Aquatic Resources had to ban the harvesting and sale of shellfish from affected areas. These bans gave rise to vehement objections from the shellfish industry whose spokesmen invariably proclaimed the safety of their produce. Available data on the cases and deaths of paralytic shellfish poisoning and the levels of toxin in shellfish samples proved unassailable.

3. *Build research capability, that is a critical mass of committed researchers.* Training programmes based in academe, in a research insti-

tute, and in the Department of Health have produced a growing number of young health professionals now skilled to undertake a wide range of epidemiological, socioanthropological, economic, and clinical research activities. Various efforts are underway to network these growing capabilities through joint projects and professional organisations.

– *Plan for sustainability.* While the present training programmes have relied heavily on external sources of support to get started, plans must be made for eventually institutionalising these programmes and providing them with adequate local budgetary support. Success in this is already proof that resources are being committed to build the infrastructure for research.

– *Integrate research priorities within the overall vision and plan for the health sector.* Because of a tendency of some researchers to focus too narrowly on issues of personal interest, it is critical that the exercise of identifying priorities be conducted in a manner that looks at the whole picture and its interlocking components. In essence this means that each country should develop its own broad agenda for health research.

4. *Synergise resources and energies.* Because of many and diverse research initiatives, it is useful to have a database to keep track of the various activities so that networking and sharing can be facilitated on the national level. Sophisticated computer linkages are necessary to make the constant updating of database easier.

– *Seek long-term international collaboration for national priority research projects.* Long-term bilateral and multilateral collaboration between institutes has resulted in successful projects on acute respiratory infections and other vaccine-preventable diseases, noncommunicable diseases, clinical epidemiology, field epidemiology training and others. These collaborative projects have resulted in technology transfer, interaction among scientists from different backgrounds and nationalities, and opportunities to solve problems together.

– *When deciding upon accepting external funding, go for long-lasting collaboration instead of 'bleed and fly' type of short-term projects.* The latter may help map out problems, but long-term collaboration provides better opportunities for capability building.

– *Be in direct personal contact with other researchers.* By presenting one's own problem

and solution to it, one renders the ground open for discussion. It is the exchange of experience that develops the mature perspective for one's own work.

5. *Stress good quality in research.* This should be a mutual concern of all parties involved. Quality assurance should be practised on every level of research activity whether or not it is a common trait in the local culture. The quality of research is assured by careful preparation and following a study protocol, which is made according to the principles of good clinical practice (GCP). Before starting the study the protocol must have been reviewed and accepted by the ethical review boards of all participating research institutes. The study procedures should be written in standard operation procedures (SOP), which, when followed carefully, require impeccable recording and monitoring.

If the quality of research cannot be assured, time and effort is wasted. Poor quality research can be regarded as unethical, because it will fail to answer the questions it was designed to tackle.

6. *Safeguard ethical standards.* All proposals to conduct research involving human subjects must be carefully reviewed and approved by one or more independent ethical and scientific review committees. All institutes involved in clinical research need to have their own ethical review boards (ERB). Requirements of the constitution and responsibilities of an ethical review board are shown in Table 46.1. In case research institutes in a given country participate in national or multinational multicentre trials, the founding of a national ethical review board is strongly recommended.

7. *Define priorities clearly with a view towards short- and long-term goals.* Remember to anchor all research efforts to the ultimate goal of promoting equity in health.

Research institutes should establish carefully set research programmes to define their priorities in line of which new research proposals may be evaluated. Research programmes should allow room for a broad-based approach; basic, more theoretically geared studies could strengthen the intellectual basis of research, strategic research could enable planning of interventions, that is applied research, which ultimately leads to health systems research when the intervention becomes common practice.

For example, when studying childhood pneumonia, research on the pathogenesis of

Table 46.1. Requirements of the constitution and responsibilities of ethical and scientific review committees (institutional review board = IRB).

IRB membership

Members should have varying backgrounds of experience and expertise to promote and adequately review, in terms of institutional commitments and regulations, applicable law, and standards of professional conduct and practice, of research activities commonly conducted by the institution; and

Members should be sufficiently representative of the community by race, cultural background, sex, and age and should include both professionals and lay people.

Basic responsibilities of IRB

To verify that all proposed interventions, and particularly the administered drugs and vaccines or use of medical devices under development, have been assessed by a competent expert body as acceptably safe to be undertaken in human subjects; and

To ensure that all other ethical concerns arising from a protocol are satisfactorily resolved both in principle and in practice.

the disease enhances the development of methods with which to map out the spectrum of causative agents. This in turn leads to improved understanding of the scope and clinical meaning of the etiology of pneumonia, which then should be linked into improving pneumonia case management strategies, policy formation on usage of antimicrobials, and planning vaccine intervention trials to ultimately prevent the disease.

INTERNATIONAL RESEARCH COLLABORATION

Successful international collaboration in research is an exercise in identifying problems of joint interest to the collaborating parties as well as in managing the ethical and cross-cultural issues that arise.

While collaboration between more developed and developing countries may bring more resources and technology into the latter, care must be taken to avoid the internal brain drain and misapplication of scarce human resources which may result if the few competent health professionals of a developing country are made to attend to less pressing health concerns.

It is important to begin with the premise that the collaborative activity is a partnership between equals. Thus responsibilities for the success of the project are shared, decision-making is collegial, and differences are resolved through negotiation.

It may be the case that one party possesses the technology and the finances necessary to implement the project. These resources must however be combined with the political and social networking, access to the field, and governmental authorisations and other support mechanisms necessary to establish it; these are usually contributed by the second party.

Also, it should not be forgotten that a third party exists: the community. It should rightly be viewed as a partner in the project. It is the community which provides the context and the subjects for study. Research planners ignore community relations at their own peril.

The mix of these three collaborators make for challenging cross-cultural interactions. For one, world-views may differ. While the researchers may hold rational, scientific explanations of the world, members of the community may be traditional and superstitious. There may be different concepts and attitudes about the human body that may make collection of blood and other specimens difficult. Also, when the community is poor, the issue of material incentives for participation in the project becomes an ethical issue: the thin line between appreciation and manipulation is easily blurred.

What are the prerequisites that make international collaboration work?

Cultural sensitivity is paramount. It thus becomes very important to pay attention to the process of arriving at decisions, making sure that objectives, methods, procedures, are understood and accepted by all people concerned.

Mechanisms for conflict resolution should be clearly established. These are not easy since people from different cultures may react differently to conflict. While some may be open and confrontational, others may be more reticent and passive-aggressive.

Facilitators who can bridge the cultures will play a major role in interpreting verbal messages and non-verbal cues. To be effective, they must enjoy the trust of all parties concerned and be able to effectively work their respective bureaucratic systems.

Additional reading

1. Feachem RG, Graham WJ, Timaeus IM. Identifying health problems and health research priorities in developing countries. J Trop Med Hyg 1989;92:133-91.
2. Murray CJL, Bell DE, DeJonghe E, Zaidi S, Michaud C. A study of financial resources devoted to research on health problems of developing countries. J Trop Med Hyg 1990;93: 229-55.
3. The Commission on Health Research for Development. Essential national health research. Executive summary of health research: essential link to equity in development. Geneva: UNDP 1990.
4. Task Force on Health Research for Development. Essential national health research; a strategy for action in health and human development. Geneva: UNDP, 1991.
5. Council for International Organizations of Medical Sciences (CIOMS) and World Health Organization. International ethical guidelines for biomedical research involving human subjects. Geneva: CIOMS, 1993.
6. Smith PG, Morrow RH, eds. Methods for field trials of interventions against tropical diseases: a 'Toolbox'. Oxford: Oxford University Press, 1991.

About the authors

Manuel M. Dayrit is a medical doctor and also holds a Masters of Science degree in Community Health from the London School of Hygiene and Tropical Medicine. He is presently Assistant Secretary of Health and Director of the Field Epidemiology Training Program. After medical school Dr Dayrit spent 4 years organising community-based health programmes in Mindanao where he worked with village health workers in remote barangays. He has published in the field of infectious disease epidemiology and community health, and has written several articles on cholera, AIDS, typhoid fever, and, paralytic shellfish poisoning.

Hanna M. Nohynek is a medical doctor, and has trained in clinical microbiology. Presently, she works in the outbreak investigation team of the Department of Infectious Disease Epidemiology at the National Public Health Institute (KTL) and is also in charge of the KTL Newsletter. Since 1988 she has collaborated in a Filipino–Finnish research team, which aims at preventing childhood acute respiratory infections by vaccination. She has edited books on travel related health and vaccinations, and has published articles in the field of infectious disease epidemiology and diagnostic microbiological methodology.

Lankinen KS, Bergström S, Mäkelä PH and Peltomaa M, eds.
Health and disease in developing countries. London:The Macmillan Press Limited, 1994:461–468.

47 HEALTH FOR ALL – OR FOR SOME ONLY?

Håkan Hellberg, M.D., D.T.M.&H.
Itälinnake 4 B 5,
FIN-02160 Espoo,
Finland

Marjukka Mäkelä, M.D., Ph.D.
STAKES, National Research and Development Centre for Welfare and Health,
P.O. Box 220, FIN-00531 Helsinki,
Finland

INTRODUCTION

The global development of health policy, emphasising primary health care and the Health for All by 2000 approach, started a long time ago but has its roots in the period after the Second World War. The shock of war and death had people asking for improved collective mechanisms to avoid war and increase the ability for joint efforts that would improve the quality of life of people all over the world. Our mutual dependency had become clear and it ought to have an impact also on the way one looked upon health and disease.

In the late 1940s and early 1950s many chairs or departments of community medicine and social medicine were established. Participatory mechanisms were asked for and the need for *intersectoral action* became evident as one looked not only for the cause of disease but also the cause of health. By necessity, this development forced health workers and thinkers to look outside the hospitals and clinics at the reality in people's normal (or abnormal) environment. Epidemiology and the social sciences became important.

PROBLEMS AHEAD

But these early attempts at new approaches to health and a global health policy did not achieve the results that many had hoped for. One of the obstacles lay in the separation of the different professions and the sectors of activity they represented. They spoke different languages and were competing rather than cooperating. Even today reasons like these hinder full *intersectoral and interprofessional cooperation* for health.

Another reason for the slow development was the rapid development of curative medicine in the 1940s and 1950s. Both clinical investigation and treatment took tremendous strides forward and deliberately or inadvertently the broader public health issues were pushed aside by politicians, the medical profession and the general public, which is easily attracted by the super remedies.

A third reason lay in the political climate. The cold war became even chillier and words or concepts that were spelled c-o-m-m-u-n-i... or s-o-c-i-a-l... were experiencing an uphill battle in the affluent and more or less capitalist countries. In the mid-fifties references to community... or social... all but disappear from the WHO library. Political pressures were applied directly or indirectly.

BUT THE PROGRESS GOES ON

It was, however, impossible to hold back the life forces at work. The reality of the human condition in health and disease was asking for broader approaches and the social forces with their corresponding political forms kept pushing for recognition. Solidarity and concern for people in health and disease were craving for expression and the next term in the international health policy 'slanguage' was Basic Health Services (BHS).

Primary health centres were built in some countries, but they never really worked. Apart from general conceptual difficulties one of the obstacles was the deficient training of health workers, particularly medical doctors. And to the extent that other health related personnel had other views, for example public health nurses, they were not allowed roles of leadership or influence at higher levels. But many such nurses and some doctors developed good community based health programmes even if they were curatively oriented. At least they were able to get the new means of examination and treatment further out towards the periphery.

Structures were created or started but could not be properly staffed (mostly literally *manned*) because the basic health services, just like primary health care services later, need cross-country runners and not tennis players. – Nothing wrong with tennis, but when doctors and others are trained to work in white, according to set rules and in a limited and sharply defined area of action, the broader demands of a people and reality-related public health approach cannot be realised.

In the early 1970s, the Director General of the WHO gave several reports on the world health situation that pointed out the disparities in stages of development of both health services and peoples' health between countries. Much of the rural population in developing countries lacked access to health services. It was suggested that priority attention should be given to PHC at the community level.[1]

In the mid-seventies the term 'health for all' was developed as a roof term for the first attempt at a more systematic global health policy. As the political significance of this approach became clear, plans for an international PHC conference developed, and it was decided to hold it in Alma-Ata, Kazakhstan. This was supposed to meet the demands for holding it in a developing country.

In 1977 the formal decision was taken to work for the goal of Health for All by the year 2000. The following year the PHC conference took place and the Declaration of Alma-Ata outlined the steps towards the attainment of an acceptable level of health for all people in the world by the year 2000 .[2]

The participants at Alma-Ata were a mixed lot. Some came there with experiences of PHC, others with plans or dreams and some came because all the others went to Alma-Ata. This was the time when some influential interna-tional health seniors told Dr Halfdan Mahler the Director General of WHO, that WHO was losing scientific credibility through its involvement in primary health care!

At Alma-Ata and in the subsequent development the two necessary prerequisites for health were emphasised, viz. *people's participation* in the activities that influence their health and the *intersectoral planning and action*. Both are so important but also so difficult to realise. They are touching life nerves of human existence and especially traditional use of power and influence.

Translating PHC into reality has been slow because it challenges so many traditional systems of training, action and technical or political leadership. Nevertheless, Alma-Ata was a very important step forward. It turned around many notions about health and disease. Among the essential elements of PHC you start with information, water, sanitation, housing, food and then proceed to MCH and family planning, immunisations and further also to the control and treatment of diseases and injuries. If these priorities are taken seriously they are bound to have a profound influence on recruitment, training and use of all categories of health and health-related personnel.

THE DECLARATION OF ALMA-ATA

The declaration acknowledges that health is dependent on economical and social factors, describes the social structures necessary for achieving health, and gives primary care a clear priority within health care.

The Declaration of Alma-Ata consists of ten paragraphs. The first three discuss the ideological background for improving health, and in the next two the main actors in the process of improvement are presented. Paragraphs six and seven define primary health care, its components and its relations to the society and the communities. Paragraph seven is often cited alone, as it is the most detailed part of the map, forming nearly half of the declaration. The last paragraphs point out the importance of national strategies, international cooperation, and peace as a prerequisite of health.

1. The conference strongly reaffirms that health, which is a state of complete physical, mental and social wellbeing, and not merely the absence of disease or infirmity, is a fundamental human right and that the attainment of the highest possible level of health is a most important worldwide social goal whose realization requires the action of many other social and economic sectors in addition to the health sector.

A health care worker in primary health care needs several years' of working experience on top of a sound training. The often unarticulated concept of the responsibilities and actions of health care, and of the interaction between health care and other sectors, will strongly formulate the content of his or her work. The highest possible level of health cannot be reached within the health sector alone.

The components of health care are traditionally divided in four categories (Table 47.1). In development cooperation, there is a long tradition of work in the historically older areas of curative and preventive services. Here the imminent need has been strong and the achievements visible within a reasonable time period. Health promotion may, however, give more lasting effects and be the most cost-effective method in the long run. To satisfy the health needs of entire populations, a combination of all four components is clearly needed.

2. The existing gross inequality in the health status of the people, particularly between developed and developing countries as well as within countries, is politically, socially and economically unacceptable and is, therefore, of common concern to all countries.

Local inequalities in service distribution are common. When morbidity grossly exceeds the supply of health services, acute needs can overshadow the wider view. People living close to

Table 47.1. The components of health care.

1. Medical care
    – cure of diseases
    – alleviating symptoms from diseases

2. Prevention
    – protecting individuals against diseases
    – decreasing health risks in populations

3. Rehabilitation
    – diminishing damages from diseases

4. Health promotion
    – supporting healthy ways of living
    – increasing health knowledge

a hospital or other health care unit use more health services, often less appropriately, than those from longer distances – this again applies to industrialised countries as well. The impression of actual morbidity in the area can be distorted and the latent need for care and prevention overlooked in the heat of action.

Health care units should have reasonably good statistics of the size, age structure, and morbidity of the population they are serving. This facilitates a coherent planning of actions for improving the health of this defined population, a follow-up of the development by selected indicators, and an effective cooperation with neighbouring units.[3]

Health professionals should also consider the many possibilities of improving health in developing countries while at home in their industrialised countries. Spreading information, opinion building, and lobbying for political and economic decisions that are fair for developing countries may improve life in developing countries more efficiently than practising medical care on-site.

3. Economic and social development, based on New International Economic Order, is of basic importance to the fullest attainment of health for all and to the reduction of the gap between the health status of the developing and developed countries. The promotion and protection of the health of the people is essential to sustained economic and social development and contributes to a better quality of life and to world peace.

Health produces prosperity and *vice versa*. The vicious circle of poverty and illness can be broken at several different points. When health care workers are familiar with the connections between socioeconomic development and health, they have a number of opportunities for promoting development on a wider scale. Multiprofessional cooperation requires an ability to communicate in lay terms, and a willingness to listen and comprehend people from all walks of life.

4. The people have the right and duty to participate individually and collectively in the planning and implementation of their health care.

The people are subjects as well as objects of health care. Many of the most successful projects in development cooperation were initiated in the developing countries and carried out together with the target population. Such approaches combine strong motivation and true health needs with familiarity of the local culture and ways of action. A small project that the people have designed themselves is

Health clinic for medical and legal assistance near Lima, Peru. Photo: UNICEF/Fran Antmann

much more likely to live and flourish than an expensive structure reflecting the values of imported industrial health care.

5. Governments have a responsibility for the health of their people which can be fulfilled only by the provision of adequate health and social measures. A main social target of the governments, international organizations, and the whole world community in the coming decades should be the attainment by all peoples of the world by the year 2000 of a level of health that will permit them to lead a socially and economically productive life. PHC is the key to attaining this target as part of development in the spirit of social justice.

Health is one of the basic requirements for socially and economically productive life. Others are peace, sufficient nutrition, education, and work. All these aims are achievable. The Alma-Ata declaration elevates PHC to the status of the most important tool for reaching and maintaining health.

6. Primary health care is essential health care based on practical, scientifically sound and socially acceptable methods and technology made universally accessible to individuals and families in the community through their full participation and at a cost that the community and country can afford to maintain at every stage of their development in the spirit of self-reliance and self-determination. It forms an integral part both of the country's health system, of which it is the central function and main focus, and of the overall social and economic development of the community. It is the first level of contact of individuals, the family and community with the national health system, bringing health care as close as possible to where people live and work, and constitutes the first element of a continuing health care process.

This paragraph includes a number of basic principles for health care: accessibility, economic efficiency, comprehensiveness, different referral levels, and continuity. Each country decides for itself how the essential health care will be provided: which methods are efficient, necessary, and accepted by the people.

7. Primary health care

Paragraph seven enumerates the minimum requirements of PHC and outlines practical actions. In some countries, the Alma-Ata declaration was taken too literally, and fully functional parts of health care were discontinued in order to bring in a better variety. This was not intended. Integration of good old structures with a variety of new actions can be achieved with less damage than an introduction of a good but totally different system.

7.1. Primary health care reflects and evolves from the economic conditions and socio-cultural and political characteristics of the country and its communities, and is based on the application of the relevant results of social, biomedical and health services research and public health experience.

To provide PHC with an exclusively biomedical background is impossible. A professional taking up work in primary health care is wise to complement his or her education with the basics of social sciences, health care organisations, anthropology, and the culture of the people one will be working with. A major part of the work may consist of planning, management, and teaching instead of cure and care. It is better to prepare for all these possible roles before the travel.

7.2. Primary health care addresses the main health problems in the community, providing promotive, preventive, curative, and rehabilitative services accordingly.

The components of health care, given in Table 47.1 in their historical order of birth, get here priorities in a more meaningful, human, and economically sounder order.

7.3. Primary health care includes at least; education concerning prevailing health problems and the methods of preventing and controlling them; promotion of food supply and proper nutrition; an adequate supply of safe water and basic sanitation; maternal and child health care, including family planning; immunization against the major infectious diseases; prevention and control of locally endemic diseases; appropriate treatment of common diseases and injuries; and provision of essential drugs.

Food, clean water, and education promote health. The next three clauses are preventive, and traditional medical care turns up in the last two parts of this paragraph.

7.4. Primary health care involves, in addition to the health sector, all related sectors and aspects of national and community development, in particular agriculture, animal husbandry, food industry, education, housing, public works, communications and other sectors, and demands the coordinated efforts of all those sectors.

The actors in society that can support health on a population level are many.[4] Unfortunately, very few health care schools offer the students any chance for practising intersectoral cooperation. Group work is more often on the schedule. Local workers know the functions and distribution of tasks in their own society. The skills a foreigner needs are listening, negotiation, and flexibility.

7.5. Primary health care requires and promotes maximum community and individual self-reliance and participation in the planning, organization, operation and control of primary health care, making fullest use of local, national and other available resources, and to this end develops through appropriate education the ability of communities to participate.

Establishing medical training in developing countries is increasingly seen as a major form of international cooperation. This is not enough! In many countries, it is easier to train sufficient numbers of indigenous community health workers than to achieve a material self-sufficiency.

7.6. Primary health care should be sustained by integrated, functional and mutually supportive referral systems, leading to the progressive improvement of comprehensive health care for all, and giving priority to those most in need.

Primary health care produces the bulk of the health care services, but its function and credibility depend on an appropriate net of (referral) hospitals. The different levels support one another, when they have a purpose-built division of responsibilities and functional channels of communication.

7.7. Primary health care relies, at local and referral levels, on health workers, including physicians, nurses, midwives, auxiliaries and community workers as applicable, as well as traditional practitioners as needed, suitably trained socially and technically to work as a health team and to respond to the expressed health needs of the community.

In developing countries, the educational background of health care workers is more miscellaneous than is common in the industrial world. A newcomer needs to get acquainted with the knowledge, skills and sphere of activities behind the new titles. Stiff definitions of rights and duties should not make the best division of labour unachievable. The ability to work as a member of a group and common goals within the group increase decisively the chances of improving health.

8. All governments should formulate national policies, strategies and plans of action to launch and sustain primary health care as part of a comprehensive national health system and in coordination with other sectors. To this end, it will be necessary to exercise political will, to mobilise the country's resources and to use the available external resources rationally.

Finland was the first European country to formulate a national policy and strategy for health. This was finished 8 years after the Alma-Ata meeting, and the accompanying research programme was completed 2 years later. In most countries political will has been a prerequisite for the development of primary care. Secondary and tertiary care find their monuments more easily – but the village health clinics named after famous politicians are few!

9. All countries should cooperate in a spirit of partnership and service to ensure primary health care for all people since the attainment of health by people in any one country directly concerns and benefits every other country. In this context the joint WHO/UNICEF report on primary health care constitutes a solid basis for the further development and operation of primary health care throughout the world.

Over decades the WHO and UNICEF achieved a wide experience of vertical health care programmes. Many carefully planned and executed programmes did not gain a permanent place in health care, and the trend has long been to support primary health care as an entity, in pursuit of lasting health effects.

10. An acceptable level of health for all the people of the world by the year 2000 can be attained through a fuller and better use of the world's resources, a considerable part of which is now spent on armaments and military conflicts. A genuine policy of independence, peace, détente and disarmament could and should release additional resources that could well be devoted to peaceful aims and in particular to the acceleration of social and economic development of which primary health care, as an essential part, should be allotted its proper share.

The achievement of health depends on the resources of individuals and societies, and the alternative ways of utilising them. At the cost of a new television set, fifty children could be vaccinated against the six most important childhood diseases.

Pollution as a consequence of western lifestyle is an ever increasing menace to the environment. The industrial countries' willingness to keep a high standard of living results in transferring the most dangerous industries to the developing world, where legislation has not yet limited the right to pollute. Such solutions are not viable. In the spirit of Alma-Ata, we need to look closely into our daily actions, their justification and effects, and evaluate them globally.

HEALTH FOR ALL – IS IT POSSIBLE?

The principles of PHC are simple. A health care professional trained in the industrial countries may feel, however, that his or her values and actions are in conflict with these principles. In most cases the conflict is caused by two deeply rooted ideas that need careful reconsideration: the difficulty of shifting the view from *patients* to *populations*, and the tacit emphasis on primary *medical* care within primary *health* care.

For decades medical education has focused upon curative aspects of medicine. Vocational training on planning, administration, and evaluation has been scanty and undervalued. The professionals have pictured their role as helping individuals in their illness. It is a long leap from such immediately rewarding work to a more abstract action, where the targets of the work are the population and their living conditions as a whole. Results appear more slowly, they are more difficult to measure, and individual achievement is not always discernible from the action of a group.

PHC is a broad concept with emphasis on promotive and preventive aspects. Primary medical care is that part of PHC which especially the doctors have been trained to produce. The imminent health needs of the population are manifested in the demand for primary medical care, which should be satisfied within reasonable limits. If health care cannot help in need, it cannot assume that the preventive services offered instead of the curative action would be very well received. But if the basics of health, such as clean water and decent food are not provided, primary medical care faces an overwhelming task.

Health care workers may not adopt the principles of PHC overnight. Intellectual and emotional acceptance is most difficult in a situation where there is plenty of illness curable by conventional doctoring once learned and internalised, i.e. by primary – perhaps even secondary or tertiary level – medical care. Even then one should ask how the available resources could produce *most* health, and lift one's eyes from the immediate individual need to the long-term development of health in populations.

There may also be resistance because different professional groups feel themselves threatened. Researchers fear for their research funds, doctors for losing their dominating influence in the older model and most health professionals are uneasy with lawyers, engineers, economists and politicians. These other groups have their preconceived ideas and behind it all is the need to find a common language for a common understanding, if this can be achieved. In the health sector itself the relationship between nurses and doctors is always influenced by the man–woman issue as long as most of the nurses are women. – In the deepest sense it is a question of willingness to change positions of power and privileges. This process is aggravated by the fact that there really are different languages, administrative structures and working cultures.

In the Health for All approach the main element is the emphasis on *all*. This means concern for justice, equity, solidarity and distribution of the possibilities for health. This will continue to be a challenge for a long time. For over 200 years we have tried to implement *liberté, egalité* and *fraternité*. This element of justice and solidarity means that health development is closely related to the overall situation in a given country. PHC and HFA/2000 approaches are challenging the human rights in a broader sense and are limited by the overall situation concerning such rights and privileges.

The time perspective of the year 2000 is mainly there as a means for prospective thinking and approaches. The retroactive factors in medicine are very powerful and important and it is not easy to get a strong enough prospective approach, but this is absolutely essential in order to have a foundation for preventive and promotive action for health. Looking back 23 years in 1977 one could see tremendous advances in medicine and health. It was not unrealistic to think that the 23 years from 1977 to 2000 also could mean great achievements.

Yes...BUT – HOW ARE WE DOING?

As soon as one starts evaluating PHC developments and the results of Health for All approaches and plans one mostly gets a yes ... *BUT* answer. A small yes and a BIG BUT. The challenge is then to try to increase the yes and decrease the BUT.

Since 1977 there are many yes-answers, although they often tend to be lost behind the big problems and the sometimes even growing BUTs. This is caused by civil unrest, wars, internal or external displacement of large groups of people, natural disasters, drought and general misery. Also in this respect the poor often get poorer.

On the other hand, in many places, the population growth has slowed down, the average life span has increased and infant mortality has gone down. But the latter is still far too high in too many places and in many countries HIV infection and AIDS have brought the mortality figures back many years.

There is food but the distribution is so bad that some die of hunger while others have too much. Provision of safe drinking water has improved somewhat but water and sanitation continue to be intersectoral challenges of a formidable nature. Child immunisation is one of the biggest 'yes-es' but has to be kept up and those that do survive the childhood diseases have to be cared for.

Medical care has become more *accessible* but not always *affordable* to large parts of the population. In spite of efforts to change habits and lifestyles the preventable diseases are increasing in the developing countries. These countries are in a unique situation in as far as they see an increasing burden of diseases of civilisation at the same time as they still have the great burden of communicable diseases – the illnesses of poverty and ignorance are both old and new. The cold war is over but has unfortunately not led to freeing of resources for the health and wellbeing of people – to the extent that one was hoping for and that should be possible.

THE FUTURE

The issue for health for all continues to be a primary demand for justice. The urge to share the possibilities for health in a given situation and between different groups of people or nations cannot be given up. Each person should have enough health to cope with her or his life situation by using one's own health resources as much and as long as possible but also to have access to the resources of other people around them as an expression of common social responsibility.

This demands a moral and ethical capital that should be both used and replenished, but many societies show signs of having used up their moral capital and the efforts to rebuild this capital in the new generations have been insufficient. Without a moral and ethical backbone in individuals and nations there will be no realisation of health for all goals or programmes however well these may be formulated or written.

There should also be a realistic view of human beings and not an unrealistic superficial belief in people who always are good and only want the good. Social policy must be realistic human policy, concerning what people really are able to do both for good and for bad. Not only rights but also responsibility. Not only *distribution of resources* but also the *creation of new resources* both outwardly and inwardly.

Realising that health for all has to do with the most fundamental processes in and between people as well as in and between their groups and societies, we then realise that the answer must always to some extent be yes... BUT. We must, however, never give up trying to enlarge the YES and diminish the but. An essential activity and emphasis is to learn to bring together and use all the intersectoral and interdisciplinary forces relating to health, accepting the complexity without falling for mistaken simplifications as we all are moving towards the year 2000 and beyond.

CONCLUSION

The definition of health as a state of complete physical, mental and social well-being from the WHO founding document starts also the Alma-Ata declaration. In a world of limited resources, this idealistic aim should perhaps be reformulated. In a world of mass unemployment, a level of health that will permit people to lead a socially and economically productive life seems to be far away indeed. Instead of the unreachable stars, we might aim at a *sufficient functional capacity for all to lead a personally and socially full and rich life.*

The 15-year-old principles of the Alma-Ata declaration are still a valid tool for health care in its widest sense. They remain open for new uses and interpretations, and will hopefully be renewed through problematisation and criticism, so that the social justice can further be implemented through these ideals.

References

1. World Health Organization. The work of WHO 1976–1977. Biennial report of the Director-General. Geneva: WHO, 1978. (Official Records of the World Health Organization No. 243)
2. World Health Organization. Alma-Ata 1978: Primary health care. Geneva: WHO 1978. (Health for All Series, No. 1)
3. World Health Organization. Development of indicators for monitoring progress towards Health for All by the year 2000. Geneva: WHO, 1981. (Health for All Series, No. 4)
4. World Health Organization. National health development networks in support of primary health care. Geneva: WHO, 1984. (WHO Offset Publication 94)

Additional reading

1. Fry J, Hasler JC, eds. Primary health care 2000. London: Churchill Livingstone, 1986.
2. World Health Organization. Intersectoral linkages and health development. Case studies in India (Kerala State), Jamaica, Norway, Sri Lanka, and Thailand. Geneva: WHO, 1984. (WHO Offset Publication 83)
3. World Health Organization. Formulating strategies for Health for All by the year 2000. Geneva: WHO, 1979. (Health For All Series, No. 2)
4. World Health Organization. Global strategy for Health For All by the year 2000. Geneva: WHO, 1979. (Health for All Series, No. 3)
5. World Health Organization. Plan of action for implementing the global strategy for Health For All and index to the Health For All series, No. 1–7. Geneva: WHO, 1982. (Health for All Series, No. 7)
6. World Health Organization. 8th general programme of work covering the period 1990–95. Geneva: WHO, 1987. (Health for All Series, No. 10)

About the authors

Håkan Hellberg obtained his medical degree from the University of Helsinki, Finland. During 1958–63 he worked in rural health care in Namibia and subsequently held several posts in international missionary organisations, most notably as an Assistant Director in the Christian Medical Commission at the World Council of Churches in 1968-74. After 6 years as a Director and Assistant Director in the National Board of Health in Finland he was posted in 1981 as the Director of Health for All Strategy Coordination and Information at the WHO, Geneva. Returning to Finland in 1987 he commenced yet another career as the Editor-in-Chief for Hufvudstadsbladet, the largest Swedish language daily newspaper in Finland. He retired from this office in 1992, but serves still as the President for the Finnish Red Cross. Marjukka Mäkelä is a specialist in general practice in Helsinki, Finland. She works at the National research and development centre for welfare and health (STAKES) as Head of research and development in primary care, and is responsible for the programmes of quality assurance and functional development in primary care. These are also the areas of her current research, with methodology from health economics. Since 1985 she has participated in a PSR-Finland collaborative primary care development project in Tanzania. She is a member of the World Organization of National Colleges, Academies and Academic Associations of General Practitioners/Family Physicians (WONCA) European group for Quality in primary care, and has acted as a Temporary Advisor for the WHO in primary care.

Lankinen KS, Bergström S, Mäkelä PH and Peltomaa M, eds.
Health and disease in developing countries. London:The Macmillan Press Limited, 1994:469–478.

48 PREVENTION OF INFECTIOUS DISEASES BY IMMUNISATION

P. Helena Mäkelä, M.D., Ph.D.
National Public Health Institute (KTL),
Division of Infectious Diseases
Mannerheimintie 166, FIN-00300 Helsinki,
Finland

Kari S. Lankinen, M.D., D.T.M.&H.
National Public Health Institute (KTL),
Department of Bacterial Respiratory
Infections,
Mannerheimintie 166, FIN-00300 Helsinki,
Finland

INTRODUCTION

The immune system is the body's most sophisticated defence against harmful external influences. Man has learned to actively utilise and enhance it, but limitations still remain: not all vaccines are optimal, and there are infections for which we do not have vaccines, most notably the HIV infection.

Vaccines have been most successful for those diseases that a person naturally experiences only once because of the lifelong immunity they leave. They are less efficient for diseases in which the microbes have found ways to resist natural immunity: e.g. influenza virus which varies its structure so rapidly that the vaccine needs to be modified and vaccination repeated annually.

The rationale of vaccination is to introduce to the body the infectious agent (or parts of it) in a harmless form and early enough in life, before it has come in contact with the natural infection. This defines clear-cut tasks for the development of vaccines: how to design the vaccine without the harmful effects of the natural infection, yet stimulating a similar immunity? Furthermore, the vaccine must immunise effectively at an *early age*, when the immune responses of the infant are not as good as in adulthood. The vaccines also need to be inexpensive enough so that all the world's children can have access to them.

The success of the smallpox eradication campaign gave much faith in vaccination (see below). At the same time it greatly boosted the image of the WHO, which in a short time had organised the eradication of a major scourge of mankind. In 1980 the world was declared free of smallpox and this was celebrated as a landmark year. At the same time it set the goals and ambitions for the WHO and for immunisation programmes very high: which disease would be the next target for eradication?

THE EXPANDED PROGRAMME ON IMMUNIZATION

In 1974, the WHO formulated a goal of increased utilisation of vaccines all over the world, especially in developing countries. The programme was named Expanded Programme on Immunization (EPI). Its starting points were that vaccination is one of the most cost-effective measures to improve health, and the fact that its possibilities were grossly underutilised.[1] It emphasised the need to enhance the use of vaccines to reach a high *coverage* of the targeted population. Although not always remembered, it is true that no matter how efficacious a vaccine is in controlled trials, its effectiveness as a public health measure depends on its wide and appropriate utilisation.

The EPI decided that high immunisation coverage could best be achieved by visible campaigns and national commitment in each country. The programme has consistently worked to enforce these two cornerstones, indeed very successfully. Thus it could boast of having achieved 80 per cent coverage world-wide by

One of the main strategies of EPI is to use all opportunities for vaccination; only few true contraindications exist for EPI vaccines. Vaccination in Rwanda. Photo: UNICEF/Bert Demmers

1990 – a dramatic improvement over the less than 5 per cent in 1977 (Figure 48.1).[1,2]

To make such a concerted campaign possible it was necessary to define the scope of the programme very precisely. The most important definition and restriction took place

in the selection of the EPI vaccines. They had to be vaccines with proven efficacy and acceptability, estimated to prevent a large number of serious infections. Obviously, some compromises were made in the final list of the six EPI vaccines (Table 48.1). The value of BCG in the control of tuberculosis is still under debate, and the importance of pertussis in developing countries has never been critically examined.

The EPI insisted on the involvement of the national health care system. Thus the WHO only contributed, if necessary, up to 20 per cent of the costs, while the national government was expected to be responsible for the infrastructures of vaccine storage and delivery, as well as for the immunisation of the people.

This emphasis on local commitment proved correct. It served to strengthen the infrastructure of PHC, within which the immunisations should be carried out, as clearly stated in the EPI Action Plan from 1982.[1] Nevertheless, EPI is not free of the criticism expressed towards centrally-decided vertical programmes that can lead to a lack of integration of work at all levels of the health care system, even in the outposts where the practical work is carried out (Chapter 58). Obviously, the ideas, principles and idealistic thinking that inspired the conception of the Programme, have not always been conveyed to the workers in the periphery.

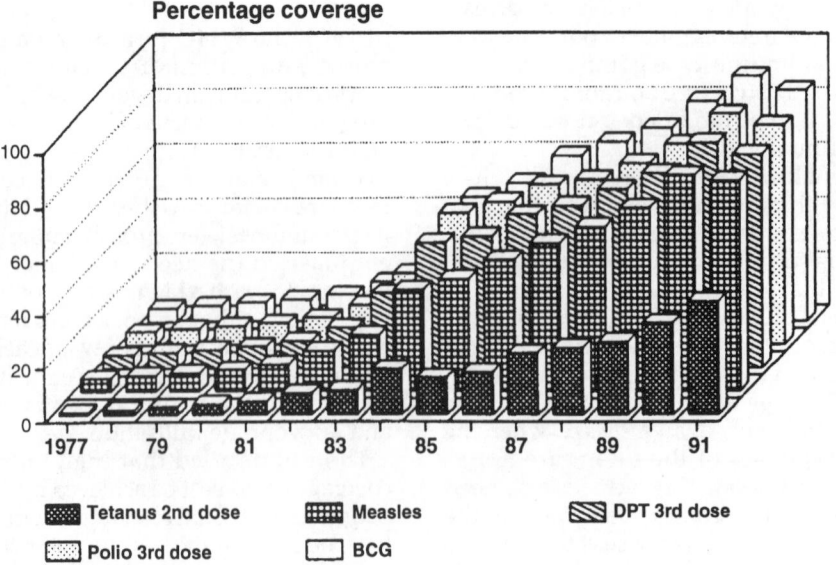

Figure 48.1. Global immunisation coverage 1977-1991.[2] Data before 1984 are estimated.

Table 48.1. The global impact of EPI target diseases, estimates from 1987.[1]

	Without vaccination annually
Measles	2.5 million deaths
Neonatal tetanus	1 million deaths
Tuberculosis	2 million deaths (only partly children)
Poliomyelitis	400 000 paralysed
Pertussis	900 000 deaths
Diphtheria	not known

THE EPI VACCINES

The choice of the original six EPI vaccines was based on the public health importance of the disease to be prevented, on the existence of a vaccine proven safe and efficacious, and on low cost of the vaccine (Table 48.1).

BCG, the vaccine to prevent tuberculosis, was included because of the importance of the disease and the long experience with the vaccine. The importance of tuberculosis is actually increasing, which speaks for continued and accelerated efforts at immunisation (Chapter 18). BCG may also afford protection from leprosy, although this was not known at the time when the inclusion of BCG was decided and is still under investigation (Chapter 26).

The present vaccine consists of live *Mycobacteria* of a species not virulent to man. In industrialised countries there is criticism against this vaccine because of the adverse – albeit rare – effects it has due to *residual virulence*: it sometimes causes local suppuration or inflammation of adjoining bones (osteitis) in apparently healthy vaccine recipients. It may cause serious disease in immune-compromised persons, especially those infected with HIV.

But the most severe criticism relates to the protection afforded by the vaccine. In many studies, especially those focusing on disease in infants and young children, the vaccine has been shown effective also on the public health level.[3,4] On the other hand, other studies, and notably those focusing on adults (who were probably already infected in childhood), have shown less or no protection.[5,6] On the basis of this, efforts at developing a new tuberculosis/leprosy vaccine are increasing, and hope is placed on vaccines based on non-living purified components of the bacteria.[7]

Poliomyelitis and measles vaccines are essential components in the EPI programme (Figure 48.2). The benefits and problems related to these vaccines are discussed in Chapters 25 and 17. **DPT**, the triple vaccine against diphtheria, pertussis (whooping cough) and tetanus, is a combination of three old bacterial vaccines. The diphtheria and tetanus components are purified proteins, and in both cases the toxin responsible for the specific disease symptoms is isolated and rendered non-toxic (toxoid) by chemical treatment (detoxification, usually with formaldehyde). Both of these components cause few adverse reactions but induce a strong and long-lasting antibody response that neutralises the respective toxins and protects efficiently from the disease.

Tetanus toxoid (TT) is also used alone to immunise mothers in order to protect the child from neonatal tetanus (Chapter 30). This is the only situation in which immunisation of pregnant women is currently recommended because of general cautiousness for possible effects on the pregnancy. However, no adverse events have been observed, and TT vaccination is currently specially emphasised as a component of EPI in order to eliminate the totally unnecessary deaths caused by neonatal tetanus.[2]

The pertussis component, on the other hand, consists of whole formalin-killed bacteria, causes fever or irritability in a large fraction of vaccinated persons and is reported to sometimes cause serious neurologic damage. The serious adverse effects are very rare – maybe 1 in 500 000 vaccinees – and the association indeed questionable, but this has caused much concern in some industrialised countries and led to decreased utilisation of the vaccine with subsequent pertussis epidemics.[8] Another problem is that the protective efficacy of this vaccine is not very good and lasts for a few years only.

So called acellular vaccines containing only some components of the pertussis bacteria are now being tested in large field trials, and may soon replace the traditional whole cell pertussis vaccine. The consequences of this to the EPI programme may be problematic, since the new vaccines are much more expensive to produce and require more sophisticated technology not readily available at the vaccine manufacturing plants in developing countries (see below).

Addition of new vaccines to the EPI has been slow, largely due to the Programme's strategy to first get the principle of childhood

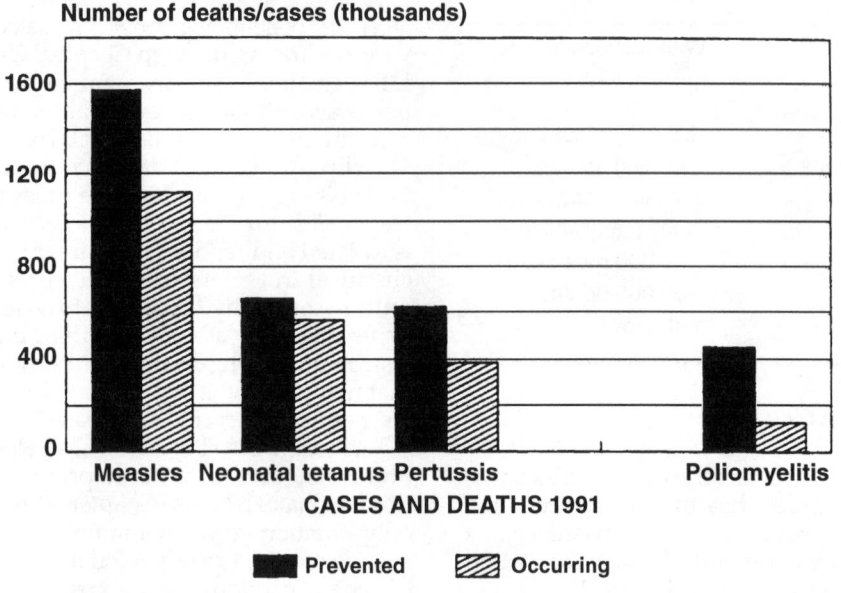

Figure 48.2. Cases and deaths occurring (black columns) and prevented in 1991 through immunisation (shaded columns).[2]

immunisation established and coverage increased before opening discussions that might sidetrack public and political attention. With the EPI accepted in principle in all countries, and the good overall coverage figures, new vaccines for the EPI are now being considered. **Hepatitis B vaccine** is recommended since 1992 for inclusion in national EPI programmes. This vaccine would be especially relevant in developing countries (Chapter 24). Its adoption is partly an economic question even with the relatively low prices at which it is manufactured in some Asian countries.

Yellow fever vaccine is also since 1992 recommended for national EPI programmes in countries where yellow fever is prevalent (Chapter 23). Many countries in Africa have already adopted it; the vaccine (one dose) is usually given together with measles vaccine at 9 months of age. The vaccine is produced in several developing countries, and its cost is very reasonable, less than 0.25 USD per dose.[2]

EPI SCHEDULE AND IMMUNISATION STRATEGY

The EPI target diseases are mostly children's diseases. Therefore immunisation should be started as early in life as possible. On the other

hand, there are two physiological factors that tend to impair the infant's ability to respond to immunisation.

One is the relatively slow maturation of the immune system. However, even at birth the child can respond to *protein* antigens with both antibody production and T cell-mediated immunity, although the responses are somewhat weaker than in the adult. There is a more important deficit in the infant's ability to respond to many *polysaccharide* antigens. The immune response to the capsular polysaccharide of e.g. *Haemophilus influenzae* type b and several (but not all) serotypes of pneumococci develops only after 2 years of age, which is a reason for the prevalence of diseases (especially ARI) caused by these bacteria in children less than 2 years old (Chapter 14 and 27). This problem has been recently overcome by conjugating the polysaccharide to a toxoid vaccine or other proteins, after which the child's immune system handles it as a protein making antibodies to it. New *conjugate vaccines* active already in infancy against pneumococci may soon prove an important tool in the prevention of ARI (Chapter 14).

Another special feature in infants is that they have received transplacentally from the mother all antibodies that she had. These antibodies will be gradually lost, so that at 6 months

Table 48.2. Situations that *are not* contraindications for vaccination.

Mild infectious disease (chesty or snuffly child, otitis, diarrhea)
Convalescence after an infectious disease
Atopy (asthma, allergic rhinitis, eczema)
Family history of convulsions
Antibiotic treatment
Local steroids (including inhaled steroids)
Small-dose systemic steroid treatment
Dermatitis, localised skin infections
Chronic heart, lung, liver or kidney disease
Rheumatoid arthritis, LED
Stable neurological disease, e.g. cerebral palsy
Mental handicap, Down's syndrome
Neonatal icterus
Preterm birth, small-for-date
Malnutrition
Breast-feeding
Mother's pregnancy
History of the same infectious disease (naturally acquired)
Incubation period of an infectious disease

of age the child has only one tenth of the antibody concentrations it had at birth. Nevertheless, these antibodies are an important factor protecting the newborn and young infant from a variety of infections until the child has had time to produce its own antibodies. Preterm babies are disadvantaged, since the placenta only becomes permeable to immunoglobulin near term.

There is also a reverse side to this: the maternally inherited antibodies act against live vaccines, prevent their multiplication and thereby reduce their ability to immunise the child. This is an important practical question regarding measles vaccine: it cannot be given before the effect of the maternal antibodies has disappeared. Since this time depends on how much antibodies the child received from the mother, and this in turn on how much antibodies the mother had, there is wide variation in the age range when a child would respond. Because of this some children will remain without protection no matter whether the vaccination was started at 9 months, when not all children respond, or at 14 months, when much better response rates are achieved but many have already contracted the disease. The inherited antibodies are not a problem with most other vaccines which do not depend on the replication of the vaccine.

Use all opportunities for vaccination

Thus all vaccination schedules and timetables are compromises between needs and possibilities. Compromises may be warranted also by the infrastructure of the health services, that is *when* the child can be reached. The practice in some areas to have only one child immunisation day each month may cause long delays in the ideal programme. Most schedules require more than one dose of vaccine to reach protection – this takes advantage of the immunological memory and consequently increased responses to a *booster dose* of vaccine.

In practice this is a difficult point: how to persuade the families to bring the child repeatedly to immunisation sessions. On this background it is easy to see the merits of the goal of the Children's Vaccine Initiative (see below) to develop new effective single dose vaccines.

An EPI principle is to use all opportunities for vaccination, i.e. to give vaccines at any contact of the child with the health services. This means immunisation whenever a sick child visits the health station or hospital. Indeed, it has been demonstrated that minor illness does not significantly reduce the immune response to the vaccine nor does the vaccination aggravate the disease (Table 48.2). Thus, there are only few true contraindications for vaccination (Table 48.3).

No vaccine is totally without adverse reactions, but the risk of serious complications from vaccines used in the EPI are much lower than the risks of the natural diseases. The decision to withhold immunisation should be taken only after serious considerations of the potential consequences for the child and the community.[9]

Table 48.3. True contraindications to EPI vaccines in developing countries.

General contraindications
– Definite sensitivity to any ingredient of the vaccine
    - very rare in childhood
– Severe reaction after previous dose
– Serious febrile illness requiring hospitalisation
    - immunise on discharge

Vaccine-specific contraindications
– BCG   immune deficiency (HIV infection)
        eczematous skin
– Measles   immune deficiency (HIV infection)

Table 48.4. Timetable of vaccinations within the EPI programme.

Disease	Vaccine	EPI timing recommendation	Comment
Tuberculosis	BCG	at birth	or as soon as possible
Hepatitis B		at birth and 1 and 6 months	or as OPV
Poliomyelitis	OPV	at birth and 6, 10 and 14 weeks	
Diphtheria			
Pertussis	DPT	6, 10 and 14 weeks	
Tetanus			
Measles		9 months	
Yellow fever		9 months (endemic areas)	
Tetanus	TT	two injections during pregnancy with one month interval	start during second trimester during subsequent prenancies one booster dose will suffice

The EPI-recommended immunisation schedule is shown in Table 48.4. In practice the timetable will be stretched because the child is not brought for vaccination when scheduled, or because vaccine or syringes and needles are not available at such a time, or for many other reasons. Good integration of the immunisation in the PHC system would be the best way to achieve an effective utilisation of the available vaccines. In many areas special campaigns, vaccination days and mop-up activities are also organised, aiming especially at the older children irrespective of whether they have been vaccinated in infancy.

These strategies apply especially to polio vaccine (which is easy to give orally), and have apparently greatly contributed to the disappearance of polio from South America (Chapter 25).[2] The inclusion of the immunisation services in the PHC should, however, not be neglected because of its lower overall costs and long-term effectiveness in reaching all children early enough in life, and also because its mutual effect on strengthening the PHC.

THE COLD CHAIN

Much emphasis has been placed on the quality of the vaccines used in EPI. Keeping the vaccines cool enough up to the point of usage has been an important aspect of the programme. The *cold chain* means controlling the temperature of the vaccine from the production unit through customs to central store, further to the health centre and finally to the village and the family receiving it.

In practice, each of these steps is vulnerable. The time when the vaccine waits for import clearance is one particularly weak point – the vaccine may stay on the airport exposed to the sun for days or weeks without protection. Another weak point may be the refrigerator at the rural health centre, subject to cuts in the supply of electricity or fuel. The travel from the most peripherally located refrigerator to the village where the vaccination session would take place may take a whole day, during which it is important to keep the vaccine in an insulated cold storage box (Figure 48.3). What to do to the vaccine left over after such a session? Transporting it back to the storage refrigerator may prevent wastage of vaccine but at the same time the vaccine may be exposed to warming up.

The vulnerability of different vaccines differs (Table 48.5).[10] As a rule of thumb, vaccines containing live viruses (OPV, measles) are the most sensitive to heat and improper storage can totally abolish their effect. On the other hand, it is also important to prevent the DPT vaccines from freezing, as this affects the adjuvant and results in reduced potency. Freezing may also disrupt pertussis cells to release endotoxins which can cause severe adverse reactions.

Compromises are obviously made everywhere: the health worker responsible for

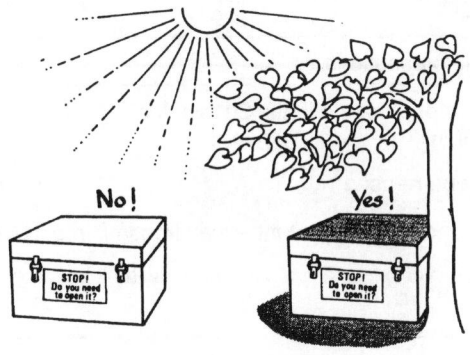

Figure 48.3. The cold chain in practice.[10]

vaccines should exercise sound judgement on what is acceptable and what is not. Both manuals and teaching materials for the upkeep of refrigerators and the principles and practice of the cold chain are available from EPI.[11,12] The EPI-recommended immunisation instruments are listed in Table 48.6.

ENSURING SUPPLIES, ASSURING QUALITY

The availability, quality and cost of vaccines are important questions everywhere, but especially in developing countries where the resources available for health care are very limited. Together with UNICEF the EPI programme has done major work to reduce the price of the EPI vaccines. Although the long-term goal of EPI is national responsibility for the programme, many poor countries still receive the majority of their vaccine supplies from UNICEF either by purchase or as donations. Currently, UNICEF procures vaccines for more than 100 countries.

Since UNICEF buys the vaccines in huge quantities, it is in a good position to negotiate very low prices as compared with the market prices in e.g. Europe and USA. It is even argued that these prices are below the production costs and not possible to maintain in the future. It is also true that UNICEF has other pressing needs for its money and its budgets have already been reduced. These should be warning signals to developing countries to be prepared for increasing costs of vaccines. On the other hand, the price of the vaccines is only a fraction of the total costs of immunising a child (Table 48.7). Thus, at UNICEF prices all the six basic EPI vaccines cost less than 1 USD per fully immunised child.

Local production

One approach to reduce the costs of vaccines and also to ensure their availability is local production. It is estimated that 60 per cent of the DPT vaccine used in developing countries already is produced there.[13] There are problems, however. Vaccine production is a specialised activity requiring a high level of expertise. Small-scale production is not cost-effective, and few developing countries have satisfactory facilities for vaccine production and quality control.[14]

Nevertheless, local production is a sound alternative to several developing countries, provided that the basic prerequisites of Good Manufacturing Practice (GMP) are met and the quality of the vaccines assured.[15,16] GMP outlines the principles of high standard manufacturing procedures. In practice, all individual production processes must then be adapted to conform with GMP.

GMP also specifies the requirements for the facilities.[14-16] Vaccine production invariably necessitates rooms that are specially designed for the purpose. It is especially important to plan the production flow so that the risk of contamination is minimised. For example in TT production it is stipulated that the cultivation of

Table 48.5. How do the EPI vaccines retain their efficacy.[10]

Vaccine	Central store	Regional store	Distribution	Health centre	Transport to vaccination site
Measles	2 yrs −20°C	3 mo −20°C	<8°C	1 mo <8°C	1 week 0–8°C
OPV	2 yrs −20°C	3 mo −20°C	<8°C	1 mo <8°C	1 week 0–8°C
BCG	8 mo 0–8°C	3 mo 0–8°C	0–8°C	1 mo 0–8°C	1 week 0–8°C
DPT	1.5 yrs 0–8°C	3 mo 0–8°C	0–8°C	1 mo 0–8°C	1 week 0–8°C
Tetanus	1.5 yrs 0–8°C	3 mo 0–8°C	0–8°C	1 mo 0–8°C	1 week 0–8°C

Table 48.6. Immunisation instruments recommended by EPI.

Syringes/needles	Handling/precautions
Sterilisable glass or plastic syringes and steel needles	autoclave or pressure kettle 20 minutes or boiling at 100°C 20 minutes
Disposable instruments[1]	may not be re-used
Jet injector	maintenance very important – may transmit infections

[1] The use of disposable instruments is currently not recommended in developing countries because the temptation for their re-use is too great.

bacteria and harvesting of toxin must take place in a facility separate from detoxification and further processing.

Vaccine production is economic when the country can spread the cost of production and quality control across large quantities of the vaccine. Speaking in broad terms, countries with more than 50 million inhabitants have a definite case for domestic vaccine production. Production sharing is a practical alternative for middle sized countries (population of 10 to 50 million). This can mean import of bulk vaccines and their local blending, filling and finishing. Production sharing may also be a good starting point for local production. For smaller countries, procurement of vaccines will always be more economic.

Quality control

Good quality is of pivotal importance for vaccines given to large numbers of healthy children; poor quality in vaccines can result in both ethically and financially unacceptable costs. Too virulent or incompletely detoxified vaccines can cause serious injury or death, whereas ineffective vaccine does not afford the protection the vaccine is supposed to give, thus giving a false impression of safety. Vaccines *must* be safe and efficient and meet their specifications.

The final release of vaccines must always depend on independent judgment of National Control Authority (NCA) which should be established in all countries, usually within the Ministry of Health.[17] The NCA should define the national requirements for each vaccine, or alternatively, adopt the international pharmacopoeia or WHO requirements. Proper national control necessitates that the authority of the implementing officials is supported by legislation. Failure to comply with the decisions of the NCA should be penalised.

ERADICATION OF INFECTIOUS DISEASES

The great success story of WHO is obviously the eradication of smallpox.[18] This once dreaded disease boasts of two landmarks in the history of vaccination. The first use of active immunisation to prevent a serious disease on record is *variolation*, the practice of inoculating skin with material from the infective lesions of a diseased person, which was exercised in Asia as early as the 17th century. The first *vaccine* introduced by Edward Jenner in 1796 consisted of pustule contents from calves infected with *vaccinia* virus, a relative of the smallpox virus. This in fact gave the group name to vaccines and the process of active immunisation.

The use of the smallpox vaccine soon greatly reduced the incidence of the disease in Europe, but a global eradication did not happen before the large-scale Smallpox Eradication Programme started by WHO in 1966. The eradication programme relied on several simultaneous actions: mass vaccination campaigns, intensive surveillance to find all cases, and effective vaccination around them. The programme succeeded in spite of the doubts expressed by most experts, and a

Table 48.7. Costs of the EPI programme per fully immunised child in developing countries.[10]

Total	5–15 USD
of which	
salaries	45%
transport	12%
vaccines[1]	12%
miscellaneous	8%
investment (equipment, facilities)	23%

[1] The six basic EPI vaccines.

turning point appeared to be the emphasis on surveillance. Effective reporting systems had to be established in countries with meagre resources; the surveillance in the field employed large numbers of reporters visiting each village in epidemic areas.

In 1980, the WHO finally declared the world free of smallpox. A few ampoules of the smallpox virus have been stored in well guarded freezers in two special laboratories in Atlanta, USA and Moscow, and in 1994 even these will probably be destroyed. General vaccination against smallpox has been discontinued, although in a few countries the army personnel are still vaccinated.

With smallpox thus in the past history, it is appropriate to ask what next. The EPI programme now aims at eradication of polio by the year 2000. Eradication seems indeed possible since an efficient vaccine is available and the virus does not have an animal reservoir. South America already shows a very promising example.[2] The year 2000 may, however, be a too optimistic estimate.

Measles has also been suggested as a possible target for eradication. This would, of course, be very desirable, but may be quite difficult to achieve, mainly because of the suboptimal efficacy of the vaccine in the age group that would need it most.

NEW VACCINES IN SIGHT

There are still many diseases against which a vaccine would be greatly needed. Two of the foremost are malaria and ARI. There are efforts to develop these vaccines, but resources devoted to them are relatively small, probably because of the fact that manufacturers cannot expect to make good profits from the sales in these countries.

The present status of these and other vaccines in sight is discussed in the relevant chapters. The feasibility of their wide use in the target populations is another matter. The infrastructure for vaccine delivery has been built within the EPI, and could incorporate other vaccines with little additional cost. The key question, no doubt, will still be money, the resources available to buy the vaccines or special efforts to expand local production capacity and expertise.

CHILDREN'S VACCINE INITIATIVE

To obtain more funds for immunisation and vaccines, the achievements, current problems

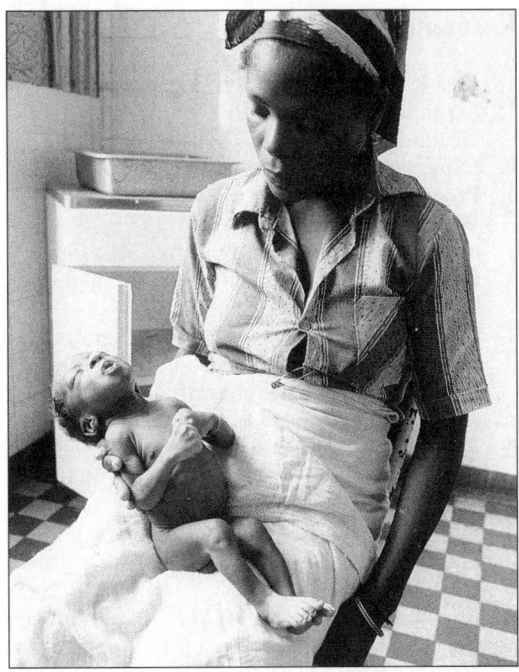

Typical posture and expression in a child with neonatal tetanus. The disease can be prevented by immunisation of pregnant mothers. Photo: UNICEF/Maggie Murray Lee

and future possibilities were presented to the Heads of State at the World Summit for Children in 1990. The idea of taking advantage of new technological capabilities to protect all children of the world from a number of infections was endorsed. The Children's Vaccine Initiative (CVI) was established as a joint activity of WHO, UNICEF, World Bank, UNDP, and the Rockefeller Foundation.[19]

A multivalent single dose orally administered Children's Vaccine was presented as the long-term goal of CVI. Specific targets listed were vaccines that would be effective as a single dose, preferably administered by the oral route soon after birth; the vaccines should be heat-stable, contain multiple antigens (component vaccines) in one dose, and protect from diseases for which currently no vaccines exist; and finally, the vaccines should be affordable to those most in need of them. The benefits thereby sought include improved acceptance and coverage, lower cost (most of the cost of vaccination is accrued in repeated contacts between the health care system and the child, Table 48.7), better quality, and prevention of new diseases.

References

1. Keja K, Chan C, Hayden G, Henderson RH. Expanded programme on immunization. World Health Stat Q 1988;41:59–63.
2. Expanded Programme on Immunization. Programme report for the year 1992. Geneva: WHO, 1993. (WHO/EPI/GEN/93.1.)
3. ten Dam HG, Toman K, Hitze KL, Guld J. Present knowledge of immunization against tuberculosis. Bull WHO 1976;54:225.
4. Styblo K. Overview and epidemiologic assessment of the current global tuberculosis situation with an emphasis on control in developing countries. Rev Infect Dis 1989;11:339–46.
5. Pio A. Impact of present control methods on the problem of tuberculosis. Rev Infect Dis 1989;11:360–65.
6. Fine PEM. The BCG story: Lessons from the past and implications for the future. Rev Infect Dis 1989;11:353–9.
7. Bloom BR, Murray CJL. Tuberculosis: Commentary on a reemergent killer. Science 1992;257:1055–64.
8. Cherry JD, Brunell P, Golden G, Karzon D. Report of the task force on pertussis and pertussis immunization – 1988. Pediatrics 1988;81:939–84.
9. Galazka AM, Lauer BA, Henderson RH, Keja J. Indications and contraindications for vaccines used in the Expanded Programme on Immunization. Bull WHO 1984;62:357–66.
10. Immunizing the world's children. Baltimore, Maryland: Population information program, Johns Hopkins University, 1986. (Population reports 1986: Series L: No 5)
11. Immunization in practice. A guide for health workers who give vaccines. Modules I–VIII. Geneva: WHO, 1984. (EPI/PHW/84/TG Rev. 1)
12. EPI Cold Chain Update. A serial information leaflet. Geneva: WHO.
13. World Bank. World Development Report 1993. Investing in health. Washington: Oxford University Press, 1993.
14. WHO. Manual for the design, equipping and staffing of facilities for the production and quality control of bacterial vaccines. Geneva: WHO, 1978. (BLG/UNDP/78.1)
15. WHO. Expert Committee on Biological Standardization. Good manufacturing practice for biological products. Geneva, WHO, 1992. (WHO Technical Report Series 822, Annex 1)
16. WHO. Expert Commitee on Specifications for Pharmaceutical Preparations. Good manufacturing practices for pharmaceutical products. Geneva, WHO, 1992. (WHO Technical Report Series 823, Annex 1)
17. WHO. Expert Committee on Biological Standardization. Guidelines for national authorities on quality assurance for biological products. Geneva: WHO, 1992. (WHO Technical Report Series 822, Annex 2)
18. Henderson DA. Smallpox eradication. Public Health Rep 1980;95:422–6.
19. Douglas RG Jr. The Children's Vaccine Initiative – will it work? J Infect Dis 1993;168:269–74.

Additional information can be obtained from

WHO, Expanded Programme on Immunization (EPI), CH-1211 Geneva 27, Switzerland

WHO, Division of Biologicals, CH-1211 Geneva 27, Switzerland

Children's Vaccine Initiative, Secretariat, WHO, CH-1211 Geneva 27, Switzerland

Both CVI, EPI and the Division of Biologicals at the WHO provide information and expert consultancy on all aspects of immunisation programmes, manufacture and quality control of vaccines. An extensive number of publications on the subjects is available from the WHO. The CVI newsletter CVI Forum can be requested free of charge from the CVI Secretariat.

About the authors

P. Helena Mäkelä is currently a research professor and Director of the Division of Infectious Diseases at KTL, the National Public Health Institute of Finland. She and her group are internationally known for research on endotoxin, pathogenesis of infectious diseases and, especially, on vaccines. She has served the WHO and CVI in several advisory positions. She is also the chairperson of Physicians for Social Responsibility (PSR) in Finland, and has participated in collaborative projects on vaccine production and field evaluation in Bangladesh and the Philippines.

Kari S. Lankinen is a research physician at the Department of Bacterial Respiratory Infections, National Public Health Institute, Helsinki, Finland. Currently, he is participating in a clinical trial conducted in the Philippines in quest of a novel ARI vaccine. Since 1987 he has been involved in setting up a vaccine quality control laboratory in Bangladesh, in collaboration with PSR-Finland and Gonoshasthaya Kendra, a Bangladeshi NGO. His special interest is development cooperation in the health sector, particularly from the perspective of NGOs.

Lankinen KS, Bergström S, Mäkelä PH and Peltomaa M, eds.
Health and disease in developing countries. London:The Macmillan Press Limited, 1994:479–484.

49 ESSENTIAL DRUGS

Juhana E. Idänpään-Heikkilä, M.D., D.M.Sc.
World Health Organization, Drug Management and Policies
20, Avenue Appia, CH-1211 Geneva 27,
Switzerland

INTRODUCTION

Availability of an appropriate selection and regular supply of affordable drugs that are efficacious, safe and of good quality, is a prerequisite for any operative health care system. In most industrialised countries a variety of drugs is usually available in sufficient quantity and some drugs may be over-used. Large segments of rural and periurban populations in developing countries – as many as about two thousand million people – have no, or only irregular, access to even essential drugs and vaccines. Drugs are expensive and often beyond the financial resources of the individual, his community or country.

The inequality in drug consumption is equally staggering; in some countries of Europe and North America the annual per capita spending is nearly 300 USD, in the developing world on average 5.00 USD, and in the poorest countries about 1.00 USD. When measured in manufacturers' prices it can be estimated that over 75 per cent of the world population living in the developing countries consume less than 20 per cent of the world's pharmaceutical market currently valued at 170 000 million USD.[1,2]

Not all countries have been able to procure low-cost generic essential drugs of good quality. Also polypharmacy and too many combination drugs and parallel preparations contribute to irrational use and prescribing practices. National morbidity and drug consumption studies in developing countries reveal mismatches between diseases and the availability of appropriate drugs to treat them. Paradoxically, in many countries, even in the developing world, there is an *over-use of drugs and non-prescription remedies*, such as tranquillisers, vitamins and tonics, but *poor compliance in the use of prescribed medications*.[3,4]

Transfer of pharmaceutical technology has met with mixed success. Some twelve to fifteen larger developing countries have the capacity to produce most of the raw materials needed for the production of pharmaceuticals and to meet most of their requirements for essential drugs and vaccines. However, some see this as part of overall industrial development, and these countries have now mainly a drug industry that produces only profitable drugs without paying much regard to the actual health needs of the population. Multi-national drug companies have subsidiaries in many developing countries, but this only rarely leads to self-reliance or to cost reduction since the mother company often owns the technology and expertise.

As more countries have started to develop the capacity to manufacture pharmaceutical products, many of the responsible governments have recognised a need for external advice on manufacturing processes, and of quality assurance in particular. Numerous small and medium-sized developing countries with formulation plants end up subsidising ineffective production or importing the same drugs at a lower cost than those produced locally. Experimental efforts to produce drugs on a large, regional or sub-regional scale have not proved to be viable alternatives to importation or domestic production.[3,4]

It was in response to this situation that WHO created in 1977 the programme on Model List of Essential Drugs, and after that

Table 49.1. List of drugs and vaccines for a village health post in an African country. Normally countries set up stepwise lists of essential drugs for different levels of health care delivery units.

Analgesics/antipyretics:	acetylsalicylic acid (tabl); paracetamol (tabl, syrup)
Antihelminthic drugs:	piperazine; niclosamide (tabl)
Antimalarials:	chloroquine (tabl and syrup)
Dermatology:	benzyl benzoate (emulsion)
Ophthalmology:	chloramphenicol (drops and ointment)
Antitussive:	any cough medication
Diarrhea:	oral rehydration salt (solution)
Disinfectants:	potassium permanganate; tincture iodine
Vitamins:	multivitamin; vitamin B complex (tabl and syrup)
Cathartics:	senna (tabl)
Vaccines:*	BCG (dried) (inj); diphtheria-tetanus-pertussis (inj); measles (inj); poliomyelitis (live attenuated) (oral solution); hepatitis B (inj); yellow fever (inj)†

* As currently recommended by WHO's Expanded Programme on Immunization (EPI) for national immunisation programmes to be available for all children (and women of child-bearing age for tetanus toxoid).
† In areas of risk of yellow fever.

the WHO Action Programme on Essential Drugs in 1981.

CONCEPT OF ESSENTIAL DRUGS

According to the World Health Organization, essential drugs are those that satisfy the health care needs of the majority of the population. Therefore, they should be available at all times in adequate amounts and in the appropriate dosage forms. This concept of essential drugs has been endorsed unanimously by the WHO Member States. It is intended to be flexible and adaptable to many different situations; exactly which drugs are regarded as essential remains a national responsibility.[5]

Model list of WHO

The WHO Model List of Essential Drugs currently has about 270 active drug substances, vaccines, diagnostics and solutions in 27 major therapy categories. Selection and updating of the list is done biennially based on the best available global expertise and scientific information in clinical pharmacology. Possibilities for local production and cost comparisons between optional drugs are also considered.[6]

The list has now been supplemented with Model Prescribing Information, and to assist countries in assurance of good quality of essential drugs WHO has prepared an Inter-national Pharmacopoeia and Basic Tests for rapid identification and screening of drugs, as well as guidelines for Good Manufacturing Practices (GMP). The WHO Certification Scheme on the quality of Pharmaceutical Products Moving in International Commerce promotes greater confidence in the quality of drugs. The consolidated information on banned and restricted products is issued regularly by WHO in the UN Consolidated List of Products whose Consumption or Sale have been Banned, Withdrawn, Severely Restricted or Not Approved by Governments.[6]

The WHO Model List does not imply that no other drugs are useful, but simply that in a given situation the listed drugs are those most needed for the health care of the majority of the population. What is essential depends on many factors, such as the pattern of prevalent diseases, the treatment facilities, the training and experience of the personnel, financial resources, and genetic, demographic and environmental factors. Where two or more drugs appear to be approximately similar in the above respects, the principle of the WHO list is to make a choice between them on the basis of a evaluation of their efficacy, safety, quality, price and availability. In cost comparisons between drugs, the cost of the total treatment, and not only the unit cost of the drug, is considered.

According to the WHO criteria most essential drugs should be formulated as single compounds. Fixed-ratio combination products are acceptable only when the dosage of each ingredient meets the requirements of a defined population group, and when the combination has proven advantage over the single components administered separately in therapeutic effect, safety or compliance. Bioavailability of each ingredient in fixed-ratio combinations also needs careful consideration.[5]

National lists

The wide applicability of the essential drugs concept is now evident from experience gained in many countries. In 1992 more than 110 countries had drawn up their own lists of the products most relevant to their needs. Most national lists are stratified to reflect requirements at different levels within the health care infrastructure, taking into consideration the training and responsibilities of the personnel charged to administer this care. In a health care system in the developing world, this usually means 6–12 drugs and 6–7 vaccines at the village level, 15–25 at the dispensary level, 40–50 at the health centre level, 100–125 at district hospital level, and in specialist hospitals rarely more than 250–300 drugs and vaccines. A list of drugs and vaccines for a village health post in an African country is described in Table 49.1. Hospital lists in the industrialised countries may contain anything from 300 to 700 different drugs.

Establishment of PHC with essential drugs should respect prevailing cultural patterns in rural communities. The work of traditional healers and use of traditional medicines (80 per cent of the world's population rely on traditional medicine) should be adapted and supplemented as required.

Other applications

The WHO List is now being used also as a model, even in highly developed countries, for basic drug selection in health centres or hospitals and for essential drugs under exceptional conditions such as war, natural catastrophes or other emergency situations. A shorter, adapted list may be of particular value in emergency situations. In collaboration with other United Nations agencies and non-governmental organisations WHO has developed an emergency health kit (including some 50 drugs) designated to cover the basic needs of a population of 10 000 for a period of about 3 months.[7]

ESSENTIAL DRUGS AT THE NATIONAL LEVEL

In order to ensure a rational basis for drug procurement, selection and use at various levels within the health care system, several steps are recommended at national level in the implementation of an essential drugs programme. The establishment of a national list of essential drugs, based on the recommendations of *a committee*, is the starting point of the programme. The committee should include individuals competent in the fields of medicine, pharmacology and pharmacy, as well as peripheral health workers. Where individuals with adequate training are not available within the country, cooperation from WHO could be sought.

The international *non-proprietary (generic) names* (INNs) for drugs or pharmaceutical substances should be used whenever available, and prescribers should be provided with a cross-index of non-proprietary and proprietary names. Concise, accurate and comprehensive *drug information* should be prepared to accompany the list of essential drugs. Competent health authorities should decide the *level of expertise* required to prescribe individual drugs or a group of drugs in a therapeutic category. Consideration should be given, in particular, to the competence of the personnel to make a *correct diagnosis*. In some instances, while individuals with advanced training are necessary to prescribe initial therapy, individuals with less training could be responsible for maintenance therapy.

Quality, including drug content, *stability* and *bioavailability* should be assured through testing or regulation. Where national or regional resources are not available for this type of control, the suppliers should provide documentation of the product's compliance with the required specifications. The success of the entire essential drugs programme is dependent upon the efficient administration of *supply*, *storage* and *distribution* at every point from the manufacturer to the end-user. Government intervention may be necessary to ensure the availability of some drugs in the formulations listed, and special arrangements may need to be instituted for the storage and distribution of drugs that have a short shelf-life or require refrigeration.

Efficient management of *stocks* is necessary to eliminate waste and to ensure continuity of supplies. *Procurement* policy should be

Table 49.2. Analgesics, antipyretics and non-steroidal anti-inflammatory drugs in the Model List of Essential Drugs. Substance in brackets is a complementary drug.

acetylsalicylic acid
paracetamol
ibuprofen
indomethacin
codeine phosphate
morphine
(pethidine)

based upon detailed *records* of turnover. In some instances, drug utilisation studies may contribute to a better understanding of true requirements. *Research*, both clinical and pharmaceutical, is sometimes required to settle the choice of a particular drug product under local conditions. Facilities for such research must be provided.

A national *drug regulatory authority* should be established along the lines recommended by WHO in the guiding principles for small national drug regulatory authorities. The authority should interact with other relevant bodies, including organisations responsible for drug procurement in the public and private sectors and the committee referred to above.[6]

ESSENTIAL DRUGS SELECTED BY WHO

The most recent version of the complete list has been published in the WHO Technical Report Series in 1992.[6] Two examples of major therapy categories from the WHO Model List of Essential Drugs are in Tables 49.2 and 49.3.

Analgesics, antipyretics and *non-steroidal anti-inflammatory drugs* include acetylsalicylic acid, paracetamol (both in tablet and suppository form), ibuprofen and indomethacin (Table 49.2). Among opioid analgesics codeine and morphine have pethidine as their complementary substance.

Antihypertensives are one subgroup of cardiovascular drugs. Since 1988 nifedipine has represented calcium-channel blockers and likewise propranolol beta-blockers among antihypertensives since 1977. Another beta-blocker, atenolol, was added to the complementary list in 1991, as well as captopril as a first example of an angiotensin-converting enzyme (ACE) inhibitors because both of these

drugs became widely used in the treatment of hypertension. Sodium nitroprusside is another complementary drug in order to treat hypertensive emergencies. Reserpine and methyldopa as complementary drugs remain on the list as low-cost well-known drugs, although neither one is commonly used any more in most of the industrialised countries. In this therapy group, hydrochlorothiazide is the only diuretic, but elsewhere in the list, under diuretics, are amiloride and furosemide. They are complemented with mannitol and spironolactone as diuretics.

The *antianginal drugs* include glyceryl trinitrate and isosorbide dinitrate as sublingual tablet, propranolol (also in injection) and nifedipine which due to its less negative inotropic effect replaced verapamil in 1988.

Antidysrhythmic drugs have on the main list lidocaine, propranolol and verapamil. The latter was added in 1988 for the treatment of supraventricular tachycardia. The complementary list now includes procainamide, quinidine and atenolol.

The list of *antiepileptics* contains almost all presently available, marketed and well-known drugs, namely, carbamazepine, diazepam, ethosuximide, phenobarbital, phenytoin and valproic acid.

The selection of *psychotherapeutic drugs* in the WHO Model List can be considered quite limited if one compares that with the large variety of drugs available today in this therapy group. From dozens of candidates in the benzodiazepine group only diazepam has qualified, based on its well-known efficacy, safety, low cost and suitability for treatment of several diseases and symptoms. Imipramine was deleted from the list in 1988 and amitriptyline has since been the only tricyclic antidepressant on the list. Lithium carbonate has been on the model list since its inception in 1977 mainly for manic-depressive illness, although the use of this drug requires specific expertise and monitoring of serum/plasma concentrations to avoid toxic reactions. Chlorpromazine, haloperidol and fluphenazine (decanoate or enantate) represent the extensive variety of neuroleptics that are available today.

Gastrointestinal drugs include as antacids and antiulcers, aluminium hydroxide, magnesium hydroxide and cimetidine. Metoclopramide and promethazine represent antiemetic drugs, atropine antispasmodic drugs, and codeine, a symptomatic drug for diarrhea. Additional drugs for diarrhea are oral rehydration salts.

Table 49.3. Anti-infective drugs. Substances in brackets are complementary drugs. For antihelminthic, antifilarial and antischistosomosis drugs see discussion in text.

Therapy category and active substance

Antibacterials, penicillins
    amoxycillin
    ampicillin
    benzathine benzylpenicillin
    cloxacillin

    phenoxymethylpenicillin
    piperacillin
    procaine benzylpenicillin

Other antibacterials
    chloramphenicol
    erythromycin
    gentamicin
    metronidazole
    spectinomycin
    sulfadimidine
    sulphamethoxazole + trimethoprim
    tetracycline
        (ciprofloxacin)
        (clindamycin)
        (doxycycline)
        (nitrofurantoin)
        (trimethoprim)

Antituberculosis drugs
    ethambutol
    isoniazid
    pyrazinamide
    rifampicin
    streptomycin
    rifampicin + isoniazid
        (thioacetazone + isoniazid)

Antileprosy drugs
    clofazimine
    dapsone
    rifampicin

A powder for reconstitution to prepare a glucose–electrolyte solution 27.9 g/l is recommended containing sodium chloride 3.5, trisodium citrate, dihydrate 2.9, potassium chloride 1.5 and glucose 20.0 g/l. In this formula trisodium citrate, dihydrate has replaced sodium bicarbonate in order to improve stability in tropical climates.

As infectious diseases are extremely prevalent, diverse factors are responsible for infections and their chemotherapy has become more complex it is understandable that the selection of globally adjusted anti-infective drugs is extensive.

The WHO Model List contains as *intestinal antihelminthics*, levamisole, mebendazole, niclosamide, piperazine, praziquantel, pyrantel, thiabendazole and albendazole. *Antifilarials* contain diethylcarbamazine, ivermectin and suramin sodium. Metriphonate, oxamniquine and praziquantel are listed as *antischistosomals*. In addition, there are *antileishmaniasis* and *antitrypanosomal drugs*.

Table 49.3 lists *antibacterials* such as penicillins, *antileprosy drugs* and *antituberculosis* drugs. Ciprofloxacin was added as a reserve antibiotic with limited indications to the complementary drugs in 1991 as a first representative of fluoroquinolones.[6]

It is becoming increasingly common for important pathogens to emerge in a country or locality that are shown on sensitivity testing to have developed resistance to all normally appropriate essential drugs. In these circumstances a *reserve antimicrobial* is needed. A reserve antimicrobial is useful for a wide range of infections, but because of the need to reduce the risk of development of resistance and because of its relatively high cost, it would be inappropriate to recommend its unrestricted use. The concept of reserve antimicrobials is of practical relevance only when information is available on the prevailing sensitivities of important bacterial pathogens. Within this context the second- and third-generation cefalosporins, the fluoroquinolones and vancomycin are most important.

The need for more systematic and coordinated international approaches to laboratory monitoring of antimicrobial sensitivity is important and urgent. It has already been emphasised that reference laboratories need to be established in developing as well as industrialised countries in order to monitor the resistance of important bacterial pathogens locally, nationally, regionally and globally. Each country should have a national reference laboratory to monitor the local resistance patterns of important micro-organisms.[6]

Antimalarial drugs have a subgroup for curative treatment and for prophylaxis. Mefloquine was added in 1988 to the complementary list and qualifies for treatment of multiple-drug-resistant falciparum malaria.

Furthermore, tetracycline was added to the complementary list and qualified for adjunctive treatment of severe falciparum malaria. In 1988 amodiaquine was deleted from the list and it was no longer recommended either for treatment or for prophylaxis.

References

1. World Health Organization. The World Drug Situation. Geneva, WHO, 1988.
2. World Health Organization. Implementation of WHO's revised drug strategy: Action Programme on Essential Drugs. Progress report by the Director-General. Geneva: WHO, 1992. (A45/12)
3. World Health Organization. Supplementary information to the WHO Programme Budget 1990–1991. Geneva: WHO, 1989. (PB 90/91)
4. World Health Organization. The rational use of drugs. Report of the Conference of Experts, 25–29 November 1985, Nairobi. Geneva: WHO, 1987.
5. World Health Organization. The use of essential drugs. Geneva: WHO, 1990. (Technical Report Series 796)
6. World Health Organization. The use of essential drugs. Geneva: WHO, 1992. (Technical Report Series 825)
7. World Health Organization. The new emergency health kit. Lists of drugs and medical supplies for a population of 10.000 persons for approximately 3 months. Geneva: WHO, 1990. (WHO/DAP/90.1)

About the author

Juhana Idänpään-Heikkilä is a senior lecturer in pharmacology and currently the Associate Director of Drug Management and Policies at the World Health Organization in Geneva. From 1971 to 1990 he was the Chief Medical Officer for Drug Evaluation in Finland. He served frequently as a Temporary Adviser to WHO, worked as a visiting scientist at the United States Food and Drug Administration (FDA) in Washington, D.C. from 1982 to 1983, and from 1988 to 1989 as a Senior Adviser to the United Nations Fund for Drug Abuse Control in Vienna, Austria. In these capacities he has worked with and visited a number of developing countries.

Lankinen KS, Bergström S, Mäkelä PH and Peltomaa M, eds.
Health and disease in developing countries. London:The Macmillan Press Limited, 1994:485–493.

50 NATIONAL DRUG POLICIES

Wilbert Bannenberg, M.D., M.Sc.
Brederodestraat 5, NL-1054 MP Amsterdam,
The Netherlands

INTRODUCTION

Although the Essential Drug Concept has been actively promoted by WHO since 1975, half of the world's population still lack regular access to life-saving and vital essential drugs.[1,2] Due to the economic crisis and the ensuing structural adjustment policies, drug budgets have been cut in many developing countries.[3] Also the rich countries are trying hard to stop the escalating costs of drugs in their health care systems. There is a worldwide need to rationalise the pharmaceutical sector: drugs should be cost-effective and serve health interests rather than business interests.

A typical developing country might suffer from two main drug problems: an abundance of expensive, non-essential, brand-name drug products often of doubtful efficacy or quality, affordable only to an urban elite; while the majority in rural areas lacks access to cheap, effective, safe, essential drugs of good quality.[1,4,5]

EXPERIENCES WITH NATIONAL DRUG POLICIES

The WHO issued its National Drug Policy guidelines in 1988 and by the end of 1991 altogether 66 countries had formulated a National Drug Policy (NDP).[2,6] But there have also been earlier examples of attempts to rationalise drug supplies.

In 1951 Egypt had 20 000 products on the market, only 10 per cent of which were produced by three local drug companies. The country then changed its drug policy to promote self-reliance and local production. By 1962, 50 per cent of the drugs were produced locally, and by 1985, 90 per cent. The number of registered drugs had fallen to less than 1500.[7] However, rational use remains a problem, drugs have recently become much more expensive, and local industries have problems competing with multinational companies.

In Asia, Sri Lanka pioneered a National Drug Policy in the early 1970s. It met with much resistance from both the medical profession and multinational drug companies. At one point the USA even threatened to stop food aid if the policy was not revised.[1]

In 1975, Mozambique had 13 000 products in a virtually uncontrolled market. Four months after independence, policies were changed, and an expert committee reduced the number of registered drugs to 2600. In 1980 another 1400 products were banned, and the National Formulary of 343 generic drugs was gaining widespread acceptance.[1] Unfortunately, the war of aggression broke out, and destroyed most of the health infrastructure. Recently, under pressure from donors, IMF and the World Bank, Mozambique was forced to accept privatisation of drug imports and distribution.

The Bangladesh experience

In June 1982 the military government of Bangladesh issued an NDP under martial law. A total of 1666 drugs were banned, based on 16 criteria drawn up in only 2 weeks by a technical committee. An Essential Drug List of 150 substances and a complementary list of 100 specialised substances were published.

The main objectives of the Bangladesh drug policy are listed in Table 50.1. The policy provoked an international controversy: it met with both praise and severe criticism. BASS, the local pharmaceutical industry association, launched an advertising campaign under the headline 'Crisis in drug industry – conspiracy against nation's drug industry must be thwarted'. The Bangladesh Medical Association, although agreeing to the policy's objectives, objected to the way it was introduced and argued that 'doctors know best what drug is good for a patient'. Multinational drug companies complained to their governments and ambassadors of six western countries made an appeal to the President to withdraw the policy.[4] The same countries had voted in Geneva during several World Health Assemblies for policies recommending PHC and the essential drug concept.[1]

NGOs organised a worldwide solidarity campaign: Bangladesh became the centre of interest for drug policy discussions. However, other countries that implemented similar policies (e.g., Ethiopia, Sudan) went unnoticed.

The ten-year experience of NDP in Bangladesh has recently been evaluated.[8] The main achievement has been the increased share of essential drugs in local production: from only 30 per cent in 1981 to 80 per cent in 1991. Drug prices have remained stable: they increased just 20 per cent in local currency, while the consumer price index rose by 173 per cent over the same period. The drug policy has saved Bangladesh an estimated 620 million USD through the reduction of import dependence and by banning useless products. The effect on rational use or quality of drugs is unclear as no reliable data exist to compare the situation before and after the introduction of the drug policy. There is probably still room for improvement, but the overall evaluation of the drug policy was positive.

NATIONAL DRUG POLICY: HOW AND WHY?

An NDP should be a written statement of intent and commitment by a country as to the drug situation it finally wants to achieve. Unfortunately, drug policies are often unwritten, out of date, inconsistent or even internally conflicting. Sometimes they are perceived as

Table 50.1. The main objectives of the Bangladesh drug policy since 1982.

– Ensure increased availability and accessibility of good quality essential drugs.

– Eliminate useless, non-essential and potentially hazardous drugs from the market.

– Encourage local manufacture of drugs and raw materials, particularly essential drugs.

– Introduce Good Manufacturing Practice (GMP) guidelines for drug producers.

– Develop appropriate legislative and administrative mechanisms.

– Take gradual steps to manufacture, distribute and sell drugs by their generic names.

– Give possibility for the government to fix maximum drug prices.

theoretical, abstract documents, drafted only to please the donor. They should, however, be a guide to action, identifying national priorities and describing the process to achieve the desired drug situation.

A National Drug Policy should state its goals, objectives, priorities and targets, and include a plan of action. It should describe the inputs (such as human resources, money and management) and the desired outputs (health and economic development). This will help to plan the pharmaceutical sector within the framework of the national health policy.

Goals and objectives

According to the WHO, the overall goal of an NDP is 'to develop, within the resources of a country, the potential that drugs have to control common diseases and alleviate suffering'.[6] Specific objectives will depend on the stage of development and the socioeconomic context of a particular country.

In Malawi, a country with a strong public sector, the first objective of the NDP is to ensure the ready and constant *availability* of high quality, acceptably safe, and proven effective essential drugs at a price the individual and the community can afford.[9] The second objective is to *rationalise use* of these essential drugs through the provision of information on improved drug utilisation. This is to be achieved by training of health professionals, and by education of the public in appropriate drug use and storage, with the aim of rationalising drug supply, management, prescribing and dispensing, and improving patient compliance.

Economic and development objectives can also be a part of the NDP: 1) to lower the cost of drugs and to reduce the amount of foreign exchange needed for drug importation; 2) to gain the necessary skills in management, pharmacy and medicine; 3) to develop a suitable infrastructure for drug procurement, storage and distribution; and 4) to develop production capacity.

Guiding principles

Drug policies cannot be isolated from health policies: therefore the NDP should support and be based upon the National Health Policy. In most countries this means support for a PHC-oriented policy. The NDP should be based on and give priority to the concept of essential drugs, as this is the most cost-effective way of guaranteeing access to vital and life-saving drugs for the majority of the population.

The NDP should be a true *national* policy, i.e. it should cover *both public and private sectors*, and be a commitment of the government as a whole, not just of the Ministry of Health. This also means that a consultative procedure with all concerned parties is needed, preferably with decisions adopted by consensus.

COMPONENTS OF NATIONAL DRUG POLICIES

Legal basis

An NDP should be officially announced by the Ministry of Health on behalf of the government. To be effective, an NDP will need a firm basis in the country's national drug legislation. Tasks such as policy coordination, drug registration, drug inspection and control, licensing of professionals and premises, and selection of essential drugs should be allocated to official bodies with clearly defined powers. Of course, laws only make sense if a country is able and prepared to enforce them. Unfortunately, many developing countries lack an effective drug inspectorate.

Drug control

Each country should decide which drug products it allows for import, production and use through a system of drug registration. The NDP should outline the criteria for drug registration: most countries have adopted efficacy, safety and good quality as criteria, but the interpretation of these data might vary from country to country.

In principle, the criteria for drug registration should be similar to those for the selection of essential drugs, but whereas the Essential Drugs List (EDL) gives priority to one or two substances within a therapeutic group, drug registration criteria define only minimum, legal requirements.

Countries must also decide how many products of the same substance they allow on their markets. The Gambia has added a *need clause* to its 1984 Medicines Act (like that in Norway).[10] This gives the authorities the right to refuse a drug on economic or policy grounds, even when it fulfils the minimum requirements of safety, efficacy and quality.

The NDP should institute a national Drug Regulatory Authority (DRA) and define its functions. WHO has produced helpful guidelines for small drug regulatory authorities.[11] The DRAs in developing countries should not unnecessarily duplicate the work of institutions in countries with more resources, and normally abstain from trying to evaluate a New Chemical Entity (NCE) unless it is specifically meant for tropical diseases. Developing countries can safely await the experiences of countries with costly post-marketing surveillance systems.

Developing countries should give priority to ensure the pharmaceutical quality of generic drugs, which form the backbone of the essential drug supply. Effective drug control also might enhance trust of the public and health workers in cheap, generic essential drugs.

Unfortunately, few developing countries have achieved effective drug control systems.[5] In most countries the political will to control and restrict the private sector is weak; the lobby of the local and importing drug merchants is very powerful. Management, financing and obtaining (and keeping!) professional staff are major problems. Developed countries and the WHO should increase support to small DRAs in developing countries, for example by providing information about the status and approved information of drugs in their countries or by twinning arrangements for training and advice. Existing information systems could also be improved and better utilised. For example, under the WHO Certification Scheme importing countries may ask DRAs in exporting countries about the status of the drug, the approved information for that drug and the GMP status of the manufacturer. Unfortunately the WHO Certification Scheme is little used.

Recent pressure from the World Bank, IMF and donors to privatise drug supply under structural adjustment programmes will probably stimulate the private sector at the expense of the public sector. Unfortunately the same donors do not help these countries to control their mushrooming private markets, and public health objectives might be compromised. Drugs should not be regarded as ordinary commodities, but should remain under strict state control in the interest of public health.

Price control

Many countries try to control drug costs for the consumer by fixing drug prices. Some use maximum prices, others use a system of fixed margins for the various levels. Some countries use the price of a drug as a criterion during drug registration. Prices differ remarkably between countries, and controlling drug prices remains a difficult issue that will depend on the socioeconomic and political orientation of the country concerned. Normally, drug companies can set the prices at a level that the market is willing to pay.

Countries probably could reduce drug costs more efficiently by applying the essential drug concept and rationalising drug procurement, prescribing, use and management through an NDP. The drug cost of a treatment episode at a typical African health centre level is 0.20 to 0.30 USD.[12] For 1.07 USD *per capita* per year Uganda can procure all the essential drugs needed up to the hospital level (Uganda 1990 quantification).[12] The fact that Africa spends an average 5 USD per capita per year shows that there is room for substantial improvement.[3,5] This could be achieved by reallocating resources from the private to the public sector in the interest of public health. However, this is not an easy issue for politicians in many countries.

Who may prescribe?

The NDP should define who has the right to prescribe. Given the lack of medical doctors it is imperative that other health workers (e.g., nurses, village health workers) are also given the right to prescribe drugs appropriate to their training and to the morbidity they face at their level. This has implications for the training and supervision of these health workers. Essential Drug Lists should be stepwise, and identify the prescribable drugs for each level. Indicators for good prescribing have been developed by the WHO and the International Network for Rational Use of Drugs (INRUD).[13]

Who may dispense?

The NDP also should define who has the right to dispense. Given the even greater lack of pharmacists, developing countries have been forced to train an intermediate level (pharmacy assistants or technicians), and to give health workers under certain conditions the right to stock, dispense and sell drugs (e.g., rural drug vendor shops).

The 'prescription only' or 'pharmacy only' systems used in developed countries do not really function under these circumstances: they rather become 'under-the-counter' systems. This means that more attention should be paid to the training of private sector drug vendors and the quality of information they provide.

Selection of essential drugs

The NDP should define the process of selecting drugs for inclusion in the Essential Drug List (including the appointment of a National Essential Drug selection Committee). Criteria for drug selection should be defined in the NDP. These have appeared in the first chapter of all WHO's Essential Drug Lists since 1977.[14]

Generic or brand names?

The use of generic names, officially International Nonproprietary Names (INN), has been advocated by the WHO since the 1950s.[15] The advantages of generic names include: standardisation of names for drug substances, clear identification of the same substance in all languages, avoidance of commercial influences, etc.

Brand names are essential for marketing activities of drug companies and are heavily promoted. A brand name identifies a specific product from a specific manufacturer whereas a generic name only defines a certain substance. Therefore drug companies try to marginalise generic names on labels and promotional material.

Countries should balance the interests of drug companies (brand names are commercial property) against the public health objectives (generic names are scientific). A compromise also exists: 'branded generics' use a generic name followed by the name of the drug company.

Quantification of therapeutic and drug needs

The NDP should rationalise the drug supply sector. For that purpose it is essential to quantify the drug needs of the various levels in the health care system. Two quantification methodologies have been developed by the WHO: the 'demand-morbidity' and the 'consumption' methods.[16] For the first method one needs the essential drug list, standard treatment guidelines, drug prices and the number of treatment episodes during a specific period. The 'demand–morbidity' method produces 'ideal' data using an epidemiological approach, as it assumes that the morbidity data are correct and that prescribers follow the standard treatment guidelines. The 'demand– morbidity' method is often used by donors to estimate the minimum budgets needed for drug supply.

The second method uses consumption data of drugs, ideally from institutions where drugs are prescribed rationally and where the supply has not been interrupted or influenced otherwise. The 'consumption' method is easier to apply but carries the risk of accepting existing bad prescribing habits. It is often used in drug ration kit systems to control the initial 'demand-morbidity' method after the first year of use.

Procurement: local production or import?

Drugs form a substantial part of health budgets. It is therefore essential that they are procured in an effective and rational way. Market intelligence is crucial: the country should monitor international price trends, reputation of manufacturers, information about drugs and product interchangeability. The traditional central medical stores under control of the Ministry of Health are gradually being replaced by independent organisations in which NGOs, donors and users may participate. The NDP should define the objectives, legal statute and the policies of such a procurement agency.

Many developing countries buy their public sector drugs in bulk under generic name through International Competitive Bidding (ICB) on the world market. This probably reduces drug costs but the quality of these generic products must be assured as enough unscrupulous drug traders exist who have no problem selling substandard or even counterfeited products. An NDP also might guide procurement policies in the private sector.

The WHO has advocated local production of pharmaceuticals for many years, but in small developing countries imported essential drugs tend to be cheaper than locally produced drugs due to economies of scale. To stimulate local manufacture, countries may allow local producers a preferential margin of 10–20 per cent. The local production of infusion fluids, syrups and ointments might be more cost-effective due to the high transport costs of water.

Equitable distribution?

The NDP should ensure an equitable distribution of drugs among the population. This means it must avoid traditional biases, such as hospitals versus health centres, urban versus rural, the rich elite versus the poor majority.

The WHO and donors pioneered the 'ration kit' concept in Kenya and Tanzania during the early 1980s.[17] This system guarantees the regular supply to peripheral health facilities of a box containing essential drugs for a given number of patients. The ration kit system bypasses the traditional drug supply chain, and some countries decided not to use the kits. They found the system inflexible and it did not stimulate active participation of peripheral health workers in their own drug supply.

Quality assurance

As the majority of developing countries import most of their drugs, they must rely on the Drug Regulatory Authority in the exporting country to certify that the manufacturer operates under GMP. For this purpose the WHO has developed the WHO Certification

The National Drug Policy in Bangladesh is exemplary. To give deprived communities greater access to basic health care, low-cost essential drugs are made available to them on a cost-recovery basis. Photo: UNICEF/Shamshuz Zaman

Scheme, which also provides the officially checked drug information and the status of registration in the exporting country. If the drug is not registered for sale in the exporting country, reasons must be given why. The certificate is only given upon request. Unfortunately, many developing countries do not yet systematically use this system.

Counterfeited drugs are becoming a serious threat to developing countries.[18] The pharmaceutical industry estimates that worldwide 6 per cent of all drug products are counterfeited: this amounts to 12 billion USD, which is more than enough to procure essential drugs for all people in developing countries. Strict drug registration might prevent some of these problems, as it involves licensing the original manufacturers and checking their quality control methods.

To increase the protection of consumers, drugs products should be tested in a quality control laboratory (QCL). However, these institutions are costly, and they require specialised expertise and equipment. The WHO has tried to promote the use of regional QCLs, but most countries want to have a laboratory of their own. Guidelines for small or medium sized QCLs are available from the WHO. The legal, administrative, financial and staff requirements of QCLs should be ensured by the NDP.

Human resources and training

The NDP should ensure that enough skilled staff is available to fulfil the tasks defined by it. Care should be taken not to train too many highly qualified professionals as they are very costly and not always suitable to solve the health problems of the majority of people. Priority should be given to an intermediate level that is more adapted to the specific needs of the health care system.

The NDP should incorporate a training policy. The curricula of the schools for health workers should include the Essential Drug Concept, the National Drug Policy and rational use of drugs. Pharmacology training should concentrate on those drugs selected by the country as essential. Established health workers should be exposed to the same topics during workshops and supervision visits.

Drug information

The NDP should ensure the accessibility of objective drug information, which is essential for both prescribers and consumers. During the registration process all drug information should be checked, including labels and package insert.

All health workers should receive a personal copy of a National Formulary that incorporates objective, comparative information about the drugs classified as essential. In addition they should have access to textbooks and an independent drug bulletin that reviews important developments in an attractive and educational way. Such an independent bulletin should ideally be produced in a national drug information centre with cooperation of the local university and the drug regulatory authority.

Control of promotion

Research-based drug companies might spend up to 10–15 per cent of their budgets on drug marketing to promote their branded products. These promotional practices have substantial influence on the prescribing habits of health workers. As this might compromise the objectives of the NDP, these practices will need to be controlled. In 1988 the WHO published 'Ethical criteria for medicinal drug promotion', and recommended all countries to incorporate them in their national drug legislation.[19] However, a recent survey showed that only a handful of countries had actually implemented them.[20]

The NDP should define the practices that are permitted. During drug registration the drug information should be screened on its scientific validity. The NDP should define a monitoring system to control marketing practices. It would be welcomed if the professional organisations and drug industry would apply some form of self-control.

Rational drug use

All efforts to bring sufficient quantities of essential drugs to a health facility will be lost if such a drug is wrongly used by the prescriber or consumer. Polypharmacy, inappropriate prescribing, excessive self-medication and overuse of antibiotics and injections are not only bad for health but also waste a lot of scarce resources. After several years of concentrating on drug selection and logistics, the WHO introduced a revised drug policy in 1986, and made rational drug use one of the priorities.[21,22]

Little is known about the knowledge, attitude and practices of consumers. Their drug-seeking behaviour often includes preference for injections, expensive antibiotics and attractive but ineffective cough syrups and tonics. The NDP should promote studies to learn more about consumers' perceptions, which could lead to interventions and campaigns for rational use of drugs.

Self-medication

Many developing countries have a shortage of doctors and pharmacists, which makes it impractical to rely on the traditional 'prescription only' system. In addition, consumers often circumvent these expensive prescribers and rely on self-medication with drugs bought 'over-the-counter' in a nearby drug store. In some countries up to 60 per cent of drugs are bought by consumers without professional advice from either prescriber or dispenser.

Therefore, the NDP should identify a list of drugs that can be obtained over-the-counter (OTC) and regulate where they can be kept and sold. The 'under-the-counter' practices should be controlled as much as possible.

Indicators, monitoring and evaluation

Besides declaring the policies, an NDP should also use indicators and a monitoring system to check whether the objectives are being achieved. INRUD and the WHO have developed indicators and monitoring systems for use at community, health facility and national levels.[13,23,24] Drug utilisation studies may provide useful information on trends in drug prescribing in both public and private sectors. A regular evaluation of the NDP itself should be programmed.

Financial resources and cost recovery

The economic crisis in many developing countries has reduced Ministry of Health budgets. As it is more difficult to lay off people, drug budgets are often chosen for drastic cuts. Cost-recovery systems where the community or the patient pay (a part of) the drug costs have become more common. The 'Bamako Initiative' launched by UNICEF in 1987 even proposed to finance some basic PHC activities from the margins made by the sale of essential drugs.[25] The NDP should take care that equity is not compromised.

SETTING UP A NATIONAL DRUG POLICY

The implementation of NDPs is often frustrated by lack of money, staff skills or political will. In structural adjustment programmes it is probably unrealistic to expect increased budgets for drugs or drug activities. Money must therefore be 'generated' by rationalising the existing systems and asking contributions from donors, NGOs, the community or the patients.

The number of skilled professionals in a country is limited. Many countries cannot offer attractive conditions to keep highly qualified professionals in government service, creating leakage towards the private sector or greener pastures abroad. Training more health professionals is very costly.

A recent WHO study found that in Africa only 22 countries had adopted an NDP. Further analysis showed that many of these NDPs were the consequence of external pressure by donors or of internal pressure due to serious lack of drugs. On the other hand, many countries had implemented NDP components without declaring an official NDP.

The government should show its political will by officially asking the Ministry of Health to prepare an NDP document. This is best prepared by a task force, consisting of representatives from the various Ministries and Organisations active in the drug sector. The draft text produced by this task force should be widely circulated and discussed at a National Drug Policy seminar, where all sectors involved should be invited. The final text should then be edited, adopted by the government, and widely distributed.

In many developing countries the plan of action will be implemented and coordinated by the National Essential Drug Programme supported by donors and NGOs. The Ministry of Health should implement the normative aspects of the NDP.

References

1. Kanji N, Hardon A, *et al*. Drugs policy in developing countries. London: Zed Books, 1992.

2. World Health Organization. Implementation of WHO's revised drug strategy. Action Programme on Essential Drugs. Geneva: WHO A45/12, 1992.

3. World Bank. Investing in health – World Development Report 1993. Washington: World Bank 1993.

4. Melrose D. Bitter pills. Oxford: OXFAM, 1982.

5. World Health Organization. The world drug situation. Geneva: WHO, 1988.

6. World Health Organization. Guidelines for developing national drug policies. Geneva: WHO, 1988.

7. Chidomere EC. Importance of national drug policies in the pharmaceutical development of developing countries. Paper presented at the DSE Drug Control Workshop April 1986. Berlin: DSE, 1986.

8. Chetley A. From policy to practice: the future of the Bangladesh National Drug Policy. Penang: International Organisation of Consumer Unions, 1982.

9. Anonymous. The Malawi National Drug Policy. Lilongwe: Malawi Ministry of Health, 1992.

10. Jallow MT. Evaluation of the national drug policy in The Gambia. Oslo: Department of Pharmacotherapeutics, University of Oslo, 1991.

11. World Health Organization. Guiding principles for small national Drug Regulatory Authorities. Geneva: WHO, 1986. Reprinted in: Technical Report Series No. 790 (annex 6) or WHO Drug Information 1989;3:43–50.

12. Hartog R, Bannenberg WJ. A review of drug quantification studies 1984–1991. Unpublished.

13. World Health Organization. How to investigate drug use in health facilities. Geneva: WHO/DAP/93.1, 1993.

14. World Health Organization. The use of essential drugs. Geneva: WHO 1992. (Technical Report Series No. 825)

15. Wehrli A. The selection and protection of international nonproprietary names (INN) for pharmaceutical substances. WHO Chronicle 1981;35(5):172–5.

16. World Health Organization. How to quantify drug needs. Geneva: WHO/DAP/88.2, 1988.

17. Haak H, Hogerzeil H. Drug supply by ration kits. Geneva: WHO/DAP/91.2, 1991.

18. World Health Organization. Counterfeit drugs – report of a WHO/IFPMA workshop 1–3 April 1992. Geneva, WHO/DMP/CFD/92, 1992.

19. World Health Organization. Ethical criteria for medicinal drug promotion. Geneva: WHO, 1988.

20. World Health Organization. Implementation of WHO's revised drug strategy. Safety and efficacy of pharmaceutical products. Geneva: WHO A45/13, 1992.

21. World Health Organization. The rational use of drugs. Report of the Conference of Experts, 25–29 November 1985, Nairobi. Geneva: WHO 1987.
22. World Health Organization. Revised Drug Strategy. Geneva, WHO A39/13, 1986.
23. World Health Organization. How to investigate drug use in communities. Geneva, WHO/DAP/92.3, 1992.
24. World Health Organization. Indicators for monitoring national drug policies in developing countries. Geneva: WHO 1993 (draft).
25. UNICEF. The Bamako Initiative. New York, UNICEF, 1987.

Additional reading

1. Blum R, Herxheimer A, Stenzl C, Woodcock J. Pharmaceuticals and health policy. London: Croom Helm, 1981. (Reprinted as paperback by Social Audit Ltd, Box 111, London NW1 8XG, 1983.)
2. Foster S. Supply and use of essential drugs in Sub-Saharan Africa: some issues and possible solutions. Soc Sci Med 1991;32(11):1201–18.
3. Hardon A, van der Geest S, Geerling H, le Grand A. The provision and use of drugs in developing countries. Amsterdam: Health Action International, 1991.
4. Management Sciences for Health. Managing drug supply. Boston MA: MSH, 1982.
5. Management Sciences for Health. Managing drug supply training series, Part 1. Policy issues in managing drug supply. Boston: MSH, 1987.
6. Pan American Health Organization. Policies for the production and marketing of essential drugs. Washington: PAHO, 1984. (Scientific Publication No. 462)
7. World Health Organization. National drug policies. WHO Chronicle 1975;29(9):337–49.

Additional information can be obtained from

World Health Organization, Action Programme on Essential Drugs (WHO/DAP), Avenue Appia, CH-1211 Geneva 27, Switzerland.

International Network for the Rational Use of Drugs (INRUD), c/o Management Sciences for Health, 165 Allandale Road, Boston MA 02130, USA.

Health Action International, Jacob van Lennepkade 334-T, 1053 NJ Amsterdam, The Netherlands.

About the author

Wilbert Bannenberg is a public health consultant based in The Netherlands. He worked for some time as a volunteer in African hospitals before specialising in public health at the London School of Hygiene and Tropical Medicine. Since 1985 he has worked as a consultant in Africa for the WHO, the Netherlands Government and the German Foundation for International Development (DSE) in essential drug policies, programmes and training. He is also active as a volunteer in Health Action International (HAI).

Lankinen KS, Bergström S, Mäkelä PH and Peltomaa M, eds.
Health and disease in developing countries. London:The Macmillan Press Limited, 1994:495–502.

51 ESSENTIAL LABORATORY SERVICES

Michael Willcox, Dr Med Sc, CBiol, MIBiol, FIMLS
Gävle County Hospital, Department of Clinical Microbiology
S-801 87 Gävle,
Sweden

INTRODUCTION

A properly functioning laboratory is as vital to health care in developing countries as it is in developed ones. Nevertheless, in the Third World laboratory services are often inadequate or simply do not exist at all, at least at the PHC level. This leaves most of the population outside the services.

Why are laboratory services important? The laboratory can aid diagnosis; the demonstration of bacteria in the cerebrospinal fluid of a child with fever and convulsions, symptoms also seen in severe malaria, sets a definitive diagnosis of meningitis. Blood glucose levels can confirm suspected diabetes or hypoglycemia. Laboratory tests can indicate the most appropriate treatment. The course of an illness can be followed and the treatment changed if necessary, for instance according to a continuing high or increasing parasite densities in severe malaria. Laboratory support is essential in antenatal clinics and in screening population groups for certain diseases. It plays an important role in surveillance and epidemiological studies; laboratory investigations may reveal the start of an epidemic and enable appropriate measures to be taken at an early stage. Finally, one of the most important functions of the hospital laboratory is the provision of blood transfusion services (Chapter 52).

A multilevel-structured programme is generally accepted as the most effective in bringing health care in developing countries to the majority of the population. There should be laboratory services at least at the health centre and district (primary), regional and central levels. The Central Laboratory is ultimately responsible for the planning, expenditure and coordination of a National Laboratory Network. The function of regional laboratories is to assist and supervise peripheral laboratory services and act as referral centres for tests not carried out in the primary level laboratories.

Although there has been much progress in establishing and expanding health care programmes, in many developing countries laboratory services have lagged behind. One explanation is a lack of interest by policy makers at government level, possibly out of ignorance of the place of laboratory services in a nationwide health service. However, the reason often is a concentration of resources in large showpiece establishments for reasons of prestige. Moreover, the setting-up of essential laboratory services in developing countries poses many challenges seldom encountered in more favourably placed countries. Among these are the scarcity of trained and experienced laboratory workers, difficulties in obtaining appropriate equipment and materials, inadequate technical back-up for maintenance of equipment and unreliable power and water supplies and poor communications. These problems are aggravated by the poor financial resources available for health services.

INDEPENDENT LABORATORIES

Laboratories independent of the government-controlled service may be found in developing

Table 51.1. Examinations performed in laboratories at rural health centres in Papua New Guinea.

Collection of peripheral and venous blood
Hemoglobin estimation
Total and differential white blood cell counts
Examination for microfilaria
Examination for malaria parasites
Gram stain
Typhoid slide agglutination test
Urine glucose and protein
Urine microscopy
Cerebrospinal fluid glucose and protein
Cerebrospinal cell count and microscopy
Examination for fecal parasites
Collection and examniation of sputum for TB
Slit-skin sampling and examination for leprosy

countries. These include laboratories in mission hospitals and clinics and the medical services of foreign concessions involved in for example oil, mining or rubber industries. Other types of laboratory are those attached to research institutes and refugee camps. Some mobile clinics may have laboratory support on field trips. There may also be private laboratories, usually situated in larger towns. All these may provide useful epidemiological information to the health services, but attrention must be paid to the utilisation of their potential.

LABORATORY WORKERS AND THEIR TRAINING

There are both locally recruited and expatriate laboratory workers in developing countries. Local laboratory workers may have a variety of different titles implying a difference in training, experience and status within the country, for example, laboratory assistant, technician or technologist. However, the laboratory assistant in one country may be the equivalent of a laboratory technician in another.

Laboratory training

Adequate training of laboratory workers is vital. Education in laboratory work should aim at both technical competence and a basic understanding of the principles behind the tests performed, their clinical purpose and the role of the laboratory in the health service.

Basic training is best formulated nationally to ensure uniformity and quality in the training.

This will also give appropriate recognition for the trainee. The initial basic training can be done centrally but a later period of on-the-job training at a suitable laboratory is essential. The course curriculum must always be in accordance with the country's health needs, resources and laboratory working conditions. It should not be a replication of a training programme of a developed country.

There is usually need for two levels of training in accordance with the type of laboratory and complexity of tests done. The basic level is the laboratory assistant who may be the only laboratory worker in a health centre. For entry to training, candidates should have a basic schooling of at least 6-8 years. In the Rural Laboratory Assistant course in Papua New Guinea at least tenth grade with a pass in English is required together with a basic health qualification such as nursing aide or community health worker. The length of a course for laboratory assistant is usually recommended as at least 6 months; in Papua New Guinea it is 16 weeks. There, the students are trained in general laboratory technique, basic hematology, malaria microscopy, basic microbiology, cerebrospinal fluid and urine examination, as well as microscopy of tuberculosis, leprosy and fecal parasites. They are also trained to keep stock lists, estimate usage of consumables and time ordering of supplies in keeping with transport delays.

At the end of the course they are able to perform a good range of laboratory examinations using a microscope and manual equipment not requiring electricity (Table 51.1). Support after training is vital. This can be given by on-site visits by a supervisor at suitable intervals and also by organising regular refresher courses and workshops at the referral laboratory. In this way competence is maintained and new skills acquired. Provision for career advancement, for example the possibility to advance to technician grade is important.

Applicants for laboratory technician training should have attained a higher level of schooling, at least up to ninth grade with passes in mathematics and a science subject. Technician training should be of 2-3 years duration in an organised institution and cover the most important disciplines. The emphasis should be on practical work but include appropriate amount of theoretical background. The training should include quality control, maintenance and supply of laboratory equipment and materials. The in-service

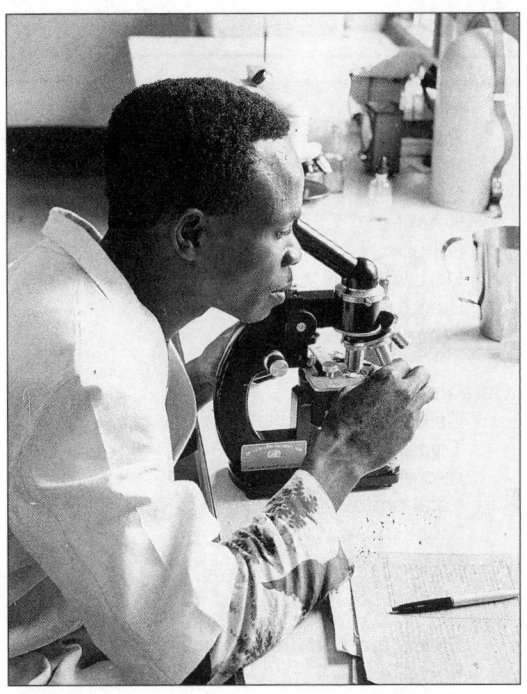

Technician examining skin biopsies in leprosy laboratory at Ossimo, Nigeria. Photo: UNICEF/ Robin Farquharson

training should in clude a period at all levels of the laboratory service including time spent at a health centre laboratory. As with laboratory assistants, both refresher courses and workshops and provision for career advancement should be arranged.

Expatriate staff in developing countries

Expatriate laboratory workers are usually recruited by organisations and agencies such as the WHO, various religious bodies, volunteer organisations, government agencies and others. They may be employed to set up new laboratory services or partake in existing ones. They usually operate in a supervisory or training capacity or as consultants.

Expatriate staff can be assumed to have a good basic education in medical laboratory work including Good Laboratory Practice. Unfortunately, working in a modern automated laboratory under ideal conditions is not the best preparation for working and living under the very demanding conditions met with in developing countries and for the professional isolation that so often leads to frustration and a sense of inadequacy.

It is the responsibility of the employing agency to see that expatriate staff are properly informed about the working conditions they will meet. This is best done by secondment to a larger laboratory in the country in which they will serve. This has both the advantage of seeing local conditions and of making useful contacts. It can also be useful to meet with persons who have had experience of working under the conditions to be encountered. Schools of Tropical Medicine in the recruiting country are often helpful.

Sometimes doctors or nursing personnel may have to keep an eye on the laboratory or even do some tests in emergencies. Orientation courses could profitably give instruction in simple laboratory procedures to all categories of health professional.

THE LABORATORY

The laboratory premises are sometimes designed and built specially for the purpose. More often it is necessary to use existing accommodation. In both cases there are several important points to consider. Bench space, ideally with a sink, should be adequate. It is important to have sufficient shelves and cupboards for storage of various items so that working surfaces can be kept uncluttered. Ventilation should be adequate. Patients and persons leaving specimens for examination should be kept out of the working areas of the laboratory. A separate room for this purpose is preferable, also separate rooms or areas for washing up and preparation of reagents. It should be possible to lock the laboratory when not in use.

Power and water supplies

Power. Most pieces of laboratory equipment need some form of power for operation. Mains electricity is lacking in many rural areas and is often unreliable even in larger towns. Power may disappear for hours or sometimes days. The voltage may also be irregular affecting the operation and even damaging some instruments. Voltage regulators protect against power surges but are ineffective with voltage drops.

In some clinics and hospitals fuel-driven generators are used to supply power and lighting but may only be used for a few hours a day during operating sessions or emergencies. The fuel for generators may run out and

Table 51.2. Essential laboratory tests for district hospitals in Africa.

Blood hematology	**Urine**
Hemoglobin	Microscopy
Hematocrit and MCHC	Parasites
Red cell morphology	Protein
Leukocyte count, differential	Glucose
Thrombocyte count	Ketones
Bleeding, clotting time	Bilirubin
Blood grouping, crossmatching	Urobilinogen
Erythrocyte sedimentation rate	Blood
Sickling test	Pregnancy test
Malaria parasites	
Microfilaria	**Cerebrospinal fluid**
Trypanosomes	Cell count
Borrelia	Trypanosomes
	Bacteria
Chemistry	Total protein
Glucose	Globulin
Urea	Glucose
Bilirubin	
Amylase	**Sputum**
Total protein	Smear for tuberculosis bacilli
Albumin	Parasites
Electrolytes	
	Pus, discharge etc.
Serology screening	Bacteria
Syphilis	Fungi
HIV	Parasites
Hepatitis B	
	Skin
Stool	Slit smear for leprosy
Blood	Snips for microfilaria
Parasites	Scrapes for fungi

Bacteriological cultures and antibiotic susceptibility tests should be done at district hospital level if possible.
Note: the range of tests done may have to be ammended according to local requirements and facilities available.

is often difficult to obtain. In remote rural areas it is rare to find power and light on a 24 hour basis. Repair and service of the generator may cause problems.

Many laboratory instruments can be adapted to run off rechargeable 12 volt storage batteries. Regular recharging is necessary. This may be done using a trickle charger if there is power from a generator for part of the day. Alternatively, a car battery can be charged from any vehicle adapted to cut out its own battery and connect the one to be charged once the vehicle has been started. Smaller instruments may be powered from small disposable batteries. However, the quality of those available in some developing countries may be poor.

A promising development is the use of solar power. Solar panels are available for charging 12 volt batteries. In Kenya, solar panels are used to power microscope lamps and hemoglobinometers in remote areas. Solar power is also used to run refrigerators and autoclaves. At present the initial installation costs of solar panels are somewhat high but maintenance is easy and running costs low.

Other forms of power which may be used for some types of equipment include bottled gas and kerosene. Disadvantages are cost, availability and the need for constant maintenance. Kerosene may be contaminated with diesel which makes the regulation of temperature in kerosene-powered incubators and refrigerators difficult.

Water. A reliable and constant supply of pure water is essential for the laboratory especially when reagents are to be produced locally. A still or deioniser is necessary to produce pure water. Stills need power for boiling water and a flow of mains water through the condenser for condensing the steam. Simple deionisers need no power and less water than a still. Ion-free water can be used for making reagents and other solutions. It is not pyrogen-free and should not be used for the preparation of intravenous solutions. Distilled water of high quality is needed for this.

The volume of pure water produced depends on the size of the deioniser cartridge and on the initial impurity of the water to be processed. Cartridges will last longer if boiled and filtered rainwater is used to produce the deionised water. The disadvantage of a deioniser is the cost and availability of replacement cartridges.

In smaller laboratories where reagents are not prepared locally, it may be possible to use clean rain or well water for such purposes as diluting stains and washing slides and coverslips. The water should be filtered before use, preferably through a ceramic filter and it is necessary to test the local water first to see if it is suitable.

Laboratory investigations

The range of tests undertaken in the laboratory should be selected according to local health needs. Suitable tests for a primary level hospital laboratory in tropical Africa are shown in Table 51.2. Appropriate technical manuals are listed in section Additional reading.

Several considerations will affect the choice of tests. These include the financial resources available, the training and experience of laboratory personnel and the facilities and equipment available. Another consideration is the volume of work possible without affecting the quality. All too often laboratories, especially at the primary health care level are given too much to do resulting in long and irregular hours of work. This inevitably leads to a reduction in standards.

Each test must be considered on its merits. Is it really needed? For instance, in a holoendemic malaria area are routine thick drops on every patient necessary? Are the likely numbers of a particular test sufficient to justify its inclusion in the laboratory's repertoire? Can the examination be done better elsewhere? Where skin slit smears for leprosy are only required occasionally it may be more practical to refer patients to a leprosy clinic with laboratory facilities if one is situated within a reasonable distance. On the other hand, there are always certain tests less commonly needed than others but when they are needed, they are often wanted urgently, for example blood glucose levels. In such instances it is important that the laboratory is kept in practice by being asked to perform the test sufficiently often.

A simple form of recording receipt of specimens and results is needed. Whether books or filing cards are used, much unnecessary writing can be saved by using rubber stamps. It should be routine practice to prepare monthly and annual reports of laboratory activities for the appropriate authorities.

Quality control

Internal Quality Control and Quality Assurance are procedures for monitoring the performance of a laboratory. The term Quality Control usually applies to the technical work of the laboratory whereas Quality Assurance is a wider and more modern concept including all aspects of laboratory investigations from the doctor ordering a test through specimen collection, transport to the laboratory, reception and analysis of the specimen and giving the answer back to the doctor. All laboratories should have some form of quality control.

Simple methods such as dividing occasional specimens in half and submitting both for testing under different names are preferable. Another simple method which is used in the assessment of leprosy smears at the laboratory at ALERT Hospital in Addis Ababa but can be applied to other types of microscopical examination, is for all involved technical staff to read one or two positive smears each week and compare the results. In time this has resulted in a satisfactory consistency in reading the smears.

Vital to internal quality control is the preparation of a local Laboratory Procedures Manual. This should include information on laboratory organisation, technical details of all methods used in the laboratory, reference values and the significance of unexpected results, advice on specimen collection and referral of specimens for investigations not done in the laboratory. The manual should include details of the maintenance and repair of equipment. One section should deal with laboratory safety and the steps to take in case of mishap. The manual should be available in a local language. It should be readily available for all and it should be reviewed and revised regularly. Above all, it should be used!

External Quality Assessment is the term used when the laboratory performance is assessed by an external agency. This may be the Central Laboratory of a national laboratory service or an international one such as the United Kingdom National Quality Assessment Schemes (NEQAS). A simple but effective External Quality Assessment scheme has been introduced in Papua New Guinea. At present it is confined to malaria, tuberculosis and leprosy slides. These are posted to rural laboratories and the returned results scored. An assessment is returned to the individual laboratories with relevant comments. The African Medical and Research Foundation (AMREF) based in Kenya is at present preparing materials for a simple external quality assessment scheme.

Referral of specimens

In a well-functioning laboratory network tests not done at the local level may be referred to a laboratory having the necessary facilities. Histopathological specimens are those most commonly referred but referral may be necessary also for other types of investigation such as some chemical tests and immunological investigations. Laboratory workers must be trained in the proper collection, preservation, packing and shipment of specimens, whether by post, road, rail or some other means of transport so that the specimens arrive at their destination in a viable condition. Those responsible for the actual transport of the specimen, drivers etc. must also be instructed in correct handling procedures. Biological safety practices must always be strictly adhered to.

Local conditions, the location of the laboratory, bad roads, inclement weather and other factors may make referral of specimens impracticable. It must always be remembered that a referral scheme no matter how well organised at the peripheral level is only justified if *results are available in time to benefit the patient or are part of an epidemiological study*. In the latter case, an explicit protocol of the study must be available and approved.

Table 51.3. Major equipment for laboratories at primary health level.

Balance
Battery, 12 volt storage and charger*
Centrifuge, general purpose
Centrifuge, microhematocrit
Colorimeter (or comparator Lovibond type)
Distilled water unit or deioniser
Hemoglobinometer (colorimeter can be used)
Incubator
Microscope
Oven, hot air
Refrigerator
Steriliser, pressure cooker type
Waterbath or heating block
Water filter

* if mains electricity is not available

Laboratory safety

This is of paramount importance. Persons working in a laboratory environment are exposed to biological, chemical and physical agents with a consequent risk of infection, poisoning or injury. Laboratory personnel must be aware of the various pathways by which infections are acquired in the laboratory. These include direct contact, ingestion, accidental injection and inhalation of aerosols released by various procedures, e.g. centrifugation. Laboratory workers should be trained to minimise the risks of infection by using good laboratory techniques. Dangerous procedures such as mouth pipetting, smoking or eating in the laboratory must be forbidden. The proper use of rubber gloves, when available, should be encouraged although in some circumstances wearing rubber gloves can introduce further hazards. Training in the handling and disposal of infected and dangerous materials is vital. Neither the environment nor other persons must be exposed to risk of infection, poisoning or injury.

The dangers associated with the faulty use of certain equipment such as centrifuges and autoclaves must be made clear. Also the possibility of explosion risks from smoking in the laboratory and the wrong storage and handling of inflammable chemicals such as ether. Faulty use of gas burners and sparking centrifuges because of worn brushes from lack of maintenance are also sources of explosion risks. There should be guidelines for the handling and storage of chemicals and reagents. Precautions and procedures to be adopted in the case of any mishap in the laboratory should be clearly defined and recorded in the Laboratory Manual.

LABORATORY EQUIPMENT

There is a shortage of laboratory equipment suitable for use in developing countries. Lack of maintenance, spare parts and repair facilities together with unreliable power supplies and extreme climatic conditions have resulted in graveyards of unusable instruments in some laboratories. Other equipment is inappropriate, for instance the automatic blood staining machine gathering dust in a laboratory in West Africa because its daily need of reagents would last a month using manual methods. Moreover, the machine cannot process thick drops for malaria, the laboratory's main output.

Despite some progress in designing equipment specially for use in developing countries, the financial returns are not sufficient to interest most manufacturers. Appropriate equipment does not have to be sophisticated. What is needed is simple, rugged and good

Table 51.4. Minor equipment for laboratories at primary health level.

Bunsen burner if gas is available, otherwise
 spirit lamp
Hotplate or kerosene stove
Insulated container
Hand tally counter
Counting chamber and coverslip
Interval timer
Dispensing and pipetting devices
Racks and trays
Staining equipment (racks, staining jars,
 drop bottles)
Slides and coverglasses
Syringes, needles
Blood lancets
Forceps
Tourniquet
Blood taking sets and units or bottles
Dressings
Cleaning materials
Markers, glass writing material
Thermometer
Glass and plastic ware (test tubes, beakers,
 cylinders, flasks etc)

---

quality instruments. Two important priorities are a low cost microscope with good optics and a simple, reliable and reasonably priced hemoglobinometer. Items of equipment essential for use in primary level hospital laboratories are shown in Tables 51.3 and 51.4. Technical details of this equipment can be found in publications listed under Additional reading. Before buying new equipment there are several factors to consider:

Needs. is the piece of equipment really necessary? Is it compatible with the type and volume of tests performed in the laboratory? Is it appropriate, that is, is it the right piece of equipment for the local conditions of use? Note that needs must be distinguished from wants. A want may arise from a whim, seeing a new piece of equipment in a catalogue or in another laboratory.

Cost. Do the purchase price and operating costs, including servicing, fall within the available financial limits? Are there other equivalent but cheaper instruments that will perform as satisfactorily under local conditions? It may be useful to consult others that are using equipment for the same purpose. It is always important to inspect the market and obtain estimates including the cost of servicing.

Maintenance. Are spares readily available and is a comprehensive operating and repair manual provided with the instrument? Are the instructions simple and readily understandable by local staff? Are they available in a more understandable language when this is not English?

Operation. Is the instrument suitable for use by personnel with limited training and experience?

Power requirements. Does the piece of apparatus require a stable electricity supply? Can it be used with a voltage stabiliser or an alternative power supply such as a battery?

Safety. Is the apparatus safe to use under local conditions?

Laboratory stores and supplies

Obtaining laboratory supplies is often a major logistic problem in developing countries. In a well-run national laboratory service, peripheral laboratories are supplied with necessary materials through the Central and Regional laboratories. In other cases, the responsibility lies with the individual laboratory.

Consumables and items needing replacing fairly often, such as chemicals, reagents, test kits where used, glassware, microscope lamp bulbs etc. are often difficult to obtain quickly especially in remote rural areas where it may take several months to obtain materials. It is essential that a proper record of stocks maintained and used be kept and needs anticipated well in advance. This is especially important for reagents with a limited shelf life.

Training of all laboratory workers should include anticipation of supply needs and ordering procedures. In practice, one person in the laboratory should be given this responsibility. Theft of desirable items is not uncommon in laboratories. Laboratory stores must be safeguarded. This applies especially to items such as pregnancy test kits which may be used in private business. Even major items of equipment such as microscopes have been known to disappear mysteriously.

Reagents can be prepared locally from the various chemicals or bought ready-made. Although it is often better to buy ready-made and standardised reagents this will depend on the cost and availability and also on the level of ability of the local laboratory worker.

Chemicals and reagents must be stored correctly both from the point of view of safety and also keeping qualities. Expiry dates should be noted and storage temperatures adhered to. If a blood bank is maintained, laboratory specimens and, where possible, reagents should be stored in a separate refrigerator.

Additional reading

1. Cheesbrough M. Laboratory health care in developing countries. Proceedings of the 17th Congress of International Association of Medical Laboratory Technologists; 1986 August 3–8; Stockholm, Sweden. Cambridgeshire: Tropical Health Technology, 1986.
2. Cheesbrough M. Medical laboratory manual for tropical countries. Volume I. Second edition. Cambridgeshire: Tropical Health Technology, 1991
3. Cheesbrough M. Medical laboratory manual for tropical countries. Volume II: Microbiology. Cambridgeshire: Tropical Health Technology, 1991.
4. Johns W. Establishing a refugee camp laboratory: A practical guide. London: Save the Children, 1987.
5. King M. A Medical laboratory for developing countries. London: Oxford University Press, 1973.

6. Mitchell FL, Martinez-Silva R, Vardhan H, et al. Supply, maintenance and repair of health care equipment in developing countries. Geneva: WHO, 1983. (WHO/LAB/83.8)
7. Nilsson T, Sparell G. Skin smears for leprosy. Würzburg: German Leprosy Relief Association, 1989.
8. Program for Appropriate Technology in Health. Major equipment for peripheral laboratories. Seatlle: Program for Appropriate Technology in Health, 1991. (Health Technology Directions 11; No 1)
9. Program for Appropriate Technology in Health. Small equipment and supplies for peripheral laboratories. Seattle: Program for Appropriate Technology in Health, 1992. (Health Technology Directions 12; No 1)
10. Vandepitte J, Engbaek K, Piot P, et al. Basic laboratory procedures in clinical bacteriology. Geneva: WHO, 1991.
11. World Health Organization. Laboratory services at the primary health care level. Geneva: WHO, 1987. (WHO/LAB/87.2).
12. World Health Organization. Manual of basic techniques for a health laboratory. Geneva: WHO, 1980.
13. World Health Organization. Basic laboratory methods in medical parasitology. Geneva: WHO, 1991.
14. World Health Organization. Basic malaria microscopy. Part I: Learners guide. Geneva: WHO, 1991.
15. World Health Organization. Basic malaria microscopy. Part II: Tutor's Guide. Geneva: WHO, 1991.

Additional information

For a list of information sources and providers of appropriate technology laboratory equipment see Appendix in Chapter 53.

About the author

Michael Willcox has many years' experience of laboratory work in the tropics. During 1968–1973 he worked in Liberia as a Laboratory Chief. Since 1976 he has participated regularly in field studies in Liberia, Somalia and Tanzania on the epidemiology and development of drug resistance in malaria. His major research interest is hemoglobinopathies and the malaria hypothesis. He teaches regularly on the Uppsala University Course in Tropical Health Care and the Karolinska Institute Diploma Course in Tropical Medicine in Stockholm.

Lankinen KS, Bergström S, Mäkelä PH and Peltomaa M, eds.
Health and disease in developing countries. London:The Macmillan Press Limited, 1994:503–511.

52 BLOOD TRANSFUSION SERVICES

Jukka Koistinen, M.D., Ph.D.
Finnish Red Cross Blood Transfusion
Service
Kivihaantie 7, FIN-00310 Helsinki,
Finland

Nandrani De Zoysa, M.B.B.S., D.T.M.&H.
National Blood Transfusion Service, Central
Blood Bank
General Hospital, Colombo 8,
Sri Lanka

INTRODUCTION

Blood transfusion is today a routine hospital function, and transfusions are given in every hospital with surgeons, obstetricians or pediatricians. Whole blood and red cell concentrates are needed for the management of anemia and hemorrhage, while other components, such as plasma, coagulation factors and white cell and platelet concentrates are used in the management of patients with burns, hemophilia and hematological disorders (e.g. leukemia and aplastic anemia).

Blood and blood components should be available to all patients who need them and the clinicians should be able to plan the treatment of their patients without fearing lack of blood. This can be best taken care of by organising a blood transfusion service at least within the hospital, but preferably within a region or country as part of the national health care structure. However, more than half of the developing and least developed countries still have only uncoordinated hospital-based blood banks (Figure 52.1).

BLOOD TRANSFUSION SERVICES IN THE NATIONAL HEALTH PLAN

Recognition

The organisation and the degree of development of the blood transfusion services (BTS) should fit into the national health plan. The government has the ultimate responsibility for the BTS regardless of the organisation that

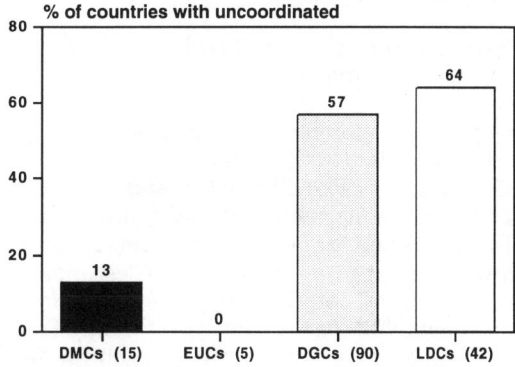

Uncoordinated hospital based BTS

Figure 52.1. Proportion of countries in which the blood transfusion services are the responsibility of individual hospitals. Numbers in parenthesis indicate the number of countries which have replied to the WHO/GBSI questionnaire. DMC = industrialised developed countries, EUC = Eastern European (economies in transition) countries, DGC = developing countries, and LDC = least developed countries. Classification according to World Economic Survey.

is responsible for the implementation of the blood programme. – Transfusion medicine consists of donor recruitment and retention, collection, testing, processing, and storage of blood as well as training of physicians in appropriate use of blood. In order to gain adequate support for all this the national authorities should recognise BTS as a distinct entity in the medical care system.

Annual blood donations

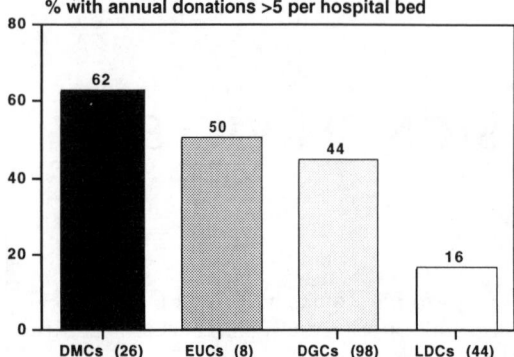

Figure 52.2. Proportion of countries with five or more blood donations per hospital bed. Only beds in the acute hospitals have been included (excluding e.g. mental hospitals). Classification of countries as in Figure 52.1. Number of reporting countries in parentheses.

Estimation of the need of blood and blood components

As many developing countries have shortage of blood, it is usually difficult to assess the need. In most cases all blood that is collected is transfused immediately, and there is usually no demand for blood components because they have not been available. It is estimated that an annual collection of *five units of blood per hospital bed in acute care is sufficient*. This has been achieved by only 44 per cent of developing and 16 per cent of the least developed countries (Figure 52.2). The degree of sophistication of a BTS should be based on an estimation of the need for blood products in the country. It is a waste of resources to prepare *blood components* if the hospitals are not equipped to diagnose or treat patients who would benefit from them. For example, preparing cryoprecipitate cannot be justified if it is not possible to diagnose hemophilia.

Formulation of a national blood policy

Every country should have a *national blood policy* which should be integrated into the national health plan, for implementation by the authority responsible for managing the BTS system. This policy should define: 1) the organisation that is responsible for the implementation of the blood programme; 2) the method of funding the BTS; 3) the concept of

blood donation (voluntary non-remunerated blood donation system is preferable to a replacement system and a paid system should be avoided); and 4) the appropriate regulations and legislation for blood donation and transfusion.

The establishment of a national blood policy has been one of the most important recommendations at the WHO regional blood safety workshops, and in many regions good progress has been made towards reaching this elementary target. Already 61 per cent of the developing and 32 per cent of the least developed countries have adopted a national policy (Figure 52.3). – Leaving the BTS system unorganised leads to uncontrolled operations with risks of exploitation of the blood donors and unsafe practices which may endanger the lives of patients by exposing them to transfusion-transmissible agents.

National blood policy

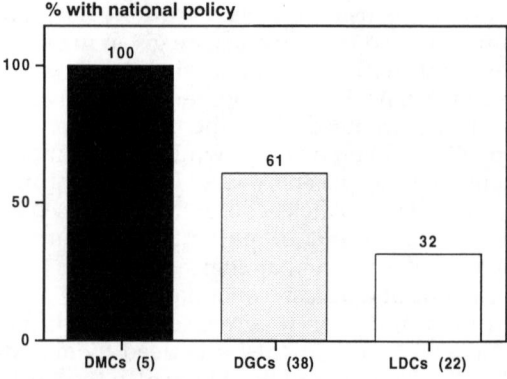

Figure 52.3. Proportion of countries in which a national blood policy has been adopted. Classification of countries as in Figure 52.1. Number of reporting countries in parentheses.

RESPONSIBILITY FOR THE ORGANISATION OF TRANSFUSION SERVICES

The Ministry of Health in each country has the responsibility of ensuring that there is a functioning BTS system. The responsibility of the organisation can be delegated to a governmental agency or a non-governmental organisation (NGO). The Red Cross is the NGO that is most often associated with BTS. Blood banks operating for profit are not recommended, because they may have a temptation to save costs at the expense of adequate quality assurance.

In many countries national BTSs operated by the government collaborate with NGOs, usually the Red Cross Societies. The Red Cross is often responsible for donor recruitment and the national or hospital BTS takes care of blood collection, component preparation, testing and storage of blood.

PROVISION OF FUNDING

Recognition of a need to have a BTS system is not enough, sufficient funding should also be provided. It is the responsibility of the national authorities to do this regardless of the methods of implementation of the blood programme, because the Red Cross or any other NGO will not be able to provide funds for BTS on a permanent basis. Funding should be provided as an annual allocation to the BTS, or on a cost recovery basis by the hospitals for reimbursement later by the government.

BTS should provide information on the principles of the cost recovery system to blood donors to enable them to understand the reasons for charges levied on blood which has been donated without remuneration. The activity is readily accepted if it can be shown that the expenditure of the BTS exceeds the allocation from the national budget and no profit is made.

NATIONAL BLOOD TRANSFUSION SERVICE

The 28th World Health Assembly passed in 1975 a resolution (WHA 28.72), which urges WHO Member States to promote the development of national blood transfusion services based on voluntary non-remunerated blood donations. In small countries (e.g. with a population less than ten million) it may be more feasible to have a National Blood Transfusion Service (NBTS), where one single organisation takes care of the BTS in the whole country. In large densely populated countries regional organisation may be better.

The degree of centralisation will depend on factors such as the economy of the country, historical background of the BTS, geography, the development of the general infrastructure and also the political realities. It may be necessary to create a network of regional BTSs, which can work under the supervision of the NBTS. Some of the advantages and the disadvantages of a centralised national blood transfusion service system are listed in Table 52.1. If a country has uncoordinated hospital-based BTSs, their work should be coordinated for instance through a national blood transfusion committee which would be able to agree on the guidelines, practice and national quality assurance of transfusion medicine in the country.

RECRUITMENT AND SELECTION OF BLOOD DONORS

Voluntary unpaid blood donation

Voluntary non-remunerated (unpaid) blood donation is preferred. It is safer because *it does not attract persons in acute need of money*, e.g. drug abusers, who often are carriers of transfusion-transmissible infectious agents. It also *eliminates the risk of exploitation of the poor* as it removes remuneration as a motive for blood donation. Small tokens (pins, awards etc.) given in recognition of repeated donations can be used, but they must be of no commercial value.

Many developing countries rely on replacement donations, which means that patients have to find blood donors to replace the amount of blood which they may need (Figure 52.4). Replacement donation can sometimes be a prerequisite for a surgical operation, but this system is not recommended. If the

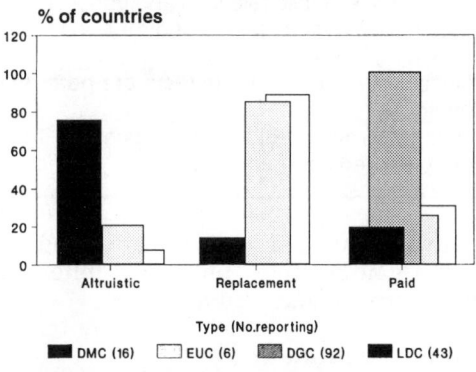

Type of blood donation

Changes are being introduced in EUC

Figure 52.4. Proportion of countries having altruistic (voluntary, non-remunerated), replacement (e.g. family) and paid blood donation systems. Numbers in parenthesis indicate the number of countries which have replied to the WHO/GBSI questionnaire. Classification of countries as in Figure 52.1.

Table 52.1. Advantages and disadvantages of a centralised national blood transfusion service system.

Advantages

- Good national coordination
    - cost-effectiveness (bulk purchases, centralisation of some functions, more efficient use of personnel
    - better capacity to provide blood in emergencies
    - better national quality assurance
    - uniform training of personnel
- Possibility to create a strong national blood transfusion service centre, which:
    - can provide wider expertise to develop the blood transfusion service and to serve the clinicians
    - can establish national reference laboratories (e. g. blood group serology, hematology, HLA, coagulation, etc.)
    - can support research (which may serve as an incentive for hiring talented professionals)
- A unified image and high profile nationally, which is important in donor recruitment and in the professional community.

Disadvantages

- Requires good communication (telephone, telefax, for laboratory results) and transportation (for samples and blood products) systems.
- Greater distance to the hospitals if they have to contact the national blood transfusion service for assistance.
- Greater distance to the blood donors, if the mobile units, public relations and donor recruitment operate from a central blood transfusion service only.
- Delay in test results if the tests are performed centrally.
- Delay in provision of blood components if they are prepared only centrally.

relatives are not willing to donate blood or if there are no relatives, unknown donors are often recruited and paid for.

Donor recruitment

Some problems associated with blood donor recruitment are listed in Table 52.2. The director and other professional staff of the BTS are important in the recruitment of donors, for example in gaining the support of community leaders. The BTS professionals should make public appearances, write and be interviewed about blood donation and blood transfusion and in this way educate the public. Lack of knowledge about human physiology is often a cause of fear of blood donation. Potential blood donors like to hear about the importance of their blood gift also from the doctors, scientists and clinicians who process and use their blood. Also political, religious and other leaders should understand the importance of blood donation and, if possible, become blood donors. Because of their position in the community, this actually often facilitates blood donor recruitment.

Blood donors must feel that their needs are attended to at the blood transfusion service, that their questions are taken seriously and answered and that their gift to the patient is appreciated also by the personnel of the BTS. Friendliness and ability to deal with prospective donors are important characteristics of the donor room personnel. A friendly and positive attitude alleviates also the fears the blood donor may have.

Adequate information about the need of blood and about blood donation is important in getting support to blood donation. The recruitment strategies must also comply with the possibility to donate blood. Sometimes it may be costly to organise blood donations at remote places, but they are important to gain the support of the public as everyone should have a feeling that he/she has an opportunity to donate blood. *Satisfied blood donors are always the best donor recruiters*.

Regardless of the efforts of the medical professionals special personnel are necessary for donor recruitment and public relations. Donor recruitment material must be produced, contacts with the press developed and maintained. Once the press understands the importance of the work of blood transfusion service and the need of the support of the public, it is usually willing to help.

Selection of blood donors

Good health is the basic requirement for a blood donor. There must be standard selection criteria, based on epidemiological surveys, so that the donor room personnel can judge who will be eligible to donate blood. The reason for rejection of a blood donor should be explained to ensure his/her positive attitude towards the BTS in spite of the rejection.

Fear of being rejected from blood donation and this being noticed by other donors may inhibit some people from attending the session. Confidentiality must always be maintained, and blood donors should have an opportunity to refrain from donation without undue publicity or stigmatisation. These issues should receive appropriate attention also at mass blood donations, where there may be peer pressure to donate blood.

Either hemoglobin or hematocrit should be measured and donors who do not meet the requirements should not be accepted. The simple copper sulphate method for screening of hemoglobin concentration is acceptable, but must be properly controlled.

COLLECTION AND PROCESSING OF BLOOD

Blood collection

Whether blood is collected at blood centres or mobile blood donation sessions the facilities for blood collection should be made as convenient as possible for the donors. For instance, it may be necessary to keep the centres open after normal working hours, even if this requires flexibility from the donor room personnel and the staff responsible for processing the blood.

Mobile donation sessions are useful in that the service is taken to the donors and many employers allow their personnel to donate blood during working hours if the donation is organised at the work place. Blood donations organised in cafeterias, gymnasiums, and halls are usually more successful and cost effective than those organised in mobile donation vans. The vans are also expensive to purchase and maintain.

Table 52.2. Often mentioned causes for unsuccessful blood donor recruitment.

- Insufficient participation by the Director and other professional staff of the BTS
- Lack of support from community leaders
- Improper handling of blood donors
- Weak and unconvincing recruitment efforts
- Fear of the donation process
- Fear of any 'medical' action in general
- Religious objections
- Fear of being rejected from donation
- Indifference
- Egoism (e.g. give only to family members)
- Poor general state of health of the population

Testing

It is essential to do blood grouping (ABO and Rh groups) and screening for HIV and other markers of transfusion-transmissible infections of every blood unit collected. Blood grouping on both red cells and serum (reverse grouping) are necessary, because the latter is part of the quality control system, particularly in those circumstances in which storage conditions for reagents are not ideal. The necessity of Rh grouping in populations where the Rh negative group is rare (e.g. in China and the Far East) must be decided locally, depending on available resources. Compatibility testing (cross matching) must be done with the patient's blood sample and the unit of blood to be transfused, in order to detect serological incompatibilities or identification errors which could result in transfusion reactions which may cause severe illness and may even be fatal.

If the number of samples to be tested is small, it is advisable to use rapid assays such as particle agglutination, which becomes cheaper than the enzyme-linked assays (EIA). Simple tests do not need expensive equipment requiring power supply. HIV-positive blood units must be disposed of safely. If blood donors are informed of positive results, appropriate facilities for counselling must be available. Donors should be informed only after confirmation of the positive result by another method and also from a new blood sample.

The WHO currently recommends that all donated blood should be tested for hepatitis B markers and for anti-hepatitis C. In some countries where hepatitis B is endemic, but which cannot afford to purchase hepatitis B antigen (HBsAg) test kits, this test is not done. This could be argued for also on medical grounds – if the carrier rate of HBsAg is 20 per cent and as much as 70 per cent of the population have antibodies to HBsAg, the risk of transfusion hepatitis is small in comparison with other mechanisms of transmission. Currently, hepatitis C carriage rates appear to be low both in developing and industrialised countries and the practical significance of hepatitis C testing is not quite clear yet (Chapter 24). The complex testing issue has been discussed in detail in a recent WHO document (WHO/LBS/91.1).

The causative agent for syphilis dies in blood at +4 °C storage within 3 days. Although storage of blood in a refrigerator eliminates the risk

Figure 52.5. Safety of blood transfusion is maximised by selection of safe donors, appropriate testing, processing and storage of blood and by giving transfusions only when necessary.

of transmission, testing for syphilis is also recommended. It is cheap, easy to perform and serves as an additional surrogate marker for other transmissible diseases. Testing for Chagas disease is important in endemic areas. treatment of blood after collection with gentian violet eliminates the causative agent of Chagas disease. In malaria-endemic areas treatment for malaria following blood transfusion is recommended, but the drug selected should be appropriate to local conditions and a curative dose should be used.

Processing and storage

Production of blood components must correspond to clinical needs, which may be different in different parts of the country. Sophisticated products are needed only if the hospitals have appropriate diagnostic and other resources to justify their use.

Whole blood and red cell concentrates must be stored at +4 °C and plasma at –20 °C. If special blood bank refrigerators are not available, normal household refrigerators may be used if suitably monitored. Solar-powered refrigerators are useful in some circumstances despite of the high purchase price. The

temperatures of refrigerators and freezers should be monitored and recorded and insulated transport boxes should be used for transport of blood and blood products.

COSTING OF BLOOD TRANSFUSION SERVICES

It should be realised that operating a blood transfusion service is costly and it is better to budget separately for it than to include the costs in other budgets (e.g. laboratory). This facilitates monitoring expenditure and the processing of requests for further development. This applies even if the BTS is run by the Red Cross or by some other NGO: the BTS budget should be separated from the budget of the rest of the organisation. This allows the decision makers and those who ultimately pay (e.g. the government) a better opportunity to monitor the use of funds.

Estimates of the production price of a unit of blood must include the capital and overhead costs for fuel, telephone, utilities, insurance and building and equipment maintenance, as well as allowances for depreciation and inflation. These costs vary in different parts of the world, but usually the production price is 25–35 USD per blood unit. This is about the same in developing countries despite lower labour costs, because blood bags and reagents for screening of transfusion-transmissible agents and for blood grouping and other supplies form the major part of the costs.

In many countries purchase of all medical equipment, material and supplies is centralised to the Ministry of Health. This may allow more economical bulk purchasing also for BTS material. At least the most expensive items, blood collection bags and reagents, should be purchased in bulk.

APPROPRIATE USE OF BLOOD

A classical statement by a surgeon is 'when my patient bleeds he bleeds whole blood and I want to give him whole blood'. This is still echoed by some surgeons, but modern transfusion therapy is not transfusion of whole blood, not even in an acute hemorrhage. In most cases restoration of blood volume with crystalloids and colloids suffices. Sometimes red cell replacement is also necessary, but this should preferably be done with red cell concentrates. In some developing countries blood is often easier to obtain than other intravenous solutions. However, blood should be transfused only when it is clearly indicated because of the associated risks. Crystalloids and colloids like glucose, sodium chloride, dextran 70 and polygeline are included in the WHO list of essential drugs and should be made available in all countries.

Blood transfusion services have the responsibility of educating the clinicians on the appropriate use of blood including information on the characteristics and advantages of blood components. – It should also be emphasised that dividing one unit of whole blood into a red cell concentrate and plasma or into four pediatric units of blood gives an opportunity for optimal use. Preparation of more sophisticated components like cryoprecipitate, cryodepleted plasma, platelets and leukocytes, further optimises the use of each single unit of blood.

BLOOD TRANSFUSION SERVICE IN A SMALL HOSPITAL

In a small hospital in remote areas far from the nearest BTS it may not be feasible to organise a separate blood transfusion service. The collection, testing and processing of blood must then be taken care of by the department of surgery, pathology or laboratory. In this case it is necessary to obtain support from a larger BTS and a reference laboratory, which can provide the rarely needed blood components and solve difficult laboratory problems. Ideally the blood collection and training of the personnel responsible for it should be supervised by the national or regional BTS.

Often in these cases it is better to collect blood only when needed, for instance in emergency cases. For such purposes a register should be established of potential blood donors who have been tested for infectious agents and who can be asked to donate blood. However, it must be remembered that in many so called emergency cases where large amounts of blood are needed, it is often better to start with crystalloids and colloids and to bring blood from larger blood banks than to start calling the blood donors, bleed them, test the blood and send it to the wards.

RECRUITMENT AND TRAINING OF PERSONNEL

It is important to remember that the blood donors of a BTS are different from the patients in a hospital. This sets different standards to the qualifications and personality of the BTS personnel when compared with the hospital staff.

There must be continuous training of all categories of the personnel, starting from the donor recruiters, donor room personnel, laboratory technicians and including the physicians of the BTS. In developing countries it may be difficult to allow the trained personnel a leave of absence for participation in further training. The WHO is in the process of producing distance learning material to assist in training in situations where the manpower resources do not allow attendance in training courses away from the hospital.

Since the career opportunities in blood banking are limited, the special knowledge achieved through training must be acknowledged by other means. The personnel should be compensated for reaching higher levels of expertise. Because the career opportunities for the medical doctors are also limited, incentives should be found in order to attract talented professionals. An opportunity for research and for personal development in the profession through e.g. training abroad may guarantee recognition among peers and may serve as a good incentive.

INTERNATIONAL ORGANISATIONS DEALING WITH BLOOD TRANSFUSION

The World Health Organization

The Global Blood Safety Initiative (GBSI) in the unit of Health Laboratory Technology and Blood Safety (LBS) aims at provision of adequate and safe blood supplies in all countries which are also accessible to all and are appropriately used. This objective can be achieved by well organised integrated blood transfusion services that are strengthened by a sustained cooperative worldwide effort.

The main activities are: 1) promotion of donor recruitment and retention of safe blood donors; 2) promotion of improvement in processing and storage of blood; 3) promotion of measures to reduce the risk of transfusion-transmissible infections; 4) encouragement of appropriate use of blood and blood products; and 5) support and facilitation of relevant research. Guidelines, reports and manuals on different aspects of transfusion medicine have been written and books published on management, organisation and quality assurance of BTS (Appendix).

GBSI participates in the organisation of regional blood safety workshops in all WHO regions, communicates with other international organisations in the field and participates in different training exercises during their planning and implementation. It has a country database which helps in the assessment of the development of blood transfusion services in all WHO member states. GBSI also acts as a clearing house for bilateral development activities. Its database of potential consultants provides assistance when consultancies in the field are needed.

International Federation of Red Cross and Red Crescent Societies (IFRCS)

IFRCS has a blood programme department (BPD), the purpose of which is to advise and support the Secretary General of IFRCS in the efforts of the organisation to promote non-remunerated blood donations throughout the world. It maintains information on assistance programmes and facilitates the follow-up of the development of Red Cross blood services and helps professional contacts between sister societies. It also maintains a liaison with WHO and other organisations and conducts and maintains a programme of public information and education that assists national societies in achieving self-sufficiency in blood and blood products. The department publishes regularly a newsletter 'Transfusion International'.

Other organisations

The International Society of Blood Transfusion (ISBT) is a scientific society in transfusion medicine, which organises international conferences on blood transfusion and publishes a scientific journal *Vox Sanguinis* and a scientific newsletter *Transfusion Today*. In 1980 ISBT published ethical guidelines for blood transfusion which have been accepted by many international organisations as general guidelines for blood donation and transfusion.

The World Federation of Hemophilia (WFH) is a society for hemophilia patients. The society has close relations with blood transfusion professionals because part of the plasma needed for the production of the coagulation factor for hemophilia treatment (FVIII) is derived from the plasma of donated whole blood.

The Commission of European Communities (CEC) through its AIDS Task Force (ATF) is active in assisting developing countries in their efforts to increase the safety of blood transfusion. CEC supports or is planning to support development programmes for blood transfusion services in 30 developing countries.

The Council of Europe has traditionally developed recommendations and standards for European blood transfusion services through its expert committees and is now active in finding out means to support the upgrading of blood transfusion services in Eastern and Central Europe.

Acknowledgement

We thank Dr W.N. Gibbs and Ms P. Corcoran, WHO/LBS, for helpful discussions and comments during the preparation of the manuscript and Ms N. Kachouri for skillful technical assistance.

Additional reading

1. Beal RW, Bontinck M, Fransen L, eds. Safe blood in developing countries. A report of the EEC's expert meeting. Brussels: EEC AIDS Task Force 1992, 124 p.
2. Contreras M, ed. ABC of transfusion. London: British Medical Journal 1990, 66 p.
3. Council of Europe. Guide to the preparation, use and quality assurance of blood components. Strasbourg: Council of Europe 1992, 129 p.
4. Genetet P, Andrew G, Bidet J-M. Aide-memoire de transfusion. 2nd ed. Paris: Medecine-Sciences Flammarion, 1991, 385 p.
5. Global Programme on AIDS. Recommendations for the selection and use of HIV antibody tests. WHO Wkly Epidemiol Rec, 67:145–152, 1992.
6. McClelland DBL ed. Handbook of transfusion medicine. United Kingdom blood transfusion services. London: Her Majesty's Stationery Office 1989, 88 p.
7. Määttä T, Laulajainen T, eds. Optimal use of resources. Follow-up course. Helsinki: Finnish Red Cross 1991, 242 pp.
8. Pisciotto PT, ed. Blood transfusion therapy. A physician's handbook. Third edition. American Association of Blood Banks. 1989, 105 pp.
9. Smit Sibinga CT, Das PC, Cash JD, eds. Transfusion medicine: Fact and fiction. Dordrecht/Boston/London: Kluwer Academic Publishers 1992, 207 pp.
10. Sondag D, Fournel JJ, Beal RW, Bontinck L, Fransen L. Securite transfusionnelle dans les pays en voie de developpement. Rapport de la

reunion des experts de la CCE. Bruxelles: Task Force SIDA de la CCE 1992, 13O p.

11. Wendel S, Brener Z, Camargo ME, Rassi A, eds. Chagas disease (American trypanosomiasis): Its impact on transfusion and clinical medicine. Sao Paulo: ISBT Brazil 1992, 271 p.

About the authors

Jukka Koistinen is Director of Total Quality Management at the Finnish Red Cross Blood Transfusion Service, and Docent of Immunology at the University of Helsinki, Finland. During 1990–93 he worked as the Coordinator of Global Blood Safety Initiative in the Unit of Health Laboratory Technology and Blood Safety at WHO in Geneva. Before that he served as Director of Laboratory Services of the FRC Blood Transfusion Service, was the Coordinator of the Finnish Red Cross development projects in blood transfusion, a Temporary

Advisor in blood transfusion for the WHO and member of the Expert Advisory Group for the Blood Programme Department of the League of Red Cross and Red Crescent Societies. He has published extensively on immunodeficiency and blood transfusion as well as on development and organisation of blood transfusion services in developing countries.

Nandrani de Zoysa has a 30 year career in blood transfusion, first as Medical Officer and Senior Medical Officer and since 1980 as the Director of the National Blood Transfusion Service in Colombo, Sri Lanka. She has trained in transfusion medicine in Great Britain, India, Australia, Hungary, Canada and West Germany and has served for the WHO on several occasions as a Temporary Advisor on expert panels and in informal consultations on blood transfusion. Her publications have dealt with production of blood grouping reagents and distribution of blood groups in Sri Lanka.

APPENDIX

WHO/GBSI guidelines, recommendations, reports and publications can be ordered from WHO, 20 Avenue Appia, CH-1211 Geneva 27, Switzerland.

From the Unit of Health Laboratory Technology and Blood Safety (LBS):

– Minimum targets for blood transfusion services (WHO/LAB/89.5)
– Consensus statement on accelerated strategies to reduce the risk of transmission of HIV by blood transfusion (WHO/LAB/89.6)
– Essential blood components, plasma derivatives and substitutes (WHO/LAB/89.7)
– Essential consumables and equipment for a blood transfusion service (WHO/LAB/89. 8)
– Use of plasma substitutes and plasma in developing countries (WHO/LAB/89.9)
– Guidelines for appropriate use of blood (WHO/LAB/89.10)
– Consensus statement on screening of blood donations for infectious agents transmissible through blood transfusion (WHO/LBS/91.1)
– Autologous transfusion in developing countries (WHO/LBS/91.2)
– Suomela H. Viral inactivation of blood and blood products. (WHO/LBS/92.5)
– Report of the GBSI informal consultation on assessment of training needs in transfusion medicine (WHO/LBS/92.6)
– Report of the GBSI informal consultation on collaboration in training in transfusion medicine (WHO/LBS/92.7)
– Report of GBSI informal consultation on costing of blood transfusion services (WHO/LBS/92.9)
– Blood group serology and preparation of blood grouping reagents (being processed)
– Consensus statement on how to achieve a safe and adequate blood supply by recruitment and retention of voluntary, non-remunerated blood donors. (WHO/LBS/93.2)

From WHO/Sales and Distribution (DSA):

– Gibbs WN, Britten AFH, eds. Guidelines for the organization of a blood transfusion service. Geneva: WHO 1992, 150 p., (Price: CHF 25.-; CHF 17,50 for developing countries).
– Hollan SR, Wagstaff W, Leikola J, Lothe F, eds. Management of blood transfusion services. Geneva: WHO 1990, 229 p., (Price: CHF 41.-; CHF 28.70 for developing countries).
– World Health Organization. Guidelines for quality assurance programmes for blood transfusion services. Geneva: WHO 1993, 50 p., (Price CHF 12.-; CHF 8.40 for developing countries).

Lankinen KS, Bergström S, Mäkelä PH and Peltomaa M, eds.
Health and disease in developing countries. London:The Macmillan Press Limited, 1994:513–522.

53 MEDICAL EQUIPMENT MANAGEMENT

Gerald Bloom, B.Phil. (Economics), MDCM
University of Sussex, Institute of
Development Studies, Health Unit
Brighton BN1 9RE,
United Kingdom

Caroline Temple-Bird, B.Sc. (Eng.) Hons., M.Sc., AMIEE, ACGI
Ziken International Consultants
Carlton House, 11 Marlborough Place,
Brighton BN1 1UB,
United Kingdom

INTRODUCTION

Health services use a number of different kinds of equipment. For example, health facilities contain boilers to heat water, ovens to cook patients' meals, and operating theatre lights to illuminate surgical activities; in addition they have special medical equipment such as chemical analysers for laboratory tests, X-ray machines to aid diagnosis and ultrasound for physiotherapy treatment. Health professionals in both industrialised and developing countries are trained to depend on equipment, although there are differences between rich and poor regions in the variety and sophistication of the technologies that are available. Health services need to manage their equipment to ensure that effective care is provided.

Many countries suffer from severe shortages of functioning medical equipment. One reason is simply lack of money. This is illustrated in Figure 53.1, which compares the levels of expenditure on medical equipment per person in Sub-Saharan Africa, Great Britain and the United States in 1985. Of the estimated 30 billion USD worth of medical equipment that was produced globally that year, much less than 1 per cent went to Sub-Saharan Africa. That region spent under 0.5 USD per person, while Great Britain and the United States spent 21 USD and 66 USD, respectively.

The money that countries spend on medical equipment is often not used well: many items are inappropriate to a harsh environment; inadequately trained operators do not use equipment safely and effectively; items stand idle because there are no chemical reagents or X-ray films and expensive equipment cannot be used due to minor faults. These examples are common in developing countries, but also arise in industrialised ones which do not manage their resources effectively.

The effectiveness of a health service is severely diminished when it does not have functioning medical equipment. This was illustrated in a recent study carried out in a country where health services have faced severe resource constraints for a number of years. Among the hospitals' problems were

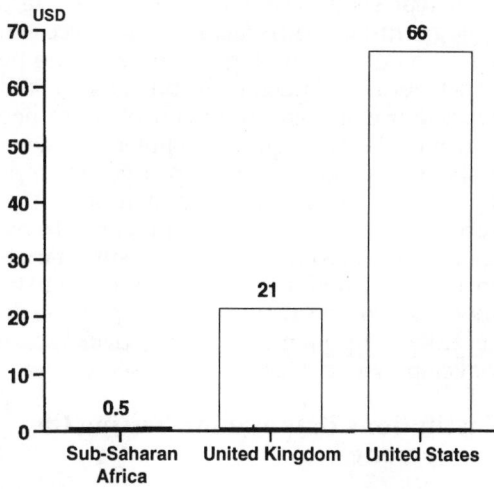

Figure 53.1. Expenditure on medical equipment *per capita*, 1985.

Table 53.1. The medical equipment technology package.

- establishment of a management system
- planning expenditure on the equipment service
- selection of technology
- procurement in the international market
- installation and operation
- maintenance and repair
- training in use, maintenance and management
- technology assessment and research
- local production

an inability to sterilise equipment due to lack of steam and difficulties in making diagnoses due to non-functioning laboratory equipment. Another problem was that decayed teeth had to be extracted because there were no drills.

The international community has just begun to address the issue of medical equipment management in developing countries. Since 1986 the WHO has recommended every health service to establish a health care technical service to oversee the management of its medical equipment.

However, there are no internationally agreed guidelines on how such a unit should function. Nor would it be appropriate simply to copy what has been done in the industrialised countries.

INSTITUTIONS IN THE MEDICAL EQUIPMENT SECTOR

The acquisition of a piece of medical equipment represents the introduction of a new technology into a health facility. The successful adoption of a technology involves a number of activities in addition to the purchase of hardware. For example, staff need to be trained, consumables are required, maintenance needs to be organised and safety procedures must be written. The full range of activities is referred to as the 'medical equipment technology package'. Its components are summarised in Table 53.1 and discussed in more detail below. Some of the institutions that provide different components of the package in developing countries are discussed below.

Institutions in the country using the equipment

Ministries of Health often do not have an effective system of medical equipment management. Many different departments, including those responsible for supply, finance, personnel, training, planning, aid and maintenance, may be involved in equipment-related matters, often with little coordination.

Maintenance of medical equipment is undertaken by a mixture of institutions. In many countries, the Ministry of Health has its own workshops. Other Ministries, such as Telecommunications and Construction, may also play a role.

Private firms, including subsidiaries of international suppliers, agents of foreign manufacturers and local companies with expertise in maintenance, also repair medical equipment. Private facilities have been more successful in keeping equipment in running order than public ones. For example, both the Zambian mining hospitals and the Kenyan private hospitals have been able to keep their equipment in running order at a time when the public sector has experienced problems.

The consequences of a weak industrial sector. One reason why it is so difficult and expensive to keep equipment in operation in developing countries is the small size of their industrial sectors. In this situation, a firm (or health facility) which uses imported technology must develop all the necessary skills for supporting equipment itself, or identify an alternative source of specialised inputs. It is often difficult to obtain a specific component or find an engineer with a particular skill when required. Even if a person has been given special training, there is always the danger that he or she will seek alternative employment. This is a problem for the public sector in many countries.

These problems are made worse by the small size of many national economies, which provide companies with little incentive to develop the capacity to maintain complex machinery or make spare parts. One way to deal with this situation is to increase regional integration. Another is to reduce the variety of imported technologies in order to make it easier to establish a stable market for spare parts, after-sales services and locally manufactured items (see below).

Suppliers of health care technology

Organisations involved in the export of medical equipment technology to developing countries include manufacturers, suppliers, packaging agents, turnkey operators, consultants, import/export merchants, maintenance contractors, training facilities and public health service institutions. They sell a mixture of hardware, services and management advice. In addition, a number of organisations provide information and advice as well as equipment and technical support; several of them are listed in the Appendix.

Suppliers of medical equipment frequently provide their customers in industrialised countries with a full range of after-sales services, but usually do not give this kind of service to purchasers in developing countries. It is often difficult for them to find local companies with the facilities and staff required to perform the necessary tasks. They will have to invest a great deal of money in order to establish a support network. However, they have not had much incentive to do so. Expenditure on medical equipment has fluctuated a great deal and the market has been very uncertain. Furthermore, Ministries of Health have not appreciated the need for after-sales support and have been unwilling to pay for it. This has reinforced the tendency of the manufacturers to concentrate their efforts on their major markets in the industrialised world.

MEDICAL EQUIPMENT DEVELOPMENT STRATEGY

Managing the equipment sector

The first step which Ministries of Health need to take, once they recognise the importance of equipment management, is to establish a unit with the capacity and authority to manage all aspects of the medical equipment service as outlined in Table 53.1. One of its first tasks is to formulate a medical equipment development strategy.

In order to plan the medical equipment service it is necessary to have information about existing stocks and future needs. The health service can establish how much equipment it owns and its state of repair by carrying out an inventory. This inventory can be compared with standard equipment lists, which include the minimum complement of equipment necessary for each kind of facility to provide an appropriate mix of services, in order to estimate the shortfall. It is then possible to estimate how much additional equipment needs to be purchased and what resources will be required to keep it operational. Attention should turn to more sophisticated technologies only

when these core equipment needs have fully been met.

Planning expenditure

It is possible to discern a recurring cycle in the equipment sector in a number of countries: new equipment is purchased; its effectiveness decreases rapidly due to unskilled use and poor maintenance; a crisis occurs and a rehabilitation operation is carried out. The purchases may be funded locally, during a period of relative prosperity, or by an international donor. This cyclical approach to funding is costly and provides little benefit to patients.

In order to avoid this waste, health services need to prepare an expenditure plan which estimates annual requirements over a period long enough to achieve rationalisation – perhaps 10 years. Resources need to be allocated to cover the life-time cost of the equipment, which includes purchase, installation, operation and maintenance. All of this information can be summarised in a core medical equipment expenditure plan (Table 53.2).

The expenditure plan should provide for maintenance and replacement of worn out equipment (depreciation). Experts suggest that maintenance costs ought to be about 6–15 per cent of purchase price each year. Most equipment needs to be replaced within 5–20 years. However, the useful life of equipment can be shortened by a harsh environment, frequent use, unskilled handling and neglect of maintenance. A reasonable estimate of the combined annual costs of maintenance and replacement is 20 per cent of current purchase price.

Many pieces of equipment use consumable items such as X-ray film and chemical reagents. It is quite common for hospitals to be unable to function effectively during much of the year because they cannot obtain these inputs, many of which are imported. Their cost should be included in the expenditure plan.

The core expenditure plan needs to be accepted by all those who provide funds for the health service. The Ministry of Finance needs to integrate it into Ministry of Health budgets. The decision to allocate adequate funds to keep the medical equipment service fully operational will create the financial basis for the establishment of a maintenance capacity and for the negotiation of longer-term commitments by suppliers.

Table 53.2. Formulation of a core medical equipment service expenditure plan.

Identifying the equipment stock and equipment needs
- undertake an inventory of the stock of equipment and document its state of repair
- clarify the functions of each level of health care service delivery
- establish standard lists of equipment for each kind of facility
- calculate the size of the shortfall in existing facilities
- assess the equipment needs of new facilities

Calculating expenditure required
- estimate the cost of maintenance and the replacement of worn out equipment
- estimate the cost of consumable items
- define a core expenditure plan which estimates the amount of money required to ensure that all facilities are provided with functioning equipment at the level defined by the standard lists by the end of a specified period.

Donors should also explore alternatives to their preference for equipping new facilities. The purchase of equipment could be coupled with the commitment of funds to keep it in running order for a number of years. For example, a recent agreement by the Finnish Government to supply laboratory equipment to the Pakistani health service included the supply of consumables and manuals, user and maintenance training and the establishment of maintenance workshops.

Selection

Many factors need to be taken into consideration in the selection of equipment including: safety, ease of use, appropriateness to priority health problems, the purchase price and the life-time cost. There is no point in buying an expensive piece of equipment that has capabilities that are hardly ever utilised, or in acquiring an item that will be almost impossible to keep in running order and operate safely and effectively.

The selection of suitable equipment requires significant investment of time and resources. Advice is required from a number of disciplines including health workers, technical personnel, architects, planning officers, procurement officers, administrators and financial planners. They need to define the functions which equipment will serve in the different kinds of facilities. Standard lists that use generic specifications rather than brand names should be prepared. Those who are responsible for procurement can then look for the equipment that meets these needs at the most attractive terms. The best choice is not always the cheapest option. For example, the ability of a supplier to provide a package of accessories, training and maintenance support should be taken into account.

Advice on selection can be obtained from a variety of publications. In addition, when a major re-assessment of the health service's stock of equipment is carried out, it may be worth investing some money in the services of an experienced consultant.

Procurement

Many Ministries of Health have little expertise in procuring equipment. They rarely remember that they need a package of inputs including accessories, training and maintenance support when they acquire hardware. There are numerous examples of hospitals that have purchased inferior products or have neglected commissioning and after-sales services. As a result, within a few years they have little to show for their substantial investment. More attention needs to be paid to the management of the procurement process and the negotiation of contracts with suppliers.

Standardisation of equipment. Ministries of Health need to limit the variety of equipment that they buy. For example, they might decide on one or two brands of a particular kind of equipment for the entire health service. This would mean that health workers would not have to learn how to use a different model each time they move to a different facility. It would also make it easier to provide spare parts and maintenance.

The establishment of standard equipment lists is a key step in the rationalisation of procurement. It makes it possible to invest more

Table 53.3. Procedures for the operation of medical equipment.

Introduction into the health service

– provide correct facilities to house equipment taking into account room size and design, electricity, gas and water
– install the equipment to fix it in place
– commission it to ensure proper operation
– undertake acceptance testing to confirm that it is safe
– calibrate it to ensure that readings are accurate
– enter the item into the records for use by planners and the maintenance service
– train users in operation and care

Day-to-day operation

– supply with consumable inputs, such as X-ray film, ECG recorder paper and gas
– establish safety procedures and a schedule of safety checks
– institute a system of periodic testing to identify items which need to be repaired or replaced
– carry out a programme of planned preventive maintenance

management effort on each purchasing decision. It also establishes a situation whereby suppliers compete for relatively large contracts which have the potential of establishing a long-term market. This gives them greater incentive to provide after-sales support at a reasonable cost.

Contracts with suppliers. Contracts with equipment suppliers often concern only the supply of hardware. This leads to inadequate documentation, poor installation and commissioning, an inability to obtain accessories and spare parts, and difficulty in obtaining maintenance. Tender procedures rarely encourage suppliers to offer these services and adjudication boards often simply award contracts to the lowest bidder. International donors, who fund a large proportion of equipment imports into the least developed countries, have not adequately taken these issues into account.

Contracts between suppliers of medical equipment and purchasers should specify both hardware and services. This can be difficult where they concern only one hospital or a few items. This is one reason why it is important to standardise equipment.

Operation

A number of tasks must be undertaken when equipment first arrives at a health facility and throughout its lifetime in order to ensure that it is effective and safe. These are outlined in Table 53.3. In the first place, it is necessary to provide equipment with the conditions to function properly. Common problems include inadequate space, a fluctuating electricity supply and insufficient water pressure. Care must be taken to install, commission and calibrate equipment properly or it may never function accurately.

Throughout its lifetime, steps must be taken to ensure the daily running of equipment and keep it in working order. Equipment can be dangerous when it is not performing well (inaccurate anesthetic machines), when it is misused (using adult suction pumps on children) and when it is in poor condition (electrical faults from fraying leads). There must be regular supervision and monitoring in order to achieve good equipment working practice.

Maintenance

There are a number of reasons why it is important to establish an effective maintenance service. When equipment breaks down the lives of patients are put at risk. Unreliable or inaccurate equipment is often worse than none at all. For example, an autoclave has to be hot enough to sterilise its contents and an X-ray machine must produce diagnostic quality radiographs. In addition, users and patients can be at risk of exposure to radiation or electric shock. The maintenance and repair service should include a 'planned preventive maintenance programme', which is a schedule of simple procedures to be undertaken at regular intervals. This will diminish the amount of time during which equipment is out of service.

Who should maintain the equipment? In contrast to the situation in industrialised countries, health services in many developing countries can rely on neither in-house units nor private companies to maintain their equipment. They will have to make substantial investments in order to establish effective maintenance services. The relative roles of the public and private sectors will vary for different kinds of equipment.

Relatively simple equipment can be maintained by personnel with basic skills. The first priority for a medical equipment service should be to keep this equipment in running order. Most of the work can be accomplished by a team of technicians employed by the public sector. In addition it may be possible to utilise private sector firms with the requisite skills, such as metal workshops and electrical companies.

Equipment of medium complexity requires attention from skilled technicians. In some cases, Ministry of Health personnel can be trained to undertake the necessary work. Alternatively, local private firms may already have skilled technicians. These may be representatives of international companies or they may be local firms which have relevant skills, such as boiler makers for sterilisers and television repairmen for basic X-ray machines. Where the private sector is used, a system of monitoring contracts has to be established to ensure that services of a reasonable quality are provided at an acceptable price.

Sophisticated equipment usually has to be maintained by the manufacturer. It is difficult to train a local engineer to the same level as an employee of the manufacturer and the cost is high where there are only a few units to be maintained. Health services often have to choose between paying large bills to a foreign contractor, accepting that equipment will be frequently out of order and not purchasing the item at all.

The development of maintenance capacity. The establishment of an in-house team requires a substantial investment of management effort. It will not be enough to train basic technicians. They have to be provided with adequately equipped workshops and work within an organised service which provides reasonable levels of pay and a well defined career structure.

There are a number of ways in which suppliers could develop a long-term presence in developing countries. They could establish relationships with local private firms which include: providing access to technical information and experienced personnel, training personnel and transferring systems for managing maintenance. However, excessive reliance on the private sector can create problems for the public health service. The most immediate ones are the high cost in foreign exchange and the use of skilled personnel. If scarce resources, often donor supplied, were allocated largely to the creation of a private after-sales service network, it might

not be possible to retain adequate technical expertise within the public sector. This might discourage the creation of preventive maintenance programmes for basic equipment. Furthermore, if the public sector does not have technical staff of its own, it will be unable to monitor the activities of private contractors.

Direct links could be established between manufacturers and the public sector maintenance service. This relationship would be defined in contracts that cover supply of spares, training of technicians, access to technical manuals, provision of back-up advice and so forth. A considerable amount of work is needed to define the appropriate content of such agreements and the financial relationship which might be entailed.

The role of regional maintenance centres. It may be possible for a single regional centre to maintain some kinds of equipment in several countries. Subsidiaries of transnational companies function in this way. There is a need to define the relationships that could be established between manufacturers, in-house maintenance services and regional private sector or parastatal firms.

The success of regional initiatives does not depend on health sector policies alone. A considerable amount of regional collaboration would be necessary to deal with questions such as customs duties on spare parts, cross-border payment for services and the coordination of procurement policy. It will be impossible to establish regional self-sufficiency in maintenance of medical equipment if such developments do not take place.

Training

A training programme for health workers, technicians and administrators is a necessary part of a medical equipment management development plan. The skills that need to be developed include: selection, writing and adjudication of tenders, procurement, operation, maintenance and management. Several different levels of skill are required. Most countries need to provide training for users of equipment, basic technicians, middle level technical cadres and a small number of professionally trained engineer/managers.

Training can be provided by a number of institutions: formal training courses abroad, short updating workshops run by manufacturers, in-country courses and long-term technical assistance. Theoretical training has to be combined with practical work in the health service. Formal training should be followed by a period of supervised work in a well organised technical service. It is not enough to send cadres away to acquire technical skills. At the same time, work has to be underway in establishing a functioning maintenance service.

Furthermore, a programme of continuing education is needed. This enables users and technicians to upgrade their skills and keep up with developments in the field. This is specially important in countries with a relatively small health care technical service and a high turnover of personnel.

Technology assessment, research and development

The medical equipment industry is evolving rapidly. Until recently health services have not adequately assessed the safety and cost of new technologies. In recent years there have been an increasing number of technology assessment studies. However, few of them have concerned the use of equipment in developing countries.

Investment in research brings about changes in the design of medical equipment. Virtually no such expenditure is being made in developing countries and most manufacturers do not have an economic incentive to develop equipment appropriate to the needs of poor countries. There is a need for international support for this kind of activity.

A number of topics require research as part of an international programme to support the more effective use of health care technology in developing countries. These include: the development of appropriate equipment; assessment of existing technologies; and research into alternative ways of structuring the relationship between suppliers of medical equipment and the health sector.

Local production

A number of products could be manufactured in countries with relatively weak industrial sectors. These include basic consumables, furniture, prosthetics and simple laboratory equipment. In addition, parts can be produced, or there can be assembly of entire units from imported components. However, a stable market for health care products must be established before local production can be economically viable.

CONCLUSIONS

Health facilities cannot provide effective services if they do not have a reasonable amount of functioning medical equipment. Unfortunately, many health services do not adequately recognise the importance of this issue. Too little money is allocated for the purchase, operation and maintenance of equipment and the resources which are available are not used to best effect. It is particularly difficult to make effective use of medical equipment in developing countries, where public health services have limited resources and little management expertise and private companies do not have the capacity to provide the specialised services which are required.

The medical equipment industry has been successful in meeting the needs of health services in the industrialised countries, but less so in the developing ones. The correction of this failure will require concerted action by private companies, governments and international donors. Exporters of medical equipment need to re-assess their relationship with customers in developing countries. They could play an active role in the development of appropriate models of after-sales support. However, they cannot be expected to invest in these services until they are confident that enough resources have been committed to establish a stable market for essential equipment and ancillary services.

Donors, who finance a substantial share of purchases of medical equipment for the health services of many countries, can also contribute. New forms of support need to be developed which encourage the establishment of a sustainable cost-effective service.

Public health services have to establish units to take responsibility for making better use of medical equipment technology. Each country will have to prepare a medical equipment development strategy as outlined above. The resources required to implement this strategy will have to be committed for a number of years. If policy-makers and health service managers do not make the necessary investment, patients will be denied the benefits of this powerful technology.

Additional reading

1. American Hospital Association. Medical equipment management in hospitals. Chicago: American Hospital Association, 1982. Clinical

Engineering Section, American Society for Hospital Engineering, AHA, 840 North Lake Shore Drive, Chicago, Illinois 60611, USA.

2. American Hospital Association. Estimated useful lives of depreciable hospital assets. Chicago: American Hospital Association, 1983. Available from AHA, see reference 1.

3. Battersby A. How to assess health services logistics with particular reference to peripheral health facilities. Geneva: WHO, 1985. (SHS/85.9)

4. Berg H. Medical equipment in developing countries. Two neglected issues: planning and financing. SHS Current Concerns Series, Paper No 6. Geneva: WHO, 1992. (WHO/SHS/CC/92.2)

5. Bloom GH. Round table: The right equipment...in working order. World Health Forum 1989;10(1):3–27.

6. Bloom GH, Temple-Bird C. Medical equipment in Sub-Saharan Africa: a framework for policy formulation. Brighton: Institute of Development Studies, 1988. (Research Report Rr19; reprinted by the WHO as document WHO/SHS/NHP/90.7)

7. British Medical Journal. Appropriate technology: Articles published in the BMJ, 1985. London: British Medical Association, 1985. BMA, Tavistock Square, London WC1H 9JR, UK.

8. Cooper-Poole J. Equipping hospitals and other health facilities in developing countries. In: Kleczkowski BM, Pibouleau R. Approaches to planning and design of health care facilities in developing areas. Volume 3. Geneva: WHO, 1979. (WHO Offset Publication Number 45).

9. England R. How to make basic hospital equipment. Rugby: Intermediate Technology Publications, 1979. Intermediate Technology Development Group, 103 Southampton Row, London WC1B 4HH, UK.

10. Knebel P. Furniture and equipment in relation to activities, personnel, and architecture, primary and secondary health care in developing countries. Paris: Club du Sahel, OECD, 1984. Organization for Economic Co-operation and Development (OECD), Club du Sahel, OCDE-OECD, 2 rue Andre Pascal, 75775 Paris CEDEX 16, France.

11. Neureiter J, Tschank A. Technician's handbook on hospital engineering. Kenyan-Austrian Development Co-operation Programme, 1989. Geneva: WHO, 1990. (WHO/SHS/NHP/90.6)

12. Palmer PES. Radiology in basic-care hospitals and clinics. In: Kleczkowski BM, et al., eds. Approaches to planning and design of health care facilities in developing areas, Volume 3. Geneva: WHO, 1979. (Offset Publication Number 45)

13. Prage L. Procurement, operation and maintenance of scientific equipment in developing countries. Stockholm: International Foundation of Science, 1987. c/o Dr L Prage, International Foundation for Science (IFS), Grev Turegatan 19, S–114 38 Stockholm, Sweden.

14. Prage L. Support to research equipment in developing countries – a critical look at the present mechanisms and some ideas on how to improve them. Stockholm: International Foundation of Science, 1987. Available from IFS, see reference 13.

15. Steele PA, Little FA, Littlewood P. Commissioning health care facilities. In: Kleczkowski BM, Pibouleau R. Approaches to planning and design of health care facilities in developing areas. Volume 4. Geneva: WHO, 1983. (WHO Offset publication Number 72).

16. World Health Organization. Inter-regional meeting on the maintenance and repair of health care equipment. Nicosia, November, 1986. Geneva: WHO, 1987.

17. World Health Organization. Inter-regional meeting on manpower development and training for health care equipment management, maintenance and repair. Campinas, November, 1989. Geneva: WHO, 1989.

18. World Health Organization. District hospitals: guidelines for development. WHO Regional Publication. Geneva: WHO, 1992. (Western Pacific Series No 4)

About the authors

Gerald Bloom, a medical doctor and health economist is a Fellow of the Institute of Development Studies at the University of Sussex. He has worked in a number of African countries on issues of resource planning and health service financing. In addition to his work on the management of medical equipment, his research interests include rural health finance in China and strengthening of health sector management in Southern Africa.

Caroline Temple-Bird is a biomedical engineer. She was employed by the Government of Zimbabwe for several years in its programme for upgrading public sector hospitals. She has worked as a consultant on medical equipment management in a number of countries and organises an annual course on the subject at St Bartholomew's Hospital Medical College in London. Her principal research interest is medical equipment management in developing countries.

APPENDIX

Several organisations provide information, advice, equipment, technical assistance, training and international support for the medical equipment sector. In addition some non-profit making organisations and charities supply equipment, materials, learning aids, books and other items at low cost to developing countries. A number of these organisations are reviewed here.

AFRICAN MEDICAL AND RESEARCH FOUNDATION (AMREF) has produced a textbook 'A Practical Laboratory Manual for Health Centres in East Africa'. A re-edited version will be available shortly. AMREF also tests appropriate equipment and provides refresher training for laboratory workers. AMREF is preparing materials for a simple external quality assessment scheme.

AMREF Laboratory Programme, P.O. Box 30125, Nairobi, Kenya.

ASSOCIATION OF ANAESTHETISTS OF GREAT BRITAIN AND IRELAND has produced a booklet 'Checklist for Anaesthetic Machines' detailing full check procedures which should be performed at the beginning of each operating theatre session. Association of Anaesthetists of Great Britain and Ireland, 9 Bedford Square, London WC1B 3RA, UK.

DEPARTMENT OF HEALTH OF THE UK GOVERNMENT critically evaluates equipment currently on the market, publishes reports of their findings, and registers manufacturers:

– Health and Equipment Information Series,

– Evaluation Series, and

– Ultrasound Equipment Evaluation Project Series, from DH (Leaflets), P.O. Box 21, Stanmore, Middlesex HA7 1AY, UK.

– The DH Register of Manufacturers, from Medical Devices Directorate, Department of Health, 14 Russell Square, London WC1B 5EP, UK.

DEUTSCHE GESELLSCHAFT FUR TECHNISCHE ZUSAMMENARBEIT (GTZ) is the technical assistance branch of the German Government Development Program. They are currently working in many developing countries in the field of medical equipment maintenance and training. They produce valuable reports from international information-gathering workshops:

– Hospital Engineering in Developing Countries, GTZ Symposium, Giessen, Germany, November 1983.

– Maintenance Strategies for Public Health Facilities in Developing Countries, GTZ workshop, Nairobi, Kenya, 1989.

– Spare Parts and Working Materials for the Maintenance and Repair of Health Care Equipment, GTZ workshop, Lübeck, Germany, August 1991. c/o H Halbwachs, GTZ GmbH, Dag-Hammarskjöld-Weg 1 & 2, D-6236 Eschborn, Germany.

EMERGENCY CARE RESEARCH INSTITUTE (ECRI) is the WHO Collaborating Centre for Information Transfer on Medical Devices. It critically evaluates equipment currently on the market, publishes reports of their findings, and publishes the WHO Newsletter *Health Care Equipment Management*. It has also developed planned preventive maintenance software.

ECRI, 5200 Butler Pike, Plymouth Meeting, PA 19462, USA.

HANDS TO CLINICAL LABS OF THIRD WORLD COUNTRIES INC offers several types of technical assistance to laboratories in developing countries including training for laboratory personnel, short term assignment of volunteer US laboratory workers as consultants and supplying of surplus equipment from US laboratories.

c/o Dr Sharon Roberts, California State University, Bakersfield, CA 93311–1099, USA.

HULP AAN MEDISCHE LABORATORIA IN ONTWIKKELINGSLANDEN (HAMLO) is a committee of the Dutch Association of Medical Laboratory Technologists which gives assistance to laboratories in developing countries. This includes technical advice and supplying literature, acquiring new equipment and materials also surplus equipment from Dutch laboratories and adapting this to the needs of the country requiring the equipment. HAMLO also assists laboratory technologists who wish to work in developing countries by putting them in touch with development agencies and helping them to attain the necessary knowledge and experience for work in developing countries.

HAMLO, Wilhelminapark 52, 3581 NM Utrecht, The Netherlands.

INTERNATIONAL ATOMIC ENERGY AGENCY (IAEA) has over 1000 projects worldwide concerned with nuclear medicine and related equipment. To address the problems of maintenance they have initiated several programmes in developing countries with which governments can collaborate: training fellowships, training programmes, running training workshops, providing spare parts and manuals, setting up a Nuclear Instrumentation Network (NIN) for users and coordinating a research programme in quality control.

c/o Dr A Benini, Division of Life Sciences, IAEA, Vienna, Austria.

INTERNATIONAL DISPENSARY ORGANISATION (IDA) is a non-profit organisation whose objective is to improve the availability of essential drugs and medical supplies including laboratory equipment in developing countries.

IDA, P.O. Box 3098, NL–1003, AB Amsterdam, The Netherlands.

INTERNATIONAL FOUNDATION FOR SCIENCE (IFS) supports scientific projects worldwide making use of instruments and laboratory facilities. To address the problems of maintenance they have initiated several programmes in developing countries with which governments can collaborate: running training workshops, providing spare parts and manuals, setting up a Network of Users of Scientific Equipment in Southern Africa (NUSESA), compiling a regional database of existing equipment in SADCC, and producing a directory of persons in the SADCC region with skills for operation and maintenance of scientific equipment. c/o Dr L Prage, IFS, Grev Turegatan 19, S-114 38 Stockholm, Sweden.

ECHO INTERNATIONAL HEALTH SERVICES LIMITED, Equipment to Charity Hospitals Overseas (ECHO) provides high quality low cost medical and surgical equipment, pharmaceuticals, teaching aids and solar-powered items to charitable and government hospitals and clinics in developing countries. Both new and reconditioned laboratory and other equipment is available.

ECHO, Ullswater Crescent, Coulsden, Surrey CR5 2HR, UK.

PROGRAM FOR APPROPRIATE TECHNOLOGY IN HEALTH (PATH) is an international organisation devoted to the development of appropriate health technology for primary health care programmes. PATH is at present assisting in the development of a low-cost direct readout hemoglobinometer. PATH also supplies a bibliography on laboratory equipment and publishes *Health Technology Directions* at irregular intervals (see Additional reading list in Chapter 51).

PATH, 4 Nickerson Street, Seattle, WA 98109, USA.

TROPICAL HEALTH TECHNOLOGY supplies training manuals, medical textbooks and learning materials such as colour bench aids, wall charts and colour transparency sets. A Tropical Medicine Microscope is available from Tropical Health Technology. The organisation formerly sold other equipment and materials; this has been taken over by SOLMEDIA Tropical Laboratory Supplies.

Tropical Health Technology, 14 Bevill's Close, Doddington, March, Cambridgeshire, PE15 0TT, UK.

Solmedia Tropical Laboratory Supplies, 6 The Parade, Colchester Road, Romford, Essex RM3 0AQ, UK.

UNITED NATIONS EDUCATIONAL, SCIENTIFIC AND CULTURAL ORGANISATION (UNESCO) is involved in educational and scientific projects worldwide. They have initiated several programmes in developing countries with which governments can collaborate: running training workshops, initiating the African Network of Scientific and Technological Institutions (ANSTI), surveying Instrument Maintenance Courses available in African institutes, and investigating the possibility for local production of chemistry equipment.

UNESCO, 31 Rue Francois Bonvin, 75015 Paris, France.

UNITED NATIONS CHILDREN'S FUND (UNICEF) has a Supply Division which prepares kits of equipment and supplies for primary health care facilities; this has enabled many countries to standardise and has simplified ordering. The Division's Procurement and Assembly Centre, UNIPAC publishes a catalogue which can be obtained through UNICEF offices.

UNICEF Plads, Freeport, DK-2100 Copenhagen, Denmark; and UNICEF, United Nations, New York 10017, USA.

UNITED NATIONS INDUSTRIAL DEVELOPMENT ORGANISATION (UNIDO) supports many projects relating to instrumentation and has a special programme on medical equipment. Its Engineering Industries Branch supports projects specifically directed towards maintenance, manufacture, repair workshops and tropicalisation. The Training Branch covers the management and technical aspects of maintenance work, including computer aided methods for maintenance.

Department of Industrial Operations, UNIDO, P.O. Box 300, A-1400 Vienna, Austria.

WEST OF SCOTLAND HEALTH BOARDS' Department of Clinical Physics and Bio-engineering produces a series of booklets detailing operation, safety, maintenance, and testing for specific items of medical equipment:

– Test and Check Procedures Series (Books 1–8), from Physicare, 11 West Graham Street, Glasgow G4 9LF, Scotland

WORLD HEALTH ORGANIZATION (WHO) has launched a Global Action Plan to coordinate and promote medical equipment management issues internationally. This initiative is led by Dr A Issakov of the Division for the Strengthening of Health Services. Documents are available on the organisation and planning of medical equipment services (see Additional reading list in this chapter). WHO can also supply information on equipment, supplies and the establishment of services in a variety of key equipment areas:

Radiology Applications. Information is available on the Basic Radiological System (BRS) and other imaging systems:

– Manual of Radiographic Technique.

– Manual of Darkroom Technique.

– Manual of Radiographic Interpretation for General Practitioners.

– Future Use of New Imaging Technologies in Developing Countries, WHO Technical Report Series 723, 1985.

Laboratory Services. There is a series of manuals on laboratory procedures (see Additional reading list in Chapter 51) and Bench Aids for the Diagnosis of Malaria and Intestinal Helminth Infections.

– Health Laboratory Technology and Blood Safety, WHO/LAB.

Expanded Programme on Immunization. Information includes:

– Expanded Programme of Immunization, Refrigerators Use, Maintenance and Repair Series, EPI/LOG/84/1–27 and EPI/TECH.HB/A–H, 1984–1987.

– EPI Product Information Sheets, WHO/UNICEF/EP.TS/86.1.

– Selection of Injection Equipment for EPI, WHO/UNICEF/EP.TS/86.2.

– Guide on the Implications of Solar Energy for EPI, WHO/UNICEF/EP.TS/86.3.

– EPI Training Information Sheets, WHO/UNICEF/EP.TS/86.4.

Anesthesia. Information includes:

– Anesthesia at the District Hospital, Dobson MB, 1988.

Appropriate Technology. There is a Global Program on Appropriate Technology for Health Care.

Further information can be acquired from WHO country representatives, as well as from Dr A. Issakov of the Division for the Strengthening of Health Services, and the Publications Office, WHO, CH-1211 Geneva 27, Switzerland.

Lankinen KS, Bergström S, Mäkelä PH and Peltomaa M, eds.
Health and disease in developing countries. London:The Macmillan Press Limited, 1994:523–529.

54 ORAL HEALTH SERVICES

Paavo Luukkonen, L.D.S., D.D.P.H.
City of Jyväskylä, Centre for Health and
Social Services
Kauppakatu 21 A, 6th floor, FIN-40100
Jyväskylä, Finland

Clement Luhanga, D.D.S. (Oslo),
Dipl. Oral Surg. (Tor)
Jwaneng Hospital
P.O. Box 569, Jwaneng,
Botswana

INTRODUCTION

Many oral disease conditions are caused by
poverty, malnutrition, ignorance and margi-
nality. In destitute conditions enough resources do not exist for prevention and treatment of
oral diseases. In many of the developing countries there is at most one dentist for 100 000
people.

When serious efforts are made to bring
about oral health services in developing countries, there is always a risk of taking primary
recourse to such technology as is dominant in
the industrialised world. It is often ignored
that the systems and technologies for health
care, particularly oral health care, are specific
to certain social, political and economic conditions. Therefore, direct transfer of technology
is doomed to fail.

ORAL HEALTH PROBLEMS IN DEVELOPING COUNTRIES

The spectrum of oral diseases in developing
countries is different from the one observed
in the industrialised world. The prevalence
and trends of dental caries vary considerably
in different parts of the world (Figure 54.1).
A few decades ago it was a rare disease in
most developing countries, but with a 'westernisation' of cities and urbanisation of rural
areas it has rapidly become a significant public health problem. The change is particularly
evident in higher-income groups, whose food
regimes and dietary practices have 'west-
ernised'.

In broad outline during one generation, the
approximate average of decayed teeth per
young person at 12 years of age has at least
doubled in most developing countries; tripled
in Uganda, Indonesia and the Philippines; increased sevenfold in Ethiopia and Guatemala;
and even more in Zambia and the Central
African Republic.[1] In India the proportion of
the caries-free population plummeted from
60 per cent down to 15 per cent within a few
decades.[2,3]

These developments seem to concur with
objectives in the resolution of 1977 by the
International Sugar Association, which is 'To
increase sugar consumption and in particular
to promote measures to encourage consumption in countries where per capita consumption is low. The potential for promoting the
consumption of sugar is greater in underdeveloped countries because they are low
sugar consumers and most developed countries have either reached a saturation level of
sugar consumption or switched to sugar
substitutes.'[4]

A number of positive developments have
also emerged, especially among countries with
high initial values of caries index. In French
Polynesia the 10.5 average of decayed teeth
per person at 12 years of age in 1977 dropped
to about three in 10 years. Similar positive
trends have also surfaced in other countries
e.g. Thailand and Sri Lanka, during the past 10
years. The positive trends are mostly due to
enhanced levels of primary education, increased awareness of the importance of oral
health and health education, and lack of

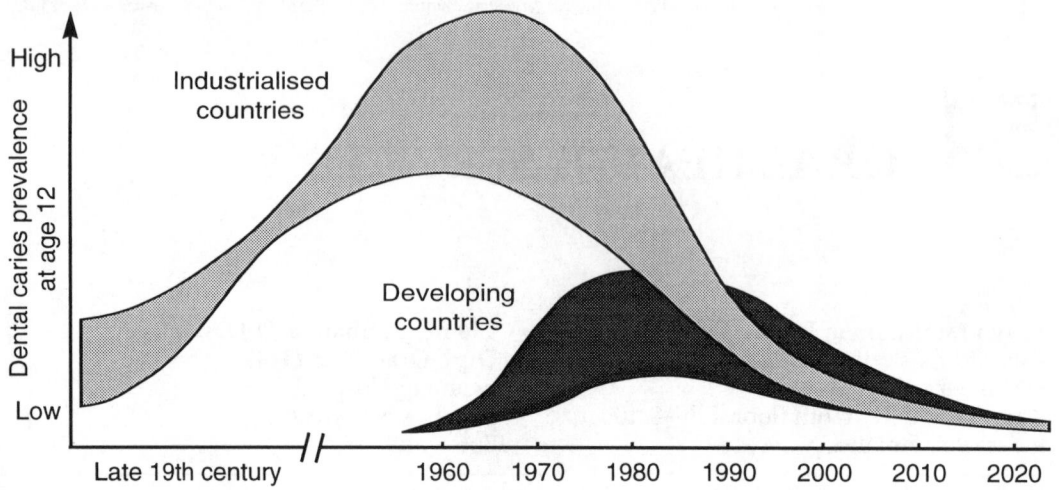

Figure 54.1. Schematic representation of the global prevalence of dental caries at 12 years of age since the late nineteenth, with a forecast into the first quarter of the twenty-first century. The upper and lower limits of the shaded areas give an idea of the ranges of prevalence found across different regions of the world falling broadly into two groups i.e. industrialised countries and developing countries. While caries prevalence is still rising in some developing countries, in others the falling trend has set in. (From Evolution in Dental Care, reproduced by kind permission of Professor R J Elderton, and Clinical Press, Bristol).

exposure to aggressive mass-media advertising, especially in rural areas. Organised community efforts such as preventive programmes for children, including various methods of fluoridation and oral hygiene, have undoubtedly contributed to improved oral health in those areas.

In industrialised countries, the descending trend for caries and periodontal disease began much earlier, about the middle of this century, showing in recent years very dramatic falls in incidence figures.

If the trends persist, further dental caries will be reduced to very low levels by the year 2020 at the global level. Although the developing countries, as a whole, seem to lag behind, they are gradually overtaking the developed countries, and hence the difference in the frequency of dental caries is expected to disappear within about three decades.[5]

In contrast to dental caries, *the periodontal and gum diseases* have at all times been very prevalent in developing countries, more widespread than in the developed countries, albeit great differences have been registered between population groups.[5-8] The higher prevalence is thought to be associated with ignorance, poverty and low socioeconomic status. In Nigeria, Ghana and Uganda children aged hardly

more than 10 years present pathological changes in their periodontium, and middle-aged people suffer much from these diseases, regardless of their socioeconomic status.[7]

Necrotising ulcerative gingivitis (NUG) may affect, though rarely, young adults and adolescents in the industrialised world. In Africa and India it is a disease attacking children under 10 years of age, and especially the poorest ones. Children with kwashiorkor are the ones most afflicted with the disease. In common with other periodontal diseases NUG is associated with poor oral hygiene. As additional etiological factors there may be certain anaerobic microbes, stressful conditions and immunological disturbances.[9,10]

Cancrum oris (noma) is a gangrenous stomatitis of the mouth and face particularly in debilitated children. In the industrialised countries noma is almost unknown, but it still occurs in many developing areas. Malaria and measles in conjunction with protein energy malnutrition (PEM) are regarded as its predisposing and aggravating factors.[9]

Odontogenic and other tumours of the oral cavity continue to be a serious health problem in developing countries. India has the greatest frequency of oral cancer in the whole world. Especially those chewing betel nuts or using tobacco in various ways are at risk. Approximately one third of these tumours are malignant.

Oral manifestations of systemic diseases including AIDS, maxillofacial trauma, benign tumours, acute and chronic infection of the oral tissues, handicapping malocclusions and fluorosis (in some countries) are also a cause of serious concern. Typical disorders associated with nutritional problems are developmental defects of tooth enamel.[10]

Burkitt's tumour is most frequently seen in children under the age of 10 years. Malpositions of teeth and malocclusions are quite few in comparison with other diseases of the mouth.[11]

ORAL HEALTH SERVICES

Levels needed

The realistic level of oral health services in a developing country is closely related to the resources, infrastructure and technology allocated for health care, public health strategy and priorities adopted by the government, and the degree of self-reliance in higher learning and research in dentistry and oral health.

Availability of foreign exchange determines whether a country can afford to import indispensable materials for restorative and rehabilitative dental service. Hence there exists glaring social inequality because the low income earners, particularly in the rural population, do not have access to restorative treatment provided by the relatively few dental practitioners in the urban areas.

In consequence, it is realistic or even mandatory to *focus mainly on prevention and health promotion* which will ultimately give the desired results in the developing countries. A lot of effort should also be directed at incorporating oral health care into other PHC programmes for synergetic benefits. Apart from the overall level of service, serious attention should be paid to optimal, economic and need-related staggering of dental services. The model outlined below, when modified by the local politicocultural conditions, could function as a pattern suitable for many poor developing countries.

The family should form the very basic milieu for support of home dental care in relation to oral hygiene, proper nutrition with particular reference to sugar controlled diet, and the use of fluoride when appropriate.

Proven and effective indigenous methods of dental care should be identified, researched and disseminated for home care.

The community should organise programmes for health education, oral hygiene techniques, and various uses of fluoride supplements. School dental screening is a typical activity featuring the community level. Non-operative oral health workers should be responsible for the above tasks.

The *primary or district level* should provide for the diagnosis of oral disease and provision of emergency care e.g. extraction, scaling, and emergency treatment of mandibular fractures. The dental therapist, or in his absence the medical assistant of the district hospital, can be responsible for prevention and emergency care. This level forms the first tier of the referral system to more specialised or advanced treatment.

The *secondary level*, to be staffed by dentists at the regional hospital should be responsible for more advanced restorative and rehabilitative care, in particular diagnosis of oral disease, and reinforcement of the referral system. The *tertiary level* should enable the diagnosis and performance of specialist procedures to be undertaken by dental practitioners in various clinical specialities. This level could be provided at the national referral hospital.

Present status

Oral health care facilities are unevenly distributed in many developing countries. The bulk of the resources are concentrated in major cities, leaving the urban fringe and the rural areas unattended. This disparity is also seen in manpower distribution which mismatches community needs as over 80 per cent of trained professionals live in affluent urban areas, providing services to less than a quarter of the total population. Recent observations indicate that less than 2–3 per cent of the total budgetary allocation goes to oral health (Thorpe, personal communication).

The rapid increase of oral diseases in many countries has inevitably resulted in an increasing demand for dental care. Insufficient resources and the inadequate number of trained manpower have not been able to meet this challenge. Many developing countries have also fallen victim to a hasty training of manpower, often without relevant planning.

Many developing countries have been made to establish expensive and inappropriate

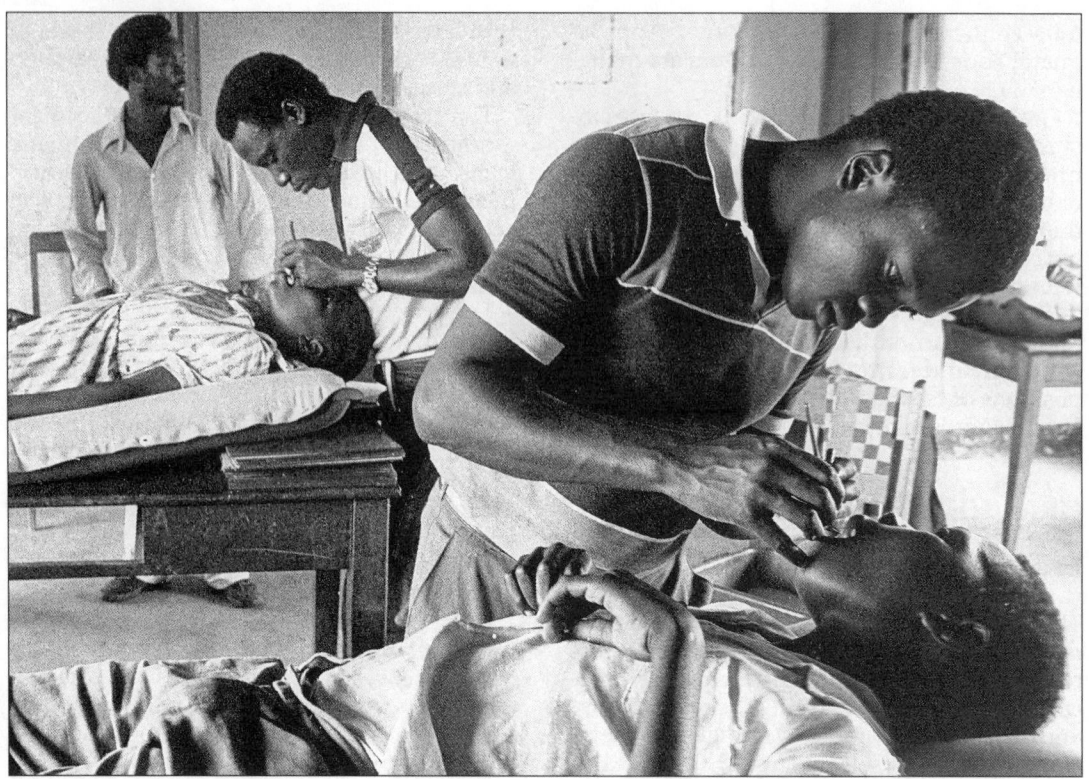

Dental students examining children's oral health status in a classroom in Morogoro, Tanzania.
Photo: Jorma Pyykkö

services which have been unable to promote the oral health of the people. A frequent mistake has been placing too much emphasis on restorative care at the expense of health promotion activities.[12,13]

In most developing countries the number of dentists is not sufficient for community-based dental services to be organised for the whole population. In Africa the dentist-to-population ratio is in the order of 1:100 000, in South-East Asia about 1:80 000, while in the Eastern Mediterranean and the Western Pacific territories the ratios average 1:10 000 and 1:13 000, respectively. In the European countries the ratio is about 1:2000, in some of them even less.

In Latin America several countries, in the sixties, moved in the direction of creating more manpower to combat increasing caries. Thus more new faculties were opened, reaching the current total of 201 in all of Latin America and the Caribbean. By today the number of dentists has considerably increased, while the caries problem still remains. Rather, a new problem has emerged, that is, the plethora of professionals and the underutilisation of this resource, since in some countries only ten percent of the population can be treated.

Furthermore, when the public does have access to health services, whether private or state-run, they will attend a practice which aims at rehabilitation, not prevention. This results in a vicious circle reproducing diseases and, therefore, does not succeed in fostering good health. To reorient the services health authorities and professional organisations have taken measures to create a new and truly alternative dentistry in the region, admitting the need for changes in the education, accepting a new profile for professionals based on primary health care with emphasis on prevention, assuming the importance of integrating teaching, treatment and research, and encouraging community participation.[13]

Strategies for improvement

In Africa experts at dental services met in Brazzaville in 1978 to make object-oriented plans for the development of oral health services in the African continent. At that juncture it was realised that, if the occurrence of dental caries could be kept at a low level (1.5 decayed teeth at age 12), services could be restricted to preventive care and emergency treatment. The plan was based on two objectives: in the beginning the dentist-to-population ratio should be raised to 1:80 000, and at the next stage up to 1:40 000, while the growing number of dentists would concur with training of sufficient auxiliary personnel. However, the target for the initial stage has not been reached yet.

As early as the mid-1950s Tanzania and the Sudan, some of the poorest countries (LDC), grew acutely aware of the health problems caused by dental diseases, and therefore embarked upon an organised dental service by beginning to train *dental assistants* (dental therapists) and posting this new cadre to regional hospitals. The dental assistant, trained to do a large number of routine dental procedures acceptable to the community, is a professional person who very seldom needs to refer their patients to the dentist.

Previously Tanzania had at its disposal only five dentists who only catered for the dental care of the colonial staff. The 3-year training of dental assistants, begun in the fifties, is still continuing and has proved very appropriate for the needs and conditions of the poor country. Other developing countries have also increasingly started to utilise manpower with non-university training (dental therapists).[14]

Strategic planning for public health care is crucial, also for oral health care. Emphasis should be placed upon the principles of primary health care (PHC), preventive approach and community involvement.

It is particularly important to make dental services available to the rural population by generating new appropriate technology and re-training dental staff for preventive work. Moreover, much emphasis should be put on health education and the role of primary school teachers and other non-dental personnel in carrying it out.

TRAINING OF DENTAL PERSONNEL

After independence, many African countries endeavoured to create their own reserves of academic manpower for training, research and services. The best educated people had opportunities for further training e.g. dental degree courses abroad. The academic nuclei formed by these professional people have later enabled the governments to begin their own schools of dentistry at different levels.

However, developing countries often need to cooperate with foreign countries so as to secure adequate financial and personnel support for academic training programmes. For instance, the French government has given support to the dental school in Senegal, and Germany has aided in establishing the Nairobi dental school in Kenya. The support of the United Kingdom to the dental schools in Nigeria has been of great importance.

Unfortunately, the donor–recipient relationship has often mirrored the very ideals and models that the foreign cooperating partners have been applying in their home countries. Foreign curricula, teaching methods and other forms of technology have often been transferred to local conditions, with no critique and with little or no modification at all.

The argument presented to vindicate this direct transfer of technology has been that of maintaining high academic standards, international acknowledgement and equivalence with study requirements for degrees awarded by foreign universities.

The legitimacy of this belief, however, can be questioned by demonstrating that *scientific knowledge and technology may be specific for or solely applicable to certain conditions*. This aspect of technology should be emphasised in the training of dental personnel; socioeconomic and political realities should be recognised and the training objectives made compatible with changing developmental phases of the country.

TRAINING OF DENTAL PERSONNEL IN TANZANIA

Starting the educational programme for the degree of Doctor of Dental Surgery at the University of Dar es Salaam in the year 1979 was part and parcel of a plan for training competent manpower in accordance with the national plan for oral health. Although the dental assistants with intermediate professional training no doubt constituted the mainstay of the service system, crucial importance was attached to educating *national experts in oral health planning and management* for all levels of the public health administration. Special emphasis was laid on self-reliance in strategic planning, development of appropriate technology, as well as maximising the use of available resources.

The Doctor of Dental Surgery programme was designed to be a degree course of 5 years' duration, geared to the needs of Tanzania with an express aim of producing dentists fit for Tanzania. Besides the theoretical studies and basic clinical training at the university clinic, the course included a lot of practical field work and extramural training e.g. in health centres, schools, mother and child health (MCH) clinics, villages, farms, industrial plants, teacher training seminars, dental clinics and wards of district hospitals, and other establishments of health care.

The fundamental idea aimed at training dental students in exactly those conditions in which they would be working as dental officers. This training approach was emphasised by establishing a special extramural training centre in the rural area (the Morogoro Project), not only for sheer training but also for service and teaching-related research activities. Teaching, service and research functions were considered inextricable in this approach designed to produce community and prevention-orientated dentists.[14,15]

The first batch of Tanzanian dentists completed their five-year course and were awarded the D.D.S. degrees in 1984. Some of the newly graduated dentists were appointed to posts of junior academic staff at the dental school, with an objective to embark on potential academic careers.

The next great challenge to the dental school in the University of Dar es Salaam was scientific and professional postgraduate education. It was started in 1984 in close cooperation with the University of Kuopio in Finland and the University of Nijmegen in the Netherlands. Its primary objective was to create a competent teaching staff for the university dental school. Emphasis on national strategies and principles of primary health care was also demanded of this education.[16]

The above programmes were considered most appropriate especially because of their preventive and community dentistry oriented curricula. The much desired self-reliance in undergraduate training was gained rapidly as didactic training was incorporated into postgraduate courses, and the responsibility for teaching gradually shifted from expatriate teachers to the local postgraduates.

From the early 1990s onwards the undergraduate and postgraduate programmes will continue to produce teachers and researchers who are expected to generate such new knowledge and technology as is appropriate to solving major health problems in a developing country.

Optimal utilisation of a developing country's innate resources and potential for development, combined with respect for politicoeconomic realities and decision-making processes have made the Muhimbili Project a unique and exemplary project of successful cooperation. Hence it must be regarded as only a beginning of further joint cooperation in the health sector.[16]

References

1. WHO Oral Health. Dental caries levels at 12 years, May 1992. Paper prepared at Geneva, WHO Oral Health, 1992.
2. Moller IJ. Impact of oral diseases across cultures. Int Dent J 1978;28:376–82.
3. Mistry KM. Dental health in India. A brief report on its development, its constraints, its needs, and a suggested programme of action. Paper presented at a Symposium on Assisting Dental Education and Dental Public Health in Developing Countries, CIBA Foundation, London, 1980.
4. Luhanga CM. Dentistry for the nineties: Can developing countries escape the impact of confectionery advertisement? Paper presented at a Symposium of the Sri Lanka College of General Dental Practitioners 28–30 Jan. 1989.
5. Elderton RJ, ed. Evolution in dental care. Bristol: Clinical Press, 1989.
6. Nyyssönen V. Oral health research in East Africa. Publications of the University of Kuopio. Community Health. Statistics and Reviews 1/1987.
7. Enwonwu CO. Review of oral disease in Africa and the influence of socioeconomic factors. Int Dent J 1981;31:29–38.
8. Miyazaki H, Pilot T, Leclercq MH. Periodontal profiles: An overview of CPITN data in the WHO Global Oral Data Bank for the age groups of 15–19 years, 35–44 years and 65–74 years as of 1 August 1992. Geneva, World Health Organization, 1992.
9. Enwonwu CO. Epidemiological and biochemical studies of necrotizing ulcerative gingivitis and noma (cancrum oris) in Nigerian children. Arch Oral Biol 1972;17:1357–72.
10. Enwonwu Co. Influence of socioeconomic conditions on dental development in Nigerian children. Arch Oral Biol 1973;18:95–107.
11. Mugonzibwa E. Occlusal variations among 7–14-year-old children in Ilala district. Research pro-

posal. Ilala Oral Health Survey. Publications of the University of Kuopio. Community Health. Statistics and Reviews 2/1987.

12. Tala H, Barmes DE. Health manpower out of balance: Conflicts and prospects for oral health. XX CIOMS Conference 7–12 Sept. 1986, Acapulco, Mexico. CIOMS Geneva 1987.

13. Gomez AO. Latin America in the time of cholera: Dentistry and the search for alternatives. In the FDI News, Sept/October 1991, No 179.

14. Lembariti BS, Luukkonen P. Professional dental training at the University of Dar es Salaam. In: Report of the Curriculum Development Workshop on Dentistry Teaching at All Levels. The Commonwealth Regional Health Secretariat, Arusha, Tanzania, 1987.

15. Luukkonen P. Development cooperation in dental education – The anatomy and development of a process of collaboration. In: Proceedings of the Third African Dental Research Conference, 1988. Publications of the University of Kuopio. Community Health. Statistics and Reviews 3/1988.

16. Tuutti H. Development of local self-reliance in academic education in developing countries. In: Honkala E, ed. Themes. Health research and developing countries. Helsinki: National Agency for Welfare and Health, 1992.

Additional reading

1. Hobdell MH, Sheiham A. Barriers to the promotion of dental health in developing countries. Soc Sci Med 1981;15A(6): 817-23.

2. Barmes DE, Leous PA, Infirri JS. Global trends on oral disease. Prevention of oral diseases. Report of a WHO Workshop on Community Oral Health Services, Erfurt, 11–16 December 1983, pp. 81-9.

3. Luukkonen P. Prevalence of oral diseases and the manpower situation in developing countries. In: Development cooperation between universities. Kuopio: University of Kuopio, 1984 (Publications of the Centre for Continuing Education 1/1984).

4. Bakilana PB. Histological distribution of oral tumours in Tanzania. Trop Dent J 1988;11:7–10.

5. Hassan H. Primary prevention of oral cancer by the year 2000 in Tanzania. In: Proceedings of the Second East African Dental Research Conference. Kuopio: University of Kuopio, 1986.

6. Luhanga CM. Dental education in developing countries. Paper presented at the 50th Conference of the Sri Lanka Dental Association 1982.

7. Muya RJ, Rambush E, Fejerskov O, Hobdell MH, Normark S. Changing and developing dental services in Tanzania 1980–2000. Central Dental Unit, Ministry of Health, Tanzania, 1984.

8. World Health Organization. Accelerating the achievement of oral health for all Africans. The three-phase health development scenario. Brazzaville: WHO/AFRO, 1989.

9. Luukkonen P, ed. Tenth anniversary of the Division of Dentistry, University of Dar es Salaam. Dar es Salaam: University of Dar es Salaam, 1989. (Publications of the Division of Dentistry 1/1989).

10. Honkala E, Nyyssönen V, Lembariti BS, Tuutti H, Muya RJ, Luukkonen P. Oral health research and postgraduate training project in Tanzania. In: Proceedings of the International Symposium on Health and Environment in Developing Countries. Haikko: Finland, 1986.

About the authors

Paavo Luukkonen obtained his degree of Licentiate in Odontology from the University of Helsinki, Finland in 1972. He also holds a Specialist Diploma in Dental Public Health, and Administrative Qualifications in Public Health. He has held a number of posts in the public health service in rural and urban Finland, and had several consultant or academic positions at the dental faculties of the University of Kuopio (Finland) and the University of Dar-es-Salaam (Tanzania). Dr Luukkonen has written a number of professional articles and technical reports dealing with oral public health and training of dental personnel.

Clement Luhanga graduated in dentistry from the University of Oslo, Norway in 1966. In 1967 he returned to Tanzania where he was appointed Dental Surgeon in charge of the Muhimbili Medical Centre. Dr Luhanga was the first to establish the training of assistant dental officers in 1969. In 1976 he was requested to establish the first Dental School in Tanzania. Since 1983 Clement Luhanga has been working in Botswana. His main interests are centred on contemporary socioeconomic issues and their impact on oral health in developing countries. Currently, he is involved in establishing a Regional Academic Oral Health Centre in Southern Africa to be based in Zimbabwe.

Lankinen KS, Bergström S, Mäkelä PH and Peltomaa M, eds.
Health and disease in developing countries. London:The Macmillan Press Limited, 1994:531–542.

55 DISABILITY PREVENTION AND REHABILITATION

Padmani Mendis, M.C.S.P., O.N.C., Dip.T.P. (U.K.) M.D. (H.C. Uppsala)
University of Kelanya, Faculty of Medicine
P.O. Box 06, Ragama
Sri Lanka

INTRODUCTION

Past perspectives

The scope of the terms disability prevention and rehabilitation has undergone a significant expansion over the last decade or two. Before 1979 and the Alma-Ata Declaration on PHC, health systems of developing countries were largely hospital-based and disease-oriented. In this context measures for disability prevention were generally seen to be those that restricted or eliminated the immediate sequelae of illness or disorders of the locomotor system such as, for instance, secondary contracture and deformity which could follow poliomyelitis or trauma. Immunisations and accident prevention campaigns were seen as the most important means to prevent disease and disorders. Rehabilitation generally included those services provided in special institutions for people who had problems with mobility and orientation such as those who had severe paralysis, paraplegia or amputations and those who had lost their sight.

With PHC came a change in the perspective of health from the absence of disease to a state of physical, social and mental well-being. Health systems were called upon to shift their focus from disease to its impact on the individual and on those with whom the individual interacts. The term disability came to be used extensively to describe the more permanent effects. Its meaning widened to encompass the consequences of all diseases, including chronic heart and respiratory diseases, alcoholism and drug abuse, cancer, chronic pain, epilepsy, mental illness and mental retardation.

Present concepts

The conventional medical view of illness is illustrated in Figure 55.1. However, the model does not describe the full impact that disease has on an individual. This is the various sequelae that interfere with the ability to carry out daily functions and social obligations. The conventional view of illness therefore needs to be expanded to take into account its

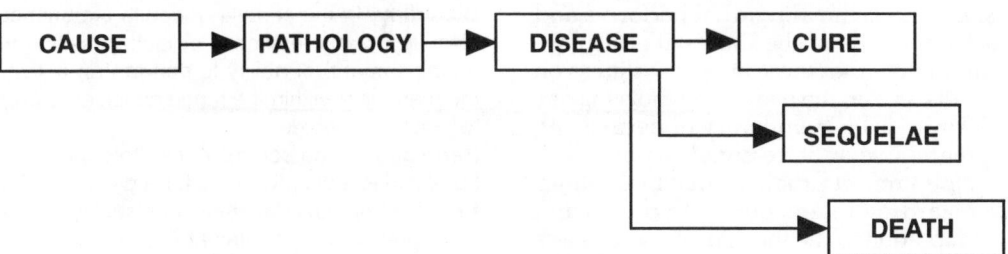

Figure 55.1. Conventional medical view of illness.

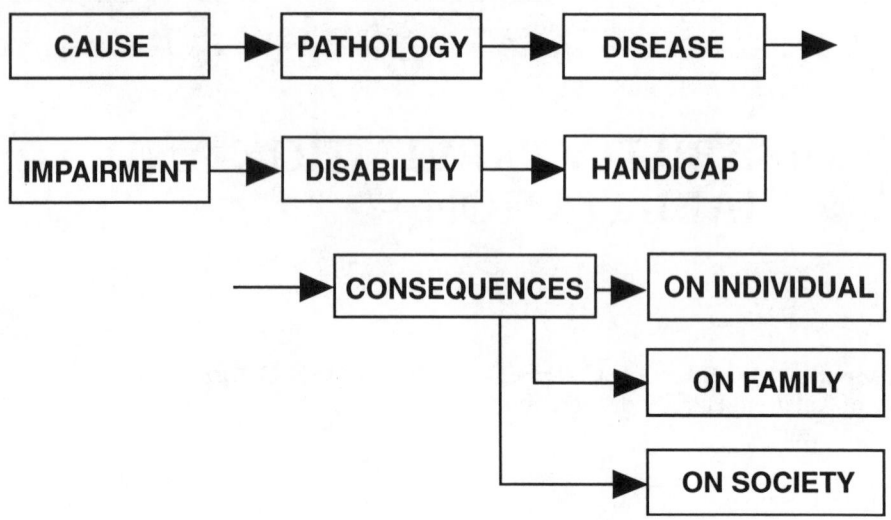

Figure 55.2. Socioeconomic effects must be included to get a more complete view of illness.

socioeconomic effects. This is illustrated in the model in Figure 55.2.

A consideration of the circumstances leading to disease and of the possible effects of disease on an individual illustrated in the model above, gives an indication of the current scope of disability prevention and rehabilitation. Thus, disability prevention includes all measures aimed at the limitation or elimination of disease and its effects, whereas rehabilitation seeks to prevent or reverse handicap, or reduce its consequences.

The definitions of the sequelae of disease used by the WHO relate to the context of health experience (Table 55.1).[1] Example 1 shows how these definitions apply to a practical situation.

A significant corollary of these definitions is that *impairments* refer to disturbances at the organ level, that is, apply to parts of the body and their functions. *Disabilities* describe the effect of these disturbances at the level of the person, being concerned with integrated activities of the body as a whole, such as the tasks, and skills the individual performs and the behaviours he or she shows. It is also important to note that these effects of illness on body parts and on the body as a whole may be visible or invisible, temporary or permanent, and progressive or regressive.[2]

Handicaps reflect problems that individuals have regarding interaction with others and with adaptation to the their surroundings as a result of impairment or disability. Handicap therefore depends on the demands, values and attitudes that society imposes on people who have impairment and disability. It is a social phenomenon.

Disability patterns

Prevalence. It has recently been estimated that the global prevalence of moderate and severe disability is about 5.2 per cent.[3] This is an aggregate of prevalence of 7.7 per cent for the more developed regions and of 4.5 per cent for the less developed regions. Further, based on data from screening procedures carried out in the Community-Based Rehabilitation (CBR) programmes cautious estimates of prevalence rates for moderate and severe disability in developing countries have been suggested (Table 55.2).

Table 55.1. Definition used by the WHO to describe the sequelae of disease.[1]

Impairment. In the context of health experience, an impairment is any loss or abnormality of psychological, physiological or anatomical function.

Disability. In the context of health experience, a disability is any restriction or lack (resulting from an impairment) of ability to perform an activity in the manner or within the range considered normal for a human being.

Handicap. In the context of health experience, a handicap is a disadvantage for a given individual, resulting from an impairment or disability, that limits or prevents the fulfilment of a role that is normal (depending on age, sex, and social and cultural factors) for that individual.

Table 55.2. Estimate of prevalence based on observed ranges of moderate and severe functional limitations among people in the developing countries.[3]

Type of limitation	Prevalence (%)
Moving difficulty	2.0 – 2.5
Seeing difficulty	0.5 – 0.8
Hearing/speech difficulty	0.5 – 0.8
Learning difficulty	0.2 – 0.4
Chronic fits	0.3 – 0.6
Strange behaviour	0.1 – 0.2
Feeling difficulty (in hands or feet)	0.1 – 0.2
Combinations of the above	0.2 – 0.3

Table 55.3. Causes of disability and estimated prevalence (suggested ranges) of moderately and severely disabled people in the world, world population at 5300 million.[3]

Causes of disability	millions
Congenital or perinatal disturbances	
Mental retardation	10 – 20
Somatic hereditary defects	10 – 15
Non-genetic disorders	15 – 20
Communicable diseases	
Poliomyelitis	5 – 10
Trachoma	8 – 10
Leprosy	3 – 4
Other communicable diseases	30 – 40
Non-communicable somatic disease	70 – 80
Functional psychiatric disturbances	15 – 20
Chronic alcoholism and drug abuse	25 – 30
Trauma/injury	
Traffic accidents	15 – 20
Occupational accidents	10 – 12
Home accidents	15 – 20
Other	2 – 3
Malnutrition	7 – 10
Other	2 – 3
ESTIMATED TOTAL	250 – 300

Causes. There are only few statistical studies on the causes of disability in developing countries. Available data suggest that the four major worldwide contributors to moderate and severe disability are congenital and perinatal disturbances (15–20 per cent), communicable diseases (about 20 per cent), non-communicable somatic and mental conditions (40–45 per cent), and trauma/injury (about 15 per cent) (see Table 55.3 for details). These estimates should, however, be taken with a great deal of caution.[3]

It is generally believed that communicable diseases, low-quality perinatal care and accidents or violence are the major causes of disability in developing countries. The link between disability and poverty is clear.

DISABILITY PREVENTION

The wide spectrum of (preventive) measures is classified at three levels, as shown in Figure 55.3.[4]

First-level prevention

One of the most important preventive programmes is the Expanded Programme on Immunization (EPI) affording children protection from measles, poliomyelitis, whooping cough, diphtheria, tetanus and tuberculosis (Chapter 48). Measles alone is estimated to kill two million children (Chapter 17). In association with malnutrition, it is a major cause of mental retardation, loss of sight and loss of hearing.[5]

Poor perinatal and child care are associated with birth trauma, low birth weight, brain damage, and infections, and are a major cause of life-long disability. Effective Mother and Child Health Programmes will reduce impairment from these causes (Chapters 30 and 32). At the same time, improved perinatal care increases survival of infants with disability from genetic and developmental defects.

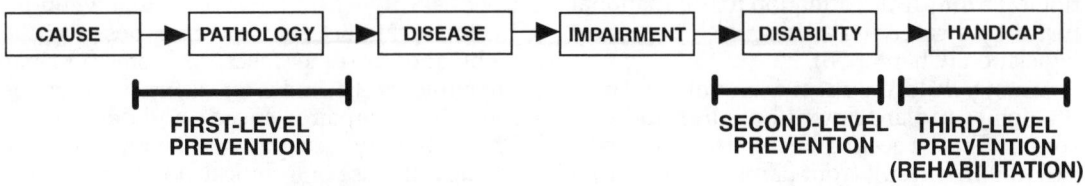

Figure 55.3. Possible levels of disability prevention.

EXAMPLE 1. Nela, aged 7, lost the sight in both her eyes when she was 3 years old, as a result of vitamin A deficiency. She spends most of her time indoors, sitting alone because she cannot move outside by herself. She has not been to school. Cause–effect relationships could be illustrated as follows:

vitamin A deficiency —> affectation of eye tissue —> xerophthalmia —> destruction of eye tissue
    cause   *pathology*   *disease*   *impairment*

—> loss of vision —> no schooling —>   no access to a child's rights
    disability   *handicaps:*   *consequences:*

                inadequate play   lack of stimulation
                poor social integration   impaired development
                poor orientation   disadvantaged & deprived
                poor mobility   discriminated against
                etc.   etc.

Other first-level preventive measures are discussed in separate chapters of this book. They include health education, safe housing, adequate food supply, proper nutrition, safe drinking water, sanitation, good personal and community hygiene, legislation and education to reduce the intake of alcohol, drugs and tobacco, reduction of vector populations, treatment of endemic diseases (such as iodine deficiency diseases and malaria) and high risk groups, and genetic counselling, particularly in areas where consanguine marriages are common. Once disease has occurred permanent impairment can be prevented by early detection and management of complications, education, early treatment of emergencies and provision of essential medicines.

Prevention of accidents. In some countries of South America and Africa *road traffic accidents* exceed disease as the first cause of death and disability among people of working age. Legislation (and its effective application) regarding the use of seat belts and helmets, speed restrictions, vehicle maintenance and learner drivers, and public education have had a major impact on reducing traffic injuries in some developed countries. Accident prevention is yet to have a significant impact in developing countries. – Rapid industrialisation calls for greater attention to occupational health and safety measures, with necessary legislation (Chapter 56).

Among children, most accidents occur in the home, and are caused by burns and poisoning. Traffic accidents are also a common cause. Burns result from flames such as from overturning of oil lamps, and from hot liquid which the child pours over himself. Poisoning is from medicinal drugs and from household products. Other causes of child accidents are drowning in rivers and unprotected water points, falls from heights and suffocation by inhaling small objects. *Simple precautions such as the use of stabilised lamps, storing of medicines, detergents, pesticides and other poisons away from the reach of children, and protection of fireplaces, electric sockets and water points can significantly reduce the risk of these accidents.* More than half of the accidents to children happen with an adult present, and often originates from faulty supervision.

Reduction of disability resulting from accidents calls for a much greater consciousness about accidents and particularly their consequences to a child. This calls for health education for the general public, directed especially at parents, school teachers and school children, driving-school instructors, and health personnel.

Second-level prevention

The provision of appropriate drugs for chronic diseases (e.g. for tuberculosis, ear infections, leprosy, epilepsy, mental illness, diabetes, hypertension, and trachoma) is an important area of second level prevention. The provision of essential surgery for the treatment of wounds, fractures, cataracts, etc. and early postsurgical ambulation are other measures. Some possible impairments of a stroke, for example, are loss of movement, impaired speech, and depression. Physiotherapy, occupational therapy, speech therapy, the use of technical aids and psychological counselling are important second-level measures to prevent disability.

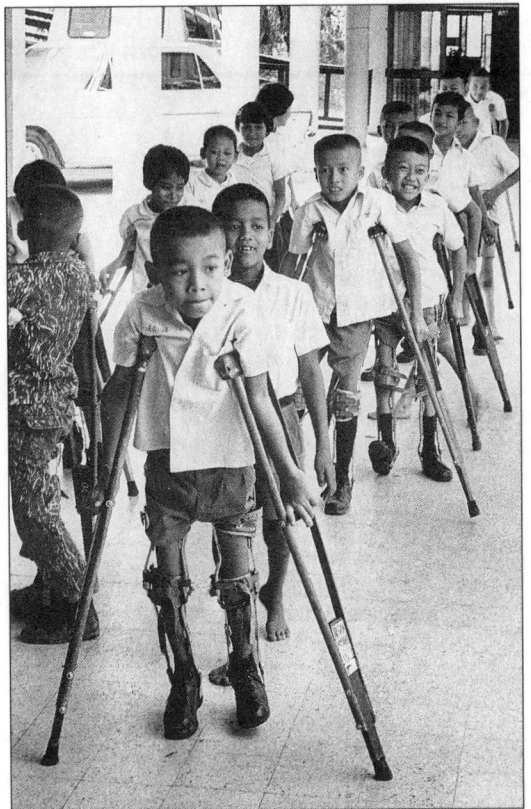

Over 200 000 children a year are still being crippled by polio. Immunisation has reached about 80 per cent of developing world's children and is preventing estimated 400 000 cases of polio annually. Photo: UNICEF/J. Danois

Third-level prevention

This includes all measures directed at preventing a disability from causing handicap, and at reducing the consequences of the handicap. The word handicap describes the possible negative experience of individuals who have impairments or disabilities because they are unable to fulfil their role in the society. This refers to feeding, dressing, personal hygiene and moving around in one's surroundings, and also communication, social interaction and relationships, play, sports, recreation and leisure, schooling, household activity, sexual activity and socioeconomic activity.

Third-level prevention aims at enabling the individuals to perform the varying roles expected by the family, community, and society-at-large to the extent possible. At the same time it seeks to influence attitudes and environment so that the limitations imposed by

disease are recognised for what they are, and taken into account. In effect this is the same as rehabilitation, and will be considered as such in this chapter.

REHABILITATION

Recent changes

A radical change has quite recently taken place in the field of rehabilitation. Some aspects of the depth of this change can be seen when one compares WHO definitions of rehabilitation within the span of just over a decade:

WHO 1969: 'As applied to disability, this is the combined and coordinated use of medical, social, educational and vocational measures for training or retraining the individual to the highest possible level of functional ability.'[6]

WHO 1981: 'Rehabilitation includes all measures aimed at reducing the impact of disabling and handicapping conditions, and at enabling the disabled and handicapped to achieve social integration. – Rehabilitation aims not only at training disabled and handicapped persons to adapt to their environment, but also at intervening in their immediate environment and society as a whole in order to facilitate their social integration. The disabled and handicapped themselves, their families, and the communities they live in should be involved in the planning and implementation of services related to rehabilitation.'[2]

From these definitions it is clear that the earlier view of rehabilitation held that it was impairment and disability *per se* that caused handicap. Conventional rehabilitation implemented as institutional and outreach approaches, therefore focused on bringing about changes in the impaired or disabled individual (and sometimes in the immediate family). Consideration of the demands of the international disability movement and of the situation of people who have disability even in those developed countries where institutional and outreach services have been more or less universally accessible, leaves no doubt that such services have not brought about the equalisation of opportunities for people who have disability.

The 1981 definition recognises the fact that the greater cause of handicap lies with the attitudes of the individual's family and community. However, this definition, seeing 'social integration' as the final goal of rehabilitation, now appears to be outdated.

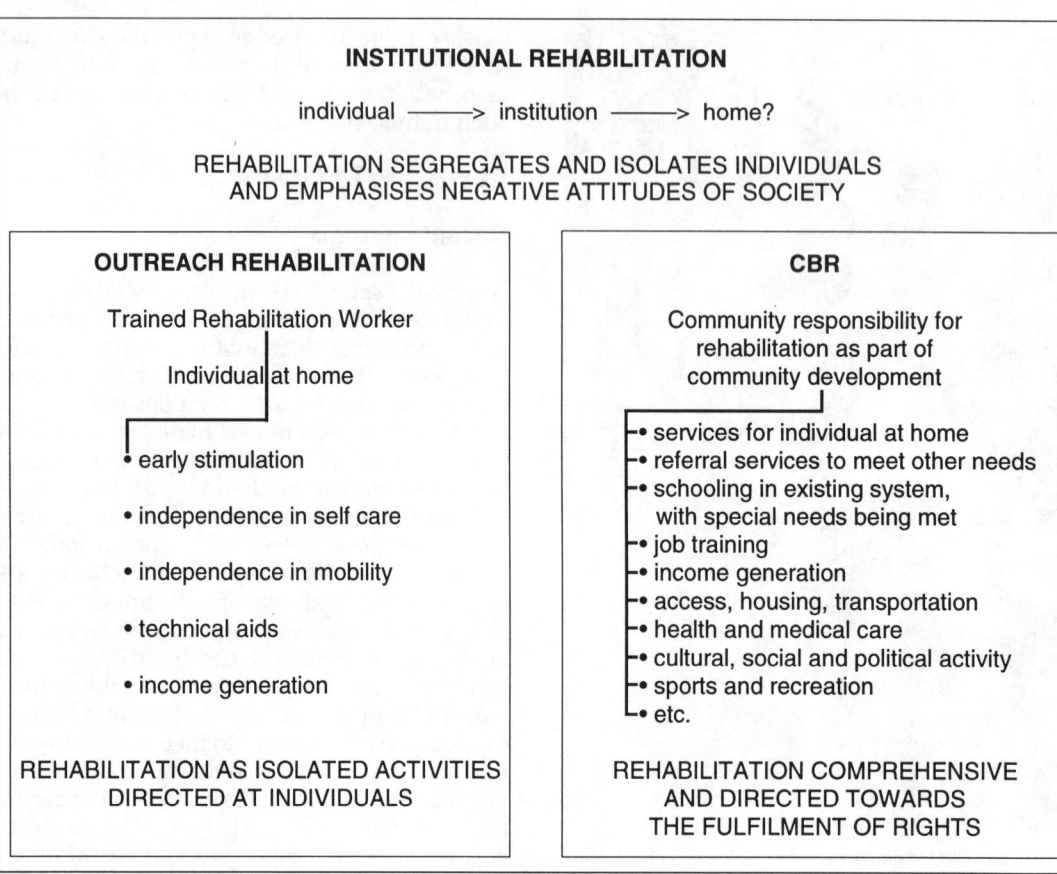

Figure 55.4. Community based rehabilitation in perspective.

The United Nations Decade of Disabled Persons (1983–1992) had as its theme 'Full Participation and Equality'. The Decade did much to stimulate the growth of organisations of people with disability both at national and international levels, as a result of which consumers are at last beginning to have a say in the development of their services. Their demands are for 'equal rights to education and training: to health and medical services; to be included in national economic planning and employment; to have access to information, research and buildings, both private and public, places of sports, leisure and recreation and entertainment; to politics and political participation, citizenship and equality in the eyes of the law.'[7]

The Independent Living Movement, currently at the centre of activity of the disability movement in the developed countries, and which is now being thought about in some developing countries as a kind of self-directed living movement, focuses on the process of empowerment, enabling people who have dis-

abilities to exercise choices and control over their lives, and thus fulfil themselves as human beings.

However functionally independent individuals may be, they cannot avail of their rights or fulfil themselves unless their families and communities recognise and accept the concept of equality. Recognition of the equality of people who have disabilities calls for a radical change in attitudes towards disability in individuals, families, communities and society-at-large. This has been the basis for the shift away from institutional and outreach approaches to rehabilitation, and the development of community-based rehabilitation.

COMMUNITY-BASED REHABILITATION (CBR)

Social change cannot be imposed from outside. The experience of other development activities has shown that a positive attitude change is encouraged when people partici-

Table 55.4. Review of rehabilitation needs among a group of 77 disabled people participating in a CBR project in Vietnam.[3]

Need/training for	With this need (per cent)
Information about the disability	90
Eating and/or drinking	51
Washing/keeping clean	78
Latrine use or similar	55
Dressing/undressing	68
Understanding simple instructions, etc.	53
Expressing thoughts, needs, feelings, etc.	51
Communicating with others	49
Getting up from lying	39
Moving hands and arms	42
Moving legs	53
Mobility around house	49
Mobility around village	60
Play activities	19
Schooling (includes adults)	84
Participation in household activities	77
Participation in community activities	84
Income-generating activities (adults only)	29

pate actively in the processes calling for change. Attitude change must come from within, people need to be aware of the change called for and take responsibility for that change, participating in the processes relating to the change, if it is to be effective and lasting. The emphasis that *social change must come from within the families and communities in which people with disability live* has been one of the underlying principles of CBR.

CBR aims at strengthening relationships and promoting interaction between individuals who have disability, their families and their communities. The role of rehabilitation services at all levels, beginning with community level services, is to strengthen relationships and promote interaction between all three units. To do this, the concept envisages that the community, through its leadership, takes on the responsibility. This is the base in CBR.

However, communities cannot do this without support. CBR calls for, and encompasses, the participation of all other available sectors and services within that society, that could contribute to the community's efforts. Services provided by institutions are vital supportive components of CBR.

CBR has also evolved on the basis that it is only when issues related to disability are con-

sidered to be a part of overall community development, that equalisation of opportunities and fulfilment of rights are possible. When issues related to disability are taken as a community responsibility and social development activity, services for people with disability are integrated in other development activities.

Consider some needs of disabled people in relation to community development. Educational provision for children with disability is considered within the existing school system with resources and inputs to meet their special needs. Health services include a system for early detection of persons with disability and for making services to overcome the consequences of their disability accessible to them. Transportation, design and construction should consider easy access. Housing, employment creation, poverty alleviation and other social welfare programmes should consider needs of people with disability. Within these concepts, disability-related programme development keeps pace with overall community development, whatever the level of development and resource availability. Figure 55.4 illustrates the CBR concept in the perspective of conventional approaches to rehabilitation.

Needs met

CBR is being developed to meet comprehensively, as one system, the needs of those with the most prevalent disabilities in developing countries, namely difficulties in seeing, hearing, speaking, moving or learning (mental retardation), loss of sensation (leprosy), fits (epilepsy), strange behaviour (schizophrenia) or combinations of these disabilities. In the context of the CBR philosophy, and with the technology available today, there is really no justification for single-disability programmes.

The focus of early field trials of CBR was on the analysis of rehabilitation needs expressed by people with disability, their families and communities. Table 55.4 lists the rehabilitation needs among a group of people in a CBR project in Vietnam in 1988.[3] CBR programme development takes into account these needs in people with varying disabilities and all age groups (see further below).

Service structure

CBR has basically two levels of services, namely home and community level and the referral level. Besides meeting the needs of disabled

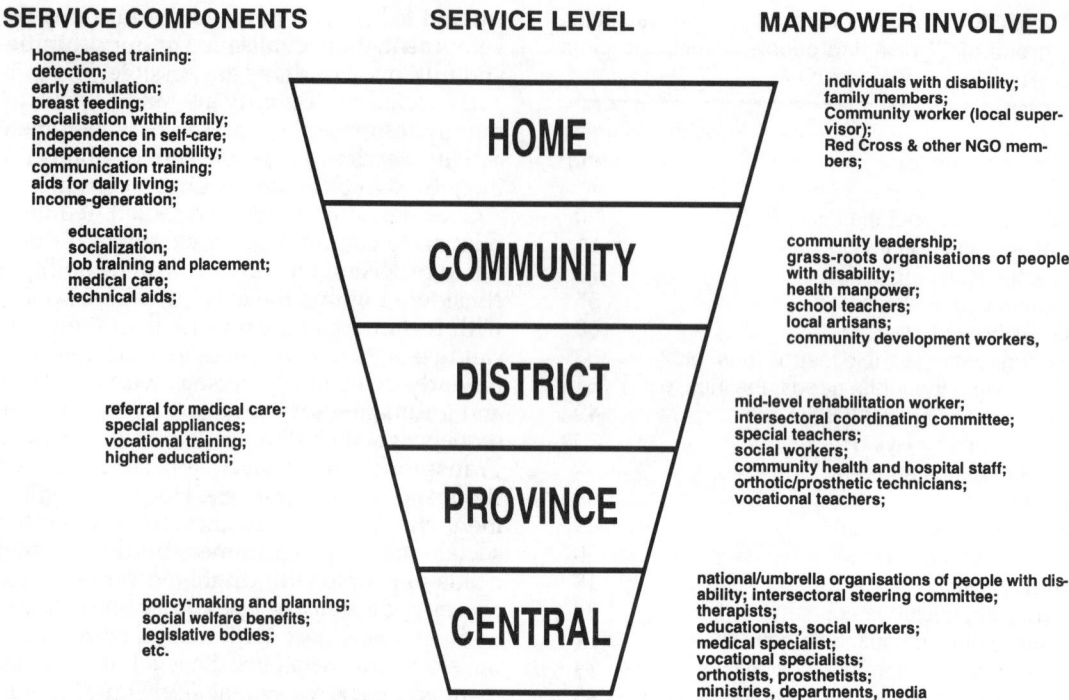

Figure 55.5. Some aspects of the CBR delivery system.

people the service should also be cost-effective.

Programme development should begin in the homes of individuals who have rehabilitation needs. Interventions in the home include detection, early stimulation for children, advice on breast feeding of infants, socialisation, training in communication, physical independence, orientation and mobility (including the making of simple technical aids), and income generation. Within the community, socialisation, education, health and medical care, job training and placement, and the making of technical aids by local artisans take place. At the grass roots non-governmental organisations, self-help disability groups and parent-support groups stimulate CBR, and are stimulated by it.

Referral services enable the use of interventions that cannot be implemented cost-effectively in the home and community. Some examples of referral services include those for diagnosis, medication and surgery (mental illness, leprosy, epilepsy, cataract etc.), specialised rehabilitation therapy, assessment of hearing and vision and provision of eyeglasses, higher education, specialised vocational training, and special technical aids (prostheses, wheelchairs, tricycles etc.). Referral services are made available at successively higher

service/administrative levels according to their cost and frequency of use. At the central level responsibility must be taken for the formulation and adoption of specific policies and strategies for the recognition and fulfilment of rights and for the empowerment of consumer organisations, including necessary legislation and information campaigns. Figure 55.5 illustrates some aspects of the CBR Delivery System.

Manpower roles

The CBR Delivery System calls for the deployment of specific manpower categories at the different levels of the service structure. Both its focus within community development and its multisectoral nature demand that all persons working within these areas should have orientation in disability issues related to their activities.

At the same time, a core group of technical manpower takes specific responsibility for making the system work (Figure 55.6). Whereas multipurpose community development workers such as PHC workers appear to suit best the concept at the community level, the intermediate level has called for specific fulltime rehabilitation workers. Programme

Figure 55.6. Manpower involved in the CBR process.

development to date has utilised a variety of categories to fill this role; social workers (Ghana), physiotherapists (Myanmar) occupational therapists (Argentina). Programme output appears to depend greatly on this level. Where no specific cadre has taken on this role, programmes remain small. On the other hand, when suitable manpower cadres have been available and their role well defined, programme output both in terms of quality and coverage has increased. This has been so in Vietnam, where the role and curriculum of physiotherapists has been adapted for CBR.

Technology

One of the first findings of early field trials of CBR was that for programmes based in the community to be successful, the community must have access to necessary technology (knowledge and skills). In response to this, the manual Training in the Community for People with Disabilities[8] was developed. This has evolved to an essential tool to promote the self-reliance and empowerment of communities, and documents technology to meet the needs of the most prevalent disability groups. Translated and adapted for local conditions, it is now being used by people with disability, their families, community workers, pre and primary school teachers, as well as formal and informal community leaders.

Technology for other levels is being developed, based on the analysis of referral needs of

communities. Some works are suitable for the intermediate level, e.g. Disabled Village Children[9], Handling the Cerebral Palsied Child at Home[10], Essential Action to Minimise Disability in Leprosy Patients[11], and CBR of the Rural Blind[12].

Management

In CBR effective management is necessary at every level of the service structure, beginning with the home of the individual with disability to the most specialised level, so that the system will be of maximum benefit to each individual. The quality of management has greatly influenced programme quality. Direct managerial responsibility is being taken by different sectors. While in Zimbabwe and Kenya for instance, CBR is managed by the Health Ministry, in Ghana, Ivory Coast and Benin it is the responsibility of the Social Welfare Ministry. The situation in Mauritania is an example to be followed, where an organisation of people with disability manages the CBR programme in partnership with the State.

Implementation

The Eighth General Programme of Work of the WHO (1990–1995) has the following Rehabilitation Programme targets: 1) at least half of all developing countries will have initiated community-based rehabilitation activities within primary health care; and 2) 25 per cent will have taken action to set up manpower training programmes at the district level in order to expand population coverage.

The level of achievement of the first target may be assessed on the basis of statistics from 1992: in a sample of 51 countries scattered in the Western Pacific Region, South Asia and Africa, 25 countries are reported to have initiated CBR projects or programmes. In 13 of these countries CBR is part of the government plan for rehabilitation.

Achievement of the second target appears to be woefully lagging behind, and is a severe constraint to programme development. Very few countries have formal ongoing mid-level education for CBR in any of the lead sectors of health, social welfare or education. Vietnam, Mauritius and Zimbabwe have established mid-level education in the health sector.

The CBR concepts discussed in this chapter can be adapted to varying social, cultural and

EXAMPLE 2. CBR AS A PARTNERSHIP.

An international NGO donor, having an allocation for childhood disability, initiated discussions with its counterpart in country A, the Ministry of Health, regarding the development of rehabilitation services. The Ministry immediately requested the provision of a well-equipped children's rehabilitation centre, while the donor suggested a project initiating CBR through the relatively well-developed PHC structure. Negotiations continued for 3 years until the Ministry agreed to an experimental project.

A joint feasibility study was carried out by the Ministry and the donor, with the participation of five communities in one province (total population about 50 000) who expressed interest in the project, and representatives of the district and provincial local governments and the three-tiered PHC system. The study outlined a plan of action for initiating the project. A National Steering Committee was set up within the Ministry for central level management. The WHO Manual was translated and adapted for use at community level.

Project activities began with orientation of the support sectors through seminars for professionals and administrators at the various levels. Next, mid-level professionals selected by the project communities and those selected by the supportive PHC administrations participated in a training course in CBR. At the end of the course community middle-level workers returned to their communities, and together with the community development committees, made preliminary plans of action for initiating CBR. Technical expertise for the seminars and training course was made available by the donor through an outside consultant.

Community-level activities continued with training courses in each community for PHC workers selected by the Development Committee and conducted by the trained mid-level workers. Costs were met by the Community Development Committees. The overall objective was that they should be able to adapt and use the knowledge and skills described in the National Manual, of which each worker had a copy, and empower individuals with disability and families with this technology. This was followed by the location and identification of all people who had a disability of any kind, and determination of their rehabilitation needs, if any. Home and community level interventions were begun for each individual with needs. Grass-roots non-governmental organisations were informed and they participated particularly in counselling families and in promoting social interaction for individuals. Referrals were made to district, provincial and central level services when necessary.

Workshops were organised for school teachers to equip them with basic special education knowledge and skills, and children with mild and moderate disability were registered in ordinary classrooms. Adults with disability joined in income generation activities, which, being rural agricultural communities, were by and large, family activities. All recurrent costs are met locally while the donors main role is to support training in CBR.

The project was assessed after a year and enlarged. Today, after 6 years, it has become a national programme extending to nine provinces and covering a total population of over two million. Curricula of middle-level health professionals has been restructured for CBR, and CBR has been included in other health curricula. The same donor has now an agreement also with the Ministry of Education to support the development of integrated education for children who have disabilities.

political environments and levels of development. It is also interesting to note that, though the concepts were designed for the developing countries, some industrialised countries have also recently started to consider CBR. Early in 1993 CBR was formally launched as an experimental project in Sweden.

It follows then that the manner in which CBR is being implemented varies from country to country. Some have been successful, and others not (Examples 2 and 3). Another observation needs to be made here. That is the alarming tendency to stretch the flexibility of implementation that the CBR philosophy allows beyond its possible limit, and describe blatant outreach approaches as CBR (Example 4).

Constraints to programme development

Three major constraints to CBR development can currently be identified. The first is the dearth of appropriately trained manpower in the main sectors of health, education and social welfare. Conventionally, categories in these sectors have been educated for segregated, institutional services. CBR calls for a

EXAMPLE 3. WHY CBR MAY FAIL?

An International NGO with its own country office, expatriate project manager and local staff had a mandate for supporting community development in country B and had been doing so for many years. Having decided to embark on CBR, it appointed a CBR coordinator and gave her the use of a motor cycle and the task of setting up CBR in three villages to begin with. After some community preparation, community rehabilitation volunteers were selected and given a one-week training by the coordinator and medical personnel from the local hospital. None of these had any knowledge of CBR, while the CBR coordinator herself had some previous informal institutional training in a home for disabled children. She was, however conscientious and committed, and did well to benefit many children in the three villages. Most of the work with the families was done by her since the volunteers had inadequate knowledge and skills. After some time the project was enlarged to three more villages. All costs were met by the NGO. This included meeting the costs of public transport for children to get to school and back, and for hospital visits.

The project continued for two years. At the end of this time the NGO had a drastic reduction in its grant from its own government, and its programme in country B had to be stopped. The expatriate manager left for home, the office was closed, services of local staff terminated and the motor cycle sold off.

The question is, was this CBR?

EXAMPLE 4. WHY IS THIS CALLED CBR?

A large national NGO in country C with activities in the disability field decided to adopt the CBR strategy. A CBR Centre was built and equipped with foreign aid, to serve as a base for training. Selected communities were then the recipients of education in disability. The PHC system was the entry point. When the communities were thought to be ready, primary health workers were trained to identify children who had disability and refer them to the mobile centre staff for advice, therapy and stimulation programmes. Knowledge, and therefore control is maintained by the CBR centre and its staff. There is no empowerment of individuals who have disability, their families and communities.

radical new approach to curriculum development for these cadres.

The second constraint is the inadequate participation as yet of consumer organisations. Their involvement, particularly in planning, monitoring and evaluation is essential if CBR is to continue to be relevant and achieve desired long-term goals.

The third constraint is the lack of interest in disability issues generally among policy makers in developing countries. CBR calls for a firm commitment from Governments because it is only through the use of coordinated multisectoral government infrastructures that all people with disability can be reached with the best possible level of service.

The development of CBR to date has been a truly cooperative effort between the developing and industrialised countries. There is no doubt that continued cooperation focusing on overcoming these major constraints will strengthen CBR approaches as a powerful strategy towards achieving the rights of people who have disabilities.

References

1. World Health Organization. International classification of impairments, disabilities and handicaps. Geneva: WHO, 1980.
2. World Health Organization. Disability prevention and rehabilitation. Geneva: WHO, 1981. (Technical Report Series 668)
3. Helander E. Prejudice and dignity. An introduction to community-based rehabilitation. Geneva: UNDP, 1993 (in press).
4. World Health Organization. Disability prevention and rehabilitation. Geneva: WHO, 1976. (A29/INF.DOC/1)
5. IMPACT. Data on disability. United Kingdom IMPACT Foundation Brighton, England, and American IMPACT Foundation, Washington D.C., USA (undated)
6. World Health Organization. Expert Committee on Medical Rehabilitation. Second report. Geneva: WHO, 1969. (Technical Report Series 419)
7. Chandran-Dudley R. Disabled peoples international activities: history and philosophy. In:

Asia Pacific Regional Council DPI, Equalization of Opportunities. Bangkok, 1988.

8. Helander E, Mendis P, Nelson G, Goerdt A. Training in the community for people with disabilities. Geneva: WHO, 1989.

9. Werner D. Disabled village children. Palo Alto: The Hesperian Foundation, 1987.

10. Finnie N. Handling the cerebral palsied child at home. London: Heineman, 1974.

11. Watson J. Essential action to minimise disability in leprosy patients. Brentford, Middlesex, UK: The Leprosy Mission International, 1986.

12. Horton JK. CBR of the rural blind. New York: Helen Keller International, 1986.

Additional reading

1. Helander E. Rehabilitation for All: a guide to the management of CBR. Geneva: WHO, 1984. (WHO RHB/84.1)

2. Hindley-Smith R. Helping disabled people at home; a new approach to rehabilitation. New York: WHO, 1981. (PAHO Scientific Publication 411)

3. United Nations. World Programme of Action Concerning Disabled Persons. Department of Public Information, New York 1983. United Nations Economic and Social Commission for Asia and the Pacific. Community-based disability prevention and rehabilitation. Guidelines for planning and management. New York: UN, 1989.

4. UNESCO. UNESCO Consultation on special education. Final report. Paris: UNESCO, 1988. (ED-88/WS/45)

5. O'Toole BJ. Guide to community-based rehabilitation services. Paris: UNESCO, 1991. (Guides for Special Education No 8)

6. World Health Organization. Report of a WHO consultation on community-based rehabilitation, 28 June – 3 July 1982. Colombo, Sri Lanka. Geneva: WHO, 1982. (RHB/IR/82.1.)

7. World Health Organization. The education of mid-level rehabilitation workers. Geneva: WHO, 1992. (WHO/RHB/92.)

8. World Health Organzation. Report on planning and management of community-based rehabilitation programmes in the South Pacific. Suva, Fiji, 4–8 November 1991. Manila: WHO/WPRO, 1992.

About the author

Padmani Mendis is a specialist in rehabilitation. She has been a member of the WHO Expert Advisory Panel on Rehabilitation since 1980 and was a member of the WHO Expert Advisory Committee convened in 1981 to provide guidelines and recommend strategies for implementing Disability Prevention and Rehabilitation through existing national health services at all levels, especially as part of PHC. She is a co-author of the WHO Manual 'Training in the Community for People with Disabilities' and a visiting lecturer on the course 'Rehabilitation in Developing Countries' at Uppsala University Sweden. She currently serves as a consultant in community-based rehabilitation to WHO and other international agencies. She has visited over 25 developing countries in Africa, Asia and Central and South America, to promote overall CBR programme development including planning, monitoring and evaluation, and conducting seminars, workshops and training courses, and has presented papers at an equal number of international conferences and meetings.

Lankinen KS, Bergström S, Mäkelä PH and Peltomaa M, eds.
Health and disease in developing countries. London:The Macmillan Press Limited, 1994:543–548.

56 OCCUPATIONAL HEALTH CARE

Matti Tuppurainen, M.D.
Institute of Occupational Health,
Department of Occupational Medicine,
Topeliuksenkatu 41 a A, FIN-00250
Helsinki, Finland

Kari Kurppa, M.D., Ph.D.
Institute of Occupational Health, Department
of Epidemiology and Biostatistics
Topeliuksenkatu 41 a A, FIN-00250 Helsinki,
Finland

Jorma Rantanen, M.D., Ph.D.
Institute of Occupational Health
Topeliuksenkatu 41 a A
FIN-00250 Helsinki
Finland

INTRODUCTION

While traditional occupational diseases, such as fatal pneumoconiosis or heavy metal and pesticide poisonings, have largely disappeared from industrialised countries, they still have a great impact on the health, working capacity and productivity of workers in developing countries.

Due to haphazard notification systems in the developing countries, occupational accidents and diseases are only sporadically recorded. Because of the underdevelopment of occupational health and medical services in general, the majority of occupational diseases remain undiagnosed.

The most important occupational health problems in developing countries are related to accidents, toxic chemicals (particularly pesticides), mineral and organic dusts, metals, and noise, as well as zoonotic infections and parasitic diseases.

ORGANISING OCCUPATIONAL HEALTH SERVICES

Of the world's population 77 per cent live in developing countries, and 69 per cent of the labour force is located there. About 60 to 80 per cent of the workers in the developing countries are employed or self-employed in agriculture. Manufacturing employs less than 10 per cent in the least developed countries (Table 56.1).

The population growth will increase the world total from the present 5.2 billion to 8 billion by the year 2025 and up to 90 per cent of this growth takes place in the poorest developing countries. Thus, the young working population mainly in the developing countries will increase by 1.5 billion, creating a corresponding need for new jobs.

Only 16 per cent of the workers in Africa, 43 per cent in Latin America, and 23 per cent in Asia are socially protected, and the majority lack social security and sickness insurance schemes. In traditional large families the number of dependent members is usually three to four times the number of those formally employed. In these circumstances the consequences of an occupational accident, disease, or unemployment can be catastrophic for the worker and his dependants.

Occupational accidents

An estimate of the total annual number of occupational accidents in the world amounts to 100 million, of which 180 000 are fatalities. Of about 200 000 fatal pesticide poisonings, more than 90 per cent occur in developing countries. The proportion of occupational pesticide

Table 56.1. Distribution of the labour force among various sectors of economy in industrialised and in developing countries.

Sector of economy	Industrialised countries (%)	Developing countries (%)
Agriculture and forestry	5–10	65–90
Manufacturing industry	30–50	5–10
Building and construction	5–8	6–10
Trade	12–20	10–20
Community and social service	15–30	1–18

poisoning has been estimated to 10–30 per cent but the number of cases indirectly related to occupational uses may be much higher (Figure 56.1). The figures are probably underestimates due to poor reporting systems.

Although the total number of occupational accidents is still increasing in many countries, the number of fatalities has declined in industrialised countries. In developing countries, *both the total number of accidents and the number of fatalities are increasing*. The highest accident rates are seen in young, inexperienced workers in construction, mining and logging activities. The transfer of modern second-hand technology is also likely to increase accident risk.

Occupational diseases

The most important occupational diseases are respiratory diseases caused by organic and inorganic dusts, acute and chronic intoxications by chemical compounds, noise-induced hearing loss, and skin disorders. Due to climatic and hygienic conditions, zoonotic infections and parasitic diseases are also common.

In China silicosis is the most important occupational disease. Carbon disulphide poisoning in the Korean viscose rayon industry, and manganese intoxications in battery manufacturing in Thailand are common. Prevalence of byssinosis, caused by exposure to inhalable cotton dust, amounts to 60–80 per cent in many textile mills of Egypt and Sudan. Gasoline, which contains benzene, a potent leukemogen, is still widely used as a general

solvent in many countries of Africa and Asia. Mercury poisonings still occur in South American gold recovering activities. One pattern of industrial exposures in a developing country is shown in Figure 56.2.

In industrialised countries, mortality from occupational causes is no longer a quantitatively important public health issue, although occupational exposures may be an important determinant of the overall health in limited risk groups, like among asbestos-exposed workers. In developing countries work-related health problems may be a major contributive cause to ill health in large groups, either alone or together with other health risks like chronic infections, nutritional deficiencies, and poor hygienic conditions.

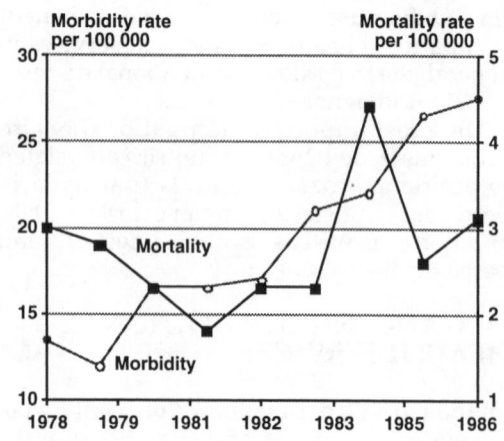

Figure 56.1. Annual morbidity and mortality caused by pesticides in Antioquia, 1978–1986.[1]

Table 56.2. Organisational models of occupational health services.

1. Totally voluntary (India, USA, Venezuela)
2. Based on collective agreements (Sweden)
3. Guiding legislation
4. Binding legislation (Finland, the Netherlands)
   a) specific
   b) in connection with health legislation
   c) in connection with safety legislation
   d) in connection with social security legislation

Occupational health personnel

The distribution of occupational health professionals in developing countries is geographically uneven; most of the available services are provided for the workers of big industries. Occupational health services on the average cover only 5–10 per cent of the work force. Agricultural workers, workers of the informal sector, and bonded labour are typically left without any services.

OCCUPATIONAL HEALTH AND LEGISLATION

It is important to realise that the development of occupational health services will not be effective without a strong legislative support. While some companies, usually the largest, may establish health services for their workers, comprehensive services will always be delayed until legal obligations are introduced. Currently, the legal basis of occupational health services varies from one country to another and depends strongly on local conditions and national traditions (Table 56.2).

The different models have certain implications pertinent to the provision of services, the contents of services, and the relation of occupational health services with other parallel activities, such as public health services. Irrespective of the adopted model, the accepted ultimate goal of occupational health services is to promote working conditions that guarantee the highest degree of quality in working life by protecting the workers' health, and enhancing their physical, mental and social well-being.

FUNCTIONS AND INTEGRATION OF OCCUPATIONAL HEALTH SERVICES

The traditional functions of occupational health services have focused on the provision of primary health care, compensating or substituting for inadequate public health services. In many developing countries this is still the case, while workers still lack specific health examinations necessary for the identification of special health hazards in their work.

In industrialised countries the functions of occupational health services now include three

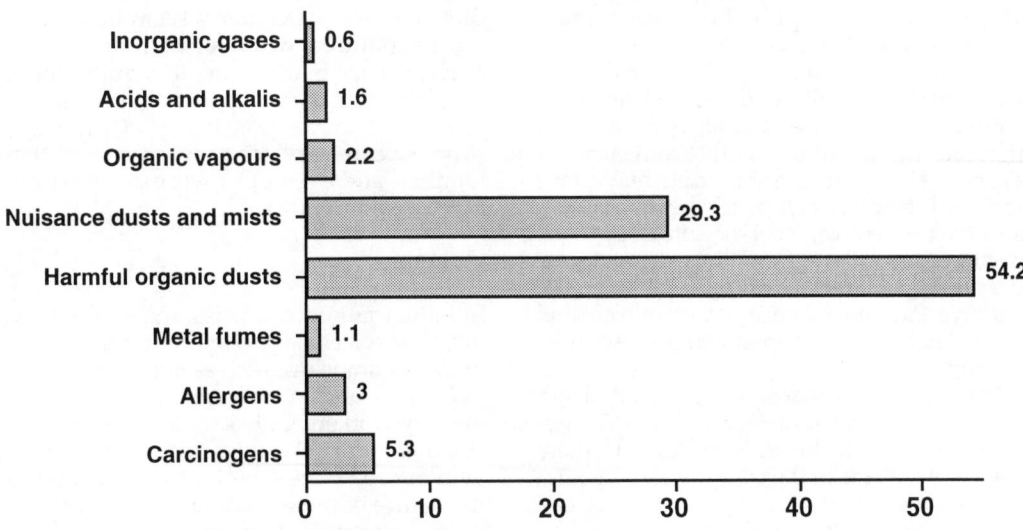

Figure 56.2. Workers' exposures in 65 Tanzanian industries, N=6164, TLV = Treshold Limit Value.[2]

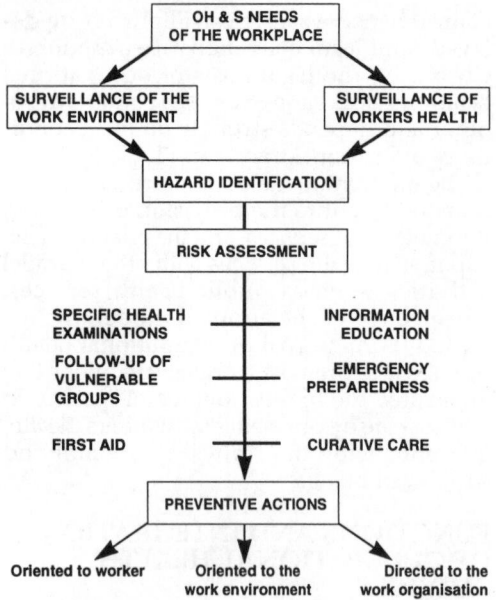

Figure 56.3. Model for comprehensive occupational health services.

main elements: 1) the prevention of occupational hazards, 2) the provision of first aid at the workplace, and 3) certain curative activities depending on the needs and local conditions. Occupational health services may also comprise full primary health care for workers. In some other countries primary health services are allowed but not stipulated by law. There are also examples of countries where the services are exclusively preventive.

Full integration of occupational health services within PHC allows the establishment of comprehensive workers' health programmes that encompass all preventive and curative aspects. However, these models may place too much emphasis on public health aspects, and the preventive, work-oriented approach becomes secondary. In models stressing the preventive aspects the fruitful combination of curative and preventive aspects is missed, and early detection of occupational diseases may be jeopardised.

For historical reasons, occupational health services in many countries are clearly demarcated from public health services, and there may be problems in the communication of information to and from public health services. Such concept leads to the ineffective use of resources through poor coordination and duplicate work. Important information may be

lost and a holistic approach to the workers' health becomes difficult. Thus, irrespective of the administrative model of occupational health services, functional coordination and integration are essential elements between occupational health and safety and primary health care.

At the workplace level, strictly health-oriented occupational health services, when provided by the health care system, may be too far from the actual problems of the workplace. Day-to-day work in occupational health necessitates close functional and informational links with the production, as well as with the safety experts at the workplace. This can provide valuable information to the safety personnel and to the technical design of workplaces and work organisation.

In developing countries the integration of occupational health into the primary health care system appears to be the only feasible solution in order to achieve sufficient coverage of services. It can, however, be effective only if the health personnel receive appropriate training also in occupational health. The outline of comprehensive OHS is shown in Figure 56.3.

PROBLEMS IN THE DEVELOPMENT OF OCCUPATIONAL HEALTH SERVICES

The content of occupational health services varies from one country to another, and rigid directives for the contents seem inappropriate. In countries where primary health care networks are inadequate, it is quite understandable that the occupational health services assume the responsibility of providing primary care services to workers and their families, and even of providing services for nearby communities.

Coverage

In industrialised countries, the occupational health services have been first organised in high-risk branches, such as mining and metal industries, and in big companies with thousands of workers. Only later has it been understood that the risks at work are not primarily determined by the size of the company but by the nature of the work and the quality of the work environment. Small industries and the self-employed, e.g. in agriculture, typically have more risks than workers in well

Improving safety in the workplace is one of the main issues of the occupational health care in developing countries. Photo: UNICEF/Ingeborg Lippman

organised big industries. Still, at present many developing countries still exclude small workplaces and agriculture from occupational health legislation. – In countries with well-developed OHS the coverage of services varies between 50–90 per cent of the workforce.

A special problem is posed by the uncontrolled expansion of informal sector in developing countries. The formal sector cannot absorb the ever increasing work force and the legislators and administrators are often not interested in conditions in which the informal sector is functioning. The use of child labour is common – as many as 100 million children may be employed currently, often in miserable conditions like coal mines. It is important to realise that slavery still occurs in many developing countries, even if in different forms.

In most developing countries agriculture, often run by women, is the backbone of the national economy. Agricultural workers have high accident risks and problems of pesticide poisonings, infectious and parasitic diseases, organic dusts and allergies. These hazards have been reasonably solved only in countries with a relatively high standard of living. Additional problems for occupational health in agriculture are created by the seasonal nature of the work, and by the migrating work force.

Manpower development

In several developing countries industrialisation has proceeded more rapidly than has the understanding of the importance of occupational health and safety. As a result, the number of professional and auxiliary personnel trained in occupational health and safety is inadequate.

Due to the interdisciplinary character of occupational health and safety, the professionals come from many different backgrounds. Some have received formal academic training, others have acquired the necessary capabilities from their work experience. Similarly, the functions and tasks range from routine safety work in factories to high-level decision making. An important problem of occupational health and safety is to train personnel with the relevant skills and attitudes to do the right tasks at an affordable cost.

In addition to training core groups of occupational health professionals, it is necessary to disseminate a variety of information to a wide range of people in the society, including employers, workers, authorities and the general public. Professionals working in primary health care should not be ignorant of the possible risks at work and should be able to interfere by offering advice for curbing the detected hazards at work.

FUTURE DEVELOPMENT
OF OCCUPATIONAL HEALTH

The future development of occupational health in developing countries, the creation of effective manpower development plans, and the redistribution of the scarce resources in an effective way necessitate a thorough evaluation of the national needs and expectations related to industrial and economic activities.

It would be a mistake to introduce in the developing countries the same type of occupational health care system that has been built up in the industrialised countries through a long process. A realistic model could be an integrated one, in which occupational health services would be provided by primary health care units, and thus occupational health services would be an integral part of the public health care system. In order to retain the interdisciplinary character of occupational health, special emphasis should be given to strengthening of the collaborative links between the primary health care and the workplaces.

References

1. Reich MR, Okubo T, eds. Protecting worker's health in the Third World. National and international strategies. New York: Auburn House, 1992
2. Tuppurainen M, Kurppa K, eds. Proceedings of the First ILO-Finnish-Tanzanian Symposium on Occupational Health 8–10 October 1984. International Labour Organization, Geneva, Ministry of Labour and Manpower Development, Dar-es-Salaam, Institute of Occupational Health, Helsinki, 1985

Additional reading

1. Jeyaratnam J, ed. Occupational health in developing countries. Oxford: Oxford University Press, 1992
2. Phoon WO. Practical occupational health. Singapore: PG Publishing, 1988.
3. Waldron HA. Occupational health practice. London: Butterworth, 1988.

About the authors

Matti Tuppurainen is a specialist in occupational health and in occupational medicine, and currently working as consultant at the Department of Occupational Medicine, Finnish Institute of Occupational Health (FIOH), Helsinki, Finland. Since 1983 he has conducted training and research in his specialty in East and Central Africa. In 1988-89 he worked as an expert in Kenya and Tanzania in the context of the East African Programme on Occupational Health and Safety.

Kari Kurppa is Assistant Departmental Director of the Department of Epidemiology and Biostatistics at the FIOH and senior lecturer in occupational health at the University of Helsinki. Since 1991 he has worked at the ILO in Geneva as a Senior Expert on Occupational Health for an ILO/FINNIDA technical development programme for 20 countries, Asia-Pacific Regional Programme on Occupational Safety and Health. Since 1976 he has been involved with the institute's projects in Africa.

Professor Jorma Rantanen is a specialist in occupational health and has been the Director General of the FIOH since 1974. His special research interests are toxicology and risk assessment. He has participated in the development of occupational health services in Finland, in developing countries, and within international organisations (ILO, WHO). Presently, he is the Chairman of the Programme Advisory Committee of the ILO-FINNIDA Programmes on Occupational Safety and Health for Africa and Asia.

Lankinen KS, Bergström S, Mäkelä PH and Peltomaa M, eds.
Health and disease in developing countries. London:The Macmillan Press Limited, 1994:549–555.

57 HEALTH PROJECTS WITHIN THE HEALTH CARE SYSTEM

Marjatta Blanco Sequeiros, M.D.
Provincial Government, Province of Oulu
Linnakatu 3, FIN-90100 Oulu,
Finland

INTRODUCTION

There is not, fortunately, one health project which could be referred to as *the* health project; all of them are different as the environments and reasons that led to their planning, acceptance, implementation and evaluation differ. The role of a health project can therefore be very different even in the same country in different times and different areas. Even the role of a single project varies with time. In this chapter an attempt is made to evaluate health projects from several viewpoints in order to find general characteristics of their role in health care systems.

Health projects can be classified by the size of the project, its funding sources, target area or target group (Table 57.1). Many of these standpoints are interrelated and some of them will be discussed in detail in order to define the different roles of the projects in health care systems.

SIZE OF A PROJECT

Small project and the health care system

A project can be small in size from the point of view of the recipient or the donor. A small project seldom attracts great political interest or pressures in either recipient or donor country. Therefore the project has freer hands and an experimental approach is easier to achieve. Voluntary contributions and direct involve-ment of the population in restricted areas of implementation are more probable. The same is true of genuine interest on the donor's side. On the other hand, the restricted area of coverage of a small scale activity and its limited sociopolitical value can make such projects non-interesting and reduce their official support or necessary back-up.

Visible results necessitate a long-term personal involvement on both sides. This can produce a useful personal partnership and a learning process, which at its best could be later utilised on a larger scale. In real life a paternalistic approach easily develops when the experience, training and economic possibilities of both partners differ greatly. If a long-term attachment of staff with experience in partnership work is available a small project offers a challenge e.g. for work in a remote area or for testing new working methods and active local participation.

Large projects

A large project usually has significant sociopolitical implications locally or nationwide both in the country of implementation and the assisting country. This interest evokes both national and local pressures that should be anticipated in planning, monitoring and evaluation of the project. The organisational structure of a large project is more important than that of a smaller activity, in which success depends on fewer people and a smaller number of interested parties. A large project should

Table 57.1. Determinants of health projects.

Magnitude of the project:
- small/large for the recipient
- small/large for the donor

Origin of funds:
- voluntary contributions from donor and/or recipient country
- funding through state budgets
- combination of both

Principal implementor:
- NGO
- government(s)
- bilateral agency
- multinational organisation

Geographic target area:
- rural
- urban

Target group:
- preschool children
- pregnant women
- families
- handicapped
- patients with a specific disease
- men or population as whole only in exceptional cases

Working method:
- experimental, research or routine methods
- immunisation
- screening
- treatment with drugs
- upgrading of facilities
- training of personnel, or lay workers
- health education

Working approach:
- vertical, horizontal
- multisectoral collaboration
- pure health projects
- combined projects (education, health, water, economic activities)

---

be organisationally well balanced between the recipient and the donor to ensure cooperation with national structures. Also the methods of negotiation between the participating agencies should be well developed in advance both at national and local level.

However, there are usually considerable differences between the cultures of parties in acceptance of structures, methods, definitions of financial terms etc. During the preparation phase of a project mutual enthusiasm or human interest can hide the differences that eventually cause disappointment and misunderstanding during the implementation,

monitoring and evaluation. It is therefore important to pay sufficient attention during the planning of a project to the exact management rules to be applied.

A horizontal approach at the local level should include other sectors of the society as supporters of the project and thus prevent them from feeling that they are outsiders. This will also enhance the development of useful infrastructures outside the health care system. Integration in the existing health care system is very important as a way to extend positive results into areas outside the project. It is also of importance in the education of health personnel and modifications of staff organisation, which are often needed in a large project.

A large project also attracts public attention on the donor side, which should be remembered both in advance and during the implementation. More time is needed for reporting, evaluation, studies and research of the process itself and its results. Great openness is very important, keeping in mind that the media have a considerably greater acceptance of criticism in western cultures than in the developing world. The need for developed structures and methods of negotiation can prove to be valuable from this point of view too.

A large project offers a chance to reach visible results by targeting a significant part of the population, but the time needed for the effects to show cannot be substituted by a large size. In fact, the effect of a large project can take more time to show up. In comparison to small ones, a large project is more difficult to manage and keep together, and the stability of staff is usually not given the importance which it deserves.

Even in a large project personal interaction with mutual learning between different staff members is the most valuable way of learning and development. It has a lasting effect longer than any economic input alone. The learning process is often understood as important for the recipient country only, but the different experiences in the health field and understanding between cultures are equally valuable to the donor country and for the development of its health care system.

FUNDING SOURCES AND FINANCIAL VIABILITY

In development cooperation the major part of funding for health projects comes from outside the country of implementation. The foreign input is mostly from public funds either bilaterally or through multinational agencies (Chapter 58). Since the financial resources of a donor are of different magnitude than those of the developing country, it can be difficult for a donor to estimate the economic capacity of the recipient. Sometimes e.g. political pressures in the donor side can lead to a superficial estimation of the partner's capacity to sustain the activities.

It is tempting for the recipient to pursue the greatest possible foreign inputs, whereas long term sustainability seems to be the sorrow of tomorrow. When statistics are old or difficult to obtain, facts tend to be replaced by optimistic wishes, and the assessments become inaccurate. As a consequence, both short term capacity of local inputs and long term capacity to sustain health activities may be overestimated. A well-wishing health project may end up by deteriorating the existing health care system.

During the economic recession of the Western World also the reliability of the donor funding has been variable. It would be better to be cautious in the initial planning of the budgetary inputs than to be forced to cut down on plans at a later stage. Health care projects are long term exercises, which need consistency also financially.

There is, however, usually at least a nominal involvement of the recipient in the funding of a project. The recipient participation has to be realistic in the beginning, and develop gradually within the life span of the project to facilitate the handing over of the activity to the local structures. The necessary input of capital costs is usually regarded less important for the ability to sustain the activity. Nevertheless, the scale of the project should not be too large and the creation of unnecessary new structures and increasing running costs should be avoided. In fact, *a proportional input in capital costs can prevent investments that later could be hard to keep running by the recipient alone.*

The *running costs of the local staff should be included in the budget of the recipient* and this rule should be regularly monitored. In order to avoid unnecessary disagreements later, monitoring of financial inputs should be formulated in the initial agreement. The integration of a project into existing infrastructures is economically valuable, since the running costs can be reduced with proper use of existing personnel and physical facilities.

The local involvement is mostly regarded as funding from state budget, but the possibilities of using direct local resources should be examined too. This input is usually limited and might include e.g. a small fee of utilisation or a fee for annual subscription to services, or more substantially, an involvement of the population to support of the activities in the form of labour. However, because only in a few cases, if any, can regular voluntary work of a few persons maintain any activity, a broad participation of all beneficiaries should be aimed at. There are numerous examples of projects counting on voluntary work by those already overburdened with daily duties and most in need of any kind of paid job – usually poor women with large families. In these cases it is not surprising if, after the initial enthusiasm, the project tends to fail. On the other hand, when the participation is regarded as a social duty at all levels of the community, the viability of the activities is more realistic.

TARGET AREA

The target area of a project defines its size, funding possibilities and working approach. In most countries the majority of the population has hitherto lived in rural areas. The rural population has been exposed to hazards of environment, insufficient schooling and training, and underdeveloped infrastructure in all fields of the modern state. In many countries the traditional way of life is disappearing, bringing completely new problems to which the people have no ways to respond. It is therefore natural that the rural population has been regarded as socially deprived and in need of help and health projects.

There are many examples of rural projects of different size and target areas. The results have been encouraging, if the initial assessment of the situation has taken the local social structure into account and the local population has taken the activity in their own hands. Necessarily, this means that they have to influence the forms of activity, accept them and implement them in the project. Anything coming from outside, even from a national level, without local involvement turns to sad examples of vanishing efforts or creates unrealistic expectations and results in frustration among both the population and the implementers.

However, we should realise that rapid urbanisation is a fact in most developing countries and that the situation of the urban poor is

Waiting for food supply in Aweil, Sudan. Photo UNICEF/Jeremy Hartley

at least as desperate than that of the rural poor (Chapter 10). The dangers of the environment are many in urban slums. It seems necessary to consider opportunities to improve the physical environment of deprived urban areas from the health point of view. In such cases the involvement of the recipient population becomes of utmost importance. The local community tends to have, besides the official structure, a strong informal and largely unnoticed infrastructure of its own. Unfortunately, in urban projects the inputs required are large and their planning and implementation demand a highly developed cooperation.

TARGET GROUPS AND WORKING METHODS

It seems easier to define a narrow group of individuals as a target than the whole population living in a certain area or several subgroups of the population. It is human to want to help the weak: children or handicapped or pregnant women. Regrettably the projects often do not give them many possibilities to get involved, the approach tends to be top-down. Vertical approaches seem to be preferred in order to eliminate the most pressing problems as quickly as possible. The integration into existing structures is overlooked or becomes

very difficult if these aspects are not emphasised. Lasting results are hard to achieve without integration.

The acceptance of weak population subgroups as partners is essential for long term results. It might be a good exercise to think how we would proceed if the target group consisted of healthy young working men? Would we ignore their possible partnership? This mental exercise is useful for planners and decision makers both on the donor and on the recipient side.

If the whole population of an area is targeted, the need for integration is obvious and is not easily overlooked, although there are always pressure groups in favour of separation of the project from the normal health service structure. In an integrated project the success is a result of the whole structure. The project staff has not the merit coming from a vertical project nor has it a status among the population or the politicians; also this applies to both sides, donor and recipient.

COMBINED PROJECTS AND PURE HEALTH PROJECTS

During the last years an increasing amount of lip-service has appeared in favour of multisectoral projects. However, practical examples are not easy to find, and intra-sectoral and vertical thinking tends to penetrate attempts to do the things together. The western society has developed into narrowly specialised fields and a true multisectoral approach is not common in the developed world; no wonder this kind of approach is not achieved in assisted projects. The official structures of developing countries have a similar narrow field approach.

The population that would benefit from a more comprehensive view has few means to participate in the decision-making. It is therefore a challenge to all interested parties to develop new multisectoral projects. Utilisation, search and provision of water together with environmental, preventive and curative health services are some examples of the many choices. Possibilities to join education of the young and information of the general public and decision makers may offer an asset to a project.

A multisectoral project needs support from official and unofficial structures; society has to accept the approach and see that the benefits outweigh the possible restrictions on sectoral independence. The positive multisectoral partnership should be encouraged and supported with negotiations, training and joint targets.

In the long run, respect for different professional skills, experience and special abilities are necessary for a good partnership. A balanced structure of the project allows participation in decision-making, implementation and evaluation, but it also defines sufficiently the methods of negotiation in case of divergence of opinions during the implementation.

A multisectoral project needs more time in all phases, but especially in the preparatory stage. The support of the teamwork has to be constant and able to solve problems at the earliest possible moment. All this extends the life span of such a project and if time is limited to a few years only, results are difficult to see, even if new patterns of thought and action may be dawning. An the other hand, a long life-span of a project has a negative effect on integration into normal services, reduces the affinity to new working methods, and increases the dependence from foreign input. Therefore a 10-year period could be recommended as the maximum, including a gradual transition to non-assisted work within existing structures.

The preparation of a multisectoral project also requires more work and time for intersectoral assessment which is often forgotten in spite of its crucial significance. One year of preparative multiprofessional and multinational team work is not much if the project is planned to last 10 years and use human and material resources in several fields of society. According to some reports the effect of combined sanitation, water and health projects on diarrhea in children was more visible than that of a separate water project alone; unfortunately the process of participation and degree of partnership at local level are not emphasised in the reports that concentrate on demonstration of a health effect.

A multisectoral approach brings a new dimension also to the research of effects of multi-sectoral health projects. The effects on the health of the population and individuals are only one aspect of the possible changes just as they are only one part of the inputs. More research of health projects and their effects on health and social wellbeing is clearly needed. The environment, climate and populations vary a lot between the continents and even within one country and results of one project are only seldom directly transferable to another setting. This type of research should be a part of each project of a moderate or larger size in order to learn more of the positive and negative effects of the projects.

PLANNING OF HEALTH PROJECTS

In the beginning of project planning, it is essential to clarify the purpose of and the justification for the project, to identify information requirements and to define the key elements and the time frame of the project. It is also necessary to analyse the project setting and to identify how the success or failure of the project should be measured (Table 57.2).

Planning documents are generally detailed concerning physical and financial inputs, personnel, activities and expected physical results. The assessment of development objectives and immediate objectives is often in need of improvement; indicators should be specified and their monitoring system agreed upon. External factors (outside the direct control of the project) affecting the project should also be specified.

Objectives-oriented project planning can be a useful tool for analysing health problems of target groups, the alternative project designs and the possible effects of the project. It is a target group oriented and participatory method

Table 57.2. Main stages in the development of a project.

---

1. PROJECT IDENTIFICATION
The initial project proposal is conceived and formulated with regard to development policy and priorities of the partner countries:
- justification for the project,
- potential target groups,
- external factors influencing the project.

2. FEASIBILITY STUDY
Data necessary for preparation of alternative project designs and for selection of one of the alternatives as project strategy are collected, analysed and assessed:
- perspectives, development and immediate objective
- needs of target groups
- anticipated positive/negative effects of the project
- external factors influencing the success/failure.

3. PROJECT DESIGN
The basic project structure, the main external factors, main elements of monitoring system are identified:
- life-span of the project
- development objective and its indicators
- immediate objective and its indicators
- output and indicators
- activities and inputs broadly
- collecting and monitoring of indicators
- monitoring system of activities and inputs
- positive/negative external factors, their monitoring.

4. DETAILED PLANNING
Detailed implementation plan is agreed, specified indicators chosen, time schedule and budget fixed, monitoring, review and evaluation system agreed, related external factors specified:
- time schedule realistic in relation to external factors, immediate objectives and project inputs
- few specified indicators
- inputs – activities – outputs chosen to achieve objectives.

5. MONITORING
Continuous or periodic surveillance of the implementation ensures that the project is proceeding according to plan:
- time schedule of monitoring
- inputs, activities, outputs
- indicators of immediate and development objectives
- indicators of external factors.

6. PROJECT REVIEW
The purpose is to provide guidance and make recommendations regarding the strategy and management of the project.

7. EVALUATION
An independent assessment of the impact, efficiency, effectiveness, sustainability and relevance of the project, undertaken by external collaborators:
- review of existing information
- discussions with involved parties
- impact studies.

---

of planning emphasising the structured analysis of the project effects. NORAD has recently published a handbook on the subject.[1] The international agencies as well as national development agencies usually have their own guidelines and specific formats for planning.

If a large project is composed of several parts, which have different immediate objectives, it is advisable to divide the project to several subprojects or components. Outputs of subprojects/components then form the immediate objectives of the whole project.

Planning terminology

Development objective is the main overall goal to which the project is intended to contribute in the long run, it explains the reason why the project is implemented (e.g. safer confinement on rural areas of a district). The achievement is measured with *specified indicators* (e.g. infant mortality, maternal mortality, crude death rate, birth rate, prevalence of malnutrition in children aged less than five) and related to *external factors* (adult or female literacy rate, GNP per inhabitant, production of staple crops per inhabitant)

Immediate objective is the immediate reason for a project. It defines the effect which the project is expected to achieve if completed successfully *and* in time (e.g. decease of puerperal infections in a district). *Indicators of immediate objectives* specify the level of achievements in given time and area (e.g. increase in births assisted by trained traditional midwives, decrease in incidence of neonatal tetanus and decrease in hospital puerperal admissions). The achievements are regarded *in context with external factors* (e.g. change in female literacy, change in health facility network, increase/decrease of GNP).

Outputs are the results that are produced by the project (e.g. 100 trained TBA/year, 30 midwives trained on TBA training, 30 hospital nurses retrained on sterility techniques).

Indicators monitor in which degree the planned outputs are produced. External factors influencing the results are recorded (e.g. famine due to delay of rains, collapse of road network, increase in hygiene instruction at school).

Activities are the actions taken or work performed within the project in order to transform inputs (personnel, funds, materials) into outputs (e.g. 25 TBA courses arranged/year, three trainers' training courses arranged, five refreshing courses on sterility techniques performed, procurement of training material, procurement/production of health education material).

Inputs consist of the number of working years of project personnel and defined amount of funds in given time. Possible positive and negative external factors are taken in count (e.g. initiative of women's groups for assistance during training, fuel not available).

References

1. NORAD. The logical framework approach (LFA). Handbook for objectives-oriented project planning. Oslo: NORAD, 1990.

Additional reading

1. Bridger GA, Winpenny JT. Planning development projects. A practical guide to the choice and appraisal of public sector investments. Overseas Development Administration. London: HMSO, 2nd edition 1987, 2nd impression 1991.
2. Pendreigh DM. The management and planning of health services. Copenhagen: WHO/EURO, 1982. (R 4/48/2 (32) C, 3557 D)
3. Mach EP, Abel-Smith B. Planning the finances of the health sector. A manual for developing countries. Geneva: WHO, 1983.
4. Economic evaluation in the health field. WHO Health Stat Q 1985;38;4.
5. Epidemiological and statistical methods for rapid health assessment. WHO Health Stat Q 1991;44;3.
6. Urbanization and health in developing countries, a challenge for health for all. WHO Health Stat Q 1991;44;4.
7. Lee K, Mills A, eds. The economics of health in developing countries. Oxford: Oxford University Press, 1983.
8. Health and development with special reference to Africa. (Special issue) Soc Sci Med 1983;17;24.
9. Health Policy and Planning 1992;7(2).

About the author

Marjatta Blanco Sequeiros is a specialist in pediatrics, public health and health service administration. She is currently Provincial Medical Officer at the Provincial Government of Oulu Province. She has undertaken planning tasks for FINNIDA (development of health sector resources for development cooperation, health sector project preparation) and served as temporary adviser in planning and evaluation missions of FINNIDA. She served as a short term consultant for the Health Resource Management Section of WHO in 1985 and during 1989–1991 worked as Medical Officer of Kenya–Finland Primary Health Care Programme in Kenya. She lectures on district health administration at the Public Health Department, University of Oulu, and has initiated a new system of monitoring and distribution of selected health data from Province of Oulu. Currently she is involved in research of health impact of improved water supply in Western Kenya.

V TOWARDS BETTER HEALTH

Lankinen KS, Bergström S, Mäkelä PH and Peltomaa M, eds.
Health and disease in developing countries. London:The Macmillan Press Limited, 1994:559–570.

58 INTERNATIONAL COOPERATION IN DEVELOPMENT

Kari S. Lankinen, M.D., D.T.M.&H.
National Public Health Institute, Department of Bacterial Respiratory Infections
Mannerheimintie 166, FIN-00300 Helsinki,
Finland

INTRODUCTION

To achieve and maintain health requires concerted efforts of governments and individuals, both on national and international level. Presently, global health challenges are being tackled by two types of organisation: intergovernmental and non-governmental organisations (IGOs and NGOs, respectively). Both groups include a number of organisations with significantly different foundations, organisational structures, working methods and, above all, objectives.

While most of the IGOs were established already decades ago, the number of NGOs is steadily increasing both in industrialised and developing countries. It has been suggested that this development reflects the inability of IGOs to respond to global challenges in the health sector. On the other hand, many critics have pointed out that the activities of NGOs tend to be short-sighted and their sustainability questionable.

CURRENT SCOPE OF DEVELOPMENT COOPERATION

In 1991 the total net resource flow to developing countries was 131 billion USD, official development assistance (ODA) and all credits

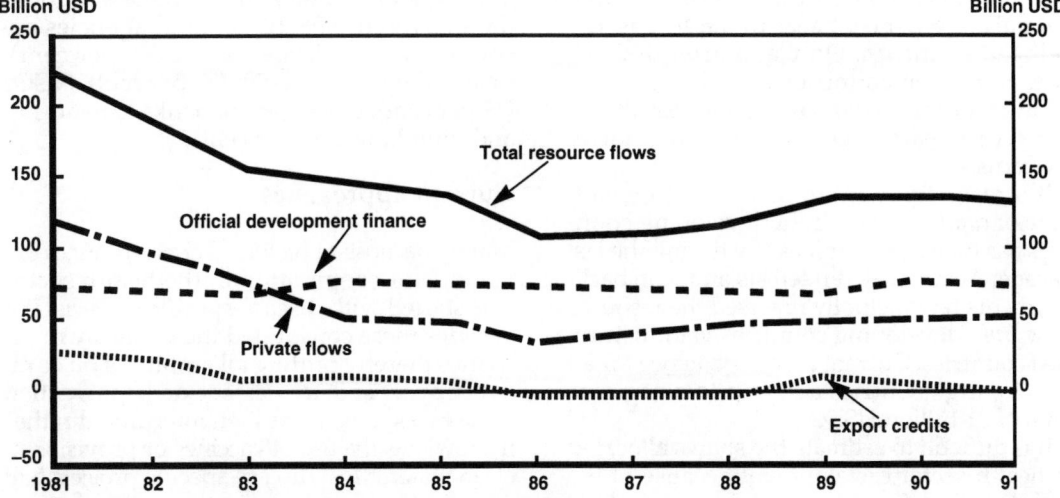

Figure 58.1. Breakdown of total resource flows to developing countries, at 1990 prices and exchange rates. Private flows include direct investments, international bank lending, bond lending, and grants by non-governmental organisations.[1]

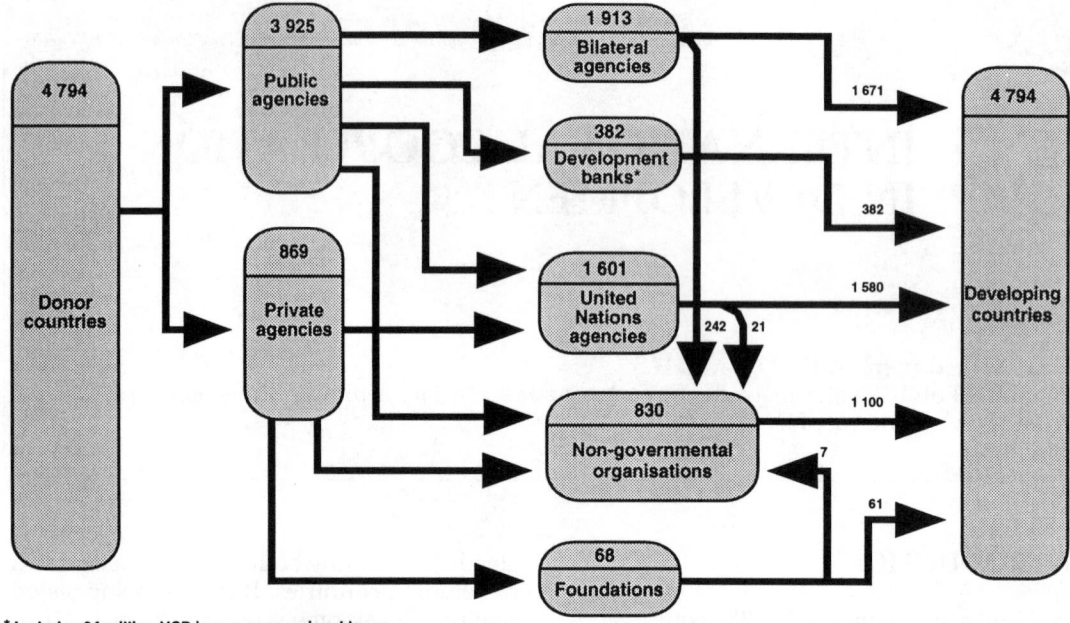

* Includes 84 million USD in non-concessional loans.

Figure 58.2. Disbursements of external assistance for the health sector (millions of USD) 1990.[3]

included. This is down from some 200 billion USD annually at the beginning of the 1980s. The decrease is mostly due to cuts in private flows and export credits, while ODA allocations have remained relatively stable (Figure 58.1).[1]

Aid inputs are still substantial, but the allocation may be biased. The mean of OECD Development Assistance Committee (DAC) member states' ODA is 0.35 per cent of GNP but only 0.08 per cent goes to the 44 least developed countries. Only a quarter of ODA goes to the ten countries containing three-quarters of the world's poor, and less than 7 per cent is earmarked for human priority concerns.[2]

It is also important to realise that the volume of *capital exports* from developing countries has increased significantly during the last decade. Accumulated interests and loan back-payments have actually reversed the resource flow *from* developing countries *to* industrialised countries. Current account balance for all developing countries adds up to a negative total of 21 billion USD.

It is difficult to estimate the shares allocated to health sector development because of the different classification principles currently in use: some group water and sanitation projects as health development, some do not. DAC

classifies all health related items under 'social administrative infrastructure' the share of which amounted to 22 per cent of all ODA in 1990. The sub-class 'health and population' received only 3.7 per cent.[1]

On a global scale, the World Bank estimates that health sector has received 6–7 per cent of aid during the 1980s. Total aid flows to health were 4.8 billion USD in 1990, almost 4 billion in ODA and 0.8 billion from NGOs and foundations (Figure 58.2). Bilateral agencies accounted for the largest share (40 per cent), followed by UN agencies (33 per cent), NGOs (17 per cent), development banks (8 per cent), and foundations (2 per cent).[3]

Current approaches

Mainly because of historical circumstances development cooperation in the health sector was started with disease-specific projects. For decades these constituted the mainstay of activities thereby putting all emphasis on curative services and, to a lesser extent, prevention of diseases which was then interpreted rather narrowly as the use of vaccines or provision of clean water. Most disease-specific projects had a vertical approach.

During the last 10 years the goal of *sustainability* has been emphasised in development projects. Sustainability refers to the ability of project activities to remain functional after the actual implementation of the project has been finished. It expresses how well the knowledge, attitudes and practices introduced can root in the target population or community.

Vertical project denotes an activity or an approach that is limited in scope, limited in sector and implemented in a top-down fashion. Plans for the project are made centrally in project headquarters (often abroad) and the broad involvement of communities is largely neglected. Typically, also the project personnel are all outsiders. The projects have their own infrastructures, separate administration, own vehicles etc.

Vertical programmes have advantages, most importantly a higher level of cost-efficiency. At best vertical programmes have been able to eradicate diseases at national, regional or even global level. What has not necessarily been achieved, is sustained improvement of public health as a whole. – Even if measles incidence in some countries may have been dramatically reduced, the overall child mortality rate may not have changed as a result.

Nevertheless, vertical programmes are not redundant. What is needed is a better integration of activities, and enough consideration to the priority order of the interventions.

Horizontal project denotes an integrated activity that typically involves many sectors and is implemented in cooperation with the local people. Often, pre-existing infrastructures (administration, transport, communications) are utilised and local personnel involved, which should provide better starting points towards sustainability. PHC projects often have a horizontal approach.

Because of their obvious advantages horizontal programmes have been forcefully promoted. However, there are also problems. Even if the programmes result in improvements, their cost-efficiency may be very difficult to measure due to complex involvement of several sectors. The successful implementation of horizontal projects requires a highly competent, strong leadership which may not always be available.

Admittedly, many improvements in public health in industrialised countries have been achieved through vertical programmes. At the same time the direct application of these programmes in developing countries has often failed. What has not been remembered is that in industrialised countries the efforts in the health sector were always supported by another vertical programme, primary schooling obligatory for all people. Obviously, also improved incomes facilitating better living standards were a crucial factor.

Much of the effort will be in vain if the general level of training and knowledge is not improved. Think just of the whole bulk of helminthoses: they would be almost completely preventable by just increasing public awareness of the modes of transmission.

The road to improved health goes neither via horizontal nor vertical programmes but via *integrated* primary health programmes encompassing both horizontal and vertical elements. Health systems are always embedded in the local culture and its original features should always be taken into account as an asset (Chapter 6).

INTERGOVERNMENTAL ORGANISATIONS

The importance of international cooperation in the health sector has been well recognised for over a hundred years, starting with the First International Sanitary Congress 1851 in Paris. The first treaties and organisations dealt mostly with quarantine regulations etc., but already the Health Organization of the League of Nations (established in 1923) had services in epidemiology, standardisation and technical help.[4]

For practical reasons, intergovernmental cooperation is further divided into bilateral (government to government) and multilateral levels (channelled through intergovernmental organisations). An intermediate form also exists: multi-bi cooperation means assistance channelled through an international organisation so that the donor has specified the recipient.

Multilateral cooperation

Within the UN system there are 30 organisations and specialised agencies working in health-related sectors, including social and economic development.[5] Organisations like WHO, UNDP and UNICEF have a high level of expertise in their field and are influential both on national and international levels. Usually they also try to remain neutral and pursue diplomacy in order to gain universal recognition and credibility. Sometimes this has not been possible, giving rise to bitter

Table 58.1. Major functions of the WHO.

- Acting as a forum for international health discussions.
- Providing advice on health to the UN system.
- Providing impartial health advise to governments.
- Establishing and maintaining quarantine and sanitary regulations.
- Setting standards and establishing international agreements (through expert committees, study groups etc.).
- Establishing and maintaining reference laboratories.
- Providing authoritative information on health matters, through international health statistics, journals and other publications.
- Establishing and maintaining technical cooperation programmes to provide assistance of national governments.
- Establishing and maintaining international campaigns for disease control and eradication (smallpox, malaria, yaws etc.).
- Undertaking research (providing leadership through a number of specific research programmes including tropical diseases research, human reproduction research).
- Assisting governments with national health programming and training.

political battles in the venues of multilateral organisations as well.

The World Health Orgazation

Since its inauguration in 1948 the WHO has grown into an international authority in health. The organisation has currently about 4600 employees, distributed in six regional offices, country representations and the headquarters in Geneva.[6]

Initially, the functions of the WHO followed the traditional concept of international health. The work concentrated on epidemiology of communicable diseases and on standardisation of biological and pharmaceutical products. During its first decade the WHO launched campaigns to control diseases such as yaws, a programme that reduced the burden of this crippling disease from some 50 million infected to almost nil.[6]

During the first three decades, numerous other vertical disease-specific projects and programmes were started. While many of these were undoubtedly successful, their long-term sustainability was often questioned. Also

growing international concern over gross inequities in health promoted a discussion on alternatives and more integrated approaches in health care.[6]

Objectives. The objectives of the WHO have not been changed since its constitution was formulated. Thus, the organisation has always advocated health as something more than just the absence of disease. The WHO emphasises health as a *fundamental right* of all peoples. *Equity* both on national and international levels should be a goal for both promotion of health and control of disease. The benefits of medical knowledge should be made *accessible* worldwide. Healthy development of the child is recognised as of basic importance.[4,6,7]

Throughout its activities the WHO stresses its impartiality and advisory functions. National policy decisions should remain the responsibility of each national government since the improvements will depend on national legislation and local infrastructures.

Strategies. The turning point of the health strategies of the WHO was reached in the international congress held in Alma-Ata in 1978 (Chapter 47). The congress laid out the principles of PHC and marked a definite new approach to the operations of the world organisation. Since then the WHO has advocated *integrated* development in health, with intersectoral action.[7]

Notwithstanding, combatting major diseases in the field is still a major task of the WHO. This is quite appropriate as the organisation has acquired considerable expertise in e.g. implementation of immunisation programmes and research on communicable diseases. The AIDS pandemic has also a prominent part on the WHO agenda, although the policies adopted have been under much debate. The most important functions of the WHO are listed in Table 58.1.

Achievements. The eradication of smallpox is evidence of the strength of the WHO. Polio and measles are the next potential candidates for successful eradication as a part of the ambitious EPI programme that already has reached about 80 per cent immunisation coverage worldwide (Chapter 48). The international standards created by the WHO benefit the work of health professionals every day. The organisation has an extensive publication programme, and provides expert consultancy to governments.

The WHO has achieved an eminent role in world health. However, simultaneously the organisation has grown into vast dimensions and become increasingly difficult to manage. Some of the strengths and weaknesses of the organisation are listed in Table 58.2.

Problems and challenges. A recent review of the activities of the WHO demonstrates that the organisation adequately performed the *situation analysis* of essential worldwide health problems.[8] It has organised innumerable studies, meetings and conferences on a multitude of subjects. However, the priorities at the operational level are not clear-cut. The Health for All by the Year 2000 policy, while undoubtedly full of good ideas, remains too superficial. The vertical programmes still receive a substantial share of the organisation's budget.

Vertical programmes are an especially vulnerable part of WHO's activities. They depend to a large extent on extrabudgetary resources which often contradicts the overall objective of sustainability. They typically have separate administrations which certainly does not result in improved efficiency.

In the 1990s, the WHO is facing severe financing difficulties which have resulted in significant cuts in resources of many divisions. Thus, dependence on special programme funding has been further increased. But even the extrabudgetary funds have faced unexpected

Table 58.2. Strengths and weaknesses of the WHO.

STRENGTHS
– internationally acknowledged expert agency
– emphasis on primary health care
– community participation
– intersectoral cooperation
– emphasis on developing countries
– support of research activities

WEAKNESSES
– role poorly defined (normative vs. operative functions)
– overlapping functions with other IGOs
– unresponsiveness to novel challenges (economic and political)
– less than optimal operational abilities of the regional offices and country representatives
– vertical programmes
– benefits to industrialised countries seem distant as most emphasis is on programmes in developing countries, this has a negative influence on the industrialised countries' willingness to donate funds to the organisation.

---

cuts, because of the economic crisis in Europe and the consequent significant reductions in allocations.

Setting priorities within the limited resources is a challenge for the work of the WHO. Coordination must be improved both within programmes and at all levels of the organisation. The WHO should be more responsive to the rapid economic and political changes in the world situation. It should be realised that in the immediate future narrow vertical projects will not be generally acceptable. Health issues related to urbanisation and the increasing numbers of people in the slums should be tackled urgently.[8]

UNICEF

United Nations International Children's Emergency Fund was established in 1946 with the task of providing emergency help to the children of a war-torn Europe. Since 1950 the emphasis of the organisation has been on long-term aid to children in developing countries. In 1953 the UN General Assembly accepted the Fund as a permanent body of the world organisation. The official name was changed to United Nations Children's Fund, but the well-known UNICEF acronym was kept.[7]

UNICEF is a specialised agency of the UN, that also plays a partially free role. The funding is based on voluntary contributions, currently 25 per cent from governments and the rest from private sources through national UNICEF committees and sales of greeting cards and other materials.

Currently, the target groups for UNICEF's activities are children, youth and women. Its programmes concentrate on health, nutrition, clean water and education. About half of the total expenditure is used for provision of food, pharmaceuticals, medical equipment, water pumps and vehicles. The organisation supports programmes in 127 countries and has established an efficient distribution apparatus.[9,10]

Objectives. The main task of UNICEF is to cooperate with developing countries in their efforts to improve the condition of children and to give the children chance to participate in the development of their society.

The major goals of UNICEF for the 1990s (Table 58.3) include reduction by 50 per cent of infant mortality, under-five mortality and maternal mortality rates, and then annually by 3.5 per cent, virtual elimination of severe

Table 58.3. The operational targets of UNICEF during the four development decades of the UN.

Development decade	Operational targets
1960s	Accelerate elimination of hunger and disease.
1970s	Improve nutrition; mount a worldwide effort to eradicate one or more diseases; establish a health services infrastructure for prevention, treatment and health promotion; safe water supply coverage target to be specified by each country.
1980s	Eliminate hunger and malnutrition; universal child immunisation by 1990; primary health care: essential drugs, education, immunisation, environmental health; safe water and sanitation for all by 1990; life expectancy of 60 plus; lower IMR of poorest to less than 120 by 1990 and IMR in all countries less than 50 by 2000.
1990s	To allow the survival, development and protection of today's children through sustainable development that also protects the environment for future generations.

malnutrition, universal access to safe drinking water and to sanitary means of excreta disposal, and eradication of the guinea worm.[9,10]

Strategies. Entering the developing world, much alike the WHO, UNICEF began programmes in the 1950s for control of infectious diseases such as yaws, tuberculosis and leprosy, provision of clean drinking water, education, and various maternal and child health activities. From the 1960s through the middle of 1970s the emphasis was still on vertical programmes.[9,10]

Basic Health Services (BHS) strategy was pioneered by UNICEF in the mid-1970s, and the PHC approach was endorsed in Alma Ata also by UNICEF which co-sponsored the conference. These two strategies represent a major shift in the way of addressing health problems in developing countries.

Although the objectives have evolved over the years, the programmes of UNICEF reflect the priorities set by the contributors. Some countries would like UNICEF to have a more independent role in determining its policies, relying mostly on the expertise of its own professionals and not on the whims of political decision-makers in donor countries.[9,10]

The World Bank

The World Bank Group consists of the International Bank for Reconstruction and Development (IBRD), the International Development Association (IDA), the International Finance Corporation (IFC) and the Multilateral Investment Guarantee Agency (MIGA). The agencies have separate statutes but function within the same administration. The Group forms the largest development financing organisation in the world.[11]

Objectives. IBRD was originally established to fund reconstruction after the Second World War, but its current objective is to finance projects and programmes that would eventually be profitable to the developing countries. It requires the participation of the recipient government in its programme financing, or at least government securities for the credits. IDA serves the least developed countries by providing donations or loans on reasonable terms (interest-free loans, loan time 50 years). IFC has the special task of funding profitable private sector projects if these will eventually enhance the national economic development in the Third World. IFC can provide credit even without government securities.

The World Bank has formulated health sector policies and financed health components since the early 1970s but it did not start providing direct loans for health programmes until 1982.[12,13] Currently, it is the biggest lender in the sector and the allocations are still on the increase. Projects for health, population and nutrition grew from less than 1 per cent of new World Bank lending in 1987 to nearly 7 per cent in 1991.[3]

Strategies. Most of the projects continue the Bank's traditional support for basic health services, but there is an increasing focus on broad policy reforms in the health sector. The loan agreements have to fit into ongoing structural adjustment programmes (Chapter 2).[3]

Themes in the Bank's health sector work have included strengthening of management systems, developing peripheral health care systems, training of health sector staff and establishing appropriate strategies for health sector financing. Cost-effective approaches are emphasised.[3,13]

The involvement of the World Bank in health sector activities has generally met a warm welcome. In contrast to the WHO that struggles in financial difficulties the World Bank group still has access to considerable financial resources. Critics have considered the Bank's policy shift just a face-washing exercise, in response to the criticism provoked by the structural adjustment programmes.

Other development financing organisations

Although dwarfed by the huge dimension of the World Bank Group, regional development financing agencies are still significant lenders in their respective areas. The African Development Bank (AfDB) finances mainly technical cooperation in development projects. The Asian Development Bank (AsDB) serves the Asian and Southern Pacific regions focusing its activities on agriculture, forestry and related industries.[11]

The Inter-American Development Bank has assumed the special task of mapping the environmental problems in Latin America. The International Fund for Agricultural Development (IFAD) wants to help the poorest of the rural people by supporting agriculture and food production.[11]

The World Bank works in close association with the International Monetary Fund (IMF). IMF is not a development financing agency but strives for stabilisation of world currencies. It can, however, provide short-term financial assistance in efforts to correct the negative balance of payments of individual countries. The IMF consultancy has specialised in developing structural adjustment programmes.[11]

There is now general agreement that the regional development banks, while remaining primarily project-oriented, should develop policy-based lending systems for programmes and work together the World Bank and IMF in concerted efforts.

Bilateral cooperation

Bilateral organisations implement development projects on country-to-country i.e. government-to-government basis. Most industrialised countries have international development agencies, usually organised within the ministry of foreign affairs. In 1991 all DAC members allocated 75 per cent of their ODA in bilateral disbursements.[1]

Bilateral organisations are restricted in their actions by the policies of their governments: political or military objectives may influence the resource allocations more than determinants of poverty or the perceived needs in the target country. The organisation of the ministry of foreign affairs as a rule has expertise in international diplomacy but not necessarily in the crucial problems of the target countries. Lack of specialist knowledge and experience is recognised as a major constraint in the functional capacity of the development agencies.

DAC

The Development Assistance Committee (DAC) of OECD has become a major policy formulator for development cooperation. Currently DAC strives for more coherence in its members' policy approaches to development cooperation. Participatory development and good governance are acknowledged as essential conditions for a broad-based development and poverty reduction. DAC has repeatedly emphasised the need for increased aid resources and, more recently, started to focus on reducing excessive military expenditures.

The general principles of DAC member countries' development cooperation follow closely the principles jointly approved by the UN member states. Regarding the objectives of the health sector, the members have recognised the principles advocated by the WHO and UNICEF, and mainly support activities emphasising the PHC concept. The basic strategy is to give individuals and countries the knowledge and tools for self-sustained development in health.[1,8]

Nordic countries

Since 1980s, the Nordic countries (Denmark, Finland, Norway and Sweden) have set an example to other DAC countries by allocating a mean of about 0.8 per cent of their GNP to official development assistance. However, in the beginning of 1990s the economic recession has been used as an excuse for significant cuts in ODA in both Finland and Sweden. The reduction was most dramatic in Finland, coming down from 0.7 per cent to 0.4 per cent of GNP – a policy change demonstrating more opportunistic budgeting than true commitment to development cooperation.[1]

A recent review of the development cooperation policies in the health sector disclosed no major differences between the four Nordic countries.[8] The objectives have been formulated to comply with those already internationally acknowledged, and set forward by the UN, UNICEF and WHO. Even the operational strategies are to a large extent similar.

However, there are definite differences at the project level. DANIDA is one of the very few development agencies that have ever financed projects relating to mental health (Chapter 34). FINNIDA has pioneered in supporting research and prevention of non-communicable diseases in developing countries. Furthermore, FINNIDA has successfully effected the principle of combining development in health and social sectors in order to achieve better sustainability.

NON-GOVERNMENTAL ORGANISATIONS

NGOs can be either religious or secular, but they usually have an ideology as a driving force. They rely on volunteer work and derive a substantial share of their funding from voluntary contributions and donations. Sometimes the NGOs have grown into the scale of IGOs, as in the case of the International Red Cross.

Distinction is sometimes made between people's organisations (POs) and NGOs. POs can be defined as democratic organisations representing the interests of their members working together for a common cause. NGOs, on the other hand, work on issues and people beyond their own membership.[2] The trade unions are among the largest POs in any country. The distinction is rather vague, and in development cooperation the differentiation does not offer any benefits, as both have very similar objectives and ways of action.

There are at least 2500 NGOs in the 25 OECD countries, but the organisations are really flourishing in the South: 23 000 women's groups in Kenya, at least 12 000 local groups in Bangladesh, and 18 000 registered NGOs in the Philippines.[2]

The NGOs in developing countries offer a number of outstanding examples of success, often in areas neglected by the government. Self-help groups and cooperatives have become increasingly popular. By joining forces and the meagre resources even poor people have increased productivity and achieved better incomes.

Getting bank loans for major investments remains a problem for poor people as they are not able to provide collateral. The Grameen Bank, founded on a private initiative in Bangladesh, has proved that the landless poor are dependable loan customers. The bank's policy is to organise people into groups of five and ask each person to guarantee the repayment of a loan to the others. By 1991, the bank had services in 23 000 villages through its 900 branches. The average loan is 60 USD, and the interest rate (16 per cent) contains no subsidy. The loans have generated a great deal of employment, especially for women.[2]

The value of NGOs in international development cooperation is being increasingly acknowledged. Most DAC members are allocating substantial funds in their support. Nevertheless, the total share of NGOs from all ODA from DAC countries amounted to only some 17 per cent in 1991.[1] UNDP estimated that in 1990 only 2.5 per cent of the total resource flows to developing countries were channelled through NGOs.[2]

NGOs usually fly their colours proudly as they work with enthusiasm for their cause. The people involved are usually hard-working and quite often also recognised professionals. Their advantages include flexibility and ability for rapid response in moments of acute need. Often NGOs are well financed (although there are many NGOs that because of their principles function on minimal subsistence). On the other hand, their operations may often rely on the performance of few dedicated individuals with insufficient organisational support. Thus the sustainability may be severely compromised.[8]

Many NGOs have religious or political ideologies that may not be acceptable in the target country. Some NGOs have then adopted a policy of hidden agendas, e.g. claiming to work for education or housing projects while their activities really are concealed missionary

Table 58.4. Factors affecting the policy formulation and actions of NGOs.

- own government
- media
- affiliations (religious, political)
- funding sources
- charity laws
- field workers and projects
- supporters
- host governments

actions aiming at the maximal number of converts.[8]

In any case, the NGO activities are very popular in most countries. It has even been suggested that the NGOs should be given the main responsibility of helping the poorest of the poor and ensuring development towards equity on global scale. In face of the current ODA allocations to NGOs this seems hardly a feasible alternative. How could the 80 per cent of the people in developing countries be helped with less than 20 per cent of the ODA?

In the latest Human Development Report UNDP analysts pointed out that, compared with official aid donors, NGOs often take on much tougher tasks in very inhospitable environments. Tackling poverty, providing credit to the poor, reaching the poorest, empowering marginal groups, challenging gender discrimination and delivering emergency relief are essential themes on the NGO agendas.[2]

The NGOs have a definite role in health development worldwide. But the working methods of NGOs are not without problems. Their accountability and responsibilities may not be clearly defined. Often, there is a significant lack of coordination, both between different NGOs, and within the organisations themselves that are often run by non-professionals in management.[8] The most biting criticism, however, has been aimed at the hidden agendas of the NGOs. Of course, this is most obvious for missionary organisations. There are a number of external factors affecting the NGOs that may complicate the operations (Table 58.4).

ACHIEVEMENTS

Cynics have often claimed that development cooperation is a useless activity and there are no visible changes for better. Development critics of developing countries have pointed out that continued aid and technical assistance

may inhibit the innate potentials of the target country. In the face of opinions like this it is necessary to list some of the major improvements in the global situation.

The average life expectancy in developing countries has increased by over one-third during the past three decades. During same period the infant and under-five mortality rates were more than halved. Twenty-three countries have achieved a life expectancy of 70 years or more.[2]

In the developing world, more than 70 per cent of the population has access to health services and nearly 60 per cent has access to sanitation. Safe water has been brought to 300 million Africans during 1981–90. Between 1965 and 1990, the number of countries that met their daily *per capita* calorie requirements doubled, from about 25 to 50.[2,14]

Several disease-specific examples of substantial improvement in health have been recorded in other chapters of this book. Taken together, there is a definite case for optimism in development cooperation in the health sector.

AGENDAS FOR ACTION

At the same time it is noteworthy that the progress has been uneven and especially the poor are lacking behind. The available resources are being used in less than optimal way.[3] The ongoing *epidemiological transition* in developing countries will pose quite new challenges for the health care (Chapter 33). Thus, new strategies need to be planned.

World Summit for Children

In 1990, the heads of state met in New York in the historical summit dedicated for children and their future. The health goals of the summit's plan of action included increasing the immunisation coverage of 1-year-old children to 90 per cent by 2000, and several disease-specific targets, all very much in line with the EPI goals of the WHO.[3,14]

As the health of mothers is essential to the development of the fetus and the neonate, the agenda includes goals of reducing iron deficiency anemia among women by one-third and providing access for all women to prenatal care, trained attendants during childbirth, and referral for high-risk pregnancies and obstetric emergencies.[3,14]

In fact, the agenda did not provide any new approaches to the health sector development,

Tackling the pathology of poverty remains our common challenge on the road towards better health.
Photo: UNICEF/Roger Lemoyne

but the summit itself increased the momentum of the efforts. The 71 heads of state who attended and the 77 more who subsequently signed the declaration committed their countries to developing national programmes of action to achieving these goals. In 1993, about 85 countries had drawn up national programmes, and another 60 were in process of preparing them.[3]

The World Bank health agenda

The 1993 World Development Report 'Investing in Health' proposes a three-pronged approach to government policies for improving health. Governments should foster an environment that enables households to improve health. It is recognised that household decisions shape health and that these decisions are constrained by the income and education of the household members. Government spending on health should be improved. In many countries the spending on health and social services is in gross imbalance with the military spending.[3]

Characteristically to the World Bank, the promotion of diversity and competition is encouraged. Certainly, diversity and competition between different care providers often results in an improved supply of services, but the supply of public health services should always be secured by the government. Where control is lacking, free competition can easily generate unwanted profit-seeking activities.[3]

UNDP agenda

The Human Development Report 1993 outlined five new pillars of a people-centred world order: new concepts of human security; new models of sustainable human development; new partnerships between state and markets; new patterns of national and global governance; and new forms of international cooperation.[2]

UNDP insists that the concept of security must change from an exclusive stress on national security to individual security, from territorial security to food, employment and environmental security. Such change in policies would liberate substantial resources to foster human development.[2]

Emphasising the evolving interdependence of the North and South, UNDP proposes that the principles of development cooperation should be revised: focusing aid on human priority issues, basing ODA allocations on levels of poverty and linking ODA with mutual concerns.[2]

PIVOTAL ISSUES

Currently, twice as much ODA per capita goes to high military spenders as to more moderate spenders. More than half of the US bilateral assistance in 1991 was earmarked to five strategically important countries: Israel (which is industrialised), Egypt, Turkey, the Philippines and El Salvador (none of which belongs to the least developed countries). With five million people and a *per capita* income of 1000 USD, El Salvador received more US assistance than Bangladesh, with 116 million people and a *per capita* income of only 210 USD.[2]

Fears of political insecurity are still stronger motivators for aid than purely humanitarian concerns. But in an era after the cold war there are clear options for different policies.

Towards peace

Working for peace and disarmament will increase regional political stability, finally on the global scale. Once people have the experience of peaceful coexistence, the disproportionate spending on military buildup will cease by itself, and aid allocations will be less skewed. It would, of course, not be realistic to expect complete disarmament in the foreseeable future, but working for peace must be on the agenda of health professionals, as too much of their legitimate resources are wasted on rearmament.

An example of the grassroots power, International Physicians for the Prevention of Nuclear War (IPPNW) has worked actively since 1980 for disarmament. Gaining supporters rapidly both in East and West, North and South, the movement started several high-profile action programmes contributing to the process that led to the ending of the cold war. As an outstanding peace-promoting initiative IPPNW was awarded the Nobel peace prize in 1985. The movement has currently 250 000 members in 72 countries.[14] Recognising that there are already signs of reduced nuclear

armament, IPPNW is currently reviewing its general plan of action and orienting towards development issues, especially reduction of military expenditure and conversion of resources to the health sector.

Economic development

In the long run, economic development and increased income generation are prerequisites for sustainable development in health. Structural adjustment programmes have been designed to help developing countries to balance their economies. Unfortunately, they often involve adverse effects on the spending on the public sector. This may be unavoidable, but with proper consideration of the priorities the financing of health sector could be secured. In any case, the insufficient funding for health is mostly not due to structural adjustment, but to deliberate government choices of investing more in arms than health.[2,3]

CONCLUSION

Organisations involved in development cooperation have met with variable results, but none of them could be singled out as outstandingly successful. Most problems identified relate to sustainability, regardless of the type of the organisation. Thus, the perfect channel for development assistance remains to be found, but also the working methods need to be developed further.

Needs of coherence in policies and coordination of efforts have already been underscored by several expert agencies in development cooperation. Similarly, research is needed on the effectiveness of the implemented programmes. To date their weaknesses have not been thoroughly investigated. Evaluation should be a part of all development projects.

The NGOs have an important role in search for novel approaches in development cooperation. They can set examples and influence the public opinion and formulation of policies. On the global scale, individual organisations will have little means of eradicating poverty or effecting permanent change in health of a nation. It is the governments that have decisive powers to reallocate the necessary resources for health. Addressing the pathology of poverty remains our common challenge.

References

1. Organisation for Economic Co-operation and Development. Development co-operation. 1992 report. Paris: OECD, 1992.
2. United Nations Development Programme. Human development report 1993. New York: Oxford University Press, 1993.
3. World Bank. World development report 1993. Investing in health. New York: Oxford University Press, 1993.
4. Basch PF. A historical perspective in international health. In: Velji AJ, ed. International health. Infect Dis Clin North Am 1991;5(2): 183–96.
5. Umhau TH, Umhau JC, Morgan RE. National and international health agencies. Profile of key players. In: Velji AJ, ed. International health. Infect Dis Clin North Am 1991;5(2):197–220.
6. World Health Organization. Four decades of achievement 1948–1988. Highlights of the work of WHO. Geneva: WHO, 1988.
7. Basch P. Textbook of international health. New York: Oxford University Press, 1990. 423 pages.
8. Furu P, Haglind P, Lankinen KS, Johansen OL, Mäki-Kerttula A. International organizations and community health. Review of strategies. In: Staugård F, Lundborg M, Assaf G, eds. International health problems and strategies for health promotion. Gothenburg: The Nordic School of Public Health, 1993: 48-91. (International Health 1993:1)
9. United Nations Children's Fund. Development goals and strategies for children in the 1990s. New York: UNICEF, 1990.
10. United Nations Children's Fund. Strategies for children in the 1990s. New York: UNICEF, 1989.
11. Finnish International Development Agency. Finnish development assistance 1992. Annual report. Helsinki: FINNIDA, 1993.
12. World Bank. Health sector policy paper. Washington: World Bank, 1975.
13. World Bank. Health sector policy paper. Washington: World Bank, 1980.
14. Velji AM. International health. Beyond the year 2000. In: Velji AJ, ed. International health. Infect Dis Clin North Am 1991;5(2):417–28.

Additional reading

1. Velji AJ, ed. International health. Infect Dis Clin North Am 1991;5(2):435 pp.
2. The Nordic UN Project. Perspectives on multilateral assistance. A review by The Nordic UN Project. Stockholm: The Nordic UN Project, 1991.
3. The Nordic UN Project. The United Nations in development. Reform issues in the economic and social fields. A nordic perspective. Final report by The Nordic UN Project. Stockholm: The Nordic UN Project, 1991.
4. The Nordic UN Project. The United Nations issues and options. Five studies on the role of the UN in the economic and social fields commissioned by The Nordic UN Project. Stockholm: The Nordic UN Project, 1991.
5. Sachs W, ed. The development dictionary. London: Zed Books, 1992.
6. Lankinen KS, Karvonen JT, Mäkelä PH, Peltola H, Peltomaa M, eds. Health and disease in developing countries (in Finnish: Kehitysmaiden terveys ja sairaus). Helsinki: Kandidaattikustannus, 1989. 590 pp.

About the author

Kari S. Lankinen is a research physician at the Department of Bacterial Respiratory Infections, National Public Health Institute, Helsinki, Finland. Currently, he is participating in a clinical trial conducted in the Philippines in quest of a novel ARI vaccine. Since 1987 he has been involved in setting up a vaccine quality control laboratory in Bangladesh, in collaboration with PSR-Finland and Gonoshasthaya Kendra, a Bangladeshi NGO. His special interest is development cooperation in the health sector, particularly from the perspective of NGOs.

Index

Page numbers in **bold** indicate the text parts with most extensive discussion of the subject; numbers in *italics* refer to illustrations or tables.

France
  alcohol consumption, *106*
  HIV infection, 191
French Guinea, malaria, 148
French Guiana, yellow fever, 233
French Polynesia, oral health, 523
French West Africa, 105
Friday, *Aedes aegypti*, 231
full term infants, 288
fund raising systems, for health care,
  421, *422*
funding systems, for health care,
  417-26
fungal infections, *272*, **275-6**
fungi, in respiratory infections, 128
furazolidone, *142*, 227
furosemide, 482

G6PD, 153, 154
Gabon
  gross national product, *4*
  hepatitis C, 245
  infant mortality rate, *4*
Galenic theory, 49
gallstones, 383
Gambia, 160, 309
  chloroquine-resistant malaria, *156*
  artemisinin, 157
  drug policy, 487
  malaria, *149*; prophylaxis, 159
  maternal mortality, 311
  measles, *164*, *166*
gametocyte antigen, 161
gametocyte, of malaria parasites, *147*
Gandhi, Mahatma, 105
gas gangrene, 364, **382**
Gastrodiscoides hominis, 196
gastrointestinal drugs, 482
gastrointestinal damage, in malaria,
  154
gastroscopy, 336
gender, 95
generators, 497
Geneva Conventions, 118
gentamycin, 358
gentian violet, 276,277, 279
geohelminths, 201
gerbils, *217*, 218
Germany
  alcohol consumption, *106*
  measles, 168
gestational age, definition, *294*
Ghana, 14, 65
  Ga tribe, 297
  oral health, 524
  social workers, 538
giant cell pneumonia, 163
Giardia lamblia, 226-7
Giemsa stain, 155
gingivitis, 524
Glasgow coma score, *153*
glaucoma, 342, 351
  congenital, 350
Global AIDS Policy Coalition, 189
Global Blood Safety Initiative, 509
Global Programme on AIDS, 186
Global Strategy for the Prevention
  and control of AIDS, 186

Glossina, 214
glucose
  blood g. in malaria, 156
  infusion for severe malaria, 158
glycerol, 269
glyceryl trinitrate, 482
gluten-sensitive enteropathy, 143
Gonoshasthaya Kendra, 428
Good Clinical Practice, 457
Good Laboratory Practice, 497
Good Manufacturing Practice, 475,
  480, *486*, 488
Grameen Bank, 566
Great Britain
  alcohol consumption, *106*
  lung cancer, 335
  medical equipment, 513
Greek medicine, 49
Greenland
  HIV infection, 185
  measles, 171
gross national product, *4*, 10, 15
  Africa, *10*
  Asia, *10*
  growth, *14*
  Latin America, *10*
  Middle East, *10*
  see also individual countries
ground itch, 202
growth failure, 297, 299
  patterns, 299
growth retardation, asymmetrical, 288
Guatemala, 54, *143*
  health care staff, *428*
  measles, *164*
  oral health, 523
Guillain–Barré syndrome, 250
Guinea–Bissau, 173
  measles, *164*, *166*
gum diseases, 524
gynecophoric canal, 196

Haemophilus influenzae, 128, 131,
  132, 265, 276, 358, 472
Haiti, 173
  leprosy, 262
  malaria, 148
  measles, 172
halofantrine, 157
haloperidol, 482
handicap, 532
  hearing, 356
hanging groin, in onchocercosis, 206
Hansen, Armauer, 4, 255
harmattan 266, *267*
Hartling, Poul, 117
Hausa, 55
Hawaii, cancer incidence, *332*
healers, **49-58**
  religious, 52, spiritual, 53
healing, 49
health, 50
  and economic development, 569
health assistants, 427
health care
  levels of, **393-401**
  organisation, **393-401**
health care delivery systems, 49

health care managers, self-
  assessment tools, 411-15
health care systems, 50
  components of, *463*
  financing, **417-26**; sources, *421*
  functional problems, 399
health care technology, **513-22**,
  see also medical equipment
health cultures, **56-7**
  regional, 51
health education, 44, **59-66**, 310,
  321, *463*
  and ARI control programmes, 132
  campaigns, 59
  dengue, 232
  HIV infection, 192
  in health programmes, 59
  oral health, 525
  in primary schools, *63*
  in school curricula, **62-3**
  and tobacco, 113
Health for All by 2000, **461-8**
health indicators, **64-6**
health management, information
  support, 407
health officers, 427
health planning, 50
health policy, 461
health projects, 432, **549-55**
  combined, 552-3
  determinants, *550*
  funding, 550-1
  multisectoral, 553
  planning, 553-5
  target area, 551-2
  working methods, 552
health promotion, *463*, see also
  health education
health research, **453-9**, 569
  constraints, *455*
  international collaboration, 458
health sector
  financing, 9
  disbursements of aid, *560*
health service records, 446
health services, segmentation of, 57
health systems, **393-401, 403-15**
  financing, **417-26**
  parallel, 440
health visitors, 397
health workers, 445
  multipurpose h.w. in India, 396
  training, **427-32**
healthy life, 62
hearing
  disorders, **355-62**
  handicap, 356
  impairment, classification of, 356;
    grades of, *356*, etiology, *357*, iden-
    tification, 361, prevention, 356-60
  loss, 533; classification of, 355
  disorders; rehabilitation, 377
heart failure, malaria, 153
heat
  cramps, 386-7
  disorders, 386-7
  exhaustion, 387
  stroke, 387